DICTIONARY OF
AMERICAN BIOGRAPHY

American Council of Learned Societies

American Philosophical Society, Philadelphia, Pennsylvania
American Academy of Arts and Sciences, Cambridge, Massachusetts
American Antiquarian Society, Worcester, Massachusetts
American Oriental Society, New Haven, Connecticut
American Numismatic Society, New York, New York
American Philological Association, Swarthmore, Pennsylvania
Archeological Institute of America, New York, New York
Society of Biblical Literature and Exegesis, Haverford, Pennsylvania
Modern Language Association of America, New York, New York
American Historical Association, Washington, District of Columbia
American Economic Association, Evanston, Illinois
American Philosophical Association, Middletown, Connecticut
American Anthropological Association, Chicago, Illinois
American Political Science Association, Evanston, Illinois
Bibliographical Society of America, Albany, New York
Association of American Geographers, Minneapolis, Minnesota
American Sociological Society, Washington, District of Columbia
American Society of International Law, Washington, District of Columbia
College Art Association of America, New York, New York
History of Science, South Hadley, Massachusetts
Linguistic Society of America, Washington, District of Columbia
Mediaeval Academy of America, Cambridge, Massachusetts
Population Association of America, Washington, District of Columbia

Dictionary of

American Biography

PUBLISHED UNDER THE AUSPICES OF

American Council of Learned Societies

EDITED BY

Dumas Malone

Sewell — Stevenson

VOLUME XVII

NEW YORK

Charles Scribner's Sons

MCMXLIII

Prompted solely by a desire for public service the New York Times Company and its President, Mr. Adolph S. Ochs, made possible the preparation of the manuscript of the Dictionary of American Biography through a subvention of more than $500,000 and with the understanding that the entire responsibility for the contents of the volumes rests with the American Council of Learned Societies.

CONTRIBUTORS TO VOLUME XVII

Thomas P. Abernethy	T. P. A.	Louise Fontaine Catterall	L. F. C.
James Truslow Adams	J. T. A.	Zechariah Chafee, Jr.	Z. C., Jr.
Nelson F. Adkins	N. F. A.	Hope S. Chamberlain	H. S. C—in.
Robert Greenhalgh Albion	R. G. A.	Joseph Edgar Chamberlin	J. E. C.
William F. Albright	W. F. A.	Henry S. Chapman	H. S. C—an.
Edward E. Allen	E. E. A—n.	Wayland J. Chase	W. J. C.
William H. Allison	W. H. A.	Arney R. Childs	A. R. C.
Gertrude L. Annan	G. L. A.	Francis A. Christie	F. A. C.
George B. Arbaugh	G. B. A.	Arthur E. Christy	A. E. C.
John Clark Archer	J. C. A.	Jane Clark	J. C.
Newton Arvin	N. A.	Oral Sumner Coad	O. S. C.
Edwin Ewart Aubrey	E. E. A—y.	Frederick W. Coburn	F. W. C.
John Bakeless	J. B.	Fannie L. Gwinner Cole	F. L. G. C.
Frank Collins Baker	F. C. B.	Fay-Cooper Cole	F-C. C.
Thomas M. Balliet	T. M. B.	Rossetter G. Cole	R. G. C.
Thomas S. Barclay	T. S. B.	Florence Converse	F. C.
Adriaan J. Barnouw	A. J. B.	E. Merton Coulter	E. M. C.
Harold K. Barrows	H. K. B.	Jesse H. Coursault	J. H. C.
Clarence Bartlett	C. B.	William C. Covert	W. C. C.
Ernest Sutherland Bates	E. S. B.	Isaac J. Cox	I. J. C—x.
William G. Bean	W. G. B—n.	Esther Crane	E. C.
C. C. Benson	C. C. B—n.	Katharine Elizabeth Crane	K. E. C.
S. Stillman Berry	S. S. B.	Edward E. Curtis	E. E. C.
Julius August Bewer	J. A. B.	Stuart Daggett	S. D.
William C. Binkley	W. C. B.	Arthur Kyle Davis, Jr.	A. K. D., Jr.
Robert Emory Blackwell	R. E. B.	Clive Day	C. D.
Edith R. Blanchard	E. R. B.	Richard E. Day	R. E. D.
Wyndham B. Blanton	W. B. B.	D. Bryson Delavan	D. B. D.
Willard Grosvenor Bleyer	W. G. B—r.	Herman J. Deutsch	H. J. D.
Louise Pearson Blodget	L. P. B.	Bernard DeVoto	B. D-V.
Louis H. Bolander	L. H. B.	Edward H. Dewey	E. H. D.
Charles K. Bolton	C. K. B.	Everett N. Dick	E. N. D.
Robert W. Bolwell	R. W. B.	Mary LeGrand Didlake	M. L. D.
Sarah G. Bowerman	S. G. B.	Irving Dilliard	I. D.
Julian P. Boyd	J. P. B.	Charles A. Dinsmore	C. A. D.
John E. Briggs	J. E. B.	Frank Haigh Dixon	F. H. D.
Robert C. Brooks	R. C. B.	Eleanor R. Dobson	E. R. D.
Robert Preston Brooks	R. P. B.	Leonidas Dodson	L. D.
C. A. Browne	C. A. B.	Randolph C. Downes	R. C. D.
G. MacLaren Brydon	G. M. B.	William Howe Downes	W. H. D.
Solon J. Buck	S. J. B.	Carl S. Driver	C. S. D.
C. C. Burlingame	C. C. B—e.	Edward A. Duddy	E. A. D.
Edmund C. Burnett	E. C. B.	Andrew G. Du Mez	A. G. D-M.
William H. Burnham	W. H. B.	B. A. Dunbar	B. A. D.
Lester J. Cappon	L. J. C.	Harold H. Dunham	H. H. D.
Charles F. Carey	C. F. C.	George Matthew Dutcher	G. M. D.
Irving J. Carr	I. J. C—r.	Edward Dwight Eaton	E. D. E.
William Glasgow Bruce Carson	W. G. B. C.	Walter Prichard Eaton	W. P. E.
		Edwin Francis Edgett	E. F. E.

Contributors to Volume XVII

EVERETT E. EDWARDS	E. E. E.
CLARA EGLI	C. E—i.
ELIZABETH BRECKENRIDGE ELLIS	E. B. E.
MILTON ELLIS	M. E.
CARL ENGEL	C. E—l.
AMOS A. ETTINGER	A. A. E.
PAUL D. EVANS	P. D. E.
JOHN O. EVJEN	J. O. E.
ELLSWORTH FARIS	E. F.
PAUL PATTON FARIS	P. P. F.
HALLIE FARMER	H. F.
ETHEL WEBB FAULKNER	E. W. F.
HAROLD U. FAULKNER	H. U. F.
JAMES WALDO FAWCETT	J. W. F.
FELIX FELLNER	F. F.
NORMAN FENTON	N. F.
ROBERT S. FLETCHER	R. S. F.
HARRY W. FOOTE	H. W. F.
JEREMIAH D. M. FORD	J. D. M. F.
W. FREEMAN GALPIN	W. F. G.
PAUL N. GARBER	P. N. G.
WINFIELD R. GAYLORD	W. R. G.
GEORGE HARVEY GENZMER	G. H. G.
W. J. GHENT	W. J. G.
BLAKE-MORE GODWIN	B-M. G.
ARMISTEAD CHURCHILL GORDON, JR.	A. C. G., JR.
HERBERT H. GOWEN	H. H. G.
DOROTHY GRAFLY	D. G.
WILLIAM CREIGHTON GRAHAM	W. C. G.
VIRGINIA GEARHART GRAY	V. G. G.
FLETCHER M. GREEN	F. M. G.
ANNE KING GREGORIE	A. K. G.
BERENICE ELAINE GRIEVES	B. E. G.
FRANK W. GRINNELL	F. W. G.
CHARLES BURTON GULICK	C. B. G
SIDNEY GUNN	S. G.
LE ROY R. HAFEN	L. R. H.
GORDON S. HAIGHT	G. S. H.
J. EVETTS HALEY	J. E. H.
COURTNEY R. HALL	C. R. H.
J. G. deR. HAMILTON	J. G. deR. H.
TALBOT FAULKNER HAMLIN	T. F. H.
JOSEPH MILLS HANSON	J. M. H.
EDWARD ROCHIE HARDY, JR.	E. R. H., JR.
ALVIN F. HARLOW	A. F. H.
RALPH V. HARLOW	R. V. H.
GEORGE MCLEAN HARPER	G. M. H.
IDA HUSTED HARPER	I. H. H.
SAMUEL G. HEFELBOWER	S. G. H.
SAMUEL J. HEIDNER	S. J. H.
ELIZABETH WILTBANK HEILMAN	E. W. H.
J. F. HELLWEG	J. F. H.
JOHN L. HERVEY	J. L. H.
JOHN DONALD HICKS	J. D. H.
JOHN HAYNES HOLMES	J. H. H.
WALTER HOUGH	W. H.
JOHN TASKER HOWARD	J. T. H.
LELAND OSSIAN HOWARD	L. O. H.
HARRISON E. HOWE	H. E. H.
EDWARD BUELL HUNGERFORD	E. B. H.
J. RAMSAY HUNT	J. R. H.
RAY W. IRWIN	R. W. I.
JOSEPH JACKSON	J. J.
EDNA L. JACOBSEN	E. L. J.
T. CARY JOHNSON, JR.	T. C. J., JR.
HORACE LEONARD JONES	H. L. J.
RUFUS M. JONES	R. M. J.
LOUIS C. KARPINSKI	L. C. K.
PAUL KAUFMAN	P. K.
HERBERT ANTHONY KELLAR	H. A. K—r.
HOWARD A. KELLY	H. A. K—y.
RAYNER W. KELSEY	R. W. K.
JOHN KIERAN	J. K.
MARIE GOEBEL KIMBALL	M. G. K.
JAMES O. KNAUSS	J. O. K.
ERNST C. KROHN	E. C. K.
LEONARD B. KRUEGER	L. B. K.
WILLIAM PALMER LADD	W. P. L.
GORDON J. LAING	G. J. L.
WILLIAM G. LAND	W. G. L.
WILLIAM CHAUNCY LANGDON	W. C. L.
HERBERT S. LANGFELD	H. S. L.
CONRAD H. LANZA	C. H. L.
FRED V. LARKIN	F. V. L.
KENNETH S. LATOURETTE	K. S. L.
EDWIN A. LEE	E. A. L.
ANNA LANE LINGELBACH	A. L. L.
WALTER LEE LINGLE	W. L. L.
CHARLES SUMNER LOBINGIER	C. S. L.
WARFIELD T. LONGCOPE	W. T. L.
ELLA LONN	E. L.
FREDERIC B. LOOMIS	F. B. L.
HARRY MILLER LYDENBERG	H. M. L.
THOMAS McCRAE	T. M.
ROGER P. McCUTCHEON	R. P. M.
W. J. McGLOTHLIN	W. J. M.
REGINALD C. McGRANE	R. C. McG.
SETH SHEPARD McKAY	S. S. M.
BLAKE McKELVEY	B. McK.
EDWARD McMAHON	E. M.
WILLIAM McNAMARA	W. M.
T. F. McNEILL	T. F. M.
JOHN H. T. McPHERSON	J. H. T. M.
CAREY McWILLIAMS	C. McW.
HELEN JO SCOTT MANN	H. J. S. M.
ASA EARL MARTIN	A. E. M.
JEAN WEST MAURY	J. W. M.
WILLIAM R. MAXON	W. R. M.
ROBERT DOUTHAT MEADE	R. D. M.
FRANKLIN J. MEINE	F. J. M.
CLARENCE W. MENDELL	C. W. M—l.
A. HOWARD MENEELY	A. H. M.
NEWTON D. MERENESS	N. D. M.
GEORGE P. MERRILL	G. P. M.
RAYMOND C. MILLER	R. C. M.

Contributors to Volume XVII

Broadus Mitchell	B. M.
Stewart Mitchell	S. M.
Carl W. Mitman	C. W. M—n.
Frank Monaghan	F. M.
Robert E. Moody	R. E. M.
Charles Moore	C. M.
George T. Moore	G. T. M.
Louise M. Moore	L. M. M.
Warren King Moorehead	W. K. M.
Theodore H. Morgan	T. H. M.
Samuel Eliot Morison	S. E. M.
Richard B. Morris	R. B. M.
Frank Howard Neff	F. H. N.
Allan Nevins	A. N.
Clinton Andrew Neyman	C. A. N.
Jeannette P. Nichols	J. P. N.
Robert Hastings Nichols	R. H. N.
W. A. Noyes	W. A. N.
A. J. Olmsted	A. J. O.
Francis R. Packard	F. R. P.
John McAuley Palmer	J. McA. P.
Mildred B. Palmer	M. B. P.
John I. Parcel	J. I. P.
Stanley M. Pargellis	S. M. P.
Arthur C. Parker	A. C. P—k—r.
Edd Winfield Parks	E. W. P.
Charles O. Paullin	C. O. P.
Frederic Logan Paxson	F. L. P.
James H. Peeling	J. H. P.
Dexter Perkins	D. P.
Frederick T. Persons	F. T. P.
A. Everett Peterson	A. E. P.
Caroline S. Pfaff	C. S. P—f.
James M. Phalen	J. M. P.
Francis S. Philbrick	F. S. P.
Ulrich B. Phillips	U. B. P.
John E. Pomfret	J. E. P.
David deSola Pool	D. deS. P.
Alfred C. Potter	A. C. P—t—r.
Charles Shirley Potts	C. S. P—s.
Richard J. Purcell	R. J. P.
Lowell Joseph Ragatz	L. J. R.
James Garfield Randall	J. G. R.
Belle Rankin	B. R.
Albert G. Rau	A. G. R.
P. O. Ray	P. O. R.
Thomas T. Read	T. T. R.
Herbert S. Reichle	H. S. R—e.
J. E. Retherford	J. E. R.
Charles Dudley Rhodes	C. D. R.
Edward E. Richardson	E. E. R.
Leon B. Richardson	L. B. R.
Robert E. Riegel	R. E. R.
Donald A. Roberts	D. A. R.
James Alexander Robertson	J. A. R.
Burr Arthur Robinson	B. A. R.
Herbert Spencer Robinson	H. S. R—n.
William A. Robinson	W. A. R.
William M. Robinson, Jr.	W. M. R., Jr.
Nicholas R. Rodionoff	N. R. R.
Victor Rosewater	V. R.
Earle Dudley Ross	E. D. R.
Henry Kalloch Rowe	H. K. R.
William Sener Rusk	W. S. R.
Verne Lockwood Samson	V. L. S.
David J. Saposs	D. J. S.
Joseph Schafer	J. S.
Israel Schapiro	I. S.
Richard C. Schiedt	R. C. S.
A. Arthur Schiller	A. A. S.
Louis Bernard Schmidt	L. B. S.
H. W. Schoenberger	H. W. S.
Hamilton Schuyler	H. Sc—r.
Louis Martin Sears	L. M. Se—s.
Robert Francis Seybolt	R. F. S.
Fred A. Shannon	F. A. S.
William Bristol Shaw	W. B. S.
William E. Shea	W. E. S—a.
Solon Shedd	S. S.
William R. Shepherd	W. R. S—d.
Guy Emery Shipler	G. E. S.
Lester B. Shippee	L. B. S.
Eleanor M. Sickels	E. M. S.
Kenneth C. M. Sills	K. C. M. S.
Francis Butler Simkins	F. B. S.
St. George L. Sioussat	St. G. L. S.
Theodore Sizer	T. S.
Constance Lindsay Skinner	C. L. S.
William Adams Slade	W. A. S—e.
David Stanley Smith	D. S. S.
Edward Conrad Smith	E. C. S.
William E. Smith	W. E. S—h.
William Roy Smith	W. R. S—h.
Harriet Smither	H. Sm—r.
Herbert Solow	H. So—w.
E. Wilder Spaulding	E. W. S.
Oliver L. Spaulding, Jr.	O. L. S., Jr.
Thomas M. Spaulding	T. M. S.
Robert E. Spiller	R. E. S.
James Duane Squires	J. D. S.
C. P. Stacey	C. P. S.
Harris Elwood Starr	H. E. S.
J. M. Steadman, Jr.	J. M. S., Jr.
Bertha Monica Stearns	B. M. S.
Wendell H. Stephenson	W. H. S.
John A. Stevenson	J. A. S.
Tracy E. Strevey	T. E. S.
Lionel M. Summers	L. M. Su—s.
William A. Sumner	W. A. S—r.
William U. Swan	W. U. S.
William W. Sweet	W. W. S.
Charles S. Sydnor	C. S. S.
Thomas E. Tallmadge	T. E. T.
Lucy Lucile Tasher	L. L. T.
Ernest Trice Thompson	E. T. T.
Frederic L. Thompson	F. L. T.

Contributors to Volume XVII

R. P. TOLMAN . . . . R. P. T.

HARRISON A. TREXLER . . . . H. A. T.

ALONZO H. TUTTLE . . . . . A. H. T.

LEONARD TWYNHAM . . . . . L. T.

ROLAND GREENE USHER . . . R. G. U.

GEORGE B. UTLEY . . . . . . G. B. U.

CARL VAN DOREN . . . . . . C. V-D.

HENRY R. VIETS . . . . H. R. V.

HAROLD G. VILLARD . . . . . H. G. V.

ALEXANDER J. WALL . . . . . A. J. W.

D. D. WALLACE . . . . D. D. W.

JAMES ELLIOTT WALMSLEY . . . J. E. W.

EDITH E. WARE . . . . E. E. W.

ROBERT A. WARNER . . . . . R. A. W.

CHARLES H. WARREN . . . . . C. H. W.

W. RANDALL WATERMAN . . . W. R. W.

FRANCIS P. WEISENBURGER . . F. P. W.

ALLAN WESTCOTT . . . . A. W.

COURTLAND Y. WHITE, III . . . C. Y. W., III

JEROME K. WILCOX . . . . . . J. K. W.

WALTER F. WILLCOX . . . . . W. F. W—x.

MARY WILHELMINE WILLIAMS . M. W. W.

SAMUEL M. WILSON . . . . . S. M. W.

ALBERT T. WITBECK . . . . . A. T. W.

ALLEN E. WOODALL . . . . . . A. E. W.

ROBERT H. WOODY . . . . . . R. H. W.

THOMAS WOODY . . . . T. W.

JOHN W. WRIGHT . . . . J. W. W.

WALTER L. WRIGHT, JR. . . . . W. L. W., Jr.

LAWRENCE C. WROTH . . . . . L. C. W.

WILLIAM F. WUNSCH . . . . . W. F. W—h.

MARY ALICE WYMAN . . . . . M. A. W.

KIMBALL YOUNG . . . . K. Y.

CASIMIR DOUGLASS ZDANOWICZ . C. D. Z.

ADOLF EDWARD ZUCKER . . . . A. E. Z.

DICTIONARY OF

AMERICAN BIOGRAPHY

Sewell — Stevenson

SEWELL, WILLIAM JOYCE (Dec. 6, 1835–Dec. 27, 1901), soldier, railroad executive, politician, was born in Castlebar, County Mayo, Ireland, the son of William and —— (Joyce) Sewell, and came to America as an orphan in 1851. After working in a New York shipping office, he was a clipper-ship officer (Prowell, *post*) and then engaged in business in Chicago. In 1860 he moved to Camden, N. J., which was thereafter his home. Commissioned captain in the 5th New Jersey Infantry, Aug. 28, 1861, he became lieutenant-colonel of his regiment after the Seven Days and colonel after Second Bull Run. On the morning of May 3, 1863, at Chancellorsville, he led his regiment against three heavy Confederate attacks, and then led his brigade in counter attacks, capturing eight colors and a thousand prisoners, but finally having to retire when ammunition gave out (*War of the Rebellion: Official Records*, 1 ser. XXV, 392, 473–76). Sewell was wounded there and at Gettysburg and was invalided after Spotsylvania, but returned to duty shortly as colonel of the 38th New Jersey Infantry and served until June 30, 1865. He was brevetted brigadier-general of volunteers for his gallantry at Chancellorsville.

For the rest of his life, he was prominently associated with the railroads of southern New Jersey, first with the Camden & Amboy Railroad and particularly with its subsidiary the West Jersey, which grew from thirty-seven miles in 1867 to 309 miles in 1896. After 1870, it was an autonomous part of the Pennsylvania system, controlling several subsidiaries of its own. Sewell was its general superintendent until 1881, when he succeeded A. J. Cassatt [*q.v.*] as vice-president, becoming a director in 1885. In 1899 he was made president of the West Jersey & Seashore Railroad, formed in 1896 by consolidating the West Jersey and its subsidiaries.

The Pennsylvania Railroad was a real power in New Jersey politics at that time. It was particularly interested in checking charters to rival lines and preventing local taxation. As state senator from Camden County from 1872 to 1881 and president of the Senate in 1876, 1879, and 1880, Sewell showed tactical skill in the events leading up to the general railroad law of 1873 and in time became virtual Republican boss of New Jersey. In 1873 he was a member of Governor Parker's staff with the rank of major-general, and that same year he secured a charter for the Camden Safe Deposit & Trust Company, of which he was an incorporator and thereafter a director. In 1881 he was elected to the United States Senate in place of Theodore Fitz Randolph [*q.v.*]. He sought reëlection in 1887, opposing Gov. Leon Abbett [*q.v.*], but after weeks of deadlock the choice fell on a dark horse, Rufus Blodgett. Sewell returned to the Senate in 1895, however, and was a senator until his death. It is interesting to note that he voted for the Interstate Commerce Act in 1887. He enjoyed considerable influence in Washington, particularly with President Harrison. During these years he retained his interest in military affairs. He commanded a brigade of the National Guard and ably handled the situation at Phillipsburg, N. J., in the railroad strike of 1877. In 1898 he was appointed major-general of volunteers, but did not see active service.

Sewell was married twice; his first wife died in 1861 and at the close of the war he married Helen L. Heyl, who with five children survived him. Two of his sons became army officers. He died at his home in Camden. His portrait, showing a mild expression and drooping moustache, gives no indication of the overbearing, masterful and vehement disposition sometimes ascribed to him. He had the faculty of summing up a complicated situation in a few words; he seldom made orations, and was doubtless at his best in the informal gatherings where the real decisions were made.

[E. C. Stokes, *Memorial Address upon Wm. J. Sewell* (1902); W. E. Sackett, *Modern Battles of Trenton* (1895); H. V. Poor, *Manual of the Railroads of the U. S.*, 1867–1901, esp. under "West Jersey"; J. Y. Foster, *N. J. and the Rebellion* (1868); *Manual of the Legislature of N. J.*, 1901; G. R. Prowell, *The Hist. of Camden County, N. J.* (1886); *Who's Who in America*, 1901–02; *Social Register, Phila.*, 1902; *Biog. Dir. Am. Cong.* (1928); *N. Y. Times, N. Y. Tribune, Daily State Gazette* (Trenton), *Daily True American* (Trenton), *Pub. Ledger* (Phila.), Dec. 28, 1901.]   R. G. A.

SEYBERT, ADAM (May 16, 1773–May 2, 1825), physician, scientist, congressman, was born in Philadelphia, the son of Sebastian and Barbara Seybert. After receiving instruction in the classics privately, he was prepared by Caspar Wistar [*q.v.*] for the medical department of the University of Pennsylvania, which granted him the degree of M.D. in 1793. His inaugural dissertation was an attempt to disprove experimentally the theory that in certain diseases the blood of living animals undergoes putrefaction. In his experiments Seybert used dogs, subjecting them to all the conditions, so far as he could simulate them, which famous physicians, among them, Herman Boerhaave of Leyden, had asserted induced the deterioration of the blood composition. This work, published in 1793 under the title *An Inaugural Dissertation, Being an Attempt to Disprove the Doctrine of the Putrefaction of the Blood of Animals*, attracted some attention and was reprinted in a collection of outstanding theses of American medical institutions, published by Charles Caldwell in 1805; it appeared, also, in a German translation in 1816.

Seybert continued his studies at London, Edinburgh, and Göttingen, but most intensively, in mineralogy, at the École des Mines, Paris, under the Abbé Hauy, the "father of crystallography." Returning to Philadelphia in 1797, Seybert was that year elected to membership in the American Philosophical Society. To the sessions of the Society he contributed pioneer papers upon marsh air, and land and sea air, which were published in its *Transactions* (vol. IV, 1799). In 1799 he became one of the secretaries of the Society, serving as such until 1808; in 1810 and 1811 he was elected a counselor. He married, in 1798, Maria Sarah, daughter of Henry Pepper. Two children were born to them, a daughter who died in infancy and Henry Seybert [*q.v.*].

To his interest in chemistry, Seybert added a striking ability to analyze minerals correctly, becoming in this respect perhaps the earliest American expert. To the Philadelphia Academy of Sciences he sold his collection of European minerals, enabling that institution to begin, in 1814, a series of lectures upon mineralogy and crystallography. Upon the death, in 1809, of James Woodhouse, professor of chemistry at the University of Pennsylvania, Seybert was strongly recommended for the position by his old teacher, Caspar Wistar, but the position eventually went to John R. Coxe [*q.v.*] through the influence of Benjamin Rush [*q.v.*]. During the first few years of the century, Seybert ran a drug and apothecary shop in Philadelphia, to which was attached a laboratory for the manufacture of chemicals. In this early commercial laboratory were manufactured, it is claimed, the first mercurials in America (Scharf and Westcott, *post*, III, 2273).

In 1809 Seybert was elected to fill the congressional seat made vacant by the resignation of Benjamin Say [*q.v.*] and served as a Democratic member from 1809 to 1815 and again from 1817 to 1819. During this period he interested himself chiefly in the collection of elaborate statistical data concerning the revenues and expenditures of the federal government, publishing in 1818 *Statistical Annals . . . of the United States, 1789–1818*. Careful tables accompanied the book, tabulating the expenditures for the mint, the army, the navy, and other governmental departments; the national revenues and expenditures and the public debts were also summated therein. This work was translated into the French in 1820, and its appearance was noted in the British Isles by an article in the *Edinburgh Review* (January 1820) from the pen of Sydney Smith. Upon the conclusion of his last term in Congress Seybert returned to Europe for a two-year period, and again in 1824. He died in Paris and was buried in Père La Chaise cemetery.

The versatility of Seybert's mind is reflected by the breadth of his interests and activity. To whatever he turned his attention he brought the patience and persistence which exhibited the true scientist and friend of humanity. In chemistry and mineralogy he was one of the American pioneers, worthy to rank with Silliman, Hare, Woodhouse, and Mitchill. In his will he bequeathed the sum of $1000 for the education of the deaf and dumb, $500 to start a fund for discharged prisoners, and other sums to the Philadelphia Dispensary and to its Orphan Asylum. It was his belief, expressed in his will, that the poor unfortunates leaving the penitentiary might be prevented from the commission of further crimes by the donation to them of funds for two days' food and two nights' lodging; hence his provision for discharged prisoners. Besides the American Philosophical Society, he was a member of the American Medical Society, of the Chemical Society of Philadelphia, and of the Royal Scientific Society of Göttingen.

[J. T. Scharf and Thomson Westcott, *Hist. of Phila.* (1884), vols. II, III; E. J. Nolan, *A Short Hist. of the Acad. of Natural Sci.* (1909); W. S. W. Ruschenberger, *A Notice of the Origin, Progress and Present Condition of the Acad. of Natural Sci. of Phila.* (1852); E. P. Oberholtzer, *Phila.: A Hist. of the City and Its People* (1912), vol. II; E. F. Smith, "Early Scientists of Phila.," in *Pa. Mag. of Hist. and Biog.*, Jan. 1923 and "Early Science in Phila.," *Ibid.*, Jan. 1927; *Autobiog. of Charles Caldwell, M.D.* (1855), ed. by H. A. Warner; *Nat. Gazette* (Phila.), July 8, 1825; parents' names derived from Abstract of Federal Census of 1790 and Abstracts of Phila. wills.]   C. R. H.

SEYBERT, HENRY (Dec. 23, 1801–Mar. 3, 1883), mineralogist, philanthropist, was born in Philadelphia, the son of Adam [*q.v.*] and Maria Sarah (Pepper) Seybert. His early education was supervised by his father, whose traveling companion and scientific assistant he became. Later he studied at the École des Mines at Paris, and upon his return to Philadelphia he was made, at the early age of twenty-one, a member of the American Philosophical Society.

Having acquired a keen interest in science, he began a short but productive period as a contributor to the *Transactions of the American Philosophical Society*, the *Journal of the Academy of Natural Sciences of Philadelphia*, and Silliman's *American Journal of Science and Arts*. In his papers he analyzed tourmalines, manganesian garnets, glassy actynolite, crysoberyls, pyroxene, tabular spar, chromite, colophonite, fluosilicate of magnesia, and bog iron ore. In communications to Silliman's *Journal* (January, May 1823) he engaged in a controversy with Thomas Nuttall [*q.v.*] and other mineralogists over the identity of certain specimens previously classified by Cleaveland and Bruce. In the chondrodite of New Jersey he independently discovered fluorine (*American Journal of Science and Arts*, April 1883, p. 320). Though after his father's death in 1825 he seems to have lost something of the eager interest in mineralogy which had formerly characterized him, occasional papers by him appeared. He analyzed (*Ibid.*, January 1830) the meteorite which was first described by Bowen, and his analysis of the hydraulic lime used in the construction of the Erie Canal is historically interesting (*Transactions of the American Philosophical Society*, n.s., vol. II, 1825).

For the last half of his life Seybert devoted his attention and a large fortune to the promotion of human welfare and to the encouragement of an interest in science. In 1876 he gave to the city of Philadelphia the clock and bell for Independence Hall. He never married and became greatly concerned as to the proper disposal of his wealth, consulting on this question a number of the high church dignitaries of Europe. The mysteries of the future awakened in him a keen interest in psychical research and led him to bequeath to the University of Pennsylvania the sum of $60,000 to endow a chair of philosophy, on the condition that an additional sum be used to support the activities of a commission of the University appointed to investigate modern spiritualism. The condition was duly met, and the commission, which included such prominent persons as S. Weir Mitchell, William Pepper, and H. H. Furness [*qq.v.*], published a preliminary report of their findings four years after the donor's death, exposing many of the common frauds practised by the slate writers and invokers of spirits. Seybert was not a "blind believer in spiritualism," but "his desire was to have a fair, searching, and, as far as possible, scientific examination" of its claims (Pepper, quoted by Thorpe, *post*, p. 232).

His will contained 160 specific bequests to individuals and welfare or educational institutions. The negro, the Indian, prisoners, the sick and aged, poor children, and indigent families all received recognition. The residue of the estate was given to the city of Philadelphia to assist in providing clothing, maintenance, and practical education to the poor children of the community, until they could by their own labor enter the trades or engage in other useful employment. By 1906 this residual sum had increased to more than $1,000,000 and was at first used to support charities already established. In 1914, however, the Adam and Maria Sarah Seybert Institution for Poor Boys and Girls was established, which in addition to independent activities cooperates with all private, state, and city institutions.

[*A Living Hand: Ten-Year Report of the Seybert Institution* (1930); *Preliminary Report of the Commission . . . to Investigate Modern Spiritualism in Accordance with the Request of the Late Henry Seybert* (1887); F. N. Thorpe, *William Pepper* (1904); W. S. W. Ruschenberger, *A Notice of the Origin, Progress and Present Condition of the Acad. of Natural Sci. of Phila.* (1852); E. P. Oberholtzer, *Phila.: A Hist. of the City and Its People* (1912), vol. II; *Am. Jour. Sci.*, Apr. 1883; *Proc. of the Am. Philosophical Soc.*, vol. XXI (1884); Max Meisel, *Bibliog. of Am. Natural Hist.*, vol. II (1926).]   C. R. H.

SEYBERT, JOHN (July 7, 1791–Jan. 4, 1860), bishop of the Evangelical Association, was born at Manheim, Lancaster County, Pa., the eldest of the four children of Henry and

Susan (Kreuzer) Seybert. His mother was a native of Württemberg. His father, a boy of fifteen at the time, came to the United States as a German conscript in the British army and was captured and interned at Lancaster, where he may have heard the Rev. J. A. C. Helffenstein [*q.v.*] preach his famous sermon to the prisoners on Isaiah, LII, 3. At the close of the Revolution he refused to be exchanged and was "redeemed" for $100 by a man named Schaffner, who taught him the tailor's trade.

John Seybert inherited a little property from his father, who died in 1806, and became a cooper. He was troubled intermittently by religious incertitude until on June 21, 1810, through the instrumentality of Matthias Betz, an Evangelical preacher, he felt himself converted fully to the life eternal—*"tief ins ewige Leben hinein bekehrt."* He joined the Evangelical Association, was licensed as an exhorter by John Dreisbach, and was elected class-leader for Manheim and Mount Joy, but for ten years he continued to work at his trade. Then, on Sept. 12, 1820, he set out as an itinerant preacher on the York circuit and devoted the rest of his laborious life to proclaiming the gospel as taught by his sect. He traveled other circuits in Pennsylvania and Ohio, was ordained a deacon in 1822 and an elder in 1824, was elected presiding elder in 1825 and assigned to the Canaan district, was reëlected in 1829 and assigned to the Salem district, and in 1833 was sent at his own request to do missionary work in the northwestern counties of Pennsylvania. At the General Conference of 1839 he was elected to the office of bishop, which had been vacant since the death of Jacob Albright [*q.v.*] in 1808. He had won and continued to hold the complete confidence of his fellows, and was reëlected unanimously every four years until his death. Under his leadership the Association became a vigorous missionary sect, extending its lines constantly to the west and north along the paths followed by German emigration.

Unencumbered by wife or child or by any concern for merely secular affairs, Seybert devoted himself to the work with apostolic singleness of purpose. He lived in the saddle. His biographer, tabulating the records of his scrupulously kept journal, found that in forty years he had traveled 175,000 miles on horseback, had preached 9,850 sermons, had held about 8,000 prayer and class meetings, and had made about 46,000 pastoral visits besides some 10,000 other calls on the sick and distressed. Like his prototype, Francis Asbury, he was an almost perfect circuit rider; even his eccentricity and uncouthness were elements of his power. In his sermons he dwelt

chiefly on the doctrine of entire sanctification in this life and denounced the sins of the world, or such of them as came to his notice, with a picturesqueness of objurgation that has been called "indescribable." He was especially hard on ostentatious dress, and such words as *Modesucht, Putzsucht, Hurenschmuck, Teufelsputz,* and *Sündenstrich* flared like rockets through the smoke of his discourse. In his fashion he was student and became deeply read not only in the Bible but in the great devotional classics. Transparent simplicity and kindliness of character were his most winning traits. He died at the house of Isaac Parker near Bellevue, Ohio, and was buried in the village cemetery at Flat Rock. The last entry in his diary was "One soul saved."

[Solomon Neitz, *Das Leben und Wirken des seligen Johannes Seybert* (1862); S. P. Spreng, *The Life and Labors of John Seybert* (1888); Reuben Yeakel, *Hist. of the Evangel. Asso.* (2 vols., 1892–95).]

G. H. G.

SEYFFARTH, GUSTAVUS (July 13, 1796–Nov. 17, 1885), archeologist, theologian, the son of Traugott August Seyffarth, clergyman, was born at Uebigau near Torgau, Germany. He received an excellent classical training at St. Afra, the *Fürstenschule* at Meissen, and then continued his studies at the University of Leipzig from 1815 to 1819, where he passed examinations for the ministry and obtained the Ph.D. degree. Later he was appointed *Docent* in his alma mater and given the charge of completing, since he was the only one in the city who knew Coptic, the two volumes of F. A. W. Spohn's *De lingua et literis veterum Ægyptiorum . . .* (1825–1831). In order to equip himself better for the task, he visited public and private collections in numerous cities, particularly in southern Europe, from 1826 to 1828, and made more than 10,000 separate copies and impressions from Egyptian monuments and Coptic manuscripts. This material, "Bibliotheca Ægyptiaca Manuscripta," in fourteen royal folio volumes and an index in quarto, became in 1885 the property of the New York Historical Society, to which he willed it. In 1830 he was promoted to the first professorship of archeology at the University, and soon became involved in a lifelong controversy with the school of the French archeologist, Champollion. It was contended by Champollion that the ancient language of Egypt was modern Coptic and that Egyptian writing was mainly ideologic. Seyffarth claimed that Egyptian literature was based on ancient Coptic, related to Hebrew, the mother of all languages; that hieroglyphic signs were mainly phonograms, or syllabic writing; that the hieroglyph represented a syllabic composite derived from the alphabet of Noah, which consisted of

eighteen consonants and seven vowels representative of the zodiac; and that all other alphabets
were derived from this one.

Seyffarth was a man of vast erudition, with a
marvelous memory for languages, but a specu-
lative-dogmatic mentality was his bane. Since
the Champollionists were given the curatorships
in large museums, and Seyffarth found it increasingly difficult to publish his works and gain
a following for his views, he resigned from the
University in 1854 and emigrated two years later
to the United States, thereby terminating at the
same time unhappy domestic relations. He
taught for three years gratuitously in Concordia
College, St. Louis, Mo., and moved in 1859 to
New York, where he preached at Yorkville.
Together with other ministers he tried in vain
to establish a theological seminary at Dansville.
His theology was severely orthodox, championing verbal inspiration and Saxon Lutheranism.
He agreed with the older "Missouri Lutherans"
except that he attacked slavery. He favored the
chronology of the Septuagint and of the Church
Fathers, which he regarded as confirmed by
mathematical fact and differing by 2,000 years
from the vocalized Hebrew text of the Old Testament. In all of his interpretations there was an
unwarrantable regard for unusual astronomical
constellations. His views on Roman Chronology
are partly expressed in the *Quarterly Review of
the Evangelical Lutheran Church,* January 1872.

Seyffarth was a busy polyhistor, maintaining
an extensive correspondence, and writing much
for publication. Twelve pages in his autobiography, *The Literary Life of Gustavus Seyffarth*
(1886), catalogue the titles of his publications in
Latin, German, and English, devoted mainly to
classical and Oriental philology, archeology, astronomy, chronology, and apologetics. Two pages
list his manuscripts, not including his "Thesau-
rus Copticus" in four volumes, 1829, and twelve
minor manuscripts, 1827-40, which are in the
library of the University of Leipzig. The New
York Historical Society possesses also his "Clavis Ægyptiaca," a collection of bilingual and
some other hieroglyphic inscriptions translated
and explained, with the syllabic alphabet in
hieroglyphic, hieratic, and demotic characters,
glossaries, and indexes. This "Clavis" was his
most mature effort in Egyptology. One of his
manuscripts is a treatise on aviation, with numerous designs for the construction of a dirigble
airship. He also contributed articles to the
Evangelical Review, July 1856, and July 1857;
*Quarterly Review of the Evangelical Lutheran
Church,* July 1886; and the *Transactions of the
Academy of Science of St. Louis,* volume IV

(1886). He contended throughout his whole life
that he had discovered that Egyptian literature
was syllable writing, and had made known this
discovery in his *Rudimenta Hieroglyphices*
(1826), which he later regarded as juvenile,
here and there absurd, but nevertheless substantially correct. He repeatedly accused the
followers of Champollion (Brugsch, Lepsius,
and De Rougé) of appropriating the substance
of his own theory, and was zealously defended in
his crusade by his pupils Prof. M. Uhlemann and
Heinrich Wuttke. The latter in his *Geschichte
der Schrift und des Schriftums* (1872) credits
him with the discovery of the syllabic hiero-
glyphs (see p. 497). Knortz claims that the first
translation of the Rosetta Stone was made possible by the use of Seyffarth's system. Seyffarth
completely overlooked the brilliant contributions
of the school he combated. His own translations
possessed a certain beauty, but were frequently
fantastic. Among theologians having a high regard for Seyffarth's knowledge of Semitics was
Franz Delitzsch, once his pupil in Hebrew. The
last nine years of Seyffarth's life were spent in
New York City.

[In addition to references cited above, see: Karl
Knortz, *Gustav Seyffarth, Eine Biographische Skizze*
(1886); Georg Ebers, a critical estimate of Seyffarth's
work, in *Zeitschrift der Deutschen Morgenländischen
Gesellschaft,* vol. XLI (1887); Curt Wachsmuth, *Ein-
leitung in das Studium der Alten Geschichte* (1895);
*Festschrift zur Feier des 500 Jährigen Bestehens der
Universität Leipzig* (1909), vol. IV, part 1; *Der
Lutheraner,* Dec. 1, 1885; and the *N. Y. Herald,* Mar.
8, 1886.]
J.O.E.

SEYMOUR, GEORGE FRANKLIN (Jan.
5, 1829–Dec. 8, 1906), Protestant Episcopal
bishop, was born in New York City, the son of
Isaac Newton and Elmira (Belknap) Seymour.
He graduated from Columbia College with distinction in 1850, and from the General Theological Seminary in 1854. Bishop Horatio Potter
ordained him deacon on Dec. 17 of the same year
in the Church of the Annunciation, New York,
and priest in Zion Church, Dobbs Ferry, N. Y.,
on Sept. 23, 1855. His first cure was at Annan-
dale-on-Hudson, Dutchess County, where he organized a church and incidentally trained students for the seminary, the latter work resulting
in the establishment of St. Stephen's College, of
which he was the first warden (1860). From
1861 he was rector in succession of St. Mary's,
Manhattanville (now a part of New York City),
Christ Church, Hudson (1862), and St. John's,
Brooklyn (1863–67). In 1865 he was elected
professor of ecclesiastical history at the General
Seminary, New York, and in 1867 became chaplain of the House of Mercy, an institution in
charge of the Community of St. Mary, founded

in 1865 and one of the first religious orders in the Episcopal Church.

Seymour was an ardent Anglo-Catholic, in full agreement with the principles taught by Pusey. He broke with the more conservative high churchmen by defending the expression of doctrine in ritual, promoting the rise of monastic communities, and pleading for toleration for those who held more advanced opinions than he did. His argumentative temper made him willing to stand for his principles, but also gave a certain personal character to the controversies in which he was engaged. The first permanent dean of the General Seminary, John Murray Forbes, installed in 1869, had returned to the Episcopal Church from the Roman communion. In several points of policy and in his attempt to discipline certain Anglo-Catholic students, he was opposed by Seymour alone among the faculty. In 1871 Seymour published *A Defence of the Professor of Ecclesiastical History against the Assault of the Dean and the Other Professors of the General Theological Seminary*; nevertheless, on Forbes's retirement, Seymour was made, in 1872, acting dean, and in 1875 was formally elected to the deanship. Meanwhile, in 1874, he had been elected bishop of Illinois. His views and actions were widely attacked, and at the General Convention the House of Deputies, after a week in executive session, refused, by a close vote, to confirm the election. As dean of the Seminary, Seymour established a refectory and made a number of minor improvements in the plant. He secured the maintenance of the institution in New York—an achievement to which he attached great importance; restored its inclusive character; and left it prepared for future progress.

In December 1877 he was elected Bishop of Springfield, one of the three dioceses into which Illinois had been divided. After confirmation of the election and a second request from the diocesan convention he finally accepted in May 1878. He was consecrated in Trinity Church, New York, on June 11, and at once went West for a visitation of his diocese. At the end of the following academic year he resigned his positions in New York and moved permanently to Springfield. After ten years he was able to report that the diocese had doubled in almost all respects capable of statistical statement. The rest of his life saw a solid, if gradual, expansion. In 1892 Seymour obtained a coadjutor, Bishop Charles Reuben Hale [*q.v.*], but after his death in 1900 resumed the entire charge of the work.

Seymour was considered to be an effective teacher, and learned in church history and canon law. His scholarly productions, however, were all controversial or occasional—often pamphlets written at a sitting to meet a particular occasion. He lived to see the Catholic principles for which he had fought everywhere tolerated and widely accepted, and many advanced practices of his youth (*e.g.*, weekly communion) common to the whole church. Towards the end of his life, however, he was inclined to take a dark view of the state of the Church, and was seriously alarmed by the rise of the broad church party. He was one of those who conscientiously opposed the consecration of Phillips Brooks [*q.v.*]. Although he had been suspicious of the revision, the Prayer Book of 1892 included much which he had supported; but the movement for changing the name of the Protestant Episcopal Church, of which he was one of the chief promoters, remained unsuccessful. In 1904 a coadjutor, Edward William Osborne, was elected and consecrated, but Seymour remained active almost until the end, performing his last official acts a month before his death, which occurred at Springfield. He was survived by his wife, Harriet Atwood (Downe) Aymar, whom he married on July 23, 1889.

[W. S. Perry, *The Bishops of the Am. Church* (1897); *Living Church*, Dec. 15, 1906; "Mother Harriet of the Sisterhood of St. Mary," in the *Church Eclectic*, June 1896; *Jour. of the Proc. of the Conventions of the Protestant Episcopal Church in the Diocese of N. Y.*, 1855–77; *Proc. of the Board of Trustees of the Gen. Theological Sem.*, 1866–79; *Diocese of Springfield, Convention Jour.*, 1879–1906; *Who's Who in America*, 1906–07; *Ill. State Reg.* (Springfield), Dec. 9, 1906.]

E. R. H., Jr.

SEYMOUR, HORATIO (May 31, 1810–Feb. 12, 1886), governor of New York, was born in the frontier village of Pompey Hill, Onondaga County, N. Y., and was named for his father's elder brother, Horatio, later (1821–33) United States senator from Vermont. His father, Henry Seymour (1780–1837), a native of Litchfield, Conn., and a descendant of Richard Seamer or Seymour who emigrated from Hertfordshire to New England in 1638 and went the next year to Hartford, Conn. (Wall, *post*, p. 1), settled at Pompey Hill about 1800, as the keeper of the first store. He was one of the political lieutenants of Martin Van Buren and his election as canal commissioner was the decisive factor in the scheme to take the patronage of the Erie Canal from DeWitt Clinton [*q.v.*]. After thirteen years in this office, in 1835 Henry Seymour became president of the Farmers' Loan and Trust Company of New York. During the panic of 1837 he committed suicide while on a summer visit to Utica, which had been his home since 1819. His widow, Mary Ledyard (Forman), mother of his six children, survived until 1859.

She was the daughter of Jonathan Forman and the niece of William Ledyard [q.v.]. Although Horatio Seymour owed the better part of his education to reading, his schooling was as good as the community afforded. Under Joshua Leonard, the academy at Pompey Hill was the nursery of more than one notable man. After the move to Utica, Horatio attended the Utica Academy, Oxford Academy, and the Geneva Academy, until he was entered in the military academy which Alden Partridge [q.v.] then conducted at Middletown, Conn. There he remained for two years. In 1826 he returned to Utica and learned law in the office of Greene C. Bronson and Samuel Beardsley, being admitted to the bar in 1832. The business cares of the involved estate of his father drew him away from his profession after 1837.

In January 1833 Seymour became the military secretary of Gov. William L. Marcy [q.v.], a post he held for six years. He lived in Albany and learned the ropes of the Regency. For twenty-four years Marcy remained his closest political friend: Seymour was his lieutenant at the Baltimore convention in 1852, and was in close touch with him during his two periods of service in the cabinet. While living in Albany, Seymour met, and married on his twenty-fifth birthday, Mary, the youngest daughter of John Rutger Bleecker, head of an old Dutch land-holding family and part owner of the site on which the city of Utica grew up. The match was childless. After living together over fifty years, Seymour and his wife died within a month of each other.

William H. Seward [q.v.] defeated Governor Marcy in the fall of 1838, and Seymour retired to Utica, just about the time that Van Buren's independent treasury policy was splitting the New York Democrats into the factions that came to be known (1844–46) as Hunkers and Barnburners. The interests of Seymour's friends and his family lay with the conservatives (later the Hunkers). In the autumn of 1841 he was elected to the Assembly and served there in 1842. In the spring of 1842 he was elected mayor of the Whig city of Utica after an exciting campaign, but a year later he was defeated by sixteen votes (Utica Weekly Herald, Feb. 16, 1886). He served again in the Assembly in 1844 and 1845. As chairman he brought in his famous "Report of the Committee on Canals" (New York Assembly Documents, 1844, No. 177), and forced its recommendations through the legislature by skill and logic, over the opposition of the strict-constructionist Democrats, under the lead of Michael Hoffman. The Erie Canal became a tradition in the Seymour family. In the fifties

and sixties, he helped promote a scheme to unite the Great Lakes and the Mississippi by means of the Fox and Wisconsin Rivers, investing heavily in the land of that region. Waterways, he always argued, would regulate the rates of railways better than laws could ever do.

Seymour's success with his canal bill led to his election as speaker in 1845, after a fierce contest among the Democrats. After Polk's nomination for president the Van Buren Democrats were disgruntled, and Silas Wright [q.v.] had been nominated for governor to appease them. He was duly elected, serving 1845–47, but quarrels over the canal, anti-rent riots, a new state constitution, and the Mexican War wrecked Seymour's legislative program. Wright was defeated for reëlection in 1846, allegedly by the defection of Hunker votes, and his death in 1847 added a martyr to the Barnburner cause. Thereafter there were actually two Democratic parties in the state, and it was Seymour's success at effecting working compromises between them that made him important. Though as early as 1845, according to Silas Wright, he declared for free soil in the southwestern territory which might be gained from Mexico (R. H. Gillet, The Life and Times of Silas Wright, 1874, vol. II, 1625), his dislike for abolitionists was equaled only by his suspicion of Southern extremists. He always opposed federal interference with slavery, which was certain to succumb, he thought, to the competition of free labor as strengthened by immigration. His intelligent distrust of both sides of the argument partly accounts for his unwillingness ever to hold federal office.

Democratic quarrels over offices in Polk's cabinet and the election of Senators John A. Dix and Daniel S. Dickinson [qq.v.] seem to have determined Seymour to retire from politics. He withdrew to Utica and took no part in the constitutional convention in 1846, although he kept in touch with Marcy at Washington. After the Democratic schism of 1848, Marcy persuaded him to help repair the damage by accepting the first of his six nominations for governor in 1850. His narrow defeat by Washington Hunt that year was followed by his victory over the same opponent in 1852. He was an industrious, conscientious governor, taking particular care to improve the administration of the penal system. But the first of his two terms coincided with the high tide of prohibition sentiment in the legislature, as evidenced in the famous Maine Law Bill, which he courageously vetoed in the spring of 1854. He was defeated for reëlection by a handful of votes in a field of four candidates. In 1856

7

a second Maine Law was thrown out as unconstitutional. Seymour never relented in his uncompromising hostility to prohibition and anti-Catholicism, both of which played a part in the confused campaign of 1854. Two years later, on July 4, 1856, at Springfield, Mass., campaigning for Buchanan, he uttered the first of his once-famous denunciations of abolition, prohibition, and nativism (*Public Record*, pp. 1–21). For four years thereafter he devoted himself to private business.

By the spring of 1860 Dean Richmond hoped to nominate Seymour for the presidency as a compromise candidate at the Charleston Democratic Convention (Alexander, *post*, II, 276, 298). Seymour remained at Utica, withdrawing his name on June 5 (*New York Tribune*, June 6, 1860) from consideration by the Baltimore convention, which met June 18. He voted for Douglas, having helped to organize the fusion electoral ticket. He was prominent at the Tweddle Hall convention which met at Albany, Jan. 31, 1861, and, although he agreed with Tilden that Lincoln's victory without a single electoral vote from the South was a political disaster, he urged loyal acceptance of the constitutional fact, begging both North and South to compromise their quarrel and submit the Crittenden Compromise to popular vote. At first he thought the conquest of the South impossible; he never thought it wise.

During the first year of the war, Seymour helped Gov. Edwin D. Morgan [*q.v.*] to raise troops and money for the Union armies. When, in 1862, the radical Republicans of the state forced the nomination of General James Wadsworth for governor, Seymour's candidacy consolidated the conservative vote, and his election expressed not only disgust with abolitionists, but also disappointment with the progress of the war. The Democratic victories of 1862 probably spared Lincoln political pressure from the most noisome supporters of the Union, but Seymour found himself pushed into the precarious position of the national leader of the opposition. Although he opposed the Emancipation Proclamation (*Public Record*, pp. 99, 369) and denounced the arrest of Vallandigham as an outrage (McCabe, *post*, pp. 136–38; Wall, p. 94), he was tireless at filling up the state's quotas in the Union armies. Assistant-Secretary of War Dana testified to his unimpeachable loyalty (New York *Sun*, Feb. 13, 1886). To the end of his life, he insisted that the extra-constitutional powers assumed by the Lincoln administration were the most serious problem arising from the Civil War (see his article, "The Political Situa-

tion," in *North American Review*, February 1883).

Seymour's participation in the most notorious incident of his whole career was clouded by partisan politics. He had opposed the enrollment act of March 1863 as both unconstitutional and unwise, believing that the raising of troops belonged to the states. The inequalities of the statute and the tactlessness of its application encouraged discontent. When the riots of July 1863 broke out, Seymour hastened to New York from a vacation in New Jersey, and directed the rapid restoration of order. The famous "My Friends" speech (*Public Record*, p. 127) was addressed, at noon, to an orderly crowd in front of the city hall, at a time when the rioters were no nearer than three miles. But Greeley denounced him as a temporizing "Copperhead," and the legend of his disloyal language followed him to the grave. Careful examination of the evidence shows that the draft riots were grossly exaggerated : claims for property damage were corruptly padded, once it was discovered that the state was liable; and the traditional estimate of a thousand deaths is sheer fiction.

In 1864 he urged the Democrats to name a civilian candidate for president (Brummer, *post*, pp. 403–04; N. Y. *World*, Aug. 29, 1864), but he presided at the Chicago convention and campaigned for McClellan. To aid the ticket in New York he unwillingly accepted his fifth nomination for governor. The manipulation and suppression of the soldier vote cast a shadow of doubt, if not dishonesty, over his defeat. After the Civil War, Seymour retired to the country home he had built at Deerfield, just north of Utica, and devoted his leisure to reading, to farming, and to the reconstruction of the Democratic party. His nomination for president in 1868, in the convention of which he was again the presiding officer, resulted from a union of eastern Democrats who would not have George H. Pendleton [*q.v.*], with western Democrats who would not have Thomas A. Hendricks [*q.v.*]. Seymour was working for Chief Justice Chase, but his second choice was Hendricks. In the end, the West got the platform and the East the candidate. The final outcome was utterly against his will, and his acceptance, he always believed, was the great mistake of his life. When he was pushed out of the hall, he supposed the convention would adjourn until the following day, when he could persuade it to reconsider its vote, but the Democrats completed their ticket with Francis Preston Blair, Jr. [*q.v.*], and went home.

Seymour's showing in the campaign astonished even as astute a politician as Blaine. Although President Johnson threw his support against Grant, Blair's utterances were made to seem to threaten a reopening of the Civil War. Seymour was described as the insane son of a suicide. Partly to offset the influence of Blair, Seymour spoke with vigor and ability throughout the North and West. Although the electoral result was overwhelmingly against him, an analysis of the popular vote makes it not improbable that he was the choice of the white voters of the nation. Mississippi, Texas, and Virginia did not take part in the election, and Alabama, Arkansas, and South Carolina were "carried" by the Republicans; yet Grant received a majority of only 300,000. The Democratic victory in New York raised the cry of fraudulent naturalization, but Seymour himself was never unready to contradict the calculations of the Republicans by means of their own figures.

After 1868 Seymour became an elder statesman of the Democratic party, opposing centralization and protection. In the seventies he helped Tilden drive Tweed from power and took part in one of the early efforts to reform Tammany Hall (Alexander, III, 270–71; *N. Y. Times,* Oct. 9, 1871). Tweed, he liked to point out, was the creature of rich men who were too selfish and negligent to share the burden of government (see his article, "The Government of the United States," in the *North American Review,* November-December 1878). In 1876 he was nominated for governor a sixth time, but he forced the state convention to re-assemble and name another candidate. In 1875 he declined to be a candidate for senator and managed the election of Francis Kernan [*q.v.*]. He was a presidential elector in 1876–77, and spoke publicly against the seating of Hayes. It was fear of his influence on his brother-in-law, Roscoe Conkling [*q.v.*], which probably cost the latter a seat on the electoral commission. Although a sunstroke and increasing deafness took him out of public life, he supported Hancock for president in 1880 and lived to see his disciple, Grover Cleveland, in the White House. Among writings of his not already mentioned the following may be cited: *A Lecture on the Topography and History of New York* (1856, reprinted in 1870), evincing his lifelong interest in the geography of his state; "Crime and Tramps," in *Harper's New Monthly Magazine,* December 1878; and "The Influence of New York on American Jurisprudence," in the *Magazine of American History,* April 1879.

Though Seymour denounced the "leprosy of hypocrisy" all his life, his own diffidence about public office laid him open to the charge of insincerity. In manners and appearance he resembled his father, the memory of whose mental breakdown haunted him throughout life; thus the "great decliner," as enemies called him, was earnest in his love of private life, in spite of his power as a public speaker and the dignity and fascination of his presence. George Clinton alone excels him in number of nominations for governor. His name was a tower of strength: twice during the seventies his nephew, Horatio Seymour, Jr., was the only Democrat elected on the state ticket. Seymour's practical failure as a statesman can fairly be attributed to his gentlemanly scorn for extreme opinions. He was, in the genuine sense, a Jeffersonian, for he always insisted on the supreme importance of local government. If his faith in the Democratic party approached religious fervor, he nevertheless made and maintained friendships with distinguished Republicans like Hamilton Fish and Andrew D. White. Yet, wide as were his cultural interests, he never visited Europe, and, aside from trips to conventions and campaigns, he made only one extensive tour of the United States. His opposition to prohibition caused this respectable "teetotaling" Episcopalian to be charged with drunkenness; attacks of dyspepsia were said to be insanity. Yet Seymour, always outwardly serene, liked to remark that the longer he observed men the less he thought of their heads, and the better he thought of their hearts. None of his bitter enemies, it is significant to notice, ever knew him.

[The chief manuscript sources are the Horatio Seymour Papers and Scrap Books, an extensive collection in the State Library, Albany, N. Y.; and a collection of letters and notes in N. Y. Hist. Soc. Better than the two campaign biographies, J. D. McCabe, Jr., *The Life and Public Services of Horatio Seymour* (1868), and D. G. Croly, *Seymour and Blair* (1868), is the *Public Record . . . of Horatio Seymour* (1868), a careful compilation of his speeches and papers from 1856 to the spring of 1868, ed. by T. M. Cook and T. W. Knox. This volume, largely financed by August Belmont and Tilden, is one of the earliest examples of a reliable campaign textbook. A. J. Wall, *A Sketch of the Life of Horatio Seymour, 1810–1886* (1929), with bibliography of his speeches and articles; and C. H. Coleman, *The Election of 1868* (1933) are valuable studies of Seymour's character and career. See also Stewart Mitchell, "Horatio Seymour of New York: A Political Biography," a doctoral dissertation in the Harvard Coll. Lib.; C. Z. Lincoln, *State of N. Y. Messages from the Governors,* vol. V (1909); D. S. Alexander, *A Pol. Hist. of the State of N. Y.,* vols. II, III (1906–09); S. D. Brummer, *Pol. Hist. of N. Y. State During the Period of the Civil War* (1911). An excellent collection of pictures of Seymour is in the N. Y. Hist. Soc. The portrait commonly published is very poor.]
S. M.

SEYMOUR, HORATIO WINSLOW (1854–Dec. 17, 1920), editor, was born in Cayuga County, N. Y. His parents, Andrew

Milliken and Louisa Maria (Goodyear) Seymour soon removed to the state of Wisconsin, where, in the public schools of Racine, the boy received his early education and where he met Annie E. Jones to whom he was married in 1876. After serving an apprenticeship in Racine as a printer, he served as a reporter, city editor, and news editor of the *Milwaukee Daily News.* While connected with the *Milwaukee Daily News* his work attracted the attention of Wilbur Storey [*q.v.*], who offered him a position with the *Chicago Times,* then a radical Democratic newspaper. From 1875 until 1879 Seymour was telegraph editor, and from the latter date until 1883 he served as night editor of the Storey paper. While on the *Chicago Times* he wrote the headline "Jerked to Jesus" concerning the hanging of a religiously fanatical negro. Severing his connection with the *Times* he immediately became connected with the *Chicago Herald* and held the position of editor and managing editor until 1895. Under the direction of James W. Scott [*q.v.*], one of the owners, and Seymour, the *Herald* became an independent Democratic paper and enjoyed growing prosperity and an enviable reputation. Seymour's editorials gave him distinction as an expert on the tariff. Among the more important of his editorials that gained national fame were those attacking the protectionist policies of the Republican party. Among them were "Protectionism Exposed and Doomed," "Pauperizing and Brutalizing Labor," "Coining Money out of Blood," "Monopoly-Ridden Agriculture," and "Republicanism and Robbery," which with twenty-two others he wrote during the campaign of 1892 were published as *The Chicago Herald, Editorials that Won* (copr. 1892). In all of them he advanced the doctrine of competitive tariffs and advocated revision downward. In 1895 he became editor and publisher of the *Chicago Chronicle,* owned by John R. Walsh, with which he remained until 1907. In that year, with the crash of several of Walsh's banks, owing to the panic, the *Chronicle* was suspended, and Seymour went to New York City as editorial writer and supervisor of the *World.* He served for ten months as editor of the *St. Louis Republic,* and then returned in 1912 as editorial contributor for the *World.*

He was the author of one book, *Government and Co., Limited* (1895), which dealt with his ideas of free trade and democratic government. In both the campaigns of 1892 and 1896 he was active in attacking the hard money and high tariff policies of the Republican party, and he assumed a position of leadership in the western states. Among his colleagues he was noted for his new and startling use of headlines, a feature that found its way into many papers throughout the nation. He died in New York City.

[*Chicago Herald and Examiner, Chicago Daily Tribune, N. Y. Times,* Dec. 18, 1920; *Who's Who in America,* 1918–19; Eugen Seeger, *Chicago, the Wonder City* (1893); *A Hist. of the City of Chicago* (1900).]

T. E. S.

SEYMOUR, THOMAS DAY (Apr. 1, 1848–Dec. 31, 1907), classicist, was born in Hudson, Ohio, the son of Nathan Perkins and Elizabeth (Day) Seymour. He was a direct descendant of Richard Seymour (or Seamer) who came from England to Hartford, Conn., in 1639; on his mother's side he was the grandson of Thomas Day of Hartford, secretary of state in Connecticut for twenty-five years. His great uncle was Jeremiah Day [*q.v.*], president of Yale College. Thomas Seymour grew up in the college atmosphere of Western Reserve, where his father's home was on the New England Green which served Hudson and the College as a reminder of their origin. His father was a professor of Greek and Latin. Seymour matriculated at Western Reserve in 1866 and graduated with the degree of bachelor of arts in 1870, being given at the same time the unusual distinction of an honorary B.A. by Yale. He was valedictorian of his class and something of a leader both in social and literary affairs. Music, however, was his greatest interest outside the curriculum, and to the development of musical activities in the college he made a permanent contribution.

Nathan Seymour resigned his professorship in 1870 and the work he had been conducting was divided. Thomas was elected professor of Greek with leave of absence for two years to study in Europe in preparation for the position. These two years were spent at Leipzig, Berlin, and Athens, and during this period he developed still further a remarkable power of concentration which was his throughout life. He began his service at Western Reserve in the fall of 1872. On July 2, 1874, he married Sarah Melissa, daughter of Henry L. Hitchcock, the president of Western Reserve; they had three children. In 1880 he was called to a professorship of Greek in Yale College, which he held until his death. He taught a wide range of courses in Greek literature to the undergraduates and took an important part in developing the graduate school. He was always actively interested in the American schools for classical studies at Athens and at Rome and played a large rôle in their foundation and development. He was chairman of the managing committee of the school at Athens from 1887 to 1901, the period during which it attained real importance and recognition from the scholars of other nations. In 1903 he was elected president of the Archæological Institute of America, which position he held until his death. He was active in the American Philological Association and its president in 1888–89, was an honorary member of the Archæological Society of Athens, to which he was elected in 1895, and in 1900 was made an associate fellow of the American Academy of Arts and Sciences. He died in New Haven, Conn.

Throughout the years of his professional activity his leading interests were the fostering of the undergraduate life of the college, the development and strengthening of the graduate work of the University in his own field, and the furthering of the closely allied activities of the Archæological Institute and the American School at Athens. In all three fields he was distinctly a leader. Publication was to him rather a means of serving his ends in these directions than an end in itself. Instead of publishing all the material that he gathered and all of his original interpretations of classical texts, he used them in his teaching or to help others to publish, while he spent himself in gathering more knowledge, producing more scholars, and improving the conditions under which classical scholars develop. His own most notable publication was *Life in the Homeric Age* (1907), an exhaustive presentation of the body of evidence presented in the Iliad and the Odyssey. It is a masterpiece of thoroughness and clarity. He edited *Selected Odes of Pindar* in 1882 and published his *Introduction to the Language and Verse of Homer* in 1885. He was for many years one of the editors of Ginn & Company's College Series of Greek Authors and himself prepared a number of the volumes. He was an editor, also, of the *Classical Review*. An excursion which he made into the field of genealogy resulted in *The Family of the Rev. Jeremiah Day,* published in 1900.

[J. W. White, *Thomas Day Seymour, 1848–1907, Memorial Address* (1908) ; *Who's Who in America,* 1906–07 ; Yale Univ. records ; *Nation,* Jan. 9, 1908 ; *Am. Jour. of Archæology,* Jan.-Mar. 1908 ; *Classical Jour.,* Feb. 1908 ; *Classical Philology,* Apr. 1908 ; personal acquaintance.]   C. W. M–l.

SEYMOUR, THOMAS HART (Sept. 29, 1807–Sept. 3, 1868), governor of Connecticut, congressman, minister to Russia, was born in Hartford, Conn., the only child of Maj. Henry and Jane (Ellery) Seymour. His father, a broker of means and a man of liberal education, was descended from Richard Seymour (or Seamer) who settled in Hartford in 1639, while his mother was descended from William Ellery of Gloucester, Mass., whose grandson had come to Hartford about 1742. Both families were so-cially prominent and noted for their military spirit. After some schooling in Hartford, Thomas was sent to Capt. Alden Partridge's military academy at Middletown, Conn., from which he graduated in 1829. Subsequently, he studied law in Hartford and was admitted to the bar in 1833, but as he was too active by nature to settle down to the routine of the profession it was not until 1839 that he appeared on the register of practising attorneys.

Meanwhile he interested himself in politics and military affairs, becoming an active member of the Hartford Light Guard and serving as its commander from 1837 to 1841. When the Democrats came into power in 1836, he was elected probate judge for the Hartford district, and showed both legal and political acumen during the three years that he held office. In 1837 and 1838 he also edited the *Jeffersonian,* and in 1842 was clerk of the superior court. Elected to the Twenty-eighth Congress (1843–45), he was as active on the floor of the House as any of his age and standing. Though renominated by his party in 1844 he declined to run and returned to Hartford.

With the advent of the Mexican War, he again became active in military affairs. In 1847 he sailed with General Scott's forces to Vera Cruz as a major of Connecticut Volunteers. On Apr. 9, he was commissioned a major in the 9th United States Infantry, and on Aug. 12, lieutenant-colonel of the 12th Infantry. In the battle of Chapultepec he led his regiment after its commander had fallen, and, with his command, was first to enter the fortress. For gallant and meritorious service in this engagement he was brevetted colonel on Sept. 13, 1847.

Acclaimed for his part in the campaign, he was nominated for governor of Connecticut in 1849, but failed of election by a small margin. He was chosen, however, in 1850 and in 1851, when the elections were thrown into the legislature, and in each of the two years following he was re-elected by popular vote. He resigned in April 1853, the month after his fourth election, since, as a reward for his active support of Pierce in the presidential election of 1852, he had been tendered the appointment as minister to Russia, but he did not relinquish the governorship until Oct. 13, and did not sail for his post until Dec. 24. His duties at St. Petersburg were neither onerous nor difficult, and after four years of residence there he resigned in 1858, toured the Continent for nearly a year, and then returned to Hartford. His years abroad had separated him from events at home and from anti-slavery propaganda. His sympathies had turned toward the

South and he thus became the leader of the Connecticut Peace Democrats. When feeling became extreme in 1862, the Connecticut Senate voted to remove his portrait until his loyalty to the Union should be affirmed. He ran for governor in 1863, but defeat was inevitable. At the National Democratic Convention at Chicago in 1864 he received thirty-eight votes on the first ballot for the presidential nomination. He died, unmarried, in Hartford four years later, and was buried there in Cedar Hill Cemetery. Throughout his life he was noted for his courtesy and his military bearing.

[F. C. Norton, *The Governors of Conn.* (1905), first printed in the *Conn. Mag.*, ser. of 1902, vol. VII, nos. 3–4; Forrest Morgan, *Conn. as a Colony and as a State* (1904), vols. III, IV; J. H. Trumbull, *The Memorial Hist. of Hartford County, Conn.* (1886), vol. I; S. F. Bemis, *The Am. Secretaries of State and Their Diplomacy*, vol. VI (1928); *Biog. Dir. Am. Cong.* (1928); F. B. Heitman, *Hist. Reg. and Dict. U. S. Army* (1903).]   W. G. L.

SEYMOUR, TRUMAN (Sept. 24, 1824–Oct. 30, 1891), soldier, was born in Burlington, Vt., the son of Truman and Ann (Armstrong) Seymour. His father was a Methodist minister. After two years, 1840–42, at Norwich University he was appointed a cadet in the United States Military Academy; he was graduated and appointed brevet second lieutenant, 1st Artillery, July 1, 1846. He served with distinction in the Mexican War and received the brevets of first lieutenant and captain for gallant and meritorious conduct at Cerro Gordo, Contreras, and Churubusco. From 1850–53 he was assistant professor of drawing at West Point. During this period he was married to Louisa, daughter of Robert W. Weir, professor of drawing at the academy. Rejoining his regiment at Fort Moultrie, S. C., he participated in the operations against the Seminole Indians in Florida, 1856–58.

As captain of artillery he took part in the defense of Fort Sumter, and was brevetted major for gallant conduct. He commanded a training camp at Harrisburg, Pa., in the autumn of 1861, served in the defenses of Washington as regimental commander and divisional chief of artillery, and was appointed brigadier-general of volunteers on Apr. 28, 1862. In the Peninsular campaign, he was engaged at Mechanicsville, bore an important part in the defensive battle at Beaver Dam Creek, and skillfully covered the withdrawal to Gaines's Mill. He commanded a division at Malvern Hill, was engaged at Manassas, at South Mountain executed the decisive enveloping movement, and at Antietam led the advance of Hooker's corps in opening that battle. He was brevetted lieutenant-colonel and colonel of the regular army for gallantry at South Mountain and Antietam respectively. Transferred in November 1862 to the Department of the South, he commanded the assaulting column in the unsuccessful attack on Battery Wagner, Charleston harbor, July 18, 1863, and was severely wounded. Early in 1864 he was placed in command of the expedition to Florida and on Feb. 20 was badly defeated near Olustee Station. On May 5, having been relieved and ordered north, he took command of a brigade of Sedgwick's corps during the battle of the Wilderness, and on the following day he was taken prisoner. Because of his kindness to Confederate wounded after Antietam President Davis directed that provision be made for his comfort. The order, however, was not fulfilled; Seymour was exposed, as a retaliatory measure, to the fire of the Federal batteries bombarding Charleston and was otherwise harshly treated (*War of the Rebellion: Official Records, Army*, 1 ser., vol. XXXV, pt. 2, p. 164; 2 ser., vol. VII, pp. 135, 185, 571). Exchanged on Aug. 9, 1864, he commanded a division of the VI Corps in the operations in the Shenandoah Valley during November and December 1864, in the Richmond campaign, and in the siege of Petersburg. He handled his division at the battle of Sailor's Creek, Apr. 6, 1865, with an energy and ability that won the commendation of General Sheridan. He was present at the capitulation of General Lee. He received three brevet commissions dated Mar. 13, 1865, as major-general of volunteers, and brigadier- and major-general, United States army. After the war he reverted to his regular army rank of major of the 5th Artillery, and served in command of various posts along the Atlantic coast. After he was retired from active service at his own request, Nov. 1, 1876, he lived at Florence, Italy, where he died, survived by his wife. He was an artist of considerable talent. Brave and steady as a leader, he was modest and unaggressive in the promotion of his own ambitions. He won the regard of his subordinates by uniform courtesy and unfailing care for their welfare. He was, however, a man of strong prejudices with a tendency to impulsive action, which retarded the advancement his training, experience, and devotion would otherwise have merited.

[G. M. Dodge and W. A. Ellis, *Norwich Univ., 1819–1911* (1911), vol. II; *Twenty-third Ann. Reunion, Assoc. Grads. of U. S. Mil. Acad.*, 1892; W. L. Haskin, *The Hist. of the First Regiment of Artillery* (1879); G. W. Cullum, *Biog. Reg. Officers and Grads. U. S. Mil. Acad.*, vol. II (1891); *War of the Rebellion: Official Records* (*Army*); obituaries in *Army and Navy Jour.*, Nov. 7, 1891, and *N. Y. Times*, Nov. 5, 1891; unpublished records of the War Department, 1840–91.]   T. F. M.

SEYMOUR, WILLIAM (Dec. 19, 1855–Oct. 2, 1933), actor, stage director, theatre manager, was born in New York City, the son of James Cunningham, who had changed his name to Seymour when he ran away from his home in Belfast, Ireland, to become an actor. He came to America in 1849 and acquired a high reputation as a comedian, his adopted name having since been retained by all members of his family. In the same year he married Lydia Eliza Griffiths of Philadelphia, who acted under the name of Mrs. Seymour for some thirty years thereafter. In 1857 in New Orleans the infant William made his first appearance on the stage in his mother's arms. His first speaking part was on his seventh birthday in *To Parents and Guardians*; afterwards he appeared occasionally with visiting stars. During this period he was receiving an elementary education in the New Orleans schools.

Returning to New York in 1865 with his mother (his father had died in 1864), he later was engaged at Booth's Theatre, being cast for the Player Queen in *Hamlet* and other rôles. After two seasons there, he went to the Globe Theatre in Boston in the fall of 1871, and on Apr. 2, 1872, he acted François in *Richelieu* with Edwin Forrest [*q.v.*] on that actor's last appearance on the stage. Following engagements at the Union Square Theatre in New York, with Lawrence Barrett on tour, with John McCullough [*qq.v.*] in San Francisco, and other actors, he joined the stock company at the Boston Museum in August 1879 where he remained for ten seasons, acting an occasional part such as the First Grave Digger in *Hamlet*. In 1889, after brief engagements in New York and elsewhere, he became house manager of the newly opened Tremont Theatre in Boston, where he remained until 1897, when he went on tour with Sol Smith Russell [*q.v.*]. He was manager of the Metropolitan Opera House, New York, in 1900–01, and in 1904 he joined the forces of Charles Frohman [*q.v.*], remaining with him for years as general stage director, actor, and historian. During his later years he lived in semi-retirement at South Duxbury, Mass., where he had long maintained a summer home, going thence frequently to Boston and New York to engage temporarily in such activities as a tour with George Arliss as actor and stage director, to appear in the all-star production of *The Two Orphans* in 1925–26, and to serve as stage director of the annual productions of the Players Club.

During many years his friends received a cordial welcome at South Duxbury and had the pleasure of looking over his notable collection of books, autograph letters, manuscripts, playbills, and other memorabilia. He was an efficient actor and an able producer of plays, whose training led many actors to success. He was of short stature and portly figure, a genial companion whose conversation was delightful and whose devotion to his family was one among his many admirable traits. On Jan. 8, 1882, he married May Davenport, daughter of Edward Loomis Davenport and younger sister of Fanny Lily Gypsy Davenport [*qq.v.*]. She had a brief career as an actress in the Boston Museum Stock Company and elsewhere, and died suddenly in New York in 1927. He died after a brief illness at the Jordan Hospital in Plymouth, Mass. Of their five children only one permanently adopted the family profession.

[M. J. Moses, *Famous Actor-Families in America* (1906) ; *Who's Who in America*, 1928–29 ; *Who's Who in the Theatre*, 1933 ; J. B. Clapp and E. F. Edgett, *Players of the Present*, pt. III (1901) ; Kate Ryan, *Old Museum Days* (1915) ; *N. Y. Dram. Mirror*, Dec. 24, 1898 ; *Boston Daily Globe*, Aug. 16, 1923 ; *Boston Herald*, Jan. 21, 1929 ; H. I. Jackson, in book section, *Boston Transcript*, Jan. 10, 17, 1931 ; obituaries in *Boston Transcript*, *N. Y. Times*, Oct. 3, 1933, and *Boston Herald*, *N. Y. Herald Tribune*, Oct. 4, 1933 ; personal acquaintance ; information from Seymour's daughter, Mrs. May Davenport Seymour Eckert, who is the authority for the spelling of Lydia Eliza Griffiths' surname.]
E. F. E.

SHABONEE (*c.* 1775–July 1859), Potawatomi chief, was born into the Ottawa tribe, possibly near the Maumee River in what is now the state of Ohio. It is said that his father was a nephew of Pontiac [*q.v.*]. His name was spelled variously as Shabbona, Shabonee, Shobonier, Shaubena, and sometimes Chambler or Chambly. It seems to have been pronounced in two syllables with the accent on the first, as though spelled Shabney. He married the daughter of a Potawatomi chief and on the death of the old chief succeeded to his place of influence in that tribe. For a time he lived in a Potawatomi village on the Illinois River near the mouth of the Fox but soon removed to a place that became known as Shabbona Grove, now in southern Dekalb County, Ill. About 1807 he became attached to the rising power of Tecumseh [*q.v.*], in 1810 went with the leader to visit the Indian villages in the northern Illinois country and on the Wisconsin River, and the next year accompanied him south to try to persuade the southern tribes to join the confederation. When war was declared between Great Britain and the United States he was loath to join in the bloody business of killing and scalping American settlers and, with Sauganash [*q.v.*], was active in saving the lives of the family of John Kinzie [*q.v.*] and others in the Chicago massacre of August 1812 ; but he fought at Tecumseh's side in the battle of the Thames.

After the War of 1812 he never wavered in his allegiance to the government of the United States and in various ways rendered important aid to the settlers. In the Winnebago outbreak of 1827 he opposed the desire of Big Foot and other Potawatomi to join the Winnebago, was made prisoner at Big Foot's Lake, now Geneva Lake, Wis., and narrowly escaped death in his efforts to protect the American settlers. When Black Hawk undertook active opposition to white encroachment in 1832, Shabonee again protected the settlers. He sent his son and nephew to warn the settlers at Holderman's Grove and on the Fox River, and himself set out on a desperate ride to the settlements near Bureau and Indian creeks. For this exploit the descendants of the settlers raised a monument in 1903 and in 1906 set aside a park to his memory, but in his own lifetime his reward was neglect and poverty. Although the treaties of July 29, 1829, and Sept. 26, 1833, seemed to grant him two sections of land at his own village, he became involved in technicalities of the white man's law of ownership and lost his lands to encroaching settlers. However, a small group of settlers bought for him a small farm in Grundy County, Ill. There in his old age he ate the bitter bread of charity and pondered on the white man's gratitude.

[G. S. Hubbard, "Addresses Delivered . . . 1868 . . . Sketches of . . . Shabonee," *Fergus' Hist. Series*, no. 10 (1877); L. A. Hatch, *The Indian Chief Shabbona* (1915); N. B. Wood, *Lives of Famous Indian Chiefs* (copr. 1906); Nehemiah Matson, *Memories of Shaubena* (1878); *Wis. State Hist. Soc. Colls.*, vol. VII (1876); *Ill. State Hist. Lib. Pubs.*, no. 12 (1908); H. L. Boies, *Hist. of De Kalb County, Ill.* (1868); *The Public Statutes at Large of the U. S.*, vol. VII (1846); *Niles' Weekly Register*, Sept. 15, 1827.] K. E. C.

SHAFER, HELEN ALMIRA (Sept. 23, 1839–Jan. 20, 1894), educator and college president, was born in Newark, N. J., the daughter of Archibald and Almira (Miller) Shafer. In her girlhood, her father, a Congregational minister of Scotch and German ancestry, moved with his family to Ohio, and Helen entered Oberlin College, where she was graduated in 1863. After two years of teaching in New Jersey, she went to St. Louis, Mo., as teacher of mathematics under William Torrey Harris [q.v.], then superintendent of the St. Louis public schools and later United States commissioner of education. In 1877, her ability and distinction as a teacher of mathematics fully established, she was offered the chair of mathematics at Wellesley, two years after the founding of the college. The department of mathematics was hers to create, and under her leadership it became one of the strongest in the college. When as yet no adequate text-

books existed in English, she gave courses in the history of geometry and in determinants, Wellesley being one of the first colleges to offer such work. In her scholarship, as later in her administrative work, there was a masculine strain; justice, integrity, intellectual vision, and practical insight were her outstanding qualities.

In 1888 she succeeded to the presidency of the college. The administration of her predecessor, Alice Elvira Freeman Palmer [q.v.], had been brilliant, and in its nature extensive. Helen Shafer's work as scholar and administrator was intensive. Under her stimulus and guidance the curriculum was completely remodeled, the requirements for admission were altered to meet the exigencies of the new plan, and sixty-seven new courses of study were opened to the students. Although there have since been further modifications of the elective system, her work, wise, far-seeing, and modern, was the basis of Wellesley's later academic instruction. But she was no pedant. The social life of the undergraduate gained in dignity and freedom during her term of office; she fostered the beginnings of the college periodicals and furthered the re-establishment of the local Greek-letter societies. In the last ten years of her life she was constantly fighting a tendency to tuberculosis. In 1890–91 she spent a winter in Thomasville, Ga., for her health. Undoubtedly her life might have been prolonged had she chosen to retire, but she gave the college two more years and died at Wellesley of heart failure following upon pneumonia. Tall and slender, with a grave and rather severe exterior, she had the kindliness of a Christian gentlewoman and an unexpected sense of humor. A Scotch keenness of mind and a German thoroughness characterize all her work. The impress of her high standards, wise leadership, and clear vision in the formative years of the college remains a part of its permanent heritage.

[Florence Converse, *The Story of Wellesley* (1915); *Wellesley Mag.*, Feb. 1894; Wellesley Coll. reports, 1888–94; *Boston Transcript*, Jan. 20, 1894.] F. C.

SHAFROTH, JOHN FRANKLIN (June 9, 1854–Feb. 20, 1922), representative, senator, governor of Colorado, was the youngest of the six children of John and Anna (Aull) Shafroth, of Swiss and German birth respectively. He was born at Fayette, Mo., where his father was a merchant. He received his primary education in the Fayette public schools and at Central College, and graduated from the University of Michigan in 1875. He then studied law in the office of Samuel C. Major of Fayette, was admitted to the Missouri bar in 1876, and practised with his preceptor until 1879, when he moved to Denver, Colo.

After some years of private practice here he was chosen city attorney in 1887 and again in 1889. Five years later he was elected to Congress on the Republican ticket. A strong advocate of free coinage of silver, he bolted the Republican National Convention of 1896 and with Senator Henry M. Teller helped found the Silver Republican Party. As a candidate of this party, and indorsed by the Democrats, he was reëlected in 1896 and 1898, and with the disappearance of the Silver Republicans he was again returned in 1900 by the Democrats. His election in 1902 was contested and the ballot boxes were taken to Washington. He requested permission to examine them, found that in certain districts frauds had been committed in behalf of the entire Democratic ticket, and immediately resigned (Feb. 15, 1904), asserting that he would not hold a tainted seat. He was generally praised for this act, which was practically unprecedented. Later that same year he ran again for Congress, but was defeated. While in the House his efforts had been largely devoted to the problems of the West. His battle for the Reclamation Act was successful, though his dream of free silver was not attained. He repeatedly introduced and supported a constitutional amendment for woman's suffrage. He also introduced (Mar. 27, 1897) a resolution to abolish the session of Congress held after the election of the succeeding Congress, popularly known as the "lame duck" session.

In 1908 and again in 1910 he was elected governor of Colorado. In the latter year he called the legislature in special session in an effort to force the enactment of the Democratic platform pledges of the previous year, and it was at that session that the direct primary, initiative, and referendum were adopted. Under him also the Highway Commission was started on its good-roads program. In January 1913 he was chosen by the legislature to the United States Senate, where he supported President Wilson in nearly all matters. He drafted and had charge of the bill providing constitutional government for Puerto Rico. In the Banking and Currency Committee, as a supporter of the President's plan, he helped frame and adopt the Federal Reserve Act. He clashed with the President, however, as he had with President Theodore Roosevelt, on the question of conservation; his speech in the Senate, Mar. 21, 1914, is the classic presentation of the Western viewpoint on that problem (*Congressional Record*, 63 Cong., 2 Sess., pp. 5224–31). During the World War,

with three sons in the service, he stood vigorously by the administration, and at its close became an advocate of the League of Nations. After his defeat for reëlection in 1918, he was for two years administrator of the War Minerals Relief Act.

On Oct. 26, 1881, Shafroth married Virginia Morrison of Fayette, Mo., who exerted a marked influence on his life and character; they had four sons and one daughter. One son and the daughter died before their father, whose death occurred in Denver in his sixty-eighth year.

[Biog. sketch by Senator C. S. Thomas in *Cong. Record*, Feb. 28, 1923 (67 Cong., 4 Sess., pp. 4944–47); Dawson Scrapbooks (State Hist. Soc. of Col.), LXI, 445–95, and LXIV, 21–47; *Portrait and Biog. Record of the State of Col.* (1899); J. C. Smiley, *Semi-Centennial Hist. of the State of Col.* (1913), vol. II; *Who's Who in America*, 1920–21; *Rocky Mountain News* (Denver), Feb. 21, 1922; data from the sons of Senator Shafroth.]   L. R. H.

SHAFTER, WILLIAM RUFUS (Oct. 16, 1835–Nov. 12, 1906), soldier, said to have been the first white male child born in Kalamazoo County, Mich., was the son of Hugh Morris and Eliza (Sumner) Shafter, who went west from Windsor, Vt. He attended the common schools of Galesburg, Mich., and at odd times helped on his father's farm and taught school. In 1861, while attending Prairie Seminary in Richland County, he enlisted for three years' Civil War service, and was commissioned first lieutenant, 7th Michigan Infantry. He took part in the battle of Ball's Bluff on Oct. 21, 1861, and in the Peninsular campaign of 1862. He was brevetted lieutenant-colonel and years later (June 12, 1895) was granted a Medal of Honor for distinguished gallantry at Fair Oaks. He was promoted major, 19th Michigan Infantry, on Sept. 5, 1862, saw service in the affair at Thompson's Station in March 1863, was taken prisoner and exchanged in the following May, and became lieutenant-colonel of his regiment on June 5, 1863. On Apr. 19, 1864, he was appointed colonel, 17th United States Colored Infantry, and took part in the battles of Dec. 15–16, 1864, in front of Nashville. He received, on Mar. 13, 1865, the brevet of brigadier-general of Volunteers. With post-war reorganization, he was assigned to frontier duty with the 24th United States Infantry, Apr. 14, 1869, with the rank of lieutenant-colonel, and ten years later was promoted colonel, 1st Infantry. He became brigadier-general, in 1897, and with the outbreak of the Spanish War was advanced to major-general of Volunteers.

Largely because of his rugged aggressiveness and ability to meet difficult situations, Shafter was given command of the important expeditionary force to Santiago de Cuba, and on Apr. 29, 1898, established his headquarters at Tampa, Fla. On June 14 he sailed for Cuba, with a fleet of thirty-two transports, carrying some 819 officers and 15,058 enlisted men, in addition to teamsters, packers, clerks, and correspondents. A landing was effected at Daiquiri on June 22, the town of Siboney was taken the next day, and the engagement of Las Guasimas was fought June 24. After a more or less hasty reconnaissance of the Spanish defenses in front of the city of Santiago, the main attack was begun against the city, July 1, with a secondary attack by the division of Henry W. Lawton [q.v.] upon the outlying suburb of El Caney. The battle was continued, July 2–3, with considerable loss to the American forces, and on the latter date Shafter demanded of Gen. José Velazquez Toral, the Spanish commander, the surrender of the city. This demand was refused, but owing to the almost total destruction of the Spanish fleet on July 3 Toral formally capitulated July 17. The surrender included some 23,500 combatants. During the armistice that preceded the final negotiations, the morale of the American troops was so seriously impaired by malaria and yellow fever that Shafter considered the advisability of withdrawing his troops to high ground, five miles from the city. However, Aug. 8–25, he embarked some 25,000 men for Montauk Point, L. I., of which about eighty per cent. were ill upon landing in the United States. A man of large size, Shafter was so ill during certain critical days of the Santiago campaign as to be able to maintain contact with his advanced troops only through his staff-officers. Although he was subjected to considerable criticism from the press of the country in regard to alleged deficiencies in subsistence and equipment, much of this may be justly charged to the country's unpreparedness for an overseas expedition in the tropics, and to the world's ignorance of tropical diseases.

In October 1898 Shafter was assigned to command the Department of the East at Governors Island, N. Y., but in a few days was transferred to his old command, the Department of California and Columbia. He remained at San Francisco until retired from active military service as a brigadier-general, Oct. 16, 1899, but retained command under his volunteer commission as a major-general, until June 30, 1901. By a special act of Congress, Feb. 2, 1901, he was advanced to the grade of major-general on the retired list, July 1, 1901. After retirement, he made his home with a daughter, on a ranch near Bakersfield, Cal., where his death occurred on

Nov. 12, 1906, after but a week's illness. His funeral and interment with high military honors took place Nov. 15, 1906, at the Presidio of San Francisco, and was attended by many distinguished persons and representatives of patriotic societies. His wife, Harriet Amelia Grimes, of Athens, Mich., to whom he was married Sept. 11, 1862, had died in 1898. On Aug. 22, 1919, there was unveiled at Galesburg, Mich., a bronze bust of Shafter, erected by the state of Michigan.

[H. H. Sargent, *The Campaign of Santiago de Cuba* (3 vols., 1907) ; Stephen Bonsal, *The Fight for Santiago* (1899) ; J. D. Miley, *In Cuba with Shafter* (1899) ; John Bigelow, *Reminiscences of the Santiago Campaign* (1899) ; George Kennan, *Campaigning in Cuba* (1899) ; S. W. Durant, ed., *Hist. of Kalamazoo County, Mich.* (1880) ; *Michigan History Magazine*, Apr.–July 1920, p. 485 ; *Who's Who in America*, 1906–07 ; *Army and Navy Journal*, Nov. 17, 1906 ; *San Francisco Examiner*, Nov. 13, 1906 ; *San Francisco Call* and *San Francisco Chronicle*, Nov. 13, 16, 1906 ; information supplied by Shafter's daughter, Mrs. Mary Shafter McKittrick, of Los Olivos, Cal., and by Dr. G. N. Fuller, Sec. Mich. Hist. Commission.]   C. D. R.

SHAHAN, THOMAS JOSEPH (Sept. 11, 1857–Mar. 9, 1932), Roman Catholic prelate and educator, was born in Manchester, N. H., to Maurice Peter and Mary Ann (Carmody) Shahan, Irish immigrants of some culture, who amassed a small competence in the mill towns of New England without acquiring a slavish obsequiousness to their "Yankee betters." Trained in the public school of Millbury, Mass., he developed a priestly vocation through association with an uncle, the Rev. Peter Shahan of Norwich, Conn. In the Sulpician College of Montreal, Shahan was thoroughly grounded in philosophy, the classics, and French literature before going to the American College and the Propaganda in Rome, where he won a doctorate in sacred theology in 1882 and was ordained to the priesthood, June 3, 1882. He was a brilliant student of prodigious memory and great versatility. He returned to Connecticut, where as a curate in St. John's Church, New Haven, chancellor of the diocese, and secretary to Bishop L. S. McMahon of Hartford, 1883–88, he obtained experience in ecclesiastical administration and an acquaintance with men and affairs in New England. Though essentially a priest, he took time to delve into the history of the diocese and its immigrant population, and supplied invaluable notes for J. H. O'Donnell's *History of the Diocese of Hartford* (1900). When in 1888 he was invited by Monsignor John Joseph Keane [q.v.] to lecture at the pontifical Catholic University at Washington in church history, Roman law, and patrology, he continued his studies at the Sorbonne and the Catholic Institute in Paris, at the Roman Seminary, which awarded him a licentiate in canon law in 1889, and at the University of Berlin, where he specialized in history and learned German. In 1891 he began his lectures. An enthusiastic and emotional teacher of vivid imagination, generous nature, and broad culture, he made history a living subject for his students. While he emphasized the German seminar method in training students, he was himself an interpretative historian whose religious intensity drove him into apologetic channels and whose Celtic fervor and fancy made his written style somewhat redundant. A voluminous writer of historical and apologetic essays for Catholic magazines over a period of forty years, author of *The Blessed Virgin in the Catacombs* (1892), *The Beginnings of Christianity* (1903), *The Middle Ages* (1904), *St. Patrick in History* (1904), *The House of God* (1905), and translator of Otto Bardenhewer's *Patrology; the Lives and Works of the Fathers of the Church* (1908), he exercised considerable influence over American Catholic thought. As a founder and an editor of the *Catholic Encyclopedia* (1907–13) to which he contributed over two hundred articles, he became known to Catholic scholars the world over.

In 1909 he was appointed a domestic prelate of the pontifical court and rector of the Catholic University. Five years later he was consecrated titular bishop of Germanicopolis, and in February 1928 he was named an assistant to the papal throne by Pius XI, with whom he had labored in the Roman archives. As head of the university, he was paternalistic but tactful; he led a harmonious, self-sacrificing faculty, protected freedom of teaching, maintained the principle of security of tenure, and popularized the university in critical circles. His vision was of a national medieval university, enriched by modern methods and science, and energized by American influences and rivalries, which should be a center for national Catholic activities and for a revival of Catholic culture. Yet he had a certain Puritan shrewdness about him. During his régime, the faculty increased fourfold; the endowment was raised to over $3,000,000; superior departments of theology, canon law, and Oriental studies were fostered; several buildings were constructed; and a score of religious communities were encouraged to establish houses of study near the university. He may be considered one of the founders or promoters of the Catholic Sisters' College, of the original summer school for teaching nuns (1913), of the Shrine of the Immaculate Conception in whose crypt he has found his tomb, of the Catholic Educational Association (1904), of the National Conference of

Catholic Charities (1910), of the American Catholic Historical Association (1917), and of the International Federation of Catholic Alumnae. With his assistance the *Catholic University Bulletin*, a literary magazine he had founded and edited, 1895–1909, gave way to the *Catholic Educational Review* (1911), the *Catholic Charities Review* (1917), the *Catholic Historical Review* (1915), and the *New Scholasticism* (1927). In 1928, having left an indelible mark on the cultural life of the Catholic Church in America, he retired from the rectorship to a quiet retreat at Holy Cross Academy.

[Ann. Reports of the Rector of Cath. Univ., 1909–28; files of *Cath. Univ. Bull.*, 1895–1909; *The Cath. Encyc. and Its Makers* (1917); *Am. Cath. Who's Who*, 1911; *Who's Who in America*, 1932–33; Speer Strahan, *The Spirit of Bishop Shahan* (1932) of which a part is printed in *Commonweal*, June 1, 1932; *Baltimore Cath. Rev.*, Mar. 11, 18, 1932; *Cath. Transcript* (Hartford), Mar. 1932; *Cath. Charities Rev.*, Apr. 1932, the *Cath. Educ. Rev.*, Apr., May 1932; *Cath. World*, Apr. 1932; obituary in *Evening Star* (Washington, D. C.), Mar. 9, 1932; personal information.]

R. J. P.

SHAIKEWITZ, NAHUM MEIR [See SCHOMER, NAHUM MEIR, 1849–1905].

SHAKALLAMY [See SHIKELLAMY, d. 1748].

SHALER, NATHANIEL SOUTHGATE (Feb. 20, 1841–Apr. 10, 1906), geologist, educator, was born at Newport, Ky., the second child of Nathaniel Burger and Ann Hinde (Southgate) Shaler. An elder brother had died in infancy; three younger children lived to maturity. The father, son of a Connecticut sea-captain and nephew of William Shaler [*q.v.*], was a graduate of Harvard College and Medical School; the mother was the daughter of a Virginian who had built up a comfortable estate in Kentucky through the practice of law and the purchase of land.

Because Nathaniel was a frail child he had little formal schooling but spent most of his time out-of-doors with imaginary companions or with older people. He was familiar with the life of the village and of the military post at Newport, and from contact with people of all degrees gained considerable acquaintance with human nature; his father encouraged his interest in plants and animals; his grandfather Southgate, during the child's long visits on Sunday afternoons, gave him "counsel and instruction," and a certain guidance in interpreting the things he saw. After he was ten he acquired the rudiments of Latin and mathematics in the garrison school, took drawing lessons from a master in Cincinnati, and a little later received a thorough training in the use of sword and pistol. In his middle teens, a German clergyman stored his receptive mind with the Greek and Latin classics, introduced him to the philosophy of Hegel and Kant, and developed in him "a way of looking . . . upon the doings of men with an amused interest which kept me then and ever since much in the attitude of spectator" (*Autobiography, post,* p. 209). Mentally mature for his years but unsystematically schooled, he was sent at seventeen to Cambridge to be prepared for Harvard College. Here he resented being required to memorize rules for scanning the Latin verse he loved, and turning away from the humanities enrolled in 1859 in the Lawrence Scientific School as a student of geology and zoölogy under Agassiz. He was a favorite pupil of Agassiz, to whom throughout his life he was devoted, although after graduation he soon broke away from his preceptor's anti-Darwinianism to uphold the theory of evolution. Mentally stimulated, and with "the inquiring motive" planted in him for all time, he took the degree of B.S. *summa cum laude* in 1862.

After two years in the Union army as captain of the 5th Kentucky Battery, his health gave way and he returned to Cambridge. In 1862 he had married Sophia Penn Page, whom he had known since childhood. For two years he was assistant to Agassiz in paleontology, then spent nearly two years abroad in study and exploration. In 1868 he returned to Harvard as lecturer and the next year was made professor of paleontology; in 1888 his title was changed to professor of geology. From 1891 until his death he was also dean of the Lawrence Scientific School.

In his nearly forty years of teaching at Harvard, Shaler left an impression upon thousands of students. His elementary course, "Geology 4," was one of the most popular in the University. His teaching "was as a rule more broadening and inspiring than minutely systematic and instructive" (Davis and Daly, *post,* p. 319). Like his master Agassiz, he had a broad conception of the purpose of science study, and was more concerned with awakening the student's mind than with imparting information. He conducted a summer school of geology in 1875 and 1876 at "Camp Harvard" in Cumberland Gap and subsequently, as director, was instrumental in developing the Harvard summer school at Cambridge. As dean, he revivified the Lawrence Scientific School which had been overshadowed by the development of the College, secured the bequest (1903) from Gordon McKay [*q.v.*] for the teaching of applied science, and fought (1904–05) the proposed merger with Massachusetts Institute of Technology. He took a keen personal interest in individual problems of the students under his care; he made a practice of visiting the infirmary, often gave financial aid, and was never too busy to receive, at home or office, a student seeking encouragement or counsel.

Characterized by William James as a "myriad-minded and multiple-personalitied embodiment of academic and extra-academic matters" (Davis and Daly, p. 320), Shaler had many activities outside the University. From 1874 to 1880 he was state geologist of Kentucky, spending most of his summer vacations with parties of students in the field. He was a member of Massachusetts state commissions on a topographic survey, the destruction of the gypsy moth, the development of a metropolitan park system, and the building of state highways; he established one of the first laboratories in the country for testing road materials. From 1884 to 1900 he was in charge of the Atlantic Coast Division of the United States Geological Survey, and in this connection traveled almost the whole length of the coast from Maine to Florida on foot. He was called into consultation in a number of mining ventures; on the basis of personal investigation advised Gordon McKay in his investments in mining properties, and himself was president of the Conroy mine in Montana.

Throughout his life Shaler was handicapped by frequent headaches, and his health was at no time robust; nevertheless, he was incessantly active. In the intervals between lectures, field trips, and the performance of administrative duties, he wrote prolifically, producing "books and essays on many subjects, in which his exceptional powers of observation, reflection, and imagination were blended" (Davis and Daly, p. 320). Besides the reports published by the Kentucky Survey, the United States Geological Survey, and the Museum of Comparative Zoölogy at Harvard, he contributed to the *Atlantic Monthly, Scribner's,* and many other periodical papers on "earthquakes, whales, the moon, climate, hurricanes, metal-mining, floods, red sunsets, altruism, the silver question," dreams, the negro problem, and other topics. He published *A First Book in Geology* (1884), *Aspects of the Earth* (1889), and a number of popular volumes on geological subjects. Most notable of his nongeological writings is a history, *Kentucky: A Pioneer Commonwealth* (copr. 1884), in the American Commonwealths series. Other titles which suggest the range of his interests are *Thoughts on the Nature of Intellectual Property* (1878); *The Interpretation of Nature* (1893), lectures delivered at Andover Theological Seminary; *Domesticated Animals: Their Relation to Man* (1895); *The Individual: A Study of Life* and Death (1900); *The Neighbor: The Natural History of Human Contacts* (1904); *The Citizen: A Study of the Individual and the Government* (1904); *Man and the Earth* (1905), an attempt to forecast the future from a study of the past. As a test of the theory, which he challenged, that scientific study impairs the imaginative faculty, he wrote *Elizabeth of England* (5 vols., 1903), a series of five romantic dramas in blank verse. A collection, *From Old Fields; Poems of the Civil War* (1906), was published after his death.

Shaler was thoroughly human. A ready speaker and brilliant conversationalist with a strong sense of humor, at times nervous and irascible, occasionally blunt and outspoken, he was generous of spirit and kind in his dealings, and was universally liked and respected. "In appearance he was striking . . . tall and well-proportioned, neither slender nor stout, . . . with erect, active carriage" (Wolff, *post*, p. 597). "If he hears you call him old man," said one of his students, "he'll walk your d—d legs off" (Memoir, in *Autobiography*, p. 369). In his later years, from the nervous intensity of his life at Cambridge he escaped at intervals to his "alleged farm" on Martha's Vineyard, where he found relaxation in exterminating field thistles with a hoe. Although he planned to retire from teaching and to write in this loved retreat, he died in harness, of pneumonia following an operation for appendicitis. His widow and two married daughters survived him.

[*Autobiography of Nathaniel Southgate Shaler with a Supplementary Memoir by His Wife* (1909); J. E. Wolff, in *Bull. Geol. Soc. of America,* vol. XVIII (1907), with extensive bibliog.; W. R. Thayer, in *Harvard Grads. Mag.,* Sept. 1906; *Science,* June 8, 1906; *Nature* (London), July 5, 1906; W. M. Davis and R. A. Daly, "Geology and Geography, 1858–1928," and other references, in *The Development of Harvard University . . . 1869–1929* (1930), ed. by S. E. Morison; G. P. Merrill, *The First One Hundred Years of Am. Geol.* (1924); *Boston Transcript,* Apr. 10, 1906.]

G. P. M.
E. R. D.

SHALER, WILLIAM (*c.* 1773–Mar. 29, 1833), sea captain, consul, and author, was born in Bridgeport, Conn., the son of Sibbel (Warner) and Capt. Timothy Shaler, who commanded the sloop *Lyon,* a privateer during the American Revolution (L. F. Middlebrook, *History of Maritime Connecticut During the American Revolution,* 1925, vol. II, p. 148). He first appears in 1800 in Mauritius, where he met Richard Jeffry Cleveland [*q.v.*] and sailed with him to Copenhagen as partner in a venture to sell coffee. At Copenhagen they purchased the *Lelia Byrd,* a brig of Portsmouth, Va., of which, by a toss of a coin, Shaler became captain. After vari-

ous adventures in South America, they bought furs for the China trade in Mexico and on the Pacific coast of North America, and reached Canton in 1803. Returning alone in 1804 to collect more furs, Shaler visited the Hawaiian Islands and gained the confidence of the brilliant native king, Kamehameha I, whom he aided in negotiating the peaceful annexation of the last independent island of the archipelago. Having sold his brig to the king, he freighted his furs on another vessel, which took him to Canton as a passenger. His "Journal of a Voyage Between China and the North-Western Coast of America" (published in the *American Register,* vol. III, 1808, pp. 137–75) gives a valuable account of his experiences and observations during more than a year of trading with Indians and Spaniards.

During the summer of 1810 he was appointed consul and agent for commerce and seamen at Havana, whither he went in September; in January 1812, he left Havana for Louisiana and Natchitoches as an official agent to report on the filibustering activities of the Mexican revolutionist, Alvarez de Toledo. He returned to New York in February 1814 and in August made a journey to Ghent, having been commissioned by President Madison to attend as observer any general European peace congress. When a quarrel arose between Henry Clay and John Quincy Adams over his function, he returned disgustedly to America in December. As joint commissioner with Commodore Stephen Decatur, 1779–1820 [*q.v.*], to negotiate a peace with Algiers, he set sail from New York in May 1815 with the squadron which Decatur was taking to chastise that state for declaring war on the United States in 1812. The American commissioners secured at the cannon's mouth the most liberal treaty ever made with Algiers by a Christian power, and Shaler immediately went ashore as consul general. The treaty of 1815 remained in force until December 1816; on Dec. 23, though the Dey wished to renew the treaty of 1795, by which the United States paid tribute, he was forced to accept the American terms and signed a treaty embodying the provisions of the treaty of 1815. After this, though he had a leave of absence from April 1821 to the summer of 1822, Shaler remained at Algiers for twelve years, enjoying great prestige with both foreigners and natives. He wrote an article, "On the Language, Manners, and Customs of the Berbers, or Brebers, of Africa" (*Transactions of the American Philosophical Society,* vol. II, n.s., 1825), and in 1826 he published *Sketches of Algiers,* a volume which contains his remarkably accurate observations of the country, its government, and its history during his residence there; the book is said to have served as guide to the French expedition of 1830. In 1828 he visited the United States on account of ill health, and resigned the Algiers consulate to accept appointment, confirmed Mar. 29, 1830, to that at Havana, where, being a bachelor, he lived with R. J. Cleveland and his wife until he died of cholera in an epidemic. A man of "superior talents, . . . calm dignity of manner, and immoveable firmness" (A. S. Mackenzie, *The Life of Commodore Oliver H. Perry*, 1840, vol. II, p. 123), he achieved success in a position more diplomatic than consular, and through his writings added much to contemporary knowledge of unfrequented countries.

[C. O. Paullin, *Diplomatic Negotiations of American Naval Officers* (1912); G. W. Allen, *Our Navy and the Barbary Corsairs* (1905); *Memoirs of John Quincy Adams*, vol. III (1874), pp. 35, 47–58, 91, and vol. V (1875), p. 393; R. J. Cleveland, *Narrative of Voyages and Commercial Enterprises* (2 vols., 1842); H. W. S. Cleveland, *Voyages of a Merchant Navigator* (1886); review of *Sketches of Algiers* in *North Am. Rev.*, Apr. 1826; *Proc. Mass. Hist. Soc.*, vol. XLIV (1911), p. 316; obituary in *Daily Nat. Intelligencer*, Apr. 15, 1833; MSS. in the archives of the State Department and in the possession of Mrs. Willoughby Webb; information on Shaler's parentage and birth from Roy F. Nichols.]   W. L. W., Jr.

SHANNON, WILSON (Feb. 24, 1802–Aug. 30, 1877), lawyer, politician, diplomat, was born at Mount Olivet in Belmont County, Ohio Territory, the ninth and youngest child of George and Jane (Milligan) Shannon. After spending his boyhood on a farm he was sent to Ohio University at Athens, 1820–22, by his elder brothers. In 1823 he went to live with two of them, George and James, at Lexington, Ky., where he read law in their office and studied at Transylvania University. He returned to Ohio in 1826, was admitted to the bar in 1830, and began to practise at St. Clairsville. In 1832 he was defeated for Congress on the Democratic ticket, but the next year he was elected state's attorney. He was chosen governor of Ohio in 1838, being the first native to attain that office. He was defeated for reëlection two years later by the popular Thomas Corwin [q.v.] but in the contest of 1842 he defeated Corwin. Shannon resigned the governorship in 1844 to become minister to Mexico (appointed Apr. 9). In that position he "blustered, blundered, threatened and undertook to argue" (J. H. Smith, *The War with Mexico*, 1919, vol. I, 86), and although Calhoun disapproved his tactless course he was not recalled until the last of March 1845 (G. L. Rives, *The United States and Mexico*, 1913, vol. I, 702). Upon his return Shannon practised law at Cincinnati, but abandoned his profession to lead an

expedition of "Forty-Niners" from eastern Ohio and western Virginia to California. Returning to Ohio in two years, he served without distinction in Congress, 1853–55, and voted for the Kansas-Nebraska bill.

Shannon was commissioned governor of Kansas Territory on Aug. 10, 1855. He was welcomed at Westport and Shawnee by members of the Missouri party, with whom he became confidential. Free-State men aroused his suspicions, however, and he accused them of maintaining a secret military organization to resist the laws and assail Southern immigrants. The first few months of his administration passed quietly as opposing factions were perfecting their plans. Shannon himself presided at a pro-slavery meeting at Leavenworth Nov. 14 which organized a "Law and Order" party. A crisis arose two weeks later with the outbreak of the Wakarusa War. Free-State men rescued one of their number whom Sheriff Samuel J. Jones of Douglas County had arrested, and that officer requested 3,000 men of the Governor to enforce the laws. The militia which Shannon ordered to report for service was only partially organized, but some 1,200 Missourians responded and assembled on the Wakarusa River, eager to destroy Lawrence. Free-State emissaries soon convinced Shannon that such was the purpose of the "border ruffians," and he sought aid of Col. E. V. Sumner, commander of federal forces at Fort Leavenworth. The Missourians, Shannon admitted, *"are beyond my power, or at least soon will be"* (quoted in W. E. Connelley, *A Standard History of Kansas and Kansans*, 1918, vol. I, 507). Sumner refused to move without orders from Washington, and Shannon went to Lawrence to prevent a collision. He signed a "treaty" with Charles Robinson [q.v.] and James H. Lane, 1814–66 [q.v.], in which the two Free-State leaders pleaded ignorance of any organization to resist the laws, and Shannon denied that he had called the Missourians to assist him. He then persuaded both factions to disband their forces. Disturbances on a smaller scale continued sporadically during the winter. When guerrilla bands again assembled before Lawrence in May 1856, Shannon refused to intervene, and on the 21st they pillaged the town and destroyed the Free-State hotel and printing presses. On June 4 he issued a proclamation commanding that armed combinations organized to resist the laws disband. Later in June he left Kansas for an official visit to St. Louis, but directed Colonel Sumner to disperse the "pretended" Topeka legislature, by force if necessary, should it reassemble on July 4. In August, Lane invaded the territory with his "Army of the North" and attacked pro-slavery strongholds. Shannon again played the rôle of peacemaker and effected a settlement which constituted his last official act. On Aug. 18 he forwarded his resignation to the President; three days later he received notice of his removal. The problems of bleeding Kansas would have perplexed any statesman; to the time-serving politician the difficulties were insuperable.

Although Shannon was frequently a delegate to state and national Democratic conventions, he never again sought office. He resumed the practice of law, first at Lecompton, later at Topeka, and finally at Lawrence, and became a leading member of the Kansas bar. He was twice married; his first wife, Elizabeth Ellis, lived only a short time after their marriage; his second, Sarah Osbun of Cadiz, survived him four years. In 1885 a son and two daughters were living.

[Biography of Governor Wilson Shannon," and "Executive Minutes," in *Transactions of the Kansas State Hist. Soc.*, vol. III (1886), pp. 279–323; "Administration of Governor Shannon," *Ibid.*, V (1896), pp. 234–64; valuable notes in A. T. Andreas, *Hist. of the State of Kansas* (1883), and D. W. Wilder, *The Annals of Kansas* (1886); for Ohio career, "Hon. Wilson Shannon," in *The U. S. Magazine and Democratic Review*, Aug. 1849, pp. 173–78; A. T. McKelvey, *Centennial Hist. of Belmont County, Ohio* (1903); death notice in *Daily Leavenworth Times*, Aug. 31, 1877; obituary, *Ibid.*, Sept. 2, 1877, and *N. Y. Times*, Sept. 1, 1877.]   W. H. S.

SHARKEY, WILLIAM LEWIS (July 12, 1798–Mar. 30, 1873), chief justice and provisional governor of Mississippi, was born in the Holston valley of eastern Tennessee. Patrick Sharkey, his father, was of Irish descent; his mother was the daughter of Robert Rhodes. Together with an older cousin who, to the confusion of several writers, was William's guardian and also bore the name of Patrick, William entered the War of 1812 and was with Jackson at New Orleans. While returning to Tennessee at the close of the war, Patrick was favorably impressed with the country and in 1816 removed to Mississippi and settled on land now covered by the southern part of Vicksburg. William did not emigrate at this time but remained in Tennessee to attend school in Greeneville and then to read law at Lebanon before following his relatives to Mississippi. After continuing the study of law under Judge Edward Turner in Natchez, he was admitted to the bar in 1822, opened his office at Warrenton, and removed to Vicksburg three years later. During 1828 and 1829 he was a member of the state House of Representatives. In 1832 he was made circuit judge but served only a few months before being elected one of the

three judges of the high court of errors and appeals. This is noteworthy because just before the election he had vigorously opposed the part of the constitution of 1832 that subjected the judiciary to popular election. His two associates on the bench at once chose him chief justice. He was reëlected at the expiration of each term, although immediately before one election he resisted the popular demand for the repudiation of the Union Bank bonds. His opponent had promised the voters a decision against the validity of the bond issue. Though Sharkey knew a good deal of law, precedents influenced his decisions less than sound judgment and common sense. This was perhaps fortunate in view of his long term of service in the formative years of the state. He declined a seat in Taylor's cabinet in 1848. In November 1851 financial pressure drove him to resign his judgeship and to resume his private practice. He settled in Jackson.

He was elected president of the Nashville convention of 1850, and with great skill he strove to block the efforts of the extreme Southern party to capture that body. He worked in the same direction in 1859, when the opening of the African slave-trade was proposed in the Vicksburg convention. Fillmore appointed him to represent the United States as consul at Havana, but he soon resigned. He refused the secretaryship of war tendered by the same president. A task more to his liking came with his selection by the Mississippi legislature to be a member of a commission to compile *The Revised Code of the Statute Laws of Mississippi* (1857). A charter member of the board of trustees of the University of Mississippi, he served from 1844 to 1865. Although in his early political life he was a state-rights Whig, before 1861 he was probably the most active anti-secession man in Mississippi. In 1863 he took the oath of allegiance to the Union. These facts, together with his birth in east Tennessee, made him an unusually suitable person to negotiate with President Johnson concerning the reconstruction of Mississippi. Following a successful conference in Washington, he and his fellow commissioner returned home. Shortly afterward, in June 1865, he was appointed provisional governor, and he served until after the election of Benjamin G. Humphreys in the fall of that year. In spite of clashes of opinion over the well-known reconstruction problems and of Sharkey's own pre-war and war records, he evidently retained the confidence of the people of the state for he was chosen United States senator, but was denied a seat in that body, when Congress repudiated Johnson's plan of reconstruction. In 1867 he and Robert J.

Walker unsuccessfully endeavored to obtain a decision of the federal Supreme Court on the constitutionality of the Reconstruction activities of Congress (*State of Mississippi* vs. *Johnson, 4 Wallace,* 475). He died before the close of Reconstruction, survived by his widow, Minerva (Hyland) Wren Sharkey. He was buried in the Greenwood Cemetery at Jackson.

His wisdom, friendly manner, and upright life, as well as his religious convictions, enabled him to remain a trusted leader of a constituency from which he differed politically on many of the outstanding issues of the day. After his death Henry S. Foote (*post*, p. 62), who had known him forty years, wrote: "I never knew a person of more integrity and honor; nor one whose general course of life was more blameless and more worthy of commendation."

[Official papers relating to governorship in Miss. Dept. of Archives and Hist.; "Judge Sharkey Papers," ed. by F. G. Davenport, *Miss. Valley Hist. Rev.*, June 1933; recollections and manuscript geneal. of Clay Sharkey, Glen Allan, Miss.; *Amer. Rev.*, May 1852; J. S. Morris, *Miss. State Cases*, vol. I (1872), pp. iii–v; H. S. Foote, *The Bench and Bar of the South and Southwest* (1876); *Hist. Cat. of the Univ. of Miss.* (1910); J. D. Lynch, *The Bench and Bar of Miss.* (1881); J. F. H. Claiborne, *Mississippi* (1880); J. W. Garner, *Reconstruction in Miss.* (1901); Dunbar Rowland, *Mississippi*, vol. II (1907); *Miss. Hist. Soc. Pubs.*, vols. IV, XIV (1901–14); date of birth from tombstone.]   C. S. S.

SHARP, DALLAS LORE (Dec. 13, 1870–Nov. 29, 1929), author, educator, naturalist, was born in Haleyville, N. J., the son of Reuben Lore and Mary Den (Bradway) Sharp. Receiving his early education in the public schools of his native district, he graduated from the South Jersey Institute in Bridgeton, N. J., before he was eighteen. He made an attempt to become a surveyor, which was unsuccessful because his interest in nature distracted his attention from his duties as chain bearer, and he also went to Georgia to engage in business. However, he decided that he needed a college education and entered Brown University, a natural choice since his interest in nature study had already brought him into contact with J. W. P. Jenks of Brown. He supported himself at college by working in the biological laboratory and by acting as pastor of a Methodist Episcopal Church at Wakefield, R. I., receiving ordination as deacon in 1895. He did not neglect undergraduate activities, including track athletics, and he was class poet on graduation in 1895. On Aug. 4 of that year he was married to Grace Hastings, of Detroit, Mich. They had four sons. He entered the theological school of Boston University and completed the course for the S.T.B. degree in 1899,

while acting as pastor for churches in Brockton and East Weymouth, Mass. In 1899, however, he became assistant librarian of the college of liberal arts of Boston University and the next year he was also an instructor in English. As assistant professor of English after 1902 and professor after 1909, he was probably the best known man in the institution both to the student body and the outside public. He gave up his regular teaching in the university in 1922 but was again scheduled to teach a non-credit course for the year 1929–30.

In 1900 he joined the editorial staff of the *Youth's Companion*, and he remained on it three years, still continuing his academic work and literary activities. In 1901 he published his first book, *Wild Life Near Home*, and this and succeeding volumes and articles gave him a considerable reputation that was not affected when President Roosevelt fulminated against "nature fakers," for John Burroughs indorsed him as a true naturalist, and the public found his work attractive and convincing. He was very thrifty in the employment of his material, using magazine articles to make books and combining published matter to make new volumes; but he has more than twenty distinct volumes to his credit, and his contributions to periodicals run into the hundreds, while two of his books, *A Watcher in the Woods* (1903) and *Beyond the Pasture Bars* (1914), are said to have been sold to the extent of more than 100,000 copies each. He wrote many striking articles for the *Atlantic Monthly*, the most characteristic one, perhaps, being "Turtle Eggs for Agassiz," published in the issue of February 1910 (also in *The Face of the Fields*, 1911), which is probably the best example of his ability to present effectively aspects of nature or the study of nature for which he had enthusiasm. In the August 1925 issue of *Harper's Magazine* he published "Five Days and an Education," which was his comment on his own educative process. He had other than literary and academic prominence. He was for years a vigorous advocate of the democracy of the public school, and, as such, disapproved of private schools, attacking them repeatedly as educationally ineffective and undemocratic. He also entered politics in 1922, seeking the Democratic nomination for federal senator, but he was defeated in the primaries. He made a trip to California by automobile, lecturing along the way, and he has left an account of this in his book, *The Better Country* (1928). The last seven years of his life were devoted to public lecturing and literary work. He died at his farm, "Mullein Hill," in Hingham, Mass., from a tumor on the brain.

[*Current Literature*, Sept. 1904; *House Beautiful*, Nov. 1921; *Bostonia*, Mar. 1931; *Year-Book of the New England Southern Ann. Conference of the M. E. Church* for 1895 to 1900; *Who's Who in America*, 1928–29; *Boston Evening Transcript*, May 5, 1928, Nov. 30, 1929; *Boston Herald*, May 27, 1916, June 6, 1920, Apr. 28, Nov. 30, 1929.]
S. G.

SHARP, DANIEL (Dec. 25, 1783–June 23, 1853), Baptist clergyman, was born in Huddersfield, Yorkshire, England, son of the Rev. John Sharp, a Baptist minister. The boy grew up under favorable home and community influences. His first church connection was with the Congregationalists, but he became a Baptist by conviction. Because he was known as a youth of ability and integrity, he was appointed American agent of a Yorkshire mercantile firm, and he became a resident of New York at the age of twenty-two. His interest in religion associated him with a Baptist church, and he engaged occasionally in lay preaching, revealing personal qualities that led his friends to urge him to enter his father's profession. Deciding at length to do so, he placed himself under the tutelage of the Rev. William Staughton of Philadelphia, and on May 17, 1809, was ordained to the ministry in Newark, N. J., where he became pastor of the Baptist Church. Three years later, he accepted a call to the Third Baptist Church of Boston, afterward known as the Charles Street Church, and there he remained until his death.

He did not draw the attention of people to himself by any tricks of publicity. He was never sensational in his methods. His preaching was deliberate and impressive. As he warmed to his theme he turned aside from his manuscript, laid his glasses on the pulpit, and with vivid gesture and kindling energy spoke extemporaneously. Not only did he gain the regard and support of his own people, he won as well the respect of the community. Baptists were not yet on a legal equality with Congregationalists in the old Puritan capital, but Sharp was invited to preach the annual election sermon in 1824 before the governor and legislature, and in 1840 he was asked to preach to the Ancient and Honorable Artillery Company. A number of his sermons were printed, and his *Recognition of Friends in Heaven* (3rd ed., 1844) was widely read.

Sharp was a leader among the Baptists of his day. He had executive ability which fitted him for such responsibilities as came to him with the presidency of the American Baptist Foreign Mission Society and of the board of trustees of the Newton Theological Institution. He was concerned with the organization of the Northern Baptist Education Society, was elected a fellow of Brown University, and Harvard made him one of its Overseers. In his later years his noble courage and white locks gave him an air of distinction. He was always dignified, and rather stern in manner as he was conservative in disposition, but he was gracious in friendliness. A biographer said of him: "God made him a perpendicular gentleman, of the noblest class, and we never expect to see him voluntarily assume, in any sense, the air and attitude of a curved and sycophantic charlatan" (*Knickerbocker*, August 1849, p. 95). He carried the responsibilities of his parish easily, and so was able to give large service to his denomination. As he approached the age of seventy his constitution weakened and he went South to visit friends and recuperate. He died near Baltimore, leaving a widow, Ann (Cauldwell), whom he had married Jan. 1, 1818, and nine of his eleven children.

[W. B. Sprague, *Annals of the Am. Pulpit*, vol. VI (1860); a collection of sermons and pamphlets in the library of the Andover Newton Theological School; Thomas Armitage, *A Hist. of the Baptists* (1895); *Christian Watchman and Reflector*, July 7, 1853; *Christian Rev.*, Oct. 1853; *Boston Transcript*, June 24, 1853.]
H. K. R.

SHARP, JOHN (Nov. 9, 1820–Dec. 23, 1891), Mormon pioneer, known as the "railroad bishop," was born in Clackmannanshire, Scotland, the son of Mary (Hunter) and John Sharp, the first Mormon convert in Scotland. At the age of eight he was sent to work in the coal pits, and he received little or no formal education. In 1847 he joined the Mormon Church and the next year left for America, although he did not finally reach Salt Lake City until August 1850. He secured work in the church quarries nearby, was shortly made superintendent, and managed the difficult task of quarrying great blocks of granite to construct the foundation of the Mormon Temple. On Oct. 7, 1856, Brigham Young [*q.v.*] ordained him bishop of the Twentieth Ward in Salt Lake City, a position he held for nearly thirty years. He was major and later colonel in the Nauvoo Legion, the Mormon militia. When federal troops under Gen. Albert Sidney Johnston [*q.v.*] threatened the Mormon settlements, he managed the removal of church property from Salt Lake City to points of safety. In 1872 he sponsored the formation of a local "institute" of young people which later gave birth to the Mutual Improvement Association, one of the most important organizations fostering social and religious solidarity among the Mormons. He held various local political offices and became intimately associated with many Mormon commercial enterprises: banking, manufacturing, merchandising, and telegraph service.

He is best known, however, as a railroad builder. In 1867, when Brigham Young took a contract to construct ninety miles of roadbed for the Union Pacific Railroad from Echo Canyon to Ogden, Sharp was one of the principal sub-contractors, and under his direction the heavy stone abutments and the tunnels in Weber Canyon were constructed. Later with Young he undertook other contracts for both the Union Pacific and the Central Pacific. Out of the financial settlement between the Union Pacific and Brigham Young, in which Sharp played an important rôle, the Utah contractors obtained a large amount of rolling stock and other railroad materials with which they developed the Utah Central Railroad, organized in 1869 to connect Salt Lake City with the transcontinental lines at Ogden. Sharp was at first assistant superintendent, later superintendent, and in 1873 president. In January 1871, when the Utah Southern Railway was incorporated, he was chosen vice-president. He later became one of the directors of the Union Pacific.

He had three wives. His first, Jean Patterson, he married in 1839; later in Utah he married two polygamous wives, Anne Wright Gibson and Sophie Smith. He was among the many Mormons brought to trial under the Edmunds Act forbidding polygamy, and when he was arraigned, Sept. 18, 1885, he was one of the first to plead guilty to "unlawful cohabitation," for which he was fined three hundred dollars and costs. Tall and impressive, with great physical endurance, he was a hard-headed man of affairs and although an ardent Mormon was never a fanatic; as one official Mormon biographer naïvely puts it, "He had a very common-sense type of mind, was, in fact, a 'man of the world,' notwithstanding he was a Bishop" (Jenson, *Biographical Encyclopedia, post,* p. 678). He possessed great tact in dealing with non-Mormons in business relations and thus admirably helped to bridge the gap of prejudice that had developed between the Mormons and the "gentile world" outside. He was survived by five sons and eight daughters.

[See H. H. Bancroft, *Hist. of Utah* (1889); O. F. Whitney, *Hist. of Utah,* vols. I, II, III (1892–98); Andrew Jenson, *Latter-Day Saint Biog. Encyc.,* vol. I (1901), and *Church Chronology* (2nd ed., 1914); obituaries in *Deseret Evening News* (Salt Lake City), Dec. 23, 1891, and *Salt Lake Tribune,* Dec. 24, 1891. For Sharp's connection with railroads, see also his testimony before the U. S. Pacific Railway Commission, *Sen. Doc. 51,* 50 Cong., 1 Sess. (1888), pts. IV, V, pp. 2154–89. Information on certain points has been supplied by relatives.]   K. Y.

SHARP, KATHARINE LUCINDA (May 25, 1865–June 1, 1914), librarian, library-school director, was born at Elgin, Ill., the daughter of John William and Phebe (Thompson) Sharp. After preparing for college at Elgin Academy and the Oakland, Cal., High School, she entered Northwestern University, Evanston, Ill., and graduated in 1885. Four years later she was awarded the master's degree. She taught school at Elgin for a couple of years, but without remarkable success, the unavoidable problems of discipline being distasteful to her. In 1888, accordingly, she accepted the proffered librarianship of the public library at Oak Park, a suburb of Chicago, and soon found that she had discovered a congenial life work. Better to equip herself for it she resigned her position after two years and took a course at the New York State Library School. Just as she graduated in 1892, Chicago was busily engaged in assembling and arranging the various exhibits for the World's Columbian Exposition, and she was placed in charge of the exhibit of the American Library Association. Her conspicuously excellent work, brought thus prominently to the attention of Chicago educators, resulted in her appointment as director of the newly established department of library science, opened in the fall of 1893 at Armour Institute of Technology. When, four years later, the library school was transferred to the University of Illinois, she continued as director and became also librarian of the University.

The founding of this school and her signally successful management of it for fourteen years brought her into the front rank of American librarians and gave her a deserved place of influence and leadership. In 1894–96 she was grand president of her college sorority, Kappa Kappa Gamma. She was director of the summer school of library science at the University of Wisconsin in 1895 and 1896, and lecturer on library economy at the University of Chicago in 1896. From 1895 to 1905 she was a member of the council of the American Library Association and in 1898 and 1907 was vice-president; she was elected a fellow of the American Library Institute in 1906 and was president of the Illinois Library Association in 1903–04. She wrote frequently for library periodicals, and her 800-page monograph, *Illinois Libraries* (5 vols., 1906–08), remains the foundation work on that subject. In the years before the establishment of a state library extension commission in Illinois, she gave much time and thought to library extension matters, she and her school serving practically as an informal bureau.

In 1907, because of impaired health, she left the professional library field—temporarily, as she thought—and became second vice-president and an executive in the Lake Placid Club in the

Adirondacks, then rapidly developing under the presidency and leadership of Melvil Dewey, who had been state librarian of New York and director of the New York State Library School when Katharine Sharp was a student there. She had been actively and happily engaged in this enterprise for seven years when she died as the result of an automobile accident. She had pronounced qualities of leadership, a well-balanced though perhaps not brilliant intellect, and an animated personality that compelled attention and recognition. She had rare administrative ability, an exceptional faculty for making wise decisions, and a happy combination of tact and forcefulness. In 1922 a portrait tablet, executed in bronze in low relief by Lorado Taft, was presented to the University of Illinois by her former students.

[*Semi-Centennial Alumni Record of the Univ. of Ill.* (1918); *Who's Who in America,* 1914–15; Frances Simpson, *Katharine L. Sharp, an Appreciation* (1914), a paper read before the Ill. Lib. Asso.; *Library Journal,* July 1914; *Public Libraries,* July 1914, May 1922; *Chicago Daily Tribune,* June 2, 1914.]   G. B. U.

SHARP, WILLIAM GRAVES (Mar. 14, 1859–Nov. 17, 1922), ambassador to France during the World War, was the son of George Snider and Mahala (Graves) Sharp of Mount Gilead, Ohio, and the great-grandson of John Sharp who emigrated from England and settled in Frederick, Md., at the end of the eighteenth century. He graduated from the high school at Elyria, Ohio, and, in 1881, from the law department of the University of Michigan. Like his father and grandfather, he first turned to journalism and edited a paper at Fargo, S. D., but he soon returned to Elyria and the bar, where at the age of twenty-five he was elected as a Democrat to the office of prosecuting attorney. However, the law was losing its attractions, so he refused a renomination and turned to manufacturing. He made a fortune in pig-iron, chemicals, and charcoal, and he built the large Lake Superior Iron and Chemical Company. In 1895 he was married to Hallie M. Clough. They had five children. He was a Cleveland elector in 1892, opposed Bryan and free silver in 1896, was nominated for Congress by the Democrats in 1900, was elected to that body in 1908, and reëlected for two succeeding terms by increasing majorities. In the House he became ranking member of the committee on foreign affairs; he introduced a pioneer air mail bill, supported the income tax and a substantial duty on the raw wool in which his own state was interested, and, more important for his own career, he spoke vigorously, on Dec. 13, 1911, in favor of denouncing the commercial treaty of 1832 with Russia be-

cause of Russian discriminations against Jewish-American citizens (*Congressional Record,* 62 Cong., 2 Sess., p. 316). In consequence he could not become ambassador to Russia some months later, when offered that post by President Wilson.

Appointed ambassador to France, to succeed Myron T. Herrick [*q.v.*], on June 19, 1914, he resigned from the House on July 23 and arrived in France in early September, while the Germans were threatening Paris and the French government was at Bordeaux. The American embassy, then representing German interests, remained at Paris. Because of the crisis Herrick remained at his post, and Sharp stayed in Paris unofficially until Nov. 28, when he was instructed to assume his duties. He spent four and a half useful years in Paris, conducting the business of the embassy, visiting German prison camps and Allied, and later American, army encampments, keeping his eye on developments in aviation, which always interested him, directing or encouraging relief work of various kinds, and ironing out the difficulties that arose between his own and the French governments. He made, for instance, a number of protests to the French authorities against the drafting of naturalized American citizens of French birth into the French army, but with meager results. However, with a French diplomat of Jusserand's experience and ability at Washington, it was only natural that many of the most important problems involving Franco-American relations should be settled directly between the state department and the French embassy, instead of through Sharp at Paris. Although a novice at diplomacy when appointed, he remained at his post until Apr. 14, 1919, long enough to become the first American dean of the diplomatic corps at Paris. An address he made at the presentation of a collection of French drawings and autographs to the American people was published in *Le Secours Américain en France* (1915), and after his death was published *The War Memoirs of William Graves Sharp* (1931). In 1919 he returned to Elyria, where he died.

[*War Memoirs, ante,* with a biographical introduction by Warrington Dawson; Beckles Willson, *America's Ambassadors to France* (1928); *Foreign Relations of the United States,* 1914–1918; *Register of the Department of State,* 1918; *Who's Who in America,* 1922–23; *N. Y. Times,* Nov. 18, 1922.]   E. W. S.

SHARPE, HORATIO (Nov. 15, 1718–Nov. 9, 1790), governor of colonial Maryland, was born near Hull, Yorkshire, England, one of a numerous and celebrated family. He had, before his appointment as governor, held a commission as captain of marines and as lieutenant-colonel of foot in the West Indies. His appointment was probably due in part to family influence and partly to the obvious expediency of placing a military man in office on the eve of a threatened attack by the French. Upon his arrival in Maryland on Aug. 10, 1753, he was immediately confronted by problems both numerous and serious. As a crown officer he had to provide men and supplies for the approaching war; as the representative of the proprietary he must resist every encroachment on his rights; but as the governor of the province he was equally bound to protect the citizens against injustice. The most immediately pressing of his problems was the French and Indian War. His correspondence shows how keenly he felt the gravity of the situation, and he promptly put himself in communication with the other governors. Commissioned royal commander-in-chief, he exerted himself with the greatest energy, consulting his colleague, Governor Dinwiddie, gathering supplies, and descending the Potomac in a canoe to inspect the military posts. When Braddock arrived to displace him in the midst of these preparations, he cooperated loyally. Upon the news of that officer's disaster, Sharpe seemed to increase his efforts, animating the people with his own courage. He strengthened Fort Cumberland and erected four small forts, and he also found time to attend military councils in New York and Philadelphia in 1755 and 1757.

In his conflicts with the lower house, he faithfully performed his duty to the proprietary under very trying circumstances. Probably the greatest tribute to his ability is the grudging admission of the Assembly that his inclination led him toward a due regard for the interest of the province. The delegates clung to their determination to pass no appropriation bills unless the revenues of the proprietor were included in the taxation proposed. In his private correspondence he deprecated the action that loyalty obliged him to take; and, when the government tried to punish the colonists for their niggardly support of the war by quartering troops in Annapolis, he remonstrated against punishing citizens instead of the real offenders, the burgesses. Some historians credit him with first suggesting the Stamp Act; certain it is that in 1754 in a communication to Lord Baltimore he outlined concisely a plan that is a prototype of the famous act (*Archives, post,* VI, 99). Yet, faced with open resistance to parliamentary taxation, his native good sense led him to warn the ministry that the act could be enforced only by troops. Especially charged to determine the boundaries of his province, he set men at work surveying the line in dispute with

Virginia and by 1760 arrived at an agreement that eventuated in the Mason and Dixon's line. In 1769, in spite of the tact he had exercised toward Lord Baltimore, he was replaced by a brother-in-law of the proprietor.

So wedded had he become to his province that he settled at "Whitehall," the country home he had created near Annapolis, to manage his estate, dispense a generous hospitality, and indulge his passion for agriculture until summoned to England in 1773 by family affairs. Though obliged to renounce the management of his estate to his friend and secretary, John Ridout, he watched the Revolution with interest and sorrow from his home in London. "Whitehall," one of the most beautiful examples of eighteenth-century architecture in the colonies, passed to John Ridout, who had married the daughter of Samuel Ogle [*q.v.*], Mary Ogle, for whom it is said that "Whitehall" was built and for whom its first master, Sharpe, remained a bachelor. On the wall of its dining-room still hangs (1935) a portrait of Sharpe painted probably by John Hesselius [*q.v.*].

[Some letters and transcripts in the Lib. of Cong.; "The Correspondence of Governor Horatio Sharpe," *Archives of Md.,* vols. VI, IX, XIV (1888–95); "Correspondence of Governor Sharpe," *Md. Hist. Mag.,* Dec. 1917; Lady Edgar, *A Colonial Governor in Md.* (1912); Jonathan Boucher, *Reminiscences of an Am. Loyalist* (1925); M. P. Andrews, *Tercentenary Hist. of Md.* (1925), vol. I; J. M. Hammond, *Colonial Mansions of Maryland and Delaware* (1914).]   E. L.

SHARPLES, JAMES (*c.* 1751–Feb. 26, 1811), portrait painter, was born in England but spent his youth in France studying for the priesthood until he realized that his bent was for art. Returning to England, where he settled after several moves at Bath, he began in 1779 to exhibit his pictures at the Royal Academy. He displayed some ability as an inventor as well. A design of his for a "steam carriage" is registered in the patent office of Great Britain (*Subject-Matter Index . . . of Patents of Invention,* 1857, pt. II, p. 761). In 1791 he published a pamphlet on *Reducing Friction in Machinery,* said to have been reprinted in 1856, and in 1804 one on *Apparatus for Surveying, Etc.* (Knox, *post,* p. 4). He was married three times. Of the first two wives little is known except that by the first he had a son, George, and by the second a son, Felix Thomas. His third wife was Ellen Wallace, a young lady of fashion and good family, whom he met through an art class he conducted in Bath. Their son James was born probably in Liverpool in 1788, and their daughter Rolinda in Bath in 1793. That year, with Felix, James, and Rolinda, they set out for America, but the journey was a difficult one and it was not until after their vessel had been captured by a French privateer and they had been interned at Brest for seven months that they finally arrived.

Sharples was soon painting portraits of men high in the military, civil, literary, and social life of the country. Noted for his ability to catch a likeness, he charged fifteen dollars for a profile and twenty dollars for a full face, and could finish a portrait in two hours. Although in England he had used oils, he now used pastels, crayons which he powdered and applied with a camel's hair pencil on a thick gray paper of soft grain and woolly texture. Making practical use of his inventive powers, he constructed a traveling carriage into which he packed his wife, the three children, and his drawing materials, and set out to travel as an itinerant painter through the New England states and into the South. In 1796 he settled in Philadelphia. There, according to Mrs. Sharples' diary, he "was generally engaged drawing in crayons the portraits of the most distinguished Americans, foreign Ministers and other distinguished visitants from Europe" (*Ibid.*, p. 13). About this time he made portraits of Washington and his wife. Copies of many of the portraits being in demand, his wife turned her talents to duplicating his efforts. The copying of their own portraits and of portraits by each other soon became a matter of course in the family, for James at fifteen and Felix at seventeen began professional art careers, and somewhat later Rolinda also turned to art. They did not sign their works, and in consequence much confusion and controversy have arisen in attempts to authenticate the work of the father. The Washington portraits were many times copied by Ellen and the two sons.

In 1798 the Sharples family were living in New York; in 1801, because of the unsettled state of English finances, they returned to Bath and three years later went to London, where the father turned again to his mechanical pursuits. Soon, however, they were in Bath again. In 1806, they started for America, but when their vessel foundered they turned back. Felix and James, however, landed in the autumn of 1806; on July 22, 1809, the others finally arrived. Sharples portraits known to have been executed in America between those dates are unquestionably by the sons (*Ibid.*, p. 25). After the return to America Sharples made his headquarters in New York but wandered through New York, Pennsylvania, and New Jersey, and often visited his son James in Albany; Felix, who was something of a rover but loved the South, seldom left that part of the country for long. The elder Sharples died of a heart attack in New York, his last wish being that his family should settle permanently in England. His wife advertised the Sharples collection of portraits for sale and in late spring sailed for England. She had a second collection of the Sharples paintings there, which she left in 1849 to the Bristol Academy for the Promotion of the Fine Arts (later the Royal West of England Academy). Felix, in the South, was after 1811 the only member of the family in America. He too had a collection of pastels which he is said to have left as security for a loan with his friend Winder of "Yardley," Northampton County, N. C., intending to reclaim his property. He was never heard of again. The collection thus left, including portraits of many patriots of the time, was subsequently sold and is thought (*Ibid.*, p. 49) to be the nucleus of the Sharples collection in Independence Hall, Philadelphia.

[In the course of the Sharples family's wanderings in America their name sometimes became Sharpless. The most detailed biog. is that of Katharine McCook Knox, *The Sharples, Their Portraits of George Washington and His Contemporaries* (1930), with bibliog. See also *The Dict. of Nat. Biog.*; J. T. Scharf and Thompson Westcott, *Hist. of Phila.* (1884), vol. II, p. 1045; William Dunlap, *A Hist. of the Rise and Progress of the Arts of Design in the U. S.* (rev. ed., 3 vols., 1918); H. T. Tuckerman, *The Character and Portraits of Washington* (1859); J. W. Palmer, in *Lippincott's Mag.*, Dec. 1871; death notice in *Public Advertiser* (N. Y.), Feb. 28, 1811; *Cat. of the Independence Hall Coll. of Paintings*; *Cat. of the . . . Loan Exhibition of Portraits of George Washington . . . at the Corcoran Gallery of Art*, Mar. 5, 1932. The diary of Ellen Sharples is in the Royal West of England Acad., Bristol.] D. G.

SHARPLESS, ISAAC (Dec. 16, 1848–Jan. 16, 1920), college president, Quaker leader, was born on his father's farm in Birmingham Township, Chester County, Pa., the son of Aaron and Susanna (Forsythe) Sharpless and the descendant of John Sharples who became a Quaker and, with his son Joseph and other children, emigrated from England to Chester, Pa., in the seventeenth century. He has told with penetration and humor of his early training, in his *Quaker Boy on the Farm and at School* (copr. 1908). He attended the little Friends' school at Birmingham and later Westtown Boarding School near West Chester, Pa. He received the B.S. degree from Harvard College in 1873, specializing in bridge building. He taught mathematics for a few years at Westtown School, and in 1875 he began his long and fruitful service at Haverford College. On Aug. 10, 1876, he married Lydia Trimble Cope, of West Chester, Pa., who survived him with six children. He held the positions of instructor in mathematics, 1875–79, professor of mathematics and astronomy, 1879–84, dean, 1884–87, and president, 1887–1917.

After 1917 he consented to continue for a time under a lighter burden and served as dean of the T. Wistar Brown Graduate School of Haverford College until his death.

He was the author of several textbooks such as *Astronomy for Schools* (copr. 1882) and *An Elementary Plane Geometry* (copr. 1879), and he wrote many articles in mathematics and astronomy. He was a founder, in 1904, and the first president of Friends' Historical Society of Philadelphia, later Friends' Historical Association. He was also the first editor of its official *Bulletin*. His writings on early Pennsylvania, especially *A Quaker Experiment in Government* (1898), are marked by a maturity of understanding and a reserve of statement that give them peculiar value. It was followed in 1899 by "The Quaker in The Revolution" as vol. II of *A History of Quaker Government in Pennsylvania*, and in 1900 the two volumes were again published under the title *A History of Quaker Government in Pennsylvania*. In 1905 he published a volume of essays *Quakerism and Politics* and in 1915 *The American College*. He was a leader of an educational revival among Friends, especially in Philadelphia and the vicinity, that resulted in progress of thought and broadening of interests. His insistent advocacy of progress was always steadied by his respect for the past. In connection with a Quaker anniversary he once wrote: "The lack of historic background, while compatible with much Christian goodness and zeal . . . seems . . . to lead to opportunism, and to destroy that continuity of principle so essential to the preservation of the type" (*Friends Meeting House, Fourth and Arch Streets, Philadelphia, A Centennial Celebration*, 1904, pp. 8–9). He was active in local projects for community betterment and in the larger civic interests of state and nation. He strongly supported the peace movement and government reform. He was appointed shortly before his death on a state commission for revising the constitution of Pennsylvania but could not serve because of failing health.

In his later years his contributions were sought for educational conventions and periodicals. By that time he was one of the most eminent exponents in the United States of the efficient small college. At Haverford College, during his administration of thirty years, he wrought a great transformation. He relieved a difficult disciplinary situation by the adoption of student government, improved physical equipment, increased the general endowment tenfold, improved faculty standards by increased salaries, by the establishment of an independent pension fund, and by a liberal system of tenure, and provided for the requirement of entrance examinations for all applicants, which was a rather courageous move for a small college. Resisting the clamor for technical and vocational courses, he held to the ideal of a liberal arts college. His own description of those years is contained in his *Story of a Small College* (1918). He was once introduced to a convention of educators as "the college President who does not lie." His great sense of justice was always impressive to his students who, though never coddled by him, came to regard him with a devotion bordering on worship. Part of his appeal lay in his inimitable humor, which frequently relieved a difficult and even a dangerous disciplinary situation. A tablet to his memory, in the science building named for him at Haverford College, bears the following inscription: *Magister amatus, dux sapiens, administrator fidelis*.

[Some unpublished MSS. at Haverford College, including "George Keith," and "Friends and Slavery"; *Quaker Biog.*, ser. 2, vol. V (1926); R. M. Jones, *Hist. of Haverford College* (1933); Gilbert Cope, *Geneal. of the Sharpless Family* (1887); *Bulletin of Friends' Hist. Soc. of Philadelphia*, May 1920, with bibliography of writings.]
                           R. W. K.

SHARSWOOD, GEORGE (July 7, 1810– May 28, 1883), judge, was born in Philadelphia, the posthumous son of George Sharswood, a lumber dealer, and Esther (Dunn). His paternal ancestors were English and old Philadelphians, though the first of the name in America, George Sharswood, settled in New London, Conn., *c.* 1665 (Hart, *post,* p. 34). He was graduated from the University of Pennsylvania with highest honors in 1828, and was admitted to the bar on Sept. 5, 1831. His practice soon became primarily that of a counselor. Nominated by the governor an associate judge of the district court of Philadelphia, and immediately and unanimously confirmed by the Senate, he served on that court, with a distinction rivaled only by that of his colleague, J. I. Clark Hare [*q.v.*], for twenty-two years (beginning Apr. 9, 1845); from 1848 onward he was president judge. In 1851 he was indorsed by five political parties for continuance on the court when the office became elective; and was reëlected in 1861 for another ten-year term; but before its expiration was elevated to the supreme court of the state. On that bench he served fifteen years (Jan. 6, 1868–Dec. 31, 1882), and then retired. From Jan. 6, 1879, onward he was chief justice by seniority.

He accomplished marvels in expediting business in the district court under rules compelling promptitude in trials. He had never been active in trial work before going on the bench, but he had prepared American editions of two English works on that field of practice, and proved to be, in the opinion of most competent lawyers, a *nisi prius* judge of unusual powers. Of immense yet exact learning, quick to grasp facts, full of practical wisdom, naturally judicial, rigidly impartial, decisive yet extraordinarily prompt in rulings, firm in controlling arguments, and remarkably lucid in his jury charges, he was unquestionably a great judge. His judgments were very sound; out of some 4,000 cases only 156 were appealed and only thirty-two reversed. In the main this extraordinary record was due to his accuracy; in part, doubtless, to his conservatism, for he was a stict constructionist, a great admirer of the common law, and little disposed to weaken the rule of *stare decisis*. Partly because of the hurry of an overburdened court, but probably also from choice, his opinions were succinct and devoid of any display of learning. Marked cooperation and mutual respect characterized his relations with the bar. His administrative talents were no less needed, and were similarly exercised, on the supreme court.

Appointed professor of law in the University of Pennsylvania in 1850, he reorganized and revivified its law school, serving it for eighteen years (as dean after May 4, 1852). Not only in private but also in public law, in politics, economics, and other fields he was continuously an earnest student, and as a teacher his ideal was "to teach young men how to study and to excite them to love to study" (Dickson, *post*, p. 123). He preserved throughout life his command of the classics. Before assuming judicial duties he served a term in the state legislature (beginning December 1837), and two terms in the select council of Philadelphia (1839–1840). A follower of Adam Smith and Thomas Jefferson, he cherished a strong antipathy to governmental interference with personal liberty and action (see, in particular, *An Address Upon the Rights of the States, delivered before the State Rights Association of Pennsylvania . . .*, 1834). His hatred of fiat money was embodied in a dissent to a decision of the district court (*Borie* vs. *Trott*, 5 *Philadelphia Reports*, 366) which held constitutional the Legal Tender Act of 1862. His report, for a stockholders committee, on the United States Bank (*The United States Gazette*, Philadelphia, Apr. 8, 1841) was a masterly legal production, quoted by Thomas H. Benton in his *Thirty Years' View* (II, 1856, pp. 365–69).

He was long a trustee of the University of Pennsylvania (1872–83), president of an institution for the deaf and dumb, a trustee of the

General Assembly of the Presbyterian Church, and a director of its theological seminary at Princeton. Sharswood was companionable and hospitable, despite a laborious life and poor health. For friends he spared no trouble; it is said that he learned Hebrew to aid one who was blind. His kindness to students and young lawyers was notable. On Nov. 27, 1849, he married Mary Chambers (d. Nov. 8, 1857), and by her had one son who predeceased him.

His opinions are in the *Philadelphia Reports*, vols. I–VI (covering 1850–68) and the *Pennsylvania State Reports*, vols. LVII–CII. His many other publications (for which see S. A. Allibone, *A Critical Dictionary of English Literature and British and American Authors*, vol. II, 1870, and Hart, Biddle, and Dickson, *post*) included: *A Compendium of Lectures on the Aims and Duties of the Profession of Law* (1854), better known by the half-title, *Professional Ethics,* and several times republished as *An Essay on Professional Ethics; Popular Lectures on Commercial Law* (1856); *Lectures Introductory to the Study of the Law* (1870); and various articles and addresses, among them *The Common Law of Pennsylvania* (1855). For three years (1843–46) he edited the *American Law Magazine*. His other editorial work included American issues, several in repeated editions, of eight English law textbooks, and of some twenty-nine volumes of collected English cases; and two volumes of United States statutes.

[*Legal Intelligencer*, June 1, 1883, vol. XL, 220; C. H. Hart, *Memoir of G. Sharswood* (1884); G. W. Biddle, *A Sketch of the Professional and Judicial Character of the late George Sharswood* (1883), also printed in 102 *Pa. State Reports*, 601–30; *Hon. George Sharswood, the Nominee for Judge of the Supreme Court of Pennsylvania. By a Member of the Philadelphia Bar* (n.d.); *Complimentary Reception and Dinner by the Philadelphia Bar to Hon. George Sharswood . . . Dec. 20, 1882* (1883); *Bar Meeting* [May 31, 1883]: *Stenographically Reported by R. A. West* (1883), also in *Legal Intelligencer*, June 8, 1883, vol. XL, pp. 230–32; H. L. Carson, "Historical Sketch of the Law Department," in *Catalogue of the Alumni of the Law Department of the University of Pennsylvania . . . 1790–1882* (1882), pp. 23–28; Samuel Dickson, "George Sharswood," in W. D. Lewis, ed., *Great American Lawyers*, vol. VI (1909), pp. 123–61; obituary in *Philadelphia Press*, May 29, 1883. In Hart, Biddle, and Dickson will be found analyses of important cases.]   F.S.P.

SHATTUCK, AARON DRAPER (Mar. 9, 1832–July 30, 1928), painter, was born at Francestown, N. H., the seventh of nine children of Jesse and Harriet (Williams) Shattuck. His grandfather, Stephen Shattuck, a Revolutionary pensioner, had settled at Francestown, but the family came originally from Massachusetts, the earliest settler having been William Shattuck, who was born in England about 1621 and died in Watertown, Mass., in 1672. Jesse Shattuck, a stone mason, worked at his trade in Francestown, at Lowell, Boston, and Worcester, Mass., and at Hartford, Conn. After having been educated in the public schools at Lowell, where his father's name appears in directories between 1844 and 1851, Aaron in 1851 began to paint portraits in the Boston studio of Alexander Ransom, later accompanying his master to New York. There he continued his art education at the National Academy of Design, perhaps through Ransom's advice. By 1855 he was already established as a portrait painter in New York. He was elected a member of the National Academy in 1861 (*Commemorative Exhibition by Members of the National Academy of Design, 1825–1925*, 1925, p. xx). He married, June 4, 1860, Marian, daughter of Samuel and Pamela (Chandler) Colman and sister of Samuel Colman [*q.v.*], the landscape painter, with whom he was closely associated. They had three sons and three daughters.

Shattuck's landscapes were specially commended in his New York period for the fidelity with which he rendered foreground objects. "He is exact, graceful, and often effective," says Tuckerman (*post,* p. 560). "There is a true pastoral vein in him; his best cattle and water scenes, with meadow and trees, are eloquent of repose . . ." He painted during the summers in the White Mountains, on Lake Champlain, and in the Housatonic valley. In 1868 he "discovered" Granby, Conn., and two years later he bought there a farm which became his permanent home during the rest of his very long life. He became a stock-breeder as well as a painter and often portrayed his own cattle and sheep in his landscapes. French (*post,* p. 144) especially commends his large painting, "Sunday Morning in New England," as "direct, simple, and truthful, without attempt to surprise by novel effects, or feats of elaborate realism." Among Shattuck's Academy pictures were "Hillside, Lake Champlain" and "Morning Light," 1869; "Lake Champlain," 1870; "The New England Farm" and "A Group of Sheep," 1871; "White Hills in October," 1872; "Sheep," 1873; "Sheep and Cattle," 1874; "The Old Homestead" and "Haying Time," 1875; "The Road to Simsbury" and "Autumn near Stockbridge," 1876; "Granby Pastures," 1877. "Down in the Meadows" became the property of the Albright Art Gallery, Buffalo, N. Y. He once devised a stretcher frame for painters' canvases which had a large sale. His later years were uneventful. He died at Granby, Conn. In the commemorative exhibition of the National Academy of Design, 1925,

he was represented by "Sheep near the Sea." His art was that of the nineteenth century academicians—scholarly, able, carefully finished; it has no considerable vogue among collectors of the twentieth century.

[The best evaluation of Shattuck as a painter is in H. T. Tuckerman, *Book of the Artists* (1867). See also Lemuel Shattuck, *Memorials of the Descendants of William Shattuck* (1855); H. W. French, *Art and Artists in Conn.* (1879); Clara E. Clement and Laurence Hutton, *Artists of the Nineteenth Century and their Works* (1879), vol. II; *Who's Who in America*, 1930–31; obit. in *Am. Art Ann.*, 1928; vital records, Granby, Conn.]

F. W. C.

SHATTUCK, FREDERICK CHEEVER (Nov. 1, 1847–Jan. 11, 1929), physician, was born in Boston, Mass., the son of George Cheyne Shattuck, 1813–1893 [*q.v.*], and Anne Henrietta (Brune) Shattuck. With his brother, George Brune Shattuck [*q.v.*], he was a member of the first class to graduate from St. Paul's School. A few months at the Boston Latin School were followed by four years at Harvard College in the class of 1868. He was very popular as a student although not a first-rate scholar. In view of the family tradition, a career in medicine naturally appealed to him and he was graduated from the Harvard Medical School in 1873. Work and research in hospitals in London, Paris, and Vienna occupied the next three years until he settled in Boston to practise in 1875. On June 19, 1876, he was married to Elizabeth Perkins Lee, the daughter of Henry Lee, of Brookline, Mass. Of his four children, one son, George Cheever Shattuck, became a physician, the fifth in direct line to practise medicine in Boston. After many years of indifferent practice, serving as an instructor in the Harvard Medical School and as a junior physician at the Massachusetts General Hospital, Shattuck was appointed James Jackson professor of clinical medicine in 1888. His private patients soon increased to a large number and, at the height of his career, he was the most noted physician in Boston. He was never primarily interested, however, in caring for patients. Teaching at the Medical School or on the wards of the Hospital, pleasant hours spent in the Massachusetts Historical Society room, at social gatherings at his beautiful manor-house in Brookline or in one of his clubs, or the writing of papers on historical subjects, were all of more importance to him. Nevertheless, he was a brilliant diagnostician, a useful consultant and a physician of wide influence. He read many papers of worth at medical meetings. Usually interpretive rather than creative, he was, nevertheless, an early advocate of adequate feeding in typhoid fever and, under his direction, the first drainage of the pericardium was successfully accomplished in Boston. He retired from his professorship in 1912. From 1913 to 1919 he was an overseer of Harvard College and for many years a trustee of St. Paul's School. An original member of the Association of American Physicians in 1886, he served as president in 1898.

In early life his youthful appearance and misunderstood levity kept him from rapid advancement, but later his sterling worth, his wit and his thorough knowledge of medicine gave him great popularity as a teacher from Maine to California. The picture of the doctor on the back seat of his small Victoria, being driven rapidly behind a pair of fast horses, and without regard for traffic rules through the streets of Boston, is one not easily forgotten. His favorite dachshund and a pile of medical journals were beside him, a cigarette was between his lips, a carnation was in his buttonhole, and a bright waistcoat and a cheery smile for all lent vivid color to the picturesque ensemble. Without revolutionizing medicine or adding greatly to the body of medical knowledge, Shattuck set a distinct stamp of vigorous scholarship and high standards upon the profession, largely through his influence on others.

[Who's Who in America, 1928–29; J. T. Morse, Jr., biog. sketch in Harvard Grads. Mag., Mar., 1929; G. G. Sears and R. I. Lee, sketches in New England Jour. of Medicine, July 4, 1929; Harvard Coll., Class of 1868, Fortieth Anniversary (1909); Index-Cat. of the Lib. of the Surgeon-General's Office, U. S. Army, vol. XII (1891); 2 ser., vol. XV (1910); Boston Evening Transcript, Jan. 11, 14, 1929.]   H. R. V.

SHATTUCK, GEORGE BRUNE (Aug. 18, 1844–Mar. 12, 1923), physician and editor, the son of George Cheyne and Anne Henrietta (Brune) Shattuck, was born in Boston, Mass. His father, George Cheyne Shattuck, 1813–1893, his grandfather, George Cheyne Shattuck, and his brother, Frederick Cheever Shattuck [qq.v.], were all physicians of note in Boston. He was graduated in the first class of the St. Paul's School along with his brother and Horatio R. Bigelow, and then entered St. James College, Md., transferring to Harvard College in 1861, where he received the B.A. degree in 1863, the M.A. in 1867, and the M.D. in 1869. Before beginning practice in Boston Shattuck traveled in Italy and voyaged around Cape Horn in a sailing ship. On his return, he established a connection with the Boston City Hospital. Later made visiting physician, he served with distinction up to the time of his death. Judicious, conservative and unusually formal on his ward-rounds, his common sense never deserted him; his comments, trenchant and discriminating,

were tempered by a pervasive humor. Particularly interested in typhoid fever, he wrote a number of papers on the subject. Teaching did not appeal to him and he served the Harvard Medical School for only a short time.

Shattuck was never vitally interested in the actual practice of medicine. He served as overseer of Harvard College for twenty-one years, president of the board of managers of the Massachusetts Eye and Ear Infirmary, president of the Boston Medical Library, director of the Boston Athenaeum, trustee of the Massachusetts Humane Society, and charter member of the Association of American Physicians. Shattuck was influential in establishing the Massachusetts State Board of Health in 1869, the first in the United States, and through the Massachusetts Medical Society rendered valuable service in influencing state and national legislation on public health measures.

Becoming a member of the board of editors of the Boston Medical and Surgical Journal in 1879, and editor-in-chief in 1881, he gave the greater part of his time to this publication until his resignation in 1912. He was an able editor, not always appreciated by his contemporaries, with a "rare capacity for literary expression, through which ran a vein of subtle humor, rendering his writings as it did his conversation, altogether charming" (Taylor, post, p. 780). The younger members of his staff, in whom he took a lively interest, were greatly influenced by his kindliness and sympathetic understanding of their problems. He wrote few papers, the most important being "Influenza in Massachusetts," a Shattuck Lecture given before the Massachusetts Medical Society in 1890, at the height of an influenza epidemic. In this lecture Shattuck gave an important account of his family and their influence on medicine in New England, his description of his grandfather being especially notable. He was married to Mrs. Amalia (Schutte) de La Valle, the daughter of William Schutte of Paris, on June 6, 1872. Two daughters survived him.

[The chief reference is the article by E. W. Taylor in the Boston Medic. and Surgic. Jour., May 17, 1923. See also, Who's Who in America, 1922–23; Report of the Secretary of the Class of 1863, Harvard College (1913); and the Boston Evening Transcript, Mar. 13, 1923.]   H. R. V.

SHATTUCK, GEORGE CHEYNE (July 17, 1783–Mar. 18, 1854), physician and philanthropist, was born in Templeton, Mass., the youngest son of Benjamin and Lucy (Barron) Shattuck. The Shattuck family, many of whom have become distinguished in New England life, have a common ancestor, William Shattuck, who was born in England and died in Watertown, Mass., in 1672. Shattuck's father, a graduate of Harvard College in 1765, a pioneer physician in Massachusetts, deeply religious, and greatly respected by his contemporaries, was a member of the fifth generation in America. He named his son for George Cheyne of Bath, England, a physician whom he greatly admired. At Dartmouth College George Cheyne Shattuck received the degree of A.B. in 1803, and M.B. in 1806. While there he was greatly influenced in medicine by Nathan Smith, 1762–1829, and Lyman Spalding [qq.v.]. He also studied for a short period at Harvard College, and finally spent a year in medicine at the University of Pennsylvania where he received the degree of M.D. in 1807. Thus equipped with the best medical teaching of his day, he started a general practice of medicine in Boston, living in a fashionable section of the city. He soon became the leading physician and one of the most important citizens. His practice was very large and he had little time to devote to public interests, but he served for a short period as consulting physician to the city of Boston, as president of the Massachusetts Medical Society from 1836 to 1840, and as president of the American Statistical Association, 1845–51.

Philanthropy was essentially a part of Shattuck's nature, but he gave without public acclaim. There are many stories about his kindness, especialy to needy students of Andover and Harvard College. Many of his fees were remitted, although in the best years his practice amounted to about $10,000, collected at a time when fees were $1.50 a visit. His larger gifts included a donation toward the building of an astronomical observatory at Dartmouth College, many books and portraits to the library, funds to Harvard College, the endowment of what is now the Shattuck Professorship of Pathological Anatomy in the Harvard Medical School, numerous benefactions to the American Statistical Association, and a grant to the Massachusetts Medical Society for the foundation of the Shattuck lectures. He assisted James Thacher [q.v.] financially with his *American New Dispensary* (1810) and his *American Medical Biography* (2 vols., 1828), and John James Audubon [q.v.] with the *Birds of America* (1827–38). Shattuck, himself, wrote little. Soon after he returned from the University of Pennsylvania, he won the Boylston medical prize two years in succession for a series of essays, published in Boston in 1808. This was his only contribution of note except "A Dissertation on the Uncertainty of the Healing Art," published in *Medical Disser-*

tations read at the Annual Meetings of the Massachusetts Medical Society (vol. IV, 1829), a stirring plea for hygienic measures "to prolong and render more comfortable human existence" (see p. 163), and a lengthy correspondence with Nathan Smith. Several honorary degrees were bestowed upon him, including one of M.D. by Dartmouth College in 1812.

He was married on Oct. 3, 1811, to Eliza Cheever Davis, the daughter of Caleb Davis of Boston. They had six children, only one of whom survived, the oldest son, George Cheyne Shattuck [q.v.]. After the death of his first wife in 1828, he was married to Amelia H. Bigelow of Cambridge, on Aug. 17, 1835. From his first wife he received a large fortune, part of which he dispensed, along with his annual income, to various charities.

[The chief references to Shattuck are a sermon by C. A. Bartol, published in Boston in 1854, and *Memoir of the Life and Character of G. C. Shattuck*, by Edward Jarvis, M.D., read before the American Statistical Association, April 12, 1854, and published as a pamphlet in that year. See also, Lemuel Shattuck, *Memorials of the Descendants of William Shattuck* (1855); H. A. Kelly and W. L. Burrage, *Am. Med. Biog.* (1920); W. L. Burrage, *A Hist. of the Mass. Med. Soc.* (1923); E. A. Smith, *The Life and Letters of Nathan Smith* (1914); and the *Boston Evening Transcript*, Mar. 18, 20, 27, 1854. Shattuck's diaries, the catalogue of his library, and his account-books, are now deposited in the Boston Medical Library.]

H. R. V.

SHATTUCK, GEORGE CHEYNE (July 22, 1813–Mar. 22, 1893), physician and philanthropist, the son of George Cheyne Shattuck [q.v.] and Eliza Cheever (Davis) Shattuck, was born in Boston, Mass. He enjoyed exceptional educational opportunities, attending the Boston Latin School, "Round Hill School" in Northampton, Mass., under Joseph Green Cogswell [q.v.], Harvard College, where he received the degree of B.A. in 1831, one year at the Harvard Law School, and four at the Harvard Medical School, receiving the M.D. degree in 1835. After he was graduated in medicine, he spent nearly three years studying in Europe. In Paris he fell under the spell of P. C. A. Louis, one of the best medical teachers of his day, whose American pupils were to influence the course of medicine in the United States to a marked degree. Louis entrusted Shattuck with the translation of his *Anatomical, Pathological and Therapeutic Researches on the Yellow Fever of Gibraltar of 1828* (1839) and sent him to England to study typhus fever at the London Fever Hospital. Shattuck's report of thirteen cases in which he differentiated typhoid from typhus fever was read before the Medical Society of Observation of Paris in 1838 and published in the *Medical Examiner*, Philadelphia, Feb. 29 and Mar. 7,

1840. It is one of the early and important contributions to the subject, contemporary with the work of Gerhard, Pennock and Stillé.

Shattuck returned to Boston in 1840 to begin to practise with his father. Although at first without hospital or school appointment, he was so imbued with the spirit of Louis that he established a private clinic, or *ambulatorium*, in his home to train young men in clinical medicine. Eminently practical, like his famous teacher, he would not tolerate medical hypothesis or "system makers." With Oliver Wendell Holmes, Henry Ingersoll Bowditch, and James Jackson, 1777–1867, [*qq.v.*], he founded the Boston Society of Medical Observation, which had a lasting influence on Boston medicine. Official recognition came at last in 1849 when he succeeded Holmes as visiting physician to the Massachusetts General Hospital. A few years later, in 1855, he succeeded Jacob Bigelow as professor of clinical medicine at the Harvard Medical School, and in 1864 he was made dean of the school. The school at this time was a private undertaking for which the faculty were entirely responsible. Shattuck woke it out of lethargy, kept the best teachers, added new ones, extended the teaching outside of the regular courses to the hospitals and to the physicians' offices, and introduced clinical conferences.

In addition to his work in medical education, Shattuck made an important contribution to general education when he founded St. Paul's School in Concord, N. H., in 1855. The school was built upon the Cogswell formula, so successful at Round Hill: "Physical and moral culture can best be carried on where boys live with, and are constantly under the supervision of the teachers, and in the country" (Coit, *post*, p. 14). To this end he gave his country estate as a site for the school, with an adequate endowment. The school and the Protestant Episcopal Church, in which he was considered the foremost layman of his time, were Shattuck's greatest interests outside of medicine, throughout the rest of his life. He was a founder and active supporter of the Church of the Advent in Boston, and a trustee of the General Theological Seminary. A simple and sincere man, Shattuck endeared himself to Boston by his sturdy and selfless devotion to the welfare of others. His death was considered almost a public calamity. Stillé felt that "perhaps no one in Boston had done more good to a greater number of people" than Shattuck, an opinion shared by many of his contemporaries (Stillé, *post*, p. lxxiv). He was married on Apr. 9, 1840, to Anne Henrietta Brune, the daughter of F. W. Brune of Baltimore, Md. She and their three children survived him. Two sons became Boston physicians, George Brune Shattuck and Frederick Cheever Shattuck [*qq.v.*].

[*Boston Medic. and Surgic. Jour.*, Apr. 6, 1893; Alfred Stillé, sketch in *Trans. Coll. of Physicians, Phila.*, 3 ser., vol. XV (1893); Samuel Eliot, *Proc. Am. Acad. Arts and Sci.*, vol. XXVIII (1893); H. A. Coit, *A Sermon in Memory of the late George C. Shattuck* (1893); C. D. Bradlee, *New-England Hist. and Geneal. Reg.*, July 1894; *Boston Evening Transcript*, Mar. 23, 1893; diaries and note books, Boston Medical Library; personal reminiscences in "Memorials of St. Paul's School" (1891); portrait in Boston Medical Library.]

H. R. V.

SHATTUCK, LEMUEL (Oct. 15, 1793–Jan. 17, 1859), statistician, genealogist, son of John and Betsy (Miles) Shattuck and descendant of William Shattuck who died in Watertown, Mass., in 1672, was born in Ashby, Mass., and brought up in or near New Ipswich, N. H. He supplemented brief formal schooling at Appleton Academy by private study, then taught school at Troy and Albany, N. Y., and later in Detroit, where he organized the first Sunday school in Michigan. At the age of thirty, he became a merchant at Concord, Mass., in partnership with his brother Daniel. As a member of the school committee he reorganized the schools of Concord, introducing annual school reports, the first of which he presented and published. This practice, required by law throughout the state as a result of his suggestion as a member of the legislature in 1838, did much to improve the school system. About 1834 Shattuck removed to Cambridge and some two years later, to Boston, where he became a publisher and bookseller. At the age of forty-six he retired to devote the rest of his life to public service.

His first publications, appearing in a newspaper, were papers on the two hundred years of Concord's history. Finding that they kindled local interest, he added to them and in 1835 published *A History of the Town of Concord,* a great improvement upon preceding town histories. In studying local genealogy he found that the Concord records of births, marriages, and deaths had been greatly neglected; accordingly, he joined in founding the American Statistical Association, 1839, and not long afterward, the New-England Historic Genealogical Society. He helped to persuade the Massachusetts Medical Society and the American Academy of Arts and Sciences to propose a more effective system of registering births, marriages, and deaths, and was thus instrumental in securing the passage in 1842 of a law requiring such registration, passed in 1842. Shattuck furnished material for the early registration reports and alone prepared the fourth report, on a novel plan. As a member of the legislature in 1849 he became chairman of a special committee on registration which through its report brought about a thorough revision of the state's registration laws.

To utilize the statistics of births, marriages, and deaths as Shattuck desired to do, further information about various classes of the population was necessary. Accordingly, he persuaded the Boston Common Council, of which he had been an active member in 1837–41, to take a census of that city in 1845, and was chosen by the committee to execute the project. His method of procedure made this census primarily one of persons rather than of families. For the first time in the United States the record included "the name and description of every person enumerated . . . among other characteristics specifying the birth place of each, and thus distinguishing the native from the foreign population" (Shattuck's autobiography, *post*, p. 308). Shattuck also wrote an interpretative introduction to the report, another innovation that later became standard practice. The federal census of 1840 had been widely and justly criticized; when it was time for the federal census of 1850, Shattuck was called to Washington for consultation. He persuaded those who were organizing it to introduce many improvements based on his Boston experience, and as a result that census marked a longer advance over its predecessor than has been made at any other date.

He became chairman in 1849 of the commission to make a sanitary survey of Massachusetts, and its *Report* (1850), written entirely by him, is a milestone in the development of public health work throughout the country. Dr. Henry I. Bowditch [*q.v.*] said of it long afterwards, "The ideas contained therein germinated slowly but surely . . . Shattuck . . . as a layman, did more towards bringing Massachusetts to its present status than all the efforts made by the Massachusetts Medical Society in its corporate capacity or by members" (*Public Hygiene in America*, 1877, pp. 31–32). Of this same report, which led to the creation twenty years later of the Massachusetts State Board of Health, another writer said in 1917, "One is amazed, first, at the far-sightedness of Shattuck, and, second, at the way in which his ideal slowly fulfilled itself; there is hardly one of his fifty recommendations which has not in one way or another been carried out in Massachusetts, and there is hardly a public health measure put into practice which was not anticipated by Shattuck, save only those relating to bacteriology—a science then unborn" (George C. Whipple, *State Sanitation*, I, 170).

Shattuck was somewhat above the medium height, precise in dress, slightly pompous in manner. He married Clarissa Baxter of Boston, Dec. 1, 1825, and they had five daughters, of whom three survived him. In 1855 he published *Memorials of the Descendants of William Shattuck,* a genealogy of his own family.

[Autobiographical sketch in *Memorials,* mentioned above; *New-England Hist. and Geneal. Reg.,* Apr. 1860; *Memoirs of the Members of the Social Circle in Concord* (2 ser., 1888); *Memorial Biogs. of the New-England Hist. Geneal. Soc.,* vol. III (1883); *Boston Daily Advertiser,* Jan. 18, 1859.]   W. F. W—x.

SHAUBENA [See SHABONEE, *c.* 1775–1859].

SHAUCK, JOHN ALLEN (Mar. 26, 1841–Jan. 3, 1918), jurist, was the son of Elah and Barbara (Haldeman) Shauck, of Swiss-English and German ancestry, respectively. He was born near Johnsville in Richland (now in Morrow) County, Ohio, to which state his paternal grandfather had migrated from Pennsylvania in 1816. John worked on the farm, attended the common schools, and entered Otterbein University at Westerville, Ohio, where he received the degree of A.B. in 1866. A year later he was graduated in law at the University of Michigan. He began practice in Kansas City, Mo., but in 1869 returned to Dayton, Ohio, where he formed a partnership with Samuel Boltin. This association lasted for fifteen years, becoming especially well known in the field of probate and estate practice. On June 1, 1876, Shauck married Ada May Phillips of Centralia, Ill.

Upon the creation of the circuit courts in Ohio in 1884, Shauck was elected a judge of the second, soon recognized as one of the ablest in the state. After ten years' service on this bench he was elected, in 1894, a member of the supreme court of Ohio, and served for nineteen years, being chief justice three times, through the system of rotation. He was without question one of the greatest of the Ohio supreme court judges. His opinions are distinguished not only for their broad scholarship and clear legal reasoning, but also for their literary style. This same command of language appeared in his occasional addresses, particularly in that delivered in Cleveland in 1910 as a tribute to his intimate friend, William McKinley. As a judge he stood firmly for what he believed to be the most important of the fundamental principles of constitutional law. He held that the state legislatures are limited to powers governmental in nature and that it is the duty of courts to declare void all acts of state legislatures which are non-governmental in character even though not forbidden by express constitutional provision. This belief, fortified by a naturally conservative attitude of mind, led him to be more than willing to declare void legislation which to his mind was subversive. As a result, the supreme court of Ohio under his dominating leadership declared void many laws passed for social betterment, including an eight-hour law and a progressive inheritance tax. Many of the amendments proposed by the constitutional convention of 1921 were framed for the purpose of making such laws constitutional and thus rendering possible in Ohio legislation which had all along found favor in the eyes of the United States Supreme Court. Shauck's most useful contribution to Ohio jurisprudence was his courageous insistence upon the unconstitutionality of various acts of special legislation, passed for local partisan purposes. Such acts had been upheld by the supreme court over a long period of years, but soon after coming to the bench Shauck set out to have these many decisions overruled, and was finally successful in having a unanimous court concur with him.

From 1900 to 1915 he taught the subject of equity in the College of Law at the Ohio State University. As a teacher of law he belonged to the old school; a textbook, supplemented with a few selected cases, was his material. After his fashion, however, he was an excellent teacher, noted for his clarity of exposition and the deep personal interest he took in each student's development. Failing in 1913 of renomination for a fourth term on the supreme court, largely because of the opposition to his conservative views, he associated himself with Edgar L. Weinland in Columbus, in the practice of law. In July 1917 the Ohio State Bar Association elected him its president. The following year he died in Columbus, survived by one daughter.

[Shauck's decisions appear in 52–91 *Ohio Reports* and 1–8 *Ohio Circuit Court Reports.* Biographical information has been drawn from 96 *Ohio Reports,* xli–xlviii; A. W. Drury, *Hist. of the City of Dayton and Montgomery County* (2 vols., 1909); *Hist. of Morrow County and Ohio* (1880), p. 831; *Biog. Annals of Ohio,* 1902–03 (n.d.); *Who's Who in America,* 1916–17; *Proc. Ohio State Bar Asso.,* 1918; *Ohio State Journal* (Columbus), Jan. 4, 1918; family records and recollections.]   A. H. T.

SHAW, ANNA HOWARD (Feb. 14, 1847–July 2, 1919), reformer, physician, minister, was born in Newcastle-upon-Tyne, England, of Scotch-English parents, Thomas and Nicolas (Stott) Shaw. Her father was descended from the "fighting Shaws" of Scotland, and from her mother's side of the family as well she inherited courage and persistence. In 1849 in the hope of recouping his fortunes her father sailed for America, followed in 1851 by his wife and their six children. They lived in Lawrence, Mass., until 1859, when the visionary Thomas Shaw

put his small savings into 360 acres of unbroken wilderness in Michigan. Having cleared a spot large enough for a cabin, he continued for a time his trade of designing wall papers in Lawrence and sent out his wife and five of the children to hold the claim. Anna, who was twelve at the time, faced with characteristic courage the difficulties of these years in the wilderness, of which there is a vivid account in her autobiography, *The Story of a Pioneer* (1915). Though she had only the rudiments of an education, she read eagerly everything that was available and at fifteen became a school teacher at two dollars a week and board among her patrons. The years of the Civil War, in which her father and older brothers served, were particularly hard, but after the war, living with a married sister in Big Rapids, she entered the high school to prepare for college.

She was now about twenty-three. Her desire to become a preacher, an ambition she had cherished from childhood, was first realized when she was invited to preach in a Methodist Church by the presiding elder of the district, who later asked her to follow him during the year in his circuit of thirty-six appointments. Her family, strict Unitarians, who objected not only to her Methodism but to her preaching, considered that she had disgraced them, and for some time there was a marked breach between them. At twenty-four she was given a license to preach by the annual conference. From the fall of 1873 until February 1876, she was a student at Albion College, Albion, Mich., where she was soon in the midst of a battle to maintain the rights of the women students, and where, though she earned a little by giving an occasional temperance lecture or preaching in the neighboring villages, her financial problems were serious. After deep consideration, however, she decided to go on to the theological school of Boston University, an act which she later described as "an instance of stepping off a solid plank and into space" (Shaw, *post,* p. 82). Living in a little attic room on Tremont Street with no light but a skylight, no heat, and no water, she cooked her food over a coal-oil lamp and almost starved. At last the Woman's Foreign Missionary Society arranged that she should have an allowance of three dollars and a half a week; with this and the two dollars granted to licensed preachers for rent, she finished the year. During the summers she served as a substitute preacher on Cape Cod and was temporary pastor at Hingham. After finishing at the university in 1878 she became pastor of a church of the Wesleyan Methodist denomination at East Dennis, where she spent seven years. Since she was not an "ordained" but only a "licensed" minister, she could not administer the sacraments or baptize or receive members into the church, although she could perform the marriage service and bury the dead. When the Methodist Episcopal denomination twice refused to ordain her, she applied to the Methodist Protestant Church, and after a rigorous examination she was ordained, Oct. 12, 1880, against strong opposition. While she was at East Dennis she not only conducted three services a Sunday, did all the necessary parish work, and often lectured in Boston, but began and completed a course in the Boston University Medical School, where she received the degree of M.D. in 1886.

During her years in Boston she made many friends, among them such prominent figures as Mary R. Livermore, Julia Ward Howe, Anna Garlin Spencer, Lucy Stone and Henry Brown Blackwell, Ralph Waldo Emerson and his wife, Amos Bronson Alcott and his daughter Louisa, John Greenleaf Whittier, and Wendell Phillips [qq.v.]. Partly through them she had come to desire a wider field for her efforts. She had become interested not only in the temperance movement but in woman's suffrage, which she saw as a requisite in all reform work for women. In 1885 she became lecturer for the Massachusetts State Suffrage Association, of which Lucy Stone was president, and until the end of her life was actively associated with the effort to secure suffrage for women. In 1886, at the urging of Frances E. Willard [q.v.], she became superintendent of franchise of the national Woman's Christian Temperance Union, a position she held, for the most part without payment, for many years. About 1887 she began to lecture independently. She was soon in constant demand; night after night the year around she lectured, at "Chautauquas" and conventions during the summer and all over the country during the winter. She later wrote of all-night journeys in freight-cars, engines, and cabooses as "casual commonplaces," and of thirty- and forty-mile drives across the country in blizzards and bitter cold.

Although she knew well the prominent reformers of New England, she did not meet Elizabeth Cady Stanton, Susan Brownell Anthony, Lucretia Coffin Mott [qq.v.], and others of that branch of the suffrage movement in New York until she had been actively engaged in it for several years. After 1888, when she and Susan B. Anthony first met at the International Council of Women in Washington, they were intimate friends; for eighteen years they campaigned together for woman's rights, attended conventions,

appeared before committees of Congress, and went to conventions in Europe. From 1892, when Miss Anthony became president of the National American Woman Suffrage Association, Anna Shaw was vice-president at large, and in 1904 she became president, an office she held for eleven years. After 1909, when national suffrage headquarters were opened in New York, she made the city the point of her going and coming. She attended the now frequent conventions for amending state constitutions and was greatly assisted in her work by Jane Addams and Katharine Dexter McCormick, who became officers of the national suffrage association. In 1915, recognizing that her object was nearly achieved, she resigned the presidency, becoming honorary president for life. Had it not been for the World War she might now have been free of some of her heaviest responsibilities. In April 1917, however, she was appointed by the Council of National Defense chairman of the women's committee, and from then until the middle of March 1919, when the committee ceased to exist, she devoted herself to it. She received the highest tributes for this work and was awarded the Distinguished Service Medal. She now saw an opportunity to take up the work for the federal suffrage amendment, which was at its most critical stage in Congress, and had arranged a long list of speaking engagements in various constituencies until May. But at the urging of William Howard Taft and of A. Lawrence Lowell, president of Harvard University, she joined them on a tour of the country to advocate the League of Nations and the treaty of peace under the auspices of the League to Enforce Peace. She surpassed the eloquence of all her former speeches, and vast crowds came out to hear her. Ill from over-exertion, she was obliged to enter a hospital in Springfield, Ill., where she was found to have pneumonia. She died several weeks later at her home in Moylan, Pa.

Her personal life was centered upon her home, her friends, and members of her family; with her lived Lucy E. Anthony, a niece of Susan B. Anthony, who was her private secretary, friend, and companion for over thirty years. As a lecturer she had no equal among women, a distinction that was acknowledged not only in the United States but abroad. Her voice was rich and musical, and she could speak for several hours without any apparent strain. The word, the phrase, the quotation she needed were always at her command, and she was mistress of all the arts of oratory. She was only five feet tall and was rather stout. Her hair, worn in a pompadour, grew white at an early age, but her black eyes sparkled and her smile won an audience immediately. Her humor, courage, and practical sense, which gave her the balance so conspicuously absent in many reformers, were invaluable aids to her in public activities. A vivid and forceful personality, she made friends and won admiration wherever she went. At the time of her death there were messages of regret from the most distinguished men and women of many countries, and many editorial tributes in the newspapers. Memorial foundations were later established at Barnard, Bryn Mawr, and the Women's Medical College of Pennsylvania.

[*Who's Who in America,* 1918–19 ; Anna H. Shaw, *The Story of a Pioneer* (1915) ; Susan B. Anthony and Ida H. Harper, eds., *The Hist. of Woman Suffrage,* vols. IV–VI (1902–22) ; Emily N. Blair, *The Woman's Committee, U. S. Council of Nat. Defense, An Interpretative Report* (1920) ; obituary in *N. Y. Times,* July 3, 1919.]   I. H. H.

SHAW, EDWARD RICHARD (Jan. 13, 1850–Feb. 11, 1903), educator, was born at Bellport, Long Island, N. Y., the son of Joseph Merritt and Caroline Amanda (Gerard) Shaw. His early education was received at Bellport Academy and the Port Jefferson High School. On July 10, 1876, he married Hulda Maria Green, by whom he had one child, a son, who died in 1889. Shaw was graduated from Lafayette College, Easton, Pa., in 1881, with the degree of Ph.B. and in 1887 received that of M.A. from the same institution. He entered the Graduate School of New York University while teaching, attending lectures and seminars after public-school hours, and in 1890 was made a doctor of philosophy.

Shaw's first teaching was done in the high school at Greenport, Long Island. In 1883 he was elected principal of the Yonkers high school. Here he made important reforms, especially in the teaching of physics and mathematics. He developed and introduced an inductive approach to geometry, which was widely adopted, and wrote two textbooks, *Physics by Experiment* (1891), and *English Composition by Practice* (1892). In his writings for educational journals he emphasized the significance of the motor factor in education, and the importance of studying educational problems in the light of biology and the theory of evolution. During his nine years at Yonkers he became known as one of the ablest high school principals in the country.

His experience in this position convinced him that teachers in secondary schools needed professional training on a higher level than that then given in normal schools, and he further believed that such training could be given only by universities, in departments established especial-

ly for the purpose. Largely through his efforts and advice, in 1887 New York University established a professorship of pedagogy in its Graduate School and in October 1890 expanded this professorship into the School of Pedagogy, a professional school on an equal basis with the Law School and the Medical School. A faculty of four full professors and three lecturers was appointed. This was the first university school of education, in distinction from a mere professorship, established in the United States, and is now one of the largest. Shaw became a professor in this school in 1892, and in 1894 was promoted to the position of dean, which he held until his resignation in 1901. In November 1902 he was elected superintendent of schools of Rochester, N. Y., but while preparing for his new duties was taken ill, and died in February following.

Shaw was deeply interested in the new educational movements of his day and appraised them with keen judgment and an unbiased mind. He made repeated journeys to Europe and to many parts of America and was thus able to bring to his students in New York University the best current thought on education in all progressive countries. He was a man of rare ability as a classroom instructor, exercising a marked influence over his students, who were mature young men and women, most of whom had had some experience in teaching. In 1901 he published *School Hygiene,* a textbook which was a standard work and widely used for many years. He also translated and edited Wilhelm Ostermann's *Das Interesse* (1895), under the title *Interest in Its Relation to Pedagogy* (1899), and published a purely literary volume, *Legends of Fire Island* (1895). A posthumous work entitled *A New Course of Study,* and containing a biographical sketch of him by Earl Barnes, was published in 1904.

[Biog. sketch by Earl Barnes, mentioned above; *The Men of Lafayette* (1891) ; *Universities and Their Sons: N. Y. Univ.* (1901), ed. by J. L. Chamberlain ; *N. Y. Univ., 1832–1932* (1933), ed. by T. F. Jones ; *Who's Who in America,* 1901–02 ; *N. Y. Times,* Feb. 12, 1903 ; records of N. Y. Univ.; correspondence with relatives and friends.]   T. M. B.

SHAW, ELIJAH (Dec. 19, 1793–May 5, 1851), pioneer minister of the Christian Connection, was born in Kensington, Rockingham County, N. H., of Scotch descent, the son of Elijah and Deborah (Nudd) Shaw. He was a farmer's boy, and the only formal education he received was that afforded by winter terms in the local school. The Shaws were Congregationalists, but partly through the influence of the father's second wife—Elijah's mother died when he was fourteen—the family became connected with the movement for a vital, undenominational Christianity inaugurated in New England by Abner Jones [q.v.]. Elijah was converted at the age of seventeen and almost immediately became an active religious worker. In the first half of the following year, 1811, he visited Newburyport, Mass., and Saratoga Springs, N. Y., to receive medical treatment, for, in addition to other infirmities, he had an affection of the right hip which incapacitated him for farm labor and gave him more or less trouble throughout his life. During the next three years he made frequent tours as an exhorter, not only in his native state but also in Maine, Vermont, and Massachusetts. On Mar. 31, 1814, he was ordained to the ministry at the "Christian" meeting house in Kensington.

From this time on his labors in behalf of the developing religious body he had joined were incessant and varied. On July 16, 1818, he married Lydia True of Andover, N. H., and soon afterward they removed to Cayuga County, N. Y., and settled at Brutus. For eight years or more Shaw cared for the congregation there and for those in surrounding towns, also making numerous missionary tours, some of which extended into Ohio and northward into Canada. Returning with his family to New England in the spring of 1828, he took charge of a church in Salisbury, Mass., but in 1830 accepted an invitation to become pastor of a church in Portland, Me. He was away much of the time, however, on preaching tours that carried him throughout New England. In 1834 he resigned and, after making his home in Amesbury, Mass., for a brief period, removed to Exeter, N. H., to take editorial charge of the *Christian Journal*. This paper was a continuation of the *Herald of Gospel Liberty*, the earliest religious newspaper in the United States, started in 1808 by Elias Smith [q.v.]. From 1818 to 1835 it was published as the *Christian Herald* by Robert Foster, from whom it was taken over by the Eastern Christian Publishing Association, organized Jan. 1, 1835, with Shaw as one of its executive committee. Shaw was sole editor of the *Journal* from 1835 to 1840 and associated with it till the end of his life. First issued as a bi-weekly, it later became a weekly. In 1840, when relieved of office work in connection with the paper, he removed to Lowell, Mass. The remaining eleven years of his life he spent in untiring labors, especially in behalf of education and organized missionary activity. For brief periods he had pastoral care of churches in Lowell, Mass., Durham, N. H., Franklin and Fall River, Mass.; he also continued his itinerant preaching. For a time (1842–43) he was agent

to secure funds for the establishment of Durham (N. H.) Academy. He published *Sentiments of the Christians* (1847), a brief work setting forth succinctly the history, beliefs, and ecclesiastical polity of the Christian Connection. The preceding year he had served as president of its General Conference. In 1840 he began in the columns of the *Christian Herald* a series of articles urging a "missionary system," and partly as a result of these articles and other efforts of his the New England Missionary Society was formed in 1845, of which Shaw was appointed agent. He traveled in its interests chiefly in New England, but in 1850 made a tour from Massachusetts to Michigan and back. This was his last great effort; for some time his health had been failing, and in May of the following year he died.

[Letitia J. S. Brown, *Memoir of Elder Elijah Shaw, by His Daughter* (1852), reprints *Sentiments of the Christians* and other of Shaw's writings; see also E. W. Humphreys, *Memoirs of Deceased Christian Ministers* (1880), and M. T. Morrill, *A Hist. of the Christian Denomination in America* (1912).]   H. E. S.

SHAW, HENRY (July 24, 1800–Aug. 25, 1889), founder of the Missouri Botanical Garden, was born at Sheffield, England, the eldest of the four children of Sarah (Hoole) and Joseph Shaw, both natives of Leicester. His father was a manufacturer of grates and fire-irons. Between the ages of ten and sixteen he attended Mill High School, near London, which a hundred years before had been the home of Peter Collinson, a merchant who was the friend and correspondent of Linnæus, John Bartram [q.v.], and other well-known botanists. Here he acquired a good knowledge of French and received excellent training in mathematics.

Emigrating to Canada with his father in 1818, he was sent to New Orleans to learn the cotton business but he remained less than a year. In May 1819 he went to St. Louis. There he set up a small hardware and cutlery business in a second-story room, where for a time he slept, cooked, and ate his meals as well as sold his goods. Social life had little attraction for him, but he read widely and applied himself diligently to his work. By the time he was forty he had accumulated what he regarded as a fortune, and he retired from business to enjoy it. Most of the next ten years he spent in travel abroad, improving his knowledge of languages and becoming, though his tastes remained sober, a thoroughly cosmopolitan gentleman. He had a great interest in plants and with advice from such men as Asa Gray, Dr. George Englemann [qq.v.], and Sir William Jackson Hooker, then the director of Kew Gardens, he established a garden in St. Louis that was in reality a scientific institution for the study of plants. Work was begun in 1857, and about 1860 "Mr. Shaw's garden," as it was popularly known, was opened to the public. There he built up the nucleus of one of the best botanical libraries, as well as one of the largest herbariums, in the United States and provided in his will for the maintenance of a scientific staff which was to conduct "scientific investigations in botany proper, in vegetable physiology, the diseases of plants, the study of the forms of vegetable life . . ." Through a special act of the legislature, the Missouri Botanical Garden, as he named it, was established under a self-perpetuating board of trustees, the income from Shaw's estate being its only source of revenue. He also endowed what came to be known as the Henry Shaw School of Botany of Washington University. After 1851 he scarcely left St. Louis but devoted his time to the development of his garden and to the planning and planting of Tower Grove Park, his gift to the city. He never married. He died in St. Louis and was buried in the garden in a place he had chosen. During his lifetime the institution he founded was the only one of its kind in the United States, and after his death it continued to be one of the important botanical gardens of the world.

[Shaw's diaries and MSS. are in the library of the Mo. Botanical Garden. See *Mo. Botanical Garden Bull.*, Sept. 1918, Apr. 1921, June 1926, May 1931, and esp. Jan. 1921, which contains a series of portraits, and Nov. 1924, which reprints a biog. sketch from *First Ann. Report Mo. Botanical Garden*, 1890; obituary in *St. Louis Globe-Democrat*, Aug. 26, 1889.] G. T. M.

SHAW, HENRY WHEELER (Apr. 21, 1818–Oct. 14, 1885), humorist, better known by his pseudonym Josh Billings, was born in Lanesboro, Berkshire County, Mass., the son of Henry and Laura (Wheeler) Shaw. His grandfather, Samuel Shaw, a Vermont physician, was sent to jail for libelling John Adams and afterward, apparently for the same reason, to Congress. His father, for many years a henchman of Henry Clay's, ended his career in the House of Representatives by voting for the Missouri Compromise, which was unpopular in the Berkshires. A maternal uncle, John Savage, after holding various political offices, was for fourteen years chief justice of New York. Shaw attended an academy kept by John Hotchin in Lenox and entered Hamilton College in 1832, but neglected his books and was dismissed in his sophomore year for removing the clapper from the chapel bell. The records of his next twenty years are scanty. Armed with letters of recommendation from John Quincy Adams, Henry Clay, and Martin Van Buren [*qq.v.*], he went west and at St. Louis joined a party of young men who proposed to explore the Rocky Mountains, but when one of his companions died on the Kansas prairie the ill-considered expedition broke up. For a year or more he sojourned in Norwalk, Ohio, where he was remembered as a practical joker. One of his reputed hoaxes was a public lecture, "On Milk," a device to which he reverted when he became a professional humorist. After some years' absence he returned home and was married on Feb. 18, 1845, at Lebanon, N. Y., to Zilpha Bradford (Palmer, *post*, p. 165), daughter of Levi Bradford of Lanesboro, by whom he had two daughters. For a few years he lived as a farmer in his native township and then set out again for the West. After a harrowing experience as proprietor of a ramshackle Ohio river steamboat, which he tried to navigate in midwinter, Shaw decided that he had been a rolling stone long enough and settled in Poughkeepsie, N. Y., as an auctioneer and dealer in real estate.

He was forty-five years old before he began to write. His earliest attempts were printed in the New Ashford, Mass., *Eagle* and in Poughkeepsie newspapers, but until he rewrote his "Essay on the Mule" in grotesque misspelling he attracted no attention. Through the kindness of Charles Farrar Browne [*q.v.*], better known as Artemus Ward, he secured a publisher for his first book, *Josh Billings, His Sayings* (1865). Similar collections followed: *Josh Billings on Ice, and Other Things* (1868); *Josh Billings' Farmer's Allminax for the Year 1870* (1869–70) —a success that he repeated each year until 1880; *Twelve Ancestral Sighns in the Billings' Zodiac Gallery* (1873); *Josh Billings, His Works Complete* (1876); *Everybody's Friend* (1874); *Josh Billings' Trump Kards* (1877), *Complete Comical Writings* (1877); *Josh Billings Struggling with Things* (1881); and *Josh Billings' Spice Box* (1881). His books were pirated extensively in England. The range of his gift was narrow. "With me," he once observed, "everything must be put in two or three lines." He had no knack for story-telling or character portrayal, and his satire was too kindly to have much edge; but as a crackerbox philosopher, issuing bucolic aphorisms by the hundred, he had no equal among his contemporaries and has been surpassed only by Edgar Watson Howe. His best work is in the *Allminax*. Like other humorists of his day, he early ventured upon the lecture platform, but success came slowly. Once he gained a reputation, he removed from Poughkeepsie and made his headquarters in New York. He was fond of travel, and the discomforts of a lecturing tour were for him excitement and pleasure. He was tall and corpulent. Long hair—a fashion he detested—concealed a birthmark on his neck. In his maturity the harum-scarum, shiftless youth had long since disappeared in the thrifty, kindly moralist. He was unaffectedly domestic in his habits, was fond of driving and of trout-fishing, and read little except the newspapers and the Bible. His fame was largely popular, but a few earnest pursuers of the autochthonous in American literature thought they saw in him a Yankee Rochefoucauld. He died of an apoplectic stroke at Monterey, Cal., while sunning himself on a hotel veranda, and was buried in Lanesboro.

[Cyril Clemens, *Josh Billings, Yankee Humorist* (Webster Groves, Mo., 1932), and Jennette R. Tandy, *Crackerbox Philosophers in Am. Humor and Satire* (1925) are the most useful references. Both have bibliographies. See also W. P. Trent, "A Retrospect of Am. Humor," *Century Mag.*, Nov. 1901; E. P. Thomson, in *New England Mag.*, Feb. 1899; F. S. Smith, *Life and Adventures of Josh Billings* (1883); *Appletons' Ann. Cyc.*, 1885; obituaries in *Evening Post* (N. Y.) and *Boston Transcript*, Oct. 15, 1885; C. J. Palmer, *Hist. of Town of Lanesborough, Mass.* (1905).]
G. H. G.

SHAW, HOWARD VAN DOREN (May 7, 1869–May 6, 1926), architect, was born in Chicago, Ill. His father was Theodore Andrews Shaw, a wholesale dry-goods merchant of Madison, Ind., whose Scotch Presbyterian ancestry went back to the settlement of Pennsylvania. His mother was Sarah Van Doren of Brooklyn, a descendant of Pieter Van Doorn, who emigrated to America from Holland in 1659 and settled at New Amsterdam. After preparing for college at the Harvard School in Chicago Shaw went to Yale College, where he graduated in 1890. After studying architecture at the Massachusetts Institute of Technology (1890–91), he spent about a year abroad and returned to Chicago and entered the office of William LeBaron Jenney [*q.v.*] and William B. Mundie, pioneers in the design and erection of the skyscraper. On Apr. 20, 1893, he married Frances Wells, daughter of a prominent Chicago merchant, who with their three daughters survived him at the time of his death. When, sometime in the following year, he opened an office of his own, his work consisted at first in designing houses for his friends. His practice soon increased, however, and as his performance and his reputation grew together he became probably the most highly regarded architect in the sphere of domestic, ecclesiastical, and noncommercial architecture in the Middle West.

His work, particularly in domestic architecture, exerted a powerful influence on younger architects and on taste in general. Though reminiscent often of English or Austrian precedent, his style was very personal. He never used French and seldom Italian motives. The buildings he erected, for the most part, were of such character and magnitude that neither his ideals nor his talents had to suffer restrictions. He designed many town houses in Chicago, and country houses in Lake Forest and other fashionable suburbs. His other buildings include the Market Square in Lake Forest; a model town, built by the Clayton Mark Manufacturing Company, Indiana Harbor, Ind.; and in Chicago the Lakeside Press buildings; the Mentor Building; the Fourth Presbyterian Church (with Cram, Goodhue, and Ferguson); the University Church of the Disciples of Christ; the Quadrangle Club, University of Chicago; the Kenneth Sawyer Goodman Memorial Theatre; apartments at 1130 Lake Shore Drive, 2450 Lakeview Ave., and 191 E. Walton Place. Of all these and a great many others it can be said that each exemplified originality, taste, and learning at its best. It is to be regretted that Shaw designed so few churches, for he was an excellent Gothicist. In his last days he was awarded the gold medal of the American Institute of Architecture for service to American architecture.

About 1898 he built a beautiful house, "Ragdale," in Lake Forest, Ill., where he lived until his death. The estate became an experimental laboratory for the testing of his taste and craftsmanship. Here, in his spare hours, he became an excellent carpenter, bricklayer, tree-surgeon, gardener, and painter; he also designed the setting, lighting effects, and scenery for an outdoor theatre, and did much of the work upon it. Throughout his life he sought recreation in travel, often in Europe. Although he was of a markedly retiring disposition, behind the scenes he exerted a powerful influence in many civic and charitable activities. He was a trustee of the Art Institute of Chicago from 1900, chairman of the state art commission, a trustee of the United Charities and of Illinois College, Jacksonville, Ill. He was a Fellow of the American Institute of Architects and active in its councils. Shortly before his death, too late for him to serve, he was appointed a member of the United States battle monument commission, and was directed to design the United States naval monument at Brest and the memorial chapel in Flanders Field. He died of anemia in Baltimore, Md.

[Shaw's work is discussed in *Architectural Record*, Apr. 1913; *Western Architect*, Oct. 1917; and *House Beautiful*, Mar. 1927. See also *Who's Who in America*, 1924–25; *Yale Univ. Obit. Record of Grads.* (1926); *Forty Year Record, Class of 1890, Yale Coll.* (1933), ed. by L. S. Haslam; *Brickbuilder*, Jan. 1916; *Western Architect*, Sept. 1926; *Am. Architect*, May 20, 1926; *Jour. Am. Inst. of Architects*, July 1926; *Architectural Forum*, June, July 1926; *Architectural Record*, July 1926; obituaries in *Sun* (Baltimore), *Chicago Daily News*, May 7, 1926; poem in *Poetry*, July 1926.]
T. E. T.

SHAW, JOHN (1773–Sept. 17, 1823), naval officer, was born at Mountmellick, Queen's County, Ireland, the son of John and Elizabeth (Barton) Shaw, and died at Philadelphia, Pa. His paternal grandfather was an English army officer who entered Ireland on service in 1690 and later married and settled there. His father also became an army officer and served in Ireland and Germany. In 1763 he returned from the Continent, married Elizabeth Barton, a member of an English family which had become established in Kilkenny, and in 1779 retired to a farm where he subsequently eked out a meager livelihood and reared a large family. Poverty ultimately led to the emigration of two sons, John and an elder brother, to America. Reaching New York in December 1790, they soon proceeded to Philadelphia to seek employment. Apparently in consequence of his recent voyage, John immediately began a seafaring career. Between March 1791 and the autumn of 1797 he made four voyages to the East Indies. He also was employed in Philadelphia counting-houses and served with the Macpherson Blues, a volunteer military organization which in 1794 helped to suppress the insurgents in western Pennsylvania. Becoming master of a brig in 1797, he spent the next year in making a voyage to the West Indies and in trying to evade French privateers. Immediately after returning to Baltimore he entered the United States navy and on Aug. 3, 1798, was commissioned lieutenant. Until October 1799 he served aboard the *Montezuma,* which was engaged in convoying merchantmen throughout West Indian waters, and displayed such marked abilities that he soon received command of the schooner *Enterprise.* With her Shaw made a brilliant record; within a few months the *Enterprise* captured eight French privateers and fought five sharply-contested actions, of which two were "with vessels of superior force" (Cooper, *post,* vol. I, p. 139).

His activities during the ensuing years were exceedingly varied. In 1801 he commanded the *George Washington* on a voyage to Algiers with tribute to that regency; the following year, having been placed on half pay, he obtained a furlough that enabled him to make a voyage as master of a merchantman to Canton. In 1804, while he was absent, he was promoted to the rank of commander and upon his return volunteered to lead a flotilla of gunboats against Tripoli. In 1805 he was placed in command of the frigate *John Adams* and, accompanied by three gunboats, sailed to the Mediterranean but soon returned to America, peace with Tripoli having been declared in the meantime. He was ordered

to New Orleans in 1806 to construct gunboats for coastal defense, and Aug. 27, 1807, he was promoted to the rank of captain. Learning about Aaron Burr's intrigues in the Southwest, he prepared to frustrate them by mobilization of a naval force in the lower Mississippi. Later he served as a witness at Burr's trial. From May 1808 until August 1810 he was in charge of the navy yard at Norfolk, Va.; from 1811 until the spring of 1814 he was actively engaged in fortifying New Orleans and in helping to capture Mobile. In 1814 he took command of the naval squadron which was being blockaded by the British in the vicinity of New London, Conn., and there remained until the end of the war. Soon after he joined Commander William Bainbridge's squadron, ordered to the Mediterranean to settle accounts with Algiers, and when peace was made he remained behind in command of a squadron to protect American interests. After December 1817, when he returned to America, he did not go to sea. During his last years he was for a time in charge of the Boston navy yard and later of the naval station at Charleston, S. C. He was twice married. His first wife was Elizabeth Palmer, a Philadelphia Quakeress; she bore him a number of children, but only two daughters reached maturity. His second wife, whom he married Oct. 13, 1820, and by whom he had no issue, was Mary Breed of Charlestown, Mass., a member of the family after which Breed's Hill, of Revolutionary fame, was named.

[R. W. Irwin, *The Diplomatic Relations of the U. S. with the Barbary Powers, 1776–1816* (1931), and G. W. Allen, *Our Navy and the Barbary Corsairs* (1905) contain numerous references to Shaw's Mediterranean activities. See also J. F. Cooper, *Lives of Distinguished Am. Naval Officers* (1846), vol. I; *Nat. Gazette and Lit. Reg.* (Phila.), Sept. 20, 1823; T. B. Wyman, *Geneal. and Estates of Charlestown . . . Mass., 1629–1818* (1879), vol. II; brief obituary in *Poulson's Am. Daily Advertiser,* Sept. 18, 1823.]   R. W. I.

SHAW, JOHN (May 4, 1778–Jan. 10, 1809), physician, poet, was born at Annapolis, Md. He entered St. John's College in that city at its opening in 1789 and graduated as Latin salutatorian in October 1796, in the same class with his close friend, Francis Scott Key. His first published poem, apparently, was "The Voice of Freedom" in the *Baltimore Telegraphe* for May 13, 1795. For two years he remained at Annapolis studying medicine under Dr. John Thomas Shaaff and reading widely in Greek and medieval medical literature. In November 1798 he went to Philadelphia to continue his studies at the University of Pennsylvania, but a boyish freak led him to take the post of surgeon on a squadron about to sail for Algiers, and on Dec. 23 he embarked with James Leander Cathcart and William Eaton [*qq.v.*] on the brig *Sophia.* For a few months he was Eaton's secretary at Tunis and was then sent to London to confer on diplomatic business with the elder Rufus King [*q.v.*]. He visited Italy, Gibraltar, and Lisbon, and learned not only Portuguese, Spanish, and Italian but also some Arabic. He returned to Annapolis in the spring of 1800 but sailed again in July 1801 to take up his medical studies at Edinburgh. In 1803 he accompanied the colony sent out by Thomas Douglas, fifth Earl of Selkirk, to Prince Edward Island, where he had to cope with a severe epidemic. Early in 1805 he returned once more to Annapolis and took up practice with his old teacher Shaaff, but after his marriage on Feb. 12, 1807, to Jane Selby (or Telby) of Annapolis he removed to Baltimore. There he gained immediate recognition. In 1807 he joined with James Cocke and John Beale Davidge [*q.v.*] to secure a charter from the state legislature for the College of Medicine of Maryland, the fifth medical school in the United States, and the forerunner of the University of Maryland. The three founders and their colleagues gave instruction in their own houses, Shaw taking charge of the work in chemistry. He taught and worked with enthusiasm. One experiment that he conducted obliged him to immerse his arms in cold water at frequent intervals throughout an entire night; this exposure brought on an attack of pleurisy, and after it tuberculosis set in. In accordance with the practice of the time, he set out for the South. He died at sea while voyaging from Charleston, S. C., to the Bahamas. He had contributed poems to Joseph Dennie's *Port Folio* between 1801 and 1805 under the name of Ithacus (A. H. Smyth, *The Philadelphia Magazines and their Contributors,* 1892), and in 1810 *Poems by the Late Doctor John Shaw* was published at Philadelphia and Baltimore, with a memoir, including selections from his journal and letters, by John Elihu Hall [*q.v.*]. His poems reveal no conspicuous talent or originality, yet they were sufficiently pleasing to gain a place in nineteenth-century anthologies of American verse from Samuel Kettell's in 1829 to E. C. Stedman's in 1900. The best of them stand comparison with the work of Francis Hopkinson and with all but the finest of Philip Freneau's.

[Hall's memoir in *Poems by the Late Dr. John Shaw* (1810) is the only authority for Shaw's life but is generally inaccessible. The best secondary account is John Ruhräh, "John Shaw—A Medical Poet of Md.," *Annals of Medical Hist.,* Sept. 1921. See also H. A. Kelly and W. L. Burrage, *Am. Medic. Biogs.* (1920); E. F. Cordell, *Hist. Sketch of the Univ. of Md. School of Medicine* (1891); E. A. and G. L. Duyckinck, *Cyc. of Am. Lit.* (1875), vol. I.]   G. H. G.

SHAW, LEMUEL (Jan. 9, 1781–Mar. 30, 1861), jurist, was born in Barnstable, Mass., the second son of Oakes Shaw and his second wife Susanna, who was a daughter of John H. Hayward of Braintree. The Shaws were descendants of Abraham Shaw, who left Halifax, England, in 1636 and settled in Dedham, Mass. Oakes Shaw (a Congregationalist minister, was pastor of the West Church in Barnstable forty-seven years. Lemuel was named for his uncle, Dr. Hayward of Boston, father of George Hayward [*q.v.*], the surgeon. Taught at home by his father except for a few months at Braintree he entered Harvard in 1796. There he taught school in winter vacations. After graduating with high rank in 1800, he taught for a year in a Boston public school, and wrote articles and read proof for the *Boston Gazette,* a Federalist newspaper. In August 1801 he began studying law in Boston under David Everett [*q.v.*]. Meanwhile he learned French proficiently from a refugee, Antoine Jay, afterwards a founder in France of the liberal *Constitutionnel.* In 1802 he moved with Everett to Amherst, N. H., where besides doing legal work he contributed a poem on dancing and translations from French to the *Farmers' Cabinet,* a local newspaper. He became engaged to Nancy Melville, daughter of Maj. Thomas Melville of Boston, the original of Holmes's "The Last Leaf," but she died soon afterwards.

Admitted to the bar in Hillsboro County, N. H., in September 1804, and in Plymouth County, Mass., in November, he began practice in Boston. When his associate left Boston after being acquitted of murder in a political quarrel, he practised alone for fifteen years; about 1822 he took Sidney Bartlett, an able trial lawyer, as his junior partner. His practice gradually became large, but he was less known as an advocate than as the adviser of important commercial enterprises. On Jan. 6, 1818, he married Elizabeth Knapp, daughter of Josiah Knapp of Boston. She died in 1822, leaving a son and a daughter, who became the wife of Herman Melville [*q.v.*], nephew of Shaw's former fiancée. On Aug. 29, 1827, he married Hope Savage, daughter of Dr. Samuel Savage of Barnstable; they had two sons. He was admirably prepared for his judicial career by numerous public positions. He was a representative in the General Court in 1811–14, 1820, and 1829, a state senator in 1821–22, and a member of the constitutional convention of 1820. He also held many offices in Boston. In 1822, with few precedents to guide him, he drew the first charter of the city, which lasted until 1913. On the death of Chief Justice Isaac Parker [*q.v.*], Gov. Levi Lincoln,

1782–1868 [*q.v.*], offered Shaw the appointment. Though it meant giving up a practice of $15,000–$20,000 a year for a salary of $3500, he accepted. His commission was issued Aug. 30, 1830, and he served thirty years, resigning Aug. 21, 1860.

His exceptionally long judicial career coincided with the development of many important industries, so that his great abilities had full scope for making the law on such matters as water power, railroads, and other public utilities. Probably no other state judge has so deeply influenced commercial and constitutional law throughout the nation. Almost all the principles laid down by him have proved sound, although his remarkable skill in expounding the unfortunate fellow-servant rule considerably delayed the replacement of that rule by workmen's compensation. An opinion by Shaw rarely lends itself to isolated quotations; its strength lies in the entire solidity of its reasoning. "His words had weight rather than brilliancy or eloquence" (Chase, *post,* p. 278), and his greatness came from his personality as well as from his intellectual powers. He was no mere writer of opinions but preëminently a magistrate. In Shaw's time the chief justice sat often at trials. In such work he was thorough, systematic, very patient, with a remarkable power to charge juries so that they understood the exact questions before them. Among his cases that excited great public interest were the trial in 1834 of the anti-Catholic rioters who destroyed the Ursuline convent in Charlestown (*Commonwealth* vs. *Buzzell,* 33 *Mass. Reports,* 153) and that in 1850 of Prof. John White Webster [*q.v.*] for murdering Dr. George Parkman (*Commonwealth* vs. *Webster,* 59 *Mass. Reports,* 295). A notable example of his courage and integrity was his refusal in 1851 to release Sims, the fugitive slave, on *habeas corpus* (61 *Mass. Reports,* 285); he was strongly opposed to slavery, but he felt bound by the Constitution and the law, and disregarded both the violence of the mob and the denunciations of the respectable.

Widely read in English literature, he was also attracted by new mechanical processes and was a member of many learned and charitable societies. He was fellow of Harvard College from 1834 until his death, and an overseer from 1831 to 1853, two offices rarely united. In politics he was a Federalist and a Webster Whig, but remained all his life a free-trader. He attended Unitarian services, though he was never a communicant. Fond of entertaining and dining out, he was simple and affectionate in his home life, his interest in the social events of his household extending to the minutest details. After his resignation from the bench, his health failed, and

he died within a few months. He was buried in Mt. Auburn cemetery.

[The best biog. is that of F. H. Chase, *Lemuel Shaw, Chief Justice of the Supreme Judicial Court of Mass., 1830–1860* (1918), reviewed by E. H. Abbot, *Harvard Law Rev.,* Dec. 1918. A pamphlet, *Lemuel Shaw, Chief Justice of the Supreme Judicial Court of Mass.* (1885), reprints articles by S. S. Shaw and P. E. Aldrich in *Memorial Biogs. New England Hist. Geneal Soc.,* vol. IV (1885) and by B. F. Thomas in *Am. Law Rev.,* Oct. 1867. See also J. H. Beale, in *Great Am. Lawyers,* vol. III (1907), ed. by W. D. Lewis; C. G. Loring, in *Proc. Am. Acad. of Arts and Sci., 1860–1862,* vol. V (1862); *The Proc. at the Meeting of the Bar at the Birthplace of Chief Justice Shaw, West Barnstable, Mass., Aug. 4, 1916* (n.d.); W. T. Davis, *Hist. of the Judiciary of Mass.* (1900); obituaries in *New England Hist. and Geneal. Reg.,* July 1861, *Boston Daily Advertiser,* Apr. 1, 1861, *Boston Transcript,* Mar. 30, 1861, *Daily Evening Traveller* (Boston), Mar. 30, Apr. 1, 9, 1861. Shaw's opinions appear in 27–81 *Mass. Reports.* The proceedings of the bench and bar on his resignation are in 15 *Gray,* 599, and on his death in 1 *Allen,* 597.]

Z. C., Jr.

SHAW, LESLIE MORTIER (Nov. 2, 1848–Mar. 28, 1932), governor of Iowa, secretary of the treasury, banker, typified in his entire career Yankee business genius developed and modified by a midwestern, frontier environment. He was born at Morristown, Vt., but his parents, Boardman O. and Lovisa (Spaulding) Shaw, soon removed to a farm in Stowe township. His youthful ambition was to become a Western landowner, and after graduating from the village academy he taught school only long enough to secure the funds to go out, in 1869, to an uncle's farm in eastern Iowa. Two years later he entered the neighboring Cornell College, where, after supporting himself by farm labor, school-teaching, and selling fruit trees, he graduated in 1874. Meanwhile his interest had shifted to the law, and in 1876 he completed the course at the Iowa College of Law, Des Moines, and started practice at Denison, where he had made friendships as a salesman. The following year, Dec. 6, 1877, he married Alice Crawshaw of Clinton County, the daughter of a pioneer farmer. They had three children, a son and two daughters.

Shaw's legal business was at first so light that he was forced to continue selling apple trees. He recognized that the chief need of his productive agricultural region was credit, and in 1880, with his partner, organized a bank and a mortgage loan business with branches in neighboring towns. For funds he turned to Vermont savings banks, persuading some of their officials to view the region at first hand. The result was the investment of several millions to the advantage of all concerned. Shaw was active in community business, educational, and religious organizations. His Methodist connections were an especial asset. His leadership in Sunday school work attracted state-wide attention, while his lay membership in four General Conferences (1888–1900) gave him national prominence in ecclesiastical circles. His political career began in 1896 when he was invited by fellow businessmen to reply to one of William Jennings Bryan's pre-convention speeches. His presentation of his argument, illustrated by charts of price and currency trends, was so convincing that he was called upon for speeches throughout the campaign. The reputation thus gained was responsible for his nomination for governor after a deadlock in the Republican convention the next year. He was elected and served two terms (1898–1902), giving particular attention to institutional expansion and reorganization, especially of the state school system in all its branches.

Shortly after his retirement, in January 1902, President Theodore Roosevelt unexpectedly named him to head the Treasury Department. The selection, remarkable in view of Shaw's small-city background and the fact that Iowa already had a cabinet member in James Wilson, the secretary of agriculture, was due to Shaw's conspicuous position as a champion of the gold standard in the campaign of 1896, as permanent chairman of the International Monetary Convention in 1898, and as a campaigner for Roosevelt in 1900, as well as to political expediency in the removal of a potential rival in 1904. As secretary, Shaw resorted to unprecedented expedients for dealing with the pressing credit stringency—liberalizing the security and waiving the reserve requirement for government bank deposits; withholding funds, for deposit in time of need; artificially stimulating gold importation; and regulating note issues by executive decree —that were condemned by unfriendly critics as legally unwarranted and economically unsound. At the same time his ultra-protectionist views made the President uneasy. Nevertheless, when the Secretary desired to resign in 1905, Roosevelt persuaded him to remain until March 1907.

Shaw then spent a few years in metropolitan banking. He was head of the Carnegie Trust Company of New York in 1907–08 and of the First Mortgage Guarantee & Trust Company of Philadelphia, 1909–13. He was an avowed candidate for the presidential nomination in 1908, but received no serious consideration. Until 1918 he retained a New York City business address, but his residence after 1913 was in Washington, where he devoted himself to writing and lecturing. As a speaker he had a quaint, racy humor and a fund of apt anecdotes, drawn largely from personal experiences, that made him effective on Chautauqua circuit and political stump. His basic ideas, national dependence

upon high protection and domestic *laissez-faire,* were well summarized in his books, *Current Issues* (1908) and *Vanishing Landmarks: The Trend Toward Bolshevism* (1919). He wrote and spoke for party measures and candidates until within a year of his death, which occurred in Washington, D. C.

[*The Messages and Proclamations of the Govs. of Iowa,* vol. VII (1905), ed. by B. F. Shambaugh; *Ann. Reports of the Secretary of the Treasury,* 1902–06; *Selections from the Correspondence of Theodore Roosevelt and Henry Cabot Lodge* (1925), vol. II; H. H. Kohlsaat, *From McKinley to Harding* (1923); G. E. Roberts, "Leslie M. Shaw," *Independent,* Jan. 16, 1902; A. P. Andrew, "The Treasury and the Banks under Secretary Shaw," *Quart. Jour. of Econ.,* Aug. 1907; *Who's Who in America,* 1930–31; *N. Y. Times,* Mar. 28, 29, 1932; *Des Moines Register,* Mar. 29, 1932.]

E. D. R.

SHAW, MARY (Jan. 25, 1854–May 18, 1929), actress, was born in Boston, the daughter of Levi W. and Margaret (Keating) Shaw, her father being a native of New Hampshire and her mother of Ireland. After being educated in the public schools of Boston, she taught there from 1873 to 1878. Obtaining an engagement as a minor member of the Boston Museum Stock Company, she made her début there in a small part in an extravaganza and remained during the season of 1879–1880. In 1881 she appeared as Lady Sneerwell in New York and for a brief period was with Augustin Daly's company, her first real opportunity coming when she joined the company of Madame Helena Modjeska [*q.v.*] in the fall of 1883. She remained with Modjeska four seasons, acting Celia in *As You Like It,* Mariana in *Measure for Measure,* Hero in *Much Ado About Nothing,* and other important rôles. She is described by Modjeska (*post,* p. 463) as "a studious, intellectual young woman, with a great deal of talent." In 1890 she supported Julia Marlowe.

She made her first starring tour in the spring of 1890 in *A Drop of Poison,* adapted from the German, but it was only a *succès d'estime.* A reviewer in the *Boston Transcript* (May 6, 1890) said that "her exquisitely trained voice, her Delsartian truth and facility of gesture, her easy mastery of the technique of her art, assure her permanent occupancy of the high position to which she has won her way by such worthy effort." Although she remained a hard-working actress for many years, this prophecy was scarcely fulfilled. Many of the plays in which she was obliged to act were of very little merit, and she was obscured in inconsequential characters; other excellent plays that she brought out had in them no marked elements of stage popularity. She soon returned to the support of stars and to acting secondary parts in traveling companies.

She acted Roxy in *Pudd'nhead Wilson* with Frank Mayo, Gretchen in *Rip Van Winkle* with Joseph Jefferson [*qq.v.*], Marian in *Tess of the D'Urbervilles* with Minnie Maddern Fiske, and she was the original Amrah in the dramatization of Lew Wallace's novel, *Ben Hur*.

In 1899 she produced Ibsen's *Ghosts,* and acted Mrs. Alving then and on future occasions during the following twenty years or more. Her interpretation of that part and of the part of Hedda Gabler brought her much praise but little substantial encouragement. In October 1905 she appeared in New York as Mrs. Warren in George Bernard Shaw's *Mrs. Warren's Profession,* which was immediately suppressed by the municipal authorities because of what they called its immorality. Feeling that the play and its motive had been misunderstood, she later revived it several times. She was twice married. Her second husband was M. de Brissac, a stage manager of French origin, but their life together was neither long nor happy. By her first marriage she had one son. She took an active part in feminist, suffragist, and humanitarian movements. She died in New York in retirement.

[Boston vital records; *Boston Museum . . . An Interesting Retrospect . . . Issued for Season of 1880–81* (pamphlet); J. B. Clapp and E. F. Edgett, *Players of the Present* (1901); T. Allston Brown, *A Hist. of the New York Stage* (1903), vol. III; Helena Modjeska, *Memories and Impressions* (1910); Eugene Tompkins and Quincy Kilby, *The Hist. of the Boston Theatre* (1908); William Winter, *The Wallet of Time* (1913), vol. II; John Parker, *Who's Who in the Theatre,* 1925; *Who's Who in America,* 1928–29; *N. Y. Dramatic Mirror,* June 26, 1897; July 15, 1899; Oct. 26, 1910; obituaries in *N. Y. Times,* May 19, 1929, and *Boston Transcript,* May 20, 1929.]   E. F. E.

SHAW, NATHANIEL (Dec. 5, 1735–Apr. 15, 1782), a leading merchant of New London, Conn., acted during the Revolution as naval agent both for Connecticut and for the Continental Congress. His father, Nathaniel, a native of Fairfield, Conn., settled in New London before 1730, became a sea-captain in the Irish trade, founded a mercantile house, and married Temperance Harris. The younger Nathaniel took over his father's business and by the early 1760's was an established merchant in the West Indian trade. Occasionally he transacted business in London and the Mediterranean, but commonly his brigs and sloops took lumber, cattle, or provisions to the West Indies and brought back sugar and molasses, either to be landed at his wharves and warehouses in New London or shipped direct to his correspondents, Peter Vandervoort of New York, Thomas and Isaac Wharton of Philadelphia, and George Erving or William Miller of Boston. A typical Connecticut Yankee, shrewd, close, a stickler for his bond, a curt letter-writer, he adhered rigidly to the high ethical code prescribed by the commerce of his age. Generous as a citizen, he presented his native town in 1767 with a fire engine, the "Compleatest ever Imported into this Continent," and was a proprietor of the Union School. He was married, July 20, 1758, to Lucretia, daughter of Daniel Harris and widow of Josiah Rogers.

The British Acts of Parliament of the 1760's found Shaw unwaveringly on the colonial side. The Sugar Act made him an avowed enemy of those "cruizing Pyrates," the revenue sloops, and as hard money became scarcer, he landed more and more cargoes without clearing at the custom house, "for In Short brown Sugars will not bear to pay dutys on" (Rogers, *post,* p. 226). In 1769 Boston custom commissioners accused him of aiding in the destruction of the revenue sloop *Liberty* and of rescuing his own vessel with prohibited goods. His safe reply was an offer to maintain his innocence before any jury in the colonies. During these troubled years he participated as a leading figure in every form of organized colonial action against British restrictive measures. By December 1774 he was negotiating the purchase of powder for the general assembly; a year later he mournfully acknowledged the end of all trade, "no Bussiness now but preparation for Warr, Ravaging Villages, Burning of Towns" (Rogers, p. 278). New duties awaited him, however. The Council of Safety of Connecticut named him agent for the colony, with the task of fitting and supplying ships and caring for sick sailors, while the Continental Congress appointed him its agent in Connecticut to take charge of prize vessels and purchase necessaries for the fleet. He procured provisions, blankets, and tents for the Continental troops, cannon and powder, pilots to guide the French fleet into the Sound; he acted as commissary for the exchange of naval prisoners; he examined the accounts and sold the prizes of colony captains. He was the man in Connecticut to whom everyone turned to get business done. In 1778 the general assembly gave him additional authority, the management and direction, as marine agent, of all armed vessels belonging to or fitted by the state. He corresponded with Washington, who once honored him with a visit. He served two terms as deputy to the assembly. Meanwhile, beyond the commissions he took on the naval business he transacted, he had an eye to his own advantage. Where once he ran a fleet of trading vessels, he now owned a string of privateers, the most pretentious, the *General Putnam,* being a brig of twenty guns. His gains by these means scarcely compensated, however, for the losses he sustained when Benedict Arnold's attack on New London in 1781 destroyed his wharves and warehouses. In that same year he opened commercial connections with Amsterdam merchants. In December his wife died from an infection caught from the sick prisoners she nursed. The following April, while hunting ducks off Lester's Rocks, Shaw was accidentally wounded by a discharge from his own gun. Three days later he died, confessing the "emptiness of this world, and the Vanity of all its Glory" (Rogers, p. 330). He left no children.

[The only full account of Shaw is in E. E. Rogers, "Connecticut's Naval Office at New London during the War of the American Revolution," *New London County Hist. Soc. Colls.*, vol. II (1933), which contains many documents, including Shaw's mercantile letter book, from the Nathaniel and Thomas Shaw Letters and Papers in the Yale Library. See also F. M. Caulkins, *Hist. of New London, Conn.* (1852) ; *The Pub. Records of the Colony of Conn.*, vol. XV (1890) and *The Public Records of the State of Conn.*, vols. I, II (1894–95), III (1922) ; *Naval Records of the Am. Revolution* (1906), ed. by C. H. Lincoln ; *Conn. Hist. Soc. Colls.*, vols. XVI (1916), XVIII–XX (1920–23).] S.M.P.

SHAW, OLIVER (Mar. 13, 1779–Dec. 31, 1848), musician and composer, was born at Middleboro, Mass., one of eight children of Hannah (Heath) and John Shaw. As a young boy, he lost the sight of his right eye through an accident. When he was seventeen he attended the Bristol Academy at Taunton, Mass., and shortly after his graduation joined his father in seafaring enterprises. At twenty-one, when he was not fully recovered from yellow fever, he helped in taking nautical observations from the sun; this affected his remaining eye, and he was totally blind for the rest of his life. Blindness determined him to become a musician rather than a mariner. He first studied with John L. Berkenhead, a blind organist of Newport, R. I.; in 1803 he had lessons with Johann Christian Graupner [*q.v.*] in Boston, and some instruction on the clarinet from Thomas Granger. In 1807 he settled in Providence, R. I., where he remained until his death. He became organist of the First Congregational Church and gave music lessons in the homes of his pupils, led from house to house by a boy employed for the purpose. In 1809 he gathered a group of fellow musicians in Providence, among them Thomas Webb, and founded the Psallonian Society, "for the purpose of improving themselves in the knowledge and practice of sacred music, and inculcating a more correct taste in the choice and performance of it" (quoted in *Memorial, post*, p. 21). The society remained in existence until 1832, and in its twenty-three years gave thirty-one concerts. On Oct. 20, 1812, Shaw married Sarah Jenckes, daughter

of Caleb Jenckes, who bore him two sons and five daughters. His son, Oliver J. Shaw, was also a composer.

Shaw was important to his time not only for his compositions, which were characteristic of the sacred music of his day and were forerunners of the work of Lowell Mason [*q.v.*], but for his teaching and his interest in the betterment of church music. As a composer he represented the emergence of the native musician after the great immigration of foreigners in the latter eighteenth century. His best known hymn-tunes were "Taunton," "Bristol," and "Weybosset." One of his most popular sacred songs was "Mary's Tears," "sung at the oratorio performed by the Handel & Haydn Society in Boston, July 5th, 1817, in presence of the President of the United States" (Howard, *post*, p. 141). This program also contained Shaw's duet, "All Things Bright and Fair Are Thine." Others of his sacred songs were "Arrayed in Clouds of Golden Light," "The Missionary Angel," "There's Nothing True But Heaven," and works which show the trend of non-liturgical church music toward the ballad type. His secular compositions include "Bristol March," "Governor Arnold's March," and "Washington's Grand Centennial March," performed at the Providence Centennial Celebration in 1832. Several libraries have copies of Shaw's *For the Gentlemen* (Dedham, Mass., 1807) : "A favourite selection of instrumental music . . . consisting principally of marches, airs, minuets, etc. Written chiefly in four parts, viz : two clarinets, flute and bassoon; or two violins, flute and violoncello."

[The most complete account of Shaw's career is given in the *Memorial of Oliver Shaw* (1884), ed. by Frederic Denison, A. A. Stanley, and E. K. Glezen. See also Thomas Williams, *A Discourse on the Life and Death of Oliver Shaw* (Boston, 1851) ; F. J. Metcalf, *Am. Writers and Compilers of Sacred Music* (1925) ; J. T. Howard, *Our Am. Music* (1931) ; death notice in *Newport Mercury*, Jan. 6, 1849.] J.T.H.

SHAW, PAULINE AGASSIZ (Feb. 6, 1841– Feb. 10, 1917), philanthropist, the youngest child of Cécile (Braun) and Jean Louis Rodolphe Agassiz [*q.v.*], was born in Neuchâtel, Switzerland. She lived there with her grandmother from the death of her mother in 1848 until she joined her father at Harvard College in 1850. As she grew up, her father formed the habit of inviting the more intimate companions of herself and her sister to his library for an afternoon each week, and she continually met his distinguished friends. She also assisted in the school for girls that her step-mother conducted in their home. In this environment she developed the charm and lovable personality that were to characterize her through

Shawlife.Whenshewaseighteensheaccompanied
herfatheronatriptoEurope,wherehewas
entertainedbyscholarsinEnglandandFrance.
OnNov.30,1860,shemarriedQuincyAdams
Shaw,presidentoftheCalumetandHeclaMin-
ingCompany.Hewasthetravelingcompanion
andfriendtowhomFrancisParkmandedicated
his*CaliforniaandOregonTrail*(1849)andwas
oneofthefirstAmericanstorecognizethemerits
oftheFrenchlandscapepaintersandtobuytheir
works,particularlythoseofMillet.Theyhadfive
children.Bothbeforeandafterherhusband's
deathin1908sheinterestedherselfinvarious
philanthropies.

Shedidnotusethefortuneacquiredbyher
husbandmerelytosupportlongacceptedtypes
ofeducationalandsocialservice;instead,she
wasaneducationalandsocialpioneer,who,in
threeseparateinstances,sawthepossibilitiesof
someformofeducationthatwastoonewand
unprovedtobesupportedbypublicfunds,main-
taineditthroughtheexperimentalperiod,and
directeditsosuccessfullythatitcametobe
recognizedandsupportedonalargescaleat
publicexpense.Thusshesupportedmorethan
thirtykindergartensinandnearBoston,afterthe
schoolcommitteeofBostonhad,inSeptember
1879,discontinuedforlackoffundsthepublic
kindergartensestablishedbytheeffortsofEliza-
bethPeabody[q.v.]andothers.By1887shehad
organizedthesekindergartenssofullyandhadso
thoroughlydemonstratedtheirusefulnessthat
theschoolcommitteeconsentedtoreconsiderthe
question.Itexaminedherkindergartens,decid-
edtoreëstablishpublickindergartensinBoston,
andacceptedfourteenkindergartensshehad
beensupporting,togetherwiththefurnitureand
materialsrequiredintheinstruction.Shegave
similarsupporttothemanualtrainingmovement
duringitsexperimentalperiod.After1883she
providedthefundstogivefreenormalinstruc-
tioninvariousmanualartstoteachersofthe
publicschoolsandtosupportchildren'sclasses
ofmanualartsinthepublicschoolsaswellas
inherNorthBennet-StreetIndustrialSchool.
Finally,in1894,theschoolcommitteeprovided
formanualtrainingasaregularpartofthe
schoolwork.ShealsofinancedtheVocation
BureauofBoston,whereFrankParsons[q.v.]
initiatedworkinvocationalguidance,being its
onlyannualcontributorfromMarch1908to
June1917,whenthebureauwastakenoverby
HarvardUniversity.Shefoundedandsupport-
edmanyotherphilanthropicandcivicworks,
suchastheRugglesStreetNeighborhoodHouse,
theCivicServiceHouse,andtheNorthBennet-
StreetIndustrialSchool.

[*Pauline Agassiz Shaw: Tributes paid her memory at the Memorial Service held April 8, 1917* (1917); *Ann. Report of the School Committee of . . . Boston, 1887* (1888), pp. 18–22; *Ibid. . . . 1888* (1889), pp. 10–12; *Ibid. . . . 1892* (1893), pp. 9–20; *Ibid. . . . 1894* (1894); p. 31; *Documents of the School Committee of the City of Boston . . . 1887* (1887), no. 21; *Ibid. . . . 1891* (1892), no. 15; *Pioneers of the Kindergarten in America* (copr. 1924); L. A. Paton, *Elizabeth Cary Agassiz* (1919); *Fifty Years of Boston* (copr. 1932); Justin Winsor, *The Memorial History of Boston, 1630–1880*, vol. IV (1881), pp. 247, 405; J. M. Brewer, *The Vocational-Guidance Movement: its problems and possibilities* (1918), p. 23; *Arena*, July 1908, pp. 5, 6; Nov. 1908, p. 499; *Boston Evening Transcript*, June 10, 1908, June 12, 1908, Feb. 10, 1917; *New York Times*, Feb. 11, 1917; information from John M. Brewer, Graduate School of Education, Harvard University.] E. C.

SHAW, SAMUEL (Oct. 2, 1754–May 30, 1794), Revolutionary officer, was born in Boston, Mass., the son of Francis and Sarah (Burt) Shaw. It is said that his grandfather, Thomas Shaw, emigrated from Scotland the third quarter of the seventeenth century. Samuel's father was a prosperous merchant, and the boy entered the counting-house early, but at the outbreak of the Revolution he obtained a commission as second-lieutenant in the artillery. He served during the siege of Boston and at its conclusion accompanied the army to New York. For a time he was stationed at Fort Washington. He participated in the battles of Trenton, Princeton, Brandywine, Germantown, and Monmouth, and shared in the sufferings of Valley Forge. During the remainder of the war, he served principally in New York and New England. He was promoted to the rank of first lieutenant in the 3rd Continental Artillery on Jan. 1, 1777, and became captain on Apr. 12, 1780. During much of the war he was aide-de-camp to General Knox. It was his fortune in the latter capacity to be present when Washington took possession of New York after its evacuation by the British and to assist in arranging for the disbandment of the Continental Army. He was secretary of the committee of officers that formed the Society of the Cincinnati. On retiring to civil life, he was commended by Washington for intelligence, activity, and bravery.

His capacity for business, demonstrated while in the army, led a group of merchants, bent upon establishing commercial relations with the Orient, to offer him the post of supercago on the *Empress of China,* the first American vessel dispatched to Canton. He set sail in February 1784 and returned in May 1785. He was appointed by General Knox to a place in the war department. He had in the meantime addressed a letter to John Jay, the secretary of foreign affairs, describing his voyage, and in 1786 he had the honor of being elected by Congress the first American consul in China. Resigning his position in the war department, he set sail for Canton in February 1786. After an absence of three years he returned to the United States. His appointment as consul was renewed by President Washington. He sailed for China again in 1790 on board the *Massachusetts,* one of the finest merchantmen of the day, which had been built at his direction near Quincy, Mass. After selling the vessel to agents of the Portuguese government in the East Indies, he invested the proceeds in a return cargo and arrived in the United States in January 1792. On Aug. 21 of that year he married Hannah Phillips, the daughter of William Phillips of Boston. The following year he embarked on his third and last voyage to the Orient. While visiting Bombay, he developed a disease of the liver. Finding no cure at Canton, he took passage for America and died near the Cape of Good Hope.

[*The Journals of Major Samuel Shaw,* with a life of the author by Josiah Quincy (1847); *Memorials of the Mass. Soc. of the Cincinnati,* ed. by J. M. Bugbee (1890); F. B. Heitman, *Hist. Register of Officers of the Continental Army* (1893); *Mass. Soldiers and Sailors of the Rev. War,* vol. XIV (1906); Amasa Delano, *A Narrative of a Voyager and Travels* (1817); J. W. Foster, *Amer. Diplomacy in the Orient* (1903); I. N. P. Stokes, *The Iconography of Manhattan Island,* vol. V (1926); mother's name from family Bible.] E. E. C.

SHAW, THOMAS (May 5, 1838–Jan. 19, 1901), inventor, was the son of James and Catherine (Snyder) Shaw, and was born in Philadelphia, Pa., where his first American ancestor had settled in 1694. Shaw was compelled to go to work at a very early age when his father, a merchant, lost everything in a coal-mining venture. This was not a hardship, for he disliked going to school and much preferred to invent and construct useful things, his favorite occupation in his spare time. He worked in grocery stores and other such places until he was sixteen, when he apprenticed himself to a machinist. His mastery of the machinist's trade was rapid and he soon began serious invention, his first patent (Apr. 27, 1858) being for a gas meter. Other inventions that he patented the following year included a press mold for glass, a gas stove, and a sewing machine. About this time he began working in the Cyclops Machine Works in Philadelphia, and in a comparatively short time became superintendent. When the William Butcher (later Midvale) Steel Works was organized in 1867, Shaw took over the superintendency of this plant as well. By this time he had a number of other inventions to his credit, including steam gages, a stone crusher, and a grinding machine. Now he turned his attention to iron and steel manufacture. In the course of the succeeding

three years he devised a process for rolling and applying steel tires to cast-iron and invented the bolster and semi-elliptic spring for railroad cars, a centrifugal shot-making machine which eliminated the usual shot tower, and a steam-power hammer, as well as several other valuable devices of general utility. One of the simplest, yet most useful of these was the spring-lock nut washer patented in 1868 and put to immediate and almost universal use on railroads.

About 1871 Shaw gave up his connections with the Midvale and Cyclops companies to devote his whole time to the development and introduction of his own inventions. He established a manufacturing plant in Philadelphia, which he maintained until his death. The scope of his inventions, which was unusually wide, involved almost two hundred patents and included tools, engineers' special appliances, oil burners, United States standard mercury pressure gages, hydraulic pumps, noise quieting nozzles and mufflers for locomotives and steamships, steam engine and pump governors, pile drivers, power hammers, miners' safety lamps, and apparatus for testing and recording mine gases. Shaw's pile driver, patented in 1868 and 1870, was unique in that it made use of the explosive force of gunpowder and in one operation could drive a forty-foot wood pile, fourteen inches in diameter, its entire length into firm ground without injuring the timber. It was successfully used in driving most of the piles for the United States Naval Station at League Island, Philadelphia. Another very original and valuable invention was an apparatus to detect and record deadly gases in mines, for which he received a series of patents between 1886 and 1890. With it gases could be automatically tested throughout the mine at five-minute intervals by a tester above ground and, through a system of high pressure air signals in the mine, workers could be warned of danger in time to seek safety. The Shaw gas tester, as it came to be known, was capable of detecting inflammable gases to within one one-hundredth of one per cent., and was officially adopted by Pennsylvania and Ohio, as well as by Germany and Russia. During his later years Shaw received many offers for his services from foreign governments, all of which he declined. He married Matilda Miller Garber, who, with a daughter, survived him at the time of his sudden death at Hammonton, N. J. He was buried in Philadelphia.

[*Biog. Album of Prominent Pennsylvanians, Phila.,* 3 ser. (1890); J. W. Jordan, *Encyc. of Pa. Biog.,* vol. I (1914); *Index to Jour. of Franklin Inst., 1826–1885* (1890); Patent Office records; obituary in *Pub. Ledger* (Phila.), Jan. 21, 1901.] C. W. M—n.

SHAW, WILLIAM SMITH (Aug. 12, 1778–Apr. 25, 1826), librarian of the Boston Athenaeum, was born in Haverhill, Mass., son of the Rev. John Shaw and Elizabeth (Smith) Shaw, the sister of Abigail Adams [*q.v.*]. Sickly and lame, he graduated at Harvard in 1798 and became for two years private secretary to President John Adams in Philadelphia. At Washington's death, in his official capacity he carried the resolution of Congress to the widow. From 1801 to 1804 he studied law in Boston with William Sullivan and became a member of the bar. His aunt, Abigail Adams, stimulated his love for books, and he soon resolved to improve the plane of American literature. He also began a collection of pamphlets that became notable. He was active in promoting literary enterprises, procuring subscriptions for a new periodical, *The Port Folio,* and for John Marshall's *Life of Washington* (5 vols., 1804–07). For Hannah Adams [*q.v.*] he worked unceasingly, by carrying books to her door, introducing new friends, procuring subscriptions to her writings, and, when age and infirmities overtook her, he raised an annuity for her support and attended to all her affairs. In 1805 he helped to found the Anthology Society, which took over *The Monthly Anthology,* a magazine of bookish miscellany founded in 1803. The Society's editors met weekly for supper, and, as treasurer, he was very active, although he seems to have retired at eleven o'clock each evening. For volumes I and II he wrote on trial by jury; and elsewhere in the first six volumes, of the ten, he had occasional contributions of minor note. An example of his style appears in his review of an oration where he says that the orator "added potency to omnipotence ... soared above the empyrean, till his wings were melted in the blaze of his own eloquence, and then tumbled and descended below the bottom of the abyss of bathos" (Aug. 1806, p. 444).

The society, having opened an Anthology Reading Room, transferred it in October 1806 to five trustees. This library the next year became the Boston Athenaeum and was so ardently fostered by Shaw as librarian from 1807 to 1822 that he became known as "Athenaeum Shaw." He gave his services. Judge William Tudor pictured his activities: "That dog Shaw goes everywhere. He knows everybody. Everybody knows him. If he sees a book, pamphlet, or manuscript —Oh Sir! The Athenaeum must have this. Well, have it he will and have it he must" (Tudor's comment on back of manuscript presented to the Library of the Boston Athenaeum). He was also secretary until 1823. He had an accurate knowledge of the value of books, coins, and medals.

Appointment as clerk of the federal district court for Massachusetts in 1806 relieved him from the strain of active practice of the law. He held the office for twelve years and devoted his leisure to building up the Athenaeum library. He aided neighboring organizations with gifts and money, being a member of many historical, scientific, and literary societies. His last years were afflicted with illness, and he died, unmarried, in Boston.

[J. B. Felt, *Memorials of William Smith Shaw* (1852) with correspondence and notes; Josiah Quincy, *The Hist. of the Boston Athenaeum* (1851); the *Journ. of the Proceedings of the Society which Conducts the Monthly Anthology,* with introduction by M. A. DeWolfe Howe (1910).]   C. K. B.

SHAYS, DANIEL (*c.* 1747–Sept. 29, 1825), soldier, insurgent, is generally said to have been born at Hopkinton, Mass., where Patrick Shay married Margaret Dempsey in 1744, although the birth records for that town do not contain his name (*Vital Records of Hopkinton, Mass.,* 1911). Most accounts give the year of his birth as 1747, but the *New York Evening Post,* Oct. 15, 1825, states his age at death as eighty-four. His origin was humble and his early life obscure. On July 18, 1772, the marriage intentions of Daniel Shay and Abigail Gilbert were recorded at Brookfield (*Vital Records of Brookfield, Mass.,* 1909). At the outbreak of the Revolution, Shays responded to the alarm at Lexington and served for eleven days. He was in the battle of Bunker Hill and was cited and promoted for gallant conduct. He also served at Ticonderoga, Saratoga, and Stony Point, and on Jan. 1, 1777, was commissioned captain in the 5th Massachusetts. He was very popular with his men, having the reputation of being considerate of his subordinates and at the same time a brave and efficient officer (Sanderson, *post,* pp. 177, 180; Warren MS.). Toward the end of the war a handsome sword was presented to him by Lafayette, which poverty led him to sell. In 1780 he resigned from the army, settling in Pelham, Mass., where in 1781 and 1782 he served as a member of the Committee of Safety. He was subsequently elected to various town offices.

Following the prosperity after the signing of peace, an acute economic depression, felt throughout all the rural districts, swept over the country. The wide-spread demand for redress of grievances, met by the obstinate non-compliance of the legislature, resulted in western Massachusetts in a resort to force, and in this phase of the movement Shays became so prominent that his name is given to the whole uprising— "Shays's Rebellion"—although others were as active as he. On Aug. 29, 1786, the insurgents prevented the sitting of the court of common pleas and general sessions, intending merely to prevent their giving judgments in debt cases before grievances were redressed; but the leaders soon began to fear that indictments would be brought against them, and they therefore determined to prevent the sitting of the supreme court at Springfield on Sept. 26. Major-General William Shepard [*q.v.*] of the Hampshire militia prepared to defend the court. On the day appointed, 800 militia faced about the same number of insurgents, and Shays made his first historical appearance as leader. He was chairman of a committee which drew up resolutions that the court should be allowed to sit, provided it dealt with no case involving indictments of insurgents or concerning debts. An agreement was reached by which both militia and insurgents disbanded, and the court adjourned.

Outbreaks continued, however, and the legislature made no real redress of the grievances, although it enraged the insurgents by suspending the writ of *habeas corpus*. By January 1787 the insurgents had given up hope of peaceful reform, and the legislature had chosen Gen. Benjamin Lincoln [*q.v.*] to suppress what had become an armed rebellion. Shays, as the leader of a force of insurgents at Wilbraham, and Luke Day, head of another band near by, intended to make a combined attack on the arsenal at Springfield, but owing to a failure of communication, Shays's force attacked alone. It was defeated by the militia under Shepard and dispersed. Lincoln, who had arrived after the attack, then marched against Day and broke up his force. Shays, with what was left of his band, at once retreated to Amherst, where he was joined by stragglers from the other party. Lincoln followed, and Shays fell back to Pelham, then to Hadley, and Hatfield. On Jan. 29, Lincoln sent word that he would recommend to the General Court for pardon any insurgents who would lay down their arms and take the oath of allegiance. He wrote to Shays offering the same terms. Shays replied that the rebellion was due to real grievances but that the people would disperse if given a general pardon, and asked for an armistice until petitions could be presented to the legislature. Lincoln, however, was without authority to delay operations, and on the night of Feb. 2, 1787, marched with his men through a snow storm, fell on Shays's troops at Petersham, and completely routed them. Shays fled to Vermont, and was one of the few exempted from the general pardon given later in the year. He was condemned to death by the supreme court, but in February

1788 petitioned for pardon, which was granted June 13.

Some time afterward, Shays moved to Schoharie County, N. Y., where he lived for a number of years, then moved on to western New York, settling in Sparta, where he died. In his old age he was allowed a federal pension for his services in the American Revolution. He was a man of no cultural background, little education, and not much ability, but he was brave and honest, and convinced that in the rebellion of 1786–87 he was fighting the same battle of the people which he had fought in the Revolution.

[The earlier general histories, such as J. G. Holland, *Hist. of Western Mass.* (2 vols., 1855), and G. R. Minot, *The Hist. of the Insurrections in Mass.* (1810), take an unfavorable view of Shays. One of the most important accounts is in the paper by Jonathan Smith, "Features of Shays' Rebellion" (1903), in *Hist. Papers Read at Meetings of the Clinton Hist. Soc.*, vol. I (n.d.). See also Grindall Reynolds, "Concord during the Shays Rebellion," in *A Collection of Historical and Other Papers* (1895); S. A. Green, "Groton during Shays's Rebellion," *Proc. Mass. Hist. Soc.*, 2 ser., I (1885); H. K. Sanderson, *Lynn in the Revolution* (1909); C. O. Parmenter, *Hist. of Pelham, Mass.* (1898); J. P. Warren, "The Confederation and the Shays Rebellion," *Am. Hist. Rev.*, Oct. 1905, and "The Shays Rebellion" (MS.), in the Harvard Library. Contemporary newspapers are cited in J. T. Adams, *New England in the Republic* (1926). There is much manuscript material in the Mass. Archives.]   J. T. A.

SHEA, JOHN DAWSON GILMARY (July 22, 1824–Feb. 22, 1892), historian and editor, son of James and Mary Ann (Flannigan) Shea, was born in New York City. His father came from Ireland in 1815, tutored in General Schuyler's household, established a private school with Eber Wheaton, taught English in Columbia College, served as a captain of militia and as a Tammany chieftain, and became a leader in Irish and Catholic affairs, though he fought Bishops Dubois and Hughes on the trustee question. His mother traced a maternal descent from Nicholas Upsall, one of Boston's earliest settlers, and also from Thomas McCurtin, an Irish schoolmaster, who established a classical school at Mount Holly, N. J., in 1762. Baptized John Dawson, Shea adopted the name Gilmary when he became a novice in the Society of Jesus. He early showed a liking for books and received his first training in the Sisters of Charity school, Mulberry Street, and in the Columbia Grammar School, graduating from the latter in 1837. Friendly connections procured him a position in the counting-house of Don Tomas, a Spanish merchant, where he gained a knowledge of Spanish and wrote a life of Alvarez Carrillo de Albornoz, but apparently learned little about the acquisition of money, if one may judge from his life of unprofitable scholarship and penury. When only fourteen years old he contributed an article to the *Children's Catholic Magazine.*

Tiring of trade, he studied law and in 1846 was admitted to the bar, but found himself more interested in reading history than in preparing briefs. Fascinated by George Bancroft's *History of the United States,* he became a member of the New York Historical Society and wrote a series of articles on "Our Martyrs" for the *United States Catholic Magazine* (1846–47), which may have led him, in 1848, into the Society of Jesus. As a novice, he studied at St. John's College, Fordham (1848–50), and at St. Mary's College, Montreal (1850–52), where he learned enough canon law to be consulted in later years by various prelates and acquired a fluent command of French. Of more vital importance was his association with the trained Jesuit historian, Felix Martin, whose biography of Father Jogues he translated in 1885. During this period he also came under the influence of the historical editor, Edmund Bailey O'Callaghan [*q.v.*]. In 1852, the year he gave up thoughts of a religious life, Shea published *Discovery and Exploration of the Mississippi Valley,* which he dedicated to Jared Sparks. This work won him the favor of contemporary historians and invitations to become a corresponding member of the historical societies of Wisconsin, Maryland, and Massachusetts—at the time a rare honor for a Catholic.

Meanwhile, he had commenced to write the innumerable articles which appeared through succeeding years in the *United States Catholic Magazine,* the *Catholic World,* the *United States Historical Magazine,* the *American Catholic Quarterly Review,* the Boston *Pilot,* and similar publications. While most of these contributions were of a popular nature, they were far better than the ordinary article of the same type, and added something to Shea's fame. Lack of money and his marriage in 1854 to Sophie Savage, of old Puritan lineage, by whom he had two daughters, compelled him to form a connection with E. Dunigan & Brother, publishers. For this firm he compiled *First Book of History* (1854), *A General History of Modern Europe* (1854), and *A School History of the United States* (1855), which were adopted rather widely in Catholic schools. Other works of his were published by D. & J. Sadlier, including *An Elementary History of the United States* (1855) and *The Catholic Church in the United States: A Sketch of Its Ecclesiastical History* (1856), a translation of the work by Henri de Courcy, revised and enlarged in 1879.

Shea, under pressure, found time to do many things: to contribute several chapters to Justin Winsor's *Narrative and Critical History of America;* to compile articles for encyclopedias; to edit Sadlier's *General Catholic Directory* (1858–90); to assist James Lenox [*q.v.*] in collecting Americana; to serve Archbishop Hughes as a diocesan historiographer with a resultant volume, *The Catholic Churches of New York City* (1878); to edit the *Library of American Linguistics* (1860–74), including some fifteen Indian grammars and dictionaries; to work on the *Historical Magazine* (1855–67); to edit without credit a pocket Catholic Bible and a patriotic volume of sketches, *The Fallen Brave* (1861); and to join John Ireland, R. H. Clarke, and Charles G. Herbermann in founding the United States Catholic Historical Society, of which he was editor (1887–89) and president (1890). Despite all these varied enterprises, he continued to work in his own field, compiling *History of the Catholic Missions among the Indian Tribes of the United States, 1529–1854* (1854); editing twenty-six volumes of Jesuit relations (published in a very small edition as Shea's Cramoisy Press Series, 1857–87) which had not been included in the collection issued by the Canadian government; publishing *History and General Description of New France* (1866–72), a translation in six volumes of P. F. X. de Charlevoix's work; and writing his monumental, critical, and impartial *History of the Catholic Church in the United States* in four large volumes (1886–92), for which he received some financial assistance from a committee of the hierarchy which had been instructed by the Plenary Council of Baltimore (1884) to cooperate with him.

An outstanding historian and the greatest American Catholic historical writer, Shea found little contemporary appreciation for his work. Catholic colleges were not teaching history beyond a stilted drill in questions and answers; American history was not recognized; the hierarchy was more interested in building churches and charitable institutions than in records and historical scholarship. The Jesuits gave him some support when he prepared the *Memorial of the First Centenary of Georgetown College* (1891), and on his death took over his rich collection of Americana. Impoverished, he wrote to Archbishop Corrigan in 1889, asking for a clerkship in the chancery office or even in Calvary Cemetery office, for he was too proud to become a pensioner. When the Catholic University at Washington was established, he vainly hoped for a call to the chair of history. Instead, he was given an editorship on Herman Ridder's *Catholic News* (1889), which enabled him to support his family in a humble home in Elizabeth, N. J., and to complete his great historical work. In that city he died.

[Peter Guilday, in *U. S. Catholic Hist. Soc. Hist. Records and Studies*, vol. XVII (July 1926); M. F. Vallette, "Dr. John Gilmary Shea," *Ibid.*, vol. I, pt. 1 (Jan. 1899); bibliog. of Shea's works, *Ibid.*, vol. VI, pt. 2 (Dec. 1912); R. H. Clarke, in *The Illustrated Catholic Family Annual* (1893); *Catholic News*, Mar. 2, 1892; *Cath. World*, Apr. 1892; *Am. Catholic Quart. Rev.*, Apr. 1913; *New York Freeman's Jour.*, Feb. 26, 1887; *The Sun* (N. Y.), Feb. 23, 1892.] R. J. P.

SHEARMAN, THOMAS GASKELL (Nov. 25, 1834–Sept. 29, 1900), lawyer and economist, son of John and Sarah Shearman, was born in Birmingham, England, and at the age of nine was brought to New York by his father, his mother arriving later. His father, who was by turns a physician, writer, and preacher, soon became an invalid, and young Shearman at the age of twelve was obliged to shift for himself. His formal education ceased at thirteen; at fourteen he was a messenger boy, earning a dollar weekly and buying books with his savings; and at twenty-four he was an expert bookkeeper in a dry-goods store. He married Ella Partridge of Brooklyn in 1859. Almost immediately afterward he determined to become a lawyer and began studying in the office of Austin and Benjamin Vaughan Abbott [*qq.v.*]. Within six months he passed his examinations and was admitted to the bar.

While a student he began writing on procedure, and in 1861 he published, with John L. Tillinghast, the first volume of *Practice, Pleadings, and Forms in Civil Actions in the Courts of Record in the State of New York*. A second volume (1865), written wholly by Shearman, completed a reference work widely used until the law was changed in 1877. In 1860 he was employed by David Dudley Field [*q.v.*] of the New York code commission to prepare a book of forms, which he completed the following year. He then assisted with the proposed civil code (which was not adopted), preparing the part relating to obligations. With Amasa R. Redfield [*q.v.*] he wrote *A Treatise on the Law of Negligence* (1869), a pioneer work which was frequently cited in judicial opinions and greatly influenced the law on the subject. It reached its sixth edition in 1913.

In 1868 Shearman, with little practical experience but with a great store of legal learning, became a partner of Field and the immediate legal adviser of the officers and directors of the Erie Railroad, then under the control of James Fisk, Jr., and Jay Gould [*qq.v.*]. In the violent legal struggles of the "Erie war" the unusual methods of the partners, particularly the invention of injunctions by telegraph and the revival of writs of assistance, provoked much adverse criticism. In 1873, as a result of friction with Field's son, Shearman withdrew from Field & Shearman and with John W. Sterling established a new firm which specialized in corporate reorganizations and the management of large estates. Beginning in 1874 he gave most of his attention for nearly two years, without compensation, to defending his pastor, Henry Ward Beecher [*q.v.*], in civil and ecclesiastical proceedings resulting from the famous suit brought by Theodore Tilton. He successfully defended Jay Gould in every one of nearly a hundred damage suits growing out of the Black Friday gold panic of 1869. His firm was counsel for the National City Bank, for James J. Hill [*q.v.*], for the builders of the Canadian Pacific Railway, and for several important railroad and industrial companies.

By nature a reformer, Shearman succeeded Field as the foremost exponent of codification in New York and kept a number of clerks employed in preparing an annotated edition of the proposed civil code, which he would have published if the code had been adopted. An active free-trader, he assembled data to prove that protective tariffs had not even nominally raised the standard of wages. In 1881 he became converted to the fiscal measures of Henry George [*q.v.*] and in 1887 suggested to him the name "single tax" (Henry George, Jr., *The Life of Henry George*, 1900, p. 496 n.). In numerous pamphlets and in his *Natural Taxation* (1895) he presented statistics to prove inductively the conclusions that George had arrived at by deduction. Shearman estimated that half the proceeds of ground rent would pay all the expenses of government; and he was opposed to having more collected because of his fear of governmental extravagance. His particular theory, which proposed the collection of ground rents for purely fiscal rather than social purposes, became known as the "single tax limited." His *Natural Taxation* went through five editions. Besides its contribution to single tax theory, it contains one of the strongest indictments of the general property tax ever written. Shearman appeared on the platform more than seven hundred times in behalf of the Indian, the Armenian, the negro, and of the poor in coal fields, factories, sweat shops, and city tenements. He frequently gave his legal services without compensation to poor clients. Most of his large earnings were used in dispensing charity, and at his death in Brooklyn, his estate amounted to but little more than

$300,000. For all his humanitarian endeavors, however, he was never popular. His lack of tact and his habit of speaking in paradoxes alienated many who might have been his friends.

[*Memorial: Thomas Gaskell Shearman* (1900), recording various services held by Plymouth Church, Brooklyn, contains several personal estimates. The 1915 edition of *Natural Taxation* has an introductory sketch by C. B. Fillebrown, which is substantially the same as an article, "Thomas G. Shearman and His Natural Taxation," in the *National Magazine*, Mar. 1915, reprinted in pamphlet form. See also J. A. Garver, *John William Sterling* (1929); A. N. Young, *The Single Tax Movement in the U. S.* (1916); H. R. Stiles, *The Civil . . . Hist. . . . of the County of Kings and the City of Brooklyn, N. Y.* (1884); *Who's Who in America*, 1899–1900; *Brooklyn Daily Eagle*, Sept. 30, 1900. For criticisms of his conduct of the Erie litigations see C. F. Adams, *Chapters of Erie* (1871); and *High Finance in the Sixties* (1929), ed. by F. C. Hicks.]

E. C. S.

SHECUT, JOHN LINNAEUS EDWARD WHITRIDGE (Dec. 4, 1770–June 1, 1836), physician, author, and botanist, was born in Beaufort, S. C. His father, Abraham Shecut, and his mother, Marie (Barbary) Shecut, were French Huguenots who were refugees first to Switzerland and later to America. In Shecut's early childhood his parents moved to Charleston, S. C., and there he made his home until his death. In 1786 he began the study of medicine under Dr. David Ramsay [*q.v.*]; later he is said to have gone to Philadelphia to study. He had an extensive practice in Charleston and was prominently identified with the cultural life of the city. As a physician, he was best known for his early experiments with the use of electricity in the treatment of disease. He had an electric machine which he used widely, and with much apparent success in cases of withered or paralyzed limbs; a number of these cases are fully described in *Shecut's Medical and Philosophical Essays* (1819). Having conceived the idea that yellow fever was in part caused by lack of electricity in the atmosphere, he wrote widely on the subject and sustained his contention by elaborate meteorological and thermometrical observations. The first of his essays on the subject was reviewed and warmly commended in the *New York Medical Repository* (vol. XIX, no. 3, 1818). He was in advance of his time in limiting the letting of blood and the use of mercury as a drug. In connection with yellow fever he said in 1819: "I have, as it regards this disease, long since sheathed my lancet. . . . Along with the lancet I have rejected mercury" (*Shecut's Medical and Philosophical Essays*, p. 128).

With unusual versatility he added to his medical practice an extensive study of botany and the publication of a number of books and pamphlets. His *Flora Carolinaeensis* (1806), of which only one volume was published, was the most extensive work on the botany of South Carolina up to that time and was intended to promote a taste for the study of botany by simplifying the Linnaean system. It is said to have cost him twenty months of work and, although it was published by subscription, over eighteen hundred dollars. In addition he wrote a number of pamphlets, *Sketches of the Elements of Natural Philosophy* (1826), and two novels, *Ishnoo-ju-lut-sche; or The Eagle of the Mohawks* (2 vols., 1841) and *The Scout; or the Fast of St. Nicholas* (1844). He is also said to have written a treatise on medicine called "Elements of Medicine." In 1813 he organized the Antiquarian Society of Charleston, which was incorporated a year later as the Literary and Philosophical Society of South Carolina, its primary purpose being the collection and preservation of specimens in natural history. The museum of the society became the nucleus of the Charleston Museum, one of the earliest public museums in the United States. In 1808 he became connected with the South Carolina Homespun Company, perhaps the earliest cotton mill in South Carolina (*Ibid.*, p. 26), which was sold at a loss about four years later. He was twice married. His first wife was Sarah Cannon, of Edisto Island, S. C., whom he married Jan. 26, 1792. He was married for a second time, Feb. 7, 1805, to Susanna Ballard, of Georgetown, S. C. He had nine children, four by the first marriage and five by the second. His books indicate that he was a man of broad culture and wide reading. His professional altruism was high, and he was eager to promote the welfare of humanity through his books and his work in medicine.

[Wilson Gee, "South Carolina Botanists: Biog. and Bibliog.," *Bull. Univ. of S. C.*, Sept. 1918; W. G. Mazÿck, *The Charleston Museum: Its Genesis and Development* (1908); *Am. Medic. Biogs.* (1920), ed. by H. A. Kelly and W. L. Burrage; death notice in *Charleston Courier*, June 2, 1836.]

A. R. C.

SHEDD, JOEL HERBERT (May 31, 1834–Nov. 27, 1915), hydraulic and sanitary engineer, was born in Pepperell, Mass., the eldest of eight children of Joel and Eliza (Edson) Shedd. He was descended from Daniel Shed, who settled in Braintree, Mass., about 1642; his great-grandfather, Joel Shedd, was a soldier of the Revolution. After his education in the public schools and at Bridgewater Academy, Shedd began his professional life in 1850 as a student in the office of Thomas and John Doane in Charlestown, Mass. He made rapid progress and before his three years of study were completed went to Indiana to engage in railroad work in a responsible capacity.

In 1856 he opened an office in Boston which he maintained for forty years. Many young engineers who later became prominent began their studies in his office. He soon became well known in the field of hydraulic engineering; in 1860 he was appointed by Gov. John A. Andrew of Massachusetts as commissioner on the Concord and Sudbury rivers and in 1876 he was made chairman of the newly established Board of Harbor Commissioners of Rhode Island, a position he retained for the rest of his life. He was later identified with many other state commissions in Rhode Island, serving as commissioner to the exposition at Paris in 1878, on the Rhode Island-Connecticut Boundary Commission and the Pawcatuck River Commission in the middle eighties, and on the Sakonnet River Stone Bridge Commission, 1902–10. His best-known works are probably those for the city of Providence, R. I. As early as 1866 he began investigations for a water supply, in 1869 he was appointed chief engineer in charge of construction, and in 1877, having completed the task, resigned, retaining a connection as consulting engineer. In 1871, while in charge of the water works, he designed and began the construction of a sewerage system which was completed between 1890 and 1897, while he was city engineer of Providence.

After this time he closed his Boston office and practised as a hydraulic and sanitary engineer in Providence for the remainder of his life. His wide reputation and proven skill in his profession brought him many important assignments. He gave special attention to damage caused by the diversion of water for public supplies, which field became an important part of his practice. Some of his notable water diversion cases included the Abbott Run–Pawtucket case; the Tatnuck and Kettle Brook diversion cases of Worcester, Mass.; and the Wachusett Reservoir cases on Nashua River in Massachusetts. He was commissioned to investigate the failure of the Diamond Hill Reservoir dam in the great freshet of 1886, which caused much damage in the valley of Abbott Run, near Pawtucket, R. I. He designed and developed the water-power project at Rumford Falls, Me., one of the larger early works of this kind. He devised and established systems for the measurement of water used for power purposes at various places in New England, including Norwich and Windsor Locks, Conn., and Lewiston, Me. In his later years he was engaged chiefly as an expert in valuation of water power and water works, and in this field, as an expert witness, he has rarely been equaled. His frankness of manner and pleasant personality were an asset when he was called to give testimony before a jury.

Shedd devised and patented the Shedd water meter (Sept. 7, 1880) and in connection with his work on the Providence sewerage project devised and patented a trap for house drains and waste pipes (Apr. 9, 1878). Later patents issued to him were for a movable dam (with O. P. Sarle, Jr.), Dec. 3, 1901, and a hydraulic air compressor, Sept. 8, 1903. He married in Medford, Mass., Aug. 26, 1856, Julia Ann, daughter of Thomas Clark of Newport, Me. She contributed widely upon art to various publications and was the author of several books, including *Famous Painters and Paintings* (1876) and *Famous Sculptors and Sculpture* (1881). She died in 1897, having borne two sons and a daughter, and on June 29, 1905, Shedd married Sarah Marble of North Smithfield, R. I., who with one son of his first marriage survived him. He died in Providence.

[*Trans. Am. Soc. Civil Engineers,* vol. LXXX (1916); *Representative Men and Old Families of R. I.* (1908), vol. III; *Who's Who in America,* 1914–15; *Who's Who in New England* (1916); F. E. Shedd, *Daniel Shedd Geneal.* (1921); *Providence Sunday Journal,* Nov. 28, 1915.]   H. K. B.

SHEDD, JOHN GRAVES (July 20, 1850–Oct. 22, 1926), merchant and philanthropist, was born on a farm near Alstead, N. H. Descended from Daniel Shed, who settled in Braintree, Mass., in 1642, he was the youngest son among the eight children of William and Abigail (Wallace) Shedd. He left the farm at seventeen to work in a small fruit store in Bellows Falls, Vt., with the prospect of receiving seventy-five dollars a year and his board. He soon entered the general store first of one Timothy Tufts and then of James H. Porter, both in Alstead. While with Porter he was induced in 1870 to go to Rutland, Vt., to work in a general store at a salary of one hundred and seventy-five dollars a year and his board. Soon after, he had an opportunity to visit Chicago in a vacation. There he sought an interview with Marshall Field [*q.v.*], who had already established himself in the retail dry-goods business. Having secured employment with Field, Leiter & Company, in 1872 he returned to Chicago to begin work as stock boy and salesman in the linen department of the wholesale house at ten dollars a week.

He was a natural salesman, a keen judge of merchandise, and a faithful worker. It was not long before he had worked out an analysis of sales as a basis for ordering goods; this drew him to the attention of his departmental superior, and from then on his rise was rapid. More intimately than anyone but Field himself, Shedd knew the conditions in the western country which were making possible the rapid expansion of the Field business. On May 15, 1878, he married Mary Roenna Porter of Walpole, N. H., daughter of Dr. Winslow Burroughs Porter, by whom he had two daughters. In 1893 he was taken into partnership, the firm having then become Marshall Field & Company by the withdrawal of Levi Z. Leiter. He had by this time made himself so essential both to the wholesale and retail branches of the business through his skill in buying that when Marshall Field died in 1906 he was chosen president. As the major executive of the company he not only continued the Field tradition of careful credit extension, quantity buying, and quality merchandise, but introduced ideas of counter display, specially built showrooms, and conveniences for customers which gave the Field organization prestige and reputation throughout the country. In order to control the quality of merchandise and to increase the earnings of the company, he embarked on a manufacturing program which led successively to the development of textile mills in North Carolina and Virginia, a rug-making factory in Philadelphia, and a lace-making industry at Zion City, Ill. In December 1922, when he retired from the presidency to become chairman of the board of directors, the Field organization had grown to proportions at which its founder might well have been amazed. He took an active interest in civic and business affairs. He was the first president of the Chicago Association of Commerce, a director in a number of insurance companies, banks, and railroads, and a member of the Chicago Plan Commission. He made liberal gifts to the Young Men's Christian Association and to the Art Institute of Chicago. In 1924 he established a fund of $2,000,000 to build the Shedd Aquarium in Grant Park, Chicago, with an additional $1,000,-000 as an endowment. He died in Chicago.

[F. E. Shedd, *Daniel Shed Geneal.* (1921); *Who's Who in America*, 1926–27; S. H. Ditchett, *Marshall Field and Company: the Life Story of a Great Concern* (1922); obituary in *Chicago Daily Tribune*, Oct. 23, 1926.]

E. A. D.

SHEDD, WILLIAM AMBROSE (Jan. 24, 1865–Aug. 7, 1918), Presbyterian missionary to Persia, was born at Mount Seir, Urmia (Urumiah), Persia, son of the Rev. John Haskell and Sarah Jane (Dawes) Shedd. His first American ancestor was Daniel Shed who settled in Braintree, Mass., about 1642. William graduated at Marietta College in 1887, and after two years in Persia entered Princeton Theological Seminary, where he graduated with the highest honors in 1892. Ordained as an evangelist by the Presbytery of Athens, Ohio, June 23 of the same year, he returned to Persia and resumed work at his father's mission to the Nestorian Christians at Urmia. He was treasurer of the mission, superintendent of schools, and teacher of theology as well as editor of a paper in Syriac. He made many friends among the Mohammedans, although able to do little mission work among them. In 1904, however, he established a school for Moslem boys which became a part of Urmia College. He was a leader in the movement for the union of the old Nestorian and Evangelical churches and effected a working agreement under which there was a free interchange of pulpits, he himself preaching constantly in both churches.

He was a frequent contributor to various periodicals and was the author of two books: *Islam and the Oriental Churches* (1904), consisting of his lectures at various American seminaries, and a biography of Dr. J. H. Cochran in Persian (1907). He was also a leading collaborator in the Syriac Concordance to the Peshitta. This labor of years, existing only in manuscript but well known to scholars, perished with the destruction of the mission in 1918.

Although his work on the Syriac Concordance gave evidence of scholarship of the first rank, it is primarily as a statesmanlike leader of men that Shedd will be longest remembered. In 1905 he became the head of the legal board of the Evangelical Church, which was the court recognized by the government for the trial of all cases between Christians except those purely criminal. He became an authority on Persian law and an arbitrator of wisdom and power. The World War brought him into marked prominence. On the withdrawal of the Russian troops from the province in January 1915, the Christian population of the entire region flocked into Urmia, where they were besieged for five months by the Turks and Kurds. Shedd's cool-headed management of the situation was a factor in saving thousands from starvation and epidemic. After a year in America in 1916, he added to his other duties the chairmanship of the Urmia Relief Committee. In 1917 he was made a member of the food commission, at the request of the Persian government. On the final withdrawal of the Russians, Jan. 1, 1918, he became honorary vice-consul of the United States, and the mission compound became the American consulate. For many months during the ensuing siege by Turks and Kurds, Shedd was the chief defender of the Christians, and when some seventy thousand of them left the city, July 31, 1918, to flee to Hamadan, he followed them and protected the rear. Most of the refugees reached the British lines, but Shedd died of cholera on Aug. 7 at Sain Kala.

He was married three times: on June 21, 1894, to Adela Ludlow Myers, who died Nov. 30, 1901; on Apr. 24, 1903, to Louise Wilbur, who had been appointed to the mission in 1900 and died of typhus May 17, 1915; and on July 5, 1917, to Mary Edna Lewis, who accompanied him in the flight from Urmia and, with two daughters of the first marriage and two of the second, survived him.

[M. L. Shedd, *The Measure of a Man; the Life of William Ambrose Shedd, Missionary to Persia* (1922), with portr.; *The Eighty-Second Ann. Report of the Board of Foreign Missions of the Presbyt. Ch. in the U. S. A.* (1919), pp. 271–72; *Marietta Coll. Biog. Record* (1928); *Princeton Theol. Sem. Necr. Report,* 1919; *Princeton Theol. Sem. Biog. Cat.* (1909); W. T. Ellis, "A Yankee Cadi," *Century Mag.,* Feb. 1919; E. A. Powell, "Unsung Heroes I Have Known," *Am. Mag.,* Nov. 1926; F. E. Shedd, *Daniel Shed Geneal.* (1921); *N. Y. Times,* Aug. 21, 1918.]   F. T. P.

SHEDD, WILLIAM GREENOUGH THAYER (June 21, 1820–Nov. 17, 1894), theologian and author, sixth in descent from Daniel Shed who settled in Braintree, Mass., in 1642, was largely a product of New England Puritan ancestry, birth and education. His father, Marshall Shedd, who had entered preparatory school at twenty-one and graduated at Dartmouth as valedictorian, was pastor of the Congregational church at Acton, Mass., when his son William was born. The boy's mother, Eliza (Thayer), was the daughter of Obadiah Thayer, a wealthy Boston merchant who, making his home with her, constantly encouraged the grandson in his ambitions. William was named in honor of a friend of the Thayer family, William Greenough, a well-known New England philanthropist. His grandfather's companionship and his father's determination that the boy should have an adequate education exerted a decisive influence on the future religious leader.

The family having moved in 1831 to Willsboro, in northeastern New York, where Obadiah Thayer owned extensive property, William was prepared for college at Westport, N. Y., and at fifteen entered the University of Vermont. The greatest personal influence he felt there was that of James Marsh [*q.v.*], professor of philosophy, who made him an ardent disciple of Coleridge, Kant, and Plato. After graduation from college in 1839 he taught school for a year in New York City. There he united with a Presbyterian church and determined to enter the ministry. After three years in Andover Theological Seminary, where he graduated in 1843, he served the

Congregational church at Brandon, Vt., 1843–45, being ordained Jan. 4, 1844. Except for eighteen months (1862–63) at the Brick Presbyterian Church, New York City, as co-pastor with the venerable Dr. Gardiner Spring [*q.v.*], he devoted the remainder of his life to teaching and writing. He was professor of English literature at the University of Vermont, 1845–52; of sacred rhetoric at Auburn Theological Seminary, 1852–54; and of church history at Andover Seminary, 1854–62. He then entered upon the most notable phase of his career as a professor at Union Theological Seminary, New York City. For eleven years he taught sacred rhetoric, but in 1874 succeeded Henry Boynton Smith in the chair of systematic theology. Then began his greatest service, which continued until failing strength forced his resignation in 1893. His impact on his generation was felt in his vigorous lectures to his students, his public addresses, his writings for the religious press, and especially in his *Dogmatic Theology,* issued in two volumes in 1888, to which he added a third in 1894. This work was at once widely recognized for its close logic, intellectual power, earnest sincerity, and cogent defense of Calvinism.

Although Shedd attained high rank among American systematic theologians of his time, he became increasingly conservative in a day of progress in theological thinking, and during his last years was an active opponent of the higher criticism represented by his famous seminary colleague, Charles A. Briggs [*q.v.*], which since then has generally won its way throughout the Church. Nevertheless, by those who knew him best, however widely they differed with him, he was revered and loved for the simplicity and sincerity of his character and for the delightful charm of his personality. Of his many published works those which attracted most attention, besides his *Dogmatic Theology,* were his *Lectures upon the Philosophy of History* (1856), *Discourses and Essays* (1856), and *Literary Essays* (1878), and his editions of *The Confessions of Augustine* (1860) and *The Complete Works of Samuel Taylor Coleridge* (7 vols., 1853), which he issued with his own introductions. He published several other translations and commentaries and contributed frequently to religious and theological periodicals. In general his writings were characterized by vigor, beauty, and clearness of style. He married, Oct. 7, 1845, Lucy Ann Myers of Whitehall, N. Y., who with their two sons and two daughters survived him. He died in New York City.

[John De Witt, in *Presbyterian and Reformed Review,* Apr. 1895; G. L. Prentiss, *The Union Theol.*

Seminary (1899); F. E. Shedd, *Daniel Shed Geneal.* (1921); *N. Y. Observer,* Nov. 22, 1894; *N. Y. Tribune,* Nov. 18, 1894.]
            P. P. F.

SHEEDY, DENNIS (Sept. 26, 1846–Oct. 16, 1923), stockman, merchant, capitalist, organizer, had a career that gives him a place in the early history of almost every state west of the Missouri River. He was born in Ireland, youngest of the twelve children of John and Margaret (Fitzpatrick) Sheedy. Both parents were educated. The father, who was a middle-class farmer, brought his family to the United States when Dennis was an infant. After settling near Rockport, Mass., they moved in 1858 to Lyons, Iowa, where the father soon died. Dennis began work by clerking in a store, but at sixteen he determined to seek his fortune farther west. He first went by wagon train to Denver, where he obtained employment in a store; two years later he was in Montana, engaged in placer mining and then in merchandising. He was very successful with freighting and trading in Utah and Montana and at nineteen had accumulated $30,000. After a winter in a commercial school in Chicago, he bought a wagon train and loaded it with stoves, which he freighted to Salt Lake City and sold at a handsome profit, taking produce in trade. This he took to the Montana mines and sold for gold dust. In 1870, after having been in Nevada, California, and Arizona, he went through New Orleans to Texas, bought 2,000 head of cattle, and drove them north to Abilene. A year later he bought 7,000 more. Having driven them north, with narrow escapes from outlaws, he sold all but 3,000. These he drove to Humboldt Wells, Nev., where he established a ranch that he held three years while he increased his stock and ran other herds in Texas, Nebraska, and Colorado. In 1878 the Cheyennes under Chief Dull Knife raided some of his herds and caused him much trouble and loss; the next year he consolidated his cattle interests on the North Platte River. He was now buying 10,000 head annually and branding 3,000 calves each year, but cold winters entailed heavy losses, about thirty per cent. in 1883. Foreseeing the end of the free range, he sold out his cattle interests—32,000 cattle and 400 horses—in 1884.

Furthermore, having been married, Feb. 15, 1882, to Catherine V. Ryan of Leavenworth, Kan., he desired to lead a more settled life. Going to Denver, he bought stock in the Colorado National Bank of Denver and became vice-president. When in 1886–87 the Holden Smelting Works of Denver, upon which the bank had made heavy loans, had financial difficulties, he was asked to work out a solution. His work in

this shows his versatility. Being entirely unfamiliar with the methods and problems of smelting he set about to learn with the help of a teacher and by private study. He reorganized the smelting company, effected economies, and placed it on a paying basis. As president and general manager of the Globe Smelting and Refining Company he rebuilt and enlarged the plant, increased the annual production from $20,000 to $16,000,000, and founded the town of Globeville, Colo. His work with the railroads for favorable rates and with Congress for a protective tariff on lead ores contributed to the success of the company, with which he retained his connection until 1910. In 1894 he became president and general manager of the Denver Dry Goods Company, which under his management became the largest department store in Colorado. After the death of his first wife in 1895, he married Mary Teresa Burke of Chicago on Nov. 24, 1898. The two children born to her died in their youth. His widow and two of the six children of the first marriage survived him. He died in Denver. His record of his experiences, *The Autobiography of Dennis Sheedy,* was privately printed in 1922.

[The principal source of information about Sheedy's life is *The Autobiog. of Dennis Sheedy* (1922). A sketch of his early years appears in J. G. McCoy, *Hist. Sketches of the Cattle Trade of the West and Southwest* (1874). See also *Who's Who in America,* 1922–23; W. N. Byers, *Encyc. of Biog. of Colo.* (1901); J. C. Smiley, *Hist. of Denver* (1901); obituaries in *Denver Post,* Oct. 16, and *Rocky Mountain News,* Oct. 16, 17, 1923.]
            L. R. H.

SHEFFIELD, DEVELLO ZELOTES (Aug. 13, 1841–July 1, 1913), missionary to China, was born in Gainesville, N. Y., the son of Asa Campbell Sheffield, a farmer, and Caroline (Murry). His early education was obtained in Warsaw, Middlebury, and Alexander academies. In 1861 he enlisted in the Union army, serving for two years. He was invalided home and to the end of his days bore the traces of his illness. He taught for about three years and for a time served as principal of the high school at Castile, N. Y. Apparently he passed through a religious crisis in his middle twenties; having been skeptical, he was converted, and united with the Presbyterian Church in Castile in 1866. In that same year he entered Auburn Theological Seminary, where he graduated three years later. On May 2, 1869, he was ordained to the ministry by the Cayuga Presbytery; on July 27 he married Eleanor Woodhull Sherrill of Pike, N. Y.; and soon afterward he sailed for China as a missionary of the American Board of Commissioners for Foreign Missions. On arriving in China he was assigned to Tungchow, a small city thirteen miles from Peking, where he spent most of the remainder of his life. He had three daughters and two sons, one of whom died in infancy.

Sheffield's achievements were mainly in education, literature, and administration. He was early attached to the school which his mission had established in Tungchow and had no small part in its development into a high school. He taught a wide variety of subjects, including courses in the affiliated Gordon Theological Seminary. When to the high school was added North China College (organized in 1892–93) he became the president of the new institution, and continued as such when by the cooperation of other missions (1902–03) the scope of the college was enlarged and its name changed to North China Union College. He retired in 1909 only because of advancing years. As president he taught and also for a long period did most of the preaching in the college church. He continued to teach until the year before his death. He had the reputation of being an excellent instructor, a strict disciplinarian, and an impressive preacher.

By dint of the persistence, diligence, and thoroughness which were characteristic of him he achieved a remarkable knowledge of the Chinese language. He was the author of several books in Chinese—on systematic theology, political economy, ethics, psychology, political science, church history, and general history—which largely grew out of his teaching. His *Universal History,* published in 1881—a pioneer in introducing modern China to that field—had a wide circulation. He devoted a large proportion of his time to the translation of the Bible into Chinese. He did much of the work on the standard Protestant co-operative revision of the New Testament in classical style, and was engaged in a similar revision of the Old Testament when, in 1912, failing health compelled him to give up his accustomed activities. He had also assisted in preparing the International Sunday School lessons in Chinese and in the revision of S. Wells Williams' Chinese-English dictionary. In addition to his exacting labors as a teacher and author he found time to serve in many administrative capacities —on the many committees which are a concomitant of Protestant missions, as secretary of his mission, and as president of the (Protestant) Educational Association of China (1896–99). He had not a little mechanical ability, and constructed a typewriter for the Chinese language as well as much of the apparatus required in college teaching.

He was slight of build and not of robust physique. He was wise in counsel, logical of mind, of a masterful spirit, ripe in judgment, and in his later years tolerant and possessed of a certain childlike simplicity. He died at Peitaiho, in North China.

[*Chinese Recorder,* Aug., Sept., 1913; *Missionary Herald,* Aug. 1913; *Ann. Report, Am. Board of Commissioners for Foreign Missions,* 1861–1912; archives of the American Board; *Who's Who in America,* 1908–09, 1910–11; *Gen. Biog. Cat. Auburn Theol. Sem.* (1918); C. H. Sherrill and L. E. deForest, *The Sherrill Geneal.* (1932).]   K. S. L.

SHEFFIELD, JOSEPH EARL (June 19, 1793–Feb. 16, 1882), merchant financier, philanthropist, was born in Southport, Conn., the son of Mabel (Thorp) and Paul King Sheffield. His father, who had moved from Stonington, had seen service on a privateer fitted out by his family during the Revolution; his mother was also a member of a seafaring family, a daughter of Capt. Walter Thorp of Southport, engaged in the West India trade. Sheffield completed his formal education at the age of fourteen, leaving the village school on a voyage to New Bern, N. C., in a vessel of his uncle's. He entered as clerk a store in that town, transferring the next year to the drug store of Dr. Thomas Webb, under whom he continued his studies. On a visit at Southport when the War of 1812 broke out, he undertook in the following spring to act as supercargo of a small vessel which ran the British blockade at Sandy Hook and brought back naval stores from New Bern. Remaining at New Bern, he conducted several similar and very profitable enterprises. In 1814, before he was twenty-one, he became the partner in New Bern of a large dry-goods firm in New York. Faced by the disastrous fall in prices after the peace of 1815, he boldly sold the dry goods below cost but turned loss into profit by the quick shipment of naval stores. On a horseback trip of over a thousand miles, which he made in 1816–17 in search of an outlet for the remainder of the stock, he was impressed by the prospects of Mobile, Ala., then a town of about a thousand inhabitants, still lacking a bank or any extensive trade, but at the outlet of two great rivers reaching into a rich cotton country. He entered the cotton trade, established important business connections in New Orleans, New York, Liverpool, and Havre, and became the largest exporter of this important port, in one year shipping 20,000 bales. He had judgment and courage, and in addition an appreciation, very unusual in that day, of the importance of accurate statistics as a basis of forecasting. He secured as detailed information as possible not only on the cotton crop but also on the harvests in Europe, and ascribed to this practice the fact that of twenty years in a very speculative trade only two were unsuccessful.

He had married on Aug. 22, 1822, Maria, daughter of Col. John T. St. John of Walton, N. Y., who bore him nine children. In 1835, influenced by considerations of health and social environment, he removed to New Haven. He gradually retired from the cotton trade, but found a larger field for his wealth, his business ability, and his craving for substantial accomplishment in the development of means of transportation. In close cooperation with an able engineer, Henry Farnam [q.v.], he helped to finance the completion of the New Haven-Northampton canal, the railroad which succeeded it, and the railroad from New York to New Haven. Although he lost money in these enterprises, he contracted with Farnam to complete the unfinished part of the Michigan Southern Railroad, about 170 miles, over which the first train from the East entered Chicago in 1852; in that year he contracted to build 182 miles for the Chicago & Rock Island Railroad completed in 1854 and extended by a bridge across the Mississippi the next year. The contractors were paid for their work on the Rock Island in bonds and stock at par; Sheffield raised all the cash, about five million dollars, and divided the profits equally with Farnam. He then retired from active business connections and devoted his energy to benefaction.

He gave a generous part of a large fortune to education. Impressed through his engineering experience with the importance of science, and with his interest probably quickened by the marriage of his daughter to Prof. John Addison Porter [q.v.], he gave steadily and wisely to the scientific department of Yale College. Without him its success would have been impossible; though it had been founded in 1847 and made a separate school in 1854, its resources were meager. His gifts and bequests to it, for which in 1861 it was renamed the Sheffield Scientific School, amounted to over a million dollars. In 1871, fifteen years before Yale College assumed the larger title of university, he expressed in a deed of gift the "hope and belief that New Haven is to be the seat of a true university, made up of many colleges having distinct though harmonious aims" (Chittenden, post, vol. II, p. 577). He also gave liberally to Trinity College, Hartford, Conn., to the Berkeley Divinity School, Middletown, Conn. (later in New Haven), and to local New Haven institutions. He died in New Haven, survived by his wife and six children.

[H. W. Farnam, in *Papers of the New Haven Colony Hist. Soc.*, vol. VII (1908); memoir in Bernard's *Am. Jour. of Educ.*, July 15, 1878; R. H. Chittenden, *Hist. of the Sheffield Sci. School of Yale Univ., 1846–1922*

(2 vols., 1928); obituary in *New Haven Evening Reg.*, Feb. 16, 1882.]   C. D.

SHELBY, EVAN (1719–Dec. 4, 1794), soldier and frontiersman, was baptized in October 1719 at Tregaron, Cardiganshire, Wales. He came to America with his parents, Evan and Catherine (Davies?) Shelby, about 1734, the family first settling in what is now Antrim Township, Franklin County, Pa. In 1739, they moved into Prince George's (later Frederick) County, Md., where the father died in June 1750. Evan, Jr., continued to reside in Maryland, near the North Mountain, Frederick County, in which locality, now a part of Washington County, he acquired, by deed or patent, nearly 24,000 acres of land. He also became interested in the Indian fur trade and was concerned in trading-posts at Michilimackinac and Green Bay. He was in Braddock's campaign in 1755, and laid out part of the road from Fort Frederick to Fort Cumberland. Having served as first lieutenant in Capt. Alexander Beall's company in 1757–58, he was commissioned by Governor Sharpe of Maryland captain of a company of rangers and also held a commission as captain under the government of Pennsylvania. He was in the advance party of the force under Gen. John Forbes [q.v.] which took possession of Fort Duquesne in 1758, and crossed the Ohio with more than half his company of scouts, making a daring reconnoissance of the fort. On Nov. 12, 1758, near Loyalhanna, in a personal ecounter, Shelby is said to have slain with his own hand one of the principal Indian chiefs (Banvard, post). In this same war, he served later as major of a detachment of the Virginia regiment. For several years he was a justice of the peace. In May 1762 he was chosen one of the managers for Maryland of the Potomac Company. He sustained heavy losses in the Indian trade from the ravages growing out of Pontiac's Conspiracy of 1763, and most of his property in Maryland was subjected to the satisfaction of his debts.

Hoping to better his fortune he moved, probably in 1773, to Fincastle County, in Southwest Virginia, which he had previously visited, where he engaged in farming, merchandising, and cattle-raising, became again a prosperous landowner and a conspicuous and influential frontier leader. In 1774 he commanded the Fincastle Company in Dunmore's War, and in the battle of Point Pleasant, Oct. 10, 1774, he succeeded near the close of the action to the chief command in consequence of the death or disability of his superior officers. In 1776 he was appointed by Governor Henry of Virginia a major in the troops commanded by Col. William Christian against the Cherokees, and on Dec. 21 he became colonel of the militia of the newly created county of Washington, of which he was also a magistrate. In 1777, he was entrusted with the command of sundry garrisons posted on the frontier of Virginia, and in association with Preston and Christian negotiated a treaty with the Cherokees near the Long Island of Holston River. In 1779 he led a successful expedition of two thousand men against the Chickamauga Indian towns on the lower Tennessee River, for which service he was thanked by the Continental Congress.

By the extension of the boundary line between Virginia and North Carolina it was ascertained that his residence lay in the latter state, and in 1781 he was elected a member of its Senate. Five years later, the Carolina Assembly made him brigadier-general of militia of the Washington District of North Carolina, the first officer of that grade on "the Western Waters." In March 1787, as commissioner for North Carolina, he negotiated a temporary truce with Col. John Sevier [q.v.], governor of the insurgent and short-lived "State of Franklin." In August 1787, he was elected governor of the "State of Franklin," to succeed Sevier, but declined the honor. Having resigned his post as brigadier-general on Oct. 29, 1787, he withdrew from public life. He married first, in 1744, Lætitia Cox, a daughter of David Cox of Frederick County, Md. She died in 1777. His second wife, whom he married early in 1787, was Isabella Elliott, who survived him. He is buried in East Hill Cemetery, Bristol, on the Tennessee-Virginia line.

Shelby was of a rugged, stocky build, somewhat low in stature and stern of countenance. He possessed great muscular strength and unbounded energy and powers of endurance. He was straightforward and, at times, rather blunt in speech, absolutely fearless, and always prompt to take the aggressive in any action or enterprise, civil or military, in which he engaged. For a man of his day, he was well educated, and he was noted for his probity and patriotism. He left many descendants, of whom the most celebrated was his son, Isaac Shelby [q.v.], the first governor of Kentucky.

["Correspondence of Gov. Horatio Sharpe" (3 vols.), being *Archives of Md.*, vols. VI (1888), IX (1890), XIV (1895); J. T. Scharf, *Hist. of Western Md.* (2 vols., 1882); Joseph Banvard, *Tragic Scenes in the Hist. of Md., and the Old French War* (1856); J. G. M. Ramsey, *The Annals of Tenn.* (1853); L. P. Summers, *Hist. of Southwest Va.* (1903) and *Annals of Southwest Va.* (1929); R. G. Thwaites and L. P. Kellogg, *Doc. Hist. of Dunmore's War* (1905); G. N. Mackenzie, *Colonial Families of the U. S. A.*, II (1911), 652–57; Zella Armstrong, *Notable Southern Families*, vol. II (1922); S. C. Williams, *Hist. of the Lost State of Franklin* (1924); T. W. Preston, *Hist.*

Sketches of the Holston Valleys (1926); Cass K. Shelby, *A Report on the First Three Generations of the Shelby Family in the U. S.* (privately printed, 1927); A. M. Moon, *Sketches of the Shelby, McDowell, Deaderick and Anderson Families* (1933); D. C. Rees, *Tregaron Historical and Antiguardian* (Llandyssul, 1934).]
            S. M. W.

SHELBY, ISAAC (Dec. 11, 1750–July 18, 1826), soldier, first governor of Kentucky, was born near the North Mountain, in Frederick (now Washington) County, Md., the son of Evan [q.v.] and Lætitia (Cox) Shelby. Brought up to the use of arms, he early became inured to the dangers and hardships of frontier life. He received a fair English education, worked on his father's plantation, was occasionally employed as a surveyor, and served as a deputy sheriff of the county. About 1773 the Shelby family moved to the Holston region of Southwest Virginia, now East Tennessee, where they established a new home.

Isaac Shelby served as a lieutenant in his father's Fincastle Company, at the battle of Point Pleasant, Oct. 10, 1774, distinguishing himself by his skill and gallantry; his report of the action is one of the best contemporary accounts now in existence (printed in Thwaites and Kellogg, *post*). He remained as second in command of the garrison of Fort Blair, erected on the site of the battle, until July 1775, when he visited Kentucky and surveyed lands for the Transylvania Company. The following year he returned to Kentucky and marked and improved lands on his own account, and also perfected military surveys previously selected and entered by his father. In July 1776 he was appointed by the Virginia committee of safety captain of a company of minute men. In 1777, Governor Henry made him commissary of supplies for a body of militia detailed to garrison frontier posts. He attended the Long Island Treaty with the Cherokees, concluded at Fort Patrick Henry, on July 20, 1777, at which his father was one of the Virginia commissioners. In 1778, he aided in furnishing supplies for the Continental Army and for the expedition projected by General McIntosh against Detroit and the Ohio Indians. The following year, he provided boats for Clark's Illinois campaign and collected and furnished supplies—mainly upon his own personal credit—for the successful campaign waged about the same time against the Chickamauga Indians. In the spring of 1779 he was chosen a member for Washington County of the Virginia legislature, and, the ensuing fall, Governor Jefferson made him a major in the escort of guards for the commissioners appointed to run the western boundary line between Virginia and North Carolina. Early in 1780, he became colonel of the militia of Sullivan County, N. C. In the spring and summer of the same year he was again in Kentucky, supervising the surveying of lands for himself and others.

News of the fall of Charleston (May 12, 1780) having reached him, he hurried home and found an urgent summons for help from Col. Charles McDowell [q.v.]. He at once organized a force and about July 25 joined McDowell at the Cherokee Ford, S. C. On July 30, 1780, at the head of a detachment, Shelby captured a formidable Loyalist stronghold, Thicketty Fort (or Fort Anderson), on the headwaters of the Pacolet River. In the second battle of Cedar Springs, Aug. 8, 1780, his command successfully repulsed a strong party sent against it by Major Ferguson, and on Aug. 18, he was largely responsible for the victory won over a superior force at Musgrove's Mill, on the north side of the Enoree River.

The report of General Gates's defeat at Camden on Aug. 16 halted further operations by the patriot forces under McDowell and Shelby. The term of enlistment of Shelby's volunteer regiment being about to expire, he proposed that an army of volunteers be raised on both sides of the mountains. A threatening message dispatched by Ferguson, instead of intimidating Shelby, fired him with greater resentment and determination. In consequence, he initiated and, in concert with John Sevier [q.v.] and others, organized and conducted the expedition against Ferguson, whose combined Provincial and Loyalist force was overwhelmingly defeated in the decisive battle of King's Mountain, Oct. 7, 1780. To Shelby, also, has been accorded credit for the scheme of attack, which led to the battle of the Cowpens, Jan. 17, 1781. In February 1781, the legislature of North Carolina adopted resolutions of thanks to Shelby and his compatriots for their services at King's Mountain, similar resolutions having been adopted by the Continental Congress on Nov. 13, 1780.

Repeated uprisings and depredations by Cherokee Indians along the western borders of North Carolina, during the first half of the year 1781, rendered it impracticable to send any considerable force from that quarter to assist General Greene. A treaty with the Cherokees having been negotiated on July 20, 1781, however, Shelby, in October, upon receipt of a delayed message of appeal from Greene, raised 500 mounted riflemen and, accompanied by Col. John Sevier in command of 200 more, marched to join Greene, by whose order they reported to General Marion on the Santee. Shelby, in joint command with Col. Hezekiah Maham, of the Carolina dragoons,

rendered conspicuous service in the capture of a strong British post at Fair Lawn, near Monck's Corner, S. C., on Nov. 27, 1781. While on this expedition, he was elected a member of the North Carolina legislature, and, obtaining leave of absence, attended its sessions in December. Many years later, he declared: "For myself, for the whole services of 1780 and 1781, both in camp and in the Assembly, I received a liquidation certificate which my agent in that country, after my removal to Kentucky, sold for six yards of middling broadcloth, and I gave one coat of it to the person who brought it out to me—indeed I was proud of receiving that" (*North Carolina Booklet,* July 1918, pp. 50–51, footnote 62). Reelected to the North Carolina Assembly in 1782, he attended the legislative sessions held at Hillsboro, in April. He was appointed one of three commissioners to superintend the laying off of the land south of the Cumberland River allotted by North Carolina for military service in the Revolution. This task was performed in the early months of 1783.

Shortly thereafter, he removed to Kentucky, where, at Boonesborough, he was married, on Apr. 19, to Susannah Hart, a daughter of Capt. Nathaniel Hart, by whom he had eleven children. In 1783 he was appointed a trustee of Transylvania Seminary (later Transylvania University). He was chairman of the convention of militia officers held at Danville on Nov. 7–8, 1784, called to consider an expedition against the Indians and separation from Virginia; he was also a member of the succeeding conventions (1787, 1788, 1789), which prepared the way for independent statehood. He helped to organize the Kentucky Society for Promoting Useful Knowledge, formed at Danville, Dec. 1, 1787. In January 1791, he was appointed a member of the board of war, created by Congress for the District of Kentucky, with power to provide for the defense of the frontier settlements and to prosecute punitive expeditions against the Indians. For several years he served as high sheriff of Lincoln County. He was a member of the convention (Apr. 2–19, 1792) which framed the first constitution of Kentucky, and in May he was elected governor, taking office on June 4, and serving four years. During his administration many events of importance to the infant commonwealth occurred, not the least being the part it took, under Shelby, in supporting Wayne's campaigns against the Indians in the Northwest Territory. At the close of his term, he declined reëlection, and for the next fifteen years gave attention to his private affairs.

The imminence of war with Great Britain

called him from retirement, and in August 1812 he was a second time elected governor. He co-operated vigorously in the prosecution of the war, and in 1813 assembled and led in person 4,000 Kentucky volunteers to join General Harrison in the Northwest for the invasion of Canada, an expedition which resulted in the decisive defeat of the British, Oct. 5, 1813, at the battle of the Thames. For his patriotic and heroic services he was awarded a gold medal by Congress on Apr. 4, 1818. In March 1817, he was tendered the portfolio of War by President Monroe, but declined the honor on the score of age. The year following he was commissioned, with Gen. Andrew Jackson, to hold a treaty with the Chickasaw Indians for the purchase of their lands west of the Tennessee River, and performed this service most acceptably. He was president of the first Kentucky Agricultural Society, formed at Lexington in 1818, and was chairman of the first board of trustees of Centre College, founded in 1819 at Danville, Ky. At his death he was buried at his historic home, "Traveller's Rest," and a monument was erected over his grave by the state of Kentucky. Counties in nine states have been named Shelby in his honor.

In person, Shelby was of a sturdy and well-proportioned frame, slightly above medium height, with strongly marked features and florid complexion. He had a hardy constitution capable of enduring protracted labor, great privations, and the utmost fatigue. Habitually dignified and impressive in bearing, he was, however, affable and winning. A soldier born to command, he nevertheless evidenced a high degree of political sagacity and executive ability. Numerous difficulties confronted him during his first administration, when the new government was passing through its formative stage, and much depended on the choice of officials then made by the executive. Shelby exhibited rare selective intelligence and an extraordinary mastery both of men and measures. Kentucky at this time experienced constant dread of the occlusion by Spain of the Mississippi River, and use was made of this situation by designing men to promote speculative ventures and political schemes hostile to the true interests of both Kentucky and the Union. Through it all, Shelby pursued a wise and moderate course which baffled the plots of all conspirators and held Kentucky firmly to her federal moorings. During his second administration, the pressure of the war with Great Britain fell with extraordinary and unremitting severity upon the state, and he showed himself not only a prudent and farseeing counselor, but an active, resourceful, and patriotic leader. His

energy, determination, and perseverance knew no bounds, and his devotion to duty was unflagging.

[James Herring and J. B. Longacre, *The Nat. Portrait Gallery of Distinguished Americans,* vol. I (1834); Autobiog. of Isaac Shelby (MS.), in Durrett Collections, Univ. of Chicago; R. B. McAfee, *Hist. of the Late War in the Western Country* (1816); W. T. Barry, *Speech on the Deaths of Adams, Jefferson, and Shelby* (1826); John Haywood, *Civil and Pol. Hist. of the State of Tenn.* (1823); Mann Butler, *A Hist. of the Commonwealth of Ky.* (2nd ed., 1836); J. T. Morehead, *An Address in Commemoration of the First Settlement of Ky.* (1840); Lewis and R. H. Collins, *Hist. of Ky.* (1874); J. G. M. Ramsey, *The Annals of Tenn.* (1853); L. C. Draper, *King's Mountain and Its Heroes* (1881); John Watts de Peyster, in *Mag. of Am. Hist.,* Dec. 1880, and *The Battle or Affair of King's Mountain* (1881); J. B. O. Landrum, *Colonial and Revolutionary Hist. of Upper S. C.* (1897); Edward McCrady, *The Hist. of S. C. in the Revolution* (2 vols., 1901, 1902); B. H. Young, *The Battle of the Thames* (1903), Filson Club Pubs., no. 18; R. G. Thwaites and L. P. Kellogg, *Doc. Hist. of Dunmore's War* (1905); C. H. Todd, in *Jour. of Am. Hist.,* vol. II (1908), no. 2; V. A. Lewis, *Hist. of the Battle of Point Pleasant* (1909); A. C. Quisenberry, *Ky. in the War of 1812* (1915); Archibald Henderson, *N. C. Booklet,* Jan. 1917, July 1918; Samuel M. Wilson, *A Review of "Isaac Shelby and the Genet Mission,"* by Dr. Archibald Henderson (1920); "Hist. Statements Concerning the Battle of King's Mountain, and the Battle of the Cowpens, S. C.," *House Doc. 328, 70 Cong., 1 Sess.;* H. J. Berkley, in *Md. Hist. Mag.,* June 1932; *Ky. Gazette* (Lexington), July 21, 28, Aug. 25, 1826; a few MSS. in Lib. of Cong.]   S. M. W.

SHELBY, JOSEPH ORVILLE (Dec. 12, 1830–Feb. 13, 1897), Confederate soldier, the son of Orville Shelby and his second wife, Anna M. Boswell, was born in Lexington, Ky. He was a descendant of the fourth generation from Evan Shelby, who came to America from Wales about 1734, and a kinsman of Evan and Isaac Shelby [*qq.v.*] When Shelby was about five years old his father died and the boy received his early schooling from his step-father, Benjamin Grantz. He entered Transylvania University at the age of fifteen and remained there for three years. After an additional year's study in Philadelphia, he returned to Lexington to engage in rope manufacturing. In 1852 he moved to Berlin and later to Waverly, Mo., where he established a rope factory. During the Kansas-Missouri border troubles, Shelby, favorable to slavery, raised and commanded a company of Kentuckians. He then returned to his business pursuits and by 1861 was accounted one of the wealthiest slave and land owners in Missouri.

When Fort Sumter was fired on, Shelby, refusing a Federal commission, joined the Confederacy and in three years rose from the rank of captain to that of brigadier-general. His cavalry force was prominently identified with the campaigns of Gen. Sterling Price [*q.v.*] in the West, fighting at Carthage, Wilson's Creek, Lexington, Springfield, Mo., Pea Ridge, St.

Charles, and Duvall's Bluff, Ark. In June 1862 he joined the forces of Gen. James E. Rains at Van Buren, Ark., to invade Missouri. Shelby's men swore at this time never to lay down arms until the war ended. At Newtonia, Mo., he organized a cavalry brigade, and during the fall of 1862 remained near Huntsville, Ark., operating throughout the winter against Gen. James Gillpatrick Blunt [q.v.]. The Confederates broke camp in Arkansas in December 1862, dashed into Missouri, captured the outer defenses of Springfield, and then retreated to Batesville, Ark. Here they rested until spring, when the ill-starred Cape Girardeau expedition was organized. This project was abandoned in favor of an attempt to interrupt Grant's communications and they attacked Helena, Ark., on July 4, 1863, not knowing that Vicksburg had fallen. Shelby was wounded in this action, but upon his recovery he raided Missouri, captured Booneville, Neosho, Bower Mills, Warsaw, Tipton, Stockton, and Humansville, and then withdrew to Camden, Ark., for winter quarters. Shelby was ordered on Mar. 3, 1864, to garrison Princeton, on the Saline River line, and to cover all roads leading into Camden. In the ensuing action, his thousand cavalrymen restrained Steele's force of fifteen thousand throughout an entire day. This engagement as well as the remarkably successful Missouri raid of the following summer demonstrated the devotion with which his men followed him and justified fully the respect he commanded from friend and foe alike. His personal courage and his mastery of cavalry tactics carried him to a conspicuous place among Confederate cavalrymen. The Confederates invaded Missouri again in the summer of 1864 to divert Grant from his hammering campaign. Shelby and Price attacked at Lexington and at the Little Blue River, then moved to Westport, Mo., where they engaged heavily late in October 1864. When Price was forced to withdraw to Newtonia, Shelby ably covered the movement. After an engagement with Blunt at Newtonia, Shelby retired to Clarksville, Tex., where he learned of Lee's surrender.

When General Buckner surrendered at Shreveport, La., Shelby urged his men to cross into Mexico, there to join forces either with General Juarez or Emperor Maximilian. Shelby's command buried their battle flag in the Rio Grande River on July 4, 1865, and crossed the border. Against Shelby's judgment, his men voted to support Maximilian, but the Emperor, suspicious of the proffered aid, held aloof. Later he repented of his folly, and gave Shelby some land upon which a colony, named Carlotta for the Empress,

was formed. As the French withdrew from Mexico, Juarez struck and Maximilian finally called for Shelby's aid, but his hour had passed and the unhappy monarch soon faced a firing squad. Shelby returned to Bates County, Mo., to rebuild his fortunes, but steadfastly refused to capitalize politically on his great personal popularity until 1893, when President Cleveland appointed him United States marshal for the western district of Missouri. While carrying out the duties of this office, he contracted an illness which resulted in his death at Adrian, Mo. He was buried in Forest Hill Cemetery, Kansas City, Mo. In 1858 he was married to Elizabeth N. Shelby, a remote cousin. They had seven children, of whom a daughter and several sons survived their parents.

[Correspondence with a member of the family; Zella Armstrong, *Notable Southern Families*, vol. II (1922); J. N. Edwards, *Shelby and His Men* (1867); B. H. Young, *Confed. Wizards of the Saddle* (1914); *Confed. Mil. Hist.* (1899), vol. IX; W. L. Webb, *Battles and Biographies of Missourians* (1900); W. R. Hollister, Harry Norman, *Five Famous Missourians* (1900); W. B. Stevens, *Centennial Hist. of Mo.* (1921), vol. II; J. N. Edwards, *Shelby's Expedition to Mexico* (1872); *St. Louis Globe-Democrat*, Feb. 14, 1897.]

C. C. B—n.

SHELDON, EDWARD AUSTIN (Oct. 4, 1823–Aug. 26, 1897), educator, was born near Perry Center, N. Y., the son of Eleazer and Laura (Austin) Sheldon. He was a descendant of Isaac Sheldon, who emigrated to America, probably in 1634, and later settled in Windsor, Conn. As a boy he worked on his father's farm and in the winters attended a district school nearby. After preparing for college at the newly established Perry Center Academy, he matriculated in 1844 at Hamilton College but withdrew in 1847 to recuperate from an attack of pleurisy and for several months lived outdoors with Charles and Andrew Jackson Downing [qq.v.], well-known horticulturists of Newburgh, N. Y. The experiences of this period influenced him to enter into a partnership in the fall of 1847 in the nursery business at Oswego, N. Y., but the venture failed. Unsuccessful as well in his search for employment in New York City in 1848, he returned to Oswego.

Moved to sympathy by conditions among the poor people of the city and learning that many were illiterate, he succeeded in bringing about the organization, on Nov. 28, 1848, of the Orphan and Free School Association of Oswego and was appointed to take charge of it. Though he saw the need and importance of making all the public schools of the city free and urged it at this time, public interest in the "Ragged School," as it was called, waned, and in 1849 he resigned to open a private school for boys and girls, in partnership with J. D. Higgins. On May 16, 1849, he married Frances Ann Bradford Stiles, daughter of Ezra and Anna (Spear) Stiles of Syracuse, N. Y. In 1851 he again urged the establishment of free schools in Oswego and had the satisfaction of seeing his suggestions embodied in a bill which became a law in 1853. In the meantime he became superintendent of public schools in Syracuse, where he improved the classification and gradation of schools, established a system of evening schools, and organized school libraries. In 1853 he returned to Oswego as secretary of the board of education, a position corresponding to that of superintendent, and organized the first system of free schools there. As in Syracuse, he reorganized courses of study, graded and classified schools, and secured better qualified teachers. His accomplishments were recognized by other educators in the state and in 1860 he was elected president of the state teachers' association; in the same year he became one of the editors of the *New York Teacher*.

In May 1861, as a result of his recommendations, the Oswego Primary Teachers' Training School was opened, the first city training school in the United States. After the first year Sheldon became principal, a position he held until the year of his death. In 1863 he secured state recognition and financial aid for the school, which in 1866 became the Oswego State Normal and Training School. His success as head of the school was immediate. Under his direction it became the most important center of Pestalozzianism and objective instruction in the United States. His methods of practice-teaching were studied widely, and many of his graduates were called to organize and take charge of city training schools. In 1866-67 six additional state normal and training schools were established in New York on the plan of the Oswego school. His publications include several spelling books, a series of readers, *A Manual of Elementary Instruction* (1862), *Teachers' Manual of Instruction in Reading* (copyright 1875), and *Autobiography of Edward Austin Sheldon* (copyright 1911). At the time of his death he was survived by a son and four daughters, one of whom was Mary Downing Sheldon Barnes [*q.v.*].

[See esp. *Autobiog. of Edward Austin Sheldon* (copr. 1911), ed. by Mary Sheldon Barnes; N. H. Dearborn, *The Oswego Movement in Am. Educ.* (1925); A. P. Hollis, *The Oswego Movement* (1898). See also *Am. Ancestry*, vol. IV (1889); H. R. Stiles, *The Stiles Family in America* (1895); W. S. Monroe, *Hist. of the Pestalozzian Movement in the U. S.* (copr. 1907); *Am. Jour. Educ.*, Sept. 1865, pp. 484-85; *Proc. Nat. Educ. Assoc., 1898* (1898); obituary in *N. Y. Tribune*, Aug. 27, 1897.]   R. F. S.

SHELDON, EDWARD STEVENS (Nov. 21, 1851–Oct. 16, 1925), philologist, lexicographer, was born at Waterville, Me., a son of the Rev. David Newton and Rachel Hobart (Ripley) Sheldon, and a brother of Henry Newton Sheldon [*q.v.*]. After preliminary studies at the Waterville (later Coburn) Classical Institute and at Colby College, Waterville, where he spent one year, Sheldon went to Harvard College and graduated in 1872. Soon after, he was appointed proctor in the College, at the same time teaching Greek in a school for young ladies in Boston, and in the spring of 1873 he was instructor in Spanish and Italian at Harvard. Later he received a traveling fellowship, which enabled him to develop an already large linguistic equipment by three years' work at the Universities of Berlin, Leipzig, and Paris, 1874-77. During this sojourn he prepared himself for his life work in English lexicology and the teaching of Romance linguistics; he also gave much attention to Germanics and the history of the Greek and Latin languages. In Germany he profited particularly by his relations with the noted professor of Romance philology, Adolf Tobler. Returning to the United States, he became in 1877 an instructor in modern languages and then a tutor in German at Harvard University. With the year 1884, when he was appointed assistant professor of Romance philology, his labors at Harvard were fixed for good and all. In that year, on Apr. 2, he married Katherine Hamlin Hinckley of Poughkeepsie, N. Y., by whom he had one daughter. In 1894 he became professor of Romance philology, a position he held until his retirement in 1921. His activities brought him very naturally into connection with various learned societies. He was a fellow of the American Academy of Arts and Sciences; and he served as president of the American Dialect Society, which he had helped to found, in 1894-95, of the Modern Language Association of America in 1901, and of the Dante Society from 1909 to 1915.

Over a stretch of years Sheldon performed scholarly work of a monumental sort, which is represented by his revision of the etymologies in *Webster's International Dictionary* for its issues of 1890 and later. For this useful learning, in which his individuality is submerged, the world will never give him the reward merited by his patient and fruitful research, which often meant invaluable correction of errors present in anterior lexicons, not excluding the great *Oxford English Dictionary* (1888–1928). His writings, apart from minor articles in various learned reviews, include *A Short German Grammar* (1879), which went through several editions,

"Some Specimens of a Canadian French Dialect Spoken in Maine" (*Transactions and Proceedings of the Modern Language Association of America*, vol. III, 1888), "The Origin of the English Names of the Letters of the Alphabet" (*Studies and Notes in Philology and Literature*, 1892), "Further Notes on the Names of the Letters" (*Ibid.*, 1893); *Concordanza delle opere italiane in prosa e del Canzoniere di Dante Alighieri* (1905), in collaboration with A. C. White, and "Some Remarks on the Origin of Romance Versification" (*Anniversary Papers by Colleagues and Pupils of George Lyman Kittredge*, 1913). He was one of the best informed of all the specialists who have ever studied the general subject of French contributions to the English vocabulary. Unfortunately, in spite of the efforts of his friends to secure a permanent record of his knowledge of Anglo-French, he died without preparing the study of the subject he had promised. The agony of his last years, in which he suffered from an extremely painful ailment, explains his failure to leave such a tangible memorial of his erudition. He died in Cambridge, Mass.

[*Who's Who in America*, 1924–25; reports of Harvard Coll. Class of 1872 esp. those published in 1898, 1912, 1917, and 1924; C. H. Grandgent, in *Harvard Graduates' Mag.*, Dec. 1925; *Harvard Univ. Gazette*, Dec. 12, 1925; obituary in "Notes and Comments," *Modern Philology*, Feb. 1926; death notice in *Boston Transcript*, Oct. 16, 1925.]   J. D. M. F.

SHELDON, HENRY NEWTON (June 28, 1843–Jan. 14, 1926), jurist, was born in Waterville, Me., son of Rachel (Ripley) and David Newton Sheldon, a Unitarian clergyman who was at one time president of Waterville (later Colby) College, and brother of Edward Stevens Sheldon [*q.v.*]. Educated in the public schools of Bath and Waterville, he went first to Bowdoin for a year and then entered the sophomore class at Harvard, where he obtained a scholarship and, partly working his way, graduated first scholar in the class of 1863. He taught school and studied law for about a year and then entered the 55th Massachusetts Regiment (colored) as a lieutenant on June 28, 1864. After active service in South Carolina and Georgia, he returned to Boston at the close of the war and was admitted to the bar in 1866. On Dec. 31, 1868, he married Clara P. Morse of Hubbardston, Mass., by whom he had two children. Until 1894 he practised law in Boston, being associated for about twenty years with Gen. Wilmon W. Blackmar. During this period he edited Joseph Bateman's *A Practical Treatise on the Law of Auctions* (1883) and published *The Law of Subrogation* (1882), which became the standard work on the subject.

In 1894 the judicial office "sought the man" in a way that shows the value to the public of the Massachusetts system of judicial appointment. Being exceptionally modest, quiet, and scholarly in his habits, Sheldon would never have attracted political attention for a position on an elective bench; he was appointed to the superior court by Gov. Frederic Thomas Greenhalge [*q.v.*], a lawyer himself and a friend of Sheldon's in college. Though he had been comparatively obscure, he quickly became a leading figure on the court, where he served for ten years, and was known for his scholarship, his quick perception, his balanced judgment, his power of clear statement, his knowledge of men, his firmness, and his natural courtesy. When he was promoted to the supreme judicial court of Massachusetts in 1905, there was general gratification at the bar throughout the commonwealth. He excelled both as a *nisi prius* and as an appellate judge, and had the ability to make the loser feel that his case had been fairly considered. During his ten years of service on the appellate court he wrote almost six hundred opinions. Although he resigned in 1915, his work was not ended. That year he was chosen president of the Massachusetts Bar Association. Under his supervision the *Massachusetts Law Quarterly* was established, and he served as a member of its publication committee until the fall of 1921. While still on the superior court, he had rendered an important service as chairman of a special commission to simplify criminal procedure, and in 1919, when he was more than seventy-five years of age, he was drafted for two important public services. He served as chairman of an investigating committee of the Boston Bar Association, a most difficult and trying task which led to the removal of two district attorneys. He also served during a period of fourteen months as chairman of the judicature commission, which was created to study and report on the entire judicial system of Massachusetts. The work of this commission resulted among other things in the creation of the first statewide "small claims" procedure in the United States, and in the recommendation of a judicial council composed of representatives of both bench and bar for the continuous study of the judicial system, a plan which was later adopted not only in Massachusetts but in about twenty other states. In 1921 Sheldon retired from active service; five years later he died, survived by a son.

[See *Who's Who in America*, 1924–25; *Mass. Law Quart.*, Jan. 1926; *Proc. in the Supreme Judicial Court of Mass. in Memory of Henry Newton Sheldon* (1927), reprinted in *Bar Bull.* (Boston), Dec. 1927; obituary in *Boston Transcript*, Jan. 14, 1926; personal acquaintance. Sheldon's opinions appear in 189–220 *Mass. Reports*.].   F. W. C.

SHELDON, MARY DOWNING [See BARNES, MARY DOWNING SHELDON, 1850–1898].

SHELDON, WALTER LORENZO (Sept. 5, 1858–June 5, 1907), leader in the ethical culture movement, was born in West Rutland, Vt., first of three sons of Preston and Cornelia (Hatch) Sheldon. His father, a lumber dealer, was a descendant of Isaac Sheldon, who lived in Windsor, Conn., as early as 1652. Intended by his father for the Episcopalian ministry, Sheldon spent two years at Middlebury College, 1876–78, and then went to the College of New Jersey (Princeton), where he took an attitude, he wrote later, that put him "far outside the pale of its theology." Graduated in 1880, he studied philosophy in Berlin, Leipzig, and Paris until 1883; the next two years he passed in New York, a disciple of Felix Adler, who in 1876 had established the first Society for Ethical Culture. In 1886, after another winter in Germany, he went to St. Louis, Mo., where he organized the Ethical Society of St. Louis and became its lecturer. Regarding ethical culture as the means of freeing people from outmoded creeds, he nevertheless looked on it as universal religion, the societies as churches, and its lecturers as the clergy. Although he was young and retiring, he was soon recognized as an intellectual leader in a community widely known for its group of Hegelian philosophers, including William Torrey Harris and Henry C. Brokmeyer [*qq.v.*], and for the *Journal of Speculative Philosophy*, to which he contributed an article on "Agnostic Realism," in July 1886.

In 1888 he founded the Self-Culture Hall Association for wage-earners, an early attempt of settlement work in the United States, for which he won the services of educators and ministers of various faiths, and the support of such citizens as William Taussig and Nelson Olsen Nelson [*qq.v.*]. Sheldon described this venture in *Ethical Addresses* (1900, 7 ser.) and in an article in *Charities and the Commons*, Sept. 5, 1908. He organized classes for negroes, whose educational needs had been neglected, and he was also so keenly concerned with the training of children that he gave much time to lessons in citizenship, ethical Sunday schools, and ethical literature for children. He established a Greek Ethics Club for discussion of current problems, which survived as the Contemporary Literature Circle of St. Louis. In 1904 he directed the social science department of the congress of arts and sciences at the Louisiana Purchase Expo-

sition. Throughout his years in St. Louis he wrote prolifically. His publications include *Ethics and the Belief in a God* (1892), *Ethics for the Young* (1894), *Story of the Life of Jesus for the Young Told from an Ethical Standpoint* (1895), *An Ethical Movement* (1896), *The Story of the Bible from the Standpoint of Modern Scholarship* (1899), *An Ethical Sunday School* (1900), *Class Readings in the Bible* (1901), *Lessons in the Study of Habits* (1903), *Citizenship and the Duties of a Citizen* (copyright 1904), *Duties in the Home and the Family* (1904), and *The Divine Comedy of Dante* (1905). Posthumously appeared *Thoughts from the Writings and Addresses of Walter L. Sheldon* (1919), edited by Cecilia Boette. After celebrating his society's twentieth anniversary, he went to Japan for his health, but he accepted so many invitations to lecture that when he returned he was worse. Bedridden, he directed his society for another season, and then died of chronic myocarditis and arterio-sclerosis in his forty-ninth year. On May 18, 1892, he had married Anna Hartshorne of Philadelphia; there were no children. His widow later married Percival Chubb, his successor in the society. Sheldon's ashes were sealed in the cornerstone of the building of the Ethical Society of St. Louis, dedicated in 1912 and named the Sheldon Memorial in his honor, a personal recognition he unquestionably would have opposed. A handsome man with scholarly brow and pointed beard, he fully looked the intellectual leader. Probably no St. Louisan has enjoyed greater esteem in both extremes of society.

[See George Sheldon, *A Hist. of Deerfield, Mass.* (2 vols., 1895–96); *Who's Who in America*, 1908–09; William Hyde and H. L. Conard, *Encyc. of the Hist. of St. Louis* (1899), vol. IV; *Centennial Hist. of Mo.* (1921), vol. V; *The Book of St. Louisans* (1906), ed. by J. W. Leonard; *Sexennial Record of the Class of 1880, Princeton College* (1887); *St. Louis Post-Dispatch*, June 5, and *St. Louis Republic*, June 7, 1907; memorial addresses in *Ethical Addresses and Ethical Record* (1908, 15 ser.). The Sheldon Memorial contains his library, his published writings, several portraits, and many unpublished MSS. Information on certain points has been supplied by Mrs. Martha E. Fischel, an associate, Percival Chubb and George R. Dodson of St. Louis, and Rex Preston Sheldon of Salisbury, Vt., a nephew.]   I. D.

SHELDON, WILLIAM EVARTS (Oct. 22, 1832–Apr. 16, 1900), educator, was born in Dorset, Vt., the son of Julius King and Harriet Newell (Sheldon) Sheldon. His earliest years were spent on his father's farm. After attending local district schools, in 1847 he entered Burr Seminary in Manchester, Vt., where he remained for a year, earning his expenses by teaching during the winter quarter in West Rupert, Vt. Apparently he undertook too much and so undermined his health that he was obliged to resign and seek a milder climate. From 1848 to 1850 he lived in Virginia and in 1849–50 taught school near Richmond. In 1850 he reëntered Burr Seminary, where he graduated in 1853. He then matriculated at Middlebury College but withdrew to become principal of the high school in East Abington (later Rockland), Mass. Here he effected important reforms in methods of instruction and in administration, and succeeded in bringing about a reclassification and gradation of schools in the town. His achievements brought him many invitations to address teachers' institutes and societies. In 1857 he was elected president of the Plymouth County Teachers' Association; in the same year in Philadelphia he helped to organize the National Teachers' Association, of which he was elected secretary. He married, July 30, 1854, Mary Ames Soule of East Abington, daughter of Josiah and Sophronia (Jenkins) Soule, who with a daughter survived him.

From 1858 to 1864 he was principal of the high school at West Newton and became increasingly active in improving conditions in public schools. He was president of the Middlesex County Teachers' Association, 1861–62, an editor of the *Massachusetts Teacher,* 1860–65, president of the Massachusetts Teachers' Association, 1862–64, and of the American Institute of Instruction, 1867. As an organizing member in 1862 of the Society of Arts (one of the three divisions of the institution that became the Massachusetts Institute of Technology), he took an active part in the intellectual life of Boston. In 1864 he became principal of the Hancock School in Boston. Appointed supervising principal of the primary schools at the same time, he succeeded in reorganizing instruction on the basis of Pestalozzian principles, of which he was an untiring advocate. The organization of the kindergarten department of the National Education Association was due chiefly to his efforts.

In 1867 he resigned to join the firm of Bailey, Jenkins, and Garrison, wool merchants of Boston, but this proved to be an unhappy adventure, from which he withdrew two years later to become principal of the Waltham Grammar School. Somewhat later he became business manager of the *Boston Daily News,* and in 1875 he helped to establish the *Journal of Education,* acting as advertising manager, a position he held until the end of his life. He was also co-editor of the *American Teacher* from 1883 to 1887. He was secretary of the National Education Association in 1882–83 and 1885–86, and president in 1887. During these years he published many articles on educational topics and gave numerous addresses before teachers' organizations. Throughout his professional life he was nationally known as a leader of progressive educational movements and reforms.

[Vital records of Dorset, Vt.; records of Burr Seminary; *Am. Jour. Educ.,* Sept. 1865, pp. 525–26; *Jour. of Educ.,* Apr. 19, 1900; *Mass. Teacher,* Jan. and Apr. 1858, May and Sept. 1861; C. Northend, *The Annals of the Am. Inst. of Instruction* (1884); *Proc. Nat. Educ. Assoc., 1900* (1900); obituary in *Boston Transcript,* Apr. 17, 1900.]   R. F. S.

SHELEKHOV, GRIGORIĬ IVANOVICH (1747–July 31, 1795), Russian merchant, the founder of the first Russian colony in America, was born in Rylsk, in the government of Kursk, Russia. His name was also spelled Shelikhov, Shelikof, and Schelechof. Nothing is known about his education, his childhood and youth. He was the son of a merchant, Ivan Shelekhov, lived with his parents in Rylsk until their death, and about 1775 left his birthplace for Siberia. He settled in Kamchatka region, the base from which Russian merchants carried on a trade in arctic furs, began to send out his boats after furs, usually in partnership with other merchants, to the Kurile and Aleutian Islands, and was successful in his very first ventures. In 1781 he was married to a wealthy merchant-woman in Irkutsk, a person of great courage, energy, and business ability. Her first and middle names were Natal'ĭa Alekseevna, her last name before her marriage to Shelekhov being unknown. In 1783 he organized in Irkutsk a fur-trading and exploring expedition to Alaska in partnership with Ivan Larionovich Golikov, a merchant of Kursk, and his nephew, Capt. Mikhail Sergĭeevich Golikov. Near the harbor of Okhotsk the company built and equipped three vessels, armed them with several cannon, engaged a crew of 192 men, and on Aug. 27, 1783, set sail with Shelekhov at the head of the expedition. His wife was with him on board the vessel, *The Three Saints,* the first white woman to sail Alaskan waters. Not until a year later, on Aug. 14, 1784, did Shelekhov reach Kadiak Island, where he founded the first Russian colony in America, naming the harbor "The Three Saints." He conquered the native tribes with ease by the use of diplomacy and with the aid of his well-armed crew.

Soon afterward Shelekhov expanded his activities and conquests to the other islands and to the mainland of Alaska. He spent about a year and eight months in the new colony, and, leaving it in charge of one of his company's employees, Samoïlov, who was later replaced by Delarov, sailed back to Siberia, where he submitted a report of his achievements to the local governor-general, followed by a petition to Empress Catharine II for financial and military assistance for his company, and, especially, for a trade monopoly in the new Russian territories discovered by the company. In spite of the very favorable support and recommendations of the governor-general and the special commerce commission in St. Petersburg, the petition was not granted by the Empress, although she gave Shelekhov and I. L. Golikov special gold medals, silver swords, and a laudatory charter, which permitted them to continue their exploits for the benefit of Russian commerce. The petitioner, however, was explicitly denied a trade monopoly (see Complete Collection of Laws, *post,* vol. XXII, p. 1106). Bancroft in his history of Alaska, *History of the Pacific States* (vol. XXVIII, 186, p. 309), and C. L. Andrews in *The Story of Alaska* (1931, p. 39), are both in error in stating that the Shelekhøv-Golikov company was granted exclusive privileges by the Empress in 1788. Shelekov established his headquarters in Irkutsk and managed his enterprises quite successfully from there, organizing several Russian fur-trading companies. In 1790 he appointed Alexander Andreevich Baranov [*q.v.*] to the position of general-manager of the new colony. The keen and ruinous competition with other Russian as well as foreign fur traders caused Shelekhov to stick to his idea of the organization of a single powerful, monopolistic colonial company, protected and assisted by the Russian imperial government. He died in Irkutsk, however, before his plans materialized, and they were carried out by his widow, his son, Ivan, and his two sons-in-law, Nikolaĭ Petrovich Rezanov [*q.v.*] and Mikhail Matvĭeevich Buldakov. Thus in 1799 the famous Russian-American Company came legally into being, and Emperor Paul ordered that the principal director of the company be selected from the members of the Shelekhov family. The Emperor prior to that had granted rank of nobility to Shelekhov's widow and children (see The General Armorial, *post,* part 4).

Shelekhov wrote and published an account of his own voyage and of the expedition in Alaskan waters of his agents, Izmaĭlow and Bocharov, in 1788, under two long titles, of which the first words are: *Rossiĭskago kuptsa Grigor'ĭa Shelekhova stranstvovanie v 1783 godu Iz Okhotska po Vostachnomu Okeĭanu k Amerikanskim beregam* (The Voyage of Grigoriĭ Shelekhov, a Russian Merchant, in the Year 1783, from Okhotsk over the Eastern Ocean to the American Shores), and *Rossiĭskago kuptsa Grigor'ĭa Shelekhova prodolzhenie stranstvovaniĭa po Vostochnomu Okeanu k Amerikanskim bere-*

gam v 1788 godu (A Sequel to the Voyage of Grigoriĭ Shelekhov, a Russian Merchant, on the Eastern Ocean to the American Shores in the Year 1788). The first editions of these works, published in St. Petersburg, appeared in 1791 and 1792. Bancroft considered Shelekhov's account of these two expeditions one of the chief authorities for that period of Alaskan history, although V. M. Golovnin, a Russian naval officer, writer, and explorer, in the report of 1818 of his official investigation of the Russian-American Company's activities during the first years of its existence pointed out striking misstatements and misrepresentations in Shelekhov's books. This report was published in the official naval magazine, *Morskoĭ Sbornik,* St. Petersburg, 1861, as a supplement to the first number. Shelekhov was undoubtedly one of the outstanding leaders of Russian commerce, a shrewd business man who organized new enterprises under extremely severe physical conditions. He can hardly be considered a statesman, for he risked his life and suffered hardships primarily for the sake of gain; but he did help to make Russia's dominion over Alaska a fact. Until his coming her control was merely nominal, endangered by other powers, especially Great Britain. Had Alaska fallen under British dominion, the opportunity for its acquisition by the United States would probably never have come.

[All dates in this article are new style. For reference see: the Russian manuscripts in the Library of Congress referring to the Russian-American Company; *Polnoe Sobranie Zakonov Rossiĭskoĭ Imperii* (Complete Collection of Laws of the Russian Empire), vol. XXII, pp. 1105–07, vol. XXIII, pp. 440, 478; vol. XXIV, pp. 670, 725, vol. XXV, pp. 699–718, 931; *Obshchiĭ Gerbovnik Dvorĭanskikh Rodov Vserossiĭskĭa Imperii* (The General Armorial of the Noble Families of the All-Russian Empire, St. Petersburg, 1798–1836); R. J. Kerner, "Russian Expansion to America. Its Bibliographical Foundations," *The Papers of the Bibliog. Soc. of America,* vol. XXV (1931); Avrahm Yarmolinsky, "Shelekhov's Voyage to Alaska, A Bibliographical Note," *Bull. of the N. Y. Pub. Lib.,* Mar. 1932; *Russkiĭ Biograficheskiĭ Slovar'* (The Russian Biog. Dict.), vol. "Shebanov-Shiuts" (1911); V. N. Berkh, *Khronologicheskĭa istorĭa otkrytĭa Aleutskikh ostrovoĭ* . . . (A Chronological Hist. of the Discovery of the Aleutian Islands, St. Petersburg, 1823); F. A. Golder, *Guide to Materials for Am. Hist. in Russian Archives* (1917); J. V. Farrar, *An Elementary Syllabus of Alaskan Hist.* (1924).]   N. R. R.

SHELTON, ALBERT LEROY (June 9, 1875–Feb. 17, 1922), missionary of the Disciples of Christ in West China and Tibet, was born in Indianapolis, Ind., the son of Joseph Oscar Shelton, at that time a carpenter, and of Emma Rosabelle (Belles) Shelton. When he was five years of age the family moved to Kansas, and his boyhood was spent there on a farm. Camp meetings and a country church were the background of his religious development and his elementary education was acquired in the district school. His first thought of becoming a missionary seems to have dated from a reading of *Ben Hur*. When he was seventeen he taught his first school, and at the age of twenty went to the Kansas State Normal College at Emporia. His course there was interrupted by a few months of service in the army during the Spanish-American War, but he resumed it after being mustered out. In 1899 he married Flora Beal, a fellow student. In 1900 he entered the medical department of Kentucky University, at Louisville, and graduated in 1903, the financial means for his course coming in part from a scholarship, in part from his wife's earnings as a teacher, and in part from his own labor.

On completing his medical course he was appointed a missionary to China by the Foreign Christian Missionary Society of Cincinnati. Shortly before sailing, in the autumn of 1903, he was ordained to the Christian ministry. The Society asked him to help Dr. Susie Rijnhart with a mission on the Tibetan border. She had lost her husband and child while undertaking a mission in Tibet, but wished to return and for two years had been looking in vain for a physician to accompany her. They arrived in Tachienlu, in Szechwan, near the Tibetan border, in 1904. Here Shelton studied Tibetan and Chinese and in due course began the varied life of a pioneer missionary, preaching, practising medicine, taking charge of a school, and itinerating, chiefly to care for the sick or for those wounded in the border skirmishes of the region. In 1908 he moved to Batang, farther inland and nearer his ultimate objective, Tibet. Here, with his colleagues, he established a mission station. Here, too, with his associates, he introduced new fruits and vegetables, partly to enlarge the menu of the staff, and partly to assist the people among whom he lived. From Batang he made long journeys in the difficult mountain region, healing and preaching. He was an ardent sportsman and an excellent shot. He won the confidence and respect of Tibetans and Chinese, partly by his friendliness and bluff manliness, partly by his sense of humor, partly by his commanding physique, but chiefly by his sterling character. He and his adventurous life made a marked appeal to the churches of his denomination in America, and during his two furloughs he spoke widely among them. Early in 1920, in Yünnan, while on the way out from Batang for one of these furloughs, he was captured by bandits, was held by them for over two months, and suffered greatly before his escape. While in America he published *Pioneering in Tibet* (1921). A few

months after his return to his post, when he was hoping that his dream of reaching Lhasa was about to come true, he was shot by robbers a few miles from Batang and died as a result of the wound.

[Flora Beal Shelton, *Shelton of Tibet* (1923) and *Sunshine and Shadow on the Tibetan Border* (1912); annual reports of the Foreign Christian Missionary Society, some printed in the *Missionary Intelligencer,* and some in the *Annual Reports of the Constituent Boards of the United Christian Missionary Society*; *World Call,* Apr., May 1922; *Missionary Review of the World,* Aug. 1921, May 1922; *N. Y. Times,* Mar. 5, 7, 1922.]
K. S. L.

SHELTON, EDWARD MASON (Aug. 7, 1846–May 9, 1928), agriculturist, was born in Huntingdonshire, England, and came to America with his parents in 1855. The family settled first in New York, but removed in 1860 to Michigan, where Edward worked his way through the Michigan Agricultural College, teaching in country schools during the winters and graduating in 1871. In this year he joined as agriculturist the commission headed by Gen. Horace Capron which had been appointed by President Grant to advise the Japanese government in matters pertaining to stock raising and agriculture. It was at first intended to establish an agricultural school at Hokkaido, but that project apparently had no great chance of success from the first, and the commissioners confined themselves to operations in the neighborhood of Tokyo, where they accomplished work of value in the selection of machinery, horses, cattle, sheep, and swine for the imperial farms. In September 1872 Shelton was much gratified to see, at the ceremonial opening of the first Japanese railway, that the Emperor rode behind a pair of bay geldings which he had himself purchased in Coldwater, Mich.

Shelton returned to America in 1872 and, after a brief experience with the Greeley Colony in Colorado, took the degree of MS. at the Michigan Agricultural College (1874), and accepted the position of professor of agriculture at the Kansas State Agricultural College. Here he remained till 1890, in which year he was called by the government of Queensland, Australia, to go thither as agricultural adviser and instructor. In this capacity he did much excellent work, achieved considerable fame locally, and in 1897 founded and was appointed the first principal of an agricultural school, Gatton College, one hall of which has been named in his honor. In 1899 he returned to the United States and settled with his family in Seattle, Wash. Here he continued his horticultural pursuits, including successful experiments in orcharding at Cashmere, Wash. By correspondence and the reading of a large literature he kept in contact with his old interests in various parts of the world and this interest he retained to the end of his life. Till his last illness, his vigor was apparently undiminished. He died in Seattle, in his eighty-second year, survived by his wife, Elizabeth (Sessons), whom he had married in 1890, together with two sons and five daughters.

[Letters and material made available by Shelton's family; *Queensland Agric. Jour.*, June 1928; *College Symposium of the Kan. State Agric. Coll.* (1891); H. H. Gowen, "An American Pioneer in Japan," *Wash. Hist. Quart.*, Jan. 1929; *Seattle Post-Intelligencer*, May 10, 1928.]   H. H. G.

SHELTON, FREDERICK WILLIAM (May 20, 1815–June 20, 1881), Protestant Episcopal clergyman, author, was born at Jamaica, Long Island, N. Y., the son of Nathan Shelton, M.D., and Eliza Henrietta, eldest daughter of Frederick William and Mary (Dundas) Starman. On his father's side he was descended from Daniel Shelton who was in Stratford, Conn., as early as 1687. He received his early education at the hands of Dr. Eigenbrodt and Professor Mulligan of Union Hall Academy, Jamaica, and graduated from the College of New Jersey in 1834. He married Rebecca, daughter of David S. and Isabella (Fletcher) Conkling, by whom he had six children, of whom only two sons survived him.

Shelton early wrote humorous sketches, but his first published work was *The Trollopiad; or, Travelling Gentleman in America* (1837), a satire by "Nil Admirari, Esq." In it he joined J. K. Paulding, J. Fenimore Cooper [*qq.v.*], and others in resenting the aspersions upon American manners and character which were then coming in great numbers from such English travelers as Capt. Basil Hall, the Rev. Isaac Fidler, and Mrs. Trollope. Both the preface and the poem itself, written in facile couplets, reveal more bitterness than humor. An admiration for Washington Irving, however, seems to have turned his pen into gentler channels. In 1838 he became a regular contributor to the *Knickerbocker,* then edited by Lewis Gaylord Clark [*q.v.*]. To this journal over a period of years he sent a series of sketches known as "The Tinnecum Papers," although they were not announced by that title. Among these were "Hans Carvel" (November 1838), "Rural Cemeteries" (December), "Peter Cram, or The Row at Tinnecum" (January 1841), "The Country Doctor" (February 1841–Jan. 1842), "Morus Multicaulis" (May 1845), and others. He contributed to the same magazine essays on the Latin poems of Vincent Bourne (October 1844) and on the writings of Charles Lamb (June 1850), and to

The Knickerbocker Gallery (1855), "Gentle Dove, an Indian Legend," a tale of Christianized Indians.

In the fall of 1844 he entered the General Theological Seminary, New York City, to prepare for the Protestant Episcopal ministry. He graduated June 25, 1847, and two days later was ordered deacon by the Rev. W. H. DeLancey, bishop of Western New York. He filled a temporary vacancy at Christ Church, Montpelier, Vt., for a few months, then served St. John's Church, Huntington, Long Island, 1848–52, being ordained priest, Dec. 3, 1848, by Bishop Whittingham. In 1852 he was appointed to Trinity Church, Fishkill, N. Y. Two years later he returned to Christ Church, Montpelier, as its rector, remaining until 1866, when he resigned. For about a year thereafter he was at St. Thomas's Church, East Somerville, Mass., and from 1869 to 1881 he was rector of St. Mark's Church, Carthage Landing, N. Y.

After his ordination, his literary work took a secondary place in his interests, but he continued to write essays somewhat in his earlier style, although more formal and moralistic in tone. Two collections of these were published: *Up the River* (1853), a series of letters, dated from Fishkill, N. Y., which run through the seasons with observant and friendly comments on men and nature; and *Peeps from a Belfry; or, The Parish Sketch Book* (1855), a record of his first winter in Vermont which reveals kindly humor and a considerable facility in the use of dialect. It also contains an essay in appreciation of Jeremy Taylor. In addition, he wrote three tales: *Salander and the Dragon, A Romance of the Hartz Prison* (1850), an allegory modeled on Bunyan's *Pilgrim's Progress*; *The Rector of St. Bardolph's* (1853), a simple tale of a country parson, similar in many respects to his sketches, and *Crystalline, or, The Heiress of Fall Down Castle* (1854), a conventional romance. The second is his most characteristic and popular work; it was reprinted in 1856 and again in 1882. Other published writings are "Clarence, A Domestic Story" (included in the volume with *Crystalline*); *Lectures before the Huntington Library Association* (1850); an historical sermon on the Montpelier parish (published posthumously in the *Vermont Historical Gazetteer,* vol. IV, 1882, pp. 413–19); and several poems (*Ibid.*, pp. 420–21). Among his unpublished manuscripts at his death were translations of several of the dialogues of Plato.

As a clergyman he was much loved by his parishioners for his gentle character, and as a writer he received extravagant praise from his contemporaries. Although his style was in the tradition of Irving, he stamped everything, but particularly his rural sketches, with the imprint of his personality. He liked best a life of semi-retirement, and seems to have devoted much of his time to miscellaneous reading and writing.

[A. M. Hemenway, *Vt. Hist. Gazetteer,* vol. IV (1882) ; E. N. Shelton, *Reunion of the Descendants of Daniel Shelton* (1877) ; E. A. and G. L. Duyckinck, *Cyc. of Am. Lit.* (1875), vol. II ; *Boston Transcript,* June 22, 1881, and *Churchman,* July 23, 1881 ; portrait in *The Knickerbocker Gallery* (1855).]

R. E. S.

SHEPARD, CHARLES UPHAM (June 29, 1804–May 1, 1886), mineralogist, was born in Little Compton, R. I., the son of Rev. Mase and Deborah (Haskins) Shepard, and a descendant of Thomas Shepard, who was living in Malden, Mass., before 1658. Most of his early education was received in the schools of Providence. In 1820 he entered Brown University but at the end of the freshman year left that institution to join the group which made up the original student body of Amherst College.

Shepard was primarily a mineralogist and his collection, or cabinet as he terms it, was the interest which determined much of his life. He began to collect minerals when he was fifteen years old, and carried his collection first to Brown University and then to Amherst. At the latter college he found disappointingly little science but came under Amos Eaton [*q.v.*], a distinguished botanist and geologist of that period. Shepard at once began making excursions to the various mineral localities, and found the tourmalines at Chester and Goshen. Eaton used Shepard's collection to illustrate his lectures, for the college had none of its own at that time. With these minerals, while still a student, Shepard began making exchanges, dealing with the Imperial Museum at Vienna and other institutions. Graduating from Amherst in 1824, the next year he accepted the position of teacher of natural science in the Boston schools, and at the same time began studying under Thomas Nuttall [*q.v.*], a botanist and mineralogist.

During the three years Shepard lived in Boston he collected in nearby places and one summer made a most profitable trip to Maine, where he discovered that the locality around Paris furnished the finest pink and green tourmalines then known. In this period, also, he began writing articles for the *American Journal of Science and Arts,* and through these he became acquainted with its editor, Benjamin Silliman [*q.v.*]. In 1827 he became Silliman's assistant at New Haven, and in 1830–31 was a lecturer in botany at Yale. The next two years he was in charge of the Brewster Scientific Institute, New Haven, and in 1833 was appointed lecturer in natural history at Yale, which position he held until 1847. As Silliman's assistant he engaged in an investigation of the sugar industry for the Southern states, work which led to his appointment, in 1834, as professor of chemistry in the South Carolina Medical College. Since his duties there required but part of his time, he continued his lectures at Yale and in 1835 assisted in making the Connecticut geological survey. He also visited all the known mineral localities east of the Mississippi River and found the rutile locality on Graves Mountain, Ga. These rutiles and the Paris, Me., tourmalines became the means by which he was able to build up his great collection. In 1839 he began a long series of trips to Europe for making exchanges.

Accepting a call to be lecturer in natural history at Amherst under Edward Hitchcock [*q.v.*] in 1844, he made an arrangement with the college for housing his collection in a fireproof building and its eventual purchase. Accordingly, such a building having been provided, in 1847 his specimens were moved to Amherst and his Yale lectureship terminated. As early as 1828, he had collected meteorites, and by the end of his life this collection was the largest in America. During the Civil War he resigned his professorship at South Carolina Medical College, but was called back at the end of the war, serving until 1869, when he was succeeded by his son. In 1877 he retired from teaching at Amherst and the college purchased his collection as agreed, though he continued to collect until his death. After his retirement the collection was moved to another building, and in 1880 a fire destroyed a large part of it. The rarest minerals and the meteorites were stored in a vault, however, and so escaped the fire. After Shepard's death his supplementary collection was given to the college, and the collection as a whole was rebuilt.

Shepard wrote some forty papers for the *American Journal of Science and Arts,* partly on new minerals discovered and partly on mineral occurrences. He also wrote a textbook, *Treatise on Mineralogy* (1832), a second part to which appeared in 1835. He was a member of many learned societies, among them the Imperial Society of Natural Science in St. Petersburg, the Royal Society of Göttingen, and the Society of Natural Science of Vienna. His scholarship was everywhere recognized, and while his methods of teaching were far from conventional, his enthusiasm and kindliness attracted many students. On Sept. 23, 1831, he was married to Harriet, daughter of Robert Taylor of New Braintree, Mass.; they had three children.

[W. S. Tyler, *A Hist. of Amherst Coll.* (1895); Edward Hitchcock, *Reminiscences of Amherst Coll.* (1863); *Amherst Coll. Biog. Record of Grads.* (1927); *Popular Science Mo.*, Aug. 1895; *Am. Jour. of Sci. and Arts*, June 1886, pub. also in *Proc. Am. Acad. Arts and Sciences*, vol. XXI (1886); W. J. Youmans, *Pioneers of Sci. in America* (1896); *New Eng. Hist. and Geneal. Reg.*, Apr. 1869; *News and Courier* (Charleston, S. C.), May 2, 1886.] F. B. L.

SHEPARD, EDWARD MORSE (July 23, 1850–July 28, 1911), lawyer, political reformer, was born in New York, the son of Lorenzo Brigham and Lucy (Morse) Shepard. His father, an able lawyer and active Democrat, died when Edward was six years old, and Abram S. Hewitt [*q.v.*] became guardian of the Shepard children. From early childhood Edward lived in Brooklyn, spending his summers at Lake George, near his mother's birthplace. He received his early education principally in the schools of Brooklyn and New York, and in 1869 was graduated with the highest distinction from the College of the City of New York. After reading law in the office of his father's former partner, he was admitted to the bar in 1871, and immediately entered upon a legal career distinguished by unusual ability and the highest ethical standards.

Although a specialist in civil practice, he, nevertheless, displayed professional mastery as special deputy attorney general in the criminal prosecution of John Y. McKane in 1893–94 for flagrant election frauds, and also in his defense of Dr. Algernon C. Crapsey [*q.v.*], whose case involved canon law. In his own field he rendered his most memorable service as counsel to the New York Rapid Transit Commission and to the Pennsylvania Railroad. His legal ability combined effectively with his concern for the public welfare in the intricate negotiations he directed for the building of the first subway and for the erection of the Pennsylvania Terminal.

A disciple of Jefferson and Van Buren, Shepard was a power in the Democratic party. The "bosses" both feared him and tried to make use of him. At a price he would not pay he might have attained high place, but at the demand of principle he readily subordinated self-interest, as his part in organizing the Young Men's Democratic Club of Brooklyn and the fact that in 1895 he was independent Democratic candidate for mayor of Brooklyn indicate. In 1896, as a "Gold Democrat," he supported John M. Palmer [*q.v.*] for president in preference to Bryan, but in 1900, believing imperialism the most important issue, he supported Bryan. He accepted nomination for mayor of New York on the regular Democratic ticket in 1901, running against Seth Low [*q.v.*]. Many criticized him for allowing himself to be used as a respectable head for the ticket by Tammany, but his action was due to his belief in party regularity and his feeling that reform should come from within. He was one of the leaders in the movement that brought about the nomination for governor of John A. Dix in 1910, and it was expected that the Democratic legislature would, in 1911, elect Shepard to the United States Senate, but opposition within the party arose and Shepard and his opponent withdrew in favor of James A. O'Gorman. By appointment he served as forestry commissioner of New York in 1884–85, a member of the Brooklyn water commission in 1889–90, and a commissioner of the Saratoga Springs Reservation in 1909. In collaboration with Everett P. Wheeler [*q.v.*], he drew the bill that applied the principles of civil service reform to New York. Upon its passage in 1883 he was appointed to the Brooklyn civil service commission, serving from 1883 to 1885 and, as chairman, from 1888 to 1890. When the application of the system became mandatory in municipalities in 1884, Shepard wrote the regulations for Brooklyn. He embodied his views in a paper, *The Competitive Test and the Civil Service of States and Cities* (1884), published by the New York Society for Political Education.

Shepard had part in several educational endeavors, but rendered his most continuous service to the College of the City of New York. A trustee from 1900 to 1911, and chairman of the board from 1904 to 1911, he gave to every detail of college business the most thorough consideration, and to larger matters of policy both vision and practical wisdom, at a time when, largely through his initiative, the college underwent basic educational as well as physical changes. Though an effective speaker and a man of broad contacts, he cherished a quiet life devoted to work, study, and the close fellowship of friends. This fact, however, indicated no inaccessibility of nature; for he was as democratic in spirit as he was patrician in manner. He never married, but enjoyed the life of the home in intimate association with his married brother and sister and their children. Although he wrote much on law and politics for periodicals he produced only one book, *Martin Van Buren* (1888), a minor classic of political biography which appeared in the American Statesmen series. He died at Lake George, N. Y., where he had been accustomed to spend his summers; he is commemorated there by a memorial park and a monument.

Shepard

[Who's Who in America, 1910–11; City Coll. Quart., Dec. 1911, Oct. 1912; Nation, Nov. 7, 1901, Aug. 3, 1911; Current Lit., Jan. 1911; Review of Reviews, Nov. 1901; Outlook, Aug. 12, 1911; N. Y. Times, July 29, 1911; D. S Alexander, Four Famous New Yorkers (1923), pp. 361–71.]   D. A. R.

SHEPARD, FRED DOUGLAS (Sept. 11, 1855–Dec. 18, 1915), physician and missionary, was born on a farm at Ellenburg, Clinton County, N. Y., the son of Rufus George and Charlotte (Douglas) Shepard. At fourteen he became practically an orphan through the death of his father and the permanent invalidism of his mother. After several years on the farm of an uncle at Madrid, N. Y., he went to live with his mother and sisters at Malone, where he attended Franklin Academy and distinguished himself both in studies and sports. After graduation he taught in a district school for a year before entering the civil engineering course at Cornell in 1876, paying his way largely with his earnings as a farm workman. After two years of study he determined to take up medicine and transferred to the University of Michigan, where he graduated in 1881, second in a class of a hundred. The next year he spent fitting himself for the varied work of medical missionary by serving as clinical assistant in the New York Ophthalmic and Aural Institute under Herman Knapp [q.v.] and in taking a course in practical dentistry.

On July 5, 1882 (Riggs, post, p. 18), he married Fanny Perkins Andrews, who had been one year behind him in medical school and was the daughter of Lorrin Andrews [q.v.], missionary in Hawaii. Sailing the same year for Turkey, he went to Aintab as professor of surgery in the newly opened medical department of Central Turkey College, an institution founded by American Board missionaries. In 1888 lack of funds led to the closing of this department after twenty-one students, who became the leading Armenian physicians of southern Asia Minor, had been graduated, but Shepard continued his connection with the college as physician in charge of the small Azariah Smith Memorial Hospital. Meanwhile he carried on an extensive practice in the town and surrounding country, often traveling on horseback to Marash, Aleppo, or even Diyarbekir when called for serious illness. He played an important part in relief work after the massacres of 1895 and quelled a cholera epidemic among the Armenians of Zeitun, whose desperate revolt had provided the excuse for widespread attacks on their co-religionists. After similar outbreaks in 1909 in Cilicia and the Amanus Mountains, he was appointed chairman of the committee for relief and rebuilding set up by Jemal Pasha, the powerful "Young Turk" gov-

Shepard

ernor of Adana. For energetic and fearless work in distributing funds and fighting disease among the refugees he was decorated by the sultan and given the medal of merit of the American Red Cross. When deportation threatened the Armenians of Aintab in 1915, he went to Constantinople in an effort to avert it. The government granted his request for Protestant and Catholic Armenians, and he stayed at the capital for two months, working in a Red Cross hospital among Turks wounded at Gallipoli. When he returned to Aintab in October, however, he found deportation in full swing. He spent the remaining months of his life in heroic work among plague-stricken refugees, from whom he contracted a fatal attack of typhus.

A man of short stature but unusual strength, Shepard was a great hunter and tireless rider, who was dismayed by no obstacle of road or weather. Famed throughout the wide provinces between the Mediterranean and the Tigris, he obtained from wealthy officials and nobles fees which helped support his hospital. Though he was whole-heartedly an evangelical missionary, patients of every faith sought his services and honored him as a surgeon of outstanding ability, strong character, and loyal friendships, and as one who sought always to promote mutual understanding among the embittered peoples of Turkey. Working under the grave handicaps of primitive equipment and insufficient helpers, he operated with remarkable skill and success on many thousands of cases. He was one of the outstanding missionaries of his generation, and one who practised both medicine and Christianity.

[Who's Who in America, 1912–13; Alice Shepard Riggs, Shepard of Aintab (copr. 1920); W. N. Chambers, in Missionary Herald, Mar. 1916; Mich. Alumnus, Feb. 1916; J. K. Greene, Leavening the Levant (1916); brief obituary in N. Y. Times, Jan. 11, 1916; manuscript records, Am. Board of Commissioners for Foreign Missions, Boston, Mass.]   W. L. W., Jr.

SHEPARD, JAMES HENRY (Apr. 14, 1850–Feb. 21, 1918), chemist, was born in Lyons, Ionia County, Mich., the son of Daniel Ensign and Lydia Maria (Pendell) Shepard. In his early childhood both his parents died and, although he was cared for by his friends, he soon undertook his own support and secured his elementary schooling by doing any work obtainable. As a mere boy he recognized his proper career to be that of a scientist. His early struggles to this end account for his plain, rugged, uncompromising character, which prompted him later to reject many financial and professional offers that he regarded as savoring of bribery or compulsion. He was largely self-educated in the basic branches. After two years at Albion College, Albion, Mich., he went to the University of Michigan, where he was graduated in 1875 with the degree of B.S. As opportunity offered, he studied chemistry at Michigan until 1881 but was financially unable to complete work for a graduate degree. Later he refused offers of honorary degrees, since he regarded as meaningless a degree not based upon resident study. He was superintendent of public schools at Holly, Marquette, and Saline, Mich., 1875–80, and instructor in science in the high school at Ypsilanti, Mich., 1882–88, where he married Clara R. Durand on June 28, 1888.

In that year he became head of the department of chemistry in the South Dakota State College of Agriculture and Mechanic Arts, and chemist of the South Dakota agricultural experiment station. He also served as vice-president of the college, 1890–1900; as director of the experiment station, 1895–1901; and as chemist of the South Dakota pure food commission, 1901–18. He was a contributing member of many scientific societies. His homely, practical, and extremely effective methods of instruction reflected his early experience as a secondary teacher. His publications, likewise, are marked by forceful and concrete presentation, and an avoidance of pure theory. He was the author of *Elements of Inorganic Chemistry, Descriptive and Qualitative* (1885), the pioneer text in placing laboratory experimentation in the hands of the student; *A Record of Laboratory Work* (1886); *Notes on Chemistry* (1886), and many bulletins and brochures. As director of the South Dakota agricultural experiment station, he conducted a survey of the surface waters of the state, a chemical analysis of its forage plants, and developed sugar beets to a sugar content in excess of 25 per cent., as capable of profitable production in South Dakota (reported in the bulletins of the United States Office of Experiment Stations). In his researches upon bleached flour, whiskey constants and food adulterants, in his exhibit of adulterated foods at the Louisiana Purchase Exposition, St. Louis, Mo., and as an expert witness in the courts of the United States and England in pure food and whiskey trust prosecutions, he won an international reputation. In 1916 failing health caused his partial retirement from active work. He died in St. Petersburg, Fla.

[*Who's Who in America*, 1916–17; U. S. Dept. of Agriculture, *Experiment Station Record*, Mar. 1918; obituary in *Daily Argus Leader* (Sioux Falls, S. D.), Feb. 23, 1918; personal acquaintance.]   B. A. D.

SHEPARD, JESSE [See GRIERSON, FRANCIS, 1848–1927].

SHEPARD, SETH (Apr. 23, 1847–Dec. 3, 1917), jurist, was born at Brenham, Tex., the son of Chauncey Berkeley and Mary Hester (Andrews) Shepard. He was trained in Texas private schools and served in the Confederate army during the last months of the Civil War. He then entered Washington College, now Washington and Lee University, and was graduated in law in 1868, began the practice of law in Brenham, and became a state senator from Washington County. During the sessions of 1874 and 1875, he was an active leader in the "Democratic readjustment" under Gov. Richard Coke [*q.v.*], and he supported the movement for a constitutional convention in 1875. He led the fight against the compromise measure proposing an award of $3,000,000 in state bonds to the International Railroad, when the radical legislature in 1870 had voted the road a bonus of $8,000,000 to build across the state, and succeeded in substituting the Coke-Shepard plan of land gifts in 1875. In 1874 and the two following election years he failed by a narrow margin to obtain the Democratic nomination for Congress, and in 1880 he was nominated unanimously in convention but was defeated by the Greenback candidate. He had removed to Galveston and was attorney for the Gulf, Colorado and Santa Fé Railroad. He made Dallas his home in 1886 and continued the practice of law. As a member of the board of regents of the University of Texas from 1883 to 1891, he worked for improvement of the high schools and for a better system of correlation and affiliation with the university, and he was a spokesman for the regents, especially upon public occasions. He wrote the introduction and a chapter on "The Siege and Fall of the Alamo" in the first volume of D. G. Wooten's *Comprehensive History of Texas* (1898).

He was a leading speaker in the fight against state prohibition in 1887, arguing against the "paternalism in government" involved, opposed establishment of the railroad commission, and in 1892 advocated the change from an appointive to an elective commission. When in the Democratic split at the state convention of 1892 the Hogg group followed the Populist doctrine of "free coinage of silver" and repudiated the demands of the National Democratic Convention, Shepard, who had been a member of the committee of resolutions of the Chicago convention to write the party platform in June, adhered to the Clark faction that declared for the Cleveland policy of a gold standard. He always insisted that the Hogg men were the bolters. Hogg was elected after an exciting campaign, and the Texas Democrats were soon reunited. Cleveland appointed him as an associate justice of the court of appeals of the District of Columbia in 1893. He was made chief justice by Theodore Roosevelt in 1905. The Texas bar association unanimously urged his appointment to the United States Supreme Court after the death of Samuel Blatchford (*Galveston Daily News,* July 28, 1893), and he was even more seriously considered in 1895 after the death of Howell Jackson (letter of Cleveland to Shepard, Dec. 2, 1895, in possession of family). He retired from the court of appeals in the spring of 1917 and died the following December. Although a member of the Protestant Episcopal Church he became lecturer in law at Georgetown University in 1895 and served twenty-one years. He was married three times, on Jan. 18, 1882, to Caroline Nelson Goree, of Alabama, who died in 1889, on Mar. 25, 1890, to Etta K. Jarvis, of Louisville, Ky., who died in 1909, and subsequently to Mrs. Julia (Bones) Towsley, of Washington, who with four children survived him.

[Shepard Papers in the possession of Nelson M. Shepard, Chevy Chase, Md.; *Who's Who in America,* 1916–17; D. C. Wooten, *A Comprehensive History of Texas* (1898), vol. II; *Galveston Daily News* and *Evening Star* (Washington), Dec. 4, 1917.]   S. S. M.

SHEPARD, THOMAS (Nov. 5, 1605–Aug. 25, 1649), New England divine, was born in Towcester, England. In his autobiography he stated that his birth occurred on Gunpowder Day, Nov. 5, 1604 (Young, *post,* p. 499). Since the gunpowder plot culminated just a year later, there is uncertainty whether he was born in 1604 or 1605. His father, William, had been apprenticed to a grocer by the name of Bland, whose daughter he married, and Thomas was the youngest of their nine children. Both parents died during his childhood and he was brought up by an elder brother. He was admitted pensioner at Emmanuel College, Cambridge, on Feb. 10, 1619/20, received the degree of B.A. in 1623/24, and that of M.A. in 1627. On July 12 of the latter year he was ordained deacon, and the following day, priest. He was an occasional lecturer at Earles-Colne in Essex, and was silenced by Laud, then bishop of London, for non-conformity in 1630. He then became tutor and chaplain in the family of Sir Richard Darley of Buttercrambe, Yorkshire, and in 1632 married Darley's cousin, Margaret Tauteville. Soon after his marriage he went to Heddon, near Newcastle, Northumberland, but was not allowed to preach publicly by Bishop Morton of Durham "because Laud had taken notice" of him earlier.

In October 1634 he sailed for Boston but was driven back by a storm and remained in hiding in England until August of the next year, when he sailed again, reaching his destination on Oct. 3, 1635. Soon after, his wife fell ill of consumption following a cold contracted on the ship and died in February 1635/36. She left one son, Thomas, another son having died in England. About this time Shepard was chosen pastor of the church at Newtown (Cambridge) constituted after Thomas Hooker [*q.v.*] had moved with his congregation to Connecticut. In 1636 a plan for an institution of learning was brought before the General Court, and there was some question as to its location. In the meantime Shepard had established his ministry so firmly that Edward Johnson [*q.v.*], in his *Wonder-Working Providence* (*post,* p. 201), speaks of it as "soul flourishing," and for this reason, as well as the fact that Shepard's congregation had been "preserved from the contagion of Antinomianism" (Albro, *post,* p. 224), Cambridge was chosen as the site. Shepard was an admirer and almost surely a friend of John Harvard, and in 1636 Harvard College became an actuality.

He took immediate and active part in the early controversies of his day. His theology was that of Calvin, and most of his early sermons illustrate the doctrine of salvation by grace. Important is his definition of Congregationalism as a *via media* between Brownism on the one hand, which placed the entire church government in the hands of the people, and Presbyterianism on the other, which lodged all power in the presbytery of the individual churches, or the combined presbytery of all of them. In his opposition to the Antinomians he was unswerving, and he was one of the active leaders in the Synod at Cambridge in 1637 which condemned them. He was particularly concerned with the education of the young. In 1644 he asked the Commissioners of the United Colonies of New England to approve a plan of his whereby each family able and willing should give "yearly but the fourth part of a bushel of Corne, or something equivolent" for "the dyett of divers such students as may stand in neede" ("Acts of the Commissioners of the United Colonies," *Records of the Colony of New Plymouth,* vol. IX, 1859, pp. 20–21). Thus he founded the tradition of scholarships in America. The last important contribution to the institutions of his time was his urgent instigation of a public confession of faith and a plan of church government which, after delays, was realized in the synod of 1647, and became part of the laws of the Commonwealth of Massachusetts and a platform for Congregational churches in America. He showed a constant interest in the conversion of the Indians, and kept a friendly guard over the first Indian mission in Cambridge, established by his friend John Eliot. In 1637 he married Joanna Hooker, daughter of Rev. Thomas Hooker, who bore him four children, one of whom died at birth, and another in infancy; Samuel and John survived their father. After the death of his second wife he married, Sept. 8, 1647, Margaret Boradel, who bore him one son, Jeremiah.

Shepard's diary was first published in *Three Valuable Pieces, Viz., Select Cases Resolved: First Principles of the Oracles of God; . . . And a Private Diary; Containing Meditations & Experiences Never Before Published* (1747); in 1832 Nehemiah Adams [*q.v.*] edited and published *The Autobiography of Thomas Shepard*. These works furnish, in addition to the usual introspective jeremiad of the Puritan, an informal narrative of hardships and hopes in the earliest Colonial days. Of particular interest among his many published works is his *Theses Sabbaticæ* (1649), which is an account of the Sabbath, its origin and observance. His *Church Membership of Children and Their Right to Baptism* (1663) bears testimony to yet another of his varied interests, the advocacy of infant baptism. Another work, *The Sincere Convert* (1641), went through twenty-one editions between 1641 and 1812, and represents most of the popular religious tenets of the early Congregational churches. Jonathan Edwards made wide use of *The Parable of the Ten Virgins Opened and Applied* (1660) in his *Treatise Concerning Religious Affections* (1746). Among Shepard's more notable tracts are a sermon on the conversion of the Indians, *The Clear Sun Shine of the Gospel Breaking Forth Upon the Indians of New England* (1648), and *New Englands Lamentation for Old England's Present Errours* (1645). Characteristic of his dogma is his *Certain Select Cases Resolved* (1648), which, while it can scarcely interest the modern student, displays the learning and careful method of the author. He was a tireless worker and preacher. Samuel Mather said of his preaching that it was "close and searching with abundance of affection and compassion to his hearers" (Preface to Shepard's *Subjection to Christ*, 1652). If in his sermons he dwells at too great length upon the wickedness and worthlessness of men, it is without contempt. He was of humble mind and had the Puritan willingness to submit himself completely to the Divine Will.

[In addition to Shepard's diary and published writings, see Cotton Mather, *Magnalia Christi Americana* (ed. of 1853), I, 380–94; Alexander Young, *Chronicles of the First Planters of the Colony of Mass. Bay* (1846), which contains Shepard's autobiography; J. F. Jameson, ed., *Johnson's Wonder-Working Providence* (1910); G. L. Shepard, *A Geneal. Hist. of William Shepard and Some of His Descendants* (1886); J. A. Albro, *The Life of Thomas Shepard* (1847); W. B. Sprague, *Annals of the Am. Pulpit*, vol. I (1857); S. E. Morison, *Builders of the Bay Colony* (1930); Alexander Whyte, *Thomas Shepard, Pilgrim Father and Founder of Harvard* (1909); M. C. Tyler, *A Hist. of Am. Lit. During the Colonial Time* (ed. of 1897), I, 204–10; *Cambridge Hist. Soc. Pubs.*, vol. III (1908); John and J. A. Venn, *Alumni Cantabrigienses*, pt. 1, vol. IV (1927).]   E.H.D.

SHEPARD, WILLIAM (Dec. 1, 1737–Nov. 16, 1817), Revolutionary officer and representative in Congress from Massachusetts, was born in Westfield, Mass., the son of Elizabeth (Noble) and John Shepard, a tanner and a deacon of the Congregational Church. He was the grandson of John Shepard who emigrated from Suffolk County, England, to Westfield about the end of the seventeenth century. There the boy attended the local school and at seventeen enlisted as a private in the French and Indian War, from which he emerged with the valuable experience of six years of warfare and the rank of captain. Settling down on a farm in Westfield with his wife, Sarah (Dewey) Shepard, to whom he was married on Jan. 31, 1760, he was chosen selectman, took his part in the agitation against Great Britain, and was a member of the local committee of correspondence. In May 1775 he became lieutenant-colonel of Timothy Danielson's Massachusetts Regiment and served through the siege of Boston. Made lieutenant-colonel of the 3rd Continental Infantry in January 1776 and in October colonel to rank from May, he was present in the fighting around New York and distinguished himself in the important but little-known battle at Pell's Point (Pelham Manor). He fought at Saratoga, endured the winter at Valley Forge, and, as colonel of the 4th Massachusetts Infantry, did recruiting service at Springfield, Mass.

When he retired on Jan. 1, 1783, he returned to Westfield, where his wife was managing the farm and taking care of the younger children in their family of nine. In 1785 and 1786 he sat in the lower house of the state legislature and in 1786 was appointed major-general of militia for Hampshire County. In that capacity he found himself responsible for the defense of the federal arsenal and the protection of the federal court in Springfield at the time of Shays's Rebellion. His judgment in dealing with the insurgents and his skill in delaying them, as well as his decision to remove arms and ammunition from the arsenal without specific authority, were important in deciding the outcome of that difficult situation. On Jan. 25, 1787, before the arrival of Benjamin Lincoln [*q.v.*], he repulsed the attack on the arsenal by a force under Daniel Shays [*q.v.*]. Under the new federal Constitution he was one of the first presidential electors and enjoyed that honor again in the election of 1793. Elected to the governor's council in 1792 he served five years and then sat for three terms, Mar. 4, 1797, to Mar. 3, 1803, in the federal House of Representatives. He spent the last fifteen years of his life quietly in Westfield, a deacon of the First Congregational Church and the town's most distinguished citizen. He had never gathered any considerable fortune, and his means were even more narrow because he was not reimbursed for all of his own money that he had spent for expenses and supplies at the time of Shays's Rebellion and because sympathizers with the uprising afterward wilfully destroyed his property for revenge. He died in Westfield.

[A few papers in Lib. of Cong.; Isaac Knapp, *A Sermon, Delivered . . . Nov. 18, 1817; at the Funeral of Maj. Gen. Wm. Shepard* (1818); J. H. Lockwood, *Westfield* (2 vols., copr. 1922); *The Hist. of the Celebration of the . . . Anniversary . . . of the Incorporation of . . . Westfield, Mass. . . . 1919* (n.d.); J. M. Bugbee, *Memorials of the Mass. Soc. of the Cincinnati* (1890); Wm. Abbatt, *The Battle of Pell's Point* (1901); J. P. Warren, "The Confederation and the Shays Rebellion," *Am. Hist. Rev.*, Oct. 1905; F. B. Heitman, *Hist. Register of Officers of the Continental Army* (1893); *Mass. Hist. Soc. Colls.*, 7 ser., vol. VI (1907); *Columbian Centinel*, Nov. 22, 1817; spelling of name from facsimile, *Proc. Mass. Hist. Soc.*, vol. XLIII (1910), p. 654, and death date from records of First Church, Westfield, through the courtesy of J. Chambers Dewey, city clerk of Westfield.]   K. E. C.

SHEPHERD, ALEXANDER ROBEY (Jan. 31, 1835–Sept. 12, 1902), territorial governor of the District of Columbia, was born in Washington, the eldest of seven children. His parents, Alexander Shepherd and Susan Davidson (Robey), were of English extraction and natives of Maryland; the former was a lumber merchant. After his father's death, Alexander withdrew from school and, as store boy, carpenter's apprentice, and plumber's assistant in turn, contributed to the support of the family. He ultimately opened his own plumbing establishment and did a lucrative business, engaging also in real estate and building operations. On Jan. 30, 1862, he married Mary Grice Young, daughter of Col. W. P. Young; they had ten children, three of whom died early in life.

Shepherd was a strong Republican and a Union man. He served as a three months' volunteer at the opening of the Civil War and then entered municipal politics, being elected to the common council for three successive years and holding the presidency in 1862. His public career began at a time when Washington was a squalid village with unpaved streets, poor lighting, a primitive system of water supply, and open sew-

ers. Agitation for the removal of the Capital to a more fitting center soon gained ground and, whether from selfish motives or civic pride, Shepherd became the ardent champion of an extensive program of modernization as a means of averting the catastrophe. In October 1867 he joined Crosby S. Noyes [*q.v.*] and three other friends in purchasing the *Evening Star,* which thereafter served as his organ. In physique, he was a giant of a man. He had indomitable courage and was never daunted by criticism of the means employed for the attainment of his objectives.

He was appointed to the levy court in 1867 and again in 1869. In 1870 he was chosen president of the Citizens' Reform Association and became alderman in the same year. He advocated a centralized government, closely connected with Congress, as a means of carrying out a broadly conceived plan of urban improvement, and his efforts bore fruit in the act of Feb. 21, 1871, creating a territorial government for the District of Columbia and constituting a board of public works with extensive powers. President Grant named him a member of the latter body and he was elected vice-president at its first meeting. He quickly overshadowed his colleagues and won the name "Boss Shepherd" by assuming complete control. Imbued with the callous philosophy of a notoriously corrupt era and carried away by his enthusiasm, he spent millions beyond the legally authorized expenditures and hopelessly involved District finances. His custom of awarding contracts to friends in casual fashion without competitive bidding led to accusations that he was sharing in the spoils. Upon the resignation of Henry D. Cooke [*q.v.*] as governor in 1873, Grant bestowed the position upon Shepherd. He expanded his projects despite mounting opposition, and transformed Washington into a metropolis with paved streets, good sidewalks, adequate water and sewerage facilities, gas lights, and spacious parks; but at staggering cost. His recklessness and unscrupulous methods led to congressional investigation and the passage of the act of June 20, 1874, which replaced territorial government by commission rule. Grant thereupon named him commissioner, but the Senate refused to confirm the appointment, although he had been found innocent of personal dishonesty.

Long neglect of private affairs had left Shepherd a poor man, but determined to start life anew, he became interested in a silver mine at Batopilas, Chihuahua, Mexico, moved there in 1880, and converted the property into a highly valuable one. Meanwhile, the importance of his old undertakings had come to be recognized and, on Oct. 6, 1887, upon a visit home, he was fêted as a public benefactor. He died of appendicitis at Batopilas fifteen years later. His remains were returned to Washington and interred in Rock Creek Cemetery.

[*U. S. Statutes at Large*, XVI, 419–29, XVIII, 116–21, XX, 102–08; *Senate Executive Jour.*, Mar. 21, 1867, Apr. 3, 1867, Dec. 15, 20, 1869, Mar. 2, 1871, Dec. 2, 8, 1873, June 23, 1874; *Report of the Joint Select Committee of Cong. Appointed to Inquire into the Affairs of the Govt. of the District of Columbia* (3 vols., 1874), being *Sen. Report 453*, 43 Cong., 1 Sess.; William Tindall, "A Sketch of Alexander Robey Shepherd," in *Records of the Columbia Hist. Soc.*, vol. XIV (1911); U. S. Grant, 3d, *Territorial Govt. of Washington, D. C.* (1929); *The Unveiling of a Statue to the Memory of Alexander R. Shepherd* (1909); *War Hist. of the "National Rifles"* (1887); F. C. Adams, *Our Little Monarchy: Who Runs It, and What It Costs* (1873); W. De Wintton, *Who Is Alexander R. Shepherd?* (1874); *N. Y. Times*, Sept. 13, 1902; *Evening Star* (Washington), Jan. 13, 15, 1870, and Sept. 13, 1902; *Boston Transcript*, Sept. 13, 1902.]
L. J. R.

SHEPLEY, ETHER (Nov. 2, 1789–Jan. 15, 1877), United States senator, jurist, the second son of John and Mary (Gibson) Thurlow Shepley, was born in Groton, Mass. He was descended from John Shepley (Sheple) who was in Salem, Mass., as early as 1637 and later settled at Chelmsford. After attending the academy in Groton conducted by Caleb Butler, he entered Dartmouth College, where he was graduated in 1811. Ill health caused him to abandon his ambition to become a physician and he turned to the study of the law, for two years in the office of Dudley Hubbard of South Berwick, Me., then with Zabdiel B. Adams in Lunenburg and Solomon Strong in Westminster. On being admitted to the bar in 1814, he opened an office in Saco, Me., where he practised for a time with William Pitt Preble [*q.v.*], and later alone. His rise in his profession was rapid, owing both to close application and to practical experience.

An ardent advocate of the separation of Maine from Massachusetts, Shepley entered politics as Saco's representative to the Massachusetts General Court in 1819. The same year he took an active part in the deliberations of the Maine constitutional convention. In February 1821 he succeeded William Pitt Preble as United States attorney for Maine, an office which he held until his election to the Senate in 1833 as the successor of John Holmes [*q.v.*]. As senator he was a vigorous supporter of Andrew Jackson, defending the removal of government deposits from the United States Bank, particularly in a long speech beginning Jan. 14, 1834, wherein he spoke warmly in favor of his college classmate, Amos Kendall [*q.v.*]. His greatest effort, however, was probably his speech on the French spolia-

tions (*Register of Debates in Congress*, 23 Cong., 2 Sess., p. 36). When Albion Keith Parris [*q.v.*] resigned from the Maine supreme court, Gov. Robert P. Dunlap [*q.v.*], on Sept. 23, 1836, appointed Shepley to the vacancy. Twelve years later, by appointment of Governor Dana, he became chief justice, a position he occupied for the seven years allowed by the state constitution. His decisions are recorded in 14–40 *Maine Reports*.

More suited to law than to politics, Shepley refused to return to political office, preferring to aid in clearing the docket of its deluge of land cases proceeding from the collapse of the speculative boom in Maine. Shortly after his retirement from the bench, he was appointed by legislative resolve, Apr. 1, 1856, sole commissioner to revise and cause to be printed—before Nov. 15 of the same year—the public laws of the state. The haste thus injudiciously forced upon him prevented *The Revised Statutes of the State of Maine* (1857) from being the complete work which his experience had prepared him to produce.

During the Civil War he took over the practice of his son, George Foster Shepley [*q.v.*], who was serving with the army. He had married, June 10, 1816, Anna Foster of Hanover, N. H., who died in 1868. They had five sons, two of whom died young. In 1822 Shepley joined the Congregational Church in Saco and thereafter took an active interest in religion. He was a trustee of Bowdoin College from 1829 to 1866. A fractured hip, resulting from a fall, caused his death early in 1877.

[William Willis, *A Hist. of the Law, the Courts, and the Lawyers of Me.* (1863); G. T. Chapman, *Sketches of the Alumni of Dartmouth Coll.* (1867); J. W. Patterson, in *Memorials of Judges Recently Deceased, Graduates of Dartmouth Coll.* (1881); E. Y. Hincks, *Sermon upon the Life and Character of Chief Justice Ether Shepley* (1877); Israel Washburn, Jr., in *Me. Hist. Soc. Colls.*, vol. VIII (1881); *Biog. Encyc. of Me. of the Nineteenth Century* (1885); M. C. C. Wilson, *John Gibson . . . and His Descendants* (1900); *Biog. Dir. Am. Cong.* (1928); *Daily Press* (Portland, Me.), Jan. 16, 1877.]
R. E. M.

SHEPLEY, GEORGE FOSTER (Jan. 1, 1819–July 20, 1878), Union soldier, military governor of Louisiana, federal judge, son of Ether [*q.v.*] and Anna (Foster) Shepley, was born in Saco, Me. At the age of fourteen he entered Dartmouth College, graduating in 1837. After reading law for a time with his father and at Harvard, he began practice in Bangor in 1839 as the partner of Joshua W. Hathaway. In 1844 he moved to Portland where he became successively the partner of Joseph Howard and of John W. Dana. He was appointed, Nov. 8, 1848, United States district attorney for Maine, but lost the position the following year with the change in national politics. President Pierce in 1853 and President Buchanan in 1857 reappointed him to the office, which he held until June 1861. As district attorney he attracted much attention in the murder case of *United States* vs. *Holmes* (*26 Federal Cases,* 349), when competent observers stated that his prosecution of the case suffered nothing from comparison with the defense conducted by George Evans [*q.v.*].

Shepley was a delegate at large to the National Democratic Convention in Charleston in 1860 and attended its adjourned session in Baltimore, supporting Douglas in the campaign. An acquaintance, begun at this convention, with Benjamin F. Butler, 1818–1893 [*q.v.*], led, after the outbreak of the Civil War, to the inclusion of the 12th Regiment of Maine Volunteers, of which Shepley was colonel, in Butler's New England division in the New Orleans campaign. After the capture of that city, May 1, 1862, Butler appointed Shepley its military commandant; in June 1862 he became military governor of Louisiana, and in July was promoted to the rank of brigadier-general. He must in some measure share with Butler the responsibility for whatever dishonesty there may have been in the army's administration of New Orleans ("Letters from George S. Denison to Salmon P. Chase," *Annual Report of the American Historical Association, 1902,* vol. II, 1903). After the election of Georg Michael Decker Hahn [*q.v.*] to the governorship, by the Unionist portion of the state, Shepley was assigned to the command of the district of Eastern Virginia, in May 1864. In 1865 he was chief of staff of the XXV Army Corps under General Weitzel and when the latter occupied Richmond, was appointed military governor of that city. Years afterward he contributed an article on "Incidents of the Capture of Richmond," to the *Atlantic Monthly* (July 1880). He resigned his commission July 1, 1865, and returned to the practice of law in Portland. On Dec. 22, 1869, he was appointed circuit judge of the United States court. Equity and patent cases made up a large proportion of those in which he gave decisions. He had a quick comprehension of the intricacies of patents but his decisions contain for the most part merely a discussion of the case at hand rather than a thorough review of principles. He was vehement and impetuous, and did not possess an exploring mind.

Shepley married on July 24, 1844, Lucy A. Hayes, who died in 1859; and on May 23, 1872, he married Helen Merrill. In 1877 he joined St. Luke's Episcopal Church in Portland. He died

the following year of Asiatic cholera, after an illness of four days. His wife and two daughters survived him.

[*Proc. of the Bench and Bar of the Circuit Court of the U. S., Dist. of Me., Sept. 28, 1878, upon the Decease of Hon. George Foster Shepley* (1878); Daniel Clark, in *Memorials of Judges Recently Deceased, Grads. of Dartmouth Coll.* (1881); G. T. Chapman, *Sketches of the Alumni of Dartmouth Coll.* (1867); A. F. Moulton, *Memorials of Me.* (1916); James Parton, *Gen. Butler in New Orleans* (17th ed., 1882), pp. 590–92; B. F. Butler, *Autobiog. . . . Butler's Book* (1892); *Private and Official Correspondence of Gen. Benj. F. Butler* (5 vols., 1917); M. C. C. Wilson, *John Gibson . . . and His Descendants* (1900); *Daily Press* (Portland, Me.), July 22, 1878.]   R. E. M.

SHERIDAN, PHILIP HENRY (Mar. 6, 1831–Aug. 5, 1888), Union soldier, was the third of six children of John and Mary (Meenagh) Sheridan, who emigrated to America from County Cavan, Ireland, about 1830. They lived for a time in Albany, N. Y., where, according to his own account, Philip was born. Hoping to provide a better maintenance for his growing family, the father took them to Somerset, Perry County, Ohio, where he sought work upon the canals and roads then under construction. The village school provided Philip with the most rudimentary kind of an education, and even this was interrupted when he became a clerk in a county-store at the age of fourteen. He was too young to follow the youths of Somerset when they enlisted for the Mexican War, a bitter disappointment which was mitigated only by his appointment to the United States Military Academy. On the day of registration, July 1, 1848, Sheridan gave his age as eighteen years and one month, which would indicate that he had been born in 1830. With the aid of his roommate, Henry Warner Slocum [*q.v.*], he succeeded in passing the examinations, but his pugnacious tendencies soon brought him to grief. An altercation with a cadet-officer, who, Sheridan believed, treated him unjustly, reached a climax when Sheridan stepped from the ranks and pursued his superior with bayonet fixed. He was suspended from the Academy for a year, but subsequently was graduated with the class of 1853, number thirty-four in a class of forty-nine.

As a brevet second lieutenant, 1st Infantry, he served for a year along the Rio Grande River, and then, with the 4th Infantry, he saw arduous service against hostile Indians in the Northwest. In the spring of 1861, he received his captaincy in the 13th Infantry, and began his war service as quartermaster and commissary of Union troops in southwest Missouri and as General Halleck's quartermaster during the Corinth campaign. His aggressive spirit chafed, however, under the restrictions of staff duty, and he therefore welcomed his appointment as colonel of the 2nd Michigan Cavalry on May 25, 1862. In a little over a month, he won the stars of a brigadier-general for his signal victory at Booneville, Mo., where he commanded a brigade. His subsequent service was brilliant; at Perryville, commanding an infantry division, he succeeded where others failed, and at Stone River, he practically saved the army of Rosecrans by his stubborn resistance to the Confederate advance. His well-merited promotion to the rank of major-general of volunteers followed on Dec. 31, 1862. In the fall of the following year, Sheridan again distinguished himself in command of the XX Corps, Army of the Cumberland, at the sanguinary battle of Chickamauga. Some two months later in the battle of Chattanooga, his command swept up the heights and over the crest of Missionary Ridge in a magnificent charge which contributed largely to Grant's defeat of Bragg and brought Sheridan into favor with Grant. Accordingly, with the latter's promotion to the rank of lieutenant-general, he gave Sheridan command of all the cavalry of the Army of the Potomac, a corps consisting of three divisions, with about 10,000 men for duty.

Sheridan initiated a complete reorganization of his cavalry command with characteristic energy, and in a little over a month was actively engaged in the battles of the Wilderness, Todd's Tavern, Spotsylvania Court House, and Cold Harbor. Beginning on the morning of May 9, 1864, and continuing until May 25, Sheridan's corps raided the Confederate communications around Richmond, destroyed about ten miles of track on three important railroads, broke up telegraph communication, captured many trains of stores, and caused great alarm and apprehension in the Confederate capital. On May 28, he fought the battle of Hawes's Shop and, soon after, the battle at Trevilian Station. During the months of May, June, and July, he was engaged in successive raids against the Confederate lines, performing brilliant service and securing decisive results. Early in August 1864, Sheridan was placed in command of the Army of the Shenandoah, and received Grant's personal instructions to drive the enemy south and to destroy all supplies in the fertile Shenandoah Valley which might enable them to use it again as a base of operations. Sheridan prepared his plans with a caution which seemed almost dilatory to his superiors at Washington, and then, with forceful initiative, accomplished the defeat of Jubal Anderson Early [q.v.], at Winchester (Opequon) on Sept. 19, and again at Fisher's Hill on Sept. 22. As a reward, he was promptly

promoted brigadier-general in the regular army. He then proceeded to lay waste the Valley, driving out its herds of domestic animals and virtually reducing its non-combatants to the state of starvation. For this, Sheridan was severely censured by Southern sympathizers, but in his eyes it was a matter of military necessity, the means calculated to be the most effective in bringing the war to an early end. For three years the Valley had sustained Confederate forces which had dealt out defeat after defeat to the Federal armies and it had supported the so-called "guerrilla bands," such as Mosby's Men, which had wrought so much damage within the Union lines.

Sheridan's little army was, however, surprised by Early at Cedar Creek, and all but routed on Oct. 19, 1864. The commander, resting at Winchester en route to his army, was twenty miles from the scene. He made his famous ride to the battle-field—immortalized in verse by Thomas Buchanan Read [q.v.]—rallied his demoralized troops, reformed his retreating lines, and decisively snatched victory from defeat. As a fitting climax to this series of accomplishments, Sheridan was made a major-general in the regular army on Nov. 8, 1864, and, with his veteran troops, received the thanks of Congress for their achievements in the Valley of the Shenandoah, and especially for the victory at Cedar Run. "Little Phil" as Sheridan was known to his soldiers, was indefatigable. He was actively engaged from Feb. 27 to Mar. 24, 1865, in a great raid from Winchester to Petersburg, in which he again defeated Early at Waynesboro. He cut three railroads and two canals, destroyed important Confederate depots of supplies, and left Lee's army with but a single line of railroad communication with the South. Of even greater military importance, perhaps, the strategic concentration of Sheridan's forces at Five Forks upon the successful conclusion of this raid, enabled him, on Apr. 1, 1865, to turn the flank of the Confederate army, force it to evacuate Petersburg and to initiate the ill-fated retreat to Appomattox. In the resultant final operations of the War, which included Sheridan's successful engagement at Sailor's Creek, his command was thrown squarely across Lee's line of retreat, and the surrender of the Confederate army to General Grant followed.

After the war, Sheridan was entrusted with the highly responsible problem of administering the military division of the Gulf, fraught with unsettled conditions along the Mexican border. He combined considerable material and moral support to the Mexican liberals with strong demonstrations of American troops north of the Rio Grande River, and practically forced the French government to withdraw its support of Maximilian (see *Memoirs, post,* II, pp. 210 ff.). Early in 1867, the Reconstruction Acts were passed, and Sheridan was made military governor of the fifth military district, Louisiana and Texas, with headquarters at New Orleans—an appointment entailing many difficult as well as delicate problems of administration, incident to the bitterness engendered by post-war conditions. His policies were characterized by severely repressive measures in the interest of Reconstruction in the South, a cause to which Sheridan was thoroughly, if sternly, devoted, and although he was strongly supported by General Grant, the disapproval of President Johnson eventually brought about his relief from this duty and his transfer to the department of the Missouri. In this new sphere of action, he embarked upon military operations against the Cheyennes, Comanches, Arapahoes, and Kiowas, and finally forced these hostile Indians to settle upon the reservations which by treaty had been allotted them. On Mar. 4, 1869, President Grant appointed him lieutenant-general, and assigned him to command the division of the Missouri.

Sheridan went abroad in 1870–71, during the Franco-Prussian war, to visit the German armies in the field, met Bismarck, von Moltke, and the German emperor, and witnessed the great battle of Sedan. After a year's absence, he returned to resume command of his military division, with headquarters in Chicago. He was tentatively selected by the president to command the American forces in 1873, when an invasion of Cuba was seriously considered in connection with the *Virginius* affair. Two years later he was again sent to the city of New Orleans to settle disturbed conditions which culminated in political rioting. He was placed in command of the western and southwestern military divisions in 1878, and in 1884 he succeeded General Sherman as commander-in-chief of the army. On June 1, 1888, Congress bestowed upon him the highest military rank, that of general. The last months of his life were occupied by the writing of his *Personal Memoirs* (2 vols., 1888), the preface being signed only three days before his death at Nonquitt, Mass., where he had gone with his family in the hope of restoring his failing health. His funeral, with imposing military and civil honors, took place in Washington, D. C., and he was interred in the National Cemetery at Arlington. He was survived by his widow and by four children, three daughters and

a son. He had been married to Irene the daughter of Gen. D. H. Rucker, later quartermaster-general of the army, June 3, 1875, while stationed in Chicago.

Sheridan was a short, slight man, of unprepossessing bearing in his later years, and even of ungainly appearance in his earlier. A pronounced reserve which characterized him at all times did not affect the magnetic quality of his personality which so impressed his military subordinates. Always just and considerate in his dealings with his men, and assiduous in promoting the health, personal comfort, and general welfare of his troops, he won from them a complete and enthusiastic confidence. When the battle waged hottest, Sheridan was at his best— cool, exact, self-possessed, the dashing and brilliant leader of men willing to follow him anywhere. He was never a profound student of military science, but his natural aptitude for command led him always to execute with great success the two rules upon which he acted: to take the offensive whenever possible, and to wring the last possible advantages from a defeated enemy. It may be noted, however, that Sheridan rose to his conspicuous military position only near the end of the war, and that his greatest successes were won from a numerically inferior and poorly mounted foe.

[*Personal Memoirs of P. H. Sheridan* (2 vols., 1888); Joseph Hergesheimer, *Sheridan* (1931); W. H. Van Orden, *Gen. Philip H. Sheridan* (1896); John McElroy, *Gen. Philip Henry Sheridan* (1896); G. W. Cullum, *Biog. Reg. . . . U. S. Mil. Acad.* (1891); J. H. Wilson, biog. sketch in *Twentieth Ann. Reunion, Asso. Grads., U. S. Mil. Acad.* (1889); *The Centennial of the U. S. Mil. Acad. at West Point, N. Y.* (1904), vol. II; Adam Badeau, *Mil. Hist. of U. S. Grant* (1881), vol. III; Horace Porter, *Campaigning with Grant* (1897); *Washington* (D. C.) *Post,* Aug. 6, 1888.]   C. D. R.

SHERMAN, FRANK DEMPSTER (May 6, 1860—Sept. 19, 1916), poet, architect, mathematician, and genealogist, was born in Peekskill, N. Y., the son of John Dempster Sherman, an educator and dealer in books, and his first wife, Lucy (MacFarland) Sherman. The eldest of his father's nine children, he was a descendant of Elder William Brewster [*q.v.*] of the *Mayflower* and of Philip Sherman, who emigrated to New England about 1633, settled at Roxbury, Mass., and in 1638 was banished to Rhode Island with the adherents of Anne Hutchinson [*q.v.*]. For the most part he was educated at home by his parents, though he studied for one year at the Peekskill Military Academy. After serving for a period as secretary to William de Caindry of Washington, he entered Columbia College in October 1879, matriculating in the mechanical engineering course but transferring in February 1881 to architecture. After being graduated from Columbia with the degree of Ph.B. in June 1884, he enrolled for graduate study at Harvard, where he took courses in philosophy, Italian, Latin, and Greek, contributed to the *Harvard Advocate* and the *Harvard Lampoon,* and became an intimate friend of Clinton Scollard [*q.v.*], the poet, who later described him as "walking at twilight under the Cambridge elms," improvising "sonnet, rondeau or ballade with an ease that was the despair of those less versatile" (*Columbia University Quarterly,* March 1917, p. 162). His father's ill health limited his life at Harvard to one year, and he was obliged to return to Peekskill to look after the family business of book dealing. On Nov. 16, 1887, he married Juliet Mersereau Durand of Peekskill, N. Y., daughter of the Rev. Cyrus Bervick and Sarah Elizabeth (Mersereau) Durand. In 1887–88 he became assistant in architecture at Columbia. He was instructor in architecture, 1889–91, adjunct professor, 1891–1904, and professor of graphics, 1904–16. Known as an extraordinarily brilliant lecturer on mathematical subjects (*Columbia Alumni News, post,* p. 123), he was able also to write several volumes of poetry and to carry on the tireless research that bore fruit in an exhaustive genealogy of the Sherman family in America.

His publications include *Madrigals and Catches* (1887), *New Waggings of Old Tales* (1888), which was written in collaboration with John Kendrick Bangs [*q.v.*], *Lyrics for a Lute* (1890), *Little-Folk Lyrics* (1892), *Lyrics of Joy* (1904), and *A Southern Flight* (1905), written with Clinton Scollard. In 1917 Scollard published, with an appreciative introduction, *The Poems of Frank Dempster Sherman,* a collected edition. Contemporaries regarded Sherman as not quite equal to Sidney Lanier, Richard Hovey [*qq.v.*], or Bliss Carman, but as nevertheless on a high plane. He possessed a graceful, cheerful muse, his poetic ancestors clearly being Herrick, Lovelace, and Carew; among the moderns he owed much to Thomas Bailey Aldrich [*q.v.*] and Austin Dobson. Living long in New York society, he expressed many sides of its life in delightful *vers de société,* but his catholic and warm humanity also found expression in poems for children, which many readers have placed on library shelves beside those of Robert Louis Stevenson. Much of his lighter verse was written under the name of Felix Carmen. Manuscripts of some unpublished fugitive verse became the possessions of his descendants. His work on the genealogy of his family, which began in 1904 in a modest way,

became his greatest hobby; after his death his manuscripts were deposited in the New York Public Library. He was also interested in designing bookplates, and in collecting stamps and coins. He was a member of the National Institute of Arts and Letters. He died in New York City, survived by his wife and a son. On June 9, 1932, the Friendly Town Association of Peekskill, N. Y., dedicated a sculptured monument and a park as a memorial to him in the village where he was born.

[F. D. Sherman, "The Sherman Geneal.," unpublished MSS. in N. Y. Pub. Lib.; *Who's Who in America,* 1916–17; *Who's Who in N. Y.,* 1914; official records, Harvard and Columbia Universities; *N. Y. Geneal. and Biog. Record,* Apr. 1917; *New England Hist. and Geneal. Reg.,* supp. to Apr. 1917; *Columbia Univ. Quart.,* Sept. 1932; *Columbia Alumni News,* Oct. 27, 1916; *N. Y. Evening Post,* Dec. 3, 1904; *Herald Tribune* (N. Y.), June 10, 1932; obituaries in *N. Y. Times* and *Boston Transcript,* Sept. 20, 1916, and *Journal* (Richmond, Va.), Sept. 21, 1916.]   A. E. C.

SHERMAN, JAMES SCHOOLCRAFT (Oct. 24, 1855–Oct. 30, 1912), vice-president of the United States, the son of Richard Updike and Mary Frances (Sherman) Sherman, was of the seventh generation in descent from Philip Sherman, who came to Massachusetts about 1633 and later settled in Portsmouth, R. I. His grandfather, Willett Sherman, accumulated a small fortune as a glass manufacturer. His father was a newspaper editor, a Democratic politician, and the holder of several minor appointive offices under the state government and at Washington. James Schoolcraft Sherman was born at Utica, N. Y., and received his early education in the public schools and at Whitestown Seminary. He then entered Hamilton College, where he won some honors in debating, made many enduring friendships, and fulfilled the requirements for the degrees of A.B. in 1878 and LL.B. in 1879. In the latter year he was admitted to the bar and entered the Utica law firm of his brother-in-law, Henry J. Cookinham. Business and politics soon claimed his attention, and, though his practice was long continued, it was confined to advising clients in business matters. He became president of the New Hartford Canning Company on the death of his father in 1895, and was president of the Utica Trust and Deposit Company from its organization in 1900.

Against his father's advice Sherman entered politics, as a Republican. He was mayor of Utica in 1884 and member of the national House of Representatives in 1887–91 and 1893–1909. He early became a close friend of Thomas Brackett Reed, Joseph G. Cannon [*qq.v.*], and others of the "regular" Republican group, and throughout his congressional career acted and voted in accord with their policies. Considering his twenty years' service, his contributions to legislation were few. He introduced the false-branding bill which protected American manufacturers of cheese; he presented a committee report in 1896, strongly advocating government aid in constructing an interoceanic canal in Nicaragua; he proposed numerous measures to ameliorate the condition of the Indians; and he sponsored bills to construct a cable to the Philippines and to reform the revenue-cutter service. Apparently he had no desire to identify his name with important measures on the statute book. He preferred to give his attention to parliamentary management, for which he was conspicuously gifted. It was popularly supposed that he evolved most of the measures proposed by the committee on rules. He was made chairman of the committee of the whole in important debates like those on the Dingley tariff and the Cuban war revenue bills, when the Speaker would entrust the gavel to no one else. His firmness and dignity made him, next to Reed, the best presiding officer in the House during his service. Upon Reed's retirement, he was an unsuccessful candidate for the speakership. He presided over three New York state Republican conventions, and in 1906 was chairman of the congressional campaign committees.

In 1908, after Theodore Roosevelt had dictated Taft's nomination for the presidency, congressional leaders agreed upon Sherman for the vice-presidency to balance the ticket. Speaker Cannon spoke for him in the convention, and he was nominated on the first ballot. During the campaign, it was insinuated (*Current Literature*, August 1908) that Sherman had diverted congressional campaign funds in 1906 to secure his own reëlection and that he was interested in dummy corporations to exploit Indian oil lands; these insinuations he ignored. After his election he presided over the Senate to the satisfaction of members of both parties. He was renominated in 1912, but died before the close of the campaign. He was married, Jan. 26, 1881, to Carrie Babcock of Utica, and had three sons.

[*James Schoolcraft Sherman: Memorial Addresses Delivered at a Joint Session of the Senate and the House* (1913); *Memorial Service . . . James Schoolcraft Sherman . . . Republican Club of the City of New York* (1913); *Biog. Dir. Am. Cong.* (1928); *Who's Who in America,* 1910–11; F. D. Sherman, *The Ancestry of John Taylor Sherman* (1915), p. 58; H. J. Cookinham, *Hist. of Oneida County, N. Y.* (1912), vol. I; *Independent,* May 28, 1908; *Review of Reviews,* Aug. 1908; *N. Y. Times,* June 21, 1908; *N. Y. Tribune, N. Y. Herald,* Oct. 31, 1912.]   E. C. S.

SHERMAN, JOHN (Dec. 26, 1613–Aug. 8, 1685), Puritan clergyman, mathematician, was born in Dedham, England, the son of Edmund and Joan (Makin) Sherman. He matriculated sizar from St. Catharine's College, Cambridge, in 1631, but declined to subscribe to the Thirty-nine Articles of the established faith and left without a degree. In 1634 he emigrated to Massachusetts Bay, where he became assistant to the Rev. George Phillips [*q.v.*] at Watertown, but in 1635, with five others, was dismissed to the church at Wethersfield in Connecticut, where settlement had begun the previous year. In April 1636, with these associates he organized the Wethersfield church. He was one of the "Free Planters" of Milford, listed Nov. 20, 1639, and was invited to become teacher of the church there as a colleague of the Rev. Peter Prudden, but declined. In 1643 when Milford came under the jurisdiction of the New Haven Colony, he was sent as a deputy to the General Court.

After 1644 he preached and taught at Branford (then Totokett) and other places in the colony, but without being regularly settled. His reputation as a preacher was spreading, for not only did he win unstinted praise from Thomas Hooker and many other New England divines, but a recall came from England, which he promptly rejected. If the eulogistic pen that wrote his epitaph is to be trusted, he was "as a preacher a veritable Chrysostom." (W. T. Harris, *Epitaphs from the Old Burying Ground in Watertown,* 1869, p. 48). Invited to return to the Watertown parish after the death of Phillips, he was dismissed from the Milford church, Nov. 8, 1647, and became pastor at Watertown, where he remained for the rest of his life.

After returning to Massachusetts, Sherman became an occasional lecturer at Harvard College on mathematics, one of the few non-religious subjects to be encouraged in the early college. His fortnightly lectures continued over a period of thirty years, during which time he published for at least three years (1674, 1676, 1677) *An Almanack of Cœlestial Motions.* In the fashion of the time, pious reflections were added to these almanacs, lest in the fascination of the sciences, attention be withdrawn from the staff of the spiritual life. When his most active days were over, he was given honorary posts at Harvard which he filled with some difficulty. On May 19, 1669, he was made a freeman of the Bay Colony. In 1672 he became an Overseer of the College and in 1677, a fellow of the Corporation. The honor of bestowing degrees was given him in 1681, but, according to the College records, because "by reason of the Infirmitys attending his Age" he might not be able to do so, Increase Mather [*q.v.*] was authorized to act in his stead. In the spring of the following year, Sherman delivered a discourse before the convened Congregational ministers of Massachusetts, his being the first recorded sermon on such an occasion. While preaching at Sudbury on July 5, 1685, he was stricken with a fever, of which he died a month later. After the death of his first wife, Mary, at Milford in 1644, he married Mary Launce, a ward of Governor Hopkins, who survived him until 1710. Cotton Mather credits him with twenty-six children, but only thirteen are mentioned in his will.

[Cotton Mather, *Magnalia Christi Americana* (1702); W. B. Sprague, *Annals Am. Pulpit*, vol. I (1856); T. T. Sherman, *Sherman Geneal.* (1920); Henry Bond, *Geneals. of Watertown* (1855), II, 935; Convers Francis, *An Hist. Sketch of Watertown* (1830); J. B. Felt, *The Ecclesiastical Hist. of New England* (2 vols., 1855–62); C. J. Hoadly, *Records of the Colony and Plantation of New Haven*, vol. I (1857); S. W. Adams and H. R. Stiles, *The Hist. of Ancient Wethersfield* (1904), vol. I; *1639: Proc. at the Celebration of the Two Hundred and Fiftieth Anniversary of the First Church . . . Milford . . . 1889* (1890), p. 10; J. R. Simonds, *A Hist. of the First Church . . . of Branford* (1919), p. 12; "Harvard College Records," vol. I, *Pubs. Col. Soc. Mass.*, vol. XV (1925); John and J. A. Venn, *Alumni Cantabrigienses*, Part I, vol. IV (1927); C. L. Nichols, "Notes on the Almanacs of Mass.," *Proc. Am. Antiq. Soc.*, n.s., XXII (1912), 23; *New England Hist. and Geneal. Reg.*, Jan. 1870, Apr., Oct. 1896, and esp. July 1897, pp. 309–13.]   E. H. D.

SHERMAN, JOHN (May 10, 1823–Oct. 22, 1900), statesman, born at Lancaster, Ohio, was the eighth child of Charles Robert and Mary (Hoyt) Sherman, and a younger brother of William Tecumseh Sherman [*q.v.*]. His father, a descendant of Edmund Sherman who came from England to Massachusetts probably in 1634 or 1635 and later settled in Connecticut, removed from the latter state in 1811 to Ohio, where he practised law. Charles Robert Sherman rose to the bench of the state supreme court, but his untimely death in 1829 required his widow to share the responsibility of educating some of their eleven children with various friends and relatives. The famous brothers, Tecumseh and John, were bound by rare ties of mutual understanding and affection. John had a lively, careless disposition, that was trying alike to teachers and foster parents; and his education, divided between Lancaster and Mt. Vernon, where he lived for four years with John Sherman, a cousin of his father, gave him little taste for the college life that was planned for him. He developed a liking for mathematics and surveying, left school at fourteen to work on canal improvements, and at sixteen had grown men working under him, constructing a dam. Fortunately for him, defeat of the Whigs by the Democrats in 1839 led to his

dismissal. After a few months of roistering, a change came over him. Helped by material influences, dormant ambitions, inherited from six generations of paternal ancestors addicted to the law and public service, were awakened; a new Sherman emerged—one who realized that Ohio, lush with expansion, was a fertile field for well-directed purpose. He substituted extreme self-control for careless abandon, and in 1840 set himself studying law under his uncle, Judge Jacob Parker, and his eldest brother, Charles Taylor Sherman, at Mansfield. In this field, his father's repute and his wide family connections proved stimulating and useful.

Thus arbitrarily shortening his period of immaturity and dependence, Sherman gained an early start on his career. Before formal admission to the bar, May 10, 1844, he was doing much of a full-fledged lawyer's work. Also he launched into business, proving competent as partner in a lumber concern and buying real estate wisely. His rise to local prominence was attested by his marriage, on Aug. 31, 1848, to Margaret Sarah Cecilia, the only child of a prominent Mansfield lawyer, Judge James Stewart. The Shermans had no children, but adopted a daughter. Not content with country-town law and business, Sherman entered state politics. Loss of a job at Democratic hands in 1839 had scarcely cooled his ardor for Whiggery in 1840; thereafter he presented himself faithfully at Ohio Whig conclaves, and he attended the national conventions of 1848 and 1852. He ran for no elective office until 1854, when the wave of anti-Nebraska sentiment carried him into the federal House of Representatives, along with many other comparatively unknown young men.

Unlike most of these, however, Sherman of Ohio remained an official part of the Washington scene continuously through nearly a half century; as representative, 1855–61; as senator, 1861–77; as secretary of the treasury, 1877–81; as senator, 1881–97; as secretary of state, 1897–98. This was an astounding feat, considering the fact that during these years Ohio four times elected a Democratic governor and thrice sent Sherman a Democratic colleague in the Senate. The explanation lies in Sherman's temperament and situation. His heritage, his mother's oft-repeated precepts, his victory over youthful excesses, and his quick success in local law and business combined to overlay his naturally hot temper with a cautious reserve that was excellently adapted to Ohio's uncertainties. Economically, the conservative, creditor point of view became his personal preference; but, politically, he understood the radical, debtor psychology that flourished among his constituents during the three major and four minor depressions that punctuated his tenure of office. He carefully studied the attitude of the Middle West and helped to stamp national legislation with the influence of that section. While he was compromising his conservative personal preferences with more radical demands from the Ohio electorate, the East was compromising with the West on each piece of major legislation. Thus he and his work in some sense became typical of his political generation.

He had been elected in 1854 because he was a compromise candidate on whom warring factions could agree; and, at Washington, his more moderate utterances on slavery, contrasted with those of men like Joshua R. Giddings and Owen Lovejoy [qq.v.], quickly aided his rise. Membership on a House committee investigating unsavory Kansas affairs was exploited; Sherman wrote a report, scoring the Democracy and all its Kansas works, which was used effectively in the 1856 campaign (House Report No. 200, 34 Cong., 1 Sess., "Kansas Affairs"). He became a hardworking and effective laborer in the young Republican vineyard and at the beginning of his third term (Dec. 5, 1859) was the caucus nominee for speaker. A forgotten indorsement carelessly given Helper's Impending Crisis deprived him of the coveted honor, and increased thereafter his leaning toward compromise and caution in legislative matters. The successful candidate, William Pennington [q.v.], adopted Sherman's committee slate and named him chairman of the ways and means committee. Here his tariff convictions insured equable relations with Eastern Republicans. From loyalty to party he never deviated.

Campaign labors of 1860 fortified Sherman further, making him, in spite of Ohio's Republican factions, the successor to Senator Chase, whom Lincoln elevated to the Treasury. On a widened stage the tall, spare, impressive junior senator was ready to play his part, especially in his favorite field of finance, for he at once became a member, and in 1867 became chairman, of the finance committee. In the din of war, with its necessities, he helped give the greenbacks the status of legal tender; but he never completely forgot that there must be a day of reckoning, that order must be wrought out of a chaotic currency. He sometimes tried to encourage a policy of "paying as you go" and led in planning, with Secretary Chase, the national banking system (embodied in the act of Feb. 25, 1863). If Sherman's program of economies and rigorous taxation, especially income taxes, had seemed politi-

cally expedient, fewer bond and greenback issues might have sprouted during the war. As it was, he quieted his uneasiness over the greenbacks by reiterating the popular doctrine that the country would "grow up to" the expanded currency.

On the reconstruction issue, war between Sherman's personal preferences and popular dicta waged unremittingly, for political rivalries in Ohio, as elsewhere, imposed irrational tests of party loyalty and defined patriotism without humanity. His desire for moderation was sufficiently well known for many Southerners to write him concerning tolerance, and he spoke out against the fiery Sumner's program. But he did not carry his efforts at moderation so far from the radical path as to stray outside the confines of dominant Republicanism. Opposing Thaddeus Stevens' drastic military reconstruction plan, he advanced a substitute little less rigorous, which became law Mar. 2, 1867; and he voted for most of the radical program. For his former friend, Andrew Johnson, Sherman openly expressed sympathy; he admired Johnson's "combative propensity," and asserted his right to remove Stanton (Congressional Globe, 39 Cong., 1 Sess., Appendix, p. 129). But, knowing the ostracism suffered by the President's supporters, he voted to convict him. When seven other Republicans prevented conviction, he felt "entirely satisfied" (Recollections, I, 432).

On post-war finance Sherman dominated national policy, because of his Senate chairmanship, his interest, and his ability; like most congressmen he was swayed by the strong tide of inflationist sentiment, although as a private individual he cherished anti-inflationist desires. He saw in cancellation of greenbacks the most direct route to specie resumption and declared that a beneficial fall in prices must mark resumption; yet on these very grounds he opposed McCulloch's currency contraction policies of 1866 and 1868. The Middle West being then strongly inflationary, he claimed that resumption would speedily come if the government merely met current obligations. The greenbacks outstanding, he thought, were not too much for the condition of the country. When public opinion blamed McCulloch's contraction policy for the stringency of 1868, Sherman said contraction should cease in deference to that opinion. It did. He realized that national credit must be safeguarded by resumption as soon as political conditions permitted; and he entertained dreams of financial reforms international in scope, aiding Emperor Napoleon III's scheme for a stable, unified currency among the great trading nations (Recollections, I, 406–12). His work on the funding act of July 14, 1870, reduced the burden of public interest and helped restore national credit. While the dollar was still at a premium, he pushed the mint-reform bill which ended the coinage of silver dollars, so that after silver fell he was labeled the arch marplot of the "Crime of '73." On the resumption act of Jan. 14, 1875, he had to yield his own excellent plan, of funding greenbacks into bonds, for the substitute of George F. Edmunds. His preëminence in financial matters, and his aid to Hayes's candidacy, made him the natural choice for the Treasury in 1877.

As secretary of the treasury, Sherman occupied a congenial place, for responsibility for the national finances gave rein to his native skill at economical management and deafened him to inflationist outcry. He strengthened the resumption act by his interpretation of it, declaring that it empowered the secretary to issue bonds after, as well as before, resumption (a position for which John G. Carlisle had reason to be grateful in 1893); and, in the face of congressional clamor, he convinced hard-headed bankers that the government would redeem its bonds in gold, thus immensely enhancing the national prestige. He disappointed bankers who were confidently expecting concessions from the government and amazed them by discarding their advice and achieving sale abroad at a bond price above that of the open market. Thoroughly informing himself beforehand, he coolly bargained with London and New York syndicates and bankers, playing them off against one another, even when they fought him in the gold market and when exchange rates and London discounts went against him. He facilitated direct sales to investors, independent of syndicates. The loans of 1878 and 1879 were especially skilful.

Sherman's statesmanship while secretary was proved by the political obstacles he surmounted. The political odds against him in Hayes's administration were terrific. Hayes's title to office was uncertain; the House was Democratic for four years, and the Senate for two; and the populace was discouraged by a wearisome depression. Business failures, especially in the West, increased in Sherman's first and second years, magnifying opposition to resumption, while mine-owners and inflationists joined hands in a concerted effort to obtain "free silver." With both parties torn sectionally on this issue, it appeared late in 1877 that inflation politics would prevent Sherman from attaining his main objectives, resumption of specie payments and funding of the public debt. The House stopped resumption operations temporarily by passing two

bills: Bland's for a silver dollar with unlimited legal tender and unlimited coinage, and Ewing's for indefinite postponement of the date of resumption (Nov. 5, 23, 1877). While these bills awaited Senate action, Sherman's Republican successor, Stanley Matthews, fathered a concurrent resolution (which lacks the force of law) declaring government bonds payable in silver; and both Houses passed it, thus humiliating Sherman.

However, divisions among inflationists ultimately gave Sherman sufficient support to defeat the more extreme objectives of Bland and Ewing. The Bland-Allison Act (Feb. 28, 1878) stipulated a limited coinage of silver, rather than free coinage; and instead of postponing resumption indefinitely Congress, on May 31, 1878, forbade further retirement of greenbacks. Sherman has been severely criticized for failure to oppose the Matthews resolution originally or to support Hayes's veto of the Bland-Allison bill finally. Faced by a fiscal and political exigency, he labored to obtain maximum concessions from the extremists. He judged resumption and funding might be achieved, in spite of Bland-Allison dollars and of 348,000,000 outstanding greenbacks; and they were.

After the passage of the silver bill, Sherman helped to rally conservative support behind the administration, and the insurgents were somewhat discredited in the 1878 elections. Henceforward comparatively free from the opposition that had been hounding him, and aided by favorable trade developments, he carefully protected the final preparations for resumption. He had the New York sub-treasury made a member of the clearing houses at Boston and New York, and made payments to the government receivable in either legal tenders or coin. Consequently, the premium on gold disappeared (Dec. 17, 1878) after nearly seventeen years; and on Jan. 2, 1879, specie payments were smoothly resumed, to the general astonishment.

Whether or not Sherman could continue specie payments thereafter depended upon the demand for gold. The law of May 31, 1878, to which he had agreed, not only had stopped cancellation of legal tenders redeemed in gold but also had directed their reissue. Later, realizing the potential drain, he fabricated a theory that notes once redeemed need not be reissued when the gold reserve became less than 40 per cent. of outstanding notes. Fortunately for him, rainswept Britain and Europe in 1879 had to buy huge quantities of American wheat, corn, and cotton, paying in gold. Trade rebounded beautifully, and specie payments seemed so secure that the Secretary described legal tenders as "the best circulating medium known" (*Annual Report of the Secretary of the Treasury . . . 1880*, p. xiv). Not so the Bland-Allison dollars. They soon worried Sherman, since their intrinsic worth was declining, business men were forcing them back on the government, and treasury channels were so choked with them as to threaten the placing of the United States on the silver standard. The Secretary made a futile plea to Congress to impose new limitations on their coinage. Then a rise in interior trade temporarily removed his apprehension and he soon returned to the Senate and to his political point of view on silver. As the end of his cabinet service approached, the United States still stood on the gold standard. Resumption was an admitted success.

The most distinguished phase of Sherman's career was closing, but he did not suspect it. He planned further achievements in the White House: refunding the public debt at lower interest, perfecting disbursements, settling the silver question without banishing gold or displacing paper, reducing taxes, freeing the civil service from "infernal scramble," breaking down sectionalism in party politics, and turning politics from outworn war issues to "business and financial interests and prosperity" (Sherman, to Richard Smith June 14, 1880, Sherman MSS.). His dreams were of the stuff that made the inner man, but his success at resumption had made him a failure as a candidate for the presidential nomination. He felt that the business class in general and the party in particular owed him the office; but the unparalleled prosperity that he had helped to create made Republican victory in 1880 so certain as to insure bitter competition for the nomination. Poorly organized Sherman forces, although they helped defeat the unit rule, could not rout the Grant phalanx, or match the Blaine magnetism. Worse, ten Ohio delegates stubbornly refused to vote for Sherman. The nomination fell to the popular and available Garfield, whose presence at Chicago Sherman had thought essential to his own success. In 1880, as in 1888 and to a less degree in 1884, Sherman failed of the nomination because he lacked unscrupulousness in the use of patronage, color in personality and appeal, cordial unity in the Ohio delegation, and skill in manipulating politicians, and because he had an abundance of inflationist opposition. In 1888 he reached the exciting total of 249 votes on the second ballot; but the thread of Ohio intrigue, tortuously unwinding through the correspondence of Foraker, Garfield, Hanna, Hayes, McKinley, and Sherman, shows how futile was his dearest hope.

Through his second period of sixteen years in the Senate (1881–97) Sherman played the rôle of prominent politician, so cast by his adaptation to the plot of the play in Ohio and in the nation at large. Ohio gave him Garfield's seat only after a contest and he had to keep watch lest he should be shelved, in 1879 and later, with the governorship. Democrats won the state thrice, but luckily Republicans controlled when he came up for re-election in 1885 and in 1892 he succeeded in postponing the candidacy of Foraker (until 1896). In national politics, also, the atmosphere was one of continual uneasiness. Neither Republicans nor Democrats obtained simultaneous control of the House, the Senate, and the presidency for more than a single period of two years during this time (Republicans, 1889–91; Democrats, 1893–95); and all the political veterans were confused by uncertainties rising from the economic revolution and by cleavages between East and West that were disruptive of party strength. In such a situation Sherman's services seemed indispensable, because of his long experience in legislative compromise, his understanding of Western demands, and his reputation for astuteness in estimating reactions. The newer group of Senate managers—Nelson W. Aldrich, Eugene Hale, O. H. Platt, and John C. Spooner [*qq.v.*]—left Sherman out of much of their basic planning, for he, unlike William B. Allison [*q.v.*], never joined them on terms of close intimacy; but when the time came to compromise with the West, they leaned heavily on him. He functioned most strikingly in connection with the anti-trust and silver-purchase laws of 1890. The final draft of the first came from the pen of Edmunds and the important purchase provisions of the second never had Sherman's hearty approval; but on the one he carried the responsibility, for the finance committee, of initiating tentative drafts during two experimental years (1888–90), and on the other he so adjusted a conference committee stalemate between the two Houses as to save his party from a silver veto and from the defeat of the McKinley tariff. Then, as often during his legislative career, the immediate political exigency faced by him and his fellow partisans warped his judgment on "sound" currency and the protection of the Treasury.

Republican colleagues honored Sherman with the position of president *pro tempore* (1885–87) and listened deferentially whenever the famous ex-Secretary spoke on finance. He was important in campaigns as keynoter on currency and tariff subjects. Insistence of Ohio wool-growers on protection led him into yeoman's service regimenting Middle-Western Republicans behind a high tariff. His assignment (1886) to the chairmanship of the foreign relations committee proved none too congenial. On minor issues he shifted his position, not always in conformity with popular trends. His economic philosophy always remained basically conservative; for example, he favored general regulation of interstate commerce but questioned the right of Congress to establish maximum and minimum rates and opposed the prohibition of pooling. After he recovered from his nomination fiasco of 1888, Sherman was content in the familiar Senate environment. There were leisure for profitable business undertakings, a never-forgotten sense of service, long evenings alone in his peaceful study and, latterly, preoccupation with the work, published in two volumes in 1895 as *John Sherman's Recollections of Forty Years in the House, Senate and Cabinet*. In 1879 he had published *Selected Speeches and Reports on Finance and Taxation, from 1859 to 1878*. Things might have drifted into the usual peaceful Senate demise if Hanna and the embarrassed McKinley had not translated Sherman to the State Department to give Hanna a Senate seat. In the unaccustomed place, under stress of Cuban excitements, it became all too evident that Sherman had a growing and humiliating weakness of memory which incapacitated him for functioning out of his usual routine. The fur-seal, Hawaiian, and Spanish negotiations were taken out of his hands. When the cabinet decided for war with Spain he rose to the defense of his anti-expansionist views, and resigned in protest. Two years of unhappy private life ensued before his final release.

[John Sherman MSS. (*c.* 110,000 letters), and William Sherman MSS., Lib. Cong.; *House Executive Document No. 9*, 46 Cong., 2 Sess., "Specie Resumption and Refunding of National Debt," containing many letters; *Annual Reports of the Sec. of the Treasury, 1877–80; Papers Relating to the Foreign Relations of the U. S.*, 1897–98; S. A. Bronson, *John Sherman; What He Has Said and Done* (1880); T. E. Burton, *John Sherman* (1906); W. S. Kerr, *John Sherman, His Life and Public Services* (2 vols., 1908); R. S. Thorndike, *The Sherman Letters* (1894); M. A. DeW. Howe, *Home Letters of Gen. Sherman* (1909); J. G. Randall, "John Sherman and Reconstruction," *Miss. Valley Hist. Rev.*, Dec. 1932; E. G. Lewis, "Contributions of John Sherman to Public and Private Finance" (unprinted thesis, U. of Ill., 1932); L. M. Sears, "John Sherman," in S. F. Bemis, ed., *The Am. Secretaries of State and Their Diplomacy*, IX (1929); T. T. Sherman, *Sherman Genealogy* (1920). A biography by J. P. and R. F. Nichols is in process of preparation.]   J. P. N.

SHERMAN, ROGER (Apr. 19, 1721 o.s.– July 23, 1793), statesman, the son of William and Mehetabel (Wellington) Sherman, was born in Newton, Mass. He was descended from Capt. John Sherman of Dedham, Essex, who settled in Watertown, Mass., about 1636 and became a freeman the next year (T. T. Sherman, *post*).

William Sherman purchased land and moved in 1723 to the part of Dorchester that was incorporated in 1726 as Stoughton (Boutell, *post*, p. 18). Roger lived there until 1743, learning the trade of cordwainer from his father and helping on the farm. He received no formal education save that offered by the common schools, but he doubtless came under the influence of the classically trained Rev. Samuel Dunbar and early acquired a habit of study that led him to read widely in theology, history, mathematics, and particularly law and politics. A plausible tradition pictures him at his cobbler's bench with an open book always before him. Surprisingly, because of his deep interest in theology, Sherman did not join the church until early manhood; this was probably due to a characteristic caution in making weighty decisions. His father died in 1741. In 1743 Roger moved to New Milford, Conn., where his elder brother William had already settled, and tradition has it that he walked the entire distance with his cobbler's tools on his back. Two years later he was appointed surveyor for New Haven County, and he continued in office when Litchfield County was organized in 1752, serving until 1758 (Boutell, pp. 24–26). This position was unusually lucrative and Sherman became a considerable owner of lands. He began at once to take an active part in town affairs, serving as juryman, gauger, town clerk *pro tem.*, clerk of the church, deacon, school committeeman, and agent to the Assembly on town business. In 1756 he became sole owner of New Milford's first store, which he and his brother had been operating. Amid all these duties he found time to publish in 1752 *A Caveat Against Injustice, or an Enquiry into the Evil Consequences of a Fluctuating Medium of Exchange*, a strong argument denying that bills of credit of neighboring provinces were legal tender in Connecticut in contracts not specifically mentioning them, and incidentally inveighing against imported luxuries and urging an excise on rum to discourage its use. More remarkable than this performance was his publication of a series of almanacs between 1750 and 1761 which were based upon his own astronomical calculations and contained, with quotations from Milton, Dryden, Pope, and others, some verse apparently of his own composition (Paltsits, *post*). In February 1754 he was admitted to the Litchfield bar and in May 1755 he represented New Milford in the General Assembly, which appointed him a justice of the peace; in 1759 he became a justice of the county court. At each election from 1755 to 1761, except in 1756–57, he was reëlected to the legislature. His experience in that body prepared him for legislative duties during the Revolution, especially in matters of military finance and supply; in 1755 he was on a committee to consider how to finance the colony's part in the Crown Point expedition and in 1759 he was appointed commissary for the Connecticut troops, his depot being in Albany.

At forty, a man of property and some political standing, he gave up his law practice and embarked upon wider mercantile enterprises by moving to New Haven. Here he imported merchandise as well as books for Yale students, and he began another store at Wallingford. In 1761 he contributed liberally to the building of the college chapel, and from 1765 to 1776 was treasurer of Yale, receiving the honorary degree of M.A. in 1768. The pressure of public duties compelled his retirement from business in 1772. From October 1764 to May 1766 he was a representative, or deputy, of New Haven in the lower house of the legislature. He was elected to the upper house, as an assistant, in May 1766, and held office in that body for nineteen years. He became a justice of the peace in May 1765, a member of the county court in October 1765, and in May 1766 he was made a judge of the superior court of Connecticut, being annually reappointed for twenty-three years. When these are added to his later offices, Sherman becomes outstanding even in a day when multiple office-holding was not uncommon. These public duties came to him during disturbances over the Stamp Act, possibly in recognition of his moderate support of the Sons of Liberty in their early phases, though he disapproved of their later "proceedings [which] tend to weaken the authority of the government" (L. H. Gipson, *Jared Ingersoll,* 1920, p. 207). When radicalism made its appearance in New Haven, Sherman issued a warrant for the arrest of the leader, Benedict Arnold. However, he served as head of the New Haven committee of correspondence in securing the non-importation agreements, and presided at a meeting of merchants who resolved to boycott New York traders for failing to uphold them (*Connecticut Journal,* Aug. 3, 1770). Though apparently not a member of the Susquehannah and Delaware companies, Sherman, as a member of Governor Trumbull's party, supported in the newspapers, in the legislature, and in the Continental Congress the idea of asserting Connecticut's charter claims to western territory (*Ibid.,* Apr. 8, 1774). Though belonging to the conservative wing of the Revolutionary party, he, with Jefferson, Wythe, and James Wilson, was one of the first to deny the supremacy of Parliament. John Adams noted in 1774 that Sherman

"thought the reverse of the declaratory act was true, namely, that the Parliament of Great Britain had authority to make laws for America in no case whatever" (C. F. Adams, ed., *The Works of John Adams,* II, 1850, p. 343). As a member of the First Continental Congress in 1774, and as a member of the committee on the Declaration of Rights, Sherman also voiced these sentiments in that body, where he spoke "often and long, but very heavily and clumsily" (*Ibid.,* II, 396). A devout Congregationalist as well as a merchant, he found additional reason to support the Revolution in his fear of an Anglican bishopric in the colonies.

Serving in the Continental Congress from 1774 to 1781, and again in 1783–84, always with faithful attention to the burdensome committee duties, Sherman gained a larger legislative experience than any other member. As a member of the committee appointed to draft the Declaration of Independence, of ways and means committees, of the board of war and ordnance, of the treasury board, and of the committee on Indian affairs, he applied himself with such characteristic industry that he was forced to write Governor Trumbull in 1777: "I must leave Congress soon . . . for my Constitution will not admit of so close an application to business much longer" (Boutell, p. 100). It was about this time that John Adams spoke of him as "an old Puritan, as honest as an angel and as firm in the cause of American Independence as Mount Atlas" (C. F. Adams, ed., *Familiar Letters of John Adams and His Wife,* 1876, p. 251). Being a member of the committee on the Articles of Confederation, he, as well as Franklin, proposed a plan of union; according to Adams, "Mr. Sherman's was best liked, but very little was finally adopted from either" (*Works of John Adams,* vol. III, 1851, p. 220). He consistently fought any attempts to weaken the credit of the new government by fiat currency or excessive loans. With a courage born of lofty indifference to popular clamor, he urged the frequent levying of high taxes by Congress and by the states (Boutell, p. 104). In 1777 he attended a convention of New England states called to consider the currency, and that body gave expression to his ideas concerning taxation and paper money. Early in 1778 he was a delegate to the New Haven convention on prices, helping to draft its detailed report. His last important actions in Congress had to do with the Connecticut cession of western lands. In making the transfer with a provision for the Western Reserve, he was accused by his old Susquehannah Company friends of abandoning them in their distress, and by others, with perhaps equal inaccuracy, of making a cession that was "nothing but a state juggle contrived by old Roger Sherman to get a side wing confirmation to a thing they had no right to" (William Grayson to James Madison, May 28, 1786, Madison Papers, Library of Congress). At all events, he was toward the end of the Revolution perhaps the most influential figure in Congress, and, according to Jeremiah Wadsworth, "as cunning as the Devil" in managing legislation (C. R. King, ed., *The Life and Correspondence of Rufus King,* I, 1894, p. 221). During his service in Congress he was also a member of the Council of Safety of Connecticut from 1777 to 1779 and again in 1782. In May 1783 he was appointed with Richard Law to revise the statutory law of Connecticut, a codification which was completed in five months (*Acts and Laws of the State of Connecticut,* 1784). From 1784 to 1786 he enjoyed comparative repose for the first time since the outbreak of the Revolution, his chief offices being those of judge of the superior court and mayor of New Haven.

In the latter part of his service in Congress, Sherman had drawn up a series of amendments designed to strengthen the Confederation, the chief of which provided that Congress should have power to regulate commerce, levy imposts, establish a supreme court, and make laws binding on the people. In 1787 he entered the Federal Convention still "disposed to patch up the old scheme of Government" but he soon saw the need of creating a new system (King, I, 221; Farrand, *post,* I, 34–35). Although he was a leading member of the compromise group in the convention, his leanings were toward a national government. On June 11 he introduced the so-called "Connecticut Compromise" (Farrand, I, 196), providing for a dual system of representation, a device he had hinted at eleven years earlier (*Works of John Adams,* II, 499); in the struggle for the adoption of this essential compromise, Sherman took a leading part. Reflecting his Connecticut background rather than an admiration for the British system, he favored an executive dominated by the legislature. His opposition to democratic tendencies was illustrated in his stand for election of congressmen and senators by state legislatures and in his opinion that popular ratification of the Constitution was unnecessary. When Sherman affixed his signature to the Constitution, he achieved the distinction of being the only person to sign that and three other great documents of the Republic—the Articles of Association of 1774, the Declaration of Independence, and the Articles of Confederation. He took a prominent part in the campaign for ratification of the Constitution. Writing under the pseudonym of "A Countryman," he contributed a series of cogent letters addressed "To the People of Connecticut" (*New Haven Gazette,* Nov. 15, 22, 29; Dec. 6, 20, 1787; reprinted in P. L. Ford, *post,* where the first letter is misdated). These letters drew him into a notable correspondence with John Adams on the nature of the government (*Works of John Adams,* VI, 1851, pp. 427–42).

In 1789 he was elected a member of Congress, and in order to take his seat he reluctantly gave up his position as judge of the superior court. He took an active part in the debates of the first session, favoring the impost and opposing amendments to the Constitution, a subject he had already discussed in the press (*New Haven Gazette,* Dec. 18, 1788). In the second session he urged the use of western lands to extinguish the national debt and favored sale to settlers rather than to speculators. He had fought since 1776 for a sound system of credit and voted for Hamilton's measure for the assumption of state debts, but he opposed the measure for locating the government on the Potomac. In 1791 he was elected to fill the place of William Samuel Johnson [*q.v.*] in the Senate, an office which he held until his death.

Always illustrating at its best the Puritan combination of piety and a desire to succeed in practical affairs, Sherman opposed the granting of commissions to "foreign Papists" (*American Historical Review,* April 1896, p. 499) during the Revolution, and likewise opposed confirmation of Gouverneur Morris as minister to France because of an inherent distrust of irreligious natures (Boutell, p. 271). In 1789 he published *A Short Sermon on the Duty of Self-Examination Preparatory to Receiving the Lord's Supper,* which gained the commendation of Ezra Stiles and others. He corresponded with various New England theologians, and his discussion, with the Rev. Samuel Hopkins, of the doctrine of disinterested submission reveals his delight in theology (*Proceedings American Antiquarian Society,* n.s., vol. V, 1889, pp. 437–61). His contemporaries fully recognized his ability, honesty, and adroitness in legislative councils, but they were also fond of recording his personal awkwardness and a certain rusticity of manner. There is a crude but masterly portrait of him by Ralph Earl in the Yale Gallery of Fine Arts. His record attests industry, integrity, devotion to public duty, even moral grandeur. He was twice married: on Nov. 17, 1749, to Elizabeth Hartwell, by whom he had seven children before her death in 1760; and on May 12, 1763, to Rebecca (or Rebekah) Prescott, by whom he had eight. His second wife survived him.

[Sherman left a large mass of MSS. but they are thought to have been destroyed; some are in the Mass. Hist. Soc., in the Trumbull MSS. in the Conn. State Lib., and in the series called "Revolutionary War, 1763–1789" in the same place. A forthcoming biography by Roger Sherman Boardman is the best study, but at present L. H. Boutell, *The Life of Roger Sherman* (1896) is the standard. In addition to sources cited in the text and the usual standard works for the period, the following are useful: *Century Mag.*, Apr. 1889, pp. 803–33; *New England Quart.*, Apr. 1932, pp. 221–36; *Yale Law Journal*, Dec. 1908, pp. 75–84; John Sanderson and Robert Waln, Jr., *Biography of the Signers to the Declaration of Independence*, III (1823), pp. 197–306; V. H. Paltsits, "The Almanacs of Roger Sherman," in *Proc. Am. Antiquarian Soc.*, n.s., vol. XVIII (1907), pp. 213–58; *N. Y. Gazette*, Jan. 22, 1749/50; *Conn. Journal*, July 31, 1793 (obituary); records of the superior court of Conn., in office of secretary of state, vols. XIII–XVIII; *Am. Lit. Magazine*, June 1849, p. 697; P. L. Ford, ed., *Essays of the Constitution . . . 1787–1788* (1892), pp. 211–41; F. B. Dexter, ed., *The Lit. Diary of Ezra Stiles* (3 vols., 1901); Max Farrand, ed., *The Records of the Federal Convention* (3 vols., 1911); E. C. Burnett, ed., *Letters of Members of the Continental Cong.*, vols. I–VI (1921–33); S. E. Baldwin, *Two Centuries of New Milford, Conn. . . .* (1907), 232–55; G. F. Hoar, *Autobiog. of Seventy Years* (1903), I, pp. 7–19; Henry Bond, *Geneals. of the Families and Descendants of the Early Settlers of Watertown, Mass.* (1855), I, p. 431; T. T. Sherman, *Sherman Genealogy* (1920).]   J. P. B.

SHERMAN, STUART PRATT (Oct. 1, 1881–Aug. 21, 1926), literary critic, educator, son of John and Ada Martha (Pratt) Sherman, belonged to an old New England family tracing its descent from Edmund Sherman who came to Massachusetts about 1634. His father, a lover of music and poetry, was, ironically, a druggist who had wandered out to Anita, Iowa, where Stuart was born. In 1882 the family moved to Rolfe, Iowa, and in 1887 to Los Angeles, seeking a more healthful climate for the father, who died in 1892. The family later returned to New England, where Sherman attended Troy Conference Academy at Poultney, Vt., and subsequently the high school in Williamstown, Mass. Entering the sophomore class of Williams College in 1900, he won prizes in Latin, French, and German, and succeeded Harry James Smith [*q.v.*] as editor of the *Williams Literary Monthly*. Graduating in 1903, he did graduate work in English at Harvard, where he was profoundly influenced by Irving Babbitt. He received the degree of Ph.D. in 1906, with a brilliant thesis on John Ford, expanded and published in 1915 as an introduction to his edition of Ford's *'Tis Pity She's a Whore, and The Broken Heart*. In September 1906 he became an instructor at Northwestern University and on Dec. 25 was married to Ruth Bartlett Mears, daughter of Leverett Mears, a

chemistry professor at Williams. In 1907 he accepted a call to the University of Illinois. A letter which he published in the *Nation*, May 14, 1908, attacking the formalism of graduate instruction in English, attracted wide attention. During the summer of 1908 he served as an editorial writer for the *Nation* and was offered a position on its staff, but the University of Illinois countered by raising him to the rank of associate professor. For the next ten years, however, he was a frequent contributor to the *Nation*, with whose policy, under the editorship of Paul Elmer More, he was for a time in almost complete sympathy. He was made a full professor in 1911 and permanent chairman of the English department in 1914. With a group of devoted colleagues, he made it one of the strongest in the Middle West. A natural teacher, he combined sound scholarship with a persuasive emphasis on the living values of literature. His best course, on Matthew Arnold, resulted in the publication of *Matthew Arnold: How to Know Him* (1917), acclaimed by the caustic Irving Babbitt as "the first good book" on the subject (*Nation*, Aug. 2, 1917). In the same year he published *On Contemporary Literature*, an application of Arnold's principles to the chief contemporary writers with devastating results.

The entrance of the United States into the World War fired his patriotism, and in an address on "American and Allied Ideals," delivered on Dec. 1, 1917, before the National Council of Teachers of English, he attacked the philosophy of Nietzsche, particularly as expressed by H. L. Mencken. This assault began an exhilarating literary quarrel with Mencken, which continued intermittently for nearly a decade, with much expenditure of wit by both combatants. Under the influence of the emotions bred by the war, Sherman for a time became almost chauvinistic in his nationalism. Believing intensely in democracy, he thought that contemporary American literature had gone astray through lack of loyalty to the national ideal and that the "spiritually alien strain in our recent literature" was due to "the later importations of European blood and culture." In "Is There Anything to be Said for Literary Traditions?" (*Bookman*, October 1920) he attacked the whole group of modernist critics. The controversy thus begun raged for several years, with a plentiful amount of misunderstanding on both sides. The younger critics in their assault on conventional moral and literary standards were led to adopt the non-moral estheticism of Benedetto Croce as a rallying-point, while Sherman confused his defense of the ethical content of literature with a defense of traditional emotion, nationalism, and Puritanism. In his polemical writings, he used to good effect Arnold's weapons of irony, understatement, and the edged epithet, and he had also acquired from Arnold the exasperating habit of rising to moral altitudes where he became invisible to his adversaries, but his victories, while sometimes real, were often merely rhetorical. He ended by being largely converted to the position of his opponents, confessing that he had erred in trying to make men good instead of happy.

His gradual turning to the left may be followed in *Americans* (1922), *The Genius of America* (1923), and *Points of View* (1924). In 1924 he contributed a series of critical essays to an edition de luxe of *Men of Letters of the British Isles: Portrait Medallions from the Life,* edited by Theodore Spicer-Stimson, and published *My Dear Cornelia,* a series of imaginary conversations with a lady of old-fashioned tastes, in defense of modernism, some of which had appeared in the *Atlantic Monthly.* In April 1924 he became editor of *Books,* the literary supplement of the *New York Herald Tribune,* and thenceforward by his weekly impressionistic essays made it the leading American critical journal of the day. Some of these essays were reprinted in 1926 under the title *Critical Woodcuts.* His death came as the result of a heart attack while swimming ashore from an overturned canoe near his summer cottage at Dunewood on Lake Michigan. He was survived by his wife and a son.

[Jacob Zeitlin and Homer Woodbridge, *Life and Letters of Stuart P. Sherman* (1929), with full bibliog.; see also, G. E. DeMille, *Lit. Criticism in America* (1931); Carl Van Doren, in *Century Mag.,* Aug. 1923; S. J. Kunitz, *Authors Today and Yesterday* (1933); *The Bookman,* June 1922, June 1926; *N. Y. Times,* Aug. 23, 1926; *N. Y. Herald Tribune: Books,* Sept. 26, 1926.]   E. S. B.

SHERMAN, THOMAS WEST (Mar. 26, 1813–Mar. 16, 1879), soldier, was born in Newport, R. I., the son of Elijah and Martha (West) Sherman. He was a descendant of Philip Sherman, who emigrated to America about 1633 and moved in 1638 to Rhode Island, where he settled at Portsmouth. After attending the public schools, Sherman saw no prospect of further education, since his parents were in humble circumstances. At eighteen, when his father disapproved of his centering his hopes on West Point and a soldier's career, he walked to Washington and appealed to President Jackson, who was so impressed by this show of determination and self-reliance that Sherman got his cadetship. He was graduated, July 1, 1836, and commissioned second lieutenant, 3rd Artillery.

In 1838, after two years' active service in the Florida War, he became first lieutenant and served in the Indian Territory, assisting the Cherokee transfer. Then came four more years of the Florida hostilities, service at Fort Moultrie, S. C., and recruiting duty. Promoted captain in May 1846, he served with Taylor's army in the Mexican War, in which he commanded a battery at Buena Vista, rendered conspicuous service, and received the brevet of major. He served at Fort Trumbull, Conn., and Fort Adams, R. I., from 1848 to 1853, when he was assigned to frontier duty in Minnesota. In 1857–58 he assisted in quelling the disturbances in Kansas. While there he married Mary, daughter of Gov. Wilson Shannon [*q.v.*]. Returning to Minnesota, he commanded an expedition to Kettle Lake in 1859 whereby the Sioux were restrained from war.

At the outbreak of the Civil War he was ordered to duties in connection with the defense of Washington. He was promoted major and lieutenant-colonel in the regular army, and brigadier-general of volunteers in rapid succession, and was placed in charge of an expedition to take and hold bases on the southern coast for the use of the blockading fleet. He occupied Port Royal Harbor, S. C., after a naval bombardment, Nov. 7, 1861, and later seized Bull's Bay, S. C., and Fernandina, Fla. His management of this enterprise was marked by skill and judgment. In 1862 he was assigned to the command of a division of Halleck's army, then operating against Corinth. His manner of exercising authority, however, resulted in complaints from some of his subordinates which led to his relief and assignment to the Department of the Gulf. After serving in command of troops above New Orleans from the fall of 1862 to January 1863, he commanded a division in the expedition against Port Hudson, La. On May 27, 1863, he was wounded while gallantly leading an assault on the Confederate works and afterwards lost his right leg by amputation. Promoted colonel, 3rd Artillery, he returned to duty after nine months' sick leave in command of a reserve brigade of artillery and of Forts Jackson and St. Philip, La. From 1864 to 1866 he was successively in command of the defenses of New Orleans, the Southern Division of Louisiana, and of the Eastern District of Louisiana. All these duties he performed with marked energy and efficiency in spite of his physical handicap. He was brevetted brigadier-general, United States Army, for gallant and meritorious service at the capture of Port Hudson, and major general of volunteers for like services during the war. He was mustered out of volunteer service in 1866. After the war he served in command of his regiment at different stations on the Atlantic seaboard until November 1870; soon afterward he was retired from active service as major-general. He died at his home in Newport, R. I., his wife's death having preceded his by a few days; one son survived them. He was an officer of unquestioned ability, but his long career in the old regular army of the Indian frontier in some ways unfitted him for handling volunteers not inured to its iron discipline, and his ingrained training and positive personality sometimes produced friction that lessened the value of his military knowledge and experience.

[*New England Hist. and Geneal. Reg.*, vol. XXIV (1870), p. 163; G. W. Cullum, *Biog. Reg. Officers and Grads. U. S. Mil. Acad.*, vol. I (1891); *Battles and Leaders of the Civil War* (4 vols., 1887–88); *War of the Rebellion: Official Records (Army)*, esp. 1 ser., vol. VI (1882), vol. XVI (1886), pt. 2; *Harper's Weekly*, Nov. 30, 1861; W. E. Birkhimer, "The Third U. S. Artillery," *Jour. Mil. Service Inst.*, Mar. 1893; J. H. Smith, *The War with Mexico* (2 vols., 1919); *Army and Navy Jour.*, Mar. 15, 22, 1879; *Appletons' Ann. Cyc.*, 1879; *N. Y. Tribune*, Mar. 17, 1879.]	T. F. M.

SHERMAN, WILLIAM TECUMSEH (Feb. 8, 1820–Feb. 14, 1891), Union soldier, was born at Lancaster, Ohio, the third son and sixth child of Charles Robert and Mary (Hoyt) Sherman. The family had been in America since about 1634 when Edmund Sherman came from Dedham in Essex, England, to Boston, Mass., with his son, Samuel, and a cousin, the progenitor of Roger Sherman [*q.v.*]. Another son was John Sherman, 1613–1685 [*q.v.*]. Tecumseh's grandfather, Taylor Sherman, of Norwalk, Conn., had served as a commissioner to settle land titles in the Western Reserve, receiving some Ohio lands as compensation. Attracted by these lands, his son, Charles Robert, moved West in 1811, and entered upon the practice of law at Lancaster. He became judge of the state supreme court in 1823 and served until his sudden death in 1829. Most of his eleven children were then distributed among relatives, friends, and neighbors to be cared for, and Tecumseh was welcomed into the family of Thomas Ewing, 1789–1871 [*q.v.*], who was indebted to the boy's father for helping him begin his career as a frontier lawyer. The red-haired lad, known intimately as "Cump," had been named by his father after the noble Shawnee chief, Tecumseh [*q.v.*], but under the influence of his devout Catholic wife, Thomas Ewing permitted him to be baptized with the name of William Tecumseh. Ewing never formally adopted him.

A sound education at a local academy was interrupted suddenly when the boy was "notified" to prepare for West Point (*Memoirs, post,* I, 14). Ewing secured an appointment for his charge in 1836, and Sherman was graduated number six in the class of 1840. He was assigned as second lieutenant, 3rd Artillery, on field service in Florida, and became a first lieutenant in 1841. The following year he was stationed at Fort Moultrie, S. C., where his duties left ample time for him to begin the study of law. During his first leave in 1843 in Lancaster, he became engaged to Eleanor Boyle Ewing (called Ellen), the daughter of his guardian. Returning from this leave, he traveled down the Mississippi River and began an acquaintance with Georgia which, supplemented by a tour of three months in 1844 and a detail at the Augusta arsenal in 1845, provided him a valuable knowledge of the countryside. During the Mexican War he was aide to Philip Kearny and later adjutant to Richard Barnes Mason [*qq.v.*], but he saw so little action that he submitted his resignation and was persuaded to withdraw it only when Persifor Frazer Smith [*q.v.*], in command of the new division of the Pacific, made Sherman his adjutant-general. He was relieved in January 1850 to carry dispatches east for General Scott. On May 1, after an engagement of seven years, he was married to Ellen Ewing in Washington, D. C., an event of great social importance in the capital because of the position of the bride's father.

Sherman served as captain in the subsistence department for a year and a half, and then resigned his commission on Sept. 6, 1853, to become a partner in a branch bank of a St. Louis concern in San Francisco, Cal. Business prospered for a while, but the period of severe depression caused the bank to close in the spring of 1857. He then represented the firm in New York for a short time, but the parent bank itself failed in October, and Sherman voluntarily assumed a heavy personal financial responsibility for losses to friends who had given him money to invest for them. His efforts to return to the army failed and he established a partnership with Thomas and Hugh Boyle Ewing [*q.v.*], practising law in Leavenworth, Kan. He lost the only case he tried. Contact with the garrison at Leavenworth increased his eagerness to rejoin the service, but after other attempts failed he applied for and received the post of superintendent of a new military college about to be opened at Alexandria, La., now Louisiana State University. He was conspicuously successful in this work, in which he was engaged from October 1859 until Jan. 18, 1861, endearing himself to his co-workers, and winning many friends.

Before the secession of Louisiana compelled him to resign he was even offered a high commission in the Confederate army. He later accepted the presidency of a St. Louis street railway. This was a very trying time for Sherman. Failure had dogged his footsteps; his industry, his honesty, his recognized abilities for mastering innumerable details had—in the army, in finance, in education, in industry—availed him nothing. He had been forced, time after time, to accept the tactful hospitality of the Ewing household for his family, and had often held off with some difficulty his particular *bête noir*—the management of the Ewing salt-works in Ohio, a means of livelihood which Thomas Ewing had offered him again and again out of genuine kindness.

The prospect of war between the Union and the South caused Sherman real anguish. He regarded the preservation of the Union and the integrity of the Constitution with the same fervor—almost religious—as did Thomas Ewing, from whose fire it had probably been kindled. He also loved the South and her people. Everything must be done to avert war; if it came, it must be brought to a conclusion as swiftly as possible, and the South must be returned to the fold with no further punishment than the sufferings which the actual conflict would mete out to her. Here lies the spring of Sherman's action from the day he parted from his Southern friends; the key to his prophetic views on the proportions of the war, to the ruthless march through Georgia, to his liberal peace terms, and to his consistent opposition to Congressional reconstruction.

At last when the regular army was increased in May 1861, Sherman was appointed colonel of the new 13th Infantry, and in July was assigned to command a brigade in General McDowell's army. With this command he shared in the disaster of Bull Run. He was advanced to the rank of brigadier-general of volunteers a month later, and became second in command in Kentucky to Robert Anderson [*q.v.*], inheriting the thankless job of trying to hold the state with little more than home guards when Anderson's poor health forced him to relinquish it. His anxiety over the raw recruits for whose lives he was responsible preyed upon his mind at this time, and his nervous temperament led him to overestimate the difficulty of his position, the forces of the enemy, and the number of troops required—although, as it was proved later, the last was moderate enough. His efforts to keep newspaper reporters out of his lines in the belief that the enemy learned valuable information from this source unfortunately aroused the enmity of the press, so that the rumour that Sherman's mind was giving way spread quickly to officials and to the public. Buell was sent to assume command in Kentucky and Sherman went to Missouri to report to Halleck. He was received with coldness and suspicion and so bitter was his resentment that he even contemplated suicide. Shortly after he returned from leave, he was assigned to the District of Cairo, Grant's former command. After the capture of the forts, he joined Grant with a division of volunteers and took a prominent part in the battle of Shiloh and the advance to Corinth. The frightful carnage at Shiloh again gave the newspapers a chance to strike at Sherman, and they reported that the Federals had been surprised in their camps. True it is, that sufficient preparation had not been made, and it may be supposed that Sherman's experience in Kentucky made him very wary of the camp rumour that Johnston's army was moving against him (see Lewis, *post*, p. 218 ff.). Sherman's command, however, was vigorous and he had four horses shot from under him during the battle. He was promoted major-general of volunteers with rank from May 1, 1862.

In July 1862, Grant succeeded Halleck in charge of the western armies and sent Sherman to Memphis to place it in a state of defense. Sherman suppressed guerrilla warfare, established civil authority on a firm basis, organized a charity drive, and would have brought the cotton trade under control had not Federal authorities obstructed him. Pillaging was strictly forbidden to his soldiers. The Mississippi was now open as far down as Memphis, and as far up from the mouth as Port Hudson. The only strong points remaining were Vicksburg, on the first high ground below Memphis, and the fortified naval base at Fort Hindman, or Arkansas Post, on the Arkansas River, which threatened the western flank of any advance. Grant proposed to move against Vicksburg. He, himself, was to hold Pemberton at the Yalobusha where the general advance of Nov. 24 had pushed him, and Sherman was sent down the river to take Vicksburg. Raids on his communications, however, forced Grant to fall back and release Pemberton, and rendered Sherman's expedition hopeless. After fruitless attempts at an assault he reëmbarked his troops on Jan. 2, 1863, and turned them over to General McClernand, who had arrived with orders from the president to command the forces on the river. These forces were reorganized into the Army of the Mississippi, with two army corps, one of which Sherman commanded. At Sherman's suggestion, McClernand, with the assistance of Porter's gunboat flotilla, proceeded to the capture of Arkansas Post, then returned to the Mississippi. Grant reorganized the whole force into the Army of the Tennessee, with four corps, Sherman retaining his own, the XV, and moved down the river to open his amphibious campaign which led to the surrender of Vicksburg on July 4, 1863. For his distinguished service in this campaign Sherman was made brigadier-general in the regular army.

In September, Sherman, with his own corps and other troops, was sent back to Memphis and thence eastward to the relief of Chattanooga. Grant's advancement to supreme command in the west placed Sherman in command of the Army of the Tennessee, but strong forces had to remain at Vicksburg and Memphis, so that he could assemble for the Chattanooga operation but little more than he had with him. His command was moved across the rear of Hooker's and Thomas' troops, already in position, and formed the left element of the general movement of Nov. 24, which raised the siege of Chattanooga. The next day Sherman's advance had reached Ringgold, when he was recalled to move to the relief of Knoxville. Starting at once, without waiting for his transport to join him, he reached Knoxville on Dec. 6 only to find that Longstreet had raised the siege and gone back to Virginia. He then placed his troops in winter quarters along the Tennessee River. This campaign, for which he received the thanks of Congress, had been fought under conditions extraordinarily distressing to Sherman. His son and namesake, nine years old, who had been with him during the quiet period after Vicksburg, died of typhoid fever at Memphis as the expedition was starting. In January he went down to Vicksburg to conduct an expedition against the Confederate base at Meridian. Arranging with Banks at New Orleans for a feint toward Mobile, he moved out with four divisions to Meridian, which he reached without serious opposition. After destroying the arsenal and depots he returned to Vicksburg.

The great event of the spring of 1864 was the appointment of Grant as lieutenant-general commanding all the armies. He went east in March, turning over his command to Sherman; McPherson succeeded to the command of the Army of the Tennessee. Grant's opinion of these two great lieutenants was expressed in a letter thanking them as "the men to whom above all others" he was indebted for his successes (Sherman, *Memoirs*, 1875, I, 399). The combined plan for 1864 called for an advance by Meade's Army of the Potomac against Lee and Richmond, and an advance by Sherman against Johnston and Atlanta. Sherman issued orders for a concentration about Chattanooga, and moved his headquarters to that place late in April. His field force consisted of the Armies of the Cumberland (Thomas), the Tennessee (McPherson) and the Ohio (Schofield)—in all about 100,000 men. Opposed was Johnston with some 60,000. His first care was to assure his supply. His base was Nashville, 150 miles north, with one single track railway, open to raids, and poorly supplied with rolling stock. He took complete possession of this road, cut off all civilian traffic, reduced military supplies to the strictest essentials, impounded all rolling stock coming in from the north, in spite of the complaints of the northern railways, and reduced field equipment and rations to a minimum. By these stringent measures he succeeded in accumulating a reserve of supplies sufficient to permit him to commence operations by May 5, the date set by Grant.

Johnston was at Dalton, holding Buzzard-Roost Gap, where the railway crossed Rocky-face ridge. Sherman moved Thomas and Schofield directly against Buzzard-Roost, and McPherson around Johnston's left through Snake Creek Gap. McPherson passed through the Gap on May 9, but failed to take Resaca or to cut the railway. Johnston then fell back upon Resaca. Leaving a detachment of the railway, Sherman moved around by McPherson's route and on May 15 took Resaca and reopened his rail communications. He then followed on to Kingston and established an advanced depot there. Johnston fell back into the rugged hills behind Allatoona Pass. Sherman moved westward off the railway again and pushed up toward the Allatoona-Kenesaw Mountain line. Allatoona Pass was occupied on June 1. Progress was now slow. Johnston was entrenched in a strong position. Every advance against it was covered by hasty field works—not as a defensive, but as an offensive weapon. Violent assaults upon Kenesaw at the end of June failed, but a new extension of Sherman's right forced the abandonment of that position. Johnston fell back to the Chattahoochee. Schofield effected a crossing beyond Johnston's right, which forced him to give up the river line on July 9 and retire to the line of Peachtree Creek, immediately covering Atlanta. Here Johnston was relieved by Hood. Sherman extended his left, swinging around Atlanta by the north and east and drew violent attacks from Hood. The defenses of Atlanta being too strong for an assault, Sherman opened a regular siege, then worked his force around by his own right, west of the city, and cut the railways to Montgomery and Macon. Hood evacuated Atlanta on the night of Sept. 1. This victorious campaign won Sherman his promotion to the rank of major-general in the regular army, Aug. 12, 1864. He at once ordered the removal of the civil population from Atlanta, and proposed to Hood an armistice for this purpose. After some correspondence, in which Hood attempted without success to represent the proceeding as barbarous, it was carried out (*Memoirs,* II, 117 ff.).

Sherman had in mind from the first a further movement from Atlanta to some point on the seacoast. After correspondence with Grant, the plan took definite shape. Thomas and Schofield were sent back to hold Hood and to protect Tennessee. On Nov. 15, after destroying installations of military value, the army of 62,000 men marched out of Atlanta, breaking all communications, and disappeared for a month. The "march through Georgia" centered upon Sherman one of the bitterest controversies of the Civil War. His purpose was to break the resistance of the South by cutting off the supply of her armies and Georgia was the only untouched source of supply. The army was under orders to live off the country, to destroy war supplies, public buildings, railroads, and manufacturing shops. Foraging was strictly defined, and the destruction of private property was authorized only upon the order of the highest commanders and when some act of violence impeded the progress of the army. The execution of the orders, however, was extremely difficult to control. The army was in the pink of condition and in a holiday mood. Thousands of stragglers, negro and white, so-called "bummers," or soldiers detached from their own regiments, fringed the marching ranks and considered themselves under no orders. Wheeler's Confederate cavalrymen, also, committed acts for which the Federals were held responsible by an undiscriminating countryside. Many acts of pillage did occur, and it appears obvious that Sherman's discipline was not strict enough, a judgment which his own men rested upon him (see Hitchcock, *post,* p. 86). Under no illusions whatsoever as to the terrible effects of his march (see *Home Letters,* p. 298), Sherman contended that wanton destruction was prevented in so far as possible, and that there was no serious personal violence to noncombatants. The principle that the war could be terminated soon by bringing it home to a civilian population by the destruction of goods rather than life was a tenet to which Sherman clung. Aside from condemnation and acclaim, it is on the basis of his deliberate exploitation of this principle that he has been called the first modern general (see Hart, preface). On Jan. 10, 1865, Sherman received for the second time the thanks of Congress.

The city of Savannah was occupied on Dec. 21. On the first of February began the march northward through the Carolinas—a march in comparison to which, as Sherman said, that through Georgia was child's play. In seventeen days the army reached Columbia, forcing the evacuation of Charleston. That night Columbia was burned, and Sherman was charged with having ordered the burning. His orders were, however, to destroy only war materials and public buildings (see Lewis, *post,* p. 501). The evidence, reviewed by a nonpartisan, indicates that the evacuating troops set cotton on fire, that a high wind fanned it, that the citizens distributed liquor too liberally, that negroes and released Union prisoners itching for revenge applied the torch further, but that the officers adopted drastic measures to save the city (see Hart, *post,* p. 366 ff.). Johnston, commanding the Confederate forces in the Carolinas, was unable to make any effective resistance. On Mar. 22 Sherman effected a junction at Goldsboro with Schofield's corps. While his troops were being resupplied, he made a hasty trip by sea to visit Grant's headquarters at Citypoint on the James River, and there held the consultation with President Lincoln which so impressed upon him the government's plan for a liberal peace (*Home Letters,* p. 336). Sherman then moved upon Raleigh, but Lee had surrendered on Apr. 9, and now Johnston also made overtures for surrender. On Apr. 17 the two generals met, and liberal terms were granted by Sherman. In his eagerness to put an end to the war he inserted in his draft terms which were political in their nature and beyond his province. This fact, however, was explicitly recognized in the agreement signed, which, in effect, was merely an engagement by the generals to do their utmost to secure approval by their respective governments. But the feeling at Washington was bitter by reason of the assassination of Lincoln, and the agreement was repudiated with a vigor and discourtesy which deeply offended Sherman. At the final grand review in Washington, he publicly refused to shake hands with Secretary Stanton, although he became reconciled later.

Sherman took up his first post-war station at St. Louis in command of the Division of the Mississippi. He lent great assistance in the construction of the transcontinental railway and in controlling and mollifying the Indian opposition accomplished, in his own opinion, more of permanent value than during the war (Hart, p.

420). In the reorganization of the army, Grant became general and Sherman succeeded him as lieutenant-general on July 25, 1866. Soon afterward, he was called to Washington to take temporary command of the army, the President proposing to send Grant on a diplomatic mission to Mexico, escorting the minister accredited to President Juarez. Grant objected to this, considering it a political maneuver to get him out of Washington and Sherman was designated for the mission. The mission went to Mexico but failed to find Juarez; it constituted, however, a part of the diplomatic pressure exerted upon France for withdrawal of support to Maximilian. Upon Grant's inauguration as president, Sherman became general commanding the army on Mar. 4, 1869. Schofield, then still secretary of war, issued an order the next day to settle the long-standing quarrel of the commanding general and the heads of the staff departments, by placing them under his orders. Rawlins, however, who now became secretary of war, saw this as a diminution of the importance of his office, and rescinded the order. Although he had favored the system announced by Schofield, Grant refused to interfere. Sherman was deeply hurt by this and after a year spent on leave in Europe, 1871–72, moved his headquarters to St. Louis in 1874. A compromise having been reached, he returned to Washington in 1876, although the political chaos of Washington had always distressed him. He was untiring in the exercise of his command up to the moment of his retirement. One of his most important contributions to the army was his establishment of the school at Fort Leavenworth in 1881 which, under various names and forms, has had a continuous existence ever since, and has developed into the most influential agency of the service in shaping doctrine and training methods.

He retired from active service on Nov. 1, 1883, established himself in St. Louis, and remained there until 1886, when he moved to New York City. Repeated efforts were made to draw him into political life, especially in the Republican convention of 1884, when only his positive veto prevented a definite move for his nomination for the presidency. He established no business connections, but lived quietly and at leisure. His correspondence was very large, and he was in frequent attendance at military reunions and celebrations, besides being in constant demand at private social affairs. He died of pneumonia in New York City at the age of seventy-one and was survived by six of his eight children. At the end, while unconscious, Sherman received the last rites of the Catholic church,

but had never been a member. Ellen Sherman had died three years before, deeply absorbed to the last in her Catholic charities. Sherman was tall and erect, with sharp, dark eyes, reddish hair and beard, and deeply lined face. His features were grave and severe in repose, but animated and expressive in conversation, of which he was no mean master. His mind was extraordinarily quick; it flashed from premise to conclusion so rapidly that his associates could not follow, and even he himself seemed unconscious of the process. This rapidity, together with his nervous temperament, gave him the reputation of an erratic, even of a mentally unbalanced, genius—a reputation totally foreign to the fact. He was a cordial and devoted friend, his relations with Grant, in particular, being of the most intimate and confidential character. In public as well as in private address, in his letters and in the *Memoirs*, first published in 1875, his characteristics were strikingly displayed. The famous statement, "war . . . is all hell," was made by Sherman in a speech at Columbus, Ohio, on Aug. 11, 1880, and was reported in the *Ohio State Journal* of the following day. Augustus Saint-Gaudens [*q.v.*] modeled a bust of Sherman during the last years of the testy old general's life. The magnificent equestrian statue in Central Park, New York City, grew out of the first effort.

[Sherman and Ewing papers, Manuscript Division, Lib. of Cong.; T. T. Sherman, *Sherman Geneal.* (1920); *Memoirs of General William T. Sherman* (2 vols., 2nd ed. revised, 1886); M. A. DeWolfe Howe, ed., *Home Letters of General Sherman* (1909); R. S. Thorndike, ed., *Sherman Letters, Corresp. between General and Senator Sherman* (1894); Lloyd Lewis, *Sherman—Fighting Prophet* (1932); B. H. Liddell Hart, *Sherman—Soldier, Realist, American* (1929); W. L. Fleming, *General W. T. Sherman As College President* (1912); Henry Hitchcock, *Marching with Sherman* (1927); J. F. Rhodes, "Sherman's March to the Sea," *Am. Hist. Rev.*, Apr. 1901; Ferdinand von Meerheimb, *Sherman's Feldzug in Georgien* (1869, Berlin); *Boston Evening Transcript*, Feb. 14, 1891. See also a critical estimate of the *Memoirs* in an article by W. B. Stevens in *Mo. Hist. Rev.*, Jan. 1931.]   O. L. S., Jr.

SHERRY, LOUIS (1856–June 9, 1926), restaurateur, was born probably in St. Albans, Vt. His father was a carpenter, born in France; his mother was of New England Anglo-Saxon stock. Young Sherry, forced by circumstances to seek work at an early age, found a place as boy of all work in a hotel in Montreal, Canada. A year or two later he went to New York and, after a period of hardship, obtained a place as "bus boy" in a large hotel. There he was so punctual and efficient that he was presently promoted to be a waiter. In this position he still further distinguished himself by careful attention to every complaint and suggestion, and by his study of the patrons' personal and gustatory eccentricities. He was about twenty-two when he was hired by a large hotel at Elberon, N. J., then a very fashionable seaside resort, to take charge of its kitchen and dining room during its summer season. He was by this time planning a restaurant and catering business of his own, and during his two summers at Elberon he was promised the patronage of many wealthy New Yorkers, guests at the hotel. At the end of the second season he had saved $1,300, and with this capital he opened his first restaurant and confectionery at Thirty-eighth Street and Sixth Avenue, New York, in 1881. From the first he insisted upon the finest of materials and the most careful workmanship in every product of his house, and his motto was, "Never disappoint a patron." After he had prospered a little, he made journeys to Paris to perfect himself in culinary lore. A rapidly growing business encouraged him to move in 1890 to a larger and finer place at Thirty-seventh Street and Fifth Avenue. Here the aristocracy of the city favored him so greatly with patronage that in 1898 he moved to still more sumptuous quarters at Forty-fourth Street and Fifth Avenue, where he remained twenty years. This last place, with its costly paintings and tapestries and its cellar full of fine wines, represented an investment of $2,000,000. Frank A. Munsey, the publisher, lived in a luxurious suite in the building throughout Sherry's tenure. During some thirty years, many of the most elaborate dinners, balls, débuts, and other social, business, and political functions took place at Sherry's. The Seeley dinner in 1896, C. K. G. Billings' dinner on horseback in 1900, and other noted and bizarre affairs were given in his rooms. To prepare a dinner for 300 guests, given by a millionaire, he once went to Savannah, Ga., traveling with his staff in a Pullman sleeper and two baggage cars, carrying all china, linen, food, and decorations with him. On another occasion he sent a staff of twenty to San Francisco, where they took over a private residence for the elder J. P. Morgan's use, and he prepared some elaborate entertainments at which Morgan was host. When the national prohibition laws went into effect he disposed of his stock of wines to favored customers and closed his restaurant in 1919. He then opened a confectionery and catering business on Park Avenue, which he operated until his death. He was survived by his widow, Marie Bertha Sherry and by their son.

[Edward Hungerford, *The Story of Louis Sherry* (1929); A. S. Crockett, *Peacocks on Parade* (1931), esp. pp. 170–71, 184–93; I. N. P. Stokes, *The Iconography of Manhattan Island* (5 vols., 1926); *Where and How to Dine in New York* (copr. 1903); *New York Times* and *World* (N. Y.), June 10, 1926; death certificate, Bureau of Records, Dept. of Health, 139 Centre St., N. Y. C.]   A. F. H.

SHERWIN, THOMAS (Mar. 26, 1799–July 23, 1869), educator, was born in Westmoreland, N. H., only son of David Sherwin and Hannah (Pritchard) Sherwin, both of whom were natives of Boxford, Mass. His father, originally a farmer, had gone into business but had failed. Seeking to retrieve his losses, he went to New Hampshire, where he lived in Westmoreland, New Ipswich, and Temple. For six years, 1807–13, Thomas lived in the home of his uncle, Dr. James Crombie, in Temple, where he earned his board by small services. He was educated in the local district school and had some private lessons from his friend, Solomon P. Miles, a Dartmouth student. In 1813 he was apprenticed to Messrs. Samuel and Sewell Rockwood, a firm of clothiers in Groton, Mass. In 1819 his employers released him from his contract so that he might teach in a district school in Harvard, Mass. A year later an appointment as teacher in the Central School in Groton enabled him to enter the academy there in the spring. In March 1821 he entered the academy at New Ipswich and, after a few months of intensive preparatory study, matriculated at Harvard College, where he earned his college expenses by teaching school each winter.

Upon his graduation in 1825 among the ten best scholars in his class he was elected headmaster of the academy in Lexington, Mass. A year later he became tutor in mathematics at Harvard, where he spent his spare time in reading Blackstone and Coke with Elias Phinney, an attorney of Charlestown. Giving up his intention of becoming a lawyer, he tried engineering and in 1827 was employed under Col. Loammi Baldwin, 1780–1838 [q.v.], on the dry docks and other works at Charlestown and at Portsmouth. Later in the same year a pulmonary affection obliged him to withdraw from this work. In December 1828 he opened a private school for boys in Boston; in the following year he was elected sub-master of the English High School, which was then under the charge of his friend, Solomon P. Miles, and in May 1836, in recognition of his important contributions to the improvement of secondary school instruction, he was elected a member of the American Academy of Arts and Sciences. On June 10 of that year he married Mary King Gibbens, daughter of Daniel L. and Mary (King) Gibbens of Boston. Upon the resignation of Miles in 1837, he became principal of the school, a position he held until his death. Under his highly efficient administration, the English High School, the first to be called high school in the United States (established 1821), became the leading educational institution of its grade in the country. He staffed it with a remarkably able group of instructors, himself teaching mathematics. As its reputation grew, it attracted many visitors from other states, and inspired the establishment of similar schools elsewhere. Sherwin was one of the founders of the American Institute of Instruction in 1830, of the Massachusetts State Teachers' Association in 1845, and of the *Massachusetts Teacher* in 1847. He was one of the original editors of the *Massachusetts Teacher* and served as a member of the editorial board at intervals throughout his life, and he was a frequent contributor to the *American Annals of Education*. He was active in the establishment of the Massachusetts Institute of Technology, of which he was a director and counselor until the year of his death. His best known works are *Elementary Treatise on Algebra* (copyright 1841) and *Common School Algebra* (1845), for many years standard textbooks.

[R. C. Waterston, *Address on the Life and Character of Thomas Sherwin* (1870) ; *Am. Jour. of Educ.,* June 1860, Sept. 1865 ; C. Northend, *Annals Am. Inst. of Instruction* (1884) ; J. D. Philbrick, in *Memoirs of Several Deceased Members New England Hist. Geneal. Soc.* (1878) ; obituary in *Boston Transcript,* July 24, 1869.]   R. F. S.

SHERWOOD, ADIEL (Oct. 3, 1791–Aug. 18, 1879), Baptist clergyman, educator, was born at Fort Edward, N. Y. His father, Adiel, who had married a second cousin, Sarah (Sherwood), was a descendant of Thomas Sherwood who had emigrated to Boston in 1634 and in 1645 had settled in Stratford, Conn. The elder Adiel was a farmer, Revolutionary soldier, member of the New York legislature, and a personal friend of George Washington. The son entered Middlebury College, Vermont, in 1813, but after three years transferred to Union College, Schenectady, N. Y., where he was graduated in 1817. He then spent one year at Andover Theological Seminary.

Threatened with tuberculosis, on the advice of physicians he removed to Georgia, taking with him recommendations to leading Baptist ministers of that state. He landed in Savannah in 1818, and was soon the ardent and effective helper of every progressive movement in the Baptist denomination. Ordained at Bethesda Church, Green County, Mar. 20, 1820, he at once began a ministry that was long and apostolic in its zeal and effectiveness. Amid the pioneer conditions of that day he devoted much time to itinerant preaching over wide areas of

Georgia. He organized churches and advocated missions, Sunday schools, and Bible societies. His laborious service is evinced by the fact that in 1828 he preached 333 sermons in forty different counties. He was at different times, and for longer or shorter periods, pastor of many country and town churches, a number of which he had established. In his church at Eatonton, in 1827, there started a revival, which spread over much of the state and resulted in the addition of 16,000 members to the churches of three Baptist associations. As a speaker he was clear, logical, and forceful.

Though first of all a preacher, he was also an organizer of ability. In 1820 he prepared a resolution, adopted by Sarepta Association, which led to the founding of the Baptist State Convention in 1822. In 1823 he introduced a resolution into the Triennial Convention, urging all the states to organize state conventions. He was clerk and treasurer of the Baptist State Convention of Georgia for many years. Greatly interested in education, he taught several years in Georgia academies and started a manual labor school and a theological school at Eatonton. He was instrumental in the establishment of Mercer Institute (later Mercer University) ; was a professor in Columbian College (now George Washington University), Washington, D. C., in 1837–38; taught sacred literature at Mercer from 1838 to 1841; and was president successively of Shurtleff College, Illinois, 1841–46, Masonic College, Lexington, Mo., 1848–49, and Marshall College, Griffin, Ga., from 1857 until the Civil War. From 1852 to 1857 he was pastor at Cape Girardeau, Mo.

A diligent and instructive writer for the religious press, he also published several pamphlets and books, the most important of which were *A Gazetteer of the State of Georgia* (1827), *The Jewish and Christian Churches* (1850), and *Notes on the New Testament* (2 vols., 1856). He was a vigorous friend of foreign and home missions, steadily opposing anti-mission propaganda, and serving as secretary of the American Indian Missionary Association. In 1865 he settled in St. Louis, Mo., where he resided until his death. He had a genius for friendship with important men, was intimate with the leading ministers of America, and was personally acquainted with many prominent national officials. He was twice married; first, May 17, 1821, to Anne Adams Smith, widow of Gov. Peter Early [*q.v.*] ; she died in November 1822 and in May 1824 he married Emma Heriot of Charleston, S. C., who with one son, Thomas Adiel Sherwood [*q.v.*], and four daughters survived him.

[J. H. Campbell, *Ga. Baptists: Hist. and Biog.* (1847); *Hist. of the Baptist Denomination in Ga.* (1881); B. D. Ragsdale, *Story of Ga. Baptists* (copr. 1932); minutes of Ga. Baptist associations and of the Baptist State Convention; William Cathcart, *The Baptist Encyc.* (1881); Julia L. Sherwood, *Memoir of Adiel Sherwood, D.D.* (1884); *Mo. Republican* (St. Louis), Aug. 20, 1879.]   W. J. M.

SHERWOOD, ISAAC RUTH (Aug. 13, 1835–Oct. 15, 1925), editor, soldier, congressman, was born in Stanford, Dutchess County, N. Y., the son of Aaron and Maria (Yeomans) Sherwood. He was of English and Scotch ancestry, a descendant of the eighth generation from Thomas Sherwood who came to America about 1634. His father enlisted for service in the War of 1812, and both grandfathers and a great-grandfather were under arms in the American Revolution. He attended the Hudson River Institute at Claverack, N. Y., Antioch College, Yellow Springs, Ohio, then under the presidency of Horace Mann, where he studied from 1854 to 1856 and the Ohio Law College, Poland, Ohio. He early developed an interest in journalism, and while a law student, he purchased a weekly paper, the *Williams County Gazette*, in Bryan, Ohio. The most distinguished episode of Sherwood's editorial career occurred when, after having dared to give a favorable review to Walt Whitman's *Leaves of Grass* in his newspaper, he received a note of gratitude from the author and an autographed portrait. He was elected mayor of Bryan and probate-judge of Williams County. Enlisting in the Civil War as a private in the 14th Ohio Infantry, he participated in one of the first engagements of the war at Philippi, W. Va. After his three months' term had expired, he joined the 111th Ohio Volunteers, and rose to the rank of lieutenant-colonel in 1864. Thereafter he was continually in command of the regiment, and in February 1865 he was brevetted brigadier-general for his gallant services at Resaca, Ga., and at Franklin and Nashville, Tenn. The explosion of a shell near him while in East Tennessee destroyed the hearing in one ear. He was then transferred to the East and served through the North Carolina campaign.

After the cessation of hostilities he resigned his commission and returned to newspaper work on the *Toledo Commercial* and then on the *Cleveland Leader*. He served as secretary of state of Ohio from 1869 to 1873, and during his incumbency organized the bureau of statistics. He was a Republican congressman from the Toledo district from 1873 to 1875, but because of his financial views did not receive a renomination. He then purchased the *Toledo Journal* which he

edited for nine years. From 1878 to 1884 he was also probate-judge of Lucas County, an office to which he was first elected by the National Greenback Party in whose ranks he was a prominent leader until he joined the Democrats in 1879. He edited the Canton *News-Democrat* from 1888 to 1898, but subsequently returned to Toledo. In 1906 he was somewhat unexpectedly elected to Congress where he served seven successive terms. For many years he was chairman of the House committee on invalid pensions. He was an aggressive advocate of large appropriations for that purpose, and sponsored the Sherwood "Dollar-a-Day" law for Civil War veterans, 1912. Nevertheless he became inclined toward pacifism before America's entrance into the World War and bitterly opposed large expenditures for preparedness (see the *New York Times,* January 5, March 8, 1916). Upon the passage of the war resolution of Apr. 6, 1917, he was the only Ohioan in Congress to vote in the negative. He was defeated in the Republican landslide of 1920 but was elected again in 1922. Failing to be returned two years later he retired from public life when almost ninety years of age, just fifty years after the completion of his first congressional term.

He was an ardent sportsman and the author of a popular humorous poem, *The Army Grayback* (1889), and his *Memories of the War* (1923). An orthodox Presbyterian and a total abstainer from the use of tobacco and liquor, he denounced the Volstead Act and the Anti-Saloon League in his later years. He was overcome by smoke during a fire in 1925 in the apartment house in which he lived in Toledo. Pernicious anemia developed afterward, and he died a few months later, survived by a son, a daughter, and a grand-daughter whom he had adopted. His wife Katharine Margaret Brownlee Sherwood [*q.v.*], to whom he had been married on Sept. 1, 1859, preceded him in death.

[Information from R. Lincoln Long, Toledo, Ohio; *Who's Who in America,* 1924–25; *Biog. Dir. Am. Cong.* (1928); Clark Waggoner, ed., *Hist. of the City of Toledo and Lucas County* (1888); Harvey Scribner, *Memoirs of Lucas County and the City of Toledo* (1910), vol. II; N. O. Winter, *A Hist. of Northwest Ohio.* (1917), vol. II; Whitelaw Reid, *Ohio in the War* (1868), vol. I; B. J. Hendrick, "Pork-Barrel Pensions," *World's Work,* Mar., Apr. 1915; *Review of Reviews* (N. Y.), June 1912; *Toledo Blade, Toledo News-Bee,* Oct. 16, 1925.]   F. P. W.

SHERWOOD, KATHARINE MARGARET BROWNLEE (Sept. 24, 1841–Feb. 15, 1914), writer, reformer, known as Kate Brownlee Sherwood, was the daughter of Judge James Brownlee, a well-educated Scotsman who rose to distinction in eastern Ohio, and Rebecca

(Mullen) Brownlee, a member of a Pennsylvania family active in public affairs. She was born in Poland, Ohio, and spent her youth there. She received her early education in the local schools and in the Poland Union Seminary. She was married to Isaac Ruth Sherwood [q.v.] on Sept. 1, 1859, and went with him to Bryan, Ohio, where he was editing the *Williams County Gazette.* With youthful enthusiasm she promptly began to act as his assistant on this country newspaper. She learned every part of a printer's trade, wrote up the local news, and often supplied editorials. During the Civil War, while her husband was serving in the army, she continued to publish the paper. They moved to Toledo, Ohio, in the period following the war and thereafter Mrs. Sherwood identified herself with many civic activities. She continued her journalistic work, contributing to Cleveland and Toledo dailies, and, after 1875, when her husband purchased the *Toledo Journal,* she assisted in the editorial management of that paper for about nine years. From 1883 to 1898 she edited the woman's department of the *National Tribune,* the official organ of the Grand Army of the Republic. After General Sherwood became congressman from Ohio she acted as Washington correspondent for a newspaper syndicate. She was an active worker in the Women's Press Club of Toledo, and in her later years was elected honorary president of the Ohio Newspaper Women's Association. In addition to her journalistic writings she published patriotic playlets for use in schools, translations from the French and German, several books of selections, and two volumes of verse: *Camp-Fire, Memorial-Day, and other Poems* (1885), and *Dream of the Ages, a Poem of Columbia* (1893). One of her compositions, "The Flag that Makes Men Free," was often used at patriotic gatherings and had a circulation of over one hundred thousand copies.

Mrs. Sherwood became most widely known for her work in national associations of women. In 1879 she organized a number of societies auxiliary to the G. A. R. in the West. In 1883 these were united with the New England societies to form the Woman's Relief Corps, of which she became the first national secretary and the second national president. She did her most important work in this organization as chairman of the committee on pensions for soldiers' widows. She was also a member of the National Council of Women, and a worker on national committees of the D. A. R. In her own city she did pioneer work for women's clubs and for suffrage. Especially valuable was her cooperation in the Education League of Toledo and in the Centre University Extension Society. The breadth of her local interests is attested by the fact that she was at the same time a member of the Presbyterian church, an honorary member of the Council of Jewish Women, and the patroness of a Catholic hospital. In the midst of an active public career she found refreshment in wide reading and in domestic life. Her home, always a center of gracious hospitality, her two children and one adopted grandchild, remained absorbing interests. She was warmly admired by her contemporaries for her beauty, her forceful public speaking, and her work for civic betterment. At the funeral service held for her in Washington, D. C., Secretary of State Bryan, a valued personal friend, read a selection from his lecture "The Prince of Peace." Her tolerant spirit, free from all animosity, received due recognition in 1887 when she was asked to write a poem for the unveiling of a memorial to Albert Sidney Johnston [q.v.] at New Orleans.

[Information from a grand-daughter; *Who's Who in America,* 1912–13; N. O. Winter, *A Hist. of Northwest Ohio* (1917); Harvey Scribner, ed., *Memoirs of Lucas County and the City of Toledo* (1910), vol. II; *Toledo Times,* Dec. 1, 1912; *Evening Star* (Washington, D. C.), Feb. 16, 1914.]   B. M. S.

SHERWOOD, MARY ELIZABETH WILSON (Oct. 27, 1826–Sept. 12, 1903), author, was born in Keene, N. H., the eldest of seven children of James and Mary Lord (Richardson) Wilson. Her great-grandfather, Robert Wilson, a Presbyterian, came to America from Ireland in the first migration of Scotch-Irish to America and fought in the Revolution. Her grandfather, James Wilson, and her father were both members of Congress. Mary attended a private school but was not a good student and was reported to her parents by the village librarian as reading too many novels. Her first story, sent anonymously to the *Social Gazette,* brought her mother's reproof. After the family became Unitarians, she was sent to the school conducted by George Barrell Emerson [q.v.] in Boston. In driving there from Keene in winter on the outside of the stage coach she contracted the rheumatism that tormented her through life. When her father went to Iowa as surveyor-general about 1842, she accompanied him, meeting Charles Dickens in Washington on the way. During her father's term in Congress, 1847–50, she acted as his housekeeper and hostess in Washington, her mother having died. She was married in Keene on Nov. 12, 1851, to John Sherwood, a New York lawyer.

After her marriage she contributed to New York and Boston newspapers, to the *Atlantic Monthly, Scribner's Monthly, Appletons' Jour-*

nal, the *Galaxy, Harper's Magazine,* and *Frank Leslie's Weekly* (Willard and Livermore, *post*). Many verses appeared under the initials M. E. W. S. Her published volumes include *The Sarcasm of Destiny, or Nina's Experience* (1878), *Amenities of Home* (1881), *Home Amusements* (1881), *Etiquette* (1884), *Manners and Social Usages* (1884), which went through many editions, *Royal Girls and Royal Courts* (1887), *Sweet-Brier* (1889), *The Art of Entertaining* (1892), and *Poems by M. E. W. S.* (1892). Her stories and verse are not noteworthy. Her popularity was due to her books on social life and etiquette, which her experience in Washington official life, in New York society, and in Europe fitted her to write. Long considered authoritative, these are practical and not uninteresting, in spite of their continual insistence on the "fashionable" and the "proper." As was perhaps natural in a social arbiter, she was very conservative. In one of her books she remarks apropos of the extravagant balls of the Four Hundred in New York: "Whose business is it how rich people spend their money?" Her *An Epistle to Posterity; Being Rambling Recollections of Many Years of My Life* (1897) and *Here and There and Everywhere; Reminiscences* (1898) show her to have felt the importance of her social opportunities and of the prominent people who were her friends or acquaintances. Her style is vivacious, conversational, often humorous.

After her marriage she lived in New York but made frequent visits to Washington, Boston, and Europe. She numbered among her acquaintances Daniel Webster, W. H. Prescott, George Bancroft, J. L. R. Agassiz, James T. Fields, Oliver Wendell Holmes, Julia Ward Howe, the poets Longfellow, Bryant, and Lowell [*qq.v.*], Thackeray, Lord Houghton, Sir John Millais, and Sir Frederic Leighton. She was presented at many European courts and was decorated in France with the insignia of Officier d'Académie on account of her literary work (*Ibid.*). In New York she engaged in much philanthropy, and was especially interested in hospitals and work for women and children. During the Civil War she worked with the Sanitary Commission. Though an invalid for some years before her death, she continued to write and was a contributor to the *N. Y. Times Saturday Review of Books.* Of her four sons, two survived her. She died in New York City.

[See C. H. Bell, *The Bench and Bar of N. H.* (1894) for information on M. E. W. Sherwood's father and grandfather. See also *Vital Statistics of the Town of Keene, N. H.* (1905); M. E. W. Sherwood, *An Epistle to Posterity* (1897), *Here and There and Everywhere; Reminiscences* (1898); Frances E. Willard and Mary

A. Livermore, *Portraits and Biogs. of Prominent Am. Women* (1897), vol. II; *Who's Who in America,* 1903–05; *N. Y. Times,* Sept. 15, 1903.]   S. G. B.

SHERWOOD, THOMAS ADIEL (June 2, 1834–Nov. 11, 1918), jurist, was born at Eatonton, Putnam County, Ga., the son of the Rev. Adiel [*q.v.*] and Emma (Heriot) Sherwood. After excellent training under the guidance of his scholarly father, he entered Mercer University, transferring later to Shurtleff College, Alton, Ill. After his graduation from the Cincinnati Law School in 1857, he was admitted to the bar in Mississippi County, Mo., and began practice at Neosho, in the southwestern section of the state. The region was virtually a frontier community and he rode the circuit, with few *Reports* and fewer books to assist him. During the Civil War he moved to Springfield, which had an able local bar, forming a partnership with his brother-in-law, H. C. Young. He disliked trial work and was at his best as counsel and before appellate courts. By 1870, he was well known throughout the judicial circuits of southwestern Missouri and a leader of its bar.

A conservative Democrat, he was in thorough accord with the party group which came into power in the state during the early seventies. Sectional influence and the support of certain party leaders resulted in his nomination in 1872 for judge of the supreme court. He was reëlected in 1882 and in 1892, serving thirty years. His entire official life was spent upon the bench and his political and social philosophy must be gleaned from his judicial opinions. These indicate clearly that he was a strict constructionist, opposing subsidies, grants, and all forms of "federal encroachment," and fearing executive "usurpation" and governmental "interference" in private enterprise. Confronted by problems of constitutional construction, he relied upon a series of fixed and rigid principles. Temperamentally a controversialist and an advocate, he frequently dissented, but had the satisfaction subsequently of having many of his dissenting opinions accepted by the majority (*Proceedings of the Missouri Bar Association, post,* pp. 220–21). His most significant contributions were in constitutional law, criminal law, and equity (74 *Mo.,* 237; 159 *Mo.,* 410; 168 *Mo.,* 133). He was an earnest defender of civil liberty and of constitutional guarantees, never hesitating to overrule in terse and vigorous language the civil and criminal verdicts of lower courts. Supported alike by important politico-legal leaders and by the party rank and file, his reëlections were marked by increased majorities. He was ambitious for a fourth term, being mentally alert and physically active (*Boonville Advertiser,* May 30, 1902). The legal and political influences of the then dominant railroad interests were very active in his support, but these were nullified by innumerable personal and professional animosities developed during a long career because of his aggressive and provocative personality, and by the contention that a younger man should be designated for the ten-year term.

Following his unwilling retirement from the bench, he practised law in Springfield for a few years, published a polemical work, *Commentaries on the Criminal Law of Missouri* (1907), and retained great interest in public affairs. He was a stanch advocate of judicial reform, both administrative and procedural. Officially, he was austere and dignified, utterly impervious to what he considered public clamor, but his intimate friends knew him as a genial companion, with a knowledge and a keen appreciation of history and of literature. He married, in June 1861, Mary E. Young, of southwestern Missouri, who, with four children, survived him. He died in California of the infirmities of age.

[50–171 *Mo. Reports* (1873–1903); A. J. D. Stewart, *The Hist. of the Bench and Bar of Mo.* (1898); H. L. Conard, *Encyc. of the Hist. of Mo.* (1901), vol. V; *Proc. of the . . . Mo. Bar Asso.,* 1919; J. O. Boyd, "Thirty Years a Justice," *Am. Law Rev.,* July–Aug. 1914; *Jefferson City Tribune,* Feb. 26, 1873; Dec. 7, 1892, Nov. 25, 1893, Nov. 26, 1918; *St. Louis Republic,* Mar. 16, 1909.]   T. S. B.

SHERWOOD, WILLIAM HALL (Jan. 31, 1854–Jan. 7, 1911), pianist, teacher, composer, was born in Lyons, N. Y., the eldest of seven children of the Rev. Lyman Hinsdale and Mary (Balis) Sherwood. On his father's side he was descended from Thomas Sherwood, who emigrated from London to Ipswich, Mass., in 1634, and settled in Fairfax, Conn., and on his mother's side from John Balis, a farmer with a large grant of land between Cairo and Catskill, N. Y. Lyman Sherwood was a man of culture, an accomplished linguist, an excellent pianist and organist. He supported his family by teaching music, being so successful that he founded Lyons Musical Academy in 1854, the second music school founded in America.

William Sherwood showed musical talent at the age of four and received his first training from his aunt who was a teacher in the Academy. At the age of seven he came under the careful training of his father, with whom he studied for ten years, taking a full course in piano, harmony, and composition. Between the ages of nine and eleven he frequently appeared in concert in New York, Pennsylvania, and Canada. From 1866 to 1871 he taught in the Academy and at the same

time acquired a literary education under his father, especially in French and German. For a short time he studied piano with Edward Heimburger in Rochester, N. Y., and Jan N. Pychowski in New York City, but in 1871 he began studying with William Mason, 1829–1908 [*q.v.*], who was conducting a normal institute at Binghamton, N. Y. In the autumn of that year, upon Mason's advice, he went to Germany, where he remained five years, at first studying piano with Kullak and theory with Weitzmann in Berlin. Within seven months he was one of the students chosen to play at the annual Kullak concert at the *Singakademie,* at which he gave a brilliant performance of the Chopin fantasia in F. Other students who took part—Scharwenka, Moszkowski, Nicodé—all became famous pianists. He studied with Deppe for a time and then went to Stuttgart, where he studied organ with Scotson Clark and composition with Doppler, but he returned to Kullak and Weitzmann. The next season he played the Beethoven E flat concerto with an orchestra conducted by Richard Wüerst before an audience of four thousand, and repeated this concerto several times that season in Berlin. In 1875 he went to Weimar to study with Liszt, who was enthusiastic over the abilities of the young artist. Sherwood had studied the Grieg concerto with the composer and his performance of it with the philharmonic orchestra in Hamburg received an ovation. This success opened the door for performances with other great orchestras of Germany. While in Berlin he was organist of the English Chapel and while in Stuttgart, of the English Church.

Sherwood returned to America in 1876 and taught for a few years in the New England Conservatory, Boston, and then moved to New York. From 1889 until his death he lived in Chicago, being connected for the first eight years with the Chicago Conservatory of Music. He resigned in 1897 and established the Sherwood Music School, and devoted himself wholly to teaching and giving concerts. He was one of the first Americans to play with the great European orchestras, but in spite of his great success abroad, was always far more interested in the appreciation of his own countrymen. After one of his European trips, Karl Reinecke, conductor of the Gewandhaus concerts, invited him to appear as soloist with this orchestra in Leipzig, at that time the musical center of Europe. But Sherwood declined the invitation in order to fulfill an obligation that he always placed above all else—the development of musical life in America. He was the first to play the Grieg concerto in America, and was the first soloist to appear with the Boston Symphony Orchestra under George Henschel. Besides making several tours with the Theodore Thomas and the symphony orchestra of New York he played with all the important American orchestras. He possessed a flawless, brilliant technique, delicacy and refinement of expression, and thorough musicianship. He rarely gave a recital without including one American composition. He had a large following as a teacher, especially through his summer courses at Chautauqua, N. Y., where for twenty-two years, from 1889 till his death, he was head of the piano department.

Essentially an interpretative artist Sherwood was not deeply drawn to composition. His best works are *Scherzo Caprice,* Opus 9, two suites, Opus 5 and 14, *Scherzo Symphonique,* and two sets of *Gypsy Dances.* He possessed a lovable nature, very affable, simple, and unpretentious. His first wife, Mary Fay, of Williamsburg, N. Y., to whom he was married in 1874 while a student in Berlin, was also a gifted student of Kullak, and they often played together successfully. His second wife, Estelle F. Abrams, of Monongahela, Pa., to whom he was married in 1887, was his student in Boston. He had three daughters by the first marriage, and two by the second. He died in Chicago. Sherwood published two articles on his European studies in the *Étude,* May and July 1908.

[Information from the family; *Who's Who in America,* 1910–11; Andrew Sherwood, *Daniel Sherwood and his Paternal Ancestors* (1929); G. L. Howe, *A Hundred Years of Music in America* (1889); J. M. Green, *Musical Biog.* (1908), vol. II; *Grove's Dict. of Music and Musicians, Am. Supp.* (1930); biographical articles in *Musician,* Apr., May 1911, July 1913; *Chicago Tribune,* Jan. 15, 1911, *Musical America,* June 27, 1925; obits. in *Étude,* Feb. 1911, *Chautauquan Weekly,* Jan. 12, 19, 1911, and *Democrat Chronicle,* Rochester, N. Y., Jan. 8, 1911.]   F. L. G. C.

SHICK CALAMYS [See SHIKELLAMY, d. 1748].

SHIELDS, CHARLES WOODRUFF (Apr. 4, 1825–Aug. 26, 1904), clergyman, university professor, author, was born at New Albany, Ind., the son of James Read and Hannah (Woodruff) Shields, and grandson of Patrick Henry Shields. His paternal forebears, of Scottish descent, were settled for some time in Delaware, Maryland, and Virginia. His maternal ancestors, originally from Yorkshire, England, lived for several generations at Elizabeth, N. J. He was prepared for college at the Newark Academy, graduated from the College of New Jersey in 1844, and from Princeton Theological Seminary in 1847. On Nov. 22, 1848, he married Charlotte Elizabeth Bain of Galway, N. Y. For a time he lived in Brooklyn, supplying various pulpits, but on Nov.

8, 1849, he was ordained to the Presbyterian ministry and became pastor of a church at Hempstead, Long Island. The year following he accepted a call to the Second Presbyterian Church, Philadelphia, in the service of which he remained for fifteen years. His first wife died in 1853, and in 1861 he married Elizabeth Kane, of Philadelphia, sister of the Arctic explorer, Elisha Kent Kane [*q.v.*].

In 1861 he published a little book, *Philosophia Ultima,* which changed the course of his life. All his subsequent writing and lecturing was really an effort to substantiate the challenge uttered in the pages of that pamphlet. It advocated as an attainable and desirable object of intellectual endeavor the production of a work which should be a survey of the whole field of science, a statement of Christian theology, and a reconcilement of their apparent conflicts. This project attracted much attention. Some of his wealthy friends in Philadelphia raised a fund to enable him to develop his idea in the free atmosphere of an undenominational college, and in 1865, he was made professor of the harmony of science and religion in the College of New Jersey, at Princeton. The subject had been taught more or less irregularly in many institutions, but the chair was new and created expressly for Shields. His lectures were finished literary productions, and it was not long before they took shape as a book, *The Final Philosophy* (1877). This work was republished with two additional volumes under the title *Philosophia Ultima* (1888–1905). The title was misunderstood in some quarters, but a sentence in the preface explains it perfectly: "The construction of the final philosophy itself, it need scarcely be said, can only be the common work and reward of many minds through coming generations."

Believing that the credal statements of Christian orthodoxy were essentially the same in all those Protestant churches which have preserved historic continuity in doctrine and polity, Shields was devoted to the cause of reunion, and wrote many essays on the subject. As a step towards union, he urged the adoption of a book of common prayer by non-liturgical churches and published, in 1864, *Liturgia Expurgata, or The Book of Common Prayer amended According to the Presbyterian Revision of 1661,* and in 1893, the Presbyterian *Book of Common Prayer.*

His two great ideals, the reconcilement of science with revealed religion, and the reunion of Protestantism on a basis of ancient practices, Shields pursued with a passion which could not be discouraged. Though he frequently conducted the plain religious services which were traditional in the college chapel, he found ritual more congenial, and on Dec. 14, 1898, he was ordained deacon of the Protestant Episcopal Church, and on May 28, 1899, priest. He held his active professorship from 1865 to 1903, when he became professor emeritus. For thirteen years, 1869–82, he conducted courses in history, while continuing to lecture in philosophy.

He was one of the last of that venerable band of clerical professors in the Eastern endowed colleges who regarded themselves and were regarded by others as no less defenders of Christian orthodoxy than teachers of literature, philosophy, and science. They were expected to dominate and color university instruction. He was extremely serious, though mild, modest, and urbane. His lectures were subtle and refined in style, with a fiery undercurrent of earnestness that showed itself in outbursts of eloquence. He was fair-minded and not at all contentious. His survey of the conflicts between religion and the sciences is candid and remarkably full, though the reconcilement for which he yearned could not have been accomplished even by a modern Aquinas combined with a modern Bacon. He died at his summer home in Newport, R. I., survived by two sons and a daughter; his second wife had died in 1869.

[Personal recollections; information from the family; W. M. Sloane, "Charles Woodruff Shields," in *Philosophia Ultima,* vol. III (1905); H. W. Rankin, *The Philosophy of Charles Woodruff Shields: An Estimate* (1905); *Necrological Report, Princeton Theological Sem.,* 1905; *Biog. Cat. Princeton Theological Sem.* (1913); *Who's Who in America,* 1903–05.] G. M. H.

SHIELDS, GEORGE HOWELL (June 19, 1842–Apr. 27, 1924), politician, jurist, born at Bardstown, Ky., was descended on both sides from Scotch-Irish Presbyterians. His father, George W. Shields, came of ancestry that had early settled in Pennsylvania, moving thence to Ohio; his mother, Martha Howell, belonged to a pioneer Kentucky family. The Shields household removed in 1844 to Hannibal, Mo., where the father, as a civil engineer, surveyed turnpikes and subsequently railroads, invested in the packing business, and amassed a comfortable fortune. Shields was educated in the schools of Hannibal, and then spent two years, 1859–60, at Westminster College, Missouri.

The Civil War interrupted his education, caused the loss of his father's fortune, and disrupted the family. George became a Republican; his father and brother remained stanch Democrats. He served as a captain in the militia, protecting the local community against bushwhackers and guerrillas, and between raids studied law in Hannibal. Graduating from the Louisville

Law School in 1865, he returned home, married Mary H. Leighton on Feb. 1, 1866, and entered practice. For several years he served as city attorney and participated as counsel in many contested election cases in an era of bitter partisanship. A strict believer in party regularity, he refused to join the Liberal Republicans in 1870, but was elected to the legislature from Marion County. He was prominent in the session as a minority member of important committees, and as spokesman for his party. Following his defeat for judge of the supreme court by Thomas A. Sherwood [*q.v.*] in 1872, he moved to St. Louis and formed a partnership with John B. Henderson [*q.v.*].

His subsequent career was a successful combination of law and politics. His lucrative practice included many cases involving the rights of bondholders in connection with defaulted county and township bond issues; he was also active in the "Whiskey Ring" prosecutions and in important public-utility litigation. He served for many years as master of chancery in the federal court of the eastern district of Missouri. An intelligent organizer, he was chairman of the Republican state committee from 1876 to 1880, and was one of the few Republicans in the constitutional convention of 1875. His demonstrated ability and integrity made him the choice of his Democratic associates for the chairmanship of the Board of Freeholders, under whose auspices the city of St. Louis was separated from the county and the first home-rule charter in the United States was framed in 1876. As assistant attorney-general assigned to the Department of the Interior during the Harrison administration, he was successful in the solution of complicated legal issues concerning Indian lands, forest reserves, and conflicts with railroads and land-hungry settlers. He enjoyed the complete confidence and respect of the secretary, John W. Noble [*q.v.*]. From 1893 to 1895 he practised law in Washington and served as counsel of the United States before the Chilean Claims Commission. Encouraged by the Republican landslide of 1894, he returned to Missouri where he formed a partnership with John W. Noble and reëntered state politics. He continued in private practice until 1906, when he was elected to the circuit bench. During his two terms, 1906–12 and 1914–20, he acquired a reputation for fairness and for wise use of judicial power. A leading member of the Presbyterian church, deeply interested in many patriotic and veterans' organizations, he was highly esteemed both by the bench and bar and by the general public. He died in St. Louis of the infirmities of age, survived by two sons and a daughter.

[*Hist. of Marion County, Mo.* (1884); A. J. D. Stewart, *The Hist. of the Bench and Bar of Mo.* (1898); William Hyde and H. L. Conard, *Encyc. of the Hist. of St. Louis* (4 vols., 1899); W. B. Stevens, *Centennial Hist. of Mo.* (1921), vol. III; *Who's Who in America*, 1922–23; *St. Louis Globe-Democrat, St. Louis Post-Dispatch*, Apr. 28, 1924.]   T. S. B.

SHIELDS, GEORGE OLIVER (Aug. 26, 1846–Nov. 11, 1925), editor, author, and pioneer in the conservation of wild life, was born in Batavia, Ohio, the son of John F. and Eliza J. (Dawson) Shields. He obtained his entire formal education, three months in public school, in Delaware County, Iowa. He enlisted in the Union Army in February 1864, was wounded in action at Resaca, Ga., in May 1864, and was discharged in July 1865. After 1865 he seems not to have returned to his home for many years. For a short time after his discharge he was an immigration agent for the Pecos Irrigation and Improvement Company at Eddy (later Carlsbad), N. Mex. About this time he began writing for newspapers and periodicals. He had successfully hunted nearly every kind of game in North America south of the arctic circle, but soon after starting his career as a writer he became an ardent conservationist. Coquina, his pseudonym, was taken from the trade name of the Florida fossil-coral building material he described in his first book, *Rustlings in the Rockies* (1883). Like the first book, *Cruisings in the Cascades* (1889), made up of articles written for periodicals, is a simple narrative in which hunting and fishing play an important part. He also wrote *The Battle of the Big Hole* (1889), a valuable account of the Nez Percé Indian battle in Montana, *Camping and Camp Outfits* (1890), and *The Blanket Indian of the Northwest* (1921); he edited *The Big Game of North America* (1890), *The American Book of the Dog* (1891), and *American Game Fishes* (1892).

In 1894 he founded the popular magazine *Recreation*, through which he carried on vigorous campaigns, first against the excessive taking of game and later against the use by sportsmen of the automatic shotgun. From 1897 until 1902 he was the tireless but autocratic head of the Camp-Fire Club of America, the idea of which originated with Dr. William T. Hornaday. In 1898 he formed the League of American Sportsmen, which appointed game wardens in a great many states; through it he also encouraged animal photography and was awarded a bronze medal by the National Photographic Society. Early in 1905 he was forced into bankruptcy by his printers, though *Recreation* itself went on. Largely through the efforts of Dr. Hornaday, the New York Zoological Society soon raised money to establish *Shields' Magazine*, which was published until August 1912. Shields now devoted his whole time to lecturing. He was influential in having game laws enacted in many states and in securing the passage of the Lacey Act, the first federal law regulating interstate commerce and importation of birds and game. A man of remarkable energy and enthusiasm, too sincere in his belief in the importance of his work to adopt politic methods in presenting his views, he unfortunately made enemies of many people who might have helped him. Yet he has been called "unquestionably our most eminent and successful pioneer in the cause of the conservation of wild life" (*Outdoor Life, post,* p. 31). In his later years he was frequently given the title of colonel, evidently merely by courtesy. He married but separated from his wife in 1892; they had no children. He spent his last years in straitened circumstances in New York, where he died in St. Luke's Hospital in the early hours of the morning, Nov. 11, 1925.

[*Who's Who in America*, 1920–21; *Who's Who in N. Y.*, 1924; *Who's Who Among North Am. Authors*, 1921; W. T. Hornaday, *Our Vanishing Wild Life* (1913), *Thirty Years' War for Wild Life* (1931); G. O. Shields, in *Shields' Mag.*, Mar. 1905; *Outdoor Life*, Nov. 1931; *Back-Log*, May 1930; obituary in *N. Y. Times*, Nov. 13, 1925; information from Miss Myra Emmons, A. L. A. Himmelwright, Dr. W. T. Hornaday, T. Gilbert Pearson, and Mrs. Sadie Latimer, Shields's niece.]   E. W. H.

SHIELDS, JAMES (May 12, 1806–June 1, 1879), soldier, senator from Illinois, Minnesota, and Missouri, was born in Altmore, County Tyrone, Ireland, the son of Charles and Katherine (McDonnell) Shields. Trained in a hedge school and later in an academy and by a retired priest from Maynooth, he received a good classical education, supplemented by some teaching in tactics and swords play. Probably in 1822 he sailed by way of Liverpool for Quebec and was wrecked on the Scottish coast with only two other survivors. As a tutor, he earned a livelihood in Scotland until he obtained a berth on a merchantman and about 1826 arrived in New York harbor. He settled in Kaskaskia, Ill., where he taught French, read law, fought in the Black Hawk War, and practised Democratic politics and law. In 1836 he was elected a member of the legislature. As state auditor, he helped correct the disordered finances of the state brought to the verge of bankruptcy by the panic and canal building, but not without sharp criticism in the Whig press. As a result of anonymous charges in the newspaper, traced to the Misses Todd and Jayne, later the wives of Abraham Lincoln and Lyman Trumbull, he challenged to a duel Lincoln, who shouldered some responsibility. The matter was compromised on explanations from the latter, and the principals became permanent friends. In 1843 Shields was named to the supreme court by Gov. Thomas Ford, whose manuscript *History of Illinois* he edited and published later, in 1854. As a jurist, he was honest, industrious, and surprisingly detached in delivering decisions that were marked by common sense and some legal erudition. He was renamed by the legislature for a full term in 1845, but he resigned soon to accept President Polk's appointment to the commissionership of the general land office in Washington.

With the outbreak of the Mexican War he resigned and was commissioned brigadier-general of Illinois volunteers on July 1, 1846. At Cerro Gordo he was dangerously wounded, was brevetted a major-general, and cited by General Scott for his gallant conduct there. At Churubusco, after initial mistakes of some importance (Smith, *post*, pp. 115–17, 384), he led the charge of New York Irish and South Carolina volunteers that is commemorated in the painting in the national Capitol. In July 1848 his brigade was disbanded, and he returned to Kaskaskia and Belleville to build up his law practice, but he was soon appointed governor of Oregon Territory. This position he resigned immediately to accept an election to the federal Senate. A Whig Senate found a technicality in that he had not been a citizen the required number of years and declared his election void. He, however, was reëlected for the same term and served from Oct. 27, 1849, to Mar. 3, 1855. Martial in carriage, scrupulously neat, urbane and courteous of manner, graceful and humorous in debate, he was well informed because of his ability, experiences, and his command of Latin, French, and Spanish. In temper he was sharp and somewhat arrogantly independent. Something of a demagogue, he was intentionally candid. A strict party man, he had the courage to disagree with fanatics on either side of the slavery issue and to fight for a free California, land grants for veterans, railroad construction, and agricultural education. In 1855 he was defeated for reëlection by Lyman Trumbull in a legislature in deadlock between himself and Lincoln.

A Douglas appointee to distribute Sioux half-breed scrip, he went to Minnesota Territory, where he settled down on his land grant. He did much to stimulate an Irish movement into the region by organizing the townships of Shieldsville, Erin, Kilkenny, and Montgomery in Lesueur and Rice counties and by establishing with Alexander Faribault the town of Faribault. Elected to the federal Senate, on the admission of Minnesota, he drew the short term that expired Mar. 3, 1859, and a Republican legislature failed to reëlect him. He went to San Francisco, where in 1861 he married Mary Ann Carr, the daughter of an old friend in Armagh, Ireland, by whom he had three surviving children. Settled in Mazatlan, Mexico, as manager and part owner of a mine, he sold his interest and offered his services to Lincoln, when he learned that Fort Sumter had surrendered. Appointed as a brigadier-general of volunteers on Aug. 19, 1861, he campaigned in the Shenandoah Valley, where he won recognition at Winchester and at Port Republic. He resigned his commission on Mar. 28, 1863, and retired to San Francisco, where he was appointed a state railroad commissioner. In 1866, he was in Carrollton, Mo. There he entered politics again, campaigning against the "ironclad oath," losing an election to Congress when a canvassing board cast out the votes of two counties, and supporting the Liberal-Republican candidates of 1872. He lectured for religious, Irish, and charitable causes such as Southern relief during the cholera epidemic. Serving in the legislature, he promoted an act for a railroad commission to which he was afterward appointed. He was elected to fill out an unexpired term in the federal Senate from Jan. 27, 1879, to Mar. 3, 1879, but lack of health forced him to decline being a candidate for reëlection. He died at Ottumwa, Iowa, while on a lecture tour, and was buried with simple Roman Catholic rites at St. Mary's Cemetery in Carrollton, Mo., where in 1910 a colossal statue was erected to his memory. In 1893 his statue was placed in Statuary Hall in the national Capitol by Illinois and, in 1914, Minnesota, at the insistence of the Grand Army of the Republic, raised a memorial in the state capitol.

[W. H. Condon, *Life of Major-General James Shields* (1900); H. A. Castle, "Gen. James Shields," and John Ireland, "Address at the Unveiling of the Statue of General Shields," *Minn. Hist. Soc. Colls.*, vol. XV (1915); *N. Y. Freeman's Jour. and Catholic Register*, May 4, 1861, June 7, 14, 1879, Jan. 1, 1887; *Jour. of the Am.-Irish Hist. Soc.*, vol. IX (1900), vol. XIV (1915); *Studies* (Dublin), Mar. 1932; W. W. Folwell, *A Hist. of Minnesota* (1924), vol. II; J. H. Smith, *The War with Mexico* (2 vols., 1919); date of birth from statement concerning original family records in Castle, *ante*, p. 711.] R. J. P.

SHIELDS, THOMAS EDWARD (May 9, 1862–Feb. 15, 1921), Roman Catholic priest, educator, son of John and Bridget (Burke) Shields, immigrants from Ireland, was born and reared on a farm near Mendota, Minn. He developed physically at a rate which retarded mental growth and was regarded by his unlettered parents and by his neighbors as a hopeless dullard or "omadhaun." Dominated by an elder brother, he became a powerful farmhand who spoke brokenly and shrank from all associations. Suddenly, however, there came a revolt from paternalistic control, and an awakening of his mind which resulted in his inventing a grubbing machine. He laboriously made his way through a book and thus learned to read. Realizing at length that he was not unlike other men, he began to display an undaunted self-confidence which he retained through life, often to the annoyance of less imaginative associates. Only his confessor, an able but odd Irishman, had faith in his ability; the bishop turned from the farm boy who knew no Latin when he presented himself as a candidate for the seminary. Shields applied himself to his books, and, untrammeled by formalism and bad teaching, his mind opened amazingly. In 1882 he gained admission to St. Francis College in Milwaukee, where he prepared for St. Thomas Seminary, which he entered in 1885. As a seminarian, his talent in philosophy and science was recognized, especially when he invented in 1888 a filing system for the accumulation of information under the title *Index Omnium.*

Ordained a priest, Mar. 14, 1891, by Archbishop Ireland, who admired his rugged integrity and brilliant mind, he was sent, after fourteen months as a curate at St. Paul's Cathedral, to St. Mary's Seminary, Baltimore, where he took a master's degree, and was permitted to take graduate work in biology at Johns Hopkins University, in recognition of which he was given the degree of Ph.D. in 1895. Such a course was a radical departure for a priest, and Shields attracted the attention of teachers and fellow students as one who correlated scholastic philosophy with science. His thesis, *The Effect of Odours, Irritant Vapours, and Mental Work Upon the Blood Flow,* a thorough piece of research, was published in 1896. As a lecturer in psychology and biology at St. Paul's Seminary, he proved an independent thinker and an inspiring teacher who sympathized with his students; but in 1898 he was removed to St. Joseph's Church, St. Paul, as second assistant. In this field of service he also showed marked ability, and incidentally invented a shoe polish.

Archbishop Ireland finally released him in 1902 to accept an instructorship at the Catholic University in Washington, D. C. A magnetic teacher, if somewhat informal, he was advanced to a professorship in education and psychology in 1909. He found time, in addition to his teaching at the University and Trinity College, to prepare scientific articles for encyclopedias and magazines; to perfect a plethysmograph (see

American Journal of Experimental Medicine, vol. I) ; and to write a number of books. Among his publications are *Psychology of Education* (1904), a series in mimeograph; *The Teaching of Religion* (1907), in multigraph; *The Education of Our Girls* (1906), with a preface by Cardinal Gibbons which disarmed critics; *The Making and Unmaking of a Dullard* (1909), which was annoyingly autobiographical; *Teachers' Manual of Primary Methods* (1912) ; *Philosophy of Education* (1917) ; and, with E. A. Pace, a couple of elementary books in religion as a protest against the stereotyped method of memorizing catechism. While his system of religious instruction was logical and practical, it found more criticism than acceptance in the parochial schools. Always a promoter, he founded and directed a Catholic Correspondence School (1904–09), apparently with the hope of bringing modern, secular methods to Catholic teachers. In 1911 he established the *Catholic Educational Review,* the first journal of its kind. As its editor for ten years, he formulated theories of teacher and child training which contributed to the improvement of methods employed in parochial and high schools. In an effort to assist nuns in meeting the higher requirements which he foresaw would be demanded by state boards of education and accrediting agencies, he started at the University with the sympathetic assistance of the rector, Bishop Thomas J. Shahan [*q.v.*], a summer school for sisters, with branches at San Francisco and at Dubuque; he was also instrumental in founding in 1911 the Catholic Sisters College as an affiliated school of the University. Both institutions were novel departures, and as such they were roundly criticized for drawing nuns from their convents. Soon, however, other Catholic universities followed the example thus set and began holding summer sessions for sisters, while various religious orders adapted themselves to teaching women and even to co-education. Shields also put into operation a scheme whereby colleges, high schools, and novitiates throughout the country were affiliated with the Catholic University as a means of improving their standards and securing uniformity without loss of school autonomy. As dean of the Sisters College, he rendered one of his most important services. He bought the site, interested influential patrons in the project, and found a faculty among his lay and clerical associates who were willing to sacrifice for an ideal. Believing that the time was ripe for a series of Catholic textbooks, he established the Catholic Educational Press (1908). Not until 1913 did he find time to visit Europe; his travels had been confined to visiting Mother Houses and schools, attending conventions, and holding institutes.

A genius and a crusader, erratic but sociable, careless of dress, uncanny in vision and hence regarded as a radical and as impractical, a hard and not unwilling fighter, Shields faced difficulties, misunderstanding, and a general lack of sympathy; but he went his way refusing to be discouraged by obstacles. For his ideals, he sacrificed personal comfort and even friends who could not follow him. Aggressively he forced his way until finally he burned himself out and died from a valvular disease of the heart. His estate went to the Sisters College, and his remains repose in a mausoleum on its campus.

[*Catholic Educ. Rev.*, Apr. 1921 (memorial number), Jan. 1929; *Am. Catholic Who's Who*, 1911; *Who's Who in America*, 1920–21; *The Catholic Encyc. and Its Makers* (1917); *Evening Star* (Washington, D. C.), Feb. 15, 1921; *Irish Monthly* (Dublin), Apr. 1934; personal knowledge and notes from a number of Shields's associates.]   R. J. P.

SHIKELLAMY (d. Dec. 6, 1748), Oneida chief, was born probably into the Cayuga tribe and early adopted by the Oneida, among whom he became a chief. John Bartram [*q.v.*] described him as a *"Frenchman,* born at Mont-real," although he also wrote that "his son told me he was of *Cayuga* nation" (*Observations, post,* p. 17). His name was spelled in various ways, such as Schickillemy, Shakallamy, Shick Calamys, Shikellamy, and sometimes after the Latin form of the Moravians, Shikellemus or Sicalamous. He was also called Swataney. About 1728 he was sent by the Six Nations to assert the right of Iroquois dominion over the conquered tribes of Pennsylvania, principally Delaware and Shawnee, and to prevent their selling land to the white governments. He established himself in a strategic position near the forks of the Susquehanna; at first he was probably about ten miles above the forks on the west branch and later at the Indian town of Shamokin, where Sunbury now stands, in Northumberland County.

He was soon engaged in the general oversight of Indian relations with the white people. Again and again he made the difficult journey through the wilderness of the upper Susquehanna Valley. To Onondaga, the seat of council for the Iroquois confederation, he took messages from the white governments, guided emissaries, and from time to time went to obtain instructions from the Six Nations concerning their subject tribes to the south. He kept the English informed of French advances of friendship to the Indians and was ever ready to discourage Iroquois participation in French plans. Through Conrad Weiser and James Logan [*qq.v.*], for whom his son James

Logan [*q.v.*] was named, he was able to influence the Pennsylvania government to support the claims of the Six Nations against the Delaware and the Shawnee. He was active in negotiating the two treaties of 1736 by which Pennsylvania agreed to pay the Iroquois an indemnity for lands already ceded by their subject tribes and to acknowledge Iroquois claims to Delaware lands on the lower Delaware River. Since the confederation had not hitherto exerted right of control over these lands, this action constituted a precedent to deny Delaware claims to any lands. His influence was important in obtaining the treaties of 1744 at Lancaster with Maryland and Virginia, which provided for the payment of indemnities and acknowledgment of Iroquois land claims within the borders of those states. Pennsylvania, actuated by the conviction of the power and importance of the Six Nations, represented by Shikellamy, continued to court that confederation and to offend the Delaware and Shawnee, thus avoiding an Iroquois war at the cost of the sullen resentment of the Delaware and Shawnee—a resentment that broke forth to ravage Pennsylvania after Braddock's defeat.

Apparently Shikellamy spoke more English than he generally acknowledged (Bartram, *post,* p. 43). He possessed a sympathy for white men, which he manifested over a period of years by protecting their personal safety, by his response to the Moravians, and by his personal relations to such men as Count Zinzendorf, Conrad Weiser, and David Zeisberger. In early life he had been baptized by a Jesuit in Canada, was for years interested in the Moravian way of life, and in his last year went down to Bethlehem to be received into that communion. Stricken with mortal illness he went home to Shamokin, where the Moravian missionaries watched with him until he died.

[C. H. Sipe, *The Indian Chiefs of Pa.* (1927); W. M. Beauchamp, "Shikellimy," *Am. Scenic and Hist. Preservation Soc., 21st . . . Report* (1916), pp. 599–611; J. S. Walton, *Conrad Weiser* (1900); *Minutes of the Provincial Council of Pa.*, vols. I–V (1852–51); *Pa. Archives*, vols. I, II (1852–53), ed. by Samuel Hazard; John Bartram, *Observations* (1751), pp. 17, 20, 43; G. H. Loskiel, *Hist. of the Mission of the United Brethren* (1794), trans. by C. I. Latrobe; E. A. De Schweinitz, *The Life and Times of David Zeisberger* (1870); W. C. Reichel, *Memorials of the Moravian Church* (1870), pp. 84–93; Witham Marshe, "Journ. of the Treaty . . . at Lancaster, Pa., June 1744," *Mass. Hist. Soc. Colls.*, vol. VII (1801), pp. 195–96.]
K. E. C.

SHILLABER, BENJAMIN PENHALLOW (July 12, 1814–Nov. 25, 1890), humorist, newspaperman, poet, was born at Portsmouth, N. H., one of six children of William and Sarah Leonard (Sawyer) Shillaber. He was a descendant of John Shillaber who emigrated from

Devonshire to Salem, Mass., toward the end of the seventeenth century. Educated in the district schools, he served his apprenticeship years as printer's devil in the Dover offices of the *New Hampshire Palladium and Strafford Advertiser,* 1829–31, and in the Portsmouth offices of the *Portsmouth Courier* and the *Christian Herald.* In the spring of 1833 he became a book-compositor with the printing firm of Tuttle & Weeks on School Street, Boston, who printed the popular Peter Parley tales of Samuel Griswold Goodrich, the *New England Farmer,* and some of the anti-slavery poetry of John Greenleaf Whittier [*qq.v.*]. At twenty-one he was rated as journeyman printer. In October 1835 violent nasal hemorrhages forced him to the tropics, where for about two years he served as compositor on the *Royal Gazette of British Guiana* (Demerara). Restored to health, he returned to Boston in July 1838 and there on Aug. 15 married Ann Tappan de Rochemont. They had eight children, of whom three daughters and one son survived their father.

Shortly thereafter he joined the *Boston Post,* then under the editorship of Charles Gordon Greene, an outstanding journalistic figure of the forties. Until 1847 he was a "manipulator of the stick and rule" without any aspirations for a literary career, when a squib he set up in the *Post* chanced to make a great hit. In this a certain imaginary Mrs. Partington, who had been described by Sydney Smith as vainly mopping back the ocean, was reported to have said that it "made no difference to her whether flour was dear or cheap, as she always had to pay just so much for a half-dollar's worth." The sayings and doings of the old lady soon made her a national figure and Shillaber an outstanding American humorist. In 1850 he became editor of the *Pathfinder and Railway Guide,* distributed by "news-butchers" on railroads and steamboats; a year later he began to edit a humorous weekly, the *Carpet-Bag,* through whose columns the nationally popular sayings of Mrs. Partington continued. Although the *Carpet-Bag* boasted the best humorous writers of the day, including in addition to the older established men the youthful Charles Farrar Browne, S. L. Clemens, Charles Bertrand Lewis, and Charles Graham Halpine [*qq.v.*], it died prematurely in 1853 after two years' struggle. It remains, however, one of the most important American humorous papers, developing as it did a whole school. To the *Boston Post* Shillaber returned that year as local reporter, remaining until 1856; from 1856 to 1866 he was on the staff of the *Saturday Evening Gazette,* and subsequently he spent two years on

the lyceum circuits giving humorous lectures. Later he retired to his home in Chelsea, Mass., where he died. Although he abandoned direct connection with the press, he was an occasional correspondent and contributor, wrote his Ike Partington juveniles, and continued the writing of poems, always referring to them as "rhymes" and to himself as a "rhymist." He was large of build, jovial, ever ready of wit, with a plain, frank face.

Chief among his separately published works are *Rhymes With Reason and Without* (1853), *Life and Sayings of Mrs. Partington* (1854), of which thousands of copies sold in a short time, *Knitting-Work* (1859), *Partingtonian Patchwork* (1872), *Lines in Pleasant Places* (1874), and the Ike Partington juveniles. His reminiscences, "Experiences During Many Years," appeared in the *New England Magazine,* June 1893–May 1894. Between the old school of American humor, which preceded the Civil War, and the new, he served as the chief connecting link. As a young newspaperman under Greene on the *Boston Post* he met and knew the humorists of the forties; as editor of the *Carpet-Bag,* 1851–53, he came into contact with and stimulated the coming generation of humorists. It was to the *Carpet-Bag* that Artemus Ward and Mark Twain sent their first contributions; and it was through Shillaber that they readily became a part of the ever-broadening stream of American humor.

[The chief source is B. P. Shillaber, "Experiences During Many Years," *New England Mag.,* June 1893–May 1894. See also *Geneal. of the Cutts Family in America* (1892), comp. by C. H. C. Howard; *A Family Souvenir: Record of Proc. at the First Gathering of Descendants of John Shillaber* (1877); *Proc. N. H. Press Assoc.* (1895); S. A. Allibone, *A Critical Dict. of Eng. Lit.,* vol. II (1870); G. W. Bungay, *Off-Hand Takings* (1854); *Appletons' Ann. Cyc.,* 1890; *Lit. World,* Dec. 20, 1890; obituaries in *Boston Post, N. Y. Tribune,* Nov. 26, 1890.]   F. J. M.

SHINN, ASA (May 3, 1781–Feb. 11, 1853), Methodist clergyman, one of the founders of the Methodist Protestant Church, was born in New Jersey, the son of Jonathan and Mary (Clark) Shinn, and a descendant of John Shinn, who emigrated from England to America and was in New Jersey as early as 1680. Both of Asa's parents were Quakers. When he was seven years of age they moved to one of the inland counties of Virginia, and seven years later to what is now Harrison County, West Virginia. In these frontier communities the boy's only schooling was received from a former sailor who wandered through the country conducting schools as opportunity afforded. In 1798, under the preaching of Rev. Robert Manly, a Methodist circuit rider, Shinn professed conversion and three years later, influenced by the scarcity of ministers in the West, he joined the Baltimore Conference of the Methodist Episcopal Church, and was assigned to the Redstone circuit in southwestern Pennsylvania. In 1803 he was transferred to the Western Conference, which included all the territory west of the Alleghany Mountains. Here he remained until 1807, serving circuits in western Virginia, southern Ohio, and Kentucky. He returned to the Baltimore Conference in 1807 and about the same time married Phebe Barnes of western Virginia, by whom he had two sons and two daughters. Until 1816, when he was forced by mental derangement temporarily to discontinue his work, he had charge of circuits in Maryland and the District of Columbia.

During the course of his life Shinn suffered four periods of insanity, resulting from a fracture of the skull in his boyhood. The first three of these, in 1816, 1820, and 1828, were of short duration; from the last, in 1843, he never recovered, and he died in an asylum for the insane at Brattleboro, Vt. Except for the short periods of inactivity caused by his ailment, Shinn continued to hold important circuits and stations in the Baltimore Conference until his transfer to the Pittsburgh Conference in 1825, where he served as presiding elder of the Pittsburgh district and as minister at Washington, Pa.

In 1824 he became greatly interested in the agitation for certain reforms in the government of the Methodist Episcopal Church. The reformers established a monthly paper in 1824 called *The Mutual Rights of Ministers and Members of the Methodist Episcopal Church,* for which Shinn became one of the most voluminous and effective contributors. He also wrote several controversial pamphlets, among them, *An Appeal to the Good Sense of the Citizens of the United States* (1826), *A Finishing Stroke to the High Claims of Ecclesiastical Sovereignty* (1827). When the Baltimore Conference in 1827 expelled a minister for circulating *Mutual Rights,* Shinn became active in his defense. Other reformers were also suspended. At the General Conference of 1828 the great issue was the appeal of these persons for restoration. Shinn presented their case in an eloquent speech which won the admiration even of his opponents, and had the vote been taken at once, the reformers would probably have been reinstated; but it was delayed until the next day and their cause was defeated.

Convinced that all chance at conciliation was past, the leading reformers now proceeded to form separate congregations and Conferences, and on Nov. 2, 1830, a convention of delegates

from the disaffected groups met in the city of Baltimore and there formed the Methodist Protestant Church. Shinn took a leading part in its organization, was chosen president of the Ohio Conference when it was constituted, and in 1833, was elected president of the Pittsburgh Conference. From 1834 to 1836 he was in Baltimore, editing with Nicholas Snethen [*q.v.*], the new denominational paper, *Mutual Rights and Methodist Protestant,* and thereafter for the next ten years held important pulpits in Cincinnati, Pittsburgh, and Allegheny City. At the General Conference of 1838 the slavery issue brought on an acrimonious debate in which Shinn took the anti-slavery view and defended that position in a speech of great power.

He was the author of two considerable books on theology. The first, published in 1812, was entitled *An Essay on the Plan of Salvation*; the second, *On the Benevolence and Rectitude of the Supreme Being,* appeared in 1840. He possessed a logical mind and was particularly impressive in public address. After the death of his first wife he married Mary Bennington (Wrenshall) Gibson, widow of Woolman Gibson, and daughter of John Wrenshall, by whom he had one son.

[J. H. Shinn, *The Hist. of the Shinn Family in Europe and America* (1903); E. J. Drinkhouse, *Hist. of Methodist Reform* (1899); W. B. Sprague, *Annals Am. Pulpit,* vol. VII (1859); A. H. Bassett, *A Concise Hist. of the Methodist Protestant Church* (2nd ed., 1882); R. F. Shinn, *A Tribute to Our Fathers* (1853); Matthew Simpson, *Cyc. of Methodism* (1878); *Daily Commercial Jour.* (Pittsburgh), Feb. 18, 1853.]

W. W. S.

SHIPHERD, JOHN JAY (Mar. 28, 1802– Sept. 16, 1844), home missionary, one of the founders of Oberlin College, was born near Granville, N. Y., the third son of Zebulon Rudd and Betsy (Bull) Shipherd. His father, a successful lawyer, served for many years as a trustee of Middlebury College and, for one term (1813– 15), as a Federalist member of Congress. When John was seventeen "the Lord mercifully revealed Himself to his mind" and he determined to become a minister. He was at that time attending Pawlet Academy, Pawlet, Vt., from which he soon transferred to Cambridge Academy, Cambridge, N. Y. He planned to complete his education at Middlebury College, but an accidental dose of poison so weakened his eyes and voice and so undermined his health generally that he was forced, for a time, to abandon the prospect of further study. After two years spent in unsuccessful ventures in the marble and whetstone industries at Vergennes, Vt., however, he entered the household of Rev. Josiah Hopkins at New Haven, Vt., to prepare for ordination.

Here he spent a year and a half, depending largely upon the eyes of others for his reading.

He was ordained as an evangelist by a Congregational council at Blanton, Vt., Oct. 3, 1827, but after preaching for a year at Shelburn, in the autumn of 1828 he accepted the general agency of the Vermont Sabbath School Union and removed to Middlebury. For the next two years he traveled about the state, founding and inspecting Sunday schools; he also published a semi-annual, *The Sabbath School Guide,* and a tiny juvenile religious magazine, *The Youth's Herald.* Middlebury College granted him an honorary master's degree in 1830. Already, however, he had decided to go as a home missionary "to Mississippi's vast valley."

Accordingly, in the autumn of 1830, without waiting to secure an appointment, he went West, stopping at Rochester, N. Y., to receive the advice and blessing of Charles G. Finney [*q.v.*]. Upon reaching Cleveland he was promptly assigned to the missionary pastorate of a Plan-of-Union Presbyterian church in the village of Elyria, Lorain County, Ohio. His experience here was checkered but generally disappointing to him, and in the summer of 1832, in collaboration with a classmate of Pawlet days, Philo P. Stewart [*q.v.*], he formulated a scheme for the evangelization of the West through a Christian colony and manual-labor school to be founded in the wilderness, far from the polluting influence of established communities. The new enterprise was christened Oberlin in honor of the philanthropist and educator, Jean Frédéric Oberlin, a life of whom had recently been published by the American Sunday School Union. In 1832–33 Shipherd traveled through New York and New England, securing money, teachers, pious settlers, and title to a tract of land nine miles from Elyria; while Stewart and other associates forwarded the enterprise on the spot. The first settlement was made in April 1833. Shipherd returned in September and presided at the opening of the preparatory and "infant" departments of the Oberlin Collegiate Institute, Dec. 3, 1833. A full staff of teachers was secured the following spring, and in the fall, the first students of college grade appeared. The initial report of the Institute, published in December 1834, was optimistic, but Shipherd knew that the funds available were insufficient to guarantee the long continuance of the enterprise.

The rebellion of the students at Lane Seminary, near Cincinnati, furnished the means of saving Oberlin. Lane, also, had been founded to promote the evangelization of the West and for this purpose had been liberally endowed by Arthur and Lewis Tappan [*qq.v.*]. Under the leadership of Theodore Weld [*q.v.*] the students had begun the discussion of the slavery question and formed an anti-slavery society. The trustees, mostly conservative Cincinnati business men, prohibited further debate of this dangerous issue and the students walked out, almost to a man. Shipherd read of the situation in the religious periodicals and hastened to Cincinnati, where he discussed with the "rebels" and Rev. Asa Mahan [*q.v.*], one of the friendly minority of the Lane trustees, the possibility of their coming to Oberlin. His proposition was favorably received, but final acceptance was conditioned upon securing the support of the Tappans and the appointment of Charles G. Finney to teach theology at Oberlin. Shipherd and Mahan therefore proceeded to New York, where they won over the Tappans and persuaded Finney to accept the appointment if the Oberlin trustees would agree to leave the internal administration of the school exclusively to the faculty. Shipherd persuaded his reluctant associates to accept this condition. In the spring of 1835 Mahan became president of the Institute and the Lane "rebels" arrived to study theology under Finney in the newly founded theological department. Oberlin was now firmly established as a center of reform and revival piety.

After 1835, the leadership having passed to Finney and Mahan, Shipherd turned to the founding of other colonies and schools. His Grand River Seminary in Michigan, announced in 1836, and his Lagrange Collegiate Institute, proposed in the spring of 1838, were stillborn. In 1844 he led personally the little group of people who established the colony and school at Olivet in Michigan. There, early in the autumn of the same year, he died. In 1824 he had married Esther Raymond of Ballston, N. Y., by whom he had a daughter who died in infancy, and six sons.

[Letters and other manuscripts in the possession of Oberlin College and privately owned; D. L. Leonard, *The Story of Oberlin* (copr. 1898); *N. Y. Evangelist,* June 18, 1831, Jan. 30, 1832, Sept. 7, 1833, Mar. 21, July 18, 1835, Sept. 17, 1836, Mar. 31, Apr. 22, 1837; *Ohio Observer* (Hudson, Ohio), June 12, July 17, 1834, Feb. 5, July 9, 1835; W. B. Williams, *A Hist. of Olivet College* (1901), and "Two Early Efforts to Found Colleges in Mich.," *Hist. Coll. . . . Mich. Pioneer and Hist. Soc.,* vol. XXX (1906); R. S. Fletcher, "Oberlin, 1833–1866," in MS.]
R. S. F.

SHIPMAN, ANDREW JACKSON (Oct. 15, 1857–Oct. 17, 1915), scholar and lawyer, son of John James and Priscilla (Carroll) Shipman, was born in Springvale, Fairfax County, Va., and reared in the desperate days of the Civil War and Reconstruction. With his father in the

Confederate forces, the boy was dubbed a "little rebel Zouave" by Unionist soldiers who occupied the region. On his father's side his ancestry was English, while the Carrolls traced their descent from Thomas, an Irishman, who settled in Maryland in 1725. Taught by his learned grandfather, Bennett Carroll, and by a succession of stranded schoolmasters, the boy Andrew was amply prepared for Georgetown Academy, Washington, where he was sent upon the recommendation of one of his teachers, a Roman Catholic and a former officer in the Austrian army, from whom he had learned some German and considerable European history. He completed the preparatory course in 1874, and four years later was graduated from Georgetown College. While a student, he joined the Roman Catholic Church, to which his mother returned. In 1879, he was back in Fairfax County, editing the *Vienna Times* and learning Czech from Stefan Melzer, who like other wandering foreigners had sought temporary refuge with the Shipmans. The following year Shipman found employment as a superintendent of the coal mines of W. P. Rend & Company in Hocking Valley, Ohio. Here he took a deep interest in the welfare of the foreign laborers and undertook to learn a number of the Slavic dialects. Among the miners were many Catholics of the Greek and Ruthenian rites, to whom the Roman Catholic service seemed as strange as that of another creed. Shipman feared that they would lose the faith if priests of their own rite and race were not provided. Hence, at a time when Catholics were woefully unconscious of the problem, he entered with a convert's zeal upon a lay apostolate in their behalf.

In 1884 he acquired a competitive clerkship in the New York Custom House, where he challenged attention as an investigator of the sugar frauds and during his free time acquired, in 1886, a degree in law from the University of the City of New York. In 1891 he became a law partner of Edmund Mooney—whose sister, Adair, he married two years later—and in 1893 the firm of Blandy, Mooney, & Shipman was formed. Shipman won recognition as a forceful, diligent advocate, and a respected counselor in labor cases, in the St. Stephen's Protestant Episcopal Church cases (1891–1900, 11 *New York Supplement,* 669), which compelled a study of ecclesiastical law, and in the business of the Greek, Ruthenian, and Slavic peoples, in whose native lands he spent all his vacations. A Democrat of influence without desire for office, he was a member of numerous clubs, president of the board of Mohansic State Hospital, a member of the Board of Regents of the University of the State of New York (1913), an associate manager of the Sevilla Home for Children, a member of the state constitutional convention of 1915, a leader in the Catholic Theatre movement, and a promoter of the Marquette League for Indian missionaries. His keenest interest remained, however, in the problem of the Eastern-rites Catholic immigrants.

No other American Catholic knew and served the Greek, Syrian, Slavic, Hungarian, and Ruthenian Catholics as did Shipman, and few Americans knew so well the peoples and languages of Eastern Europe. He persistently labored to bring about a sympathetic union between Roman and Orthodox Greek Catholics, to urge upon Catholic prelates an appreciation of the importance of this religious issue, to secure European churchmen to care for the hundreds of thousands of Eastern-rite Catholics in the industrial centers and mining regions of America, and to Americanize these immigrants in a worthy sense. He wrote of these Eastern peoples and their religious forms in the *Catholic Encyclopedia,* the *Century, McClure's Magazine,* the *Messenger,* and *Pravoslavny Viestnik,* and he spoke of their problems from numerous platforms. In 1911, he translated into English, for the first time, *The Holy Mass According to the Greek Rite.* In 1895, he was associated with Rev. Joseph Chaplinski in organizing a Ruthenian Greek Church in New York; he brought a stone from Jerusalem for the Church of St. Joachim which the Syrians were building; he was the friend and prized adviser of Bishop S. S. Ortynsky [*q.v.*] when uninformed Catholic priests were suspicious of the orthodoxy of their Ukrainian brethren; he exposed the attempts of Orthodox priests to proselytize by using Greek ceremonials; and he prevented the legislative sanction sought by the Russian Orthodox bishop for the use of the term Russian Greek Catholic Church. On his sudden death, of acute Bright's disease, he was buried from St. Patrick's Cathedral, where, after the Roman Mass, Bishop Ortynsky read the burial service according to the Greek rite, and the Ukrainian choir, which Shipman had assisted in forming, chanted the dirge.

[*A Memorial of Andrew J. Shipman: His Life and Writings* (1916), ed. by C. B. Pallen; *The Am. Cath. Who's Who* (1911); *The Cath. Encyc. and Its Makers* (copr. 1917); Coleman Nevils, *Miniatures of Georgetown* (1934), pp. 352–53; *Records of the Am. Cath. Hist. Soc.,* Dec. 1917; *Proc. N. Y. State Bar Asso.,* 1916; *N. Y. Times,* Oct. 18, 1915.] R. J. P.

SHIPP, ALBERT MICAJAH (June 15, 1819–June 27, 1887), Methodist Episcopal clergyman, educator, was born in Stokes County,

N. C., the son of John and Elizabeth (Oglesby) Shipp. Converted at Rock Spring camp meeting in August 1835, he joined the Methodist Church. In 1840 he was graduated at the University of North Carolina and in January of the following year was admitted on trial to the South Carolina Conference of the Methodist Episcopal Church. In 1843 he was ordained deacon by Bishop Andrew, and in December 1844, elder by Bishop Soule. He served two years on circuits, four years on stations, and one as presiding elder. He was a member of every General Conference of the Methodist Episcopal Church, South, from 1850 to 1886 inclusive, and of the Centennial Conference, held at Baltimore in 1884.

He early became one of the outstanding preachers in his denomination, but in 1848 his voice weakened under a chronic throat affection, making regular pulpit service thereafter impossible. His intellectual ability and his thorough scholarship pointed naturally to educational work as an alternative, and in 1848–49 he served as president of Greensboro Female College, North Carolina. For ten years (1849–59) he was professor of history in the University of North Carolina, and for the next sixteen years president of Wofford College, Spartanburg, S. C. From 1875 to 1885 he held the chair of exegetical theology in Vanderbilt University, for three years of the time serving as dean of the theological department and vice-chancellor of the University. Bishop Holland N. McTyeire, then powerful in the affairs of the institution, bluntly demanding a head of the theological department of greater ability, Shipp resigned in 1885, and was at his own request superannuated by the South Carolina Conference. The remaining two years of his life he spent at his home "Rose Hill," Marlboro County, near Cheraw, S. C.

As a teacher he won the respect and affection of his students. He was a man of correct literary taste and broad scholarship. In December 1876, his Conference requested him to prepare a history of Methodism in South Carolina. Pressure of his new duties at Vanderbilt University caused him to delay the project until the summer and fall of 1880, and the work, *The History of Methodism in South Carolina,* was published in 1883. Comprising a large amount of valuable data regarding both institutions and persons, it is still the most copious single body of information on the subject. It is less systematic, though more extensive, than Dr. A. M. Chreitzberg's *Early Methodism in the Carolinas* published in 1897. The effort expended in its preparation was a labor of love, and any profits from the pub-

lication were directed to the support of worn-out preachers and their widows and orphans. Though marked by hasty composition, it shows a realization of the part that Methodism has played in the life of the state and of its people, not neglecting the remarkable service rendered the slaves.

Dr. Shipp reared a large family; his wife was Mary, daughter of Samuel Gillepsie, a planter of Cheraw. An illness which the aged minister brought on by aiding a neighbor to fight a forest fire terminated in his death, at Cleveland Springs, N. C., where he had gone in quest of health.

[*Minutes of the . . . S. C. Ann. Conference of the M. E. Church,* 1887; *Southern Christian Advocate* (Columbia, S. C.), July 7, 14, 1887; *Christian Advocate* (Nashville), July 2, 16, 1887; K. P. Battle, *Hist. of the Univ. of N. C.* (2 vols., 1907–12); R. E. Grier, *S. C. and Her Builders* (1930), p. 335; *News and Courier* (Charleston), June 30, 1887; names of parents from Shipp's daughter.]   D. D. W.

SHIPP, SCOTT (Aug. 2, 1839–Dec. 4, 1917), soldier, educator, was born in Warrenton, Va., the son of John Shipp and Lucy (Scott) Shipp. After the death of his father in 1849, his mother married Henry Clarkson, a physician of Boone County, Mo., and the family removed there. He went to Westminster College at Fulton, Mo., and then found employment with a railroad. Attracting the attention of one of the officials of this railroad, Robert E. Rodes [*q.v.*], a graduate of the Virginia Military Institute, he was persuaded by Rodes to enter that institution, from which he graduated in 1859. From 1859 until the outbreak of the Civil War he was an assistant professor of mathematics and tactics there. He accompanied a detail of cadets to Harpers Ferry in December 1859 to witness the execution of John Brown. He was ordered in April 1861 with the entire corps of cadets to Camp Lee near Richmond to assist in the drilling of recruits for the Confederate army. Commissioned major in the 21st Virginia Infantry in July 1861, he participated in the West Virginia campaign in the late summer of 1861 under the command of Robert E. Lee and later served in the Romney campaign with Stonewall Jackson, his former preceptor and colleague. Upon the reopening of the Virginia Military Institute in 1862 he was ordered to report there as commandant of the cadets with the rank of lieutenant-colonel. He led the cadets into the field on five occasions, the most notable being the Valley campaign when the Federals under Hunter invaded the Valley of Virginia. In this campaign the cadets formed a part of Breckinridge's army and won fame at the battle of New Market in May 1864, where, though wounded, Shipp skilfully conducted the battalion of cadets across an open field against the Federals under the terrific fire of their batteries. Throughout the war he chafed at the inactive service imposed upon him and twice sought unsuccessfully to be relieved of his duties at the institute in order to join Lee's army. After the battle of Gettysburg, he obtained a two months' furlough, joined as a private the famous Black Horse Troop (4th Virginia Cavalry) and skirmished with it during July and August.

After the war he resumed his duties as commandant of the cadets, though he contemplated for a time the practice of law and in 1866 was graduated from the Lexington Law School (later the law department of Washington and Lee University. On Aug. 19, 1869, he was married to Anne Morson of Richmond. They had three children. For many years he was a vestryman of the Robert E. Lee Memorial Church in Lexington. He refused in 1880 the proffered honor of the presidency of the newly created Virginia Agricultural and Mechanical College (Virginia Polytechnic Institute), when he found himself restricted in the selection of his faculty. In spite of his denunciation of the Readjuster party he survived the proposed general change of the officers of the institute at the hands of a Readjuster board of visitors. Upon the resignation of Gen. Francis H. Smith in 1889 Shipp was elevated to the superintendency of the Virginia Military Institute in January 1890 and served in this capacity until his retirement in June 1907. As commandant and superintendent, he was noted as a strict disciplinarian. He dismissed his own son for a violation of military discipline, for which a lesser penalty than dismissal had been inflicted in the past, and he opposed, though not successfully, the boy's reinstatement later by the board of visitors. In educational matters, he was very conservative and emphasized the military feature of the institute against the wishes of a group of the alumni. Materially, his administration witnessed many changes, freedom from debt, increased appropriations from the state, an enlarged corps (to which he was on the whole opposed), and more buildings. During this period he was a member of the board of visitors at the United States Military Academy in 1890, and at the United States Naval Academy in 1894.

[J. C. Wise, *Personal Memoir of . . . Scott Shipp* (1915) and *The Military Hist. of the Va. Mil. Institute* (1915); *War of the Rebellion: Official Records (Army)*, 1 ser., XXXVII, pt. 1; F. H. Smith, *The Va. Mil. Institute* (1912); *Cat. of the Officers and Alumni of Washington and Lee Univ.* (1888).]   W. G. B—n.

SHIPPEN, EDWARD (1639–Oct. 2, 1712), mayor of Philadelphia, speaker of the Assembly, president of the provincial council, and acting governor of Pennsylvania, was born at Methley in Yorkshire, England, and was baptised in the parish church on Mar. 5, 1639. He was the son of Mary (Nunes) and William Shippen, a prosperous yeoman and an overseer of the poor and of the highways. In 1668 he emigrated to Boston, Mass., where he soon became a wealthy merchant and owner of real estate. He joined the Society of Friends about 1671 and was severely persecuted on account of his faith until about 1694, when he removed his family and his business to Philadelphia. In 1695 he was elected to the provincial Assembly of Pennsylvania and was chosen speaker. He served as an elective member of the provincial council from 1696 until the constitution was changed in 1701 and then as an appointive member until 1712. He was president of the council from 1702 to 1712 and acting governor from April 1703 until February 1704. He also served again as a member of the Assembly in 1700–01 and 1705–06. In the charter of Philadelphia, granted by William Penn on Oct. 25, 1701, he was named as mayor and held that post until October 1703. He was also city treasurer from 1705 until 1712. The tradition that he was chief justice of Pennsylvania in 1698 is probably erroneous, but he was justice of the peace for many years, presiding justice of the county courts of Philadelphia, 1698–1701, and an associate justice of the supreme court, 1699–1703 (Martin, *post,* p. 14). He died at his home in Philadelphia.

He has been described as "a man of courage, energy, integrity, intelligence and sagacity" (*Letters and Papers, post,* p. xvii). Penn was favorably impressed by his business ability, and he served as one of the proprietary commissioners of property from 1701 until his death. He was famous in his day as the biggest man and the owner of "the biggest house and the biggest coach" in Philadelphia. His home, near the northwest corner of Spruce and Second streets, was called "the Great House" or "the Governor's House." It was surrounded by "extraordinary fine and large Gardens abounding with Tulips, Pinks, Carnations, Roses (of several sorts), Lilies" and many other flowers and shrubs (Gabriel Thomas, *An Historical and Geographical Account of Pensilvania,* 1698, p. 43, spelling the name Shippey). He was married three times: at Boston in 1671 to Elizabeth Lybrand, who died on Oct. 25, 1688; on Sept. 4, 1689, to Rebecca (Howard) Richardson of New York, who died in February 1705; and in Philadelphia, about Aug. 1, 1706, to Esther (Wilcox) James, who died in August 1724. His first wife probably converted him to the Quaker faith, but the story that he withdrew from the Quakers and retired from public life because of his third marriage (*Letters and Papers, post,* p. xviii) has no foundation. The manuscript records of the Society of Friends show, however, that Shippen was subjected to discipline, because he had anticipated the marriage relation with his third wife. He was finally pardoned and was a member of the Society in good standing at the time of his death. There is also evidence that the comparative inactivity of his later years was due to lack of health ("Correspondence," *post,* I, 304, II, 302, 307). He had eleven children, of whom Joseph became the grandfather of Edward Shippen (1729–1806) and William Shippen [*qq.v.*].

[Thomas Balch, *Letters and Papers Relating chiefly to the Provincial History of Pennsylvania* (1855); "Correspondence between Wm. Penn and James Logan," ed. by Edward Armstrong, *Memoirs of the Hist. Soc. of Pa.,* vols. IX, X (1870–72); J. H. Martin, *Martin's Bench and Bar of Philadelphia* (1883); C. P. Keith, *Provincial Councillors of Pa.* (1883); T. W. Balch, *The English Ancestors of the Shippen Family and Edward Shippen of Philadelphia* (1904); material in the Shippen, Penn and Logan manuscripts in the possession of the Pa. Hist. Soc. and in the manuscript records of the Society of Friends in Philadelphia; portrait, painted by an unknown artist, in possession of family and reproduced in J. T. Scharf and Thompson Westcott, *Hist. of Philadelphia* (1884), vol. I, p. 158.]
W. R. S—h.

SHIPPEN, EDWARD (Feb. 16/26, 1728/29– Apr. 15 1806), chief justice of Pennsylvania, was the son of Sarah (Plumley) and Edward Shippen of Lancaster and the great-grandson of Edward Shippen [*q.v.*]. He was born and went to school in Philadelphia. He went to London, probably not before 1748 (letter of Feb. 25, 1748, concerning "seeing all the curiosities," Balch, *post,* p. 15), read law in Middle Temple, and was called to the English bar on Feb. 9, 1750. He also studied law in the office of Tench Francis [*q.v.*], to whose daughter Margaret Francis he was later married, on Nov. 29, 1753. They had nine children, one of whom, Margaret, married Benedict Arnold [*q.v.*]. On Sept. 25, 1750, he was admitted to practice before the supreme court of Pennsylvania, and he soon became one of the leaders of the provincial bar. He was a member of the common council of Philadelphia, 1755–56, and on May 27, 1758, was elected clerk of the council and clerk of the city court. He was prothonotary of the supreme court from about 1762 until 1776 and a member of the provincial council from 1770 to 1775. We owe to his pen the earliest published law reports of the supreme court of Pennsylvania (A. J. Dallas, "Reports of Cases . . . in Pennsylvania," printed in the first

volume of Dallas' *United States Reports,* pp. 1– 7, 29. See also vol. II–IV for Shippen's opinions). He was also a judge of the court of vice admiralty from 1752 until 1776, although the position had "little or no value" after the court was reorganized in 1768 (*Pennsylvania Archives,* ser. 1, vol. IV (1853), ed. by Samuel Hazard, p. 600).

He was a moderate Loyalist during the Revolution and for a time was practically interned on his country estate near the falls of the Schuylkill. In a letter of July 12, 1777, he pled the Test Act as an excuse for not visiting his father at Lancaster (Shippen Mss. VIII, 13). On Aug. 15, 1777, however, he and several other Loyalists who were willing to maintain an attitude of neutrality had "the bounds prescribed in their respective paroles enlarged to the whole state of Pennsylvania" (*Minutes of the Supreme Executive Council of Pennsylvania,* vol. XI, 1852, p. 269). He must have been successful in the rôle of neutral because he and his family were prominent in the social life of Philadelphia during both the British occupation and the military administration of General Arnold. His career was not seriously handicapped even by the treason of his son-in-law. He was president of the court of common pleas of Philadelphia County, 1784–91, justice of the peace, 1785–86, and president of the court of quarter sessions and general jail delivery, 1785–86. On Sept. 14, 1784, he was also appointed a judge of the high court of errors and appeals, which was at that time the highest appellate court in Pennsylvania, and he served on this court as a special judge until 1791. He was a member of the supreme court from 1791 until 1805, as an associate justice until 1799 and then as chief justice. Although he was a Federalist, he did not take an active part in politics, and his opinions were free from political bias. He and two of his associates were, however, impeached by the Democratic assembly in 1804 under charges growing out of the Passmore case, but they were acquitted by the Senate of the Commonwealth in January 1805 (William Hamilton, *Report of the Trial and Acquittal of Edward Shippen* (1805). His health was failing at this time, and later in the year he resigned from the bench. He died at his home in Philadelphia. He was noted for his kindness and generosity and for the courtesy and dignity of his manners. His conservative attitude at the time of the Revolution was probably due partly to his religious affiliations and partly to the fact that he was a member of the governor's executive council. He was born and bred in a Presbyterian atmosphere, his father being one of the founders of the College of New Jersey (Princeton), but in his early manhood he joined the Church of England.

[Letters in possession of the Pa. Hist. Soc.; sketch by Lawrence Lewis, Jr., in *Pa. Mag. of Hist. and Biog.,* Apr. 1883; *Ibid.,* Jan. 1901–Dec. 1902 with some letters to his daughter Margaret; Thomas Balch, *Letters and Papers Relating Chiefly to the Provincial Hist. of Pa.* (1855); C. P. Keith, *Provincial Councillors of Pa.* (1883); E. A. Jones, *Amer. Members of the Inns of Court* (1924); date of birth from records of First Presbyterian Church of Philadelphia and date of death from *Poulson's Am. Daily Advertiser* (Philadelphia), Apr. 17, 1806; his portrait painted by Gilbert Stuart in the Corcoran Gallery of Art, Washington, D. C.]

W. R. S—h.

SHIPPEN, WILLIAM (Oct. 21, 1736–July 11, 1808), physician and pioneer teacher of anatomy and midwifery, was born in Philadelphia, the cousin of Edward Shippen, 1729–1806, and the great-grandson of Edward Shippen, 1639–1712 [*qq.v.*]. He was the son of Susannah (Harrison) and William Shippen, who was one of the prominent medical men of his day and a member of the Continental Congress. After attending the academy kept by Samuel Finley [*q.v.*] at Nottingham, the boy went to the College of New Jersey (Princeton), from which he graduated in 1754. He then studied medicine with his father until 1757, when he went abroad to study. About 1760 he was married in London to Alice Lee, the sister of Francis Lightfoot, William, Richard Henry, and Arthur Lee [*qq.v.*]. He studied especially under William Hunter and Colin McKenzie. He won the esteem and friendship of John Fothergill, who became greatly interested in his plans to establish courses in midwifery and anatomy in Philadelphia. From London he went to Edinburgh, where he received the degree of M.D. in 1761, with a thesis *"De Placentae cum Utero Nexu"* (1761). In spite of the fact that Great Britain and France were at war, through the good offices of Sir John Pringle, the physician-general of the British Army, he was able to take an English lady suffering from tuberculosis to southern France for her health and to see something of the medical schools at Paris and Montpellier.

When he returned to Philadelphia in 1762, Fothergill sent, in his care, to the Pennsylvania Hospital a number of anatomical drawings and casts that he desired the managers to permit Shippen to use in his teaching. The pictures had been made by Jan Van Rymsdyk, the celebrated Dutch painter residing in London, who made most of the pictures for William Hunter's great work on the gravid uterus. They are still preserved in excellent condition in the hospital. Shippen began his courses on Nov. 16, 1762, in the State House. Although he made use of the Fothergill pictures and casts, he utilized chiefly the dissection of human bodies, a method taught by Hunter. This aroused the animosity of the populace, his dissecting rooms were mobbed on several occasions, and once he narrowly escaped with his life; but his courses were very successful, and the number of students increased year by year. Somewhat later he began giving courses on midwifery, not only to medical students but also to women who intended to practise midwifery. When John Morgan [*q.v.*] succeeded in getting the trustees of the College of Philadelphia to organize a medical school in connection with the college in 1765, Shippen was appointed professor of surgery and anatomy. In 1776 he was appointed chief physician and director general of the hospital in the Continental Army in New Jersey. In October of the same year he was appointed by Congress director general of all the hospitals in the west side of the Hudson River, and, after John Morgan was displaced by Congress, was appointed on Apr. 11, 1777, chief physician and director-general of the Continental Army hospital in his stead. Morgan in his published *Vindication of his Public Character* (1777) accused Shippen of having procured his discharge by underhand means in order that he might get the position. In March 1777 Shippen had submitted to Congress a plan for the reorganization of the army medical department, which had been adopted practically in its entirety; and this brought him prominently to the notice of Congress and, no doubt, had much to do with his obtaining the appointment (copy of this plan in Shippen's handwriting in the Library of Congress). Shippen himself was later subjected to a court martial on charges of financial irregularity in his department. He was acquitted and remained chief of the medical department of the Continental Army until his resignation in 1781. In 1778 he was elected physician to the Pennsylvania Hospital, but he resigned in the following year owing to the pressure of his military duties.

In 1791 he again became a member of the staff of the hospital, on which he continued to serve until 1802. He was one of the founders of the College of Physicians of Philadelphia and was president from 1805 to 1808. When the legislature repealed the charter of the College of Philadelphia in 1779 and created the University of the State of Pennsylvania, he accepted a chair in the new school. In 1791, when the University of Pennsylvania was established, he was appointed professor of anatomy, surgery, and midwifery. After the death of his only son, a young man of great promise, in 1798 he seems to have lost interest in life. His health gradually declined, his practice fell off, and he seldom lectured. He died in Philadelphia.

[A few papers and letters in Lib. of Cong.; Caspar Wistar, *Eulogium on Doctor Wm. Shippen, Delivered . . . 1809* (1818) and reprinted in *Philadelphia Journ. of the Medical and Physical Sciences,* vol. V (1822); Charles Caldwell, *Extract from an Eulogium on Wm. Shippen* (1818); G. W. Norris, *The Early Hist. of Philadelphia* (1886); J. F. Watson, *Annals of Philadelphia* (1844); T. G. Morton, *The Hist. of the Pa. Hospital* (1895); W. S. W. Ruschenberger, *An Account of . . . the College of Physicians of Philadelphia* (1887); Joseph Carson, *A Hist. of the Medical Department of the Univ. of Pa.* (1869); Roberdeau Buchanan, *Geneal. of the Descendants of Dr. Wm. Shippen* (1877); date of birth from E. W. Balch, *The Descendants of Edward Shippen* (1883).]   F. R. P.

SHIRAS, GEORGE (Jan. 26, 1832–Aug. 2, 1924), jurist, was born in Pittsburgh, Pa., one of four sons of George and Eliza (Herron) Shiras. His paternal ancestry was of Scotch origin, but American since 1750, when an earlier George Shiras settled at Mount Holly, N. J.; his maternal ancestors had also long been in the country. His general education was completed at Ohio University (Athens) and at Yale College, where he was graduated in 1853. After studying law in the office of Judge Hopewell Hepburn of Pittsburgh and in the Yale Law School, though he was not graduated therefrom, he was admitted to the Pittsburgh bar, Nov. 7, 1855. He practised first for a year in Dubuque, Iowa, in partnership with his brother, Oliver Perry Shiras [*q.v.*], then in Pittsburgh as a partner of Judge Hepburn (1858–62), and thereafter independently. He attained eminence as a lawyer and was constantly employed for many years in cases involving the railroad, banking, oil, coal, and iron interests of western Pennsylvania. In 1882 he was offered, as a compromise selection of the Pennsylvania legislature by a very close vote, an opportunity to represent his state in the Senate of the United States, but, apparently because of his own slight interest, he was not nominated.

On July 19, 1892, he was nominated by President Harrison as an associate justice of the Supreme Court of the United States. Though favored by the bar, he was opposed by the senators of his state, apparently only because, both being very insecure in office and at outs with the President, they were anxious about patronage, and Shiras was too little of a politician for them (A. K. McClure, *Old Time Notes of Pennsylvania,* 1905, II, 572–73, 579–81, 584; Carson, *post,* II, 560–63). Because of this situation, the Judiciary Committee of the Senate reported the nomination without recommendation, but it was

nevertheless speedily confirmed, July 26, 1892. His wide experience and his personal qualities of courtesy, dignity, quick apprehension, clarity of thought, and restrained judgment, well qualified Shiras for judicial service. Unquestionably, also, he was a very able man and a lawyer of ample experience and technical acquirements. Yet his work as a member of the Court, while entirely creditable, was not remarkable, unless for one unfortunate incident. In the Income Tax Case (1895, *Pollock* vs. *Farmers' Loan & Trust Co., 157 U. S. 429, 158 U. S., 601*), one of immense importance and historical interest, Shiras was long supposed to have changed his vote on reargument, thus, by a vote of five to four, causing reversal of the first decision and nullification of the federal statute as unconstitutional (Warren, *post,* II, 700). Violent criticism followed, but since the grant of a reargument concedes the propriety of changed opinions, personal criticism was necessarily unjust, particularly so if it was in truth, as intimated by Chief Justice Hughes, another of the justices who changed his vote (C. E. Hughes, *The Supreme Court,* 1928, p. 54). The criticisms directed against him Shiras met with silence. He resigned on Feb. 23, 1903, under the statute of 1869 permitting voluntary retirement on full pay at the age of seventy, after ten years of service. He had married, Dec. 31, 1857, Lillie E. Kennedy, daughter of Robert T. Kennedy, a manufacturer of Pittsburgh. Two sons, both lawyers, survived him. He died in Pittsburgh, as the result of a fall.

[Shiras' opinions are to be found in 146–188 *U. S. Reports.* For biog. data and comment see H. L. Carson, *The Hist. of the Supreme Court* (1902), II, 560–64; Charles Warren, *The Supreme Court in U. S. Hist.* (rev. ed., 1926), II, 699 and index; *Yale Univ. Obit. Record,* 1925; *Who's Who in America,* 1922–23; *Report of the . . . Pa. Bar Asso.,* 1925; *N. Y. Times,* Aug. 3, 1924.]   F. S. P.

SHIRAS, OLIVER PERRY (Oct. 22, 1833–Jan. 7, 1916), jurist, brother of George Shiras [*q.v.*], was one of four sons of George and Eliza (Herron) Shiras. The home of the family during his youth was on a farm near the Ohio River about twenty miles from his birthplace, Pittsburgh. At the age of fifteen he entered the preparatory department of Ohio University at Athens, where he graduated in 1853. Thence he went to Yale. After a year of scientific study, he decided to be a lawyer and in 1856 obtained the degree of LL.B. Attracted by the bustling character of Dubuque, Iowa, while exploring the West for professional opportunity, he was easily persuaded by old friends, the Herron brothers, to settle there in preference to Chicago.

On Aug. 9, 1856, he was admitted to the Iowa bar. Confident of the future, in February 1857 he married Elizabeth Mitchell of Springfield, Ohio, by whom he had four children. In August 1862 he was commissioned first lieutenant and quartermaster of the 27th Iowa Volunteer Infantry, but was transferred to staff duty as an aide to Brigadier-General F. J. Herron [q.v.] before his own regiment was mustered in. Service as judge advocate took him campaigning with the Army of the Frontier, but he resigned in December 1863 and returned to resume the practice of law at Dubuque. His firm maintained an enviable reputation until it was dissolved by political preferment. When the federal judicial district of northern Iowa was created, Shiras was appointed judge, in August 1882. Thereupon he made one of his partners clerk of the court, and in November of the same year the other partner, D. B. Henderson [q.v.], was elected to Congress.

On the federal bench Shiras was known for his wisdom, integrity, and precise reasoning. His little manual, *Equity Practice in the United States Circuit Courts* (1889), is perhaps as much an evidence of his own interests as it is an attempt to aid the busy practitioner and the novice. One of the most important disputes to come before him was an action in equity—the final episode in the long stream of litigation flowing from the ambiguous Des Moines River improvement land grant. The government presented a bill to confirm the title of certain settlers to land they were supposed to have obtained from the United States, but Shiras, following the precedents of previous cases, dismissed the claim, though he recognized the injustice of deciding the dispute in favor of either party and recommended that Congress compensate the injured settlers for the loss of their homesteads (43 *Federal Reporter*, 1). The Supreme Court sustained this judgment, and Congress eventually followed his advice (142 *U. S.*, 510; 28 *U. S. Statutes at Large*, 396). The occasion for his principal judicial contribution, however, arose in connection with the attempt of the railroads to avoid regulation of interstate traffic before Congress assumed control in 1887. In opposition to the doctrine of a legal vacuum created by the failure of Congress to exercise its power (*Swift* vs. *Railroad Companies*, 58 *Federal Reporter*, 858), Shiras in 1894 enunciated the conception of a national common law subject to independent application by the federal courts irrespective of state interpretation. He held that the binding force of the general system of jurisprudence as applied to the whole country by the federal government was not derived from action by the states or subject to abrogation by them. In the absence of congressional legislation, the common rules of the common law prevail. Thus the railroads could not escape responsibility in a sphere of anarchy. His elaborate opinion in *Murray* vs. *Chicago & North Western* (62 *Federal Reporter*, 24) was cited with approval by Justice Brewer of the Supreme Court (181 *U. S.*, 92), and has become the accepted view.

On Oct. 11, 1888, in St. Paul, Minn., Shiras married his second wife, Hetty E. (Spaulding) Cornwall. He retired from the bench at the age of seventy, in November 1903, and thereafter devoted his attention to civic affairs until his death in 1916.

[E. H. Stiles, *Recollections and Sketches of Notable Lawyers and Public Men of Early Iowa* (1916), 167–69; *Who's Who in America*, 1914–15.; *Proc . . . Iowa State Bar Asso.*, 1916; *Yale Univ. Obit. Record*, 1916; *Dubuque Times-Journal*, Jan. 7, 16, 1916.]

J. E. B.

SHIRLAW, WALTER (Aug. 6, 1838–Dec. 26, 1909), genre, portrait, and mural painter, and engraver, was born at Paisley, Scotland. His father was an inventor, and a maker of the handlooms used in the weaving of Paisley shawls. Before Walter was three the family came to America and settled in New York, where at the age of twelve he left school and entered the employ of a firm of real-estate agents. Soon afterward he was apprenticed for a term of five years to an engraver of banknotes, and during that time succeeded in saving about $800 with which to begin a career as a painter. His first picture was hung at the National Academy exhibition of 1861, but a few years later he found it expedient for economic reasons to return to engraving for a livelihood. For five years, until 1870, he was with the Western Bank Note and Engraving Company of Chicago. He was active in the founding of the Art Institute of Chicago, which was conceived about this time. In 1870 he went to Munich, where for about seven years he studied and painted. His first teacher was George Raab, in whose class he obtained a sound knowledge of drawing; later he came under the instruction of Alexander Wagner, A. G. Von Ramberg, and Wilhelm Lindenschmit, the younger. It was at Munich that he painted his two best pictures, "Toning the Bell" (1874) and "Sheep-Shearing in the Bavarian Highlands" (1876). Returning in 1877 to New York, where he exhibited his "Sheep-Shearing" at the National Academy, he became one of the founders and the first president of the Society of American Artists, taught in the Art Students' League, and occupied a studio in the old university building in Washington Square. In 1880 he married Florence Manchester. That year at the Doll and Richards gallery, Boston, he opened a notable "one-man show" containing fifty-eight oil paintings and a large collection of water colors and drawings. About ten years later he held another important exhibition in Boston. He became an Academician in 1888.

When mural decorations became popular he was commissioned to execute a frieze symbolizing peace and plenty for Darius Ogden Mills [q.v.] of New York. In this rich composition, which is excellent in design and felicitous in mood, he employed not only human figures but animals, birds, flowers, and fruits. A still more important decoration from his hand is the ceiling painting, "The Sciences," in the entrance pavilion of the west corridor in the Library of Congress, Washington, a series of eight female figures whose symbolic value is obvious enough but not over-emphasized. The design is conspicuously good, the play of line in the draperies being exceptionally fluid and rhythmical. He was one of the group of painters who decorated the dome of the Manufactures and Liberal Arts building of the Columbian Exposition in Chicago in 1893. He also did some minor decorative work for the house of William Thomas Evans [q.v.], including two stained-glass windows, "The Rainbow" and "The Lost Chord." He traveled much, and everywhere recorded his impressions. He made a considerable number of illustrations, usually in charcoal, for such magazines as the *Century* and *Harper's Monthly*. He was a master designer, a serious and weighty painter, an influential teacher, a man of culture and intelligence, and his success, though not phenomenal, was fairly commensurate with his merits. In the summer of 1909 he went to Spain; in December in Madrid he became ill and died after three weeks. He was buried in the English cemetery there. Soon after his death memorial exhibitions of his pictures were held in New York, Buffalo, Boston, Washington, Pittsburgh, Chicago, and St. Louis. His pictures are in museums in St. Louis, Buffalo, Chicago, Washington, and Indianapolis; and in the Century, Lotos, and Salmagundi Clubs, New York. The examples in St. Louis and Buffalo are of his best, but "Toning the Bell," probably his masterpiece, is privately owned (1934) in Chicago.

[*Who's Who in America*, 1908–09; T. H. Bartlett, in *Am. Art Rev.*, July and Aug. 1881, a full account of Shirlaw; W. H. Downes and F. T. Robinson, "Later Am. Masters," in *New England Mag.*, Apr. 1896; Royal Cortissoz, "Color in the Court of Honor at the Fair," *Century Mag.*, July 1893; A. J. Searle, in *Internat. Studio*, May 1911; S. G. W. Benjamin, *Our Am. Artists* (1879); Samuel Isham, *The Hist. of Am.*

Painting (1905); Clara E. Clement and Laurence Hutton, *Artists of the Nineteenth Century* (1885); *Handbook of the New Lib. of Congress* (1897), comp. by Herbert Small; Art Inst. of Chicago, *A Memorial Coll. of Works by Walter Shirlaw, N. A.* (1911); *Cat. of Am. Paintings Belonging to William T. Evans* (1900); *Cat. of the Private Art Coll. of T. B. Clarke* (1899); obituaries in *Am. Art News*, Jan. 1, 1910, *N. Y. Times*, Dec. 30, 1909.]　　　　　　　　　　W. H. D.

SHIRLEY, WILLIAM (Dec. 2, 1694–Mar. 24, 1771), colonial governor, was born at Preston, in Sussex, the son of William Shirley, a London merchant, and Elizabeth, daughter of John Godman of Ote Hall, Wivelsfield, Sussex. When he was seven years old his father died, leaving him with comparatively little property but with aristocratic tastes and connections. From the Merchant Taylors' School, London, he was admitted pensioner at Pembroke College, Cambridge, and received the degree of A.B. in 1714/15. On July 3, 1720, he was called to the bar. Meanwhile he had married Frances, daughter of Francis Barker of London. Five daughters and four sons were born to them. For eleven years Shirley practised law in London, gaining a substantial reputation and influential friends, but not much money. A crisis in his financial affairs decided him to emigrate to America, and with his family he landed at Boston, Oct. 27, 1731, bearing a letter from his kinsman and lifelong patron, Thomas Pelham-Holles, Duke of Newcastle, to Gov. Jonathan Belcher [q.v.].

Shirley was by nature a "prerogative man" and his earliest case in Boston of a controversial sort aligned him with that party. While Belcher yielded more and more to the colonial view of business matters, Shirley upheld the imperial. He was appointed judge of admiralty in 1733, a post he soon exchanged for that of advocate-general. He labored faithfully to enforce the Molasses Act and other measures relative to trade, while in his private capacity he became counsel for Samuel Waldo [q.v.], a large operator in timber lands and one of the richest capitalists of Boston. Unsympathetic toward Belcher's policy of permitting the exploitation of the King's Woods by colonial business men, Shirley sent to England by the hand of his wife a report which tended to weaken the confidence of the government in Belcher's administration. Frances Shirley also improved the occasion to plead her husband's cause. He had already asked for several offices without success; she now pressed the Duke of Newcastle for a salary for the Advocate-General, or for her husband's appointment as collector of customs or naval officer at Boston, and finally, for his appointment as governor. In 1739 she was joined in England by Waldo, who was anxious to be rid of Belcher. The Governor for the moment was still too strong to be displaced, but in 1740 Shirley's opportunity arose, with the necessity for raising troops in New England for the English expedition to the West Indies. Acting on Newcastle's suggestion, he was much more successful in enlisting recruits than the unpopular Belcher, and this success enabled him to supersede his rival. He was commissioned governor of Massachusetts on May 25, 1741.

One of the first difficulties he had to meet was the problem of the land bank, left to him by his predecessor. This agrarian scheme for cheap money had created much ill feeling in the colony, but Shirley handled his share in it with adroitness, winning the respect even of the defeated land bankers. On his accession to office he also found the colonial defense in a precarious condition, but eventually persuaded the General Court to make fairly liberal appropriations for the repair of Castle William and other fortifications. By the time that war with the French, which he had foreseen, was declared in 1744, he had put the colony into a fair state of defense, and adjusted the problem of paper money.

With the outbreak of hostilities he at once showed himself alive to the economic importance of the war from the standpoint of the colonies, particularly as concerned the fisheries. To protect these and to provide themselves a naval base, the French, at vast expense, had fortified Louisbourg on Cape Breton Island, but as Shirley knew, the garrison there was in a weak condition, owing to the neglect and venality of the authorities. After the beginning of war, the French governor made an attack on an outpost of New England fishermen on Canso Island which, though ineffectual, aroused the ire of New England, and Shirley conceived the desire to capture Louisbourg. Undismayed by the failure to receive encouragement from the government in England, he matured his plans and laid the proposition before the General Court of Massachusetts. That body at first would have nothing to do with it, but the governor had gained the confidence of prominent merchants and with their help succeeded in winning the Court to the support of his plans, provided the other New England colonies would cooperate in the audacious project. The other governors promptly consented, and the expedition was set under way.

Shirley ably handled the negotiations with the other governments, the Court, and the English authorities. Carefully side-stepping trouble with the touchy governor of New Hampshire, Benning Wentworth [q.v.], who desired to lead the expedition, Shirley appointed William Pepperrell [q.v.] to the command. Meanwhile Newcastle in England had been more active in their behalf than the colonists knew, and Commodore Peter Warren [q.v.], in command of the fleet cruising in the West Indies, had been ordered to cooperate with the colonial forces. After some delay, Shirley was able to dispatch some thirty-three hundred men from Massachusetts, who with the smaller forces sent by New Hampshire, Connecticut, and Rhode Island, arrived at Louisbourg a few days after the fleet had taken up its position there. The undertaking was completely successful, and the capture of the weakly defended fortress on June 17, 1745, was the one great English victory of the war. Shirley wrote an account of it which was published in *A Letter ... to ... the Duke of Newcastle: with a Journal of the Siege of Louisbourg* (1746). The government rewarded his services by making him colonel of a British regiment to be raised from the New England provincial troops, and used him as a clearing house in examining the claims of the northern colonies for reimbursement of expenditures growing out of the war. Massachusetts' share of the amount allowed by Parliament in 1748 was approximately £183,649. With this unprecedented amount in hard cash the colony was enabled to retire its paper money and place its finances on a sound basis.

Meanwhile, in 1749, Shirley had gone to England on leave. While there he was appointed a member of the commission sitting in Paris to determine the boundary line between French North America and New England. The negotiations were spun out to interminable length and it was not until 1753 that he returned to his post in Boston. His first wife had died there in September 1746, and in Paris he married a young Frenchwoman, Julie ——, the daughter of his landlord.

Shirley foresaw that war must soon begin again between England and France, and as early as January 1754, writing to the authorities in England, urged the importance of uniting the colonies and the strategic significance of Crown Point. He also did what he could to establish friendly relations with the Indians. In February 1755 he was appointed major-general and in April was one of the five governors who attended a council of war with Gen. Edward Braddock [q.v.] at Alexandria, Va., to bring about concerted action. Here he argued the importance of controlling the Great Lakes, and when the council decided to move against Niagara, Crown Point, and the forks of the Ohio, Shirley was given command of the Niagara expedition. Af-

ter the death of Braddock in July, he was the acknowledged commander of all the British forces
on the continent and in August he was formally
appointed to that position, although "his friends
saw the risk he was running, and wished he had
contented himself with his civil station" (Hutchinson, *post*, III, 38). His plans were sound, and
that they were unsuccessful must be attributed
in great measure to bickerings among the colonies, their failure to provide men and supplies,
and jealousy and lack of cooperation on the part
of individuals which Shirley had neither the capacity nor the prestige to overcome. He himself
took the field with the Niagara expedition, which
got no further than Oswego; confronted by a
strong French force at Kingston, he left a garrison—inadequately provisioned—and turned
back to Boston. His eldest son, secretary to
Braddock, had been killed in Pennsylvania with
his chief; his second son, a captain, died of fever
on the Oswego expedition.

Meanwhile, the Governor's political enemies
had been increasing in numbers and strength,
and with the failure of his military venture they
accused him of gross mismanagement and of in-
termeddling in Indian affairs, the sole province
of William Johnson [*q.v.*]. At the same time a
number of letters from some officer in the British colonies to the French were intercepted; in
England it was believed these letters might have
been written by Shirley, and the home authorities suspected him of treason. He was replaced
as commander in chief temporarily by James
Abercromby and then by John Campbell, Earl
of Loudoun [*qq.v.*]. The latter, irritated by the
evidences of Shirley's inefficiency as a military
man and carelessness in financial matters, took
an intense dislike to him and for a while seemed
to be intent on destroying him. Shirley was ordered to England early in 1756 and after unwarranted delay sailed in October, arriving as his
patron's ministry fell and was followed by that
of Pitt. Officials of the War Office wished to have
him court-martialed, but for lack of evidence
against him the matter was dropped in the fall
of 1757. Meanwhile, he had been succeeded as
governor of Massachusetts by Thomas Pownall
[*q.v.*]. He was given the rank of lieutenant-general and was promised the post of governor of
Jamaica but did not receive it; in 1761 he was
made governor of the Bahama Islands. This post
he relinquished to his only surviving son, Thomas, in 1767. Two years later he returned to Massachusetts and took up his residence in his mansion, "Shirley Place," at Roxbury, where in
March 1771 he died.

Shirley with reason has been called a "place-

hunter"—even after he became governor of
Massachusetts he expressed a desire for other,
perhaps more comfortable, appointments. Nevertheless, as an executive he showed ability and
tact, and although he steadily upheld what he
believed to be the rights of the Crown, he became one of the most popular of colonial governors. In spite of his straitened circumstances
and loose handling of army contracts and
finances, his personal integrity was unimpeachable. Although as a military commander he was
neither a tactician nor an organizer, he had more
than any other contemporary governor a broad
grasp of the whole imperial problem.

[The major published source is *Correspondence of
William Shirley . . . 1731–1760* (2 vols., 1912), ed. by
C. H. Lincoln. See also Wm. Alexander, *The Conduct
of Maj. Gen. Shirley . . . Briefly Stated* (1758), a vindi-
cation by his private secretary; "Aspinwall Papers,"
Mass. Hist. Soc. Colls., 4 ser. IX–X (1871); "The
Belcher Papers," *Ibid.*, 6 ser. VI–VII (1893–94); "The
Pepperrell Papers," *Ibid.*, 6 ser. X (1899); *Acts of the
Privy Council of England, Colonial Ser.*, vols. III–VI
(1910–12); John and J. A. Venn, *Alumni Cantabri-
gienses*, pt. 1, vol. IV (1927); Thomas Hutchinson,
The Hist. of the Province of Mass. Bay, vol. III
(1828); H. L. Osgood, *The Am. Colonies in the Eigh-
teenth Century* (1924), vols. III, IV; S. M. Pargellis,
Lord Loudoun in North America (1933); J. T. Adams,
Revolutionary New England (1923); E. P. Shirley,
Stemmata Shirleiana (1873); H. W. Foote, *Annals of
King's Chapel* (2 vols., 1882–96); G. A. Wood, *William Shirley* (1920) is an administrative study cover-
ing the years 1731–49. The sketch by J. A. Doyle in
Dict. Nat. Biog. is not very satisfactory.]   J. T. A.

SHOBONIER [See SHABONEE, *c.* 1775–1859].

SHOLES, CHRISTOPHER LATHAM
(Feb. 14, 1819–Feb. 17, 1890), printer, journalist, inventor, the son of Orrin Sholes, was born
on a farm at Mooresburg, Pa. His ancestors,
who came from England, settled in the vicinity
of Groton, Conn. He is said to have been a lineal descendant of John and Priscilla Alden, and
to have had several ancestors who served with
distinction in the Revolutionary War. When
Sholes was young his parents moved to Danville,
Pa., where he attended Henderson's school until
he was fourteen. When he had completed an apprenticeship of four years on the *Danville Intelligencer*, his parents moved to Wisconsin and
settled at Green Bay. Although he was in rather
delicate health, young Sholes went to work immediately at his trade; within a year he had become state printer and had taken charge of the
house journal of the territorial legislature, carrying it to Philadelphia to be printed. At twenty
he left home to follow his brother Charles to
Madison, Wis., where the latter had acquired
a substantial interest in the *Wisconsin Enquirer*.
After service for a year as editor of this paper
and as journal clerk of the legislature, he married Mary Jane McKinney at Green Bay on Feb.

4, 1841, and moved to Southport (later Kenosha), Wis., to become editor of the *Southport Telegraph* for four years, resigning when he was appointed postmaster of Southport, by President Polk. Through his activities as a journalist and postmaster, he was eventually drawn into politics in spite of the fact that he was very poorly fitted for it by character and temperament. He served, however, with credit to his constituents, two terms as state senator, and one term in the state assembly. In 1860 he moved with his family to Milwaukee, where he had accepted the editorship of the *Milwaukee News*. Subsequently he served as editor of the *Milwaukee Sentinel* but gave up this position to become collector of the port of Milwaukee, an appointment made by President Lincoln.

That Sholes was possessed of inventive genius in addition to his journalistic and political ability is evidenced by the fact that at an early date in his newspaper work he devised a method of addressing newspapers by printing the names of subscribers on the margin, but his extremely busy life at this time prevented his following closely his inventive bent. His less arduous duties as collector of customs presumably gave him the opportunity of exercising these talents again, for he and a machinist friend, Samuel W. Soulé, were granted a patent for a paging machine on Sept. 27, 1864, and one for a machine numbering serially the pages of blank books on Nov. 13, 1866; on Apr. 30, 1867, Sholes alone received patent No. 64,375 for an improvement on the numbering machine. Both men had space to work in a small machine-shop where there was also a third inventor, Carlos Glidden. The latter one day suggested to Sholes that as he had devised a numbering machine he ought to be well fitted to perfect a letter-printing machine, and referred him to a published account of a writing machine newly invented in London by John Pratt [*q.v.*]. The suggestion so much appealed to Sholes that he devoted the rest of his life to the perfection of the typewriter, which he lived to see definitely established and in use throughout the world. Sholes, Glidden, and Soulé were granted a patent for a typewriter, No. 79,265, on June 23, 1868, and another, No. 79,868, a month later. For the next five years Sholes struggled unsuccessfully to make and market the machine. In August 1871 he obtained a third patent for improvements. His partners one at a time relinquished their rights in the patents for working capital, and on Mar. 1, 1873, he gave up his rights to the Remington Arms Company for $12,000. This company, with its complement of fine machinery and expert mechanics, perfected the Sholes typewrit-

er and successfully introduced it as the Remington typewriter. Sholes continued making typewriter experiments with the help of two sons, giving all of the results to the Remington company. His last patent was granted Aug. 27, 1878. The strain told on his naturally frail constitution, however; he became consumptive, and spent the last nine years of his life in search of health, though he continued to work on inventions even when he was too weak to be about. He was survived by his wife, six sons, and four daughters.

[Waldemar Kaempffert, *A Popular Hist. of Am. Invention* (1924), vol. I; C. E. Weller, *The Early Hist. of the Typewriter* (1918); H. W. Roby, *The Story of the Invention of the Typewriter* (1925), ed. by M. M. Quaife; Herkimer County Hist. Soc., *The Story of the Typewriter, 1873–1923* (1923); obituary in *Milwaukee Sentinel*, Feb. 18, 1890; correspondence with family, U. S. Nat. Museum.]   C. W. M—n.

SHONTS, THEODORE PERRY (May 5, 1856–Sept. 21, 1919), railroad executive, chairman of the second Isthmian Canal Commission, was a son of Dr. Henry Daniels and Margaret Nevin (Marshall) Shonts. He was born in Crawford County, Pa., where members of the Shonts (or Shontz) family, coming from Lancaster County, had settled about 1800. As a boy he went with his parents to Appanoose County, Iowa, and there he grew to manhood Dependent on the district schools of a new country for his education, he was a schoolmaster himself at sixteen and then passed four years at Monmouth College, Monmouth, Ill., where he was graduated in 1876. Upon his return to Iowa, the distinction of his work as comptroller for an investment company at Centerville, Iowa, soon led to a demand for his services as accountant for banks in the state, but he had decided to be a lawyer and after studying in the office of Gen. Francis M. Drake [*q.v.*], later governor of Iowa, he was duly admitted to the bar and made a partner in the firm. Drake, however, was an aggressive and successful organizer and builder of railroads and after a time he persuaded Shonts to give up the law as a profession for a railroad career. The first challenge to the younger man's mettle came from the Iowa Construction Company, financed in the East, which made him responsible for building within ninety days 100 miles of road to connect with the Central Iowa Railway (later Iowa Central). Although fifty-one of the ninety days were rainy, the job was completed in the stipulated time, so that the rails could receive locomotives and trains. In 1882 Shonts was married to Harriet Amelia Drake (called in his will Milla), daughter of his senior partner in the law firm. His advance in railroading was rapid. He was general superintendent of the Indiana,

Illinois & Iowa Railroad from 1882 to 1886, when he became general manager; from 1898 to 1902 he was also president. In time he succeeded to the presidency of the Chicago & Alton Railroad (1907–12), the Iowa Central Railway (1910–11), the Minneapolis & St. Louis Railroad (1909–11), and the Toledo, St. Louis & Western ("Clover Leaf") Railroad (1904–12). He was known in the Middle West among railroad men as an outstanding example of pluck and efficiency in management, an executive who could give and take hard knocks, who somehow succeeded most completely when the odds were against him.

In 1905, at the moment of beginning work on the Panama Canal, President Theodore Roosevelt was seeking a chairman for the second Isthmian Canal Commission. He was advised by his secretary of the navy, Paul Morton [q.v.], that Shonts (of whom Roosevelt had never heard) had many of the qualities demanded by that position. An interview, in which Shonts made his acceptance conditional on his being given a free hand and absolute authority, convinced the President that he was the man for the place and the appointment was made. Shonts, who cheerfully admitted his ignorance of the technique of canal building, was saved by Roosevelt from a disastrous error at the start when he was persuaded to reverse his intention to supplant Col. William C. Gorgas [q.v.], whose supervision of sanitation on the Isthmus led to most brilliant results and so made possible the completion of the canal with the minimum loss of life. Shonts cooperated most effectively with Gorgas, putting at his disposal a force of 3,500 men as a sanitary corps. In this, as in other features of his brief canal administration, Shonts acted on the assumption that full preparation must be made before the actual digging could be started. He did this work of preparation so thoroughly that when construction was begun, under other direction, it went forward with marvelous speed.

Just what led Shonts to resign from the Canal Commission in 1907 may never be known. He was committed to the contract system of construction and when Roosevelt decided against that procedure he may have thought it impossible to continue (W. J. Abbot, *Panama and the Canal*, 1914, pp. 188–90). He was at once made president of the Interborough Rapid Transit Company (and of its parent company, the Interborough-Metropolitan) of New York City, where a consolidation of subway, elevated, and surface lines had just been effected. Although the problems of city passenger traffic were as new to Shonts

as those of canal-digging had been two years before, he faced them with no lack of confidence; by dint of hard work and intense application he mastered some of the most serious of them, but the rapid growth of demand for transportation facilities outran even the expansion that he was able to achieve. Yet the same executive ability that he had developed when a young man in western railroading scored successes for him in New York.

Shonts died of pneumonia on Sept. 21, 1919. For more than ten years he had been estranged from his wife. His will made provision for her, but a clause leaving the residuary estate to Mrs. Amanda C. Thomas gave rise to litigation extending over two years (*New York Times*, Sept. 21, Nov. 8, 1919; Apr. 11, 1920; Apr. 9, 1921). In the end the higher courts confirmed the will, but many of the securities comprising the testator's property were found to be worthless. Two married daughters shared in the bequests.

[Walter Wellman, "The New Executive of the Panama Canal," in *Am. Monthly Review of Reviews*, May 1905; letter from Roosevelt, Jan. 22, 1907, printed in W. L. Pepperman, *Who Built the Panama Canal* (1915), pp. 238–39; J. B. and Farnham Bishop, *Goethals: Genius of the Panama Canal* (1930), pp. 129–30; *The Biog. Directory of the Railway Officials of America*, 1913; *Who's Who in America*, 1918–19.] W. B. S.

SHOOK, ALFRED MONTGOMERY (July 16, 1845–Mar. 18, 1923), Southern industrialist, the eldest son of James Keith and Eliza Herndon (Green) Shook, was born near Winchester, Franklin County, Tenn. The Shooks, of German descent, had moved Westward before 1800 and finally settled in Middle Tennessee; the Greens were more recent comers from Virginia. Alfred grew up on his parents' farm and attended the country school. He joined the Confederate cavalry in June 1862 but his military career was cut short when, in February 1863, he was wounded and captured at Fort Donelson. Held as a prisoner in the North until the end of the war, he returned to Tennessee in January 1866.

Through an uncle, he was soon placed in charge of the Tennessee Coal & Railroad Company's store at Tracy City, where he rapidly worked his way to a position of responsibility in the company. The mineral resources of the South were looked upon as a possible means of economic recovery from the effects of the Civil War and attracted many an enterprising Southerner from the impoverished agricultural districts. Shook, like his older associates, engaged in coal mining without any scientific training, but his capabilities were recognized by the new manager of the company, James C. Warner [q.v.], who appointed him superintendent in 1868. Shook's account of the struggles and discouragements of these early years portrays in realistic fashion the industrial pioneering of the "New South," where the margin between success and failure was narrow indeed (see Armes, *post*). The growth of the company's business during the seventies, however, justified a venture into the manufacture of coke and convinced Shook that the future of the enterprise would be assured by utilizing this fuel in the company's furnaces. Under his management the Sewanee Furnace was built at Cowan, Tenn., in 1881, and the following year the Tennessee Coal, Iron & Railroad Company, as it was now called, absorbed a rival English concern, The Southern States Coal, Iron & Land Company, operating a furnace near Chattanooga. Shook as general manager until 1886 was in direct touch with both the metallurgical and the accounting problems of the business; he mastered the intricacies of the blast furnace and saved the company many a dollar in operating expenses.

As the business was expanded and the stock increased to $10,000,000, the control passed from the hands of the Tennessee group to speculators on the New York Exchange, and a reorganization early in 1886 cost Shook his position. At this critical moment, however, industrial affairs in Birmingham, Ala., worked to his advantage and transferred the principal activity of the Tennessee Company to that city. The Pratt Coal & Iron Company of Enoch Ensley [*q.v.*], representing the largest iron interests of that region, was suddenly brought under the control of the Tennessee company by Shook and his Tennessee associates, who enlisted enough capital to secure options previously issued on the Pratt corporation. The Tennessee company, with its prestige so suddenly enhanced, underwent another reorganization, and Shook was reinstated as general manager. Closely associated with Ensley now, he worked to carry out the latter's dream of a new industrial city near Birmingham, and in 1889 the fourth up-to-date iron furnace went into blast. The ultimate goal, however, was the manufacture of steel, if it could be made from the South's high-phosphorus ore. Shook's faith in experiments by the Southern Iron Company, in which he had been interested in Chattanooga in 1890, was justified when the first heat of steel was poured at Ensley on Thanksgiving Day 1899, and the Tennessee company's steel works began a new era in Southern industrial developments. His connection with the company was almost continuous from the time of its revival in 1866 until 1901, and no one contributed more in sound judgment and able management to establishing its preëminence in the Southern iron and steel industry.

Shook married Teresa Estill on July 17, 1871, and had five children. He was a Presbyterian and deeply interested in education. The school which he built and furnished at Tracy City at a cost of $40,000 is but one example of his widespread benefactions. He lived in Nashville during most of his life, and died there in his seventy-eighth year.

[*Tracy City News,* supplement, 1895; *Nashville Tennessean,* Mar. 19, 1923; *Who's Who in America,* 1920–21; Ethel Armes, *The Story of Coal and Iron in Alabama* (1910); Crawford Perkins, *The Industrial Hist. of Ensley Ala.* (1907); information as to certain facts from Shook's son, P. G. Shook.]   L. J. C.

SHOREY, PAUL (Aug. 3, 1857–Apr. 24, 1934), classicist, born in Davenport, Iowa, was the son of Daniel Lewis and Maria Antoinette (Merriam) Shorey. His parents moved to Chicago when he was a boy and he received his secondary education at the Chicago High School. He took his A.B. degree at Harvard in 1878. After graduation he studied law in his father's office and was called to the bar in Illinois in 1880. He practised law for a brief period in Chicago, but not caring for the life went to Europe to pursue his classical studies. From that time to the day of his death in Chicago he never swerved from his devotion to the classics or wavered in his belief that in them the world could find its best literature, its most satisfying philosophy, and its most effective instrument of education.

After attending the University of Leipzig (1881–82), the University of Bonn (1882), and the American School of Classical Studies at Athens (1882–83), he took his Ph.D. degree in Munich in 1884. His first academic post in America was at Bryn Mawr College, where he was professor of Latin and Greek from 1885 to 1892. His edition of *Horace: Odes and Epodes* (1898, 1910) was the direct outcome of one of his courses there. It is unique in the aptness and range of the illustrative material drawn from Latin, Greek, French, and English literature. He was one of the group of scholars whom President William Rainey Harper [*q.v.*] called to the University of Chicago at its founding (1892). Coming as professor of Greek, he was made head of the department in 1896 and remained in that position till 1927. In 1901–02 he was annual associate director of the American School of Classical Studies at Athens. He became professor emeritus in 1927 but was invited to continue his courses and he held classes till the summer of 1933. He was one of the founders of the periodical, *Classical Philology,* and was its editor from 1908 to 1934. In June 1895 he married Emma L. Gilbert of Philadelphia, who survived him; there were no children.

Shorey's greatest contribution to scholarship was in the field of Platonic studies. His knowledge of philosophy, his faculty of keen analysis of philosophic concepts, and his command of Greek were the chief elements in his effectiveness. His first monograph in the subject was his doctoral dissertation at Munich, *De Platonis idearum doctrina atque mentis humanae notionibus commentatio* (1884). Later appeared *The Idea of Good in Plato's Republic* (1895); *The Unity of Plato's Thought* (1903); a translation of Plato's *Republic* in the Loeb Classical Library in two volumes (1930–35); and the outstanding work, *What Plato Said* (1933). The philosophic implications of other Greek authors are considered in "The Implicit Ethics and Pyschology of Thucydides," *Trans. Am. Philological Assoc.*, vol. XXIV (1893), 66–88, and in the more general essay, "The Abiding Power of Greek Philosophy" in *Culture of the Classics* (1910).

He had no patience with modern pedagogical methods. He often said that knowledge of the subject and some degree of common sense in the organization of courses and the handling of students constituted the only equipment that a teacher needed. In his hands a course in Homer or Pindar or Plato was not merely an exercise in translation; it was a study of epic or lyric poetry or of some phase of philosophy. His intimate knowledge of French and English literature and his pertinent and witty application of ancient ideas to modern times gave his lectures a zest that is too often lacking in academic classrooms. He supervised more than fifty doctoral dissertations and many of his students became teachers of Greek and Latin in the colleges and universities of the United States and Canada. He was convinced that the movement against the classics in education was a mistake, and frequently expressed his views in essays. The best known of these are "The Case for the Classics" (*School Review*, November 1910) and "The Assault on Humanism" (*Atlantic Monthly*, June, July 1917), but there are many others.

He was a member of the American Philosophical Society, the American Philological Association (president 1910), the American Institute of Archaeology, the American Academy of Arts and Letters, and associé de l'Académie Royale de Belgique. He had unusual gifts as a public speaker. He gave the Turnbull Lectures on Poetry at Johns Hopkins and the Lane Lectures at Harvard in 1912; the Harris Lectures at Northwestern University in 1916; the Sather Lectures at the University of California (twice); the Lowell Lectures in Boston; and the Martin Lectures at Oberlin. In 1913 he was Roosevelt Exchange Professor at the University of Berlin, and in 1924 he lectured on Aristotle at four of the universities of Belgium. Honorary degrees were conferred on him by many universities. Shorey had a rare combination of qualities: he had erudition and yet fine literary appreciation; he was interested in research, but was also a teacher of unusual effectiveness; he was a classicist and a stanch protagonist of the classics as a medium of education, but his study of the ancients never dulled the edge of his interest in contemporary life.

[R. J. Bonner, "Paul Shorey," in *Classical Jour.*, June 1934; George Norlin, "Paul Shorey—The Teacher," in *Classical Philology*, July 1934, where there is also an unsigned obituary article; *Who's Who in America*, 1932–33; personal acquaintance.]   G. J. L.

SHORT, CHARLES (May 28, 1821–Dec. 24, 1886), classical philologist, was born in Haverhill, Mass., the second of the twelve children of Charles and Rebecca (George) Short, and the seventh in descent from Henry Short, who emigrated to Ipswich in 1634 and later removed to Newbury. At Phillips Academy, Andover, 1837–40, he studied Greek and Latin with passionate ardor. "I used to open my eyes very early in the morning," he said later, "waiting impatiently for daylight, that I might rise and be at my books" (*Memoir, post*, p. 4). Once, when neither his teachers nor the available books could satisfy him as to a difficult passage in a Greek author, he tramped the twenty miles to Cambridge to settle the matter in the Harvard library. After two years of teaching he entered Harvard College in 1842 and graduated fourth in the famous class of 1846. While a sophomore he acquired renown by a translation into Greek hexameters of H. H. Milman's "The Belvidere Apollo." He tarried a year at Cambridge as a pupil of Prof. Evangelinus Apostolides Sophocles [*q.v.*]. He became an assistant master at his old school in 1847, was headmaster of the Roxbury Latin School, 1848–53, and conducted a school of his own in Philadelphia, 1853–63. In 1849 he married Anne Jean, daughter of Elihu Lyman of Greenfield, Mass., who with three sons and a daughter survived him. In 1860 he visited England; he went to Europe again in 1881 and in 1884. In 1862 he and his wife were confirmed in the Episcopal Church in the first class presented by Phillips Brooks [*q.v.*]. A year later, several clergymen having declined, he was elected to the presidency of Kenyon College, at Gambier, Ohio, in succession to the late Lorin Andrews [*q.v.*]. He retained the strong faculty that his predecessor had gathered, made the beginnings of a college library, and attracted worthy students to the institution, but in 1867, as the result of squabbles among the teachers and trustees, he resigned. Almost immediately he was called to succeed Henry Drisler [q.v.] as professor of Latin in Columbia College, New York, where he remained for the rest of his life. On its organization in 1872 he was made a member of the American Committee on the Revision of the English Authorized Version of the Bible, to serve in the New Testament Company. Of his scholarly productions the most notable were the monograph on "The Order of Words in Attic Greek Prose," prefixed to Drisler's edition of Charles D. Yonge's *An English-Greek Lexicon* (1870); his work on the letter *a* in *Harper's Latin Dictionary* (1879); and his minute textual study, "The New Revision of King James' Revision of the New Testament, as Illustrated by the Gospel of St. Matthew," in the *American Journal of Philology* (vols. II–VII, 1881–86). Brander Matthews described him as "a man of many amusing peculiarities, but possessed of real learning and inspired by a genuine love of letters" (*These Many Years*, 1917, p. 110). Until the steady inroads of nephritis began to make life burdensome for him, he was an able teacher and lecturer, and he remained a conscientious one to the end. He died at his home in New York and was buried in Sleepy Hollow Cemetery.

[C. L. Short, *Memoir of the Life of Charles Short, M.A., LL.D.* (privately printed, 1892), with list of his pubs.; *Cat. of the Biblical, Classical, and Miscellaneous Lib. of the late Charles Short* (auctioneer's cat., 1887); G. F. Smythe, *Kenyon Coll.: Its First Century* (1924), with portrait; *N. Y. Daily Tribune*, Dec. 25, 1886.]

G. H. G.

SHORT, CHARLES WILKINS (Oct. 6, 1794–Mar. 7, 1863), was a physician, teacher, and botanist, who collected, preserved, classified, and generously distributed to other naturalists the plants of the little explored country west of the Alleghanies. A nephew of William Short [q.v.], he was born at "Greenfield," Woodford County, Ky., the country place of his parents, Peyton Short and his first wife, Maria (or Mary), daughter of John Cleves Symmes [q.v.]. Charles attended Joshua Fry's celebrated school in Mercer County, and later, Transylvania University, Lexington, where he was graduated with honor in 1810. He began the study of medicine with his uncle, Dr. Frederick Ridgely, and in 1813 went to Philadelphia to become the private and beloved pupil of Dr. Caspar Wistar, 1716–1818 [q.v.]. The University of Pennsylvania bestowed upon him the degree of doctor of medicine in the spring of 1815, his thesis being on the medicinal virtues of *Juniperus Sabina*. In November of the same year he married his step-

sister, Mary Henry Churchill, only daughter of Armistead and Jane (Henry) Churchill, the latter having become Peyton Short's second wife. The young couple soon returned to Kentucky, making the entire trip in a spring wagon and botanizing along the way.

After a short stay in Lexington and some years in Hopkinsville, combining the practice of his profession with botanical researches, he accepted, in September 1825, a call to the chair of materia medica and medical botany at Transylvania University, which he filled with distinction, serving as dean of the faculty from 1827 to 1837. With Dr. John Esten Cooke [q.v.], he started the publication, in 1828, of the *Transylvania Journal of Medicine and the Associate Sciences,* one of the first periodicals of its kind in the West. In this, most of his writings—descriptions of certain medical cases and contributions to botany—were published. Notable among the latter was "A Catalogue of the Native Phaenogamous Plants and Ferns of Kentucky," which he prepared in cooperation with Robert Peter and H. A. Griswold (December 1833, supplemented in the issues of December 1834, December 1835, September 1837). As an illustration of the zeal of himself and his associates, he states that within five years they had prepared and distributed 25,000 specimens among correspondents in Europe and America, who gave valuable and acceptable material in exchange (*Transylvania Journal of Medicine,* April 1836, p. 348).

In 1838 Short left Transylvania University to fill a similar position in the young Medical Institute of Louisville. After ten years more of teaching and while still in the prime of life, his own fortune having been augmented by an inheritance from his distinguished uncle, William Short [q.v.] of Philadelphia, he decided to retire, bought Col. George Hancock's beautiful estate "Hayfield" near Louisville, and indulged himself in promoting botanical research and in the enjoyment of his family, his gardens, his library, his herbarium and his correspondence. Here he died of typhoid pneumonia in the sixty-ninth year of his age, and was buried in Cave Hill Cemetery. One son and five daughters survived him. His valuable herbarium of over 15,000 species belongs to the Academy of Natural Sciences, Philadelphia. Dignity and modesty were perhaps his most noticeable qualities. A love of accuracy led him always to write out his lectures and read them to his pupils. Learned Latin phrases were frequent in his addresses. He was a member of the Presbyterian Church, and urged upon his students that "strict, unswerving, religious regard for truth which should be the prime object in every investigation."

[S. D. Gross, in *Proc. Am. Philosophical Soc.*, vol. X (1869) ; Asa Gray, in *Am. Jour. Sci.*, July 1863 ; *Louisville Jour.*, Mar. 18, 1863 ; Robert Peter, *The Hist. of the Medic. Dept. of Transylvania Univ.* (1905), Filson Club Pub. No. 20 ; H. A. Kelly, *Some Am. Medic. Botanists* (1914) ; Max Meisel, *A Bibliog. of Am. Natural Hist.*, vol. II (1926), pp. 455–57 ; *Transylvania Jour. of Medicine*, vols. I–XII (1828–38) ; Minutes Transylvania Medic. Faculty ; information from grand-daughters and the curator of the dept. of botany, Acad. of Nat. Sci., Phila.]   M. L. D.

SHORT, SIDNEY HOWE (Oct. 8, 1858–Oct. 21, 1902), electrical engineer, inventor, was the son of John and Elizabeth (Cowen) Short and was born in Columbus, Ohio, where his father was engaged in manufacturing. Like many inventors, he displayed remarkable mechanical ingenuity as a child, and was so interested in electricity that at the age of fourteen years he was an expert telegrapher and had equipped his home with a burglar alarm and many other electrical devices. After completing grade school and spending a short time at Capital University, Columbus, he entered Ohio State University, where he was a student assistant in physics and graduated with the degree of B.S. in 1880. Immediately following his graduation he accepted the position of professor of physics and chemistry and vice-president of the University of Denver, Denver, Colo., and began with enthusiasm his professional career. His departments developed rapidly ; in 1882 the work had become so great that he was relieved of chemistry to devote his whole time to teaching and research in physics. Although his earliest interests in electricity were the telegraph and the telephone —he perfected, patented, and sold a telephone transmitter in 1879—he turned his attention to arc-lighting and electric traction soon after going to Denver, and made important discoveries and improvements, many of which he patented.

After five years at the university he resigned and became associated with the United States Electrical Company, Denver, Colo., to develop and manufacture his inventions. At first he worked on improved equipment for electric arc-lighting, but about 1886 he invented a double reduction electric motor for street railways and soon engaged in building electric railways incorporating his inventions. After completing several installations and patenting additional improvements in his system, in 1889 he removed to Cleveland, Ohio, where with the financial help of Charles F. Brush he organized the Short Electric Railway Company and began the manufacture of his railway machinery. He was very successful in this but in 1892 sold his company

to the General Electric Company. In 1893 he became connected with the Walker Manufacturing Company of Cleveland, which immediately entered the electric traction field with an entirely new system of apparatus of Short's design ; by 1898 it had become such a formidable competitor of both the General Electric and Westinghouse companies that the latter felt compelled to purchase a controlling interest in it. Meanwhile Short had started negotiations with Messrs. Dick, Kerr & Company, Ltd., in England for the manufacture of his patented electric railway machinery and system. Accordingly late in 1898 he went to London, and within eighteen months the production of all kinds of equipment was under way at a new factory erected at Preston. He then became technical director of the English Electric Manufacturing Company, Ltd., organized a technical staff to undertake research and development work, and had practically completed the work he had gone to England to do when he died at the age of forty-four.

In his brief career he was granted over five hundred patents for improvements in electrical machinery both by the United States and foreign countries, and was widely recognized as an authority in electric railways and continuous current motors. He was a pioneer in the use of a conduit system of concealed feed rail to avoid the use of the overhead wire and trolley, and was also very successful with gearless motors in which all the gears between the electric motor armature and the driven car-axle were eliminated. He was a member of engineering societies in England and the United States, and was a fellow of the American Association for the Advancement of Science. He married Mary F. Morrison of Columbus, Ohio, in Washington, D. C., on July 26, 1881, and at the time of his death was survived by his widow and four children.

[*Electrical Rev.*, Nov. 1, 1902 ; *Electrical Rev.* (London), and *Electrician* (London), Oct. 31, 1902 ; Waldemar Kaempffert, *A Popular Hist. of Am. Invention* (1924), Patent Office records ; death notice in the *Times* (London), Oct. 23, 1902.]   C. W. M—n.

SHORT, WILLIAM (Sept. 30, 1759–Dec. 5, 1849), diplomatist, was born at "Spring Garden," Surry County, Va., the son of William Short, a well-to-do planter, and his wife Elizabeth, daughter of Sir William Skipwith. He was graduated in 1779 at the College of William and Mary, where he had been one of the founders of Phi Beta Kappa and was president of that society from December 1778 to January 1781. In 1783–84 he was a member of the Executive Council of Virginia, then followed Jefferson on his mission to France. Soon after his arrival in Paris, he was sent by Jefferson, Adams, and Franklin to arrange with the Prussian envoy at The Hague for a commercial treaty between Prussia and the United States. Upon the successful conclusion of this business he returned to Paris, where he acted as Jefferson's private secretary and later as secretary of legation. Of a sensitive, appealing personality, with the easy charm of the South in his manner and a perfect command of the French language, he achieved an enviable position in the highest circles of French society. Upon Jefferson's return to America in 1789, Short became chargé d'affaires, and during the next two years was busy attempting to negotiate a commercial treaty with France, handling the business of American loans in Amsterdam, and sending full reports to Jay and Jefferson on the political developments in France. An enthusiastic witness of the events of 1789, he became more doubtful of the benefits of revolution as the Jacobins rose to power, and his outburst against them after the August and September massacres of 1792 brought him a rebuke from Jefferson (*Short Papers*, 1789–92; Jefferson, *Writings*, Ford ed., VI, 153–55).

After Jefferson became secretary of state, Short nursed every hope of being appointed to succeed him as minister to France, but despite the weight of Jefferson's influence, the post went to Gouverneur Morris [*q.v.*], early in 1792, and Short reluctantly accepted appointment as minister at The Hague. With a heavy heart he set out from Paris. By this time he had become the devoted admirer of Alexandrine Charlotte de Rohan-Chabot, familiarly known as Rosalie, the young wife of the Duc de la Rochefoucauld. It was a profound attachment on both sides that was destined to last for nearly fifty years, but when the assassination of the Duke, in September 1792, left his widow free to marry again, she was restrained by an ideal duty to the aged Duchesse d'Anville, her mother-in-law. Her decision was one in which Short was bound to concur, but it added another to the list of disappointments that marked his life.

In February 1793 he went from The Hague to Madrid as joint commissioner with William Carmichael [*q.v.*] to negotiate a treaty concerning boundaries, navigation, and commercial privileges in regard to Florida and the Mississippi, and after Carmichael's recall in the spring of 1794, he was made minister resident with sole power to carry on the negotiations. Just as success was about to crown his labors, Thomas Pinckney [*q.v.*] was sent to Spain as envoy extraordinary and commissioner plenipotentiary

to conclude the treaty. The appointment for this task of Pinckney, still minister at London, was the result of the objection of the Spanish court, as a pretext for delay, that Short and Carmichael were not of sufficient rank to be acceptable; before Pinckney's arrival, however, Spain had become ready to negotiate. Although chagrined at being superseded, Short continued to handle affairs until Pinckney's arrival and then loyally cooperated with him in securing the treaty which bears Pinckney's name, signed Oct. 27, 1795. Leaving Spain the next day, he lived in Paris until 1802, when he returned to the United States. In March 1809 he was destined to receive one more rebuff. Commissioned by Jefferson in the previous August as minister to Russia, he had proceeded as far as Paris when he received word that a hostile Senate had rejected his appointment, declaring a permanent minister to Russia unnecessary.

Short remained in France until 1810, when he returned to America, settling in Philadelphia, and for the remainder of his life devoted himself to his private affairs. He had made profitable investments through the Dutch bankers with whom he had become acquainted in Amsterdam, and had made extensive purchases of land in Kentucky and northern New York. During the next years he built up a large fortune, but he never again interested himself in public office. Slightly world-weary, he seemed satisfied to look upon the realm of action from the heights of a bitter experience.

[The best account of Short's career yet published appears in S. F. Bemis, *Pinckney's Treaty* (1926). Sources include Short Papers and Jefferson Papers, Lib. of Cong.; MSS. in the possession of the Short family; *The Writings of Thomas Jefferson* (20 vols., 1903–04), ed. by A. A. Lipscomb and A. E. Bergh; *The Writings of Thomas Jefferson* (10 vols., 1892–99), ed. by P. L. Ford; *Am. State Papers, For. Rel.*, vol. I (1832). The account in L. G. Tyler, *Encyc. of Va. Biog.* (1915), II, 153, is brief and inaccurate. Marie G. Kimball, "William Short, Jefferson's Only 'Son'," *North Am. Rev.*, Sept., Oct., Nov. 1926, contains extracts from Short's correspondence with Madame de la Rochefoucauld. See also *Wm. and Mary Coll. Quart.*, Apr. 1896; *Pennsylvanian* (Phila.), Dec. 7, 1849.]

M. G. K.

SHORTER, JOHN GILL (Apr. 23, 1818–May 29, 1872), jurist, representative in the Confederate Congress, governor of Alabama, was born in Monticello, Ga., the son of Reuben Clark and Martha (Gill) Shorter. His father was a physician and planter who came originally from Virginia, settled in Georgia in his young manhood, and became a leader in the Democratic party in the state. John Gill was one of three sons who attained prominence in Alabama political life, the other two being Henry Russell, who served for some years as state railroad commissioner, and Eli Sims, who was a congressman.

John graduated from Franklin College (now the University of Georgia) in 1837 and immediately went to Eufaula, Ala., where he studied law and in 1838 was admitted to the bar. He spent four years in practice and was then appointed solicitor for the district in which he lived. He held this post until 1845, when he was elected to the state Senate. After two years in that body he declined to serve again and returned to his law practice. In 1851 he was elected to the lower house of the state legislature, but gave up his seat to accept an appointment to the circuit bench. Completing his term, he was elected to the office in 1852, and reëlected six years later without opposition.

He was an enthusiastic supporter of secession, and when Governor Moore appointed him Alabama's commissioner to the secession convention of the state of Georgia, he resigned his position on the bench to accept the appointment. Later he was chosen to represent his district in the provisional Confederate Congress, in the work of which he took an active part. An unwavering supporter of President Davis, he voted to sustain all of Davis's vetoes and favored all measures which he recommended. He was also active in the work of framing the Confederate constitution.

In August 1861, while he was in Richmond attending the third session of the provisional Congress, he was elected governor of Alabama, his election being an expression of the loyalty which the voters of Alabama accorded the Confederate government. Entering upon the duties of his office in a trying time, he was at first given enthusiastic support by the people. He exerted every effort to construct defenses where they were needed and tried especially to defend the port at Mobile. He was tireless in raising and equipping troops and in caring for the families of soldiers. Gradually, however, he lost popular support. Union troops invaded the state and devastated many parts of it. The tax burden became increasingly heavy as the war progressed. As loyal men went into the army, only the lukewarm or indifferent were left behind, and these were unwilling to endure the demands made upon them by the governor. Shorter, moreover, was stanch in his support of the Davis government and much of its unpopularity reacted upon him. His support of conscription, also, and his collection of the tax in kind brought him much criticism. In the election of 1863 he was defeated by a vote of more than three to one. He then returned to Eufaula and resumed the practice of

law, taking no further part in political life. On Jan. 12, 1843, he married Mary Jane Battle of Eufaula, by whom he had one daughter.

[A. K. Walker, *Old Shorter Houses and Gardens* (1911); T. M. Owen, *Hist. of Ala. and Dict. of Ala. Biog.* (1921), vol. IV; B. F. Riley, *Makers and Romance of Ala. Hist.* (n.d.); William Garrett, *Reminiscences of Public Men in Ala.* (1872); A. B. Moore, *Hist. of Ala. and Her People* (1927); W. L. Fleming, *Civil War and Reconstruction in Ala.* (1905); *Mobile Daily Reg.*, May 30, June 1, 1872.]   H. F.

SHOUP, FRANCIS ASBURY (Mar. 22, 1834–Sept. 4, 1896), Confederate soldier, educator, clergyman, was born in Laurel, Ind., the eldest son of the nine children of George Grove Shoup, a well-to-do merchant, and Jane (Conwell) Shoup. His father was a member of the Indiana constitutional convention and served for many years in the state legislature. His maternal grandfather, James Conwell, was also a member of the legislature, and was founder of the town of Laurel. After attending Asbury University (now De Pauw), in Greencastle, Ind., Shoup entered the United States Military Academy at West Point, N. Y., where he was graduated in 1855. He was commissioned second lieutenant of artillery and served in Florida on garrison duty and during a campaign against the Seminole Indians. In 1860 he resigned from the army, studied law, and was admitted to the Indianapolis bar. During the excitement following the John Brown raid, he organized a company of zouaves in the city and was chosen captain, but in 1861 he returned to Florida and was admitted to the St. Augustine bar. Moved by his aristocratic inclinations and admiration for the South, he volunteered for service with the Confederate army.

Upon the order of the governor of Florida, Shoup erected a battery at Fernandina. He was appointed lieutenant of artillery and in October 1861 was promoted to the rank of major. After a campaign in Kentucky, he became chief of artillery under Hardee, and at Shiloh, by effective massing of his guns, he played an important part in the capture of Prentiss' command. Subsequently, he fought under Beauregard and Hindman and was commended by the latter for his conduct at Prairie Grove, Ark. On Sept. 12, 1862, he was promoted to the rank of brigadiergeneral and, after service at Mobile, commanded a Louisiana brigade at Vicksburg. He was captured upon the fall of the city, but was soon exchanged and served with distinction as chief of artillery to Joseph Johnston [*q.v.*]. In the retreat from Dalton to Atlanta, Shoup did not lose a single gun, and the works constructed under his supervision at the Chattahoochee River were highly praised. When a court of inquiry reported regarding the loss of stores to Sherman at Atlanta in September 1864, he received mild censure. Perhaps because of his Northern birth, he seems to have been much criticized, but Jefferson Davis wrote that "the only very clear information" communicated to him regarding the establishment of munition manufactures in the Trans-Mississippi "was in the report of that much-abused officer, Brigadier-General Shoup" (*War of the Rebellion: Official Records, Army,* 1 ser., LIII, 880). After the removal of Johnston, Shoup served as chief-of-staff under Hood. He wrote a pamphlet urging the enlistment of negro troops which was submitted to the Confederate Congress.

Upon the reorganization of the University of Mississippi, Oxford, Miss., in 1865, Shoup was elected professor of applied mathematics. In 1868 he took orders in the Episcopal church, which he had joined while the Confederate army was at Dalton, and served as rector of St. Peter's in Oxford, in addition to his university duties. In 1869 he was chosen professor of mathematics at the University of the South in Sewanee, Tenn., assuming also the duties of chaplain. He became rector at Waterford, N. Y., in 1875, and later served churches at Nashville, Tenn., and New Orleans, La. He was recalled to Sewanee in 1883 as professor of engineering and physics, and later, of mathematics, remaining here until his death. As a professor, Shoup was "very stimulating upon occasion," but was unable to raise the average student to the level of his metaphysical thought and soon gave up the effort (Du Bose, *post*). He had marked intellectual ability and was the author of *Infantry Tactics* (1862), *Artillery Division Drill* (1864), *The Elements of Algebra* (1874), and *Mechanism and Personality* (1891). He was of distinguished military bearing, over six feet tall. He was married in 1870 to Esther Habersham Elliott of Sewanee, Tenn., the daughter of Bishop Stephen Elliott, granddaughter of Stephen Elliott, and sister of Sarah Barnwell Elliott [*qq.v.*]. She and three children survived him when he died at Columbia, Tenn.

[Information from Miss Laurel Conwell Thayer, Indianapolis, Ind., Bishop T. F. Gailor, and a former student of Shoup's, the Rev. W. H. Du Bose; G. W. Cullum, *Biog. Reg. . . . U. S. Mil. Acad.* (1891); *Hist. Cat. of the Univ. of Miss.* (1910), including a biographical sketch by Shoup's wife; G. R. Fairbanks, *Hist. of the Univ. of the South* (1905); *Nashville Am.,* Sept. 5, 1896.]   R. D. M.

SHOUP, GEORGE LAIRD (June 15, 1836–Dec. 21, 1904), first governor of Idaho, was born at Kittanning, Pa., the son of Henry and Mary Jane (McCain) Shoup. His father was of Dutch and his mother of Scotch-Irish descent. He obtained his education in the public schools of his native state before he started with his parents for Illinois when about sixteen years of age. The financial panic of 1857 broke soon after the family had settled and they were left with little or nothing, the parents in poor health. In 1859 George went into the territory of Colorado to do some mining and merchandising in the neighborhood of Pike's Peak and helped carve out of the rugged Rocky Mountains the future state of Colorado. When the Civil War began he enlisted in September of 1861 in a company of independent scouts working in New Mexico, Colorado, and Texas. Promotion came rapidly for him and when the 3rd Colorado Cavalry was formed he was commissioned colonel. He took part in many sanguinary skirmishes, among them, Apache Cañon and Sand Creek. He was given a leave of absence from his command long enough to act as a member of the constitutional convention when Colorado made an attempt to enter the Union in 1864.

After the war he was again in the mercantile business. He took a stock of goods to Virginia City, Mont., in 1866, and maintained a store for a short time but later in the year moved on to help found Salmon, Idaho, which he thenceforth claimed as his home. Here he was married in January 1868 to Lena Darnutzer, of Swiss descent. Three sons and three daughters were born to them. Here, also, a political career began with his appointment as commissioner to organize Lemhi County, from which, in 1874, he was elected to the territorial legislature. In 1878 he was a member of the territorial council, and in the eighties served on the Republican National Committee for Idaho. He represented Idaho at the cotton centennial at New Orleans in 1884 where he spent $35,000 of his own money to advertise the resources of Idaho. President Harrison appointed him governor of the territory of Idaho on Apr. 1, 1889. He at once repeated a call issued by his predecessor for a constitutional convention which met on July 4, 1889. When the document was finished, Shoup accompanied it to Washington to work for its ratification by Congress. In the elections that followed ratification he became governor of Idaho. The metamorphosis of Idaho from territory to state then absorbed him. He called the legislature to meet in December 1890, and was elected by this body to be the first United States senator from Idaho.

His policy in the Senate was to give a general support to all Republican measures, and a special support to those dealing with the welfare of his state. He opposed the repeal of the "purchasing clause" in the Sherman silver bill by one of his two notable speeches in the Senate, and then supported the Republican measure in 1900 to establish the gold standard (*Congressional Record,* 53 Cong., 1 Sess., pt. II, p. 1440; 56 Cong., 1 Sess., pt. II, p. 1825). He was an opponent of "free silver" in spite of the fact that Idaho was a great producer of that metal. His great interest in the territories brought him the position as chairman of the Committee on Territories, member of committees on Military Affairs, Indian Affairs, Indian Depredations, Pensions, and Education. He advocated a liberal and just treatment of the Indians, was a firm believer in a liberal pension law and introduced many of the personal bills that President Cleveland vetoed. He believed in the popular election of United States senators. He held his place in the Senate continuously for ten years, being defeated in 1901, probably because of his stand on the silver question. He died at Boise, Idaho. His statue was placed in Statuary Hall at the national capitol by his state in 1910.

[*Who's Who in America,* 1903–05; *Biog. Dir. Am. Cong.* (1928); W. B. Mathews, *Sketch of the Life and Services of the Hon. George L. Shoup* (1900); Byron Defenbach, *Idaho, The Place and its People* (1933), vol. I; J. H. Hawley, ed., *Hist. of Idaho* (1920), vol. I; *Idaho Daily Statesman,* Dec. 22, 1904; *Idaho Statesman,* Jan. 16, 18, 1910.]   J. E. R.

SHRADY, GEORGE FREDERICK (Jan. 14, 1837–Nov. 30, 1907), surgeon and medical journalist, was the son of John and Margaret Beinhauer) Shrady. His father, a schoolmate of Washington Irving and Dr. John Wakefield Francis [*qq.v.*], was the son of John Shrady, active Revolutionary patriot, and grandson of Johan Schrade of Württemberg, who came to America about 1715 and twenty years later made his permanent home in New York city. His mother was the grand-daughter of Dr. John W. Zeiss of Amsterdam and daughter of Frederic Beinhauer of Vienna. (See *New York Genealogical and Biographical Record,* Oct. 1875, p. 198.) His brother John also practised medicine in New York. Educated in both private and public schools in New York, in 1858 he received the degree of M.D. from the College of Physicians and Surgeons of New York. His appointments were many; he was connected with St. Francis Hospital, New York Cancer Hospital, Columbus Hospital, Red Cross Hospital, Home for Incurables (Fordham), Vassar Hospital (Poughkeepsie), and the Hudson River State Hospital for the Insane, and he was physician in chief of the New York health department. During the Span-

ish-American War he was assistant surgeon of the Central Park Hospital, New York, and was detailed for field duty as well. His attention was early turned towards journalism. From 1860 to 1864 he edited the *American Medical Times*; from 1866 to 1904, the *Medical Record,* which he had helped to found. As an editor he championed many important and worthy causes. He advocated the abolition of sects in medical practice, the improvement of professional education, the extension of clinical instruction, and the establishment of state examinations for license to practice.

In spite of this work, which was his most important contribution to his profession, he did not neglect his practice. He was called to attend Pres. James Abram Garfield when he was shot and Pres. Ulysses S. Grant [*qq.v.*] in his last illness, and was consulted by Sir Morell Mackenzie on the illness of the Emperor Frederick III of Germany. He served as president of the American Medical Editors Association, the New York Pathological Society, the Practitioners Society of New York, and was a member of a number of other organizations. A calm, agreeable person, with an unusual gift for mimicry and a kindly sense of humor, he won many friends. Although a skilful operator, he was inclined to be conservative and very much opposed operations except when they were absolutely necessary. His work lay mostly in the field of plastic surgery; he wrote a number of articles on that subject and in other branches of surgery. His touching account of *General Grant's Last Days* (1908), his "Surgical and Pathological Reflections on President Garfield's Wound" (*Medical Record,* Oct. 8, 1881), and the satirical "Pine Ridge" papers in the *Medical Record* directed against medical charlatanism, are perhaps among the most important. In 1860 he was married to Mary Lewis of New York City, who died in 1883; he was married again on Dec. 19, 1888, to Hester Ellen Cantine of Ulster County, N. Y. He died in 1907 from sepsis following an attack of gallstones. He was survived by his wife, two daughters, and three sons (*New York Herald, post*), of whom one became a doctor and another, Henry Merwin Shrady [*q.v.*], a well-known sculptor.

[*Who's Who in America,* 1906–07; *Am. Medic. Biogs.* (1920), ed. by H. A. Kelly and W. L. Burrage; *The Coll. of Physicians and Surgeons, N. Y. . . . A Hist.* (n.d.), vol. I, ed. by John Shrady; *Medic. Record,* Dec. 7, 1907; obituary in *N. Y. Herald,* Dec. 1, 1907.]
G. L. A.

SHRADY, HENRY MERWIN (Oct. 24, 1871–Apr. 12, 1922), sculptor, was born in New York City, the son of Mary (Lewis) and George

Frederick Shrady [q.v.]. Taking the degree of A.B. at Columbia in 1894, he was diverted from a legal career into business and for five years was with a match company, 1895–1900. After an illness and the failure of the company, he began to do sketching and modeling. One of his sketches, sent to the National Academy of Design exhibition without his knowledge, was sold, and a jeweler offered to take all the small animal bronzes he would make. What little technical instruction he had, he got from Karl T. F. Bitter [q.v.], who invited him to share a studio. Lack of early instruction prolonged all his labors and accounts for the small number of his works, of which he himself was a severe critic. He enlarged figures of a moose and a buffalo for the Pan-American Exposition of 1901 at Buffalo, and modeled a group of Indians in relief on a bronze panel for the pedestal of the Robert Fulton monument at Spuyten Duyvil. In 1901 he won a competition with his equestrian Washington at Valley Forge, placed in Brooklyn near the Williamsburg Bridge. He was elected a member of the National Sculpture Society in 1902, became an associate of the National Academy of Design in 1909, and was a member of the National Institute of Arts and Letters.

His preëminent achievement in sculpture is the Grant memorial in Union Square, forming the Capitol end of the Mall in Washington. In 1902, twenty-three sculptors and associated architects submitted designs (*The Grant Memorial, post*, p. 19). Those of Shrady and Edward Pearce Casey were chosen unanimously by a jury made up of two of Grant's officers, Generals John McAllister Schofield and Wesley Merritt; Augustus Saint-Gaudens [qq.v.] and Daniel Chester French, sculptors; Daniel Hudson Burnham and Charles Follen McKim [qq.v.], architects. The memorial represents a sweeping cavalry charge. In the center of the marble platform, 252 feet in length, rises the colossal figure of Grant, garbed according to his custom in the uniform of a soldier, without side arms. The horse, two and a half times life-size, is alertly intent, while his rider calmly watches the battle. This monument, in which there are thirteen horses in the round, places Shrady among the most prolific equestrian sculptors of all time. He spent twenty years laboring on details of action and equipment, which have passed the scrutiny of military men as well as artists, and suffered a financial loss as the result of such prolonged work. The panels on the memorial were executed by Sherry Fry from sketches made by Shrady. As a relief from his exacting labors on the Grant memorial he accepted commissions for the equestrian statue of Gen. Alpheus Starkey Williams in Belle Isle Park, Detroit, Mich., and the seated figure of Jay Cooke at Duluth, Minn. He made the bust of Grant in the New York University Hall of Fame, and for the Holland Society of New York he modeled the equestrian statue of William the Silent on Riverside Drive, New York City. His last work was on the equestrian statue of Gen. Robert E. Lee at Charlottesville, Va., which was modified and executed by Leo Lentilli. He died two weeks before the elaborate ceremonies of dedication of the Grant Memorial on Apr. 27, 1922. On Nov. 18, 1896, he had married Harrie E. Moore, with whom he made his home at Elmsford, N. Y., in a house that had been built before the Revolution. He had a daughter and three sons, all of whom, with his widow, survived him.

[*Who's Who in America*, 1920–21; R. E. Jackman, *Am. Arts* (1928); Lorado Taft, *The Hist. of Am. Sculpture* (1924); H. P. Caemmerer, *Washington, the Nat. Capital* (1932); *The Grant Memorial in Washington* (1924); Mrs. B. S. Church, in *Jour. of Am. Hist.*, Apr.–June 1913; C. H. Garrett, in *Munsey's Mag.*, July 1903; William Walton, in *Scribner's Mag.*, Mar. 1911; Helen Wright, in *Art and Archaeology*, Apr. 1922; obituary in *N. Y. Times*, Apr. 13, 1922; information from the family.]   C. M.

SHREVE, HENRY MILLER (Oct. 21, 1785– Mar. 6, 1851), steamboat captain on the Mississippi River and its tributaries, was a descendant of Thomas Sheriff [*sic*] who was in Massachusetts as early as 1641. He was born in Burlington County, N. J., where his great-grandfather, Caleb, had settled about the beginning of the century; his parents were Israel and Mary (Cokely) Shreve. The father, though a Quaker, served as colonel in the Revolutionary War, and having suffered the loss of home, crop, and stock at the hands of the British, joined the westward movement of the post-war period. Henry, scarcely three years old at the time of their migration to Fayette County, Pa., became acquainted with the frontier life and the hardships of the pioneer which rapidly developed youth into maturity. After the death of his father in 1799, he began to make trading journeys by keelboat, pirogue, or barge, down the Monongahela and the Ohio into the West. His successful fur-trading expedition, by barge, to St. Louis in 1807, started the trade between that city and Philadelphia, by way of Pittsburgh. His next new venture lay in the Upper Mississippi Valley, where the lead trade monopolized by the British had attracted his attention, and in 1810 he took a cargo of lead from the Fevre (Galena) River to New Orleans, thus inaugurating a lucrative trade. On Feb. 28, 1811, at Brownsville, Pa., he married Mary Blair, and for four years thereafter carried on a thriving trade between Pittsburgh and New Orleans by means of a 95-ton barge which he had built at Brownsville. After the death of his first wife, he married Lydia Rogers; a son and daughter of the first marriage and one daughter of the second died before their father; two daughters survived him.

In 1814, his ambition fired by the success of the *New Orleans,* Fulton's first steamboat on the Mississippi, Shreve became a stockholder in the steamboat *Enterprise,* an eighty-foot sternwheeler, built at Brownsville under the patents of Daniel French. In this vessel, laden with supplies for Jackson's army, he went from Pittsburgh to New Orleans in December of that year. While the vessel was at New Orleans, December 1814–May 1815, Shreve gave valuable service to General Jackson, running the British batteries with supplies for Fort St. Philip and later being sent to the Gulf to exchange prisoners with the British fleet. By special permission, he helped man a twenty-four-pound gun in the battle of New Orleans. In May 1815 Shreve attempted successfully to ascend the Mississippi and Ohio rivers to Louisville; the *Enterprise* was the first steamer to accomplish that trip, but it remained for his second steamboat, the *Washington,* to establish the practicability of steam navigation on the Mississippi and Ohio route. The *Washington,* built at Wheeling under Shreve's direction, differed from its predecessors in that it had a flat, shallow hull and a high-pressure engine which it carried on the main deck instead of in the hold; it was also the first of the river boats to have a second deck. Just prior to its maiden trip, an accident to one of the cylinders of the *Washington* caused the first of the western steamboat explosions in which lives were lost, but despite this catastrophe, Shreve made the voyage from Pittsburgh to New Orleans and back to Louisville in 1816, and in 1817 made the round trip between Louisville and New Orleans in the record time of forty-one days. From this time on, boats modeled upon the *Washington* continued in increasing numbers to ply the western rivers. Shreve had interests in many other boats; his *Post Boy* (1819) was one of the first steamers to carry mail on western waters. His success as a steamboat builder and operator brought him into conflict with the Fulton-Livingston interests, to which monopoly of steam navigation of its waters had been granted in 1811 by the Territory of Orleans, but he won the lawsuit brought against him by the holders of the monopoly and thus opened the navigation of the Mississippi and its tributaries to competitive enterprise.

As superintendent of western river improvements, by appointment of the President, from Jan. 2, 1827, until his retirement 1841, Shreve designed the first steam snagboat (the *Heliopolis*), by means of which he drew from the river the sunken tree-trunks—sawyers, snags, and planters—that had for so many years menaced navigation in the early days of river trade. "Uncle Sam's tooth-pullers," as the snagboats were commonly designated at the time, not only broke the logs from their moorings, but drew them on board the boat, where they were used as fuel to continue the operation of removing their fellows still in the stream. In the thirties Shreve removed the famous Red River raft, an obstruction which had encumbered its waters for hundreds of years and had prevented the development of North Louisiana. His camp, established at Bennett's Bluff during the progress of the work, had grown by 1839 to such an extent that it was incorporated under the name Shreveport. After his retirement, Shreve spent the rest of his life on a plantation in St. Louis County, Mo. He died in St. Louis.

[L. P. Allen, *The Geneal. and Hist. of the Shreve Family from 1641* (privately printed, 1901); "Journal of Col. Israel Shreve," *Mag. of Am. Hist.,* Dec. 1878; "Henry Miller Shreve," in *U. S. Mag. and Democratic Rev.,* Feb., Mar. 1848; Caroline S. Pfaff, "Henry Miller Shreve: A Biog.," *La. Hist. Quart.,* Apr. 1927; E. W. Gould, *Fifty Years on the Mississippi* (1889); Herbert Quick, *Mississippi Steamboatin'* (1926); M. L. Hartsough, *From Canoe to Steel Barge on the Upper Mississippi* (1934); *Louisiana Gazette,* Oct. 9, 24, 1816, and Mar. 3, Nov. 15, 1817; Henry McMurtie, *Sketches of Louisville* (1819); J. T. Scharf, *Hist. of St. Louis City and County* (1883), vol. II; *Daily Missouri Republican* (St. Louis), Mar. 7, 1851.]

C. S. P—f.

SHREVE, THOMAS HOPKINS (Dec. 17, 1808–Dec. 22, 1853), writer and editor, was born in Alexandria, Va., the only son of Thomas and Ann (Hopkins) Shreve. On his father's side he was descended from a Thomas Sheriff (Shreve), who first appears in the records of a suit at law in New England in 1641, and who headed a line of Shreves numerous and prominent in colonial New Jersey. His grandfather, Caleb Shreve, served in the New Jersey assembly during and after the Revolution. His granduncle, Israel Shreve, father of Henry Miller Shreve [*q.v.*], was a colonel in Washington's army. His mother, who died in 1815, was closely related to Johns Hopkins [*q.v.*], founder of the Johns Hopkins University. Both Shreves and Hopkinses were Quakers. Shreve was educated in Alexandria and in Trenton, N. J., to which his father, after the failure of his calico mills, removed in 1821. About 1830 he followed his father and sisters to Cincinnati, where they had gone in 1827.

There he promptly entered upon a literary career in which he was associated with the literary pioneers of Cincinnati: William Davis Gallagher, James Handasyd Perkins [*qq.v.*], Otway Curry, James B. Marshall, and others. With Gallagher he published the *Cincinnati Mirror,* 1833–35, and in 1835 his own firm, T. H. Shreve and Company, brought out the first five numbers of a Unitarian magazine, the *Western Messenger.* Until the spring of 1836 he and Gallagher edited the *Cincinnati Mirror,* begun in 1831. For the *Mirror* he wrote about thirty essays, tales, and sketches, and a dozen poems. His essays and poems appeared also in the *Western Messenger,* 1835; the *Western Literary Journal and Monthly Review,* 1836; the *Western Monthly Magazine and Literary Journal,* 1837; the *Knickerbocker, or New-York Monthly Magazine,* 1837–38; the *Hesperian,* 1838–39; and the *Western Literary Journal and Monthly Magazine,* 1844. In 1838, with a brother-in-law, Joshua B. Bowles, he established in Louisville, Ky., the wholesale dry goods firm of Bowles, Shreve & Company, but he continued his contributions to magazines. On Apr. 16, 1840, he was married to Octavia Bullitt, daughter of Benjamin Bullitt, of Louisville, who survived him for many years; they had three daughters, all of whom died unmarried. Two years later he gave up his interest in an agricultural warehouse—the partnership with Bowles had been previously dissolved—to become assistant editor of George Dennison Prentice's powerful newspaper, the *Louisville Daily Journal,* a position he held until his death from tuberculosis. His work on the *Louisville Journal* won him the high esteem of Prentice and other editors of his day. He made a collection of his essays which never appeared in book form, though parts of it were published in the *Knickerbocker;* he also wrote "Betterton: A Novel," unpublished, and *Drayton: A Story of American Life* (1851). He died in Louisville and was buried in Cave Hill Cemetery. His best work is to be found in his genial and lively essays, often Addisonian in style and content. *Drayton,* while it reflects something of the life of the latter eighteenth century and the current social and political cleavages, is better proof of his ability as an essayist than as a novelist. Some of his few fugitive poems (reprinted in W. D. Gallagher's *Selections from the Poetical Literature of the West,* 1841) show native poetical capacity which was never fully developed. Though his contemporaries regarded him as a highly gifted writer whose talents would gain him an important place in western American letters, he is most interesting as a member of the group that brought Cincinnati and Louisville cultural rec-ognition during the early decades of the nineteenth century.

[L. P. Allen, *The Geneal. and Hist. of the Shreve Family from 1641* (1901); W. T. Coggeshall, *The Poets and Poetry of the West* (1860); F. L. Mott, *A Hist. of Am. Mags.* (1930); W. H. Venable, "William Davis Gallagher," *Ohio Archaeogolical and Hist. Quart.,* Mar. 1888; J. S. Johnston, *Mem. Hist. of Louisville,* vol. II (n.d.); C. A. Neyman, unpublished monograph on Shreve, lib., George Washington Univ.]   R. W. B.
                                                                      C. A. N.

SHUBRICK, JOHN TEMPLER (Sept. 12, 1788–July 1815), naval officer, was born on Bull's Island, near Charleston, S. C., son of Col. Thomas Shubrick, a veteran of the American Revolution, and his wife Mary, daughter of Ezekiel Branford of Charleston. After attending school at Charleston and at Dedham, Mass., he began law study at Charleston under Col. William Drayton [*q.v.*], but soon felt a stronger call for the navy, in which he was commissioned midshipman on June 20, 1806. It was typical of his extraordinarily eventful service career that his first cruise brought him under fire in the surrender of the *Chesapeake* under Capt. James Barron [*q.v.*] to the British frigate *Leopard,* June 22, 1807. He served subsequently under Stephen Decatur, the younger [*q.v.*], in the *Chesapeake* and the *Argus,* and after challenging a fellow midshipman to a duel underwent the obviously lenient punishment of transfer to the brig *Viper,* where he became at once acting lieutenant (1810). In 1811 in the *Siren* he lost both thumbs by a single pistol shot fired by a New Orleans ropewalk superintendent whom he was about to strike with a stick for insults to himself and his men. These affairs apparently reflect merely the temper of his period and profession, for he was reputed to be of quiet, even melancholy spirit, so mild as to give a false impression of weakness.

Commissioned lieutenant in May 1812, he was in the *Constitution* in her celebrated escape from Broke's squadron, July 17–20, and in her victory over the *Guerrière,* Aug. 19; he commanded the quarter-deck guns and was in the thick of the mêlée when his ship's stern fouled the enemy. He was third lieutenant in the *Constitution's* defeat of the *Java,* Dec. 29, off Bahia. Sailing homeward in the *Hornet* under James Lawrence [*q.v.*], he was acting first lieutenant in a third famous victory on Feb. 24, 1813, the capture of the *Peacock,* which he boarded upon her surrender. Lawrence commended him highly, remarking that previous commanders could also testify to "his coolness and good conduct" (*The Naval Monument,* 1816, p. 42). After a relatively inactive period in the *United States* at New London, he shifted with Decatur to the

President, and was captured in her, Jan. 15, 1815, when she was attacked off New York by the British blockading squadron. After the death of his next superior early in the battle, Shubrick had become second in command. Through all these actions he came unscathed but with the reputation of bringing fighting to any ship in which he served. He received three medals from Congress and a sword from his native state. As first lieutenant in Decatur's flagship *Guerrière* against Algiers, he participated in the capture of the Algerian frigate *Mashuda,* June 17, 1815. After the peace he was given command of the *Epervier* to carry home the treaty. His ship passed Gibraltar early in July but was never again seen; it is believed to have gone down in a gale off the American coast.

Of the younger officers of the 1812 period none served more gallantly or gave brighter promise. He is described by Cooper as being five feet eleven in height, of strong frame, with grey eyes and brown hair, a man of intelligence and culture beyond the ordinary in his profession. His death was made more tragic by his marriage in 1814 to Elizabeth Matilda Ludlow of New York. His son, Edward Templer Shubrick, rose to lieutenant in the navy, resigning in 1852. Of the sixteen children in Col. Thomas Shubrick's family, six sons served in the War of 1812, four in the navy. Of these latter, Edward Rutledge became a captain and was lost at sea (1844); Irvine died a commander (1849); and William Branford [q.v.] became a rear admiral.

[See biog. sketch in *Analectic Mag. and Naval Chronicle,* Sept. 1816, reprinted in the *Portfolio,* May 1825; J. F. Cooper, *Lives of Distinguished Am. Naval Officers* (1846), vol. I, pp. 147–70; additional material in a sketch of W. B. Shubrick by Susan Fenimore Cooper, *Harper's Mag.,* Aug. 1876. For accounts of battles in which Shubrick took part, see E. S. Maclay, *A Hist. of the U. S. Navy from 1775–1893* (2 vols., 1894).]
A. W.

SHUBRICK, WILLIAM BRANFORD (Oct. 31, 1790–May 27, 1874), naval officer, son of Thomas and Mary (Branford) Shubrick and brother of John Templer Shubrick [q.v.], was born on his father's plantation, "Belvidere," Bull's Island, S. C. After schooling at Charleston and later at Dedham, Mass., he spent a year at Harvard and then in 1806 entered the navy as midshipman. Following a short Mediterranean cruise in the *Wasp,* he was on the American coast until 1810, serving under James Lawrence and as shipmate with James Fenimore Cooper [qq.v.], with whom he formed a lifelong friendship. Cooper dedicated to him *The Pilot* and *The Red Rover,* took brief cruises with him, and much enjoyed his seaman's comment on the lee

shore passage in the *Pilot,* "It's all very well, but you have let your jib stand too long, my fine fellow." A brief cruise in the *Hornet* early in the War of 1812 was followed by promotion to lieutenant, Jan. 5, 1813, and duty in the *Constellation* at Norfolk, during which he led a detachment of seamen in the successful defense of Craney Island, June 22, 1813, against a British boat attack. Later that year he joined the *Constitution* at Boston; he served in her as third lieutenant in her brilliant capture of the *Cyane* and *Levant,* Feb. 20, 1815, and as first lieutenant when she escaped from two ships of the line and a frigate, Mar. 11–12, near the Cape Verde Islands. His part in this cruise won him a congressional medal and mention in the vote of thanks to Commodore Charles Stewart [q.v.] and crew.

The next thirty years was a period of faithful routine service, marked by a cruise in the *Washington,* 1815–18; command of the *Lexington* and then the *Natchez,* 1826–29, in the latter of which he brought the body of Oliver Hazard Perry [q.v.] from Trinidad; promotion to captain, 1831; command of the West Indies Squadron, 1838–40; and administration of the bureau of provisions and clothing, 1845–46. At the opening of the Mexican War he applied for sea duty and sailed in the *Independence* to relieve John Drake Sloat [q.v.] in command of forces on the California coast. These orders unfortunately conflicted with similar ones to his senior, James Biddle [q.v.], who arrived at Monterey with the East Indies Squadron Jan. 2, 1847, a week later, and assumed control. Though chagrined, Shubrick remained, took charge of the Mazatlán blockade, Apr. 17–June 1, and was then recalled to California, where Biddle restored the command to him on July 19. The vigorous operations that followed included a hazardous night entry of Shubrick's squadron into Mazatlán harbor on Nov. 10, the landing of 600 men next day, and the occupation or blockade of other coastal towns. Relieved in May 1848, he became in 1849 head of the Philadelphia navy yard and later of the bureau of construction and repair, finding leisure in the summer of 1851 to visit Cooper during his last illness. In August 1852 he was made chairman of the lighthouse board, an office he held during the next nineteen years. In the ensuing summer he went to Halifax with a small squadron and made temporary arrangements with Admiral Sir George Seymour, R.N., for a fisheries treaty.

His name is now chiefly remembered through his command of the imposing expedition of nineteen ships and 2500 men sent to settle commercial and other difficulties with Paraguay. The fleet sailed in October 1858, and on Jan. 25 following reached Asunción, where Shubrick and the American commissioner, Mr. Bowlin, secured a treaty settling all points in dispute. "To the zeal, energy, discretion, and courteous and gallant bearing of Flag-officer Shubrick and the officers of his command," wrote Isaac Toucey (*Report of the Secretary of the Navy,* 1859, pp. 1137–38), "is the country largely indebted not only for the success of the enterprise, but for the friendly feeling . . . in that part of South America." His selection for these missions bears out the opinion expressed by Samuel Francis Du Pont [*q.v.*], that "he represented us abroad with men of high rank better than any officer we ever had" (S. F. Cooper, *post,* p. 406). He was a man of cultivated manners and fine presence; "feature, form, and carriage were all manly and distinguished" (*Ibid., post,* p. 403). In December 1861 he was retired after fifty-five years' service, less than ten of which were unemployed. Promoted to rear admiral (retired) in July 1862, he lived subsequently in Washington, in his last years nearly blind. His marriage in September 1815 to Harriet Cordelia, daughter of John Wethered of the Eastern Shore of Maryland, continued happily for over fifty years. His only daughter married Dr. George Clymer of the navy, and a grand-daughter became the second wife of Thomas Francis Bayard [*q.v.*].

[Susan Fenimore Cooper, in *Harper's Mag.,* Aug. 1876; *Commodore Shubrick, Speech of Hon. Andrew P. Butler of S. C. in the Senate, Mar. 18, 1856* (1856); *Correspondence of James Fenimore Cooper* (1922), containing frequent references to Shubrick and several of his letters; material on the Mexican war in *House Exec. Doc. 1,* 30 Cong., 2 Sess. (1848), on the fisheries treaty in *House Exec. Doc. 21,* 33 Cong., 1 Sess. (1854); Captains' Letters, Navy Dept. Lib., Washington, D. C., for the periods of his important activities; editorial in *Army and Navy Jour.,* May 30, 1874; obituary in *Evening Star* (Washington), May 27, 1874.]
A. W.

SHUCK, JEHU LEWIS (Sept. 4, 1812–Aug. 20, 1863), missionary to the Chinese, was born in Alexandria, then in the District of Columbia. His father died in 1816 and later his mother moved to Lewisburg, Greenbrier County, in what is now West Virginia. Here he studied privately and at the Lewisburg Academy. He read law for a time, but, after a deep religious experience, decided to enter the ministry and was licensed to preach by the Lewisburg Baptist Church on May 13, 1832. He prepared for his calling at the Virginia Baptist Seminary in Richmond. It was while there, apparently, that he determined to be a missionary. On Sept. 8, 1835, he was married to Henrietta Hall, who was then not quite eighteen years of age, and that same month sailed from Boston under the American

Baptist Board of Foreign Missions as a missionary to the Chinese.

At that time Westerners—except a few Russians at Peking—were allowed in China only secretly or in the Portuguese colony of Macao and in a restricted district at Canton, so that it was uncertain where Shuck could settle permanently. For several months in 1836 he was in Singapore studying Malay and Chinese, and in 1836 he removed to Macao. Here, with the exception of one fruitless effort to reach the island of Hainan and occasional visits to Canton and Hongkong, he remained until 1842, studying the language and, in time, preaching to the Chinese in private houses or on the streets. He and his wife were the first Baptist missionaries to reside in China. His years at Macao were not altogether happy, for his first convert apostatized after a few months and he had misunderstandings with the board which supported him. In 1842 he removed to Hongkong, which had recently come into the possession of the British. There, within the next few years, he organized a church and shared in the organization of another, built three chapels, a mission house, and a school, and baptized several Chinese. His wife died Nov. 27, 1844, and several years later, 1852, a work she had prepared, *Scenes in China; or, Sketches of the Country, Religion, and Customs of the Chinese,* was published.

In 1845 Shuck returned with his children to the United States, bringing a convert and a Chinese nurse with him. Here he spoke extensively on China, and here, in October 1846, married Lizzie Sexton. Transferring his connection to the newly formed Board of Foreign Missions of the Southern Baptist Convention, he returned to China in 1847 and after a short visit at Hongkong removed to Shanghai, where he had a share in establishing a mission of his board. In 1851 his second wife died and not long afterward he again returned to the United States, this time to remain permanently. On June 5, 1854, he married Anna L. Trotti. Appointed by the Board of Domestic and Indian Missions of the Southern Baptist Convention to carry on work among the Chinese in California, he began a Chinese church in Sacramento. For at least part of the time he served as general secretary of his denomination in the state, and organized a number of churches and edited a paper. Resigning Jan. 1, 1861, he removed to South Carolina, where he was pastor of churches at Blackville and Steel Creek. He died at Barnwell Court House, S. C. In his earlier years, at least, he was decidedly intolerant and was at times blunt in presenting his own convictions, especially to the non-Christians whom he met in the Far East. He was the author of a number of tracts in Chinese, and in English of a volume published under the title *Portfolio Chinensis* (Macao, 1840).

[Alexander Wylie, *Memorials of Protestant Missionaries to the Chinese* (Shanghai, 1867), pp. 90, 91; T. S. Dunaway, *Pioneering for Jesus, The Story of Henrietta Hall Shuck* (1930); J. B. Jeter, *A Memoir of Mrs. Henrietta Shuck* (1846); *Ann. Reports of the Am. Baptist Board of Foreign Missions; Proc. of the Southern Baptist Convention*, 1861, p. 35; *Baptist Missionary Mag.*, 1836–44; G. B. Taylor, *Va. Baptist Ministers —Third Series* (1912), pp. 45–47; manuscript files of the Am. Baptist Foreign Mission Soc.]   **K. S. L.**

SHUEY, EDWIN LONGSTREET (Jan. 3, 1857–Sept. 27, 1924), business man, director of factory welfare work, author, was born in Cincinnati, Ohio, the son of Sarah (Berger) and William John Shuey [*q.v.*], a minister of the United Brethren in Christ. In 1865 the family removed to Dayton, where the son received his early education. In 1874 he entered Otterbein College at Westerville, Ohio, where he majored in Latin and Greek, and three years later received the degree of B.A. Following a year devoted to the study of law, he turned to teaching in academies in Indiana and northwestern Ohio, and in 1881 was invited to Otterbein to organize a preparatory department, of which he became the principal. On Aug. 15, 1882, he married Effie Mitchell of Springfield, Ohio, by whom he had two daughters and a son.

In 1885, prompted by the urgings of his father, he returned to Dayton to assume charge of the retail bookstore of the denominational publishing house. Through this work he became interested in advertising, in which he afterwards became a national expert. Asked by a Bible publishing company in Philadelphia to organize commentaries on the Scriptures from an American point of view, he obtained contributions from British and American experts and secured the compilation of a "word book" for assistance to readers of the Bible; these helps were sold as the Bible Readers' Aids of the International Bible, the compiler appearing only as the American editor. After his removal to Dayton he became active in the work of the Young Men's Christian Association as chairman of a local committee with the task of arranging evening study classes for young men. Although in New York cultural subjects had been taught in free evening sessions, in Dayton technical courses were offered with a charge for tuition and were so successful that Shuey was appointed in 1893 to the International Y. M. C. A. Committee; for over thirty years a member of this committee, he assisted in the development of its educational poli-

cies. In 1899 he was president of the International Convention; from 1917 to 1920 he was a member of the National War Work Council; and in 1923 he was active in devising a new plan for the national administration of the organization.

In 1897 he became head of the welfare department of the National Cash Register Company. His success in this work led to his writing *Factory People and Their Employers* (1900) and to his being consulted by other prominent corporations interested in welfare programs. In 1900 he associated himself with the Lowe Brothers Company of Dayton, paint manufacturers, to develop advertising and promote an effective sales policy; he achieved conspicuous success and remained with the company until his retirement in 1918. In 1915–16 he served as president of the Association of National Advertisers, whose declaration of ethical standards was due in part to his efforts. A delegate to several quadrennial conferences of the Church of the United Brethren, he was a successful advocate at the last one he attended of a liberalization of the Book of Discipline. For five years he was president of the board of trustees of Otterbein College. He was an imaginative, quietly dynamic man, whose decided opinions made enemies as well as friends. He died of cancer a few months after the death of his wife.

[D. B. Shuey, *Hist. of the Shuey Family in America* (2nd ed., 1919); *Who's Who in America*, 1924–25; N. R. Best, *Two Y Men: David A. Sinclair, Secretary; Edwin L. Shuey, Layman* (1925), based on Shuey's personal papers; *Daily News* (Dayton), Sept. 28, 29, Oct. 1, 1924.]   **F. P. W.**

SHUEY, WILLIAM JOHN (Feb. 9, 1827–Feb. 21, 1920), clergyman of the United Brethren in Christ, was born in Miamisburg, Montgomery County, Ohio, the son of Adam and Hannah (Aley) Shuey. He was of Huguenot lineage, a descendant of Daniel Shuey who emigrated to Pennsylvania in 1732 and settled in what is now Lebanon County. William attended the public schools of his native town and of Springfield, his parents having moved to a farm in the latter place in 1836. A brief period of study at the Ohio Conference High School of the Methodist Church, Springfield, completed his formal education. In 1848 he was admitted to the Miami Conference of the Church of the United Brethren and the same year, Mar. 7, married Sarah Berger, by whom he had four sons, one of whom was Edwin L. Shuey [*q.v.*].

From the beginning of his ministry Shuey displayed, in addition to religious zeal, unusual administrative and business ability. He was quick to see and to indicate lines of advance, and no little of the progress of his denomination during the last half of the nineteenth century was due to his wisdom and energy. After serving on the Lewisburg Circuit (1849–51), he became pastor of the First Church, Cincinnati. In 1854, having been prominent in stimulating organized missionary activity, he was appointed by the newly constituted Home, Frontier, and Foreign Missionary Society to go to Africa and select a site for its first work abroad. Accompanied by D. C. Kumler and Daniel K. Flickinger [q.v.], he sailed in January 1855. The three fixed upon what seemed a suitable location, and Kumler and Shuey returned. Until 1864 he was engaged in pastoral work in Cincinnati and Dayton, and was for three terms presiding elder of the Miami Conference. During this period he published in collaboration with Flickinger, *Discourses on Doctrinal and Practical Subjects* (1859). In 1864 he was elected assistant publishing agent, and in 1865, agent. His more than twenty years' service in this position is regarded as an epoch in the history of the denomination. Taking charge of the publishing concern at Dayton when it was in a precarious condition, he put it on a permanent basis and greatly extended its activities. "More than any Bishop, editor, or other Church leader . . . Shuey in his position as Publishing Agent was for an entire generation the strategic center for the activities and progress of the United Brethren in Christ" (Drury, *post*, p. 581). He was an important member of the commission that formulated the revised confession of faith and constitution adopted in 1889, and in the long court contest for possession of the publishing house, inaugurated by those who held to the old constitution and separated from the majority, he carried the burden of the defense which kept the property in the hands of the latter. He was instrumental in the founding of Union Biblical Seminary (Bonebrake Theological Seminary), the first theological school of the United Brethren. Many of the institutions of the Church profited by his abilities; he was for twenty-two years a trustee of Otterbein College, for more than a quarter of a century a member of the board of missions, one of the first directors of the Church Extension Society, and a member of the Board of Education. For years he edited *The Yearbook of the United Brethren in Christ*; he prepared several editions of the denominational *Handbook*, and, with others, *A Collection of Hymns for the Use of the United Brethren in Christ* (1858); he published also, *An Outline of Our Church Troubles* (1881), and *A Manual of the United Brethren Publishing House* (1892). In 1897 he relinquished his position as publishing agent

and became business manager of Bonebrake Theological Seminary, retiring from official church service in 1901. During his long residence in Dayton he was active in civic affairs and was for many years a director of the Fourth National Bank.

[D. B. Shuey, *Hist. of the Shuey Family* (1919); Daniel Berger, *Hist. of the Ch. of the United Brethren in Christ* (1897); A. W. Drury, *Hist. of the Ch. of the United Brethren in Christ* (1924); *Who's Who in America*, 1918–19.]   H. E. S.

SHUFELDT, ROBERT WILSON (Feb. 21, 1822–Nov. 7, 1895), naval officer, was born at Red Hook, N. Y., son of George Adam Shufeldt, a prominent lawyer, and his wife Mary (Wilson) Shufeldt, and a descendant of George Shufeldt, who emigrated to New York from Holland in 1710. Entering the navy as midshipman, May 11, 1839, he cruised in the Brazil and Home Squadrons, was commissioned passed midshipman on July 2, 1845, after a year's study at the Philadelphia naval school, and then served a year in the coast survey and two years in African and Mediterranean waters. In 1849–51 he was chief officer of the mail steamers *Atlantic* and *Georgia*. He was made lieutenant in October 1853 but resigned from the navy the following June, and commanded first the Collins Line steamer *Liverpool* for two years and then the *Black Hawk* and *Catawba* between New York and New Orleans. At the opening of the Civil War, he was appointed consul general to Cuba and continued in this duty until April 1863, going to Mexico in 1862 on a hazardous secret mission at the time of the French invasion. He then rejoined the navy, his commander's commission dating from Nov. 19, 1862, and commanded first the *Conemaugh*, which participated in the capture of Morris Island, S. C., and in other operations off Charleston, and later the *Proteus* of the East Gulf Squadron, in which he was senior naval officer in joint operations, Mar. 23–27, 1865, at St. Marks, Fla. His post-bellum service included command of the *Hartford* and *Wachusett* in the Orient, with promotion to captain in 1869; of the *Miantonomah*, 1870; and of an expedition surveying the Isthmus of Tehuantepec canal route, 1870–71, his report of which was published in 1872 (*Senate Executive Document 6*, 42 Cong., 2 Sess., 1872). After a brief Mediterranean cruise in the *Wabash* and duty at the Brooklyn navy yard, he was chief of the bureau of equipment and recruiting, 1875–78; during this service he reorganized the naval apprentice system and also commanded naval forces at New Orleans during the election troubles of '76.

Having advocated the use of the navy in extending American commerce (in *The Relation of the Navy to the Commerce of the United States*, 1878) and persuaded James Gillespie Blaine [*q.v.*], then secretary of state, of the possibilities of a treaty with Korea, which had just made trade concessions to Japan but had not yet opened relations with any western power, he sailed in the *Ticonderoga* in 1878 on a combined commercial and diplomatic mission. After acting as American and British representative to settle a Liberian boundary dispute, and making a treaty with the king of Johanna, he sailed to Japan, reaching Nagasaki, Apr. 15, 1880, and Fusan, Korea, May 4. Finding Japanese mediation of very doubtful value, he secured from the Chinese viceroy Li Hung Chang a promise of aid with Korea in exchange for help in organizing a Chinese navy. After a trip home, Shufeldt was back in China in June 1881 as naval attaché and with full power to negotiate a treaty, which was finally drawn up, signed May 22, 1882, and subsequently ratified. Much more comprehensive than any previous American treaty with eastern nations, it established diplomatic relations, extraterritoriality, and privileges to Americans of trade and residence in open ports. The treaty was wholly the result of Shufeldt's initiative, pertinacity, and genuine diplomatic skill; it was the great achievement of his career. Subsequently he was president of the Naval Advisory Board, 1882–84, during the beginnings of the "White Squadron," and superintendent of the naval observatory, reaching rear admiral's rank in 1883, and retiring Feb. 21, 1884. Of gigantic frame and strong physique, he succumbed finally to pneumonia in his Washington home. His burial was at Arlington. His wife, whom he married Oct. 16, 1847, was Sarah Hutchins Abercrombie, daughter of the Rev. James Abercrombie of Philadelphia. They had six children, of whom three sons survived their parents.

[See G. N. Mackenzie, *Colonial Families of the U. S. A.*, vol. V (1915); L. H. Hamersly, *Records of Living Officers of the U. S. Navy* (4th ed., 1890); R. W. Shufeldt, *The Relation of the Navy to the Commerce of the U. S.* (1878); C. O. Paullin, *Diplomatic Negotiations of Am. Naval Officers* (1912); obituaries in *Army and Navy Jour.*, Nov. 9, and *Evening Star* (Washington), Nov. 7, 1895. The Shufeldt Papers, temporarily deposited in the Navy Dept. Lib., Washington, D. C., include a manuscript history, "The Cruise of the *Ticonderoga*," and many other docs. relating chiefly to the Korean mission.]   A. W.

SHULZE, JOHN ANDREW (July 19, 1775–Nov. 18, 1852), governor of Pennsylvania, was born in the township of Tulpehocken, Berks County, Pa. His father, Christopher Emanuel Shulze, a distinguished clergyman of the Lutheran Church, was a native of Saxony, Germany, educated at the University of Halle, who emigrated to America in 1765; and his mother, Eva Elizabeth, was the daughter of Henry Melchior Mühlenberg [*q.v.*]. The boy received a classical and theological education, studying in Lancaster, York, and New York City under the guidance of some of the most eminent educators and divines of the day. He was married to Susan Kimmell, by whom he had at least two children. In 1796 he was ordained to the ministry, was admitted to the German Lutheran Synod of Eastern Pennsylvania, and preached in Berks County. In 1802 he retired from the active ministry on account of serious rheumatism. In 1804 he established himself in the mercantile business in Myerstown, then in Dauphin County, and within a decade had accumulated a moderate fortune.

In 1806 he served in the House of Representatives of Pennsylvania. He was reëlected for the two succeeding years but refused to become a candidate for a fourth term. A stanch advocate of Republican principles in government, he played a very active and influential part in the proceedings of the legislature during his three-year tenure in that body. In 1813 he was appointed to the office of surveyor-general of the state but declined this position. He was induced, however, to accept the duties of register, recorder, prothonotary, clerk of the orphans' court, and clerk of the sessions court of Lebanon County. After serving eight years in these capacities he was elected again to the House of Representatives in 1821 and the next year was chosen a state senator from Dauphin and Lebanon counties. In 1823 he received the Republican nomination for governor and was elected by a majority of more than 25,000. Upon the expiration of his term of three years he was returned to the governorship by the unprecedented majority of approximately 72,000 votes to about 2,000 for his opponent. In dispensing the patronage, grown to enormous proportions by the public works in which the state was then engaged, he proved himself a keen judge of men and a politician of no mean merit. Although questioning at first the wisdom of having the state embark on a program of internal improvements, the chief feature of which was the construction of a canal from Columbia on the Susquehanna River to Pittsburgh with side branches to act as feeders to the main canal, he bowed to the wishes of the people and gave the project his hearty support. Before the expiration of his second term of office more than $6,000,000 had been expended on the canals alone, and a considerable portion of the program had been completed.

Especially interested in the extension of the system of public elementary education to all classes throughout the state, he repeatedly appealed to the legislature on the subject. Although the legislation enacted in response to his requests did not measure up to his expectations, something was accomplished; and the publicity given the subject paved the way for the establishment of the system of public education on a sound basis during the decade of the thirties. After the expiration of his second term in December 1829, he retired from public life and devoted himself to farming, though he continued his interest in politics and public questions in general. In 1839 he was a delegate to the state convention that assembled in Harrisburg and the following year was chosen a member of the electoral college of the state, of which he was elected president. In 1846 he removed to Lancaster, where he resided until his death.

[*Pa. Archives*, ser. 4, vol. V (1900); W. C. Armor, *Lives of the Governors of Pa.* (1872); J. B. Sutherland, *An Impartial View of the Respective Claims of Mr. Shulze and Mr. Gregg to the Office of Governor of Pa.* (1823); W. H. Egle, *Hist. of the Counties of Dauphin and Lebanon* (1883); H. M. M. Richards, "Descendants of H. M. Mühlenberg," *Proc. and Addresses Pa.-Ger. Soc.*, vol. X (1900) p. 21 giving his name as John Andrew Melchior Shulze.]   A. E. M.

SHUNK, FRANCIS RAWN (Aug. 7, 1788– July 30, 1848), governor of Pennsylvania, was born at Trappe, Montgomery County, Pa., the son of Elizabeth (Rawn) and John Shunk, a farmer. His two grandfathers, Francis Shunk and Caspar Rawn, had emigrated to America early in the eighteenth century from the Palatinate of the Rhine. Because of the poverty of his parents the boy's formal education was limited to the country school, and at the age of fifteen he became a teacher. Soon afterward he was placed in charge of the village school at Trappe, a position he continued to fill for nine years. When the school was not in session he worked on the neighboring farms and studied as much as he could. In 1812 he was appointed by Andrew Porter, the surveyor-general of the state, as a clerk. He also studied law in the office of Thomas Elder of Harrisburg and in 1816 was admitted to the bar. In 1814 he marched as a private in a local company of the state militia to the defense of Baltimore against the invasion of the British. Soon after his return he became assistant and then principal clerk of the House of Representatives. In 1820 he married Jane Findley. Nine years later he was appointed clerk to the canal commissioners and in 1839 became secretary of the commonwealth. In 1842 he began the practice of law in Pittsburgh, but in 1844

he was elected as a Democrat governor of the state. In 1847 he was reëlected by an increased majority.

He was essentially a self-made man. Though not brilliant, he was honest, industrious, and devoted. During his administration the Mexican War made many demands upon the resources of the state as did also a variety of complicated domestic problems of major importance, some of which had been inherited from the preceding decade. Especially troublesome was the serious plight of the public treasury on his accession to office. Not only had the debt of the state reached the then staggering sum of approximately $40,-000,000, much of which had been accumulated in the construction of canals and other public works, but also the revenues were insufficient to meet the regular obligations of the government. Indeed, for a period of two years the interest on the state debt had not been paid, and the credit of the state was otherwise seriously impaired. To the question of balancing the budget and restoring the credit of the state he gave his constant attention throughout his entire administration with the result that he improved conditions measurably. His early labors gave him a hearty sympathy with the poor and unfortunate, and he steadfastly opposed all measures tending to the aggregation of property in the hands of the few or to the extension of special privileges and concessions to vested interests by legislative action. He vetoed many acts of the legislature granting concessions to corporate business enterprises. Among other measures which he commended to the legislature for favorable consideration were: state control of inheritance by laws preventing entailed estates, a more careful scrutiny on the part of the legislature of the increasingly large numbers of pleas for divorce presented to that body annually, and the extension and improvement of the system of public education. On July 9, 1848, however, on account of the failure of his health he resigned his office in a simple farewell message (*Archives, post*, pp. 275–76). He died of tuberculosis three weeks later.

[*Pa. Archives*, ser. 4, vol. VII (1902); W. C. Armor, *Lives of the Governors of Pa.* (1872); Moses Auge, *Lives of the Eminent . . . of Montgomery County, Pa.* (1879); *Commemoration Biog. Encyc. of Dauphin County, Pa.* (1896).]   A. E. M.

SHURTLEFF, NATHANIEL BRADSTREET (June 29, 1810–Oct. 17, 1874), mayor of Boston and antiquary, was born in Boston, the descendant of William Shurtleff who was in Plymouth as early as 1634. He was the son of Sally (Shaw) and Benjamin Shurtleff, a physician of Carver, Mass., who had removed to

Boston to acquire a professional reputation and a fortune. The boy graduated at the Boston Public Latin School in 1822 and then went to the Round Hill School at Northampton, under Joseph G. Cogswell and George Bancroft [*qq.v.*]. At Harvard College, where he received the A.B. degree in 1831, he was an indifferent student. He took the medical degree at Harvard in 1834 and soon succeeded to his father's practice. He married on July 18, 1836, Sarah Eliza, the daughter of Hiram Smith of Boston, and had six children. Some twenty years after graduation he enhanced his growing reputation as an antiquary by editing with scrupulous care the *Records of the Governor and Company of the Massachusetts Bay in New England* (5 vols. in 6, 1853–54). He said that every word and letter in the proof sheets had been compared with the original by himself. *Records of the Colony of New Plymouth in New England* (8 vols., 1855–57) followed, and to these David Pulsifer added four volumes (1859–61) after Shurtleff's expensive methods were discontinued (see *Mass. Col. Soc. Pubs.,* vol. III, 1900, pp. 104, 114–17). His most important work was *A Topographical and Historical Description of Boston* (1871) from articles written in the midst of years of professional and political activity. It is a minute account of Boston places, well written and readable. He wrote on everything that interested him: phrenology, a perpetual calendar, a study of the Bay Psalm Book, maps, a decimal system for the arrangement of books in libraries, and accounts of the Shurtleff, Leverett, and Beal families. His list of *The Passengers of the Mayflower* (printed in *New England Historical & Genealogical Register,* Jan. 1847 and privately printed in 1849), compiled from sources known before Bradford's *History* was found, is an example of his thoroughness. He failed to mention nine minor passengers out of one hundred and one, and he included one woman and several children not on board.

He was mayor of Boston for three terms, 1868–70, as a Democrat, being reëlected by increasing pluralities. His administrations were marked by the annexation of Dorchester and Roxbury, by street improvements, and by unsuccessful attempts to economize. He was not, it was said, a good judge of character, and he knew little of the proper methods of government. His addresses, however, reveal high purposes and wide sympathies. He took pride in being the first life-long democratic mayor. His party opposed a third term but an aroused electorate returned him to office. He was chosen a member of the Massachusetts Historical Society in 1847 and held office in that society nearly all the years following until his death. He belonged to several other societies in the United States and in England. From 1854 to 1874 he served as secretary to the board of overseers of Harvard College, having been a member of the board, 1852–61, 1863–69. He was also a trustee of the public library. He lived at No. 2 Beacon Street, where his apartments were crowded with books. His library, which was sold at auction in the fall of 1875, had 1790 items, a first rate local historical and genealogical collection (*Catalogue of the Library of Dr. N. B. Shurtleff to be Sold at Auction . . . Nov. 30, 1875,* 1875).

[C. C. Smith, in *Proc. Mass. Hist. Soc.,* ser. 1, vol. XIII (1875); *New-England Hist. and Geneal. Register,* July 1878; J. M. Bugbee, "Boston Under the Mayors," *The Memorial Hist. of Boston,* ed. by Justin Winsor, vol. III (1881); Benjamin Shurtleff, *Descendants of Wm. Shurtleff* (2 vols., 1912); *Ballou's Pictorial Drawing Room Companion,* Jan. 5, 1856, with portrait.]

C. K. B.

SHURTLEFF, ROSWELL MORSE (June 14, 1838–Jan. 6, 1915), landscape painter, born at Rindge, N. H., was the fourth and youngest child of Asahel Dewey and Eliza (Morse) Shurtleff. He was a descendant of William Shurtleff, who was born in the West Riding of Yorkshire, England, and was in Plymouth, Mass., in 1634. He went to Dartmouth College with the class of 1857 but did not graduate. He took charge of an architect's office in Manchester, N. H., 1857; worked in a lithographer's shop in Buffalo, N. Y., 1858–59; went to Boston in 1859 and made drawings on wood for John Andrew, the engraver, in the meantime studying drawing in the evening classes of the Lowell Institute; and in 1860–61 was in New York, where he attended the school of the National Academy of Design and made magazine illustrations. Upon the opening of the Civil War he enlisted, as a private; in a short time he was promoted to a lieutenancy, and later he became adjutant. On July 19, 1861, he was wounded and captured. After nearly eight months in Southern hospitals and prisons, he was finally released on parole. He returned to New York, and busied himself with drawing illustrations for magazines and books. On June 14, 1867 (*Who's Who in America, post*), he married Clara Eugenia Halliday, daughter of Joseph B. and Eleanor C. Halliday, of Hartford, Conn. From 1869 to 1875 he had a studio in Hartford.

It was in 1870 that he began to paint in oils and in 1872 that he first exhibited at the National Academy. At first he specialized in such pictures of animal life as "The American Panther" (1876), "A Race for Life" (1877), "The Still Hunter," and "On the Alert" (1879), and "The

Wolf at the Door," all of which were shown at the Academy in the seventies. "The Race for Life," which depicted a pack of wolves dashing through the winter woods in pursuit of some unseen prey, was considered by contemporaries (*New York Tribune,* Apr. 28, 1877) a most remarkable picture. About 1880 Shurtleff turned to landscapes, and he won his greatest success through his paintings of the northern woods and forests. He usually went to the Adirondacks in the summer and autumn, and had a cottage and studio at Keene Valley, where he produced many excellent forest interiors that showed both thorough knowledge and fine feeling. He became an Academician in 1890. Characteristic examples of his work have been hung in several public museums. In the Corcoran Gallery, Washington, is "The First Snow." The Metropolitan Museum, New York, owns "A Mountain Stream," in which a brook flows between banks crowded by trees. The Museum of Springfield, Mass., also has a good landscape. Shurtleff regularly exhibited his wood interiors at the Academy for many years and was successful in finding a market for them. He died in New York, survived by his wife. There were no children.

[Benjamin Shurtleff, *Descendants of William Shurtleff* (2 vols., 1912); *Who's Who in America,* 1914–15; G. W. Sheldon, *Am. Painters* (1879); H. W. French, *Art and Artists in Conn.* (1879); Clara E. Clement and Laurence Hutton, *Artists of the Nineteenth Century* (1885); *Nat. Acad. Notes* and cats., 1881–1913, C. M. Kurtz, ed.; *Cat. of Am. Paintings Belonging to William T. Evans* (1900); *Met. Mus. of Art Cat. of Paintings* (1926); *Nat. Gallery of Art, Cat. of Colls.* (1926); obituaries in *Am. Art Ann.,* 1915, *Am. Art News,* Jan. 9, *N. Y. Times,* Jan. 7, 1915.]   W. H. D.

SHUTE, SAMUEL (Jan. 12, 1662–Apr. 15, 1742), colonial governor of Massachusetts, was the son of Benjamin Shute of London and his wife, a daughter of the Rev. Joseph Caryl, a distinguished nonconformist minister. Samuel received his preliminary schooling from the Puritan schoolmaster Charles Morton [*q.v.*], and was admitted to the Middle Temple, Nov. 23, 1683. On Dec. 12 of the same year he was admitted fellow commoner at Christ's College, Cambridge, but apparently took no degree. He obtained a captaincy in the army, fought in Marlborough's campaigns, was wounded at Blenheim, and in 1712 became lieutenant-colonel of the 3rd Dragoon Guards. He was selected for the governorship of Massachusetts Bay and New Hampshire in April 1716 and reached Boston on Oct. 4.

Although he was well received by Judge Samuel Sewall and the Rev. Cotton Mather [*qq.v.*], his administration was one of the stormiest suffered by any royal governor. He was insulted by the Assembly in their treatment of the salary question, a perennial cause of hostility between the executive and legislative powers. He opposed the issues of paper money, acting within his instruction and also in the light of sound business principles, but was over-powered by the Assembly, which was largely composed of men of "Small fortunes & Meane Education" (Perry, *post,* III, 121). The Assembly attempted to encroach upon the governor's rights to adjourn the General Court and to designate its place of meeting, claiming that the right of adjourning the court did not include the right of adjourning the lower House. They quarrelled with him over his right to negative the choice of a speaker, and as a result the colony was obliged in 1725 to accept an explanatory charter defining this right of the governor. There had been much trouble with the Indians on the northern frontier, and a further quarrel with the Assembly occurred when they refused to provide the fortifications which Shute considered necessary. In 1717, Shute met the Indians in a conference at Arrowsick Island, where, although he handled the negotiations without great ability, a new and useful treaty of friendship was signed, but by 1720 the relations with the more northern Indians, stirred up by French machinations, had become so serious as to necessitate war, and in connection with the military operations the Assembly made absurd and unwarranted claims to authority.

Finally, despairing of conducting the government in the face of these and other claims, Shute sailed, on Jan. 1, 1723, for England. There he presented a memorial to the Privy Council and laid his grievances before them. These were so obvious that the colony's agent, Jeremiah Dummer [*q.v.*], and other friends in England wrote to the Assembly that they were doing themselves and their cause much harm by the way they had treated Shute. The only answer that body made to their agent's candor was to refuse him an allowance (Palfrey, *post,* IV, 428, note). Shute remained in England, endeavoring to collect his arrears of salary. In the spring of 1727, when he was about to return to Massachusetts, his commission was vacated by the death of the king. He was not reappointed, but was consulted about the instructions for his successor, William Burnet [*q.v.*], and was awarded a pension of £400 a year. He remained thereafter in private life until his death.

[Inaccurate account by J. A. Doyle, in *Dict. Nat. Biog.;* J. T. Adams, *Revolutionary New England* (1923), with additional references; J. G. Palfrey, *Hist. of New England,* vol. IV (1875); W. S. Perry, *Hist. Colls. Relating to the Am. Colonial Church,* vol. III (1873), containing Shute's memorial to the King; *The Report of the Lords of the Committee upon Gov. Shute's Memorial* (1725); *George Town on Arrowsick Island*

. . . *A Conference of His Excellency the Governour with the Sachems and Chief Men of the Eastern Indians* (1717), repr. in *Me. Hist. Soc. Colls.*, vol. III (1853); *Jour. of the Commissioners for Trade and Plantations, 1714–28* (1924–28); *Cal. of State Papers, Col. Ser., America and West Indies, 1716–21* (1930–33); *Mass. Hist. Soc. Colls.*, 5 ser. VII (1882), 6 ser. II (1888), 7 ser. VIII (1912).] J.T.A.

SIAMESE TWINS [See CHANG and ENG, 1811–1874].

SIBLEY, GEORGE CHAMPLAIN (Apr. 1, 1782–Jan. 31, 1863), Indian agent, explorer, was born in Great Barrington, Mass., the descendant of John Sibley who emigrated from England to Plymouth about 1629 and later settled in Salem, Mass., and the son of John Sibley [*q.v.*] and Elizabeth (Hopkins) Sibley, the daughter of Samuel Hopkins, 1721–1803 [*q.v.*]. The boy was reared and educated in Fayetteville, N. C. Appointed a clerk in the Indian bureau, he went to St. Louis and in 1808 accompanied the military detachment sent up the Missouri to a point near the site of the present Sibley, Jackson County, Mo., to build Fort Osage. At this establishment, known also as Fiery Prairie Fort and Fort Clark, which included a government trading factory for the Indians and which for a decade was the furthermost outpost of the frontier, he was stationed as factor, and later as Indian agent, until about 1826. In June and July 1811, escorted by a band of Osage warriors, he explored the Grand Saline, in the present Woodward County, Okla. (see John Bradbury, *Travels in the Interior of America,* 1817, and H. M. Brackenridge, *Views of Louisiana,* 1814), and in August he made a tour of investigation among the Kansas Indians. Though his services in the War of 1812 seem not to have been conspicuous, they brought him the unofficial title of major, by which he was ever afterward known.

On Aug. 19, 1815, in St. Louis, he was married to Mary, the accomplished daughter of Rufus B. Easton, who accompanied him to the fort. Here the Sibleys, in a large log building, furnished with many of the conveniences and some of the luxuries of city life brought by the bride on her wedding voyage, kept open house for all voyagers and wanderers who passed that way. In 1825 Sibley served as one of the three commissioners to mark the Santa Fé trail from Council Grove to the Mexican boundary. A year or two afterward he retired from government service and made his home near St. Charles, where he developed a large and beautiful estate. In 1844 he was a delegate to both the state and the national Whig conventions and also an unsuccessful candidate for the state Senate. Though a semi-invalid in his later years, he maintained a lively interest in political and social questions. Both of the Sibleys held somewhat advanced views for their time and place, and Mrs. Sibley was one of the first avowed advocates of woman's suffrage. In 1827 they established a school for girls on a nearby tract named by them Lindenwood. This school, subsequently taken over by the presbytery of St. Louis and endowed with the gift of Sibley's estate, became Lindenwood College. Sibley died at his home. Though his criticism of the fur traders, whom he charged with swindling and corrupting the Indians, brought upon Sibley some abuse, he is generally praised for his honesty and good judgment, his hospitality and helpfulness, and his tactful relations with his savage wards.

[Sibley Papers in possession of Mo. Hist. Soc., and of Lindenwood College; R. G. Thwaites, *Early Western Travels,* esp. vols. V, VI (1904), XIV–XVII, XX (1905); J. C. Luttig, *Journal* (1920), ed. by S. M. Drumm; L. deL. Templin, *Two Illustrious Pioneers in the Education of Women in Mo. The Sibleys* (1926); Louis Houck, *A Hist. of Mo.* (1908) vols. I, III; C. J. Taylor, *Hist. of Great Barrington, Mass.* (1882); W. A. Benedict and H. A. Tracy, *Hist. of the Town of Sutton, Mass.* (1878), p. 722.] W.J.G.

SIBLEY, HENRY HASTINGS (Feb. 20, 1811–Feb. 18, 1891), fur trader, territorial delegate, governor of Minnesota, was born in Detroit, Michigan Territory. He was the descendant of John Sibley who emigrated from England to Plymouth about 1629 and later settled in Salem, Mass., and the son of Solomon and Sarah Whipple (Sproat) Sibley. His mother was the granddaughter of Abraham Whipple [*q.v.*], and his father was territorial delegate to Congress and judge of the territorial supreme court. The boy's education at the local academy was supplemented by two years of tutoring in the classics and two years of law study. In June 1828 he became a clerk in the sutler's store at Fort Brady at Sault Ste. Marie. In the spring of 1829 he entered the employ of the American Fur Company at Mackinac as clerk, a position he held for five years. During the last two winters of this service he was stationed at Cleveland, Ohio, charged with the important duty of purchasing the company's supplies of flour, corn, pork, tobacco, and other produce. In the summer of 1834 Hercules L. Dousman and Joseph Rolette, veteran fur traders in the Northwest, invited him to join them as a partner in operating one of the outfits of the American Fur Company and to assume exclusive management of the trade with the Sioux from Lake Pepin to the Canadian boundary and west to the Rocky Mountain divide. On Oct. 28 (*Autobiography, post,* p. 29, footnote), after an arduous journey by canoe and horse, he arrived at Mendota, beneath the walls of Fort Snelling.

In 1835 he built himself "a substantial and commodious stone dwelling . . . the first . . . private residence, in all of Minnesota, and Dakota" (*Autobiography, post,* p. 35) ; and here many explorers, travelers, missionaries, Indians, and other visitors to the region were entertained. His influence among the Sioux was extensive, not alone because of his position as head of the fur trade, but because of his firm and commanding personality, his remarkable physique, and his skill as a huntsman. On May 2, 1843, he was married to Sarah Jane Steele, sister of Franklin Steele.

In 1848 he was elected delegate to Congress by the inhabitants of that part of the Territory of Wisconsin not included in Wisconsin state. He promoted the organization of Minnesota Territory in 1849 and was promptly elected as delegate to Congress. When Minnesota became a state in May 1858 he took office as the first governor, having been elected as a Democrat. His administration was marked by his interest in the state militia and in the public school lands, a premature sale of which he prevented by veto. He was not a candidate for reëlection in 1859. As territorial delegate he had urged on Congress a change in Indian policy but in vain, and in the Sioux uprising in Minnesota of 1862 he led the military forces of the state against the Indians. With an ill equipped command and practically no cavalry he marched from St. Paul to the relief of the frontier posts, reënforced the soldiers and settlers after the battle of Birch Coulee, and fought the battle of Wood Lake on Sept. 23. His influence among the Indians was no doubt partly responsible for the return of the white captives after this battle. In 1863 and 1864 he commanded punitive expeditions against the Sioux in the Dakota region, and in 1865-66 he was one of the commissioners to negotiate peace treaties with the Sioux.

He removed to St. Paul, Minn., and thereafter was concerned with more prosaic public service and private business. He was president of a gas company, an insurance company, and a bank in St. Paul; he was for one term a representative in the state legislature, 1871, and was for many years president of the board of regents of the University of Minnesota and of the Minnesota Historical Society, for which he wrote several addresses and sketches (see *Minnesota Historical Society Collections,* vols. I, III, *post*). These, with *The Unfinished Autobiography of Henry Hastings Sibley, together with a Selection of . . . Letters* (1932) ed. by T. C. Blegen (also in *Minnesota History,* Dec. 1927) give a picture of his early life and of his character. He was perhaps

the most striking figure among his contemporaries in Minnesota. For years after his retirement from politics he remained an important and influential figure in the state.

[W. W. Folwell, *A Hist. of Minn.* (4 vols., 1921–30) ; *Minn. Hist. Colls.,* vols. I (1872), III (1880), VI (1894) ; *Autobiog. ante,* and in *Minnesota Hist. Bull.,* Aug. 1919 ; Nathaniel West, *The Ancestry, Life, and Times of Hon. Henry Hastings Sibley* (1889) ; and W. P. Shortridge, *The Transition of a Typical Frontier, with Illustrations from the Life of Henry Hastings Sibley* (1922) ; W. A. Benedict and H. A. Tracy, *Hist. of Sutton, Mass.* (1878) ; *Daily Pioneer Press* (St. Paul), Feb. 17, 19, 1891 ; an important collection of Sibley's papers in possession of the Minnesota Historical Society.]
S. J. B.

SIBLEY, HIRAM (Feb. 6, 1807–July 12, 1888), business man and promoter, was born at North Adams, Mass., the son of Benjamin and Zilpha (Davis) Sibley. His education was what the village school could supply. At an early age, having already practised the shoemaker's trade, he left North Adams, and went to the village of Lima, N. Y., where he entered a cotton factory. At twenty-one, he started a machine-shop in the nearby town of Mendon, and there he built up a successful business, of which he was able to dispose at a profit. He also carried on at this time an extensive wool-carding business at Sparta and Mount Morris.

In 1838, with the beginnings of a fortune already in hand, he moved to Rochester, N. Y. Here he engaged in banking and real estate, and acquired sufficient popularity to be elected sheriff of Monroe County in 1843. During his period of office he came into contact with Royal Earl House [*q.v.*], the inventor of the House printing telegraph, then in financial difficulties. With this contact began Sibley's interest in the telegraph itself. He was instrumental the next year in obtaining an appropriation from Congress for the support of the experiments carried on by Samuel F. B. Morse [*q.v.*], and in 1851 he bought up the House patents and organized the New York & Mississippi Valley Printing Telegraph Company. Before the end of the year he had built 100 miles of line. He early formed the conviction, however, that there were too many small companies, and that consolidation was demanded. Accordingly, in 1854 he formed an association with Ezra Cornell [*q.v.*], who had valuable grants under the Morse patents, and the two agreed to form the so-called Western Union Telegraph Company, which was chartered in 1856, with Sibley as president. This position he held for the next ten years. Under his administration the number of telegraph offices increased from 132 to 4,000, and the value of the property from $220,000 to $48,000,000. He was the earnest advocate of a transcontinental telegraph line, and, failing to secure the support of his co-directors in the Western Union, he undertook the project on his own account, securing from Congress in 1860 an annual subsidy of $40,000 for ten years and shrewdly coming to terms with a California rival. The line was a success from the beginning and was amalgamated with the Western Union in 1864. He now dreamed of telegraphic communication with Europe via Bering Strait and Siberia. He had thoughtfully played a leading part in the entertainment of the Russian naval squadron in 1863, and when he visited Russia, soon afterward, was cordially received by the Czar. Wires were actually strung in Alaska and Siberia when the laying of the transatlantic cable led to the collapse of the project at heavy loss.

Retiring from the Western Union Company in 1869, Sibley started an extensive seed and nursery business. He had also a large interest in railroads in the South and West, and made extensive investments in both sections. He bought a 40,000-acre farm in Illinois, and much farm land elsewhere, usually letting it out to tenants, and was in 1888 the largest owner of improved lands in the United States. He also owned timber lands and salt mines. The scale of his agricultural enterprises has hardly been appreciated. He took an active interest in experiments of all kinds for the improvement of plants; he was much interested in reclamation, as in the case of the Fox Ridge Farm, formerly a swamp, in Central New York; he cultivated the largest farm in that state. In industry and agricultural pursuits alike, he was a man of extraordinary capacity.

With his friend Ezra Cornell, he was one of the incorporators of Cornell University, and to the new institution he gave at various times the sum of $150,000 for the foundation of the Sibley College of Mechanic Arts (now Sibley College of Mechanical Engineering). He also built and presented Sibley Hall to the University of Rochester, for use as a library. To Rochester hospitals and other charitable institutions he gave at least $100,000. His personality was an agreeable one. He had much humor, and was an excellent raconteur. In his business operations he practised the methods of diplomacy rather than those of coercion. He was simple in his habits and broad in his interests. His wife was Elizabeth M. (Tinker) who, with a son and daughter, survived him. He died in Rochester.

[Encyc. of Contemporary Biog. of N. Y. (4 vols., 1878–85), vol. II; Rochester Hist. Soc. Pub. Fund Series, vol. II (1923); J. D. Reid, The Telegraph in America (1879); North Adams Transcript, July 19, 1888; N. Y. Tribune, July 13, 1888.]   D. P.

SIBLEY, JOHN (May 19, 1757–Apr. 8, 1837), physician, Indian agent, Louisiana politician and planter, was descended from John Sibley who came from England in 1629 and settled at Salem, Mass. Born at Sutton, Mass., the son of Timothy and Anne (Waite) Sibley, he studied medicine with Dr. John Wilson of Hopkinton, served in the Revolution with the Continental troops as surgeon's mate, and settled for practice at Great Barrington, where in 1780 he married Elizabeth Hopkins, daughter of the Rev. Dr. Samuel Hopkins [q.v.]. After her death in 1790 at Fayetteville, N. C., to which place he had moved with his family and where he had established the Fayetteville Gazette, he married on Nov. 10, 1791, Mrs. Mary White Winslow. In September 1802 he moved to Louisiana, leaving his family in North Carolina but keeping up a correspondence with them until the death of his wife in 1811. Two years later he married as his third wife Eudalie Malique, a resident of Louisiana. On his arrival in New Orleans, Sibley presented letters of introduction to prominent officials, and soon became a familiar visitor to the homes of some of the élite of the colony. At Natchez, where he visited many times, he met W. C. C. Claiborne [q.v.], later governor of Orleans Territory, who was impressed with Sibley's knowledge of Louisiana and of the Indian tribes and recommended to President Jefferson that he be sent into the colony to gather information. Leaving Natchez by boat and proceeding up Red River, he arrived at Natchitoches in March 1803. Upon the arrival of the United States troops after the transfer of that post from the Spanish, he was appointed contract surgeon to the army. In 1805 he was appointed Indian agent for Orleans Territory and subsequently visited most of the tribes within the area now covered by the state of Louisiana. Reporting on their condition to both Claiborne and Jefferson, he began the gathering of a vocabulary of the tribes within the territory. Whether this was ever completed is not known, but a considerable fragment of the Caddo vocabulary is printed in the American Naturalist for December 1879. Sibley's reports to Jefferson were unusually complete, and are an important source of information regarding Louisiana.

Summarily removed from the office of Indian agent late in 1814 for political reasons, he entered politics himself, becoming parish judge and serving in the legislature of the state for many years. His military training served him in good stead, for he soon became colonel of militia and joined Col. James Long's raid on the province of Texas in 1819. After the capture of Nacagdoches, he was made a member of the supreme council governing the latter post (D. G. Wooten, *A Comprehensive History of Texas,* 1898, I, 97; J. H. Brown, *History of Texas,* 2 vols., 1892–93). Returning to Natchitoches, he retired to his plantation at Grande Ecore, and engaged in the manufacture of salt at Postlewaite's salt works, a few miles away, and in the planting of cotton, in which occupations he became very prosperous. At his death he left many descendants, of whom the most prominent was his son, George Champlain Sibley [*q.v.*].

[Sibley left many diaries covering his experiences in Louisiana, and many letters, in some of which he recounts the events of his early life. See Sibley Manuscript Books, parts I, 5, 6, 7, at Lindenwood College, St. Charles, Mo.; letters of John Sibley in Jefferson Papers at Lib. of Cong., in the Mo. Hist. Soc., St. Louis, in the American Antiquarian Soc., Worcester, Mass., and elsewhere. Some of his reports appear in *Am. State Papers; Indian Affairs,* vol. I (1832). See also *A Report from Natchitoches in 1807 by Dr. John Sibley* (1922), ed. by A. H. Abel; *Official Letter Books of W. C. C. Claiborne* (6 vols., 1917), ed. by Dunbar Rowland; *Early Western Travels,* ed. by R. G. Thwaites, V (1904), 129, XVII (1905), 63–68; G. P. Whittington, in *La. Hist. Quart.,* Oct. 1927; W. A. Benedict and H. A. Tracy, *Hist. of the Town of Sutton* (1878), 722–23; C. J. Taylor, *Hist. of Great Barrington* (1882).]   A. T. W.

SIBLEY, JOHN LANGDON (Dec. 29, 1804–Dec. 9, 1885), librarian, was born in Union, Me., the eldest child of Dr. Jonathan and Persis (Morse) Sibley. After studying two years at Phillips Exeter Academy, he entered Harvard, where he partly supported himself by working in the library. On his graduation in 1825 he was appointed assistant librarian at an annual salary of $150. Resigning at the end of a year to continue studying for the ministry, he graduated from the Harvard Divinity School in 1828 and became pastor of the church in Stow, Mass., where he was ordained in 1829. In 1833 he returned to Cambridge to devote himself to various literary pursuits and for three years edited the *American Magazine of Useful and Entertaining Knowledge,* an illustrated monthly journal. In March 1841, just before the removal of the Harvard College Library to Gore Hall, he was reappointed assistant librarian; fifteen years later he became librarian, succeeding Thaddeus William Harris [*q.v.*]. He married on May 20, 1866, Charlotte Augusta Langdon Cook, daughter of Samuel Cook, a Boston merchant, with whom he lived in great happiness.

At the beginning of his long term of service in the library the number of volumes was about 41,000 and the annual income from invested funds $250; when he retired in 1877 the number of books had increased to 164,000 and the investments to $170,000. According to Sibley himself, he made so many pleas for gifts of books that he "acquired the name of being a sturdy beggar," and there must have been many a book-hunting expedition like that of Nov. 18, 1862, recorded in the "Librarian's Diary," a detailed account of the work of the library which he kept with care for years, when he "spent four hours with a lantern and cloak in the chilly cellar and found many things not in the College Library" (A. C. Potter and C. K. Bolton, *post,* p. 40). Gore Hall, which had been confidently expected to hold the accessions for the rest of the century, became inadequate, and in the last year of his librarianship, a large addition was erected which contained a book stack of six floors, said to be the first example of this familiar form of library architecture. But Sibley's service to the library was by no means confined to fostering its accessions; he introduced many administrative improvements and in every way made the books more accessible. Though at the beginning of his term the public could use only the printed catalogue of 1830, in 1861 there was begun a public card catalogue, indexed according to author and subject, in which there were introduced for the first time many features later in common use. Although he had scant sympathy for the desultory reader and has usually been pictured as a typical example of the old-style librarian, only interested in increasing his hoard of books and in protecting them from the profane touch of the reader's hands, he gave generous help to the genuinely serious seeker after knowledge and freely granted access to the alcoves, a most unusual privilege in those days.

Failing eyesight finally obliged him to resign, but he continued with his most important literary work, his *Biographical Sketches of Graduates of Harvard University* (3 vols., 1873–85), covering the lives of graduates through the class of 1689. He left to the Massachusetts Historical Society his accumulated material for later classes and a fund for the continuation of the work. He also published *A History of the Town of Union, Me.* (1851). During his librarianship he prepared twelve triennial catalogues of Harvard, 1842–75, and one quinquennial catalogue, 1880, and for twenty years, 1850–70, edited the annual catalogues. He was also an occasional contributor to magazines and to the publications of the Massachusetts Historical Society. Not a rich man, he gave to many charities, and many needy students came to him both for advice and for financial help. At Phillips Exeter Academy, in memory of his father, he established a fund of nearly fifteen thousand dollars for the aid of meritorious students; one gift to Exeter of five thousand dollars for this fund, it is reported, represented more than half of his entire property. He died after a long illness, survived by his wife.

[*Proc. Am. Acad. Arts and Sci.*, vol. XXI (1886) ; F. O. Vaille and H. A. Clark, *The Harvard Book* (1875), vol. I, with portrait ; *Lib. Jour.*, July–Aug. 1879 ; *Letters of James Russell Lowell* (1893), vol. II ; *Proc. Mass. Hist. Soc.*, 2 ser., vol. II (1886), with portrait ; A. P. Peabody, *Harvard Reminiscences* (1888) ; A. C. Potter and C. K. Bolton, "The Librarians of Harvard Coll.," *Lib. of Harvard Univ., Bibliographical Contributions*, no. 52 (1897) ; J. L. Sibley, librarian's diary and ann. reports, MSS. in Harvard Coll. Lib. ; obituary in *Boston Daily Advertiser*, Dec. 10, 1885.]

A. C. P—t—r.

SIBLEY, JOSEPH CROCKER (Feb. 18, 1850–May 19, 1926), oil refiner, congressman from Pennsylvania, was born in Friendship, Allegheny County, N. Y., the son of Lucy Elvira (Babcock) and Joseph C. Sibley, a physician. He was the descendant of John Sibley who emigrated from England and settled in Salem, Mass., about 1634. In 1866, while he was at the Friendship academy preparing for college, his father died, and until 1871 the boy was variously occupied as school-teacher, farm worker, drugstore clerk, medical student, and, toward the end of the period, as clerk in the drygoods-store of his brother-in-law, Charles Miller, of Franklin, Pa. On Mar. 17, 1870, he was married to Metta Evalina Babcock of Friendship, N. Y. They had two children. When Miller's business failed, Sibley became Chicago agent of the Galena Oil Works of Franklin, in which Miller was a partner. In 1873, after having lost his possessions in the Chicago fire, he returned to Franklin. There, after many trials, he made a signal oil superior in several respects to the oils then in use, and in 1875 he organized the Signal Oil Works, with himself as president, and arranged to have the new oil manufactured by the Galena Oil Works. By 1879 the controlling interest in both these companies had been acquired by the Standard Oil interests. Sibley also made a new valve oil for locomotives, which, under the Standard Oil management, came into use on most of the railroads in the United States and on many in South America and Europe. When in 1902 the Galena-Signal Oil Company was formed by a merger of the two companies, Sibley became a director of the new company, and he was chairman of its board of directors from 1905 to 1910 and remained on the board until 1913.

In 1879 Sibley, then a low-tariff Republican, was elected mayor of Franklin. In 1884 he left the party on the tariff question and began to vote the Prohibition ticket. He had apparently no political ambitions until in 1892 a combination of Democrats, Populists, and Prohibitionists nominated him for congressman. Elected in a district normally Republican, he voted and spoke in Congress for free silver, becoming sufficiently prominent in its support to be mentioned by members of the Bimetallic League as a possible presidential candidate in 1896. After his first term he was twice defeated for Congress, but in 1898 he was elected as a Democrat, and for three subsequent terms he was elected as a Republican. In 1906 he declined renomination ; in 1910 he was nominated but was unable to campaign because of illness. Throughout his career his interest in business and politics was paralleled by a passion for agriculture and stock-breeding. Miller and he owned jointly a large farm near Franklin, on which they conducted a profitable business. Sibley was a pioneer in breeding Jersey cattle for milk-producing records and was regarded in the nineties as one of the best judges of Jerseys in the United States. On the stock farm were probably the first silo built west of the Alleghanies and the second DeLaval separator in the United States. He was active in national agricultural and breeding associations, was for a time a member of the state board of agriculture, and in later years, by demonstrations of methods at his "River Ridge Farm" three miles from Franklin, helped to spread agricultural science among the farmers of northwestern Pennsylvania. In 1910 he retired from business and devoted himself to study and experimental agriculture at his farm. After the death of his first wife in 1911 he was married, on Dec. 6, 1913, to Ida L. Rew. He died on his farm.

[Sketches by a brother in *Hist. of Venango County, Pa.* (1890), pp. 211–17, 792–94 ; C. A. Babcock, *Venango County, Pa.* (1919), vol. I ; J. W. Jordan, *Geneal. and Personal Hist. of the Allegheny Valley, Pa. . . .* (1913) I ; H. M. Irwin, "Presidential Possibilities : Hon. Joseph C. Sibley," in *Am. Mag. of Civics*, June 1895 ; *Biog. Directory of the Am. Cong.* (1928) ; *Who's Who in America*, 1926–27 ; *Gazette-Times* (Pittsburgh), May 20, 1926 ; information from J. French Miller, secretary of the Galena Oil Corporation of Franklin, Pa., and from *U. S. . . . vs. Standard Oil Co. (N. J.) . . . In Circuit Court of U. S. for Eastern Division of Eastern Judicial District of Mo.*, esp. "Brief for Defendants on the Facts," 3 vols. (1909), "Defendants' Exhibits," vol. XIX (1909), and "Petitioner's Exhibits," vol. XXI (1909).]

S. J. B.

SICALAMOUS [Shikellamy, d. 1748].

SICARD, MONTGOMERY (Sept. 30, 1836–Sept. 14, 1900), naval officer, was born in New York City, son of Stephen and Lydia (Hunt) Sicard. His father, of a French *émigré* family settled in Philadelphia, was engaged, before his marriage, in a mercantile business that necessitated considerable residence in Mexico; his mother was a daughter of Montgomery Hunt of Utica, N. Y., and sister of Justice Ward Hunt [*q.v.*] of the United States Supreme Court. After Stephen Sicard's death, in 1840, the family moved to Utica, where Montgomery lived until his appointment to the Naval Academy, Oct. 1, 1851.

Following cruises after graduation on the Mediterranean and China stations, he was promoted to lieutenant, May 31, 1860, and saw active service throughout the Civil War. He was executive in the *Oneida* of Farragut's squadron during the engagements with the forts and flotilla below New Orleans and the ensuing campaign around Vicksburg; then, having been promoted to lieutenant commander, July 1862, in the *Susquehanna* off Mobile, from the spring of 1863 until late in 1864 he served in the *Ticonderoga,* hunting Confederate cruisers. He commanded the gunboat *Seneca* in both attacks on Fort Fisher, and had charge of the left wing, Second Naval Division, in the severe fighting of the final land assault, Jan. 15, 1865. After post-war duty as head of the Ordnance Department, Naval Academy, he commanded the *Saginaw* in the Pacific, and was wrecked, Oct. 29, 1870, on Ocean Island, remaining there two months with his crew while Lieutenant Talbot and four men—of whom but one survived—sailed for aid 1200 miles to Hawaii in the ship's gig.

Subsequently, his distinctive achievements were in the field of ordnance, and to his patient work and scientific attainments is chiefly credited the development of modern high-power naval guns before the war with Spain. He was on ordnance duty at the New York Navy Yard, 1871–72, and afterward at Washington until 1877, designing and constructing the first steel breech-loading guns for the navy (see his pamphlet, *Description of Naval 3-Inch Breech-Loading Howitzers,* 1876). With Richard W. Meade [*q.v.*] he also prepared a revised edition of the *Ordnance Instructions for the United States Navy* (1880). Having been advanced through the grade of commander (Mar. 2, 1870) to that of captain in 1881, he was head of the Bureau of Ordnance for ten years following, during which period the Washington Gun Factory was established and rapid progress made in ordnance manufacture. He was president of the Steel Inspection Board, 1890–91, and in command of the monitor *Miantonomah,* 1891–93. On July 10, 1894, he was made commodore, and subsequently his duties included administration of the New York Navy Yard, 1894–96, and, after his promotion to rear admiral, April 1897, command of the North Atlantic Squadron until March 1898. Despite his declining health, he had hoped to retain the squadron in the impending war with Spain, but on the adverse verdict of a medical

survey he was forced to relinquish it to his senior captain, William T. Sampson [*q.v.*]. The sacrifice was bitter; "I remember no more pathetic scene," writes a newspaper correspondent (W. A. M. Goode, *post,* p. 15), "than the hurried departure from Key West of this white-haired old man." Regaining strength in the North, he was made president, with A. T. Mahan [*q.v.*] and A. S. Crowninshield as associates, of the strategy board which largely directed the naval war.

He was retired for age Sept. 30, 1898. By his marriage, May 20, 1863, to Elizabeth Floyd, great-grand-daughter of William Floyd [*q.v.*], a signer of the Declaration of Independence, he had three children. After his retirement, his winters were spent in Washington and his summers in the old Floyd home at Westernville, near Utica, N. Y. His death from apoplexy occurred at Westernville, and he was buried in the Westernville cemetery. The departmental special order announcing his death spoke of him as "one of the most able, upright, and conscientious officers of the service," whose "courage, coolness, and presence of mind in time of danger were proverbial and unquestioned."

[L. R. Hamersly, *Records of Living Officers of the U. S. Navy* (1898); *War of the Rebellion: Official Records (Navy)*; G. H. Read, *The Last Cruise of the Saginaw* (1912); W. A. M. Goode, *With Sampson Through the War* (1899); J. D. Long, *The New Am. Navy* (1903); further material in annual reports of the Secretary of the Navy; *Washington Post*, Sept. 15, 1900; information from family.]   A. W.

SICKELS, FREDERICK ELLSWORTH (Sept. 20, 1819–Mar. 8, 1895), inventor, was born in Gloucester County, N. J., not far from Camden, and was the son of John and Hester Ann (Ellsworth) Sickels. He had a grade-school education in New York City, where his father, who was a practising physician, had established his residence. His chief interest in his youth was in engineering and mechanical work, and at the age of sixteen he went to work as rodman for the Harlem Railroad. A year later he began an apprenticeship as machinist in the Allaire Works in New York City and at the same time, because of his great interest in invention, studied physics and mechanics in his spare moments. In 1841, he perfected his first invention. This was the first successful drop cut-off for steam engines devised in the United States, the basic patent for which was granted him on May 20, 1842. With this mechanism the admission of steam to an engine cylinder was stopped or cut off before the end of the piston stroke, and the expansive force of the steam in the cylinder was utilized. The immediate adoption by steam-engine builders of this device, with the three improvements patented between 1843 and 1845, brought him a considerable fortune, all of which he subsequently lost in fighting infringers.

In 1846 he turned his attention to the study of steering vessels by steam engines, and on July 2, 1849, he applied for a patent on his "mode of steering ships," presenting his steam-steering apparatus. While this patent was pending (a matter of eleven years) he proceeded with the construction of a full-size steam-steering unit, and at the same time tried to find some ship owner who would permit his vessel to be used to try out the apparatus. Having been unsuccessful in this at the time the machinery was completed in 1854, he placed it as a working exhibit in the Crystal Palace, New York. At last in 1858 he succeeded in having the equipment installed on the coastwise steamer *Augusta,* plying between Savannah, Ga., and Fernandina, Fla. Two years' demonstration proved its practicability, but Sickels found no purchasers, and after he received his patent, No. 29,200, on July 17, 1860, he took the unit to England. His success there was no better than at home, although he was granted three British patents, and in 1867 he returned to the United States. His brother meanwhile had made installations on a Hudson River steamer, a United States frigate, and the steamer *Great Eastern.* During the succeeding six years Sickels continued his fruitless efforts to interest ship builders and owners. In the end, financially ruined, he abandoned the project. Turning to civil engineering, he went west to engage in railroad and bridge construction. About 1890 he was made consulting engineer of the National Waterworks Company of New York and in 1891 was detailed as chief engineer of its operations at Kansas City, Mo. In this service he died suddenly at the age of seventy-six years. He was married to Rancine Shreeves, and was survived by his widow and five children. He was buried at Paterson, N. J.

[E. W. Byrn, *Progress of Invention in the Nineteenth Cent.* (1900); R. H. Thurston, *A Hist. of the Growth of the Steam-Engine* (1891); orig. data, U. S. Museum; E. H. Knight, *Am. Mechanical Dict.* (3 vols., 1874); *Nautical Gazette,* Nov. 5, 1881; obituaries in *Kansas City Star,* Mar. 8, 1895, *Kansas City Jour.,* Mar. 8, 9, 1895, *N. Y. Tribune,* Mar. 9, 1895; Patent Office records; correspondence with family.]

C. W. M—n.

SICKLES, DANIEL EDGAR (Oct. 20, 1825–May 3, 1914), congressman, Union soldier, diplomat, was born in New York City, the son of George Garrett and Susan (Marsh) Sickles, and a descendant of Zachariah (Zacharias) Sickels, of Vienna, Austria, who entered the service of the Dutch West India Company and settled in America about 1656. He attended the University of the City of New York and later engaged in the printing trade, but changed to study law under Benjamin Franklin Butler, 1795–1858 [*q.v.*]. Admitted to the bar in 1846, he was elected to the state legislature in 1847. He was married to Theresa Bagioli, the seventeen-year-old daughter of an Italian music teacher, in 1853. The same year he was appointed corporation counsel for the city of New York, but resigned to become secretary of the United States legation at London. He held this position for two years, and then he was elected to the state Senate. He served as a Democrat in Congress from 1857 to 1861, residing with his wife and little daughter in Washington, D. C. On Feb. 27, 1859, he shot and killed Philip Barton Key, the son of Francis Scott Key [*q.v.*], on account of attentions to Mrs. Sickles. In a celebrated trial in which, for the first time, the defense pleaded temporary aberration of mind, Sickles was acquitted (see *Harper's Weekly,* Mar. 12, 19, Apr. 9, 23, 1859). Sickles subsequently forgave his young wife, who died a few years later.

Although a Democrat, Sickles offered his services to President Lincoln early in March 1861, and was authorized by him to raise troops for the Federal service. Sickles organized in New York, the Excelsior Brigade, becoming first a colonel, then brigadier-general and led it, participating in the Peninsular campaign. He was promoted to the rank of major-general early in 1863, commanding the III Corps, and had an important part in the Chancellorsville campaign. It was the III Corps that, on May 2, discovered the march of Stonewall Jackson around the Federal army. Sickles reported this fact, and after some delay was instructed to attack the enemy cautiously. He did so, but arrived too late, and was surprised by the Confederate attack launched against the XI Corps, posted on his right, which broke. Falling back with his men well in hand, Sickles attacked the victorious Jackson, and after bloody fighting stopped his advance.

The last campaign of Sickles was Gettysburg. Arriving on July 2, 1863, the second day of the battle, the III Corps was stationed by George Gordon Meade [*q.v.*] to cover the Round Tops, two hills on the left. Sickles decided he could best do this by advancing to the famous peach orchard salient in front of the Round Tops. This decision later aroused a bitter controversy (see *Battles and Leaders, post,* vol. III). Meade personally examined the new line, which Sickles had assumed without specific orders, and suggested retreat, but the discussion was interrupted by a violent Confederate attack on Sickles' forces led by James Longstreet [*q.v.*]. By nightfall the III Corps had lost one-half its men, but with belated reënforcements had stopped the enemy after slight loss of ground. At the very end of the battle, Sickles was struck by a shell, which resulted in the hasty amputation of his right leg on the field. Sickles' position would have been advantageous if an offensive battle had been contemplated, but, in the opinion of Meade, the battleground at Gettysburg favored a defensive contest for the Union forces, and he later criticized Sickles in his reports. His military career now at an end, Sickles was sent on a confidential mission to South America in 1865. He returned the same year and was appointed military governor of the Carolinas, but President Johnson found him too strenuous in the execution of his duties and relieved him in 1867. He was mustered out of the volunteer army on Jan. 1, 1868, reverting to the rank of colonel in the regular army. In 1869 he was retired as a major-general.

In May 1869 he was appointed minister to Spain where the complications of the Cuban problem and the *Virginius* affair proved too much for him. His actions were so vigorous that he was called the "Yankee King," but they were not diplomatic and he resigned in December 1873, leaving to his successor, Caleb Cushing [*q.v.*], the fruits of his efforts. Senorita Carmina Creagh became his second wife on Nov. 28, 1871, at the American legation in Madrid. Sickles then lived abroad for seven years, and when he returned to the United States his wife refused to come with him. They were reconciled more than three decades later at his deathbed, through the efforts of their son. A daughter by this marrige had died in New York City. Sickles became chairman of the New York state monuments commission in 1886, but was relieved in 1912 because of mishandling funds (see *New York Times*, Jan. 23, 26, 28, 1913). He served another term in Congress from 1893 to 1895. Separated from his family, continually involved in financial troubles and altercations, the "old, irresponsible and cantankerous" gentleman spent his last years in New York City (*Literary Digest*, May 16, 1914). His one claim to honor which remained undisputed was his successful effort in 1852 to obtain Central Park for New York City. He related some of his experiences in an article "Leaves from My Diary," in the *Journal of the Military Service Association of the United States*, June and September, 1885.

[*Who's Who in America*, 1914–15; S. A. Merriam, *The Ancestry of Franklin Merriam Peabody* (1929); *Trial of the Hon. Daniel E. Sickles* (1859); *War of the Rebellion: Official Records* (*Army*), 1 ser., vols. XIII, XXXIX, XLIII; *Battles and Leaders of the Civil War* (1887–88), vol. III; G. G. Meade, *With Meade at Gettysburg* (1930); Francis Marshal, *The Battle of Gettysburg* (1914); *Harper's Weekly*, Sept. 14, 1867; S. F. Bemis, *The Am. Secretaries of State*, vol. VII (1928); *Nat. Tribune* (Washington, D. C.), Mar. 31, 1910; *N. Y. Times*, May 4, 1914.]   C.H.L.

SIDELL, WILLIAM HENRY (Aug. 21, 1810–July 1, 1873), engineer and soldier, son of John Sidell, was born in New York City. He received an appointment to the United States Military Academy from New York on July 1, 1829, and was graduated four years later, standing sixth in a class of forty-three. He was commissioned brevet second lieutenant of the 1st Artillery, but, disappointed at not having been assigned to the engineer corps, he resigned from the army on Oct. 1, 1833, and took up the profession of civil engineer.

For four years he served successively as city surveyor in New York City, as assistant engineer on the Croton aqueduct, as division engineer of the Long Island Railroad, and as assistant engineer on projected dry docks in New York harbor. From 1837 to 1839 he was an engineer on the United States hydrographic survey of the delta of the Mississippi, and subsequently, until 1846, served as a civil engineer of various railroads in New York and Massachusetts. During the Mexican War he accepted a captaincy in the 4th New York Volunteers, but his regiment was never mustered into the federal service. From 1846 to 1849 he was with the Isthmus (of Panama) Railroad, becoming during the last year of his service its chief engineer. For the next two years he was in the United States service, exploring for a railroad route from the Mississippi to the Pacific. In 1851–52 he was engaged in the surveying of a railroad route across the isthmus of Tehuantepec in Mexico. Thereafter he was chief engineer of various railroads in Illinois and Missouri until 1858, when he returned to Mexico as chief engineer of the Louisiana Tehuantepec Company, to complete the difficult survey of the transisthmian railroad route on which he had been engaged some years earlier.

When the Civil War broke out, he at once offered his services to the Union, and, May 14, 1861, was commissioned major of the 15th Infantry in the regular army and assigned to recruiting duty in Kentucky and Tennessee. In 1862 he was appointed acting assistant adjutant-general of the department of the Cumberland, and in 1863, acting assistant provost-marshal-general for Kentucky and general superintendent of recruiting and chief mustering and disbursing officer at Louisville, Ky., which positions he held to the end of the war. On May 6, 1864, he was promoted to lieutenant-colonel, 10th Infantry. Though Sidell's accomplishments in the war were inconspicuous, they were of the greatest importance. He organized a system by which 200,000 men were mustered in and out of the armies without delay or confusion and with an exact record of each man's service. He was brevetted colonel, May 13, 1865, for meritorious and faithful services in the recruitment of the armies of the United States, and on the same date, brigadier-general for faithful and efficient services during the war. He was on frontier duty in the Dakotas and in Kansas for the most of the time until 1870, when he was retired from active service for disability contracted in line of duty. He died at the home of his sister, Mrs. Jasper Grosvenor, in New York City.

[G. W. Cullum, *Biog. Reg. Officers and Grads. U. S. Military Acad.* (1891); *Bull. Asso. Grads., U. S. Mil. Acad., Ann. Reunion, June 1873*; *War of the Rebellion: Official Records* (Army); *Am. Ann. Cyc. 1873* (1874); *Army and Navy Jour.*, July 5, 1873; *N. Y. Times*, July 2, 1873; records at headquarters U. S. Mil. Acad., West Point, N. Y.; records of Pension Bureau, Washington, D. C.]   S. J. H.

SIDIS, BORIS (Oct. 12, 1867–Oct. 24, 1923), psychopathologist, was born in Kiev, Russia, the son of Moses and Mary or Elizabeth (Marmor) Sidis. His family was in comfortable circumstances, and he was tutored at home under the direction of his father until the age of seventeen, when he was sent to a government school at Kishinev in southern Russia. While there he was arrested for political reasons along with a number of other students, subjected to solitary confinement, and then sent home where he remained under police surveillance for several years. He finally came to the United States in 1887 and settled in New York City. Being without funds, he worked in factories and gave private lessons for a living, and in his spare moments studied in the public libraries. In 1892 he entered Harvard as a special student. In 1893 he was regularly enrolled, and received the A.B. degree in 1894, the A.M. in 1895, and the Ph.D. in 1897. He was married in 1894 to Sarah Mandelbaum, and they had two children. At Harvard he attracted the attention of William James [*q.v.*], and it was undoubtedly due to James and Hugo Münsterberg [*q.v.*] that he became interested in psychology. In 1898 he published his first book, *The Psychology of Suggestion,* an attempt to explain the nature of the subconscious, especially in relation to personality. The ideas he formulated on the subject of dissociation formed the basis of his future work. William James wrote a complimentary preface to the book, describing it as an original work, although he could not agree with all of Sidis' contentions.

Sidis returned to New York to accept the position of associate psychologist and psychopathologist in the recently established Pathological Institute of the New York State Hospitals from 1896 to 1901. While there he developed the method of treatment of functional psychoses and obtained some interesting cures. In 1901 he became director of the psychopathic hospital and laboratory of the New York Infirmary for Women and Children. He published his *Psychopathological Researches, Studies in Mental Dissociation* in 1902, contributions by Drs. G. M. Parker and W. A. White being included. He advanced the theory that psychoses were due to mental dissociations. One of his most interesting cases, the reassociation of the Rev. Mr. Hanna, who was suffering from amnesia and who had acquired a second personality, is described in his book *Multiple Personality,* written in collaboration with Dr. S. P. Goodhart, and published in 1905. In 1904 Sidis returned to Massachusetts and settled in Brookline where he spent five very active years, studying medicine at the Harvard Medical School, practising psychotherapy, and continuing scientific research. Among the papers he published was "Studies in Psychopathology," in the *Boston Medical and Surgical Journal,* Mar. 14, to Apr. 11, 1907, in which he described his theory of nerve energy in connection with psychotherapeutic cures. *An Experimental Study of Sleep* (1909), based on research performed in part at the Harvard Medical School through the friendly cooperation of Dr. W. B. Cannon, attempted to prove that monotony and limitation of voluntary movements tend to raise the threshold of psychomotor activities, and thus cooperate in the induction of sleep. In 1908 he received the M.D. degree from Harvard.

In 1909 he established the Sidis Psychotherapeutic Institute at Portsmouth, N. H., where he continued to practise until his death. *The Psychology of Laughter* appeared in 1913, and expounded the Freudian idea that forms of inferiority excite laughter. In his *Symptomatology, Psychognosis, and Diagnosis of Psychopathic Diseases* (1914), however, he takes issue with the Freudian doctrine. In the same year he published *The Foundations of Normal and Abnormal Psychology,* and in 1916, *The Causation and Treatment of Psychopathic Diseases.* Sidis had a very active and forceful mentality. In addition to his special subject, he was an ardent student of political economy, philosophy, and languages. He possessed a genial and kindly nature, but was apt to express his opposition to what he considered fraudulent or dishonest with abruptness and vigor. He was of a retiring disposition, and did not seek a following of pupils. He made few contacts with his colleagues, but the few friends he did make, among them Morton Prince [*q.v.*], were his loyal admirers.

[Information from the family: *Who's Who in America, 1922–23; Harvard Coll., Class of 1894* (privately printed, 1919); H. Addington Bruce, "Boris Sidis— An Appreciation," *Jour. of Abnormal and Social Psychology,* Oct.–Dec. 1923.]   H. S. L.

SIDNEY, MARGARET [See LOTHROP, HARRIETT MULFORD STONE, 1844–1924].

SIGEL, FRANZ (Nov. 18, 1824–Aug. 21, 1902), soldier and editor, the son of Franz Moritz and Maria Anna (Lichtenauer) Sigel, was born in Sinsheim, Baden, Germany. His father was chief magistrate of a district. After completing his studies in the Gymnasium of Bruchsal, Franz entered the military academy of Karlsruhe from which he graduated in 1843 to become a lieutenant in the grand ducal service. His liberal political views brought him into conflict with the existing régime, and in 1847, after severely wounding an opponent in a duel, he resigned from the service. In the insurrection in Baden in 1848, as an associate of Friedrich Karl Franz Hecker [*q.v.*], he led an army of 4,000 revolutionists against the government but was defeated and compelled to flee to Switzerland. The next year, when a revolutionary government succeeded in establishing itself in the duchy, he was recalled and became minister of war. He took the field against the Prussian army sent to restore the old order, but his inferior force was soon overpowered and he was again forced into exile in Switzerland. His reminiscences of these years were published in Germany in 1902 under the title, *Denkwürdigkeiten aus den Jahren, 1848 und 1849.* He spent the year 1851–52 in England and then emigrated to America and settled in New York City, where he became an instructor in the private school of Dr. Rudolph Dulon. He maintained an interest in military affairs and became a major in the 5th Regiment of the New York militia. He accepted a position as instructor in mathematics and history in the German-American institute of St. Louis, Mo., in the fall of 1857 and subsequently became a director of schools in that city.

When the Civil War broke out, Sigel organized the 3rd Missouri Infantry and, on May 4, 1861, became colonel. He performed efficient service in saving St. Louis, with its important arsenal, for the Union, and was soon assigned to command the 2nd Missouri Brigade, being appointed brigadier-general of volunteers to date from May 17, 1861. During the remainder of the year he took part in a number of battles in the struggle for the possession of Missouri. At the battle of Pea Ridge, Ark., Mar. 7–8, 1862, Sigel commanded two divisions in Frémont's army, and by his gallantry and skill contributed greatly to the decisive Union victory which settled the fate of Missouri. He was promoted to the rank of major-general of volunteers on Mar. 21, 1862, and in June became commander of the I Corps in Pope's army of Virginia. In this capacity he took a prominent part in the second battle of Bull Run. In September 1862 his corps was transferred to the Army of the Potomac as the XI Corps. Later, when Burnside divided that army into grand divisions, Sigel was given the reserve grand division, consisting of the XI and XII Corps, but in February 1863, he reverted to the command of the XI Corps. Owing to bad health he gave up his command temporarily in the spring of 1863, and when he returned to duty in the summer he was given a subordinate command in the department of the Susquehanna. He was assigned to command the department of West Virginia in March 1864, but a serious defeat at the hands of Breckinridge at New Market in the Shenandoah Valley, on May 15, 1864, cost him his command and he was removed to Harpers Ferry.

When Early's raid threatened Washington in July 1864, Sigel, by skilfully occupying a strong position on Maryland Heights, delayed Early's greatly superior force. The authorities, however, at no time had considered him sufficiently aggressive and now removed him from command. He resigned his commission in May 1865 and became for two years an editor of the *Baltimore Wecker,* a German newspaper in Baltimore, Md. In 1867 he moved to New York City where he spent the remainder of his life. His great influence with the German element soon brought him into politics. From 1866 to 1869 he was pension agent in New York, and two years later he was appointed collector of internal revenue for the city, later being elected register. He was a prominent lecturer and kept himself in the public eye as publisher and editor of the *Neu Yorker Deutsches Volksblatt,* and from 1897 to 1900 as editor of the *New York Monthly.* A love for free government had been the ruling motive of Sigel's life. His military successes were not of the greatest, but his prompt and ardent espousal of the Union cause was a great factor in uniting the large German population of the North, with which he was extremely popular, solidly behind the Union. In October 1907, a bronze equestrian statue of Sigel, by Karl Bitter [*q.v.*], was unveiled with impressive ceremonies on Riverside Drive in New York City. He had been married to Elise Dulon, the daughter of his first employer, in January 1854. She and their five children survived him when he died in New York City.

[*Who's Who in America*, 1901–02; C. W. Schlegel, *Schlegel's German-Am. Families in the U. S.*, vol. I (1916); F. K. F. Hecker, *Die Erhebung des Volkes in Baden* (1848); *War of the Rebellion: Official Records (Army)*, see index; *Battles and Leaders of the Civil War* (1887–88), vol. IV; *N. Y. Times*, Aug. 22, 23, 1902, Oct. 20, 1907; *New-Yorker Staats-Zeitung*, Aug. 22, 23, 24, 1902, Oct. 13, 20, 1907.]　　S. J. H.

SIGMAN, MORRIS (May 15, 1881–July 20, 1931), labor leader, was born in Costesh, Bessarabia, Province of Hatino Uezd, the son of Samuel and Rebecca (Sikernetsky) Sigman. The son of a farmer in a small Bessarabian-Russian village, he received little schooling, and as a Jew and a subject of the czar of Russia he lived in an atmosphere of persecution and hate. At twenty-one he emigrated to London, where for a year he worked in a men's clothing shop. Initiated into the ideals of the labor movement, he journeyed to New York in 1903 and found employment on the East Side as a presser in a cloak shop, where he soon formed the Independent Cloakmakers' Union. Joining at first with those in the labor movement who favored opposition of "dual unions," he was led into the Industrial Workers of the World when it was formed in 1905; by 1908 he had come to believe that destroying existing unions by founding opposition unions was detrimental to the interests of the workers, and he helped to induce his and other I.W.W. locals of ladies' garment workers to affiliate with the International Ladies' Garment Workers' Union of the American Federation of Labor.

When the International Ladies' Garment Workers' Union undertook to control cut-throat competition and deplorably bad working conditions, the employers resisted, and the union became involved in a series of bitter strikes. In the historic strike of 1910, which established the union on a firm foundation, Sigman honorably acquitted himself in the difficult and dangerous position of chairman of the picket committee. When the employers consented to negotiate with the union he was selected as a member of the joint conference committee. This established the famous "Protocol," signed Sept. 2, 1910, which created permanent machinery consisting of representatives of labor, capital, and the public to supervise and regulate all relations in the industry. But permanent peace was not attained. During a strike in 1915 Sigman and seven other leaders were arrested and confined to jail while awaiting trial on charges of murder; with the

others, he was later acquitted by a jury. In his own Pressers' Union, Local No. 35, he served in every important post from member of the executive board to business agent and manager. He was also the organizer and manager of the Boston unions in their formative period; the organizer, 1909, and manager, 1917–21, of the New York Joint Board of Cloakmakers' Unions (the coördinating body of the local unions of this trade); and vice-president, 1920–22, secretary-treasurer, 1914–15, of the International Union. He was in charge of establishing the New York Joint Board of the Dressmakers' Unions, and acted as its first manager. In February 1923 he became general president, a position he held to October 1928, when ill health caused him to resign. During his term as president two events shook the union to its very foundations. Before the World War a difference of opinion, later known as the Left and Right controversy, had developed within the ranks; after the Bolshevik revolution the Communists assumed leadership of the Lefts and organized themselves under the auspices of the Trade Union Educational League, formed in 1920. Sigman condemned this procedure as a dual union movement which aimed to disrupt the International Union and succeeded in disbanding the opposing Lefts, but the union suffered severe losses in membership. At the same time economic conditions in the industry once more became chaotic through the appearance of the jobber, who controlled the markets. Under Sigman's leadership a new economic program for the industry was devised. Failing to win the employers through negotiation, the union induced the governor to appoint an advisory committee, which succeeded in reconciling the two elements, and temporarily at least conditions were improved.

Sigman died in Storm Lake, Iowa, survived by his wife, Mathilda Sikernetsky, who was his cousin and whom he had married on Mar. 17, 1912. Although neither an orator nor a "showman," he was an effective and logical speaker. He showed little trace of vanity and remained to the end the simple but intelligent worker. Like most Jewish labor leaders he retained his socialist ideology, but reversed the emphasis. In his youth he stressed ultimate ideals; in his later years he fostered immediate reforms, with the hope that in addition to improving the conditions of the time they might ultimately bring about the overthrow of the wage system.

[*Report of Proc. . . . Ann. Convention Internat. Ladies' Garment Workers' Union*, 1908–31; *Ladies' Garment Worker*, 1910–18, *Justice*, 1919–31, official pubs. of the union; L. L. Lorwin, *The Women's Garment Workers* (1924); *N. Y. Times*, July 21–24, 1931;

information from Sigman's widow through the courtesy of Miss F. M. Cohn, Executive Secretary, Educ. Dept., Internat. Ladies' Garment Workers' Union.] D. J. S.

SIGOURNEY, LYDIA HOWARD HUNTLEY (Sept. 1, 1791–June 10, 1865), author, the only child of Ezekiel Huntley and his second wife Zerviah (Wentworth) Huntley, was born at Norwich, Conn., in the house of Mrs. Daniel Lathrop, by whom her father was employed as gardener. On her father's side she was of Scotch descent, her grandfather having emigrated from Scotland as a young man. For old Mrs. Lathrop she formed a sentimental attachment that inspired scores of youthful poems and left its impress on her whole life. She was educated in Norwich and Hartford. From 1811 to 1813 she conducted a school in Norwich with a friend, and in 1814 went to Hartford to establish a small school for girls. For their use she wrote much of her first book, *Moral Pieces, in Prose and Verse* (1815), and her persuasive teaching and kindly personality had an enduring influence upon her young pupils. But the promising career was interrupted by her marriage, June 16, 1819, to a widower with three children, Charles Sigourney, who had come from Boston in 1800 to open a hardware business in Hartford. A man of good classical education, he was inclined to be a little over-precise and pedantic, but he commanded general respect, and Mrs. Sigourney's friends believed that the humble school mistress had made a very fortunate marriage.

Finding, however, that her husband's affluence had been exaggerated, she turned to writing to supplement her means—anonymously at first, since her husband bitterly opposed her writing under her own name. Her success was marked. By 1830 she was contributing regularly to more than twenty periodicals, and three years later she dropped her anonymity. The volumes of prose and verse that appeared regularly each year and her constant contributions to the magazines and the newly risen annuals—she herself edited *The Religious Souvenir* for 1839 and 1840 —soon brought her a good income. Such edifying volumes as *How To Be Happy* (1833) and *Letters to Young Ladies* (1833), were followed by numerous poems and sketches, reading books for children, several memoirs, even by a *History of Marcus Aurelius, Emperor of Rome* (1836). She was so popular that she was paid well by Louis Godey [*q.v.*] for the mere use of her name as an editor of the *Lady's Book*; her contributions at the same time to the rival *Ladies' Companion* brought strong protests from him. It is almost impossible to find a number of one of the popular magazines of the thirties or forties that does not contain a poem or an article by her, and though Edgar Allan Poe [*q.v.*] in a review in the *Southern Literary Messenger* for January 1836 accused her of too direct imitation of other writers he continued to solicit her contributions.

By 1840 "the American Hemans" was sufficiently prosperous to go to Europe to secure new literary material, of which she was in urgent need. Toward the end of her two months' stay in Paris, she was presented to Louis Philippe; most of the time, however, she lived in England, attending to the publication of *Pocahontas, and Other Poems* (1841), *Poems, Religious and Elegiac* (1841), and a new edition of her *Letters to Young Ladies,* cultivating "literary friendships," calling on Samuel Rogers, the Carlyles and the Wordsworths, and distributing presentation copies of her poems with a lavish hand. On her return to America the inclusion in *Pleasant Memories of Pleasant Lands* (1842) of extracts from a letter of Mrs. Robert Southey gave the world its first intimation of the Poet Laureate's mental disintegration and precipitated a storm of recrimination. Mrs. Sigourney, who had never seen Mrs. Southey, was accused of having interpolated in the letter "phrases implying intimacy and ejaculations of pathos," and in spite of the warm defense of her friends the affair was never satisfactorily explained.

She spent the rest of her life quietly in Hartford, writing, busying herself with charities, receiving the visiting celebrities who stopped to pay their respects. Her fellow citizens were proud to think that this demure lady who sewed and knitted and chatted like one of themselves was at the same time "the recipient of costly gifts from Royalty in honor of her Muse" and "the most famous of the female bards of her country." In her later years she was described as a short little woman in a full dress of black satin and a fine lace cap with wide satin ribbons, her hands soft and patrician, and her flaxen curls carefully arranged (Louise J. R. Chapman, "A Visit to Mrs. Sigourney," *Connecticut Quarterly,* Jan.-Mar. 1895, p. 47). Regularly, year after year, appeared the sentimental volumes. Among the number of pious memoirs she wrote is *The Faded Hope* (1853), an account of her son Andrew, who died in 1850, not yet twenty. The death of her austere husband in 1854 and the marriage of her daughter left her quite alone, but there was no cessation in the steady stream of books—sixty-seven all told—which her unimpeachable morality and tuneful echoing of conventional sentiments made popular. Vigorous at its best, her prose style, like her poetry, is too often spoiled by absurd circumlocutions and an affected ele-

gance. The theme of most of her writing is death.
The inevitable regularity with which her poetic
tribute followed the demise of any prominent
person led a wag to declare that she had added
a new terror to death. She herself died in Hartford, survived only by her daughter. Her autobiography, *Letters of Life* (1866), was published
after her death.

[The chief source is the correspondence of Lydia ¯¯.
H. Sigourney, Conn. Hist. Soc., Hartford. Her letters
to Theodore Dwight are in the N. Y. Pub. Lib. See
also her autobiography, *Letters of Life* (1866), *Sketch
of Conn., Forty Years Since* (1824), *Pleasant Memories
of Pleasant Lands* (1842), and *The Faded Hope* (1853);
R. W. Griswold, *The Female Poets of America* (1874);
J. S. Hart, *The Female Prose Writers of America,*
(1852); S. A. Allibone, *A Crit. Dict. of Eng. Lit. and
British and Am. Authors,* vol. II (1870); Gordon S.
Haight, *Mrs. Sigourney, The Sweet Singer of Hartford*
(1930), with portraits and bibliog.; obituary in *Hartford Daily Courant,* June 12, 1865.]   G. S. H.

SIGSBEE, CHARLES DWIGHT (Jan. 16,
1845–July 19, 1923), naval officer, son of Nicholas and Agnes (Orr) Sigsbee, was born in Albany, N. Y. Appointed to the United States
Naval Academy in 1859, he was graduated in
1863, made ensign, and assigned to the *Monongahela* and, later, to the *Brooklyn* of the West
Gulf Blockading Squadron. He participated in
the battle of Mobile Bay, Aug. 5, 1864, and was
given special mention for his gallant conduct
by his commanding officer, Capt. James Alden.
Transferred to the North Atlantic Blockading
Squadron, he took part in both attacks on Fort
Fisher. In 1865 he was assigned to the Asiatic
Squadron, and in 1869 was ordered to duty as an
instructor at the Naval Academy. Here he served,
in all, three tours of duty, 1869–71, 1882–85, and
1887–90, besides commanding the *Dale* and *Constellation* in three midshipmen practice cruises.

His most notable peace-time achievement was
his work while in command of the Coast Survey
steamer *Blake,* 1875–78. During these years,
associated with Alexander Agassiz [*q.v.*], he
was engaged in deep-sea explorations, principally
in the Gulf of Mexico, where he made a complete
deep-water survey of the Gulf. In recognition of
this work its deepest area was named Sigsbee
Deep. While on this duty he invented a deep-
sea sounding machine, based on the wire sounding apparatus of Sir William Thomson; a water
specimen cup for collecting specimens at various
depths at a single haul; a gravitating or collecting trap for obtaining animal specimens from
intermediate ocean depths; and a detaching apparatus to be used with a specimen-collecting
cylinder originally devised by Commander
George E. Belknap [*q.v.*]. These appliances practically revolutionized deep-sea sounding and
dredging. For his contributions to the advance

of scientific exploration Emperor William I of
Germany bestowed upon him the decoration of
the Red Eagle of Prussia; a gold medal, also,
was given him at the International Fisheries
Exhibition of London. He spent a total of ten
years in the hydrographic office at Washington,
and from 1893 to 1897 was chief hydrographer
to the Navy Department.

Having been advanced through the preceding
grades, he was commissioned captain Mar. 21,
1897, and was in command of the battleship
Maine from April 10 of that year until she was
blown up and destroyed in Havana Harbor, Feb.
15, 1898. The naval court of inquiry exonerated
him and his officers and crew from all blame for
the disaster. Sigsbee's temperate, judicious dis-.
patches at the time did much to avert a popular
demand for immediate reprisal against Spain.
On May 25, 1898, in command of the *St. Paul,*
he captured the British collier *Restormel* laden
with coal for Cervera's squadron. On June 22
he engaged and defeated the Spanish destroyer
Terror and the cruiser *Isabella II* off San Juan,
Puerto Rico. For his services during the war he
was advanced three numbers in rank with the
citation: "For extraordinary heroism displayed
during War with Spain and on the occasion of
the wreck of *Maine.*"

Commissioned rear-admiral Aug. 11, 1903, after a year at the League Island Navy Yard, he
was given command of the Caribbean Squadron.
On June 18, 1905, he sailed for Cherbourg,
France, with a fleet of four ships and brought
back the body of John Paul Jones in his flagship,
the *Brooklyn,* arriving at Annapolis, July 23,
1905. After commanding the second squadron
of the Atlantic Fleet for two years, he was retired Jan. 16, 1907. He wrote *Deep Sea Sounding and Dredging* (1880), and *The Maine, an
Account of her Destruction in Havana Harbor*
(1899). A veteran of two wars, in both of which
he won the recognition of his superiors, Admiral
Sigsbee achieved greater distinction for his services as an inventor and scientist than as a warrior, though his conduct at the time of the destruction of the *Maine* won him great popular
acclaim. In November 1870 he married Eliza
Rogers Lockwood, by whom he had one son and
three daughters.

[*Army and Navy Jour.,* July 28, 1923; *Army and
Navy Reg.,* July 28, 1923; L. R. Hamersly, *The Rec-
ords of Living Officers of the U. S. Navy and Marine
Corps* (1898); *Message from the President of the U.
S. Transmitting the Report of the Naval Court of
Inquiry Upon the Destruction of the U. S. Battleship
Maine* (1898), being *Sen. Doc. 207,* 55 Cong., 2 Sess.;
John Paul Jones Commemoration at Annapolis (1907),
being *House Doc. 804,* 59 Cong., 1 Sess.; J. R. Spears,
Our Navy in the War with Spain (1898); reports of
the U. S. Coast and Geodetic Survey, 1877, 1878, 1879;

Ann. Report of the Chief of the Bureau of Navigation, 1898, Appendix; Who's Who in America, 1922–23; War of the Rebellion: Official Records (Navy); N. Y. Times, July 20, 1923.]   L. H. B.

SIKES, WILLIAM WIRT (Nov. 23, 1836–Aug. 18, 1883), journalist and author, was the son of Dr. William Johnson and Meroe (Redfield) Sikes. Born in Watertown, N. Y., where he lived as a boy, he attended the local schools. At the early age of sixteen he threw himself whole-heartedly into the temperance movement and lectured frequently in Watertown and its vicinity. When his youthful enthusiasm subsided, as it did soon, he entered the office of a local paper, where he learned the printing trade, and for a time conducted a sheet of his own. In 1855 he married Jeannette A. Wilcox, by whom he had a son and daughter, and in the following year became employed on the *Utica Morning Herald*. During the past few years he had frequently contributed to home and out-of-town papers tales and poems, some of which he collected in 1858 under the title *A Book for the Winter-Evening Fireside*. A more active mode of life now presenting itself, in 1861 he accepted the position of state canal inspector of Illinois, but two years later he was working on the *Chicago Evening Journal*. A life of wandering had become a habit with him, and in 1865 he removed to New York, where in the course of the next few years he contributed to such papers as the *Youth's Companion, Oliver Optic's Magazine, Harper's New Monthly Magazine,* and the *Sun* (N. Y.). It was at this time that he also established the Authors' Union. Settling in Nyack, N. Y., about 1868, for a few years he edited *City and Country* (Nyack) and the Rockland County *Journal* (Piermont, N. Y.), in both of which he possessed a financial interest. While working in Chicago he had given much time to the study of social conditions among the lower classes, and during his residence in New York and elsewhere he continued his investigations of city slums. This interest in social problems is reflected in a number of magazine articles, but especially in two novels, "The World's Broad Stage" published serially in the *Toledo Weekly Blade*, beginning Jan. 2, 1868, and *One Poor Girl* (1869). In 1870 he was divorced from his first wife and on Dec. 19, 1871, was married in New York to the well-known actress and lecturer, Olive Logan [*q.v.*], with whom he had been previously associated as a business manager (*Evening Post*, N. Y., Dec. 20, 1871). Among his varied hobbies at this time was an interest in art. A visit he made to the Wiertz Museum, Brussels, early in the seventies resulted in a biographical and critical sketch of

Antoine Wiertz, contributed to *Harper's New Monthly Magazine* for May 1873, which was deemed worthy of being prefixed to the *Catalogue of the Wiertz-Museum . . .* (1899), a pamphlet published in English at Brussels. During his journalistic career he published much anonymously, employing, it is said, some twenty-two pseudonyms.

In June 1876 he was appointed United States consul to Cardiff, Wales. In his newly acquired leisure he turned his attention to the region surrounding Cardiff, rich in old Welsh folklore. "I have tramped the green lanes and roads of rural and the streets of urban South Wales so persistently during my residence at Cardiff," he writes, "that I almost know them inch by inch" (*Rambles and Studies in Old South Wales*, p. vii). The results of these excursions found ample expression in two interesting works, certainly the most enduring of his literary labors: *British Goblins: Welsh Folk-Lore, Fairy Mythology, Legends, and Traditions* (1880), favorably noticed in the English *Saturday Review* (Nov. 22, 1879), and *Rambles and Studies in Old South Wales* (1881). His last book, *Studies of Assassination* (1881), was a work of little permanent importance. He died at Cardiff, while still acting as consul, at the age of forty-six; he was buried in London.

[Much information has been furnished by Sikes's son, George P. Sikes. See G. P. Sikes, *By the Name of Sikes or Sykes* (1927); J. H. Redfield, *Geneal. Hist. of the Redfield Family in the U. S.* (1860); *Index to Harper's New Monthly Mag.*, vols. I–LXX (1886), for a list of Sikes's contributions; obituary by G. P. Sikes in *Sunday News* (Buffalo), Aug. 26, 1883; brief death notices in *Harper's New Monthly Mag.*, Nov. 1883, *Times* (London), and *Evening Post*, (N. Y.), Aug. 20, 1883.]   N.F.A.

SILL, ANNA PECK (Aug. 9, 1816–June 18, 1889), pioneer in women's education, youngest daughter of Abel and Hepsibah (Peck) Sill, was born in Burlington, Otsego County, N. Y. She was a descendant of Puritan ancestors, John and Joanna Sill, of England, who settled at Cambridge, Mass., about 1637; later the family removed to Connecticut and thence in 1789 to Otsego County. Her father was a farmer, quiet, industrious, and intelligent, and her mother, the daughter of Judge Jedediah Peck, a woman of great energy of character. Anna attended the district school. The early discipline of domestic duties, the inspiration of nature, and above all a "thirst for knowledge and religion" constituted the mainsprings of her life. To prayer she was so early accustomed that she regarded it as innate; the Bible and the Book of Common Prayer constituted her earliest books; and yet, she says, her soul "cried out for its God," and she "groped in the dark but did not find Him." Thus she continued till 1831, when, apparently, the "wind from the Holy Spirit" which blew over New England and surrounding territory, producing great revivals, touched her soul with peace.

At twenty she left Burlington to teach a district school at Barre, N. Y., near Albion, for which she received two dollars a week. In the vacation she attended school at Albion and entered the Phipps Union Seminary, a pioneer among institutions for girls' education. A year later she became one of the teachers at Phipps, where she continued till 1843. After considering the foreign missionary field in India, she turned to the great West, which was itself coming to be considered a fruitful field for missionary activity. Failing to find an opportunity there at the time, she went alone to Warsaw, N. Y., and in 1843 opened a seminary for ladies which, though it seems to have been an immediate success, was discontinued three years later. Between 1846 and 1849 she had charge of the female department of Cary Collegiate Institute, Oakfield, N. Y., and then accepted the invitation of Rev. Lewis H. Loss to open a school for girls at Rockford, Ill. On July 11 (*Memorials, post,* p. 15) she noted in her journal: "Today commenced school, and laid the foundation of Rockford Female Seminary. Opened with fifty-three scholars. O Lord, fit me for my work and glorify Thyself thereby." For the first two years, only preparatory work was done. The first seminary class entered in 1851, and a new building, begun in 1852, was crowded at once. To secure funds and regain failing strength, she went East and returned in 1854 with a fund of $5,000. In that year a three-year collegiate course was begun, which after 1865 became a four-year course. After 1882 collegiate degrees were conferred, and in 1892 the name of the institution was changed to Rockford College. In her work Anna Sill sought to reach the less favored classes, to combine domestic training with intellectual culture, to infuse a moral and religious culture through the school, and to foster a "missionary spirit" and "self-denying benevolence" toward all. The education of women, because of their influence in the family, she regarded as not less but more important than that of men. Though she retired from active service in 1884, she continued as principal emerita until her death, which occurred in Rockford.

[The birthplace is taken from Miss Sill's tombstone in Rockford, Ill. See G. G. Sill, *Geneal. of the Descendants of John Sill* (1859); *Memorials of Anna P. Sill, First Principal of Rockford Female Seminary* (1889); Hazel P. Cederborg, "The Early Hist. of Rockford Coll." (master's thesis, Wellesley Coll., 1926); official records of Rockford Female Seminary, 1849–84; C. A. Church, *Hist. of Rockford and Winnebago County, Ill.* (1900); Thomas Woody, *A Hist. of Women's Educ. in the U. S.* (2 vols., 1929); obituaries in *Rockford Daily Register,* June 18, 1889, and *Rockford Morning Star,* June 21, 1889.]   T. W.

SILL, EDWARD ROWLAND (Apr. 29, 1841–Feb. 27, 1887), poet and teacher, was born at Windsor, Conn., the son of Theodore and Elizabeth Newberry (Rowland) Sill. On his mother's side he was descended from a line of New England clergymen, one of whom, the Rev. David Sherman Rowland, as pastor in Providence, R. I., had taken an active part in the Revolution; and on his father's from John Sill, who emigrated from England to Cambridge, Mass., about 1637. Theodore Sill, like his father before him, was a physician widely beloved in the little community. After the death of his older son in 1847 and of his wife in 1852, he removed to Cleveland with his one child, and there, not long after opening an office, he too died in 1853. The boy now went to live with his uncle, Elisha Noyes Sill, at Cuyahoga Falls, Ohio. After a year at Phillips Exeter Academy and one at the preparatory school of Western Reserve College at Hudson, Ohio, he entered Yale in the fall of 1857, to graduate four years later with the class of 1861, in spite of the fact that at the end of his freshman year he was removed from college for neglecting his studies and was away for over a year. It was an hour of ebbing tides in the intellectual history of Yale, and he appears to have rebelled against the uninspired routine of college discipline; his poverty, however, and his native fastidiousness together imposed strict limitations on his protestantism, and he was remembered by his college contemporaries chiefly for his fine seriousness and brilliant literary promise. In his senior year he was on the editorial board of the *Yale Literary Magazine,* and the class poem he read at Commencement was long famous as one of the finest in Yale history.

On leaving college he was led, partly by the delicacy of his health, to make a sea voyage round the Horn to California. It was scarcely a nourishing atmosphere for a young poet of his type. The career of letters, if he had ever envisaged it practically, soon receded into the far distance, and, with characteristic plainness and freedom from self-pity, he turned his hand to such tasks as offered themselves. For some time he acted as clerk in the post-office at Sacramento; later he worked in a bank at Folsom. All the while he was casting about restlessly for a permanent profession. After fruitless attempts at reading law and then medicine he returned to the East in 1866, revisited Cuyahoga Falls for a few months, and in 1867 spent the early part of the year as a student at the Harvard Divinity School. It was the last of his experiments to give negative results. "Emerson could not preach," he wrote to his classmate, Henry Holt [*q.v.*], in August 1867, "and I now understand why." Strong as the hereditary bias was and constant as his own preoccupation was with essentially religious speculations, he could not ally himself with the institutionalized Protestantism of nineteenth-century America. "On religion," he wrote many years later to a young correspondent, "I doubt your ever agreeing with me that the church is a great fraud and nuisance. I am convinced it is doing infinitely more harm than good, every day and week."

He now spent several rather obscure months in New York making trial of journalism on the *New York Evening Mail*; and in the spring of 1868 he published *The Hermitage and Other Poems,* the one volume of his verse to appear publicly in his lifetime, and *Mozart, a Biographical Romance,* a translation from the German of Heribert Rau. In 1867, however, he had married his cousin, Elizabeth Newberry Sill, daughter of Elisha Noyes Sill, and he soon abandoned so unpredictable a calling, no doubt partly for economic reasons. Moreover, the desire to play a useful rôle in society was as strong in him as the desire to express himself in ideal form. He now returned to an old purpose, that of becoming a teacher. After three years of apprenticeship in Ohio, during the latter two years of which he was superintendent of schools at Cuyahoga Falls, he taught the classics and English at the high school in Oakland, Cal., 1871–74. From 1874 to 1882 he held the chair of English at the University of California, having been invited there by Daniel Coit Gilman [*q.v.*]. Undoubtedly one of the great teachers of his generation, without being a scholar in the strict professional sense, he had made himself a man of wide intellectual culture; his interest in exact science, for instance, was almost more continuous than his interest in letters, and his teaching was illuminated by his concern both for general ideas and for the realization of values in experience. Not that he substituted "inspiration" for less beguiling appeals: he is said to have been methodical even to austerity and exacting enough to antagonize the faint-hearted. But his personal distinction was so great and his high-mindedness so easily borne that only the dullest could resist his influence. Part of his impressiveness depended, superficially, on his striking appearance. Tall and very slender, he carried himself with an easy elegance; the pure and delicately cut outline of his features, the grave beauty of his dark blue-gray eyes, which

everyone spoke of as they spoke of Hawthorne's, the rich flexibility of his voice, the expressive responsiveness of his whole manner were outward facts that seemed in harmony with his essential spirit. The administrations that followed upon Gilman's were far from being so sympathetic to the humanities as his had been; the pressure from outside toward emphasis on technology and vocationalism was organized and truculent; and Sill was not happy during his last two or three years at Berkeley. Partly on this account, partly for family reasons, he resigned from his chair in March 1882, and the following year, after issuing privately a small volume of poems, *The Venus of Milo and Other Poems* (1883), he returned to his father-in-law's home in Cuyahoga Falls. He now contributed frequent anonymous essays to the *Atlantic Monthly,* as well as poems to it and other magazines, often under the pseudonym of Andrew Hedbrooke, but his last years were troubled by intellectual isolation, by private anxieties, and by ill-health. He died prematurely, following a minor operation, in a hospital in Cleveland.

As a prose-writer he can hardly be said to have an important place in literature. His essays, collected in 1900 as *The Prose of Edward Rowland Sill,* have a certain tenuous charm, and through some of them his fastidious humor shines pleasantly and mildly, but their substance is mostly of the slightest. Nor can even the best of his poetry (*The Poems of Edward Rowland Sill,* 1902) be said to loom imposingly on the horizon. It suffers from his own refusal after his earliest youth to take himself quite seriously as a writer. Nevertheless his gifts, if limited, were delicate and true, and his verse has a warm undercurrent of thoughtfulness and deep feeling. Mainly this is due to the sense it conveys of the spiritual conflicts that lay behind it. More than any other American verse of the time except that of Herman Melville [*q.v.*], it is colored by metaphysical doubt and perplexity and fatigue. Unable to accept the certainties of the Christian religion without scrutiny, he was unable also to dispense with spiritual assurance, and in consequence he is one of the authentic voices of the age's malady. Yet he was not merely a poet of low spirits, and many of his finest poems, such as "The Fool's Prayer" and "Opportunity," give expression to a humane and even humanitarian idealism which is the worthy American equivalent of Matthew Arnold's modern stoicism. The purity of his language and imagery, moreover, —its freedom, at its best, from the literary honey of his day,—accounts very largely for the pleasure with which it can still be read.

[H. R. Stiles, *The Hist. and Geneal. of Ancient Windsor, Conn.*, vol. II (1892); A. P. Stokes, *Memorials of Eminent Yale Men* (2 vols., 1914); *Obit. Record Grads. Yale Univ.* (1890); *The Twenty-Five Years' Record . . . Class of 1861, Yale Coll.* (1888), with bibliog.; W. B. Parker, *Edward Rowland Sill: His Life and Work* (1915); *A Memorial of Edward Rowland Sill . . . Together with Extracts from His Correspondence* (1887); *The Prose of Edward Rowland Sill* (1900), introduction; correspondence with Milicent W. Shinn, J. C. Rowell, and Eloise Hersey; correspondence and interview with Anna M. Sill; obituary in *Appletons' Ann. Cyc.*, 1887; death notice in *Cleveland Plain Dealer*, Mar. 1, 1887.]   N. A.

SILLIMAN, BENJAMIN (Aug. 8, 1779–Nov. 24, 1864), professor of chemistry and natural history in Yale College from 1802 to 1853, was the most prominent and influential scientific man in America during the first half of the nineteenth century. There is a tradition that his paternal ancestors were of Italian origin, Sillimandi by name, but long domiciled in Switzerland, and that from there, by way of Holland, the first of the family came to America at the time of the great Puritan migration, settling eventually near what is now Fairfield, Conn. In the records of Fairfield County he appears as Daniel Sillivant. By 1690 the name of the family had been changed to Silliman and its members were becoming people of substance and prominence. Benjamin's grandfather, Ebenezer Silliman, graduated from Yale College in 1727, as did his son, Benjamin's father, Gold Selleck Silliman, in 1752. Both followed the law as a profession. The former was a member of the Governor's Council and a judge of the superior court; the latter was a general in the Continental Army in charge of the defense of Connecticut against the British. On the side of his mother, Mary, daughter of Rev. Joseph and Rebecca (Peabody) Fish of North Stonington, Conn., Benjamin Silliman was descended from Puritan stock through the Peabodys of Rhode Island, who derived from John and Priscilla Alden.

He was born in a part of what is now Trumbull, Conn., and brought up at Fairfield. His early education was secured in the local schools. He was prepared for college by the Rev. Andrew Eliot and entered Yale in 1792 at the age of thirteen years, the youngest but one in his class. He graduated in 1796 and after two years spent partly at home and partly teaching in a private school at Wethersfield, Conn., returned to New Haven and began the study of law under Simeon Baldwin and David Daggett [*qq.v.*], leaders of the Connecticut bar. He was admitted to the bar in 1802. Meanwhile, from September 1799 he had served as a tutor in Yale College.

In September 1802, at the age of twenty-three, he was appointed to the newly established professorship of chemistry and natural history in Yale College. The next two years he devoted largely to study in preparation for his new duties, chiefly in Philadelphia, where he attended lectures in chemistry, botany, anatomy, and surgery at the medical school. Of greater importance to him, however, was an opportunity to work in the laboratory of the able chemist and physicist Robert Hare [*q.v.*], and of more value still were occasional visits to Dr. John Maclean [*q.v.*], professor of chemistry at Princeton, a very able and scholarly man from whom he learned much and received many valuable suggestions regarding the teaching of that science.

He began the duties of his new position in April 1804 with a course of experimental lectures in chemistry, the first ever given at Yale. In the spring of 1805 he sailed for England, partly for the purpose of purchasing books for the college library and scientific apparatus for his laboratory, but chiefly to extend his knowledge of science through study and association with foreign scholars. He traveled through England, Wales, and Scotland, and also visited Holland, but the disturbed condition of the Continent prevented him from visiting other countries. The greater part of his time was spent in London and Edinburgh, where he met on intimate and informal terms the most distinguished scholars of the times, among them Sir Humphrey Davy, Sir David Brewster, Dr. John Murray, and Dr. Thomas Hope. His associations with the last two and his attendance on their lectures in geology were especially significant in their influence on his subsequent career as a scientist. Murray and Hope were ardent supporters, respectively, of the then current and radically opposed theories of Werner and Hutton regarding the origin of rock formations of the earth's crust. Their discussions provided Silliman's first real contact with geology, and the interest thus aroused in him continued throughout his life, with a far-reaching and important effect on the development of the science in America. His analysis of the merits of these two rival theories, as given in his personal journal (Fisher, *post,* I, 167–72), bears evidence of his remarkable powers of observation, criticism, and sound judgment. Although he was still in his twenties, his scholarly attainments, his character, and his great personal charm did much to produce in the British seats of learning a favorable impression of Americans. He remained abroad a year. In 1810 he published, in two volumes, *A Journal of Travels in England, Holland and Scotland,* a full account of his visit with many interesting observations on British and Scottish university life and customs and the characteristics and achievements of the scholars he met. This book, celebrated in its day and still well worth reading, went through three editions and was widely and favorably read in both England and America.

On his return to New Haven he resumed his lectures in chemistry, enriched in material and scope by his studies abroad. He was now desirous of giving a new and full course of lectures in mineralogy and geology for which he had collected some illustrative material. During the summer of 1807, which he spent in Newport, R. I., he became acquainted with Col. George Gibbs [q.v.], a gentleman much interested in mineralogy and the possessor of what was then the finest mineral collection in America; later Colonel Gibbs lent his collection to Yale College for Silliman's use. Arranged and catalogued in rooms specially provided for it in South Middle College, the Gibbs Collection excited wide interest and also made it possible for Silliman to begin (1813) the full course of illustrated lectures in mineralogy and geology which he had planned. It was a significant event in American science. Later (1823) this celebrated collection was purchased by the College from funds raised for the purpose through Silliman's efforts.

During the period immediately following his return from abroad he was made a member of a committee representing the college to consider the organization of a school of medicine at Yale. If not, indeed, the originator of this proposal, Silliman was the one who worked out most of the details, won the cooperation of the state and local medical associations, and in the end secured a charter for the new medical school from the state legislature. The Yale Medical School was formally opened in 1813 with a faculty consisting of four professors of medicine and Silliman as professor of chemistry.

As early as 1808 Silliman introduced what was an innovation for a professor in the college when he began to give occasional scientific lectures open to the public of New Haven. In succeeding years he delivered similar lectures in New York and various New England cities. During March and April 1835 he delivered by invitation a series of geological lectures before the Boston Society of Natural History. He was at this time at the height of his powers as a lecturer and the Boston series created nothing less than a sensation and firmly established his reputation as a public speaker; he thenceforth experienced an ever increasing demand for his services. In 1836 he lectured in Boston on chemistry and in New York on geology. In 1838 he was invited to open the Lowell Institute, newly

founded by John Lowell of Boston, and in the winter of 1839–40 he delivered the first series of lectures on this celebrated foundation. These dealt with geology and were followed during the next three years with lectures on chemistry. Although he spoke in the Odeon, seating 1500 people, the largest auditorium in the city, the demand for tickets was so great that each lecture was repeated. During his entire stay he received marked attentions from the intellectually and socially prominent people of Boston and Cambridge. It is doubtful if any series of scientific lectures has ever aroused greater interest, and Silliman justly regarded them as the crowning success of his professional life. Subsequently he lectured in all of the important centers of the country, going as far south as New Orleans and as far west as St. Louis. He had become a national scientific figure.

His college courses, interesting and stimulating as they were, with their wealth of experiments and material illustration, were nevertheless essentially cultural in character. There was no opportunity for advanced study or for laboratory work for any except those whom the professor employed as his personal assistants. Incidentally, the position of assistant was eagerly sought after by young men attracted by Silliman's reputation, and to mention the names of these assistants would be to enumerate many of the leaders of American science and education in the following generation. Silliman was particularly anxious to extend the opportunities for scientific study in the college, but it was not until 1847 that he succeeded, aided by his son, Benjamin Silliman, Jr. [q.v.], and his son-in-law, James Dwight Dana [q.v.], who had by this time taken over part of the instruction in geology, and doubtless also by some pressure from outside sources, in persuading the Corporation to establish a "Department of Philosophy and the Arts," under which the natural and physical sciences could be studied intensively. Even then he, his friends, and associates had to support the work of the department unaided by the college. From this modest beginning, however, within a few years, grew the Yale Scientific School which subsequently, aided by the generous support of Joseph E. Sheffield [q.v.], became the Sheffield Scientific School. This school, which rapidly became a center of scientific culture and perhaps Yale's most distinctive contribution to American education, was the direct fruitage of Silliman's influence.

In July 1818, Silliman issued the first number of *The American Journal of Science and Arts,* of which he was the founder, proprietor, and first editor. Devoted to the publication of original papers, notices, and reviews in the broad field of the natural and physical sciences, it became, under his skilful management, one of the world's great scientific journals. It brought him wide recognition throughout the scientific world and is one of his most enduring monuments. In the first hundred years of its history it had only four editors—Silliman himself, his son, his son-in-law, and his grandson.

In addition to the heavy burden of work entailed by the many activities already mentioned, Silliman found time for numerous scientific investigations and for writing. He edited, with some additions of his own, *The Elements of Experimental Chemistry* (2 vols., 1814), an American edition of William Henry's standard English textbook; he edited (1829) Robert Bakewell's *An Introduction to Geology*; and in 1830–31 he published his own excellent treatise, *Elements of Chemistry,* in two volumes. All of these went through several editions. In 1820 he published *Remarks Made on a Short Tour between Hartford and Quebec in the Autumn of 1819,* a volume which contained much of both general and scientific interest. This was widely read and went through two editions. Some sixty papers contain the results of his scientific investigations, among which may be mentioned one written in 1806 on the geology of New Haven and vicinity, a paper describing exhaustively the celebrated "Weston Meteor" (Conn.) of the fall of 1807, and several dealing with his experiments with the "Voltaic" current produced by a powerful deflagrator which he had developed with improvements along lines of one earlier made by his lifelong friend, Robert Hare. He also investigated gold deposits in Virginia and coal in Pennsylvania, and directed an investigation for the government on sugar culture. It is probably true, however, that the results of his original researches were less important than the contributions included in the vast scientific correspondence with distinguished scientists throughout the world which he carried on independently or in connection with his editorial work for *The American Journal of Science.* The influence of this correspondence, although difficult to measure, was very great. His letters also contain much of value dealing with public, political, and religious questions.

In 1805 he had been made a member of the American Philosophical Society; in the spring of 1840 he was elected the first president of the Association of American Geologists, forerunner of the American Association for the Advancement of Science; and in 1863 he became an original member of the National Academy of Sciences.

On Sept. 17, 1809, Silliman married Harriet Trumbull, second daughter of the second Governor Trumbull of Connecticut. He thus allied himself with one of the most distinguished and talented families of New England, a matter of no small importance to the rising young scholar. Incidentally it was through this connection that he secured for Yale College the historical paintings of Col. John Trumbull [*q.v.*] which now form the Trumbull Gallery of the Yale School of Fine Arts. Of the nine children of this marriage, one son and four daughters lived to maturity. Mrs. Silliman died on Jan. 18, 1850, and on Sept. 17, 1851, he married a relative of hers, Sarah Isabella (McClellan) Webb, who survived him.

In 1849 he indicated his desire to withdraw from his teaching duties at the close of the year, but was persuaded to continue in active service until 1853, when he retired as professor emeritus, having served the college for nearly fifty-four years, fifty-one as professor. During a considerable part of this period he had been the most distinguished and influential member of the Yale faculty. It can be said that he had established science at Yale and had exerted a most profound influence on collegiate education. After his retirement he enjoyed another decade of life, during which he made a second visit to Europe—an account of this trip was published in book form, *A Visit to Europe in 1851* (2 vols., 1853)—and occupied himself with compiling memoirs covering his life and work, with editorial work, and with his extensive correspondence. He died suddenly after a brief and painless illness at his home in New Haven, in his eighty-fifth year.

Benjamin Silliman was as richly endowed by nature physically as he was mentally. Tall, well-proportioned, and of vigorous physique, with handsome face and animated expression, he was a man of striking appearance. His unfailing dignity and courtesy of demeanor, his gentleness, kindliness, and generosity, and his noble integrity of character brought him a degree of regard and affection both at home and abroad seldom accorded to any man. His counsel and help in both public and private matters were constantly sought and freely given. To the members of his immediate family and to his intimate friends he appears to have been an object of love that was almost worship. Throughout his life he was deeply and sincerely religious. This was apparent in his daily life and is strikingly evident in his writings. Indeed, it was this combination of a scientific mind with deep, religious conviction that enabled him to exert such a profound influence in the interests of science on a generation that itself was dominated by strong religious convictions.

Silliman was an able scientific investigator and as such would doubtless have attained even greater distinction than he did, had he not chosen instead to be before all else the interpreter, promoter, and defender of science. To study science was, to him, to learn of the wonderful manifestations of God in the natural world, which it was man's duty to interpret reverently and by which it was his privilege to improve the conditions of his life; as told by him the story of the earth, revealed by geology, was a profoundly moving picture of the work of God. When he lectured, he conveyed much of his enthusiasm to his hearers. Speaking always extemporaneously, he drove home his point with a dignified but compelling eloquence. The experiments which were an important part of his chemistry lectures were ingenious, carefully prepared, and performed with remarkable elegance and skill. A rare and gifted teacher, whether in the college classrooms or on the public platform, he opened up new vistas of thought and inspired others with his own love of knowledge. In the course of his lifetime, despite vigorous opposition on the part of many who regarded scientific investigations and teaching as a menace to sound learning and even to morality and religion itself, he established the study of science on an equality with the older traditional educational culture, and made a whole nation conscious of its value to mankind.

[The major source is G. P. Fisher, *Life of Benjamin Silliman* (2 vols., 1866). Fisher was a student of Silliman's and later a warm personal friend and associate on the Yale College faculty; his biography is chiefly a compilation from reminiscences, diaries, and correspondence, suitably selected, arranged, and connected by brief biographical comments; a great part of the extensive original material is to be found in the Yale University library. See also Alexis Caswell, in *Nat. Acad. Sci. Biog. Memoirs*, vol. I (1877); J. M. Hoppin, in *Memorial Biogs. of the New Eng. Hist. Geneal. Soc.*, vol. VI (1905); *Proc. Am. Acad. Arts and Sci.*, vol. VI (1866); F. B. Dexter, *Biog. Sketches Grads. Yale Coll.*, vol. V (1911); R. H. Chittenden, *Hist. of the Sheffield Scientific School of Yale Univ.* (1928), vol. I; E. H. Schenck, *The Hist. of Fairfield, Fairfield County, Conn.*, vol. I (1889); *Morning Journal and Courier* (New Haven), Nov. 26, 1864.]
C. H. W.

SILLIMAN, BENJAMIN (Dec. 4, 1816–Jan. 14, 1885), chemist, was born and died in New Haven, Conn. His father was Benjamin Silliman [*q.v.*], for more than fifty years professor of chemistry and geology at Yale; his mother was Harriet (Trumbull), daughter of Jonathan Trumbull, governor of Connecticut, 1798–1809, and grand-daughter of Jonathan Trumbull [*q.v.*], governor of Connecticut during the Revolution. On May 14, 1840, Silliman married Susan Huldah Forbes of New Haven, who died in 1878. Of their seven children, four daughters and a son survived them.

Probably because of the influence of his distinguished father, Silliman's major interests throughout a very active life were scientific. Graduating from Yale in 1837, he began teaching immediately as assistant to his father. In 1838 he became an associate editor of the *American Journal of Science,* founded by his father twenty years earlier, and he continued in this capacity, or as editor, later assisted by his brother-in-law, James D. Dana [*q.v.*], until his death, a period of almost fifty years. Nearly all his scientific publications, numbering over fifty and concerned chiefly with chemistry and mineralogy, appeared in this journal, beginning in 1841. His best-known books were two college texts, *First Principles of Chemistry* (1847) and *First Principles of Physics* (1859). Both went through several editions. In 1846 he was appointed professor of practical chemistry and the following year, with John P. Norton [*q.v.*], he established a school of applied chemistry at Yale in the new Department of Philosophy and the Arts which later became the Sheffield Scientific School. In 1853 he was appointed to succeed his father, who had just retired, in the professorship of chemistry in the Yale Medical School and Yale College. He maintained his connection with the Scientific School until 1869, with Yale College until 1870, and with the Yale Medical School until his death. For a number of years also (1849–54) he spent a portion of his time in Kentucky as professor of chemistry in the medical department of the University of Louisville. He was one of the fifty original members of the National Academy of Sciences, incorporated in 1863.

Silliman frequently acted as a consultant in chemical and mining problems, and in this capacity made one major contribution to the petroleum industry the importance of which has not been generally appreciated. This was his *Report on the Rock Oil, or Petroleum, from Venango County, Pennsylvania* (1855), based on an investigation made for the company which owned the land on which Edwin L. Drake [*q.v.*] later drilled the first oil well in Pennsylvania. In this report, printed as a copyrighted pamphlet at the time and some years later republished in full in the *American Chemist* (July 1871), Silliman showed from his own researches that petroleum was essentially a mixture of hydrocarbons, entirely different in character from vegetable and animal oils, and that it could be separated, by fractional distillation and simple means of purification, into a series of distillates making up about ninety per cent. of the whole. He estimated that about fifty per cent. of the distillate (the intermediate fractions) could be used for illuminating purposes, and he found by quantitative measurements with a photometer devised for the purpose that the light was superior to that from any other of a number of illuminants. From the high-boiling oily fraction he extracted paraffine, purified it, and found it made excellent candles. The high-boiling oil he characterized as valuable for lubrication because it did not become rancid, did not freeze, and did not tend to form a gum. Finally, he found that crude petroleum, when passed through heated coke, decomposed into a gas of very high illuminating power suitable to enrich illuminating gas. In short, in this investigation Silliman discovered the chief uses which were to be made of petroleum products for the next fifty years and outlined the principal methods of preparing and purifying those products. Adequate uses for the low-boiling (gasoline) fraction were not discovered by Silliman, or by anyone else, until the development of the internal combustion engine, but the rapid growth of the industry along the lines laid down by Silliman is ample testimony to the usefulness of his discoveries.

[For biographical data, see *Am. Jour. of Sci.*, Feb. 1885; *Nat. Acad. Sci. Biog. Memoirs*, vol. VII (1913); *Record of the Class of 1837 in Yale Univ.* (7th ed., 1887); *Obit. Record Grads. Yale Coll.* 1885; R. H. Chittenden, *Hist. of the Sheffield Scientific School of Yale Univ.* (1928), vol. I; *New Haven Evening Register*, Jan. 15, 1885. A copy of the rare pamphlet: *Report on the Rock Oil, or Petroleum, of Venango County, Pa.* (1855), is in the Yale Univ. Library.]

H. W. F.

SILLS, MILTON (Jan. 12, 1882–Sept. 15, 1930), actor, was born in Chicago, Ill., the son of William Henry and Josephine Antoinette (Troost) Sills. His full name was Milton George Gustavus Sills, the middle part of which he later dropped. He was graduated from the University of Chicago in 1903 with the degree of A.B., and for a year and a half remained there as a scholar and fellow in philosophy. His experiences in college dramatic performances prepared him to some extent for his professional début at New Palestine, Ohio, in 1906, in an old melodrama entitled *Dora Thorne*. A season of barnstorming through towns of the Middle West followed, and then he went to New York, where he was soon playing conspicuous rôles under the Frohman, Shubert, Belasco, and other managements. An engagement with Charles Coburn's repertory company gave him valuable experience in Shakespearian plays. He was for a time leading man with Blanche Bates in *The Fighting Hope*. During this period he acted for the most part in plays of the hour that soon vanished from the stage; among them were *This Woman and This Man, Just Married, The Governor's Lady, The Law of the Land,* and *A Happy Marriage,* the last mentioned being one of the minor comedies of Clyde Fitch [*q.v.*]. In 1914 he deserted the stage for the screen, and in 1916, after preliminary experience in the ill-equipped studios of New York, he went to Hollywood, and there began a new era of success as a motion picture star. His first appearance on the screen was made in association with Wilton Lackaye in a motion picture version of Frank Norris's novel, *The Pit.* Later he played leading characters in *The Barker, Burning Daylight, The Sea-Hawk, Men of Steel* (of which he was part author), and *Paradise.* All of these were marked by the forceful acting in which he excelled both on the screen and the stage. He was, it is said, far removed from the popular idea of the film idol when he was outside of the studios. His library contained books in Greek, French, and Russian, all of which he read; his chess game was well above the average, and his talk ranged from philosophy or the experimental sciences to the fine points of tennis or golf (*New York Herald Tribune, post*).

He was tall, of fine figure, and with a resonant voice that served him well when the silent screen became vocal. His marriage to Gladys Edith Wynne in London on May 26, 1910, resulted in divorce in 1925, and on Oct. 12, 1926, he married an actress, Doris Margaret Kenyon. He died suddenly while playing tennis with his wife at their home in Santa Monica, Cal. With her survived a daughter by the first marriage and a son by the second. His work as an actor and motion picture performer did not fill all his active hours, for he remained interested in philosophy and art. He never abandoned his academic studies, and delivered occasional lectures at colleges and universities on various subjects connected and unconnected with the stage; in 1927 he spoke at the Harvard school of business administration on conditions in the motion picture world. He was the co-author with Ernest S. Holmes of a book, published (after his death) in 1932, entitled *Values: a Philosophy of Human Needs,* and he was one of the organizers of the Academy of Motion Picture Arts and Sciences. Unlike most actors, he became a wealthy man and left an estate of several hundred thousand dollars.

[*Who's Who in America*, 1930–31; obituaries in *Variety*, Sept. 17, 1930, in *Boston Transcript, Sun*

(N. Y.), *N. Y. Times,* and *N. Y. Herald Tribune,* Sept. 16, 1930.]   E. F. E.

SILSBEE, NATHANIEL (Jan. 14, 1773–July 14, 1850), seaman, merchant, statesman, was born in Salem, Mass., and was the oldest of the eight children of Nathaniel and Sarah (Becket) Silsbee. Both his parents, all of his grandparents, and all of his great-grandparents were born in Salem of English stock. His father, fourth in descent from Henry Silsbee who was in Salem in 1639, was a prominent and prosperous sea captain who met with financial reverses that forced his eldest son to withdraw from school and in 1787 to go to sea to assist the family, of which he became the sole support on his father's death in 1791. His first voyages were as clerk or supercargo, but in 1790 he was second mate of a brig, and the next year he commanded a sloop which he brought safely back from the West Indies after a survey there had declared her unseaworthy. Before he was twenty-one, and with a chief mate who was also a minor, he took command of the ship *Benjamin,* and in her completed one of the outstanding voyages in Salem annals, modifying the plan of the owners to take advantage of conditions arising from the outbreak of war between England and France, and by transactions in foreign exchange and merchandise bringing back a profit of over one hundred per cent. He made other noteworthy voyages to the Orient, the Mediterranean, and Russia. On one occasion, when brought as a prize into Malaga, he remained in the office of the French consul for forty hours continuously, refusing to leave till his case was decided, and secured by this means not only immediate trial but the release of both ship and cargo; in another instance, through determination and skillful bargaining, he prevented his ship's being conscripted to carry Napoleon's troops to Egypt. So uniformly successful was he that he accumulated a sufficient fortune to retire from the sea in 1801 to become a ship-owner and leading figure in the commercial and financial activities of Salem and Boston.

Silsbee was a Jeffersonian in a strong Federalist section, but the Era of Good Feeling made a man of his moderation and prominence politically strong. Against his wishes he was nominated for the federal House of Representatives in 1816 and induced to serve two terms as a public duty. On retiring from Congress, he was drafted for one term in the lower house of the Massachusetts legislature, 1821–22, and three terms in the upper house, 1823–26, acting as president of the latter body while he was in it. In 1826 he was made United States senator by legislative election, and in 1829 was elected for a six-year term by the legislature. His senatorial colleague from 1827 was Daniel Webster, and he somewhat overshadowed Silsbee, who, however, was a member of the committees on finance and commerce, and acted as chairman of the latter from 1833 to 1835. In the House, too, he exerted influence on legislation affecting the navy, merchant marine, and other matters on which he had special knowledge, and in the Senate he had a good deal to do with a bill, passed Mar. 2, 1833, that marks a stage in the development of the customs service. He served continuously as a director of the Boston branch or the main division of the Bank of the United States in Philadelphia, 1816–32; he was a presidential elector, 1824 and 1836; and he was regarded as more important in both political and economic circles than the offices he held would indicate.

On Dec. 12, 1802, he was married in Salem to Mary Crowninshield, who died in 1835; one of his daughters was the second wife of Jared Sparks [*q.v.*], and his son Nathaniel held such offices as mayor of Salem, representative in the Massachusetts legislature, and treasurer of Harvard University. He died in Salem, survived by three of his children. His autobiography appeared as "Biographical Notes" in the *Essex Institute Historical Collections,* January 1899.

[M. W. F. Duren, *Three Generations of Silsbees and Their Vessels* (privately printed, 1924); J. A. Emmerton, in *Essex Inst. Hist. Colls.,* July 1880; Nathaniel Silsbee, *Ibid.,* Jan. 1899; R. J. Cleveland, *A Narrative of Voyages and Commercial Enterprises* (2 vols., 1842); R. D. Paine, *The Ships and Sailors of Old Salem* (1909); *Biog. Directory Am. Cong. 1774–1927* (1928); obituary in *Salem Reg.,* July 18, 1850; death notice, *Boston Daily Jour.,* July 22, 1850.]   S. G.

SILVER, THOMAS (June 17, 1813–Apr. 12, 1888), civil engineer, inventor, was of American Quaker parentage and was born at Greenwich, Cumberland County, N. J. It is recorded that he was educated in Greenwich and Woodstown, N. J., and in Philadelphia, Pa., and then engaged in civil engineering practice in Philadelphia. He became well known locally as a young man because of the unusual mechanical ingenuity he displayed in designing such contrivances as a grain-dryer, a gas-burner, a stove, and a window-tightening device to prevent rattling, patented June 13, 1854, No. 11,092. In 1854 the loss of the United States steamship *San Francisco,* bound to California with troops, turned his attention to devising a governor for marine engines. The ordinary steam engine governor was slow in action. When it was used with marine steam engines driving side-wheel steamships, it was unable to control the speed of the engine quickly, consequently, when a ship rolled, one of the paddle wheels was brought out of the water, and often much damage was caused. The first patent to correct this condition, No. 13,202, was issued to Silver on July 3, 1855. The contrivance was a very simple one, like the ordinary two-ball governor except that it was kept from being affected by the force of gravity by the use of four balls of equal weight placed at equal distance from the axis of motion. Furthermore, it could be used in any position—horizontal, vertical, or inclined. In 1856 Silver succeeded in having his governor installed on the United States mail steamship *Atlantic,* as well as on the engines of the United States mint at Philadelphia, the *Public Ledger* (Philadelphia) and the *New York Tribune,* where they operated with entire success. He failed to interest the United States navy, however, and in 1857 went to Europe in the hope of introducing his governor there. After obtaining an English patent on May 23, 1857, he went to France and succeeded in having it adopted by the French navy. He obtained a second United States patent on Apr. 26, 1859, a reissue of his original patent on July 25, 1865, and still another improvement patent on Oct. 2, 1866. Meanwhile, in 1864, he succeeded in having his governor ordered into general use in the British navy. This was followed by its adoption by most of the naval authorities of the world, though not by the United States. About 1870 he returned to take up residence at Nyack, N. Y., where he lived for the rest of his life. He obtained four additional patents between 1871 and 1885, one for a hoisting apparatus and three for a completely inclosed oil lamp, in which air was furnished to the burning oil by a revolving fan operated by a clock movement. He became a member of the Franklin Institute, Philadelphia, in 1855. He was awarded the James Watt medal by the Royal Polytechnic Society, London, in 1866, and received a medal from Napoleon III for his "regulateur marine." In 1887 he published a pamphlet on *The Scientific Explanation of the Polar Tides, and the Formation of Icebergs.* He married the daughter of James M. Bird, Philadelphia, and at the time of his death in New York was survived by his widow and a daughter.

[E. H. Knight, *Knight's Amer. Mech. Dict.,* vol. II (1875) ; *Sci. Amer.,* Apr. 28, May 19, 1888 ; *Jour. of Franklin Inst.,* June 1855, Mar. 1857 ; obituaries in *N. Y. Times, N. Y. Tribune,* Apr. 14, 1888 ; Patent Office records.]　　　　　　　　　　C. W. M—n.

SILVERMAN, JOSEPH (Aug. 25, 1860–July 26, 1930), rabbi, was born at Cincinnati, Ohio, the son of Michael Henry and Ulrika (Piorkowsky) Silverman. His parents came to America from Russia, and his early surroundings were poor and humble. He was educated in the public schools, at the University of Cincinnati (A.B. 1883), and at the Hebrew Union College (Rabbi 1884, D.D. 1887). On Dec. 5, 1886, in Galveston, Tex., he married Henriette Block, by whom he had four daughters. After serving as minister of Temple Emanu-El in Dallas (1884–85) and Congregation B'nai Israel in Galveston (1885–88), he was called to the leading reform Jewish congregation of the country, Temple Emanu-El, New York, as junior rabbi, and on the retirement of Gustav Gottheil [*q.v.*] in 1897, he was elected rabbi. He filled this position for thirty-four years, becoming, in 1922, rabbi emeritus. He died in New York at the age of seventy.

Besides articles in the press, Silverman published some Jewish religious textbooks, pamphlets, and a volume of sermons, *The Renaissance of Judaism* (1918) ; he was also a contributing editor of the *Jewish Encyclopedia.* His strength, however, lay less in homiletic and literary work than in his community service. He was the founder (1903) and first president of the Emanu-El Brotherhood, and served as secretary of the Emanu-El Theological Seminary Association and as president of the Central Conference of American Rabbis (1900–03), the New York Board of Jewish Ministers (1906–07), the Order B'nai Brith, District I (1913–15), the Eastern Council of Reform Rabbis (1917–19), and the Association of Reform Rabbis of New York and Vicinity (1919–21). He also served as a governor of the Hebrew Union College and as a member of the American Jewish Committee. The breadth and variety of his interests is suggested by the fact that he was a member of the Congress of Religions at the World's Columbian Exposition, Chicago, in 1893; vice-president of the International Peace Forum; a member of the executive committee of the Lake Mohonk Peace Conference on International Arbitration (1912), and of the executive committee of the National Association for the Advancement of Colored People (1909–12). In 1892, and again in 1904, he delivered the opening prayer in the House of Representatives at Washington.

Though a liberal in religion, he was conservative in his social and political views. He was opposed to the feminist movement, and held that socialism was based on false theories and constituted a menace to American institutions. In the last eight years of his life, he allied himself with Zionism, energetically throwing himself into the work of raising funds and securing adherents. His conversion to this movement after many years of uncompromising opposition to it attracted wide attention. He became an honorary vice-president of the Palestine Foundation Fund, and a member of the national executive committee of the Zionist Organization of America.

Silverman was a good-looking man, especially in his later years, when his silvery hair and full beard added a venerable impressiveness to his appearance. His was a kindly and sympathetic nature, and he took real delight in participating in philanthropic movements. He is remembered as a man who was steadfast in his friendship, loyal to his convictions, and a messenger of intercreedal good-will.

[N. Y. Times, July 27–30, 1930; Am. Hebrew, Aug. 1, 1930; Reform Advocate, Aug. 2, 9, 1930; Central Conference of Am. Rabbis, Year Book, vol. XLI (1931); Am. Jewish Year Book (1903–04), p. 100; Who's Who in Am. Jewry, 1928; Who's Who in America, 1929–30.]
D. deS. P.

SILVERMAN, SIME (May 18, 1873–Sept. 22, 1933), editor and publisher, was born in Cortland, N. Y., son of George and Rachel (Ganz) Silverman. His mother was a native of Bristol, England, and a life-long lover of music. Educated in the public schools of Cortland and Syracuse, N. Y., and at a business college, he began active life with his father in business in Syracuse, but his interest in the theatre led him to New York, where he secured work with the *Morning Telegraph,* a racing and theatrical daily. On Mar. 1, 1898, he married Hattie Freeman, daughter of George Freeman of Syracuse. When he lost his job in 1905 because of some adverse criticism he wrote of a variety performance, he immediately borrowed enough money from his father-in-law to start his own paper, a weekly which he named *Variety.* It started humbly with sixteen pages and a total staff of three, Silverman and two assistants. Incidentally, it was written in correct English. When its founder died nearly thirty years later it was often issued with 100 pages, had 225 employees, and was almost entirely written in the worst, as well as often the most entertaining and lively English to be found anywhere in print. From 1905 until his death Silverman's story was entirely the story of his paper. He gave his entire time and life to it. Its success was due to his labors and to the qualities he put into it. It was honest, it kept well abreast of the times, and it was remarkably vivid. Unlike theatrical trade papers which had gone before, *Variety* never changed an opinion out of consideration for its advertisers or the influence of those whom it criticized, and the editor supported his staff against every outside pressure so well that there was general respect for the paper's opinions and

reliance on its statement of facts. It was first, largely because of Silverman's foresight, in what turned out to be the highly remunerative fields of motion picture and radio reviewing, and made other innovations that were highly successful. Its style, furthermore, came to be one that reflected with curious fidelity the argot of Broadway—its slang, its verbal short cuts, and its "hard-boiled" humor. Though Silverman meant only to make his paper more effective with his professional readers, more and more people in the outside world bought it, and read and studied it to try the flavor of its odd language, which was often astonishingly effective in its brevity and vividness. In *Variety* verbs became nouns and nouns verbs; an actor "vowed" or "panicked" an audience.. Its headline on its story of the great financial debacle of 1929 was "Wall St. Lays an Egg" (Oct. 30, 1929); "Went for a Grand on Dust" meant that the producer had lost $1000 on a play called "Watch my Dust." *Variety* became, and remained, a place where philologists could study the popular language in evolution. In 1922 Silverman bought the old *New York Clipper;* he published it separately until 1924, when some features were absorbed by *Variety,* and then sold the name to the *Billboard* (Cincinnati). In 1923 he attempted to issue a daily paper of Broadway news, the *Times Square Daily,* but this soon failed. He did succeed, however, with a daily issue of *Variety* in Hollywood, Cal., begun Sept. 6, 1933. He died in Los Angeles a few weeks later.

After his death it was found that he had left fifty-one per cent. of *Variety* to his wife and son, and forty-nine per cent. to his employees, a gift of great value. The act was characteristic. Tall, spare, with white hair in later years, modest to a degree, even shy of any public appearance, but blunt and slangy and "hard-boiled" of speech, he yet possessed a strong strain of sentiment for his paper, for the world of Broadway, and for the men who worked with him. He tolerated no reporters he did not like, but those he kept found him raising their pay unasked, looking after their investments, and backing them up in all critical controversies. His staff, consequently, had for him unlimited devotion, which they expressed in the same Broadway lingo that he used; the old man was a "swell egg" to them. Though his paper so vividly reflected Broadway, he was not a Broadway playboy. He found his recreation in work and in convivial meetings with his staff late at night after work. He lived simply and left a large estate, with his son well trained for the editorial chair he vacated.

[Allene Talmey, in *Stage*, Mar. 1935; *Variety*, Sept. 26, 1933; *N. Y. Times*, *N. Y. Herald Tribune*, Sept. 23, 1933; information from Mrs. Silverman.] W. P. E.

SIMMONS, EDWARD (Oct. 27, 1852– Nov. 17, 1931), mural painter, was born at Concord, Mass., where his father, George Frederick Simmons, was a Unitarian minister. He was a descendant of Moses Simmons, who arrived in America in 1621. His mother, Mary Emerson (Ripley) Simmons, was a grand-daughter of Ezra Ripley [*q.v.*] and through her grandmother, Phoebe (Bliss) Emerson Ripley, was connected with the family of Ralph Waldo Emerson [*q.v.*]. Edward's name was originally Edward Emerson Simmons, but in his later life he dropped the middle name. Only three when his father died, he was reared at the Old Manse in Concord under the supervision of his mother and his grandmother Ripley, who knew some Sanskrit and read Greek and Latin with ease. In his boyhood he was a naturalist companion of Henry David Thoreau [*q.v.*]. Prepared in the local schools and by relatives for college, he went to Harvard, where he studied under Francis James Child and Asa Gray [*qq.v.*], and could have led his class but saw no reason to do so. He was a founder of the *Harvard Crimson* and, according to his autobiography, one of those who introduced Rugby football as an intercollegiate sport in the United States. Graduated in 1874, he first became an oil salesman in Cincinnati and then a clerk in a store in San Francisco, where he also wrote dramatic and literary criticisms for the *San Francisco Chronicle*. After teaching school in Strawberry Valley, Cal., 1876–77, and teaching painting in Bangor, Me., 1877–78, he studied painting at the Boston Museum of Fine Arts, where he came under the influence of Dr. William Rimmer [*q.v.*].

In 1879, assured of a small income, he took steerage passage to Europe, registered at the Académie Julian, and studied under Gustave C. R. Boulanger and Jules Joseph Lefebvre. His portrait of a highlander was in the Salon, 1881, and in 1882 his "La Blanchisseuse" had honorable mention. He joined the artist colony at Concarneau, Brittany, during 1881–86, where he had as friends Jules Bastien-Lepage and Marie Bashkirtseff. The novel *Guenn: a Wave on the Breton Coast* was written by Blanche Willis Howard [*q.v.*] in his Brittany studio, and a legend of his being its hero persists. In London, on Dec. 4, 1883, he married Vesta Schallenberger, author of several books of fiction. He later had a studio at St. Ives, Cornwall, for several years.

In 1891 a commission to design a window for Harvard University brought him back to the United States, where in 1893 he painted with great success the decorations of the dome of the Manufactures and Liberal Arts Building at the World's Columbian Exposition in Chicago, assigned him by Francis Davis Millet [*q.v.*]. Later he painted murals for the appellate division of the supreme court of New York; the criminal court building, courts of oyer and terminer, New York; the state capitols of Minnesota and South Dakota; court houses at Des Moines, Ia., and Mercer, Pa.; the Waldorf-Astoria Hotel, New York; the residences of John D. Rockefeller at Pocantico Hills and Frederick Vanderbilt at Hyde Park, N. Y.; and the Panama Pacific International Exposition at San Francisco in 1915. For the Library of Congress, Washington, D. C., he painted the nine muses in the corridor leading to the north from the entrance hall; for the Massachusetts State House, representations of "Concord Bridge, Apr. 19, 1775" and "The Return of the Colors . . . Dec. 22, 1863." Resident at New York from 1891 onward, he enjoyed social as well as professional popularity, for he was picturesque in person, an entertaining speaker and writer, and a clever amateur actor. He was of the group who called themselves Ten American Painters. In September 1903 he married Alice Ralston Morton. He died in Baltimore after a brief illness, survived by two sons by his first marriage and one by his second.

His autobiography, *From Seven to Seventy, Memories of a Painter and a Yankee* (1922), tells his story brilliantly and wittily, with many anecdotes of his celebrated contemporaries. His article on "The Fine Arts Related to the People," a statement of his philosophy of art which appeared in the *International Studio* for November 1917, lacks the vividness of the autobiography. Strong and direct, his paintings had both simplicity and dignity. He was what is called a "clean painter," not given to fumbling or hesitant strokes, but he lacked profound originality whether in composition or execution. His panels for the Massachusetts State House were criticized when unveiled as somewhat wanting in dramatic appeal and in unusual motivation, and when they are compared with the work in the same building of Robert Reid [*q.v.*], more poignantly interesting, that criticism may still appear just. He was at his happiest in the decorations of the Waldorf-Astoria ballroom, in which the gaiety and brilliance of his own personality are reflected.

[H. S. Bradford, *One Branch of the Bradford Family* (1898); L. A. Simmons, *Hist. of the Simmons Family* (1930); *Who's Who in America*, 1930–31; *Seventh*

Report . . . Class of 1874 of Harvard Coll. (1899);
Samuel Isham, *The Hist. of Am. Painting* (1905);
Handbook of the New Lib. of Cong. (1901), compiled
by Herbert Small; Ellen M. Burrill, *The State House,
Boston, Mass.* (1907); Arthur Hoeber, in *Brush and
Pencil*, Mar. 1900; obituaries in *Art News*, Nov. 21,
1931, *Art Digest*, Dec. 1, 1931, and *N. Y. Times*, Nov.
18, 1931.]   F. W. C.

SIMMONS, FRANKLIN (Jan. 11, 1839–Dec.
6, 1913), sculptor, was born in Lisbon (later
Webster), Me., the son of Loring and Dorothy
(Batchelder) Simmons. John and Priscilla
Alden of Plymouth, as well as Samuel Simmons,
a Revolutionary veteran, were among his ancestors. He spent his boyhood at Bath and early
showed an interest in art. He undertook modeling
while he was employed in a mill at Lewiston,
eventually reached the Boston studio of John
Adams Jackson [*q.v.*], and later opened a studio
of his own in Lewiston. "The Newsboy," modeled
from life, was one of his early works. He studied
at the Lewiston Falls Academy and, for a time
at least, at the Maine State Seminary (later
Bates College). Becoming an itinerant artist, he
went from Waterville, the seat of Waterville
(later Colby) College, where several of his early
busts are preserved, to Brunswick, where he
received the patronage of the Bowdoin faculty;
in 1859 or 1860 he went to Portland, where he
portrayed leading citizens in medallions and
busts, and received his first commission for a
statue, that of Maj.-Gen. Hiram Gregory Berry
[*q.v.*] at Rockland. On Dec. 27, 1864, he married Emily J. Libbey of Auburn, Me. In the
winters of 1865 and 1866 he was in Washington,
making portraits of such leaders in political and
military life as Ulysses S. Grant, William Tecumseh Sherman, and David Glasgow Farragut
[*qq.v.*]. He also designed the war memorial for
Lewiston. As a result of securing a commission
for a statue of Roger Williams [*q.v.*], which was
later placed by Rhode Island in Statuary Hall,
Washington, he went to Italy with his wife, probably in the latter part of 1867, and thereafter
lived in Rome, though he made occasional visits
to America. A replica of the Williams statue
was unveiled in Providence in 1877, with the
addition of a figure representing history. Simmons' other works in Washington include the
Naval Monument at the foot of Capitol Hill,
erected in 1877; an equestrian statue of John
Alexander Logan; statues of William King, the
first governor of Maine, and Francis Harrison
Pierpont, governor of the "restored" state of
Virginia [*qq.v.*]; and the heroic Grant, which
was placed in the rotunda of the Capitol in 1900.
Meanwhile he made for Portland, Me., in 1888
the seated Longfellow in bronze and in 1891 the

Civil War monument, "The Republic." Of his
ideal works the "Penelope" in marble, of which
four replicas were made, is considered his best;
it is now in the Portland Society of Art.

His first wife died in 1872; twenty years later,
June 9, 1892, he married Ella, Baroness von
Jeinsen, daughter of John F. Slocum of Providence, who died in 1905. There were no children.
During his last years he traveled much of the
time and worked on his symbolic group, "Hercules and Alcestis," which he finished not long
before his death. He died suddenly in Rome just
as he was about to return to America, and was
buried in the Protestant Cemetery there, the
grave marked by a replica of his "Angel of the
Resurrection." He left his estate to the Portland
Society of Art, where a collection of his works
is preserved as the Franklin Simmons Memorial.
Other examples are to be seen in the Portland
public library, the Maine Historical Society, and
the Greenleaf Law Library in Portland. His
statues are distinguished by an idealism that at
its best becomes simple and sculptural, as in the
Roger Williams and the equestrian Logan, which
in spite of its heavy bronze base has both grace
and power. Possessed of tireless energy, he
executed about a hundred portrait busts, about
fifteen public monuments, and a number of ideal
figures.

[*Who's Who in America*, 1912–13; *Maine Hist.
Memorials* (1922); W. D. Spencer, *Maine Immortals*
(1932); Lorado Taft, *The Hist. of Am. Sculpture*
(1924); "A Veteran Sculptor," *Outlook*, May 27, 1911;
Lilian Whiting, in *Internat. Studio*, May 1905, supp.;
C. E. Fairman, *Art and Artists of the Capitol of the
U. S. A.* (1927); obituary in *La Tribuna* (Rome), Dec.
10, 1913.]   W. S. R.

SIMMONS, THOMAS JEFFERSON (June
25, 1837–Sept. 12, 1905), soldier, jurist, was
born at Hickory Grove, Crawford County, Ga.,
the son of Allen G. and Mary (Cleveland) Simmons. His grandfather, William Simmons, was
a native of North Carolina. Poverty prevented
Thomas from receiving even the scanty educational advantages afforded by the county schools,
but with borrowed money he was at length enabled to attend Bromwood Institute at Lagrange,
in Troup County. Later he studied in the law
office of A. D. Hammond, of Forsyth, and in
August 1857 was admitted to the bar and began
practice at Knoxville in his native county. In
1859 he married Pennie Hollis.

At the beginning of the Civil War he entered
the Confederate army. Enlisting in the Crawford Greys, the first troops to leave the county,
he was made a lieutenant. His company became
a part of the 6th Georgia Infantry under Col. A.

H. Colquitt [*q.v.*], and Simmons was soon in Virginia, where he fought until Lee's surrender. He was attached to the 45th Georgia Infantry in the 3rd Brigade in A. P. Hill's division of Longstreet's corps; in 1862, he was promoted to lieutenant-colonel; and near the end of the year he was made a colonel. He was recommended by General Lee for a brigadier-generalship, but the surrender came before his commission could be delivered. At the battle of Seven Pines, he received a severe wound which disabled him for six months.

After the war, he returned to Georgia and soon thereafter was chosen a delegate to the constitutional convention which met in November 1865. Under the new government set up, he was elected to the state Senate. In 1867 he became solicitor of the Macon circuit; but, being a Conservative, he was replaced with a Republican a few months later by the incoming Radicals. He then moved to Macon and in 1871 served again in the state Senate. With the Radicals now displaced from power, he played a conspicuous part as chairman of the committee on finance and bonds. By proving many of the Reconstruction bonds to be fraudulent, he prevented their validation and thereby saved the state millions of dollars. The amount the legislature repudiated was $7,957,000. He was reëlected to the Senate in 1873, and in 1875 he was made its president. In 1877 the Conservatives, having the state securely in their hands, called a constitutional convention, to which Simmons was elected and in which he became the chairman of the committee on finance. He reported the financial provisions of the new document and saw them adopted without material change.

The next year he was elected to the superior court of the Macon circuit, where he continued as judge for nine years. In 1887 he was elected to fill a vacancy on the state supreme court, and the following year was elected to a full term. In 1894, when the chief justice, Logan E. Bleckley [*q.v.*], retired, Simmons succeeded him and continued in that position until his death eleven years later. It is for his work as a judge, extending over a period of twenty-seven years, that he is best remembered. He was an indefatigable worker, as is well attested by the large number of decisions which he wrote. Though not brilliant, he had a tenacious memory and was a patient listener. In religion he was a Primitive Baptist. After the death of his first wife, in 1864, he married, in 1867, Lucille Peck, who died in 1882. Six years later he married Mrs. Nannie R. Renfro, who with three of his children, survived him.

[A. D. Candler and C. A. Evans, *Georgia* (1906), vol. III; W. J. Northen, *Men of Mark in Ga.*, vol. IV (1908); *Who's Who in America*, 1903–05; A. O. Park, *Report of the Twenty-Third Ann. Session of the Ga. Bar Assoc.* (1906); *War of the Rebellion: Official Records (Army)*; 79–123 *Ga. Reports*; "In Memoriam," 124 *Ga.*, 1083–98; *Jour. of the Senate of the State of Ga.*, 1871–77; I. W. Avery, *The Hist. of the State of Ga. from 1850 to 1881* (copr. 1881); *Weekly Banner* (Athens, Ga.), Sept. 15, 22, 1905; *Atlanta Constitution*, Sept. 13, 1905.]   E. M. C.

SIMMS, WILLIAM ELLIOTT (Jan. 2, 1822–June 25, 1898), lawyer, soldier, congressman, Confederate senator, was born near Cynthiana, Harrison County, Ky. His parents were William Marmaduke Simms, born in Henry County, Va., who emigrated to Kentucky in 1809, fighting in the War of 1812 under the command of William Henry Harrison, and Julia (Shropshire) Simms, a daughter of James Shropshire, a Kentucky pioneer. He had one brother, Edward, who died in 1840. His father died in 1844, and his mother, in her twenty-first year. The family had moved in 1828 to Bourbon County, with which Simms was thereafter identified. He received a scanty education in the county schools, and after his father's death began reading law in Lexington in the office of Judge Aaron K. Wooley. In 1845, he entered the law department of Transylvania University, and the next year he completed his course of study with distinction. He had scarcely begun the practice of his profession in Paris, the county seat of Bourbon, before war with Mexico broke out. Raising a company of the 3rd Kentucky Regiment of Infantry and becoming its captain, he served in Mexico under Gen. Winfield Scott, and at the end of the war brought back at his own expense the bodies of his comrades who had fallen. As was true of many other veterans of this war, he capitalized in politics his military career. In 1849, he was elected as a Democrat to the Kentucky House of Representatives, where he served one term, and then returned to his law practice in Paris.

In 1857 he began editing the *Kentucky State Flag*, largely to promote the election to Congress of James B. Clay. Two years later he was nominated by the Democrats to succeed Clay, in the famous Ashland district, and after a heated campaign he succeeded in defeating John Marshall Harlan [*q.v.*] by sixty votes. In this campaign he became embroiled with Garret Davis [*q.v.*], who challenged him to a duel, but mutual friends were able to prevent their meeting. In the Thirty-sixth Congress Simms took an active part in the bitter sectional debate, showing unusual ability as an orator, both in the selection of effective words and phrases and in delivery. He strongly opposed the election of John Sherman to the speakership, and he solemnly charged the North with a fanaticism which had already expressed itself in the Kansas struggle and in the John Brown raid and which was about to drive the South from the Union. He also opposed polygamy in Utah and spoke against sectional tariff measures which, he argued, protected the capital of the New England states but ignored labor in the South and the West. On Christmas Day, 1860, he issued a message to the citizens of his district, *To the People of the Eighth Congressional District of Kentucky,* advising Kentucky to be ready to join the South if coercion should be used against any Southern state. On Feb. 9, 1861, after the Southern Confederacy had been formed, he delivered a powerful attack against the Republican party, in which he charged it with being the author of all the woes which were besetting the country. Apparently his Southern sympathies were too much for the Ashland district, for he was defeated for reëlection by John J. Crittenden [*q.v.*].

Being unable longer to remain neutral, he joined, in September 1861, the Confederate forces of Humphrey Marshall, 1812–1872 [*q.v.*], and as a colonel fought through eastern Kentucky and western Virginia. In November he was selected by the Confederate government of Kentucky to be one of the three commissioners to treat with the Confederacy for the admission of the state, and upon its entry into the Confederacy, he was elected to the Confederate Senate, where he served until the end of the war. At the close of hostilities he fled to Canada and there remained a year before returning to Kentucky. Laboring under political disabilities, which were not removed until about three years before his death, he henceforth eschewed politics and devoted himself to agriculture. In his new occupation he became one of the wealthiest men in Bourbon County, living on his estate near Paris, which he called Mount Airy. On Sept. 27, 1866, he married Lucy Ann Blythe, a daughter of James Blythe of Madison County, and to them were born three children.

[For biog. data, see *The Biog. Encyc. of Ky.* (1878); Lewis and R. H. Collins, *Hist. of Ky.* (2 vols., 1882); *Daily Leader* (Lexington, Ky.), June 25, 1898. The *Biog. Dir. Am. Cong.* (1928) gives Simms's middle name as Emmet, but James Blythe Anderson, Esq., of Lexington, Ky., in a letter to Dr. Allen Johnson, Aug. 17, 1929, stated that the name is recorded as Elliott, in the handwriting of Simms's father, in the family Bible in Mrs. Anderson's possession. In most other places only the initial appears.]   E. M. C.

SIMMS, WILLIAM GILMORE (Apr. 17, 1806–June 11, 1870), novelist and man of letters, was born in Charleston, S. C., the son of a Scotch-Irish William Gilmore Simms who had come from Ireland shortly after the Revolution, and of Harriet Ann Augusta (Singleton) Simms, a member of a family which had left Virginia for South Carolina before the Revolution. On neither side was the child allied by birth with the ruling class in South Carolina, then the most compactly governed as well as the most feudal of the American states. There was, moreover, no wealth to bring him such advantages as it could. His father, an unsuccessful merchant, lost everything during the winter of 1807–08 and his mother died at almost the same time. The elder Simms turned his disheartened back on Charleston to wander and settle in what was still the territory of Mississippi, and to be a volunteer soldier in the forces of Andrew Jackson. The younger, brought up in Charleston by his maternal grandmother, a widow who had remarried and was now Mrs. Gates, was sent to public and private schools, all of which he later remembered as useless, and was apprenticed to a druggist at some unknown date. At eighteen he was called upon to decide between South Carolina and Mississippi, to which he had gone to visit his father. Much as the youth seems to have been impressed by the rough humors and violences of the frontier, and strongly as he was urged by his father to give up Charleston, he chose to be loyal to a more venerable tradition. He studied law in his native city, married Anna Malcolm Giles there on Oct. 19, 1826, and the next year was admitted to the bar.

Law from the first was for Simms only a way to literature. Beginning with Byronic impulses, he wrote and published a good deal of verse, of which his fifth volume was *Atalantis* (1832), a kind of epic-romance concerned with the fabulous lost continent. A journalist almost as soon as he was a poet, he gave his energy also to magazines and newspapers, and as editor of the *City Gazette* of Charleston took a vigorous, unpopular stand against nullification. Though too much a South Carolinian not to insist upon state rights, he was too much an American, as late as 1832, to look with favor on disunion. That year saw the breakup of his life as he had so far planned it. His wife died, soon after the deaths of his father (1830) and his grandmother, and he was left without money or a newspaper and with a small daughter. Having nothing but literature to sustain him, he set out for the North, where in New York he formed a permanent friendship with Bryant and a new taste for the theatre, and in New Haven wrote a tale of crime, *Martin Faber* (1833), which by 1837 appeared in the customary two volumes. It was so well received that he followed it with *Guy Rivers*

(1834) and *The Yemassee* (1835), much as Cooper a dozen years before had followed his first experiment with more successful and more characteristic ventures. Simms, however, could not feel at home in the North. Again he returned to Charleston, which took hardly a greater interest in the novelist than it had taken in the boy.

Circumstances aided him. In 1836 he married Chevillette Roach, the daughter of Nash Roach of "Woodlands" plantation, in Barnwell County, and thereafter for a quarter of a century lived in a handsome house on a dignified plantation from October to May of every year, and spent the summers in Charleston with his family or in New York on his own literary business. As Nash Roach trusted his son-in-law, and increasingly depended upon him, Simms was soon in effect the master of the household. He passed long mornings in his library, but by dinner he was at the disposal of the guests who were likely to be present, and his afternoons and evenings were spacious and genial. Charleston, as conservative in its literary inclinations as in its social standards, still largely disregarded him. In Barnwell County he was a man of mark and influence. For six or seven years after his second marriage he felt himself free to be a romancer, and he produced ten substantial novels and a collection of short stories. *Richard Hurdis* (1838) had its melodramatic scene in Alabama, *Border Beagles* (1840) in Mississippi, *Beauchampe* (1842) in Kentucky. Others went still further afield, most of all *Pelayo: A Story of the Goth* (1838). But Simms was unmistakably at his best when he kept at home in South Carolina, as in *The Partisan* (1835), *Mellichampe* (1836), and *The Scout,* originally called *The Kinsmen* (1841).

Writing romances, however, was not enough for a story-teller who had a strong bent toward public affairs, a warm local patriotism, and a passion to defend South Carolina, with the whole South, against those who, he thought, maligned or misunderstood them. To say that Simms from being a beneficiary of slavery became an apologist for the institution is to speak, no doubt, with a logic too cold and short to be entirely true. But he did lose all his union sentiments, chiefly because he held that slavery was "an especially and wisely devised institution of heaven" which the North, without true consideration for the negroes, would destroy. Both the South and slavery must be saved. Simms was not satisfied to be the formal advocate of a doctrine, though he did contribute an essay, published as a pamphlet in 1838, to the influential volume, *The Pro-Slavery Argument, as Maintained by the Most Distinguished Writers of the Southern States*

(1852). With a powerful if uncritical industry he undertook to do whatever a man of letters could do for South Carolina, not only by compiling a *History* (1840) and a *Geography* (1843) of the state but by delivering orations, writing poetry, tragedies, criticism, biographies of Francis Marion (1844), Captain John Smith (1846), the Chevalier Bayard (1847), and Nathanael Greene (1849), and even editing the apocryphal plays of Shakespeare (1848). By the quantity and diversity of his output he made himself an impressive figure in whom many of his contemporaries saw a Southern Cooper and some an American Scott. In all Simms wrote there was something generous, earnest, and high-minded. If nothing of his miscellaneous work survives it is because such moral qualities are less lasting than the literary qualities which he did not have or use. The most ardent local patriotism cannot make a good general man of letters of a man who is untrained, formless, diffuse, and extravagant in conception and execution.

From 1842 to 1850 Simms wrote comparatively little fiction, employing what then seemed the heavier guns of history, biography, oratory, and disquisition in his literary siege of Charleston. During the decades before the Civil War he turned again to romantic novels, the best of them, as before, celebrating the valors and endurances of South Carolina in the Revolution. To the *Partisan* series he added *Katharine Walton* (1851), *The Sword and the Distaff* (1853), later (1854) known as *Woodcraft, The Forayers* (1855), and its sequel *Eutaw* (1856), and half a dozen other novels, among them the sensational *Charlemont* (1856), and the neglected but stirring and varied romance of seventeenth-century Carolina, *The Cassique of Kiawah* (1859).

Simms experienced to the full the cataclysm of the war. In 1856 he undertook to explain the South to the North in lectures delivered in New York, and found his audiences first hostile and then absent. His tour was abandoned. That same year, when a convention at Savannah appointed a committee to prepare for the South a "series of books in every department of study, from the earliest primer to the highest grade of literature and science" (Trent, *post,* p. 246), his name was omitted from the list, though in the North Simms was regarded as the leading Southern man of letters. He seemed to himself, at times, a man without any true country, and he declared that he should long ago have followed his father's advice and left Charleston altogether. Yet during the war he was as Southern in his sympathies as in his adversities. His house at "Woodlands" was burned by accident in 1862.

His wife died in 1863, and two more of the nine children whom he survived had died in 1865. That part of his house which had been rebuilt was destroyed by Sherman's raiders, and Simms witnessed the dreadful burning of Columbia in which he had taken refuge. Though a young Northern officer who admired Simms's novels protected him and his family in Columbia, it cast but a momentary light upon his black fortunes. And after the war was over Simms could do nothing to restore himself and his lost country but edit the *War Poetry of the South* (1867), busy himself with helpless journalism, and write bad serials for worse magazines in New York and Philadelphia. He died in Charleston.

Only the curious now read Simms's poetry or plays or criticisms or biographies or consult any of the varied books by which he showed himself a man of letters if not of genius. Though certain of his novels have continued to be read, and a collection of *Border Romances* has been several times reprinted, the selective process had been much stricter in his case than in, say, Cooper's. His novels with a foreign setting, *Pelayo, The Damsel of Darien* (1839), *Count Julian* (1845), and *Vasconselos* (1853), are practically extinct. His novels of the Southern Border, like *Richard Hurdis, Border Beagles, Beauchampe,* and *Charlemont,* have been kept half-alive, at best, by a sporadic interest in their materials. The novels of South Carolina alone still have such vitality as may be felt in the romances of an out-moded fashion.

Little of course is to be gained by insisting that romances which most people find unreadable deserve to be read or by accusing an indifferent posterity of unjustly overlooking a writer who did not please many even of his contemporaries. Yet, Simms's novels dealing with the frontier are full of a rich picaresque energy, of the rogues whom he magnificently enjoyed drawing to the life with all their eccentric vulgarity and swaggering ruthlessness. If the young man could only have left Charleston and its traditions, he might in the Southwest, fugitive and rebel like his father who somehow appears the younger of the two, have made himself the realist which the region called for and which he was fitted by a whole set of impulses to become—although in the Southwest he might not have written at all. Dealing with South Carolina, he could seldom forget the stiffening presence of its aristocracy. His gentlemen and ladies are generally too great to be convincing. He was obliged to assign to a lower class most of the characters who still remain alive because they were created lifelike rather than correct and noble and eloquent. On

the whole a more veracious novelist than Cooper, Simms wrote almost no novels which seem so clearly to be of the same material throughout as some of Cooper's. This is because Cooper's actions take place in the forest where none but the persons of the story live at all. Simms's novels are crowded with life, and a life which besides being romantic is often robust and comic.

His best-remembered novel, *The Yemassee,* happens to be perhaps his most romantic. It is a chronicle of the Yemassee War of 1715, hardly known except for Simms's story. He chose to give his Indians a dignity and courage which he thought becoming to their heroic age. He invented a mythology for them. He made the action turn upon a high dramatic moment in which a renegade Indian, having betrayed his tribe, is denounced by his father and with a more than Roman fortitude is killed by his mother who thus saves him from a final shame which could be inflicted only upon a living man. All the changes of taste since 1835 have not been able to deprive this episode of its moving power. But *The Yemassee,* however well remembered, displays a narrower range of Simms's abilities than is to be found in the *Partisan* series.

The first of the series, itself called *The Partisan,* was designed as the first member of a trilogy which was to celebrate the Revolution in South Carolina. Simms did not keep to his scheme, and though he finally called *Mellichampe* and *Katharine Walton* the other members of the trilogy, he used more or less the same material in four more novels which belong to the same cycle. *The Partisan* traces events from the fall of Charleston to Gates's defeat at Camden; the action of *Mellichampe,* which is nearly parallel to that of *Katharine Walton,* the real sequel to *The Partisan,* takes place in the interval between Camden and the coming of Greene; *The Scout* illustrates the period of Greene's first victories; *Woodcraft* furnishes a kind of comic afterpiece to the series. Simms later returned to the cycle and produced *The Forayers* and *Eutaw* to do honor to the American successes of the year 1781. Of these seven *The Scout* is perhaps the worst, because of the terrific melodrama into which Simms always tended to run. *Woodcraft* is on many grounds the best, by reason of its close-built plot and the high spirits with which it tells of the pranks and courtship, after the war, of Captain Porgy, the most truly comic character produced by this school of American romance.

But neither of the two books is quite representative. Neither has the full dignity which Simms imparted to his work when he was most under the spell of Carolina. That always warmed him. He had a tendency to overload his tales with fact in a passionate antiquarianism which made him forget his own belief that "the chief value of history consists in its proper employment for the purposes of art." He was too much stirred by actual events in the history of Carolina to perceive that they needed to be colored into fiction. Simms never looked upon his art as a mere contemporary enterprise. He held that "modern romance is the substitute which the people of the present day offer for the ancient epic," and he aspired to be another Homer. The *Partisan* novels are his epic of the Revolution. Marion, "the Agamemnon of these wars," had already become a legend in the popular memory with the help of Weems's fantastic life; Simms exhibited the whole society of South Carolina as engaged in Marion's task.

Simms relied too often upon one plot for his tales—a partisan and a loyalist as rivals in love —and he repeated stock scenes and characters over and over. But he handled warfare with interest and power and he managed to multiply episodes with a rich invention. His epic was decidedly nearer to Froissart than to Homer. He was both sanguinary and sentimental. His women, at least his gentlewomen, seem now almost all of them fragile and colorless. His comedy is successful chiefly in the words and deeds of the gourmand Porgy and such rowdy playboys. Simms could be admirable in dealing with landscapes. His natural descriptions are full of reality and gusto but have agreeably little to say about the "poetry" or "philosophy" of nature.

All the students of Simms's character, as a man and as an author, have found themselves admiring him for his integrity and force and deeply regretting his misfortunes. His misfortunes were not all external, not all the result of the strife which led to the Civil War, not all the consequences of his allegiance to a state which refused to recognize him or admit him to the rank which he deserved. He suffered most from the conflict in him between his nature and the tradition which he inherited. By nature a realist, with the heartiest appetite for general human life seen with his own eyes, he let himself be limited by a romantic tradition which did not call for all his powers and which indeed gave him over to inflation and often to sensationalism. It was in spite of his conscious aims and his deliberate theories that he now and then wrote about convincing characters and situations through vivid pages in a simple, nervous, racy style. The most accomplished and typical man

of letters of the Old South was often, though perhaps not often enough, a good writer judged by any standard.

[The *Border Romances* were collected in an edition of 17 vols. in 1859 and were several times reprinted, but little of his miscellaneous work survives. The standard biography is that by W. P. Trent, *William Gilmore Simms* (1892). Bibliographies are A. S. Salley, Jr., "A Bibliography of William Gilmore Simms," in *Pubs. Sou. Hist. Asso.*, vol. I, Oct. 1897, and "Additional Simms Bibliography," *Ibid.*, vol. XI, Nov. 1907; Oscar Wegelin, *A List of the Separate Writings of William Gilmore Simms of South Carolina* (1906); *The Cambridge Hist. of Am. Literature*, vol. I (1917), pp. 540–44. An excellent critical discussion of his work appears in V. L. Parrington, *Main Currents in Am. Thought*, vol. II (1927), pp. 125–36. An obituary appeared in *Charleston Daily Courier*, June 13, 1870.]

C. V—D.

SIMONTON, CHARLES HENRY (July 11, 1829–Apr. 25, 1904), soldier, jurist, was born in Charleston, S. C., of Scotch-Irish parents, Charles Strong and Elizabeth (Ross) Simonton. His father was a merchant of Charleston and his mother had emigrated from Ireland. Educated at the public high school, the College of Charleston, and South Carolina College (October 1846–December 1849), from which he was graduated with first honor, he served for one year as assistant in the private academy of William J. Rivers, Charleston; meanwhile, he studied law in the office of William Munro and was admitted to the bar in 1851. In 1852 he married Ella, daughter of Thomas W. Glover.

For a brief period (1851–52) Simonton was assistant clerk of the House of Representatives, and from 1858 to 1860 he was a member of that body. An ardent secessionist, he entered the service of his state as captain of the Washington Light Infantry; for a few weeks during the summer of 1861 he was acting adjutant and inspector general of South Carolina. On Feb. 24, 1862, he was mustered into the Confederate service as commander of the Eutaw Battalion, which soon afterwards was consolidated with the 25th Regiment, South Carolina Volunteers, with Simonton as colonel. Until April 1864 he saw service on the islands commanding the approaches to Charleston. He then rejoined his regiment in Virginia, but was again detached and placed in command of Fort Caswell. After the forced evacuation of that post, Simonton was captured at Town Creek, N. C., Feb. 20, 1865. He was sent first to a Washington prison, and then to Fort Delaware, where he remained until Aug. 6, 1865.

He was a member of the South Carolina constitutional convention of 1865 and of the legislature of 1865–66, and on Dec. 18, 1865, was elected speaker of the House to fill an unexpired term. He was chairman of the state Democratic convention of 1868 which declared for a "white man's government," and, the same year, was a member of the Democratic national committee and a delegate to the national convention. In the decisive political campaign of 1876, he was chairman of the important executive committee of Charleston County. With the overthrow of Radical rule, he again became a member of the House, 1877–86; in 1882 he was one of the codifiers of the general statutes of the state.

In 1865 Simonton became the senior partner in a very successful law practice with Theodore G. Barker of Charleston, a connection which continued until he was commissioned judge of the United States district court of South Carolina, in September 1886. This position he occupied until his elevation to the circuit court of appeals, Dec. 19, 1893. He was assigned to the fourth circuit and served until his death. In 1857 he compiled and published, with James Conner, *A Digest of the Equity Reports of the State of South Carolina,* covering decisions of the court of chancery from 1784 to 1856. In 1896 he delivered some lectures before the law school of Richmond College, which were afterwards published as *The Federal Courts, Their Organization, Jurisdiction and Procedure* (1896).

As a lawyer, legislator, and judge, he was distinguished for his calm and even temperament; tact and common-sense and a pleasing personality rather than eloquence or brilliance accounted for his professional advancement. In politics he was essentially conservative and was noted for his ability to effect compromises. Combined with unusual industry and a great love for the law, he had a quick and logical mind with a gift for clear expression. A life-long resident of Charleston he was greatly interested in civic and educational improvements. He died in Philadelphia, survived by his widow and daughter, and was buried in Magnolia Cemetery, Charleston.

[*Who's Who in America,* 1903–05; Edward McCrady and S. A. Ashe, *Cyc. of Eminent and Representative Men of the Carolinas of the Nineteenth Century* (1892), vol. I; U. R. Brooks, *S. C. Bench and Bar,* vol. I (1908); *Memorial Proc. on the Life and Character of Charles Henry Simonton Had in the U. S. Circuit Court of Appeals* (1904); *Relics, Mementos, Etc., of the Washington Light Infantry* (n.d.), catalogue of a display in the W. L. I. armory; *War of the Rebellion: Official Records (Army)*; memorial proceedings of the Washington Light Infantry Veterans (MS.) and memorial resolutions of Camp Sumter No. 2, United Confederate Veterans (MS.) in possession of Simonton's grand-daughter, Caroline S. Alston; *House Journals* of the S. C. General Assembly; *Jour. of the Convention of the People of S. C. Held in Columbia, S. C., Sept. 1865* (1865); *House Misc. Doc. 31,* 44 Cong., 2 Sess., pt. 2, pp. 125–30; 28–119 *Federal Reporter*; *News and Courier* (Charleston), Apr. 26, 1904.]   R. H. W.

SIMONTON, JAMES WILLIAM (Jan. 30, 1823–Nov. 2, 1882), journalist, was born in Co-

lumbia County, N. Y. His family moved to New York City when he was a boy, and there he attended the public schools until the poverty of the family obliged him to become apprenticed to a tailor. He was eager for a journalistic career, however, and at the age of twenty he secured a position as reporter on the *Morning Courier and New-York Enquirer.* For this work he displayed such aptitude that in the next year he was sent by his paper to Washington with Henry Jarvis Raymond [*q.v.*] as congressional correspondent. He remained until 1850, steadily winning the respect and confidence of leading statesmen in the capital. With the opening of California in the fifties he conceived the plan of establishing a Whig paper in San Francisco, and he accordingly set out across the continent with a complete printing-press outfit. On his arrival, finding that he had been anticipated in his purpose, he joined the staff of the *California Daily Courier.* When the *New York Times* was founded in 1851 he became one of the proprietors, and soon afterward returned to Washington to serve as correspondent for the *Times* and for papers in New Orleans, San Francisco, and Detroit. His weekly letters entitled "The History of Legislation," 1855–58, which were almost a political history of these years, won for him wide recognition. In 1857 he performed the most distinguished feat of his career: an exposure in the *Times* for Jan. 6, 1857, of a congressional bill ostensibly granting public lands for the provision of necessary rights of way to the Pacific railroad but actually surrendering a large part of the territory of Minnesota. The congressional investigation that resulted ended in the expulsion of four members from the House of Representatives. In the course of the hearings before the investigating committee Simonton, subpoenaed as a witness, steadfastly refused to disclose the sources of his information, resting upon the principle of journalistic ethics that the origin of facts revealed to a representative of the press in confidence must not be divulged. Piqued by this persistent stand, the committee forthwith excluded him as reporter from the floor of the House.

In 1859 he became part owner of the *San Francisco Evening Bulletin* and afterwards of the *Morning Call.* In 1867 he was recalled to New York as the general agent of the Associated Press, a capacity in which he served fourteen years. During this period he was instrumental in exposing some of the corruption of Grant's administration through the press, but not without arousing bitter attacks upon his own integrity. In 1873 appeared an anonymous pamphlet of forty-seven pages, *One of the Reasons for*

Telegraphic Reform. Power and Tyranny of the Associated Press. The Character of its . . . Manager James W. Simonton . . . Shall He Continue to be the Sole Telegraphic Historian of the Country? Quoting at length from the record of the hearings of the investigating committee in 1857, but interlarding this text with distorted scurrilous headings, this broadside accused Simonton of perjury and of admitting that he had acted as a paid lobbyist. He was called the "sole telegraphic historian of the country" because of the preference which the Associated Press enjoyed in transmission of dispatches through the Western Union Telegraph Company. Says the discreetly anonymous author of his pamphlet, "The object of its publication is to arouse . . . the people generally to the real character of this small and vicious tyrant who prepares for the public the only telegraphic record they can have of the hurrying events of the times . . ." (*One of the Reasons*, p. 4). But apparently the public remained apathetic, for the "tyrant" came through the ordeal unscathed. Retiring in 1881, Simonton purchased a large tract of land in the Sacramento valley and devoted his time to various agricultural and civic enterprises. He died suddenly in the following year on his estate at Napa. About a year and a half before his death he married Minnie Bronson, who was his second wife. He was survived by his widow, two sons, and a daughter.

[*Frank Leslie's Illustrated Newspaper*, Sept. 10, 1859; J. P. Young, *Journalism in Cal.* (1916); Augustus Maverick, *Henry J. Raymond and the N. Y. Press* (1870); E. H. Davis, *Hist. of the N. Y. Times, 1851–1921* (1921); J. M. Lee, *Hist. of Am. Journalism* (1917); *Cong. Globe*, 34 Cong., 3 Sess., pp. 274–77, for land-grants investigation; editorial in *San Francisco Call* and obituary in *N. Y. Times*, Nov. 4, 1882.]

P. K.

SIMPSON, ALBERT BENJAMIN (Dec. 15, 1843–Oct. 29, 1919), clergyman, founder of the Christian and Missionary Alliance, was born at Bayview, Prince Edward Island, of Scottish ancestry, the son of James and Jane (Clark) Simpson. The father, a miller, shipbuilder, and exporter at Bayview and, after 1847, an Ontario farmer, was a Presbyterian elder deeply interested in foreign missions. Sensitive and imaginative, Albert was early molded by the religious training of his home, nine miles from Chatham, Ontario, and at fourteen he determined to enter the ministry. After a few months in the Chatham high school and of study under tutors, he taught for a term, and in 1861 entered Knox College, Toronto, graduating in 1865. On Sept. 12 of that year he was ordained by the Hamilton Presbytery as pastor of Knox Church, Hamilton. In 1874 he accepted a call to the Chestnut Street Church, Louisville,, Ky. In this city he led a united evangelistic campaign and later conducted Sunday evening services of his own in public halls. A deepening of his own spiritual life led to his emphasizing sanctification in his preaching. Dissatisfaction in his congregation followed, and this, together with his desire to reach a larger number with his message, resulted, late in 1879, in his undertaking the pastorate of the Thirteenth Street Church, New York City. For two years he endeavored to lead his new congregation into evangelistic work for neglected people, but in November 1881 he asked to be released, and soon embarked on the independent movement which he was to carry on until his death.

He first held meetings in a hall, preceding his evening services with street preaching. Growing attendance soon compelled him to utilize a theatre and later, Steinway Hall. Within eight years twelve places of worship were used until, in 1889, a tabernacle, with which were connected a book store, the six-story Berachah Home of divine healing, and quarters for his missionary training college, was opened at Eighth Avenue and Fourteenth Street. Here he continued an increasing work until the end of his life, at which time five additional buildings were also in use, at Nyack, N. Y. In 1882 he organized an independent church, especially for people of the middle class who had no church connection; later he added many rescue mission activities to his work.

His outstanding achievement was the founding, in 1887, of the Christian Alliance, which, in 1897, was combined with the International Missionary Alliance, under the name Christian and Missionary Alliance. Of this organization Simpson became president and general superintendent. At his death it reported between 300 and 400 branches and connected churches in the United States and Canada, with about 200 pastors and local superintendents and twenty-five evangelists. In the foreign mission field it was active in sixteen countries. More than 1,000 missionaries had been sent out, who had been educated, with nearly 3,000 other Christian workers, at the Bible and missionary training schools of the Alliance.

A feature of Simpson's ministry was the conducting of conventions, with the aid of numerous associates, throughout the United States and in several foreign lands. These combined characteristics of camp meeting, Bible conference, evangelistic campaign, Second Coming retreats, and missionary conventions. In 1871 he visited Europe for his health; in 1885 he attended a conference in Great Britain on the spiritual life; and beginning in 1893 made many tours which took him to Europe, Asia, Africa, and South America, to visit mission fields and recruit new supporters.

Literary work consumed much of his energy. He published more than seventy religious books, including poems, some of which have had wide and continued circulation. Among the best known were *The Fullness of Jesus* (1886), one of many sermon volumes; *The Christ Life* (1892), the second of four small books explaining the Alliance movement; *The Holy Spirit in the Old and New Testaments* (1899); and *Christ in the Bible* (1888–1909), a sixteen-volume commentary. He also composed words and music of many hymns. Periodicals which he founded and edited included *The Gospel in All Lands* (1881–1903), a pioneer illustrated missionary monthly, and *The Word, Work and World,* a monthly first issued in 1882, which later became *The Alliance Weekly.*

He was no extremist, whatever follies or fanaticisms some of his followers may have fallen into. Though a believer in divine healing, he gave first place to his evangelistic message. He was a man of commanding personality, and his resonant voice and gracious manner gave added force to the intellectual and spiritual power of his preaching and of his spoken prayers. He took little sleep, usually working from twelve to fifteen hours a day. When he died he left no estate. Having voluntarily surrendered all his business affairs to others in 1918, he lived on an allowance from the Alliance. On Sept. 13, 1865, he married Margaret, daughter of John Henry of Toronto, by whom he had six children.

[A. E. Thomson, *The Life of A. B. Simpson* (1920) quotes from a brief manuscript autobiog. of Simpson's earlier years, and includes appraisals of his life by religious leaders; it also gives evidence that his birth was in 1843 rather than in 1844 as stated elsewhere; see also *Who's Who in America,* 1918–19; *N. Y. Times,* Oct. 30, 1919.]   P. P. F.

SIMPSON, EDMUND SHAW (1784–July 31, 1848), actor, theatrical manager, was English born. Although educated for a mercantile life, he had, as he phrased it, " 'a soul above buttons,' " so he "ran away, and took to the stage" (Dunlap, *post,* p. 356). He made his bow in May 1806, with a barn-storming troupe in the village of Towcester, Northamptonshire, England, appearing as the Baron in August F. F. von Kotzebue's then famous play, *The Stranger.* He soon shifted his allegiance to a company at Buckingham, where, he wrote, "we had the pleasure of playing in a larger stable" (*Ibid.,* p. 356). Subsequently he acted at Dover, Margate, and Brighton, and then undertook an engagement at

Dublin, whence he was brought to the United States by Thomas Abthorpe Cooper and Stephen Price [*qq.v.*], managers of the Park Theatre, New York. His American début occurred at that house on Oct. 25, 1809. On this occasion, as Harry Dornton in *The Road to Ruin* by Thomas Holcroft, and later in such rôles as Jack Absolute in *The Rivals* and Joseph Surface in *The School for Scandal* he gave convincing evidence of distinct gifts for high comedy. He was at once warmly received by the playgoers and praised by the critics, who pronounced him "easy, natural, and graceful," with a "modulant and sonorous" voice (*Ramblers' Mag., post,* pp. 103, 104) and a "glowing and animated expression of . . . countenance" (Odell, *post,* II, 351). That he displayed ability also in other departments of the theatre is seen in his appointment as "acting manager" by 1812 (*Ibid.,* p. 387), and some half dozen years later he replaced Cooper as Price's partner. Because of the latter's frequent absences abroad much of the burden of management fell upon Simpson, but, despite a disastrous fire at the Park on May 24, 1820, and increasing competition, he kept the theatre in a prosperous state for several years. The popularity of the house was greatly enhanced by the many celebrities of the British stage brought over by the partners for brief starring visits, and by the introduction of Italian opera to New York in 1825 through the engagement of the admirable Garcia company.

Perhaps because of permanent lameness, resulting from a serious stage accident in December 1827, and because of his waning popularity as a player, Simpson practically withdrew from acting about 1833 and confined himself largely to his duties as director. As a result of the panic of 1837 and of the enterprise of young and progressive competitors, the fortunes of the Park and its managers declined so much that when Simpson became sole lessee of the theatre upon the death of Price in 1840 he found himself master of a tottering house. For some years he struggled on doggedly and not always hopelessly, thanks to the efforts of a good company. But it was a losing battle. His methods were outmoded, the building was in an advanced state of dilapidation because of the proprietors' niggardliness, and the public had formed the habit of going elsewhere. On June 5, 1848, the ruined manager surrendered, forfeiting his interests to Thomas Sowerby Hamblin [*q.v.*] of the Bowery Theatre for a small annuity. Less than two months later he died—of a broken heart, his contemporaries believed. He left a widow—the former actress Julia Elizabeth Jones, whom he married Mar. 9, 1820—and several children, one of them Edward Simpson [*q.v.*]. For their relief a highly profitable benefit was held at the Park on Dec. 7, in which many leading actors of the day participated. This was followed by five other dramatic benefits in the city, indisputable testimony to the high esteem in which Simpson was held by his fellow-townsmen for his long years of able public service in the theatre, his valiant struggle against adversity, and his unblemished character.

[William Dunlap, *A Hist. of the Am. Theatre* (1832); G. C. D. Odell, *Annals of the N. Y. Stage,* vols. II, III, IV, V (1927–31); T. A. Brown, *Hist. of the Am. Stage* (1870) and *A Hist. of the N. Y. Stage* (1903), vol. I; J. N. Ireland, *Records of the N. Y. Stage,* vols. I, II (1866–67); *Ramblers' Mag.,* and *N. Y. Theatrical Reg.,* vol. I (1809–10?); Joseph Cowell, *Thirty Years Passed Among the Players in England and America* (1844); newspaper notices in the *Albion* (N. Y.), June 10, Aug. 5, 1848, and in *Evening Post,* (N. Y.), Aug. 1, 1848; date of marriage from records of Grace Church, N. Y. City.]   O. S. C.

SIMPSON, EDWARD (Mar. 3, 1824–Dec. 1, 1888), naval officer, was born in New York City, son of Edmund Shaw Simpson [*q.v.*] and Julia Elizabeth (Jones) Simpson. The mother was of Welsh parentage, the father an Englishman who had come to New York in his twenties and was for years manager of the Park Theatre. The son entered the navy as midshipman on Feb. 11, 1840, served five years in the Brazil and Mediterranean Squadrons, and after nine months' study at the United States Naval Academy, then just established at Annapolis, was made passed midshipman, July 1846. Through the Mexican War he was in the small steamer *Vixen* "wherever a shot was fired on the east coast" (Harrington, *post*), including the attacks on Tabasco, Tampico, and Túxpan, and the siege of Vera Cruz, where the *Vixen* made a celebrated reconnaissance under the guns of the fort, remaining there till ordered back by Perry. During the next decade he was in the coast survey, 1848–49 and 1855–56; in the *Congress,* Brazil Squadron, 1850–53; instructor in gunnery, Naval Academy, 1853–54; and after promotion to lieutenant in 1855, in the *Portsmouth,* Asiatic Squadron, participating under Andrew Hull Foote [*q.v.*] in the capture of the barrier forts below Canton. From September 1858 to May 1862 he had charge of ordnance instruction at the Naval Academy, being made first head of that department in 1860. His *Treatise on Ordnance and Naval Gunnery* (1859) was long an academy textbook. After promotion to lieutenant commander in 1862 and another year at the academy as commandant of midshipmen, he secured sea service in command of the *Wabash,* and

shortly afterward of the ironclad *Passaic,* which figured in the attacks on Forts Wagner and Sumter and in the whole arduous 1863 campaign off Charleston, S. C. He commanded the steamer *Isonomia* on the southeast coast, May–December 1864, and subsequently joined the West Gulf Squadron, with promotion to commander, March 1865, acting as fleet captain under Rear Admiral Henry Knox Thatcher in operations below Mobile until after its capitulation. His generous, kindly nature is illustrated by his loan of $100 to surrendered Confederate officers, his former students, with the words "Repay it when you are able; never, if not" (Harrington, *post*). His post-bellum sea commands included the *Mohican* and *Mohongo* in the Pacific, 1866–68, *Franklin* and *Wabash* in the Atlantic, 1873–74, and *Omaha* in the south Pacific, 1875–77. More noteworthy, in view of his eminence in the field of ordnance, were his shore assignments, especially as assistant chief of the ordnance bureau, 1869–70. In 1873 he published his *Report on a Naval Mission to Europe Especially Devoted to the Material and Construction of Artillery,* in two volumes. Made captain in 1870, commodore in 1878, and rear admiral in 1884, he commanded the New London, Conn., station, 1878–80, and the League Island navy yard, 1880–83. He was president of the gun foundry board, 1883–84, for which he wrote a report of a mission abroad (*House Executive Document 97,* 48 Cong., 1 Sess.); president of the naval advisory board, 1884–85; and president of the board of inspection and survey from October 1885 until his retirement Mar. 3, 1886. His publications include "A Proposed Armament for the Navy" (*The Proceedings of the United States Naval Institute,* vol. VII, 1881), "The Navy and its Prospects of Rehabilitation" (*Ibid.,* vol. XII, 1886), and *Modern Ships of War* (1888), with Sir Edward Reed. His high service reputation is evidenced by his selection as president of the United States Naval Institute, 1886–88, and of the association of naval academy graduates from its organization until his death. His wife was Mary Ann, daughter of Gen. Charles Sterett Ridgely, whom he married at Oak Ridge, Md., in 1853, and by whom he had a son, who became a rear admiral, and four daughters. His death from Bright's disease occurred at Washington; he was buried in Cypress Hills Cemetery, Long Island.

[L. H. Hamersly, *Records of Living Officers . . . U. S. Navy* (4th ed., 1890); obituaries in *Army and Navy Jour.,* Dec. 8, 1888, and *Evening Star* (Washington, D. C.), Dec. 1, 1888; papers in the possession of Simpson's grandson, E. R. Simpson, Ruxton, Md., including a biog. sketch in MS. by Rear Admiral P. F. Harrington.]   A. W.

SIMPSON, JAMES HERVEY (Mar. 9, 1813–Mar. 2, 1883), soldier, engineer, author, was born in New Brunswick, N. J., the son of John Neely and Mary (Brunson) Simpson. After a common-school education he entered the United States Military Academy, West Point, N. Y., at fifteen and graduated creditably in 1832. Commissioned in the artillery, he served as aide to Gen. Henry Lawrence Eustis during the Seminole War, 1837–38, and was in action at Locha-Hatchee. In 1838 he was transferred to the topographical engineers, and during the following ten years was engaged in engineering projects in the East and the South. In 1849 he was in charge of the exploration of a route from Fort Smith, Ark., to Santa Fé, N. Mex. (*Report from the Secretary of War Communicating the Report and Map of the Route from Fort Smith, Ark., to Santa Fé, N. Mex.*, 1850), serving as chief topographical engineer, Department of New Mexico. About this time, too, he reconnoitered a route from Santa Fé to the Navajo Indian country, which he reported in *Journal of a Military Reconnaissance from Santa Fé, N. Mex., to the Navajo Country* (1852). He was promoted captain, Mar. 3, 1853, and served five years on road construction in Minnesota and two years on coast survey duty. In 1858 he accompanied the Utah Expedition, and submitted a valuable report on a new route from Salt Lake City to the Pacific coast.

With the outbreak of the Civil War he attained the rank of major and for a few months was chief topographical engineer, Department of the Shenandoah, when he was commissioned colonel, 4th New Jersey Volunteers. With his regiment he saw service in the Peninsular campaign, and was engaged at Westpoint, Va., and at Gaines's Mill, where he was taken prisoner. After being exchanged he resigned his volunteer commission on Aug. 27, 1862, and served as chief topographical engineer and chief engineer, Department of the Ohio, 1862–63. Until the end of the war he was in general charge of fortifications and engineering projects in Kentucky. For faithful and meritorious services during the war, he was brevetted colonel and brigadier-general, Mar. 13, 1865. He became chief engineer, Department of the Interior, 1865–67, and was charged with general direction and inspection of the Union Pacific Railroad (*Report on the Union Pacific Railroad and Its Branches*, 1865), as well as of all government wagon-roads. He was promoted colonel of engineers on Mar. 7, 1867. His subsequent active military service covered road construction, river and harbor improvements, and lighthouse supervision in the

South and the Middle West. At his own request he retired on Mar. 31, 1880, and made his home in St. Paul, Minn., where he died of pneumonia, and where he was buried with military honors. He was married first to Jane Champlin, and second, in 1871, to Elizabeth Sophia (Borup) Champlin, widow of Raymond Champlin. He was survived by his wife, two daughters, and two adopted daughters. He published a number of interesting reports, descriptive of his explorations in the West (listed in *Centennial of the United States Military Academy*, 1904, vol. II, p. 356), including *Route From Fort Smith, Ark., to Santa Fé, N. Mex.* (1850), *The Shortest Route to California* (1869), *Coronado's March in Search of the Seven Cities of Cibola* (1871), and *Exploration Across the Great Basin of the Territory of Utah* (1876).

[G. W. Cullum, *Biog. Reg. Officers and Grads. U. S. Mil. Acad.* (3rd ed., 1891), vol. I; *Fourteenth Ann. Reunion Assoc. Grads. U. S. Mil. Acad.* (1883); C. L. Andrews, *Hist. of St. Paul, Minn.* (1890); obituaries in *Army and Navy Jour.*, Mar. 17, 1883; *N. Y. Times, Daily Globe* (St. Paul), Mar. 3, 1883.]   C. D. R.

SIMPSON, JERRY (Mar. 31, 1842–Oct. 23, 1905), congressman from Kansas, was born in the old Scotch settlement in Westmoreland County, New Brunswick, Canada, the son of Joseph Simpson. His mother's maiden name was Washburn. He was probably named Jeremiah. His father, a sawmill owner and sailor, decided in 1848 to remove the family to Upper Canada, and, though the journey was interrupted near Syracuse, N. Y., by 1852 they were established east of the Saint Clair River. Probably they subsequently removed to Indiana. The boy had almost no formal education, but home influence and books in part compensated. At the age of fourteen he became cook on a lake boat and ultimately became captain. At the opening of the Civil War he enlisted for three months in Company A, 12th Illinois Infantry. After 1869 his home was in Porter County, Ind., where he met Jane Cape, a native of Cumberlandshire, England, whom he married on Oct. 12, 1870, at Buffalo, N. Y. About 1879 he abandoned the Lakes for a farm and sawmill near Holton, Kan.; after five years he took advantage of increased prices to sell out and invested his savings, about $15,000, in a cattle ranch near Medicine Lodge, Kan. His hopes for speedy profits from this new "boom" were ended, when an especially severe winter wiped out his herd, and he found himself under mortgage and without resources. He was glad to accept appointment as marshal of Medicine Lodge at forty dollars a month. In a sense, his prosperity, his disaster, and his courageous efforts at recovery were typical of the big majority of his fellows. Ruinous prices made the mortgage burden impossibly large, and "booming" gave way to despair; in 1888–89, the Farmers' Alliance swept through the state until, with its allies, it numbered a third of the voters, and in 1890 as the People's Party it entered politics. Simpson was named for Congress from the seventh district.

He was prepared to lead such a movement. Originally a Lincoln Republican, he had deserted that party to work for Peter Cooper and his monetary program. He had followed his principles into the newer Union Labor party and was twice defeated for the state legislature, 1886 and 1888, in spite of Democratic support. In this campaign for Congress, his wit and clever, telling illustrations were very effective before audiences that accepted agrarian doctrines and needed only the emotional stimulus to break past allegiances. A reporter twisted a statement to mean that, in contrast to his wealthy banker opponent who wore silk socks, he, Simpson, wore none, and the name "Sockless Jerry" was his for life. The Populist state ticket was narrowly defeated in 1890, but Simpson was elected. In 1892 the Democrats were eager to draw Kansas from the Republican presidential column, and their indorsement gave victory to the state ticket; he was again elected. In 1894 the allies divided, and he went down with his ticket in defeat. National fusion in 1896 meant the practical absorption of the Populists by the Democrats, and, after his reëlection of that year, he called himself a Demo-Populist. In 1898 he was defeated for the second time by Chester I. Long, whom he had twice defeated, and, after a vain attempt to obtain Populist convention indorsement for senator, he retired to private life. He accepted Populist doctrine completely and combined with it a belief in the single tax. In Congress he delivered few speeches and proposed few bills; his weapon was a shrewd question or witty comment directed at effort that he thought false or insincere, and he was a feared and respected opponent. He advocated a paper money system and accepted free silver coinage as only a step. His belief in simple democracy and his monetary program are the two consistent threads through his career. On the Spanish War he was uncertain, but he was an ardent opponent of army expansion and imperialism. After retirement he lived a short time in Wichita and Kansas City. On May 8, 1899, he began to publish *Jerry Simpson's Bayonet,* which he continued to publish until Sept. 17, 1900. In 1902, partly on account of his health, he removed to Roswell, N. Mex., where he associated with a land and colonization

corporation. His health grew steadily worse, and he returned to Wichita, where he died and was buried. He was survived by a wife and one son.

[A. L. Diggs, *The Story of Jerry Simpson* (copr. 1908), a slight memoir by a co-worker assisted by Simpson's wife; *Biog. Directory Am. Cong.* (1928); T. A. McNeal, *When Kansas was Young* (1922); Hamlin Garland, "The Alliance Wedge in Congress," *Arena,* Mar. 1892; S. J. Buck, *The Agrarian Crusade* (1920); J. D. Hicks, *The Populist Revolt* (1931); *Leavenworth Times,* Oct. 24, 1905.]   R. C. M.

SIMPSON, JOHN ANDREW (July 4, 1871– Mar. 15, 1934), farm leader, was born near Salem, Nebr., the son of William J. and Sarah Catharine (Cornell) Simpson; his father died when John was seven years old. He attended the district school and later the Auburn high school, where he completed the four years' course in one year and graduated as the honor student of his class. After some teaching he entered the University of Kansas, from which he received the degree of LL.B. in 1896. On June 21 of the same year he married Millie Berlet.

He began the practice of law in Auburn, but the political upheaval of the nineties brought him into the ranks of the Populist party and in 1897 he was appointed accountant in the state auditor's office in Lincoln, a position which he held for four years. He then resumed the practice of law in Auburn, but within a year the pioneer spirit that led his father and mother to move westward impelled him to go to Oklahoma, which had been opened to settlement, and in 1901 he drew a claim at the El Reno drawing. Taking possession of his land, which lay near the town of Alfalfa in Caddo County, for some nine years he engaged in farming and also became a country banker. He was a member of the Oklahoma legislature in 1915–17, the only official position he ever held in public life, except that of membership on the school board.

About this time he became interested in the Farmers' Union, joining that organization in Custer County, Okla., in 1916. The following year he became state president and held this office until 1930, during which period the membership increased from 500 to 200,000, and more than 200 cooperative institutions were established with headquarters and warehouses in Oklahoma City valued at $100,000. Meanwhile, he founded and edited the *Oklahoma Union Farmer.* In 1930 he was elected president of the Farmers' Educational and Cooperative Union of America, which office he held until his death. His twenty years of farm leadership were characterized by bitter controversies, activity in political campaigns, attacks on the national administrations, and numerous stumping tours. He advocated violence in the form of farm strikes and holidays when such measures were deemed necessary. He was a caustic critic of the Hoover administration; advocated the election of Smith to the presidency in 1928; was one of Franklin Roosevelt's earliest supporters for that office in the Southwest; and was mentioned for the secretaryship of agriculture in the Roosevelt cabinet. He was a zealous champion of the enactment of a law to guarantee cost of production prices for farm products consumed in the country, and stressed the impossibility of regulating the production of 30,000,000 farm occupants. He maintained that the government should treat agriculture as it treats industry, and that it should refinance the farmer's mortgage indebtedness on as favorable terms as it accords to industry. He urged currency inflation, the remonetization of silver, and paper money. The national Farmers' Union, under his influence, put forward the Swank-Thomas bill, which provided that the farmer should be guaranteed cost of production plus a reasonable profit for his products consumed in the home market; the Frazier-Lemke bill, to refinance the farmer at 1½ per cent.; and the Wheeler free coinage bill. To the furtherance of these measures he devoted practically all his time. He died in Washington, survived by his wife, two sons, and four daughters. After his death a collection of excerpts from his speeches and writings, *The Militant Voice of Agriculture* (1934), was published.

[*Who's Who in America*, 1932–33; *N. Y. Times*, Mar. 16, 1934; *N. Y. Herald Tribune*, Mar. 16, 1934; *Cong. Record*, Apr. 2, 1934; *Okla. Union Farmer*, Feb. 1, Mar. 1, Apr. 1 and 15, 1934; data supplied by Mrs. John A. Simpson of Oklahoma City.]   L. B. S.

SIMPSON, MATTHEW (June 21, 1811–June 18, 1884), bishop of the Methodist Episcopal Church, was the son of James Simpson, who at the time of Matthew's birth was manufacturing weaver's reeds and running a store in Cadiz, Ohio, of which town he had been one of the first settlers. His widowed mother had migrated with her family from Ireland to the United States in 1793 and settled in Huntington County, Pa., whence her sons later moved westward. James died when Matthew, the youngest of three children, was a year old, and the latter was brought up by his mother, Sarah, a native of New Jersey, daughter of Jeremiah Tingley. He had little schooling, but, naturally inclined to books, mastered with practically no other aid the ordinary school subjects, German, and Latin; acquired some knowledge of Greek during a summer term at an academy in Cadiz; and spent two months at Madison College, Unionville, Pa., being unable financially to stay longer. He also learned something of the printing business in the office of an uncle who was editor of the county paper, of the law by frequenting the court of which another uncle, Matthew Simpson, was a judge, and of public affairs from the same uncle, who was for ten years a member of the Ohio Senate. He supported himself by reed-making, by copying in the office of the county court, of which a third uncle was clerk, and by teaching. In 1830 he began the study of medicine under Dr. James McBean of Cadiz and after three years qualified as a practitioner.

In the meantime, having been reared under strong Methodist influences, he had become active in religious work and had been licensed to preach. Deciding at length to devote himself to the ministry, he was received into the Pittsburgh Conference on trial in 1834, and in 1836 admitted into full connection. On Nov. 3 of the preceding year he had married Ellen Holmes Verner, daughter of James Verner of Pittsburgh. On the Cadiz circuit, in the neighborhood where he had been reared, a tall, plain-faced, somewhat ungainly and diffident young man, he began a career of swiftly increasing responsibility and prominence which culminated in his being the best known and most influential Methodist of his day in the United States, a counselor of statesmen, and a public speaker of international reputation. His promise was soon recognized and after a year on the Cadiz circuit he was stationed at Pittsburgh (1835–36), and then at Williamsport (Monongahela). Elected professor of natural sciences in Allegheny College in 1837, he entered the educational field and in 1839 became president of Indiana Asbury University, now De Pauw, Greencastle, Ind., chartered in 1837. During the nine years he served in this capacity he did valuable pioneer work in the development of the institution. Invitations to the presidency of Northwestern University, Dickinson College, and Wesleyan University, Middletown, Conn., were later declined.

As a member of the General Conferences of 1844 and 1848 he became prominent in the deliberations of his denomination. The General Conference of 1848 elected him editor of the *Western Christian Advocate*. Through this medium his frank and forceful utterances on public questions, especially those relating to slavery, attracted wide attention and brought him to the favorable notice of Salmon P. Chase. A delegate to the General Conference of 1852, he was by that body elected bishop. His patriotism was as deep and sincere as his religious convictions and during the Civil War he was a tower of strength for the Union cause. Both his knowledge and his oratorical powers were employed in behalf of the Union, and his address on "The Future of Our Country," delivered in many places, had great effect on large audiences. Already known to Secretary Chase, he soon stood high in the esteem of Secretary Stanton, and was consulted by both Stanton and Lincoln. He preached a notable sermon in the House of Representatives the day after Lincoln's second inauguration and delivered the eulogy at his burial in Springfield, Ill. His episcopal residence was first Pittsburgh, later Evanston, Ill., and finally Philadelphia, but his duties carried him all over the United States, to Mexico, Canada, and Europe. In 1857 he was a delegate to the British Wesleyan Conference, Liverpool, attended the Conference of the Evangelical Alliance at Berlin, and visited the Holy Land. In 1870 and again in 1875 he made official visits to Europe, and in 1881 he delivered the opening sermon at the Ecumenical Methodist Conference, London. His address in Exeter Hall at a meeting in commemoration of President Garfield, presided over by James Russell Lowell, evoked an unusual response from an audience of three thousand, the most of whom were English.

The high place which he held both officially and in popular esteem was due to the character of the man himself, to a well balanced if not brilliant endowment, and particularly to his extraordinary power over audiences. He was not preëminent as a theologian, as a scholar, or as an innovator, but he was well informed and combined conservatism, open-mindedness, practical wisdom, ability to discern the adjustment conditions called for, and unadulterated religious devotion in an exceptional degree. While remaining strictly orthodox, he was sympathetic toward science and in general progressive. He early favored higher education for Methodist ministers, and was influential in the movement to secure lay representation in the General Conference. Judged by the effect upon the hearers, few public speakers of the day were his equal. Having remarkable facility of expression and an imagination of wide sweep, he took great subjects and portrayed them on a big canvas with a fervid evangelical earnestness. His aim was not to instruct but to persuade. Thoroughly sincere, he felt profoundly the truths which he expounded, so that his preaching had in it the note of testimony. People believed in him and surrendered themselves to him. Such was his power over them that frequently large numbers rose to their feet, clapped their hands, laughed, or

wept. Too busy with many things for much literary work, he nevertheless wrote *A Hundred Years of Methodism* (1876) and edited the *Cyclopædia of Methodism* (1878). His *Lectures on Preaching Delivered before the Theological Department of Yale College* was published in 1879. After his death *Sermons* (1885), from shorthand reports by G. R. Crooks, appeared.

[H. A. Simpson, *Early Records of the Simpson Families* (1927) ; *Minutes of the Annual Conferences of the M. E. Church* (1884) : E. A. Smith, *Allegheny—A Century of Education, 1815–1915* (1916) ; G. R. Crooks, *The Life of Bishop Matthew Simpson* (1890) ; E. M. Wood, *The Peerless Orator* (1909) ; C. T. Wilson, *Matthew Simpson* (1929) ; *National Mag.,* Oct. 1855 ; *Meth. Quart. Rev.,* Jan. 1885 ; *Zion's Herald* and *Western Christian Advocate,* June 25, 1884. Many of Simpson's MSS. have been deposited in the Lib. of Cong.]
H. E. S.

SIMPSON, MICHAEL HODGE (Nov. 15, 1809–Dec. 21, 1884), capitalist, manufacturer, inventor, was born in Newburyport, Mass., the son of Paul Simpson and his wife, Abigail (Johnson), widow of J. S. Hodge; his father was a sea-captain who became a merchant. Michael was educated in the schools of Newburyport until he was fifteen, when he went to Boston and entered the employ of a shipping firm. In the small ventures clerks were allowed to make, he and a fellow employee named Coffin were so successful that before either was twenty-one they owned one-third of the cargo of a ship bound for Calcutta and had established their own business. Much of it consisted in the importing of wool from South America. This wool was cheap but not suitable for spinning because of the dirt and burrs embedded in it, and constant efforts were being made to devise machinery for combing out these foreign materials. By 1831 Simpson had bought out his partners, and later he disposed of the business to the New England Worsted Company, of Saxonville, Mass.

His contacts with this concern brought the mechanical problems of manufacture more directly to his attention, and in 1833 he happened to see a machine for burring wool designed by a French inventor named Samuel Couillard. This he bought and improved, patenting the improvements July 7, 1837. The English rights to it he then sold for ten thousand pounds. The panic of 1837 threw the Saxonville mills into the hands of their creditors, of whom he was one, and he became their agent, commencing, in 1839, the manufacture of bunting, in addition to blanket and worsted yarns. On July 4, 1848, at the inauguration of work on the Washington Monument at the capital, he presented the Washington National Monument Society with what is said to have been the first American bunting flag made in the United States. The mills did not prosper, however, and so Simpson bought a two-thirds interest and assumed their management and most of the financial responsibility for their operation. With machinery improved or invented by him they gradually became extremely profitable, and in 1854 he bought a carpet factory in Troy, N. Y., moved it to Roxbury, Mass., equipped it with machinery that gave it an advantage over its competitors till the patents had expired, and conducted it in conjunction with the Saxonville mills. As an employer of labor he was remarkably considerate and generous, allowing the grounds of his extensive Saxonville estate to be used as a park by his employees, and on one occasion, when the mills were burned down, paying wages to all of his force who applied for work, even when there was nothing for some of them to do.

He gave liberally to educational and civic enterprises. He contributed $50,000 in 1880 to build a jetty at the mouth of the Merrimac River; to Wellesley College he donated in 1881 an infirmary, Simpson Cottage; he made by far the largest donation towards the building of an addition to the Newburyport Public Library, which was opened in 1882 and called The Simpson Annex; he also gave sums for the construction of roads, the sprinkling of the streets in summer, and other public purposes. He was married, Dec. 24, 1832, to Elizabeth Kilham, of Boston, by whom he had several children; after her death, he married, June 1, 1882, Evangeline Marrs, of Saxonville. He died in Boston.

[*Boston Morning Jour.*, and *Boston Post*, Dec. 22, 1884; J. J. Currier, *Hist. of Newburyport, Mass., 1764–1909* (2 vols., 1905–09); A. H. Cole, *The Am. Wool Manufacture* (1926), vol. I; J. L. Hayes, *Am. Textile Machinery* (1879); M. D. Leggett, *Subject-Matter Index of Patents for Inventions Issued by the U. S. Patent Office ... 1790 to 1873* (1874).]
            S. G.

SIMPSON, STEPHEN (July 24, 1789–Aug. 17, 1854), author and editor, was born, lived, and died in Philadelphia. Following the occupation of his father, George Simpson, who had been an official in the Bank of North America, the Bank of the United States, and Girard's Bank, Stephen became a note clerk in the second Bank of the United States and afterwards cashier of Girard's Bank. His father had been assistant commissary-general in the Revolution; Stephen enlisted for the War of 1812 and distinguished himself at the battle of New Orleans, at the same time forming an admiration for Andrew Jackson which motivated much of his political writing a decade later. After the war, with his brother-in-law Tobias Watkins, he founded the *Portico,* Baltimore, a miscellany discussing every topic

from Russian literature to nervous diseases, of which he was joint editor from January 1816 to June 1817. The financial failure of this magazine did not deter him from becoming co-proprietor with John Conrad in 1822 of the weekly *Columbian Observer,* Philadelphia, in which Jackson was as extravagantly praised as Calhoun was extravagantly condemned. He wrote for the *Aurora* and contributed an essay on "The Waywardness of Genius" to *The Philadelphia Book; or Specimens of Metropolitan Literature* (1836). He was the first, but unsuccessful, candidate for Congress of the initial political organization of workers in the United States, the Workingmen's Party of Philadelphia; paradoxically, for he was opposed to several leading principles of the old Hamiltonians, he was at the same time (1830) the candidate of the Federal Party.

The chief expression of his views is to be found in *The Working Man's Manual: a New Theory of Political Economy on the Principle of Production the Source of Wealth* (Philadelphia, 1831). This was written at the time of his political candidacy, and is informed by the philosophy of Robert Owen as made specific in the advocacies of Robert Dale Owen and Frances Wright [*qq.v.*]. It owed much also to the nationalist economic demands of Mathew Carey [*q.v.*] and others among the Philadelphia protectionist writers. Simpson's "American Theory" discountenanced "the profound dissertations of [European] writers bewildered in the fogs of Gothic institutions," and gave place "to the elucidation of obvious principles, of practical utility or equitable application" (p. 4). In holding that "all wealth is produced by labor" (p. 67) he borrowed from Adam Smith, but in amplifying the doctrine to the contention that labor should therefore receive the whole of its production he placed himself among the important anticipators of Marx. The chief filchers of labor's just rewards were the fund holders and the land monopolists, upheld by outworn legal sanctions. He wanted, instead of "personal parties," political division according to economic allegiance. "The party of the producers," he maintained, opposing "the party of stockholders and capitalists" and gaining the ascendency, "could not fail to shed a genial, and prosperous beam upon the whole society. Such a party would merely exhibit the interest of society, concentrating for the true fulfilment of the original terms of the social compact" (p. 23). Simpson resembled in America the Chartists in England. He desired to improve the condition of labor through parliamentary means. "Let the producers . . . but once fully comprehend their injuries, and fully appreciate their strength at the polls," he said, "and the present oppressive system will vanish" (p. 20). Political action by the workingmen, however, required a system of free public education. Simpson resented the economic exploitation of workers hardly less than the cultural patronage to which they were treated by the rich and learned, although, unlike Frances Wright, he opposed literary education for women because he thought it would take them from the circle of the family and make them labor competitors of men. Simpson was an economic optimist, as befitted one viewing the productivity of a new country; it was not the niggardliness of nature, but the injustice of social institutions which held down the standard of living. He espoused the protective tariff to encourage manufactures. In an appendix to his *Manual* he retreated from his former objections to the United States Bank and its notes, thus losing influence among the working men whom he had led. In 1832 he published a *Biography of Stephen Girard* which displayed the financier's foibles with more humor than hostility, and the following year issued *The Lives of George Washington and Thomas Jefferson: with a Parallel* (1833); the biographies contained in the latter volume were reprinted separately in 1844.

[Besides the publications mentioned above, see J. R. Commons and others, *Hist. of Labour in the U. S.* (1918), vol. I; Henry Simpson, *The Lives of Eminent Philadelphians, Now Deceased* (1859); F. L. Mott, *A Hist. of Am. Mags.* (1930); *Pennsylvania* (Phila.), Aug. 19, 1854.]   B. M.

SIMPSON, WILLIAM DUNLAP (Oct. 27, 1823–Dec. 26, 1890), governor and chief justice of South Carolina, was born in Laurens District, S. C. He was the son of Elizabeth (Saterwhite) and John W. Simpson, a successful physician, and the grandson of John Simpson, a Scotch-Irish Presbyterian who emigrated from Belfast, Ireland, to Laurens shortly after the American Revolution and became a wealthy planter and merchant. After studying at the Laurens academy he entered South Carolina College, now the University of South Carolina, and graduated in 1843. He entered the Harvard Law School but withdrew after a single session and returned home, where he continued his studies in the office of Henry Young. Admitted to the bar in 1846, he became Young's partner and in March 1847 married his daughter Jane. They had eight children. He was successful in law and was elected to the state legislature. Appointed an aide to M. L. Bonham [*q.v.*] at the secession of South Carolina, he participated in the siege of Fort Sumter and the first battle of Manassas. He aided Samuel McGowan [*q.v.*] in the organization of the 14th South Carolina Volunteers, which became a part of Gregg's Brigade, became a major and subsequently lieutenant-colonel, and fought in important battles in Virginia. He was slightly wounded at Germantown, and the bow of his cravat was shot away at Cold Harbor. His popularity among the soldiers and the men at home led to his election in 1863 to the Confederate Congress, in which he served until the end of the war.

After the war he practised law at Laurens with his brother, John Wistar Simpson. In 1868 he was a delegate to the National Democratic Convention and was elected to the federal Congress but was denied a seat on the grounds that he was disqualified under the Fourteenth Amendment. In 1876 he became Democratic candidate for lieutenant-governor and accompanied Wade Hampton [*q.v.*] on a memorable tour of the counties of South Carolina. As the presiding officer of the Senate he refused to take the oath of office a second time at the behest of the Republican majority of the Senate, and he engineered the organization of that body in such a way as to obtain a Democratic majority. In 1878 the Democrats obtained his reëlection without serious opposition. Immediately thereafter he became acting governor as a result of the illness of Governor Hampton and became governor, when Hampton resigned at the beginning of the following year to become United States senator. In his messages to the legislature he urged educational progress, and he aided in the creation of a state agricultural bureau (for his principal address as governor see *Journal of the House of Representatives of S. C. . . . 1879,* 1880, pp. 11–30). In August 1880, two months before his term as governor expired, he resigned to become chief justice of the state and served until his death. Although well trained in the knowledge of adjudicated cases he sought also to analyze the underlying principles of the law. During his service on the supreme court his convictions and example were important in upholding the constitutional provision that forbade circuit judges to instruct juries as to their own opinions on the facts in any case. His career was like that of many other Southerners of his class and age. Well born and handsome, pious and patriotic, competent but not brilliant, he accepted the opinions of his class and justified the series of honors conferred upon him because of conscientious service.

[*Cyc. of Eminent and Representative Men of the Carolinas* (1892), vol. I; J. F. J. Caldwell, *The Hist. of . . . "Gregg's" and subsequently . . . "McGowan's Brigade"* (1866); "Tribute of Respect," *33 S. C. Reports,* app. pp. 613–27; *Confederate Military Hist.* (1899) by C. A. Evans, vol. V, pp. 841–45; *News and Courier* (Charleston), Dec. 27, 1890.]

F. B. S.

SIMPSON, WILLIAM KELLY (Apr. 10, 1855–Feb. 6, 1914), laryngologist, was born at Hudson, N. Y., the youngest of nine children of George Nicholas and Caroline (McCann) Simpson. He attended school at Hudson and at the Episcopal Academy (later the Cheshire School), Cheshire, Conn., and graduated from Cornell in 1876 with the degree of B. A. and from the College of Physicians and Surgeons, New York, in 1880. After serving as interne in the Presbyterian Hospital until 1882, he became a specialist in laryngology through the influence of Dr. Clinton Wagner [*q.v.*], the celebrated laryngologist. On Oct. 25, 1882, he married Anna Farrand of Hudson, N. Y., who with a daughter and a son survived him. He early identified himself with dispensary and hospital practice. He was attending surgeon to the Northern Dispensary, and to the throat department of the Presbyterian Hospital and of the New York Eye and Ear Infirmary. As attending physician to the outdoor department of the New York Foundling Asylum, he became associated with Dr. Joseph O'Dwyer [*q.v.*] in his work on intubation; he was among the first after O'Dwyer to advocate the method in the application of intubation to chronic stenosis of the larynx. He was assistant surgeon to the Metropolitan Throat Hospital and instructor in laryngology in the New York Post-Graduate Medical School, in association with Dr. Wagner, 1885–87. He became an assistant in the throat department of the Vanderbilt Clinic in 1887, chief of clinic and instructor in 1898, and in 1904 succeeded Dr. George Morewood Lefferts [*q.v.*] as professor of laryngology at the College of Physicians and Surgeons, Columbia University, a position he held until his death. He was consulting laryngologist to a number of hospitals, a fellow of the American Laryngological Association, of the New York Academy of Medicine, and of the Hospital Graduates' Club, and secretary of the executive committee of the Congress of American Physicians and Surgeons.

An excellent practitioner and lecturer, his contributions to the literature of his specialty were of distinct value. The most important are *Sequelae of Syphilis of the Larynx* (1896), "A Study of . . . Intubation in Chronic Stenosis of the Larynx" (*Transactions of the American Laryngological Association,* 1901), "A Case of Laryngeal Diphtheria in an Adult" (*Ibid.,* 1905), "Stenosis of the Trachea" (*Ibid.,* 1906), "Laryngeal Stenosis in the Adult" (*Ibid.,* 1908), and

"Two Cases of White Exudative Laryngeal Growths" (*Ibid.,* 1912). He was a lover of music and excelled as a vocalist; he was a leading member and one of the best tenors of the Musurgia Society for many years. He was a man of attractive personality and highly social nature.

[*Who's Who in America,* 1914–15; *The Coll. of Physicians and Surgeons, N. Y.* (n.d.), vol. I, ed. by John Shrady; H. A. Kelly and W. L. Burrage, *Am. Medic. Biogs.* (1920); *Trans. Am. Laryngological Assoc.* (1914); *Medic. Record,* Feb. 14, 1914; obituary in *N. Y. Times,* Feb. 7, 1914.]

D. B. D.

SIMS, CHARLES N. (May 18, 1835–Mar. 27, 1908), Methodist Episcopal clergyman, college president, was born in Fairfield, Ind., the son of John and Irene (Allen) Sims. He had no middle name, but for some reason used the initial N. Brought up on a farm, he obtained his early education in neighboring district schools. Itinerant preachers of the Methodist Church stopping at his father's house acquainted him in his boyhood days with religious and ecclesiastical matters. One of these, the zealous John P. Durbin [*q.v.*], took an interest in the lad and urged him to prepare for the ministry. At the age of seventeen he began to teach school and two years later he entered Indiana Asbury University (De Pauw University), from which he graduated in 1859. During the latter part of his course he served as principal of Thorntown Academy and was admitted on trial (1857) to the Northwest Indiana Conference of the Methodist Episcopal Church, being ordained deacon the year of his graduation, and elder in 1861. In 1860 he was made president of Valparaiso College, but the outbreak of the Civil War hampered its work and he remained but two years. Entering the active ministry, he was in charge of churches in Indiana and Illinois until he was called East in 1870, where he held important pastorates in Baltimore, Newark, and Brooklyn. In 1881 he was elected chancellor of Syracuse University.

This institution at that time was poorly equipped and in financial straits. "The indomitable perseverance of Chancellor Sims, his tireless industry, his undying faith in the college and its future saved the plant, and an upward progress was slowly begun" (*The Golden Jubilee, post,* p. 12). He virtually "lived in a carpet bag," and his pursuit of funds was notably successful. During the twelve years of his administration the indebtedness of the college was decreased, its endowment enlarged, and a building era inaugurated. He was instrumental in securing from John Crouse funds for the erection of Crouse Memorial College at a cost of approximately

$250,000; and a library, an observatory, and a gymnasium were erected. He was also active in denominational affairs, being a member of the General Conferences of 1884 and 1888, and one of the speakers at the Centennial Conference held in Baltimore in 1884. The state of New York utilized his abilities by making him one of a commission of three, established by the legislature in 1882, to investigate the condition of the Onondaga Indians, and his name heads the report presented in 1883 (*Documents of the State of New York . . . 1883, No. 35*). A commission was appointed to negotiate a new treaty with the Indians, upon which, also, he served.

After resigning the chancellorship of the University in 1893, he was pastor of the Meridian Street Church, Indianapolis (1893–98), and of the First Church, Syracuse (1898–1904). Two years later, having in the meantime been general secretary for the Methodist Hospital, Indianapolis, he retired to Liberty, Ind., where he died. Of his several publications the most important was *The Life of Rev. Thomas M. Eddy* (1879). On Aug. 12, 1858, he married Eliza A. Foster of Tippecanoe County, Ind.

[C. A. Martin, *Alumnal Record, DePauw Univ.* (1910); *The Golden Jubilee of Syracuse Univ., 1870–1920* (n.d.), ed. by Frank Smalley; *Minutes of the Seventy-seventh Session of the Ind. Ann. Conf. of the M. E. Ch.* (1908); obituary in *Christian Advocate* (N. Y.), Apr. 9, 1908.]   H. E. S.

SIMS, JAMES MARION (Jan. 25, 1813–Nov. 13, 1883), gynecologist, was born in Lancaster County, S. C. His father, John Sims, descended from the English colonists of Virginia, was a tiller of the soil, the village hotel keeper and sheriff, a great hunter and cock fighter; his mother was Mahala (Mackey), of Scotch-Irish origin. Marion grew up in a variety of schools and attended the South Carolina College, Columbia, during the presidency of Thomas Cooper [*q.v.*], a man of remarkable learning, who, Sims thought, "exerted a very bad influence," because he was a pronounced infidel and denied the Mosaic authorship of the Pentateuch. Graduating in 1832, Sims reached home two months after his mother's death. She had counted on his entering the Presbyterian ministry, while his father wanted him to study law. He therefore turned to medicine, although his father reckoned it a profession "for which I have the utmost contempt" (Sims, *post*, p. 116).

With the local Dr. Churchill Jones as preceptor, Sims entered the Charleston Medical School in November 1833, where John Edwards Holbrook [*q.v.*], celebrated herpetologist, was his professor of anatomy. Here he found his billet and pitched in zealously. The following October, in true medical peripatetic fashion, he traveled by stage to Philadelphia and matriculated in the Jefferson Medical College. While he was there smallpox broke out, contracted from a dissecting-room subject, and several of the students died; Sims, who nursed one of them, was protected by a vaccination he had forgotten. He graduated in May 1835, and returned home with a full set of surgical instruments.

Settling in Mount Meigs, Ala., he attracted attention, after eight or nine other doctors had been consulted to no avail, by urging an abdominal incision for an abscess, although a consultant had diagnosed cancer. A layman-arbiter siding with Sims, he performed the operation, and the patient recovered. In 1840, Sims moved to Montgomery. One of his early achievements here was the complete rectification of a cleft palate with a hideous snout-like protrusion; the patient came to him wearing a double-thick blue veil to hide her face even from her own family, but the new presentable mouth effected by the operation made of her a really pretty woman. Chapin A. Harris [*q.v.*], of the Baltimore College of Dental Surgery, visiting Montgomery, insisted on the publication of the case, and although Sims protested that he had never written anything in his life, the article appeared in the *Journal of Dental Surgery* for September 1845.

In June of that year a call to a colored girl of seventeen, Anarcha, three days in labor, proved the turning point in Sims's life. Impaction and extensive sloughing resulted in a large bladder fistula and a wreck of a patient, unfit for all social relationships—a burden for life on her master's hands. This was his first fistula case, but two others shortly appeared, all being regarded as incurable. In spite of strenuous objections, the third patient was sent to Sims's small negro hospital. At that very juncture, an accident to a patient causing a uterine displacement revealed to him a new approach and suggested a way of treating his fistula patients, on whom, with a newly devised speculum, he now inaugurated a long-drawn-out series of operations. Anesthesia was not yet known; doctor friends, enthusiastic coadjutors in holding the patients so long as there was a bright hope of relieving the incurable malady, could no longer be commandeered when weeks and months brought only slight improvement, and Sims had to depend upon the poor sufferers themselves for any assistance. After many failures, his brother-in-law, Dr. Rush Jones, pleading the waste of time and labor and the consequent injustice to his family, begged him to drop the whole matter. Sims replied: "I am as sure that I shall carry this thing through to success, as I am that I now live. . . . I am going on with this series of experiments to the end. It matters not what it costs, if it costs me my life" (Sims, pp. 242–43). Subsequently, in a moment of inspiration, he had a local artisan make some silver wire for sutures which were passed and tightened with perforated shot. This was the crucial step; the thirtieth operation on Anarcha was crowned with success. The silver sutures and the unparalleled deftness and skill the surgeon had acquired in the long, patient years of repeated efforts had transformed the situation. This operation took place in the late spring of 1849; two weeks later, Betsey and Lucy were also cured. Sims was now fully justified in declaring, "Then I realized the fact that . . . I had made, perhaps, one of the most important discoveries of the age for the relief of suffering humanity" (*Ibid.*, p. 246).

Six weeks later he collapsed with an old intestinal complaint and had to quit work and spend several years moving from place to place in search of relief. His weight dropped to ninety pounds. Lying in bed at home, desperately ill, in the fall of 1850, he wrote the history of the vesicovaginal fistula operation, which appeared in the *American Journal of the Medical Sciences* for January 1852 and was reprinted separately in 1853. At the time he thought it "my last free-will offering to the medical profession, before I should quit this world" (Sims, p. 259). In 1853, dismissing his negro servants and selling out all his interests in Montgomery, he journeyed to New York with his family and bought a house on Madison Avenue. Valentine Mott, Francis, Stevens, Delafield, and other leaders of his profession, astounded by his claims, began to seek him out. The first New York fistula cases brought no remunerative practice, since some of his colleagues even borrowed his instruments for their own use. This situation finally forced him to consider the establishment of a hospital, where poor patients could be received and visiting doctors instructed. Henri L. Stuart assisted at the beginning of the project by using the city papers to invite the physicians of New York to hear Sims speak on the need of a woman's hospital. When the day arrived in the spring of 1854, no less than 250 doctors filled the hall. From that time on, with the further effective cooperation of the leading women of the city, chief among them Mrs. William E. Dodge, the hospital plan advanced to its inauguration at 83 Madison Avenue, May 1, 1855, with about thirty beds—all charity. The state charter for the Woman's Hospital of the State of New York was obtained in 1857, the city bargaining for fifty free beds and giving in exchange the old Potter's Field with its memories of the cholera epidemic of 1832.

In June 1861, Sims, never vigorous physically, sailed for Europe for a rest. Wherever he went he was royally received. Sir James Y. Simpson of Edinburgh was especially interested in his work. In Paris, he met Jobert de Lamballe, writer of the *Traité de Fistules* (1852), and Velpeau and Nélaton. The elderly Civiale complimented him before a group of students; the King of the Belgians made him a Knight of the Order of Leopold I. In Paris, he cured one of Jobert's patients after sixteen futile efforts. Doctor Mungenier brought him a woman with an enormous fistula of more than twenty years' duration, whom he cured by a single operation; some seventeen or eighteen of the leaders in the profession were present at this *tour de force*. These, with five previous successful operations in Paris within three or four weeks, "created a furore among the profession."

He returned to New York in January 1862, but, unhappy there because of his sympathy with the South, took his family back to Paris in July to find abundant work awaiting him. In 1863, the Empress Eugénie was under his care for several weeks, and for the next two years Paris yielded him a comfortable living. In London, in 1866, he published his *Clinical Notes on Uterine Surgery* (brought out in an American edition the same year). This book was a potent factor in the formation of the nascent specialty of gynecology. Hearing of the destitution in his native county following Sherman's march to the sea, he sent five thousand francs to relieve the most needy, later giving enough to buy a large house and sixty acres of land for the helpless indigent, to be known as The J. Marion Sims Asylum for the Poor.

After the Civil War he returned to New York, but upon the outbreak of the Franco-Prussian War in 1870, went again to France to organize and become surgeon-in-chief of the Anglo-American Ambulance Corps. For distinguished professional services, France bestowed on him the Order of the Commander of the Legion of Honor. In 1872, again in New York, he was made a member of the board of surgeons of the Woman's Hospital, where work had been maintained efficiently by Thomas Addis Emmet [*q.v.*], but two years later he resigned, offended by the ruling of the managers limiting to fifteen the spectators admitted to any operation. In 1876, he was president of the American Medical Association. His last visit to the South, in March 1877, was the occasion of a triumphal entry into

Montgomery where he was met by the medical and surgical societies, his old friend W. O. Baldwin delivering a notable address (published with Baldwin's memorial tribute, *post*). In 1880, he presided over the American Gynecological Society. Happy memories and many friendships drew him to revisit Paris in 1882. On returning, in August 1883, he bought a building lot in Washington, where he intended to settle, but pneumonia claimed him on the morning of Nov. 13, three days after the execution of the title deed.

Sims's wife was Eliza Theresa Jones of Lancaster, to whom he had been devoted since they were respectively eleven and nine years old. She took him in spite of strong parental opposition, married him while poor (Dec. 21, 1836), lived in log cabins with him and the rapidly arriving children, guided him in all but his professional activities, and cared for and clung to him through years of harassing, exhausting illnesses, herself ill part of the time. Repeatedly she made the crucial decisions of life. With a son and four daughters, she survived him. Sims's autobiography, *The Story of My Life,* edited by his son, was published in 1884.

[J. M. Sims, *The Story of My Life,* mentioned above; W. O. Baldwin, *Tribute to the Late James Marion Sims* (1884); Ely van de Warker, in *Trans. Am. Gyn. Soc.,* vol. IX (1885); J. A. Wyeth, in H. A. Kelly and W. L. Burrage, *Am. Medic. Biogs.* (1920); *Boston Medic. and Surgic. Jour.,* Nov. 22, 1883; *Am. Jour. Obstetrics,* Jan. 1884; *N. Y. Times,* Nov. 14, 1883.]
H. A. K—y.

SIMS, WINFIELD SCOTT (Apr. 6, 1844–Jan. 7, 1918), inventor, was born in New York City, the son of Capt. Lindsay D. and Catherine B. Sims. He was graduated from the Newark, N. J., high school in 1861; soon after this he enlisted in the 37th New Jersey Regiment and served in the Civil War, 1861–65. On June 11, 1867, he married Lida Leek of Newark, who died in 1888; on June 27, 1891, he married Mrs. Josephine Courter French of Newark. He invented various devices in electro-magnets. In 1872 he constructed a small electric motor for light work, with a battery of twenty half-gallon Bunsen cells, which would propel an open boat sixteen feet long, with six persons on board, at four miles an hour. He was the first to apply electricity for the propulsion of torpedoes. His "fish torpedo," on which he secured patent No. 319,633 in 1882, was a submarine boat with a cylindrical hull of copper, conical ends, and a screw propeller and rudder. Within it was a coil of cable two miles long, by means of which it was propelled, guided, and exploded, the power being electrically generated on shore or shipboard. Ten

of these, purchased by the United States government in 1885, were experimented with for a number of years by army officers, and for a time were seriously considered for adoption as a principal means of coast defense. These torpedoes were twenty-eight feet long, twenty-one inches in diameter, and attained a speed of eleven miles an hour when tested by the government in 1885. Subsequently he designed a boat with a speed of twenty-two miles an hour, capable of carrying a five hundred pound charge of dynamite.

He also invented an apparatus for coiling ropes and for preventing ropes from kinking and twisting while they were being paid out, patent No. 374,209, and the Sims-Dudley powder pneumatic gun, patent No. 619,025, which was used by the Cuban insurgents and by the Rough Riders at the battle of Santiago. This was a very light field gun, intended to be drawn by one horse, or by three or four men, and consisted of two tubes, one of which carried the projectile and the other the powder charge of from six to eight ounces of powder. The projectile was a vaned cylinder with a Merriam fuze and a charge of explosive gelatin, pencil of gun cotton, and fulminate of mercury; when the projectile struck an object, a steel ball, acting as a hammer, was driven forward by the sudden retardation of the flight of the shell and struck one or more percussion caps, which ignited the charge. He also invented a breech mechanism for cannon, patent No. 619,026; the Sims-Merriam projectile, patent No. 667,407; a wireless dirigible torpedo, of which he sold five to the Japanese government in 1907; a dynamite gun for use with dirigibles, and a dynamite gun for aeroplanes. At the time of his death he was engaged in designing a dynamite cruiser to carry one hundred tons of high explosive, controlled by an operator on shipboard or on shore. He died in Newark, where he had made his home for years.

[See *Who's Who in America,* 1916–17; obituary in *N. Y. Times,* Jan. 8, 1918. Sims's "fish torpedo" is treated in *Harper's Mag.,* Nov. 1885, *World* (N. Y.), Dec. 19, 1885, and *Iron Age,* Dec. 31, 1885.]
C. F. C.

SINGER, ISAAC MERRIT (Oct. 27, 1811–July 23, 1875), inventor, was born in Pittstown, Rensselaer County, N. Y., the son of a millwright, who a few years later moved to Oswego, N. Y., to work at his trade. Here Singer spent his boyhood and received a bit of schooling. At twelve he left home, went to Rochester, N. Y., and for seven years worked at all sorts of unskilled labor. He finally entered a machine shop as an apprentice machinist, but after four months he left and began nine years of wandering from state to state, making a good living because of his mechanical cleverness and gaining wide experience. On May 16, 1839, while he was living in Lockport, Ill., he obtained his first patent, for a rock-drilling machine; however, he soon squandered the money he made when he sold it. In 1849, when he was in Pittsburgh, he secured a patent on a wood and metal-carving machine that he had begun five years before in Fredericksburg, Ohio. He went immediately to New York and secured the help of A. B. Taylor & Company to finance the development of his invention. After unavoidable delays lasting over a year, he completed a machine that was commercially practicable and operated it for a short time. Then a boiler explosion in the manufactory completely destroyed it and left him penniless.

In 1851 he was at work in a machine shop in Boston when a Lerow and Blodgett sewing machine was brought in for repairs. He was called upon for suggestions and was told incidentally that if he could make a practical sewing machine his fortune would be made. Within twelve hours he had prepared a rough sketch and within eleven days had built a machine incorporating his ideas. He immediately applied for a patent, which was granted Aug. 12, 1851, patent No. 8294, and with a few hundred dollars borrowed from friends he organized the I. M. Singer & Company and began the manufacture of his machine. Though the sewing machine of Elias Howe [q.v.] was supreme at that time Singer's had one feature that Howe's lacked, the ability to do continuous stitching; because of this his machine came into immediate demand. When Howe brought suit for $25,000 because he refused to pay royalties, Singer fought it for three years, but in July 1854, losing the case, he was forced to pay $15,000 in settlement. By that time, however, his company had reached a commanding position in the sewing-machine industry, and took a leading part in bringing about the subsequent combination of manufacturers and the pooling of patents. Singer received twenty patents between 1851 and 1863 for improvements on his machine; the most important were the continuous wheel feed, the yielding presser foot, and the heart-shaped cam as applied to moving the needle bar. His greatest service, however, was in developing the first practical domestic sewing machine and in bringing it into general use. In 1863, with forty per cent. of the stock in his name, he withdrew from active connection with the company and went to Europe to live. Early in life he married Catherine Maria Haley, from whom he was divorced in 1860; in 1865 he married Isabella Eugenia Summerville in New York. At the time of his death at his home in Torquay, Devonshire,

England, he was survived by his widow and two daughters.

[F. L. Lewton, "The Servant in the House," *Ann. Report . . . Smithsonian Inst.*, 1929; Henry Howe, *Adventures and Achievements of Americans* (1858); *Genius Rewarded or the Story of the Sewing Machine* (1880); *N. Y. Atlas*, Mar. 20, 1853; obit. in *N. Y. Tribune*, July 26, 1875; Patent Office records.]
C. W. M—n.

SINGERLY, WILLIAM MISKEY (Dec. 27, 1832–Feb. 27, 1898), editor and publisher, the eldest of five children of Joseph and Catherine (Miskey) Singerly, was born in Philadelphia, Pa., where his father was a successful carpenter and builder. Graduating from high school in 1850, he secured a job with a produce commission house on the water front. After ten years in this school of long hours and hard work, he became associated with his father in the development of street railways, especially in Germantown, Pa. In 1870 he removed to Chicago to engage again in the commission business, but he was soon recalled. During this period of interest in street railways he dipped into politics, and in 1877 he purchased the *Public Record,* buying it very cheaply at a time when its circulation had ebbed to 5,200. Though he then knew nothing of newspaper publishing, he improved paper and typography, introduced display headlines, added new departments, and enlarged the Saturday issue. In 1879 he changed the name to *Philadelphia Record,* cut the price in half, and made it the pioneer morning daily in Philadelphia sold at one cent and giving complete news. In 1882 he launched a Sunday edition. He went roughshod after the theft of bodies by the coroner's underlings, exposed bogus medical colleges, laid bare registration frauds, assailed corruption in office. Warring against excessive coal prices, he organized a direct sales scheme in 1881 that undercut the established rate by seventy-five cents a ton and saved hard-pressed householders thousands of dollars. In 1882 he moved the *Philadelphia Record* into a new building that was among the first in which incandescent electric lighting was used. The circulation of the paper grew rapidly from the start and rose to nearly 200,000 during his lifetime. To assure the necessary supply of paper, he ran his own paper mill at Elkton, Pa.

He was soon the recognized Democratic leader of Pennsylvania. He championed Cleveland in each of his presidential campaigns, espoused tariff reform when that doctrine was particularly unpopular in Pennsylvania, and helped to secure the election of Robert Emory Pattison [q.v.], the only Democrat chosen governor in Pennsylvania after the Civil War until 1934. In

1894 he himself was nominated for governor but was not elected; otherwise he refused office except honorary appointment to the Fairmount Park Commission. In 1896 he withdrew his support from Bryan and gave it to John McAuley Palmer and Simon Bolivar Buckner [qq.v.]. His boundless energy found many other outlets. In 1878 he inherited his father's shares in the Germantown Passenger Railway, appraised at $750,000, which he subsequently sold for $1,500,000. In addition to the paper mill, he owned a gleaner and binder factory at Norristown and knitting mills in Philadelphia, at one time the largest producer of "jerseys" in the land, and had a model stock farm, which was his suburban home. In the biggest single building operation in Philadelphia to that date, he erected over a thousand dwellings. After the destruction by fire of the Temple Theatre he erected a building on its site for the Chestnut Street National Bank and its savings fund affiliate, which he had organized under the presidency of Ex-Governor Pattison and of which he became president in 1891. The disastrous collapse of these banks in the aftermath of the 1893–96 depression gave his brilliant career a tragic ending. Struggling to meet his obligations, he arranged to divert the earnings of his *Record* holdings equitably to his creditors. His signature on the indenture scarcely dry, he died suddenly in Philadelphia from an aneurism ascribed to "tobacco heart." Of imposing appearance, with the air of one born to command, Singerly was reckless of consistency and fearless of consequences, the embodiment of enterprise and open-handedness. He was twice married, first on June 4, 1854, to Pamelia Anna Jones of Philadelphia and second on Aug. 12, 1872, to Mary Ryan of Chicago, both of whom died. He was survived by one of his two daughters.

[T. W. Bean, *Hist. of Montgomery County, Pa.* (1884); J. T. Scharf and Thompson Westcott, *Hist. of Phila., 1609–1884* (1884), vol. III; George Morgan, *The City of Firsts* (1926); J. R. Young, *Memorial Hist. of the City of Phila.*, vol. II (1898); *A Gallery of Eminent Men of Phila.* (copr. 1887), ed. by E. C. Savage and William Anderson; obituaries in *Phila. Record, Public Ledger* (Phila.), Feb. 28, 1898.] V. R.

SINGLETON, ESTHER (Nov. 4, 1865–July 2, 1930), author, editor, and music critic, was born in Baltimore, Md., the daughter of Martha Colgate (Morling) and Horace Leonard Singleton. Her father was a grandson of John Singleton of Norfolk, who fought in Daniel Morgan's rifle regiment and in the Virginia line under Washington, and a direct descendant of Edward Rawson, secretary of the Massachusetts Bay Colony, and Nathaniel Reynolds, a captain in King Philip's War. Her mother was the daughter of a near relative of Jane Austen. Educated in private schools and by private teachers in Baltimore, for several years she studied with Sidney Lanier [q.v.], who was a friend of her parents. In her early teens she spent much time in the Naval Observatory studying with her cousin, Edward Singleton Holden [q.v.], the astronomer. In 1887 she went to New York to prepare for a musical career. Although she became a proficient violinist, she lacked confidence in her ability and turned to writing for a living; music, however, remained one of the chief enthusiasms of her life. One of her earliest books is *A Guide to the Opera* (1899); later appeared *A Guide to Modern Opera* (1909) and *The Orchestra and Its Instruments* (1917).

The subtitle of her first book, *Turrets, Towers and Temples: The Great Buildings of the World as Seen and Described by Famous Writers* (1898), suggests the nature of most of her books: prose anthologies of love, famous women, notable pictures, statues, cathedrals, various interesting cities, countries, natural wonders, and the world's great events. The vogue for collecting antiques stimulated her own lively interest in the historical associations of things, and led her to write several books and numerous articles on antiques. In *The Furniture of our Forefathers* (1900), *Social New York under the Georges* (1902), and *Dutch New York* (1909), she built up historical backgrounds, reconstructed homes, and gave glimpses of the family and social life of the times by quoting freely from old inventories, wills, newspaper advertisements, letters, diaries, and travel books, and by describing and giving illustrations of heirlooms and museum treasures of those periods. Her careful research, historical insight, and artistic selection make the books both interesting and authentic. From 1923 until 1930 she was editor of the *Antiquarian*. The writing of *The Shakespeare Garden* (1922) gave her keen satisfaction, for she knew, word for word, most of the comedies and the greatest of the tragedies. Her last published book, *Shakespearian Fantasia: Adventures in the Fourth Dimension* (1929), and a story for girls, *A Daughter of the Revolution* (1915), are the only ones that are not the result of research, compilation, or translation. She was an ardent French student and used the language with facility. In addition to translating from the French many of the selections in her anthologies, she published two translations, *Musical Education* (1903) and *The Music Dramas of Richard Wagner* (1898), from the French of Albert Lavignac. She also wrote *États-Unis d'Amérique* for the first part of the *Encyclopédie de la Musique et Dictionnaire du Conservatoire* (1922).

During 1904 she traveled abroad, but she did not welcome either change or motion and lived in New York almost continuously for over forty years. She enjoyed the society of brilliant people and was herself a gifted conversationalist. Her interest in music, art, literature, and history was keen, her memory remarkable, and her appetite for reading omnivorous. In searching out facts for her books and articles she was both accurate and indefatigable. She contributed to many magazines, among them the *Saturday Evening Post, Garden and Home, International Studio,* and the *Musical Courier.* She died at Stonington, Conn., where she was spending the summer.

[*Who's Who in America,* 1930–31; *Woman's Who's Who of America,* 1914–15; Esther Singleton, preface to *The Shakespeare Garden* (1922) and *"Die Meistersinger* under Anton Seidl," *Musical Courier,* Feb. 1, 1930; *N. Y. Times,* Aug. 31, 1930, pt. VIII (appreciation) and July 5, 1930 (obituary); obituary in *Musical Courier,* July 12, 1930; correspondence with Charlotte Austen Carrington, a sister.]   V. L. S.

SINGLETON, JAMES WASHINGTON (Nov. 23, 1811–Apr. 4, 1892), congressman, was an Illinois political leader of Southern antecedents. He was born at "Paxton" in Frederick County, Va., the estate of his father, Gen. James Singleton, who served in the Revolutionary War and the War of 1812. Through his mother, Judith Throckmorton (Ball), he had ancestral connections in common with George Washington. After attending the academy in Winchester, Va., he struck out for the West, "read medicine," practised as youthful physician, then turned to legal studies, and became a circuit-riding lawyer. About 1834 he settled at Mount Sterling, Ill. In the "war" against the Mormons (1844) he served as brigadier-general of militia. He also served his state in constitutional conventions, 1847 and 1862, and in the legislature, 1850–54, 1860–62. Having removed to Quincy about 1854, he lived on a large estate, "Boscobel," combining the grand life of a gentleman planter with law and politics and being widely known as a gracious Southerner at whose mansion prominent men gathered. In 1862 he served on an international commission to investigate water communication between the United States and Canada.

During the Civil War he labored persistently for peace. Pursuing the political aims of the "Sons of Liberty," he opposed Lincoln's arbitrary measures and took prominent part in peace conventions at Peoria and Springfield in August 1864. In November 1864 he was in Canada conferring with Clay and Tucker, Confederate "commissioners." Seeking interviews with Lincoln for his plans to end the war, he reached the President both directly and through intermediaries and claimed to have been told by Lincoln that abolition would not be demanded as a condition of peace (O. H. Browning, *post,* I, 694, 699), though this was inconsistent with Lincoln's terms as given in the Greeley peace episode. Late in the war he made several trips to Richmond bent on peace projects and being associated with O. H. Browning and James Hughes [*qq.v.*] in a scheme to buy Southern products with greenbacks, get them through Grant's lines with presidential permission, and sell them in the North at enhanced prices. Lincoln approved this scheme as a means to shorten the war by getting federal money into Southern hands. As to the peace efforts, however, Lincoln withheld official sanction while standing ready to step in if satisfactory Confederate proposals should emerge from Singleton's informal "negotiation." After the war Singleton continued his political activities, serving as a Democrat in Congress from 1879 to 1883, but gave increasing attention to railroad promotion. Interested particularly in transportation advantages for his own city, he directed the building of two roads, the Quincy & Toledo, which merged with the Wabash, and the Quincy, Alton & St. Louis, which was absorbed by the Chicago, Burlington & Quincy. Political animosities did not mar his friendships, and "Boscobel" remained during this period a scene of generous entertainment. He was married three times: first probably to Catherine McDaniel, second to Ann Craig of Kentucky, and third, in 1844, to Parthenia McDonald, who bore him seven children. About 1891 he removed to Baltimore, where he died.

[Information from his daughter, Mrs. Lily Singleton Thomas Osburn of Charles Town, W. Va.; "The Diary of Orville Hickman Browning," ed. by T. C. Pease and J. G. Randall, *Ill. State Hist. Colls.,* vols. XX, XXII (1927–33); *The Biog. Encyc. of Ill.* (1875); E. C. Kirkland, *The Peacemakers of 1864* (1927); *Hist. Encyc. of Ill. and Hist. of Schuyler County* (1908), ed. by Newton Bateman; "The Constitutional Debates of 1847," ed. by A. C. Cole, *Ill. State Hist. Colls.,* vol. XIV (1919); P. H. Redmond, *Hist. of Quincy* (1869); D. F. Wilcox, *Quincy* (1919), vol. I; H. E. Hayden, *Va. Geneal.* (1891); *Ill. State Jour.* (Springfield), Aug. 6–25, 1864; editorial, *N. Y. Tribune,* Jan. 13, 1865; M. P. Andrews in *N. Y. Times,* Feb. 12, 1928; *Whig* (Quincy, Ill.), Apr. 5, 1892; *Sun* (Baltimore, Md.), Apr. 5, 1892.]   J. G. R.

SIRINGO, CHARLES A. (Feb. 7, 1855–Oct. 19, 1928), cowboy, detective, and author, was born in Matagorda County, Tex. His father, an Italian emigrant, died when the boy was only a year old, and his mother, herself an emigrant from Ireland, brought up the little family. At the age of four Charlie started to school. At twelve he rode out as a full-fledged cowboy, accoutred in all the habiliments of the range. He worked on the coast for the colorful "Shanghai" Pierce, drove on the trail with cattle in 1876, spent some time in the Kansas cowtowns, and in the spring of 1877 helped, as a cowboy, to establish the LX's, an extensive ranch in the Texas Panhandle fostered by eastern capital. There he remained until sent to New Mexico in the fall of 1880 with a posse of Texas cowboys to help run down "Billy the Kid." He took the company money to Las Vegas for the purpose of buying provisions, fell into a game of monte, lost all, and rejoined the posse with an empty chuck-wagon. Leaving the search for the Kid to bolder spirits, he turned south to the mining camp called White Oaks and back to the LX range after the outlaw band was dispersed. After a mercantile venture at Caldwell, Kan., he drifted into Chicago. Probably in the summer of 1882 at Wellington, Kan., he was married to Mamie Lloyd of Shelbyville, Ill., who died six years later leaving one daughter.

In 1885, "being in need of money," and he was always in need, he published his first book, a racy little volume called *A Texas Cowboy, or Fifteen Years on the Hurricane Deck of a Spanish Pony.* Bound in paper and peddled by "butcher boys" upon the trains, its sale is said to have run to near a million copies. The next year he joined the Pinkerton detective agency in order "to study the world" and record his "experiences in book form." After about twenty-two years he had collected the necessary copy. *A Cowboy Detective*, the stirring account of his connection with the agency, resulted in the raising of legal barriers to publication by his former employers. The text was modified, the Pinkertons fictitiously alluded to, and in 1912 the volume appeared —an account of the suppression of Haymarket riots, strikes, express banditry, cattle rustling, and anarchical outbreaks—though the agency later obtained a permanent injunction and suppressed the book. In 1915 he issued a homely little pamphlet in a glowing paper cover called *Two Evil Isms: Pinkertonism and Anarchism,* merely outlining the *Cowboy Detective* and telling what he first wanted to tell about his late employers and a good deal he had thought of since. In 1919 he published *A Lone Star Cowboy* to take the place of his first book, then out of print, and issued a pamphlet of ballads called *The Song Companion of a Lone Star Cowboy.* Next year he compiled his *History of "Billy the Kid"* (1920). In 1927 he saw the best of his stories on cowboys and detectives issued in dignified format by a standard publisher under the title of *Riata and Spurs.* Again the Pinkertons objected, and the volume was radically revised

(1927), eleven chapters being replaced with fresh material from what was to have been Siringo's last book, "Bad Men of the West." The "Bad Men" failed to appear. He left no fluent narrative or polished works, but he traced honest chronicles in a simple and direct style. Though he was uncritical of careless sources, his works will probably live for their vivid portrayal of the cattle range and cowboy characters, and for their rollicky cowboy style. No single writer typifies the achievement of cowboy literature, from the plane of the dime novel to one of character and distinction, so well as Charlie Siringo. Much of his later life was spent in New Mexico, at Roswell and Santa Fé, though he died at Hollywood, Cal.

[Letters of Siringo to author, Mar. 4, 1928, Jas. H. East to author, 1927, and letters from Siringo in the East Collection in possession of author; Harrison Leussler to author, May 17, 1934; writings, *ante*; *Publishers' Weekly*, Nov. 17, 1928; *Fort Worth Star-Telegram*, Oct. 20, 1928; *Houston Post-Dispatch*, Oct. 21, 1928.]

J. E. H.

SITTING BULL (1834?–Dec. 15, 1890), a Hunkpapa Sioux chief, leader in the Sioux war of 1876–77, was born on Grand River, S. D. His father, also named Sitting Bull, was a subchief. The son earned a reputation as a warrior in the sixties, but at a comparatively early age he retired to the safer and more lucrative occupation of medicine man and political leader. Always hostile to the whites, he spent most of his time off the reservation. His camp in the buffalo country became the rallying point for all Sioux, Cheyenne, and Arapaho hostiles; and as he had become wealthy, in an Indian way, he was enabled to make presents that greatly extended his influence throughout the Sioux confederacy and the allied tribes. Though not a war chief, he had become by 1875 the head of the war council. The certainty of war, in the spring of 1876, brought to his camp numbers of well-armed warriors until he had a fighting force estimated at from 2,500 to 4,000 men and boys. When, on June 25, George A. Custer [*q.v.*] made his disastrous attack on the consolidated Indian village at the Little Big Horn, Sitting Bull did no fighting but spent the time in "making medicine," while Gall and Crazy Horse [*qq.v.*] took the leading parts. His following soon afterward broke up into small bands, and, under the relentless pursuit of the military, thousands returned to the reservations. By the end of the year his own band had been pushed across the Canadian border. He remained there until the defection of all his leaders and the increasing destitution of his people caused him to return. At Fort Buford, in July 1881, with 187 men, women and children, he surrendered. He was taken to Fort Randle and was later settled on the Standing Rock reservation. To the end he remained a bitter irreconcilable. In 1890 he took an active part in the Messiah agitation. On Dec. 15 he was arrested by Indian police and in the fight that followed was shot and killed. He was buried in the military cemetery at Fort Yates.

He was a heavy-set, muscular man, about five feet eight inches in height. James McLaughlin, who was Indian agent at the Standing Rock reservation during the Messiah agitation of 1890, credited him with a knowledge of men and a deep insight into affairs among Indians, but wrote that he was wily, untrustworthy, and in his rôle of medicine man "had all the tricks of the fake spiritualist" (*My Friend . . . post,* pp. 180–81, 203). His fame during the years from 1875 to 1881 had a disturbing effect on the unstable imaginations of a number of whites, and many fantastic myths about him were created. He was asserted to be a white man, a graduate of West Point, as well as of other institutions, a linguist, a scholar, a Mason, and a Catholic; and much was written and published in support of these assertions. A book that appeared in 1878, *The Works of Sitting Bull,* credited him with the authorship of French and Latin poems. In reality his sole achievement in letters, won by him during his exile in Canada, seems to have been the ability to write his name, which he spelled "Seitting Bull."

[Jas. McLaughlin, *My Friend the Indian* (1910) and his report in *Sixtieth Ann. Report of the Commissioner of Indian Affairs, 1891* (1891), pp. 325–38; James Mooney, "The Ghost Dance Religion and the Sioux Outbreak of 1890," *14th Annual Rept. of the Bureau of Ethnology,* pt. 2 (1896); W. F. Johnson, *The Red Record of the Sioux* (1891); J. M. Hanson, *The Conquest of the Missouri* (1909); unsigned sketch in *Handbook of Am. Indians* (1910), ed. by F. W. Hodge; a wholly different interpretation of character and achievement in Stanley Vestal, *Sitting Bull* (1932) and *New Sources of Indian Hist.* (1934); C. A. Eastman, *Indian Heroes* (1918).]   W. J. G.

SIZER, NELSON (May 27, 1812–Oct. 18, 1897), phrenologist, was descended from Anthony de Zocieur, a French sailor from the island of Terceira, who took the name Sizer after he settled in Middletown, Conn., in 1726. His grandfather, William Sizer, was an ingenious Jack-of-all-trades whose most notable exploit occurred during the Revolution when he inoculated four men with a jack-knife, and carried them through smallpox with butternut physic made into pills by boiling the juice. His father, Fletcher Sizer, was married to Lydia Bassett, of Westfield, Mass., and moved to Chester, Mass., where Nelson was born. Reared among the Berkshire Hills, he wrote for country news-

papers until he came under the influence of the phrenologist, J. G. Spurzheim, who came to the United States in 1832. He studied phrenology, lecturing after 1839 in the South and East, and in 1849 he became examiner in the famous phrenological cabinet of Orson Squire Fowler and Samuel Roberts Wells [*qq.v.*] in New York City. He examined the heads of nearly three hundred thousand persons. From 1859 to 1863 he edited the *American Phrenological Journal,* which, under his editorship, was a dignified periodical. He became president of the American Institute of Phrenology, founded in 1866, with Amos Dean and Horace Greeley among the corporate members. Sizer was the principal lecturer at the Institute, which, at the time of his death, had graduated 731 students.

He was the author of many articles in the *Phrenological Journal,* and of ten pamphlets on phrenology and related subjects, published in the *Human-Nature Library.* His first known publication was *An Address on the Life and Character of Washington* (1842). The most important of his many books expounded the principles of phrenology, and developed the phrenological theses in respect to the reading of character, education, vocational choice, and marriage. Of the first sort are *Heads and Faces, and How to Study Them* (1885), and *How to Study Strangers by Temperament, Face, and Head* (1895). On education, he published *How to Teach According to Temperament and Mental Development* (1877). On vocational guidance, he contributed *What to Do, and Why* (1872), and *The Road to Success* (1885). His contributions on marriage were *Thoughts on Domestic Life* (1850), and *Right Selection in Wedlock* (n.d.). His *Forty Years in Phrenology* (1882) is a volume of recollections of his life work. Although not so important a figure in the history of phrenology as Gall, Spurzheim, the Combes, and the Fowlers, Sizer was one of the leading popularizers and practitioners of the pseudo-science. The basic assumptions of the phrenologists were unsound, but their efforts to analyze character, their discussions of the problems relating to sex, vocational choice, prison reform, and educational reform, stimulated progressive thought. Their influence was felt by such men as Edgar Allan Poe, Walt Whitman, Horace Mann, and Henry Ward Beecher. There is ample testimony that Sizer exerted a helpful influence on the men and women whom he advised. Perhaps the same skill which permitted his grandfather to cure smallpox with butternut physic aided the phrenologist to cure souls by measuring the cranial protuberances. He was married at Suffield,

Conn., on Mar. 12, 1843, for the second time, and had two children by his first wife, and one by his second.

[On the Sizer family, see bound manuscript data in the Newberry Library, C. W. Hayes, *William Wells of Southold and His Descendants* (1878), F. W. Bailey, *Early Conn. Marriages*, vol. II (1896), and *Vital Records of Chester, Mass.* (1911). For Nelson Sizer, see his *Forty Years in Phrenology* (1882), obituaries in the *N. Y. Times* and *N. Y. Daily Tribune*, Oct. 19, 1897, and the *Phrenological Jour. of Sci. and Health*, Dec. 1897.]

E. B. H.

SKANIADARIIO (*c.* 1735–Aug. 10, 1815), Seneca sachem, religious leader, was born at the village of Ganawaugus, on the west side of the Genesee River opposite the present town of Avon, N. Y. He was also known to his own people as Ganiodaiio, and his name is translated Handsome Lake. He led a dissolute life until about 1796, when he suffered a severe illness brought about by his dissipation. According to native accounts he wasted away in a hut near the present Warren, Pa., and passed into a condition of coma. Arising from this, he declared that he had been visited by four messengers of the Creator of Life and had been instructed in certain principles that were to constitute a new religion to be called the Gaiwiio. According to the code that he later proclaimed, he afterward had other revelations. His great work was in recrystallizing a declining faith and giving it new vigor by means of his revelations, thus giving to the Iroquois a new philosophy and religion about which to rally. Wandering from one Indian village to another he preached his doctrine with considerable success, demanding that his people abstain from drunkenness, witchcraft, and infidelity, practise industry and thrift, and hold faith in his revelations. For fifteen years, from 1800 to 1815, he conducted his ministry, at one time visiting Thomas Jefferson to whom he explained his teachings. He succeeded in blotting out much of the older religion of the Iroquois and in blocking missionary efforts, but during his last years he seems to have been assailed with doubts, for he had obtained a clearer view of Christianity. He died at Onondaga, near Syracuse. In 1900 the followers of his religion among the Iroquois of New York and Ontario numbered more than one fourth of all these people, and at the present time (1935) there are groups of his followers meeting in "long houses" on every reservation of the Iroquois except at Tuscarora, Saint Regis, and Caughnawaga.

[A. C. Parker, "The Code of Handsome Lake," *N. Y. State Museum Bull.*, no. 163 (1913); L. H. Morgan, *League of the . . . Iroquois* (1851); F. W. Hodge, *Handbook of Am. Indians*, pt. II (1910).]

A. C. P—k—r.

SKENANDOA (1706?–Mar. 11, 1816), Oneida chief, was said to have been born into some other tribe, possibly the Conestoga, and adopted by the Oneida at an early age. His name is often written differently, Scanondo, Schenandoah, Shenandoa, and even Johnko' Skeanendon. Traditionally, he was a drunkard until about 1755, when, finding himself to have been robbed in a drunken stupor, he resolved to change his way of life and succeeded in doing so. Shortly after that he was converted to Christianity by Samuel Kirkland [*q.v.*]. A firm friend of the colonists, he fought against the French in the French and Indian War, and at the outbreak of the Revolution, with Samuel Kirkland and Thomas Spencer, he was responsible for keeping the Oneida and Tuscarora from joining the rest of the Iroquois Confederation in fighting for the British. Instead, he was able to persuade the Oneida to adopt an address of neutrality in May 1775 and, when they abandoned neutrality, to influence many of the Oneida and Tuscarora to join the Americans. He is said to have prevented the massacre of many settlers at German Flats, now in Herkimer County, N. Y.

After the war he shared the fate of the rest of his people, living on year after year in a situation gradually becoming more narrow and more uncomfortable. He grew to be a very old man, perhaps past the century mark, blind and feeble, "an aged hemlock . . . dead at the top" (Campbell, *post,* App. p. 30), and he died at his home near Oneida Castle strong in the white man's faith. According to his often expressed wish he was buried by the side of his friend Samuel Kirkland in the latter's garden at Clinton, N. Y., and later removed with Kirkland to lie in the graveyard of Hamilton College. There the Northern Missionary Society erected a monument to him, who, "wise, eloquent and brave . . . long swayed the Councils of his Tribe . . . remained a firm friend of the United States . . . and . . . adorned by every Christian virtue . . . fell asleep in Jesus."

[Consult: obituary from Utica *Patriot,* Mar. 19, 1816, reprinted as Note D in App., W. W. Campbell, *Annals of Tryon County, N. Y.* (1831); *Documentary Hist. of Hamilton College* (1922); Wm. Gordon, *The Hist. of the . . . Independence of the U. S.* (3rd Am. ed., 1801), I, 359–61; S. K. Lothrop, "Life of Samuel Kirkland," *The Lib. of Am. Biog.,* ser. 2, vol. XV (1848), ed. by Jared Sparks; Pomroy Jones, *Annals and Recollections of Oneida County* (1851), pp. 865–68; H. R. Schoolcraft, *Hist. of the Indian Tribes* (1857), pt. 6, p. 136; "Skenandoah" was a pseudonym used by Lewis H. Morgan, see his *League of the . . . . . . Iroquois,* new ed. (2 vols. in 1, 1904), ed. by H. M. Lloyd, II, 164, 195.]

K. E. C.

SKENE, ALEXANDER JOHNSTON CHALMERS (June 17, 1837–July 4, 1900), pioneer gynecologist, was born in Fyvie, Aberdeenshire, Scotland, of a family well known in Scottish history (see W. F. Skene, *Memorials of the Family of Skene of Skene*, Aberdeen, 1887). His parents were Johnston and Jean (McConachie) Skene. He spent his boyhood in his native village, acquired an education in the local schools, and began to study medicine at Kings College. At nineteen years of age he left home and came to America. He studied medicine in Toronto in 1860 and attended the University of Michigan in 1861 and 1862. The following year he received the M.D. degree from the Long Island College Hospital Medical School. His practice, begun in Brooklyn in 1864, was interrupted by active duty in the Federal army as assistant surgeon in the volunteer corps. He taught gynecology at the New York Post-Graduate Hospital from 1883 to 1886, and was consultant to a number of dispensaries and hospitals. He was for many years attached to the Long Island College Hospital, where he served as teacher, operator, dean, and president. He was a founder of the American Gynecological Society (president, 1886–87), and the International Congress of Gynecology and Obstetrics (honorary president, Geneva, 1896), and acted as president of the Medical Society of Kings County, 1874–75, the New York Obstetrical Society, 1877–79, and the Brooklyn Gynecological Society, 1891–92. He was associate editor of the *Archives of Medicine*, 1883–84, the *American Medical Digest*, 1884–89, and the *New York Gynaecological and Obstetrical Journal*, 1891–1900. He has to his credit more than one hundred medical papers (see Browning and Schroeder, *post*), and he was the author of *Diseases of the Bladder and Urethra in Women* (1878); *Education and Culture as Related to the Health and Diseases of Women* (1889); *Electro-haemostasis in Operative Surgery* (1889); *Medical Gynecology* (1895); and *Treatise on the Diseases of Women* (1888). One mediocre novel, *True to Themselves,* published in 1897, came from his pen.

He entered the field of gynecology at a critical moment, when great leaders were in demand to direct the investigations which were bringing about startling and important developments. His discovery in 1880 of what are now called Skene's urethral glands gave him an international reputation and an assured place in the history of gynecology. He also is known to have devised thirty-one surgical instruments. He opened a private sanitarium in 1884 in Brooklyn with Dr. W. M. Thalon, and, in 1899, Skene's Hospital for Self-supporting Women.

His tremendous physique, his ruddy face, glowing with a kindly heartiness, his firm chin, and compelling eyes, reflected a vigorous and commanding personality. Intense in his work, he was equally so in his emotions, a stanch friend and formidable enemy. His lectures were lucid, terse, and to the point, and he never missed an opportunity to assist and encourage younger men in special lines of work. A skilful operator, the leading physician of Brooklyn of his time, he rose early, operated all morning, and saw as many as fifty patients in the afternoon. He never became resigned to city life and resorted frequently to his country home in the Catskills where he enjoyed to the full the freedom of outdoor life. Here he could devote himself to his artistic talents, for had he not been a physician, he might well have made a name for himself as a sculptor. Many examples of his work may be seen at Kings County Medical Society. He was married to Annette Wilhelmine Lillian Van der Wegen of Brussels, Belgium. They had no children but adopted a daughter. After completely disregarding repeated warnings, he succumbed to an attack of angina pectoris at a comparatively early age and at the height of his career. A bust of him stands in Prospect Park, Brooklyn, an unusual honor and tribute to a physician.

[Some obituaries and biographies give 1838 as Skene's birth date, see, however, *Who's Who in America*, 1899–1900. For further data, consult: H. A. Kelly and W. L. Burrage, *Am. Med. Biogs.* (1920); William Browning, "Alexander . . . Skene," *Brooklyn Med. Jour.*, Apr. 1897; R. L. Dickinson, "Alexander . . . Skene," *Trans. Am. Gynecological Soc.*, vol. XXVI (1901); J. C. MacEvitt, "Alexander . . . Skene," *Am. Jour. of Surgery*, Mar. 1928; William Schroeder, "Alexander . . . Skene," *Brooklyn Med. Jour.*, Sept. 1900; *Brooklyn Daily Eagle*, July 5, 9, 1900.]   G. L. A.

SKILLERN, ROSS HALL (Nov. 13, 1875–Sept. 20, 1930), laryngologist, was born in Philadelphia, Pa., the son of Dr. Samuel Ruff Skillern and his wife, Sarah Hall Ross. He received his preliminary education in George F. Martin's academy, studied in the school of biology at the University of Pennsylvania, 1892–93, then entered the medical department, from which he was graduated in 1897. After practising general medicine for several years with his father he began to specialize in laryngology. In 1905 he suffered an attack of epidemic cerebrospinal meningitis which he had contracted from a patient. He recovered after a prolonged illness and then went abroad to study rhinology and laryngology in Vienna for a year and a half. He returned to Philadelphia in 1907 and began giving private courses in the anatomy and pathology of the nasal accessory sinuses. In 1913 he was professor of laryngology in the Medico-Chirurgical College of Philadelphia and continued to serve in that capacity after the institution became part of the graduate school of medicine of the University of Pennsylvania in 1919. He was an enthusiastic and gifted teacher, and an excellent operator, and his classes attracted many students. He was a frequent contributor to current medical literature, his bibliography enumerating the titles of forty-six contributions to medical journals. His most important work, *The Catarrhal and Suppurative Diseases of the Accessory Sinuses of the Nose,* was published in 1913 and reached four editions within ten years.

During the World War he served first as a major in the medical corps, chief of the division of surgery of the head, in the base hospital at Camp Sheridan, Ala. He was promoted to the rank of lieutenant-colonel in July 1918, and acted as commanding officer of United States base hospital No. 89, American Expeditionary Force, at Mésves-sur-Loire, France. In 1912 he organized the Philadelphia Laryngological Society and became the first president. He was a member of the American Academy of Ophthalmology and Otolaryngology, and served as president in 1926; he was chairman of the section on otolaryngology of the American Medical Association in 1920, and president of the American Laryngological, Rhinological and Otological Society in 1929. He was a member of the American Laryngological Association, and when the American Board of Examiners in Otolaryngology was organized in 1924, was chosen as one of the delegates to represent the Association on the Board, a position to which he was reëlected every year until his death. He was also a fellow of the College of Physicians of Philadelphia and of other local medical societies. He was married to Eliza Michler Porter, of Hackettstown, N. J., on June 3, 1903. She, with two daughters and two sons, survived him when he died suddenly in Philadelphia.

[*Who's Who in America, 1930–31; Who's Who in Am. Med., 1925;* memoir by G. M. Coates, M.D., in *Trans. . . . of the Am. Laryngological Asso.* (1931); personal acquaintance; *Public Ledger* (Phila.), Sept. 21, 1930.]   F. R. P.

SKINNER, AARON NICHOLS (Aug. 10, 1845–Aug. 14, 1918), astronomer, was born at Boston, Mass., the son of Benjamin Hill and Mercy (Burgess) Skinner. He attended the schools in the vicinity of his home, and early developed habits of study which in his later life became dominant characteristics. He continued his education at Beloit College, Beloit, Wis., and pursued a special course in astronomy at the

University of Chicago from 1868 to 1870. He was married to Sarah Elizabeth Gibbs, of Framingham, Mass., on Feb. 9, 1874, and they had two children, a daughter and a son. While studying at the University of Chicago, he held a position as assistant at the Dearborn Observatory, and after completing his course he became assistant astronomer at the United States Naval Observatory, a position which he held for twenty-eight years. He then passed a competitive examination and in 1898 was commissioned in the naval service as a professor of mathematics. From 1893 to 1902 he was in charge of the twenty-six-inch equatorial. From 1903 until his detachment from the Naval Observatory in 1909, he had charge of the equatorials.

He discovered four variable stars in the course of his observations with the meridian circles. The transit circle observations of the sun, moon, planets, and meridian stars were carried out under his direction, first as an assistant astronomer and then as a professor. From these observations he determined the places of approximately 8824 stars in the zone from 14 degrees, south declination, to 18 degrees, south declination, as a contribution to the *Katalog der Astronomischen Gesellschaft* of Leipzig, Germany. This work was published as the Washington Zone Catalogue in 1908 under the title: *Catalogue of 8824 stars between 13° 50' and 18° 10' south declination.* He was placed in charge of the expedition which was sent to the island of Sumatra to observe the total eclipse of the sun on May 18, 1901. He took with him six members of the Observatory staff and five scientists from other observatories in the United States. The expedition was ably handled by Skinner, who carefully arranged to cover all possible contingencies. In addition to the observations made of the total solar eclipse, observations were made at newly erected, outlying stations; at Solok one member of the expedition (W. W. Dinwiddie) discovered a bright comet on the night of May 3.

Skinner was retired from the United States naval service with the rank of commander, United States Navy, Professor Corps, in 1907, but remained in active service in the Naval Observatory until 1909. He was a member of the American Association for the Advancement of Science, the Astronomische Gesellschaft of Leipzig, Germany, and of the Astronomical and Astrophysical Society of America. His writings, in addition to the Washington Zone Catalogue, include results of observations, published by the United States Naval Observatory, the *Naval Observatory Expedition to Sumatra* (1902), printed first in *Popular Astronomy,* January 1902, and numerous articles on variables and minor planets for scientific periodicals. He died at Framingham, Mass.

[*Who's Who in America,* 1918–19; *Pubs. of the U. S. Naval Observatory,* 2 ser., vol. VI (1911); *Washington Post,* Aug. 15, 1918.]   J.F.H.

SKINNER, ALANSON BUCK (Sept. 7, 1886–Aug. 17, 1925), anthropologist and ethnologist, was born in Buffalo, N. Y., the son of Frank Woodward Skinner, a civil engineer, and Rachel Amelia (Sumner) Skinner. When he was a small boy, the family moved to Staten Island, where Alanson became interested in natural science and made collections of Indian relics. During a school vacation (1902) he worked for the American Museum of Natural History, New York, in the excavation of an ancient shellheap near Shinnecock Hills, Long Island, and two years later accompanied an archeological expedition of the Peabody Museum of Harvard to western New York, where he made his first visit to an Indian reservation. After finishing his high school course, he occupied a position in a commercial establishment for a time, but ultimately devoted himself to scientific work.

From 1907 to 1913 he was connected with the American Museum of Natural History, finding opportunity in the meantime to take courses at Columbia and Harvard. During this period he led two expeditions (1908, 1909) to Hudson Bay, to study the Cree Indians; carried on investigations in Wisconsin; visited the Florida Everglades to make collections from the Seminoles; and spent much time in explorations on the archeological sites of the Algonquian Indians in New York State. This last work led him to make studies of the material culture of these Indians and of the Siouan tribes in contact with them, in which field he became an authority. In 1916 he joined the staff of the Museum of the American Indian, Heye Foundation, and took charge of an archeological expedition to Costa Rica. Two years later he accepted the position of curator of anthropology at the Public Museum of Milwaukee. Returning to the Museum of the American Indian in 1924, he remained with that institution until his death in an automobile accident near Tokio, N. Dak., the following year.

Beginning in 1903, he published rapidly the results of his investigations; a bibliography of his writings contains more than a hundred titles. Among these papers may be mentioned the following: "A Short Account of the Algonkin Indians of Staten Island" (*Proceedings of the Natural History Society of Staten Island,* Jan. 6, 1904); "Notes on the Eastern Cree and Northern Saulteaux" (*Anthropological Papers of the American Museum of Natural History,* vol. IX, 1911); with Max Schrabisch, a preliminary chapter on the types of Indian remains found in New Jersey (*Geological Survey of New Jersey, Bulletin IX,* 1913); "Social Life and Ceremonial Bundles of the Menomini Indians" (*Anthropological Papers of the American Museum of Natural History,* vol. XIII, 1913); *The Indians of Greater New York* (1915); "Exploration of Aboriginal Sites at Throgs Neck and Clasons Point, New York City" (*Contributions of the Museum of the American Indian, Heye Foundation,* vol. V, 1919); in collaboration with John V. Satterlee, "Folklore of the Menomini Indians" (*Anthropological Papers of the American Museum of Natural History,* vol. XIII, 1915); *Ethnology of the Ioway Indians* (1926); *The Mascoutens or Prairie Potawatomi Indians* (3 parts, 1924–27), and a posthumous work in which Skinner returned to archeology, *Certain Mounds and Village Sites of Shawano and Oconto Counties, Wisconsin* (1932), all published as bulletins of the Milwaukee Public Museum.

He was a man of athletic figure, but suffered from ill health. During the World War he tried several times to enlist, but was rejected on physical grounds. As a member of the New York Guard, however, he served in the 9th Coast Artillery. His good nature and friendliness won him the confidence of the Indians. His wife, Dorothy Preston, who, with a small daughter, survived him, was part Wyandotte. He confined his work to the observational field and did not undertake the intangibles, yet the gatherings of his short but busy life are of the greatest value and importance to anthropology.

[*Am. Anthropologist,* vol. XXVIII (1926); M. R. Harrington, in *Indian Notes* (New York), Oct. 1925; *Explorers Jour.,* July–Dec. 1925; *N. Y. Times* and *N. Y. Herald Tribune,* Aug. 19, 1925.]   W.H.

SKINNER, CHARLES RUFUS (Aug. 4, 1844–June 30, 1928), politician, educator, librarian, was born on a farm in Union Square, Oswego County, N. Y., the son of Avery and Charlotte Prior (Stebbins) Skinner. Educated in the district school and at Mexico Academy and Clinton Liberal Institute, both in Oswego County, he went to New York City in 1867 and spent three years there in business. From 1870 to 1874 he was city editor and manager of the *Daily Times,* Watertown, N. Y. He married, Oct. 16, 1873, Elizabeth Baldwin of Watertown, daughter of David W. and Laura (Freeman) Baldwin. In 1876 he published *Watertown, N. Y., A History of Its Settlement and Progress.* He served on the Watertown board of education, 1875–84. A member of the state legislature from 1877 to 1881, he was chairman of the committee on railroads and advocated a five-cent fare on the New York elevated railway. In 1881 he was elected as representative to Congress, succeeding Warner Miller, who had resigned in order to fill the unfinished term of Thomas Collier Platt [*qq.v.*]; he was reëlected and served until 1885, his chief interest being in postal matters. He originated and secured the passage of a bill providing for special delivery letters.

After another year of editorial work, he became deputy state superintendent of public instruction in 1886, supervisor of teachers' institutes and teachers' training classes in 1892, and state superintendent of public instruction in 1895. During these years he compiled and edited a teachers' manual, books on school libraries and school architecture, an *Arbor Day Manual* (1890), and a *Manual of Patriotism* (1900). He also compiled *The Bright Side* (copyright 1909), a scrapbook of quotations. He was president of the National Education Association, 1896–97. To the end of his life he believed that the state should concentrate its educational efforts on the elementary schools, leaving the high schools and colleges to private enterprise and endowment. In 1904, when the department of public instruction was merged with the state board of regents through legislation that Skinner himself sponsored, his position ceased to exist.

From 1906 to 1911 he was assistant appraiser of merchandise for the port of New York. He was librarian of the state assembly, 1913–14, and in 1915 was given the newly created post of legislative librarian. Under him the legislative library became a quick reference library in which everything was arranged alphabetically, apple orchard cultivation and arbitration in labor disputes following each other in the same section. The librarian personally knew where material could be found, and there he ruled, tall, handsome, and commanding, until Oct. 31, 1925, when he reached the legal retiring age. Not quite three years later he died while he was visiting his son in Pelham Manor, N. Y. He was survived by three sons and a daughter.

[*Who's Who in America*, 1928–29; *Biog. Directory of the Am. Cong., 1774–1927* (1928); C. E. Fitch, *The Pub. School; Hist. of Common School Educ. in N. Y., 1633 to 1904* (n.d.), prepared for N. Y. State Dept. of Pub. Instruction; N. Y. (State) Univ., *Bull. to the Schools*, Sept. 15, 1928, p. 10; obituaries in *Watertown Daily Standard*, June 30, 1928, *N. Y. Times*, July 1, 1928.]   E. E. W.

SKINNER, HALCYON (Mar. 6, 1824–Nov. 28, 1900), inventor, the son of Joseph and Susan (Eggleston) Skinner, was born in Mantua,

Ohio, where his parents had gone from Massachusetts upon their marriage. When he was eight years old his parents removed to Stockbridge, Mass., and there he received a common school education, working at the same time on neighboring farms and in his father's shop. After his parents removed to West Farms, N. Y., in 1838, he helped his father in the making of violins and guitars for seven years. He then engaged in general carpentry work for himself until 1849, when he was hired by Alexander Smith, a carpet manufacturer in West Farms, to design and construct a hand loom that would weave figured carpet instead of the striped sort prevailing at the time. The machine, which was completed in a year, was so successful that by 1851 Smith had one hundred looms at work to supply the demand for the new "tapestry ingrain" carpet. For forty years Skinner was retained by Smith as mechanical expert and consultant. In 1856 he devised and patented jointly with Smith a power loom to weave Axminster or tufted carpets, but it was not until 1860 that a satisfactory machine was put into operation. He then turned his attention to inventing and patenting a power loom for weaving ingrain carpets and developed a very successful machine, first installed in 1864 in Smith's new manufactory at Yonkers, N. Y., and used until ingrain carpet weaving was discontinued. Around 1870 Smith began the manufacture of tapestry carpet, using looms imported from England; these, however, were not satisfactory until after Skinner had completely altered them and had doubled their output.

Probably his most important invention was a power loom for weaving moquette carpets, first conceived in 1876 and patented on January 16, 1877. In the course of five or six years, Skinner and his two sons secured a series of patents. The machines built in accordance with these placed Smith's company in the lead among American manufacturers of moquette carpets. It is said that the origination of the moquette loom stamped Skinner as a creative genius and placed him in a high position among the inventors of the world. In 1889 he severed his connections with the Smith company and lived more or less in retirement in Yonkers. He perfected some further improvements of the moquette loom, however, and occasionally served his former employer in an advisory capacity. He was twice married; his first wife, Eliza Pierce, died in 1869, and subsequently he married Adelaide Cropsey of Brooklyn, N. Y. His death occurred when he was struck by a train. He was survived by his widow, and two sons and three daughters, all by his first marriage.

[J. T. Scharf, *Hist. of Westchester County, N. Y.* (1886), vol. II; *Am. Carpet and Upholstery Jour.,* Dec. 1900; *Carpet and Upholstery Trade Rev.,* Dec. 1, 1900; obituaries in *N. Y. Times* and *N. Y. Herald,* Nov. 29, 1900; Patent Office records.]   C. W. M—n.

SKINNER, HARRY (May 25, 1855–May 19, 1929), representative from North Carolina, was born in Perquimans County, N. C., and came of a family prominent in state affairs through several generations. His parents were Elmyra (Ward) and James C. Skinner, a prosperous planter. He received his preparatory education at the Hertford academy, and in 1875 he received the LL.B. degree from Kentucky University. He returned to North Carolina and, having been admitted to the bar in 1876, began practice in Greenville. On June 5, 1878, he was married to Lottie Monteiro of Richmond, Va., who died ten years later leaving four children. Devoting himself to his profession for some years, he was very successful. He was also interested in politics as a rather uncompromising Democrat, and in 1891 he was a member of the lower house of the legislature. Already well and favorably known, he was prominent in spite of inexperience, was chairman of the committee on internal improvements and of the house branch of the committee on redistricting the state, advocated the appointment of a committee to codify the corporation laws, and worked enthusiastically for the establishment of a state college for women and for other educational improvements.

His mind had for some years been much occupied with the problem of improving the condition of the farmer and laborer, and he had become convinced that the evils which oppressed them were due chiefly to a faulty financial system. He joined the Farmers' Alliance and was prominent in its political councils. In *Frank Leslie's Illustrated Newspaper,* for Nov. 30, 1889, he published "The Hope of the South," an exposition of a plan for the federal government to fix the price of cotton at thirteen cents a pound by providing warehouses and issuing negotiable warehouse certificates to the cotton growers. He always claimed that his ideas formed the basis for the "sub-treasury" plan that the Alliance and, later, the People's party advocated. Later he introduced a bill in Congress providing for the establishment of the system and a somewhat similar plan to care for the cotton crop of the South. His name was proposed to the Democratic state convention for lieutenant-governor, but he refused to let it be considered because he thought his financial views made his selection unwise and nothing must be done to endanger party success, since he was strongly opposed to the plan of separate party organization. When the Populists elected him a delegate to the Omaha Convention in 1892, he repudiated their action. He also declined the Populist nomination by acclamation for governor and for Congress.

However, in 1894 he was elected by the Populist party to the Fifty-fourth Congress and re-elected two years later. In that year he was permanent president of the Populist state convention and, as a "middle-of-the-road" Populist, opposed further fusion with the Republicans. He split with the leaders of his party who wanted to break the agreement made in 1895 to reëlect Jeter C. Pritchard to the federal Senate, and he helped obtain the election. In Congress Skinner was true to his party faith. He labored under the handicap of belonging to a minority, but, an eloquent speaker, able debater, and an impressive figure, he gave a good account of himself (for his financial and tariff theories see such speeches as *The Coin Redemption Fund. Remarks ... in House ... Dec. 27, 1895,* 1896, and *Equitable Protection and Bimetallism ... Speech ... in the House ... Mar. 25, 1897,* 1897). Apart from his work for Populist policies, he was active in his support of a system of inland waterways. He was defeated in 1898 and returned to the practice of law. In 1900 he was still a Populist and a supporter of Bryan, and he favored the ratification of the constitutional amendment disfranchising the bulk of the negroes; but shortly thereafter he became a Republican. In 1902 he became federal district attorney and served ably for eight years. He was president of the North Carolina Bar Association in 1915 and for several years vice-president for North Carolina of the American Bar Association. He was a member of the Episcopal Church. He died in Greenville survived by three children and by his second wife, Ella (Monteiro) Skinner, to whom he was married on Oct. 26, 1895.

[*Cyc. of Eminent and Repres. Men of the Carolinas* (1892), vol. II; *N. C. Bar Ass. Proc. ... 1929* (1929), pp. 77–79; J. G. deR. Hamilton, *Hist of N. C.* (1919), vols. III and IV ed. by special staff; J. D. Hicks, *The Populist Revolt* (1931); *Greensboro Daily Record,* Mar. 14, 1892; *News and Observer* (Raleigh), May 20, 1929.]   J. G. deR. H.

SKINNER, JOHN STUART (Feb. 22, 1788–Mar. 21, 1851), agricultural editor and writer, was born in Calvert County, Md., and spent his early years on the family plantation established by Robert Skinner, who emigrated from England in the early part of the seventeenth century. His father, Frederick, was an officer in the American Revolution and later managed his own plantation and one inherited by his wife, who was a sister of the well-known "Jack" Stuart, companion of Lafayette. Skinner was educated in local schools and at Charlotte Hall, a classical academy in St. Mary's County. At eighteen he became an assistant to the clerk of the county court and later began to study law at Annapolis. Here he was appointed reading clerk in the legislature and made a notary public for Annapolis by Governor Wright. At the age of twenty-one he was admitted to the bar.

Following the outbreak of the War of 1812, President Madison made him inspector of European mail at Annapolis, and he was also designated an agent for prisoners of war. Skinner successfully performed these responsible duties, incidentally making life-long friends among the British officers. In 1813 his headquarters were removed to Baltimore, where, Mar. 26, 1814, he was commissioned a purser in the navy, a position held throughout the war and for a number of years thereafter. While visiting the fleet of Admiral Cockburn, Skinner and Francis Scott Key [q.v.] were detained during a furious night bombardment of Fort McHenry, Sept. 13–14, 1814, following which they were released and returned to Baltimore. They then went to the "Fountain Inn," where Key wrote "The Star Spangled Banner." Skinner, impressed with the beauty of the song, took the manuscript and arranged to have it printed. From 1816 to 1837 he was postmaster at Baltimore. In 1841 President Harrison appointed him third assistant postmaster general, in which capacity, through his attention to detail he was able, it is said, to reduce by $200,000 the expenditures of the United States post office department. In 1845, under President Polk, he was removed from office for political reasons.

Perceiving the worn-out state of much of the soil in Maryland and stimulated by the writings of John Taylor of Caroline [q.v.], Skinner decided in 1819 to establish an agricultural paper, with a view to disseminating knowledge respecting the best methods of farm practice. Accordingly, on Apr. 2, he offered to the public the initial number of the *American Farmer,* the issue being held over a day lest the paper be taken for an April Fool joke. Although David Wiley published the *Agricultural Museum* at Georgetown in 1810, to Skinner belongs the honor of establishing the first continuous, successful agricultural periodical in the United States. The *American Farmer* quickly became the principal organ of expression for all those who took an active interest in agricultural improvement. In its pages one finds communications from such men as John Taylor of Caroline, Thomas Jefferson, Timothy Pickering, John Hare Powel, James Garnett, James Madison, Richard Peters, John H. Cocke,

and others of like standing. Among foreign contributors were Sir John Sinclair, Thomas W. Coke, and General Lafayette. Throughout the twenties the paper offered the best available information on field crop cultivation, fertilization of soil, horticulture, new agricultural machines, agricultural organizations, fairs, prices, internal improvements, and similar subjects. In August 1829 Skinner started the monthly publication of the *American Turf Register and Sporting Magazine,* devoted to the improvement of American thoroughbred horses, and to veterinary knowledge, racing, shooting, hunting, fishing, and the habits of American game. It was the first magazine of its kind in the United States and was more influential than any other factor of its day in improving the breed of American horses. Finding the dual editorship too great a demand upon his time, he sold the *American Farmer* in 1830 for $20,000, remaining thereafter an occasional contributor. In 1835 the *American Turf Register* was sold for $10,000 to Gideon B. Smith, who, four years later, sold it to William Trotter Porter [q.v.]. Greeley and McElrath, proprietors of the *New York Tribune,* engaged Skinner in 1845 to edit, in New York, the *Farmers' Library and Monthly Journal of Agriculture,* the first issue of which was dated July of that year. A portion of each number consisted of a reprint of some celebrated agricultural work, frequently foreign; the remainder was devoted to material on domestic and foreign farming, experiments, new machines, inventions, and similar subjects. The publication eventually proved too technical for popular subscription and at the conclusion of a three-year contract, Skinner bought the rights and established, at Philadelphia, a periodical of his own entitled *The Plough, the Loom, and the Anvil,* the first number of which appeared in July 1848. Its pages were devoted to domestic agriculture and industry, and to advocating a protective tariff for both. The magazine soon attained wide popularity and Skinner continued as editor until his death.

In cooperation with officials of the Maryland Agricultural Society he established a stock farm a few miles from Baltimore, where the Society observed the scientific breeding of horses and mules, various types of cattle, Tunis sheep, and other animals. He was also active in developing the Western Shore branch of the Maryland Agricultural Society, and a society to improve the breed of horses. At the time of General Lafayette's visit to Baltimore in 1824, Skinner arranged a special meeting of the Maryland Agricultural Society which Lafayette attended. The two became friends, corresponded extensively, and Skinner acted as business agent for Lafayette in the United States, and later for the Lafayette family. In the course of his career he became an honorary member of practically every important agricultural organization in his own country and abroad. Several of these presented him with costly sets of silver, and the South Carolina Agricultural Society voted him a gold medal. Making use of his extensive acquaintance among officers in the United States Navy, he was instrumental in having brought into the United States useful plants, improved livestock, and valuable agricultural books from various parts of the world. As early as 1824 a quantity of guano was thus introduced, but he did not succeed in popularizing this type of fertilizer.

Skinner wrote *The Dog and the Sportsman* (1845), and a number of monographs on agricultural subjects. He also contributed agricultural articles to leading newspapers such as the *Albion* (New York), and the *Philadelphia Courier,* and edited a number of agricultural works. Among the latter were *Memoirs of the Pennsylvania Agricultural Society* (1824); *The Horse* (1843) by William Youatt; *Every Man His Own Cattle Doctor* (1844) by Youatt and Francis Clater; *Every Man His Own Farrier* (1845) by Clater; and *Mason's Farrier and Stud Book* (1848), by Richard Mason. He also added supplementary material to François Guénon's *A Treatise on Milch Cows* (1846), and John Badcock's *Farriery* (1848); and subsequently printed, with a preface written by himself, *Sheep Husbandry in the South* (1848) by H. S. Randall [q.v.], which had appeared in the *Farmers' Library* in 1847. Skinner's activities as an agricultural publicist were chiefly carried on for over twenty-five years outside of his working hours as a public official. On Mar. 10, 1812, he married Elizabeth G. Davies, by whom he had three sons, one of whom, with his widow, survived him. Skinner's death, at the height of his powers, was occasioned by an accidental fall in the post office at Baltimore.

["Memorial of J. S. Skinner, Praying the Establishment of an Agricultural Department of Government," *Senate Misc. Doc. 120,* 30 Cong., 1 Sess.; *The Plough, the Loom, and the Anvil* (N. Y.), Apr., Dec. 1851, July 1854; B. P. Poore, *Biog. Sketch of John Stuart Skinner* (repr. 1924); *Am. Farmer* (Baltimore), Apr. 1851; *Ohio Cultivator* (Columbus), Apr. 1, 1851; *Prairie Farmer* (Chicago), May 1851; *Am. Agriculturist* (N. Y.), May 1851; *Cultivator* (Albany), May 1851; *Am. Hist. Rev.,* Jan. 1928; *Minn. Hist.,* Dec. 1933; W. E. Ogilvie, *Pioneer Agricultural Journalists* (1927), privately printed; E. G. Swem, "A Contribution to the Bibliog. of Agriculture in Va.," *Bull. Va. State Lib.,* Jan.–Apr. 1918; *Baltimore Clipper,* Mar. 22, 1851; Myrtle Helfrich, "A Baltimore Pioneer of Farm and Turf," in *The Sun* (Baltimore), Feb. 17, 1935.]

H. A. K—r.

SKINNER, THOMAS HARVEY (Mar. 7, 1791–Feb. 1, 1871), Presbyterian clergyman, educator, and author, seventh of the thirteen children of Joshua and Martha Ann Skinner, was born at Harvey's Neck, N. C. The mother, reared an Episcopalian, became a member of the Baptist Church, and her husband, a Quaker, followed her into that communion. Their dwelling served as the neighborhood schoolhouse, the elder Skinner employing the schoolmaster. Here Thomas received his early education; later, he attended two other schools, and eventually enrolled as a student at Edenton Academy. The rapid progress which he made induced his eldest brother, Joseph, an Edenton attorney, to assume in 1804 the direction of Thomas' further education, and for three years the boy was a member of the brother's home. Entering the College of New Jersey in 1807, he won distinction in mathematics, and was graduated in 1809. For a year and a half he read law in his brother's office, serving also as clerk of the superior court.

About to be admitted to the bar, he decided in 1811, partly as a result of the death in a shipwreck of his youngest brother, John, to enter the Presbyterian ministry. Accordingly, he studied theology at Princeton, N. J., under President Samuel Stanhope Smith [q.v.] of the College of New Jersey; at Savannah, Ga., under Dr. Henry Kollock; and at Elizabethtown, N. J., in the home of Dr. John McDowell [q.v.]. On June 10, 1813, he was ordained at Philadelphia and became co-pastor with Dr. Jacob J. Janeway of the Second Presbyterian Church. He served in this capacity until 1816, vigorously preaching New School theology. Opposition developing, he resigned, and became pastor of the Fifth Church, to which small congregation on Locust Street about seventy members of the Second Church followed him. Seven years later a new edifice was dedicated at a more desirable location on Arch Street. Here his doctrinal sermons attracted crowded evening audiences. He remained with this congregation, except for a few months when he was in charge of the Pine Street Church, Boston, for nearly sixteen years.

After repeated invitations, in 1832 he accepted the professorship of sacred rhetoric in Andover Theological Seminary. Here he labored arduously in the then new task of teaching homiletics. His love of active preaching, however, together with the fact that his health had become impaired, led him in 1835 to undertake the pastorate of the new Mercer Street Presbyterian

Church, New York. Here he remained more than twelve years, a period in the church's history characterized by able preaching and religious revival. He also gave much aid in the work of establishing and stabilizing Union Theological Seminary. From its founding, in 1836, he was a director, and in 1848, when poor health compelled him to relinquish his pastorate, a parishioner endowed a chair of sacred rhetoric there, with special reference to its occupancy by Skinner.

He remained connected with Union until his death, at New York, twenty-three years later. In 1854 he was elected moderator of the General Assembly (New School). He had earlier published several books, of which *Aids to Preaching and Hearing* (1839) was perhaps the most notable, and during his years at Union he issued several others, among them *Pastoral Theology* (1853) and *Homiletics* (1854), both editions of Alexandre R. Vinet's works, prepared with much care and evidence of learning. He was also the author of *Discussions in Theology* (1868) and of a biography of his brother, *The Life and Character of the Late Joseph B. Skinner* (1853). During his career he did noteworthy work in systematizing the teaching of homiletics and in promoting broader theological views and closer interdenominational relations. Personally he was a man of cultivation, sincerity, simplicity, and deep spirituality. He was married and one of his children, Thomas Harvey Skinner (1820–92), was professor of theology at McCormick Seminary, Chicago.

[G. L. Prentiss, *A Discourse in Memory of Thomas Harvey Skinner* (1871) ; E. F. Hatfield, *The Early Annals of Union Theological Sem.* (1876) ; *Gen. Cat. of the Coll. of N. J.* (1896) ; *Princeton Theological Sem. Biog. Cat.* (1909) ; *N. Y. Observer*, Feb. 9, 1871 ; *N. Y. Tribune*, Feb. 2, 1871.]   P. P. F.

SKINNER, WILLIAM (Nov. 14, 1824–Feb. 28, 1902), silk manufacturer, the son of John and Sarah (Hollins) Skinner, was born in London, England. He received some private instruction, but at an early age went to work in the silk dyeing establishment where his father was employed. In 1843 his employer's son, who had started a dyeing establishment in Florence, Mass., sent to England for a foreman and William came to the United States to take the position. When his employer failed, Skinner took over the business, out of which grew the Nonotuck Company. In 1848, with Joseph Warner, he started the manufacture of sewing silk. This partnership was short-lived, however, and Skinner then built a mill between Haydenville and Williamsburg, Mass., on a site later called Skinnersville. There his business flourished and of-

fices were opened in New York and other cities. He built houses for his employees and a substantial home for himself, but all were destroyed, with the exception of his own home, when, in the flood of 1874, the Mill River dam gave way. Undaunted by this disaster, he set about looking for another location and finally decided upon Holyoke, Mass., where the Holyoke Water Power Company offered him a large tract of land if he would erect a mill. His credit being good and his personal integrity well known, he had no difficulty in reëstablishing his business. When his two sons were taken into partnership in 1883, the name of the concern became William Skinner & Sons. The firm gave special attention to broad-silk weaving, and its cotton-back satins and linings were popular throughout the country, "Skinner's Satin" being accepted as the hallmark of excellence in lining material.

Skinner was married on Apr. 12, 1848, to Nancy Edwards Warner of Northampton, Mass., the sister of his partner. She died about two years later and on May 15, 1856, he married Sarah Elizabeth Allen, daughter of Capt. Joseph Allen of Northampton. They were the parents of seven children, five daughters and two sons. He took a keen interest in the affairs of the city in which he lived, was president of the Manufacturers Association of Holyoke, and of the board of directors of the Holyoke City Hospital, which he founded and in which he took a keen interest until his death. He gave generously to the Holyoke Young Men's Christian Association and to the public library, and made gifts to Vassar College and to Mount Holyoke College, of which he was a trustee. From the time of its formation in 1872 he was a director of the Silk Association of America. Known as the "Old Roman" to his intimates, he had a rugged personality and his word was never questioned.

[*Am. Silk Jour.*, Apr. 1902; *XXX Ann. Report of the Silk Asso. of America* (1902) ; *Hist. of the Conn. Valley in Mass.* (1879), II, 926; *Springfield Daily Republican*, Mar. 1, 1902; information as to certain facts from Joseph A. Skinner, a son.]   B. R.

SLADE, JOSEPH ALFRED (c. 1824–Mar. 10, 1864), reputed "bad man," variously known as "Jack," "Alf," and "Cap" Slade, was born at or near Carlyle, Clinton County, Ill. The earliest available record concerning him is of May 22, 1847, when he enlisted in the army. After more than a year's uneventful service in New Mexico, he was mustered out at Alton in October 1848. He is next heard of, in the late fifties, as a freighter and wagon-train boss in the employ of Russell, Majors & Waddell. In the spring of 1860, after the firm had organized its overland stage service, he was made a division agent at

Julesburg, in what is now Colorado, with instructions to rid the region of bandits preying upon the company's property. In an encounter with "Old Jules" Reni (or Réné Jules, as one writer insists) Slade shot his antagonist to death, cut off his ears, and nailed them up to dry, later, it is said, wearing one of them as a watch-charm.

Transferred to a more westerly division, he continued to prove a scourge to evil-doers. Mark Twain, who in August 1861 met him at a Wyoming station, says that he then bore the reputation of having killed twenty-six men. In 1862 the stages were withdrawn to a more southerly line, and Slade was transferred to a new station, Virginia Dale, a hundred miles north of Denver. Unaccountably, he had by this time become a brawling drunkard, and in the fall of the year was discharged. With his companion, a dashing and attractive frontier woman whose given name was Maria Virginia and whose surname may have been Dale, he set out in the spring of 1863 at the head of a small freighting outfit for the Montana gold diggings. Settling on a small ranch near Virginia City, he conducted a number of freighting expeditions and for a time was peaceful. Later, he again began drinking heavily and indulging in outbursts of drunken rowdyism. When arrested, in March 1864, he defied the People's Court, and subsequently, revolver in hand, made threats against the judge. A joint meeting of the Vigilantes of Virginia City and the miners of the adjoining camp of Nevada decreed his execution, and though he begged pitifully for his life, he was promptly hanged. The body was embalmed in alcohol and buried in Salt Lake City.

Slade was of sturdy build. When sober he was genial and friendly, according to Mark Twain "the most gentlemanly-appearing, quiet and affable officer" found along the road (*post*, p. 87); but when drunk he was a ferocious ruffian. Though the accounts of his numerous killings have been disputed by some writers, they were fully accepted by Frank A. Root, who entered the company's service in Colorado only a few months after Slade's departure and who had every opportunity to learn the facts.

[*Record of the Services of Ill. Soldiers in the Black Hawk War . . . and in the Mexican War* (1882); Granville Stuart, *Forty Years on the Frontier* (1925), I, 151; F. A. Root and Wm. E. Connelley, *The Overland Stage to Cal.* (1901); N. P. Langford, *Vigilante Days and Ways* (1890), vol. II; T. J. Dimsdale, *The Vigilantes of Mont.* (2nd ed., 1882); Emerson Hough, *The Story of the Outlaw* (1907); Hoffman Birney, *Vigilantes* (1929); E. L. Sabin, *Wild Men of the Wild West* (1929); Mark Twain (S. L. Clemens), *Roughing It* (1872).]   W. J. G.

SLADE, WILLIAM (May 9, 1786–Jan. 16, 1859), statesman and educator, was born at Cornwall, Vt., the son of Capt. William Slade, a veteran of the Revolution, who had moved to Vermont from Washington, Conn., about 1783. He was a descendant of William Slade who was in Lebanon, Conn., as early as 1716. The youngest William's mother was Rebecca (Plumb). After preparatory work in the Addison County grammar school at Middlebury and four years at Middlebury College, where he was graduated in 1807, Slade studied law in the office of Judge Joel Doolittle of Middlebury. Admitted to the bar in the summer of 1810, he at once opened an office in the same village. Clients, however, were few, and the excitement of a bitter political contest in his state drew him into politics.

Like his father he was an ardent Democrat and he now devoted himself heart and soul to the interests of his party. Speeches and pamphlets were puny weapons against the Federalist press of Middlebury; Slade, therefore, in 1813, helped to found the *Columbian Patriot,* a weekly newspaper, which two years later became the *National Standard* (*Proceedings of the American Antiquarian Society,* n.s. vol. XXXV, 1925, p. 125). Soon he was its proprietor and editor, conducting in connection with it a book printing and selling establishment. The *Patriot* was a decided political success and it was partly responsible for the Democratic triumph in Vermont in 1815; as a business venture, however, it was a failure and by 1817 Slade was ruined. Refusing bankruptcy, he was saddled with a heavy debt which he struggled the rest of his life to repay; hence, in part, his eager search for political office.

Fortunately, the Democratic triumph of 1815 carried him into the office of secretary of state, a post which he filled with credit until 1823. Meanwhile (1816–22), he was judge of the court of his county. Having relinquished his state offices, he served as a clerk in the Department of State, at Washington (1824–29), until discharged at the beginning of Jackson's administration. He had married Abigail Foote of Middlebury, Feb. 5, 1810, by whom he had nine children, and he now sought to support his family by resuming his practice of law; but politics remained his prime interest and the main source of his livelihood. While serving as state's attorney for Addison County he was elected in 1830 to Congress, where he sat for twelve years, in the course of time joining the Whig party. He distinguished himself as an uncompromising opponent of slavery, and with John Quincy Adams fought tenaciously against the gag rules. Though not a great orator, he was a quick-witted and a ready debater with a command of searing phrases which enraged the Southern representatives. With an eye to the Vermont woolen industry he was a persistent champion of protective tariffs.

For one year (1843–44) after his retirement from Congress he was reporter of the state supreme court, resigning to become governor, in which office he served from 1844 to 1846. Under his leadership the legislature provided for a geological survey of the state and for a thorough reorganization of the public school system. He bitterly opposed the admission of Texas to the Union and the policy which led to war with Mexico. Before the end of his second term as governor he had lost the support of many influential Whig leaders, partly because of his bitter public controversy with Samuel S. Phelps, Whig senator from Vermont, whom, it was charged, Slade wished to supersede. His political career ended, he became corresponding secretary and general agent of the Board of National Popular Education. Indefatigable in this congenial work, which he continued until a few weeks before his death, he traveled through most of the Northern states, founding local societies and recruiting teachers in the East for service along the Western frontier. Besides many speeches in and out of Congress and his annual reports to the educational board, he published the *Vermont State Papers* (1823), a volume of documents on the early history of the state, and *The Laws of Vermont of a Publick and Permanent Nature* (1825). He died in Middlebury.

[T. B. Peck, *William Slade of Windsor, Conn., and His Descendants* (1910); *Cat. of the Officers and Students of Middlebury Coll.* (1928); Lyman Matthews, *Hist. of the Town of Cornwall, Vt.* (1862); Samuel Swift, *Hist. of the Town of Middlebury* (1859); M. D. Gilman, *The Bibliog. of Vt.* (1897); J. M. Comstock, *A List of the Principal Civil Officers of Vt.* (1918); J. G. Ullery, *Men of Vt.* (1894); W. H. Crockett, *Vermont,* vol. III (1921); *Biog. Dir. Am. Cong.* (1928); *Memoirs of John Quincy Adams,* vols. VII, IX, X (1876).]
                                              P. D.·E.

SLAFTER, EDMUND FARWELL (May 30, 1816–Sept. 22, 1906), Protestant Episcopal clergyman, author, was born at Norwich, Vt., the seventh of the ten children of Sylvester and Mary (Johnson) Slafter, and a descendant of John Slaughter (Slafter) who emigrated from England to Massachusetts in 1680, and later went to Connecticut. Edmund's great-grandfather, Samuel, was one of the original proprietors of Norwich, Vt. The boy grew up on his father's farm in Thetford, preparing for college at the local academy. He graduated from Dartmouth in 1840, and studied at the Andover Theological Seminary in 1840–41 and 1842–44. On July 12, 1844, he was ordained a deacon of the Protestant Episcopal Church, and on July 30 of the following year, priest. He served as rector of St. Peter's Church, Cambridge, Mass. (1844–46), and of St. John's Church at Jamaica Plain (1846–53). Meanwhile, he had married, Aug. 16, 1849, Mary Anne Hazen of Boston, who brought him sufficient wealth to permit him to retire from pastoral work when his health weakened in 1853. His vigor restored by 1857, he became superintendent, for his denomination, of the American Bible Society. This post he held for twenty years. Since its duties were not burdensome, he had ample leisure for the quiet activities of the scholar which he pursued for the rest of his long life.

From the time he joined the New England Historic Genealogical Society in 1861 he was one of its most active members. From 1867 to 1887 he was its corresponding secretary; from 1867 to 1889, a director; from 1879 to 1889 a member of its committee on publication; and to the end of his life a frequent contributor to its *Register.* His interest in genealogy, evinced by the study of his own family, *Memorial of John Slafter* (1869), soon ripened into historical research. The results of his labors appeared in the publications of the Prince Society, an organization formed in 1858 to preserve and extend the knowledge of American history by editing and printing important source material. Slafter served as its secretary in 1865–66 and as its vice-president from 1866 to 1880, when he became its president, which position he held until his death. Of its monographs he edited *Sir William Alexander and American Colonization* (1873), *Voyages of the Northmen to America* (1877), *Voyages of Samuel de Champlain* (3 vols., 1878–82), and *John Checkley, or, The Evolution of Religious Tolerance in Massachusetts Bay* (2 vols., 1897). He also contributed a well documented chapter on Champlain to the fourth volume (1885) of Justin Winsor's *Narrative and Critical History of America.* Among his minor publications were contributions to the journals of other New England societies.

Slafter maintained an active interest in the work of his Church long after he gave up preaching. From 1884 until his death he was registrar of the diocese of Massachusetts; and to him is due the foundation and development of the rich diocesan library. During a considerable period he was also assistant to the rector of Trinity Church, Boston. Absorbed as he was in historical and religious work, he yet found time for the successful management of his moderate fortune, which he increased considerably. Having no children, he bequeathed his estate to various educational and charitable institutions. The portrait of himself, which he left to the Massachusetts Historical Society, shows a kindly, sensitive face, and a strong, firm chin. He died at Hampton, N. H.

[*Who's Who in America*, 1906–07; C. K. Bolton in *New England Hist. and Geneal. Reg.*, Apr. 1907; M. D. Gilman, *The Bibliog. of Vt.* (1897); *The Prince Society*, 1903; *Boston Daily Advertiser*, Sept. 24, 1906.]
P. D. E.

SLATER, JOHN FOX (Mar. 4, 1815–May 7, 1884), manufacturer, philanthropist, was born in Slatersville, R. I. His father was John Slater who emigrated from England to the United States about 1804 after having familiarized himself with machinery for the making of yarns and cloths. His mother was Ruth (Bucklin) Slater of Pawtucket, R. I., where Samuel Slater [*q.v.*], an uncle, had established the first cotton mill in the United States. Young Slater received a good education and attended academies in Plainfield, Conn., and at Wrentham and Wilbraham, Mass. When he was seventeen, he began work in his father's woolen mill at Hopeville, Conn., of which he was placed in full charge by the time he was twenty-one. He was next entrusted with the management of his father's cotton mill in the nearby village of Jewett City. About 1842 he removed to Norwich, Conn., where he died some forty years later. On May 13, 1844, he married Marianna L. Hubbard, by whom he had six children. On the passing away of his father in 1843 he came into a modest fortune. He at once formed an equal partnership with his brother William S. Slater to manufacture cotton and woolen goods. In the course of a few decades he became very wealthy. When he and his brother dissolved their partnership in 1872 he retained the Jewett City mill and also an interest in the Ponemah mill at Taftville, a suburb of Norwich. This cost $1,500,000 to build and when opened on Nov. 16, 1871, was probably the second largest plant of its kind in the world.

He was of a devout disposition and contributed liberally both to the erection and upkeep of the Park Congregational Church of Norwich, of which he was a member. Always interested in educational questions, he in 1868 helped to found and endow the Norwich Free Academy. Influenced by the successful working of the Peabody Education Fund for negroes he finally decided, probably without any outside suggestion, to give a million dollars toward conferring Christian education upon the lately emancipated population of the Southern states. On Apr. 28, 1882, the New York legislature passed an act incorporating the John F. Slater Fund, and in the following month he transferred the promised million to its first board of trustees, of which the president was Rutherford B. Hayes. This munificent gift was widely acclaimed, and Congress passed a resolution thanking the donor and bestowing on him a gold medal. Slater, disliking publicity, did not even strive for the perpetuation of his own name. He expressly directed that his fund might be wound up after thirty-three years should there be no serious need for it. However, the fund still (1935) exists and in the fifty years following its establishment it distributed nearly four million dollars, mainly in aiding the training of teachers for the colored race.

[*Documents relating to the origin and work of the Slater Trustees 1882 to 1894* (1894); S. H. Howe, "A Brief Memoir of the Life of John F. Slater," *The Trustees of the John F. Slater Fund Occasional Papers*, No. 2 (1894); D. C. Gilman, *Memorial Sketch of John F. Slater* (1885); *Proc. of the Trustees of the John F. Slater Fund, 1884* (1885); *Vital Records of Norwich*, pt. 2 (1913), p. 907; *Appletons' Ann. Cyc. . . . 1884* (1885); *N. Y. Daily Tribune*, Mar. 8, 1884.]
H. G. V.

SLATER, SAMUEL (June 9, 1768–Apr. 21, 1835), founder of the American cotton industry, was born at "Holly House" in Belper, Derbyshire, England, where his father William Slater, a respected, educated independent farmer, lived and tilled his own land. His mother was Elizabeth (Fox) Slater. Young Slater received the ordinary English education, in which he manifested a particular interest in mathematics. Appreciating this, his father arranged that upon the completion of his education Samuel should enter the employ of a neighbor, Jedediah Strutt, who was in partnership with Richard Arkwright in the development of cotton manufacturing machinery. When he was fourteen his father died suddenly, and on Jan. 8, 1783, he was apprenticed to Strutt for six and a half years. Strutt's natural interest in his friend's son, coupled with Slater's unusual aptitude, created an affection between the two which Strutt showed in advice and help. Although Strutt believed that cotton manufacturing in England would always yield a living to the individual manufacturer, he saw no great future for it. Influenced by this opinion and by the advertisements of bounties offered by the state legislatures in America for experienced textile men and machines, Slater decided to go to America. Since at that time the exportation from England of any data relative to textile machinery was prohibited, he set out first to acquaint himself thoroughly with cotton machinery as made by Arkwright, James Hargreaves, and Samuel Crompton. After completing his apprenticeship when he was a little over twenty-one, he remained for a short time to supervise Strutt's mill and the erection of new works, and to get a general knowledge of the business, and then in September 1789 embarked for America—in disguise, since the emigration of textile workers was forbidden—carrying all of his information in his head. He reached New York in November and was first employed by the New York Manufacturing Company. In January 1790 he met Moses Brown in Providence, R. I., and on Apr. 5, 1790, signed a contract with Almy & Brown to reproduce Arkwright's cotton machinery for them. Brown had a wooden spinning-frame that was not satisfactory and was quite ready to agree to the building of new machinery. Almost a year passed before the first machines were put into operation, for Slater was handicapped by lack both of skilled mechanics and of tools, but sales of American-made cotton yarn began almost immediately thereafter. In 1793 they built their first factory in Pawtucket under the firm name of Almy, Brown & Slater. On Oct. 2, 1791, Slater married a daughter of Oziel Wilkinson, Hannah Wilkinson, who is said to have conceived the idea of making sewing-thread of fine cotton yarn instead of linen and to have produced thread so satisfactory that her brothers established a factory to make it. In 1798, still continuing his relationship with Almy & Brown, he formed a partnership with his father-in-law and brothers-in-law, known as Samuel Slater & Company. Manufacturing their own machinery, they erected their first cotton manufacturing plant near Pawtucket; subsequently they began the spinning of yarn in Smithfield, R. I. (later called Slatersville), and at East Webster, Mass. They reëstablished a defunct cotton mill at Jewett City, Conn., and finally erected a mill at Amoskeag Falls, N. H., on the Merrimac River, which was the foundation of the great manufacturing industries now located at Manchester. Besides these large mill operations, which he directed until his death, Slater was an incorporator and for fifteen years president of the Manufacturers' Bank in Pawtucket. After the death of his first wife in 1812, he married Esther, widow of Robert Parkinson of Philadelphia, Nov. 21, 1817. There were nine children by the first marriage (White, *post*, p. 242), of whom six sons were living in 1817.

[G. S. White, *Memoir of Samuel Slater, the Father of Am. Manufactures* (1836); Henry Howe, *Memoirs of the Most Eminent Am. Mechanics* (1844); W. R. Bagnall, *Samuel Slater and the Early Developments of the Cotton Manufacture in the U. S.* (1890); F. L. Lewton, "Samuel Slater and the Oldest Cotton Machinery in America," *Ann. Report Smithsonian Inst., 1926; The Slater Mills at Webster* (n.d.); *The Biog.*

Cyc. of Rep. Men of R. I. (1881); J. D. Van Slyck, *Representatives of New England* (2 vols., 1879); Massena Goodrich, *Hist. Sketch of the Town of Pawtucket* (1876); "The Slater Cotton Centennial, 1790–1890," *Providence Daily Jour. and Evening Bull.*, Sept. 29, 1890; obituary in *Manufacturers and Farmers Jour.*, Apr. 23, 1835.]   C. W. M—n.

SLATTERY, CHARLES LEWIS (Dec. 9, 1867–Mar. 12, 1930), bishop of the Protestant Episcopal Church, was born at Pittsburgh, Pa., son of the Rev. George Sidney Leffingwell and Emma McClellan (Hall) Slattery. He was a descendant of Thomas Slattery who emigrated from Ireland and was in Westerly, R. I., some time before 1780. Charles's father, a clergyman of the Episcopal Church, died in early life, leaving his family little more than an inspiring tradition. Returning to Maine with his widowed mother, young Slattery grew up in an environment of culture and natural beauty. The Rev. Harry P. Nichols of Brunswick, and, later, Bishop Phillips Brooks, were the mentors of his youth. He graduated with honors from Harvard in 1891 and from the Episcopal Theological School, Cambridge, in 1894. On June 20 of the same year he was ordained deacon by Bishop Lawrence, and on June 8, 1895, priest.

From 1894 to 1896 he was a master at Groton School and rector of St. Andrew's Church, Ayer, Mass. In the latter year he became dean of the Cathedral of Our Merciful Saviour, at Faribault, Minn., while Bishop Henry B. Whipple [*q.v.*], "Apostle to the Indians," was still living. In 1907 he was called to Christ Church, Springfield, Mass., where he served until 1910, when he became rector of Grace Church, New York City, in succession to the Rev. William R. Huntington [*q.v.*]. He was elected bishop coadjutor of Massachusetts on May 3, 1922, and was consecrated at Trinity Church, Boston, on Oct. 31, of the same year. When Bishop Lawrence retired, May 30, 1927, Bishop Slattery automatically succeeded him. He died at his home in Boston after a brief illness, and he was buried in Mount Auburn Cemetery, Cambridge.

Slattery was preëminently a scholar and a pastor. "He had a consuming love of books and of sound learning. He combined a sensitiveness to truth with a fine appreciation of beauty" (*Churchman*, Apr. 5, 1930, p. 10). During the thirty-five years of his busy ministry he wrote a total of some twenty-five volumes as well as countless occasional papers for the periodical press. Among his best known works were: *The Master of the World: A Study of Christ* (1906); *Life beyond Life: A Study of Immortality* (1907); *The Historic Ministry and the Present Christ: An Appeal for Unity* (1908); *The Au-*

thority of Religious Experience (1912); *Why Men Pray* (1916); *The Holy Communion* (1918); *The Ministry* (1921); *Following Christ* (1928), and biographies of Felix Reville Brunot, Edward Lincoln Atkinson, Alexander Viets Griswold Allen, William Austin Smith, and David Hummell Greer. To the Church at large his supreme contribution was his devoted labor during fifteen years toward the revision and enrichment of the Book of Common Prayer, a task which he lived to complete and the fruits of which he saw generally accepted. In all his work he combined liberality of outlook with great spirituality. As a parish priest and guide he showed real genius. Equipped with an abundant natural love for pastoral duty, he conceived it a privilege to maintain close personal touch with his people, and was tireless in his endeavor to be a true shepherd to his flock.

The calls made upon him, however, were numerous and varied. For many years he was general chairman of the Church Congress in the United States. He served on the Church commissions on the hymnal and the lectionary, and was chairman of the commission on the revision of the Book of Common Prayer. He lectured at the Seabury Divinity School, 1905–07, and at the Berkeley Divinity School, 1909–10, and gave the Paddock lectures at the General Theological Seminary, 1911–12, and the West lectures at Stanford University, 1915. He was an overseer of Harvard College, a trustee of Boston University and of Brooks School, Andover, and president of the board of trustees of Wellesley College. On Nov. 19, 1923, he was married to Sarah, daughter of Bishop Lawrence, by whom he was survived.

[H. C. Robbins, *Charles Lewis Slattery* (1931); *Boston Transcript*, Mar. 13–15, 1930; *N. Y. Times*, Nov. 20, 1923, June 2, 1927, Mar. 13, 1930; *Churchman*, Mar. 22, Apr. 5, 1930; *Living Church*, Mar. 22, 29, 1930; the files of *Church Militant*, 1922–30; *Who's Who in America*, 1928–29; and information from personal friends.]   J. W. F.

SLAUGHTER, PHILIP (Oct. 26, 1808–June 12, 1890), Episcopal clergyman, historian, was born at his father's home, "Springfield," in Culpeper County, Va., a descendant of a family that had been prominent in Culpeper County since the earlier years of its settlement; his parents were Philip Slaughter, a captain in the American Revolution, and his wife, Elizabeth, daughter of Col. Thomas Towles, of Lancaster County, Va., and widow of William Brock. After preliminary training at an academy in Winchester, in 1825 the younger Philip entered the University of Virginia, finishing his course in 1828. For five years he practised law, giving up this profes-

sion in order to prepare himself for the ministry of the Protestant Episcopal Church at the Theological Seminary in Virginia, at Alexandria.

Ordained deacon in May 1834 and advanced to the priesthood in July 1835, he was in active pastoral work for about twelve years, serving the Church in Middleburg, Va.; Christ Church, Georgetown, D. C.; Meade and Johns parishes, Fauquier County; and for the last five years of this period, St. Paul's Church, Petersburg.

He quickly came into prominence as a remarkably effective preacher of the intensely evangelical type, and his services were in constant demand in series of meetings, called "Associations." In connection with these, he preached in many of the city churches and rural parishes of Virginia. Though brief, writes a biographer, his active ministry was "brilliant and effective. He had all the personal magnetism, the fire and spiritual power of Whitefield. Great crowds attended on his ministry and conversions were numbered by the hundred" (Brock, *post*, p. xii).

His health failing, he spent the years 1848 and 1849 in travel in Europe, and was then compelled to give up the hope of further continuous pastoral work. Returning to Richmond, he established in 1850 the *Virginia Colonizationist,* a periodical published in the interests of the colonization of negro slaves in Africa. For five years he edited this periodical with signal ability, and was successful in enlisting the interest of the Virginia legislature and in securing large appropriations for the project. He then removed to his own home on Slaughter's Mountain in Culpeper County. With the aid of friends he erected a church building upon his father's farm in which he preached as his health permitted. The church was destroyed during the Civil War. Driven from his home by invading forces, he found refuge with his family in Petersburg. While sojourning here he published a religious paper, the *Army and Navy Messenger,* for distribution among the soldiers of the Confederate army. At the close of the war he returned to his home in Culpeper County and devoted the remainder of his life to historical and genealogical studies, in which from early life he had been interested.

In 1846 he published *A History of Bristol Parish,* and the following year, *A History of St. George's Parish,* both of which were revised and republished, the former in 1879 by Slaughter himself, and the latter in 1890 by Dr. R. A. Brock. The publication of these doubtless did much to arouse interest in the preservation of the original records of many other parishes and the protection of the historic records of the state.

Slaughter had formulated a plan for the preparation of a general history of the old parishes and families of Virginia and for years had been gathering material, but his declining health compelled him to relinquish the task and to turn over the material to Bishop William Meade [*q.v.*], who after years of research published in 1857 his monumental work, *Old Churches, Ministers, and Families of Virginia.* Slaughter himself wrote *A History of St. Mark's Parish* (1877) and had practically completed, at the time of his death, *The History of Truro Parish,* which was published in 1908 by Rev. Edward L. Goodwin. In addition to his parish histories, Slaughter was the author of many historical books, pamphlets, and addresses, among the most important being: *The Virginian History of African Colonization* (1855); *A Sketch of the Life of Randolph Fairfax* (1864); *Memoir of Col. Joshua Fry* (1880); *Christianity the Key to the Character and Career of Washington* (1886). His more significant monographs include his address at the semicentennial celebration of the Theological Seminary in Virginia (1873); a paper on historic churches of Virginia printed in W. S. Perry's *The History of the American Episcopal Church* (1885); "The Colonial Church in Virginia," published in *Addresses and Historical Papers Before the Centennial Council of the Protestant Episcopal Church in Virginia* (1885); and a biography of the Rt. Rev. William Meade, in *Memorial Biographies of the New England Historic and Genealogical Society* (vol. IV, 1885).

The Diocese of Virginia elected him historiographer of the diocese in 1879, and after his death honored him by giving his name to a parish in that part of Culpeper County in which he lived. On June 20, 1834, he married Anne Sophia, daughter of Dr. Thomas Semmes, of Alexandria, Va., who with one daughter survived him.

[Biog. sketch by R. A. Brock in Slaughter's *History of St. George's Parish* (2nd ed., 1890); *Southern Churchman,* June 19, 26, July 10, 1890; *Richmond Dispatch,* June 15, 1890; reports of the historiographer and other records in the council journals of the Diocese of Va.]   G. M. B.

SLEEPER, JACOB (Nov. 21, 1802–Mar. 31, 1889), merchant, philanthropist, son of Jacob and Olive (Dinsdale) Sleeper, was born in Newcastle, Me. He received his early education in the common schools and at Lincoln Academy. When he was fourteen, his parents died and he was placed in the care of his uncle in Belfast, where he worked in the latter's store and subsequently in a store of his own. Seeking medical relief from a lameness which troubled him all through life, though it did not noticeably affect

him, in 1825 he went to Boston, where he was a bookkeeper for True & Brodhead, dealers in naval supplies. Here he received the business training which in 1835 led him to form a partnership with Andrew Carney, a clothier. Carney's contracts for furnishing clothing to the navy, made before the panic of 1837, proved especially profitable in a period of falling prices and the firm prospered steadily. When Sleeper withdrew from business in 1850, his fortune was estimated to be $250,000, a sum which investments in real estate increased considerably.

After his retirement he became interested for a brief time in politics. He was a member of the state House of Representatives in 1851 and 1852; of the Governor's Council from 1859 to 1861 inclusive; and an alderman of Boston in 1852 and 1853. As candidate for mayor in the latter year on the Young Men's League ticket, he was defeated. His greatest interest, however, was the Methodist Episcopal Church, of which he became a member at the age of twenty-one. For fifty-nine years he was superintendent of the Sunday School of the Bromfield Street Methodist Episcopal Church, in Boston, and for forty-six years treasurer of the church's board of trustees. He was an original member of the Boston Wesleyan Association, frequently serving as its president, and was a liberal supporter of the New England Methodist Historical Society, of which, also, he was president. As a trustee of Wesleyan University from 1844 to 1878, and as an overseer of Harvard from 1856 to 1868, he became greatly interested in education, and devoted much time to the study of it, both in the United States and in England. This interest led to his becoming, in 1869, one of the three founders of Boston University, the other two being Lee Claflin and Isaac Rich [*q.v.*]. Sleeper's total benefactions to this university exceeded $500,000, nearly all of it given during his lifetime. He was its treasurer, 1869–73, and vice-president of its corporation, 1875–89. Among his other educational interests were Wilbraham Academy, Wilbraham, Mass., the New England Female Medical College, which in 1873 united with the Boston University School of Medicine, and the New England Conservatory of Music. His private philanthropies were innumerable, his practice being to give away yearly the bulk of his income. He himself followed the advice he proffered a friend, "Do as much good as you can, and don't make a fuss about it." He was married twice: first, May 7, 1827, to Eliza Davis; and second, Apr. 7, 1835, to her sister Maria. He had three daughters and a son. His death occurred in Boston.

[*Boston Jour.* and *Boston Transcript*, Apr. 1, 1889;
Zion's Herald, Apr. 3, 1889; Abner Forbes and J. W.
Green, *The Rich Men of Mass.* (1851); *The Twenty
Years of Boston Univ. 1869–1889. Fifteenth Ann. Report
of the President* (1890); John C. Rand, *One of a
Thousand* (1890); *Methodist Rev.*, Sept.-Oct. 1889;
D. L. Marsh, *The Founders of Boston University*
(1932).]   R. E. M.

SLICER, THOMAS ROBERTS (Apr. 16,
1847–May 29, 1916), Unitarian clergyman, was
born in Washington, D. C., the son of Henry and
Elizabeth Coleman (Roberts) Slicer. His father, of Scotch descent, was a prominent minister of the Methodist Episcopal Church and several times chaplain of Congress. Thomas was
educated in the public schools of Baltimore and
in Baltimore City College. When he was twenty
years old he was admitted on trial to the East
Baltimore Conference of the Methodist Church;
he was ordained deacon in 1869 and elder in
1871. He then transferred to the Colorado Conference and was pastor at Denver (1871) and
Georgetown (1872). Returning East, he became a member of the New York Conference in
1873. After serving churches within its bounds
for several years, he was impelled by changes in
his theological views to sever his Methodist connections and to unite with the Unitarians. Pastorates in Providence, R. I. (1881-90), and Buffalo, N. Y. (1890-97), were followed by one at
All Souls Church, New York City, which continued until his death. On Apr. 5, 1871, he married Adeline E. Herbert, daughter of Theodore
C. Herbert of the United States Navy.

Slicer achieved prominence in three ways:
through his preaching, through his writings, and
as a civic reformer. He had the ability, though
speaking extemporaneously, to express ideas co-
gently, consecutively, and in a manner that held
the close attention of his hearers. Many of his
sermons and addresses, stenographically reported, appeared in print, and his church is said to
have been one of the few to which strangers
in New York City asked to be directed. His
theological views are set forth in such publications as *The Great Affirmations of Religion*
(1898), *The Foundations of Religion* (1902),
One World at a Time (1902), and *The Way to
Happiness* (1907). They are an attempt to guide
those emancipated from the bonds of orthodoxy
to a rational religion, and the fundamental ideas
they elaborate are that religion is a natural function of the human soul, since the mind is so constituted that it cannot conceive of the causeless;
that, consequently, the assumption that what is
best in man's mind and feeling has its counterpart at the heart of the universe, is inescapable;
and that the religious life consists in the devel-

oping of this best to its perfection in the individual and in society. There was a poetic strain
in his temperament and his interest in the field
of literature led him to publish *Percy Bysshe
Shelley, an Appreciation* (1903) and *From Poet
to Premier: the Centennial Cycle 1809–1909*
(1909), which offers commentaries on Poe, Lincoln, Holmes, Darwin, Tennyson, and Gladstone,
all born in 1809. After his death, a volume of selections from his writings, which he himself had
put together as an aid to devotion, was published
under the title, *Meditations: a Message for All
Souls* (1919).

Although convinced that an ideal society can
be achieved only through the regeneration of the
individual, he believed that those who sought that
ideal were called to combat social evils. To many,
therefore, he was best known as a militant leader
of civic reform. While at Buffalo he was in the
thick of the fight for clean politics and better
municipal institutions. Upon going to New
York, he became a member of the City Club, organized to aid in securing permanent good government for the city, and was later placed on its
board of trustees. As chairman of one of its committees he formulated the charges against District Attorney Asa Bird Gardiner in 1900. These
were dismissed by Gov. Theodore Roosevelt,
who, however, later in the year removed Gardiner from office (*Public Papers of Theodore
Roosevelt, Governor, 1900*, pp. 186–87, 200–05).
Slicer also carried on a warfare against gambling institutions, which brought him much publicity. He was chairman of the National Commission on Prison Labor, a member of the council of the Immigration League, and a trustee of
the People's Institute, to which he was especially
devoted. His varied exertions broke down his
health and for two or three years before his
death, in New York City, he was comparatively
inactive.

[*Minutes* of the East Baltimore, Colorado and N. Y.
Conferences of the M. E. Ch.; *Who's Who in America*,
1916–17; obituary of Henry Slicer in *Christian Advocate* (N. Y.), Apr. 30, 1874; *Christian Register*, June
8, 22, 1916; *N. Y. Times, Sun* (N. Y.), and *Buffalo
Express*, May 30, 1916.]   H. E. S.

SLIDELL, JOHN (1793–July 29, 1871), Louisiana politician, diplomat, was born in New
York City. His mother, Margery (called May)
Mackenzie, was a Scotswoman; his father, for
whom he was named, became a respected merchant and president of the Tradesmen's Insurance Company and the Mechanics' Bank. His
younger brother, Alexander Slidell Mackenzie
[*q.v.*], adopted the name of a maternal uncle,
and his sister Jane married Matthew C. Perry
[*q.v.*]. After graduating at Columbia College

in 1810, John went into a mercantile business with James McCrea, but this was ruined by the Embargo policy and the War of 1812. In 1819, partly because of this failure, and partly because of the scandal resulting from a duel (Scoville, *post*, pp. 258–60), he removed to New Orleans, equipped with a knowledge of law and commercial principles; by 1833 he boasted that his practice yielded him $10,000 annually. Two years later he was married to Mathilde Deslonde, a Creole girl of twenty.

Slidell was defeated for Congress on the Jackson ticket in 1828, but he was appointed district attorney at New Orleans the following year. His rival, Martin Gordon, soon procured his dismissal, and neither Jackson nor Van Buren was sympathetic when he suggested a diplomatic post in 1833, though he continued to support Van Buren for a decade longer. In 1834 and again in 1836 he was an unsuccessful candidate for the United States Senate. As a member of Congress from 1843 to 1845, he advocated the use of the civil law in federal courts in Louisiana, a reduction of the tariff, except the duty on sugar, and remission of the fine levied against Jackson in 1815. In the election of 1844 he and other Democrats transported "floaters" from New Orleans to Plaquemines parish under doubtful legal authority, and thereby assured a majority for Polk in Louisiana (*Congressional Globe,* 28 Cong., 2 Sess., pp. 233, 243; Greer, *post,* p. 31). Late in 1845 he was appointed commissioner to Mexico to adjust the Texan boundary and Mexican claims, and to purchase New Mexico and if possible California. Although the Mexican government had agreed to receive an agent, it refused to treat with him upon the technical ground that his credentials were faulty. Withdrawing to Jalapa to wait and observe, he remained until April without accomplishing his major object, and apparently without justifying the American cause to other powers. His mission did, however, help to prepare the American conscience for a war to secure what could not be acquired through diplomatic channels. In 1853 he declined the Central American mission but accepted an agency to sell bonds of the New Orleans and Nashville Railroad in London.

Slidell had a twofold ambition, to attain a seat in the Senate for himself and the presidency for Buchanan. His rival in the Louisiana Democracy, Pierre Soulé [*q.v.*], whose ultra-Southern position contrasted with his own rôle as a moderate national Democrat, defeated him for the Senate in 1848, but Soulé's appointment as minister to Spain in 1853 opened the way for Slidell's entrance into that body, where he remained

until 1861. He favored repeal of the Missouri Compromise, credited Buchanan with the Ostend Manifesto, and blamed Pierce with the failure of the movement to acquire Cuba. After two unsuccessful attempts to secure the Democratic nomination for Buchanan, he widened his activities as campaign manager in 1856 and materially promoted Buchanan's nomination and election. Accepting responsibility for the success of the incoming administration, he recommended numerous cabinet and diplomatic appointments though he himself preferred to remain in the Senate as its spokesman. In 1858 he presented a resolution to grant the president limited authority to suspend neutrality laws, with a view to promoting filibustering, and the next year he introduced a bill to appropriate thirty millions to purchase Cuba (*Congressional Globe,* 35 Cong., 1 Sess., pp. 461–62; 35 Cong., 2 Sess., p. 277). He urged admission of Kansas under the Lecompton constitution as a test of the abstract principle of non-intervention, and questioned whether the Union would long endure if the bill should fail to pass. Never a friend of Douglas, he headed the movement to read him out of the party in 1858, managed the redistribution of the federal patronage in Illinois, and opposed his nomination at the Charleston convention. Although Slidell supported the Breckinridge-Lane ticket in 1860, he was a moderate Union man until Lincoln's election was interpreted as a cause for secession. Returning to Congress for the session of 1860–61, he found himself at odds with the administration, though he did not break with Buchanan until John B. Floyd was replaced in the War Department.

Slidell's Mexican mission and residence in Louisiana made him a logical appointee to represent the Confederacy in France. He reached Nassau safely and, with James M. Mason [*q.v.*], newly appointed agent to England, took passage on the British mail steamer *Trent.* Their removal and detention at Fort Warren, Boston, caused a tense diplomatic situation and delayed their arrival in Europe until Jan. 30, 1862. Reaching Paris early in February, Slidell was enthusiastically greeted by Confederate sympathizers. Napoleon III received him cordially at Vichy in July, and avowed sympathy for the Confederacy, but found difficulty in giving it material expression. Slidell proposed recognition of independence and a Franco-Confederate treaty which would admit French products duty free and provide a cotton subsidy for naval convoys of merchant vessels. He left with the impression that if Great Britain did not soon favor joint action, France would move by herself. In a second interview at St. Cloud on Oct 28, Napoleon proposed a six months' armistice with Confederate ports open, which if refused by the North would justify recognition and perhaps intervention. The Emperor also suggested a Confederate navy and implied that vessels might be built in French shipyards. In 1863 Slidell and James D. Bulloch [q.v.] arranged with Arman and Voruz for the construction of two ironclads and four corvettes at Nantes and Bordeaux. Although the scheme had the approval of the Emperor, protests from William L. Dayton [q.v.] led to official notification that the vessels could not enter Confederate service. Meanwhile it appeared that the rams for which Bulloch had contracted at Liverpool would not be delivered. An ingenious scheme was concocted with Bravay & Company of Paris to purchase them for delivery to the Sultan of Turkey, but this plan also failed. Early in 1863 a contract was arranged with Emile Erlanger, whose son married Slidell's daughter, to lend the Confederacy £3,000,-000 secured by cotton to be delivered within six months after the war closed. The sale of bonds netted little more than one-sixth of the amount because of high commissions and discounts and the necessity for "bulling" the market. On numerous occasions Slidell approved Napoleon's Mexican venture and attempted unsuccessfully to use it, along with a belated offer of emancipation, as leverage to secure recognition of the Confederacy.

Slidell and his family continued to reside in Paris with occasional visits to England until the Empire fell. He had a son, two daughters—both of whom married Frenchmen, and possibly another daughter. Although he did not seek pardon, he applied to President Johnson in 1866 for permission to visit Louisiana, but received no reply. Mrs. Slidell died in 1870, and he died at Cowes the following year. As a diplomat Slidell performed creditably, although with few exceptions Confederate agents in Europe distrusted him. As a politician he was a shrewd manager and skilful wire-puller. His control of men came from great capacity for political intrigue rather than from oratorical effort. He possessed more ingenuity than ability, but shallowness was in part offset by good breeding. From the thirties he wielded a potent influence in Louisiana politics; in the fifties he was political boss of his state; and during the first three years of Buchanan's administration he was the power behind the presidency.

[L. M. Sears, *John Slidell* (1925), contains much material published earlier in *Am. Hist. Rev.*, Jan. 1921, July 1922, and in *So. Atlantic Quart.*, Jan. 1913. Valuable notes are available in Beckles Willson, *John Slidell and the Confederates in Paris* (1932); F. L. Owsley, *King Cotton Diplomacy* (1931); J. H. Smith, *The War with Mexico* (1919), vol. I; S. F. Bemis, ed., *The American Secretaries of State and their Diplomacy*, vol. V (1928); Pierce Butler, *Judah P. Benjamin* (1907). The Buchanan Papers in the Pa. Hist. Soc. Lib. and the James M. Mason Papers in the Lib. of Cong. contain Slidell letters. For his Mexican corres. see Washington *Union*, Apr. 18, 1846, *et seq.* See also John Bigelow, *France and the Confederate Navy* (1888); J. A. Scoville, *The Old Merchants of N. Y. City*, II (1863); J. K. Greer, *Louisiana Politics, 1845-1861* (1930), reprinting articles in *La. Hist. Quart.*]
W. H. S.

SLOAN, JAMES FORMAN (Aug. 10, 1874–Dec. 21, 1933), popularly known as "Tod" Sloan, the most celebrated jockey of the early twentieth century, was born at Bunker Hill, near Kokomo, Ind., and died at Los Angeles, Cal. Like that of most followers of his calling, his origin was humble and obscure, his father having been a barber. James was so small a child that his father called him "Toad," a name which was transformed into "Tod" by his playmates. In later life he signed himself James Todhunter Sloan, in order more ornamentally to account for the nickname which was his universal designation. He was the youngest of three children and his mother died when he was five; soon after, the father, a veteran of the Civil War and no longer able to support himself or keep his family together, was placed in a soldiers' home. The boy was adopted by a woman named Blauser, of Kokomo, where he lived until he was about fifteen. He then ran away and joined the troupe of a so-called "Professor" Talbot, who made balloon ascensions at county fairs. After varied adventures he finally joined fortunes with an elder brother, Cassius, who had become a professional jockey. According to Sloan's own statement he was as a child much afraid of horses and did not overcome this fear entirely for a long while. Eventually, however, he was able to master powerful and rebellious horses and became celebrated for his ability to win the confidence and obedience of his mounts.

For a number of years he knocked about in the lower circles of the turf, making little progress, until he obtained employment from John S. Campbell, of Kansas City, Mo., one of the ablest trainers of his time, who encouraged him to persevere. A boy of quick mentality, he was attracted by the problem of wind-resistance, then just becoming a moot one among athletes, and in view of it adopted the seat in the saddle that was to revolutionize modern race-riding. Lying along the neck and shoulders of his mounts, he rode in what was jeered at as a "monkey-on-a-stick" attitude until his success became so great that imitation followed and finally his way of riding was everywhere adopted. Being ambitious, daring, and of unlimited self-confidence and egoism, after several seasons of glittering success in America, he decided to go abroad, where he made his first appearances in the saddle in England in 1897. There, on account of his peculiar seat, he was the subject of unlimited ridicule, but after he had ridden twenty-one winners in his first season the ridicule ceased. At home he had become the principal rider for William C. Whitney, then the owner of the most powerful racing stable in America. In England he was employed by the leading turf magnates and finally was selected to ride the horses of King Edward VII. He also became a spectacular figure upon the Parisian courses. Thereafter he was seen in America but seldom until his career came to a sudden and sensational end by the announcement in 1901 that he had been refused a license to ride in England by the Jockey Club, an action which led to his being banned by all other turf bodies of repute the world over.

The reasons assigned for the action of the Jockey Club were his activities in the betting ring and other conduct "prejudicial to the best interests of the sport." Many and powerful efforts were made to have him restored to good standing but they were unsuccessful. In the perspective of time it has become the impression that the extreme and severe punishment allotted him was out of all proportion to any misdemeanors that he may have committed. Prior to his disgrace, Sloan had accumulated a fortune said to have approximated $300,000, but it was dissipated in a few years of prodigal living and futile efforts to establish himself in various enterprises. He returned to America and thereafter until his death led a hand-to-mouth existence, finally dying penniless after a long illness. Always a diminutive personage, at his death he was reported to have weighed but sixty pounds. He was twice married, in each case to an actress: first, in 1907 to Julia Sanderson, from whom he was divorced in 1913; second, in 1920, to Elizabeth Saxon Malone, from whom he was divorced in 1927. By his second wife he had one daughter. Sloan is generally accorded, by the best authorities, the credit of being an epochal man in his profession, not only because of his peculiar seat (in which he had been anticipated by an earlier American jockey, Edward H. Garrison), but also because he introduced the practice of forcing the pace from the fall of the starter's flag, instead of "waiting to win," the system consecrated by immemorial custom previously. In 1915 he published, in London, *Tod Sloan by Him-*

self, an autobiography, written in collaboration with A. Dick Luckman.

[In addition to his autobiog. sources include: L. H. Week, *The Am. Turf* (1898); George Lambton, *Men and Horses I Have Known* (1924); *Idler,* Apr. 1899; *Times* (London), Dec. 22, 1933; *N. Y. Times,* Dec. 22, 1933; data in author's possession.]   J. L. H.

SLOAN, RICHARD ELIHU (June 22, 1857–Dec. 14, 1933), judge, governor, author, was born on a farm in Preble County, Ohio, the son of Dr. Richard and Mary (Caldwell) Sloan. His ancestors on both sides were of Scotch-Irish origin, and settled first in South Carolina. After graduating A.B. at Monmouth College, Illinois, in 1877, he taught in a preparatory school for about a year, meanwhile beginning the study of law in an office at Hamilton, Ohio. He then went to Denver, Colo., where he worked as a reporter on the *Daily Rocky Mountain News* while continuing his law studies. From 1879 to 1882 he tried his fortune in the mining regions of Leadville and Breckenridge, Colo., but in the last-named year returned to his native state and entered the Law School of the Cincinnati College (now University of Cincinnati), where he received the degree of LL.B. two years later.

Planning to practise in the West, he went to San Francisco, but upon the advice of a friend to "try Arizona," opened an office, with a classmate, at Phoenix, where he was enrolled as a member of the territorial bar in January 1885. After about two years he removed to Florence, distant some seventy-five miles, upon the promise of appointment as district attorney of Pinal County, an office which he held for two years. In 1887 he returned to Ohio and married, Nov. 22, Mary Brown of Hamilton, by whom he had three children, a son who predeceased his father, and two daughters who survived him. In 1888 he was a delegate from Pinal County to the Republican territorial convention, where he was chosen temporary chairman and made the "keynote speech." Later in the same year he was elected a member of the Territorial Council and served one term, being on several committees and chairman of that on the judiciary.

His most noteworthy service began in October 1889, when he was appointed by President Benjamin Harrison as a judge of the territorial supreme court—the first *bona fide* resident of Arizona to receive such an appointment. He thereupon removed to Tucson and, like his associates, exercised *nisi prius* as well as appellate jurisdiction. In his appellate court work, his first important opinion was in *Cheyney* vs. *Smith* (3 *Ariz.*, 143), Mar. 24, 1890, holding that the limit of "sixty days duration" fixed by the federal statute for territorial legislative sessions, meant sixty working, but not necessarily consecutive, days. In *Porter* vs. *Hughes* (4 *Ariz.*, 1), he held that the governor's affixing of his signature to an appropriation bill constituted approval of the whole measure, even though he disapproved a specific item; and in *Carroll* vs. *Byers* (4 *Ariz.*, 158), he held unconstitutional a territorial statute authorizing verdicts by nine jurors in civil cases and misdemeanor prosecutions. Toward the close of his term he was obliged to commit for contempt an editor and his attorney for falsely charging in the former's paper that the judge was closeted with the prosecuting attorney following the argument of a demurrer to the editor's indictment for criminal libel. Friends of the convicted parties thereupon sought Judge Sloan's removal; but President Cleveland not only permitted him to serve the balance of his term but for some eight months thereafter (until June 1894), before he appointed a successor. Sloan then reëntered the practice of his profession, at Prescott; but, after three years he was restored to the bench by President McKinley (July 8, 1897), and was twice reappointed by President Theodore Roosevelt. He served in all seventeen years—longer than any other Arizona judge up to his time. His first important opinion during his second period was that in *Gage* vs. *McCord* (5 *Ariz.*, 227), wherein he construed the federal act authorizing the obligations of the territory and its subdivisions to be refunded. In 1908 he was elected a delegate to the Republican National Convention, where he secured the adoption of a plank favoring statehood for Arizona. In the following year he was tendered by President Taft the post of governor, which he accepted, qualifying May 1, 1909. Thus within a quarter century he served with distinction in all three branches of the Arizona government—legislative, judicial, and executive—and was its last territorial governor. In March 1911 he presided at the dedication of the Roosevelt Dam and in February 1912 he surrendered his office to the recently elected governor of the new state.

The remaining years of his life were devoted to professional and literary labors. He will be long remembered as the supervising editor of the four-volume *History of Arizona* (1930) as well as for his *Memories of an Arizona Judge* (Stanford University Press, 1932). He died at Phoenix as the result of a fall.

[*Memories* above mentioned; *Journals of the Fifteenth Legislative Assembly of the Territory of Ariz.* (1889); 3–12 *Ariz. Reports*; *Portrait and Biog. Record of Ariz.* (1901); *Hist. of Ariz.*, mentioned above, III, 10–13; *Who's Who in America*, 1932–33; *Arizona Independent Republic* (Phoenix), Dec. 15, 1933; middle name from a daughter, Mrs. Blake C. Wilbur.]

C.S.L.

SLOAN, SAMUEL (Dec. 25, 1817–Sept. 22, 1907), railroad executive, was a son of William and Elizabeth (Simpson) Sloan of Lisburn, County Down, Ireland. When he was a year old he was brought by his parents to New York. At the age of fourteen, the death of his father compelled Samuel to withdraw from the Columbia College Preparatory School, and he found employment in an importing house on Cedar Street, with which he remained connected for twenty-five years, becoming head of the firm. On Apr. 8, 1844, he was married, in New Brunswick, N. J., to Margaret Elmendorf, and took up his residence in Brooklyn. He was chosen a supervisor of Kings County in 1852, and served as president of the Long Island College Hospital. In 1857, having retired from the importing business, he was elected as a Democrat to the state Senate, of which he was a member for two years.

Sloan at forty was recognized in New York as a successful business man who had weathered two major financial panics, but it could hardly have been predicted that twenty years of modest achievement as a commission merchant would be followed by more than forty years of constructive and profitable effort in a wholly different field—that of transportation. As early as 1855 he had been made a director of the Hudson River Railroad (not yet a part of the New York Central system). Election to the presidency of the road quickly followed, and in the nine years that he guided its destinies (including the Civil War period), the market value of the company's shares rose from $17 to $140. Resigning from the Hudson River, he was elected, in 1864, a director, and in 1867, president, of the Delaware, Lackawanna & Western Railroad, then and long after known as one of the small group of "coal roads" that divided the Pennsylvania anthracite territory. Beginning in the reconstruction and expansion era following the Civil War, Sloan's administration of thirty-two years covered the period of shipping rebates, "cut-throat" competition, and hostile state legislation, culminating in federal regulation through the Interstate Commerce Commission. Sloan's immediate job, as he saw it, was to make the Lackawanna more than a "coal road," serving a limited region. Extensions north and west, and, finally, entrance into Buffalo, made it a factor in general freight handling. Readjustments had to be made. It was imperative, for example, that the old gauge of six feet be shifted to the standard 4' 8½". This feat was achieved in 1876, with a delay to traffic of only twenty-four hours. The total cost of the improvement was $1,250,000. Great changes in the road's traffic ensued. In the decade 1881–90, while coal shipments increased thirty-two per cent., general freight gained 160 per cent. and passenger traffic, eighty-eight per cent. Dividends of seven per cent. were paid yearly from 1885 to 1905.

Although Sloan resigned the presidency in 1899, he continued for the remaining eight years of his life as chairman of the board of directors. At his death, in 1907, at the age of ninety years, he had been continuously employed in railroad administration for more than half a century and had actually been president of seventeen corporations. He died in Garrison, N. Y., survived by his wife and six children.

[*Evening Post* (N. Y.), and *N. Y. Tribune*, Sept. 23, 1907; *Railroad Gazette*, Oct. 11, 1907; *Who's Who in America*, 1906–07; J. I. Bogen, *The Anthracite Railroads* (1927); annual reports of the Del., Lackawanna & Western Railroad Company; information as to certain facts from a son, Benson Bennett Sloan.]

W. B. S.

SLOAN, TOD [See SLOAN, JAMES FORMAN, 1874–1933].

SLOANE, WILLIAM MILLIGAN (Nov. 12, 1850–Sept. 11, 1928), historian and educator, was born at Richmond, Ohio, where his father, a native of Topsham, Vt., was principal and half the faculty of a combined academy and college. His parents, James Renwick Willson Sloane and Margaret Anne Wylie (Milligan), were of Scotch Covenanter ancestry; both his grandfathers were Presbyterian ministers. When William was five years old, his father became pastor of the Third Reformed Presbyterian Church in New York City, and here the boy received his early education. A graduate of Columbia College (1868) at the age of eighteen, he taught for some five years in a private school. He became interested in history while acting (1873–75) as private secretary and research assistant to George Bancroft [*q.v.*], who for a part of that time was American minister at Berlin. From the University of Leipzig he received the degree of doctor of philosophy in 1876. In the same year he was called to the College of New Jersey at Princeton. There he taught Latin from 1877 until 1883, when he was appointed professor of history and political science. In 1896 he accepted the Seth Low professorship of history at Columbia, continuing in that position until his retirement with the title of professor emeritus twenty years later. In 1912–13 he held the Roosevelt exchange professorship at Berlin and also gave lectures at Munich. Among the other honors he received were election to the presidency of the National Institute of Arts and Letters, the American Historical Association (1911), and

the American Academy of Arts and Letters (1920).

Of his writings, that which attracted most attention was his *Life of Napoleon Bonaparte*. It was published originally in the form of a serial in the *Century Magazine*, beginning in November 1894, was enlarged into four massive volumes in 1896, and appeared in a revised edition in 1910. The product of many years of elaborate investigation, it was sumptuously illustrated and composed in a fashion to appeal to the general reader rather than the historical student. His other works include: *The French Revolution and Religious Reform* (1901); *Party Government in the United States of America* (1914); *The Balkans: A Laboratory of History* (1914); *The Powers and Aims of Western Democracy* (1919); and *Greater France in Africa* (1924). He also published *The Life of James McCosh* (1896) and his father's autobiography, with supplementary material, *Life and Work of J. R. W. Sloane* (1888).

Powerful in build, hearty in manner, genial, urbane, Sloane resembled the diplomat and man of affairs rather than the typical professor. To the duties of presiding officer on public occasions he imparted a gracious dignity. Fluent in conversation, abounding in pithy anecdote and witty allusion, possessed of an extraordinary knowledge of unusual things, he moved always in a circle of friendship and appreciation. He was married, Dec. 27, 1877, to Mary Espy Johnston and they had two sons and two daughters. He died at his home in Princeton, N. J.

[*Who's Who in America*, 1928–29; *Columbia Univ. Quart.*, Sept. 1911; *A Bibliog. of the Faculty of Political Science of Columbia Univ., 1880–1930* (1931); commemorative tribute by Henry van Dyke, in *The Am. Acad. of Arts and Letters: Publication No. 67* (1929); *New Eng. Hist. and Geneal. Reg.*, July 1929; *N. Y. Times*, Sept. 12–16, 1928; critical reviews of Sloane's *Napoleon* in the *Nation* (N. Y.), Nov. 25, 1897; *Am. Hist. Rev.*, Jan. 1898, Apr. 1911, and of other works of his in *Am. Hist. Rev.*, July 1902, Jan., Apr. 1915, Apr. 1925; obituary note, *Ibid.*, Oct. 1928.]   W. R. S—d.

SLOAT, JOHN DRAKE (July 26, 1781–Nov. 28, 1867), naval officer, was the posthumous son of Capt. John Sloat, an officer of the Revolution, who was accidentally killed by a sentinel. His father's family was of Dutch stock; that of his mother, Ruth (Drake) Sloat, English. He was born near Goshen, N. Y., where he attended the country schools. Appointed a midshipman in the navy, Feb. 12, 1800, he served until the end of the naval war with France, chiefly in the West Indies on board the *President,* flagship of Commodore Thomas Truxtun [*q.v.*]. Discharged from the navy under the peace establishment of 1801, he entered the merchant service as commander of his own vessel and made several voyages, losing heavily on his ventures. On Jan. 10, 1812, he returned to the navy with the rank of master and went to sea on board the frigate *United States* under the younger Stephen Decatur [*q.v.*], participating in that ship's successful fight with the *Macedonian*. This cruise ended his active service in the War of 1812, however, for on the arrival of his ship at New London she was blockaded there and kept in port until the end of the war. On July 24, 1813, he was commissioned lieutenant. On Nov. 27, 1814, he was married to Abby Gordon (1795–1878), who bore him two sons and a daughter.

Obtaining a furlough, he made a voyage to France in 1815 as master of the schooner *Transit*. It is said that there he was a party to a plan that miscarried to convey Napoleon and his suite to the United States. Returning to the navy in 1816, he was on duty alternately at the New York navy yard and the Portsmouth navy yard until 1820–21. In 1821–22 he served in the Pacific on board the *Franklin,* and in 1822–23 in South American waters on board the *Congress*. At the age of forty-two he received his first naval command, the schooner *Grampus,* and in 1824–25 he cruised among the Windward Islands, engaged in the hazardous work of suppressing piracy. On Mar. 21, 1826, he was promoted master-commandant and on Mar. 6, 1837, captain, taking rank from Feb. 9. A period of service at the New York naval rendezvous was interrupted in 1828–31 by a tour of duty in the Pacific as commander of the *St. Louis*. At Callao during a revolution in Peru he gave refuge to several leading Peruvian officials. In 1840–44 he was commandant of the Portsmouth navy yard.

On Aug. 27, 1844, he was chosen commander of the Pacific Squadron, a position of much responsibility by reason of the uncertain relations between the United States and Mexico. He arrived at Mazatlán, Mexico, on Nov. 18, 1845, and remained there seven and a half months with his flagship *Savannah*. In February 1846, he received from George Bancroft [*q.v.*], secretary of the navy, secret and confidential orders, dated June 24, 1845. These were decidedly unwarlike. The ships of the squadron were to be assiduously careful to avoid any act that might be construed as an act of aggression. In case of a declaration of war by Mexico, however, he was to occupy San Francisco and blockade or occupy such other ports as his force might permit (Sherman, *post,* p. 51). Later he was ordered, in the event of hostilities, to dispose of his whole force so as to carry out most effectually the objects specified in the earlier instructions. Receiving word on June

7 that the Mexicans had invaded Texas and had attacked the American forces there, he sailed for California the next day on board the *Savannah,* convinced that the hostilities of the Mexicans would justify "commencing offensive operations on the west coast" (*Ibid.,* p. 82). He arrived at Monterey on July 2; five days later, after consulting with the American consul, who counseled the postponing of action (Smith, *post,* vol. I, p. 334), and after examining the defenses of the town and preparing various official documents, he landed a detachment of seamen and marines under Capt. William Mervine [*q.v.*], who hoisted the American flag over the custom-house and read a proclamation taking possession of California and extending over it the laws of the United States. Sloat has been severely criticized for delaying action for five days, but it has also been held that in annexing California he exceeded his orders (*Ibid.,* vol I, p. 531). On July 6 he sent one of his officers to take possession of San Francisco; a few days later all California north of Santa Barbara was in the possession of the Americans. Suffering from ill health, he turned over the squadron to Commodore Robert Field Stockton [*q.v.*] on July 23 and returned to the United States by way of Panama, arriving at Washington in November. His conduct of affairs in the Pacific was warmly commended by Bancroft, who described the military movements of Sloat and his successor as "ably conceived and brilliantly executed" (Sherman, p. 85). He was commandant of the Norfolk navy yard, 1848–51; on special duty, 1852–55, with the bureau of construction and repair, part of the time in charge of the building of Stevens' Battery at Hoboken, N. J.; and on Sept. 27, 1855, he was placed on the reserved list. In 1862 he was promoted commodore and in 1866 rear-admiral, both on the retired list. He died at Staten Island and was buried in Greenwood Cemetery, Brooklyn. There is a statue to his memory, unveiled in 1910, at the Presidio, Monterey, Cal.

[E. A. Sherman, *The Life of the Late Rear-Admiral John Drake Sloat* (1902), an amateurish book, contains most of the essential facts. See also J. H. Smith, *The War with Mexico* (2 vols., 1919) ; G. L. Rives, *The U. S. and Mexico, 1821–1848* (1913), vol. II ; J. C. Frémont, *Memoirs of My Life,* vol. I (1887) ; Record of Officers, 1798–1871, Bureau of Navigation ; obituary in *Army and Navy Jour.,* Mar. 7, 1868 ; death notice in *N. Y. Tribune,* Nov. 29, 1867. Sloat's official dispatches for July 1846 appear in *House Executive Doc. 1,* 30 Cong., 2 Sess., pp. 1006–34.]   C. O. P.

SLOCUM, FRANCES (Mar. 4, 1773–Mar. 9, 1847), Indian captive, was born in Warwick, R. I., the descendant of Anthony Slocum who was one of the early settlers at Taunton, Mass., in 1637, and became the ancestor of Samuel,

Henry Warner Slocum and Margaret Olivia (Slocum) Sage [*qq.v.*]. She was the daughter of Jonathan and Ruth (Tripp) Slocum. In 1777 the Slocums with their seven children removed to the upper Susquehanna frontier near Wyoming, Pa. Disregarding the warning of the Wyoming massacre in July 1778, the Slocums fell victims to an attack by Delaware on Nov. 2, when, in the absence of the adult males, Frances was captured. She was adopted by a Delaware family to take the place of a dead daughter, Weletawash, whose name Frances was given. Her home changed with the fortunes of the Delaware, and she accompanied her family from the Sandusky, to Niagara, to Detroit, and finally at the close of the Revolution to the Maumee on the site of what became Fort Wayne. At the latter place she married a Delaware named Little Turtle. When he went west after the defeat of Wayne, she remained behind. She then married a Miami named Shepancanah, or Deaf Man, by whom she had four children. She spent the rest of her life at Deaf Man's Village on the Wabash near what is now Peru, Ind., to which she and her husband moved about the year 1810.

The country of the defeated Miami nation was gradually surrounded by white settlements, and by the treaty of St. Mary's in 1818 the tribe was confined to a reservation on the Wabash; and she and her family shared in the annuities paid by the United States to her adopted nation. In 1835 a chance traveler found her living among the Miami, communicated with the postmaster at Lancaster, Pa., and established her identity. When visited by her white relatives in 1837, she and her family were not dependent upon the hunt and the chase but lived the agricultural life. They had over fifty horses, one hundred dogs, seventeen head of cattle, and many geese and chickens. Although she knew no English and spoke the Miami tongue and adhered to the Miami ways of life, she preferred, with the permission of the United States government, to remain with her family on the Wabash, when the tribe was removed to the west in accordance with the treaty of 1840. She would not, however, return to her relatives on the Susquehanna. Mentally alert, she was an able administrator of her home establishment both before and after her husband's death. Although short of stature, she was exceedingly sturdy, a fact symbolized by her Miami name, Maconaquah, which means "little bear." She died among her Indian children and grandchildren.

[John Todd, *The Lost Sister of Wyoming* (1842); J. F. Meginness, *Biog. of Frances Slocum* (1891); M. B. Phelps, *Frances Slocum* (1905); C. E. Slocum, *Hist. of Frances Slocum* (1908) and *A Short Hist. of the*

Slocums (1882); date of birth from monument; photograph of monument in Phelps, *ante*, p. 146.] R. C. D.

SLOCUM, HENRY WARNER (Sept. 24, 1827–Apr. 14, 1894), Union general, was born at Delphi, Onondaga County, N. Y., the son of Matthew Barnard and Mary (Ostrander) Slocum. He was of the eighth generation in descent from Anthony Slocombe, who came from Taunton in England to Taunton, Mass., in 1637. His early education was in the local district school and in Cazenovia Seminary. For several years he taught school, attending the state normal school during some of his vacations. An early interest in military reading was stimulated by the Mexican War, and he sought an appointment to the United States Military Academy. He secured it in 1848 and was graduated in 1852, number seven in a class of forty-three, being commissioned second lieutenant in the 1st Artillery. He went first to Florida, then, in 1853, to Fort Moultrie. On Mar. 3, 1855, he was promoted first lieutenant, but resigned on Oct. 31, 1856, to engage in the practice of law, for which he had been preparing himself while at Moultrie. He was admitted to the bar in 1858 and established himself at Syracuse, N. Y. He soon gained local prominence; in 1859 he was a member of the New York assembly, and, in 1860, treasurer of Onondaga County. He also served as colonel and artillery instructor in the New York militia.

On May 21, 1861, he became colonel of the 27th New York Infantry. At the battle of Bull Run on July 21, he was severely wounded, but won promotion as brigadier-general of volunteers, on Aug. 9, 1861. Reporting for duty again in September he was assigned to the command of a brigade in Franklin's division, and went with it to the Peninsula. This division became part of the VI Corps; Franklin was assigned to command the corps, and Slocum succeeded him in the division, which he commanded through the rest of the campaign. On July 4, 1862, he was promoted major-general of volunteers. Upon the withdrawal of McClellan's army from the Peninsula, Slocum's division was transported to Alexandria. From there it moved forward to assist in covering Pope's withdrawal. Slocum remained in command during the ensuing campaign in Maryland, and was engaged at South Mountain and Antietam. In October he assumed command of the XII Army Corps, which took part in the Fredericksburg campaign, but was not engaged in the battle. In the following spring it bore a very active part in the campaign and battle of Chancellorsville. At Gettysburg Slocum had command of the extreme right of the

Union line—the "point of the fish-hook," from Culp's Hill southward. Until Meade's arrival early in the morning of July 2, Slocum exercised command, as senior officer present, of all the troops as they arrived, and supervised the formation of the lines.

In the autumn of 1863, after the battle of Chickamauga, it became necessary to reënforce Rosecrans by troops from the east. On Sept. 24, Howard's XI Corps and Slocum's XII were designated to move by rail to Tennessee. General Hooker was assigned to command the two corps. Slocum had been hostile to Hooker ever since the battle of Chancellorsville, and now, rather than serve under him, tendered his resignation. This was not accepted, but dispositions were made so as to avoid in so far as possible personal contact between the two officers. This transfer of troops was the largest ever made by rail up to that time. It involved the transportation of 24,000 men, with artillery and trains, for a distance of 1200 miles, with three changes of trains, and was completed in nine days. Slocum with half his corps was stationed on the Nashville-Chattanooga Railway; the rest of the corps served directly under Hooker. In April 1864, he was assigned to command the district of Vicksburg. The XI and XII Corps were consolidated into the XX Corps under Hooker. In July, after McPherson's death, Howard was assigned to command the Army of the Tennessee in his place. Hooker, being senior to Howard, asked to be relieved, and Slocum returned to his old command as now enlarged. He joined it before Atlanta on Aug. 26, and his troops were the first to enter the city on Sept. 2. On the march to the sea and up through the Carolinas, Slocum commanded the left wing of Sherman's army, consisting of the XIV and XX Corps. Toward the end of the campaign the two wings became separate armies, Howard's resuming its old title as the Army of the Tennessee, and Slocum's, taking that of the Army of Georgia.

At the end of the war Slocum was assigned to command the department of the Mississippi with headquarters at Vicksburg. He resigned on Sept. 28, 1865, and returned to Syracuse. He was nominated as Democratic candidate for secretary of state of New York, but was defeated by Francis Channing Barlow [q.v.]. In the spring of 1866 he moved to Brooklyn, and began the practice of law in that city. He was a Democratic presidential elector in 1868. He was elected to Congress in 1868, and again in 1870. In 1876 he was commissioner of public works in Brooklyn. In 1882 he was returned to Congress, and served until March 1885. He was active in the case of Fitz-John Porter [q.v.], and in that officer's interest delivered one of his strongest speeches in Congress on Jan. 18, 1884. Slocum maintained an active interest in military matters, and was a member of the Board of Gettysburg Monument Commissioners. His wife, Clara Rice, of Woodstock, N. Y., to whom he had been married on Feb. 9, 1854, survived him, with three of their four children, when he died in New York City.

[C. E. Slocum, *A Short Hist. of the Slocums, Slocumbs and Slocombs of America*, vol. I (1882), vol. II (1908), *The Life and Services of Major-General Henry Warner Slocum* (1913); *In Memoriam, Henry Warner Slocum 1826–1894* (1904); G. W. Cullum, *Biog. Reg. . . . U. S. Mil. Acad.* (1891); *Biog. Dir. Am. Cong.* (1928); *War of the Rebellion: Official Records (Army)*, see index; *Brooklyn Daily Eagle*, Apr. 14, 16, 1894.]
O. L. S., Jr.

SLOCUM, JOSHUA (Feb. 20, 1844–*c.* 1910), mariner, author, lecturer, was born in Wilmot Township, Nova Scotia, on a little farm close to the Bay of Fundy, the son of Sarah Jane (Southern) and John Slocomb [*sic*]. His father came from a line of mariners but was himself a farmer. His earliest American ancestor was apparently Simon Slocomb, who was in Boston in 1701, but the Slocombs, Loyalists at the time of the Revolution, had been in Nova Scotia for three generations. While he was still a boy Joshua shipped as cook on a fishing schooner and later made deep-sea voyages that carried him to many parts of the world. Except for some later studies in navigation and marine architecture his schooling was scanty, but he took advantage of his leisure at sea to become widely read. On the California coast in 1869 he secured his first command. For several years he sailed from San Francisco to China, Japan, Australia, and other parts of the Pacific. In January 1871 he was married at Sydney, Australia, to Virginia A. Walker, by whom he had three sons and a daughter. In 1874 he built an eighty-ton steamer at Subig Bay in the Philippines; about that time, too, he secured command of the *Northern Light,* which he maintained to be one of the finest ships of her day; and he had a career as a shipmaster that was on the whole successful and prosperous until 1886. At that time he invested his savings in the purchase of a 326 ton bark, the *Aquidneck,* and set out with his second wife, Henrietta M. Elliott, whom he had married in Boston in February 1886, and two of his sons to trade along the South American coast. In the last days of 1887 the *Aquidneck* was wrecked on a Brazilian sandbar. From the wreckage Slocum built a thirty-five foot sailing canoe that he called the *Liberdade,* and in this he sailed with his wife and sons all the way to New York. For the next few years he tried various ventures without success. In December 1893 he took the Ericsson *Destroyer* from New York to Brazil for use against the revolutionists, but the Brazilians sank her at Bahia and Slocum was not paid for his services.

His chief adventure started when he acquired the dilapidated hulk of a sloop at Fairhaven, near New Bedford, Mass., and rebuilt it almost completely. In the *Spray*, which now was nearly thirty-seven feet long and measured nine tons net, he started from Boston on Apr. 24, 1895, for what he asserted to be the first solitary cruise around the world. The *Spray*, built like a fisherman, was such a good sea boat that in normal weather he could lash the tiller and sleep soundly while she made good progress through the night; for a tender, he carried a dory sawn in half. From Boston he sailed to Nova Scotia and then to Gibraltar by way of the Azores. He had at first intended to go through the Suez Canal but, being warned of Red Sea pirates, recrossed the Atlantic to Pernambuco and worked his way down the coast, encountering his roughest weather in the Straits of Magellan. Finally clear, he reached Juan Fernandez and, after forty-three days on the Pacific, Nukahiva. He spent nine months in Australia, crossed the Indian Ocean to Durban and Cape Town, and spent three months visiting South Africa. After leaving St. Helena and Ascension, he met the *Oregon* on her famous run and finally reached Newport, June 27, 1898, by way of the Leeward Islands, having covered 46,000 miles. Although he had started the trip with no capital at all, he received generous gifts and assistance throughout the voyage. In Australia he began to reap substantial profits by lecturing and charging admission to the *Spray*. In 1900 he published *Sailing Alone Around the World*, which had appeared in the *Century Magazine*, Sept. 1899–Feb. 1900.

He had become a naturalized American citizen early in his life and now, retiring for a while from the sea, he made his home at West Tisbury, Martha's Vineyard, Mass. His writings include *Voyage of the Liberdade* (1890), which also appeared in *Outing*, Nov. 1902–Apr. 1903, as "The Voyage of the Aquidneck"; "The Voyage of the 'Destroyer' from New York to Brazil," in *McClure's Magazine*, March 1900; "Lines and Sail-Plan of the Spray," in *Century Magazine*, March 1900; and "Bully Hayes, the Last Buccaneer," in *Outing Magazine*, March 1906. On Nov. 14, 1909, he sailed in the *Spray* once more and was never heard from again. Rumors occasionally drifted back that he had been seen on a South American river, but he was finally declared le-

gally dead as of the date on which he sailed. Bald-headed and bearded, he looked like a typical shrewd Yankee skipper.

[C. E. Slocum, *A Short Hist. of the Slocums, Slocumbs and Slocombs of America* (2 vols., 1882–1908); *Who's Who in America*, 1908–09; Clifton Johnson, in *Outing*, Oct. 1902; private correspondence.]

R. G. A.

SLOCUM, SAMUEL (Mar. 4, 1792–Jan. 26, 1861), inventor, manufacturer, was the son of Peleg and Anne (Dyer) Slocum and was born on Canonicut Island, Jamestown Township, Newport County, R. I. He was a descendant of Anthony Slocum (or Slocombe), one of the first purchasers of Cohannet, New Plymouth (later Taunton, Mass.), in 1637. After a rudimentary education, he learned the trade of carpentry and for upwards of twenty years engaged in construction work in various parts of Rhode Island. He apparently accumulated in the course of these years quite a sum of money. Shortly after his marriage in 1817 to Susan Stanton in Richmond, Washington County, R. I. (Slocum, *post*, p. 291) he accepted the office of justice of the peace of Richmond. His movements after this are not clear. Probably about 1823 he removed from Richmond to Bristol, but just what his occupation was there is not known. Some eight or ten years later he sailed with his family for England and for upwards of five years lived in London and in Newport on the Isle of Wight. Although up to this time he had given no indication of an interest or talent in invention, in 1835 he perfected and patented in London a machine to make wrought-iron nails, and the same year devised and patented a machine for making pins with solid heads.

It is thought that, being unable to find a financial backer in England, he returned to the United States shortly after obtaining his pin-machine patent, and after establishing his residence in Providence, R. I., sought a partner to engage in making pins for the market. At all events, the firm of Slocum and Jillson was a going concern in 1840 at Poughkeepsie, N. Y., and was one of the two pin-making companies in the United States. Meanwhile the question of packaging pins held Slocum's attention, and on Sept. 30, 1841, he obtained patent No. 2,275 for a machine for sticking pins in paper. Shortly after this Slocum and Jillson joined forces with John Ireland Howe [*q.v.*], and from Slocum's pin-sticking machine and Howe's paper-crimping device evolved a sticking machine superior to that of their competitor, Fowler Brothers of Northford, Conn. The latter, however, had the better pin-making machine, and in 1842 this organization was purchased by Brown and Elton of Waterbury, Conn., who subsequently purchased a third interest in Slocum and Jillson's works and acquired control of Howe's paper crimper as well. Slocum continued operating his plant at Poughkeepsie for the succeeding four years, however, and then sold out to the newly established American Pin Company. This company retained Slocum for some years, and he secured an extension and reissue of his patented machine for sticking pins on paper, Oct. 1 and Dec. 4, 1855. About this time he retired to his native Rhode Island and lived first in Smithfield, and last in Pawtucket, where he died. He was survived by his widow and three sons.

[C. E. Slocum, *A Short Hist. of the Slocums . . . of America* (1882); *Vital Record of R. I., 1636–1850,* vol. IV (1893); W. G. Lathrop, *The Brass Industry in Conn.* (1909); J. L. Bishop, *A Hist. of Am. Manufactures* (1864), vol. II; Patent Office records.]

C. W. M—n.

SLOSS, JAMES WITHERS (Apr. 7, 1820–May 4, 1890), industrialist, the son of Joseph and Clarissa (Wasson) Sloss, was born at Mooresville, Limestone County, Ala. His father, an immigrant to Virginia in 1803 from County Derry, Ireland, had served in the War of 1812. James's education was limited. At fifteen he was working as bookkeeper for a butcher, which position he held for seven years. He married Mary Bigger, Apr. 7, 1842, and opened a store in Athens, Ala., that same year. His business grew, and by the fifties he had mercantile establishments at several points in northern Alabama. He continued to prosper and bought a number of plantations in the Tennessee Valley about Decatur. From early years he was deeply interested in railroads, seeking to extend them through southern Tennessee and northern Alabama, and after the Civil War he combined a number of short lines into the Nashville & Decatur Railroad, becoming the president of the combine in 1867. This line now forms that portion of the Louisville & Nashville system which connects the Cumberland and Tennessee rivers. His ambitions drove him to encourage the extension of the line southward, through the new and booming coal and iron center of Birmingham, to Montgomery, where it made connection with a line from the Gulf.

Thus brought into contact with the rising Birmingham district, Sloss, in 1876, together with James Thomas, leased the Oxmoor iron furnaces, a few miles south of the new industrial city. In January 1878, with Truman Aldrich and H. F. De Bardeleben [*q.v.*], he formed the Pratt Coal & Coke Company, the first big concern organized in the Birmingham district. The Company exploited the Browne Seam, a large body

of coal just west of Birmingham, later called the Pratt Seam in honor of Daniel Pratt [*q.v.*]. In 1879 Sloss withdrew from this company and concentrated his interests in the Eureka Mining Company, the first concern to make pig iron with coke instead of charcoal in the Birmingham district.

In 1881 he organized the Sloss Furnace Company and put up two furnaces on the eastern edge of the growing city. His plant was well located with relation to the railroads, and prospered. After some years of operation he sold his control, in 1886–87, to J. W. Johnston of the Georgia Pacific Railway and others having New York capital, and the plant later became one of the units of the Sloss-Sheffield Steel & Iron Company.

By his first wife, Mary Bigger, Sloss had nine children, of whom six died young; and by his second, Martha Lundie, he had three, all of whom survived him. He was highly respected as one of the great men of the Birmingham district in the days when it had to find its own capital, and his railroad enterprises were of inestimable value to that growing industrial center of the South.

[T. M. Owen, *Hist. of Ala. and Dict. of Ala. Biog.* (1921), vol. IV; E. M. Armes, *The Story of Coal and Iron in Ala.* (1910); G. M. Cruikshank, *Hist. of Birmingham and Its Environs* (2 vols., 1920); *Daily Register* (Mobile), May 6, 1890.]

H. A. T.

SLOSS, LOUIS (July 13, 1823–June 4, 1902), San Francisco capitalist and philanthropist, was born in Bavaria, of a Jewish family. Endowed with ambition and self-reliance, he left the overcrowded community of his birth and emigrated to America in 1845. He first settled in Mackville, Ky., where he opened a country store. In 1849 he joined the gold-seekers, crossed the plains, and reached Sutter's Fort, Cal., on Sept. 13. He traded in some of the flourishing mining towns for a time, but early in the fifties moved to Sacramento and for ten years (1852–61) was engaged in the wholesale grocery business with Lewis Gerstle [*q.v.*], another Bavarian emigrant, and Simon Greenewald, under the firm name of Louis Sloss & Company. The great flood of 1861 brought heavy losses and led the firm to move to San Francisco early in 1862, where they opened a stock brokerage office. In 1866, Sloss obtained a seat on the San Francisco Stock and Exchange Board, and soon acquired a commanding position as a broker, especially in connection with the silver discoveries in Nevada. During the period of frenzied mining speculation and widespread business dishonesty and treachery in the seventies, he commanded universal public confidence as "the most honest man that ever handled mining shares" (*San Francisco Chronicle*).

Leaving the Stock Exchange in 1873, the firm engaged in the wool, fur, hide, and commission business, and became one of the most extensive shippers in the port of San Francisco. Their tannery became the largest in the city, manufacturing more sole leather than any other establishment of its kind on the Pacific coast. Along with his partners, Sloss was one of the prime movers in the organization of the Alaska Commercial Company, and for many years was a director and the president of the company. In 1869 or 1870, he went to Washington and negotiated the lease from the government of the exclusive right for twenty years, beginning May 1, 1870, to conduct seal-fishing on the Pribilof Islands. After the discovery of gold in Alaska, the company developed into a great trading enterprise.

Among the notable commercial investments of Sloss was the Alaska Packers Association, owning large salmon canneries in Alaska. He was also interested in fire and marine insurance and served as first president of the Anglo-Nevada Assurance Association. Directly or indirectly, he had a substantial interest in numerous mercantile enterprises, as well as extensive landholdings in Southern California. A handsome fortune resulted from his varied activities, and after it had reached a certain amount, he systematically endeavored to prevent its attaining huge proportions by means of pensions and charities to carefully selected individuals and societies. He took especial delight in helping worthy persons to start in business and become permanently self-sustaining. The orphans and sick, the aged and feeble, also elicited his special interest and care; he actively supported almost every charity and philanthropy in San Francisco. He was a member of the Congregation Emanu-El, twenty-eighth president of the Society of California Pioneers (1884–85), treasurer of the Republican state central committee, trustee of the Free Public Library, and treasurer of the University of California (1885–1902). On July 19, 1855, in Philadelphia, he married Sarah Greenebaum, whose sister later married his partner, Gerstle. Mrs. Sloss, with five of their six children, survived her husband, who died at his summer home in San Rafael and was buried in Home of Peace cemetery, San Mateo County. Although he was a business genius of the first order, the *San Francisco Chronicle* said of him at the time of his death, "Modesty was his cardinal virtue, and [he] knew no distinction between rich and poor, the favored and un-

fortunate. . . . No man was ever more considerate of his fellow-beings."

[See *San Francisco Call,* June 5, 1902; *San Francisco Chronicle,* June 5, 1902; W. F. Swasey, *The Early Days and Men of Cal.* (1891), pp. 277–82; J. A. Graves, *My Seventy Years in Cal.* (1927), pp. 87–88; A. W. Foster, "Louis Sloss," in *Univ. Chronicle* (Univ. of Cal.), July 1902; J. S. Hittell, *The Commerce and Industries of the Pacific Coast* (1882), p. 493. On the early history of the Alaska Commercial Company, see "Hist. of Alaska, 1730–1885," *The Works of H. H. Bancroft,* XXXIII (1886), 637–59, 746–47; "Fur Seal Fisheries of Alaska," *House Report No. 3883,* 50 Cong., 2 Sess. (1889); *Reply of the Alaska Commercial Company to the Charges of Gov. Alfred P. Swineford, of Alaska, against the Company in his Annual Report for the year 1887* (n.p., n.d.). This reply is signed by Louis Sloss as president of the Company and Appendix 3 is a letter of Sloss to U. S. Treasury Agent George R. Tingle, dated Dec. 10, 1887.]   P. O. R.

SLOSSON, EDWIN EMERY (June 7, 1865–Oct. 15, 1929), chemist, author, lecturer, was born at Albany, later called Sabetha, Kan., the son of William Butler Slosson and Achsa (Lilly) Slosson. His father, of Puritan ancestry, had moved from Maine, N. Y., to what was then a border community and became a pioneer merchant. Slosson attended the high school at Leavenworth, Kan., and then chose a European trip rather than to attend college. He managed, however, to enter the University of Kansas when he returned and received the B.S. degree in 1890 and the M.S. degree in 1892. He became an assistant professor in chemistry at the University of Wyoming, but continued his studies, spending his summers studying organic chemistry at the University of Chicago, where he received the Ph.D. degree in 1902. On Aug. 12, 1891, at Centralia, Kan., he was married to May Gorsline Preston, the first woman to receive a Ph.D. from Cornell University. While teaching at the University of Wyoming, Slosson began to write, and many of his contributions appeared in the *Independent.* So successful was this effort, and he derived such pleasure from it, that he soon combined journalism with his study of the natural sciences, and in this unique field achieved his greatest distinction. In 1903 he became the literary editor of the *Independent,* serving that organization in various capacities until 1921, when he became director of Science Service of Washington, D. C. He remained in this position until his death in Washington. His interests were of the broadest, and by dint of hard study, he equipped himself to discuss advances in numerous fields of science, as well as in philosophy, politics, and religion, and to write on various cultural topics.

He was a man of more than average size, being almost six feet in height and of rather heavy build, blond, broad-featured, energetic, restless. He was a keen observer, an excellent reviewer, a successful reporter, an experimentalist in politics and social theory, a philosopher, and a humorist who enjoyed any play on words, including puns. He had a unique knack of associating ideas in his discussions in an unexpected way which emphasized his points and crowded his sentences full of facts. He was humble, almost diffident or shy, and yet, besides his achievement as a writer and an editor, he was in great demand as a lecturer. His engagements were limited only by his physical strength which was affected by an ailing heart. As an editor he was fearless, always telling the whole truth frankly as he found it, while his humor enabled him to place telling emphasis on important points and to retain always the interest of his audience. He was especially prolific in ideas for books, articles, and projects so numerous that he was physically unable to carry them all to completion. He was fond of the library as well as the laboratory, the theatre, the museum, and the opera. His amazing interest in all things made it a pleasure for him to search out details, and this always led to a number of suggestions for still further writing. He was a kindly, generous soul, and interested in promising youths, several of whom he assisted in obtaining a college education.

At his death, Slosson was easily the outstanding interpreter of sciences to the non-technical public. He was able to interest anyone, not only in the accomplishments of science, but in science itself, without offending the purest of the scientists. A bibliography of his works includes eighteen books, more than eighty pamphlets of reprinted articles and addresses, twenty technical bulletins based on his research in chemistry, and about 2,000 articles, editorials, and essays. The best known of his books, some based upon his articles, are *Major Prophets of Today* (1914), *Six Major Prophets* (1917), *Creative Chemistry* (1919), *Easy Lessons in Einstein* (1920), *The American Spirit in Education* (1921), *Plots and Personalities* (1922), *Chats on Science* (1924), *Sermons of a Chemist* (1925), *Snapshots of Science* (1928). In addition to his doctorate, he held many honorary degrees, and when he died had been about to accept the title of "Professor of Things in General" at Rollins College, Winter Park, Fla. One of his two sons, Preston William Slosson, survived him.

[Private correspondence with the family; *Who's Who in America,* 1928–29; C. H. Preston, *Descendants of Roger Preston* (1931); biographical memoir by Preston W. Slosson in E. E. Slosson, *A Number of Things* (1930); *Bibliog. of the Writings of Edwin E. Slosson,* compiled by Science Service (1929); *Jour. of the Washington Acad. of Sci.,* Nov. 4, 1929; Hamilton Holt, memorial article in *Book League Monthly,* Dec. 1929; *Washington Post,* Oct. 16, 17, 1929.] H. E. H.

SMALL, ALBION WOODBURY (May 11, 1854–Mar. 24, 1926), sociologist, teacher, university administrator, was born at Buckfield, Me., the eldest son of the Rev. Albion Keith Parris Small, a Baptist minister, and Thankful Lincoln (Woodbury) Small. He was a descendant of Edward Small who emigrated from England, probably before 1640, and settled at Kittery, Me. The family at first owned by title from the Indians all the northern part of the county of York. On his mother's side he was descended from Samuel Lincoln of Hingham, Mass., the earliest American ancestor of Abraham Lincoln. After ten years at Bangor, the family moved in 1868 to Portland. Graduated from the high school in Portland, Small entered Colby University (later Colby College), Waterville, Me., where he was an outstanding figure. Receiving the degree of B.A. in 1876, he entered Newton Theological Institution the next year and was graduated in 1879. At Newton, under the influence of Ezra P. Gould, he developed an ambition for a life of scholarship. Devoting himself to history and political economy, he spent a year at the University of Berlin and another at Leipzig, and then returned to take the chair of history and political economy at Colby, where he taught from 1881 to 1888. Before returning to America he married, June 20, 1881, the daughter of a German general, Valeria von Massow, who died in 1916. In 1889 he received the degree of Ph.D. at Johns Hopkins University in the graduate school of history and political economy. In the same year he became president of Colby University.

As college presidents in those days were also teachers, Small began a course in the new field of sociology, his interest in the subject due chiefly to the conviction that history was tending to be a mere chronicle of events and that economics was neglecting essential aspects of social life. In 1892 he became head of the department of sociology at the new University of Chicago, the first department of its kind. He served also as dean of the College of Liberal Arts, and from 1904 to his retirement in 1924 as dean of the Graduate School of Arts, Literature and Science. He was vice-president of the Congress of Arts and Sciences at the Louisiana Purchase Exposition at St. Louis in 1904, president of l'Institut International de Sociologie at Paris, one of the leaders in the organization of the American Sociological Society in 1905, and its president, 1912–14. He exerted his strongest influence, however, through the *American Journal of So-*

ciology, which he founded, and of which he was editor from July 1895 to March 1926. The first journal devoted exclusively to the subject, it became the forum for sociological discussion for America and Europe, and Small admitted to its pages all shades of opinion. He himself was for years the most prolific contributor not only of articles but of reviews of sociological literature.

The bibliography of his writings includes some three hundred titles. His *General Sociology* (1905) is a systematic treatment that shows the influence of the Germans, especially of Gustav Ratzenhofer, and reveals the profound ethical interest which characterized his whole life and work. In *Adam Smith and Modern Sociology* (1907) and *The Meaning of Social Science* (1910) he set forth his conviction of the unity of the social sciences, one of his ruling passions. In *The Cameralists* (1909), his most scholarly volume, he discussed with profound insight the application of social theory to political institutions. It was in 1913 that his most remarkable book appeared, *Between Eras: From Capitalism to Democracy.* This brilliant discussion was published as a dialogue, which may account for its lack of influence in academic circles, but perhaps its indictment of capitalism is sufficient reason for the relatively scant attention it received. His last book was *Origins of Sociology* (1924), a history of tendencies in social science in Germany during the nineteenth century.

As a teacher he was distinguished for the rare charm of his personality. His whimsical humor never deserted him, even during the last years when he was suffering from a painful malady. As a scholar he possessed the outstanding merit of intellectual hospitality. At Chicago he built up a large and important department, purposely assembling men of divergent views, and he is one of four men who may be said to have founded American sociology. He died in retirement at Chicago, survived by a daughter. He bequeathed his estate to the University of Chicago to found a journal devoted to the application of moral and Christian principles to society.

[L. A. W. Underhill, *Descendants of Edward Small of New England* (rev. ed., 1934), vol. I; *Who's Who in America,* 1924–25; articles by T. W. Goodspeed, H. E. Barnes, Annie M. Maclean, and F. N. House, in *Am. Jour. of Sociology,* July 1926; T. W. Goodspeed, in *Univ. Record* (Univ. of Chicago), vol. XII (1926); E. C. Hayes, in *Social Forces,* June 1926; *Am. Masters of Social Sci.* (1927), ed. by H. W. Odum; obituary in *Chicago Daily Tribune,* Mar. 25, 1926.]   E.F.

SMALL, ALVAN EDMOND (Mar. 4, 1811–Dec. 31, 1886), homeopathic physician, was born in Wales, Me. His father was Joseph Small, who served several terms in the state legislature. His mother was Mary (Jackson) Small, the daughter of Bartholomew Jackson, a Revolutionary soldier. Small was one of a large family of children, and received his earliest education in the public schools of his state. He then entered the Monmouth Academy, Monmouth, Me., and at the age of sixteen began to teach in the district schools. After four years he was made principal of one of the city schools of Bath, Me., a position which he held for two years. During this period he was a private pupil of Benjamin Randall under whom he pursued studies in the classics and in English literature. He started the study of medicine in the office of Dr. Israel Putnam, of Bath, in 1831, continuing his studies later under the preceptorship of Dr. H. H. C. Greene, of Saco, Me. In 1834 he was married to Martha Mary Sloan of Bath. In 1840 he entered the Pennsylvania Medical College from which he was graduated in 1842. He began his practice in Upper Darby, Delaware County, Pa., but moved to Philadelphia in 1845. When the Homoeopathic Medical College of Pennsylvania was organized in 1848, he was appointed professor of physiology and pathology.

He moved to Chicago in 1856 to take over the practice of Dr. David S. Smith. The Hahnemann Medical College of Chicago was organized three years later and Small was elected the first dean. From 1850 to 1869 he served as professor of theory and practice of medicine. In accordance with the peculiar educational methods in medical colleges of the period, he was forced at times to teach unrelated subjects during the same session. He resigned as dean in 1865 and became president of the institution in 1869. The same year he was elected a life member of the Chicago Historical Society. He delivered his last lecture to the students of Hahnemann Medical College in 1885, but maintained his private and other institutional activities and interests to the day before his death. In addition to his private and institutional work, he possessed intense literary interests. He was general secretary of the American Institute of Homoeopathy, 1849–50, and president in 1850. He was co-editor of the *Philadelphia Journal of Homoeopathy,* 1854–60, and of the *United States Medical and Surgical Journal* from 1870 to 1874. His contributions to medical literature were numerous. In 1854 he published a *Manual of Homoeopathic Practice,* for the use of families and private individuals, which went through fifteen editions and was translated into German by K. J. Hempel in 1856. In 1856 he published *Diseases of the Nervous System,* and in 1886 appeared his voluminous work of 900 pages, *A Systematic Treatise on the Practice of Medicine.* He was survived by his wife, and three of their four children. Two sons became homeopathic physicians.

[H. H. Cochrane, *Hist. of Monmouth and Wales* (1894), vol. I; *Biog. Sketches of the Leading Men of Chicago* (1868); T. L. Bradford, *Hist. of the Homoeopathic Med. Coll. of Pa.* (1898); *Trans. . . . Am. Inst. of Homoeopathy, 1887* (1887); *Med. Visitor,* and *Hahnemannian Monthly,* Feb. 1887; *U. S. Med. and Surgical Jour.,* Oct. 1872; *Chicago Tribune,* Jan. 1, 1887.]
C. B.

SMALLEY, EUGENE VIRGIL (July 18, 1841–Dec. 30, 1899), journalist, editor, was the son of Jared Frost Smalley and his wife, Cordelia Lewis, who moved from New York to settle on the Western Reserve. He was born at Randolph, Portage County, Ohio, but after the death of the father returned with the family to Blackrock and then Fredonia, N. Y. At the age of eleven, he started to learn the printer's trade and at fourteen went to Painesville, Ohio, where he was joined by his mother a year later. Between 1856 and 1861 he wandered east as far as New York City and west to Louisville and Harrodsburg, Ky. Between short periods of formal education, he set type or taught school, and, on the eve of the Civil War, bought, with a friend, two papers in Painesville, which they consolidated and published. Smalley enlisted in the 7th Ohio Infantry and remained in service until he was wounded at Port Republic. Letters from the field, written to his paper and copied in others, opened a place for him on the Cleveland *Herald.* In 1863 he was in Washington, D. C., holding a minor clerkship in the treasury department. He made the acquaintance of James A. Garfield, whom he much resembled in appearance and who was responsible for his obtaining the clerkship of the House Committee on Military Affairs. In 1868 he bought the *Mahoning Register,* a paper published in Youngstown, Ohio, but after a short time he sold it and became a free-lance journalist. He traveled in Europe in 1869–70, and then began contributing articles to the *New York Tribune,* becoming a regular member of the staff in 1871. During this period he investigated Ku Klux Klan activities in North Carolina, reported the Vienna world's fair in 1873 and the Centennial Exhibition at Philadelphia for the *Tribune,* and wrote extensively for the periodicals, *Forum, Atlantic Monthly,* and *Century.* For the last of these he made a trip west from Lake Superior and wrote about northwestern states and territories.

Henry Villard, when he was preparing for the formal opening of the Northern Pacific Railroad, engaged Smalley to edit the *History of the Northern Pacific Railroad* (1883), and thus began a long connection with the advertising department of that road. In 1883 he started *The Northwest Illustrated Monthly Magazine* designed to acquaint people with the resources of the region traversed by the railroad. In 1884 Smalley and the magazine moved from New York to St. Paul, Minn., where the editor resided until his death. He traveled in the Northwest and wrote profusely of the area he knew so well. In 1889 he published *The Great Northwest; a Guide Book and Itinerary.* He took an active part in Republican politics through his writings, publishing in 1880 *The Republican Manual; . . . with Biographical Sketches of James A. Garfield and Chester A. Arthur,* and, in 1884, *A Brief History of the Republican Party,* the latter being elaborated in 1896 to include a history of Republican Minnesota and Minnesotians. He also wrote *American Journalism—An Appendix to the Encyclopædia Britannica* (1884). He was a member and, for many years, president of the St. Paul Chamber of Commerce. He was also active in G. A. R. circles and the Sons of the American Revolution. At his death he was survived by his wife, Mrs. Josephine M. Conday, to whom he had been married in 1873, a son and a step-son.

[*Who's Who in America,* 1899–1900; St. Paul *Daily Pioneer Press,* St. Paul *Globe,* Dec. 30, 1899; *Memoirs of Henry Villard* (2 vols., 1904); *Northwest Magazine,* Jan. 1900.]
L. B. S.

SMALLEY, GEORGE WASHBURN (June 2, 1833–Apr. 4, 1916), journalist, was born at Franklin, Norfolk County, Mass., "of good Old Colony stock," and grew up there and at Worcester, Mass., whither he went with his parents, the Rev. Elam and Louisa Jane (Washburn) Smalley, in 1840. In 1849 he entered Yale University, where he won his chief laurels as an athlete, rowing stroke in the first Yale-Harvard race on Lake Winnepesaukee. He received the A.M. degree in 1853, and read law for a year at Worcester in the office of George Frisbie Hoar [q.v.]. He studied at the Harvard Law School, 1854–55, was admitted to the bar in 1856, and practised law in Boston until 1861. In Boston he became closely associated with Wendell Phillips [q.v.], with whom he several times shared the danger of mob violence. When Smalley wished to go South in the autumn of 1861, partly for his health and partly to see something of the war, Phillips obtained for him an assignment from the *New York Tribune* to do a series of papers on South Carolina negro life. From November 1861 to October 1862 he served as war correspondent at the front, notably with Frémont in the Shenandoah Valley and with the Army of the Potomac. On the field of Antietam, Sept. 17, 1862, he acted as impromptu aide to "Fighting

Joe" Hooker, carrying orders for him under fire. After the battle Smalley commandeered a horse (his own had two bullets in it), rode in the night thirty miles to the nearest telegraph, and wired in a summary of the engagement. The operator, on his own initiative, sent the dispatch to Washington instead of to New York. Smalley then took a night train to New York and wrote his longer story standing under a dim oil lamp. This earliest account of Antietam, which appeared on Sept. 19, was a notable triumph for the *Tribune,* and Smalley's feat was, in the opinion of Henry Villard [*q.v.*], the greatest single journalistic exploit of the war (*Memoirs of Henry Villard,* 1904, I, 335). Smalley was married to Phoebe Garnaut, adopted daughter of Wendell Phillips, on Dec. 25, 1862. She was the "only child of an estimable friend of Welsh birth who had married a native of France and come to Boston, where her husband soon died" (Lorenzo Sears, *Wendell Phillips, Orator and Agitator,* 1909, p. 87n). They had five children, two boys and three girls. In October 1862 Smalley took a regular place on the *Tribune* staff in New York, and when the *Tribune* building was attacked by the draft rioters in 1863 he was prominent among the armed defenders.

The beginning of Smalley's distinguished career as a foreign correspondent came in 1866, when he was sent to Europe on two days' notice to report the Austro-Prussian War. Although the fighting was practically over when he arrived, he made use of the newly-laid transatlantic cable to send from Berlin what was probably the first of all cabled news dispatches. In 1867 he was again sent abroad to organize a London bureau which should receive and coordinate all European news. This move marked a revolution in journalism. At the outbreak of the Franco-Prussian War in 1870 Smalley formed the first international newspaper alliance, with the London *Daily News,* and organized his bureau on the basis of a free use of both telegraph and cable hitherto unknown on either side the Atlantic. Combining this policy with an adaptation of his own procedure at Antietam, he scored, through the exploits of his correspondents with both armies, triumph after triumph, notably the famous "scoop" of Sedan. Smalley remained in charge of the *Tribune's* European correspondence until 1895, when he returned to America to act as American correspondent of the London *Times.* This position he held for ten years (1895–1905), living either in New York City or in Washington, D. C. Then, retiring from active journalism except for weekly letters to the *Tribune* and occasional contributions to reviews, he

made his home in London until his death in 1916.

Smalley's letters to the *Tribune,* both before and after the *Times* interlude, added greatly to the reputation he had gained by his revolutionary handling of war news. The initialed signatures G. W. S. became widely familiar, and without doubt Smalley did excellent service to the cause nearest his heart, the cementing of Anglo-American friendship and understanding. His style is vigorous and lucid. Moving freely in the upper strata of English society, he knew everybody of importance in both England and America, and was, perhaps, even too eager to let his high connections be known. He is at his best in his brief portrait sketches, always chatty and anecdotal but invariably discreet. Indeed, many readers have been distinctly annoyed by his rather ostentatious discretion, his attitude of "I could an I would." This somewhat superior air, his violent likes and dislikes, his "cold irony," and his toryism, made him numerous enemies on both sides of the ocean. Yet he won the respect of people as diverse as Gladstone, Lowell, Whistler, and Arnold. The best of the *Tribune* letters, with some other material, were collected in a series of books which still hold considerable interest: *A Review of Mr. Bright's Speeches* (1868); *London Letters* (2 vols., 1891); *Studies of Men* (1895); and *Anglo-American Memories* (1911, second series, 1912). He also published in 1909 *The Life of Sir Sydney H. Waterlow, Bart.*

[There is incidental autobiographical material in most of Smalley's books, notably *Anglo-American Memories,* in particular the first series. Other sources include: *Who's Who in America,* 1906–07; *Who Was Who,* 1916–28 (London, 1929); *Worcester Births, Marriages and Deaths* (1894); obituaries in the London *Times,* the *N. Y. Tribune, N. Y. Herald, Evening Post, Sun,* and *World,* Apr. 5, 1916; *N. Y. Tribune,* Apr. 6, 1916; *N. Y. Jour.,* May 29, 1900; *N. Y. Herald,* Oct. 1, 1895; *Mail and Express* (N. Y.), Apr. 20, 1898; F. L. Bullard, *Famous War Correspondents* (1914); *Obit. Record of Grads. of Yale Univ.,* July 1, 1916.]

E. M. S.

SMALLS, ROBERT (Apr. 5, 1839–Feb. 22, 1915), negro congressman from South Carolina, was born at Beaufort, S. C., the son of Robert and Lydia Smalls and a slave of the McKee family. He was kindly treated by his master and allowed to acquire a limited education. In 1851 he moved with his master to Charleston and became successively a hotel waiter, a hack driver, and a rigger. In 1856 he married his first wife, Hannah, who died in 1883. In 1861 the Confederate authorities impressed him into service and made him a member of the crew of *The Planter,* a dispatch and transportation steamer doing service in Charleston Harbor. In the early morning of May 13, 1862, taking advantage of the absence of the white officers, with his wife, two children, and twelve others aboard, he carried *The Planter* beyond the Charleston forts into the lines of the blockading Federal squadron outside the harbor. This daring exploit gave him national fame. He was made a pilot in the United States Navy and given a share of the prize-money. His knowledge of Charleston Harbor and its fortifications was of great service to the Federals. On Dec. 1, 1863, when the commander of *The Planter* deserted his post under Confederate fire, Smalls took command of the steamer and led it out of danger. For this act he was promoted to the rank of captain and placed in command of *The Planter,* holding this post until September 1866, when his craft was put out of commission.

His rise to political importance in South Carolina during Reconstruction was inevitable. He was good-humored, intelligent, fluent, and self-possessed. His moderate views and kindness toward the family of his former master made him to the whites the least objectionable of the freedmen with political aspirations. The fact that he was the pet of their liberators led the freedmen to believe that he was "the smartest *cullud* man in Souf Car'lina" (*The Trip of the Steamer Oceanus to Fort Sumter and Charleston,* 1865, p. 86). His modesty and lack of education were the only circumstances which prevented him from becoming preëminent among the directors of the state during Reconstruction. As early as May 1864, a meeting of negroes and northerners at Port Royal elected him a delegate to the National Union Convention. He was one of the less prominent delegates to the state constitutional convention of 1868. From 1868 to 1870 he served in the state House of Representatives and in the latter year was elected to the state Senate, where he served through the session of 1874. From 1875 to 1887, except during 1880 and 1881, he served in Congress.

His congressional career was not notable. His most important speeches were attacks on the election tactics of the South Carolina Democrats and in support of a bill to provide equal accommodations for the races on interstate conveyances. A thorough partisan, he opposed civil service reform and favored pension bills. He made an unsuccessful attempt to have $30,000 voted him as additional compensation for his part in *The Planter* escapade. He was a conspicuous figure in the Republican national conventions of 1872 and 1876. From 1865 to 1877 he served in the state militia, rising to the rank of major-general. In December 1889 he was appointed collector of the port of Beaufort, holding this position until 1913 except during Cleveland's second term. In 1877 he was convicted of accepting a bribe of

$5,000 while state senator and was sentenced to three years in prison, but while his case was under appeal he was pardoned by Gov. William Dunlap Simpson [*q.v.*] as part of the policy of amnesty which the state Democratic administration deemed wise. His last conspicuous service was as one of the six negro members of the state constitutional convention of 1895. Before that body he made a vain but gallant attempt to prevent the practical disfranchisement of his race. The last twenty years of his life were spent quietly at Beaufort, where he enjoyed the confidence of both races, cooperating with white leaders in efforts to advance the material interests of the community. On Apr. 9, 1890, he was married a second time, to Annie E. Wigg.

[The best sketches of Smalls are in *Who's Who in America,* 1912–13; J. H. Brown, *The Cyc. of Am. Biogs.,* VII (1903), 103–04; and the *Union Herald* (Columbia, S. C.), Nov. 1, 1873. The episode of *The Planter* is described in *War of the Rebellion: Official Records* (*Army*), 1 ser. XIV, 13–14, and in *Report of the Secretary of the Navy,* 1862, pp. 227–28. His political career is traced in F. B. Simkins and R. H. Woody, *S. C. during Reconstruction* (1932); S. D. Smith, "The Negro in Congress, 1870–1901" (MS.), the library of the Univ. of N. C.; A. A. Taylor, *The Negro in S. C. during the Reconstruction* (copr. 1924); *Biog. Dir. Am. Cong.* (1928). An obituary appeared in *News and Courier* (Charleston, S. C.), Feb. 25, 1915. Sir George Campbell, *White and Black; the Outcome of a Visit to the U. S.* (1879), pp. 346–47, 356–57, and *Letters and Diary of Laura M. Towne* (1912), ed. by R. S. Holland, pp. 240–41, give personal impressions. Mr. William Elliott of Columbia, S. C., and Mr. and Mrs. Niels Christensen of Beaufort, S. C., have furnished information concerning Smalls's relations with the whites.]   F. B. S.

SMALLWOOD, WILLIAM (1732–Feb. 12, 1792), soldier and governor, was the great-grandson of James Smallwood, who arrived in Maryland in 1664, settled in Charles County, became a large planter, served as sheriff and as county commissioner, received the rank of colonel with authority to raise a regiment for fighting Indians, and during nearly the entire period of the royal government of Maryland, 1692–1715, was a representative of his county in the Maryland Assembly. William Smallwood's father was Bayne Smallwood, a delegate for Charles County in the Maryland Assembly in 1738 and several succeeding years. His mother was Priscilla (Heaberd), who was born in Virginia. William, born in Charles County, is said to have been sent to school in England. He began his military career as a soldier in the French and Indian War. He took his seat in the Maryland Assembly in 1761 as a delegate for Charles County and became one of the liberal leaders of that body, speaking and voting on important questions with Thomas Johnson and William Paca [*qq.v.*]. He joined the Maryland non-importation association in June 1769, and as a delegate to the Maryland

Convention of 1775 he joined the Association of the Freemen of Maryland which advocated "opposition by arms, to the British troops, employed to enforce obedience to the late acts and statutes of the British parliament, for raising a revenue in America" (*Proceedings of the Conventions of the Province of Maryland, 1774, 1775 & 1776*, 1836, pp. 17–18).

In January 1776, commissions were issued to raise a regiment of Maryland troops under Smallwood's command. The Maryland Convention withdrew its objections to a declaration of independence June 26, and five days after the famous declaration by the Continental Congress, Smallwood marched northward with a battalion of nine companies. Reinforcements followed, and in the battle of Long Island, although Smallwood was absent, the Maryland line established a reputation for valor. Under Smallwood the survivors covered Washington's retreat. They fought with like valor at White Plains, where Smallwood was wounded. The Continental Congress elected him a brigadier-general Oct. 23, 1776, and two months later he was ordered to Maryland to promote the raising of new levies. His men fought at Fort Washington, Trenton, Princeton, and Germantown. In 1778–79 he was at Wilmington, Del., covering Washington's stores at the head of the Elk River, watching for operations of the enemy on the Chesapeake, and suppressing a Tory uprising on the Eastern Shore of Maryland. He was ordered to the South in April 1780, was promoted to the rank of major-general in September of that year, and for brave fighting near Camden he and his men received the thanks of Congress. Upon the death of Baron de Kalb [*q.v.*] three days after the battle of Camden, Smallwood was placed in command of a division, but when Horatio Gates [*q.v.*] was removed, his position was that of a subordinate to Baron Steuben [*q.v.*]. He protested and threatened to resign rather than serve under a foreigner, but Washington expressed his displeasure at this attitude, Congress was firm, Greene sent him to Maryland to aid in procuring supplies and reinforcements, and he continued in the service until Nov. 15, 1783.

Smallwood made himself disagreeable by repeated complaints that he was not promoted as rapidly as he deserved, by complaints that his state was not accorded recognition in proportion to its services, and by his offensive attitude toward foreigners. The sacrifice of his men during battle seemed not to disturb him. His greatest service in the war was as a drill master, in raising men and supplies, and in administering other military affairs of his state. When the war had ended, he enjoyed some of the usual popularity of a military hero. The Maryland Assembly elected him a delegate to the Continental Congress (Dec. 4, 1784), but he declined to serve. He was elected governor the following year and served three consecutive terms of one year each. As governor he called the convention in which Maryland ratified the constitution of the United States, and he promoted the movement for the improvement of the navigation of the Potomac. Smallwood never married. He died in Prince George's County and was buried in Charles County.

[*Archives of Md.*, vols. XII, XVI, XXI, XLIII, XLV, XLVII, XLVIII (1893–1931); *Md. Hist. Mag.*, Sept. 1924, June 1927; *Papers Relating Chiefly to the Md. Line during the Revolution* (1857), ed. by Thomas Balch; H. E. Buchholz, *Governors of Md.* (1908), critical but inaccurate; M. P. Andrews and H. F. Powell, *Tercentenary Hist. of Md.* (1925), vols. I, IV; *Maryland Journal and Baltimore Advertiser*, Feb. 1792.]

N. D. M.

SMART, JAMES HENRY (June 30, 1841– Feb. 21, 1900), school superintendent, president of Purdue University, was born at Center Harbor, N. H., the son of Dr. William Hutchings Smart, a successful physician, and Nancy (Farrington) Smart, of old New England stock. Educated at home and at the Concord high school, he began his career as a teacher when he was eighteen years of age. After one year in a district school he became the principal of a graded school at Laconia, N. H., in 1860 and taught in this and other local schools for three more years, becoming meanwhile an associate editor of the *Journal of Education* published at Manchester, N. H. He removed in 1863 to Toledo, Ohio, where he was so successful as a school principal that in 1865 he was named superintendent of schools at Fort Wayne, Ind. Here he successfully dealt with problems involving the relations of public and parochial schools, and thereby confirmed a reputation as an able administrator. On July 21, 1870, he married Mary H. Swan, daughter of a professor in Grinnell College, Iowa. In swift succession he now harvested the honors of his profession. He was president of the Indiana State Teachers' Association, 1871; state superintendent of public instruction, 1874–80; president of the National Education Association, 1880; a trustee of Indiana University at Bloomington, 1882; and president of the American Association of Agricultural Colleges and Experiment Stations, 1890. He was a trustee of the state normal school for six years and a member of the Indiana state board of education for twenty-seven years. In 1873 he was assistant commissioner of Indiana to the Vienna exposition; in 1878 United States commissioner to the Paris exposition; and in 1891 commissioner from the United States Department of Agriculture to the argricultural congress at The Hague.

In 1883 he became president of Purdue University, a land-grant college that had been established nine years before. Its initial years had been weak and struggling, but under its new administrator it gained new lease of life. Though not indifferent to agriculture, its teaching and research, Smart fostered especially the schools of engineering, which henceforth were subdivided. The university became widely known in the field of locomotive testing, and new housing, the finest of the time, was provided for the school of mechanical engineering. A school of pharmacy was started. There were notable increases in faculty, student body, and corporate income. Smart worked so indefatigably to build up the university that he brought on his own death by overwork. Among his publications are *The Indiana Schools and the Men Who Have Worked in Them* (n.d.), which he edited, and *Commentary on the School Law of Indiana* (copyright 1881).

[*Who's Who in America*, 1899–1900; *Encyc. of Biog. of Ind.*, vol. I (1895), ed. by G. I. Reed; *A Biog Hist. . . . of the State of Ind.* (1880), vol. II; W. M. Hepburn and L. M. Sears, *Purdue Univ.: Fifty Years of Progress* (1925); *Purdue Exponent* (Lafayette, Ind.), Mar. 1, 1900; obituaries in *Nat. Educ. Asso. Jour. of Proc. and Addresses*, 1900, and *Indianapolis Jour.*, Feb. 23, 1900.]   L. M. Se—s.

SMEDLEY, WILLIAM THOMAS (Mar. 26, 1858–Mar. 26, 1920), portrait painter and a leading illustrator of his time, was born in West Bradford, a township of Chester County, Pa., of Quaker stock. He was the second of six children of Peter and Amy Anna (Henderson) Smedley, and a descendant of George Smedley, who emigrated from Derbyshire, England, about 1682. His father was a miller and had operated mills in various places. At fifteen Smedley left school to enter a newspaper office. After studying for a time at the Pennsylvania Academy of the Fine Arts, he went to New York in 1878 as a draftsman for the illustrated periodicals; later he went to Paris and studied painting under Jean-Paul Laurens. From about 1880, when he opened a studio in New York, until 1906, when he turned to portrait painting, he divided his time between painting and illustrating. His work in black and white for *Harper's Monthly Magazine* and other illustrated magazines soon brought him a well-earned reputation for subtle interpretation of character, and he became one of the most important illustrators of contemporary social life. Not even Charles Dana Gibson portrayed the social characteristics of his day more lovingly and completely than Smedley. In 1882, commissioned by the publishers of *Picturesque Canada*, he traveled through the western part of the dominion for the purpose of making a series of illustrations, and in 1890, after several sketching tours in the United States, he went around the world, pausing in Australia long enough to make some interesting drawings for an illustrated publication on that country. At the exhibition of the American Water Color Society in the same year, his "A Thanksgiving Dinner" was awarded the William T. Evans prize and with his "One Day in June" became part of the Evans collection. On Nov. 27, 1892, he married May Rutter Darling, daughter of Edward Payson Darling of Wilkes-Barre, Pa., by whom he had two daughters and one son. A member of the National Institute of Arts and Letters, the American Water Color Society, and the National Academy of Design (1905), he received medals at the International Exposition at Paris in 1900; at the Pan-American Exposition, Buffalo, 1901; and at the National Academy exhibitions, 1906 and 1907. A book of his drawings was published in 1899 under the title, *Life and Character*. He died on the sixty-second anniversary of his birth at his home in Bronxville, N. Y. A large collection of his original drawings is in the Library of Congress, Washington, D. C.; other examples of his work are in the Metropolitan Museum of Art, New York, and the National Gallery of Art, Washington.

Prolific as he was, his work never suffered from lack of thought or preparation. His portraits were satisfying likenesses, skilfully and pleasingly done in academic style, but he was preëminently the illustrator and the historian of the middle class. His water-color drawings exhibited at the Avery Galleries, New York, in 1895 included many diverting glimpses of fashionable life at Bar Harbor, Narragansett Pier, Washington, and New York. As records of the American scene in the nineties such drawings as his "Afternoon at the Country Club," "Christmas Shopping on West Twenty-Third Street" and "The Meadowbrook Races" have an undeniable authenticity and historical value. "The pretty girls . . . in wonderful toilettes, and the well-groomed old gentlemen in their offices or clubs," his customary types, were depicted admirably, with a faint touch of humor. Perhaps no American illustrator has understood better than he the manners and customs of his period as exemplified by typical groups of the genteel class.

[Gilbert Cope, *Geneal. of the Smedley Family* (1901); *Who's Who in America*, 1918–19; *Who's Who in N. Y.*, 1917–18; W. T. Smedley, *Life and Character* (1899), preface by Arthur Hoeber; P. G. H., Jr., in *Book Buy-*

er, Mar. 1895; F. H. Smith, *Am. Illustrators* (1892); Ripley Hitchcock, *Some Am. Painters in Water Colors* (1890); Frank Weitenkampf, *Am. Graphic Art* (1912); C. M. Kurtz, *Am. Acad. Notes* (1883); Samuel Isham, *The Hist. of Am. Painting* (1905); obituaries in *Am. Art News*, Apr. 3, 1920, *Am. Art Ann.*, 1920, and *N. Y. Times*, Mar. 27, 1920; information from William Patten, Rhinebeck, N. Y.]   W.H.D.

SMIBERT, JOHN (1688–Apr. 2, 1751), one of the earliest artists of any importance to settle in America, was born in Edinburgh, Scotland, where his baptism was recorded in the Southwest District on the "First Aprill 1688." He was the son of John Smibert, a "litster" or dyer, and his wife Alison (Bell) Smibert. Endless confusion has arisen over the spelling of his name, which has been given as Smibert, Smybert, and even Simbert. The first of these alone appears in the Edinburgh records, in all contemporary Boston newspaper notices, in the dozen or more paintings the artist signed, and in his letters. His father was a lay member of the ecclesiastical council, and it is said that he destined his son for the ministry. His friend George Vertue (1684–1756) says he was "first apprentice at Edenbourough servd 7 years to a house painter and plaisterer. in all that time tho' he had a strong inclination to drawing and studying but no oppertunity to improve came to London" (*Proceedings of the Massachusetts Historical Society*, vol. XLIX, 1915–16, p. 25). There he was first employed in coach painting and later in copying pictures for dealers. He attended an academy, probably the original and short-lived one which opened in the autumn of 1711 on Great Queen Street. After three or four years he went to Edinburgh to try his hand at portraiture, but finding little demand for it and feeling the need of further training he returned to London and left for Italy in 1717.

In Florence, where he came under the protection of the gloomy and degenerate Medician grand duke, Cosimo III, he spent three years in copying portraits of Raphael, Titian, Rubens, and Van Dyck, and thus acquired a feeble Venetian technique and a certain facility at "face painting" in the grand manner. In Rome he painted several persons from life. It was during this Italian sojourn that he met George Berkeley, later bishop of Cloyne, then a tutor of Trinity College, Dublin. Leaving Italy in 1720 he returned probably to Edinburgh, and thence to London with something of a reputation. Although he soon found employment as a portrait painter, only a few examples of this period are known. He was a member of the Rose and Crown Club (usually confused with the Society of Virtuosi of St. Luke and referred to as Van Dyck's

Club) of which he did, according to Vertue, a "large painting peice"; this has disappeared, though a rough sketch of it exists in the Vertue manuscripts. The painter's studio, to quote Berkeley (letter to Thomas Prior, Fraser, *post*, p. 132), was "next door to the King's Arms tavern, in the little piazza, Covent Garden." Berkeley, then dean of Derry, often used his friend's quarters as a convenient place to stop when in London, and it was during these visits that he induced Smibert to accept the post of professor of drawing, painting, and architecture in the proposed "universal college of science and arts in Bermudas" (Walpole, *post*, IV, 29). Smibert, "a silent and modest man, who abhorred the finesse of some of his profession, was enchanted with a plan that he thought promised him tranquility and honest subsistence in a healthful Elysian climate ... glowing with scenery, which no pencil had yet made cheep and common" (*Ibid.*).

After four years of preparation Berkeley, accompanied by his wife and friends, embarked at Gravesend early in September 1728, landed in Virginia, and thence proceeded to Newport, R. I., Jan. 23, 1729, where he intended to remain until the £20,000 voted by Parliament for the college in Bermuda was forthcoming. The little company was painted by Smibert in Newport shortly after landing; the picture, which is at Yale, is one of the earliest group portraits painted in America. It is said that on shipboard Smibert taught Berkeley's wife, Anne Forster, to paint passable portraits. If this was so, she was among the first woman artists in British America. The "indifferent wooden house" on Berkeley's farm, "Whitehall," three miles from Newport, is sometimes said to have been designed by Smibert, but it had been built more than five years before the dean's arrival. Both philosopher and artist were much interested in the Narraganset Indians and in the strange signs on Dighton Rock. The story of their visit to the Indians, which has been called the first ethnological anecdote in American history, has been often cited, but a careful drawing which Smibert is said to have made of the pictograph writing on Dighton Rock is unfortunately lost. (See *Colonial Society of Massachusetts Publications*, vol. XVIII, 1916, p. 27.) In the fall of 1731, after waiting well over two years for the promised funds, the disappointed Berkeley returned to London.

Smibert had settled in Boston early in 1730, living first in the house of Capt. James Gooch in Green Lane, whose portrait and that of his wife he painted (now in the Brooklyn Museum with a third painting by Smibert, that of Gooch's second wife). On July 30, 1730, he married Mary, the twenty-three year old daughter of Dr. Nathaniel Williams [q.v.], physician and schoolmaster. She brought her husband a dowry of £400 and a residence in the west half of the Williams mansion, which with the land was valued at £3,000. In 1743 the Smiberts acquired the whole house, which was "in Queen Street, between the Town House and the Orange Tree" (*Bostonian Society Publications,* vol. II, 1917, p. 113). With the best location that the town afforded, a foreign reputation, and local social prestige, Smibert began to paint the "best" people in the Bay Colony—colonial officials, divines, eminent magistrates, prosperous merchants and their wives. He must have turned out some two hundred canvases in his nineteen or twenty active working years in America. Many are, of course, lost; others are miscatalogued and are masquerading under the names of other painters. The large group portrait of Berkeley and his fellow passengers, and a painting in the Essex Institute, Salem, Mass., of Sir William Pepperrell [q.v.], done about 1745, are his most ambitious pieces. One of his London portraits, of his friend Allan Ramsay, the author of *The Gentle Shepherd,* was engraved by Vertue. Some halfdozen of those painted in America were engraved by Peter Pelham, the step-father of John Singleton Copley [qq.v.].

Discovering in spite of his success that portraiture did not bring him sufficient income for his rapidly growing family, Smibert opened a store in his house for the sale "of Colours, dry or ground, with Oils and Brushes," and "the best Metzotinto, Italian, French, Dutch and English Prints, in Frames and Glasses, or without, by Wholesale or Retail, at Reasonable Rates . . ." (Dow, *post,* p. 3). The next year he advertised "a collection of valuable PRINTS, engrav'd by the best Hands, after the finest Pictures . . . done by Raphael, Michael Angelo, Poussin, Rubens, and other the greatest Masters . . ." (*Ibid.*). Judging from his correspondence with Arthur Pond, business prospered. About 1740 he took in his nephew, John Moffatt, as a partner. He had a number of copies of pictures in European galleries, besides "a collection of good busts and statues, most of them antiques, done in clay and paste, among the rest Homer's head and a model of the Venus of Medicis" (Hamilton, *post,* p. 139). The great tradition of the Renaissance was thus carried to American shores.

On May 31, 1735, Berkeley, who had been elevated to the bishopric of Cloyne, wrote and suggested to Smibert "to embark with your busts, your prints, and your drawings, and once more cross the Atlantic," and settle in Cork, a "city four times as populous as Boston, and a hundred times as rich" (*Gentleman's Magazine,* Feb. 1831, p. 100). He remained, however, in the Bay Colony, continuing with the shop and his painting. His name occurs occasionally upon the Boston town records. He furnished the designs for Faneuil Hall, which was built in 1742 from funds provided by Peter Faneuil [q.v.], whom he painted. (The picture is now in the collections of the Massachusetts Historical Society; a copy is in Faneuil Hall). Because of his failing eyesight his professional career ended about 1748. In a letter to Arthur Pond in 1749 he says, "my eyes has been sometime failling me, but is stil heart whole and hath been diverting my self with something in the Landskip way which you know I always liked" (*Proceedings of the Massachusetts Historical Society, op. cit.,* p. 34), which places him as one of the earliest landscape painters in America. Unfortunately, no examples remain or have been identified. Thirteen were listed in the inventory of his estate, though some of these might have been his copies after European masters. He died at sixty-three and was buried in the tomb of his father-in-law in the Granary Burying Ground. The grave, however, no longer bears his name but has the inscription, Thomas and John Bradlee'[s] Tomb 1816 (*Proceedings of the Massachusetts Historical Society, op. cit.,* p. 38). There is a self-portrait of Smibert in the left-hand corner of the group picture at Yale, and a portrait of his wife in the collections of the Massachusetts Historical Society.

His estate was appraised by a fellow-artist, John Greenwood, ten months later at £1,387 4s. 9d. (*Proceedings of the Massachusetts Historical Society,* vol. IX, 1866–67, pp. 208–09). His wife and his nephew, John Moffatt, succeeded to his artist's materials and print business, which they conducted for many years. About his children there is much uncertainty. According to Walpole, he left a widow with two children. Smibert himself wrote in 1743, "I am happy in 4 clever Boys . . .," and four sons are named in the records of Suffolk County, in which Nathaniel is listed as the fourth. He is also said to have had "nine children, two daughters and seven sons, the second, Nathaniel" (*Antiques, post,* p. 120). Nathaniel or Nathanael (Jan. 20, 1734– Nov. 3, 1756) is given as "the second son of the late Mr. John Smibert" in a contemporary obituary notice. The son showed considerable promise as a painter; three portraits are known by his hand, those of John Lovell at Harvard, Pres.

Ezra Stiles [*qq.v.*] at Yale, and Dorothy Wendell in a private collection in Boston.

Smibert's influence persisted long after his death. Charles Willson Peale [*q.v.*] visited his "painting-room" in 1765 and heard there of young Copley. It is doubtful if Copley received any instruction from Smibert, "but it is very probable that he was the recipient of some attention, if not information" (*Proceedings of the Massachusetts Historical Society*, IX, 209). John Greenwood occupied the premises, which had already become Boston's art center, and was followed by John Trumbull [*q.v.*] after he resigned from the Continental Army in 1777. Succeeding generations of artists—Samuel King [*q.v.*], John Mason Furnass, John Johnston, and Samuel Minot, the goldsmith—continued to occupy the celebrated Smibert House. (See W. K. Watkins, "The New England Museum and the Home of Art in Boston," *Bostonian Society Publications*, 2 ser., vol. II, 1917.) Smibert's style was much like that of the best of his contemporaries in England, which was none too good. A provincial painter in spite of his European training, he is often awkward, but there is a sincerity, honesty, and vitality about his work which many regard as peculiarly characteristic of early American painting. His importance is due to his precise, faithful, and often grim records of New England worthies, and to the fact that his work served as an early link between the art of Europe and that of the colonies.

[The chief source concerning Smibert's life in England is Horace Walpole's *Anecdotes of Painting in England* (2nd ed., 4 vols., 1765–71), an abridged and not wholly exact version of the Vertue papers in the British Museum (Add. MSS. 23,076, fol. 13, 18), which are being published by the Walpole Society of London; portions of the Vertue papers have appeared in the *Proc. Mass. Hist. Soc.*, vol. XLIX (1915–16) and in W. T. Whitley, *Artists and Their Friends in England, 1700–1799* (1928), vol. I. See Alexander Hamilton, *Itinerarium Being a Narrative of a Journey . . . 1744* (privately printed, 1907), ed. by A. B. Hart, for a description of Smibert's studio; G. F. Dow, *The Arts & Crafts in New England 1704–1775, Gleanings from Boston Newspapers* (1927) for Smibert's advertisements in *Boston Gazette*, Oct. 21, 1734, and Sept. 16, 1746, and in *Boston News-Letter*, Oct. 10/17, 1734, May 15/22, and June 5/12, 1735, and Sept. 4, 1746, as well as for obituaries of Smibert from *Boston News-Letter*, Apr. 4, 1751, and of Nathaniel Smibert from *Boston Gazette*, Nov. 8, and *Boston News-Letter*, Nov. 11, 1756; *Proc. Mass. Hist. Soc.*, vol. XLIX (1915–16), for five of Smibert's letters and for obituaries from the *Boston Gazette*, Apr. 9, *Boston Evening Post*, Apr. 8, and *Boston Post-Boy*, Apr. 8, 1751. Later sources are William Dunlap, *A Hist. of the Rise and Progress of the Arts of Design in the U. S.* (3 vols., 1918), ed. by F. W. Bayley and C. E. Goodspeed; Justin Winsor, ed., *The Memorial Hist. of Boston*, vol. II (1881), for Smibert's signature and a map showing the location of his house; Wilkins Updike, *A Hist. of the Episcopal Church in Narragansett, R. I.* (3 vols., 1907), ed. by Daniel Goodwin; F. W. Bayley, *Five Colonial Artists of New England* (privately printed, 1929); H. W. Foote, *Robert Feke, Colonial Portrait Painter*

(1930); *Dict. of Nat. Biog.* Among articles in periodicals are "Am. Artists and Am. Art," *Mag. of Art*, vol. II, 1879; R. R. Wilson, in *New England Mag.*, Mar. 1902; Lawrence Park, in *Bull. Worcester Art Museum*, Oct. 1917; L. P., in *Bull. Cleveland Museum of Art*, Jan. 1921; F. W. Coburn, *Art in America*, June 1929; Cuthbert Lee, in *Antiques*, Aug. 1930; Theodore Sizer, in *Parnassus*, Feb. 15, 1929; *Handbook of the Gallery of Fine Arts, Yale Univ.* (1931), and *Bull. of the Associates in Fine Arts*, June 1934; H. W. Foote, *New Eng. Quart.*, Mar. 1935. For Berkeley's connection with Smibert, see A. C. Fraser, *Life and Letters of George Berkeley, D.D.* (1871); Noah Porter, *The Two-Hundredth Birthday of Bishop George Berkeley* (1855); Benjamin Rand, *Berkeley's Am. Sojourn* (1932); and Theodore Sizer, "Bishop Berkeley as a Patron of Art," MS. in Yale Univ. Lib.; Andrew Burnaby, *Travels through the Middle Settlements in North-America, In the Years 1759 and 1760* (1775). For lists of Smibert's work see A. T. Perkins, in *Proc. Mass. Hist. Soc.*, vols. XVI (1878) and XVII (1879–80), incomplete, and Theodore Bolton, in *Fine Arts*, Aug. 1933. There are a number of contemporary portraits (probably English) bearing the forged signature of Smibert. A new list is being prepared by the Rev. Henry Wilder Foote, Belmont, Mass., who is also preparing a book on Smibert.]   T. S.

SMILEY, ALBERT KEITH (Mar. 17, 1828– Dec. 2, 1912), educator, humanitarian, was born in Vassalboro, Me., the son of Daniel and Phebe (Howland) Smiley. From his early boyhood on his father's farm his life was closely linked with that of his twin brother, Alfred Homans Smiley (d. Jan. 25, 1903). In their infancy the resemblance between the two was so strong that even their mother found it difficult to distinguish them, and they retained a striking similarity of feature throughout their lives. After attending a local academy the brothers went to Haverford College, where in 1849 they constituted the graduating class. They remained at Haverford as instructors in English and mathematics until 1853, when they established an English and classical academy in Philadelphia. After four years in this school Albert K. Smiley returned to Maine to serve as principal of the Oak Grove Seminary near his birthplace. In 1860 he went to Friends' School in Providence, R. I., and as teacher and principal remained until 1879. On July 8, 1857, at a Friends' meeting-house in New York City, he married Eliza Phelps Cornell. A few years after their marriage they were greatly saddened by the death of their only child.

In 1869, while Smiley was teaching in Providence, he bought a tract of land on Lake Mohonk in Ulster County, N. Y. He made over an old inn on the tract and in 1870 it was opened to guests under the management of his brother. Smiley continued to teach, in order to pay for the property, until 1879, when he left Providence to devote himself to the hotel project, taking pride, especially, in developing the natural scenery about the establishment. The unwritten regulations concerning guests, which included a ban on card-playing and the use of liquor as well as a strict observance of Sunday, apparently did not lessen the popularity of the place, which became a well-known resort.

In 1879 Smiley was appointed to the Board of Indian Commissioners by President Hayes. He remained a member of the board until his death. Of humane spirit and interests, he entered seriously into the work of the commissioners and served on various special committees within the organization. In the fall of 1883, in an effort to bring together groups and individuals concerned with Indian problems, he invited legislators, administrators, and persons interested in the welfare of the American Indians to attend a conference at Lake Mohonk. The meetings thus begun, known first as the Lake Mohonk Conferences of Friends of the Indian, were held annually, and the scope of the discussions in time widened to include the negro and inhabitants of the dependencies of the United States. Annual reports of the meetings were published from 1883 to 1913. Smiley also identified himself with the movement for world peace and in the spring of 1895 instituted another series of discussions, similar in organization to the Indian conferences, known as the Lake Mohonk Conferences on International Arbitration. The meetings were held annually, and reports of the proceedings were published.

In 1889 Smiley was appointed by the Secretary of the Interior to serve as chairman of a commission delegated to select reservations for the Mission Indians of California. In the same year he bought about two hundred acres of land south of Redlands, Cal., where he and his brother built winter homes. They were generous in their benefactions to the community and allowed their property, beautified by many rare and exotic plants, to be used as a public park. The Albert K. Smiley Library, named for its donor, and a park adjoining the library property, were gifts of permanent value to Redlands. After the death of the brothers the little city began to celebrate Smiley Day, Mar. 17, in affectionate remembrance of the two. Albert Smiley retained his interest in education throughout his life. He served as a trustee of Brown University, Bryn Mawr College, and Pomona College, and at the time of his death was president of the board of trustees of the New York State Normal School at New Paltz. He died at his California home at the age of eighty-four. His wife survived him by only a few days.

[*The Golden Day,* a memorial published upon the celebration of the fiftieth wedding anniversary of Albert K. Smiley and his wife, July 8, 1907; Lyman Abbott, *Silhouettes of My Contemporaries* (1921); *Hist.*

of San Bernardino and Riverside Counties (3 vols., 1922), ed. by John Brown, Jr., and James Boyd; J. S. McGroarty, *California of the South* (4 vols., 1933); L. A. Ingersoll, *Ingersoll's Century Annals of San Bernardino County* (1904); F. E. Partington, *The Story of Mohonk* (1911; 2nd ed., 1932); *Biog. Cat. of the Matriculates of Haverford Coll., 1883–1900* (1900); *Phi Beta Kappa Gen. Cat.* (1922); *Bull. of the Pan American Union,* Jan. 1913; scrapbooks of newspaper clippings at the Albert K. Smiley Library, Redlands, Cal.]

M. B. P.

SMILLIE, GEORGE HENRY (Dec. 29, 1840–Nov. 10, 1921), landscape painter, was born in New York, son of Katharine (Van Valkenbergh) and James Smillie [*q.v.*], and younger brother of James David Smillie [*q.v.*]. He was educated in private schools, received his first lessons in art from his father, and later became the pupil of James MacDougal Hart [*q.v.*], who, like himself, was a landscapist of Scotch descent. He spent his professional life in New York, where he had his studio, but sought his subjects from New England to Florida and west to the coast. On June 28, 1881, he married Nellie Sheldon Jacobs, a painter of genre pictures, who had been a pupil of James D. Smillie and was a member of the American Water Color Society. A year later he was made a member of the National Academy of Design. In 1884, with his wife, he made an extended tour of Europe. He was recording secretary of the National Academy from 1892 to 1902, and treasurer of the American Water Color Society for four years. With James D. Smillie, he and his wife shared a studio in East Thirty-sixth street; their home was in Bronxville, N. Y.

The merits of his pictures were recognized by amateurs of discernment. Three good specimens were included in the famous collection of Thomas B. Clarke, "Low Tide," "From Grindstone Neck," and "Landscape, Easthampton, L. I."; in the collection of William T. Evans [*qq.v.*] were his "Long Island Farm" and "Gray Autumn." The museums were not slow in following the example of the collectors. "A Long Island Farm" and "Autumn on the Massachusetts Coast" were acquired by the Corcoran Gallery, Washington, D. C.; other examples are to be seen in the Metropolitan Museum of Art, New York; the Rhode Island School of Design, Providence, R. I.; the Lotos Club, New York; and the Union League Club of Philadelphia, which owns his "Light and Shadow along Shore."

Among his important works is the "Lake in the Woods," first shown at the National Academy in 1872, and subsequently exhibited at the Centennial Exhibition, Philadelphia, 1876, together with several water colors. The summing-up of his qualities as a landscape painter in the catalogue of the Clarke collection is fair: "His pictures combine artistic skill and poetic feeling in a high degree and are marked by agreeable cheerfulness of color . . ." He won the first prize of the American Art Association, New York, 1885, and received medals at the Louisiana Purchase Exposition, St. Louis, 1904, and from the Society of American Artists, 1907. He died of heart disease at his home in Bronxville in his eighty-first year, leaving his wife and three sons.

[*Who's Who in America*, 1920–21; *Who's Who in N. Y.*, 1917–18; Clara E. Clement and Laurence Hutton, *Artists of the Nineteenth Century* (1885 ed.); Samuel Isham, *The Hist. of Am. Painting* (1905); catalogues of the Corcoran Gallery of Art, 1908, the Thomas B. Clarke collection, 1899, and the William T. Evans collection, 1900; obituaries in *Am. Art News*, Nov. 19, 1921, and *N. Y. Herald*, Nov. 11, 1921.]
W. H. D.

SMILLIE, JAMES (Nov. 23, 1807–Dec. 4, 1885), engraver, was born in Edinburgh, Scotland, the son of David and Elizabeth (Cummins) Smillie. His father was an amateur lapidary and is said to have been an authority on the flora and fauna of the Hebrides. James was apprenticed to James Johnston, a silver-engraver, with whom he worked for nearly a year; later he worked for a time with an engraver on steel, Edward Mitchell. In 1821 the Smillie family moved to Quebec, Canada, where the father and an elder brother William, also an engraver, are believed to have carried on a jewelry business. James worked with them as an engraver until 1827, when he went to London and thence to Edinburgh, returning to Quebec only to proceed to New York about 1829. At the outset he had some difficulty in obtaining employment, but Robert Walter Weir and Asher Brown Durand [*qq.v.*] lent him their assistance and influence to such good effect that by 1830 he was settled there permanently as a busy banknote engraver, a pioneer in this work. As opportunity offered, he also engraved on steel the works of some of the leading figure painters and landscapists of the period. During the early years in New York he was associated with George W. Hatch; among other things they reproduced some views of New York City (1831), after C. Burton, and a plate in one of the annuals, "The Equinoctial Storm," which William Dunlap [*q.v.*] considered "of exceeding beauty."

The first of his line engravings to attract favorable notice was "The Convent Gate," after the painting by Robert W. Weir. Other excellent reproductive plates are "Dover Plains," after Durand; "Evening in the New York Highlands," after Weir; "The Bay and Harbor of New York," after John Gadsby Chapman; "Mount Washington from Conway Valley," after John Frederick Kensett; "American Harvesting," after Jasper Francis Cropsey; and "The Land of the Cypress," after Daniel Huntington [*qq.v.*]. But the most important undertaking of all was the series of large plates after the "Voyage of Life," of Thomas Cole, a set of four allegorical paintings that met with great popularity and drew an eloquent eulogy from William Cullen Bryant [*qq.v.*]; few were the genteel parlors of the fifties that were not adorned with one or more of these works. It was the period of the gift books known as annuals, and Smillie from time to time contributed line engravings to these flowery publications. He supplied prints after sketches by Thomas Addison Richards [*q.v.*] for a volume called *Georgia Illustrated* (1842), engraved the landscape background for Durand's historical picture entitled "The Capture of Major André" (1845), in collaboration with Robert Hinshelwood, and for the American Art Union reproduced "The Dream of Arcadia" after Thomas Cole's painting. Another important plate which elicited much commendation was "The Rocky Mountains," after one of the big scenic compositions of Albert Bierstadt [*q.v.*] which was famous in its day (1864).

Smillie was outstanding among engravers of landscape; it is therefore difficult to explain why, after 1861, he should have devoted all his time to engraving banknote vignettes, with the exception of 1864, when he was working on the Bierstadt. It may have been due to prudential considerations, or possibly to changes in the public taste for landscape work. He was elected a member of the National Academy of Design in 1851, one of the few engravers to have won that distinction. He married Katharine Van Valkenbergh of New York in 1832. Three of their sons, James David, George Henry [*qq.v.*], and William Main, following in their father's footsteps, became engravers of note. He died at Poughkeepsie, N. Y., survived by his widow, four sons, and two daughters.

[Frank Weitenkampf, *Am. Graphic Art* (1912), *How to Appreciate Prints* (1921 ed.), and "The Evolution of Steel Engraving in America," *Book Buyer*, Sept. 1901; W. S. Baker, *Am. Engravers and Their Works* (1875); Clara E. Clement and Laurence Hutton, *Artists of the Nineteenth Century* (1885 ed.); William Dunlap, *A Hist. of the Rise and Progress of the Arts of Design in the U. S.* (1918), ed. by F. W. Bayley and C. E. Goodspeed; D. M. Stauffer, *Am. Engravers upon Copper and Steel* (1907), vol. I; obituaries in *Appletons' Ann. Cyc.*, 1885, and *N. Y. Tribune*, Dec. 6, 1885; family information from Smillie's grand-daughter.]
W. H. D.

SMILLIE, JAMES DAVID (Jan. 16, 1833–Sept. 14, 1909), engraver and etcher, born in New York, the eldest son of Katharine (Van Valkenbergh) and James Smillie [*q.v.*] and the brother of George Henry Smillie [*q.v.*], was educated in private schools and the academic department of the University of the City of New York (later New York University). Under his father's tutelage he began work in engraving very early, and became one of the most finished masters of the craft in America. He made his first plate when he was only eight years old, and until 1864, when he turned to painting, he collaborated with his father in much of his work, which included the making of banknote vignettes for the American Bank Note Company. But Smillie was not satisfied to confine his efforts to the mechanical phases of engraving, and he soon turned from line engraving on steel to etching, dry point, aquatint, mezzotint, and lithography, achieving in all of them originality, freedom, and richness of effect. His first oil painting to be exhibited was a landscape sent to the National Academy of Design in 1864. Two years later he helped to found the American Society of Painters in Water Colors (later the American Water Color Society), of which he was treasurer, 1866-71, and president, 1871-77. He was elected an Academician in 1876, and served both as a member of the council and as treasurer. During the seventies and eighties he was foremost in the movement to promote painter-etching as an art, and with a few other artists he organized the New York Etching Club in 1877. The catalogue of its first exhibition, 1882, contains an interesting account by Smillie of the making of the first little etched plate, now in the collection of the New York Public Library. On May 7, 1881, he married Anna Clinch Cook (d. 1895) of New York, by whom he had two sons. Throughout his life he continued to engage in the most diverse artistic activities. For his landscape subjects he traveled widely, paying special attention to mountain scenery in both the eastern and western United States. He died in New York.

His engravings include illustrations for the novels of Charles Dickens and James Fenimore Cooper [q.v.] after the vignettes by Felix O. C. Darley [q.v.]. They have been called "the most pleasing and satisfactory examples of the employment of steel-engraving for book-illustration" (Weitenkampf, post, p. 101). He also made a series of line engravings for The National Gallery of American Landscape (copyright, 1869), illustrations of the Saguenay River and the Yosemite Valley for Appletons' Picturesque America (2 volumes, 1872-74), some small plates after artists of the day for the American Art Review, 1880, and a reproduction of "The Goldsmith's Daughter" of Daniel Huntington [q.v.], 1884. Typical examples of his landscapes are "Evening, High Sierras, California," exhibited at the National Academy, 1876, "Cathedral Rocks, Yosemite," 1883, and "The Lifting of the Clouds, White Mountains." His "Cliffs of Normandy," which belongs to the Corcoran Gallery, Washington, D. C., dates from 1907. His etchings, dry points, and aquatints, however, are his most personal contributions to the art of his day, and reveal great versatility and technical mastery. Complete collections may be seen in the print departments of the Boston Museum of Fine Arts and the New York Public Library.

[Who's Who in America, 1908-09; Who's Who in New York, 1909; Frank Weitenkampf, Am. Graphic Art (1912); Samuel Isham, The Hist. of Am. Painting (1905); S. R. Kochler, in Am. Art Rev., Oct. 1880; obituaries in Am. Art News, Sept. 20, 1909, and N. Y. Times, Sept. 15, 1909.]   W. H. D.

SMITH, ABBY HADASSAH (June 1, 1797–July 23, 1878), and her sister, Julia Evelina (May 27, 1792–Mar. 6, 1886), advocates of woman's rights, were born in Glastonbury, Conn., where their earliest American ancestor, Benjamin Smith, had settled about 1693. Their father, Zephaniah Hollister Smith, a graduate of Yale, was at first a Congregationalist minister, but, becoming a Sandemanian, he soon decided it was wrong to preach for hire and turned to the law, which he practised the rest of his life. He was an abolitionist. Their mother, Hannah Hadassah (Hickock) Smith, was acquainted with Latin, Italian, mathematics, and astronomy, and wrote verse. The sisters were well educated. Julia, like her mother, had a scholarly bent. She knew Latin, Greek, and Hebrew, and made a translation of the Bible from the original, which was published in Hartford, Conn., in 1876. For a time she taught in the Emma Willard school in Troy, N. Y., but spent most of her life with her sister on the family homestead at Glastonbury. After the death of their parents and three other sisters, Abby, practical, spirited, and energetic, became manager of the home and farm, while Julia, who was rather dependent and retiring, devoted more time to scholarly pursuits. They lived simply, did their own housework, made butter and cheese, and in speech and manner reflected rural New England. Locally they were noted for their geniality, kindliness, and honesty, their hatred of slavery, and their many deeds of charity.

Their interest in woman's suffrage began about 1869 when, indignant at having to pay a highway tax twice, they went to a suffrage meeting in Hartford. In 1872-73 they were again aroused by having their taxes and those of some other women increased, while men's were not, and in October 1873 Abby, then seventy-six, attended the Woman's Congress in New York. The next month she spoke at the Glastonbury town-meeting against taxing unenfranchised women; later, denied another hearing by that body, she mounted an ox-cart outside and addressed the crowd. From 1873 until her death she refused to pay local taxes without a vote in town-meeting, and Julia joined her in resisting. A tract of their land worth $2,000 was once disposed of at public sale for a $50 assessment, and repeatedly their cows were sold at the sign-post for delinquent taxes. In 1877 Julia published *Abby Smith and Her Cows, with a Report of the Law Case Decided Contrary to Law.* The sisters became active also in general work for woman's suffrage. They wrote letters to the press, and spoke at local meetings and at suffrage conventions; almost annually they petitioned the Connecticut legislature for the vote, and in January 1878 they attended a hearing on the equal suffrage amendment before a committee of the United States Senate, at which Julia spoke. The Smith sisters and their cows soon became known in foreign lands as well as throughout the United States, and gave new publicity and added impetus to the cause of woman's rights. After the death of Abby, Julia, who had leaned on her in many ways, on Apr. 9, 1879, married Amos A. Parker, aged eighty-six (with whom she had become acquainted when he wrote to sympathize with her over her sister's death), and soon thereafter went to Hartford to live.

[F. B. Dexter, *Biog. Sketches of the Grads. of Yale Coll.*, vol. IV (1907), for Zephaniah Smith's life and family background; L. W. Case, *The Hollister Family of America* (1886); *Hist. of Woman Suffrage,* vol. III (1887), ed. by Elizabeth C. Stanton, Susan B. Anthony, and Matilda J. Gage; journal of the Conn. State House of Representatives and of the Conn. State Senate, 1874–79; *Woman's Jour.*, Jan. 26, Mar. 2, Apr. 20, Aug. 3, 1878, and Mar. 13, 1886; *Hartford Daily Courant,* Dec. 11, 1873, July 25, 1878, Mar. 8, 1886; *Boston Daily Advertiser,* July 27, 1878; private information.]

M. W. W.

SMITH, ALBERT HOLMES (July 19, 1835–Dec. 14, 1885), obstetrician and gynecologist, was born in Philadelphia, Pa., a descendant of Quakers from Yorkshire who settled in Pennsylvania in 1685. He was the youngest of seven children of Moses B. and Rachel (Coate) Smith, his father being a prominent physician. He was educated at the Friends' school at Westtown and in private schools in Philadelphia. Although he passed the entrance examinations of the University of Pennsylvania at the age of thirteen years, he did not enter at once; he was graduated with the degree of A.B. in 1853 and of M.D. in 1856, his preceptor being Prof. George Bacon Wood [*q.v.*]. He was assistant physician in the Frankford Asylum for eighteen months, and then an interne in the Pennsylvania Hospital for an equal

period of time; in 1859, after finishing his term there, he began practice.

He soon showed a decided skill in obstetrics, to which he gave especial attention. Appointed in 1859 assistant physician to the Philadelphia Lying-in Charity, he was promoted in 1862 to be attending physician, a position he held for over twenty years. For a short time he was obstetrician to the Philadelphia Hospital. In 1867 he became consulting physician to the Woman's Hospital of Philadelphia. He was also a manager of the Wills Ophthalmic Hospital, 1863–71. His interest in obstetrics led to the invention of various instruments and to the modification of others, among them a pessary that bears his name. His modification of the Hodge pessary, known as the Smith-Hodge pessary, probably did more to extend his reputation than his writings; among other inventions were a uterine speculum, urethral dilators, and modifications of obstetrical forceps. His writings dealt almost entirely with obstetrical and gynecological subjects, and he was regarded as one of the leading obstetricians of his day. He was a founder of the Philadelphia Obstetrical Society and its president, 1874–76; a founder of the American Gynaecological Society and its president in 1884; an honorary member of the British Gynaecological Society; president of the Philadelphia County Medical Society, 1880–81; and a member of the American Philosophical Society. He seems to have gained his eminence rather by patient study and hard work than by brilliance or genius; he was evidently a safe reliable man in all that he did.

He played a prominent part in advocating the recognition of women in medicine at a time when support of this view was unpopular with the majority of men in the profession. His acceptance of the post of consulting physician to the Woman's Hospital exposed him to much criticism and alienated some of his friends; the feeling was so strong that it was even suggested that he be expelled from the College of Physicians. A particularly bitter controversy arose over the proposal to admit women physicians to membership in the county medical society, for which Smith carried on an active but unsuccessful campaign. He taught for many years in the Lying-in Charity, which students of both sexes attended, and the statements of his contemporaries bear testimony to the soundness and value of his instruction. In 1860 he married Emily Kaighn, daughter of Charles Kaighn of Camden, N. J.; they had seven children, five of whom survived him. His death occurred from malignant disease of the prostate after an illness of several years, during part of which he carried on his work despite the handicaps of pain and weakness.

[H. A. Kelly and W. L. Burrage, *Am. Medic. Biogs.* (1920); *Medic. News,* Dec. 19, 1885, with bibliog.; *Am. Jour. of Obstetrics,* Feb. 1886; *Trans. Am. Gynaecological Soc.,* vol. XI (1887); *Proc. Am. Philosophical Soc.,* vol. XXIII (1886); *Trans. Coll. of Physicians of Phila.,* 3 ser., vol. IX (1887); *Phila. Enquirer,* Dec. 15, 1885.]   T. M.

SMITH, ALEXANDER (Sept. 11, 1865–Sept. 8, 1922), chemist, educator, author, was born in Edinburgh, Scotland, the son of Alexander and Isabella (Carter) Smith. His grandfather was a sculptor and his father a musician. In preparation for the University of Edinburgh he studied for seven years at the Edinburgh Collegiate School. While he received the degree of B.S. in chemistry in 1886, he devoted a good part of his four years at the university to the study of astronomy and published four semipopular articles on it before he was graduated. Finding that there was little prospect of a successful career in that subject, however, he turned to the study of chemistry under Adolph Ritter von Baeyer at the University of Munich, where his principal subject was organic chemistry. After securing the degree of Ph.D. at Munich in 1889, he was assistant in analytical chemistry at Edinburgh for a year and gave a course of lectures on organic syntheses. During a visit to the United States in the summer of 1890 he was appointed professor of chemistry and mineralogy at Wabash College, Crawfordsville, Ind., a position he held for four years. He also continued his researches in organic chemistry, following the lines of his work in Munich. In 1891 he became a member of the Royal Society of Edinburgh.

In 1894 he was invited by John Ulric Nef [*q.v.*] to take charge of the work in elementary inorganic chemistry at the University of Chicago. He was assistant professor, 1894–98; associate professor, 1898–1904; and professor, 1904–11. From 1900 to 1911 he was dean of the junior colleges. Partly because of his field of teaching, but quite as much because he thought it wise to devote his energies to inorganic and physical chemistry rather than to compete with the brilliant work Nef was doing in organic chemistry, he very soon began important investigations on quite other topics than those on which he had been working. Thoroughly trained in physics and mathematics, he soon made for himself a distinguished name in physical chemistry, which was rapidly coming into vogue in America through the influence of chemists who had received their inspiration in the laboratory of Wilhelm Ostwald in Leipzig. His most important studies in the new field were on the forms of sulfur, for which he was awarded the Keith prize and medal by the Royal Society of Edinburgh in 1912, and on vapor pressure measurements at comparatively high temperatures. In a series of masterful, experimental researches, he threw a flood of light on the conditions for the formation and existence of the different solid and liquid forms of sulfur. He also devised new methods for the determination of vapor pressures and through them demonstrated that the vapor above solid calomel consists of a mixture of metallic mercury and mercuric chloride. As a teacher he made a very careful study of the best methods for presenting chemistry to beginners. His ideas were crystallized in a book on *The Teaching of Chemistry and Physics in the High School* (1902), written with Edwin H. Hall. In 1906 he published his *Introduction to General Inorganic Chemistry,* which probably had a greater success than any other textbook of inorganic chemistry published during the first quarter of the twentieth century. It was translated into German, Italian, Russian, and Portuguese. Its phenomenal success was due to the fact that it presented adequately for the first time in a textbook written in English the theories of ionization and equilibria which lay at the foundation of the rapid advances then in progress in physical chemistry.

On Feb. 16, 1905, he married Sara (Bowles) Ludden, daughter of William Bowles of Memphis, Tenn.; they had a son and a daughter. Six years later, in 1911, he became head of the department of chemistry at Columbia University, a position he held until 1919, when he retired because of failing health. He became president of the American Chemical Society, 1911; a member of the Society of Physics and Chemistry of Madrid, 1911, and a member of the National Academy of Sciences, 1915. He died in Edinburgh.

[*Who's Who in America,* 1920–21; *Am. Men of Sci.* (3rd ed., 1921), ed. by J. M. Cattell and D. R. Brimhall; W. A. Noyes, "Biog. Memoir of Alexander Smith, 1865–1922," *Memoirs of the Nat. Acad. of Sci.,* vol. XXI (1926), with bibliog.; James Kendall, in "Proc. Am. Chem. Soc.," issued with *Jour. Am. Chem. Soc.,* Dec. 1922; obituaries in *Weekly Scotsman* (Edinburgh), Sept. 16, 1922, and *N. Y. Times,* Sept. 10, 1922; personal acquaintance.]   W. A. N.

SMITH, ALFRED HOLLAND (Apr. 26, 1863–Mar. 8, 1924), railroad president, was born on a farm near Cleveland, Ohio, the son of William and Charlotte (Holland) Smith. He attended the Rockwell Grammar School until he completed its course. At the age of fourteen, because of his father's death, he obtained employment as a messenger out of school hours with the

Lake Shore & Michigan Southern Railway. Entering upon regular employment in 1879, he continued with the railroad for forty-five years. After advancing to a chief clerkship he sought relief from the narrowing restraints of office work by joining a bridge gang. He became bridge foreman, then general foreman of construction work; in 1890, reports of his energy, resourcefulness, and gift for leadership having reached headquarters, he was made superintendent of the Kalamazoo division of the Lake Shore. After a series of similar positions, in April 1901 he was made assistant general superintendent with headquarters at Cleveland, and in a few months general superintendent. Transferred in 1902 to the New York Central and Hudson River Railroad as general superintendent, less than two years later he became general manager; by 1912 he had become vice-president; and by 1913 senior vice-president of the railroad and its subsidiary lines in charge of operation, construction, and maintenance. In 1913, because of his generally recognized sense of fairness, he was made a member of the arbitration board that settled the controversy with conductors and trainmen in Eastern territory. When the railroad and its subsidiaries were amalgamated as the New York Central Railroad, he became president, taking office on Jan. 1, 1914.

He was then in his fifty-first year, the chief executive of a system of 13,000 miles, serving the richest traffic territory in the country. Under his guidance widely scattered and loosely joined lines were welded into an efficient and smoothly operating system. At the time the problem of railroad regulation was an acute public question. He was frequently a witness before the Interstate Commerce Commission, and, although he was not enthusiastic over the steady increase in the commission's powers, he was not an obstinate opponent, for he felt regulation to be politically unavoidable. In 1916 he was made chairman of a royal commission on railways and transportation in Canada. Following the recommendation of the majority of this body Canada entered upon its experiment in government ownership, but Smith's minority report suggested a plan of relief that would have left the railroads in private hands. His counsel was again sought in aid of the problem of consolidation of the Cuban railroads, and he was engaged upon the problem at the time of his death. With the outbreak of the World War he was faced with the need of swift mobilization for war service. Under national control of individualized railroad systems he was made assistant director general of railroads in trunk-line territory east of Chicago and north of

the Ohio, and in January 1918 he was appointed regional director of the eastern district. When he assumed charge the port of New York was blocked as a result of freezing weather and a series of blizzards that made water transport impossible, and there was great congestion on the railroads. Taking personal direction of the situation, he finally cleared up the confusion in a way that showed plainly his indomitable energy and persistence, and his leadership in the face of difficulties.

After the war he handled new problems with a grasp of their significance that amounted to genius. He dealt successfully with matters of equipment, rehabilitation, electrification, and grade-crossing elimination in New York City, re-location of lines, consolidation, and the problem of terminals in New York and Chicago, and at the time of his death he was completing for his company the most favorable annual report in its history. His manifold accomplishments as a railroad executive were due to his abundant energy, his vision and imagination, his intimate knowledge of all phases of railroading, and a remarkable understanding of people. He died as the result of a fall from a horse which he was riding in Central Park, New York City. He was survived by his wife, Maude Emery of Adrian, Mich., whom he had married Sept. 9, 1885, and one son.

[Who's Who in America, 1922–23; Railway Age Gazette, Dec. 12, 1913; Railway Age, Mar. 15, 1924; Railroad Trainman, Apr. 1924 (editorial tribute); N. Y. Central Lines Mag., Apr. 1924, memorial issue; obituaries in N. Y. Herald, N. Y. Times, N. Y. Tribune, Mar. 9, 1924; information from Smith's wife.]

F. H. D.

SMITH, ANDREW JACKSON (Apr. 28, 1815–Jan. 30, 1897), soldier, was the son of Samuel Smith, who had been a lieutenant under Montgomery at the assault on Quebec and a captain at the siege of Yorktown. Samuel Smith married a daughter of one John Wilkinson and spent the rest of his life as a farmer in Bucks County, Pa., except while commanding a brigade of militia during the War of 1812. When his youngest son was born in the township of Buckingham soon after the battle of New Orleans, he "had no other means in his power of Showing his regard for the Hero, who achieved the Victory, than calling his son for him" (War Department records, post). This son, who is described as "intelligent and sprightly" (Ibid.), was appointed a cadet at West Point, July 1, 1834, and on his graduation, July 1, 1838, was commissioned second lieutenant in the 1st Dragoons (now the 1st Cavalry). His early service was practically all in the West, including some minor Indian campaigns. He was promoted first lieutenant, Mar. 4, 1845; captain,

Feb. 16, 1847; and major, May 13, 1861, all in the 1st Dragoons.

At the outbreak of the Civil War he was stationed in California. He was appointed colonel of the 2nd California Cavalry, Oct. 2, 1861, but resigned, Nov. 3, 1861, and was sent to Missouri, where he became chief of cavalry under Henry Wager Halleck [q.v.] and served as such through the Corinth campaign in 1862. He was appointed brigadier-general of volunteers, Mar. 17, 1862. He commanded a division in the expeditions against Chickasaw Bluffs and Arkansas Post in the following winter, and throughout the Vicksburg campaign in 1863. In the Red River campaign, March to May, 1864, he had a command made up of troops drawn from the XVI Corps (his own) and the XVII Corps. He was appointed major-general of volunteers, May 12, 1864. He spent the next few months in Tennessee and Mississippi in service which, overshadowed by the great Atlanta campaign, would have been as inconspicuous as it was necessary, had it not been illuminated by his defeat of Nathan Bedford Forrest [q.v.] at Tupelo, July 14, 1864. His command was then sent to Missouri for the defense of that state, and returned in haste to reinforce George Henry Thomas [q.v.] and take part in the battle of Nashville in December. Its wanderings had become so extensive that Smith now referred to his troops as the "lost tribes of Israel." As commander of the XVI Corps he took part in the Mobile campaign of 1865. He was mustered out of the volunteer service, Jan. 15, 1866, and reverted to his regular army rank of lieutenant-colonel, to which he had been promoted, May 9, 1864; but on July 28, 1866, he was appointed colonel of the 7th Cavalry. He resigned from the army, May 6, 1869, when he was appointed postmaster at St. Louis, Mo.; he was city auditor from 1877 to 1889, and commanded a brigade of militia during the strikes in St. Louis in 1877. Under a special act of Congress he was appointed colonel on the retired list of the regular army, Jan. 22, 1889. His wife was Ann Mason Simpson, daughter of Dr. Robert Simpson of St. Louis. Smith "was of small stature, with rather brusque, abrupt manners, sometimes verging on irascibility, yet was popular with his troops, and shunned none of the hardships to which they were subjected" (Perry, Twenty-Eighth Annual Reunion (post, p. 53). Constantly shifted from place to place to meet emergencies, he did not remain long enough with any one army to become identified with it, and as a consequence the confidence his superiors had in him did nothing to enhance his popular reputation.

[War of the Rebellion: Official Records (Army); Battles and Leaders of the Civil War (1887–88), vols. III, IV; G. W. Cullum, Biog. Reg. Officers and Grads. U. S. Mil. Acad. (3rd ed., 1891); L. J. Perry, in Twenty-Eighth Ann. Reunion... Assoc. Grads. U. S. Mil. Acad. (1897) and N. Y. Sun, Feb. 21, 1897; St. Louis Globe-Democrat, Jan. 28, 31, 1897; unpublished records in the War Dept.] T. M. S.

SMITH, ARCHIBALD CARY (Sept. 4, 1837–Dec. 8, 1911), marine painter, designer of yachts, commonly known as Cary Smith, was born in New York City, one of several children of the Rev. Edward Dunlap Smith, a Presbyterian minister, and Jane B. (Cary) Smith. After a grammar-school education he learned boat building at Pamrapo, N. J., in the shop of Robert Fish, a designer of large fast yachts, and under W. W. Bates, a shipwright of the old school. He built for himself several small boats, including the Comet in 1860, and came to be regarded as the best racing helmsman and handler of small yachts on New York Bay (Outing, post, p. 227). Later, however, he gave this up for marine painting, which he studied under Mauritz F. H. de Haas in New York. By 1867 he had produced his first picture, "Off Little Gull," a lighthouse scene on eastern Long Island Sound. This was followed by "Sunrise" (1869), "The Last of the Old Ships" (1871), "Nor' Wester, Coast of Maine" (1871), "Windy Day" (1876), and "Perils of the Sea" (1878). He also made paintings of five large schooner yachts, "Columbia," "Sappho," "The Wanderer," "The Yacht Dauntless" (1877), and "Peerless."

One of his first efforts in naval architecture resulted in the building of the cutter Vindex in 1871, among the first deep-craft iron yachts to be built in America. The next year he designed the sloop Vision for J. Joseph Alexandre. About this time he discarded the long accepted method of whittling out the model in wood, and began to work out his ideas on a drawing-board. For some years he was known scornfully as a "paper boatman," but his methods of yacht and boat design have become standard. After 1877 he seems to have done little painting. A few years later he designed the sloop Mischief (1879), said to have been the first scientifically designed yacht employed for cup defense, an example of what was called the "compromise" type. He designed well over a hundred yachts. Among the most notable were the schooners Prospero (1877), Intrepid (1878), Fortuna (1882), Meteor (1902), built for the German emperor, Wilhelm II, and Enchantress (1911); the sloops Mischief (1879), which was the successful defender of the America's Cup in 1881, Priscilla (1885), and Banshee (1887); the cutters Kestrel (1882), Rajah (1884), and Vera (1885); the auxiliary schooners *Free Lance* (1895) *Genesee* (1900), *Tekla* (1902), *Vergemere* (1903), and *Resolute* (1903); the steam yachts *Cayuga* (1899), *Twinkle* (1901), and *Continental* (1905). His principal commercial productions were the Long Island Sound steamers *Richard Peck, City of Lowell,* and *Chester W. Chapin,* and the pilot boats *New York* and *Espadon*; in these he increased both speed and economy of operation. He was a member of the New York Yacht Club, and of the Society of Naval Architects and Marine Engineers. In September 1904 he published "Yacht-Racing Recollections and Reflections" in *Scribner's Magazine.* A confirmed vegetarian, he was a man of medium height and somewhat spare build, quick and nervous in his movements. He died at his home in Bayonne, N. J., of Bright's disease, the oldest and best-known naval architect in America. He had been married and was survived by a daughter.

[*Who's Who in America,* 1910-11; Clara E. Clement and Laurence Hutton, *Artists of the Nineteenth Century* (ed. of 1885); W. P. Stephens, *Am. Yachting* (1904) and "The Evolution of the Yacht Designer: Pt. II—The Am. Designers," *Outing,* Nov. 1901, with portrait; W. M. Thompson and T. W. Lawson, *The Lawson Hist. of the America's Cup* (1902); H. G. Peabody, *Rep. Am. Yachts* (1893); obituaries in *Evening Post* (N. Y.) and *Newark Evening News,* Dec. 9, 1911.]   W. U. S.

SMITH, ARTHUR HENDERSON (July 18, 1845–Aug. 31, 1932), missionary to China, author, was born in Vernon, Conn., the son of the Rev. Albert Smith, a Congregational minister, and of Sarah Tappan (Stoddard). As a boy he went with his parents to Illinois. From May to September 1864, he served as a member of Company B, 40th Wisconsin Infantry and in 1867 he graduated from Beloit College as valedictorian of his class. While in college, he publicly declared himself a Christian and about the same time decided to become a foreign missionary. At Beloit he met his future wife, Emma Jane Dickinson, to whom he was married Sept. 8, 1871. There, too, he formed an intimate friendship with a classmate, Henry Dwight Porter, with whom he later spent many years in China. From 1867 to 1869 he was a student in Andover Theological Seminary; in 1870 he graduated from Union Theological Seminary, New York City; and during the following winter, 1870–71, he attended lectures at the College of Physicians and Surgeons, New York, in further preparation for his work as a missionary. The next year, for short terms, he supplied churches in Ann Arbor, Mich., Appleton, Wis., South Chicago, and Clifton, Ill. On May 29, 1872, he was ordained to the Congregational ministry and in July sailed for China as an appointee of the American Board of Commissioners for Foreign Missions. The Smiths

and the Porters were first stationed in Tientsin, where they remained eight years; in 1880 they were sent to a pioneer post in a rural community at P'ang Chia Chuang in Shantung. Here Smith spent most of the next quarter-century helping to found a Christian community. While on a furlough to the United States in 1885–86 he was acting pastor of the First Congregational Church of Pasadena, Cal. During the Boxer storm in 1900, he and his wife were among those who were in the besieged legations in Peking. Later, in 1906, in an interview with President Theodore Roosevelt, he made a suggestion which possibly contributed toward the remission by the United States, in 1908, of a portion of its share of the Boxer Indemnity and the allocation of the funds so released to the education of Chinese youths (*American Historical Review,* October 1926, p. 65). From 1906 until his retirement from active service, in March 1925, he was missionary-at-large under his board, a position which left him free to interpret the missionary movement by voice and pen and to share in interdenominational cooperation, but with his assignment still to North China and his residence usually in T'ungchow near Peking (Peiping). In 1926 he made his home in Claremont, Cal.

One of the most widely and highly esteemed missionaries in the China of his day, Smith was prominent in denominational and interdenominational activities. He was the American chairman of the notable China Centenary Conference (of Protestant Missions) in 1907; he attended the epoch-making (Protestant) World's Missionary Conference at Edinburgh in 1910; was a member of the important China Continuation Committee, which coordinated most of the Protestant activities in China and prepared the way for the National Christian Council of China; and served on the editorial board of the *Chinese Recorder.* He was alert, quick of observation, rapid of speech, and possessed a keen sense of humor. His pungent witticisms were extensively quoted and he was very popular as a speaker. Humble and devoted, he made many friends among both the lowly and the powerful. He was probably most distinguished for his books on China. Some of these went through many editions and had large sales, two of them over a considerable space of time; two were translated into a number of foreign languages. His first venture was *Proverbs and Common Sayings from the Chinese* (Shanghai, 1888). His next two, *Chinese Characteristics* (1890) and *Village Life in China* (1899), depicted life in North China as he had observed it, the former probably being his most famous work; *China in Convulsion* (1901) was an account of the Boxer outbreak. His *Rex Christus, An Outline Study of China* (1903) and *The Uplift of China* (1907) were primarily texts for mission study classes in the churches. His *China and America Today* (1907) and *A Manual for Young Missionaries to China* (Shanghai, 1918) which he edited and to which he was the chief contributor were not so widely known. He died in Claremont, his wife and three children having predeceased him.

[*Who's Who in America*, 1932–33; *Chinese Recorder*, Dec. 1932; *North-China Herald* (Shanghai), Sept. 21, 1932; *Missionary Herald*, Sept. 1924, Jan. 1925, Nov. 1932; *The Year Book of the Congregational and Christian Churches*, 1932; *N. Y. Times*, Sept. 2, 1932; annual reports and manuscript files of the American Board of Commissioners for Foreign Missions.]
K. S. L.

SMITH, ASA DODGE (Sept. 21, 1804–Aug. 16, 1877), Presbyterian clergyman, college president, was born in Amherst, N. H., the son of Dr. Rogers and Sally (Dodge) Smith. Most of his childhood was spent at Weston, Vt., but at sixteen he was apprenticed to a printer in Windsor. During his apprenticeship his religious interests were aroused and he began to look forward to a career in the ministry. At the age of twenty he entered Kimball Union Academy; in 1830 he graduated from Dartmouth College; and in 1834, from the Andover Theological Seminary. At once he accepted a call to the only pastorate he ever held, that of the newly formed Brainerd Presbyterian Church in New York City. During his leadership of twenty-nine years this church came to be one of the important organizations of the city, building successively two edifices and receiving fourteen hundred new members. In addition to his pastoral work, Smith was active in the affairs of his denomination, serving as a trustee of the Union Theological Seminary and as a member of the controlling boards of several Presbyterian societies.

In 1863 he became seventh president of Dartmouth College. At that time the institution was at a low ebb both with respect to student attendance and to finances. It was also in some disrepute on account of the pro-slavery attitude of its retiring president, Nathan Lord [*q.v.*]. In meeting these conditions Smith was in many respects successful. Feeling against the institution was assuaged by his tact, the student attendance more than doubled, and the Thayer School of Engineering and the New Hampshire College of Agriculture were established in accord with the president's policy of making the institution a university—a policy which was abandoned by his successors. Financially, however, the administration was less fruitful. The scholarship

funds were substantially increased and large donations were received for other purposes, but many of the gifts were restricted to special uses and were in the form of accumulating funds not immediately available; consequently, the institution had the utmost difficulty in meeting current obligations. The burden on the president increased from year to year, and finally, Mar. 1, 1877, his health having given way, he resigned his office.

Tall, erect, of great dignity and urbanity of manner, he looked the part of the college president. He was remarkably fluent of speech, self-possessed, and never at a loss for a telling phrase. He was genuinely solicitous for the students and sincerely charitable, his personal donations being large in proportion to his income. Withal, he was not soft as an administrator and there was no relaxation of discipline during his term of office. Most striking was his tact, which tided over many difficult situations, but was thought by some to be overdone, and brought upon him the reproach of insincerity. His point of view was ultra-conservative, and no innovations from established practice marked his administration. While he was a student at Andover he published *Letters to a Young Student* (1832), many of his sermons and addresses appeared in pamphlet form, and he was a frequent contributor to the periodical press. On Nov. 9, 1836, he married Sarah Ann Adams of North Andover, Mass. His death occurred at Hanover, N. H.

[For biographical information, see E. B. Coe, *An Address in Commemoration of Asa Dodge Smith* (1882); J. K. Lord, *Hist. of Dartmouth Coll.* (1913); L. B. Richardson, *Hist. of Dartmouth Coll.* (1931); *Concord Daily Monitor* (Concord, N. H.), Aug. 18, 1877. The greater part of Smith's correspondence during his presidency is deposited in the library of Dartmouth College.]
L. B. R.

SMITH, ASHBEL (Aug. 13, 1805–Jan. 21, 1886), surgeon-general and secretary of state of the Republic of Texas, was born in Hartford, Conn., the son of Moses and Phoebe (Adams) Smith. Through his father he was descended from Richard Seymour who came to Hartford in 1639; through his mother, from George Adams who died in Watertown, Mass., in 1696, and from René Cossitt, who settled in Granby, Conn., about 1720. He graduated at Yale in 1824 with Phi Beta Kappa honors, and four years later received his medical degree. Having taught school in Salisbury, N. C., from 1824 to 1826, he returned to that place to begin the practice of medicine. He continued his medical studies in Paris in 1831–32, and in March 1832 began his attendance at Neckar Hospital during an epidemic of Asiatic cholera. For his services

Smith   Smith

during this plague he was publicly thanked by the director of the hospital. Returning to North Carolina in 1832, he continued his practice and became identified with political affairs as editor and part owner of the *Western Carolinian,* a Nullification paper.

In 1837, Ashbel Smith went to Texas and was made surgeon-general of the new republic. He was one of the commissioners to negotiate a treaty with the Comanches in 1838 and was minister to England and France, 1842–44. In 1843, he made known to his government certain plans of the British and Foreign Anti-Slavery Society for the abolition of slavery in Texas and in the Southern states (Garrison, *post,* vol. II, pt. 2, pp. 1098–1103, 1116–19). These facts he also communicated to the Texan minister at Washington, who placed them in the hands of Calhoun and other Southern leaders. On the basis of the evidence thus revealed, President Tyler, in 1844, offered annexation to Texas in the form of a treaty, which was rejected by the Whig Senate. Texas desired to secure annexation if possible by honorable means, and if not, to secure peace and permanent independence. To the latter end, Ashbel Smith, appointed secretary of state by President Anson Jones [*q.v.*] in February 1845, negotiated with Mexico the Smith-Cuevas Treaty by which that nation acknowledged the independence of its former province. Tyler, meanwhile, signed on Mar. 1, 1845, the joint resolution offering annexation to Texas. The issue now rested with the people of Texas, who voted overwhelmingly in favor of annexation. A torrent of abuse swept upon Smith because of the Smith-Cuevas Treaty and twice he was burned in effigy.

After a brief period of service in the Mexican War, Smith retired to his plantation. In 1848, he was appointed on the board of visitors to West Point. As a member of the legislature in 1855, he sponsored legislation aiding railroad construction within the state, the common schools, and the payment of the public debt. During the Civil War he served as captain of the Bayland Guards and as lieutenant-colonel and colonel of the 2nd Texas Volunteer Infantry. He was cited for gallantry at Shiloh and at Vicksburg. As brevet brigadier-general he commanded the forces at the head of Matagorda Peninsula which saved the rich coast counties from invasion, and later was placed in command of the defenses of Galveston. When the war closed he was one of the commissioners sent to New Orleans to surrender the district.

Smith was elected to the Texas legislature in 1866 and again in 1878. Regarded as a leader in all movements for the advancement of education in the state, he was president of the board of trustees of the Galveston Medical School and was one of the commissioners to locate the Agricultural and Mechanical College for colored youths. As president of the board of regents in 1881, he undertook the chief labor of organizing the University of Texas, endeavoring to get the best men that could be induced to go to Texas in order that the institution might start with an established reputation for scholarship. After his entrance into political life, he practised his profession for the most part only in times of emergency, such as the epidemics of yellow fever in Houston and Galveston. He was the author of several scientific and historical treatises: *The Cholera Spasmodica as Observed in Paris in 1832* (1832); *An Account of the Yellow Fever which Appeared in the City of Galveston, 1839* (1839); and *Reminiscences of the Texas Republic* (1876). He died, unmarried, at "Evergreen," his plantation home, and was buried in the State Cemetery at Austin.

[J. D. Lynch, "Life and Character of Ashbel Smith," *Daniel's Texas Medic. Jour.,* Apr. 1886; A. G. Clopton, *An Eulogy on the Life and Character of Dr. Ashbel Smith* (1886); *Obit. Record Grads. Yale Univ. . . . 1880–90* (1890); E. D. Adams, *British Diplomatic Correspondence Concerning the Republic of Texas, 1838–1846* (1917); G. P. Garrison, "Diplomatic Correspondence of the Republic of Texas," *Ann. Report Am. Hist. Asso.* for 1907 and 1908 (3 vols., 1908–11); Anson Jones, *Letters Relating to the History of Annexation* (1848; 1852) and *Memoranda and Official Correspondence of Texas* (1859); E. D. Adams, *British Interests and Activities in Texas, 1838–46* (1910); J. H. Smith, *The Annexation of Texas* (1911); "The Service of Texan Troops in the Armies of the Southern Confederacy," in D. G. Wooten, *A Comprehensive Hist. of Texas* (1898), vol. II; J. J. Lane, *Hist. of the Univ. of Texas* (1891); *Western Carolinian* (Salisbury, N. C.), 1826–36; *Journal of Commerce* (New York), 1845; *Telegraph and Texas Register* (Houston), 1839–46; *Houston Telegraph,* 1860–69; *Houston Daily Post,* 1881–86; *Galveston News,* 1875–86; *Austin Statesman,* 1884–86; Ashbel Smith Papers, and O. M. Roberts Papers in the Univ. of Texas Lib.; W. D. Miller Papers and Official Records of the Republic and State of Texas in the Texas State Lib.]   H. Sm—r.

SMITH, AZARIAH (Feb. 16, 1817–June 3, 1851), medical missionary, first cousin of Judson Smith [*q.v.*], was born at Manlius, Onondaga County, N. Y., where his father, Azariah, was proprietor of a cotton-spinning factory. His mother, Zilpah, was a daughter of David Mack of Middlefield, Hampshire County, Mass. After studying at local schools, Smith attended Yale College and graduated in 1837. During a memorable revival at the College in March 1835 he decided to become a medical missionary and thenceforth devoted himself to preparation for this work. From September 1837 to May 1839 he attended the Geneva Medical College at Geneva, N. Y., then spent several months at a dispensary and hospital in Philadelphia, and in the autumn of 1839 returned to Yale for a final year in medicine (M.D. 1840) and for theological training. While studying in the Divinity School, from which he graduated in 1842, he also attended lectures on law, astronomy, and meteorology, besides finding time to write for the *American Journal of Science and Arts* an article on "Electricity in Machinery" (April–June 1840, pp. 134–36), based on observation in his father's factory.

On Aug. 30, 1842, he was ordained by the Presbytery of Onondaga at Manlius, and on Nov. 19 sailed from Boston for Constantinople, as a missionary of the American Board of Commissioners for Foreign Missions. From the first his work was primarily among the Gregorian Armenian and Nestorian Christians, and from 1843 to 1845 he traveled extensively throughout Asiatic Turkey, preaching and practising medicine in Trebizond, Brusa, Smyrna, and many interior cities, including Mosul. In 1844 he visited the pioneer Assyriological excavations of Botta and described them in an article, "Ruins of Nineveh," in the *American Journal of Science and Arts,* April–June 1845. In 1845 he settled in Erzurum, where in the following year an Armenian mob plundered his house and seized a Gregorian priest with Protestant leanings who had sought refuge there. John Porter Brown [*q.v.*] of the American legation in Constantinople was sent with a Turkish commissioner to investigate the incident and obtained for Smith a payment for damages and a formal apology from the Gregorian Patriarch.

In 1847 Smith was transferred to Aintab, and in the following spring returned to America to marry, on July 6, his first cousin, Corinth Sarah Elder of Cortlandville, N. Y. Accompanied by his wife, he immediately returned to Aintab, where he devoted himself and his small private fortune to such missionary activities as preaching, writing tracts, and practising medicine. One of his last accomplishments was the organization under the Ottoman law of a civil community for the Protestant Armenians of Aintab. On a journey in the spring of 1851 to Arabkir, Malatya, and Diyarbekir, where he founded a Protestant church, he contracted typhoid fever, of which he died shortly after his return to Aintab.

Always a careful student and the possessor of an immense fund of general information, Smith excelled as a writer and organizer rather than as a linguist and evangelist. His continuing interest in science is attested by "Abstract of Thermometrical Records Kept at the Missionary Stations of the American Board of Commissioners for Foreign Missions in Western Asia" (*Ameri-*

can Journal of Science and Arts, July 1846), which comments on records kept by a number of mission stations. The present mission hospital at Aintab is a memorial to him and bears his name.

[*Record of the Class of 1837 in Yale Univ.* (7th ed., 1887); F. B. Dexter, *Biog. Notices Grads. Yale Coll.* (1913); *Eighth Gen. Cat. of the Yale Divinity School* (1922); G. S. S. Martin, *Mack Geneal.* (1903); many long letters from Smith, in the *Missionary Herald, passim;* brief biography, *Ibid.,* Jan. 1852.]

W. L. W., Jr.

SMITH, BENJAMIN ELI (Feb. 7, 1857– Feb. 24, 1913), editor, was born at Beirut, Syria, the posthumous son of Eli Smith [*q.v.*] by his third wife, Hetty Simpkins (Butler) Smith, a native of Northampton, Mass. After the birth of her son Mrs. Smith returned home and established herself at Amherst as keeper of a boarding-house. Smith attended the local high school and graduated in 1877 from Amherst College. Julius Hawley Seelye [*q.v.*] evidently thought well of his pupil, for he engaged him to prepare a revised, extended edition (1880) of his translation of Albrecht Schwegler's *A History of Philosophy in Epitome.* Smith remained at Amherst as a postgraduate student, 1877–78, and as instructor in mathematics, 1878–80, and then went to Germany for a year of university study. After spending a term at Göttingen, as was still all but obligatory for Americans, he went to Leipzig to hear Wilhelm Wundt. He was an assistant in philosophy in the Johns Hopkins University for another year before joining, in 1882, the staff of *The Century Dictionary and Cyclopedia,* which was then organizing under the supervision of William Dwight Whitney [*q.v.*]. His original appointment he probably owed to his family connection with Roswell Smith [*q.v.*] of the Century Company, but he soon discovered an extraordinary aptitude for the work, and to it the rest of his life was devoted. Credit for the plan and scope of the *Dictionary,* and for the high standard of scholarship set for it, belongs primarily to Whitney, but as managing editor Smith had direct charge of the endless details involved in the preparation, revision, and publication of the *Dictionary,* which began to appear in 1889. He also had a large share in the work of defining terms, an undertaking for which he was well qualified by his wide knowledge, logical habits of thought, and command of a clear, terse English. On Whitney's death in 1894 he succeeded him as editor-in-chief. He had charge of *The Century Cyclopedia of Names* (copyright 1894), *The Century Atlas* (1897), the *Century Dictionary* supplement (2 vols., 1909), and the successive issues of the *Dictionary,* culminating in a thorough revision of the *Dictionary,* the *Cyclopedia of Names,* and the *Atlas* in twelve volumes in 1911. As recreation from this strenuous and illimitable task, he edited a series of pocket-size volumes of wisdom literature: a translation of Cicero's *De Amicitia* (1897); Franklin's *Poor Richard's Almanack* (1898); *Selections from the Meditations of Marcus Aurelius* (1899); *Epictetus: Selections from His Discourses* (1900); and *Selections from the Thoughts of Pascal* (1902). Smith was married Oct. 13, 1883, to Cora (Shelton) Cheesman, daughter of George Wellington Shelton of Derby, Conn., who with one daughter survived him. He made his home in New Rochelle, N. Y., and took an active part in civic affairs as a member of the board of education and of the public library board. Years of intense work on the *Dictionary* resulted in a breakdown of his health in 1911; a fatal disease of the kidneys developed; and he died at his home in New Rochelle at the beginning of his fifty-seventh year.

[*Who's Who in America,* 1912–13; *Obit. Record of Grads. of Amherst Coll.* (1913); *Amherst Coll. Biog. Record ... 1821–1921* (1927); obituary in *N. Y. Times,* Feb. 25, 1913.]   G. H. G.

SMITH, BENJAMIN MOSBY (June 30, 1811–Mar. 14, 1893), Presbyterian clergyman, educator, was born at "Montrose," Powhatan County, Va., the son of Josiah and Judith Micheau (Mosby) Smith. He was educated by private tutors and at Hampden-Sidney College, from which he graduated with first honors in 1829. For two years he taught in an academy at Milton, N. C., where he organized one of the first educational associations in the South. From 1832 to 1834 he was a student at Union Theological Seminary in Virginia and spent the next two years there as an assistant instructor. In the meantime, Apr. 19, 1834, he was licensed to preach by the West Hanover Presbytery, and on Oct. 19, 1835, he was ordained. After leaving Union Seminary he traveled abroad for two years, chiefly in Prussia, making a special study of Semitic languages.

Returning to America, he held pastorates in Danville, Va. (1838–40), Tinkling Spring and Waynesboro—where he also taught a classical school (1840–45), and at Staunton (1845–54). At the end of this last pastorate he served for a year as secretary of the Presbyterian Board of Publication, in Philadelphia. He then accepted a call to Union Theological Seminary, at Hampden-Sidney, Va., as professor of Oriental literature, which position he occupied until 1889, when he became professor emeritus. He has been called with some justification the second founder of the seminary, for during the Civil War the school's endowment was largely destroyed and the rapid recovery of the institution and its subsequent prosperity was due to him more than to any other single individual. For sixteen years (1858–74) he was co-pastor with Robert L. Dabney [*q.v.*] of the college church. In 1876 he was elected moderator of the General Assembly of the Southern Presbyterian Church (Presbyterian Church in the United States).

Smith also rendered a large service to public education in Virginia, of which he was one of the earliest and most active advocates. In 1839 his thoroughgoing report on the Prussian primary school system, which he had studied at first hand, was submitted by Governor Campbell to the Virginia House of Delegates (Document 26, *Journal of the House of Delegates . . . of Virginia,* 1839). This report is recognized as one of the most significant educational documents of the period. With Thomas Ritchie and R. G. Scott, he presented a report on primary schools to the Richmond Educational Convention of December 1841. This report was published the following year in the form of an appeal, "To the People of Virginia" (*Richmond Enquirer,* Nov. 22, 1842). He took an active part in the Educational Association of Virginia (organized 1863), and sought unsuccessfully in 1869 to have it indorse the system of common schools inaugurated by the unpopular Underwood Reconstruction Convention of that year. At the initial meeting of the new board of education (1870), twelve county superintendents were chosen, of whom the first to take the field was Smith. He continued to serve as superintendent of Prince Edward County, in spite of many annoying difficulties, till 1882, when a political revolution in Virginia swept Dr. William H. Ruffner [*q.v.*], state superintendent, and his appointees out of office.

Smith wrote frequently for the papers and for religious and educational journals. A report of his, "The Merits and Defects of Prevailing Schemes of Common School Education in the United States," appeared in *The Educational Journal of Virginia* (August 1870). He published *Family Religion* (1859); *The Poetical Books of the Holy Scriptures* (1867), prepared in cooperation with A. R. Fausset, a reprint in large part from the Jamieson, Fausset, and Brown series of commentaries; and *Questions on the Gospels* (1868). On Oct. 31, 1839, he married Mary Moore Morrison, a daughter of Rev. James Morrison of New Providence. Five daughters and one son survived him.

[Autobiog. fragment covering the years 1811–32 and a diary in possession of a daughter, Mrs. A. J. McKelway; published sermons and addresses in library of Union Theological Sem. in Va., and in library of Presbyterian Foundation at Montreat, N. C.; *Union Sem. Mag.*, V (1893–94), 73–84; *Minutes of the Synod of Va.*, 1893, pp. 266–68; minutes of board of trustees of Washington and Lee Univ., Jan. 19, 1894; *Gen. Cat. of Union Theological Sem. in Va., 1807–1924* (1924); W. A. Maddox, *The Free School Idea in Va. before the Civil War* (1918); R. L. Morton, *Hist. of Va.*, vol. III (1924).]   E. T. T.

SMITH, BUCKINGHAM (Oct. 31, 1810– Jan. 5, 1871), lawyer, politician, antiquarian, was born on Cumberland Island, Ga., the son of Josiah and Hannah Smith (cousins), of Watertown, Conn. He was christened Thomas Buckingham Smith. His father had moved to East Florida during the British occupation, and after the cession of Florida to the United States, went to Mexico on business, leaving his wife, Buckingham, and a daughter, in St. Augustine, where Buckingham received his early education. He visited his father in Mexico when he was about fourteen years of age after the latter had been appointed United States consul in Mexico. At the death of the elder Smith in 1825, Buckingham became the ward of his uncle, Robert Smith, and was placed in Washington (later Trinity) College in Hartford, Conn., where he remained three years. In 1836 he was graduated from the Harvard Law School and then spent some time in the law office of Judge Fessenden of Portland, Me. On his return to St. Augustine, he practised law for a time and in 1839–40, acted as secretary to Gov. Raymond Reid. He was a member of the Florida territorial legislature in 1841, serving one term. On Sept. 18, 1843, he was married to Julia G. Gardner of Concord, N. H. Through the influence of Senator Jackson Morton, he was appointed secretary of legation in Mexico on Sept. 9, 1850, and served until February 1852. On June 5, 1855, through the influence of William Pitt Fessenden [*q.v.*], he was appointed secretary of legation in Spain, where he formed a lasting friendship with the great Americanist, Pascual de Gayangos, and other influential men of letters. He continued the archival research begun in Mexico, with special reference to the history of Florida, and aided various American historians, including Sparks, Bancroft, and Parkman. He was recalled in 1858 and returned to St. Augustine two years later. Although a slave owner, he sided with the North during the Civil War, and in May 1864 was a delegate to the Democratic convention held in Baltimore, Md. Shortly afterwards he went again to Spain to make further investigations in the archives and to select improved stocks for

his orange grove. He returned to Florida in 1868 and was appointed tax commissioner. In 1870–71, he resided in New York City, but the northern climate did not agree with him and it is said that he contracted tuberculosis. On Jan. 4, he suffered a stroke near his home and never regained consciousness. A policeman, thinking him intoxicated, locked him in a cell at the police station. In the morning he was taken to Bellevue Hospital, where he died. His body was removed to the morgue and was about to be buried in the potter's field when it was identified by an acquaintance. He was buried at St. Augustine.

He bequeathed his valuable papers to the New York Historical Society, and his library was purchased for the Society by John David Wolfe. He left his property to be administered for the negroes of St. Augustine by the Buckingham Smith Benevolent Association. He was a large portly man, somewhat overbearing in his manner, but his opinions were highly regarded by his friends. An Americanist of note, he stimulated study in the early history of Florida and nearby regions. His writings and books are many and varied, ranging from studies of the Everglades of Florida, and the expedition of Verrazano, to Indian linguistics, and a geographical description of Sonora (the first publication in its original or any language of a Spanish document of the eighteenth century). In 1852 he supplied extracts translated from three unpublished Spanish journals to the third volume of the monumental work on the American Indian by Henry Rowe Schoolcraft [*q.v.*]. His most important publications were: *The Narrative of Alvar Nuñez Cabeça de Vaca* (1851), translated from the Spanish with a revised translation in 1871 and published after his death by Henry C. Murphy, and the *Narratives of the Career of Hernando de Soto in the Conquest of Florida, as told by a Knight of Elvas,* translated from the Portuguese, first published as a whole in 1866. This translation was republished in two volumes under the editorship of E. G. Bourne in 1922. A de luxe edition of the de Vaca narrative based on the 1871 edition of Smith's translation was privately printed in 1929. Of considerable importance also are his *Letter of Hernando de Soto and Memoir of Hernando de Escalante Fontaneda* (privately printed, 1854), and his *Colección de Varios Documentos para la Historia de la Florida y Tierras adyacentes* (1857). With his Elvas he published also the memoir by Luis Fernandez de Biedma (written about 1544) and other materials. A number of his books were published in small editions under the patronage of George W. Riggs, Jr., of Washington, D. C.

[J. G. Shea, Introduction to the 1871 edition of the narrative of Alvar Nuñez Cabeza de Vaca; R. H. Rerick, *Memoirs of Florida* (1902), vol. I (to be used with caution); *A Jour. of the Proc. of the Legislative Council of the Territory of Fla. at its Nineteenth Session* (1841); various items in contemporary newspapers of Florida, especially the *St. Augustine Examiner*; manuscript notes received from J. C. Yonge of Pensacola, Fla.; letter from A. J. Wall, librarian, New York Historical Society; letter written in 1823 by Andrew Anderson of Florida (in the possession of Mr. Yonge); some letters and other MSS. in Lib. of Cong.; *N. Y. Times*, Jan. 9, 1871.]   J. A. R.

SMITH, BYRON CALDWELL (Aug. 28, 1849–May 4, 1877), philologist, was born at Island Creek, Jefferson County, Ohio, the eldest child of George P. and Margaret (Caldwell) Smith. He was of German descent on his father's side and of Scotch-Irish on his mother's. His father was colonel of the 129th Illinois Volunteers at the outset of the Civil War and later was proprietor of newspapers in various towns in Illinois and Kansas. Byron entered Illinois College at Jacksonville, Ill., as a preparatory student in 1863 and remained in residence until 1868. His father's means permitting, he then went to Germany, intending to study Greek philology, philosophy, and other subjects for six years and to take the degree of Ph.D. as the preliminary to an academic career. He studied at Heidelberg, Berlin, and Munich, lived for a short period in Vienna, and finally spent six months at Athens. His plans were disrupted by the death of his only sister, and in the spring of 1872 he returned to the United States and joined his parents at Humboldt, Kan. The next autumn he was appointed instructor in Greek at the recently founded University of Kansas. He was a brilliantly successful teacher and was advanced the next year to the rank of professor. Meanwhile he became engaged to Kate Stephens, who was one of his pupils. In the winter of 1874 he went to Philadelphia to be treated for an ailment there diagnosed as renal neuralgia. Regaining his health, but losing his position at the University, he joined the editorial staff of the Philadelphia *Press* and devoted his leisure to the study of economics. He developed tuberculosis after an attack of pneumonia and died, in his twenty-eighth year, at Boulder, Colo., where he had gone in hope of benefiting by the mountain air. He was buried at Humboldt.

His friends mourned him as an heir of unfulfilled renown, and his scholarly attainments and gracious personality have become something of a legend. Two collections of his letters have been published: *A Young Scholar's Letters: Being a Memoir of Byron Caldwell Smith* (1897), edited by D. O. Kellogg, consists of the letters written to his parents from Europe; his

letters to his fiancée were first published as *The Professor's Love-Life: Letters by Ronsby Maldclewith* (1919), with various alterations in the text, and were republished, without the alterations, as *The Love-Life of Byron Caldwell Smith* (1930). At the University of Kansas he showed some kindness to Frank Harris (1855?–1931), who praised him extravagantly and maligned him obscenely.

[Besides the published letters, see A. I. Tobin and Elmer Gertz, *Frank Harris: A Study in Black and White* (1931); Hugh Kingsmill Lunn, *Frank Harris* (1932); Kate Stephens, *Lies and Libels of Frank Harris* (1929), ed. by Gerrit and Mary Caldwell Smith. Dean R. L. Lacey of Illinois College has supplied some additional information.]   G. H. G.

SMITH, CALEB BLOOD (Apr. 16, 1808–Jan. 7, 1864), lawyer, congressman, cabinet officer, was born in Boston, Mass., but when six years old was taken by his parents to Cincinnati, Ohio. He was enrolled as a student at the College of Cincinnati, 1823–25, and at Miami University, 1825–26, but did not graduate. Commencing the study of law in Cincinnati, he soon removed to Connersville, Ind., where he continued his law studies in the office of Oliver H. Smith [q.v.]. He was admitted to the bar, and commenced practice in the fall of 1828. His eloquence before juries contributed no little to his advancement in his profession.

Entering politics, he was an unsuccessful candidate for a seat in the Indiana House of Representatives in 1831, but the following year he purchased an interest in the *Political Clarion*, changed its name to the *Indiana Sentinel*, used it as a medium for the publication of his Whig policies, and was elected. He was reëlected each year until 1837 and was again elected in 1840. In the sessions of 1835–36 and 1836–37 he was speaker of the House and in 1840–41, chairman of the committee on canals. During his legislative career he was one of those who took the lead in procuring an order for the survey, by the federal government, of routes in Indiana for canals and railroads, and in otherwise promoting projects for internal improvements. When those projects were more or less wrecked by the panic of 1837, Smith was appointed a commissioner to collect assets and adjust debts. He accepted and served, but not without a temporary loss of popularity. In a triangular election in 1840 he was defeated as a candidate for a seat in Congress, but he won in a clear field in 1842, was reëlected in 1844, and again in 1846. In the Twenty-ninth Congress (1845–47) he was a member of the committee on foreign affairs, and in the Thirtieth (1847–49), chairman of the committee on the Territories. At a Whig caucus preceding the opening of the Thirtieth Congress he was proposed for nomination as speaker of the House, but failed of nomination by fifteen votes. His first speech in the House was made Feb. 8, 1844, in favor of excluding from membership the men who, in four states, had been elected by general ticket. He participated in debates on the Oregon question, the independent treasury bill, slavery in the Territories and the District of Columbia, the tariff, and the Dorr rebellion, but his principal efforts were directed against the annexation of Texas and the war with Mexico. He supported Taylor in the presidential campaign of 1848, and was proposed for the position of postmaster general in Taylor's cabinet, but was given, instead, a seat on the board of commissioners to adjust claims against Mexico, serving in that capacity until 1851, when he removed to Cincinnati and resumed the practice of law. Three years later he was made president of the Cincinnati & Chicago Railroad Company, which was soon in financial difficulties, and in 1859 he removed to Indianapolis, Ind.

Smith was one of the leaders of the Indiana delegation to the Republican National Convention in Chicago in 1860, and when, in behalf of that delegation, he had seconded the nomination of Lincoln, the convention broke into its greatest demonstration. In the campaign that followed, he was one of the most effective speakers, especially in Indiana, a doubtful state. In recognition of his services or in fulfillment of a promise, Lincoln appointed him Secretary of the Interior, but when failing health would no longer permit his administration of that office, the President accepted his resignation, December 1862, and immediately appointed him judge of the United States district court for Indiana. A little more than a year later he was fatally stricken while in the court house in Indianapolis, and died the same day. On July 8, 1831, he married Elizabeth B. Walton, daughter of William Walton, a pioneer from Ohio; they had three children.

[L. J. Bailey, "Caleb Blood Smith," in *Ind. Mag. of Hist.*, Sept. 1933; Charles Roll, "Indiana's Part in the Nomination of Abraham Lincoln for President," *Ibid.*, Mar. 1929; G. J. Clarke, "The Burnt District," *Ibid.*, June 1931; *Biog. and Geneal. Hist. of Wayne, Fayette, Union and Franklin Counties, Ind.* (1899), vol. I; C. W. Taylor, *Biog. Sketches and Review of the Bench and Bar of Ind.* (1895); *Biog. Dir. Am. Cong.* (1928); *Am. Whig Rev.*, Dec. 1850; *Indianapolis Daily Jour.*, Jan. 9, 1864; Caleb Blood Smith Papers (8 vols.), MSS. Div., Lib. of Cong.]   N. D. M.

SMITH, CHARLES ALPHONSO (May 28, 1864–June 13, 1924), educator and author, was born at Greensboro, N. C., the son of the Rev. Jacob Henry Smith, Presbyterian minister, and his second wife, Mary Kelly (Watson) Smith,

both Virginians. His father's family, though of German ancestry, had been in Virginia for several generations, and Jacob Smith had been educated at Washington College (later Washington and Lee University, of which another of his sons afterwards became president). In the Greensboro public schools Smith was prepared for Davidson College (Davidson, N. C.), and meanwhile became a friend of the Greensboro drug clerk, William Sydney Porter [*q.v.*], better known as O. Henry. From Davidson he received the degrees of A.B., 1884, and A.M., 1887. After four years of teaching in three little North Carolina towns, he went to Johns Hopkins in 1889 and in 1893 received the degree of Ph.D., his dissertation being on *The Order of Words in Anglo-Saxon Prose* (1893). At Louisiana State University, 1893–1902, his gifts as lecturer and teacher clearly emerged. Two small books, *Repetition and Parallelism in English Verse* (1894) and *An Old English Grammar* (1896), with various articles, represent the literary and scholarly output of these years. In 1902 he became a professor in the University of North Carolina and soon after first dean of its graduate department. Here he founded and edited *Studies in Philology,* published by the university, to encourage graduate scholarship. He married, Nov. 8, 1905, Susie McGee Heck, of Raleigh; they had two daughters and a son. During these years he produced a series of grammars for school use, a thin volume of *Studies in English Syntax* (1906), *An English-German Conversation Book* (1902), with Dr. Gustav Krüger, and performed editorial work for the *Library of Southern Literature* (17 vols., 1907–23).

A superb raconteur and a very able and stimulating lecturer, he reached the fullness of his power and popularity as first Edgar Allan Poe Professor of English in the University of Virginia, 1909–17. On leave of absence for 1910–11, he served as Roosevelt Professor of American History and Institutions at the University of Berlin, lecturing on American literature in German and conducting a seminar on Poe. Back in Virginia, he was not merely the genial professor. He lectured widely; he wrote his most characteristic and widely circulated little book, *What Can Literature Do for Me?* (1913), and his most ambitious literary work, the *O. Henry Biography* (1916); and he founded in 1913 the Virginia Folk-Lore Society, which under his enthusiastic leadership brought together an exceedingly rich collection of genuine folk ballads, published after his death under the editorship of A. K. Davis, Jr., as *Traditional Ballads of Virginia* (1929). This ballad quest has been termed "the activity for which in the long run he may be best remembered" (Barr, *post,* p. 10). In 1917 he left Virginia to become head of the English department at the United States Naval Academy at Annapolis, Md. There he employed his gifts as expounder and interpreter of literature in winning future naval officers to the love of letters. He also continued his editorial and literary activities. In 1924, suffering a comparatively sudden illness, he died at Annapolis, survived by his wife and children, and was buried in Greensboro. His *Southern Literary Studies* (1927) was published after his death under the devoted anonymous editorship of his widow (d. Apr. 24, 1933). He was a member of the Modern Language Association and of the American Dialect Society. His eminence was not primarily that of the critical scholar; though he illuminated many fields and greatly stimulated graduate study in the South, the very diversity of his interests limited his achievement in pure scholarship. He was essentially the apostle of letters and, in the better sense, the popularizer of literature. The basis of his power lay in the fact that he was a delightful human being and that a sure psychological instinct enabled him to communicate his enthusiasms vividly. In the words of his memorial tablet at Annapolis, truer than most, "He gave back as rain what he received as mist."

[C. A. Smith, *Southern Lit. Studies* (1927), contains bibliog. and biog. study by F. S. Barr. See also *Who's Who in America,* 1924–25; Archibald Henderson, in *Greensboro Daily News,* Nov. 20, 1927; J. C. Metcalf, in *Va. Jour. of Educ.,* Feb. 1925; J. E. Routh, in *Alumni Bull. Univ. of Va.,* Apr. 1911; bibliog., *Ibid.,* Apr. 1924; Susie M. H. Smith, *The Love that Never Failed* (1928); A. K. Davis, Jr., intro. to *Traditional Ballads of Va.* (1929); Julian Street, *Am. Adventures* (1917), pp. 165–68; K. P. Battle, *Hist. of the Univ. of N. C.,* vol. II (1912); P. A. Bruce, *Hist. of the Univ. of Va., 1819–1919,* vol. V (1922); obituary in *Greensboro Daily News,* June 14, 1924. A large collection of letters and newspaper clippings is in the possession of Smith's daughter, Mrs. L. Dee York, Charlottesville, Va.]   A. K. D., Jr.

SMITH, CHARLES EMORY (Feb. 18, 1842–Jan. 19, 1908), journalist, diplomat, postmaster-general, was a son of Emory Boutelle and Arvilla Topliff (Royce) Smith, representatives of old New England families. He was born at Mansfield, Conn., but when he was seven years old his father, a manufacturer of silk, moved to Albany, N. Y. Charles attended the public schools and Albany Academy, from which he was graduated at the age of sixteen. While still in school he began his journalistic career by writing for the *Albany Evening Transcript.* In 1859 he entered Union College as a junior, graduating in 1861. His college years were chiefly noteworthy for his leadership in student jour-

nalism and in an organization formed to promote the success of the Republican party in the election of 1860. At the beginning of the Civil War he became military secretary to Brigadier-General John F. Rathbone, assisting him in the administration of the recruit depot at Albany and later was in the office of the adjutant-general. Toward the end of 1862, he resigned and became an instructor in Albany Academy, at the same time contributing two columns of editorials daily to the *Albany Express,* the staff of which he joined in 1865. Five years later he became associate editor of the *Albany Evening Journal,* the leading Republican newspaper of up-state New York, and in 1874, editor. During the next six years he wrote nearly all the state Republican platforms and in 1876, most of the national platform. In 1879 he was elected a member of the board of regents of the University of the State of New York.

He was called to Philadelphia in 1880 to become editor of the Philadelphia *Press,* which had declined considerably in circulation and influence after the retirement of John W. Forney [*q.v.*]. Chiefly by his own efforts he reëstablished it within four years as the leading Republican newspaper of the city and the state. The editorial page, written from his wide acquaintance with men and affairs, presented clear interpretations of the course of public events. Toward local matters his attitude was progressive; but he was generally conservative in his discussions of national questions. He advocated the nomination and election of Blaine in 1884 and stressed the benefits of the protective tariff, the gold standard, and other favorite measures of the Eastern Republicans.

The position of the *Press,* combined with first-rate skill in estimating the movement of public opinion and in political management, gave him an important influence in state and national affairs. For two years, beginning Feb. 14, 1890, he was minister to Russia, and won popularity both there and in the United States by his distribution of American relief funds to famine sufferers. In 1898 President McKinley appointed him postmaster-general in order, it was supposed, that he might have his advice on the political problems of the Spanish-American War period. According to one of his colleagues, he contributed to the cabinet counsels "generous and progressive views on all political questions" (John D. Long, *The New American Navy,* 1903, II, 146). In the management of his department he was active in preventing the use of the mails by vendors of quack remedies and worthless securities, and for fraudulent purposes generally,

He greatly extended and popularized the rural free delivery service, with which the previous administration had experimented. Though admitting its expensiveness, he justified it as a means of promoting good roads, enhancing farm values, and making rural life less isolated and more attractive. He supported the efforts of a subordinate to stamp out corruption in the postal service which his department had established in Cuba. Unfortunately, some irregularities of long standing in the service at home were allowed to continue and become a serious problem for his successor.

During his absence in Washington his business interests suffered and he resigned in 1901 to give them his full attention. In person he was described as a man of medium height and slender build with a round face and piercing black eyes. He won a considerable reputation as an effective and accomplished public speaker. He was married first, June 30, 1863, to Ella Huntley; after her death he was married, Oct. 3, 1907, to Nettie Nichols. He died in Philadelphia.

[*Leslie's Hist. of the Republican Party* (n.d.); *The New International Year Book . . . 1908* (1909); *Who's Who in America,* 1908–09; Charles Morris, *Makers of Phila.* (1894); S. W. Pennypacker, *The Autobiog. of a Pennsylvanian* (1918); J. T. Scharf and Thompson Westcott, *Hist. of Phila.* (1884), vol. III; *Press* (Phila.), *N. Y. Times,* Jan. 20, 1908.]
E. C. S.

SMITH, CHARLES FERGUSON (Apr. 24, 1807–Apr. 25, 1862), soldier, was born in Philadelphia, Pa., the son of Samuel Blair Smith, surgeon in the United States Army, and Mary (Ferguson) Smith. He was admitted to the United States Military Academy as a cadet, July 1, 1820, and was graduated and appointed second lieutenant, 2nd Artillery, July 1, 1825. After four years of garrison service he returned to the Military Academy as an instructor in 1829, and remained there for more than thirteen years as instructor of infantry tactics, adjutant, and finally commander of cadets. It was there, under Sylvanus Thayer [*q.v.*], that the qualities of discipline and precision, and the martial bearing and spirit that so distinguished his later career were developed and fixed. He was promoted first lieutenant in 1832 and captain in 1838. He was married, Mar. 24, 1840, to Fanny Mactier of Philadelphia. After 1842 he served at Fort Columbus, Governors Island, N. Y., and the arsenal at Frankford, Pa., until 1845, when impending war with Mexico called him to duty with Gen. Zachary Taylor's army in Texas. In command of a battalion of artillery serving as infantry he participated in the battles of Palo Alto and Resaca de la Palma, Tex., and was brevetted major for gallant conduct in those battles, May 9, 1846. With the same "red-legged infantry" at Monterey he stormed the works on Loma Federacion, a key position commanding the city. For this action he was brevetted lieutenant-colonel, Sept. 23, 1846. Transferred to Gen. Winfield Scott's army in command of an independent battalion composed of two artillery and two infantry companies, which became known as Smith's Light Infantry, he took prominent part in all the operations of that army from the siege of Vera Cruz to the capture and occupation of Mexico city. For gallant and meritorious conduct at Contreras and Churubusco he received his third brevet, that of colonel, Aug. 20, 1847.

From 1849 to 1855, in addition to garrison duties, he served on important boards dealing with the training and administration of the army. Promoted major, 1st Artillery, Nov. 25, 1854, and lieutenant-colonel, 10th Infantry, Mar. 3, 1855, in 1856 he led an expedition to the Red River of the North. The next year he served in the Utah expedition, and was in command of the Department of Utah, 1860–61. At the outbreak of the Civil War, after temporary service in Washington, he was appointed brigadier-general of volunteers (and colonel, regular army) and assigned to command the District of Western Kentucky. He commanded the 2nd Division of Grant's army in the operations against Fort Henry, Tenn., Fort Heiman, Ky., and Fort Donelson, Tenn. At a critical stage of the battle at Fort Donelson he personally led an assault against the Confederate outworks and secured a position within the defenses, the immediate cause of the surrender of the garrison. For this he was promoted major-general of volunteers, Mar. 21, 1862. He was placed in command of the expedition up the Tennessee River, but an injury resulting from an accident developed into an illness that caused his death at Savannah, Tenn., a month later. He was survived by his wife and three children.

[G. W. Cullum, *Biog. Reg. . . . Officers and Grads. U. S. Mil. Acad.* (1891), vol. I; J. H. Smith, *The War with Mexico* (2 vols., 1919); *War of the Rebellion: Official Records (Army)*; *Battles and Leaders of the Civil War,* vol. I (1887); unpublished records of the War Dept., 1845–62; records of U. S. Pension Office, for name of wife and date of marriage; J. H. Wilson, *Under the Old Flag* (1912), vol. II, for remarks about Smith attributed to Sherman and Grant; obituaries in *Phila. Inquirer, Pub. Ledger* (Phila.), and *Daily Nat. Intelligencer* (Washington, D. C.), Apr. 28, 1862.]
T. F. M.

SMITH, CHARLES FORSTER (June 30, 1852–Aug. 3, 1931), professor of Greek and classical philology, born in that part of Abbeville County which is now Greenwood County, S. C., came of fine colonial stock. His father, James Francis Smith, was a Methodist clergyman; his mother, Juliana Forster, was the daughter of a distinguished preacher and educator of the same denomination. His grandfather, John Smith, was a wealthy planter and merchant of the Abbeville section, to which region his father, William Smith, had emigrated from Virginia about 1790.

Fifth of eleven children, of whom the youngest, James Perrin Smith [q.v.], became a well-known professor of geology, Charles Forster was reared in a cultured home, attended the neighboring schools described in his *Reminiscences and Sketches,* and entered Wofford College at the age of sixteen. There he came under the inspiring influence of President James H. Carlisle, "the best man I have ever known and most potent human influence in my life" (Dedication of *Reminiscences and Sketches*). Receiving the degree of A.B. in 1872, he taught at Greenwood, S. C., until January 1874, then had a semester at Harvard University and a year at Leipzig, returning in 1875 to teach classics and German at Wofford. In 1879 he had saved money enough to go back to Leipzig with his bride, Anna L. Du Pré of Spartanburg, S. C., and in 1881 he obtained the degree of Ph.D., offering as his dissertation *A Study of Plutarch's Life of Artaxerxes, with Especial Reference to the Sources,* published (1881) in English at Leipzig.

After a year as assistant professor of Latin and Greek at Williams College, he went in 1882 to Vanderbilt University, Nashville, Tenn., as professor of modern languages, taking the chair of Greek the following year. His sound scholarship and stimulating influence on his students brought reputation as a teacher, and he was a leader in the intellectual life of the city. He formed lasting friendships, and, in later years, looked back on this period as the happiest in his life. In 1893 his wife died, leaving him with five small children. The next year he accepted the chairmanship of the Department of Greek and Classical Philology at the University of Wisconsin. Becoming professor emeritus in 1917, he regretfully relinquished active teaching, for he believed profoundly in the dynamic effect of the personality of the teacher and was eager to fire young minds with his own enthusiasm. The declining interest in the classics and their omission from the list of required studies caused him bitter regret, and he voiced his opinions with outspoken frankness.

He was president of the American Philological Association in 1902–03, and associate editor of *Classical Philology* from its founding in 1906 until his death. Although retired, he was, by exception, appointed annual professor for 1920–21 at the American School of Classical Studies in Athens. His leisure was employed in completing his accurate and very readable translation of Thucydides for the Loeb Classical Library, and his biography, *Charles Kendall Adams* (1924), for the University of Wisconsin. Besides editions of college texts (Thucydides, Bks. III, VI, VII, Xenophon's *Anabasis,* Herodotus, Bk. VII) and contributions to classical journals, marked by thoroughness and learning, he published many essays on various subjects in other periodicals, especially studies of favorite authors or great personalities; some of these were collected in the volume *Reminiscences and Sketches* (1908). In them appear his love of poetry, his fondness for the mountains, where he liked to tramp, his appreciation of character and personality, and his strong attachment to his friends. His style was decidedly personal and subjective. A citation from the introduction by President E. A. Birge to a volume of studies published in his honor by his colleagues, in 1919, fittingly portrays him: "We recognize in him one who lives among us the life of letters, who has made literature—not only Greek but all great literature —a vital influence for us as well as for his students."

He died at the home of a daughter in Racine, Wis. During his last years he was working on an unfinished book on the Old South, of which he was an excellent representative.

[*Who's Who in America,* 1930–31; *Classical Studies in Honor of Charles Forster Smith* (1919, Univ. of Wis. Studies in Lang. and Lit.); R. G. Thwaites, *The Univ. of Wis.* (1900); family records; faculty minutes of Univ. of Wis.; personal acquaintance of more than forty years.]   C. D. Z.

SMITH, CHARLES HENRY (June 15, 1826–Aug. 24, 1903), journalist, humorist, known as Bill Arp, was born at Lawrenceville, Ga., the son of Asahel Reid Smith, a native of Vermont, and Caroline Ann (Maguire) Smith, whose father had emigrated from Dublin, Ireland, and settled in Georgia. He attended a manual labor school, clerked in his father's store, and at nineteen entered Franklin College (later the University of Georgia). In 1848 his father's illness forced him to return home and manage his father's store. In the following year he married Mary Octavia Hutchins, daughter of Judge Nathan L. Hutchins, of Lawrenceville. After a brief study of law he was admitted to the bar. Moving to Rome, Ga., in 1851, he formed a partnership with John W. H. Underwood. He enlisted in the Confederate Army in 1861, served on the staffs of Gen. Francis S. Bartow and Gen. George Thomas Anderson [q.v.], and in 1864 became judge advocate at Macon. In the early years of the war there appeared in the *Southern*

Confederacy (Rome, 1861–62) four letters, addressed to "Mr. Abe Linkhorn" and signed "Bill Arp," written in the illiterate dialect employed by many early American humorists. Bill Arp—the name was that of a local wag—was first portrayed as a sympathizer with the North (*Bill Arp: From the Uncivil War to Date,* 1903), but the later sketches dropped the rôle of Yankee sympathizer and transformed Bill Arp into the uneducated but wise, humorous rustic philosopher. Dialect was gradually used less and less, and Bill Arp became more like his creator in his language, thoughts, feelings, and experiences. The popular reception accorded these letters encouraged Smith later to devote most of his time to writing. For over twenty-five years he contributed to the *Atlanta Constitution* weekly letters, which were reprinted in *Home and Farm* (Louisville, Ky.), the *Sunny South* (Atlanta), and other papers. These were a blend of humor, genial but forceful satire, and common-sense philosophy. After the war he formed a law partnership with Joel Branham, served as state senator, 1865 and 1866, acted as mayor of Rome, 1868–69, and for a time edited the *Rome Commercial.* Meanwhile he published *Bill Arp, So Called* (1866) and a little later *Bill Arp's Peace Papers* (1873), collections of the weekly letters in the *Constitution.* About 1877, giving up the practice of law, he moved to "Fontainebleau," his farm near Cartersville, Ga. Eleven years later he moved into Cartersville, where he spent the rest of his life in study and writing. His later books were *Bill Arp's Scrap Book* (1884), *The Farm and Fireside* (1891), and *Bill Arp: From the Uncivil War to Date* (1903). He also wrote *A School History of Georgia* (1893). He died at his home in Cartersville after an emergency operation following an illness of several weeks. He was survived by his wife and ten of his thirteen children.

He was a man both witty and tolerant, and his lovable personality appears plainly in his writings. Through lecture tours he widened his circle of friends and won for himself the title of "the best loved man in all the Southland"; the *Savannah Press* once said of him, "In the dark days he kept southern hearts from breaking" (quoted in *Atlanta Constitution,* Aug. 28, 1903). For many reasons his writings continue to be interesting. His handling of the negro and the Georgia cracker dialects is trustworthy and accurate. His war-time sketches are valuable for the facts presented and for the insight they give into Southern attitudes and sentiments. The outspoken courage and the vigor of his satire are blended with good-humored tolerance. "I joined the army and succeeded in killing about as many of them as they of me," he once remarked (*Scrap Book,* p. 378). At times he shows a remarkable gift for narration and for character delineation, as in "Uncle Tom Barker" in *The Uncivil War.* His opinions on woman's suffrage, the graduated income tax, the one-crop system of farming, and the negro question are still worthy of consideration.

[*Who's Who in America,* 1903–05; C. H. Smith, *Bill Arp: From the Uncivil War to Date* (1903) and *Bill Arp's Scrap Book* (1884); Marian C. Smith, *I Remember* (privately printed, 1931), and biog. sketch in memorial ed. of *Bill Arp: From the Uncivil War* (1903); L. L. Knight, *A Standard Hist. of Ga. and Georgians* (1917), vol. III, pp. 1416–20 and 1761; G. H. Aubrey, in *Men of Mark in Ga.* (1911), vol. III, ed. by W. J. Northen; *Atlanta Constitution,* Aug. 25–28, 1903; obituary in *N. Y. Tribune,* Aug. 30, 1903; family papers.]
J. M. S., Jr.

SMITH, CHARLES HENRY (Nov. 1, 1827–July 17, 1902), soldier, the son of Aaron and Sally (Gile) Smith, was born in Hollis, Me. He was graduated from Waterville (now Colby) College at Waterville, Me., in 1856, and three years later received the A.M. degree from that institution. From 1856 to 1860 he was principal of the high school at Eastport, Me., and studied law there. When the Civil War broke out he volunteered and became a captain in the 1st Maine Cavalry. His regiment was assigned to the Army of the Potomac early in 1862, and during that year he fought on a reconnaissance to Front Royal, Va., in the battle of Cedar Mountain, and in the second battle of Bull Run. From September 1862 to January 1863 he was provost-marshal at Frederick, Md., remaining thereafter on almost continuous duty with the cavalry of the Army of the Potomac. He was rapidly promoted in 1863 through the grades of major and lieutenant-colonel to colonel. During this year he commanded the 1st Maine Cavalry on Stoneman's raid into Virginia, in the Gettysburg campaign where he was cited for distinguished conduct, and in the Mine Run campaign.

The year 1864 was an active one for the cavalry; skirmishes, reconnaissances, raids, and long marches were the order of the day. Two horses were shot from under him at St. Mary's Church, Va., on June 24, 1864, and Smith was himself shot through the thigh early in the afternoon, but he did not relinquish command of his regiment until the day was over. For his heroism on this occasion he was brevetted brigadier-general of volunteers, and was awarded the Congressional medal of honor in 1895. He commanded a cavalry brigade through most of the Richmond campaign from August to December 1864 and again received special mention for distinguished service. In 1865 he fought through the Appomattox campaign to the end of the war and won renown at Sailor's Creek, Va., on Apr. 6, for a bold attack with his brigade against the flank of a retreating Confederate column. He was mustered out of the army on Aug. 11, 1865, returned to Machias in his native state, was admitted to the bar, practised law, and in 1866 became a state senator. On July 28, 1866, he accepted the appointment of colonel of the 28th Infantry in the regular army. He served at various posts in Missouri, Louisiana, Colorado, and Texas until Nov. 1, 1891, when he retired from active duty and settled in Washington, D. C. He was married to Mary Richards Livermore of Eastport, Me., on July 28, 1864. Besides the brevet rank already mentioned, he was brevetted major-general of volunteers in 1865, brigadier-general in the regular army, 1867, for his action in the battle of Sailor's Creek, and major-general for gallant service during the war. This modest officer fought in sixty-three battles and skirmishes and was three times wounded. He died in Washington, D. C., and was survived by a son and a daughter.

[*Who's Who in America,* 1901–02; W. E. Thwing, *The Livermore Family of America* (1902); *Gen. Cat. of Officers and Grads. of Colby Univ.* (1882); *War of the Rebellion: Official Records (Army),* see index; F. B. Heitman, *Hist. Reg. and Dict., U. S. Army* (1903); *Men of Progress . . . State of Me.* (1897); *Army and Navy Reg.,* July 19, 1902; *Washington Post,* July 18, 20, 1902.]   S. J. H.

SMITH, CHARLES PERRIN (Jan. 5, 1819–Jan. 27, 1883), New Jersey politician, editor, genealogist, was born in Philadelphia. His father was George Wishart Smith, of distinguished Virginia ancestry, and his mother, Hannah Carpenter (Ellet) of Salem County, N. J. The former died shortly after Charles was born and the child was taken by his mother to her home in Salem. Here, in the common schools, he received a rudimentary education, richly supplemented later by his own efforts. At the age of fifteen he entered the printing office of the *Freeman's Banner,* where he learned the practical work of newspaper publishing. In 1840, having reached his majority and inherited some property, he bought the *Banner* and renamed it the *National Standard.* This paper he edited for eleven years in the interests of the Whig party. Later, he also edited the *Harrisonian,* a campaign periodical. In 1843 he married Hester A. Driver of Caroline County, Md. He held several local offices, was active in advocating the construction of a railway in West Jersey for the development of that section of the state, and was interested in improving the life-saving stations on the Jersey coast, toward which

end he was instrumental in securing action by Congress. In 1851 he retired permanently from regular newspaper work and thenceforth devoted his time to travel, political activities, and literary and antiquarian pursuits.

Elected to the state Senate from Salem County in 1855, he served two years, and then was appointed clerk of the supreme court of New Jersey, which office he held for three terms of five years each, meanwhile making his home in Trenton. His political activities during this period were strenuous and, according to his own estimate, important. In 1856 he was appointed a member of the National American state committee and also the same year was a delegate to the Fusion Convention and a member of the committee to select permanent officers. He nominated William L. Dayton [*q.v.*] as president of the convention and secured his election, thus bringing him into national prominence and so preparing the way for his subsequent nomination by the Republican party for the vice-presidency of the United States. In 1859 Smith was appointed a member of the "Opposition" state executive committee and was successively reappointed for ten years with the exception of one year, when he declined the position. For part of the time he was chairman, and he was active in securing the election as governor of Charles S. Olden [*q.v.*]. He was opposed to the candidacy of William H. Seward for the presidency in 1860 and through his efforts induced the state convention to indorse Dayton with a view to blocking Seward's nomination at the national convention, by withholding the New Jersey vote until it could be thrown to a more eligible candidate. During the Civil War period he was active in bringing New Jersey into line with the policies of the Federal government. He advocated the nomination of General Grant for president in 1867 and arranged for a great mass meeting in Trenton, at which Grant was enthusiastically indorsed.

Retiring from office in 1872, Smith continued to live in Trenton until his death eleven years later, devoting much of his time to travel and writing. He prepared "The Personal Reminiscences of Charles Perrin Smith, 1857–1875," a large folio volume in manuscript, which was given to the New Jersey state library after his death by his daughter, Elizabeth A. Smith. This work includes his autobiography, with full genealogical records of his ancestry, and comments on political events in the state and nation with which he was actively concerned or personally familiar. Based apparently upon a carefully kept diary, it is notable for its accuracy, urbanity, and fair-mindedness. Besides narratives of his travels, political writings, and speeches, his publications include *Lineage of the Lloyd and Carpenter Family* (1870, 1873), privately printed; and *Memoranda of a Visit to the Site of Mathraval Castle, Powys Castle, Valle Crucis Abbey, Pilar of Elisig, with a Genealogical Chart of the Descent of Thomas Lloyd* (1875). He died at Trenton, N. J., survived by his wife and two daughters.

[*Report of the Proceedings of the Numismatic and Antiquarian Society of Phila. for . . . 1883* (1884); Thomas Cushing and C. E. Sheppard, *Hist. of the Counties of Gloucester, Salem, and Cumberland, N. J.* (1883); E. M. Woodward and J. F. Hageman, *Hist. of Burlington and Mercer Counties, N. J.* (1883); C. M. Knapp, *N. J. Politics During the Period of the Civil War and Reconstruction* (1924); Hamilton Schuyler, *A Hist. of St. Michael's Church, Trenton . . . 1703 to 1926* (1926); *Daily True American*, Jan. 29, 1883.]
H. Sc—r.

SMITH, CHARLES SHALER (Jan. 16, 1836–Dec. 19, 1886), bridge engineer, was born in Pittsburgh, Pa., the son of Frederick Rose and Mary Anne (Shaler) Smith. During his childhood his father died; and his mother, when he was sixteen. He attended private schools in Pittsburgh until his mother's death, when his formal education ended. After serving as rodman with a surveying party on the Mine Hill & Schuylkill Haven Railroad in 1852, and subsequently with a railroad survey in the mining regions of Lake Superior, he was made assistant engineer under George McLeod, chief engineer of the Louisville & Nashville Railroad, in 1855. The next year he became resident engineer on the Memphis branch of the Louisville & Nashville, and in 1857, he was transferred from the field to the office as assistant to Albert Fink [*q.v.*], engineer of bridges and buildings for the line. This early association had an important effect in shaping Smith's career. In 1859, he was placed in charge of track and bridge construction for the Memphis division, but he left shortly to become chief engineer of bridges and buildings for the Wilmington, Charlotte & Rutherford Railroad in North Carolina. Here he remained until the outbreak of the Civil War, when he entered the Confederate army as captain of engineers, serving with distinction throughout the conflict. One of his outstanding achievements was the building, in the Augusta district, of a powder mill with a daily capacity of 17,000 pounds—one of the largest ever built up to that time.

Immediately after the war, he built a number of bridges in the South, among them Fink truss spans over the Catawba and Congaree rivers on the Charlotte & South Carolina Railroad. In 1866, he entered partnership with Benjamin H. and Charles H. Latrobe [*qq.v.*] under the style

Smith, Latrobe & Company, soon changed to Baltimore Bridge Company. Smith was the bridge expert of the firm, which built a number of the most important structures in the country. Among these were a series of iron trestles on the Louisville, Cincinnati & Lexington and the Elizabethtown & Paducah railroads, the first metal viaducts of modern type to be built; a large bridge over the Missouri River at St. Charles, Mo.; one over the Kentucky River at Dixville, Ky.; one over the Mississippi River at Minneapolis for the Chicago, Milwaukee & St. Paul Railroad; and one over the St. Lawrence River at the Lachine Rapids (near Montreal) for the Canadian Pacific Railway. In addition, Smith served as consultant to James Buchanan Eads [*q.v.*] on the great St. Louis arch bridge, and as consulting engineer in an advisory capacity on difficult bridge problems for nearly every important Western railroad.

The Kentucky River bridge, built for the Cincinnati Southern Railway in 1876–77, was probably his greatest engineering achievement. At the point of crossing, the river was over twelve hundred feet wide, running through a canyon 275 feet deep and subject to tremendous freshets, during which a rise of as much as forty feet in one day had been recorded. Smith's plan originally contemplated spanning the three main openings of 375 feet each by a fully continuous Whipple truss, but in deference to the opinion of L. F. G. Bouscaren, chief engineer of the Cincinnati Southern, the plan was modified to the extent of providing hinges in the outside spans, thus transforming the structure into a cantilever bridge. Cantilever construction on this scale had at the time no precedent anywhere in the world, and by most engineers was viewed with profound suspicion, so that Smith (who assumed the duties of contractor as well as designer) staked both his professional reputation and his fortune on the venture. Carried through to completion strictly according to plans, without the use of falsework in the cantilever spans, and without serious mishap, it was a technical achievement second to none of its time, and the cantilever soon was widely adopted and became the dominant type for long-span construction.

Smith began preparing plans for the Lachine Bridge in 1880, using a deck truss over two side spans of 270 feet and through trusses over the two 408-foot central spans. The transition from deck to through truss was achieved by graceful lines which gave the structure an unusually beautiful appearance. It was erected largely without falsework by the cantilever method and was designed to function as a cantilever under dead load and as a full continuous truss under live load. The actual construction of this bridge was begun about the time Smith was stricken with his fatal illness, but he retained direction of the work until the critical stages were past. It was completed a few months after his death, and remained for many years the only continuous bridge of importance in America. Later (1917) this type of design was revived and became widely adopted.

Smith died in his early prime, accepted as the foremost bridge engineer in America and one of the greatest of the century. This judgment rested less upon the number of great bridges he had built (brilliant as this record was) than upon the boldness and originality of the ideas he introduced. Though his comparatively brief professional life was too crowded to allow much time for writing, he prepared a short treatise, *Comparative Analysis of the Fink, Murphy, Bollman, & Triangular Trusses* (1865), and contributed several important papers to the *Transactions of the American Society of Civil Engineers,* including "Draw-Spans and Their Turn-Tables" (vol. III, 1874), "Proportions of Eye-bar Heads and Pins, as Determined by Experiment" (vol. VI, 1877), and "Wind Pressure upon Bridges" (vol. X, 1881).

Smith moved to Missouri in 1868 to supervise the construction of the St. Charles Bridge, and upon its completion in 1871 established his home in St. Louis, where he resided until his death. He was married on May 23, 1865, to Mary Gordon Gairdner, of Augusta, Ga., who with several children survived him. He possessed a nobility of character matching his intellectual gifts. His courtesy, his utter frankness and honesty, his generosity in all matters, won him the complete loyalty of all who served with him (or for him) in any capacity.

[*Proc. Am. Soc. Civil Engineers,* vol. XIII (1887); J. A. L. Waddell, *Bridge Engineering* (1916), vols. I, II; J. B. Johnson, C. W. Bryan, and F. E. Turneaure, *The Theory and Practice of Modern Framed Structures* (augmented ed., 1904); *Railroad Gazette,* Dec. 31, 1886; *St. Louis Globe-Democrat,* Dec. 20, 1886.]

J. I. P.

SMITH, CHARLES SPRAGUE (Apr. 27, 1853–Mar. 30, 1910), educator, was born at Andover, Mass., the son of Charles and Caroline Louisa (Sprague) Smith. His childhood and youth were precocious. He graduated from Phillips Academy, being valedictorian and class poet, at the age of fifteen, but delayed his entrance to college for two years. In 1874 he received the degree of bachelor of arts from Amherst College. Going abroad in 1875, he spent five years in the study of languages and literature: first at the

University of Berlin, where he delivered a "Centenary Poem" at a gathering of American students and residents, then at the Sorbonne; later at various institutions in Italy and Spain; and finally at Oxford University, from which he received a certificate stating that "No one of his years had accomplished as much as he in his chosen field of language and literature."

In 1880 he returned to the United States to become an instructor at Columbia, where he gave the first course in Icelandic ever offered in an American university. In the same year he was raised to the Gebhard professorship of German, a position which he retained for eleven years. On Nov. 11, 1884, he was married to Isabella Jane, daughter of Benjamin Woodbridge Dwight [*q.v.*] of Clinton, N. Y. After resigning from Columbia in 1891, he continued to lecture there occasionally, as well as at Harvard and elsewhere, but he was more and more impressed with the inadequacy of the American educational system in so far as the cultural development of the masses was concerned. In 1895 he organized the Comparative Literature Society in an effort to maintain and integrate the different racial cultures of immigrants to the United States. A more important undertaking was his founding, in 1897, of the People's Institute, at Cooper Union, an institution established by Peter Cooper [*q.v.*] in 1857–59 for the education of the working classes but until Smith's time never effectively organized to that end. Smith succeeded in making the People's Institute a community center which exercised great influence, by its example, on like movements in other places, while in New York City itself it was the parent of many similar local enterprises. Lecture courses were offered, and work in music and drama; the Cooper Union Forum, the People's Church, the People's Lobby, and the Wage Workers' Social Club were established within the Institute.

Although keenly alive to questions of social justice, Smith was humanitarian rather than socialistic in his outlook. He was a fervent patriot and intensely religious in an unorthodox manner, being considerably affected by Hindu literature. He considered that the United States possessed a divine cosmic mission to realize the gospel of liberty and fraternity. Idealistic and romantic, he exerted an influence based more upon generosity and sweetness of character than upon intellectual power. He published *Barbizon Days* (1902), the record of a summer in the Forest of Fontainebleau with sketches of Millet, Corot, and others; *Working with the People* (1904), an account of the People's Institute;

and *Poems* (1908), a collection of mediocre verse mostly written in earlier years. In addition to his work at the People's Institute, in 1908 he organized the Ethical Social League and served on the Wall Street Commission to investigate the stock exchange, and in 1909 organized the National Board of Censorship of Motion Pictures, acting as its executive chairman until his death in the following year.

[R. S. Fletcher and M. A. Young, *Amherst Coll. Biog. Record* (1927); *Civic Jour.*, Apr. 30, 1910; *Who's Who in America*, 1908–09; J. A. Riis, "The People's Institute of N. Y.," *Century Mag.*, Apr. 1910; John Collier, "The People's Institute," *Independent*, May 30, 1912; records of the People's Institute, through the courtesy of Everett Dean Martin, director.]
E. S. B.

SMITH, CHAUNCEY (Jan. 11, 1819–Apr. 5, 1895), lawyer, was born at Waitsfield, Vt., the son of Ithamar and Ruth (Barnard) Smith, and a descendant of Samuel Smith who emigrated to Wethersfield, Conn., in 1634. While Chauncey attended the village school and, for a time, an academy at Gouverneur, N. Y., working and teaching to pay his expenses, it was the daily life on his father's farm that supplied the chief factor in his early development. After two years at the University of Vermont, 1845–47, he left college to study law in the office of Henry Levenworth in Burlington. He was admitted to the bar in 1848, and soon thereafter in Boston formed a partnership with Samuel W. Bates, which continued for many years. On Dec. 10, 1856, he married Caroline E. Marshall of Cambridge. They had three children, and lived for many years at 121 Brattle Street, Cambridge, adjoining the home of the poet Longfellow. During the 1850's Smith edited *English Reports in Law and Equity* (40 vols., 1851–58), the first thirty volumes in collaboration with E. H. Bennett; these reports covered the period 1850–57. Smith also edited, with Samuel W. Bates, *Cases Relating to the Law of Railways, Decided in the Supreme Court of the United States and in the Several States* (2 vols., 1854–56), and compiled *Digest of the Decisions of the Courts of England, Contained in the English Law and Equity Reports* (1857); and in 1853 he prepared an American edition of James Stamford Caldwell's *Treatise of the Law of Arbitration*. During the Civil War he held a confidential position with the War Department, acting as counsel to the provost marshal in Washington. After the war he returned to his practice in Boston.

His most eminent service was as one of the lawyers of the Bell Telephone Company and its successors in the great telephone litigation of 1878 to 1896. In 1877 he had approved as counsel the policy of Gardiner G. Hubbard [*q.v.*] to rent telephones instead of selling them and to issue all licenses subject to that condition. This policy was an essential factor in the development of the Bell System. The telephone litigation comprehended four groups of legal proceedings. Practically though not technically a part of it were the telephone interferences (1878–89), cases to determine whether the two telephone patents issued to Alexander Graham Bell in 1876 and 1877 interfered with the patent rights of certain other claimants. Smith and his associate James J. Storrow [*q.v.*] took an active part as counsel in these cases and all were decided in favor of the Bell patents.

The telephone litigation itself consisted of about 600 cases in the United States courts. The first of these stands in a class by itself. This was *Bell Telephone Company* vs. *Peter A. Dowd*, the so-called Western Union Case. Smith and James J. Storrow were the counsel for the company, which, on Sept. 12, 1878, sued Dowd, the agent of a telephone subsidiary of the Western Union Telegraph Company, for infringement. That company contended that Bell had simply invented an instrument and that the instruments invented by Elisha Gray, Amos E. Dolbear, and Thomas A. Edison, which it was using, were not infringements of the Bell patents. As the evidence was put in, George Gifford, the chief counsel for the Western Union, became convinced that the Bell patents were valid and that they covered any use of electricity in the transmission of speech. He so advised his clients, and Smith and Gifford spent most of the summer of 1879 negotiating a settlement, with the result that on Nov. 10, 1879, the court approved an agreement by which the field of electrical communications was divided between the two companies, each undertaking not to encroach on the field of the other.

There soon sprang up a great many infringing telephone companies, whose chief purpose was to break or circumvent the Bell patents. It became a matter of unavoidable routine to sue every one of these companies. The resulting tangled network of litigation finally reached the United States Supreme Court in the form of five cases, which were considered together and decided in favor of the Bell Company on Mar. 19, 1888 (*The Telephone Cases*, 126 *U. S.*, 1). These cases demanded of Smith and Storrow the utmost skill in meeting the devious technicalities of the opposing attorneys, and here Smith's penetration, forensic ability, and caustic wit had full play. In a fourth group of cases the infringing companies, beginning in 1885, assumed the offensive and attacked the telephone company in a series of suits, culminating in the so-called Government Case, *United States of America* vs. *American Bell Telephone Company et al.,* to annul the Bell patents. This dragged through the courts until, in 1896, the managing counsel for the infringers died, and the case was abandoned.

For Smith and his associates the long contest had been a triumphant but also a life-draining struggle. In his latter years recurrent attacks of rheumatism frequently prostrated him, and before the litigation had ended, he himself died in a heart attack at his home in Cambridge. Smith was of heavy build, nearly six feet tall, square-shouldered, round-headed, and square-jawed. He wore his heavy hair cut round and long like an old-fashioned wig. His expression was belligerent but the frequent twinkle in his blue eyes gave assurance of a very kindly disposition and sense of humor. He was actively interested in civil service reform and in a lower tariff. His attitude toward industry and science amounted to reverence. He advanced considerable sums of money to inventors to enable them to work out their ideas, frequently declining to accept repayments of these loans even when himself financially embarrassed. It was his conviction, in his own words, that "the inventor is the chief agent in the progress of the world."

[M. B. Jones, *Hist. of the Town of Waitsfield, Vt., 1782–1908* (1909); autobiographical fragment by Chauncey Smith (MS.) and Julia H. Caverno, "Reminiscences of my Uncle" (MS.), in the Chauncey Smith Collection, Am. Telephone Hist. Library, N. Y. City; C. H. Swan, "Narrative Hist. of the Litigation on the Telephone Patents, 1878–1896" (MS. 1903), in the same library; *Boston Journal,* Apr. 6, 1895; *Boston Transcript,* Apr. 6, 1895; information as to certain facts from the family.]   W. C. L.

SMITH, DANIEL (Oct. 29, 1748–June 16, 1818), soldier, Tennessee official, was born in Stafford County, Va., the son of Henry and Sarah (Crosby) Smith. He received his education at the College of William and Mary, and became a surveyor. On June 20, 1773, he was married to Sarah Michie of the Eastern Shore of Maryland. After his marriage he settled in Augusta County, Va., on the Clinch River at Fort Christian, and received an appointment as a deputy surveyor in 1773. In 1774 he fought as company commander at the battle of Point Pleasant and in other engagements with the Indians. On Jan. 20, 1775, he signed the Fincastle County Resolutions, protesting against the oppressions of the British government. In 1777 he aided in the organization of Washington County and became a major in the county militia. In 1779 he and Thomas Walker [*q.v.*] acted as representatives of Virginia who, with Richard Henderson [*q.v.*] and two others from North Carolina, extended the

boundary between the two states. This resulted in the establishment of the disputed Walker's Line. Smith advanced rapidly in the Washington County militia, becoming a colonel in 1781. He was appointed sheriff of the county in 1780 and also participated in the battle of King's Mountain. As a surveyor, he acted as attorney for Thomas Walker in the sale of lands.

In 1783 he moved to the Cumberland settlements and settled in what is now Sumner County near the present town of Hendersonville, Tenn. The North Carolina Legislature appointed him a director for laying out the town of Nashville in 1784, and, the next year, trustee of Davidson Academy. In 1787 the North Carolina Assembly made him a commissioner for the new county of Sumner, and in 1788 elected him brigadier-general of the Mero District militia. He was a member of the North Carolina convention which ratified the United States Constitution in 1789. He served as the secretary of the territory southwest of the Ohio under the governorship of William Blount [*q.v.*], and, as acting governor during Blount's absences from the territory, he promoted the interests of the westerners in their conflicts with the Indians. He also made the first map of Tennessee, which was published in 1794 in the *General Atlas for the Present War,* by Mathew Carey [*q.v.*], and wrote *A Short Description of the Tennassee Government* (1793), and a journal of his experiences on the boundary commission. The original manuscript of the journal and the map are in the Draper collection of the Historical Society of Wisconsin. The journal was printed in the *Tennessee Historical Magazine,* March 1915.

In 1796 he was a member of the convention which drew up the first constitution of Tennessee, and, in 1798, he succeeded Andrew Jackson in the United States Senate. Although he served only a short time, he was later returned to that body for a term from 1805 to 1809. In ability, education, and usefulness Smith ranked with the ablest men who moved to the West in this early period. He engaged in business as a planter and distiller, but he always evinced a primary interest in public affairs. He died at his home, "Rock Castle," in Sumner County. He had two children; his daughter married Samuel Donelson and was the mother of Andrew Jackson Donelson [*q.v.*].

[*Biog. Dir. of the Am. Cong.* (1928); J. G. Cisco, *Historic Sumner County* (1909); R. G. Thwaites, L. P. Kellogg, *Doc. Hist. of Dunmore's War* (1905); R. G. Thwaites, *Early Western Travels,* vol. III (1904); L. P. Summers, *Hist. of Southwest Va.* (1903), and *Annals of Southwest Va.* (1909); *Annals of Congress,* 1797–1810; *Colonial and State Records of D. C.,* see index; "Papers of General Daniel Smith," *Am. Hist. Mag.,* July 1901.]   C. S. D.

SMITH, DANIEL B. (July 14, 1792–Mar. 29, 1883), pharmacist, philanthropist, educator, was born in Philadelphia, Pa., the son of Benjamin Smith and Deborah (Morris) Smith, and a descendant of Daniel Smith who emigrated from Bramham, Yorkshire, England, to New Jersey in 1691, one of the first of several brothers who settled there. Smith's baptismal certificate gives his name simply as Daniel; he evidently inserted the initial later. When Daniel was about a year old his father died, and his mother moved to Burlington, N. J. There he attended the school conducted by John Griscom [*q.v.*], a distinguished Quaker educator, who had a liking for the sciences. It was his influence, no doubt, that led young Smith to take up pharmacy as a career. After leaving school he returned to Philadelphia and entered the drug store of John Biddle on Market Street between Fourth and Fifth Streets. On the completion of his term of apprenticeship, he was taken into partnership under the firm name of Biddle & Smith. About a year later, in 1819, he opened his own store at the corner of Arch and Sixth Streets. He was married in 1824 to Esther Morton, daughter of John Morton, a merchant of Philadelphia. They had one daughter. In 1828 he took in William Hodgson, Jr., a young English apothecary, as a partner, and the firm thus established remained in existence until 1849, when the property was sold. He was actively associated with the movement that resulted in the establishment of the Philadelphia College of Pharmacy (incorporated, Mar. 30, 1822) and served it as secretary, 1821–27; as vice-president, 1828; as president, 1829–54; and as chairman of the committee on publications. On Mar. 28, 1826, about nine months after he assumed this chairmanship, there was published the first issue of the *Journal of the Philadelphia College of Pharmacy* (later the *American Journal of Pharmacy*), to which he was a liberal contributor of original articles until 1857. Through his position in the college and his contributions to its journal he attained national reputation, and when the pharmacists of the country met in Philadelphia in 1852 to organize the American Pharmaceutical Association he was unanimously chosen to be its first president. His early business life as an apothecary was contemporaneous with an era of great progress in chemistry and pharmacy, and he took a keen interest in the various discoveries made, reading the foreign reports as soon as they became available. His interest in these records of progress was scientific rather than commercial,

and was not limited to the field of pharmacy and chemistry.

Having a strong interest in education and in social problems, he was an originator of the Apprentices' Library, 1820, one of the corporators of the Philadelphia Savings Fund, 1819; of the Historical Society of Pennsylvania, 1826, of which he was the first corresponding secretary, and of the House of Refuge, 1828. He was actively associated with the Franklin Institute. In 1834 he accepted the chair of moral philosophy, English literature, and chemistry at Haverford School (later College), where he taught for twelve years. During this time he prepared and published *The Principles of Chemistry for the Use of Schools, Academies and Colleges* (1837) and numerous lectures on ethics, and the lives and doctrines of the early members of the Society of Friends. He resigned his position at Haverford in 1846 to return to the practice of pharmacy, from which he did not retire fully until 1853. In 1849 he removed to Germantown, Pa., where he lived until his death. One of the most learned and public-spirited pharmacists of his day, he was outstanding for the versatility of his attainments.

[R. M. Smith, *The Burlington Smiths* (1877); *Am. Jour. of Pharmacy,* July 1883; *The First Century of the Phila. Coll. of Pharmacy* (1922); *Proc. of the Am. Pharmaceutical Assoc.,* vol. XXXI (1884); obituary in *Pub. Ledger* (Phila.), Mar. 31, 1883.]   A. G. D–M.

SMITH, EDGAR FAHS (May 23, 1854–May 3, 1928), chemist, provost of the University of Pennsylvania, was born in York, Pa., the son of Gibson and Susan (Fahs) Smith, of Dutch and German ancestry. After preparing at York County Academy, he entered Pennsylvania (later Gettysburg) College at Gettysburg, where he received the degree of B.S. in 1874. Here he came under the influence of Samuel Philip Sadtler [*q.v.*], who stimulated his interest in chemistry and encouraged him to complete his education under Friedrich Wöhler at the University of Göttingen, Germany. He received the degree of Ph.D. from Göttingen in 1876 and again in 1926, according to the custom at Göttingen, upon the fiftieth anniversary of his promotion to the doctorate. From 1876 to 1881 he was assistant in analytical chemistry to Prof. Frederick Augustus Genth [*q.v.*] of the University of Pennsylvania. He told charmingly of his experiences during this period in his article on mineral chemistry in "A Half-Century of Chemistry in America, 1876–1926" (*Journal of the American Chemical Society; Golden Jubilee Number,* Aug. 20, 1926). On Apr. 10, 1879, he married Margie A. Gruel of Gettysburg, Pa. He was professor of chemistry at Muhlenberg College, Allentown,

Pa., 1881–83, and at Wittenberg College, Springfield, Ohio, 1883–88. It was during this period that he published *A Text-Book of Inorganic Chemistry* (1883) and *Chemistry of the Carbon Compounds, or Organic Chemistry* (1886), both translations from the German of Victor von Richter, which were used for several decades as textbooks in American colleges.

In 1888 he returned to the University of Pennsylvania to accept the professorship of analytical chemistry, from which Genth had retired; four years later he became head of the department of chemistry. During his years at Pennsylvania he carried on with his pupils a large number of investigations upon methods of electrochemical analyses, in which he was a pioneer, upon atomic weight determinations, compounds of the rarer metals, and complex salts of various inorganic acids. His *Electro-Chemical Analysis* (1890) went through six editions and was translated into several foreign languages. He won wide attention for his work upon molybdenum, and upon tungsten and its compounds; his research on tungsten led to its extensive use in scientific and artistic work. Appointed vice-provost of the university in 1898 and provost in 1911, he carried on a very successful administration; not only were millions of dollars raised, but there was a great quickening of the intellectual and spiritual life of the university. Resigning as provost and teacher in 1920, he devoted the remainder of his life to promoting an interest in the humanistic and cultural aspects of chemistry, which he felt were being neglected in the industrial stress of American civilization. He was influential in establishing the divisions of chemical education and historical chemistry in the American Chemical Society. He wrote numerous biographical sketches of prominent American chemists and amassed a private collection of prints, autograph letters, medallions, rare books, and other memorabilia of prominent chemists that was one of the most extensive ever assembled; endowed by his wife after his death, it is preserved intact as the Edgar Fahs Smith Memorial Collection of the University of Pennsylvania. His writings include thirteen chemical textbooks, five of which were translations, seven volumes and thirty-six brochures upon historical-chemical subjects, and 169 chemical papers. He died of pneumonia in Philadelphia, survived by his wife; there were no children. Among the chemists of his time he was unsurpassed as a conversationalist, lecturer, and public speaker. His genial, affable personality and strong capacity for friendships made him loved in every circle.

He won many distinctions for his scientific and educational work. He was president of the American Chemical Society, 1895, 1921, and 1922; of the American Philosophical Society, 1902–08; and of the History of Science Society at the time of his death. He was a member of the National Academy of Sciences, an officer of the Legion of Honor of France, and an honorary member of the American Chemical Society, the American Electrochemical Society, the Société de Chimie Industrielle de France, and the American Institute of Chemists. He was awarded the Elliott Cresson medal by the Franklin Institute in 1914, the Chandler medal by Columbia University in 1922, and the Priestley medal by the American Chemical Society in 1926. From 1914 to 1920 he was a trustee of the Carnegie Foundation, and from 1917 to 1922 president of the Wistar Institute of Anatomy. He served upon the jury of awards of the Columbian Exposition at Chicago in 1893 and was a member of the United States Assay Commission, 1895 and 1901–05. In 1917 and in 1925 he was a member of the Electoral College, serving as its president in the latter year; in 1919 he was a member of the commission for the revision of the constitution of Pennsylvania, and in 1921 was appointed by Pres. Warren Gamaliel Harding a member of the board of technical advisors to the disarmament conference.

[*Who's Who in America*, 1926–27; *Jour. of Chem. Educ.*, Apr. 1932, a memorial number with bibliog. and photographs; C. A. Browne, in *Ibid.*, June 1928, and in *Isis*, Dec. 1928; W. T. Taggart, in *Science*, July 6, 1928; F. X. Dercom, M. T. Bogert, and J. H. Penniman, in *Memorial Service for Edgar Fahs Smith . . . Dec. 4, 1928*, Univ. of Pa.; obituary in *Pub. Ledger* (Phila.), May 4, 1928; information from Miss Eva V. Armstrong.]   C. A. B.

SMITH, EDMUND KIRBY [See KIRBY-SMITH, EDMUND, 1824–1893].

SMITH, EDMUND MUNROE (Dec. 8, 1854–Apr. 13, 1926), professor of legal history, editor, and writer, nephew of Henry Boynton Smith [*q.v.*], was born in Brooklyn, N. Y., the son of Dr. Horatio Southgate and Susan Dwight (Munroe) Smith. He received the degree of A.B. from Amherst in 1874, and subsequently did graduate work in politics and jurisprudence under Prof. John W. Burgess who was then teaching there. Entering the Columbia Law School, he received the degree of LL.B. in 1877. At the suggestion of Burgess, who had become professor at Columbia, he then began to prepare himself for a proposed chair of Roman law and comparative jurisprudence by going abroad and attending the lectures of Jhering, Bruns, Windscheid, Gneist, and other famous jurists, at the universities of Göttingen, Berlin, and Leipzig.

His manuscript notes (now at Columbia) attest a thorough comprehension of the ancient and modern fields of law which these scholars presented. In 1880 he received the degree of doctor of civil and canon law at Göttingen. From 1880 to 1883 he was instructor, and from 1883 until 1891, adjunct professor, of history and political science at Columbia. On Apr. 17, 1890, he married Gertrude, daughter of Gen. Henry Shippen Huidekoper, of Philadelphia; one daughter of this marriage survived him. The following year he was appointed to the chair for which he had prepared himself, that of Roman law and comparative jurisprudence, and in 1922 he became Bryce Professor of European Legal History, retiring in 1924 as professor emeritus. From its establishment in 1886 he was for many years managing editor of the *Political Science Quarterly*. Among honors that he received were the presidency of the American Political Science Association (1917) and the vice-presidency of the International Academy of Comparative Law (1924).

Munroe Smith will be remembered by his contemporaries as one of the leaders in the development of Columbia from a college to a university, as a guiding spirit in the early years of the *Political Science Quarterly,* and by his students, as an inspiring lecturer; but posterity must look to his written works to evaluate him. His first work of merit was "State Statute and Common Law," which first appeared in the *Political Science Quarterly* (March 1887–March 1888) and was reprinted in *A General View of European Legal History and Other Papers* (1927). It is a severe criticism of codification when applied to the common law system. Another early work of significance comprised a series of articles entitled "Four German Jurists" which also appeared in the *Quarterly* (1895–1901) and was reprinted in *A General View*. It presents a study of the interrelation of the juristic thoughts of his four teachers mentioned above. Smith had studied in Germany at a time when Bismarck towered over Europe; in his *Bismarck and German Unity* (1898, 3rd ed. 1923), which soon became a classic, youthful impressions are substantiated by careful scholarly thought. In fact, Bismarck influenced Smith's later writings, particularly his war books, and it can be said that no American knew Bismarck as well as did Smith. The first years of the twentieth century he devoted to various studies in constitutional law, Roman law, legal education, and jurisprudence generally. Of his writings in these fields, "Customary Law" (*Political Science Quarterly,* June 1903) and "The Japanese Code and the Family" (*Law Quarterly Re-*

view, January 1907), both reprinted in *A General View*, well illustrate his wide scholarly interests. With the outbreak of the World War, he became an anti-German propagandist, and though his writings reflect careful thinking, they are of less scientific value than his earlier works. The volume *Militarism and Statecraft* (1918) incorporates the best of the articles of this period; in addition he compiled *Out of Their Own Mouths* (1917), a collection of statements by Prussian officials and others revealing the principles by which their political activities were governed. After the war Smith perfected his lectures in Columbia Law School, published posthumously as *The Development of European Law* (1928), which with his *A General View of European Legal History* (1927) are among the best treatises upon this subject in English. These works, in which he stresses the homogeneity of European law, place his name among those of the great legal scholars.

[C. M. Fuess, "Edmund Munroe Smith," *Amherst Grads. Quart.,* Nov. 1926; *Obit. Record of Grads. and Non-Grads. of Amherst Coll.,* 1925–26; F. J. Goodnow, Foreword, in *A General View,* etc.; H. F. Stone, "Edmund Munroe Smith," *Actorum Academiae Universalis Iurisprudentiae Comparativae,* vol. I (1928); L. B. Chapman, *Monograph on the Southgate Family of Scarborough, Me.* (1907); J. B. Moore, Foreword, in Smith's *The Development of European Law* (1928); *A Bibliog. of the Faculty of Political Sci. of Columbia Univ., 1880–1930* (1931); *Who's Who in America,* 1926–27; *N. Y. Times,* Apr. 14, 1926.]   A. A. S.

SMITH, ELI (Sept. 13, 1801–Jan. 11, 1857), missionary and Orientalist, was born at Northford, Conn., the son of Polly (Whitney) and Eli Smith, who was a farmer and a manufacturer of tools, shoes, and leather. In 1821 he was graduated from Yale, after which he taught for two years in Georgia. Entering Andover Theological Seminary, he was graduated in 1826 and was ordained in Springfield, May 10, 1826. Several months before graduation, he was appointed by the American Board of Commissioners for Foreign Missions (Congregational) as associate editor of its publishing house at Malta, then the center of all printing operations carried on by the American missionary societies working in the Mediterranean. He arrived in Malta after a two months' journey from New York, which he had left in May. A few months later he left for Syria in order to study Arabic and prepare himself for translating the Bible into Arabic, but after the battle of Navarino in October 1827 he was forced to leave Syria with other American missionaries, and he returned to Malta. In early 1829 he made a tour through Greece, and in March 1830 with Harrison Gray Otis Dwight [q.v.], who had recently arrived from America, he undertook an extended journey of exploration through Asia Minor, Armenia, and Georgia into Persia, from which he returned by way of Constantinople early in 1831. The results of the journey, made with a view to opening mission stations, were published by the two travelers under the title *Researches of the Rev. E. Smith and Rev. H. G. O. Dwight in Armenia: Including a Journey through Asia Minor and into Georgia and Persia, with a Visit to the Nestorian and Chaldean Christians of Oormiah and Salmas* (2 volumes, 1833). In this journey the two missionaries explored much unknown territory and gave an extremely valuable account of conditions in Armenia, about which little was then known to the West. Their description of the poverty and ignorance of the Nestorian Christians led to the establishment of the American mission at Urumiah, one of the most important in the Near East.

Shortly after his return from this journey, Smith went back to America. There he prepared the account of his travels for publication and published a volume of *Missionary Sermons and Addresses* (1833). On July 21, 1833, he married Sarah Lanman Huntington, daughter of Jabez Huntington, who accompanied him to Syria that fall and died at Smyrna in September 1836. In January 1838 at Cairo he joined Edward Robinson, 1794–1863 [*q.v.*], who had been his teacher at Andover, and accompanied him on his epoch-making explorations in Sinai, Palestine, and southern Syria. Robinson's critical and scholarly training was supplemented by Smith's knowledge of the East and its people, and his thorough familiarity with Arabic; without these Robinson could have accomplished but little. In the fall Smith accompanied his friend to Germany, where he arranged for the casting of fonts of Arabic type for the mission press at Beirut, and then went back to America. In 1841 he returned to Beirut, accompanied by his second wife, Maria Ward Chapin, a daughter of Judge Moses Chapin of Rochester, N. Y., whom he married Mar. 9, 1841, and who died the following year. They had one son. Since his own health was now seriously undermined, he was forced to leave for America again in 1845. About a year later, after his recovery from a dangerous illness, he married his third wife, Hetty Simpkins Butler of Northampton, Mass., on Oct. 23, 1846, and returned with her to Syria in January 1847. They had two daughters and three sons, one of whom, Benjamin Eli Smith [*q.v.*], was born after his father's death. Smith devoted the last decade of his life to the translation of the Bible into Arabic, for which everything else had been preparatory. He was well equipped for

this work both by his wide linguistic training and by his long experience in Arabic presswork. Besides knowing Greek, Latin, and Hebrew, and the principal European languages, he was well acquainted with Turkish and knew Arabic so well that it had become almost a second vernacular to him. In 1856 ill health compelled him to give up his work, and he died of cancer at Beirut the following January.

[S. W. Phoenix, *The Whitney Family of Conn.* (1878), vol. I, pp. 685–88; F. B. Dexter, *Biog. Notices Grads. of Yale Coll.* (1913); Edward Robinson, *Biblical Researches in Palestine, Mount Sinai and Arabia Petraea* (3 vols., 1841); *Am. Congreg. Year-Book*, 1858; obituary in *Missionary Herald*, July 1857.]
W. F. A.

SMITH, ELIAS (June 17, 1769–June 29, 1846), clergyman, associated with the movement that led to the establishment of the Christian Connection, author, editor of the first religious newspaper in the United States, was born in Lyme, Conn., a son of Stephen and Irene (Ransom) Smith. In his fourteenth year the family moved from a Connecticut farm to the much harder conditions of the frontier settlement of South Woodstock, Vt. Elias' meager educational advantages ended with this change, but he was a thoughtful boy and fond of reading. His father was a Baptist, but the mother was a "strict" or "separatist" Congregationalist, a fact which accounted for his being baptized by "sprinkling"—to his lasting resentment—in his eighth year. At the age of eighteen he attended school for a few weeks and then began teaching, which occupation he followed for two years. About this time he experienced a profound religious awakening and, after much mental conflict over the subject of baptism, joined the Baptist Church in 1789. He now devoted himself to the study of the Bible and theology and, though greatly distrustful of his own worthiness and ability, began to preach in 1790. His success was marked and he was ordained by the Baptists as an evangelist at Lee, N. H., in August 1792. On Jan. 7 of the following year he married Mary Burleigh, established his home in Salisbury, N. H., and became a successful itinerant preacher throughout the towns of New Hampshire and Massachusetts. In 1798 he was installed pastor of the Baptist church in Woburn, Mass., but was unhappy in the relations of the settled pastorate, largely because he found no precedent for the installation in the New Testament.

Meanwhile his theological opinions underwent a radical change. He rejected the Calvinistic system held by the Baptists, repudiated the doctrine of the Trinity, and disowned all systems of church order and all denominational names not found in the New Testament. After a brief business venture which failed, he moved to Portsmouth and founded a church acknowledging no creed but the Bible and having no denominational name but Christian. He was unsparing in his criticism of other churches with their settled and tax-supported clergy and their theological systems, which he regarded as having no Biblical foundation. His denunciations, coupled with his strong anti-Federalist political views, created for him a host of enemies who pursued him for many years, and often he narrowly escaped mob violence. In order to reply more effectively to his opponents, he began to write, and his *History of Anti-Christ* (1803? 1811), *The Clergyman's Looking-Glass* (1803), *The Whole World Governed by a Jew* (1805), *A Short Sermon to the Calvinist Baptists of Massachusetts* (1806), only added fuel to the flames. In 1805 he began a quarterly, *The Christian's Magazine, Reviewer and Religious Intelligencer,* which continued for two years. On Sept. 1, 1808, he issued the initial number of the *Herald of Gospel Liberty,* the first weekly religious newspaper in the United States. This organ of the growing Christian fellowship was published in Portsmouth, Portland, and Philadelphia during Smith's residence in these places and was later continued under various names. In 1818 Smith sold the paper, and became a Universalist. He formed a business connection with Dr. Samuel Thomson [q.v.] of Boston, originator of the Thomson system of medicine and therapeutics, mastered the system, and soon built up a lucrative practice, establishing, about 1830, a private sanitarium. In 1823 he renounced Universalism, but his restoration to the Christian fellowship was only partial.

In addition to the works already mentioned and several volumes of sermons and hymns, Smith's more important books were: *Twenty-Two Sermons on the Prophesies* (1808); *The New Testament Dictionary* (1812); *The American Physician and Family Assistant* (1832); *The People's Book* (1836). In 1816 he published an autobiography, *The Life, Conversion, Preaching, Travels and Sufferings of Elias Smith.* His first wife died in Philadelphia, Feb. 27, 1814, and in the latter part of the same year he married Rachel, daughter of Samuel Thurber of Providence, R. I. There were a number of children by the first marriage.

[In addition to Smith's autobiog., see J. P. Barrett, *The Centennial of Religious Journalism* (2nd ed., 1908); Charles Burleigh, *The Geneal. of the Burley or Burleigh Family of America* (1880); M. T. Morrill, *A Hist. of the Christian Denomination in America* (1912); E. W. Humphreys, *Memoirs of Deceased Christian Ministers* (1880); F. L. Mott, *A Hist. of*

Am. Mags. (1930); *Portsmouth Jour.* (N. H.), July 11, 1846. A résumé of Smith's teachings from a hostile viewpoint is found in Thomas Andros, *The Scriptures Liable to be Wrested to Men's Own Destruction, and an Instance of this Found, in the Writings of Elias Smith* (1817).]

F. T. P.

SMITH, ELIHU HUBBARD (Sept. 4, 1771–Sept. 19, 1798), physician, author, and editor, was the only son of Dr. Reuben Smith, a Yale graduate and a prominent and public-spirited citizen of Litchfield, Conn., and Abigail (Hubbard) Smith. His American ancestry went back to William Smith, who settled in Wethersfield, Conn., about 1644, and to George Hubbard of Hartford, Conn., born in England in 1601 (Bailey, *post,* p. 11). From a cultured home in a town of unusual intellectual and humanitarian activities he entered Yale in 1782. Only a youth of fifteen, at graduation, he was sent for two years' further study at the academy at Greenfield Hill, Conn., under Dr. Timothy Dwight, the elder [q.v.], later president of Yale. At seventeen he had written, among other things, a group of five sonnets that are nearly the earliest extant in American literature. He next returned to Litchfield for two years' medical study with his father, supplemented by attendance on the medical lectures of Dr. Benjamin Rush [q.v.] in Philadelphia during the winter and spring of 1790–91. Here he became intimate with Joseph Bringhurst, Jr., and Charles Brockden Brown [q.v.], on whose life and work he exerted a continued and helpful influence. With Bringhurst he carried on for several months during 1791 in the *Gazette of the United States* a fanciful verse correspondence modeled on that of Robert Merry and Mrs. Hannah Parkhouse Cowley (Bailey, *post,* pp. 44–50).

As a practising physician at Wethersfield from the fall of 1791 to the spring of 1793, he became associated with the literary group at Hartford, which then comprised Richard Alsop, David Humphreys, and Theodore Dwight, and his fellow physicians Lemuel Hopkins [qq.v.] and Mason Fitch Cogswell. To the "Echo" series of satiric skits produced by the group between 1791 and 1800, and published in the *American Mercury* (Hartford), Smith contributed one number, "Extracts from Democracy, an Epic Poem, by Aquiline Nimblechops," and unidentified portions of others. Withdrawing from Wethersfield in the spring of 1793, he spent several happy months at Litchfield in the company of Brockden Brown, who may have assisted him in publishing during the summer the first volume of *American Poems,* the earliest anthology of American poetry. Of its 304 pages, 188 were devoted to the verse of his Connecticut friends, especially John Trumbull (1750–1831), Joel Barlow [*qq.v.*], Dwight, and Humphreys. Several other volumes were projected but never published.

Instead, early in September, he settled as a physician in New York City, and despite his years soon won an enviable professional reputation, strengthened by the publication in 1795 of his *Letters to William Buel on the Fever . . . in New-York in 1795,* in which he contended that the disastrous series of yellow-fever epidemics in Philadelphia and New York was due to crowded and unsanitary living conditions. After 1794 he lived with a fellow bachelor and lover of letters, a young lawyer, William Johnson. Their house, at first on Cedar Street, later on Pine, became the headquarters of the Friendly Club, with William Dunlap, Dr. Samuel Latham Mitchill, Edward and Samuel Miller, 1769–1850, James Kent [*qq.v.*], William Walton Woolson, George Morrison Woolson, and Anthony Bleecker as members. His closest friends, besides Johnson, were Dunlap, the dramatist and theatre manager, and Brockden Brown, whose *Alcuin* he saw through the press in March 1798, with a preface of his own writing. Dunlap staged Smith's *Edwin and Angelina,* originally written as a drama but revised as a ballad opera, at the John Street theatre, Dec. 19, 1796; it had a moderate success and was published by Swords in New York the following year and later republished in London, with a collection of other plays. Smith in turn assisted Dunlap in the publication of *André* (1798) and wrote the address for the opening of the Park Theatre, Jan. 29, 1798. He was also active as a member of the New York Society for Promoting the Manumission of Slaves, a trustee of the colored school in the city, and one of the organizers of the American Mineralogical Society in 1798. With Dr. Mitchill and Dr. Edward Miller he projected the first American medical journal, the *Medical Repository,* and edited it with them from the summer of 1797 to his death, contributing extensively to it himself.

His last literary ventures were his American edition of Erasmus Darwin's *The Botanic Garden* (1798), prefaced with a long verse epistle to Darwin, and a noteworthy series of critical and biographical sketches of contemporary American writers in the *Monthly Magazine* (London), July–October, 1798. With Brown, who became an occupant of his home in the summer of 1798, he was planning a magazine and review to be undertaken in New York. The disastrous yellow fever epidemic of 1798, however, intervened. Smith, already exhausted with conscientious attendance upon many patients, took into his household Dr. Joseph B. Scandella, an Italian physician dying with the disease, contracted it himself (as did Brown also), and died on Sept. 19, 1798, about a fortnight after his twenty-seventh birthday. He is described by his contemporaries as a man of lovable character and great talents, and his zeal and enthusiasm for literature, science, and the advancement of humanity knew virtually no limit.

[See Marcia Edgerton Bailey, *A Lesser Hartford Wit, Dr. Elihu Hubbard Smith* (1928), Univ. of Me. Studies, 2 ser., no. 11, with portrait and bibliog.; *Diary of William Dunlap* (3 vols., 1930), N. Y. Hist. Soc. Colls.; William Dunlap, *The Life of Charles Brockden Brown* (2 vols., 1815), and *A Hist. of the Am. Theatre* (1832); biog. sketches in *Medic. Repository,* vol. II (1798), and *Am. Medic. and Philosophical Reg.,* Jan. 1814; F. B. Dexter, *Biog. Sketches Grads. of Yale Coll.,* vol. IV (1907); obituary in *Commercial Advertiser* (N. Y.), Sept. 20, 1798. Some of Smith's letters are in the Yale and Harvard Univ. libraries. For a discussion of *Am. Poems,* see Milton Ellis, "Aaron Stockwell's Book," *Tex. Rev.,* Oct. 1917; for Smith's influence on Brown's work see D. L. Clark, *Charles Brockden Brown, a Crit. Biog.* (1923).]
M. E.

SMITH, ELIZA ROXEY SNOW [See Snow, Eliza Roxey, 1804–1887].

SMITH, ELIZABETH OAKES PRINCE (Aug. 12, 1806–Nov. 15, 1893), author, lecturer, reformer, was born at North Yarmouth, Me., the second daughter of David and Sophia (Blanchard) Prince. On her father's side she was a descendant of John Prince, who was in Watertown, Mass., before 1633; Thomas Prince [*q.v.*], the colonial chronicler of New England, was a member of the same family. Her ancestors on her mother's side were French Huguenots, and her grandfather was a prosperous ship owner in the East India trade. Her early childhood was dominated by strong religious discipline, against which she later rebelled. After her father's death her mother remarried, and in 1814, the family moved to Portland. There, in deference to her mother's wishes, she abandoned her hopes for a higher education and a career as head of a school for girls, and married, Mar. 6, 1823, Seba Smith [*q.v.*], editor of the *Eastern Argus.* Her husband had her admiration and respect, but there is a pathos in her statement that he was "nearly twice my age, wore spectacles, and was very bald." They had five sons. Apropos of her lack of daughters she once said, "Mr. Smith rather prefers boys," but her autobiography reveals that, too well aware of the limitations imposed on women, she was secretly glad not to produce daughters.

During the early years of her marriage she devoted her energies chiefly to her home and young children. When their fortune was lost in the speculation that culminated in the panic of 1837, the family moved in 1839 to Charleston, S. C., where Smith hoped to sell cotton-cleaning machines to planters. The venture failing, they went after a short time to New York, where they lived until 1860. To assist her husband Mrs. Oakes Smith, as she was known, contributed sketches, essays, and poems to such popular periodicals of the day as the *Ladies' Companion,* the *Southern Literary Messenger, Godey's Lady's Book,* and *Graham's American Monthly Magazine.* One Wordsworthian poem, *The Sinless Child* (1843), evoked surprisingly laudatory comment from such critics as Edgar Allan Poe and Rufus Wilmot Griswold [*qq.v.*]. She edited several annuals or Christmas gift books, had two plays produced, and wrote seven novels, in addition to numerous didactic books for children. Four of the novels—*The Western Captive* (1842), *Black Hollow* (1864), *Bald Eagle, or the Last of the Ramapaughs* (1867), and *The Sagamore of Saco* (1868)—show the influence of James Fenimore Cooper [*q.v.*] and probably owed some of their popularity to his fame; her *Bald Eagle* was one of the best sellers in Beadle's dime novel series. Her interest in the supernatural is revealed in *The Salamander, A Legend for Christmas* (1848); *Bertha and Lily* (1854), romantic and sentimental, shows her concern with social, moral, and religious questions, while her sentimental story, *The Newsboy* (1854), seems to have done much to arouse concern in New York over conditions in the slums. A considerable amount of her work appeared under the name Ernest Helfenstein. Some articles on woman's suffrage written for the *New York Tribune* in 1850 led her into lyceum lecturing, 1851–57, at which she was very successful. In 1851 these articles were published, with some of her speeches, as *Woman and Her Needs,* a plea for the recognition of the abilities of women. Her autobiography, part of which has been published as *Selections from the Autobiography of Elizabeth Oakes Smith* (1924), is filled with personal observations and anecdotes of the leading figures of public life before the Civil War. Because of the illness of Seba Smith the family moved about 1860 to Patchogue, Long Island. After his death in 1868, Mrs. Oakes Smith lived much of the time with her eldest son in Hollywood, N. C. In 1877 she became for a year pastor of the Independent Church at Canastota, N. Y. She died in North Carolina and was buried at Patchogue. Her children bore the name Oaksmith, the change having been made legally in their childhood.

[The autobiog. of Elizabeth Oakes Smith is in the manuscript dept. of the N. Y. Pub. Lib., N. Y. City. See Mary A. Wyman, *Selections from the Autobiog. of Elizabeth Oakes Smith* (1924) and *Two Am. Pioneers, Seba Smith and Elizabeth Oakes Smith* (1927), with bibliog.; *Old Times in N. Yarmouth, Me.,* Mar. 1877, Apr. 1879, Jan. 1882; E. A. Poe, in *Godey's Lady's Mag.,* Dec. 1845; R. W. Griswold, *The Female Poets of America* (1848); E. A. and G. L. Duyckinck, *The Cyc. of Am. Lit.* (1855); obituary in *Appleton's Ann. Cyc.,* 1893); editorial in *Daily Eastern Argus* (Portland, Me.), Nov. 21, 1893. The date of death has been supplied by Miss Geraldine Oaksmith, Newport, N. C., grand-daughter of Mrs. Oakes Smith.]

L. M. M.
R. W. B.

SMITH, ERASMUS DARWIN (Oct. 10, 1806–Nov. 11, 1883), jurist, was the son of Hubbard Smith, a physician, and Eunice (Jones) Smith, who moved about 1801 from Rensselaer County to Madison County, N. Y., while it was still part of the frontier. He was born at De Ruyter, N. Y., and obtained his early education in the district schools. At the age of fifteen he began to teach, using his earnings for further schooling. Completing his preparatory studies at Hamilton Academy in three summers, he entered Hamilton College in 1826, but did not remain for graduation. In 1829 he went to Rochester and began studying law in the office of Gregory & Humphrey. The next year he was admitted to the bar, and began practising in partnership with Ebenezer Griffin, whose daughter, Janet Morrison, became in 1831 his first wife.

He held the minor positions of master of chancery, 1832–35; injunction master for the eighth district, 1840; and chancery clerk for that district, 1841–47. The Democratic party nominated him for the Assembly and for Congress but, the districts being strongly Whig, he was defeated. For a short time in 1849 he was the political editor of the Rochester *Daily Advertiser.* In 1855 he was elected justice of the supreme court and served by subsequent reëlections until he was retired on account of age, Jan. 1, 1877. After 1872 he was a general term justice of the fourth department. The state constitution then provided that supreme court justices might be designated to sit on the court of appeals, and Smith was so designated in 1862 and again in 1870. With these exceptions his judicial service was wholly in the inferior courts of the state.

During his tenure of twenty-two years he had an important influence upon the development of the law. His decision in *Clarke* vs. *The City of Rochester* (24 *Barbour,* 446), a case involving many millions in investments, settled the right of cities to subscribe to the stock of railroad corporations after a referendum to the people. In 1863 he upheld the legal tender act as an incident to the war powers of Congress and the right of the national government to preserve its existence (*Hague* vs. *Powers, 39 Barbour,* 427). Secretary Chase said that the decision was, in its influence on the credit of the government, equal to a victory in the field (Peck, *post,* p. 680). His best-known decision was in the case of *People* vs. *Albany & Susquehanna R. R.* (55 *Barbour,* 344) in which he settled the main point involved in the "Erie War," a controversy that had menaced the state's police authority and the reputation of its courts.

He had a ready and extensive acquaintance with legal principles and authorities which he supplemented when occasion required by industrious research. The tendency of his decisions was to uphold legislative acts whenever possible. In both law and equity cases he was unsympathetic toward artificial rules. He approached every inquiry in a large spirit. Having arrived at a conclusion, it was his custom to write his opinions with great vigor and positiveness. Sometimes his enthusiasm led him into dicta which the higher courts would not approve. After his retirement from the bench he was frequently employed as a referee. His death followed an apoplectic stroke in his seventy-eighth year. He was survived by his second wife, Emilie Maria (Perkins), widow of Erastus T. Smith, whom he married June 6, 1879, and by several children.

[For sources, see W. F. Peck, *Semi-Centennial Hist. of the City of Rochester* (1884) ; *Appletons' Ann. Cyc. . . . 1883* (1884) ; *Landmarks of Monroe County, N. Y.* (1895) ; C. E. Perkins, *The Descendants of Edward Perkins* (1914) ; *Rochester Post Express,* Nov. 12, 1883 ; *Rochester Morning Herald,* Nov. 12, 14, 1883. An extended discussion of Smith's decision in the Albany & Susquehanna case may be found in *High Finance in the Sixties* (1929), ed. by F. C. Hicks.]
E. C. S.

SMITH, ERMINNIE ADELLE PLATT, (Apr. 26, 1836–June 9, 1886), geologist, ethnologist, was born at Marcellus, N. Y., the daughter of Joseph Platt. She attended the Troy Female Seminary at Troy, N. Y., and was graduated in 1853. Within a year she was married to Simeon H. Smith, of Jersey City, N. J., and became absorbed in a rigid and exacting domestic routine. Her interest in geology and botany, which she had demonstrated from childhood, did not wane, however, and received new impetus when she took advantage of an opportunity to study geology, mineralogy, crystallography, and other branches of science, while educating her four sons in Germany. She studied crystallography at Strasburg, German language and literature at Heidelberg, and visited and investigated the amber industry on the coast of the Baltic Sea. Mineralogy interested her and she gath-

ered one of the largest collections of her time. She also pursued courses in the famous Bergakademie at Freiberg and was graduated from that institution. Upon her return to the United States she lectured on scientific and cultural subjects and attained a reputation for lucid and eloquent address.

She became interested in the New York Indians of her neighborhood, and was led to study ethnology. In 1880 she received an appointment on the staff of the Bureau of American Ethnology of the Smithsonian Institution, Washington, D. C. The director, John Wesley Powell [*q.v.*], detailed her to study the language, customs, and myths of the Iroquois Indians. She spent two summers among the Tuscaroras in Canada and completed an Iroquois-English dictionary, now with her papers in the archives of the Smithsonian Institution. The Tuscaroras adopted her as a member of the tribe, giving her the name "Beautiful Flower." Her book, *Myths of the Iroquois,* published in the *Second Annual Report of the Bureau of Ethnology* in 1883, was an outgrowth of these studies of tales which she obtained from older informants possessing the fast-fading lore of the tribe. A complete bibliography of her contributions is to be found in J. C. Pilling's *Bibliography of the Iroquoian Languages, Bulletin 6, Bureau of American Ethnology* (1889). In recognition of her attainments she was the first woman to be elected a fellow of the New York Academy of Sciences, and also became a member of the American Association for the Advancement of Science. She held the secretaryship of the section of anthropology at the time of her death. She founded the Aesthetic Society of New Jersey and became the first president. One of the pioneers of the woman's movement, she was very active in promoting the organization of cultural societies and clubs. She was a member of the London Scientific Society, Numismatic and Antiquarian Society of Philadelphia, and others. In 1883 a geological prize was founded in her honor at Vassar College.

[Information from Mrs. Everett Griffith, Forest Glen, Md., and J. N. B. Hewitt, Bureau of Am. Ethnol., Smithsonian Institution, Washington, D. C.; *In Memoriam. Mrs. Erminnie A. Smith, 1837–1886* (privately printed, 1890) ; *Emma Willard and Her Pupils or Fifty Years of Troy Female Seminary* (1898) ; *N. Y. Times,* June 10, 1886.]
W. H.

SMITH, ERWIN FRINK (Jan. 21, 1854–Apr. 6, 1927), botanist and bacteriologist, was born at Gilberts Mills, Oswego County, N. Y., the son of R. K. and Louisa (Frink) Smith, and spent his boyhood and young manhood on farms in New York and Michigan. Since he was forced to work his way through both high school and college, it was not until 1886 that he received the degree of B.S. from the University of Michigan, where three years later he received the degree of Sc.D. In 1886 he joined the scientific staff of the United States Department of Agriculture and began the remarkable career that was terminated only by his death. In 1901 he became pathologist in the bureau of plant industry, and in 1902 pathologist in charge of the laboratory of plant pathology, a position he held until 1927. His early work dealt with yellows and other obscure peach diseases, and while he did not solve these problems completely he labored with such thoroughness that little of importance has since been added to the sum of his studies on the subject. Turning to the fungus diseases of other economic plants, he gave attention to the *Fusaria* as plant parasites and carried out fundamental studies on which other workers later based the development of disease-resistant varieties of melons, cotton, cowpeas, potatoes, cabbage, and other crops. He early became interested in what was then the very new field of the bacterial diseases of plants and advanced the theory that bacteria caused plant diseases, an idea that was rejected in scorn by European workers, Alfred Fischer and Robert Hartig in particular. With his usual thoroughness and persistence, however, Smith soon firmly established the truth of his statements and completely silenced his critics.

About 1904 he took up the study of plant tumors and the so-called crown-gall disease. His paper, "A Plant Tumor of Bacterial Origin" (*Science*, Apr. 26, 1907), written in collaboration with C. O. Townsend, established the latter disease as of bacterial origin, and was followed by many publications dealing with the etiology and other phases of the disease. His conviction that there was a striking analogy between crown-gall of plants and cancer of animals was not only accepted by plant pathologists but by the medical profession as well, as was evidenced by his election to the presidency of the American Association for Cancer Research in 1925. His work on plant tumors included studies of formative stimuli, conditions of growth, the mechanism of tumor formation, and problems of histogenesis. In the course of his professional career he contributed to American and foreign scientific journals over a hundred and fifty original papers and many reviews. His outstanding scientific publications are the exhaustive treatise, *Bacteria in Relation to Plant Diseases* (3 vols., 1905–14), of which there were other volumes in preparation at the time of his death; his textbook, *An Introduction to Bacterial Diseases of Plants* (1920);

and the series of crown-gall and cancer papers published in English, French, and German in a wide range of technical journals.

On Apr. 13, 1893, he married Charlotte M. Buffett of Cleveland, Ohio, who died Dec. 28, 1906. In 1914, on Feb. 21, he married Ruth Annette Warren of Springfield, Mass., who survived him. He died in Washington. He was a member of the National Academy of Sciences, the American Academy of Arts and Sciences, the American Philosophical Society, as well as numerous other American and European learned societies in several fields. His non-scientific interests were wide. Music and art had a great appeal for him, and he was a skilled linguist, reading French, German, Italian, Greek, and Latin. His literary ability is evidenced by his poems, by his *Pasteur, the History of a Mind* (1920), translated (with Florence Hedges) from the French of Émile Duclaux, and by his translation of the sonnets of José Maria de Heredia. By temperament an artist as much as a scientist, he stands out as a creative genius who not only did the work of a pioneer but throughout a lifetime acted as a leader in the development of the science of plant pathology. In his field he was without an equal; what Louis Pasteur and Robert Koch were to animal pathology, he was to bacterial plant pathology.

[*Who's Who in America*, 1926–27; J. M. Cattell and D. R. Brimhall, *Am. Men of Sci.* (3rd ed., 1921); R. H. True, in *Phytopathology*, Oct. 1927, with portrait and full bibliog.; L. R. Jones and F. V. Rand, in *Jour. of Bacteriology*, Jan. 1928; F. V. Rand, in *Mycologia*, July–Aug. 1928, with portrait; E. W. Brandes, in *Science*, Oct. 28, 1927; *Evening Star* (Washington, D. C.), Apr. 7, 1927.]   J. A. S.

SMITH, EUGENE ALLEN (Oct. 27, 1841– Sept. 7, 1927), state geologist of Alabama for fifty-four years, was born in Washington, Autauga County, Ala., the son of Samuel Parrish and Adelaide Julia (Allen) Smith, both of New England ancestry. The boy's early training was obtained at a private school in Prattville, Ala., but in 1856, at the age of fifteen, he entered the Central High School of Philadelphia where he remained until the autumn of 1859. The year following he entered the University of Alabama, Tuscaloosa, with advanced standing, graduating with the degree of A.B. in 1862. Throughout the Civil War he served as drill master and instructor in tactics at the University. In 1865 he went to Europe and for the next three years was in attendance at various German universities, including Berlin, Göttingen, and Heidelberg, receiving from the last named the degree of Ph.D. *summa cum laude* in 1868.

Returning to America in that year, he was

appointed assistant professor of chemistry in the University of Mississippi, where he came under the influence of Professor Eugene W. Hilgard [*q.v.*], from whom he apparently derived his first special interest in geology. In 1871 he was elected professor of chemistry and mineralogy in the University of Alabama, with the proviso that he was to devote such of his time as could be spared from his teaching to investigating the natural resources of the state. This arrangement led naturally to his appointment as state geologist in 1873, though with no immediate increase in salary. In this position he served continuously during the remaining fifty-four years of his life, a term as state geologist believed unequaled in America; for forty years he also retained his University professorship, resigning it in 1913 to give his whole time to the survey.

Smith was of a modest and retiring disposition, devoted to the interests of the state and of the survey, and with no thought of personal gain. He was of slight stature and build, wiry, and very active both physically and mentally. As a geologist he made no startling discoveries and was not given to theory, but worked steadily and faithfully, respected and loved by all who knew him. He was president of the Geological Society of America in 1913. Of the more than 100 titles given in his bibliography, many were the regular reports of progress of the survey; other papers worthy of mention are "The Iron Ores of Alabama," in *Proceedings of the American Association for the Advancement of Science* (vol. XXVII, 1879); "The Iron Ores of Alabama in Their Geological Relations" (*Mineral Resources of the United States, 1882*, 1883); "Physicogeographical and Agricultural Features of the State of Alabama," in *Report on Cotton Production in the United States*, being vol. VI (1884) of the Reports of the Tenth Census; *On the Phosphates and Marls of Alabama* (1892), a bulletin of the state survey. To the study of the coastal region he gave most of his personal energies after 1880, noteworthy papers in this field being "The Post-Eocene Formations of the Coastal Plain of Alabama" (*American Journal of Science*, April 1894); *Report on the Geology of the Coastal Plain of Alabama* (1894), published by the Alabama survey; and "On Some Post-Eocene and Other Formations of the Gulf Region of the United States" (*Proceedings of the American Association for the Advancement of Science*, vol. LV, 1906). His most original contribution was perhaps a short paper, "Underthrust Folds and Faults," published in the *American Journal of Science* for April 1893.

Smith was married, July 10, 1872, to Jane

Henry Meredith Garland, daughter of Landon Cabell Garland [*q.v.*], a professor at the University of Mississippi and subsequently first chancellor of Vanderbilt University. Smith died in Tuscaloosa, survived by his widow and three sons.

[Charles Butts, "Memorial of Eugene Allen Smith," with bibliography, *Bull. Geol. Soc. of America*, Mar. 1928; W. B. Jones, in *Engineering and Mining Journal*, Dec. 17, 1927, and in *Science*, Jan. 6, 1928; *Who's Who in America*, 1926–27; *Montgomery Advertiser*, Sept. 8, 1927.]

G. P. M.

SMITH, FRANCIS HENNEY (Oct. 18, 1812–Mar. 21, 1890), soldier and educator, was the son of Francis Smith, merchant of Norfolk, Va., and Ann (Marsden) Smith. Commissioned 2nd lieutenant, 1st artillery, Nov. 30, 1833, after his graduation from the United States Military Academy in July, he was on garrison duty for a year and then taught geography, history, and ethics at the Academy for a year. In 1834 he married Sarah Henderson, daughter of Thomas Henderson; they had seven children. Resigning his commission in 1836 to accept the professorship of mathematics at Hampden-Sidney College in Virginia, in June 1839 he became principal professor and after 1840 superintendent of the newly organized Virginia Military Institute at Lexington, to the service of which he devoted the remainder of his life. On Nov. 11, 1839, the Institute was opened with two instructors, Smith and John T. L. Preston, and twenty-eight cadets. The six thousand dollars appropriated annually by the legislature for its support was a sum so far from sufficient to warrant the adoption of the full course of instruction of West Point, as had been intended, that a system of exchange of instruction was arranged with Washington College (later Washington and Lee University), also at Lexington. In 1846 the system of cooperation with Washington College was discontinued. The growth of the Institute was accompanied by many difficulties. Local merchants resented the establishment of a commissary; Washington College sought to circumscribe its instruction; and Presbyterian Lexington not only looked with disfavor upon the founding by Smith of an Episcopal church in the community but also charged him with sectarian favoritism in the administration of the Institute. So unfriendly was local sentiment that in 1849 the legislature contemplated the removal of the Institute to another location, whereupon the local attitude toward the Institute changed. In the fifties appropriations for buildings were increased, and the faculty was enlarged; in 1859, after a six months' inspection of scientific schools in Europe, Smith recommended the expansion of the

Institute into a general scientific school, publishing a report of his trip as *Special Report of the Superintendent of the Virginia Military Institute: Scientific Education in Europe* (1859). But before final action was taken the Civil War was upon the country.

When, alarmed by the invasion of John Brown (at whose execution Smith was the commanding officer), the state appropriated one-half million dollars for armament, Smith was a member of the commission to supervise the expenditure of the money. With the cadets called into active service at the outbreak of the war, he was appointed a member of the governor's advisory board. At its dissolution in the summer of 1861 he was placed in command of Craney Island, near Norfolk, with the rank of major-general of Virginia Volunteers; he remained there until the reopening of the Institute, January 1862. Although in June 1864 the Institute was burned by the army of Gen. David Hunter [*q.v.*], for part of 1864–65 he carried on its work in Richmond, and in October 1865 saw it reopened in Lexington. In September 1865, just before its reopening, he urged the immediate rebuilding and reorganization of the institution. When a promise of an annual appropriation for current expenses had been secured from the legislature, bonds were issued to the amount of fifty thousand dollars, for the security of which Smith pledged his small estate and the faculty agreed to contribute one-third of its meager salaries. By 1870 the restoration was completed upon a scale superior to that existing before 1864, and in 1884 the bonded debt was assumed by the legislature. After fifty years as superintendent, Smith retired, Dec. 31, 1889. As an educator he attacked the classical type of education prevalent in the South before the war, emphasized the utilitarian aspects of education, and advocated military organization because of its system of discipline. Intensely religious, he presented every graduate with a Bible along with his diploma. He published a series of mathematical textbooks, *An Elementary Treatise on Analytical Geometry* (1840), translated from the French of J. B. Biot, *Best Methods of Conducting the Common Schools* (1849), and *College Reform* (1851). He died in Lexington.

[G. W. Cullum, *Biog. Reg. Officers and Grads. U. S. Mil. Acad.* (1891), vol. I; *In Memoriam: Francis H. Smith, Father and Founder of the Va. Mil. Inst.* (1890); *Reg. Officers and Cadets Va. Mil. Inst., 1860–1873;* F. H. Smith, *The Va. Mil. Inst., Its Building and Rebuilding* (1912); J. C. Wise, *The Mil. Hist. of the Va. Mil. Inst. from 1839 to 1865* (1915); obituaries in *Richmond Dispatch*, Mar. 22, 1890, and *Rockbridge County News* (Lexington, Va.), Mar. 27, 1890.]

W. G. B—n.

SMITH, FRANCIS HOPKINSON (Oct. 23, 1838–Apr. 7, 1915), engineer, artist, writer, was born in Baltimore, Md., the son of Francis and Susan (Teackle) Smith, and a great-grandson of Francis Hopkinson [*q.v.*], poet and signer of the Declaration of Independence for New Jersey. His father, whom he later portrayed in the character of Richard Horn, was a student, a musician and inventor of a musical instrument, a mathematician, and a philosopher. Smith was brought up in the society of quiet Baltimore and received an academic education in preparation for college, but reverses in the family fortunes sent him to work instead, first as a shipping clerk in a hardware store and then as an assistant superintendent in an elder brother's iron foundry. Then came the Civil War, and he removed to New York, where again he worked in the office of a foundry until the unmerciful treatment accorded an unfortunate contractor by his employer so outraged his sense of fair play that he left without the formality of a written resignation. The act was characteristic; years later he sympathized with another under-dog, and after the Dreyfus case refused to exhibit his pictures in Paris. After leaving the foundry he set up independently as an engineer, soon taking as a partner one James Symington, who like himself dabbled in art. Shortly afterwards, on Apr. 26, 1866, he married Josephine Van Deventer of Astoria, N. Y. For about thirty years the firm was engaged in construction work, the greater part of which was for the government. For this exacting client they built the Race Rock lighthouse (an experience later recorded in *Caleb West, Master Diver*), the Block Island breakwater, the sea wall at Tompkinsville, Staten Island (where their contractor was Mary Morgan, the original of the heroine of *Tom Grogan*), and the foundations for the Statue of Liberty, and filled many other marine contracts. Of them all Smith considered the Race Rock lighthouse his greatest achievement. Eight miles out at sea, at a point where the rip raced seven miles an hour, it was enough to stimulate every ingenuity and tax the courage of the engineer. Smith began work on it in 1871; on Jan. 1, 1879, it was finally completed (*Annual Report of the Light-House Board*, 1879, p. 19), a monument to the pertinacity and resourcefulness of its builder.

All this time, in the few spare moments his profession allowed him, he pursued his hobby of painting. He was thankful for whatever time he could snatch, for he believed that a man who has "a passion for art for its own sake and not as a mere means of making money" should enter an occupation that would earn him a livelihood, and should then "in his evenings and on his Sundays . . . take down his Aladdin's lamp and give it a rub," for in this way he kept his art "high and noble, his worthiest and best expression" (*Literary World, post*, 246). He had always had an interest in painting, though except for a few lessons while he was still a schoolboy he was substantially self-taught. In New York he readily made friends among the younger artists and became a member of the famous Tile Club, which included such men of prominence as Edwin Austin Abbey, Elihu Vedder, and William Merritt Chase [*qq.v.*]. He had already illustrated verse from Lowell, Holmes, and Whittier in *Old Lines in New-Black-and White* (copyright 1885), and to *A Book of the Tile Club* (1886), published anonymously, he contributed not only sketches, as did his fellows, but also stories of their adventures. More important than these, since it led directly to his literary life, was *Well-Worn Roads of Spain, Holland, and Italy* (1887), in which he first supplemented his drawings by recollections of the varied life before his canvas. Asked by his publishers for a similar accompaniment to his second series of travel sketches, he produced *A White Umbrella in Mexico* (1889), delightful both in its prose and in its pictures of Mexican life. With the recognition that came to him through these books he found more and more time for painting, and with his wife and daughter spent summers in Spain, in Italy, in Constantinople, always in search of the picturesque. He worked with a rapidity amazing even to professional artists; one summer in Venice, working ten hours a day, he painted a picture a day for fifty-three days (*Ibid.*, p. 245), yet his execution was sure and confident. Haste, of course, was principle to one who believed that the artist must finish his picture before the sun, or his mood could change. His water-colors, especially those of Venice, are wholly charming, and in their delicate tints buoyant with sunny luminescence. But if his most popular work was in water-color—he seldom used oils—perhaps his most effective was in such charcoal studies as those in *Charcoals of New and Old New York* (1912), *In Thackeray's London* (1913), and *In Dickens's London* (1914). These compositions in the contrast of light and shade, faithful to the architecture yet not conventionalized by it, interesting in their deep blacks, and vividly suggestive of the character of the cities, are among the best things he ever did.

Some promise of his literary work is to be found in the descriptions of people and places, and in the stories of tourist luck recorded in an early journal that tells of a trip made through the Virginia mountains in the summer of 1857, when he was eighteen years old. He was over fifty, however, when he published his first book of fiction. The writing of *Colonel Carter of Cartersville* (1891) grew almost by accident out of a decision to put into print some of the after-dinner stories for which he was famous. This delightful story of the old Virginia gentleman, impoverished but not disheartened by the war, was so successful that he abandoned his engineering career as one whose risks and hazards were hardly suited to a man of his advancing years, and the Aladdin's lamp so carefully polished on Saturday afternoons and Sundays now took the place of sea-walls and lighthouses. There followed in a succession quick for one no longer young a long line of travel books, of tales, of short stories, and of longer works of fiction. He was by no means restricted for subject matter to the post-war life of the South but found in his wide experience great variety. The picturesque scene as the traveling artist saw it he portrayed in *A Day at Laguerre's* (1892), *Gondola Days* (1897), and *The Veiled Lady* (1907); artist life in *The Fortunes of Oliver Horn* (1902), partly autobiographical, and *The Wood Fire in No. 3* (1905); the romance of the engineer's profession in *Tom Grogan* (1896), and *Caleb West, Master Diver* (1898); the problem of the effect of divorce upon children in *The Tides of Barnegat* (1906); the Old South during the thirties and forties in *Kennedy Square* (1911); and social contrasts in *The Other Fellow* (1899). His special talent lay in the anecdote, the local-color sketch, and the tale, forms he handled with a sure sympathy for what was picturesque and human. Even his longer stories —save *The Tides of Barnegat,* which alone among them has a tight construction—are simply extensive developments of these forms. Among his many well-rounded characters Colonel Carter, symbol of the patrician Southerner, generous, lovable, genuine, will live as one of the great figures of American literature.

His achievements in such varied fields as engineering, painting, writing, and lecturing—he was one of the most popular lecturers of his time —would have been impossible to one less versatile, less vigorous of mind and body. Thomas Nelson Page [*q.v.*], his old friend, speaks of him as ever in his prime, a man to whom fatigue was unknown and to whom the "infinite capacity for taking pains" was second nature. Revealed in "The Virginia Mountains: A Journal," as a normal, healthy boy, fond of society, yet quite independent, in later life he not only was capable of easy friendliness toward any fellow being but

Smith

also had the ability to retreat into himself in crowded railway stations or in busy London streets. Beneath his distinguished appearance, which suggested the banker or the prosperous merchant more than the artist or author, beneath the brilliance and the wit, he was a steadfast friend, invincibly cheerful, hearty in frequent and breezy laughter, possessed of a quality that was like the sunlight he loved and reflected in all his work. He died in New York, survived by his wife and two sons (*American Art News, post,* p. 5).

[*Who's Who in America,* 1914–15; F. H. Smith, "The Virginia Mountains: A Journal," MS. in the possession of H. V. D. Moore, N. Y. City, and *Capt. Thomas A. Scott* (1908); T. N. Page, in *Scribner's Mag.,* Sept. 1915; E. F. Harkins, in *Lit. World,* Sept. 1904; Clara E. Clement and Laurence Hutton, *Artists of the Nineteenth Century* (1885); Buffalo Fine Arts Acad., *Acad. Notes,* Apr. 1915; *Bookman,* May 1915, with portrait; *Outlook,* Apr. 21, 1915; *Am. Art News,* Apr. 10, 1915 (by Smith's son); *Am. Art Ann.,* 1915; *N. Y. Times,* Apr. 8 (obituary), Apr. 9 (editorial), Apr. 13, 1915 (letter); G. E. Schilling, in *Publisher's Weekly,* Dec. 2, 1922.] C.Y.W., III.

SMITH, FRANCIS MARION (Feb. 2, 1846–Aug. 27, 1931), capitalist, known as "Borax" Smith, was born at Richmond, Wis., the son of Henry G. and Charlotte (Paul) Smith, who had moved to Wisconsin from Rochester, N. Y., in 1842. After attending Milton Academy (later College) at Milton, Wis., in 1863, he remained on his father's farm until 1867, when with a few hundred dollars he went West and for about five years followed mining camps from Montana to Idaho, and then to Nevada and California. In 1872, while cutting timber for mines at Columbus, Nev., he and his partner, William Tell Coleman [*q.v.*], discovered in Teel's Marsh the mineral (colemanite) from which borax is derived. These mines soon became and for many years remained the world's chief source of borax. It was then used mainly by blacksmiths and druggists, and cost between thirty and thirty-five cents an ounce. The partners organized the Pacific Coast Borax Company and through it succeeded in controlling the borax market for a long period. By greatly reducing the price they made borax a household staple. Later Smith acquired colemanite deposits in Death Valley, Cal. From there the product was hauled by mules 164 miles to Mojave, Cal., and the "twenty-mule-team" became a familiar borax trade-mark. In 1910 he settled in Oakland, Cal. There, investing his great profits in public utilities, he brought about a merger of all street-car lines in Alameda and Contra Costa counties, which with the addition of a ferry system from Oakland to San Francisco became the Key Route system. He also opened up large tracts of land for residen-

tial and industrial uses in East Bay cities. In these new activities, however, he soon met financial disaster, and the $20,000,000 fortune that he had accumulated rapidly disappeared. Owing to his crude financial methods and reckless borrowing on short-time notes, he became involved in extended litigation that ended in his bankruptcy. Between 1921 and 1925 he strove, with only partial success, to recoup his fortunes through the acquisition of a newly discovered deposit of colemanite in Clark County, Nev. He also became a political storm center in Oakland and Berkeley through his attempts to acquire rights upon the waterfronts of those cities.

He married Mary R. Thompson of New Jersey in 1875, and in 1901 established in her name the Mary R. Smith Trust to maintain a home for Friendless Girls in Oakland; she died on Dec. 31, 1905. They had no children of their own but had adopted several. Two years later, Jan. 23, 1907, he married Evelyn K. Ellis of Oakland, by whom he had one son and three daughters. For some years he was a trustee of Mills College in Oakland. He founded a magazine, the *Blue Mule,* edited by H. A. Laffler, which flourished for a time. In politics he was a Republican, and served as a presidential elector in 1904 and 1908. He took an active interest in outdoor sports and was a devotee of yachting, especially when at his New York home at Shelter Island; in 1906 he won the cup offered by King Edward VII in the national race off Newport, R. I. He was believed to be on the way to new wealth at the time of his death in Oakland.

[*Who's Who in America,* 1924–25; J. E. Baker, *Past and Present of Alameda County, Cal.* (1914), vol. II; J. M. Guinn, *Hist. of the State of Cal. and Biog. Record of Oakland and Environs* (copr. 1907), vol. II; H. G. Hanks, in *Cal. State Mining Bureau. Third Ann. Report . . . State Mineralogist* (1883), pt. II; *San Francisco: Its Builders, Past and Present* (1913), vol. II, pp. 107–09; obituaries in *San Francisco Chronicle,* Aug. 28, and *Oakland Tribune,* Aug. 27, 1931.] P.O.R.

SMITH, GEORGE (Feb. 10, 1806–Oct. 7, 1899), banker and financier, was born in the parish of Old Deer, Aberdeenshire, Scotland. He appeared in the village of Chicago about the year 1834 and invested what little money he had in lots and wild lands. Following the boom in land values in 1835 and 1836, he had the sagacity to sell his holdings before the slump came in 1837. In 1836 he became associated with, and was in a sense the founder of, the Chicago Marine and Fire Insurance Company. The following year he went back to Scotland and organized the Scottish Illinois Land Investment Company. On his return to America in 1839, he found that the legislature of Illinois had passed a law

267

which suppressed the banking operations of his Chicago corporation. He therefore went to Wisconsin and prevailed upon some friends in the legislature to charter a similar organization. Following the panic of 1837, nearly all the legislatures in the Midwest were dominated by Jackson Democrats, and it was therefore necessary for Smith to obtain a bank charter by stealth. It contained nearly all the powers usually conferred upon insurance companies, but contained a clause that the "corporation may receive money on deposit, and loan the same on 'bottomry, respondentia,' or other satisfactory security, at such rates of interest as may be done by individuals by the law of this territory." The same section, however, contained a proviso that nothing therein contained should give the said company banking privileges. The Wisconsin Marine & Fire Insurance Company was chartered Feb. 28, 1839.

Smith made Alexander Mitchell [q.v.], then a young Scotchman twenty-two years of age, secretary of the company. He soon became the active managing head of the organization. From the beginning the company began doing a general banking business. Its certificates of deposit, which were in fact bank notes, totaled $11,918 in June 1840, but by Dec. 1, 1852, the total outstanding amounted to $1,470,235. Throughout the forties the territorial legislature endeavored to repeal its charter. Mitchell's contention that the legislature could not determine the rights of a company while "acting in the three-fold capacity of a party interested, a jury, and a court" did not fall upon deaf ears, and the matter was never carried to the courts. After Wisconsin became a state, in 1848, the attorney general began *quo warranto* proceedings to test the legality of the charter, but on the promise of either Smith or Mitchell to incorporate as a state bank in the event that the Wisconsin free-banking law was adopted by a vote of the people, proceedings against the company were dropped. In 1853 the Wisconsin Marine & Fire Insurance Company became a state bank. Under the Wisconsin law no bank could issue notes in excess of its capital stock. Smith soon saw that this provision would deprive him of the enormous profits he had made under the old charter, and in 1854 he sold his stock to Alexander Mitchell, and proceeded to Georgia. Here he obtained from the state a charter incorporating a bank of issue located at Atlanta, a rather inaccessible place at that time. He had hoped to make his Chicago institution and Mitchell's bank at Milwaukee the fountainhead of his Atlanta bank, but following the adoption of free-banking in Midwest states, "George

Smith's money" could no longer win the field, and in 1856 he closed out his banking business.

Between that date and the outbreak of the Civil War he made several trips to Scotland. On his last return to America in 1860 he invested his huge fortune in Chicago real estate and the securities of the Rock Island, Northwestern, and St. Paul railroads, which at the time were greatly depreciated, and retired from active business life. His investments were wisely chosen, for at his death in 1899 estimates of his fortune ran as high as $100,000,000. None was lower than $50,000,000. Although a man's fortune may be no test of his worth to society, Smith's contributions to the development of the West were very great. During the troublesome days of wildcat money, the credit of George Smith & Company was as good as the government's and better than that of most states. The rapid economic expansion of Wisconsin and Illinois in the forties would not have been possible without the aid of "George Smith's money." From 1860 to his death, he divided his time between his castle in the Scottish Highlands and the Reform Club of London. He never married and had no close relatives. He died at the Reform Club in London.

[Horace White, "An Elastic Currency," in *Proc. of the Nineteenth Ann. Convention of the Am. Bankers' Asso.* (1893); *Milwaukee Sentinel,* Aug. 18, 1893, Oct. 9, 1899; *Chicago Tribune,* Oct. 9, 1899; A. T. Andreas, *Hist. of Chicago,* vol. I (1884); J. D. Butler, "Alexander Mitchell, the Financier," in *Colls. of the State Hist. Soc. of Wis.,* vol. XI (1888); J. J. Knox, *A Hist. of Banking in the U. S.* (1900); E. B. Usher, *Wis. Its Story and Biog.* (1914); original record books of the Wis. Marine & Fire Insurance Company in State Hist. Library, Madison.]
                            L.B.K.

SMITH, GEORGE HENRY (Oct. 20, 1873–Jan. 9, 1931), newspaper writer and author of humorous juvenile stories, was born at Knoxville, Tenn., the son of George Henry Smith, a jeweler, and his second wife Annie (Ramage) Smith. He was a grandson of the Rev. Richard and Maria (Stribley) Smith of London, England, who settled in Horseheads, N. Y., about 1828, and is said to have been a descendant of Sir Richard Grenville. His grandparents on his mother's side were Mary (Cowan) and Joseph Ramage of Philadelphia, the latter a descendant of French Huguenots who settled in the north of Ireland. When he was three years old his father died; five years later his mother remarried, and he was sent to boarding school. He later attended University School, Knoxville, studied under private tutors, traveled in America and the British Isles, and after four years at Yale received the degree of B.A. in 1899. At seventeen he was a reporter on the *Knoxville Journal,* and before he entered college he was writing for the

Knoxville Sentinel and the *Chattanooga News.* He became traveling representative for the Lyman D. Morse Advertising Agency of New York, 1899, and a year later established an independent advertising and publishing business. He founded and was president of the Writer's Aid Association, 1901–03. For four years, 1903–07, he was solicitor for schools with the advertising department of the *New York Times.* He then became New York representative of the Chronicle Publishing Company of Orange, N. J., 1907–09.

On Apr. 8, 1901, in New Haven, Conn., he married Harriet Clarke Sanford, daughter of Rev. Elihu Turney Sanford and Harriet Ford (Clarke) Sanford. His success in entertaining the eldest of his four children with droll bedtime stories disclosed an unsuspected talent for interesting children and led him directly into a special field of newspaper work. His stories, which first began to appear in the *Globe* (New York) in 1909, were syndicated and appeared daily in many newspapers throughout America under the pen name of "Farmer Smith" and "Uncle Henry." He became children's editor on the *Globe,* 1909–15, and held similar posts successively on the *New York Evening Mail,* 1915; the *Public Ledger* (Philadelphia), 1915–17; the *Philadelphia Record,* 1918–19; the *Newark Ledger,* 1920–23; the *Daily Graphic* (New York), 1925–27; and the *Brooklyn Standard-Union,* 1928–31. During these years he also contributed special articles to the *Evening World* (New York), 1905–30, and reviewed motion pictures for the *Newark Ledger,* 1923–25. He published three collections of his early stories: *Daddy's Goodnight Stories* (1910), *Oh, Look Who's Here* (1911), and *The Dollie Stories* (1912). In 1915, while he was children's editor of the *Ledger,* he formed the "Farmer Smith Rainbow Club," which he developed from a clever advertising stunt into an organization providing wholesome occupation and amusement for its many thousands of youthful members. At the entrance of the United States into the World War he was asked to aid in the mobilization of children in war work. In 1917 he founded the National Children's Committee and assisted in the organization of the Junior Red Cross; in 1918 he conducted a speaking campaign in the South to increase membership in the Junior Red Cross. He died in Maplewood, N. J., of heart disease, survived by his wife, two daughters, and one son.

[*Hist. of Class of Eighteen Hundred Ninety-Nine, Yale Coll.,* vol. IV (1919); *Obit. Record Grads. of Yale Univ.,* 1930–31; *Editor & Publisher and the Journalist,* Apr. 22, 1916; obituary in *N. Y. Times,* Jan. 10, 1931; unpublished diaries, 1890–94, and undated newspaper clippings in the possession of Mrs. R. H. Smith; correspondence with Mrs. Smith.]   V. L. S.

SMITH, GERALD BIRNEY (May 3, 1868–Apr. 3, 1929), theologian, was born at Middlefield, Mass., the son of Metcalf John and Harriet Louise (Eldredge) Smith, and a descendant of Matthew Smith who emigrated to Massachusetts from England in 1637. He was a nephew of Judson Smith [*q.v.*]. His early training was in the public schools of Middlefield, and in the home of his father, a man of college education, with advanced views but trusted in his community, given to philosophizing. After graduating with the degree of A.B. from Brown University in 1891, he taught Latin in Oberlin Academy for one year, and mathematics and foreign languages at Worcester Academy for three years. On July 10, 1894, he married Inez Michener of New Sharon, Iowa. Entering Union Theological Seminary, he was graduated with the degree of B.D. in 1898 and awarded a traveling fellowship for the next two years in Europe. These years of study took him to Berlin, Marburg, and Paris. Upon his return he was called to the divinity school of the University of Chicago, where he passed through the ranks from instructor to professor. On Nov. 23, 1902, he was ordained to the Baptist ministry.

In his early years, following the German study, he was greatly influenced by the Ritschlian point of view, especially as that was infused with the mystical piety of his own teacher, Herrmann. His stress upon experience rather than on Biblical teaching as a basis for theology led him, however, more and more into a recognition of the claims of scientific and democratic ideals. In a monograph entitled *Practical Theology* (1903) he still insisted that the interests of science and of practical religion are in conflict and urged a new department to adapt the scientific findings of critical theology to the religious needs of men. He made an essay in this direction, collaborating with two Biblical scholars, E. D. Burton and J. M. P. Smith, in a study of the Atonement (*Biblical Ideas of Atonement: Their History and Significance,* 1909), in which he wrote the final section on the value of these critical findings for vital religious experience.

In 1912 he delivered the Taylor Lectures at Yale, published the following year under the title *Social Idealism and the Changing Theology* (1913), the purpose of which was "to show how and why the change from aristocratic to democratic ideals has taken place, and to indicate wherein an understanding of the significance of this ethical evolution may aid in the reconstruction of theology" (p. x). Here he threw down the glove to authoritarianism, and from that time on his efforts were constantly to find a vital religion which should not rest upon authoritative dogma. He initiated the project of the volume which he edited, *A Guide to the Study of the Christian Religion* (1916), in order to help pastors "to keep in sympathetic touch with the latest scholarship." Later, he brought this task up to date by editing what in a way was a supplementary volume, *Religious Thought in the Last Quarter-Century* (1927). His own chapter in the *Guide* is really a systematic prolegomenon to an empirical theology which is throughout set over against the method of authority. What this chapter does for theology his *Principles of Christian Living* (1924) does for Christian ethics. "The ethical life," he affirms, "is one of inquiry as well as one of obedience to formal principles" (p. 4). His last book was a brief but meaty work called *Current Christian Thinking* (1928), in which, after a trenchantly critical survey of various contemporary appeals to authority, he offered a thoroughly empirical approach to theological reconstruction.

As a theologian Smith was scrupulously honest in research and penetrating in his grasp and criticism of controversial literature, but he always united these qualities with a rare sense for spiritual power from which he ever feared that scholarship might be divorced. He never developed a system of theology, feeling that the fluid state of scientific research did not permit this; and he sought to give his students a method of critical and constructive thinking rather than a body of conclusions. As a teacher he was systematic and incisive, patient but intolerant of humbug, and inspired his students to do independent thinking. As a man he was genial and endowed with a rich sense of humor, extremely broad in his interests and always conveying the impression of balance and humaneness. He was very fond of sports. For several years he was chairman of the University Orchestral Association; he was president of the board of the University of Chicago Settlement, a sponsor of a history of his native town, and adviser to the Religious Education Association. With Shailer Mathews, in 1921, he edited *A Dictionary of Religion and Ethics*. As managing editor of the *American Journal of Theology* from 1909 to 1920, and editor of the *Journal of Religion* from 1921 until his sudden death at the height of his powers, he struck a balance between sound scholarship and concern for popular religious needs. He was survived by his wife and one son.

[Sources include P. M. Smith and E. C. Smith, *A Hist. of the Town of Middlefield, Mass.* (1924); S. S. Martin, *Mack Geneal.* (2 vols., 1903–04); *Alumni Cat. of the Union Theological Seminary* (1926); *Hist. Cat. of Brown Univ.* (1905); *Who's Who in America, 1928–29*; *Baptist* (Chicago), Apr. 13, 1929; *The Divinity Student* (Univ. of Chicago Divinity School), vols. VI (1929), VIII (1931). For revelation of Smith's personality see his article, "The Professor and the Fundamentalist," *Christian Century*, Nov. 11, 1926.]
E. E. A—y.

SMITH, GERRIT (Mar. 6, 1797–Dec. 28, 1874), philanthropist and reformer, was born at Utica, N. Y., the grandson of James Livingston [*q.v.*] and the son of Elizabeth (Livingston) and Peter Smith [*q.v.*]. In 1806 the family moved to Peterboro, Madison County, N. Y., where Smith spent the greater part of his adult life. He graduated from Hamilton College in 1818 and helped his father manage the substantial fortune, the product of shrewd land purchases. On Jan. 11, 1819, he married Wealthy Ann Backus, the daughter of Azel Backus [*q.v.*]. She died the next August, and on Jan. 3, 1822, he married Ann Carroll Fitzhugh. Of their four children, only two lived to maturity. In 1826 he became a member of the Presbyterian Church.

He succeeded to the entire control of his father's property, which, real and personal, was valued at about $400,000, and was able to increase it in amount and in value. His father, melancholy and later estranged from his second wife who had gone back to Charleston, S. C., to live, withdrew into himself more and more. Smith used his wealth, in so far as he could find guidance on the subject from prayer and from his own conscience, for what he considered the good of mankind. For a time he helped to build churches, and he gave generously to several theological schools and to various colleges. He experimented with systematic charity on a large scale, giving both land and money to needy men and women throughout his own state (see sketch of James McCune Smith); but his carefully selected "indigent females" made poor farmers, and the blacks whom he tried to colonize in the Adirondack wilderness found the environment unsuited to their needs. Much of the property he disposed of in this work was subsequently sold for non-payment of taxes.

His greatest reputation was made in the field of reform. He labored in the cause of the Sunday School and of Sunday observance; he was an anti-Mason; he advocated vegetarianism; and he opposed the use of tobacco and alcoholic beverages; he joined the national dress reform association and the woman's suffrage cause; he believed in prison reform and in the abolition of capital punishment. He contributed to home and foreign missions and to the causes of the oppressed Greeks, the Italians, and the Irish. Through his influence his cousin, Elizabeth Cady Stanton [q.v.], was interested in temperance and abolition movements. He was vice-president of the American Peace Society and advocated compensated emancipation of slaves. He joined the anti-slavery crusade in 1835 with his customary enthusiasm, and he became one of the best-known abolitionists in the United States. Although on terms of intimate friendship with William Lloyd Garrison, he never went to the extremes of the Garrison group; but he was always ready to help escaped slaves to Canada and in 1851 participated in the "Jerry rescue" in Syracuse. After the enactment of the Kansas-Nebraska law he joined the Kansas Aid Societies in New York, and he helped Eli Thayer's New England Emigrant Aid Company in Massachusetts. This work cost him at least fourteen thousand dollars; how much more it is difficult to determine. In spite of his advocacy of peace, he urged the use of force against the pro-slavery contingent in Kansas, and forcible resistance to the federal authorities there, because, as he said, the federal government upheld the pro-slavery cause. In February 1858 John Brown went to Smith's home in Peterboro, not to plan his campaign in Virginia but to obtain Smith's moral and financial support for plans already made. On this occasion, at a second visit in April 1859, and in several letters, Smith gave Brown assurance of his approval and some money. After the raid at Harpers Ferry, Smith became temporarily insane. He made a quick recovery, however, and six months later he was in his usual good health. From then on to the end of his life he denied complicity in Brown's plot, but the available evidence bears out newspaper charges made at the time, that he was an accessory before the fact.

Unlike the Garrisonians, he believed in political action as a means of reform, and for a full fifty years, from 1824 to 1874, he took an active part in politics. He was one of the leaders in forming the Liberty party; in 1840 he was its candidate for governor. In 1848 the "true" Liberty party men, those who refused to indorse the Free Soil "heresy," nominated him for the presidency, though he declined. In 1852 he was elected a member of Congress on an independent ticket and served from Mar. 4, 1853, to Aug. 7, 1854, when he resigned. In 1858 he ran for governor on the "People's State Ticket," advocating temperance, anti-slavery, and land reform. During the Civil War he wrote and spoke often in support of the Union cause. This work led him gradually into the Republican party, so that he campaigned for Lincoln's reëlection in 1864

and for Grant in 1868. In reconstruction he advocated a policy of moderation toward the Southern whites with suffrage for the blacks. In 1867 he was one of the signers of the bail bond to release Jefferson Davis from captivity. He published many of his speeches and letters on important subjects. Of his published books the more important are: *Religion of Reason* (1864), an exposition of his later religion of Nature or Rationalism; *Speeches of Gerrit Smith in Congress* (1856); and the two volumes (1864–65) of his *Speeches and Letters of Gerrit Smith on the Rebellion*. He died in New York City.

[Family papers in Lib. of Syracuse Univ.; O. B. Frothingham, *Gerrit Smith* (1878); 2nd ed. (1879) "corrected" by Smith's daughter in order to bring it into harmony with the family belief that Smith was not an accomplice of John Brown; C. A. Hammond, *Gerrit Smith* (1900); K. W. Porter, *John Jacob Astor* (2 vols., 1931); *Appletons' Ann. Cyc.*, 1874; R. V. Harlow, "Gerrit Smith and the John Brown Raid" and "Rise and Fall of the Kansas Aid Movement," *Am. Hist. Rev.*, Oct. 1932, Oct. 1935; *N. Y. Tribune*, Dec. 29–30, 1874.]   R. V. H.

SMITH, GILES ALEXANDER (Sept. 29, 1829–Nov. 5, 1876), Union soldier, was born in Jefferson County, N. Y. He was the son of Cyrus and Laura (Wales) Smith and a brother of Morgan Lewis Smith [q.v.], and was descended from Ignatius Smith, who emigrated to Cape Cod probably in the first half of the eighteenth century. About 1847 he went to London, Ohio, but soon afterwards moved to Cincinnati, where he engaged in the dry-goods business. Shortly after his marriage, July 31, 1856, to Martha McLain of London, Ohio, he removed to Bloomington, Ill., continuing in the dry-goods business until 1859, when he became the proprietor of a hotel. On June 4, 1861, he entered the military service as captain of Company D, 8th Missouri Volunteers, his brother's regiment, and took part in the capture of Forts Henry and Donelson, in the battle of Shiloh, and in the siege of Corinth. He was promoted lieutenant-colonel, June 12, 1862, and, on the promotion of his brother to brigadier-general, succeeded him, June 30, as colonel of the regiment. In Sherman's expedition against Vicksburg, December 1862, the command of a brigade devolved upon Smith during the assault on Chickasaw Bluffs, and he retained that command during the operations terminating in the capture of Arkansas Post, his soldierly conduct in that capacity drawing commendation from Sherman. In Grant's operations against Vicksburg he particularly distinguished himself by the rescue of the gunboat flotilla which, while trying to force a passage to the Yazoo, had been trapped in Steele's Bayou by the Confederates. He was promoted brigadier-general of volunteers, Aug. 4, 1863, for gallant and meritorious conduct in the field. On Nov. 24, 1863, at Chattanooga, he seized a position on the south bank of the Tennessee River by a skilful maneuver and covered the crossing of Sherman's corps. Later in the day, in the first assault on Missionary Ridge, he was severely wounded. In the Atlanta campaign he distinguished himself at Resaca, and on July 20, 1864, he was transferred to command the 2nd Division, XVII Corps. When two days later the battle of Atlanta was fought, the brunt of the attack fell on his division, and the repulse of the Confederates was largely due to its heroic conduct. He led his division in the march to the sea and in the Carolina campaign, and was brevetted major-general of volunteers, Sept. 1, 1864. After the collapse of the Confederacy he was stationed in Texas. He was promoted major-general of volunteers, Nov. 24, 1865. When the volunteer forces were disbanded he declined a commission as colonel of cavalry in the regular army and returned to his home in Bloomington.

He was appointed second assistant postmaster general in 1869 but resigned in 1872 because of failing health. Though he removed to California in 1874 in the hope of checking the progress of disease, he returned to his old home in Bloomington two months before his death. He possessed a natural soldierly aptitude. Under the tutelage of his brother and the experience of war he advanced rapidly by merit alone, and won esteem for his gallantry and completeness as an officer. His superiors generally took it for granted that any mission assigned him would be well performed, and there was no occasion when this confidence was not justified by the result.

[F. A. Virkus, *The Compendium of Am. Geneal.*, vol. V (1933); F. B. Heitman, *Hist. Reg. and Dict. of the U. S. Army* (1903); *Report of Proc. Soc. of the Army of the Tenn. Eleventh Ann. Meeting, 1877* (1885); *Memoirs of Gen. W. T. Sherman* (2 vols., 2nd ed., revised, 1886); *War of the Rebellion: Off. Records* (*Army*); *Battles and Leaders of the Civil War* (4 vols., 1888); U. S. Pension Office records, for name of wife and date of marriage; obituaries in *St. Louis Globe-Democrat* and *Daily Inter Ocean* (Chicago, Ill.), Nov. 6, 1876; family records.] T. F. M.

SMITH, GUSTAVUS WOODSON (March 1822–June 24, 1896), civil and military engineer, Confederate officer, was born in Georgetown, Scott County, Ky., the son of Byrd and Sarah Hatcher (Woodson) Smith. His grandfather, John Smith, had emigrated to Kentucky from Virginia with Daniel Boone. On the maternal side he was a descendant of John Woodson who came to America before 1679. He entered the United States Military Academy from Virginia and was graduated in 1842 as a second lieutenant, Corps of Engineers. He was assigned to duty at New London, Conn., where he served two years as an assistant engineer on the construction of fortifications, and was then ordered to West Point as an instructor in civil and military engineering. On Oct. 3, 1844, he was married to Lucretia Bassett, the daughter of Capt. Abner Bassett, of New London, Conn. They had no children. Upon the outbreak of the Mexican War, he was detailed to assist Capt. Alexander J. Swift to recruit and train the sole company of engineers in the army. Shortly after reaching Mexico, Captain Swift was invalided and the command devolved upon Smith. The engineer-soldiers were employed in converting the infamous mule paths of northern Mexico into passable roads until March 1847, when they joined Scott's expedition at Vera Cruz. Smith was cited for distinguished services at Vera Cruz, Cerro Gordo, Contreras, Churubusco, and Mexico City, and was brevetted, successively, first lieutenant, captain, and major, the last brevet being disapproved by the war department. Upon the conclusion of peace he returned to West Point as assistant professor of engineering.

He resigned on Dec. 18, 1854, to join, it is said, the Cuban filibustering expedition of John Anthony Quitman [*q.v.*]. This expedition proved still-born, and Smith accepted a treasury department appointment to supervise the repairs to the mint and the construction of the marine hospital in New Orleans, La. A year later he became associated with the engineering firm of Cooper and Hewitt in New York City, and served them as chief engineer of the Trenton Iron Works. He was appointed street commissioner for New York City in 1858, served until 1861, and soon achieved prominence in the councils of the Democratic party. He served on a board to revise the program of instruction at West Point in 1860. He participated in the Pine Street meeting of citizens of New York to devise measures to avert civil war, and favored the Crittenden Compromise. In the late summer of 1861, having been stricken with paralysis in April, he set out for Hot Springs, Ark., upon the advice of his physician. At Lexington, Ky., he learned that his arrest as a disloyal person had been ordered from Washington. This determined him to join the Confederacy, and he proceeded at once to Richmond, where he was appointed, Sept. 19, 1861, a major-general in the provisional army.

He commanded one wing of the Army of the Potomac until the conclusion of the Peninsular Campaign. After General Johnston was wounded during the battle of Seven Pines on May 31, 1862, he commanded as senior officer until General Lee's arrival on June 1. On June 2, he suffered another attack of paralysis. His relief by Lee caused the renewal of a quarrel with President Davis, which had originated over the appointment of his aide-de-camp the previous year. In August 1862 he was placed in command of the sector from the right of Lee's theatre of operations on the Rappahannock to the Cape Fear River, with headquarters in Richmond. He acted as secretary of war from Nov. 17 to Nov. 20. In consequence of the promotion of six officers over his head and presidential interference with details of his command, he resigned on Feb. 17, 1863. He served a short time as a volunteer aide to Beauregard in Charleston, and then became superintendent of the Etowah Mining and Manufacturing Company in north Georgia. In June 1864, he accepted an appointment as major-general to command the 1st Division, Georgia Militia, which was attached to the Army of Tennessee. After the fall of Atlanta, his division was employed in observation of Sherman's army, falling back before it during the famous march to the sea. On Dec. 30, 1864, he was assigned a sector in the defenses of the department of South Carolina, Georgia, and Florida. He surrendered to the Wilson raiders at Macon, Ga., in April 1865.

After the war, he gave testimony on Jan. 30, 1867, before the Congressional committee investigating the affairs of Southern railroads. He was employed as general manager of the Southwestern Iron Company at Chattanooga, Tenn., from 1866 until 1870, when he was appointed as the first insurance commissioner of Kentucky. He held this office for five years, and then moved to New York City, where he resided until his death. He was the author of *Notes on Life Insurance* (1870), *Confederate War Papers* (1884), *The Battle of Seven Pines* (1891), *Generals J. E. Johnston and G. T. Beauregard . . . at Manassas* (1892), and *Company "A," Corps of Engineers, U. S. A., . . . in the Mexican War* (1896).

[H. M. Woodson, *Hist. Geneal. of the Woodsons* (1915); G. W. Cullum, *Biog. Reg. . . . U. S. Mil. Acad.* (1891); *U. S. Army Register*, 1839; C. S. Stewart, in *Ann. Reunion, Asso. Grads., U. S. Mil. Acad.*, 1897 (1897); C. M. Wilcox, *Hist. of the Mexican War* (1892); *War of the Rebellion: Official Records (Army)*, see index; M. J. Wright, *Gen. Officers of the Confed. Army* (1911); *Confed. Mil. Hist.* (1899), vol. I; *House Report No. 34*, 39 Cong., 2 Sess. An obituary article in *Appletons' Ann. Cyclop.*, 1896 (1897), gives June 23 as the date of Smith's death. See, however, the Augusta *Chronicle*, June 26, 1896.]   W. M. R., Jr.

SMITH, HAMILTON (July 5, 1840–July 4, 1900), mining engineer, was the grandson of Valentine Smith, a judge at Durham, N. H.,

where the family had been established for over a century. His father, also named Hamilton Smith, was trained in the law and went to Louisville, Ky., where he practised with brilliant success. He married Martha, daughter of William Hall of Bellows Falls, Vt., and their son, the second Hamilton Smith, was born near Louisville. His mother died when he was small, his father married again, and at the age of six the boy was sent back to his grandfather at Durham, where he attended the village school. Meanwhile his father had established a cotton factory and coal mines at Cannelton, Ind., and there Hamilton was sent, in his fourteenth year, to acquire a mastery of those enterprises through experience in their engineering and accounting departments. Industrious, competent, and with unusual aptitude for mathematics, he soon demonstrated his ability, and at an early age was recognized as the chief of the engineering and accounting departments of the Cannelton coal mines.

During the sixties, he was engaged in developing other collieries in Kentucky and Indiana, but in 1869 was attracted to the Pacific Coast by its apparently greater opportunities. His first work there was as engineer and manager of the Triunfo mine in Lower California, but his most notable was at the North Bloomfield and Milton gold mines in Nevada County, Cal., which were worked by hydraulic methods. There he became the recognized authority on hydraulics in California. He was also active in efforts to reduce the cost of high explosives and in the establishment of the Vulcan Powder Works. Attracting the favorable attention of Baron Rothschild, who made a visit of inspection to the properties, he became consulting mining engineer for the Rothschild interests. For them he reported on the El Callao mine, Venezuela, in 1881, and then developed it and supervised its operation. In 1885 he opened a consulting office in London, in partnership with Edmund de Crano, and there in 1886 published his notable treatise, *Hydraulics: The Flow of Water through Orifices, over Weirs, and through Open Conduits and Pipes*. The same year he married Mrs. Charles Congreve (*née* Jennings, of New Orleans), and also, with his partner, organized the Exploration Company, Ltd. His paper, "Costs of Mining and Milling Free Gold Ores," published in the *Engineering and Mining Journal*, Sept. 4, 1886, attracted wide attention, and the Exploration Company soon became an important factor in the development of mines throughout the world, but notably in South Africa, where gold had been discovered in 1885. Many of the engineers who built up the gold industry in Africa entered that field through their previous association with Hamilton Smith's earlier mining ventures. His own work was done mostly in London, but he visited South Africa in 1892 and 1895, and was the author of important papers on conditions there, especially on the possibility of mining at deep levels. Subsequent events showed his views to be sound. He introduced into the British market the securities of notable American mining enterprises, he participated in the organization of many important mines, formed the Fraser & Chalmers mining machinery company, at Erith, England, and also organized the Central London Railway. After the death of Edmund de Crano in 1895, he took H. C. Perkins into partnership and soon moved the firm's offices to New York, though he spent much time in Washington, D. C., California, and New Hampshire. At the time of his death at Durham, N. H., from accidental drowning, he was engaged in attempting to develop the Mariposa grant in California, acquired by John Charles Frémont [q.v.] a half-century before, but long in litigation. Besides his treatise on hydraulics, he contributed three important papers on hydraulics to the *Transactions of the American Society of Civil Engineers:* "The Flow of Water through Pipes" (vol. XII, 1883), "Water Power with High Pressures and Wrought-Iron Water-Pipe," and "Temperature of Water at Various Depths in Lakes and Oceans" (vol. XIII, 1884). An accomplished engineer himself, he is perhaps more notable as an outstanding factor in bringing about the employment of American engineers at mines in the British dominions and in securing the participation of British capital in financing mines in the United States and Alaska.

[*Trans. Am. Soc. Civil Engineers,* vol. XLVI (1901); *Minutes of Proc. of the Inst. of Civil Engineers* (London), vol. CXLII (1900); *Trans. Am. Inst. Mining Engineers,* vol. XXXI (1901); *Engineering and Mining Journal,* July 7, 14, 28, 1900; *Manchester Union* (Manchester, N. H.), July 5, 1900.]   T. T. R.

SMITH, HANNAH WHITALL (Feb. 7, 1832–May 1, 1911), author, religious interpreter, reformer, was born in Philadelphia, Pa., the daughter of John Mickle and Mary (Tatum) Whitall. Her first known American ancestor was James Whitall, who in 1688 was living near Philadelphia. Both branches of her family had for many generations been members of the Society of Friends (Quakers). Her home was characterized by a blending of broad culture with spiritual piety of an unusual depth, the double effect of which was apparent in her throughout her life; her biography is in large degree the story of the development of an interior life. In 1848 at the age of sixteen she had a mystical

awakening which she described in her "spiritual autobiography" as the "first epoch" in her religious life, and which she later came to regard as a period of "morbid self-introspection." It lasted until her marriage, June 25, 1851, to Robert Pearsall Smith of Philadelphia, son of John Jay Smith [q.v.]. He was a glass manufacturer who also had a deep interest in religion and in later life became a noted religious leader and widely read author. Their children, in addition to a daughter who died young, were Franklin Whitall, Logan Pearsall, Alys, who married Bertrand Russell, and Mary Logan, who married Bernhard Berenson. The death of her son Franklin Whitall in 1872 was the occasion of her writing *The Record of a Happy Life: Being Memorials of Franklin Whitall Smith* (1873). In 1858, after a period of scepticism, she passed through the second epoch of her religious life. Coming under the influence of the Plymouth Brethren she entered into an "assurance of faith," which at the time gave her peace and serenity, and freedom from self-examination. In her "third epoch," not many years later, she made a momentous discovery, which she described as the discovery of "the unselfishness of God." It carried with it for her a belief in a final restitution of all things and every person, and gave her a temporary reputation of being a heretic. In 1865, when the family moved from their home in Germantown, Pa., to a small New Jersey town, Millville, where they were cut off from the associations they had enjoyed, she went through a period of great dissatisfaction and unhappiness. This in 1865 brought her to the fourth and final "epoch," a religious stage which she called the "higher life" or the "life of faith," a life of "absolute consecration, entire obedience, and simple trust" (*The Unselfishness of God,* p. 276). It was out of this ripe experience that she produced somewhat later the book that was always associated with her name, *The Christian's Secret of a Happy Life* (1875). Translated into every language of Europe and into a number of Oriental languages, it went through numerous editions, had an almost fabulous circulation, and made the writer known around the world. A few years later she published *John M. Whitall, the Story of His Life* (1879).

She and her husband had both begun to preach. They now had remarkable non-sectarian meetings "for the deepening of the spiritual life" in America, in England, and on the continent of Europe, their work in Europe reaching its highest point during the years of 1873 and 1874. As a preacher she was practical, explicit, and simple. Throughout her life she had a marked capacity, based largely on the practical character of her own nature, for recognizing what was insincere, fanatical, perverted, or misguided in religious enthusiasm, and she left an interesting collection of papers in which she recorded her observations, published in 1928 as *Religious Fanaticism: Extracts from the Papers of Hannah Whitall Smith.* She was an ardent reformer, working zealously for peace, for temperance, and for the widening of the sphere and scope of the influence of women. In 1886 the family settled permanently in England, and there she continued to live after the death of her husband in 1898. In 1903 she published her book on *The Unselfishness of God and How I Discovered It,* ner "spiritual autobiography." Growing in breadth and wisdom with the years, she came to see that it was a mistake to expect all persons to pass through any one path of religious experience. The later years of peace and tranquillity were marked by an influence not less impressive than in the period of prominent public service at home and abroad. She died at Iffley, where she had lived since 1905.

[C. E. Pearsall, H. M. Pearsall, and H. L. Neall, *Hist. and Geneal. of the Pearsall Family* (1928), vol. II; R. M. Smith, *The Burlington Smiths* (1877); H. W. Smith, *The Unselfishness of God and How I Discovered It* (copr. 1903), *John M. Whitall, the Story of His Life* (1879), and *The Christian's Secret of a Happy Life* (1875); Ray Strachey, *A Quaker Grandmother: Hannah Whitall Smith* (copr. 1914) and *Religious Fanaticism: Extracts from the Papers of Hannah Whitall Smith* (1928), ed.; *Am. Friend,* May 11, 1911; death notices in *Pub. Ledger* (Phila.), May 4, and the *Times* (London), May 3, 1911.]   R.M.J.

SMITH, HAROLD BABBITT (May 23, 1869–Feb. 9, 1932), electrical engineer, educator, was born in Barre, Mass., the son of Samuel Francis and Julia Asenath (Babbitt) Smith. He claimed descent in the sixth generation from Capt. Joseph Smith who led a company of Sudbury Minutemen at Lexington, and in the ninth, from Richard Smith who settled in Ipswich, Mass., about 1640. From the Barre High School, Smith went to Cornell University and was graduated in 1891 with the degree of mechanical engineer. After further study at Cornell, he became in 1892 professor of electrical engineering at the University of Arkansas, but resigned after about a year to become head designer and electrical engineer for the Elektron Manufacturing Company of Springfield, Mass. A few months later he was appointed professor of electrical engineering at Purdue University, where he founded the department and served as director of the School of Engineering until 1896. In that year he joined the faculty of Worcester Polytechnic Institute, where he established the elec-

trical engineering department and continued as its head until his retirement on account of ill health in January 1931. Under his able direction this department flourished and received national recognition; the electrical engineering laboratories constructed and installed at Worcester under his supervision were the finest of their kind in the country. Smith was a pioneer in electrical engineering education; a number of his students became heads of electrical engineering departments in other institutions, and many achieved distinction in the engineering field.

While successfully carrying on his academic work, Smith became prominent in the electrical manufacturing industry. He maintained an active practice as consulting engineer and traveled extensively. From 1905 to 1913 he held the double position of engineer and designer for the Westinghouse Electric & Manufacturing Company of Pittsburgh, Pa. An innovator in the development of high-voltage power transmissions and equipment, he carried on extensive research in dielectric phenomena and electric stress distribution. He was also concerned with the design of direct-current generators and motors and alternating-current transformers, and held many patents. During the World War he was an associate member of the Naval Consulting Board, and a consulting engineer for the special board on anti-submarine devices.

Smith's was a strong character, ambitious, and sometimes considered ruthless. He made bitter enemies and loyal friends. He was chosen president of the American Institute of Electrical Engineers in 1929, the highest honor his national society could confer upon him. He was a member of the American Engineering Council and belonged also to a number of other professional organizations. He was the author of numerous monographs and shorter articles contributed to engineering societies and periodicals, one of his best-known papers being "The Development of a Suspension-Type Insulator" (*Journal of the American Institute of Electrical Engineers,* August 1924). He was twice married: first, at Ithaca, N. Y., June 15, 1894, to Laura Bertha, daughter of Samuel and Ann (Saunders) Smith, and after her death in April 1910, to Persis Helen Smith of New York City, Sept. 28, 1911. The second marriage was ended by a divorce in 1930. There were three children. Smith was a member of the Unitarian Church.

[*Jour. Am. Inst. Elec. Engineers,* July 1929; *Electrical World,* Sept. 24, 1927 and Dec. 15, 1928; *Jour. Worcester Polytechnic Inst.,* Feb., Apr. 1932; *Who's Who in America.* 1930–31; *Who's Who in Engineering,* 1931; *N. Y. Times,* Feb. 10, 1932; information from friends and associates in Worcester.] T.H.M.

SMITH, HARRY JAMES (May 24, 1880–Mar. 16, 1918), playwright, novelist, seventh of nine children of John B. and Lucy F. (Nichols) Smith, was born in New Britain, Conn. He attended the public schools there, taught for a few months in the district school at Cornwall Hollow, Conn., and in 1898 entered Williams College. There he specialized in biology, studied one summer at Woods Hole, and the year after graduation (1902–03) was assistant in the biological laboratory. This scientific training was far from wasted, as it served later to balance his romantic zest in life and to supply an underlying realistic attitude in his writing. After a year's post-graduate work in English at Harvard, where he received the degree of M.A. in 1904, he became instructor in English composition (1904–05) at Oberlin. He proved to be a brilliant teacher, intuitively dramatizing his work and carrying his classes with him by his spontaneous enthusiasm. His purpose was set toward writing, however, and after a year he gave up teaching and declined every later inducement to return to it. A year of free lancing in New York City was followed by one on the editorial staff of the *Atlantic Monthly* and several more in New York. In 1909, however, after a severe illness, he retired from the city, whose thrill he loved while its din tormented his exacerbated nerves, to the peaceful surroundings of home in Berlin, Conn. Here, while still near enough to permit frequent visits to the metropolis, he was able to be with his family, to which his unusually tender devotion drew him all the closer through the fact that he never married.

Meanwhile, in 1908 appeared his first novel, *Amédée's Son,* an idyllic tale of the Cape Breton coast which he had visited, to escape from severe hay fever, nearly every summer after boyhood. This was followed in 1910 by *Enchanted Ground,* a novel of New York City, turning on the contrast between the bleak morality of New England and the morally dissolvent fascination of New York. Then, in 1910–11, came the extraordinary success of his comedy, *Mrs. Bumpstead-Leigh,* written for Mrs. Fiske. After this there were lean years; partially because of managerial incompetence, his plays *Blackbirds, Suki,* and *Oh! Imogen* were not successful; but in 1917 *A Tailor-Made Man* repeated the success of *Mrs. Bumpstead-Leigh*—two of the wittiest comedies America has produced—and *The Little Teacher,* produced in 1918, was also successful.

These dramas were all comedies of manners, the flash of wit playing over not too profound situations of human interest. While Harry Smith could appreciate Ibsen and Shaw, in his own work he deliberately avoided every semblance of the problem play. Battling with constant ill health, he had won a degree of fame and fortune, and, what was more dear to him, a command of the playwright's craft, when the World War interrupted his career. Always an intense admirer of French culture from the days of a bicycle trip through France in the summer of 1903, a constant reader of French literature, with Molière, whose picture he kept above his desk, as his dramatic ideal, he sympathized from the outset with the Allies. Soon after the entrance of the United States into the war he gave up writing and, incidentally, an early opportunity to have *The Little Teacher* produced, in order to devote himself to the study of Nova Scotian sphagnum moss for use in surgical dressings. As a result he became convinced of the utility of this material and, almost single-handed, secured its adoption. He "employed helpers, found and prepared the moss, arranged hospital demonstrations, raced to Washington at every chance of a hearing, and finally won out" (Tompkins, *post,* p. xiii). Having investigated Canadian resources, at his own expense, he discovered several fields of the moss in British Columbia, harvested it, and shipped it to France where it was used in military hospitals. While engaged in this work, he was killed near Murrayville, B. C., in a collision between his automobile and a train. Altogether characteristic of the charm of his conversation was the testimony of his chauffeur that he had not noticed the train because he was listening to what Smith was saying.

[*Letters of Harry James Smith* (1919) with an introduction by Juliet Wilbor Tompkins, and a brief sketch; *Who's Who in America,* 1916–17; *The Record of the Twenty-fifth Reunion of the Class of 1902, Williams College* (n.d.); obituaries in the *N. Y. Times, N. Y. Herald, N. Y. Tribune.* Mar. 18, 1918; personal acquaintance.]

E.S.B.

SMITH, HENRY AUGUSTUS MIDDLETON (Apr. 30, 1853–Nov. 23, 1924), jurist, local historian, born in Charleston, S. C., was descended through his father, John Julius Pringle Smith, from Robert Smith, 1732–1801 [*q.v.*], the first Protestant Episcopal bishop of South Carolina, and through his mother, Elizabeth (Middleton), from Thomas, brother of Arthur Middleton [*q.v.*], a signer of the Declaration of Independence, whose famous seat, "Middleton Place," came into Smith's possession. Much of his early childhood was spent at "Beech Hill Plantation." A schoolboy during the Civil War, he witnessed the chaos that it brought; he was in Columbia the morning that Sherman's army entered, and he never forgot the destruction of the

Old South into which he had been born. After some years in Aiken, he returned to Charleston for his later education, and was graduated from the College of Charleston in 1872. Having read law in the office of McCrady & Sons, he was admitted to the bar in 1874, and for thirty-four years (1877–1911) was one of the leading lawyers of Charleston in the firm of Mitchell & Smith. On June 24, 1879, he married Emma, daughter of Maj. Arthur Middleton Rutledge of Franklin County, Tenn. She, with a son, survived him.

Although a consistent Democrat and never an office-seeker, in 1911 he was appointed by President Taft judge of the United States court for the Eastern District of South Carolina, in which capacity he served till 1923. Tending always to independence, his decisions in admiralty and citizenship cases were noteworthy, and he attracted considerable attention when he denied citizenship to a Syrian on the ground that the applicant was not white within the meaning of the law. Although he was austere and exacting on the bench, and reserved with those whom he had not admitted to intimacy, he possessed a subtle sense of humor and his judgments were mellowed by a secret vein of human sympathy. As a sportsman, he loved the out-of-doors; and as owner of several plantations, he planted successfully both rice and sea-island cotton. He was also a good botanist, and during several years of poor health made a hobby of studying the grasses of the coast. Always modest and unassuming, he frequently amazed specialists with his knowledge of widely diverse subjects, for he was an expert accountant, delighted in Italian and other languages, and was widely read in literature, theology, ethnology, anthropology, and Egyptology. He also wrote creditable verse. Always interested in history, he was an organizer and member of the South Carolina Historical Commission, and for twenty years a vice-president of the South Carolina Historical Society.

It is for his contributions in the field of South Carolina history that he is chiefly remembered. A lover of the land—and himself one of the largest land-owners in the state—he constituted himself its historian. His writings might well be called the Domesday Book of the South Carolina tidewater. Beginning with "The Colleton Family in South Carolina" in the first volume of the *South Carolina Historical and Genealogical Magazine* (October 1900), they concluded with "Goose Creek" in the twenty-ninth volume (October 1928). Drawn from manuscript sources, they all dealt with the land, tracing the original plans and following the histories of the settlers

of early towns and baronies, and the chain of ownership of river seats and settlements. All were illustrated with maps the author had constructed from ancient plats. Of most general interest, perhaps, was his series, "The Baronies of South Carolina" (April 1910–January 1917), reprinted by the South Carolina Historical Society in 1931. Often legal in style and detailed in evidence, sometimes repetitious, but always clear and painstaking, his writings are a mine of information to the student of social history and second only to the original records in value.

[Recollections of Mabel L. Webber and Langdon Cheves; *Charleston Evening Post*, Nov. 24, 1924; *S. C. Hist. and Geneal. Mag.*, Jan. 1928; for genealogy, *N. Y. Geneal. and Biog. Record*, Oct. 1897; *Who's Who in America*, 1924–25; *News and Courier* (Charleston), Nov. 24, 1924.]   A. K. G.

SMITH, HENRY BOYNTON (Nov. 21, 1815–Feb. 7, 1877), Presbyterian clergyman and theologian, was born at Portland, Me., the son of Henry Smith, a merchant, and Arixene, daughter of Judge Robert Southgate of Scarborough, Me., and niece of Rufus King, 1755–1827 [q.v.]. He was descended in the fourth generation from John Smith who was married in Plainfield, Conn., in 1699. In his senior year at Bowdoin College, Henry Boynton Smith went through a religious experience which caused him to forsake Unitarianism, in which faith he had been reared, and to decide to be a minister. Graduating in 1834, he spent a year at Andover Theological Seminary and the following year at Bangor Seminary. After a year's teaching at Bowdoin (1836–37), he went to Europe because of ill health. Here he studied philosophy, theology, and church history at Halle and Berlin, laying the foundation for the knowledge of German thought and historical criticism by which he contributed much to American intellectual life. Returning in 1840, he taught another year at Bowdoin, and at length, on Dec. 29, 1842, was ordained to the Congregational ministry in West Amesbury, Mass. On Jan. 5, 1843, he was married to Elizabeth Lee Allen, daughter of William Allen, 1784–1868 [q.v.], sometime president of Bowdoin. His effective ministry to the congregation at West Amesbury ended in 1847 with his appointment to the professorship of philosophy in Amherst College. During the last two years of his pastorate he had also been instructor in sacred literature at Andover Seminary.

Smith's chief work began in 1850, when he went to Union Theological Seminary to teach for twenty-four years, first in the field of church history and after 1854 in that of theology. His reputation, steadily heightened by his writing, gave prestige to the young institution. He greatly enriched its library, of which he had charge during his whole service. By his teaching, character, and personal interest he deeply impressed the students. In theology he was of the school of Jonathan Edwards, but his encyclopedic knowledge, his contact with the intellectual currents of the world, his reconciling temper, and his endeavor to develop independent thought in his students made his influence broadening and awakening, so that he became a conspicuous representative of an orthodoxy of liberal tendencies. His conversation, abounding in original views, learning, and quaint humor, quickened the thinking of a wide circle of friends. The acknowledged intellectual leader of the New School Presbyterian Church, he was moderator of its General Assembly in 1863. To him more than any other was due the reunion of the two branches of the Presbyterian Church in 1869.

Much of Smith's best writing appeared in periodicals. For many years he contributed regularly to the *New York Evangelist*. From its establishment in 1859 he was editor of the *American Theological Review*, later published under several different titles. His many essays and reviews greatly enlarged his influence. One of his best-known articles was that ironically entitled "British Sympathy with America," published in the *Review* in July 1862, and later separately, which expressed the indignant disappointment of Northerners over what they considered British desertion of the cause of human freedom for financial gain, and powerfully vindicated the course of the United States in the Civil War. The most important examples of his service in introducing German theological work to Americans were his *Textbook of Church History* (5 vols., copr. 1855–79), a translation and revision of Johan K. L. Gieseler's work, and *A Textbook of the History of Doctrines* (2 vols., 1861–62), a revision and enlargement of C. W. Buch's translation of Karl R. Hagenbach's work. In his *History of the Church of Christ in Chronological Tables* (1859) much excellent writing on church history is obscured by a cumbrous form. From his manuscripts there were compiled *Apologetics* (1882), *Introduction to Christian Theology* (1883), and *System of Christian Theology* (1884).

In 1869–70 Smith was in Europe in search of health. He taught and carried on the *Review* under difficulties until 1874, when he resigned his professorship. Three years later he died in New York City, survived by his wife and four children.

[H. S. Munroe and A. D. Smith, *Ancestry of Henry Boynton Smith, Frederick Southgate Smith, and Horatio Southgate Smith* (1922); L. B. Chapman, *Mono-*

graph on the Southgate Family of Scarborough, Me. (1907); E. L. Smith, *Henry Boynton Smith: His Life and Work* (1881); L. F. Stearns, *Henry Boynton Smith* (1892); G. L. Prentiss, *Union Theological Sem. in the City of N. Y.* (1889); R. E. Thompson, *Hist. of the Presbyt. Churches in the U. S.* (1895); *New York Evangelist*, Feb. 15, 1877; *Presbyterian Quart. and Princeton Rev.*, Apr. 1877; *N. Y. Tribune*, Feb. 8, 1877.]

R. H. N.

SMITH, HENRY PRESERVED (Oct. 23, 1847–Feb. 26, 1927), clergyman, Biblical scholar, was born at Troy, Ohio, the son of Preserved Smith and Lucy (Mayo) Smith, and the brother of Richmond Mayo-Smith [*q.v.*]. He was of Puritan descent, on his father's side going back to the Rev. Henry Smith, a graduate of Cambridge University, who came to New England about 1637 and a few years later became the first settled pastor at Wethersfield, Conn.; on his mother's side, to the Rev. John Mayo, first pastor of Second Church, Boston, 1650. His parents, who were New England Congregationalists, moved to Ohio, where they joined the New School Presbyterians. After his graduation from Amherst College in 1869 he studied theology at Lane Theological Seminary in Cincinnati, Ohio, where he graduated in 1872. He was licensed to preach in 1871 and was ordained in 1875 by the Presbytery of Dayton. He studied at the University of Berlin, Germany, in the winters of 1872–73 and 1873–74, with a trip to Palestine in the intervening spring. On his return to America he first taught church history at Lane Seminary for a year; in 1875 he became an instructor in Hebrew, and in 1876–77 went to the University of Leipzig in order to prepare himself more thoroughly for his professorship. On Dec. 27, 1877, he married Anna Macneale of Cincinnati. They had four children, two of whom survived their father. From 1877 to 1893 he was professor of Old Testament at Lane. Conservative by nature and training—even in Germany he had selected conservative teachers—he did not at first touch Biblical criticism in his teaching. But inevitably his study led him to see that the Bible text was corrupt, the Bible itself not infallible, the tradition about it untenable, and the use of textual, literary, and historical criticism inescapable. In order not to disturb the peace of the church he did not publish these views at once; although his article on "The Critical Theories of Julius Wellhausen" in the *Presbyterian Review* for April 1882 aroused some suspicion of his orthodoxy, nothing came of it. For himself it was momentous, for he had become convinced by Wellhausen's brilliant exposition of the truth of higher criticism. It was not till he felt impelled to speak out publicly in the General Assembly of the Presbyterian Church in defense of Charles

Augustus Briggs [*q.v.*], the great protagonist of higher criticism in the United States, that he was to feel the opposition of the conservatives. In November 1892 he was tried for heresy by the Presbytery of Cincinnati and suspended from the Presbyterian ministry because he denied the doctrine of the verbal inspiration and inerrancy of the Bible; the decision was upheld on appeal to the General Assembly of 1894. He gave up his professorship and his home at Cincinnati, and from 1893 to 1898 was without official position. He now wrote his *A Critical and Exegetical Commentary on the Books of Samuel* (1899) for the celebrated International Critical Commentary on the Holy Scriptures and gave the Ely Lectures at Union Theological Seminary on *The Bible and Islam* (1897). From 1898 till 1906 he was professor of Biblical literature and associate pastor at Amherst College; from 1907 to 1913 he taught the history of religions at Meadville Theological School; and from 1913 to 1925 he was chief librarian at Union Theological Seminary. In 1917 he was also made professor of Hebrew and cognate languages at Union, but he gave little of his time to teaching. After his resignation he lived in Poughkeepsie till his death.

His position in the history of American scholarship is secure not only because he was one of the pioneers who introduced modern Biblical criticism into the United States but also because he made important contributions to it. His *Samuel, Old Testament History* (1903), and *The Religion of Israel* (1914) are standard works; his *The Bible and Islam* and *Essays in Biblical Interpretation* (1921) rank high. In the bibliography appended to his autobiography, *The Heretic's Defense* (1926), there are sixty-five titles, many of great value. He had a singularly charming spirit. Though he was not eloquent or inspiring as a speaker or teacher, he was always clear and keen in thought and speech. A fearless fighter for truth and liberty, he dealt chivalrously, fairly, and sincerely with his opponents.

[H. R. Stiles, *The Hist. of Ancient Wethersfield* (1904), vol. II; *Who's Who in America,* 1926–27; H. P. Smith, *The Heretic's Defense* (1926); J. A. Bewer, in *Am. Jour. of Semitic Languages and Literatures,* July 1927, with portrait; obituary in *N. Y. Times,* Feb. 27, 1927.]   J. A. B.

SMITH, HEZEKIAH (Apr. 21, 1737–Jan. 24, 1805), Baptist clergyman, was born in Hempstead, Long Island, the son of Peter and Rebecca (Nichols) Smith (F. C. Torry, *The Ancestors and Descendants of Humphrey Nichols of Newark, New Jersey,* 1917, pp. 11–12, 18–19). In his youth the family moved to Morris County, N. J. Here, in 1756, he was baptized by John Gano

[*q.v.*] and immediately began to contemplate entering the ministry, notwithstanding the opposition of his father, who, however, yielded his consent at the solicitations of an older son and Gano. After preparatory studies at Hopewell Academy, he entered the College of New Jersey as a sophomore, graduating in 1762. Partly in the interest of his health, he started southward on horseback, preaching constantly during an itinerancy of fifteen months, during which time he covered over four thousand miles. At Charleston, S. C., he united with the Baptist Church, where he was ordained Sept. 20, 1763.

After his return north, he accompanied James Manning [*q.v.*] to Newport, R. I., and became associated with the founding and development of Rhode Island College (Brown University). Continuing his itinerant preaching, on July 27, 1764, he reached Haverhill, Mass., which was to become his home. After preaching for some weeks at a Congregational Church, he was invited to become its pastor. He thereupon acknowledged his views as to baptism, which terminated negotiations; but he had already stimulated the New Light elements in the community, and soon there was organized the First Baptist Church of Haverhill. On Nov. 12, 1766, he was installed as its pastor. According to his diary (Guild, *post*), he was married to Hephzibah Kimball of Boxford on June 27, 1771, though the vital records of Haverhill give the year as 1770. Four of their six children lived to maturity.

Smith exerted a wide and varied influence. His pastorate at Haverhill was distinguished by evangelistic preaching and pastoral ministration of marked effectiveness. Its routine was frequently interrupted by missionary journeys, especially into southern New Hampshire and the province of Maine, where he was instrumental in the organization of many churches. In the developing life of his denomination he was a positive factor, notably in the counsels of the Warren Association, of which he was one of the organizers (1767). Through his membership on its committee of grievances he played a part second only to that of Isaac Backus [*q.v.*] in the persistent effort of Baptists to secure separation of church and state. He was selected to go to England to confer with eminent Baptists there, with a view to obtaining from the British government relief from the intolerable situation in which the Baptists felt themselves placed, but other responsibilities compelled him to decline this mission. In the field of education, his great work was done for Rhode Island College. From his own student days the intimate friend of President Manning, he was one of the first fellows appointed and for some forty years attended assiduously to his duties. He devoted eight months, including the winter of 1769–70, to traveling in the South in behalf of the college, securing for its needs about $2,500. At the last meeting of the Corporation which he attended, only a few months before his death, Asa Messer [*q.v.*], one of several young men whom Smith had in part prepared for college while carrying on his ministerial duties at Haverhill, was elected to the presidency. As regimental (1775–78) and later as brigade chaplain (1778–80) in the Continental Army, Smith gained a wide fame and thereafter was generally known as Chaplain Smith. His character and ability won for him the esteem of the higher officers, including Washington himself. Evidences of his contemporary significance abound, justifying the epithet so often used, "the great man of Haverhill," an allusion to his place of residence rather than to his sphere of influence.

[R. A. Guild, *Chaplain Smith and the Baptists* (1885), gives copious selections from Smith's journal and from other papers, most, if not all, of which are now at the Lib. of Cong.; the account in W. B. Sprague, *Annals Am. Pulpit*, vol. VI (1860), which is largely followed in William Cathcart, *The Baptist Encyc.* (1881), records family tradition, which, as Guild points out, is incompatible with the statements in the journal. See also, A. S. Train, *Centennial Discourse . . . on the One Hundredth Anniversary of the Organization of the Baptist Church, Haverhill, Mass.* (1865); A. E. Vanderpoel, *Hist. of Chatham, N. J.* (1921); F. B. Heitman, *Hist. Reg. Officers of the Continental Army* (1914).]   W. H. A.

SMITH, HIRAM (Feb. 19, 1817–May 15, 1890), agriculturist, was a descendant of a long line of Quaker colonial ancestors, the first of whom came to America with William Penn. He was born in Tinicum, Bucks County, Pa. In 1820 his father, Jonas Smith, moved to New York state. Until 1847 Hiram and his brother A. J. Smith, who later became associate editor of *Hoard's Dairyman,* carried on the business of farming, foundry work, and plow-making at the family home in Lowville, N. Y. On Mar. 20, 1845, Hiram married Catherine A. Conover, by whom he had a son and a daughter. Two years later he moved to Sheboygan Falls, Wis., where he spent the rest of his life.

Buying a tract of government land, he ultimately developed it into one of the outstanding dairy farms of the state, being among the first in that section to turn from wheat farming to dairying. By the time of the Civil War, he had become one of the leading dairymen in Wisconsin. He was active in the early history of the Wisconsin Dairymen's Association, the group most largely responsible for the shift from grain farming to dairying. He was its president for

two years, 1875–76, and its vice-president from 1878 until his death. He was also influential in starting the Dairy Board of Trade at Sheboygan Falls in 1872 and was its first president, serving a second time in that capacity in 1889. In 1871–72 he was a member of the state legislature. He was appointed a regent of the University of Wisconsin in 1877 by Gov. William E. Smith, taking office the next year, and served continuously by successive appointments until his death. He was chairman of the agricultural committee of the regents and vice-president of the board in 1889–90.

While listening to a talk which Smith was giving before the farmers at the Manitowoc county fair, Assemblyman Charles E. Estabrook conceived the idea of having a series of talks given by successful farm leaders at gatherings similar to teachers' institutes. Accordingly, he introduced into the legislature and secured the passage, in 1885, of a bill providing for the establishment of farmers' institutes. The establishment at the University of Wisconsin of the first dairy school in the United States was also largely the work of Smith while one of the regents. The school opened in 1890, the year of his death, with two students; the next winter the enrollment reached seventy, partly as a result of reports of the famous milk tests made at the University under the direction of Stephen M. Babcock. A new dairy building was opened in January 1892 and was later named Hiram Smith Hall. Besides helping to establish the dairy school, Smith took an active part in forming the Wisconsin Agricultural Experiment Station and in building up the Wisconsin College of Agriculture.

[*Sheboygan County News,* May 21, 28, 1890; *Hoard's Dairyman,* May 23, 30, 1890; R. G. Thwaites, *The Univ. of Wis., Its Hist. and Its Alumni* (1900); J. F. A. Pyre, *Wisconsin* (1920); H. C. Adams, "In Memoriam," *19th Ann. Report of the Wis. Dairymen's Asso.* (1891); "Seven Wise Men of Wis.," in *Dairy Farmer,* Aug. 1, 1919; *Milwaukee Sentinel,* May 16, 1890; records of Univ. of Wis. Board of Regents, Doc. No. 101.]   W. A. S—r.

SMITH, HOKE (Sept. 2, 1855–Nov. 27, 1931), secretary of the interior, governor of Georgia, United States senator, was born in Newton, N. C., his parents being Hosea Hildreth Smith and Mary Brent (Hoke) Smith. Hosea Smith was a native of New Hampshire and a graduate of Bowdoin College; his wife was a North Carolinian; both were of Revolutionary ancestry. The elder Smith went to North Carolina in 1850 to become president of Catawba College at Newton. Six years later he was made professor of Greek and Latin at the University of North Carolina. Forced out during the troublous Reconstruction time, he set up a private school at

Lincolnton, N. C., in 1868, and in 1872 removed to Atlanta, where he was connected with the public-school system. The son, Hoke, growing up during the Civil War and Reconstruction period, received little formal education, but having a first-class mind and the advantage of the tutelage of such a father, he suffered little handicap from lack of conventional schooling. He read law in the offices of Collier, Mynatt, & Collier of Atlanta, and was admitted to the bar in 1873.

Smith took naturally to politics. Before reaching his majority he was chairman of the Fulton County Democratic executive committee. With the purchase in 1887 of the *Atlanta Journal,* he acquired an organ, edited and managed personally, which enabled him to build up a wide following for the liberal and reform movements associated with his name. In Cleveland's third contest for the Democratic presidential nomination (1892), Smith carried Georgia for him against David B. Hill. Smith was a delegate that year to the National Democratic Convention. In recognition of this service, Cleveland appointed him secretary of the interior. As secretary (1893-96), Smith was active in furthering the cause of conservation of natural resources in the West and in purging the pension list of fraud. In the silver agitation of the nineties, he upheld Cleveland's effort to maintain the gold standard. In the summer of 1896, before Bryan's nomination at Chicago, Smith stumped the state of Georgia in opposition to the candidacy of Congressman Charles F. Crisp [*q.v.*], a leading silverite, for a seat in the Senate. However, with the subsequent nomination of Bryan for the presidency, Smith took the position that preservation of white control in the South demanded that his section support the regular Democratic nominees. Feeling uncomfortable in Cleveland's cabinet, he resigned on Sept. 1, 1896.

Ten years elapsed before Smith was again in politics. During those years he advocated, in the columns of the *Journal* as long as he controlled it (until 1900) and later through his friend and supporter, James R. Gray, the new owner, the more effective control of railways, and the extension of the powers of the railroad commission. He urged the establishment of a highway department, denounced the convict-lease system, and in general allied himself with and became the leader of the progressive and reform element in the state. In 1906 he offered himself as a candidate for governor, along with four others, including Clark Howell, editor of the rival daily, the *Atlanta Constitution.* Smith appealed against ring rule and railroad domination of politics. The state railroad commission, he held, was

serving the railroads instead of the people and was stifling the state by maintaining excessive intrastate rates, especially between Atlanta and other interior points and the Georgia ports. With a view to the elimination of a purchasable element in the electorate, he advocated what amounted to the disfranchisement of negroes. In the Democratic primary, which was equivalent to election, he carried 122 of the 145 counties, and received a larger popular vote than all the other aspirants combined. He had two non-consecutive terms as governor, from July 1907 to July 1909, and from July 1911 to November 1911. In the primary of 1908 he was defeated by Joseph M. Brown, son of the war-time governor, Joseph E. Brown [*q.v.*], whom he had suspended from his office as state railroad commissioner. Smith and Brown again contested for the Democratic nomination in 1910 and Smith was victorious by a narrow margin. His two terms were marked by legislation of a distinctly progressive type. He accomplished more in extending the scope of social control in Georgia than any other governor in recent times. Under his leadership the General Assembly created the highway department and inaugurated the good-roads movement; it established the Department of Commerce and Labor; it uprooted the convict-lease system, long a reproach to the state; it passed a new suffrage law, imposing educational and property qualifications for the privilege of voting—a law which for many years operated principally to deprive negroes of the suffrage; and it increased the railroad commission from three to five members, and extended its jurisdiction over power, telephone and telegraph, express, street railway, and dock and wharf companies. The legislature also passed the first Southern state-wide prohibition law, though Smith preferred local option.

Shortly after Smith's second inauguration (July 1, 1911) he was elected by the legislature to fill the unexpired term of United States Senator A. S. Clay, who had died in the preceding fall. He did not, however, vacate the governorship until November, preferring to continue in office until his reform program could be enacted into law. In 1914 he was reëlected for the long senatorial term, defeating his old opponent, Joseph M. Brown. He served until 1921, being defeated for renomination in 1920 by Thomas E. Watson [*q.v.*]. Watson was an uncompromising opponent of the League of Nations; another candidate, Hugh M. Dorsey, supported the Wilson position; Smith favored the Senate reservations. Hoke Smith's prime interest as a senator was in furthering the cause of education, and more especially education of the vocational type. He was chairman of a Commission on National Aid to Vocational Education created by joint-resolution of Congress on Jan. 20, 1914. This commission made an exhaustive survey (published in 1914) out of which developed the Smith-Lever bill (May 8, 1914), which resulted in a nationwide extension service devoted to the improvement of rural life; and the Smith-Hughes bill (Feb. 23, 1917), which provided for instruction in the common schools in agriculture, home economics, trade, and industry, and for the vocational rehabilitation of disabled civilians. He also secured the passage of a bill setting up a division of markets in the Department of Agriculture. While the country was still neutral in the World War, Smith made a fight to force all belligerents to respect American rights in the matter of international trade. After the entrance of the United States into the war, he was a powerful and effective supporter of all measures making for the more efficient conduct of the struggle. He disagreed with President Wilson on a number of issues, notably with reference to the League of Nations.

Hoke Smith was a man of impressive characteristics. He was uncommonly large and strong; as a public speaker he was forceful, even eloquent; as a leader he was fearless; in manner he was kindly and agreeable; he made friends easily and held them securely. Throughout his long career he played an important part in the civic development of Atlanta. He served for years as chairman of the Board of Education; he and his associates organized the Piedmont Hotel and the Fulton National Bank; it was largely through his efforts that the Federal Reserve Bank was located in Atlanta. On his death, the *Constitution*, which so long opposed him, said in an editorial (Nov. 28, 1931): "In going Senator Smith leaves an indelible imprint upon the history of the State which he served long and well." On Dec. 19, 1883, he married Birdie Cobb, daughter of Gen. Thomas R. R. Cobb [*q.v.*]. They had four children, a son and three daughters. Mrs. Smith died in 1919, and on Aug. 27, 1924, he married Mazie Crawford of Cordele, Ga. He was an elder in the North Avenue Presbyterian Church in Atlanta.

[A. D. Candler and C. A. Evans, ed., *Georgia* (1906), vol. III, 315–16; Clark Howell, *Hist. of Ga.* (1926), vol. I; *Who's Who in America*, 1930–31; *Who's Who in the South*, 1927; platform of first gubernatorial contest, *Atlanta Journal*, Sept. 5, 1906; Smith's address outlining his accomplishments as governor, *Ibid.*, July 1, 1911; obituary articles, in *Atlanta Journal*, Nov. 27, 1931, and *Atlanta Constitution*, Nov. 28, 1931; his gubernatorial messages in *Jour. of the Senate of the State of Ga.*, 1908, pp. 10–42; 1909, pp. 12–58; 1911, pp. 172–98; A. C. True, *A Hist. of Agric. Educ.*

in the U. S., 1785–1925 (1929), pp. 281–82, 361–62, 365, 368; "Report of the Commission on National Aid to Vocational Education," *House Document No. 1004, 63 Cong., 2 Sess.* (2 vols., 1914).]   R. P. B.

SMITH, HORACE (Oct. 28, 1808–Jan. 15, 1893), inventor, manufacturer, was born in Cheshire, Mass., and was the son of Silas and Phoebe Smith. When he was four years old his father, who was a carpenter by trade, moved with his family to Springfield, Mass., where he found work in the United States armory. Upon completing the public school curriculum in Springfield young Smith, then sixteen years old, entered the armory as a gunsmith's apprentice and spent eighteen years there becoming an expert gun maker. He then went to Norwich, Conn., and worked for a year with Charles Thurber [*q.v.*], the noted manufacturer of small arms. After spending a number of months in the armory of Eli Whitney at New Haven, Conn., making tools for the manufacture of rifles, he returned to Norwich and worked three years, 1843–46, in the pistol factory of Allen and Thurber. For three years he was in business for himself, manufacturing guns, but in 1849 gave it up to work for Oliver Allen in Norwich manufacturing whaling guns.

About this time he turned his attention to invention, particularly to the improvement of the breech-loading rifle, and obtained his first patent, No. 8317, Aug. 26, 1851. Before undertaking its manufacture, however, he took a position with Allen, Brown & Luther, manufacturers of rifle barrels in Worcester, Mass. While there, about 1852, he met Daniel Baird Wesson [*q.v.*], a gunsmith like himself, with whom he worked successfully, in spare time, on perfecting a repeating rifle. In 1853 they entered into partnership to manufacture the rifle in Norwich, and secured a patent on it, Feb. 14, 1854. In 1855 they were induced to sell out to the Volcanic (later the Winchester Repeating) Arms Company of New Haven. Smith returned to Springfield and for two years operated a livery stable with his brother-in-law. Meanwhile Wesson worked on the construction of a revolver to use a central-fire metallic cartridge he and Smith had devised and patented Aug. 8, 1854, which contained not only the requisite charge of powder but also a lubricant placed within the case between the powder and ball. In 1857 the two men reëstablished their partnership to make the new firearm and cartridge in Springfield, applying the principle of interchangeable parts in the manufacture. They produced their first revolvers late in 1857, before receiving their patents, which were issued July 5, 1859, and Dec. 18, 1860, respectively. From the beginning the demand for their revolver in the United States was very great, for it was adopted by the Federal military authorities; to meet it the partners were compelled to build a new plant in 1860, which had to be further enlarged periodically thereafter as the business grew. After 1867, when they exhibited their products at the international exposition at Paris, they secured large contracts with Japan, China, England, Russia, Spain, France, and most of the South American countries. In the succeeding years Smith and Wesson worked continually to better their revolver and cartridge, and not only patented a number of improvements of their own invention but also purchased the improvements of others—notably the invention of W. C. Dodge for extracting empty shells from the revolver cylinder, which they bought in 1869. Smith continued as executive head of the business for upwards of sixteen years. In July 1873 he sold his interest to Wesson and retired. He served two terms as an alderman of Springfield and was a director of a number of industrial enterprises; at the time of his death he was president of the Chicopee National Bank. He was married three times: first, to Eliza Foster, who died in 1836; second, to Mrs. Eliza Hebbard Jepson, who died in 1872, and third, to Mary Lucretia Hebbard, of Norwich, Conn., who died in 1887. He died leaving no direct descendants.

[C. W. Chapin, *Sketches of the Old Inhabitants and Other Citizens of Old Springfield* (1893); C. B. Norton, *Am. Inventions and Improvements in Breech-Loading Small Arms* (1880); J. W. Roe, *Eng. and Am. Tool Builders* (1926); obituary in *Springfield Republican*, Jan. 16, 1893; Patent Office records.]   C. W. M—n.

SMITH, ISRAEL (Apr. 6, 1759–Dec. 2, 1810), lawyer, politician, was born in Suffield, Conn., the son of Daniel and Anna (Kent) Smith, and during his childhood moved with his parents to Rupert, Vt. The family apparently was interested in securing adequate education and Israel graduated in 1781 at Yale, where an older brother, Noah, also to be prominent in the early politics of Vermont, had graduated three years before. After reading law with this brother in Bennington, Israel was admitted to the Vermont bar in 1783, and began practice in Rupert. Between 1785 and 1790 he served four terms in the legislature, its journals showing that he was active in the routine work of that body but throwing little light on his character or interests. In 1789 he served on a joint commission for adjusting boundary and title disputes with New York, and two years later took part in the convention which ratified the Constitution of the United States.

In 1791 he was elected to the federal House of Representatives, having removed to the larger and more prosperous town of Rutland in the same year. His term of service, extending from Oct. 17, 1791, to Mar. 3, 1797, was not characterized by any notable achievements. Party alignments were still fluctuating and Smith, in spite of his Yale training, moved into the Jeffersonian ranks, supporting the opponents of the administration in their effort to block the Jay Treaty by withholding the necessary appropriation. Throughout the remainder of his career he was identified with the Republican party. Defeated for Congress in 1797, he returned to Rutland, resumed practice, reëntered the legislature, and became chief justice, being ousted as a result of the Federalist victory of 1798. With the growth of Republican sentiment in Vermont he was elected to the Seventh Congress, serving from Mar. 4, 1801, to Mar. 3, 1803, when he entered the United States Senate, serving until Oct. 1, 1807. The scantily reported debates of that era fail to show the extent of his activity in the latter body, although he spoke with ability and vigor in support of Jefferson's foreign policy, denouncing British aggressions on neutral commerce (*Annals of Congress*, 9 Cong., 1 Sess., cols. 94–96). He resigned from the Senate in 1807 upon being elected governor, but held this office for one term only. His message to the legislature showed that in one matter, a more humane treatment of convicts, he was somewhat in advance of public sentiment. A year later his strength, mental and physical, having begun to deteriorate, he retired from public life. His unfortunate condition and early death deprived the state of a leader whose ability and temperate views would have been very useful in the disturbed era which accompanied the War of 1812.

Smith was married in his twenties and had two sons, one of whom died in childhood. His widow, Abiah, was married in 1811 to Col. William C. Harrington.

[*Records of the Gov. and Council of the State of Vermont*, esp. V (1877), 147–48, 393–96; W. H. Crockett, *Vermont*, V (1923), 70–71; F. B. Dexter, *Biog. Sketches Grads. Yale Coll.*, vol. IV (1907); A. M. Hemenway, *The Vt. Hist. Gazetteer*, III (1877), 1061–62; *Biog. Dir. Am. Cong.* (1928); *Rutland Daily Herald*, Oct. 12, 1867; date of birth and names of parents from the Suffield Vital Records through the courtesy of the Connecticut State Library; information concerning Smith's marriage from American Antiquarian Society, Worcester, Mass.]   W. A. R.

SMITH, JAMES (*c.* 1719–July 11, 1806), signer of the Declaration of Independence, was born in northern Ireland, the second son in a large family. His father, John, was induced to migrate to Pennsylvania (*c.* 1729) by his brothers, who had settled previously in Chester County. John Smith purchased a tract of land west of the Susquehanna in York County and became an enterprising farmer. James attended school in Philadelphia under the Rev. Francis Alison [*q.v.*], studying Latin, Greek, and surveying, and then read law in the office of his elder brother, George, at Lancaster. Shortly after his admission to the bar in 1745 he moved to Cumberland County, near Shippensburg, where he engaged in surveying and practised law when chance offered. After four or five years on the frontier he returned to York, which became his residence for the rest of his life. Although the only resident practising lawyer in town until 1769, he found little business during his early years there. Possibly it was this fact that encouraged him to take up iron manufacturing on the Codorus Creek in 1771. The venture cost him £5,000 before he sold out in April 1778. Of the two managers who brought about this loss he once remarked, with his accustomed drollery, that "the one was a knave, and the other a fool" (Carter and Glossbrenner, *post*, p. 172).

From the outbreak of trouble with the mother country, Smith assumed a rôle of leadership in the backcountry. In the provincial conference, July 1774, he read an "Essay on the Constitutional Power of Great Britain over the Colonies in America" (mentioned in *Three Signers, post*) and urged the non-importation of British goods and a general congress of the colonies as a means of securing redress for colonial grievances. Inspired by the proceedings of the conference, he returned to York and the following December raised a volunteer company of which he was chosen captain. The company later grew to a battalion, and he accepted the honorary title of colonel, leaving active command to younger men. He was a delegate to the provincial convention at Philadelphia in January 1775 and to the provincial conference, June 18-25, 1776. An ardent exponent of backcountry protests against the hegemony of the eastern counties, in the latter revolutionary body he helped to draft resolutions recommending independence and to set the wheels in motion for improving provincial defenses and for securing a new government. In the constitutional convention of 1776 he was a member of the committee to draft a new frame of government. Before the convention had been in session a week he was elected to Congress (July 20), and thus became a signer of the Declaration of Independence. Although left out of the delegation sent to Congress in February 1777, he was reëlected, Dec. 10, 1777, and served for the following year, declining election after that term.

He was a state-rights man, vigorously opposing all measures which might interfere with domestic police. While Congress met in York the meetings of the board of war were held in his office. After retiring from Congress he held but few political posts: he served one term in the assembly (1779); as judge of the Pennsylvania high court of errors and appeals (Nov. 20, 1780-May 10, 1781); as brigadier-general of militia (1782); and as counselor for Pennsylvania in the Wyoming controversy. In 1785 the assembly again honored him by electing him to Congress, but he declined on account of his age. From 1781 to 1801 he was chiefly engaged in the practice of law, and by the time of his retirement in 1801 he had acquired a substantial estate. Fire destroyed his office and practically all of his papers in the fall of 1805. Though regarded as somewhat eccentric, Smith was noted for his sharp wit, lively manner, and unusually retentive memory. An excellent conversationalist with a large store of anecdote, he drew around him many friends, especially prospective lawyers who read law in his office. He was married about 1760 to Eleanor, daughter of John Armor of New Castle, Del., who with two of their five children survived him.

[An adequate appraisal of Smith's life remains to be written. Material bearing on his career may be found in the following: W. C. Carter and A. J. Glossbrenner, *Hist. of York County* (1834), new ed. (1930), ed. by A. M. Aurand; W. H. Egle, in *Pa. Mag. of Hist. and Biog.*, IV (1880), 362-64; J. R. Harris, "The Peculiar Mr. Smith," in *Pa. Soc. Sons of the Am. Rev.: Papers . . . 1912-13-14 upon Pa. Signers of the Declaration of Independence* (n.d.); J. C. Jordan, "York, Pa., in the Revolution," *Pa. Mag. of Hist. and Biog.*, Oct. 1908; *James Wilson, James Smith and George Ross, Three Signers of the Declaration of Independence* (pamphlet, 1902); *Pa. Archives*, 2 ser., III (1875); and *Minutes of the Supreme Exec. Council of Pa.*, vols. XI, XII (1852-53).]

J.H.P.

SMITH, JAMES (*c.* 1737-*c.* 1814), pioneer, soldier, and author, was born in the Conococheague settlement in what is now Franklin County, Pa. He received only a limited education, but was well versed in woodcraft and hardened to the rigors of frontier life. While helping to cut a road from Shippensburg to join Braddock's road at the Youghiogheny in 1755, he was captured by Indians and adopted into one of their families. He subsequently accompanied his captors in their wanderings through the Ohio country until his escape, near Montreal, in 1759. Early in 1760, he returned to the Conococheague region, settled at his old home, and engaged in farming.

Following his marriage, in 1763, he entered upon an adventurous career, embracing leadership in 1763, 1765, and 1769 of the so-called "Black Boys"—self-constituted rangers whose purpose was to defend the frontier settlements against Indian attacks, service as an ensign in

1763, and service as a lieutenant in Bouquet's expedition against the Ohio Indians in 1764. In 1766–67, with a small party, he made an exploration into southern Kentucky and Tennessee, which, with the exception of tours made by Henry Scaggs, a hunter, is said to have been the first made by Anglo-Americans into the country west of the Cumberland Mountains in Tennessee. About 1769 Smith removed to a farm on Jacob's Creek, a branch of the Youghiogheny, in the region that became first Bedford, then Westmoreland County, Pa. He was a member of the board of commissioners of Bedford County in 1771, and of Westmoreland in 1773, and was a captain of militia in 1774; he was a member of the Westmoreland County convention in 1776, and of the Pennsylvania Assembly, 1776–77. During the next two years he was engaged in fighting Indians in western Pennsylvania, in 1778 being commissioned colonel of militia.

After the close of the war, he spent most of the summer of 1785 in Kentucky, looking after some land claims, and thither he removed in 1788, settling on Cane Ridge, in Bourbon County, about seven miles from Paris. That same year he was elected a member of the convention which sat at Danville, Nov. 4, 1788, to deliberate about separation from Virginia. He was a member of the constitutional convention of 1792, and afterwards, until 1799, with the exception of the session of 1796, he represented Bourbon County in the General Assembly of Kentucky.

Smith was somewhat of a religious enthusiast and for some time took an active part in the reform movement headed by Barton W. Stone [*q.v.*] but he eventually returned to the Presbyterian Church, from which he had withdrawn, and, receiving licensure, spent much time in his later years as a missionary among the Indians. On returning from one of his missionary excursions into Tennessee, he found that his son James had joined the Shakers and had taken his family to the Shaker settlement on Turtle Creek, near Lebanon, Ohio. After sojourning for a short time with that sect, the father poured out his wrath upon their leaders in a pamphlet entitled *Remarkable Occurrences Lately Discovered among the People Called Shakers; of a Treasonous and Barbarous Nature; or Shakerism Developed* (1810), of which a second edition soon appeared. This brought a rejoinder from Richard McNemar, one of the Shaker leaders; Smith again appeared in print, in a pamphlet entitled *Shakerism Detected; Their Erroneous and Treasonous Proceedings ... Exposed to Public View* (1810); and was answered by McNemar in the following year.

The book which constitutes Smith's chief title to fame as an author, however, was *An Account of the Remarkable Occurrences in the Life and Travels of Col. James Smith, During His Captivity with the Indians, in the Years 1755, '56, '57, '58 & '59,* printed and published by John Bradford in Lexington, Ky., in 1799. This valuable work has been reprinted several times, and much or all of it has been reproduced in various publications relating to the Indians and pioneers of the Ohio Valley. In 1812, Smith published *A Treatise on the Mode and Manner of Indian War, Their Tactics, Discipline and Encampments,* drawn largely from his previous *Account.*

Smith was a man of quiet and taciturn character, and much given to religious study and meditation. He had the courage of his convictions, however, and, when roused, displayed more than ordinary talent in debate. In May 1763, he married Anne Wilson, by whom he had seven children. She died about 1783, in Pennsylvania, and some two years later he married Margaret (Rodgers), widow of Abraham Irvin. She died in 1800, in Bourbon County, Ky., survived by her husband and several children born of her first marriage.

[Biog. sketch by Robert Clarke and notes by W. M. Darlington, in the 1870 edition of *An Account of the ... Travels of Col. James Smith;* biog. introduction to 1834 edition; Lewis and R. H. Collins, *Hist. of Ky.* (2 vols., 1874); Henry Howe, *Hist. Colls. of Ohio* (3 vols., 1891); J. N. Boucher, *Hist. of Westmoreland County, Pa.* (1906); P. G. Thomson, *A Bibliog. of the State of Ohio* (1880).]   S. M. W.

SMITH, JAMES (June 12, 1851–Apr. 1, 1927), United States senator, Democratic boss of New Jersey, was born in Newark, N. J., the son of Irish immigrants, James and Mary (Lyndon) Smith. After attending private schools and St. Mary's College, Wilmington, Del., he embarked upon a business career. Beginning as a clerk in his father's grocery store, he subsequently became a member of the J. H. Halsey & Smith Company, engaged in manufacturing patent and enameled leathers, and built up one of the largest establishments of its kind in the country. In 1904 he became president of the Federal Trust Company of Newark, and for several years owned the *Newark Advertiser* and its successor, the *Star.* These and other important financial interests gave him prominence in the business community, but it was chiefly through his position as Democratic overlord that he became a powerful influence in the affairs of New Jersey.

He rose to this estate as a result of many years of participation in local, state, and national politics. Beginning as an alderman (1883–87), he served as president of the board of works of

Newark and was chairman of the state's delegations to the Democratic National Convention in 1884, 1892, and 1896. In 1892 he swung his delegation from David B. Hill to Cleveland, and the following year, "with money as plentiful as ugly rumors" (Kerney, *post,* p. 20), he was elected to the United States Senate. There during his single term his services were undistinguished. He spoke infrequently and in voting generally reflected the views of "big business." The belief that he, along with other senators, had speculated in sugar stocks while the Wilson tariff bill was pending resulted in a Senate investigation. Smith denied the accusation (*Senate Report 606,* 53 Cong., 2 Sess.), but a strong suspicion against him remained long after he left the Senate.

Although his close alliance with the vested interests of New Jersey was well known and subject to much criticism, it was not until 1910 that his domination of the Democratic organization was threatened. Then he was prevailed upon by George Harvey [*q.v.*] to accept Woodrow Wilson as the Democratic candidate for governor, and by "steam-roller" methods in the state convention he forced Wilson's nomination. After the party's triumph at the polls in November, Smith put himself forward as a candidate for the Senate, despite previous assurances that he would not enter the contest. Wilson stood by the winner of the September primary, however, and succeeded in defeating Smith when the legislature balloted in January 1911. In revenge the latter fought the Governor's legislative program, but without much success. Another effort in 1912 to return to the Senate also failed, when he was beaten in the primary by Wilson's choice, William Hughes. These reverses, together with the collapse of his private business interests in 1915, destroyed his power and forced his retirement from public life.

In 1874 Smith was married to Katherine R. Nugent of Newark, who died in 1910. Ten children were born to them, of whom six survived their father. His death occurred in Newark, in his seventy-sixth year.

[*Biog. Dir. Am. Cong.* (1928); *Who's Who in America,* 1926–27; James Kerney, *The Political Education of Woodrow Wilson* (1926); R. S. Baker, *Woodrow Wilson,* vol. III (1931); R. E. Annin, *Woodrow Wilson* (1924); *N. Y. Times, Newark Star-Eagle, Newark Evening News,* Apr. 2, 1927; name of Smith's mother from his daughter.]   A. H. M.

SMITH, JAMES ALLEN (May 5, 1860–Jan. 30, 1924), political scientist, was born at Pleasant Hill, Mo., the son of Isaac James and Naomi (Holloway) Smith. His ancestors were Virginians and Kentuckians who became large land owners and slave-holders in Missouri. As a boy he grew up amid the bitter political and social antagonisms growing out of the Civil War and Reconstruction. He prepared for college in the schools of Kansas City and graduated from the University of Missouri in 1886. As an undergraduate he took a prominent part in discussion groups interested in economic and political subjects, and was influenced by the writings of Henry George.

Immediately after graduation he entered the law school, received the degree of LL.B. in 1887, and then began practice in Kansas City. He was not happy in his profession, however; the narrow limits of the legal life annoyed him. On Nov. 26, 1890, he married Doris J. Lehmann, of Kansas City, who appreciated his scholarly abilities and urged him to pursue work in the social sciences. Entering the University of Michigan, he came under the influence and guidance of Henry Carter Adams [*q.v.*]. Smith's dissertation for the doctorate was a theoretical study of money which refuted many of the basic contentions of the gold standard advocates; fundamentally it was an exposition of the ideas since made familiar by Irving Fisher's "Compensated Dollar." The thesis was vigorously opposed by some members of the faculty but Smith successfully defended his view and received the degree of Ph.D. in 1894. In 1895 he was elected professor of economics and sociology at Marietta College. In March 1896 his dissertation was published, under the title "The Multiple Money Standard," in *Annals of the American Academy of Political and Social Science.* It at once became the subject of controversy in the bitter monetary discussions of that year, and the following year he was dropped from the faculty, ostensibly for reasons of economy, although a successor was immediately elected in his place. In 1897 he became professor of political science at the University of Washington, with which institution he remained until his death. He was dean of the graduate school from 1909 to 1920, relinquishing the duties because of declining health.

On the eve of another political upheaval he published his best-known work, *The Spirit of American Government* (1907), which profoundly influenced Theodore Roosevelt, LaFollette, and many of the leading Progressives. It is a presentation of the underlying principles of American government which emphasizes the undemocratic features, laying particular stress on the arrangement of checks and balances, party organization, judicial review, and the general confusion and irresponsibility of political parties. Because of his views Smith became the storm center of hostile criticism, and repeated efforts were made to remove him from his professorship; but all were unsuccessful. Personally he was a large, handsome man, but extremely modest and retiring except among intimate friends. He never sought a quarrel but having been engaged in one he pursued it to the bitter end. In his classroom he was an inspiring, fearless, and stimulating teacher. He was at his best, as his students soon learned, when his views were stiffly opposed. Repeatedly denounced as a radical, he was, in fact, a Jeffersonian democrat who insisted upon teaching the truth as he saw it, in his own field, irrespective of criticism. He more than once declined administrative college positions; in 1912, he could have been nominated for governor of Washington by the Progressive party; in 1922, he was urged to become a candidate for the United States Senate; none of these opportunities appealed to him; he was a scholar interested in teaching.

Despite recurring attacks of heart trouble, he worked steadily to complete his last book, to which, with the aid of his daughter, he was giving final revision at the time of his death. This volume, *The Growth and Decadence of Constitutional Government* (copr. 1930), is a protest against the centralization of administration in the federal government, and against the concept of the modern state as a dominating influence rendering popular control ineffective; it is also a plea for increased freedom of initiative and authority on the part of the local government.

[V. L. Parrington, *Main Currents in Am. Thought,* vol. I (1927), and introduction to *The Growth and Decadence of Constitutional Government*; *Am. Pol. Sci. Rev.,* Feb. 1909, p. 138, May 1930, p. 524; *Who's Who in America,* 1923–24; T. S. Barclay, in *Mo. Alumnus,* Apr. 1931; *Seattle Daily Times,* Jan. 30, 1924; *N. Y. Times,* Jan. 31, 1924; private letters and papers.]

E. M.

SMITH, JAMES FRANCIS (Jan. 28, 1859–June 29, 1928), soldier, lawyer, colonial administrator, was a native of San Francisco, Cal., the son of Patrick and Ann Smith. After a common-school education, he graduated from Santa Clara College in 1877 with the degree of B.S.; in 1878 he received the degrees of B.A. and M.A. After studying law at Hastings College of the Law, San Francisco, he was admitted to the bar in January 1881 and began the practice of his profession. On Aug. 13, 1885, he married Lillie A. Dunnigan of Santa Clara (d. March 1910). During early manhood he became actively interested in local military affairs, and on May 6, 1898, was commissioned colonel, 1st California Volunteer Infantry, and commanded that regiment in the early expedition to the Philippine

Islands that followed the outbreak of the War with Spain. His regiment played a brilliant part in the first day's fighting at the capture of the city of Manila (Blount, *post,* pp. 193–94). Upon occupation of the city by the American forces, he was appointed deputy provost marshal, and in October was placed in command of the 1st Brigade, 1st Division, VIII Army Corps. Early in January 1899 he was appointed a member of the military commission to confer with commissioners designated by Emilio Aguinaldo regarding peace between the American forces and the Filipino insurgents. Soon afterward he took part in the engagement at Santa Ana, Feb. 5, and in the subsequent fighting at San Pedro Macatí, Pateros, and Taguig, Feb. 15–Mar. 1, 1899. He was officially commended in dispatches for gallantry in these actions, and was placed in command of the island of Negros as a sub-district of the insular military government.

Advanced to the grade of brigadier-general, United States Volunteers, Apr. 24, 1899, he was designated military governor of Negros and subsequently military governor of the Visayas. So successful was he in winning the good-will and the respect of the Filipinos that during the so-called Philippine Insurrection the island groups under his control gave little or no trouble to the American authorities (Blount, *post,* p. 557; Le Roy, *post,* II, 108–10). Rather against his personal wishes, he was made collector of Philippine customs at Manila, and applied to a troublesome problem of the new American government administrative methods that were both wise and efficient. With the inauguration of civil government in the islands under William Howard Taft, he was discharged from the military service and appointed an associate justice of the supreme court of the Philippines, June 17, 1901, an office he filled most creditably. In January 1903 he resigned to accept the portfolio of secretary of public instruction. A member of the Philippine Commission, which was virtually the cabinet of the governor-general, he was appointed as vice-governor in January 1906. On Sept. 20, 1906, he succeeded Henry Clay Ide [*q.v.*] as governor-general and served with great ability and marked success until May 1909, when he went to the United States. During this visit he resigned to practise law in the United States, his resignation taking effect Nov. 11, 1909. It was during his term of office that the Philippine legislature met for the first time, Oct. 16, 1907, and it was largely due to his tactful as well as practical assistance that the two houses that formed the legislature worked in comparative harmony (Worcester, *post,* I, 353). In March

1910 he was appointed an associate justice, United States court of customs appeals, an office he held for some eighteen years. (For his reports see *Court of Customs Appeals Reports,* vols. I–XVI, 1911–1929.) He served also as relief justice for the District of Columbia supreme court and court of appeals. He died at Washington after a severe heart attack that occurred while he was on the bench in an important case. He was survived by his son (*Evening Star,* Washington, *post*).

[*Who's Who in America,* 1928–29; *Eighth Ann. Report of the Philippine Commission to the Sec'y of War, 1907* (3 pts., 1908); *Report of the Philippine Com. to the Sec'y of War, 1908* (2 pts., 1909); J. A. LeRoy, *The Americans in the Philippines* (2 vols., 1914); D. C. Worcester, *The Philippines Past and Present* (1914), vol. I; J. H. Blount, *The Am. Occupation of the Philippines, 1898–1912* (1912); *Court of Customs Appeals Reports,* vol. XVI (1929), pp. 1–14; obituary in *Evening Star* (Washington, D. C.), June 30, 1928.]

C. D. R.

SMITH, JAMES McCUNE (Apr. 18, 1813–Nov. 17, 1865), negro physician and writer, was born in New York City, the "son of a slave, owing his liberty to the Emancipation Act of the State of New York and of a self-emancipated bondswoman" (Frederick Douglass, *My Bondage and My Freedom,* 1855, see the introduction by Smith). Both were of mixed blood. In the *Matriculation Albums of the University of Glasgow* (1913) is the notation in his own hand, "*Filius natu maximus Samuelis, Mercatoris apud New York.*" He was educated in the African Free School on Mulberry St., between Grand and Hester. Here, on Sept. 10, 1824, Lafayette addressed the pupils and young Smith, aged eleven, was chosen to make the reply. He entered the University of Glasgow in 1832, receiving the degrees of B.A. in 1835, M.A. in 1836 and M.D. in 1837. Following a short period in the clinics of Paris, he returned to New York City to practise medicine, and shortly thereafter opened a pharmacy on West Broadway, said to be the first in the country to be operated by a negro.

For twenty-five years he was a skilful and successful practitioner of medicine and surgery but his claims to remembrance rest upon his writings and his public service in the interest of his race. For twenty years he was on the medical staff of the Free Negro Orphan Asylum. In 1846 Gerrit Smith [*q.v.*], of Peterboro, N. Y., donated 120,000 acres of land in that state for distribution among the negroes of New York City. Smith, with two prominent negro clergymen, was chosen to select the names of about 2,000 heads of families to receive plots of land. The committee issued an address in pamphlet form (1846) ex-

tolling the project and the generosity of the donor. For a variety of reasons the venture was not a success. He was a consistent opponent of the American Colonization Society, formed for the purpose of repatriating negroes in Africa. In 1852 at a meeting of colored people in Albany, N. Y., he induced the assembly to adopt a resolution of protest against Governor Hunt's proposal to the state legislature for an appropriation in support of the colonization project. Interested in every phase of negro welfare, he was prominent in New York activities of the Underground Railroad. As early as 1833 Smith was a contributor to *Emancipator* and from January to May 1839, he was an editor of the *Colored American.* To this journal he contributed "Abolition of Slavery and the Slave Trade in the French and British Colonies," June 9, 1838. In 1841 he issued in pamphlet form *A Lecture on the Haytien Revolutions; with a Sketch of the Character of Toussaint L'Ouverture,* and in 1844, "Freedom and Slavery for Africans" in the *New York Tribune* (reprinted in the *Liberator,* Feb. 16, 23, 1844). During the short life of the *Anglo-African Magazine* (1859–60) he contributed: "Civilization: Its Dependence on Physical Circumstances," January 1859; "The German Invasion," an article on waves of immigration and their effects upon American life, February 1859; "Citizenship," a discussion of the Dred Scott decision, May 1859; and "On The Fourteenth Query of Thomas Jefferson's Notes on Virginia," a discourse upon the comparative anatomy of the white and black races, August 1859. Throughout his career he was engaged in controversy in support of the physical and moral equality of the black race. He contributed to *Hunt's Merchants' Magazine,* April and May 1846, an article on "The Influence of Climate upon Longevity" in reply to an attack upon the race by John C. Calhoun. He wrote one essay for each of the two volumes of the collection, *Autographs for Freedom* (1853, 1854). His writings show high scholarship, with a knowledge of the sciences, of history, and of foreign languages and literature. He was thought to be the most scholarly negro writer of his day by Henry Highland Garnet [*q.v.*]. At the request of the congregation of the Fifteenth Street Presbyterian Church of Washington, D. C., he wrote the introduction on the "Life and Labors of Rev. Henry Highland Garnet" for Garnet's *A Memorial Discourse* (1865). In 1863 he accepted an appointment as professor of anthropology at Wilberforce University, but failing health prevented his teaching, and he died after a prolonged illness from heart disease at his home in Williamsburg, Long Island, whither he had moved in 1864. He left a widow and five children.

[*Medic. Reg. of the City of N. Y.*, 1866; *Jour. of Negro Hist.*, Apr. 1916, Apr. 1921; G. W. Williams, *Hist. of the Negro Race in America* (2 vols., 1882); C. G. Woodson, *The Negro in Our History* (5th ed., 1928); D. A. Payne, *Recoll. of Seventy Years* (1888); Vernon Loggins, *The Negro Author* (1931); *New York Tribune*, Nov. 18, 1865.]   J. M. P.

SMITH, JAMES PERRIN (Nov. 27, 1864–Jan. 1, 1931), paleontologist, geologist, and teacher, was born near Cokesbury, Abbeville County, S. C., the son of the Rev. James Francis and Juliana (Forster) Smith. The Smith family was of English origin and had settled in Virginia, moving later to South Carolina. The boy received his early education at home until the family moved to Spartanburg where he entered the preparatory school of Wofford College. From 1876 to 1879 he was tutored by his brother, Charles Forster Smith [*q.v.*], and in 1884 was graduated with the B.A. degree from the college. Two years later he received the M.A. degree from Vanderbilt University, Nashville, Tenn. He then taught in the Nashville high school until 1888 when he was appointed assistant chemist and geologist for the newly organized Arkansas Geological Survey.

A desire for further study led him to resign his position and to go to Germany in 1890. He worked at the University of Göttingen in paleontology under Professor von Koenen and in mineralogy under Professor Liebisch, receiving the Ph.D. degree in 1892. After a brief period of study under von Zittel at Munich he returned to the United States to accept a position as the associate of John Casper Branner [*q.v.*] in the department of geology at Leland Stanford University, Palo Alto, Cal. He taught historical geology, paleontology, mineralogy, crystallography, and petrography until 1905 when he was made professor of paleontology. The study of the ammonites particularly absorbed his interest while at Stanford. He made numerous collecting trips to study the stratigraphy of various parts of western United States. He also came to be regarded as an authority on the geology of California and in 1916 superintended the compilation of a geological map of the state and prepared a descriptive report to accompany it.

From 1895 to 1906 he was assistant geologist in the United States Geological Survey and, from 1906 to 1924, geologist. His life-time work on the ammonites group culminated in the publication of a notable series of studies by the Survey: *The Carboniferous Ammonoids of America, Monographs of the United States Geological Survey*, volume XLII (1903); *The Triassic Cephalopod Genera of America, Professional Paper 40* (1905); *The Middle Triassic Marine Invertebrate Faunas of North America, Professional Paper 83* (1914); *Upper Triassic Marine Invertebrate Faunas of North America, Professional Paper 141* (1927); and *Lower Triassic Ammonoids of North America, Professional Paper 167* (1932). He published more than fifty other papers in various scientific journals and collections. In 1925 he was elected to membership in the National Academy of Sciences, and on Apr. 24, 1928, received the Mary Clark Thompson Gold Medal for his work in geology and paleontology. During thirty-seven years of teaching, Smith built up a solid following of students and took an intimate part in the life of the university. The social as well as the academic atmosphere of the college classroom appealed to him; he was fond of sports and possessed an unfailing sense of humor. At his death he was survived by his wife, Frances Norris Rand, to whom he had been married on Aug. 19, 1896, a daughter and three sons.

[Personal knowledge; information from the family; *Who's Who in America*, 1930–31; *Science*, Apr. 10, 1931; *Stanford Illustrated Rev.*, Feb. 1931; *San Francisco Examiner*, Jan. 2, 1931.]   S. S.

SMITH, JAMES YOUNGS (Sept. 15, 1809–Mar. 26, 1876), manufacturer, governor of Rhode Island, was born in Poquonoc village, in the town of Groton, Conn., the son of Amos Denison and Priscilla (Mitchell) Smith, the latter a descendant of Priscilla Mullins who came to Plymouth in the *Mayflower*. Born in humble surroundings, Smith rose to positions of prominence and responsibility by reason of native ability, indefatigable industry, and a securely founded reputation for unquestionable integrity. His formal education was such as could be obtained by intermittent attendance at a district school, and it ended when he was thirteen years old. At that time he became a clerk in the general store of his native town. In 1826, having exhausted the opportunities of this limited position, he moved to Providence and entered the counting-room of Aborn & Smith, lumber dealers. In 1830 he had made himself sufficiently important in the business to be admitted to partnership, and in 1837 he assumed full proprietorship. On Aug. 13, 1835, he married Emily Brown, daughter of Thomas Brown of Providence. They had three children, a son who died young, and two daughters. Brown was a successful cotton manufacturer and through him Smith began to turn his attention and his investments from the lumber business to that of cotton. In 1843 he entered into a partnership with his brother Amos, under the firm name of A. D. & J. Y. Smith, and engaged in the manufacture of cotton goods, and in carrying on a wholesale merchandise business. To these enterprises, as to all his financial ventures, he gave the most careful and constant personal attention. Some of the mills being at a considerable distance from Providence, he frequently made long journeys at night to avoid encroaching on the working hours of the day. In 1862 he withdrew from partnership with his brother and organized the James Y. Smith Manufacturing Company, which, with the admission of his sons-in-law, became James Y. Smith, Nichols & Rogers.

Smith found time for official public service. He was long a member of the Providence school committee, and for two years (1855, 1856) he was mayor of the city. In 1861 he was nominated for governor by the Republican party but was defeated in the election. Two years later he was renominated and this time was successful. He held the office from 1863 to 1866, declining to serve longer. In 1865 he had established an unequaled record when he received a majority vote in every town and ward of the state. His period of service as governor fell within the difficult period of the Civil War, and though he gave himself unsparingly to furthering the purposes and orders of the federal government, he did not escape criticism. Rhode Island had refused to draft its citizens to complete the quotas required of it, and it was necessary to hire recruiting officers and offer bounties, a method which required the raising and handling of large sums of money. In some instances fraudulent practices developed and Governor Smith's political enemies endeavored to lay upon him a certain measure of responsibility. It proved impossible to attach any real blame to him, however, and his reputation as a disinterested leader in public affairs was undisturbed.

To an unusual degree he enjoyed the respect and confidence of his fellow citizens, evidenced, among other ways, by the frequency with which his services as director were sought by local banks and insurance companies and as a member of committees to carry out public works. He was a man of sensitive sympathies, and his philanthropies were extensive. No intermediary was permitted to act for him, his contacts with those whose poverty or distress had brought them to his notice were always personal. For years he was the outstanding figure of Rhode Island.

[*Representative Men and Old Families of R. I.* (1908); *The Biog. Cyc. of Representative Men of R. I.* (1881); Charles Carroll, *R. I.: Three Centuries of Democracy* (1932), vol. II; *Providence Jour.*, Mar. 27, 1876.]   E. R. B.

SMITH, JEDEDIAH STRONG (June 24, 1798–May 27, 1831), trader, explorer, was the son of Jedediah Smith, a native of New Hampshire. Born in Bainbridge, Chenango County, New York, he received a fair English education, acquired a little Latin, and learned to write a good hand. At thirteen he became clerk on a Lake Erie freighter, learning business methods and presumably meeting traders returning from the Far West to Montreal from whom he imbibed an ambition for adventurous wilderness trade. Testimony concerning the time of Smith's arrival at the frontier is conflicting. He may have been in St. Louis as early as 1816, or he may have gone there several years later.

Gen. William Henry Ashley [q.v.], who organized his Rocky Mountain trade in 1822, probably had Smith in his employ from the first. It is certain that the latter was on the upper Missouri with Ashley in 1823, and continued with him thereafter until, at Great Salt Lake in the summer of 1826, Ashley sold his business to Smith, David E. Jackson, and William L. Sublette, all trusty lieutenants of the previous years' campaigns. These three men now carried on the Rocky Mountain trade till the summer of 1830, when they sold out to other mountain men, among them James Bridger [q.v.].

It was in the period 1826–30 that Smith made the journeys on which his fame as an explorer rests. He had already become familiar with the trade of the Columbia region, contested by the British, and he now proposed to investigate the Southwest and the practicability of penetrating the Oregon country from California. Leaving Great Salt Lake in August 1826, with seventeen men, he passed through the nations of the Utes, the Paiutes, and the Mohaves, and entered California from the Mohave desert, on Nov. 27, reaching the Mission San Gabriel, where he was kindly received. The governor of California was suspicious of him, however, and it was only through the intercession of Capt. W. H. Cunningham of the ship *Courier,* of Boston, that he escaped imprisonment and received permission to lead his party back across the mountains. His plan to go north into Oregon was temporarily frustrated.

Smith proceeded eastward and northward to the valley of King's River whence, in February 1827, he tried to cross the mountains and failed. He then moved farther north, to the American River, established camp for his main party, and, taking with him two companions, in May crossed the mountains, probably on the line of the present railway (Merriam, *post*). He did not chance upon the Humboldt River, and made his dreary way to Salt Lake over the unrelieved desert. About a month later he retraced the previous year's route, this time with a company of eighteen men, but the Mohave Indians, probably instigated thereto by the Californians, attacked the party treacherously, killing ten and plundering goods and papers.

With the remaining eight, Smith reached San Gabriel Mission, secured a few necessaries, and turned northeast to join the men left on the American. He found them in sad plight, which he was unable to relieve. Jeopardizing his own liberty, which would have been lost had not a group of American skippers at Monterey come to his aid, he now put himself in the hands of Governor Echeandía and finally gained permission to purchase supplies and leave the country. He wintered in the Sacramento Valley, but in April 1828, instead of crossing the mountains eastward or directly northward, he headed northwest and on June 8 reached the seacoast at the mouth of Klamath River. On July 14, he had already crossed the Umpqua on the way to the Willamette, his chosen route to the Columbia, when the Umpqua Indians massacred all his men save two. Smith and John Turner followed the Willamette route to Fort Vancouver, where they found Arthur Black, the other survivor. Dr. John McLoughlin [q.v.] aided Smith to recover his property, kept him as guest till March, and gave him a passage up the river to the Spokane, whence he made his way, over ground already familiar, to Pierre's Hole, the new rendezvous.

Smith retired from the Rocky Mountain trade the following year. In 1831 he entered the Santa Fé trade and toward the end of May, at a water hole near the Cimarron, he was surrounded by a body of hostile Comanches and killed. He was the first explorer of the Great Basin, the first American, so far as is known, to make his way into California from the east and out of California from the west. His road to Oregon is in part identical with the modern Roosevelt Highway along the coast. Smith was a gentlemanly character and a devout Christian, reared under Methodist influences.

[The chief source is H. C. Dale, *The Ashley-Smith Explorations and the Discovery of a Central Route to the Pacific, 1822–1829* (1918); M. S. Sullivan, *The Travels of Jedediah Smith* (1934), prints a more recently discovered transcript of a narrative of Smith's, and a fragment of his journal, together with other previously unpublished documents; see also H. D. Fisher, "The First Smith of California," *Am. Mercury*, Sept. 1928. For Smith's route east from California, this sketch follows the interpretation of C. H. Merriam in "First Crossing of the Sierra Nevada: Jedediah Smith's trip from California to Salt Lake in 1827," *Sierra Club Bull.*, vol. XI, no. 4 (1923), which differs from that of Dale and Sullivan. The date of birth given above is from a eulogy in the *Illinois Magazine*, June 1832; another date, Jan. 6, 1799, appears in a photographic facsimile of a family Bible record, dated 1834, printed in Sullivan, *ante*.]   J. S.

SMITH, JEREMIAH (Nov. 29, 1759–Sept. 21, 1842), congressman, governor of New Hampshire, jurist, was born in Peterborough, N. H., one of the younger members in a typical pioneer family of ten children. His parents were William Smith, an emigrant from the North of Ireland, and Elizabeth (Morison) Smith. From his Scotch-Irish ancestry Jeremiah derived habits of thrift, capacity for hard work, caustic wit, and a tendency to hardness and austerity. His early education was scanty but he possessed a native fondness for books and profited from such opportunities as the itinerant teachers of the day provided. After further study under more competent preceptors he entered Harvard College in 1777 and remained two years, his studies interrupted by a tour of duty with the New Hampshire contingent sent to oppose Burgoyne's invasion. During this term of service he was wounded at Bennington. Because of the unsatisfactory conditions at Harvard, due to the Revolution, he completed his course at Queen's College (Rutgers College), graduating in 1780.

For some years thereafter he served as a teacher in various localities in New Hampshire and Massachusetts, studying law meanwhile. In 1786 he was admitted to the bar at Amherst, in Hillsborough County, N. H. The unsettled conditions following the war and the opportunities afforded by the establishment of new institutions provided a rare opportunity for constructive work. He spent ten years at Peterborough, during which period he entered political life through the familiar school of town government. In 1790 he was elected to the Second Congress and a year later served in the New Hampshire constitutional convention which did so much to establish the governmental system of the state. He was an industrious but not particularly prominent member of Congress until his resignation, July 26, 1797. He took advantage of the enlarged opportunities for study provided by Philadelphia, followed the work of courts and government departments, became an intimate of many of the great Federalist leaders, imbided a fair share of their distrust of democratic institutions, learned to hate French influence and Jeffersonian doctrines, and on Mar. 8, 1797, married Eliza Ross of Maryland, whom he met at the capital.

He gave up his congressional career to accept appointment as United States attorney for the New Hampshire district, and bought a home at Exeter. In 1800 he became judge of probate for Rockingham County, and his legal knowledge enabled him to improve and clarify the unsatisfactory administration of this branch of New Hampshire law. He prepared a treatise on probate law, which, while it was not published, had considerable influence, being frequently consulted, it is said, by members of the New Hampshire bar. On Feb. 20, 1801, on the recommendation of John Marshall, he was appointed circuit judge by President Adams, but his tenure of office was soon terminated by the repeal of the act establishing these courts by the Jeffersonian majority in Congress. On May 17, 1802, he became chief justice of New Hampshire and for the next seven years rode on circuit, studied indefatigably, and worked to raise the standards of bench and bar in what was, in many respects, a pioneer community. Jeremiah Mason testified that Smith had done much to remedy the "most intolerable evil of a bad administration of justice" resulting from vague and uncertain judicial decisions, "by establishing and enforcing a more orderly practice, and by strenuous endeavors to conform all judicial decisions to known rules and principles of law" (Morison, *post*, p. 210); and the competent historian of the New Hampshire bar declares that "Judge Smith did more, perhaps, for the improvement of the jurisprudence of the State than any other man" (C. H. Bell, *post*, p. 61).

In 1809 he resigned the chief justiceship to serve a single term as governor, but without satisfaction either to the Federalist party, the state at large, or himself, his talents being judicial rather than political. He then resumed private practice but again served as chief justice from 1813 to 1816 during a stormy period when the courts were undergoing a reorganization, of dubious constitutionality, at the hands of the Federalist majority. With the defeat of the Federalists he returned to private life. Immediately he became associate counsel—with Daniel Webster and Jeremiah Mason [*qq.v.*]—for the trustees of Dartmouth College in his most celebrated case, *The Trustees of Dartmouth College* vs. *Woodward*. (For Smith's argument before the superior court of New Hampshire see Timothy Farrar, *Report of the Dartmouth College Case*, 1819.) In 1820 he retired from practice.

He had lived frugally and accumulated a competence sufficient to maintain him comfortably according to the modest standards of the time. His life in retirement was saddened by the death of his wife and the last of their five children. On Sept. 20, 1831, he married, second, Elizabeth Hale of Dover, N. H., and a son, Jeremiah [*q.v.*], was born on July 14, 1837. In his declining years Smith showed no diminution of mental vigor,

and he gave time and energy to local enterprises and causes, rendering valuable service to Phillips Exeter Academy, and attracting interest and attention as one of the last surviving Elder Statesmen of the Washington era. In 1842 he sold his Exeter estate, in order to lighten the responsibilities of his executors and dependents, and moved to Dover, where his death occurred a few months later.

[J. H. Morison, *Life of the Hon. Jeremiah Smith, LL.D.* (1845), based on original sources; some copies of letters in the William Plumer Papers, Lib. of Cong.; Jeremiah Smith, Jr., *Decisions of the Superior and Supreme Courts of N. H., from 1802 to 1809 and from 1813 to 1816 . . . with Extracts from Judge Smith's Manuscript Treatise on Probate Law* (1879), reviewed in *Granite Monthly*, Mar. 1879; C. H. Bell, *The Bench and Bar of N. H.* (1894); Albert Smith, *Hist. of the Town of Peterborough, . . . N. H.* (1876); C. H. Bell, *Hist. of the Town of Exeter, N. H.* (1888); *Biog. Dir. Am. Cong.* (1928); *Boston Daily Advertiser,* Sept. 24, 1842.]
W. A. R.

SMITH, JEREMIAH (July 14, 1837–Sept. 3, 1921), jurist and law teacher, was born in Exeter, N. H., son of Jeremiah Smith [*q.v.*], then in his seventy-eighth year, and his second wife, Elizabeth Hale, daughter of William Hale of Dover. His father had been a congressman, governor of New Hampshire, and chief justice of the New Hampshire supreme court. In 1843 the widowed mother settled on a farm in Lee, N. H., where the boy was taught by her and at a district school. From 1849 to 1853 he attended Phillips Exeter Academy. Entering Harvard College as a sophomore, he graduated in 1856 with high rank. He studied law under Daniel M. Christie of Dover and for a year at Harvard Law School, 1860–61. After admission to the bar in Strafford County, N. H., in 1861, he practised in Dover. On Apr. 5, 1865, he was married to Hannah M., daughter of Daniel K. Webster of that city. She died in 1904, leaving a daughter and a son.

On Oct. 16, 1867, when only thirty, Smith was appointed associate justice of the supreme court of New Hampshire, then a very strong court which included Ira Perley [*q.v.*] as chief justice and Charles Doe [*q.v.*]. Smith's decisions often dealt with questions on which there was little precedent. Instead of limiting himself to the immediate issue, he endeavored to solve general problems. His mind was greater than his task. As he said later to his students, "I know judges make law—I've done it myself." His decision, for example, in *Eaton* vs. *Boston, Concord & Montreal Railroad* (51 *N. H. Reports,* 504) established the meaning of "taking" by eminent domain. His opinions are "learned without prolixity, full of common sense, but searching first for legal principles, lawyer-like, convincing, sane" (Beale, *post,* pp. 2–3).

The heavy, confining trial work then required of his court so wore upon Smith that he was threatened with tuberculosis and resigned on Jan. 26, 1874. He restored his health by several winters in Minnesota. Meanwhile, he prepared his father's judicial opinions for the press and occasionally participated in legal consultations and briefs. In 1882 he reopened his office in Dover and at once became a leader of the state bar, frequently acting as referee and arguing many cases before the supreme court.

In 1890, at the age of fifty-three, chance brought an abrupt change in his work. A lecture he gave on Legal Ethics to Harvard students so impressed President Eliot, who happened to be in the audience, that a month later, Mar. 31, Smith was appointed Story Professor of Law. In September 1890 he settled at 4 Berkeley St., Cambridge, a house formerly owned by Richard H. Dana [q.v.], and began twenty years of teaching at the Harvard Law School. His subjects were torts, agency, corporations (then a new course), persons, and interpretation of statutes. He had a wide experience in the application of law and an illuminated common sense which checked the excess of mere theory. The personality of "Jerry" Smith furnished as large an inspiration to his pupils as his direct instruction. "The beauty of his character and the charm of his kindly smile and noble face attracted all with whom he came in contact. He was simple and direct of speech and manner, courteous and unfeignedly democratic in his dealings with all" (Williston, post, p. 158). "A class, however large, was never to him merely a collective unit" (Williston, quoted by Beale, post, p. 5). He had a remarkable gift for remembering persons, and he recognized and cultivated the separate individualities of his students. Precise and thorough as he was in defining legal rights and duties, he had little respect for the man who always insists on those legal rights, and will not do more than law requires. It was his wont each year, after showing how few positive acts were demanded by law, to recommend the students to read the last part of the twenty-fifth chapter of St. Matthew, and thus to call to mind the obligations above and beyond law. His case books in torts and other subjects display sagacity in finding significant decisions. His numerous legal articles broke new ground on several important questions, particularly "Crucial Issues in Labor Litigation" (Harvard Law Review, February–April 1907).

In the summer of 1910 he retired from teaching but not from work. Several hours of each day he spent in the Law School library, "learning the law all over again." Several of his best articles were written in this period. Though he taught students no longer, his younger colleagues delighted in learning from him. His powers remained unbroken until past the age of eighty-four. After a week's illness he died at St. Andrews, New Brunswick, which had long been his summer home. His son Jeremiah (1870–1935) was a noted lawyer, prominent in international affairs, whose work as financial adviser to Hungary after the World War is regarded as saving that country from the consequences of financial ruin.

[J. H. Beale, "Jeremiah Smith," Harvard Law Rev., Nov. 1921; Samuel Williston, "Jeremiah Smith," Harvard Graduates' Mag., Dec. 1921; Boston Transcript, Sept. 6, 1921; Eugene Wambaugh, "In re J. S.," Green Bag, Dec. 1904; secretary's reports, Harvard Coll., Class of 1856; The Centennial Hist. of Harvard Law School (1918); Who's Who in America, 1920–21; Smith's opinions in 47–54 N. H. Reports.]   Z. C., Jr.

SMITH, JOB LEWIS (Oct. 15, 1827–June 9, 1897), physician, was born in the township of Spafford, Onondaga County, N. Y. He was descended from John Smith, one of the founders of Milford, Conn.; his grandfather, Job Smith, and his father, Lewis Smith, served as officers in the Revolution; the latter was also active in the political life of Onondaga County and was a member of the state legislature in 1829. He married Chloe Benson, a descendant of a Massachusetts Puritan, and she bore him five children, one of whom, Stephen Smith [q.v.], was later a distinguished surgeon in New York City. Job Lewis Smith was the youngest child.

The boy passed the early years of his life on his father's farm and attended the village school. Thence he went to Homer Academy in Homer, Cortland County, N. Y., to prepare for Yale College, where he obtained the degree of B.A. in 1849. In accordance with the custom of his times, he entered a medical apprenticeship under the tutelage of a practising physician, and attended lectures at the Buffalo Medical College, coming under the influence of the famous clinician, Austin Flint, 1812–86 [q.v.]. Through him Smith obtained an internship in the Buffalo Hospital of the Sisters of Charity, spent one year there, and then entered the College of Physicians and Surgeons in New York City, receiving his degree of doctor of medicine in 1853. He immediately began a private practice which he pursued with great devotion for forty-four years. His first office was at 137 West Forty-ninth Street, then considered far uptown in New York, and his first patients were the poor, from whom he received little or no material remuneration but to whom he gave faithful service even at the height of his career. In the course of general practice, he developed an especial interest in the diseases of children. He is an excellent example of the specialist of the nineteenth century to whom a special field was often merely one chapter, albeit one more affectionately studied, in the book of general medicine. In 1869 he incorporated the fruit of his studies and personal experience in a textbook, *A Treatise on the Diseases of Infancy and Childhood,* which passed through eight editions in the next twenty-seven years. It is apparently one of the earliest of American publications dealing with the diseases of children in their entirety and as a specialty, and sixty years later is still interesting because its shrewd observations of disease were drawn from a wealth of personal experience controlled and amplified by an intimate contact with scientific literature. Its many editions were not merely reprints, but followed faithfully, though critically, the essential changes in medical opinion.

Smith's skill as a clinician and teacher brought him fame as one of America's leading pediatricians, a preëminence which he shared with Abraham Jacobi [*q.v.*]. He was called to the service of eight prominent New York hospitals, lectured on the diseases of children at the Bellevue Hospital Medical College, was professor of morbid anatomy there in 1871–72, and in 1876 became clinical professor of the diseases of children at Bellevue, sixteen years after the first special chair of pediatrics had been created for Jacobi at the New York Medical College. Smith held his professorship for twenty years, retiring in 1896 as professor emeritus. He was a founder of the American Pediatric Society, and in 1890 was elected its second president. He married, Apr. 22, 1858, Mary Anne, daughter of George Hannah, by whom he had seven children. A son died in 1889, shortly after entering upon the practice of medicine; four daughters survived their father.

[F. H. Garrison, "History of Pediatrics," in I. A. Abt, *Pediatrics,* vol. I (1923); E. H. Grandin, in H. A. Kelly and W. L. Burrage, *Am. Medic. Biogs.* (1920); Ellsworth Eliot, in *Trans. N. Y. Acad. of Medicine, 1896–1901* (1903); John Shrady, in *Trans. N. Y. State Medic. Asso.,* vol. XIV (1897), with portr. and bibliog. of Smith's publications; *Obit. Record Grads. Yale Univ.,* 1897; *Record of the Graduated Members of the Class of 1849 of Yale Coll.* (1875); *Gen. Alumni Cat., N. Y. Univ. . . . Medic. Alumni* (1908); *Archives of Pediatrics,* July 1897; *N. Y. Times,* June 10, 1897.]
H. S. R—e.

SMITH, JOEL WEST (Sept. 17, 1837–May 9, 1924), educator of the blind, was of New England stock and was born in East Hampton, Conn., to Delia Elliot (West) Smith, a minister's daughter, and John William Burke Smith, a

farmer. He was educated in the public schools and at a local academy. Having a bent for business, he became postmaster and manager of the village store. At the age of twenty-four, while celebrating the Fourth of July, he was blinded for life. Entering the Perkins Institution for the Blind, he learned piano tuning and became instructor in that subject there in 1866. In 1872 he was called to London to open a department of tuning in the new Royal Normal College for the Blind. After three years he returned to Perkins, where he so built up his department that he secured and held for it the yearly contract of keeping in tune and repair the pianos of the Boston public schools. Being an ingenious mechanic he worked out such devices for the use of the blind as tangible maps and improved writing appliances, one of which was a machine for typewriting in Braille letters. His scientific revision of Braille's alphabet, known as American Braille, received increasing recognition until the demand for world-wide uniformity caused it to be superseded. For four years he edited, published, and largely financed the *Mentor,* 1891–94, the first magazine published in the United States for the blind. He introduced the use of the typewriter at Perkins, working out for himself the now common touch method of using it.

In 1894 he left Massachusetts permanently for his native East Hampton, where he owned property and where he voted. A public-spirited citizen, he served repeatedly on church and village improvement committees, was one of the prominent men of his town, and became a trustee of the Connecticut School for the Blind. His geniality and humor made people forget that he was blind, and at Perkins he was counselor and popular leader. He had, however, a mercurial temperament, his periods of depression becoming pronounced as distressing disabilities came upon him. In one of these he took his own life, an act said by his intimates to be due to his morbid fear of becoming a burden to his friends. His death occurred at Middletown, Conn. He left an estate of some $25,000, partly inherited but mostly accumulated through thrift and careful investment. Some of this was left to his relatives and friends, some to church and town enterprises, and some to organizations for the blind.

[Perkins Institution and Mass. School for the Blind, ann. reports for 1872, 1895, and 1924; *Ann. Reports Board of Educ. of the Blind* (Conn.), 1924; *State of Conn. Pub. Doc.,* No. 35 (1924); *The Outlook for the Blind,* June 1924, Dec. 1928; obituary in *Hartford Courant,* May 10, 1924; autobiog. notes, letters, and other data, Perkins Inst.; personal acquaintance.]
E. E. A—n.

SMITH, JOHN (1579/80–June 21, 1631), adventurer, explorer, author, is popularly one of the best and historically one of the least known figures in early American history. With regard to many events in his life the evidence is still conflicting. Born in Willoughby, Lincolnshire, England, and baptized there Jan. 9, 1579, o.s., he was the son of George Smith, a member of the Smith family of Crudley, Lancashire, and his wife Alice. John's father died in 1596 and left him a modest property. After a grammar-school education he was apprenticed to a prominent merchant, Thomas Sendall of Lynn, whom he soon left to seek adventure. Four years of soldiering on the Continent followed. After a brief visit to Scotland, he went to the Continent again to engage in the war against the Turks. After various unverifiable adventures he succeeded in joining the military forces on the Hungarian and Transylvanian frontier. He claims that he fought three single combats with leading Turkish warriors and that his military exploits so impressed Prince Sigismund Bathori that that leader granted him a coat of arms and a pension of three thousand ducats annually. In the subsequent fighting in Transylvania, he says that he was taken prisoner and was sent to Constantinople as a present for the Turkish Pasha's wife, Tragabigzanda; she fell in love with him and, in order to protect him, sent him to her brother who ruled over a somewhat vaguely defined country between the Caspian and Black seas. There, however, he was made a slave. He killed his master, Timor, and escaped, finding his way back to Transylvania and to Bathori, who gave him a safe-conduct. With this in his possession, he claims to have wandered over a large part of Europe, with his customary adventures. He returned to England, probably in 1604. With his other travels, real or imaginary, before his connection began with American history, we need not be concerned. (For a severe analysis of Smith's story, see L. L. Kropf, *Notes and Queries,* 7 ser., vol. IX, 1890, and *American Historical Review,* July 1898, pp. 727–38; for a more favorable estimate, see Fletcher and Wroth, *post.*)

In 1606 the Virginia Company of London received its patent and Smith claims to have taken an active part in the promotion and organization of the enterprise. In December of that year three ships set sail for Virginia with 144 colonists, among them Smith. They proceeded by way of the Canaries and West Indies, entering Chesapeake Bay Apr. 26, 1607. Only 105 disembarked at Jamestown, May 24. When the instructions from England were opened it was found that the government for the first year was to consist of a council of seven, including Smith.

Owing to charges of mutiny on the voyage, he was not permitted to serve on the council until June 20, but from the first he engaged in exploration. Wingfield was chosen as president. Trouble began soon after the ships sailed back for England, leaving the colonists. There was great sickness and within the first seven months nearly two-thirds of the settlers died. Feeling ran high against the local government for various reasons. The leaders fell out among themselves, and Smith was never good at acting in concert with others. He showed at his best in the expeditions he made among the Indians to procure corn and other food for the half-famished colony. On one of these he and his companions were taken prisoner by some of the savages and, according to his story in the *Generall Historie* (1624), he was condemned to death. It was on this occasion that he is supposed to have been saved by the intercession of Pocahontas [*q.v.*], the young daughter of the chief Powhatan [*q.v.*]. Around this incident, as around most of the more spectacular adventures of Smith, controversy has long raged. Such intercession, however, was quite in accord with the customs of Indian life and there is nothing inherently improbable in the story. In any case, Smith returned to Jamestown in January 1608 to find his enemies, John Ratcliffe and Gabriel Archer, in command of the turbulent settlement; he was promptly arrested, tried for the loss of two of his men, and condemned to be hanged. Fortunately for him, Captain Christopher Newport [*q.v.*], with supplies and new settlers from England, arrived that evening. Smith was released and restored to his place in the council.

He spent much of the summer in exploring the Potomac and Rappahannock rivers and Chesapeake Bay. Newport sailed back to England after three months. In June, on the *Phoenix,* Smith sent to England the account published that year as *A True Relation of Such Occurrences and Accidents of Noate as Hath Hapned in Virginia since the First Planting of That Collony.* The "sickly season" again took its toll at Jamestown and about forty-five men out of ninety-five died. On his return on July 21 from one of his exploring trips, which interested him much more than administration at Jamestown, he effected the deposition of President Ratcliffe, and, leaving in charge Matthew Scrivener, started out again. In the autumn, however, elected president by the council, he settled down to governing the colony. That winter, 1608–09, starvation again faced the settlers and Smith saved them by getting corn from the Indians. He had a far clearer notion of the value of a colony than the company in England, which wished the settlers to waste themselves in trying to find gold, but unfortunately he was not always practical; as spring came it was found that rats had been allowed to eat a large part of the stores. Smith divided the colony into three parts, each to go where food might be found. In 1609, following the granting of a new charter, some supplies and new colonists, with whom came Ratcliffe and Archer, reached Virginia. After much wrangling about authority, Smith, who had been wounded by an explosion, sailed for England in October 1609. George Percy [q.v.] succeeded him. Complaints, mostly unfounded, were made against him at home, and in London he severely criticized the Virginia Company and its methods. In 1612 he published *A Map of Virginia, With a Description of the Countrey, the Commodities, People, Government and Religion.*

In comparison with Smith's brief, spectacular career in Virginia, the substantial contributions that he made in his later years to the founding of New England have not been sufficiently stressed. In March 1614 he was sent to the region by London merchants and, though he failed to take whales or discover gold, he brought back a valuable cargo of fish and furs. More valuable still was his map, which was printed in *A Description of New England* (1616) and several of his later works and served to establish the name of the region. He emphasized the importance of fishing and continued to the end of his life to proclaim the favorable prospects of New England for permanent settlement. Sent by Sir Ferdinando Gorges and others of the "west country," as well as the London merchants, he started on another voyage, but was captured by pirates and then by the French, and spent months at sea until landed at La Rochelle in November 1615. He managed to get back to Plymouth, where he had been given up for dead. Except for the sending of fishing vessels, his hopes of another venture were disappointed. The Pilgrims made use of his books and maps, but had no desire that he should join them (*Generall Historie*, 1907 ed., vol. II, 182). In 1620 he published *New Englands Trials* (republished later, with additional matter on the Pilgrims), and in 1624 *The Generall Historie of Virginia, New-England, and the Summer Isles,* in which much of his early writing and narratives by others were incorporated. On seamanship and his own adventures he published *An Accidence or the Path-way to Experience* (1626), which he republished in an enlarged edition as *A Sea Grammar* (1627); and *The True Travels, Adventures, and Observations of Captaine John Smith, in Europe, Asia, Affrica,*

and America (1630). The year of his death there appeared his *Advertisements for the Unexperienced Planters of New England, or Anywhere* (1631), which is full of sound and sometimes amusing suggestions based on his own experiences. Apparently he had gained, as he deserved, high repute among those engaged in American colonization.

[The best collection of Smith's writings is Edward Arber, *Capt. John Smith . . . Works* (1884), reprinted with the same pagination and with some corrections as *Travels and Works of Capt. John Smith* (2 vols., 1910), with introduction by A. G. Bradley. Valuable also are J. G. Fletcher and L. C. Wroth, eds., *The True Travels, Adventures, & Observations of Captaine John Smith* (1930), with introduction by Fletcher and bibliographical notes by Wroth; and Wilberforce Eames, *A Bibliography of Capt. John Smith* (1927), reprinted from Sabin, *Dict. of Books Relating to America.* None of the biographies is thoroughly satisfactory from the scholarly point of view. The two latest are E. K. Chatterton, *Capt. John Smith* (1927), which is strongly biased in his favor; and J. G. Fletcher, *John Smith— Also Pocahontas* (1928). J. A. Doyle, in *Dict. Nat. Biography,* is a good brief account. The strong skeptical criticism of Smith and his adventures started by Charles Deane in his ed. of E.-M. Wingfield, "A Discourse of Va.," in *Am. Antiquarian Soc. Trans.,* vol. IV (1860), was continued by him in his ed. of *A True Relation* (1866); by Henry Adams, in *No. Am. Review,* Jan. 1867, a review of Deane's ed.; by Alexander Brown, in *The Genesis of the U. S.* (2 vols., 1890), and other writings; and by Justin Winsor, in *Narrative and Critical Hist. of America,* vol. III (1885). The danger of impugning all of Smith's writings because of the extravagance of some of them, however, has been pointed out by recent scholars and there is an increasing recognition of the value of his services; see, especially, C. M. Andrews, *The Colonial Period of Am. Hist.,* vol. I (1934), p. 142 n., and Fletcher and Wroth, *ante.*]   J. T. A.

SMITH, JOHN (c. 1735–c. 1824), clergyman, merchant, United States senator, was supposedly born in Virginia. In 1790 he was ministering to a Baptist congregation on the forks of the Cheat River, in what is now West Virginia. The following year he moved to Columbia, Ohio, later a part of Cincinnati, where he took charge of a recently organized church, and for several years combined preaching with the more lucrative operations of merchant and farmer. His gifts as a speaker early brought him into public life. In 1798 he entered the first legislative assembly of the Northwest Territory and in this and the succeeding assembly was noted for his opposition to Governor St. Clair (Burnet, *post,* p. 288). As a reward for his activity in promoting statehood he was selected, in April 1803, as one of the two senators from Ohio. In addition to local connections, Smith expanded his trading and speculative activities into West Florida, where he followed the usual practice of taking an oath of allegiance to the Spanish king, and where for a time Reuben Kemper [q.v.] represented him. Smith took his seat in the Senate in the fall of 1803. He was credited with one speech only, but conferred frequently with President Jefferson, whom he had consistently supported, concerning claims to West Florida (Pickering Papers, *post*; also Burnet, *post,* pp. 294–95). He busied himself principally with army contracts, land deals, and the interest of his constituents.

Smith is best known for his association, altogether too intimate, with Aaron Burr [*q.v.*]. He furthered the latter's project for a canal around the falls of the Ohio and when the former vice-president visited the West in 1805, entertained him at Cincinnati; and again, in 1806. When contemporary reports concerning Burr's purpose aroused the Western country, Smith became alarmed and obtained from Burr a statement specifically denying any intention to separate the Western states from the Union. Smith later visited Frankfort while a grand jury was investigating Burr's conduct, and his prompt departure indicated a wish to avoid witnessing against his former associate. To the measures taken by Jefferson and the local authorities to break up Burr's project he contributed freely the necessary provisions and credit and thus helped keep the Ohio militia in the field. Later he went to New Orleans to provide Gen. James Wilkinson [*q.v.*] with provisions for his forces there. While in that city Smith learned that he also had been indicted for complicity with Burr. He immediately withdrew to West Florida and later surrendered himself to the governor of the Mississippi territory, and was allowed to go to Richmond, under escort, by way of Cincinnati. When Burr was acquitted in the Virginia court, the bill against Smith was quashed.

Rumors of Smith's complicity with Burr and his obvious neglect of his senatorial duties had stirred up his enemies in the Ohio assembly and in Cincinnati to demand his resignation. When he arrived in Washington, January 1807, his colleagues in the Senate appointed a committee headed by John Quincy Adams to investigate the charges against him. He was able to explain most of the charges acceptably but not to clear himself of the suspicion that he and his sons knew more of Burr's plans than they chose to divulge. The committee favored his expulsion but its recommendation failed of passage by one vote less than the required two-thirds. Smith thereupon resigned his seat. For a time he carried on his business operations in Cincinnati and vicinity but the notoriety gained in connection with Burr led to delay in settling his government contracts and ultimately forced him into bankruptcy. Removing to West Florida in 1812, he resided for a time in Pensacola and later retired to St. Francisville (now in Louisiana), where he carried on his clerical and business activities until his death.

[A number of letters written by Smith in his own defense are to be found in the Pickering Papers of the Mass. Hist. Soc. (see "Hist. Index to the Pickering Papers," *Mass. Hist. Soc. Colls.*, 6 ser. VIII, 1896); many facts relating to his life and his connection with the Burr conspiracy are brought out in "Testimony in Connection with Investigation of Senator John Smith . . . Queries Addressed by the Committee, Dec. 9, 1807, to Mr. Smith," ordered printed Dec. 31, 1807; *Annals of Cong.*, 10 Cong., 1 Sess., pt. 1, contain the proceedings in the Senate against him, and should be supplemented by *Memoirs of John Quincy Adams*, vol. I (1874); see also William Plumer's *Memorandum of Proceedings in the United States Senate, 1803–1807* (1923), ed. by E. S. Brown; Jacob Burnet, *Notes on the Early Settlement of the North-Western Territory* (1847); C. T. Greve, *Centennial Hist. of Cincinnati*, vol. I (1904); I. J. Cox, *The West Florida Controversy, 1798–1813* (1918).]

I. J. C—x.

SMITH, JOHN AUGUSTINE (Aug. 29, 1782–Feb. 9, 1865), physician, college president, teacher, author, and editor, was born in Westmoreland County, Va., the second son of the Rev. Thomas Smith of Cople Parish and Mary Smith, who was the daughter of John Smith of Shooter's Hill, a member of the House of Burgesses and cousin of George Washington. After graduating from the College of William and Mary, Williamsburg, Va., in 1800, he went abroad for a medical education and studied at St. Thomas' Hospital, London. On his return to the United States he practised first in Gloucester County, Va., but shortly moved to New York City. In 1809 he married Letitia Lee, by whom he had nine children. He was assigned a place on the first faculty of the College of Physicians and Surgeons in 1807 as adjunct lecturer on anatomy; he became professor of anatomy and surgery in 1808, and professor of anatomy, surgery, and physiology in 1811. When the school was merged with Columbia College (later Columbia University), he and Wright Post [*q.v.*] became joint professors of these subjects. In 1814 he was elected to the presidency of the College of William and Mary. The faculty of the college consisted of but four professors, including the president, who in addition to performing the duties of his office taught moral and political philosophy. It was not a prosperous period in the history of the college, which reached its low ebb in 1824. Not unnaturally some of the opprobrium was heaped on Smith. His enemies said he had injured the college by abolishing the honor system and instituting a plan of discipline too harsh for Virginia youths; it was alleged that he was a Deist, and that he was fonder of hunting than of teaching. But the opposition to Smith at this time was chiefly due to his attempt to move the college to Richmond. Before the legislature in 1824 he cited the alarming shrinkage in the student body of the college and predicted that the expected opening of the University of Virginia would seriously reduce even this small number; he proposed not only to move the college but to enlarge it by the creation of theological and medical departments, declaring that they "would give utility, dignity and importance to the institution" (*Journal of the House of Delegates of the Commonwealth of Virginia,* 1824, p. 4). As there was no medical school in Virginia at this time his proposal was warmly supported by the physicians of the state. The scheme, however, ran athwart the maturing plans of Thomas Jefferson for a great state university at Charlottesville, incurred his opposition, and failed.

Fortunately at this juncture (1825) a reorganization of the faculty of the College of Physicians and Surgeons in New York was in process. Invited to resume his old chair, Smith accepted, and six years later, 1831, he succeeded John Watts as president. After Valentine Mott [*q.v.*] joined the faculty in 1834 as professor of anatomy, Smith confined himself to the teaching of physiology. Three years later he was influential in moving the college to a new location on Crosby Street. The curriculum of the college was now materially broadened, and many new features were introduced which have continued to the present time. In 1841 he inaugurated a spring course of clinical lectures with the cooperation of such men as Willard Parker [*q.v.*] and Alonzo Clarke. One unpleasant incident occurred. A controversy with James R. Manley, lecturer on obstetrics, whose appointment Smith had opposed, and whose eviction from the faculty he secured, led in 1841 to the sharp strictures of a forty-eight page pamphlet entitled *Exposition of the Conduct and Character of Dr. Smith.* Smith retired to private life in 1843, devoting his leisure to a philosophical work entitled *Prelections on Some of the More Important Subjects Connected with Moral and Physical Science* (1853). His other published works consist of an *Introductory Discourse at New Medical College, Crosby Street* (1837), *Select Discourses on the Functions of the Nervous System in Opposition to Phrenology, Materialism and Atheism* (1840), *The Mutations of the Earth* (1846), *Moral and Physical Science* (1853). In 1809 he was editor of the *Medical and Physiological Journal,* and in 1828 co-editor of the *New York Medical and Physical Journal.*

[L. G. Tyler, *Encyc. of Va. Biog.,* vol. II (1915), and *Coll. of William and Mary in Va.* (1907); John Shrady, ed., *The Coll. of Physicians and Surgeons, N. Y.* (n.d.), vol. I; J. J. Walsh, *Hist. of Medicine in N. Y.* (1919), vol. II; *Am. Medic. and Philosophical Reg.,* Apr., July, 1813; *William and Mary Coll. Quart.,* Jan. 1932; *Circulars of Information Bureau of Educ.,* no. 1 (1887); death notice in *N. Y. Times,* Feb. 10, 1865; Family records in the possession of Miss Ellen Bagby, Richmond, Va.]   W. B. B.

SMITH, JOHN BERNHARD (Nov. 21, 1858–Mar. 12, 1912), entomologist, was born in New York City of German parentage. His father was John and his mother Elizabeth (Scheuerman) Smith; the father came to America in 1853, from Bavaria. The younger John was educated in the public schools, studied law, and was admitted to the bar. He established himself as a lawyer in Brooklyn, where he practised between 1880 and 1884. As a young man he became interested in the study of insects and joined the Brooklyn Entomological Society. At first *Coleoptera* attracted him, but later he took up the *Lepidoptera* and became especially interested in the large group known as the owlet moths (*Noctuidae*). In 1882 he became an editor, and later sole editor, of the *Bulletin of the Brooklyn Entomological Society,* which afterwards developed into a journal known as *Entomologica Americana.* The latter journal, which he edited from April 1885 to September 1890, was for a time the most prominent American periodical in its field for the publication of short papers and notes. Giving up his law in 1884, Smith became a field agent of the United States Department of Agriculture and spent two years in investigating insects affecting the hop and the cranberry. In 1886 he was made assistant curator of insects in the United States National Museum, and held this post until 1889, when, with the founding of the state agricultural experiment stations, he was appointed entomologist of the New Jersey station. Here he began his most important economic work, which lasted until his fatal illness.

Smith took a high rank among the rapidly growing body of state entomologists, was given the honorary degree of Doctor of Science by Rutgers in 1891, and was president of the Association of Economic Entomologists in 1895, and the Entomological Society of America in 1910. He was prominent in the early work against the San Jose scale, and conducted many other important investigations of injurious insects. His greatest triumph, however, was in the discovery of the breeding habits of the salt-marsh mosquitoes, a discovery which made it possible for summer resorts and other communities near large areas of salt marsh greatly to improve conditions. On the basis of his early biological work with these forms, he succeeded in impressing the New Jersey people, and especially the New Jersey legislature, with the possibility of the control of the salt-marsh mosquitoes, and started a movement which has gone on ever since and which has rendered the New Jersey coast infinitely more desirable for residence than it was before his time. He was the author of two excellent books, *Economic Entomology for the Farmer and Fruit Grower* (1896) and *Our Insect Friends and Enemies* (1909). He was also the author of a long list of papers, a number of them monographic in character. In addition to his research work, he was state entomologist of New Jersey, and professor of entomology in Rutgers College from 1889 until his death. He married Marie H. von Meske, of Albany, in 1886. She was a daughter of Otto von Meske, a well-known lepidopterist.

[J. A. Grossbeck, "Bibliog. of the Published Writings of Prof. John B. Smith," *Proc. Staten Island Asso. of Arts and Sciences,* vol. IV (1913), and sketch in *Entomological News,* May 1912 (portr.); L. O. Howard in *Science,* Apr. 19, 1912; Herbert Osborn, in *Jour. Economic Entomology,* Apr. 1912 (portr.); *Proc. Entomological Soc. of Washington,* vol. XIV (1913); *Proc. . . . Soc. for the Promotion of Agric. Sci., 1912* (1913); C. R. Woodward and I. N. Waller, *N. J.'s Agric. Station* (1932); *N. J. Experiment Station Record,* 1930; *Experiment Station Record,* Apr. 1912; *Who's Who in America,* 1910–11; spelling of middle name from Lib. of Cong. Second Official Cat., citing as authority information from Smith himself, Dec. 1903.]   L. O. H.

SMITH, JOHN BLAIR (June 12, 1756–Aug. 22, 1799), Presbyterian clergyman, college president, was born at Pequea, Lancaster County, Pa., the son of the Rev. Robert Smith, an emigrant from Londonderry, Ireland, and his wife, Elizabeth Blair, sister of the Rev. Samuel Blair [*q.v.*]. Robert Smith was a prominent Presbyterian clergyman of his day, the founder of a classical and theological seminary at Pequea which had great popularity, an overseer of the College of New Jersey, and the second moderator of the Presbyterian General Assembly. John Blair Smith was prepared at the classical school conducted by his father and in 1773 was graduated from the College of New Jersey. In 1775 he accepted the position of tutor in the Academy of Hampden-Sidney, Virginia, which in 1783 was rechartered as the College of Hampden-Sidney, and in 1779, having been ordained to the ministry by the Hanover Presbytery on Oct. 26 of that year, he succeeded his brother, Samuel Stanhope Smith [*q.v.*], as president of that institution and pastor of the churches of Cumberland and Briery. He married Elizabeth, daughter of Col. John Nash of "Templeton," in Prince Edward County, Va., by whom he had five sons and one daughter. In 1787 his preaching was accompanied by a great religious awakening which spread from the vicinity of the college throughout Virginia south of the James River and was carried by converts into the Valley of Virginia

and into North Carolina. Two years later, in order to enjoy to the fullest the delight of preaching the Presbyterian gospel, he resigned the college presidency. In 1791 he was called to the Third Presbyterian Church of Philadelphia, usually referred to as the Pine Street Church. Here he served acceptably and in the yellow fever epidemic of 1793 was conspicuous for heroism. In 1795 he was made the first president of Union College, at Schenectady, New York. Three years later he was chosen moderator of the Presbyterian General Assembly. He returned to his Pine Street pastorate in Philadelphia in 1799, and died there of yellow fever on Aug. 22 of that year.

He was of medium height, slender, and delicate in appearance. Remarkably vivacious and quick in movement for a Presbyterian of the dour Scotch-Irish breed, he was an attractive and popular man, a fervid and animated preacher. "It was one of his peculiar properties to put out his strength in everything he undertook, and to do nothing by halves" (Rev. Wm. Hill, quoted by Foote, *post,* p. 411).

At the age of twenty-three he became the leader of Presbyterian thought in Virginia. He was the able defender of "an entire and everlasting freedom from every species of ecclesiastical domination, a full and permanent security of the inalienable rights of conscience and private judgment" (quoted by Eckenrode, *post,* p. 77, from one of Smith's memorials to the Virginia legislature). He had supported the American cause from the beginning of the struggle with Great Britain, and for a short time had served in the field as captain of a militia company composed of Hampden-Sidney students. His enthusiastic devotion to the Revolution won for him the confidence of the triumphant patriot politicians. Moreover, he had been a Princeton classmate of "Light-Horse Harry" Lee. When, in 1783, the new and enlarged charter for Hampden-Sidney was obtained from the legislature, Madison, Henry, and other non-Presbyterians of prominence accepted appointment as trustees. In 1784–85 Smith successfully opposed Henry's General Assessment Bill (Foote, p. 431; Eckenrode, p. 113); and in 1788 opposed Henry again, this time by urging the adoption of the new federal constitution. During the fifteen years he lived in Virginia, Presbyterianism first emerged from the group of sects tolerated by the gentry as perhaps suitable for people of no particular importance, and became popular with the ruling class. The dogmatic temper and the humorless deadly logic of Presbyterianism as exemplified by Smith were to be of rapid growth in the South.

[The chief authority on Smith's life is W. H. Foote, *Sketches of Va.*, 1 ser. (1850) ; H. J. Eckenrode, *Separation of Church and State in Va.* (1910) treats of his importance as a leader of his denomination from 1780 to 1790 ; see also H. O. Gibbons, *A Hist. of Old Pine Street* (1905) ; W. B. Sprague, *Annals Am. Pulpit*, vol. III (1858) ; A. J. Morrison, *Coll. of Hampden Sidney Dictionary of Biog., 1776–1825* (1921).] T. C. J., Jr.

SMITH, JOHN COTTON (Feb. 12, 1765–Dec. 7, 1845), governor of Connecticut, was born in Sharon, Conn., a son of the Rev. Cotton Mather Smith (Oct. 16, 1731–Nov. 27, 1806), a chaplain in the Revolution and the Congregational minister of Sharon for fifty years, and his wife, Temperance, daughter of the Rev. William Worthington of Saybrook and widow of Dr. Moses Gale of Goshen. Through his father, Smith traced his descent from the Rev. Richard Mather [*q.v.*], through his son Timothy, and from the Rev. Henry Smith, the first settled pastor in Wethersfield, Conn. Prepared by his mother and local divines, he spent the later years of the Revolution in quiet study at Yale College, where he was graduated in 1783. After reading law under John Canfield of Sharon, he was admitted to the bar in 1786 and settled down to practise his profession; on Oct. 29 of the same year he married Margaret Evertson of Amenia, N. Y. (d. May 10, 1837), by whom he had a son, William Mather Smith.

Cotton Smith commenced his political career in 1793 with a term in the legislature, to which he was reëlected for the sessions of 1796–1800; he served as clerk in 1799, and as speaker in 1800. A sturdy Calvinist and a conservative with a violent hatred for French Jacobins and American Republicans, he endeared himself to the Federalist-Congregational party which ruled the state. This party he served well as a representative in Congress from Nov. 17, 1800, until his resignation in August 1806; as a member of the legislature in 1808–09; as a judge of the superior court in 1809; as lieutenant-governor in 1811, acting governor on the death of Roger Griswold [*q.v.*] in 1812, and governor from 1813 through 1817. It was as the last governor of the old "Standing Order" that Smith challenged attention. He favored the agricultural and shipping interests, half fearing that manufactures had been fostered too generously. An opponent of the War of 1812, he supported his predecessor's refusal to place the state militia under federal officers, yet he maintained that he was ready "to defend the state at every hazard, and to fulfil his Federal obligations up to the spirit and letter of the Constitution" (Andrews, *post*, p. 33). He urged Connecticut representation in the Hartford Convention, which he defended to the end of his life on the score of its distinguished membership. A bitter enemy of reform and of liberal revision of the old royal Charter, Smith went down to defeat in 1817 before the combined forces of Republicans, non-Congregationalists, and ungodly men, led by Oliver Wolcott, who demanded a new constitution granting complete toleration, universal suffrage, and the separation of Church and State.

At the close of his governorship Smith retired to an estate in Sharon to observe with misgivings the revolutionary changes wrought by a new generation and a horde of immigrants. He maintained an interest in the historical societies of Connecticut and Massachusetts and in the Royal Society of Northern Antiquaries of Copenhagen, Denmark. He was also the first president of the Connecticut Bible Society, president of the American Bible Society from 1831 to 1845, and president of the American Board of Commissioners for Foreign Missions from 1826 to 1841. A senatorial gentleman, courteous and punctilious, full of honest prejudices against Catholics, Freemasonry, and Methodists, he outlived his age, dying in 1845, in his eighty-first year.

[W. W. Andrews, *The Correspondence and Miscellanies of the Hon. John Cotton Smith . . . with an Eulogy* (1847) ; Smith's published *Oration Pronounced at Sharon . . . 4th of July 1798* (n.d.) ; *Biog. Dir. Am. Cong.* (1928) ; R. J. Purcell, *Conn. in Transition* (1918) ; C. F. Sedgwick, *A Hist. of the Town of Sharon* (1842) ; H. R. Stiles, *The Hist. of Ancient Wethersfield* (1904), vol. II ; G. H. Hollister, *The Hist. of Conn.* (1855), vol. II ; *Proc. Am. Antiquarian Soc.*, IV (1888), 375–78 ; Bayard Tuckerman, *A Sketch of the Cotton Smith Family of Sharon, Conn.* (1915) ; F. B. Dexter, *Biog. Sketches Grads. Yale Coll.*, vol. IV (1907) ; *Norwich Weekly Courier*, Dec. 17, 1845 ; a few letters in Lib. of Cong.] R. J. P.

SMITH, JOHN COTTON (Aug. 4, 1826–Jan. 9, 1882), Protestant Episcopal clergyman, editor, author, was born in Andover, Mass., son of the Rev. Thomas Mather Smith and Mary Greenleaf (Woods). His father, a Congregational minister who later entered the Episcopal Church and was president of Kenyon College, 1850–54, was a nephew of Gov. John Cotton Smith [*q.v.*] of Connecticut and a descendant of the Rev. Richard Mather [*q.v.*], from 1636 until his death pastor of the church in Dorchester, Mass.; his mother was a daughter of the Rev. Leonard Woods [*q.v.*], professor at Andover Theological Seminary. John Cotton Smith attended Phillips Academy, Andover, and was graduated from Bowdoin College in 1847, where he was first honor man of his class. After taking a course in theology at Kenyon College, he was ordained deacon by Bishop McIlvaine of Ohio in 1849; the following year he was ordained to the priesthood by Bishop Burgess of Maine. He became rector of St. John's Church, Bangor, Me., and two years later, 1852, was appointed assistant minister of Trinity Church, Boston, Mass. In 1860 he was instituted rector of the Church of the Ascension, New York, where he remained until his death. In 1867 he became associate editor of *The Protestant Churchman,* later *Church and State*—of which he subsequently became editor in chief, serving in that capacity until his periodical was absorbed by *The Churchman.*

Smith was distinguished as a scholar, theologian, preacher, and philanthropist. During the years of his ministry there were four major issues in the religious field, all of which enlisted his active interest, as editor, author, and preacher —foreign missions, social problems, adjustment of new knowledge in theological and scientific fields to traditional theological concepts, and church union. For twenty-two years he was a member of the foreign committee of the board of missions of the Episcopal Church. In the field of social problems his chief interest lay in the direction of tenement-house reform. He was a stanch and pioneer advocate of model housing and it was under his auspices that the first model tenement was erected in New York City. His book, *Improvements of the Tenement House System of New York* (1879), consisting of extracts from the report of the Ascension Association, created a sensation. In considering the socalled conflict between science and theology, his motto was, "What is true is safe." The adaptability of his mind to new knowledge is indicated by an earlier and a later essay on evolution— the second revealing a marked change in point of view from the first—published by him in his volume, *Miscellanies, Old and New* (1876). His interest in church union was evinced by his assertion that his devotion to the Episcopal Church came from his conviction that "it offered the best available basis for the unifying of American religion." In the earlier years of his ministry in New York he took the position that reunion would be possible only through purging the church of non-Protestant characteristics, *i.e.* as represented by the high church party. Later he modified this position, convinced that such a solution was impractical. From then on he emphasized the comprehensive character of the Episcopal Church, stressing his conviction that there must be room in it for all three parties (high, broad, and low). This point of view he emphasized in a sermon preached before the diocesan convention of New York, later published in his *Briar Hill Lectures* (1881). His influence with clergymen of Christian bodies outside his own gave him a strong position of leadership among the clergy of New York. He was a delegate to the General Convention of the Episcopal Church of 1880, served as a trustee of General Theological Seminary, and for twenty years was a member of the Protestant Episcopal Society for the Promotion of Evangelical Knowledge. He was one of the early promoters of the Church Congress, an annual meeting of members of the Church, lay and clerical, to discuss matters religious, moral, and social. While the rector of a wealthy parish, he was emphatically a pastor of the poor. He was known as an earnest, attractive preacher, giving impressive delivery to strong thoughts clearly expressed. Among his published works not already mentioned were *A Plea for Liberty in the Church* (1865); *The Church's Law of Development* (1872); *Limits of Legislation as to Doctrine and Ritual* (1874); *The Church's Mission of Reconciliation* (1880). He was married, Dec. 19, 1849, in Portland, Me., to Harriette, daughter of Gen. James Appleton [*q.v.*]. Two sons and four daughters survived him; one of the sons, Roland Cotton Smith (1860–1934), was for a number of years rector of St. John's Church, Washington, D. C.

[Wm. R. Huntington, *The Counsellor of Peace: A Sermon Commemorative of the Late Rev. John Cotton Smith* (1882); Bayard Tuckerman, *A Sketch of the Cotton Smith Family of Sharon, Conn.* (1915); W. S. Perry, *A Memorial of the Rev. Thomas Mather Smith, D.D.* (1866); Nehemiah Cleaveland, *Hist. of Bowdoin Coll.* (1882), ed. by A. S. Packard; *Churchman,* Jan. 14, 1882; *Living Church,* Jan. 21, 1882; *N. Y. Tribune,* Jan. 10, 1882.]   G. E. S.

SMITH, JOHN EUGENE (Aug. 3, 1816– Jan. 29, 1897), soldier, was born in the canton of Berne, Switzerland. His father, John Banler Smith, was an officer in one of the Swiss regiments which accompanied Napoleon from his ill-fated Moscow campaign to Waterloo. Before John Eugene was a year old his parents emigrated to America and settled in Philadelphia, Pa. There he received an elementary education and learned the jeweler's trade. In 1836, after having followed his trade for a few years in St. Louis, Mo., he removed to Galena, Ill., and established a jewelry business. During the same year he was married to Aimee A. Massot of St. Louis. In 1860 he was elected treasurer of Jo Daviess County, Ill. When the Civil War broke out he at once offered his services to Governor Yates, and, after serving on the staff of the latter for a few months, he organized the 45th Illinois Infantry, known as the "Washburne Leadmine Regiment," and became colonel on July 23, 1861. During 1862 he led his regiment with bravery and distinction in the operations against Forts Henry and Donelson, was in the thickest of the fight at Shiloh, and temporarily commanded a brigade at the siege of Corinth. He was appointed brigadier-general of volunteers on Nov. 29, 1862.

In the spring of 1863 he was given command of a division, under General Grant, which he led ably throughout the Vicksburg campaign, participating in the expedition to Yazoo Pass, the battles of Port Gibson, Raymond, Jackson, Champion's Hill, Big Black River, and the final siege and capture of Vicksburg. Smith, with his division, was then transferred to the Army of the Tennessee, made a brilliant charge at Missionary Ridge, Tenn., and accompanied General Sherman on his march to the sea. A prompt and effective deployment of his division at Savannah, Ga., on Dec. 20, 1864, was instrumental in causing the Confederates to evacuate the city. In June 1865 he was assigned to command the district of western Tennessee where he remained until he was mustered out of the service on Apr. 30, 1866. The following July he was commissioned colonel of the 27th Infantry in the regular army. He served at various frontier posts, and by his coolness and prompt action at Fort Laramie, Wyo., helped to quell an outbreak of the Sioux Indians under Spotted Tail [q.v.]. Smith retired from active service in May 1881, and settled in Chicago, Ill., where he died. His body was taken to his old home at Galena for interment. He had been three times honored with brevet rank: in 1865, as major-general of volunteers for service and gallantry in action; in 1867, as brigadier-general in the regular army for gallantry at the siege of Vicksburg; and again in the same year, as major-general in the regular army for action at Savannah, Ga. He was survived by three sons.

[*War of the Rebellion: Official Records (Army)*, vols. I, VII, X, XVII, XXII, XXIV, XXX–XXXII, XXXVIII, XXXIX, XLIV, XLVII–XLIX, LII; F. B. Heitman, *Hist. Reg. . . . U. S. Army* (1903); *Memorials of Deceased Companions . . . Commandery of the State of Ill., Mil. Order of the Loyal Legion* (1901); *The Forty-Fifth Ill.* (1905); Newton Bateman, Paul Selby, J. S. Currey, *Hist. Encyc. of Ill.*, vol. I (1925); *Army and Navy Reg.*, Feb. 6, 1897; *Chicago Tribune, Chicago Times-Herald*, Jan. 30, 1897.]   S. J. H.

SMITH, JOHN GREGORY (July 22, 1818–Nov. 6, 1891), railway organizer and executive, governor of Vermont, was born at St. Albans, Vt., the eldest son of John and Maria (Curtis) Smith, and a cousin of William Farrar Smith [q.v.]. Established position and affluence were his birthright. For nearly two centuries his paternal ancestors had flourished in Massachusetts. His grandfather, Samuel, a pioneer settler in St. Albans (1789), had acquired a leading position in the community and during the lad's youth his

father gained success alike in law, business and politics. Educated at the local grammar school and at the University of Vermont, where he was graduated in 1838, young Smith then studied law in his father's office and at Yale until 1841. The next year he was admitted to the bar and joined his father in legal practice.

Soon thereafter a period of railway building in Vermont began. The Vermont Central Railroad, commenced in 1846, was completed to Burlington in 1849. Meanwhile, the elder Smith was promoting the Vermont & Canada Railroad to connect the Central near Burlington with Canada. The new line, built as far as Swanton between 1848 and 1851, was leased before completion to the Central, the elder Smith subsequently holding positions with both roads. The son early joined his father on the legal staff of the railways and after his father's death in 1858, he became president of the Vermont Central, or rather of the board of trustees which was managing the road for the bondholders. He took control at a time when the physical condition of the railroad demanded heavy expenditures for rebuilding. During the boom period following the Civil War he succeeded in financing this work by large issues of trust bonds. These necessitated increased revenue, which Smith endeavored to obtain by extending his line to the Canadian border (1863) and persuading Canadian capitalists to build the connecting link to Montreal (1868). By 1872 the railroad property was undoubtedly in much better shape than a decade before, but it was in serious financial difficulties. Some of these Smith hoped to overcome by the formation in that year of a new corporation, the Central Vermont Railroad Company, which in 1873 became receiver for the Vermont Central and the Vermont & Canada companies. Smith was its president from the beginning until his death in 1891. Harrowed by interminable legal suits and constant financial difficulties, he succeeded, by leases and otherwise, in extending his line into an imposing system with terminals at Ottawa and New London and with dependent freight lines on the St. Lawrence and on Long Island Sound. Though the original investors in the Vermont railroad companies complained bitterly, Smith at least kept the lines in operation and augmented his own fortune. His enemies charged that he manipulated the state legislature and courts with entire lack of scruple.

His vision of the Vermont lines as a part of a great system which should tap the developing resources of the West undoubtedly accounts for his interest in the Northern Pacific Railroad. He succeeded Josiah Perham [q.v.] as president of that embryo concern in 1866. It was largely due to his initiative and his determination that the company was broadened, in 1867, to include most of the leading railroad men of the East. Though much occupied at home, he found time to devote to the building of the new line. He was doubtless over-optimistic and extravagant in the enterprise, and has been charged with neglect and the intrusting of important matters to incompetent and dishonest persons, but by the time friction between him and Jay Cooke brought about his resignation in 1872, nearly 500 miles of the railroad had been built and the main lines of its development fixed.

His multifarious business enterprises did not exhaust his abounding energy. He found time to play a leading part in the politics of his state; indeed, his political activity was a counterpart of his business in a day when the state legislature could make or break the railroads within its borders. After two years in the Senate (1858–59) and three in the lower house (1860–62), of which he was speaker in 1862, he served as governor of the state in 1863 and 1864. An ardent Republican and protectionist, he gave warm support to Lincoln's administration. For many years after his retirement from office he remained a power in state politics. He married, Dec. 27, 1843, Ann Eliza Brainerd of St. Albans, who with five of their six children survived him.

[L. A. Brainard, *The Geneal. of the Brainerd-Brainard Family in America* (1908), vol. II, pt. 4, pp. 162–63; J. G. Ullery, *Men of Vt.* (1894); *Gen. Cat. of the Univ. of Vt.* (1901); *Burlington Daily Free Press,* Nov. 7, 9, 1891; E. V. Smalley, *Hist. of the Northern Pacific Railroad* (1883); E. P. Oberholtzer, *Jay Cooke, Financier of the Civil War* (1907).]   P. D. E.

SMITH, JOHN JAY (June 16, 1798–Sept. 23, 1881), editor and librarian, a grand-nephew of Richard Smith [*q.v.*], was a grandson of John Smith, one of the founders of the Philadelphia Contributionship (1752), the first fire-insurance company instituted in America, and of Hannah (Logan) Smith, daughter of James Logan, 1674–1751 [*q.v.*]. Born on a farm at Green Hill, Burlington County, N. J., the sixth of seven children of John and Gulielma Maria (Morris) Smith, John Jay attended the Friends' boarding school at Westtown, Pa., and was given some courses in languages at an early age. He was then apprenticed to a druggist in Philadelphia. After a brief partnership with Solomon Temple in the wholesale drug business, he entered business on his own account, and on Apr. 12, 1821, married Rachel Collins Pearsall, of Flushing, L. I., daughter of a New York merchant. About this time he was active in the establishment of a line of Conestoga wagons, operating as regu-

lar carriers between Philadelphia and Pittsburgh, but the enterprise was short-lived.

From his early years he was interested in literature, and occasionally wrote short pieces for the local newspapers. In 1827, in partnership with George Taylor, who had published a newspaper in Mount Carbon, Pa., he inaugurated the *Pennsylvania Gazette,* purchasing the subscription list of the *Aurora* from John Norvell. Two years later he withdrew from this firm to become librarian of the Library Company of Philadelphia; he was a hereditary trustee of the Loganian Library, one of its component parts. Through his taste and industry, he gathered for the institution a large collection of autographs and manuscripts relating to the history of New Jersey and Pennsylvania.

In the early thirties Smith suggested to Adam Waldie, a Philadelphia printer, the republication of important foreign books in the form of a cheap weekly, which could be circulated through the mails; this project was realized on Oct. 1, 1832, when the first issue of *Waldie's Select Circulating Library* appeared, under Smith's editorship. This was the first effort in America to take advantage, on an extensive scale, of the absence of international copyright. Within three months the work had a circulation of 6,000 copies a week, and for some years it enjoyed great success. The covers of *Waldie's* carried literary news, edited by Smith, under the title, "The Journal of Belles-Lettres." During 1835, for Eliakim Littell [*q.v.*], he also edited the *Museum of Foreign Literature, Science, and Art.* He was treasurer of the Philadelphia Museum and a founder of the Girard Life Insurance, Annuity, and Trust Company and of Laurel Hill Cemetery. During the laying out of the cemetery, his interest in landscape gardening was deepened, and he afterwards edited (1850–51) *The North American Sylva* by François André Michaux [*q.v.*], and the eleventh edition (1857) of *The American Gardener's Calendar* by Bernard McMahon [*q.v.*]. He also published *Designs for Monuments and Mural Tablets . . . With a Preliminary Essay on the Laying Out, Planting, and Managing of Cemeteries* (1846) and *Guide to Laurel Hill Cemetery* (1844), which went through seven editions in his lifetime.

To *The National Portrait Gallery of Distinguished Americans* (1834–39), edited by James Herring and J. B. Longacre [*q.v.*], Smith contributed articles on Benjamin Franklin, David Rittenhouse, William Augustine Washington, and Simon Kenton. In 1847, assisted by John F. Watson [*q.v.*], he edited *American Historical and Literary Curiosities,* of which, in 1860, a second series was issued in New York, under Smith's editorship. Meanwhile, in 1845, his son, Lloyd Pearsall Smith [*q.v.*], had begun the publication of *Smith's Weekly Volume,* a successor to *Waldie's,* and this publication was edited by the elder Smith from January 1845 to Mar. 25, 1846. He made four trips to Europe, describing one in *A Summer's Jaunt across the Water* (2 vols., 1846). In 1851 he retired from his librarianship so that his son Lloyd might be appointed to the place. His later literary work included the editing of *Letters of Dr. Richard Hill* (1854) and the authorship of a volume of entertaining gossip, written for his children, which was edited by his daughter and privately printed in 1892 under the title, *Recollections of John Jay Smith Written by Himself.* His paper, "The Penn Family" (1867), was used as an introduction to the first volume (1870) of *Correspondence between William Penn and James Logan.* Smith died at his estate, "Ivy Lodge," Germantown, at the age of eighty-three. He had had four sons and three daughters; Hannah Whitall Smith [*q.v.*] was his daughter-in-law.

[Smith's *Recollections,* ed. by E. P. Smith; J. T. Scharf and Thompson Westcott, *Hist. of Phila.* (1884), II, 1183–85, III, 2359; autobiographical touches in Smith's "Journal of Belles-Lettres"; G. M. Abbot, *A Short Hist. of the Library Company of Phila.* (1913); *Centennial Meeting of the Phila. Contributionship* (1852); Thompson Westcott, *The Historic Mansions and Buildings of Phila.* (1877); R. M. Smith, *The Burlington Smiths* (1877); *Public Ledger* (Phila.), Sept. 24, 1881.]   J. J.

SMITH, JOHN LAWRENCE (Dec. 17, 1818–Oct. 12, 1883), chemist and mineralogist, was born near Charleston, S. C. His father, Benjamin Smith, born in Virginia, was a merchant of Charleston. Prepared in private schools and in the College of Charleston, he entered the University of Virginia in 1835 and for two years studied chemistry, natural philosophy, and civil engineering under John P. Emmet, W. B. Rogers, and Charles Bonnycastle. After leaving the University, he was for a year an assistant engineer on the projected Charleston and Cincinati railroad and then entered the Medical College of South Carolina, where in 1840 he was graduated with the degree of M.D. For several years after graduation he studied abroad. Liebig, Orfila, Dumas, and Élie de Beaumont were perhaps his most influential teachers.

In 1844 he returned to Charleston to establish himself as a medical practitioner and as a lecturer. In January 1846, with Dr. S. D. Sinkler, he founded the *Southern Journal of Medicine and Pharmacy,* which later became the *Charleston Medical Journal and Review.* Meanwhile he had published some researches on certain soils of South Carolina, which led to his selection by James Buchanan, then secretary of state, to go to Turkey in response to the request of the Turkish government for an adviser on cotton culture. In this capacity he sailed, but was soon appointed to investigate the mineral resources of the Empire, and spent three years thus engaged. His discovery of emery and coal deposits made his services profitable to his employer; moreover, his observations regarding the minerals found in association with emery and corundum, communicated to the younger Benjamin Silliman [*q.v.*], resulted in the discovery of several emery deposits in the United States. He published several papers on his findings, notably "Memoir on Emery" in two parts (*American Journal of Science,* November 1850, January 1851).

In the summer of 1850, while in Paris, Smith conceived the idea of the inverted microscope, which he later perfected (*American Journal of Science,* September 1852). By December 1850 he was back in the United States. For the next two years he lived in New Orleans, studying, and lecturing before a group of scientific students, and enjoying the titular professorship of chemistry in the University of Louisiana, an institution which then existed largely on paper. On June 24, 1852, he married Sarah Julia, daughter of James Guthrie [*q.v.*] of Louisville, Ky. They had no children.

In the fall of 1852, Smith succeeded Robert E. Rogers [*q.v.*] as professor of chemistry at the University of Virginia. Here he and his assistant, George J. Brush [*q.v.*], prepared their "Reexamination of American Minerals," an important contribution to the study of the chemistry of minerals, published as a series of papers in the *American Journal of Science,* 1853–55. His own means and his wife's now made him independent, and in 1853 he resigned his professorship. The following winter he passed in Washington as the guest of his father-in-law, now secretary of the treasury. Here Smith spent his time working and lecturing in the Smithsonian Institution. In 1854 he succeeded Benjamin Silliman, Jr., as professor of medical chemistry and toxicology in the University of Louisville, holding this chair until 1866. Although he traveled frequently, visiting Europe many times, he made his home in Louisville until his death.

During his years there, Smith was especially interested in meteorites. His collection of meteoric stones, one of the finest in America, was sold, just before his death, to Harvard University. During these years he was also something of a man of affairs. He was for a time president of the Louisville Gas Works, was associated with E. R. Squibb [*q.v.*] in a pharmaceutical laboratory, and was the founder and a liberal benefactor of the Baptist Orphanage of Louisville. For more than forty years, from the time of his graduation from medical college in 1840 until his death, he was a frequent contributor to scientific journals. His bibliography (Marvin, *post*) lists 145 separate papers. Many of these were collected and published in 1873 as *Mineralogy and Chemistry: Original Researches.* Benjamin Silliman the elder considered Smith the first noteworthy organic chemist in America (*Journal of the Elisha Mitchell Scientific Society,* June 1906, p. 33). He was president of the American Association for the Advancement of Science in 1872, was a member of the National Academy of Sciences, in 1879 succeeded Sir Charles Lyell as corresponding member of the Academy of Sciences of the Institute of France, and was decorated by the governments of France, Russia, and Turkey. Although he was neither magnetic, charming, nor eloquent, and never a great teacher, he was a bold thinker and one of the ablest American chemists of his time.

[Smith's *Mineralogy and Chemistry* (1873) was reprinted as *Original Researches in Mineralogy and Chemistry by Prof. J. Lawrence Smith* (1884), ed. by J. B. Marvin, with a list of Smith's published papers prepared by Marvin, and biographical sketches by Marvin, B. Silliman, Jr., and Middleton Michel. See also *Popular Science Monthly,* Dec. 1874; H. A. Kelly and W. L. Burrage, *Am. Medic. Biogs.* (1920); *Year Book of the City of Charleston, S. C., 1883* (1884); *Louisville Medic. News,* Dec. 6, 1879; *Proc. Am. Acad. Arts and Sci.,* vol. XIX (1883); *Nat. Acad. Sci. Biog. Memoirs,* vol. II (1886); *Proc. Am. Asso. for the Advancement of Science,* vol. XLVIII (1899); *Am. Jour. Sci.,* Nov. 1883; *Courier-Journal* (Louisville), Oct. 13, 1883.]   T. C. J., Jr.

SMITH, JOHN MERLIN POWIS (Dec. 28, 1866–Sept. 26, 1932), Biblical scholar, was born in London, England. His parents, William Martin Smith and Anne (Powis), were natives of Shropshire. The boy's early education was obtained in private schools at Leominster, Hereford, and at Dawlish, Devon. In 1881 he successfully passed the entrance examination for Cambridge. Throughout his life he displayed an extraordinary tenacity of purpose. During adolescence he had chosen a scholarly career as his goal and his interest had turned to Bible study. Finding further progress blocked in his native land, he emigrated in 1883 to Denison, Iowa. Here he worked for a time on the farm of an uncle but soon became teacher of the local school. In 1889 he found his way to Des Moines College, where he joined the Baptist Church. Here he

supported himself by teaching Greek to beginners and by arduous manual toil; yet he took a prominent part in extra-curricular activities and graduated with the degree of A.B. in 1893.

With his ultimate goal still in mind he became instructor in Greek in Cedar Valley Seminary, Osage, Iowa, but in the summer of 1894 enrolled as a graduate student in Semitics in the first summer session of the new University of Chicago. A year later he gave up his teaching post and enrolled at Chicago as a candidate for the degree of Ph.D. in Semitics. On July 1, 1899, he was awarded that degree *cum laude* and was appointed to the teaching staff of the department of Semitics as docent. His marriage to Catherine McKlveen of Chariton, Iowa, followed on Sept. 19 of the same year. Already the "tawny-haired young Englishman" had attracted the attention of President William Rainey Harper [*q.v.*], who shortly made him his literary secretary. He now entered upon a period of approximately seven years devoted almost exclusively to research under the direction of this brilliant scholar and commanding personality. The fruitful association which ensued came as a direct result of Smith's tenacity of purpose and devotion to exact knowledge in which he had schooled himself during the early years of his rigorous self-discipline. Soon the personnel of the original Semitics group at Chicago was tragically and rapidly depleted by the untimely deaths of George S. Goodspeed, the Oriental historian, President Harper, and his brother, the Assyriologist, Robert Francis Harper [*q.v.*]. These calamities made Smith's rapid advancement imperative. He became assistant professor in 1908, associate professor in 1912, and in 1915 was made professor and charged with the editorship of the *American Journal of Semitic Languages,* in succession to R. F. Harper. He fulfilled the duties of both positions with distinction till the day of his death.

His contribution to Biblical scholarship was of a double order. He developed into a highly stimulating classroom teacher who played a most important part in undermining the foundations of obscurantism and prodding the religious leadership of his generation to adjust itself, morally and intellectually, to expanding horizons. His contribution to the scientific literature of his field was also notable. His more important works include commentaries on Micah, Zephaniah, Nahum, and Malachi in the International Critical Commentary Series; *The Prophet and His Problems* (1914); *William R. Harper's Elements of Hebrew* (1921) and *Harper's Hebrew Method and Manual* (1921); *The Religion of the Psalms*

(1922) ; *The Moral Life of the Hebrews* (1923) ; *The Prophets and Their Times* (1925) ; *The Old Testament: An American Translation* (1927), of which he was general editor as well as translator of large sections of the text; and *The Origin and History of Hebrew Law* (1931). More than seventy technical and popular articles also came from his pen. Nor was his productivity significant in bulk alone; it was a positive and stimulating contribution to the reconstruction of the history of Hebrew life and thought. Smith had a fine command of the historical background of the whole ancient Near Eastern world, and he displayed great insight in relating the Hebrew experience to the total picture of the development of civilization in that world. Better still, he made his public conscious of the contribution of that world to the life of the West.

His standing was recognized by the fraternity of Orientalists in his appointment in 1927 as annual professor in the American School of Oriental Research in Jerusalem and by his election in 1931 as president of the Society of Biblical Literature and Exegesis and vice-president of the American Oriental Society. His death occurred as the vessel which carried him home from a sojourn in England and Europe was docking in New York harbor.

[*Am. Jour. of Semitic Languages and Literatures*, Jan. 1933; *Univ. Record* (Chicago), Jan. 1933; *Who's Who in America*, 1932–33; *N. Y. Times*, Sept. 28, 1932.]   W. C. G.

SMITH, JOHN ROWSON (May 11, 1810–Mar. 21, 1864), painter of panoramas, was born at Boston, Mass., the son of Elizabeth Pepperal (Sanger) and John Rubens Smith [*q.v.*]. After the family's removal in 1814 to Brooklyn, N. Y., John Rowson studied at a private school and in his father's drawing academy, which was later moved to Philadelphia, Pa. While living there he made sketches at Pottsville which his father engraved and published, but because of a family misunderstanding he left home and apprenticed himself to the scenic artist of the National Theatre, Philadelphia. Although he painted much scenery for theatres in New Orleans, La., St. Louis, Mo., and other cities from 1832 on, he became interested in experimenting with the panorama, invented probably by Robert Barker, an Edinburgh artist, about 1787. His panorama of Boston, designed to give people of interior towns successive views of a seaport, was mechanically but not financially successful; in "The Conflagration of Moscow," his next attempt, he used transparent colors on muslin and ingenious devices to simulate fire. Meantime, he had made carefully detailed sketches of Missis-

sippi river scenes, which were worked up at Boston into a huge panorama. It was burned after a brief exhibition in Boston in 1839, but the artist cherished the idea of repainting it. He married in Philadelphia, Jan. 5, 1841, Emma Louise Broughton, and in 1843 he became scenic artist at Castle Garden Theatre, New York, where he had prosperous years. He was one of those interested in the socialistic plans of Robert Dale Owen [*q.v.*], serving as president of the New York society for their furtherance.

In 1844 he completed his panorama of the Mississippi from the Falls of St. Anthony to the Gulf of Mexico. Shown at Saratoga, it earned $20,000 in six weeks, and, after touring the United States with it, in 1848 in partnership with John Risley, acrobat, he took it abroad. In London the work was in spirited competition with another Mississippi panorama, painted by John Banvard [*q.v.*], who had credentials as to its fidelity to nature from a United States engineer, the mayor of Louisville, Ky., and many steamboat men (*Description of Banvard's Panorama of the Mississippi River,* 1847). Smith in turn secured letters, which are extant, from Baron Friedrich Wilhelm von Humboldt and George Catlin [*q.v.*] affirming the scientific and artistic superiority of his panorama. By invitation of Queen Victoria he showed the piece at Balmoral, and thereafter to huge audiences in England and on the Continent. This panorama has been credited with greatly stimulating emigration toward the Mississippi Valley. While showing his panorama in Europe he made for American use a "Panorama of the Tour of Europe," which inspired a long poetic tribute in the *Philadelphia Inquirer,* Nov. 11, 1853. To it was added, in 1854, "The Siege of Sebastopol." After his return from Europe, he bought and occupied a large farm at Carlstadt, N. J., where he entertained many guests. According to Smith, he was the originator of the moving panorama in America. A brilliant and industrious artist, he painted scenery for a number of New York theatres: the Broadway in 1847, the Bowery and the National in 1856, and the Bowery again in 1862. He also had much employment winters at southern theatres. Thus employed at Mobile in 1861 at the outbreak of the Civil War, he escaped via New Orleans on the last boat carrying northerners home. In 1864, while at work at the Arch Street Theatre of Louise Lane Drew [*q.v.*] in Philadelphia, he fell victim to pneumonia. He was buried at Laurel Hill Cemetery, Philadelphia. From the nature of scene painting little of his work has been preserved, but it was highly esteemed by managers and theatre-goers of his time. A few examples of his painting and of his early engraved work are in the possession of his son, also trained in scenic art. The panorama, however, in the making of which he was a past master, was his great contribution to American social history.

[The chief source for the life of John Rowson Smith is the MS., "Recollections of John Rowson Smith" by his son, Edward S. Smith, a copy of which is in the N. Y. Pub. Lib.; this contains biog. data, announcements of panoramas, press notices, and photographs. See also Wilberforce Eames's continuation of Joseph Sabin, *A Dict. of Books Relating to America*, vol. XX (1927), pp. 298–99; G. C. D. Odell, *Annals of the N. Y. Stage*, vols. IV–VII (1928–31); death notice in *Pub. Ledger* (Phila.), Mar. 23, 1864. For a complete story of Am. panoramas, dioramas, and cycloramas consult the extensive coll. of documents in the Boston Pub. Lib.]

F. W. C.

SMITH, JOHN RUBENS (Jan. 23, 1775–Aug. 21, 1849), drawing master, engraver, painter, was born in Covent Garden, London, a son of John Raphael and Hannah (Croome) Smith, and a grandson of Thomas Smith, known as "Smith of Derby," landscape painter. From his father, an eminent mezzotinter, John Rubens learned sound draftsmanship, and between 1796 and 1811 he had nearly fifty paintings in the annual exhibitions of the Royal Academy. He came to America at least as early as 1809, for on Apr. 14, 1809, he married Elizabeth Pepperal Sanger in Boston, Mass. (*A Volume of Records Relating to the Early Hist. of Boston*, 1903, p. 273). Like other English artists, he probably emigrated because of the depression caused in Great Britain by the Napoleonic wars. In Boston, where he lived in Milk Street, he made a series of topographical water colors of local landmarks, these including Beacon Hill, then in process of partial demolition, the Old South Church, and Pawtucket Falls in the Blackstone River.

An assertive personality is said to have made him unpopular in Boston, and he presently removed (1814) to New York, where, as well as for a time in Philadelphia, Pa., he gained the reputation of being a good teacher and a quarrelsome person. He is described as being a man of "short figure, large head, peculiar one-sided gait, and indescribable expression of countenance" (*Crayon*, Nov. 7, 1855, p. 287). Among his pupils were Eliab Metcalf, Anthony De Rose, Thomas Seir Cummings [*q.v.*], George Washington Tyler, and Frederick Styles Agate [*q.v.*]. His alleged unethical attacks upon the work and character of John Vanderlyn and his shabby treatment of Francis Alexander [*qq.v.*] were indignantly denounced by Dunlap. Even the tolerant Cummings, who characterized him as "a teacher of the highest order of excellence," could

not forgive his master for "his untiring animosity and open hostility to the [National] Academy of Design and its members" (Cummings, *post,* p. 32), evidently provoked by the fact that he was not invited to become a member. Twenty years or more after these misunderstandings of the Academy's first period, Smith expressed deepest regret for his scurrilous writings and admitted that throughout life "his own temper had been his worst enemy and ruin" (*Ibid.,* 33). It is also on record (*Ibid.,* 174) that in 1843 he applied for a professorship of perspective at the Academy and that, though his request was not granted, he was offered three months' use of a room in which to exemplify some apparatus he had invented.

His last days were rendered uncomfortable by poverty which, as Cummings relates, was "in some degree alleviated by those who had suffered most from his pungent pen." He died in New York. One of his children was John Rowson Smith [*q.v.*]. During his years as a teacher of art in America he published *The Juvenile Drawing-Book* (8th ed., 1847), *A Compendium of Picturesque Anatomy* (1827), and *A Key to the Art of Drawing the Human Figure* (1831), besides engaging under the pseudonym of "Neutral Tint" in many literary controversies. His extant works, such as his mezzotints of portraits of Benjamin Lincoln [*q.v.*] and James Patterson, and his aquatint of the fire that nearly destroyed the Old South Church, Boston, are the work of an able draftsman who had an acute perception of individual character and dramatic effect; their antiquarian interest is considerable.

[Julia Frankau, *An Eighteenth Century Artist and Engraver, John Raphael Smith* (1902); William Dunlap, *A Hist. of the Rise and Progress of the Arts of Design in the U. S.* (1918), vols. II, III, ed. by F. W. Bayley and C. E. Goodspeed; T. S. Cummings, *Historic Annals of the Nat. Acad. of Design* (1865); "Saving the Old South," *Boston Sunday Globe*, Sept. 1, 1929, Frank Weitenkampf, *Am. Graphic Art* (1912); Boston Museum of Fine Arts, *A Descriptive Cat. of an Exhibition of Early Engraving in America* (1904); D. M. Stauffer, *Am. Engravers upon Copper and Steel* (2 vols., 1907); letter from Edward S. Smith, New York, a descendant, who has many unpublished documents concerning J. R. Smith.]

F. W. C.

SMITH, JONAS WALDO (Mar. 9, 1861–Oct. 14, 1933), civil engineer, son of Francis and Abigail Prescott (Baker) Smith, was born at Lincoln, Mass. At the age of fifteen he had his first engineering experience upon the small water-works system of his home town, showing such aptitude that at the age of seventeen he became chief engineer of the plant, acting as operator and general superintendent of outside work. He graduated from Phillips Academy, Andover, in 1881 and then for some three years was an assistant in the office of the Essex Company at Lawrence, proprietors of the water power of the Merrimac River at that place. In 1887 he graduated in the civil engineering course at the Massachusetts Institute of Technology. During his course, he had spent two summer vacations with the Holyoke Water Power Company, and after graduation he served from 1887 to 1890 as their assistant engineer.

In 1890 Smith became assistant engineer for the East Jersey Water Company, and for the next dozen years was engaged in the construction or maintenance of a succession of water-supply systems in northern New Jersey; he was made principal assistant engineer of the company in 1891 and ultimately chief engineer. In this capacity, in 1901, he directed the design and construction of the Little Falls mechanical filtration plant, a pioneer, and, at the time of its completion, the largest of its kind. The following year he supervised the completion of the new $7,500,000 water-supply system for Jersey City, including the Boonton dam, a concrete aqueduct, and pipe lines.

In 1903 Smith accepted the position of chief engineer of the Aqueduct Commission of New York City, taking charge of the construction of the new Croton dam then under way—in that day the largest masonry dam in the world. At this time he also made surveys for the Cross River and Croton Falls reservoirs, which were subsequently constructed. Two years later, when the Board of Water Supply of the City of New York was created to provide an additional water supply for that city, Smith became its chief engineer and began the most important work of his life as director of the Catskill Water Supply System. The initial program for this project included the Ashokan Reservoir, of 128,000,000,000 gallons capacity, upon Esopus Creek, about ninety miles from New York City, controlled by a masonry dam some 250 feet high and 1,000 feet long, and the Catskill Aqueduct, capable of supplying 500,000,000 gallons of water daily from the reservoir to the city. One of the most difficult problems was the crossing under the Hudson River near Storm King Mountain. Shafts were sunk on each side of the river to a depth of 1,114 feet below river level, and 14-foot tunnels were bored through solid rock to meet under the river. The Aqueduct, which is large enough for a railroad train to pass through, terminated at Kensico Reservoir, thirty miles from the city, where another masonry dam 307 feet high was completed in 1918.

As the demand for water by the city increased it became necessary in 1916 to commence the second step in this great project, developing an added supply from Schoharie Creek, north of Esopus Creek. Here the Gilboa dam, another massive masonry structure, was constructed, to form another large reservoir from which by the Shandaken tunnel—some eighteen miles long, the longest tunnel in the world when it was built—the waters of Schoharie Creek are taken into Esopus Creek and Ashokan Reservoir to supplement the initial supply and bring it up to the planned amount of 500,000,000 gallons a day. In 1922, when the project was nearing completion, Smith resigned as chief engineer of the Board of Water Supply, but he continued to act as its consultant and also as consulting engineer upon new water supply systems for Boston, Hartford, Providence, Kansas City, San Francisco, Kingston, Ont., and Vancouver, B. C., as well as upon the Moffat Tunnel near Denver. He continued actively engaged in his work until his sudden death, from heart disease, at his residence in New York City.

In 1918 Smith was awarded the John Fritz Medal—the highest honor in the engineering profession—by the four national engineering societies, for "achievement as engineer in providing the City of New York with a supply of water." He was also made an honorary member of the American Society of Civil Engineers, the American Water Works Association, and the New England Water Works Association. His exceptional abilities and character were well epitomized by the *Engineering News-Record* in an editorial at the time of his death: "Engineering judgment and intuition of highest order were essential parts of his equipment, of course, but to these he joined a great power over men— an almost magical ability to inspire loyalty and affection in all who worked for him, and at the same time to disarm and convince his opponents. Integrity, simplicity and justice, and a homely New England shrewdness combined to create this power. . . . The Catskill aqueduct stands as a monument to Smith, one of the greatest engineers of his time and a master of human arts."

[*Civil Engineering*, Nov. 1933; *Engineering News-Record*, Oct. 19, 1933; *N. Y. Times*, Oct. 16, 1933; *New York's Catskill Mountain Water Supply* (Report of Board of Water Supply, 1928); *Who's Who in America*, 1920–21, 1932–33; *Who's Who in Engineering*, 1931.]

H. K. B.

SMITH, JONATHAN BAYARD (Feb. 21, 1742–June 16, 1812), merchant, member of the Continental Congress, was born in Philadelphia, the second of three sons of Samuel Smith, a native of Portsmouth, N. H., and a prominent Philadelphia merchant. Jonathan received a liberal education, graduated from the College of

New Jersey in 1760, and entered business. One of the first of the younger Philadelphia business men to voice emphatic protests against the measures of the mother country, he played a prominent part in the movement leading up to separation. He was a member of the provincial conference of June 1774, secretary to the provincial convention, January 1775, and secretary to the provincial conference of June 18–25, 1776. In this last capacity he helped to engineer the overthrow of the old provincial government. In the meantime he was appointed a member of the committee of safety (1775) and later of the council of safety (1777). A believer in firm measures to insure independence, when Howe's army approached Philadelphia in the fall of 1776 he presided at a meeting of "Real Whigs" (Dec. 1) which passed resolutions recommending that every man between sixteen and fifty be ordered under arms for the defense of the state until the assembly should pass a militia law. On Feb. 5, 1777, he was elected to Congress, but on Sept. 13 following, with the British again approaching Philadelphia, he resigned to assist actively in the defense of the city. At first a captain (1775), later colonel, he was now made lieutenant-colonel of a battalion of "Associators" and participated in the Brandywine campaign, winning recognition as an "intrepid militia officer."

Smith was reëlected to Congress on Dec. 10, 1777, and served for the following year. He was made a member of the board of war on Jan. 14, 1778, and was a member of the committee to supervise publication of the journals of Congress. He stanchly defended the Articles of Confederation, prosecuted with zeal measures designed to eradicate irregularities and inefficiency in government boards and the army, and while belonging to the more liberal Whig faction, favored a minimum of acts of force as a means of keeping Whigs solidly together. An indefatigable worker, he was constantly in the heart of things in Congress, despite the handicap of serious illness during the spring and summer of 1778. From Apr. 4, 1777, to Nov. 13, 1788, he was prothonotary of the court of common pleas for the city and county of Philadelphia, and on July 6, 1778, he was commissioned justice of that court. Beginning with 1792 he served two years as alderman of Philadelphia and in the latter year was auditor-general of Pennsylvania under Gov. Thomas Mifflin [q.v.].

After 1800 Smith aligned himself with the Republicans of the more moderate stamp in Pennsylvania's factional politics, and in 1805 threw in his lot with the group opposing a constitutional convention. While no longer in public office, he continued his interest in civic affairs and politics. Throughout his life, especially in the Revolutionary period, he earned an enviable reputation for keeping records with scrupulous care. William Findley [q.v.], commenting in 1812 on the need for an accurate history of Pennsylvania, declared that years before he had fixed on Smith as the man to write it (*Pennsylvania Magazine of History and Biography,* October 1884, p. 345), but though Smith apparently at one time considered writing such a history, he abandoned the idea in later life. He was a member of the Society of the Sons of St. Tammany, a grand master of Masons of Pennsylvania, a trustee of the University of Pennsylvania and of the College of New Jersey, and a member of the American Philosophical Society. His wife was Susannah, daughter of Col. Peter Bayard of Maryland and cousin of John Bubenheim Bayard [q.v.]; after his marriage he adopted Bayard as his middle name. His son, Samuel Harrison Smith [q.v.], was the founder of the *National Intelligencer* of Washington, D. C.

[Jonathan Bayard Smith and Samuel Harrison Smith Papers in Lib. of Cong.; J. G. B. Bulloch, *A Hist. and Geneal. of the Families of Bayard, Houstoun of Ga., and the Descent of the Bolton Family* (1919); F. V. Cabeen, "The Society of the Sons of St. Tammany, of Phila.," in *Pa. Mag. of Hist. and Biog.,* Oct. 1902; J. H. Martin, *Martin's Bench and Bar of Phila.* (1883); E. C. Burnett, *Letters of Members of the Continental Cong.,* vols. II–IV (1923–28); *Pa. Archives,* 1 ser., V, VI (1853), XI (1855), 2 ser., III (1875); *Minutes of the Supreme Exec. Council of Pa.,* vols. XI, XII (1852–53); J. G. Wilson, "Col. John Bayard (1738–1807) and the Bayard Family," *N. Y. Geneal. and Biog. Record,* Apr. 1885; *Poulson's Am. Daily Advertiser,* June 17, 1812.]   J. H. P.

SMITH, JOSEPH (Mar. 30, 1790–Jan. 17, 1877), naval officer, was born in Hanover, Mass., second son of the nine children of Albert and Anne Lenthall (Eells) Smith. He was a descendant of John Smith of Barnstable and Sandwich, Mass., who came to America before 1640, and his great-grandfather was the Rev. Thomas Smith of Pembroke, Mass. On the maternal side he was descended from John Eells who was in Massachusetts as early as 1634, but who later returned to England and is reported to have fought in Cromwell's army. At an early age Joseph learned shipbuilding, his father's business. On Jan. 16, 1809, he entered the navy as a midshipman and was soon ordered to the *Chesapeake,* then at Boston. Later in the same year he was furloughed in order that he might make a voyage in the merchant service. On Oct. 13, 1812, he was ordered to Lake Champlain and in the following year, on July 24, he was commissioned lieutenant. As first lieutenant of the *Eagle,* he assisted her commander, Robert Henley [*q.v.*], in building and manning that vessel, and in the battle of Lake Champlain there fell to him the duty of winding ship and bringing to bear on the enemy an uninjured broadside. Although wounded he stayed at his post, and was commended by Henley for his gallantry and voted a silver medal by Congress.

In the war with Algiers he served on board the frigate *Constellation* and participated in engagements with the Algerines. During the long period of peace following the war, he was often on leave from the navy because there were not enough billets for his continuous employment. He was several times stationed at the Boston or Portsmouth navy yard, occasionally as commander of a receiving ship. He was a lieutenant on board the *Guerrière* in the Mediterranean in 1818–19, and, in 1828–31, again served on that vessel when it was attached to the Pacific Squadron. On Mar. 3, 1827, he was promoted master commandant. He became a captain—at this time the highest rank in the navy—on Feb. 9, 1837. The same year he aided in fitting out the Wilkes exploring expedition. From 1838 to 1840 he commanded the *Ohio* of the Mediterranean Squadron and from 1843 to 1845 he commanded that squadron with the *Cumberland* as his flagship—his last sea duty. From 1846 until 1869 he was chief of the Bureau of Navy Yards and Docks, one of the longest terms of service for a bureau chief in the history of the navy department and exceedingly important by reason of the revolution in naval construction and the naval activities of the Civil War. On Aug. 8, 1861, President Lincoln chose him as the ranking naval officer of a naval board authorized to examine plans relating to ironclad vessels. From many competing drawings the board chose three, of which one was the plan of the *Monitor,* submitted by John Ericsson [*q.v.*]. This choice of the board, made in opposition to naval tradition and expert naval opinion, proved to be epoch-making. Secretary of Navy Welles wrote that Smith beyond any other person in the department was deserving of credit for the *Monitor* (*Diary of Gideon Welles,* 1911, vol. I, p. 214).

Smith was placed on the reserved list in 1855, but was restored to the active list in 1858, being made a rear-admiral on the retired list in 1862. From 1870 to 1871 he was president of the retiring board. For many years before his death he resided in Washington, D. C., where he was a regular attendant at St. John's Episcopal Church, serving as senior warden for twenty-one years. On Mar. 1, 1818, he was married to Harriet Bryant of Nobleboro, Me. They had two sons and two daughters. One of the sons,

Joseph Bryant Smith, commanded the *Congress* when she was attacked by the *Merrimac* in March 1862, and was killed in the battle.

[S. A. Smith, *A Memorial of Rev. Thomas Smith* (1895); F. F. Starr, *The Eells Family of Dorchester, Mass.* (1903); W. H. Brooks, *A Sermon Commemorative of the Life and Character of Joseph Smith* (1877); Jedediah Dwelley, J. F. Simmons, *Hist. of the Town of Hanover, Mass.* (1910); *New-Eng. Hist. and Geneal. Reg.,* Oct. 1877; Bureau of Navigation, *Record of Officers,* 1809–78; *Navy Register,* 1815–77; *Army and Navy Jour.,* Jan. 20, 1877; *Evening Star,* Washington, D. C., Jan. 18, 19, 1877.]   C.O.P.

SMITH, JOSEPH (Dec. 23, 1805–June 27, 1844), Mormon prophet, was born at Sharon, Windsor County, Vt., the fourth of ten children of Joseph Smith and Lucy (Mack) Smith. Both families, established in New England since the middle of the seventeenth century, had declined to the status of frontier-drifters when Smith's parents were married at Tunbridge, Vt., in 1796, and they made at least ten moves in nineteen years. They went to Palmyra, N. Y., in 1816 and remained in that general vicinity till Joseph was grown. His boyhood was spent among a footloose class, excitable, semi-illiterate, and superstitious, in a part of the country (frontier New England and New York) that produced a great many of the irregular sects and experimental societies of the first half of the century.

An attack of melancholy in his fifteenth year, coincident with one of his family's periodic conversions, conditioned his whole life. His first vision occurred in the spring of 1820 (*History,* I, 5), and was followed by similar experiences on Sept. 21, and 22, 1823. The accounts of them we possess are based on one which he wrote for the *Times and Seasons* in 1842 and represent an evolution, fragments of contradictory versions being on record. The burden of the visions, conveyed to him by the angel Nephi (later corrected to Moroni), was that no existing sect represented God's will, that the church of Christ had been withdrawn from the earth, and that God had selected Smith to restore it. The vision was renewed annually and on Sept. 22, 1827, he was allowed to take from their repository at the Hill Cumorah (near Manchester, Ontario County, N. Y.) certain "plates" of gold which recorded the history of the true church on the American continent, following its migrations from Jerusalem. The history was written in ancient characters, which he contradictorily described, and during the next three years he was engaged in translating it by miraculous means. The result was published at Palmyra, N. Y., in July 1830, as *The Book of Mormon.* This volume with *A Book of Commandments* (Jackson, Mo., 1833, later and now *Doctrine and Covenants,* 1835, consisting of sermons by and divine relations to Smith) forms the basis of the Mormon Church.

That *The Book of Mormon* was based on a historical novel by Solomon Spaulding was long a favorite theory but cannot be established. That it could be work of so ignorant a man as Smith appears strange and yet he cannot be shown to have met Sidney Rigdon [*q.v.*], the most likely source of its doctrinal matter, until after its publication. It contains much autobiographical matter and its entire material is indigenous to the society in which he grew up. Probably the book is in the main Smith's composition, slowly built up from fantasy, an anthology of religious and historical ideas to which all of his associates contributed. It is a "catch-all" of frontier Protestant doctrine and touches on practically every controversial belief of the time. It also deals with many social questions that excited his neighbors, and it capitalized the wide current interest in the origins of the American Indians. It is crammed with anachronisms and, as a literary production, was summed up by Mark Twain in the epithet, "chloroform in print."

Before its publication Smith had founded the Church of Jesus Christ of Latter-Day Saints on Apr. 6, 1830, at Fayette, Seneca County, N. Y. The communicants were Smith's relatives and neighbors; not until the baptism, on Nov. 14, 1830, of Sidney Rigdon, did the extraordinary growth begin. Borrowing from most ephemeral sects of the age, the church was "at once millenial, restorationist, and perfectionist" (De-Voto, *post,* p. 12). It took over much material from contemporary communistic experiments and much theology, also, from the Campbells. Both its organization and its doctrines, however, represent an evolution over a good many years. In this evolution and in the extension of his kingdom, the prophet Joseph was the dominant personality but by no means the leading intelligence or even the chief architect. He was a dynamic despot holding authority from God, to whose service the energies of better minds were devoted. It is certain that much of the doctrine and most of the ecclesiastical organization must be ascribed to Rigdon, W. W. Phelps, and similar minds; and that such exegetes, apologists, organizers, and propagandists as Phelps, Heber C. Kimball [*q.v.*], and Brigham Young [*q.v.*] were decisive influences in its spread and preservation. The church became a cooperative society ruled by an ecclesiastical oligarchy. It was a system excellently adapted to success on the farthest frontier but one which brought the Mormons into continual conflict with their neighbors in the communities they occupied during Smith's lifetime.

The growth of Mormonism, essentially a frontier phenomenon, made Smith an important force in frontier life. He very early contemplated removal to the Rocky Mountains or beyond, but first, in 1831, took his flock to Kirtland, Ohio, where Rigdon had a church. A fugitive from justice as the result of "wildcat" banking, Smith in 1838 fled to Missouri, where he had already established an outpost on what he declared to be the site of the Garden of Eden. Political and social friction with the Missourians drove the Mormons from Jackson County to less settled parts of the state and eventually (1839) to Commerce, Ill., which Smith renamed Nauvoo. Converts from Europe as well as America swelled the population of the settlement, and, owing to the desire of both political parties to gain the solid Mormon vote, the city was chartered and the Nauvoo Legion authorized by the state legislature. Extraordinary powers were granted the local government and practical independence was permitted the military establishment. The growing church was vouchsafed five years of prosperity, and Smith ruled gaudily, enjoying power, publicity, and worship, one of the most famous Westerners of his day, a prophet, an author, a lieutenant-general of the Nauvoo Legion, and finally a candidate for the presidency of the United States. Formal announcement of his candidacy was made Feb. 15, 1844, and Mormon campaigners were scattered through the country at the time of his sudden death (Linn, *post,* pp. 253–54). His increasing megalomania had enhanced the unpopularity of his sect, and with the scandal of his business affairs and the gradual discovery of polygamy (foreshadowed as early as 1831, declared as a revelation July 12, 1843), it produced schism within the church. On June 7, 1844, appeared the first and only issue of the *Nauvoo Expositor,* containing a vigorous attack on Smith. On June 10, in compliance with his order as mayor backed by his authority as lieutenant-general, the printing-press was tyrannically destroyed. The flight of his critics was followed by an uprising among the non-Mormons in neighboring districts. Smith and his brother were arrested and lodged in the jail at Carthage, Ill., whence they were taken on June 27 and then shot. Had he lived much longer it is likely that his church would have split up; his martyrdom, however, served the usual function of consolidating his followers.

Smith had intense religious suggestibility and a jovial earthy ebullience, both of which were important elements in his leadership, but the mania of his later years seems to have been less religious than egoistic. He ruled quite as much by personality as by the acknowledged divinity of his message. He was witty, athletic, vigorous, and virile; in appearance he was tall, light-haired, blue-eyed, distinguished. He was at his best in situations that could be personalized and dramatized, but he lacked intelligence and his judgment was almost uniformly bad. He was married to Emma Hale of Harmony, Pa., on Jan. 18, 1827. She bore him five children, among them Joseph Smith, 1832–1914 [*q.v.*]. The number of his polygamous wives is officially set at twenty-seven; unofficial claims have been made on behalf of several others. No polygamous issue has been proved. Joseph Fielding Smith [*q.v.*] was his nephew.

[Mormonism has called forth an enormous literature, practically all of it controversial. The prophet's autobiography, "The History of Joseph Smith," is available in B. H. Roberts, ed., *Hist. of the Church of Jesus Christ of Latter-Day Saints,* vols. I–IV (1902–08). *Biographical Sketches of Joseph Smith,* by Lucy Smith, his mother (Liverpool, 1853), was not edited, as the autobiography was, but is only of indirect value. E. D. Howe, *Mormonism Unveiled* (Painesville, 1834), the earliest of the anti-Mormon books, is almost unique in containing trustworthy source material. J. H. Evans, *Joseph Smith* (1933), the work of a devout Mormon, is important because of its study of Smith's ancestry; see also M. A. S. Anderson, *Ancestry and Posterity of Joseph Smith and Emma Hale* (1929). The best modern biography is contained in M. R. Werner, *Brigham Young* (1925), though it does not supersede that of W. A. Linn in *The Story of the Mormons* (1902). I. W. Riley, *The Founder of Mormonism* (1903), is unacceptable as an interpretation but contains much valuable material. H. M. Beardsley, *Joseph Smith* (1931) is comprehensive but superficial. For a discussion of Smith's mental state and the relation of his church to contemporary social movements see Bernard DeVoto, "The Centennial of Mormonism," in *The American Mercury,* Jan. 1930. This is criticized by G. B. Arbaugh, *Revelation in Mormonism* (1932), app. II.]

B. D—V.

SMITH, JOSEPH (Nov. 6, 1832–Dec. 10, 1914), Mormon prophet, president of the Reorganized Church of Jesus Christ of Latter Day Saints, son of Joseph Smith, 1805–1844 [*q.v.*], was born at Kirtland, Ohio, while that place was the headquarters of the Church of Jesus Christ of Latter Day Saints which his father had founded two years before. Both his father and his mother, Emma (Hale) Smith, were of New England ancestry. The boy's early years were spent at Kirtland; he then experienced the Mormons' brief and stormy sojourn in Missouri and saw the mushroom growth of Nauvoo, Ill. His father thrice "blessed" him, though apparently not to prophetic succession. After the elder Smith's death at the hands of a mob in 1844, the mother, instead of going west with the followers of Brigham Young [*q.v.*], remarried and continued to operate the Nauvoo hotel. Jo-

seph studied law, but soon gave it up and turned to farming. On Oct. 22, 1856, he married Emmeline Griswold.

In this same year he was asked to head the Reorganized Church of Jesus Christ of Latter-Day Saints (later known as "non-polygamous Mormons"), started in 1852 by Mormons who had left the sect of James Jesse Strang [*q.v.*]. These claimed that the presidency of the Church must pass from father to son, realizing that only thus could their branch be popularized. Smith hesitated, but through "divine direction" timidly accepted office in 1860. In 1865 he moved to Plano, Ill., as editor of the *Saints' Herald.* His wife died in 1869 and on Nov. 12 of that year he married Bertha Madison. This period was filled with zealous activity; most Mormons in the Middle West joined his church. Smith always opposed polygamy, refusing to admit that his father had ever preached or practised it and maintaining that the doctrine had been fastened on the Church by Brigham Young [*q.v.*]. He did not actively defend his father's memory until many of the founders of the Church were no longer living. When, however, in 1879 his mother, on her deathbed, apparently to satisfy her son's hopes, said that to her knowledge Joseph Smith had neither practised nor taught polygamy, Smith went to Utah, challenged any one to prove his father's guilt, and insisted that even if his father were responsible for introducing the doctrine, the practice was not thereby justified. He denounced it in tracts and periodicals, one of his chief opponents in the controversy being his cousin, Joseph Fielding Smith [*q.v.*]. With H. C. Smith he also wrote a large, apologetic treatise, *History of the Church,* in several volumes, the first issued in 1897. He fostered legal suppression of polygamy and convinced two courts that the Utah church had become heterodox. His lesser writings on polygamy and other subjects include: *Who Then Can be Saved?* (1866); *One Wife, or Many* (n.d.); *Reply to L. O. Littlefield, in Refutation of the Doctrine of Plural Marriage* (1885); and articles in the *Arena* (August 1902, May 1903) and the *North American Review* (March 1903).

In 1881 the church leaders moved to Lamoni, Iowa. Here Smith strengthened his church, fought alcohol, tobacco, tea, and coffee (in conformance with "revelation"), helped found Graceland College, and opposed Mormonism's late doctrines of polytheism and baptism for the dead. Physically strong, he enjoyed plowing and haying and continued to farm. Though color-blind he was a close observer of nature. His second wife died in 1896 and on Jan. 12, 1898, he married Ada Rachel Clark. By each wife he had several children. His private life was cheerful but his friendship was not quickly extended. He had a clear, untrained tenor voice and loved familiar melodies but cared nothing for classical music. He wrote several hymns. He was a poor financial administrator but by personality and appearance was fitted for his patriarchal position. He was of large frame, and his white hair and beard lent his unusual face impressiveness. In advancing his positions he was cautious and yet firm. He disliked flattery, ostentation, and dispute, and was at times more coldly logical than persuasive; his straightforwardness of speech caused some to think him unapproachable. Under his leadership the church grew from a handful to 70,000, and he was able to visit missions in England and Hawaii. As a prophet—to the disappointment of his church, which expects continuous revelation—he translated no "hidden books" but merely explained former scriptures or designated persons for office. In 1906 he moved to Independence, Mo. During his last years he was blind and quite deaf, though he remained an interesting companion, drawing on a wealth of remembered poetry and wit. After his son and successor, Frederick, had relieved him of actual church leadership, he dictated his "Memoirs," publication of which was begun in the *Saints' Herald*, Nov. 6, 1934. Until his death the charge on his father's honor was his heaviest cross.

[*Saints' Herald*, Dec. 16, Dec. 23, 1914; *Journal of History* (pub. by the Reorganized Church), 1908–25, esp. Jan. 1915, and Oct. 1918 ff., Apr. 1925; "My Father's Letters," *Vision*, Jan. 1932 ff.; E. W. Tullidge, *Life of Joseph the Prophet* (1880); S. W. Traum, *Mormonism Against Itself* (1910); G. B. Arbaugh, *Revelation in Mormonism* (1932); M. A. S. Anderson, *Ancestry and Posterity of Joseph Smith and Emma Hale* (1929); information from M. A. (Smith) Anderson of Lincoln, Nebr., Smith's daughter.] G. B. A.

SMITH, JOSEPH FIELDING (Nov. 13, 1838–Nov. 19, 1918), sixth president of the Utah branch of the Mormon church and nephew of Joseph Smith, 1805–1844 [*q.v.*], the founder of Mormonism, was born in the town of Far West, Mo., the son of Hyrum and Mary (Fielding) Smith. His father and uncle, with other Mormon leaders, were in prison at the time. His whole childhood was spent during the period of the violent and bitter conflict between Mormons and non-Mormons in Missouri and Illinois. He had little or no schooling beyond that given him by his mother. In the crisis following the death of his father and uncle at the hands of a mob in June 1844, his mother followed the majority of the Mormons under the leadership of Brigham Young [*q.v.*], migrating to Utah in 1848.

Two months before Joseph Fielding was fourteen he was left an orphan by the death of his mother. At fifteen he was sent on a mission for his church to Hawaii. Recalled in the autumn of 1857 because of the impending "invasion" of Utah by federal troops under General Albert Sidney Johnston [*q.v.*], he enlisted in the "Nauvoo Legion" and served in the so-called "Utah War" until a truce was concluded between the Mormons and federal officials. In April 1860, he set out on a mission to Great Britain, where he served until 1863. In March 1864, with other Mormon leaders, he was dispatched on a special mission to Hawaii, where he remained for nearly a year in charge of church interests.

Rising rapidly in the hierarchy of Mormondom, he was made an apostle July 1, 1866, a few months before he was twenty-eight years old. He had been active in various home missions or colonization schemes in Utah for a decade when in 1874–75 he was sent to England to be president of the European mission; in 1877 he filled this position again for some months. Upon his return in September of that year, he was sent to take charge of the Mormon interests in the eastern part of the United States. In October 1880, he was made second counselor to John Taylor [*q.v.*], the president of the church.

In the early sixties he became active in politics. He served on the municipal council of Salt Lake City, and for seven consecutive terms (1865–74) was a member of the lower house of the territorial legislature. In 1880 and again in 1882 he sat in the upper house, during the second term being president. In 1882, also, he presided over the constitutional convention of Utah, but was legally disqualified under the Edmunds law because of his plural marriages. During his lifetime he had six wives, of whom the five polygamous ones bore him forty-two children. In September 1884, chiefly to prevent his prosecution for polygamy under the federal law, he was sent to Hawaii on another mission and remained there in voluntary exile until the summer of 1887. The next year he was busy in Washington with other Mormon leaders, urging Congress to grant Utah her statehood. On Apr. 7, 1889, he became second counselor to president Wilford Woodruff, and nine years later, on Sept. 13, 1898, second counselor to Lorenzo Snow [*q.v.*], who had become president. On Oct. 4, 1901, he moved into the position of first counselor to Snow, and on Oct. 17, a week after the death of the latter, Smith was chosen president and "Prophet, Seer, and Revelator" of his church.

The agitation concerning Mormon polygamy did not cease in spite of official pronunciamentos by Mormon officials following the so-called "Manifesto" of 1890, and in February 1904, as president of his church, Smith was subpœnaed to appear in Washington, D. C., before the Senate Committee on Privileges and Elections, then sitting on the Reed Smoot case (*Senate Document No. 486,* 59 Cong., 1 Sess., vol. I, pp. 80 ff.). He contended that, contrary to hearsay, the Mormon church no longer sanctioned plural marriages; and at the annual conference of the church on Apr. 3 he issued an official statement to this effect. In the decade that followed, the conflict of the Mormon church with the federal government and with sectarian elements having been dissipated, Smith turned his attention to strengthening its work in various Mormon communities and in foreign countries. He made two trips to Europe (1906, 1910), several trips to Hawaii, and one to Canada in 1913, when he dedicated a site for the first Mormon temple to be erected outside the United States. In his eightieth year his health became enfeebled, and he died six days after his eightieth birthday. He was buried in Salt Lake City.

Joseph Fielding Smith was the first among the presidents of the Utah Mormons to be born within his own church, and, as the official eulogy put it, "to have spent every day of his life under its ægis and influence" (*Deseret Evening News,* Salt Lake City, Nov. 19, 1918). Rather than the initiation of any important changes in the church, his chief contribution was the strengthening of the organization itself, and, through his kindly spirit of compromise, the fostering of more friendly relations with non-Mormons both in Utah and outside. In 1919, the year after his death, *Gospel Doctrine: Selections from the Sermons and Writings of Joseph F. Smith* was published.

[Andrew Jenson, *Latter-Day Saint Biog. Encyc.,* I (1901), 66–74, III (1920), 781–84; *Hist. Record* (Andrew Jensen, editor), VI (1887), 183–95; B. H. Roberts, *A Comprehensive Hist. of the Church of Jesus Christ of Latter-Day Saints* (1930), vols. V, VI; O. F. Whitney, *Hist. of Utah,* vol. IV (1904); Noble Warrum, *Utah Since Statehood* (1919), II, 66–70; *Improvement Era,* vol. XXII, Dec. 1918, Jan. 1919.]
K. Y.

SMITH, JUDSON (June 28, 1837–June 29, 1906), educator, missionary secretary, was born at Middlefield, Mass., where his parents, Samuel and Lucina (Metcalf) Smith, reared a family of seven sons and three daughters on a farm among the Berkshire hills. He was a descendant of Matthew Smith who settled at Woburn, Mass., in 1637, and a first cousin of Azariah Smith [*q.v.*]; Gerald Birney Smith [*q.v.*] was his nephew. Judson was fitted for college at home and at Williston Seminary, Easthampton, Mass., and

after taking part of his college course at Oberlin, graduated at Amherst in 1859. He taught in 1862 at Monson Academy, Mass. He graduated at Oberlin Theological Seminary in 1863, having also had a year at Union Seminary, New York. He was tutor in Latin and Greek at Oberlin, 1862–64, and instructor in mathematics and mental and moral philosophy at Williston Seminary, 1864–66. On Aug. 1, 1865, he married Jerusha Augusta, daughter of Seth A. Bushnell of Hartford, Ohio.

In 1866 Smith was called to Oberlin as professor of Latin, and on Oct. 17 of that year was ordained a Congregational minister. In 1870 he was transferred to the chair of ecclesiastical history in Oberlin Seminary, which he held until 1884. He also was lecturer on modern history at Oberlin, 1875–84, and lecturer on history at Lake Erie Seminary, Painesville, Ohio, 1879–84. From 1871 to 1884 he served as president of the Oberlin board of education. During the early eighties he was largely instrumental in the founding in China of the Shansi Mission of the American Board, which was at the outset manned by his pupils, several of whom lost their lives during the Boxer uprising of 1900.

In 1884 Smith was called from Oberlin to Boston as a secretary of the American Board of Commissioners for Foreign Missions, where he served with widening influence throughout the rest of his life. Entering upon his new duties at a time when the educational work of the Board was rapidly expanding, he brought much valuable experience to aid in this development, with which he was in hearty sympathy, as he was also with the quickening sense of the responsibility of missions for social service. He visited the missions of the Board in Turkey in 1888, and was chairman of a deputation inspecting its missions in China in 1898. He was of dignified bearing, punctilious courtesy, and abounding enthusiasm. His statement when chairman of the General Committee of the Ecumenical Conference of Foreign Missions at Carnegie Hall, New York, in 1900, that the story of missions is "a record more thrilling and more significant than any epic which man has produced," was characteristic of his habitual attitude. He served as trustee of Oberlin and of Williston Seminary and was president of the board of trustees of Mount Holyoke College. He lectured on missions at Oberlin and Hartford seminaries and was associate editor of the *Bibliotheca Sacra.* He was author of *Lectures in Church History and the History of Doctrine* and *Lectures in Modern History,* both published in 1881.

[*Ecumenical Missionary Conf., N. Y., 1900: Report of the Ecumenical Conference on Foreign Missions* (2 vols., 1900); *Amherst Coll. Biog. Record* (1927); *Who's Who in America,* 1906–07; *Missionary Review of the World,* Aug. 1906; *Congregationalist,* July 7 and 14, 1906; *Bibliotheca Sacra,* Oct. 1906; *Missionary Herald,* Aug. 1906; *Boston Transcript,* June 30, 1906.]

E. D. E.

SMITH, JULIA EVELINA (1792–1886) [See SMITH, ABBY HADASSAH, 1797–1878].

SMITH, JUNIUS (Oct. 2, 1780–Jan. 22, 1853), lawyer, merchant, promoter, has been called the "father of the Atlantic liner." He was born in Plymouth, then part of Watertown, Conn., third of the four sons of David and Ruth (Hitchcock) Smith. His father, a major in the Revolution and a general in the Connecticut militia, was a prosperous storekeeper. Junius was prepared for college at Bethlehem near by, and went as a sophomore to Yale. After graduating in 1802, he became a fellow student of John C. Calhoun at Tapping Reeve's law school, Litchfield, and in 1804 opened a law office in New Haven. Sent to London in 1805 by his brother's firm, he secured from the Court of Admiralty Appeal the award of liberal damages for the seizure of the New Haven ship *Mohawk.* He settled in London as a merchant, making his home there, except for a brief sojourn in Liverpool, until 1843. On Apr. 9, 1812, he married Sarah, daughter of Thomas Allen of Huddersfield, Yorkshire. She died in 1836, leaving one daughter. Smith dealt chiefly with New York, corresponding with his nephew Henry Smith, and constantly suggesting additional articles of export, clover seed being a favorite. In spite of reverses during the War of 1812, he became quite prosperous.

Smith's principal distinction arises from his share in establishing regular steamship service across the ocean. The single voyage of the *Savannah* in 1819, sponsored by Moses Rogers and William Scarborough [qq.v.], had been premature. In 1829, the *Curaçao* had made several trips from Holland to the Dutch West Indies, and in 1833 the *Royal William* went from Quebec to England, but none of these ventures developed into regular permanent service. The "liners" of the day were the highly efficient New York sailing packets. Smith seems to have conceived the idea of a line of transatlantic steamers about the time of his fifty-four-day voyage to New York in a British sailing vessel in 1832. He actively devoted the next few years to creating public opinion and raising capital for the support of his project. Kind, generous, and very hospitable, the little man, barely five feet six, went at the task with great energy of purpose and perseverance. Rebuffed in New York, he returned to London and in February 1833 pro-

posed his idea to the directors of the London & Edinburgh Steam Packet Company without success. He issued several prospectuses, with no immediate response. In 1836, however, having secured a powerful ally in Macgregor Laird [see *Dictionary of National Biography*] of the great Birkenhead shipbuilding family, he organized the British & American Steam Navigation Company.

Great Britain's conversion to ocean steamships, once Smith had overcome the prevailing skepticism, was rapid, and in quick succession a number of rival companies were formed. Smith and Laird, in fact, had only a few hours to spare in being the first to reach New York. Isambard K. Brunel [*Ibid.*], engineer of the Great Western Railway, persuaded its Bristol backers in 1836 to form a transatlantic steamship company. Their 1340-ton steamship, *Great Western,* was launched July 19, 1837. Smith and Laird, in the meantime, were encountering disheartening delays. They had ordered a 1700-ton steamship in October 1836, but the failure of the contractor postponed even the laying of the keel until Apr. 1, 1837. Eager to be the first across the Atlantic, they decided not to wait for this vessel to be completed, so chartered from the Cork Steamship Company the little 700-ton *Sirius,* which left Cork on Apr. 4, 1838, and reached New York, on the voyage that marked the start of permanent transatlantic steam service, on the evening of Apr. 22, a few hours ahead of the *Great Western,* which had left Bristol on Apr. 7. Smith's vessel, the *British Queen,* was finally launched on May 24, 1838, and first reached New York July 27, 1839. Smith was the hero of the hour. It was declared in *Hunt's Merchants' Magazine* (October 1840, p. 298) that to him "more than to any other individual, is the final and successful accomplishment of this great enterprise doubtless to be attributed." Yale gave him the degree of LL.D. in 1840 and he had visions of knighthood (Pond, *post,* p. 187).

Then came reverses. Under Laird's supervision, his company, in December 1839, launched the *President,* the "largest ship in the world." She sailed on a return voyage from New York Mar. 11, 1841, and disappeared without a trace. This disaster, coupled with the successful competition of the line established by Samuel Cunard, who received the lucrative British mail subsidy in 1839, soon brought the British & American Steam Navigation Company to a close, and Smith in 1843 ended his long London residence. Back in America, he purchased a plantation near Greenville, S. C., and tried to relieve the country from dependence upon China for tea by growing it in the Southern states. The idea apparently came to him through his daughter, who was married to an army chaplain in India. He wrote numerous articles on the domestic growing of tea, celery, and broccoli, and made experiments which, according to later reports of the Department of Agriculture, indicated promise of a successful American supply of tea. This work, however, came to a tragic close. Smith's anti-slavery sentiments aroused his neighbors, and on Dec. 23, 1851, he sustained a fractured skull from a beating at the hands of "patrollers." These injuries hastened his death, which occurred at Bloomingdale Asylum, after some months of illness in his nephew's home, Astoria, L. I.

Smith's publications included: *An Oration, Pronounced at Hartford, before the Society of the Cincinnati, for the State of Connecticut* (1804); *Letters upon Atlantic Steam Navigation* (1841); *Essays on the Cultivation of the Tea Plant, in the United States of America* (1848); agricultural papers in the reports of the commissioner of patents; articles in the *Merchants' Magazine,* notably "Origin of Atlantic Ocean Steam Navigation" (February 1847); "Letters on Atlantic Steam Navigation" and "Steam Ships, and Steam Navigation," in *American Journal of Science and Arts* (January, July 1839).

[E. L. Pond, *Junius Smith, A Biog. of the Father of the Atlantic Liner* (1927), utilizing source material and reproducing much correspondence between Smith and his nephew; F. B. Dexter, *Biog. Sketches Grads. Yale Coll.,* vol. V (1911); *Hunt's Merchants' Mag.,* Oct. 1840; W. S. Lindsay, *Hist. of Merchant Shipping and Ancient Commerce,* vol. IV (1876); *Brief Memoirs of the Class of 1802* (1863); article by Henry Smith in *Evening Post* (N. Y.), June 24, 1882; *Evening Post* (N. Y.), Jan. 24, 1853; *Jour. of Commerce* (N. Y.), Jan. 25, 1853.]   R. G. A.

SMITH, JUSTIN HARVEY (Jan. 13, 1857–Mar. 21, 1930), historian, was born at Boscawen, N. H., the youngest of the three sons of Ambrose and Cynthia Maria (Egerton) Smith. On the death of the father, a Congregational minister, the family moved first to Pembroke, N. H., and then to Norwich, Vt. From Norwich, Justin walked each day the three miles to Hanover, N. H., where he attended Dartmouth as his father had done; he graduated in 1877, the valedictorian of his class. He was a serious student, keeping somewhat to himself. After graduation he visited the Paris Exposition, accompanying as private secretary, John D. Philbrick, who was in charge of the United States educational exhibit. Perhaps this experience implanted in young Smith that love of journeying abroad which later made of him a world traveler. The years 1879–81 he spent at the Union Theological

Seminary; but, instead of proceeding to the ministry, he entered the employ first of Charles Scribner's Sons and then of Ginn & Company. After holding positions of responsibility, both on the business and on the editorial side, he became in 1890 a member of the latter publishing firm, highly valued by his associates. His marriage, May 22, 1892, to Mary E. Barnard of Chico, Cal., the daughter of Allyn and Sarah Barnard, who, like Smith himself, had entered into the musical circle of Boston, was followed after two years by a separation and later by a divorce in Paris (private information).

In 1898 Smith, now possessed of ample means, retired from the publishing business. He became next year professor of modern history at Dartmouth College. One of his students recalled him as "a man of flexible dignity, kindness, judgment, and scholarly taste," whom "the classroom never succeeded in narrowing" (private letter to author). Here began his work as a productive scholar with the publication in 1899 of *The Troubadours at Home* (reviewed in *American Historical Review,* April 1900). All of his later work lay in the field of American history. *Arnold's March from Cambridge to Quebec* appeared in 1903, as did also *The Historie Booke,* edited by Smith for the Ancient and Honorable Artillery Company of Massachusetts. For this he wrote the historical narrative. He also published *Our Struggle for the Fourteenth Colony: Canada and the American Revolution* (1907). In 1908 he resigned his professorship to devote his time entirely to historical research. *The Annexation of Texas,* appeared in 1911. In respect to this it has been said, "Few books of history have more decisively settled controversy on their subject" (*American Historical Review,* July 1930, p. 942). His *magnum opus, The War with Mexico* (2 vols., 1919) brought to Smith the Pulitzer Prize for 1920 and the first Loubat Prize (1923) for the best book in English published during the previous five years on the history, geography, archeology, ethnology, philology, or numismatics of North America. Both books evidenced the author's characteristics as a scholar: a tireless searching for all possible sources, consultation of the originals themselves, knowledge through travel of the regions to be described, critical discernment, and a cumulative presentation of voluminous footnotes. Smith wrote also many articles in historical journals. For the Historical Manuscripts Commission of the American Historical Association, of which he was chairman from 1917 to 1923, he edited "Letters of General Antonio López de Santa Anna Relating to the War Between the United

States and Mexico, 1846–1848" (*Annual Report of the American Historical Association for the Year 1917*, 1920). In his many reviews of books, his trenchant criticism occasionally elicited controversy, as with Prof. E. D. Adams (*American Historical Review*, Oct. 1910, pp. 151–54; Jan. 1911, pp. 402–06; Apr. 1911, p. 683).

Tall, with a somewhat ruddy countenance and keen eyes, and, at least in later life, a full beard, Smith presented a commanding figure. He was a member of many societies and clubs, professional and social, and received several honorary degrees. He derived pleasure from cruising in power boats, constructed after plans of his own which resulted in more comfort than beauty. To house what he had collected in his extensive travels he built on Parker Hill, Boston, a bungalow where, at a huge three-sided desk, constructed for the purpose, he did much of his writing. In November 1929, he was shocked and weakened by a taxicab accident. On Mar. 21, 1930, having returned from the South, where of late years he had spent his winters, he reached New York, and late that afternoon, while taking a walk in Brooklyn, where he lived, he suffered a heart attack in front of Borough Hall and died instantly. After some delay his body was identified by his friend and former associate, George A. Plimpton of Ginn & Company. The funeral service was held at Trenton, N. J., where one of his nephews lived. His remains were buried in the town of his birth.

[Sketches in *Who's Who in America*, 1901–02, and later editions; obituary in *N. Y. Herald Tribune*, Mar. 24, 1930; biographical sketch in *Dartmouth Alumni Magazine*, May 1930; *Semi-Centennial Record of the Class of 1877. Dartmouth College 1877–1927* (n.d.); letters from friends and associates; personal knowledge.]　　　　　　　　　　　　St. G. L. S.

SMITH, LLOYD PEARSALL (Feb. 6, 1822–July 2, 1886), librarian, publisher, editor, eldest child of John Jay Smith [*q.v.*] and Rachel Collins (Pearsall) Smith, was born in Philadelphia. After his graduation from Haverford College in 1837, he was placed in the counting house of Walm & Leaming, importers, to learn the business. In 1845 he began publishing *Smith's Weekly Volume*, edited by his father, a successor of *Waldie's Select Circulating Library*. This publication continued until the spring of 1846, and during part of this period young Smith also published *The Medical Library* and some law books. In 1847 he issued *A Plan of the District of Spring Garden, Philadelphia*.

In 1849 he became assistant librarian of the Library Company of Philadelphia, of which his father was librarian, and two years later succeeded him. With this ancient library, founded by Franklin and his friends, he remained identified until his death. Under his direction the third volume of *Catalogue of the Books Belonging to the Library Company of Philadelphia* was issued in 1856, for which work he supplied a copious index. When the Confederate forces invaded Pennsylvania in 1863, Smith enlisted for three months in a volunteer regiment, and closing the library, went forth to the defense of Gettysburg. During the war, he also joined with others in collecting money for the relief of those in East Tennessee who remained loyal to the Union, and published a report of a commission that was sent there to investigate conditions. He was the first editor of *Lippincott's Magazine*, conducting that periodical from January 1868 to December 1869. Under his editorship the magazine published Anthony Trollope's novel, "The Vicar of Bullhampton"; one by Robert Dale Owen, "Beyond the Breakers"; also contributions from Bayard Taylor and from George H. Boker.

In 1876 he contributed to *Public Libraries in the United States of America*, issued by the United States Bureau of Education, the section entitled "Public Libraries of Philadelphia." A paper of his read before the American Library Association and published in 1892 under the caption *On the Classification of Books*, was a pioneer discussion of the subject. Another paper, read before the Germantown Science and Art Club appeared in 1885 as *Symbolism and Science*. That same year he published *A Bibliography of that Ancient and Honourable Order, the Society of the Cincinnati*. Upon the appearance of the first volume of *Histoire de Jules César*, by Napoleon III, in 1865, Smith reviewed it in the *United States Service Magazine*, later issuing the review in pamphlet form—*Remarks on the Apology for Imperial Usurpation Contained in Napoleon's Life of Caesar* (1865). He was regarded as a most scholarly man and as better acquainted with library management than any one else of his time. He was one of the original associate editors of the *American Library Journal*, begun in September 1876. As an after dinner speaker he was much in demand. On Oct. 13, 1844, he married Hannah E. Jones, daughter of Isaac C. Jones, a Philadelphia merchant engaged in the East India trade; no children were born to them, but they adopted a daughter.

[G. M. Abbot, "Some Recollections of Lloyd P. Smith," *Library Journal*, Dec. 1887; *Public Ledger* (Phila.), July 3, 1886; J. T. Scharf and Thompson Westcott, *Hist. of Phila.* (1884), II, 1185; G. M. Abbot, *A Short Hist. of the Lib. Company of Phila.* (1913); *Biog. Cat. of the Matriculates of Haverford Coll.* (1922); information from a member of the family.]　　　　　　　　　　　　J. J.

SMITH, MARCUS (Jan. 7, 1829–Aug. 11, 1874), actor, better known as Mark Smith, was the son of the well-known comedian and theatre manager, Solomon Franklin Smith [q.v.], and his first wife, Martha (Mathews) Smith. He was born in New Orleans, La., but was educated chiefly in schools in and near St. Louis, Mo., the family home. As a child he was sometimes seen on the stage of the Ludlow and Smith Theatre in St. Louis, playing Tom Thumb in Henry Fielding's burlesque, *Tom Thumb,* as early as 1836. But his father was opposed to his adopting the stage as a profession, and sought to train him first as a printer, then as a navigator, and later as a mechanic. In 1848, however, he went to New York, where he secured a position in the Chatham Theatre. A year later he joined his father's company at the St. Charles in New Orleans, making his début as Diggory in *Family Jars.* He continued at this theatre under the management of Ben De Bar after the dissolution of the firm of Ludlow and Smith in 1853. After a season under Joseph M. Field in Mobile he became a member of the stock company of William Evans Burton [qq.v.] in New York. There he soon began to make a name for himself as an interpreter of the "good old English gentlemen" in the "good old English comedies" and became a great favorite. He remained with Burton until the closing of his theatre in 1858 (Odell, *post,* VII, 163–64).

After this he at different times supported such stars as Laura Keene, Edwin Forrest, and Edward Loomis Davenport [qq.v.]. In March 1862 he first appeared with the company of Lester Wallack, playing Sir William Fondlove in J. S. Knowles's comedy of *The Love Chase.* During the summer of 1863 he managed with Emily Thorne a brief season at the Winter Garden. After another year with Wallack he again tried his hand at management, becoming in 1866 joint-manager with Lewis Baker of the New York Theatre. February 1869 found him stage-manager for Edwin Booth [q.v.] at the latter's theatre, and the following year, after supporting Mme. Franziska Janauschek [q.v.] and Mrs. Scott-Siddons, he went abroad, there to play at the St. James's Theatre, London, under Mrs. John Wood. But he soon returned to the United States and, for a time, to Booth's Theatre in New York. The season of 1872–73 he spent under Albert Marshman Palmer [q.v.] at the Union Square Theatre. There he scored such a success in *One Hundred Years Old* that he bought the acting rights to the piece and toured the country as the centenarian. The following spring he went abroad to attend the operatic début of his daugh-

ter, and died after a stroke in Paris, Aug. 11, 1874. His death elicited many eulogies both of his artistry and of his personal character. When Mark Smith was playing one of his old gentlemen, wrote William Winter [q.v.], "the observer of him felt that every trait of manliness, kindly worth, gracious serenity, and human feeling that warmed and beautified the fictitious character had its native source in the heart of the man himself" (*Vagrant Memories,* 1915, p. 131). He was survived by his widow, Elizabeth McKenney, his daughter Kate (who as Catarina Marco became a successful opera singer), and two sons, Mark and Percival.

[See T. A. Brown, *Hist. of the Am. Stage* (1870); Laurence Hutton, *Plays and Players* (1875) and *Curiosities of the Am. Stage* (1880); S. F. Smith, *Theatrical Management* (1868), pp. 221–22; N. M. Ludlow, *Dramatic Life As I Found It* (1880); G. C. D. Odell, *Annals of the N. Y. Stage,* vols. V–VII (1931); obituary in *N. Y. Times,* Aug. 27, 1874. Many of Smith's letters to his father are in the estate of his nephew, the late Sheridan S. Smith, Webster Groves, Mo.]

W. G. B. C.

SMITH, MARGARET BAYARD (Feb. 20, 1778–June 7, 1844), society leader, author, was the daughter of John Bubenheim Bayard [q.v.] and his wife, Margaret Hodge. On Sept. 29, 1800, she married her second cousin, Samuel Harrison Smith [q.v.]. Soon after her husband became President Jefferson's political editor, she found herself a leader in Washington society. In this capacity she was hardly excelled. She was a charming hostess, happy in her married life, capable, intelligent, vivacious, energetic, sympathetic, and positive. She read the best books, and conversed with distinguished men on subjects of domestic, national, and international import. Among her guests were statesmen, philosophers, poets, musicians, and diplomats. Although the wife of a stanch Jeffersonian, she remained true to her Federalist rearing, and welcomed Whigs to her home. Men of opposite political faith associated there on friendly terms. Although she professed to think little of balls and parties, she played well at chess and whist, and participated gaily in the whirl of society during the winter season when she had left her country seat, "Sidney," for her city residence.

In addition to her social activities she baked her own bread, took great pride in making her own butter, reared four children, aided the poor, attended church regularly, and won a contemporary reputation as an author. She contributed to Godey's *Lady's Book,* the *Southern Literary Messenger, Peter Parley's Annual,* and Herring and Longacre's *National Portrait Gallery,* and wrote a novel in two volumes entitled, *A Winter in Washington; or, Memoirs of the Seymour*

Family (1824), and another tale, *What Is Gentility?* (1828). Her "Domestic Sketches" and other stories in Godey's *Lady's Book* were pitched high in moral tone, as were all her contributions to magazines; her novel is valuable to history for its true stories of Washington characters. Her most valuable contribution to literature, however, lies in her delightfully refreshing, informative, and truthful letters to her friends. These, edited by Gaillard Hunt [*q.v.*] and published in 1906 under the title, *The First Forty Years of Washington Society,* form a record, by a keen observer, of events from Jefferson to Harrison. They also reveal the writer's personal opinions. She saw no incompatibility between politeness and republicanism, but she believed that democracy was more jealous of power and privilege than despotism. Influenced undoubtedly by Jackson's fight against the United States Bank, of the Washington Branch of which her husband was president, she deplored the influence of Jackson's "Kitchen Cabinet," and the spoils system, and finally decided that the old General was in his dotage when he championed Peggy O'Neale [*q.v.*] against the ladies of the cabinet.

[In addition to Mrs. Smith's letters, ed. by Hunt, mentioned above, see: J. G. Wilson, "Col. John Bayard and the Bayard Family," *N. Y. Geneal. and Biog. Record,* Apr. 1885, repr. separately (1885); Helen Nicolay, *Our Capital on the Potomac* (1924); W. B. Bryan, *A Hist. of the National Capital,* vol. I (1914); *Daily National Intelligencer* (Washington), June 8, 1844. The important Margaret Bayard Smith Papers (28 vols., covering the period 1798–1845) are in the Library of Congress.]   W. E. S—h.

SMITH, MARTIN LUTHER (Sept. 9, 1819–July 29, 1866), Confederate soldier, was born at Danby, Tompkins County, N. Y., to which place his father, Luther Smith, had removed from Maine. He entered West Point as a cadet in 1838, and upon his graduation in 1842 was commissioned in the topographical engineers, then a separate corps of the army. His service was entirely in the Southern states, except for a brief period in Mexico, when he reconnoitered and mapped the valley of the city of Mexico. He executed surveys of several rivers and harbors in Florida and Georgia, and examined into the possibilities of a projected ship-canal across the Florida peninsula. For five years, 1856–61, he also acted as chief engineer of the Fernandina & Cedar Key Railroad. In 1846 he married Sarah, daughter of John and Harriet (Cooper) Nisbet of Athens, Ga. He was promoted first lieutenant in 1853 and captain in 1856.

Owing to his marriage and his long residence in Florida and Georgia, "his associations, feelings and interests are with the South" (Senator Yulee to Jefferson Davis, Mar. 1, 1861, War Department records); and he tendered his resignation from the army, hoping to serve the Confederacy but determined in any event not to serve against it. His resignation was accepted, Apr. 1, 1861. He had already, Mar. 16, 1861, been appointed a major of engineers in the Confederate regular army, being recorded as a citizen of Florida. Though occasionally commanding troops in the field—at one time a division —it was as an engineer that he was chiefly employed. He had a large part in the planning and construction of the fortifications of New Orleans and those of Vicksburg, and commanded troops in the defense of both of those places when they were taken in 1862 and 1863. He was appointed colonel, 21st Louisiana Infantry, in February 1862; brigadier-general (provisional army) in April 1862; and major-general in November 1862. After the surrender of Vicksburg in July 1863 he was a prisoner on parole until his exchange some seven months later. From April to July 1864 he was chief engineer of the Army of Northern Virginia, and from July to October, of Hood's Army of Tennessee. In that capacity he was responsible for the construction of the field-works used in the campaigns of those armies. Thereafter he was chief engineer to Beauregard, who was in administrative command in the western theatre; his principal service there was in the preparation of the defenses of Mobile to receive the attack which was delivered against them in the last days of the Confederacy. He was paroled at Athens, Ga., in May 1865 and took up the practice of engineering as a civilian for the few remaining months of his life. He died in Savannah.

[*War of the Rebellion: Official Records* (Army); *Battles and Leaders of the Civil War* (4 vols., 1887–88); G. W. Cullum, *Biog. Reg. Officers and Grads. U. S. Mil. Acad.* (3rd ed., 1891); C. A. Evans, *Confed. Mil. Hist.* (1899); unpublished records in the War Dept.]   T. M. S.

SMITH, MELANCTON (May 7, 1744–July 29, 1798), merchant, lawyer, member of the Continental Congress, son of Samuel and Elizabeth (Bayles) Smith, was born at Jamaica, L. I. His education was home training of a sort to reflect credit upon his obscure parents. At an early age he was placed in a retail store at Poughkeepsie. He soon owned land in various parts of Dutchess County, and had acquired a reputation for wide reading, honesty, and ability. He early manifested a life-long interest in metaphysics and religion; in 1769 he helped organize the Washington Hollow Presbyterian Church and purchased one of the pews. He was one of ten delegates from Dutchess County in the First Provincial Congress in 1775 and was made a member of a committee to raise a regiment of the line in Dutchess County. He also organized and was captain of the first company of Rangers of that county, a home guard so effective in controlling Loyalists that the First Committee for Detecting Conspiracies adopted it as a model and on Dec. 20, 1776, appointed Smith, with the rank of major, to the command of all such companies.

On Feb. 11, 1777, he was made one of three members of a commission for "inquiring into, detecting and defeating all conspiracies . . . against the liberties of America" (*Journals, post,* I, 803), under which broad phraseology he served almost daily for the next six months at twelve shillings *per diem,* administering oaths of allegiance, arresting suspects, informing upon and examining Loyalists. While wielding this powerful civil and military authority, he was also serving as high sheriff of Dutchess County, to which position he was elevated in 1777 and again in 1779. He extended his land holdings by purchasing some of the forfeited Loyalist estates (Ledger of Forfeited Estates in Dutchess County, MS., New York Public Library).

As a merchant and as one enjoying the confidence of Gov. George Clinton [*q.v.*], he naturally gravitated to the commissary department in the last years of the Revolution, and, though he came out of the war a man of considerable property, one whose word is usually reliable said he was "as pure a man as ever lived" (Hammond, *post,* I, 61). In 1782 Washington appointed him to a commission to settle disputes between the army and contractors at West Point and elsewhere (Washington Papers, Library of Congress, vols. LV-LVII, *passim*). Smith charged contractors with bad faith and in turn was charged with inducing soldiers to spend their pay in his store (*Ibid.,* LXIII, 146, 150; B. XVI, pt. 2, p. 47). He shared the indignation of other patriots over the decision in *Rutgers* vs. *Waddington* which in 1784 invalidated an act of the legislature proscribing Loyalists.

About 1785 he moved to New York City and entered upon extensive mercantile enterprises and a lucrative law practice, though it is not known where he secured his legal training. He served in the Continental Congress from 1785 to 1788. His most conspicuous public service was in the Poughkeepsie convention called in 1788 to consider ratification of the Federal Constitution. Basing his campaign on an anti-Loyalist issue, he was unable to secure election in Federalist New York County but represented Dutchess County in the convention as an Anti-

Federalist. In the convention he bore the brunt of the Federalist attack and was so successful in opposing even Hamilton that he has been characterized as "one of the ablest debaters in the country" (Alexander, *post,* I, 34). He held out for a Bill of Rights until Hamilton's eloquence and news of Virginia's ratification impelled him to announce his support of the Constitution, an action which broke the Anti-Federalist ranks and brought down Clinton's wrath upon his head. Although he was one of the few important landowners and merchants among the Anti-Federalists, Smith continued in the Clintonian party and helped in 1789 to sponsor a movement for a second constitutional convention. He was elected to the legislature in 1791 and canvassed the state for Clinton in 1792. He was one of the first victims of the yellow fever epidemic in New York City in 1798. Melancton Smith [*q.v.*], distinguished naval officer, was his grandson.

[Surprisingly few records of Smith exist for one who played such an able part among the Anti-Federalists. A few letters are in the N. Y. Hist. Soc., the N. Y. Pub. Lib., the N. Y. State Lib., and among the Force Transcripts in the Lib. of Cong. See also *Journals of the Provincial Cong. . . . of the State of N. Y.* (1842), vol. I; *Minutes of the Committee and of the First Commission for Detecting and Defeating Conspiracies* (2 vols., 1924–25); *The Debates and Proc. of the Convention . . . at Poughkeepsie* (1788); J. W. Poucher, "Melancton Smith," *Year Book Dutchess County Hist. Soc.,* 1925; *N. Y. Hist. Soc. Colls.* for 1906; *Names of Persons for Whom Marriage Licenses Were Issued by the Secretary of the Province of N. Y. Previous to 1784* (1860); D. S. Alexander, *A Pol. Hist. of the State of N. Y.,* vol. I (1906); A. C. Flick, *Loyalism in N. Y. during the Am. Rev.* (1901); J. D. Hammond, *The Hist. of Pol. Parties in the State of N. Y.* (1842), vol. I; Frank Hasbrouck, *The Hist. of Dutchess County, N. Y.* (1909); C. E. Miner, *The Ratification of the Federal Constitution by the State of N. Y.* (1921); E. W. Spaulding, *N. Y. in the Critical Period* (1932). The year of Smith's birth is often given as 1724; Poucher, *ante,* is authority for the date here given.]   J. P. B.

SMITH, MELANCTON (May 24, 1810–July 19, 1893), naval officer, was born in New York City, the third of his name, his grandfather, Melancton Smith [*q.v.*], having been prominent in early New York politics and his father, a colonel in the War of 1812. His mother was Cornelia Haring Jones. On Mar. 1, 1826, he entered the naval service, and after three years in the Pacific and study at the naval school in New York he was made passed midshipman in April 1832. During the next decade his sea duty was chiefly in the West Indies and his shore duty in New York, with promotion to lieutenant in 1837 and active participation (June 1839–March 1840) in the Seminole War in Florida. He was in the Mediterranean, 1841–43; in the *Vandalia,* Home Squadron, 1844–46; executive of the Pensacola yard during the Mexican War;

and again in the Mediterranean in the *Constitution,* 1848–51. In 1855 he was made commander, but save for a few months as executive of the *Potomac* in 1855 he had no further sea service until the opening of the Civil War, when he was sent to the mouth of the Mississippi in command of the *Massachusetts.* Here he had a long-range cannonade with Confederate batteries on Ship Island, July 9, 1861, and another with the *Florida* on Oct. 19. Speaking of his "efficient service," the Navy Department ordered him north at the close of 1861, but soon sent him back to command the side-wheeler *Mississippi* in Farragut's force against New Orleans. The *Mississippi,* as third ship of the first division, was heavily engaged in the night passage of the forts below New Orleans on Apr. 23–24, 1862, had a seven-foot gash cut in her side by the ram *Manassas,* and at daybreak drove the ram ashore and riddled it with two broadsides.

Continuing in Farragut's squadron through the ensuing year, the *Mississippi,* on the night of Mar. 14, 1863, participated in the attempt to pass the batteries at Port Hudson. At a bend in the narrow channel she grounded directly under the enemy guns, and after desperate efforts to save his ship Smith was forced to fire and abandon her, drifting with his men in boats to the Union vessels below. Admiral George Dewey [*q.v.*], who as a youthful officer was executive under Smith throughout this period, pictures vividly in his *Autobiography* (*post,* p. 51) the personality of his commander, whom he greatly esteemed. "He was a pronounced character," writes Dewey, "absolutely fearless, with something of Farragut's grim determination in the midst of battle. He smoked continually, lighting one cigar with the butt of another, whether shells were bursting around him or he was lounging on the deck.... His hobby, except in the matter of cigars, was temperance." An earnest, religious man, without humor, he was a dogged fighter, and when he went north in June, after some further service in the *Monongahela,* Farragut wrote, "I hope the department will appreciate your services as highly as I do" (June 23, 1863, Personnel Files, Navy Library). In the monitor *Onondaga* he was afterward a divisional commander in the James River, and in May–June 1864 he commanded a half dozen or more wooden gunboats in Albemarle Sound during efforts to destroy the ram *Albemarle.* His flotilla on May 5 had a desperate mêlée with the ram, in which, though driven back up the Roanoke River, the latter suffered somewhat less than her light-built opponents. The department congratulated him on "this remarkable contest"

and on his "vigilant and gallant use of the means" at his disposal (*Official Records, post,* 1 ser., IX, 761). He commanded the *Wabash* in Porter's fleet against Fort Fisher, and was warmly commended by Porter for his handling of his ship during the two heavy bombardments in December–January 1864–65. Made captain in 1862, commodore in 1866, and rear admiral in 1870, he was chief of the Bureau of Equipment and Recruiting, 1866–70, and was subsequently in charge of the New York Navy Yard until shortly after his retirement, May 24, 1871. He was governor of the Philadelphia Naval Asylum, 1871–72. In 1837 he married Mary Jackson, daughter of Thomas Jones of Long Island, N. Y.; she died at South Oyster Bay, Long Island, Apr. 4, 1885, and Smith died some eight years later at Green Bay, Wis.

[L. H. Hamersly, *Records of Living Officers of the U. S. Navy* (4th ed., 1890); *Autobiog. of George Dewey* (1913); Personnel Files, Navy Dept. Lib.; *Official Records of the Union and Confederate Navies in the War of the Rebellion* (see general index); *Army and Navy Journal,* July 22, 1893; *N. Y. Tribune,* July 21, 1893.]   A. W.

SMITH, MERIWETHER (1730–Jan. 24, 1794), statesman, was born at "Bathurst," Essex County, Va., the son of Col. Francis and Lucy (Meriwether) Smith. His father, grandson of Nicholas Smith of Petsworth Parish, Gloucester County, was a member of the House of Burgesses, 1752–58. Meriwether Smith was one of the signers of the Westmoreland Association (Feb. 27, 1766) in opposition to the Stamp Act and wrote "several spirited pieces" relating to that and other British measures (Rind's *Virginia Gazette,* Aug. 24, 1769). From 1774, when he became a member of the Essex County Committee, he was seldom out of public office during the period of the Revolution. He was a member of the Virginia House of Burgesses in 1775, of the conventions of 1775 and 1776, of the House of Delegates in 1776, 1778, 1781–82, 1785–88, of the convention of 1788, occasionally of the council, and he was three times (1778, 1779, 1780) elected a delegate to the Continental Congress.

In the Virginia convention of 1776 he was chosen to the important committee on privileges and elections and second on the committee to prepare a declaration of rights. On May 15 he was one of three members, the other two being Edmund Pendleton and Patrick Henry, who drafted resolutions of independence; Pendleton's draft, however, was accepted. Although Madison recorded a tradition (Rives, *post,* I, 164) that Smith prepared a first draft of the Virginia constitution of 1776, the weight of evidence assigns the authorship of that document to George Mason (K. M. Rowland, *The Life of George Mason*, 1892, I, 228, 254–56). John Augustine Washington classed Smith among the five best speakers in the convention (*Southern Literary Messenger*, November 1858, p. 330).

In the Continental Congress, in which he took his seat Sept. 28, 1778, he played an active, and at times a conspicuous, part in the proceedings. Like several other Virginia delegates he declined to espouse the cause of the Lees in the notorious Deane-Lee controversy, and his course in that fiery contest brought down upon him the sharp criticism of Richard Henry Lee and those aligned with him. "Mr. Smith (alias Dogberry)," Lee wrote to Henry Laurens (from Virginia, June 13, 1779), "has been famous here for being a very vain and a very troublesome man" (Ballagh, *post,* II, 70). Marbois said of him, "He has much sagacity but too much subtlety, and in seeking to penetrate he misses the goal" (Affaires Étrangères, États-Unis, Mem. et Doc., 1). He impressed members of Congress no less than his Virginia contemporaries with his eccentricities, and was dubbed with such nicknames as "the Oddity of Virginia," "Fiddle," "Fiddlehead," "Base Viol," "Ugly Instrument," etc., the origin of which remains in obscurity. For his part he was by no means averse to throwing fat into the fire when occasion offered; accordingly, when a letter of Henry Laurens severely criticizing Congress was intercepted and printed in Rivington's *New York Royal Gazette* (May 5, 1779)—he and Laurens had already more than once crossed swords—Smith eagerly brought the matter to the attention of Congress (*Journals of the Continental Congress,* May 14, 15, 18; Burnett, *post,* IV, 212–15). Friendly to the French alliance, he was of course at odds with the whole anti-Gallican party.

Although reëlected to Congress in June 1779, he did not take his seat. On his return to Virginia in the autumn of that year he became involved in a controversy with the Assembly over his account as a delegate, a controversy revolving, in part at least, around his commercial connections, but engineered no doubt by his political opponents. In June 1780, however, he was for a third time elected to Congress and attended from February to September 1781. Some of his colleagues feared that he would again indulge in trouble-making, but his course appears to have been one of acceptable placidity. Always interested in the financial problems of Congress, in April 1781 he offered a "Scheme of Finance," to which was appended this injunction: "Let Congress adopt and pursue this plan and be great

and happy." Congress honored the scheme with a first reading but chose to seek greatness and happiness by other means.

In the Virginia House of Delegates in 1785 Smith opposed the proposition to grant Congress control over commerce, and again, in 1786, he was among the irreconcilable opponents of the Annapolis convention; nevertheless, he was chosen a delegate, but declined to attend. Characteristically, in the convention of 1788 he opposed the adoption of the Federal Constitution, aligning himself with his former political enemy, Richard Henry Lee.

He was twice married: first, about 1760, to Alice, daughter of Philip Lee of Maryland and widow of Thomas Clarke; second, Aug. 3, 1769, to Elizabeth, daughter of Col. William Daingerfield of Essex. There were two children by each marriage; a son by the first, George William Smith, succeeded James Monroe as governor of Virginia (Dec. 5, 1811), but lost his life when the Richmond theatre was burned on Dec. 26 following. Meriwether Smith died at "Marigold," Essex County.

[*William and Mary Coll. Quart. Hist. Mag.,* July 1897 (which contains authority for date of death), July 1916, July 1903; H. B. Grigsby, *The Hist. of the Va. Federal Convention of 1788* (2 vols., 1890–91); J. C. Ballagh, *The Letters of Richard Henry Lee* (2 vols., 1911); E. C. Burnett, *Letters of Members of the Continental Cong.,* I–VII (1921–34); W. C. Rives, *Hist. of the Life and Times of James Madison* (3 vols., 1859–68); E. G. Swem and J. W. Williams, *A Reg. of the Gen. Assembly of Va., 1776–1918* (1918); W. G. and M. N. Stanard, *The Colonial Va. Reg.* (1902); some letters in Lib. of Cong.; Smith's accounts for services in Congress (MSS.), Va. State Lib.]
E. C. B.

SMITH, MILTON HANNIBAL (Sept. 12, 1836–Feb. 22, 1921), railroad official, spent over half a century in the employ of the Louisville & Nashville Railroad, of which, for almost forty years, he was chief executive. The son of Irulus and Almira (Blakeslee) Smith, he was born in Windham Township, Greene County, N. Y., and at the age of fourteen accompanied his family to Cook County, Ill. After a meager common-school education he went South in 1858 to make his fortune. In 1860 he became an operator for the Southwestern Telegraph Company at Oxford, Miss.; later the same year he became telegraph operator and assistant agent for the Mississippi Central Railroad at Jackson, Tenn. In 1861 he was transferred to the superintendent's office at Holly Springs, Miss., as telegraph operator and chief clerk. He was drawn into the Civil War in connection with the Federal military railroad service, being stationed successively at Stevenson, Ala., Chattanooga, Tenn., Huntsville, Ala., Knoxville, Tenn., and Atlanta, Ga. After the war (1865) he worked for a time for the Adams

Express Company at Louisville and then (1866) as division superintendent of the Alabama & Tennessee River Railroad.

Smith's connection with the Louisville & Nashville began in August 1866, when he went to Louisville as the local agent of that road. In 1869 he became general freight agent, and in 1878 he resigned because of a disagreement with his superiors in which his orders had been overruled. He was not one to accept interference kindly. Immediately after his resignation he became assistant to vice-president John King of the Baltimore & Ohio Railroad, and in the following year was made general freight agent. For a short time late in 1881 he was general agent of the Pennsylvania Railroad at New York City. In 1882, however, he returned to the Louisville & Nashville, to renew an association which was to continue unil his death. His first position upon his return was one created specially for him—that of third vice-president in charge of traffic. On July 6, 1882, he became the chief executive, a position which he retained for approximately forty years, even though the title changed from time to time. At first he was called vice-president; in 1884 he was made president; from 1886 to 1891 he was again titled vice-president so that one of the New York officers could be given the higher official rank; from 1891 to 1921 he was again president, except for the period of the World War, during which he was federal manager.

When Smith took charge of the Louisville & Nashville it was in poor condition, not having recovered from the effects of the Civil War and the panic of 1873. By an immense amount of effective work he converted his road into one of the stronger and more important railroad properties of the country. Personally he was rough in appearance, a hard but fair fighter, a hard worker who took almost no recreation, and averse to publicity. He was interested primarily in the construction and operation of his railroad and apparently but little concerned with its financial control (H. D. Dozier, *A History of the Atlantic Coast Line Railroad*, 1920, pp. 147–51). He was proud of the great expansion of the road, of the improvement of its properties, and of the excellent dividend record. As a nineteenth-century railroad man he was an exponent of practices which came to be questioned in later years. Between 1914 and 1917 he had difficulties with the Interstate Commerce Commission over its investigation of the use of passes and the participation in politics of the Louisville & Nashville. Abuses had certainly existed, but Smith insisted, with earnest conviction, that the com-

mission should not have access to his records and that the railroad's activities were entirely proper. Upon his death he was justly mourned as one of the last members of the group responsible for the rapid expansion of the American railroad net during the last half of the nineteenth century. He died in Louisville, survived by his wife, Annette (Jones) Smith, and by two sons and two daughters.

[Obituary in *Railway Age*, Mar. 4, 1921, based on Smith's dictated statements; *Who's Who in America*, 1920–21; obituaries in *Courier-Journal* and *Evening Post* (both of Louisville, Ky.), Feb. 23, 1921; *Railroad Gazette*, Oct. 25, 1878, p. 518; *Railway Age*, Feb. 6, 1879, p. 66, Mar. 22, 1883, p. 162; *Railroad Gazette*, Mar. 13, 1891, p. 188; *Railway Age Gazette*, Feb. 20, 1914, p. 393, July 17, 1914, p. 103, Mar. 5, 1915, p. 413, Oct. 6, 1916, p. 607, Dec. 15, 1916, p. 1101, Nov. 9, 1917, p. 849; *Railway Age*, Mar. 1, 1918, p. 446; 31 *Interstate Commerce Commission Reports*, 261; 33 *I. C. C.*, 168; 245 *U. S.*, 33; 49 *I. C. C.*, 320; *Poor's Manual, passim.*]   R. E. R.

SMITH, MORGAN LEWIS (Mar. 8, 1821–Dec. 28, 1874), Union soldier, was born in the town of Mexico, Oswego County, N. Y., the son of Cyrus and Laura (Wales) Smith, and elder brother of Giles Alexander Smith [*q.v.*]. His father, a farmer, soon afterwards moved to Jefferson County, N. Y., with his family. Leaving home in 1842, Smith settled in Meadville, Pa., but before long went to New Albany, Ind., and there taught school for about two years. He enlisted in the United States army in July 1845 under the name of Mortimer L. Sanford, and served for the five-year period of his enlistment as sergeant and drill instructor at the recruit depot, Newport, Ky. From 1850 to 1861 he held various positions on steamboats running between Cincinnati, Ohio, St. Louis, Mo., and New Orleans, La., and at the outbreak of the Civil War he organized the 8th Missouri Volunteer Infantry, composed mainly of rivermen and recruits from the rough element in the population of St. Louis. Appointed colonel, July 7, 1861, he soon brought his regiment to a high state of discipline, training, and combat efficiency. After conducting an expedition against guerrillas in southern Missouri, he joined the army of Ulysses Simpson Grant [*q.v.*], and at Fort Donelson, Tenn., in command of a brigade composed of his own and another regiment, he successfully stormed a strong position held by the enemy. Gen. Lew Wallace, in reporting Smith's conduct of this attack, wrote: "Words cannot do justice to his courage and coolness" (*War of the Rebellion: Official Records (Army)*, 1 ser., vol. VII, p. 240). He commanded a brigade in the expedition up the Tennessee River, and in the Shiloh and Corinth campaigns. His command bore the principal part in the battle at Russell's House, May 17, 1862, where his conduct won commendation from Gen. William Tecumseh Sherman [*q.v.*]. He was appointed brigadier-general of volunteers, July 16, 1862. He took part in Sherman's expedition against Vicksburg after active service in Tennessee and northern Mississippi. While reconnoitering the enemy's position on Chickasaw Bluffs, Dec. 28, 1862, he received a gunshot wound that disabled him until Oct. 6, 1863. On that date he returned to duty as commander of the 2nd Division, XV Corps, and bore a distinguished part in the assault and capture of Missionary Ridge, and the subsequent movement for the relief of Knoxville. He further distinguished himself for skill and gallantry in the operations against Atlanta, and was temporarily in command of the XV Corps, July 23–28, 1864. The rigors of this campaign caused such irritation of his old wound as to permanently incapacitate him for field service. He was on sick leave from Aug. 17 to Sept. 27, 1864, when he was placed in command of the District of Vicksburg. There his firm administration of martial law quickly stopped the disorders that had become prevalent. He remained at Vicksburg until the close of the war, resigning his commission, July 12, 1865.

For about two years after his marriage to Louise Genella, Dec. 18, 1866, he was United States consul general in Honolulu. Resigning, he declined the governorship of the Colorado Territory and engaged in business in Washington, D. C. He acted as counsel for the collection of claims, held contracts for the delivery of United States mails on various southern and western routes, and at the time of his death was connected with a building association. He died suddenly at Jersey City, N. J., where he was a visitor. He was survived by two daughters. He was a natural leader, magnetic, resolute, and extraordinarily brave and cool in battle, and he had in an unusual degree the ability to establish discipline in volunteer troops. The official records show that such distinguished generals as Grant, Sherman, and Wallace held him in high esteem as an able and dependable officer.

[F. A. Virkus, *The Compendium of Am. Geneal.*, vol. V (1933) ; *War of the Rebellion: Off. Records (Army)*; unpublished records of the War Dept.; *Report of Proc. Soc. of the Army of the Tenn. . . . Sept. 29, 1875* (1877) ; *Battles and Leaders of the Civil War* (4 vols., 1888) ; U. S. Pension Office records; obituaries in *Evening Star* (Washington, D. C.), *Washington Chronicle*, and *Nat. Republican* (Washington), Dec. 30, and *N. Y. Times*, Dec. 31, 1874; family records.]

T. F. M.

SMITH, NATHAN (Sept. 30, 1762–Jan. 26, 1829), surgeon, physician, professor of theory and practice of physic and of surgery in Yale College, was born at Rehoboth, Mass., the son of John Smith by his second wife, Elizabeth (Ide) Hills, widow of Benjamin Hills. The Smith family had lived at Rehoboth for four generations, Henry Smith, the great-great-grandfather of Nathan, having come to the colonies from England in 1638. Shortly after Nathan's birth the family moved to Chester, Vt., where the boy helped his father farm, received meager education in the district schools, and served in the militia towards the end of the Revolutionary War. While still a youth he was called upon to help Dr. Josiah Goodhue at an operation. The experience, it is said, made such an impression upon him that he determined to be a surgeon. After a year's preparation with the Rev. Dr. Whiting of Rockingham, Vt., and three years as pupil, assistant, and apprentice to Dr. Goodhue, he began to practise in 1787 at Cornish, N. H. Soon realizing the inadequacy of his training, he spent the year 1789–90 at the institute of medicine at Harvard College, under John Warren, Benjamin Waterhouse [*qq.v.*], and Aaron Dexter. At the termination of the year 1790, having presented a dissertation on "The Circulation of the Blood," he received the degree of bachelor of medicine. Shortly after resuming his practice in Cornish, he married, Jan. 16, 1791, Elizabeth, daughter of Gen. Jonathan Chase of Cornish; two years later she died without issue, and in September 1794 he married her half-sister, Sarah Hall Chase.

Though Smith's practice grew, he was not entirely content. He gave some private instruction, one of his pupils being Lyman Spalding [*q.v.*], but wished to teach more extensively. He was only too well aware of the difficulties of obtaining an education in medicine. At that time the only three medical schools in the United States were at Harvard, Columbia, and Pennsylvania, all at a considerable distance from the center of New England. Dartmouth College was not far from Cornish, and he became imbued with the idea that he might himself teach students medicine and surgery at this institution. With a directness which characterized many of his actions, he applied to the trustees, asking their approval and support "of a plan he had devised to establish a Professorship of the Theory and Practice of Medicine in connection with Dartmouth College" (Hubbard, *post*, p. 12). His plan in general was approved by President John Wheelock, but final action by the trustees was postponed for one year. Undaunted by this delay, he proceeded to fit himself for the post which he fully intended to occupy and spent a year abroad in study, traveling at considerable financial sacrifice, during the winter of 1796–97, to Glasgow, Edinburgh, and London. In the autumn of 1797 he returned with books for the library at Dartmouth and apparatus for anatomy, surgery, and chemistry.

Promptly thereafter, at the age of thirty-five, he delivered a course of lectures on medicine at the College, although it was not until August 1798 that the trustees formally approved his plan and elected him professor. It was his duty "to deliver public lectures upon Anatomy, Surgery, Chemistry and the Theory and Practice of Physic." He was the entire medical faculty; as Oliver Wendell Holmes expressed it, he filled a "Settee of Professorships" (quoted in *Life and Letters of Nathan Smith, post,* p. 97). Among his students was George C. Shattuck [*q.v.*] of Boston, with whom he formed an intimacy that lasted through his entire life. In 1801 Dartmouth conferred upon Smith the degree of M.D., rarely given in those days, and in 1811 he received that degree from Harvard College.

These years were crowded with many activities. From his letters one gathers that he expended much thought upon the preparation of his lectures and devoted much time to teaching. He traveled from Worcester, Mass., to Brattleboro, Vt., and from Concord, Mass., to Wethersfield, Conn., couching for cataract with great success; performing operations for necrosis of bone; attending children with "spotted fever," a disease which ravaged the Connecticut Valley in 1811; and caring for patients with "Typhus Fever." He practised vaccination shortly after Waterhouse first introduced it into the United States in July 1800. He went to state medical meetings and was elected president of the Vermont State Medical Society in 1811. He was constantly writing to his friend Shattuck in Boston for new books to add to his rapidly growing library; for chemicals; for apparatus, which he wanted built according to pattern; and for "air thermometers," for the construction of which he gave directions. He engaged Dr. Alexander Ramsay [*q.v.*] to give a course in anatomy in 1808. He visited the legislature repeatedly in efforts to obtain funds for the medical school, and was so far successful as to obtain a grant of $600 for chemical apparatus in 1803, and, after much perseverance, $3,450 for a medical building, for which he himself donated the land. He became exasperated at the slowness of the legislature to act, at its lack of support, and at proposed laws which, if passed, would restrict dissections and thus materially hamper the teaching of anatomy. He wrote to Shattuck in May

1810 of his discouragement and, finally, of his determination to leave Hanover.

It was at about this time that President Timothy Dwight, 1752–1817 [*q.v.*], of Yale College became actively engaged in a project, long under contemplation, to furnish instruction in medicine to students at Yale. In 1811 the lieutenant governor of Connecticut, Professor Silliman of Yale, and Dr. Nathan Strong were appointed a committee to act with the medical convention in establishing a chartered medical school (Steiner, *post,* p. 24). The previous year Jonathan Knight, 1789–1864 [*q.v.*], a tutor at Yale, had received a letter from Timothy L. Gridley, who was then a student under Smith, in which the writer pointed out the desirability of appointing Smith to the professorship of surgery in the proposed institute of medicine at Yale. He wrote of his originality of mind, of his success in operative surgery, of his "general information," and of his "dignified deportment," adding "in fact, wherever he is known he is admired and beloved" (*Ibid.*). Gridley had learned from Smith that should Yale College require his services, he would accept a position there without hesitation. The corporation and president were convinced, however, that his religious beliefs were unorthodox, and, since they could not countenance the appointment of an "infidel," the committee selected Dr. Mason F. Cogswell of Hartford as professor of anatomy and surgery. Cogswell was loath to accept the appointment and asked that it be reconsidered. There ensued a correspondence between Cogswell and Smith, and between Silliman and Smith, with the result that the committee was assured that Smith "had fully renounced his infidelity"; whereupon he was elected professor of theory and practice of physic, surgery, and obstetrics. Although instruction in medicine at Yale College began in the autumn of 1812, Smith was unable to leave Dartmouth until the autumn of 1813 and his resignation was not actually accepted until 1814. He was reëlected professor there in 1816 and, though he declined, he gave a final course of lectures at Dartmouth that year, so that it was not until 1817 that he permanently removed with his family to New Haven.

Smith went to Yale at the age of fifty-one, vigorous, energetic, and with wide clinical experience. He was known throughout New England as an able surgeon; he had acquired a wide reputation as a teacher, and had gained the admiration and respect of his associates. He rapidly assumed a position of importance in the community. It was largely through his personal efforts that the Connecticut legislature in 1814 appropriated $20,000 to the institute for the purchase of land, the erection of a new building, and the development of a botanical garden. In addition to his teaching, he practised medicine and surgery throughout the state and in the neighboring parts of New England. He showed an ability and resourcefulness in his methods of practice which were unsurpassed in that day. In 1821 he performed successfully ovariotomy, unaware of the fact that Ephraim McDowell [q.v.] of Kentucky had previously done that particular form of operation for the first time in the United States. It is said that he had never lost a patient from post-operative hemorrhage. In 1821 he assisted President Allen of Bowdoin College in the organization of a medical department, where he delivered a course of lectures each summer until 1826. He also lectured during the summer months at the medical department of the University of Vermont in Burlington, where his son, Nathan Ryno Smith [q.v.], had been active in developing a department of medicine.

Smith's reputation does not rest entirely either on his success as a practical surgeon and physician or on his ability as a teacher. These were what gave him eminence in his day, but for succeeding generations the importance of his work is to be found in the fresh and original manner in which he attacked problems in medicine and surgery. His approach to them is indicated by the following statements in his letters: "However we may class diseases we must study them in detail"; and in reference to theorizing, "This mode of proceeding tends to substitute idleness for industry and dogmatism for patient inquiry" (*Life and Letters,* pp. 35, 36). Dr. William H. Welch said of Smith: "Famous in his day and generation, he is still more famous today, for he was far ahead of his times, and his reputation, unlike that of so many medical worthies of the past, has steadily increased, as the medical profession has slowly caught up with him. We now see that he did more for the general advancement of medical and surgical practice than any of his predecessors or contemporaries in this country. He was a man of high intellectual and moral qualities, of great originality and untiring energy, an accurate and keen observer, unfettered by traditions and theories, fearless, and above all blessed with an uncommon fund of plain common sense" (*Yale Medical Journal,* November 1901, pp. 141–42). His writings attest the fact that he had a conception of disease which is eminently modern. In a day when the etiology of infectious diseases was unknown, when speculation as to the classification of disease processes was rife, and when doubt was being cast upon the specific nature of many diseases, he let no

opportunity pass to emphasize his belief in their specific character. He dwelt with emphasis upon the necessity of accurate observation and the importance of factual experience as opposed to thin-spun theory. Elaborate hypotheses, not susceptible to practical test, aroused his sharp criticism, for he looked upon them as obscuring clear vision. His *Practical Essay on Typhous Fever* (1824) is a classic. Typhoid fever, for it is that disease which he describes, had never before been so clearly defined or so accurately depicted. His statement, "I consider Typhous fever a disease *sui generis,* arising from a specific cause, and that cause contagion, and seldom affecting the same person more than once," is entirely modern. He also had the courage to pronounce it a self-limited disease, unaffected in its course by drugs. "His "Observations on the Pathology and Treatment of Necrosis" (*Medical and Surgical Memoirs, post,* pp. 97 ff.) is of almost equal importance.

In 1816 he published an edition of *A Treatise on Febrile Diseases,* by A. P. Wilson Philip, with an introduction, notes, and additions. He commented especially in these notes on typhous and spotted fever; devoted some attention to an epidemic of "pneumonia typhoidea"; described in all probability an epidemic of German measles; and wrote on dropsy. He also gave an account of experiments which he seems to have devised to determine whether the cutaneous surfaces absorb fluid. Two of his students immersed themselves for several hours in a warm bath of water colored with madder, and afterwards examined their urine for the coloring matter. The urine was in small degree colored with madder, but Smith concluded that this slight effect might have been caused by conditions other than absorption of the dye through the skin. From 1824 to 1826, with his son Nathan Ryno and others, Smith edited the *American Medical Review.*

He had four sons and six daughters; all his sons became practitioners of medicine. There is a striking portrait of him, by Samuel F. B. Morse [q.v.], in the possession of the Yale Medical School. He appears as an elderly gentleman, dignified in his mien, with keen penetrating eyes and a sensitive mouth. When President Woolsey of Yale was a child, he saw much of Smith in his father's house and said of him, "He was the most delightful, unselfish and kind-hearted man I ever knew, and we children all loved him" (*Life and Letters,* p. 90). He died in his sixty-seventh year and was buried in New Haven.

[E. A. Smith, *The Life and Letters of Nathan Smith, M.B., M.D.* (1914), with an introduction by Dr. William H. Welch; O. P. Hubbard, *The Early Hist. of the N. H. Medic. Institution, with a Sketch of Its Founder*

Nathan Smith, A.M., M.D. (1880); W. R. Steiner, "The Evolution of Medicine in Conn., with the Foundation of the Yale Medic. School as its Notable Achievement," *Memorial of the Centennial of the Yale Medic. School* (1915); W. H. Welch, "The Relation of Yale to Medicine," *Yale Medic. Jour.,* Nov. 1901; S. C. Harvey, "The Education of Nathan Smith," *Yale Jour. of Biology and Medicine,* May 1929; H. S. Burr, "The Founding of the Medic. Institution of Yale Coll.," *Ibid.,* Jan. 1934; William Allen, *An Address Occasioned by the Death of Nathan Smith, M.D.* (1829); N. R. Smith, *Medic. and Surgic. Memoirs of Nathan Smith, M.D.* (1831); J. A. Spalding, *Dr. Lyman Spalding* (1916); H. A. Kelly and W. L. Burrage, *Am. Medic. Biogs.* (1920).]   W. T. L.

SMITH, NATHAN (Jan. 8, 1770–Dec. 6, 1835), Connecticut jurist and politician, United States senator, son of Richard and Annis (Hurd) Smith, was born in Woodbury, Conn. On account of the poverty of his parents, he received little formal schooling. A shrewd trader and a wandering Yankee peddler in his younger days, he soon followed in the footsteps of his brother Nathaniel [*q.v.*] and read law with Judge Tapping Reeve [*q.v.*] at Litchfield. Overcoming the obstacles of poverty and a fragmentary knowledge of books, he was admitted to the Litchfield County bar in 1792, and commenced the practice of law in New Haven. He soon won a reputation as an able lawyer of sound judgment, and a clever politician, but was recognized as a man of high principle who would not plead an obviously unrighteous case. In 1808 he was given the honorary degree of M.A. by Yale College. A prominent Episcopalian, a vestryman of Trinity Church in New Haven, a participant in the sturdy fight for a charter for Washington (later Trinity) College in Hartford, of which he became an incorporator, Smith was an outstanding Tolerationist who fought stoutly for the separation of Church and State in the tedious campaign leading to the defeat of the Congregational-Federalist ascendency in 1817. The following year he was one of the framers of the reformed constitution of 1818. He disagreed, however, with the policy of popularizing the state judiciary, for he was no democrat and was completely unsympathetic with the experiments of the radical group.

He was prosecuting attorney for New Haven County from 1817 to 1835, an unsuccessful candidate for the governorship against Oliver Wolcott in 1825, and United States attorney for Connecticut by appointment of President John Quincy Adams in 1828, removed in the following year by President Jackson. In May 1832 he was chosen as a Whig to the United States Senate, to succeed Samuel A. Foot [*q.v.*], but his senatorial career was cut short by a heart attack, in Washington, three years later. President Jackson and his cabinet attended the funeral

services in the Senate chamber, and in New Haven his obsequies at Trinity Church, presided over by the Rev. Harry Croswell [*q.v.*], brought together state and local officials and officers of Yale College, regardless of their political affiliations, for Smith had not been so aggressive a partisan as to arouse personal hostility. It was generally agreed that he deserved well of his community as a prudent counselor, a civic benefactor, and a Christian gentleman. He was the father of six children.

[*Proc. at New Haven, in Relation to the Demise of the Hon. Nathan Smith* (n.d.); R. J. Purcell, *Conn. in Transition* (1918); *Biog. Dir. Am. Cong.* (1928); G. H. Hollister, *The Hist. of Conn.* (1855), II, 655; P. K. Kilbourne, *A Biog. Hist. of the County of Litchfield* (1851); Wm. Cothren, *Hist. of Ancient Woodbury,* vols. I (1854), III (1879); *Daily National Intelligencer* (Washington, D. C.), Dec. 7, 1835; year of birth supported by most reliable accounts, although others give 1769.]   R. J. P.

SMITH, NATHAN RYNO (May 21, 1797–July 3, 1877), surgeon, teacher of anatomy and surgery, was born in Cornish, N. H., the second son of Dr. Nathan Smith [*q.v.*] by his second wife, Sarah Hall (Chase). The boy's middle name was selected by his mother from one of Ossian's poems, and throughout his life he was called Ryno by his family and intimate friends. He received his early education from tutors, but later was sent to school in Hanover. In 1813 he entered Yale College and in the autumn of the same year his father moved to New Haven, where he had been called to assume the duties of professor of theory and practice of physic, surgery, and obstetrics in Yale College.

Young Ryno, from contemporary accounts, was one of the leading members of his class, but appears to have been more attracted by literature than by medicine, for in 1816 he wrote a commencement play, "The Quixotic Philosopher," in which he also acted. After receiving the degree of A.B. in 1817, he went to Virginia as tutor for the family of Thomas Turner of Fauquier County. After about a year and a half, he returned to New Haven to study medicine under his father, and in 1823 he was graduated with the degree of M.D. from the medical school at Yale. A few months later he moved to Burlington, Vt., where, the following year, he married Juliette Octavia Penniman, daughter of Dr. Jabez Penniman. The intense interest which the father had always had in the education of young men for the medical profession soon became a predominant characteristic of the son; for one of the first matters to attract his attention was the possibility of establishing a medical school at the University of Vermont. With the aid of his father, this project was accomplished and, at the age of twenty-seven, Smith assumed the duties of professor of anatomy and physiology in the new institution.

Burlington was then a comparatively isolated community, however, and Smith soon realized that he needed wider experience than was afforded there. Accordingly, he spent the winters of 1825 and 1826 at the University of Pennsylvania, then the leading medical school in the United States, acquainting himself with methods of instruction and obtaining more knowledge of anatomy and surgery. Here he met the "bold, brilliant and energetic surgeon," Dr. George McClellan [q.v.], who gave private courses in anatomy and surgery. McClellan, who was not associated with the University of Pennsylvania, contemplated, in the face of much opposition, the formation of another medical school in Philadelphia. Impressed by the ability of young Smith, he invited him to take the chair of anatomy in the proposed institution and Smith became a member of the first faculty of Jefferson Medical College, teaching anatomy there for two sessions. Among his pupils were Dr. Samuel D. Gross [q.v.], who later became a well-known surgeon, and Washington L. Atlee [q.v.], the distinguished ovariotomist. During his short stay in Philadelphia, Smith devoted some time to writing; with his father and others he edited the *American Medical Review* and in 1825 he published *A Physiological Essay on Digestion.* He also founded, in 1827, and edited the *Philadelphia Monthly Journal of Medicine and Surgery,* which the following year was merged with the *American Journal of the Medical Sciences.*

His activities in Burlington and Philadelphia gave him more than a local reputation, and when the chair of anatomy became vacant at the University of Maryland, through the resignation of Prof. Granville Sharp Pattison [q.v.], Smith was asked, in 1827, to occupy it. Accepting the position, he soon became a leading member of the faculty and also engaged in the practice of medicine and surgery. In 1829, after the death of Dr. John B. Davidge [q.v.], founder of the school, Smith was transferred to the chair of surgery, which he held, except for one comparatively short interruption, for almost half a century. That same year he published *An Essay on the Diseases of the Middle Ear,* from the French of J. A. Saissy, with a supplement of his own on diseases of the external ear. He founded the *Baltimore Monthly Journal of Medicine and Surgery,* the first number of which appeared in February 1830 with Smith as editor; it survived for only a year, however. About the same time he collected and edited, with a biographical note, addenda, and some of his own papers, the *Medical and Surgical Memoirs of Nathan Smith M.D.* (1831). In 1832 he published *Surgical Anatomy of the Arteries,* a second edition of which appeared in 1835.

Owing to his skill, ingenuity, and constant practice in the field of surgery, he gained national prominence in that branch of his profession. He made original contributions to the art of surgery that were of considerable practical importance, among them a new instrument for the operation of lithotomy. He wrote several papers on the management of fractures, the most important of which dealt with a new principle in the treatment of fractures of the thigh and leg. To put this principle into operation he constructed a form of splint, known as the anterior suspensory apparatus, or anterior splint, which was far superior to any device used for this purpose at that time and in modified form is in general use today. Begun at this period but not published until 1867 was his *Treatment of Fractures of the Lower Extremity by the Use of the Anterior Suspensory Apparatus.* He was also a pioneer in the extirpation of the thyroid gland.

In 1837 Smith was invited to give lectures on medicine and surgery at the Transylvania University, Lexington, Ky., and from 1838 to 1840 he acted as professor of surgery at this institution. Though he never relinquished his permanent residence in Baltimore, he severed his connection temporarily with the University of Maryland, since his new duties required him to spend about four months of every year in Lexington. While on one of his visits to Kentucky, he met Henry Clay and a friendship sprang up between them. He was frequently called to pay professional visits to Washington, and there formed an acquaintance with Daniel Webster, who became an occasional visitor at the Smith house in Baltimore. This house, in which he had his office and surgery, was, in fact, a center to which many visitors were constantly welcomed, and to which his students were in the habit of coming. He had eight children, one of whom, Alan Penniman Smith (1840–1898), became a prominent surgeon of Baltimore and was instrumental in obtaining from Johns Hopkins the gift to found the Johns Hopkins Hospital. Tall and impressive in appearance, Smith was called by his students "The Emperor," and the sobriquet soon gained such popularity that, in later life, he was known generally by this name. His imperial appearance was tempered, however, by a courtesy and charm of manner which endeared him to friends and patients. His duties as teacher and practitioner left him little time for other forms of occupation, but he took much pleasure in his country place "Wilton," not far from Baltimore, where he amused himself by conducting farming operations along original lines that proved expensive and entirely unsuccessful. When the press of work permitted, he read with pleasure Homer, Virgil, and Plutarch. In 1869 he published *Legends of the South,* containing tales connected with White Sulphur Springs, Mammoth Cave, and other places. After 1869 his connection with the University of Maryland was nominal, and in 1870 he became professor emeritus. Ill health forced him to reduce his practice but he did not relinquish it until shortly before his death. In 1867, at the age of seventy, he made his first journey to Europe, where he was received as a distinguished visitor by the surgeons of England and the Continent. On his return he began to write a treatise on surgery, which, however, was never completed.

[E. A. Smith, *The Life and Letters of Nathan Smith* (1914); S. C. Chew, *An Address Commemorative of Nathan Ryno Smith, M.D., LL.D.* (1878); E. F. Cordell, *Hist. Sketch of the Univ. of Md. School of Medicine* (1891), and *The Medical Annals of Md.* (1903); S. D. Gross, *Autobiog.* (1887), I, 385–87; H. A. Kelly and W. L. Burrage, *Am. Medic. Biogs.* (1920); Alexius McGlannan, "The Surgical and Anatomical Works of Nathan Ryno Smith," *Univ. of Md., Bull. of the School of Medicine,* Apr. 1925; *Sun* (Baltimore), July 4, 1877; letters of Nathan Ryno Smith in the possession of the author.] W. T. L.

SMITH, NATHANIEL (Jan. 6, 1762–Mar. 9, 1822), Connecticut jurist, was born in Woodbury, Conn., the son of poor parents, Richard and Annis (Hurd) Smith. He received little formal schooling and began working in his early years, traveling as a Yankee peddler throughout New England. On one occasion while waiting for his brother, Nathan [q.v.], who was to join him in Rutland, Vt., he visited a court room and was so struck by the ineptitude of lawyer and judge that he was moved to test his own talents in a study of the law. Indomitable of will, he succeeded in gaining admission as clerk and student to the law office of Judge Tapping Reeve [q.v.]. After some time in hard study, he was admitted to the bar (1787) and began practice in Woodbury, rapidly demonstrating ability as a clever advocate and a magnetic stump-speaker.

Smith represented Woodbury in the General Assembly, 1790–95, taking an aggressive leadership in the gradual abolition of slavery and in the foundation of a common-school system financed in part by the sale of the state's western land claims. In recognition of his service, Yale College bestowed upon him an honorary master's degree in 1795. A stout Federalist, he was elected a representative in Congress for two terms

(1795–99), but at the expiration of the second he declined to stand again as a candidate, since he had lost popularity by his support of the Jay Treaty. Returning to his practice in Woodbury, he represented that town in the state council from 1800 through 1804. In 1806 he was appointed associate judge of the superior court, in which capacity he served with considerable distinction until he was retired in 1819 after the overthrow of the Old Order in the Republican-Tolerationist sweep of the state. As an appointed member of the Hartford Convention (1814), he won the undying hostility of the Republican nationalists despite the fact that he was of the persecuted Episcopalian minority and assuredly of no disloyal turn of mind. The last three years of his life were marred by a painful illness bravely borne. He was survived by his wife, Ruth, daughter of the Rev. Noah Benedict, and by one son.

[Wm. Cothren, *Hist. of Ancient Woodbury*, vols. I (1854), III (1879); P. K. Kilbourne, *A Biog. Hist. of the County of Litchfield* (1851); D. C. Kilbourn, *The Bench and Bar of Litchfield County* (1909); R. J. Purcell, *Conn. in Transition* (1918); *Biog. Dir. Am. Cong.* (1928); *Conn. Courant* (Hartford), Mar. 19, 1822; *American Mercury* (Hartford), Mar. 18, 1822.]

R. J. P.

SMITH, OLIVER (Jan. 20, 1766–Dec. 22, 1845), philanthropist, was born at Hatfield, Mass., the son of Samuel and Mary (Morton) Smith. On his father's side, he was a descendant of Samuel Smith who emigrated from England on the ship *Elizabeth* in 1634, settled in Wethersfield, Conn., and later moved to Hatfield. Mary Morton's ancestry went back to George Morton [q.v.], one of the organizers of the voyage of the *Anne* and the *Little James* to Plymouth. The year after Oliver, the youngest of six sons, was born, his father died of an "apoplectic fit," occasioned by overwork in the hay field on a hot July day. The boys were brought up by their mother, a woman noted in the community for her frugality, vigor, and piety. One of them was Joseph, father of Sophia Smith [q.v.], founder of Smith College.

Oliver began life with a capital of $500; when he was middle aged, the boys of Hatfield expressed their ambition for wealth by saying they wished they could be as rich as Oliver Smith; at his death he left what for the place and time was a large fortune—almost $400,000. He engaged in farming, fattened cattle for market, and in his later years made profitable investments in Wall Street securities. He wasted nothing, spent little, and rarely gave anything away. A contemporary wrote regarding him: "During the thirty years or more of my recollection of him, he wore the same overgarments; but by reason of a certain trimness and neatness, he always appeared respectably dressed" (S. D. Partridge, in Wells, *post*, p. 263). When stoves were put in the meeting house, he was leader of a protesting group who withdrew from the ecclesiastical society. He was strictly honest in his dealings with others, but managed to avoid paying taxes on all his property, probably feeling that the money would be wasted. He was opposed to liberal education, believing it a hindrance rather than a help to success in life, and carried about in his pocket statistics to support his conviction. In politics he was originally a Jeffersonian Democrat, but later became a National Republican. He was a member of the Massachusetts constitutional convention in 1820, a presidential elector in 1824, voting for John Quincy Adams, and twice represented his town in the state legislature (1827–28). For many years he was a director of the bank in Northampton. He never married.

Penurious in the extreme throughout his life, he nevertheless provided that the greater part of his wealth should be devoted to charitable and educational purposes after his death. By his will —a remarkable document—he established an accumulating fund, which, when it had reached a certain amount, was to be used for three objects. Brought up by a widowed mother and mindful of the straitened circumstances of his early days, he directed that the major portion of the fund should be utilized to provide grants for indigent young people and widows. Boys selected by the trustees were to be bound out in good families, taught husbandry or a trade, and when twenty-one, if worthy, receive a grant of $500; similarly, girls were to be bound out, instructed in domestic duties, and given $300 as a marriage portion. Smaller amounts were to be given under certain conditions to young women about to be married, for household equipment, and to needy widows with dependent child or children. Smith's interest in agriculture led him to stipulate that another portion of the fund be used to establish an agricultural school in Northampton. The remainder, $10,000, was to go to the American Colonization Society. The will was contested by the heirs-at-law and a notable legal battle in the supreme judicial court of Massachusetts followed, opening July 6, 1847, with Rufus Choate counsel for the contestants, and Daniel Webster for the executor; but the will was sustained (54 *Mass.*, 34). The amount expended by the trustees in carrying out the terms of the will reaches into the millions, and on Mar. 15, 1907, the Smith's Agricultural School and Northampton School of Technology was established.

[D. W. and R. F. Wells, *A Hist. of Hatfield, Mass.* (copr. 1910), appendix containing portion of Smith's will; C. A. Wight, *The Hatfield Book* (copr. 1908); E. D. Hanscom and H. F. Green, *Sophia Smith and the Beginnings of Smith Coll.* (1926); Mass. Board of Educ., *Seventy-Third Ann. Report* (1910).] H. E. S.

SMITH, OLIVER HAMPTON (Oct. 23, 1794–Mar. 19, 1859), lawyer, representative and senator, was of Quaker descent. His ancestors accompanied William Penn to America; his grandparents occupied Smith's Island in the Delaware River about twelve miles above Trenton; and here, in Bucks County, Pa., Oliver, the son of Thomas and Letitia Smith, was born. He had six brothers and two sisters. He obtained an elementary education at a neighboring country school. When he was in his nineteenth year his father died, and Oliver soon lost the small fortune which he had inherited. In 1816 he set out for the West, and at Pittsburgh engaged to take two coal boats to Louisville. He struck a snag and lost one of them, but succeeded, in the spring of 1817, in reaching Rising Sun, Ind., where he engaged in a small business with seventy-five dollars as his capital. A year later he was in Lawrenceburg, studying law, and in March 1820 he was admitted to the bar.

He commenced practice at Versailles, but soon removed to Connersville, where he rapidly rose to prominence. In August 1822 he was elected to the Indiana House of Representatives. He was made chairman of the judiciary committee and served until 1824, when the governor appointed him prosecuting attorney for the third judicial district. During two years of service in this capacity he successfully prosecuted four notorious frontiersmen charged with the murder of Indians. In 1826 he was elected to Congress as a Jackson Democrat. He rode to Washington on horseback and took his seat at the opening of the Twentieth Congress, Dec. 3, 1827. He was a member of the committee on Indian affairs, and on Feb. 19, 1828, made a vigorous plea for an Indian policy "marked with justice, humanity, and a magnanimity of purpose, that will atone, as far as possible, for the great injustice which we have done them." In another address, Jan. 28, 1829, he presented cogent arguments in favor of appropriations for the construction of the Cumberland road. Defeated for reëlection to Congress, he was engaged in the practice of law and in farming when, in December 1836, the General Assembly elected him as a Whig to a seat in the United States Senate. He was a member of the committee on the militia in 1837, and of the committee on the judiciary in 1839, and was made chairman of the important committee on public lands in 1841. His principal

speeches in the Senate were on measures relative to the public lands, banking, bankruptcy, the
Cumberland road, and the abolition of slavery
in the Territories. He rose to leadership in
evolving a federal land policy in the interest of
the actual settlers (*Congressional Globe*, 27
Cong., 1 Sess., App., p. 456), and supported the
Whig plan for the federal assumption of state
debts to the extent of the proceeds of the sales
of the public lands within the states.

Failing of reëlection to the Senate, Smith retired to private life in Indianapolis, projected
the Indianapolis & Bellefontaine Railroad, became its first president, and subsequently participated in a project for a line from Indianapolis to Evansville. In July 1857 he commenced
writing for the *Indianapolis Daily Journal* a series of sketches and reminiscences of frontier life
in Indiana which in the following year was published in book form under the title, *Early Indiana
Trials and Sketches* (1858). Although crude in
style, the volume is a vivid presentation of various phases of early Indiana history.

Smith was a rough-hewn frontiersman, five
feet ten inches in height, with standing black
hair, shaggy eyebrows and a strong voice; he
was diffuse but convincing in speech, and one
of the most respected of Indiana pioneers. He
married Mary Bramfield, a Quaker, in 1821,
and they had three children. He died in Indianapolis and was buried in Crown Hill Cemetery.

[W. W. Woollen, *Biog. and Hist. Sketches of Early
Indiana* (1883) ; *Biog. Dir. Am. Cong.* (1928) ; *A Biog.
Hist. of Eminent and Self-Made Men of the State of
Indiana* (1880), vol. II ; *Indianapolis Daily Journal*,
Mar. 21, 1859 ; *Lafayette Daily Journal*, Mar. 22, 1859.]

N. D. M.

SMITH, PERSIFOR FRAZER (Nov. 16,
1798–May 17, 1858), soldier, was born in Philadelphia, Pa., the son of Jonathan and Mary Anne
(Frazer) Smith. He was a descendant of Joseph Smith who emigrated from Ireland to Chester County, Pa., probably in 1720, and of Persifor Frazer, 1736–1792 [*q.v.*]. Graduating from
the College of New Jersey (later Princeton University) with the degree of A.B. in 1815, he
studied law and toward the end of 1819 removed
to New Orleans, La. There his ability and attractive personal qualities quickly won him success and popularity, and he held several civil
and judicial offices. At the same time he commanded successively a company and a battalion
of militia, and became adjutant-general of Louisiana. On Jan. 19, 1822, he was married to
Frances Jeanette Bureau, daughter of François
Bureau of New Orleans, by whom he had a son
who became a physician in New Orleans. In
1836 he raised a regiment of Louisianians for the

Seminole War and served with distinction in
the campaigns of 1836 and 1838. After his return he became judge of the city of Lafayette,
and later of the parish of Jefferson.

At the outbreak of the Mexican War he was
commissioned colonel, United States Army, May
27, 1846. After commanding a brigade in the
army of Zachary Taylor [*q.v.*] in the battles
around Monterey, in which he directed the successful attacks against the forts on the south
flank of the city and for his gallant conduct was
brevetted brigadier-general, Sept. 23, 1846, he
was transferred to Winfield Scott's army in command of the new regiment of mounted rifles.
During the siege of Vera Cruz he defeated near
Vergara a Mexican force that advanced to harass
the besiegers ; on the advance to Mexico city
he commanded the first brigade of the division
under David Emanuel Twigg [*q.v.*], and at Contreras, assuming command of three American
brigades trapped between the superior forces of
Santa Anna and Valencia, he conceived and executed a surprise attack in the early morning of
Aug. 20, 1847, which resulted in the destruction
of Valencia's army. He further distinguished
himself at Churubusco, Chapultepec, and the
capture of the Belen gate of the Mexican capital, and was brevetted major-general for gallant
and meritorious conduct. A member of the armistice commission that arranged for suspension
of hostilities, he later served as military governor of Mexico city, and as commanding officer
at Vera Cruz he prepared the embarkation of
the American forces leaving Mexico, discharg-
ing all these difficult offices with characteristic
efficiency. After the war he was assigned according to his brevet rank to command first the
Pacific Division; then, 1850–56, the Department
of Texas ; and in 1856 the Western Department,
with headquarters at St. Louis. The absence of
civil authority in California, Indian uprisings
in New Mexico, and border warfare in Kansas
made each of these posts in turn difficult. He
was commissioned brigadier-general, Dec. 30,
1856. In April 1858 he was assigned to command the Department of Utah, where the Mormons were opposing Federal authority, but he
died in the early hours of the morning, May 17,
at Fort Leavenworth, Kan., where he had gone
to organize his forces. He was buried in Laurel
Hill Cemetery, Philadelphia. After the death
of his first wife in 1852, he married, Apr. 18,
1854, Anne Monica (Millard) Armstrong, widow of Maj. Francis W. Armstrong of the United
States Army, whose son Frank C. Armstrong
[*q.v.*] was a Confederate officer.

Although he was prepossessing and soldierly

in appearance, his remarkably magnetic personality was based on mental and moral qualities; few men have been able so to command the implicit trust of all ranks and classes of men. His arrival on the field of Contreras was welcomed by the soldiers with cries of "Here he is!" and "Now we'll have them!" (Smith, *post,* II, 108). Nicholas Philip Trist [*q.v.*] writes of him as "one of the most beautifully balanced characters that I have ever known" (*North American and United States Gazette,* May 25, 1858). Gen. Winfield Scott [*q.v.*] as early as Aug. 3, 1847, refers to him in a letter as "the gallant and judicious General Smith," and wherever he has occasion to refer to him does so in terms of affectionate admiration. Simple, scholarly, conciliatory, but vigilant and sure, he united daring with imperturbable composure and control of all his resources in the most critical circumstances.

[J. S. Harris, *Record of the Smith Family* (1906); F. B. Heitman, *Hist. Reg. . . . U. S. Army* (2 vols., 1903), *Gen Cat. Princeton Univ.* (1908); J. T. Sprague, *The Origin, Progress, and Conclusion of the Florida War* (1848); D. H. Maury, *Recollections of a Virginian in the Mexican, Indian, and Civil Wars* (1894), pp. 84–85; J. H. Smith, *The War with Mexico* (2 vols., 1919); G. L. Rives, *The U. S. and Mexico, 1821–1848* (1913), vol. II; *House Exec. Doc. 17,* 31 Cong., 2 Sess., pp. 703 *et seq.,* for reports of Smith on Cal.; *Gen. Scott and His Staff* (1848), pp. 117–24; War Dept. records, 1836–58; *Living Age,* June 5, 1858; *Pennsylvanian* (Phila.), May 29, 1858; *Daily Picayune* (New Orleans), May 20, 1858; some letters in Lib. of Cong.]   T. F. M.

SMITH, PETER (Nov. 15, 1768–Apr. 14, 1837), land-owner, was born near Tappan, N. Y., son of Gerrit P. and Wyntje (Lent) Smith, descendants of Dutch emigrants to America in the seventeenth century. At an early age Peter became a clerk in the New York house of Abraham Herring. From 1785 to 1788 he conducted a general store in New York selling books, library, school, and theatrical supplies. He met John Jacob Astor [*q.v.*] and formed a partnership in the fur trade that lasted only about a year. However, they cooperated in the purchase and sale of land in upstate New York for a number of years thereafter. In 1789 Smith moved to what is now Utica and established the first general store on the site of the old Baggs Hotel. There he lived for several years selling supplies and groceries to traders and Indians, receiving in return grain, pelts, and furs. At the same time he speculated in land. In 1794 he obtained a lease from the Oneida Indians for a large tract extending roughly over Oneida and Onondaga counties, and, after the state acquired title by the treaty of 1795, he was able to obtain ownership from the state. In the center of this holding he built the "Homestead," calling the village that

developed Peterboro and the township Smithfield. Further purchases increased his holdings to nearly a million acres, scattered through most of the counties of the state. He was also interested in agricultural activities, engaged in the manufacture and sale of grindstones, and for a time managed a glass factory at Peterboro. His relations with the Indians were cordial. He named his eldest son Peter Skenandoah in honor of Skenandoa [*q.v.*]. He was the second sheriff of Herkimer County and the first "first judge" of Madison County as well as holding other minor offices. He was a member and officer of the New York Tract Society.

He married twice. On Feb. 5, 1792, he married Elizabeth Livingston, the daughter of James Livingston [*q.v.*], who died in 1818. They had six children of whom the most important was Gerrit Smith [*q.v.*]. His second wife was Sarah Pogson of Charleston, S. C., though of English birth. This marriage ended in bitterness and separation. The wife returned to South Carolina, and the husband gave himself up to the religious and personal peculiarities of his earlier years. In 1819 he had made arrangements to hand over his business to his son Gerrit but retained the income from $125,000. His earlier letters and journals reflected his gloomy religious ideas, and his business dealings revealed both decided financial abilities and equally decided penurious tendencies. Growing more morose, he brooded morbidly over what he considered the neglected religious opportunities of his active years. He lived most of the time at his Schenectady home, "a trouble to himself and a vexation to those about him" (Frothingham, *post,* pp. 20–21). He died there.

[Family papers in Lib. of Syracuse Univ.; K. W. Porter, *John Jacob Astor* (2 vols., 1931); O. B. Frothingham, *Gerrit Smith* (1878); L. M. Whitney, E. C. and L. M. Hammond, *Hist. of Madison County* (1872); J. E. Smith, *Our County . . . Madison County* (1899); date of death from *Albany Argus,* Apr. 14, 1837, although Frothingham, *ante,* gives Apr. 13.]   W. F. G.

SMITH, RICHARD (Mar. 22, 1735–Sept. 17, 1803), lawyer, diarist, member of the Continental Congress, belonged to a Quaker family which was transplanted to America from its original home, Bramham in Yorkshire, by the migration of several brothers during the last decade of the seventeenth century. His grandfather, Samuel Smith, settled in West Jersey in 1694. Richard was born in Burlington, N. J., youngest of the five children of Richard and Abigail Rapier (or Raper) Smith. The elder Richard was a merchant and for many years sat in the colonial Assembly; his son Samuel, secretary and treasurer of the colonial council, published *The His-*

tory of the Colony of Nova-Caesaria, or New Jersey (1765), which is still a valuable source. Young Richard was educated by tutors and at a Friends' school, and later studied law with Joseph Galloway [*q.v.*] of Philadelphia. About 1760, he was admitted to the bar and became recorder of Burlington or clerk of the county; on June 5, 1762, he married Elizabeth Rodman, who bore him five sons. He apparently served as clerk of the colonial Assembly for several years. Following the Treaty of Fort Stanwix (1768), he was one of a group of proprietors who received a grant of land, the "Otego Patent" of 69,000 acres, in the present Otsego County, on the upper Susquehanna in New York. With several companions, Smith visited the tract in 1769, keeping a journal of the trip, with interesting observations on the valleys of the Hudson, Mohawk, Susquehanna, and Delaware. Smith helped to promote settlement in the grant, which he visited again in 1773, 1777, and 1783 before making his home there in 1790. In 1773 he built "Smith Hall" in what is now the town of Laurens.

On July 23, 1774, Smith was elected one of New Jersey's five delegates to the Continental Congress. He was twice reëlected and served until June 1776. He was a member of the committee on claims, but the chief interest attaching to his service in the Congress arises from his detailed diary of the proceedings from Sept. 12 to Oct. 1, 1775, and from Dec. 12, 1775, to Mar. 30, 1776. This diary supplies much information not available in the *Journals* or elsewhere, being more detailed than Samuel Ward's and covering periods when John Adams was absent. Smith signed the "olive branch" petition to the King (July 8, 1775) but evidently was not yet ready to consider independence. Burlington had Loyalist leanings, and on June 12, 1776, with ill health as a reason or an excuse, Smith resigned. Ten days later New Jersey sent to the Congress an entirely new delegation, more definitely in favor of independence. On Oct. 17, 1776, Smith was elected to the state treasurership, recently vacated through his brother's death, but after five months resigned that office and retired to "Bramham Hall" near Burlington.

In 1790, he moved from Burlington to the "Otego Patent," whither his son, Richard R. Smith, had already followed William Cooper of Burlington, founder of Cooperstown and father of James Fenimore Cooper [*q.v.*]. The younger Smith became the first sheriff of the new Otsego County. The father settled at "Smith Hall," remaining until 1799, when he removed to Philadelphia. Four years later, while traveling in the

Mississippi Valley, he died of fever at Natchez. His son described him as "a man of incorruptible integrity, of gentle and amiable manners, of almost unexampled temperance," with "a strong mind, enriched with a variety of knowledge, collected from judicious observations upon men and manners, and from intimate acquaintance with almost every author of note in the ancient or modern languages" (Halsey, *post,* p. xx).

[Smith's journal of his trip in 1769 was edited, with a biographical foreword, by F. W. Halsey, as *A Tour of Four Great Rivers* (1906). The Continental Congress journal (now in Lib. of Cong.) is reproduced, also with a biographical sketch, in *Am. Hist. Rev.,* Jan., Apr. 1896; and, in the form of extracts, in E. C. Burnett, *Letters of Members of the Continental Cong.,* vol. I (1921). See also R. M. Smith, *The Burlington Smiths* (1877), p. 115, table 26; V. L. Collins, *President Witherspoon* (1925), I, 212–13; R. E. Spiller, *Fenimore Cooper* (1931), 12, 18; H. W. Boynton, *James Fenimore Cooper* (1931), pp. 8–10; *Archives of the State of N. J.,* 1 ser. XIX (1897), XXIX (1919), XXXII (1924); *Biog. Dir. Am. Cong.* (1928); C. H. Jones, *Geneal. of the Rodman Family* (1886); *Poulson's Am. Daily Advertiser* (Phila.), Oct. 18, 1803.]

R. G. A.

SMITH, RICHARD PENN (Mar. 13, 1799–Aug. 12, 1854), lawyer, author, playwright, was born in Philadelphia, the son of William Moore Smith and his wife, Ann Rudulph. His grandfather, the Rev. William Smith, 1727–1803 [*q.v.*], had been the first provost of the College of Philadelphia; his father was a lawyer and a man of slight poetic gifts, interested in letters and the arts. Penn Smith, as the son was usually called, was reared in a home of refinement and culture. He received his early education under a private tutor, John Sanderson [*q.v.*], and at Joseph Neef's grammar school. When in his teens, he was placed under the care of John Johnson, a Presbyterian clergyman, who had established a school at Huntingdon, Pa., but in 1818 he returned to Philadelphia to study law in the office of William Rawle, and in 1821 was admitted to the Philadelphia bar. His inherited taste for letters now began to take possession of him, and in the columns of *The Union* he published a series of moral and literary essays under the title of "The Plagiary." He also contributed a biography of Francis Hopkinson to John Sanderson's *Biography of the Signers to the Declaration of Independence* (vol. II, 1822). Late in 1822, he purchased the Philadelphia *Aurora,* with which in 1824 he merged the *Franklin Gazette,* but in 1827, finding the duties of an editor too onerous, he sold the paper and resumed the practice of law.

He had already begun a period of unusual literary activity. In the decade 1825–35 he wrote twenty plays, of which fifteen were performed. He was a practical playwright who depended mainly upon foreign writers for his inspiration. Five of his acted plays were inspired by French originals: *The Eighth of January* (1829), a melodrama of the battle of New Orleans, is a clever adaptation of *Le Maréchal de Luxembourg* (1812), by Frédéric and Boirie; *The Disowned* (1829) is a slightly changed version of *Le Caissier* (1826), a drama by La Salle and Maurice; *The Sentinels* (1829, not published) is a faithful translation of a poor melodrama, *Les deux Sergents* (1823) by D'Aubigny; *Is She a Brigand?* (1833) is an adaptation of a French comedy, *Clara Wendel* (1827) by Theaulon, Dartois, and Francis; *The Actress of Padua* (1836) is an adaptation of Victor Hugo's romantic drama, *Angelo, Tyran de Padoue*; it was published by Smith as a narrative, with other tales, in 1836. Four of his five unacted plays also had French sources: *The Last Man, The Bombardment of Algiers, Shakespeare in Love,* and *The Daughter.* His first acted play, *Quite Correct* (1828, published 1835), is a comedy based upon an English story by Theodore Hook, who in turn borrowed the idea from a French comedy, *L'Hôtel garni,* by Désaugiers and Gentil. Besides *The Eighth of January,* his plays dealing with American history were *William Penn,* played in 1829 but not printed, and *The Triumph at Plattsburgh* (1830). Probably his two best plays are *The Deformed* (1830) based on the second part of *The Honest Whore* by Thomas Dekker, and *Caius Marius,* which was produced by Edwin Forrest in 1831. Contemporary criticism was high in praise of this last play, which unfortunately has not survived. Smith did not confine himself wholly to the writing of plays; he published a novel, *The Forsaken* (1831), his most pretentious literary production, and wrote a large number of tales and sketches and considerable verse. To him has also been ascribed *Col. Crockett's Exploits and Adventures in Texas* (1836), which purported to have been written by the gallant Tennessean prior to the massacre at the Alamo. In a single year over 10,000 copies were sold in the United States and in 1837 the book was reprinted in England and favorably received there. To Smith's early training in journalism was doubtless due his facility in composition, a facility which often resulted in serious blemishes in his work. His writings are marred by confusion of plot, unconvincing characterization, and a lack of ease.

Smith married, first, on May 5, 1823, his cousin, Elinor Matilda Blodget, daughter of Samuel [*q.v.*] and Rebecca (Smith) Blodget and widow of Abel Lincoln. Of the five children born to this union only one, Horace Wemyss

Smith, lived to maturity. Smith's first wife died in 1834, and two years later, in 1836, he married Isabella Stratton Knisell who also bore him five children. After this marriage, he retired to his family seat at the Falls of the Schuylkill, near Philadelphia, where he lived until his death.

[Smith's papers are in the library of the Hist. Soc. of Pa. The principal printed sources are Morton McMichael, Introduction, in *The Miscellaneous Works of the Late Richard Penn Smith* (1856), ed. by H. W. Smith; H. W. Smith, *Life and Correspondence of the Rev. William Smith, D.D.* (2 vols., 1879–80); B. W. McCullough, *The Life and Writings of Richard Penn Smith, with a Reprint of His Play, "The Deformed,"* 1830 (1917), Univ. of Pa. thesis. See also *Burton's Gentleman's Mag.* (Phila.), Sept. 1839; *Daily Pennsylvanian* (Phila.), Aug. 14, 1854; and A. H. Quinn, *A Hist. of the Am. Drama from the Beginning to the Civil War* (1923), containing critical estimate and complete bibliography of Smith's plays.]   H. W. S.

SMITH, RICHARD SOMERS (Oct. 30, 1813–Jan. 23, 1877), soldier and educator, was born in Philadelphia, Pa. In early life he was commonly called, and called himself, Richard S. Smith, Jr., although the name of his father, a prominent merchant and city councilor, was Francis Gurney Smith. His mother was Eliza (Mackie) Smith. On his father's side he was descended from early settlers of Long Island. Entering the United States Military Academy at West Point in 1829, he graduated in 1834 and was commissioned in the infantry, but was employed on topographical duty until 1836, when he resigned from the army to take up engineering in civil life. He was employed by the Philadelphia and Columbia Railroad, 1836–37; by a projected Charleston-Louisville-Cincinnati railroad, 1837–38; and by the Chesapeake and Ohio Canal, 1839–40. Reappointed in the army as a second lieutenant of infantry, Dec. 31, 1840, he was promoted first lieutenant in 1846 and transferred to the artillery in 1848, but served only at West Point, where he was an instructor and assistant professor of drawing from 1840 to 1855, serving also as quartermaster, 1846–51, and treasurer, 1852–55. He resigned in 1856 to become professor of mathematics, engineering, and drawing in the Brooklyn Collegiate and Polytechnic Institute (later the Polytechnic Institute of Brooklyn) where he remained until 1859. During these years he published his *Manual of Topographical Drawing* (1853) and *Manual of Linear Perspective* (1857). He was teacher of freehand drawing and then director of Cooper Union, New York City, until 1861, when, after a few weeks' service as quartermaster with New York volunteers, he was for the third time appointed to the regular army, being commissioned as major in the 12th Infantry, a newly organized regiment. After being on detached service as a mustering and disbursing officer in Maryland and in Wisconsin until December 1862, he joined his regiment with the Army of the Potomac and remained with it until after the battle of Chancellorsville.

On May 30, 1863, he resigned from the army once more to accept the presidency of Girard College, Philadelphia, for which a man who was both an experienced educator and a strict disciplinarian had been sought. In some respects his administration was a success, but it was marred by lack of harmony and finally by violent contention. Eventually he was removed by the board of directors, Nov. 1, 1867. The city councils took a hand in the dispute, directed an investigation, and on Feb. 20, 1868, received a report, published at great length in the *Journals of Councils* of that year, which "probably gave aid and comfort to both sides in the controversy; it also probably satisfied neither side" (Herrick, *post*, p. 58). From 1868 to 1870 Smith was professor of engineering in the Polytechnic College of Pennsylvania in Philadelphia. In the latter year he was called to the United States Naval Academy and spent the rest of his life in Annapolis, Md., at first as professor of mathematics and after 1873 as professor of drawing. He married Ellen Clark, who died about fourteen months before him. They had six children.

[J. W. Jordan, ed., *Colonial and Revolutionary Families of Pa.* (1911), vol. II; G. W. Cullum, *Biog. Reg. Officers and Grads. U. S. Mil. Acad.* (2nd ed., 1891), vol. I; *Eighth Ann. Reunion Asso. Grads. U. S. Mil. Acad. . . . 1877* (1877); *Sixteenth Ann. Report Bd. of Directors, Girard Coll.* (1864); C. A. Herrick, *Hist. of Girard Coll.* (1927); obituaries in *Army and Navy Jour.*, Jan. 27, 1877, and the *Sun* (Baltimore, Md.), Jan. 24, 1877; unpublished records in the War Dept.]

T. M. S.

SMITH, ROBERT (*c.* 1722–Feb. 11, 1777), colonial architect and builder, is said to have been born in Glasgow, Scotland, and to have come to Philadelphia at an early age, but he emerges from obscurity only about the middle of the eighteenth century as a builder in Philadelphia and a member of the Carpenters' Company of that city. His first recorded commission was the construction of Nassau Hall, built to house the College of New Jersey at Princeton (later Princeton University). The trustees' minutes refer to the design of the building (begun in 1754) as the work of Smith and "Doct. Shippen" (possibly Dr. William Shippen, Sr., 1712–1801, who had family connections with the college), but *An Account of the College of New Jersey* (1764) gives the credit to Smith alone. Nassau Hall, one of the largest buildings in the colonies, served as a pattern for University Hall at Brown University and Dartmouth Hall at Dartmouth

College, and seems to have been the progenitor of a whole school of American college architecture. Only the walls of the building now standing at Princeton are Smith's work. The house he built for the president of the college still stands nearby. His next major task, the erection of St. Peter's Church, Philadelphia, was undertaken in 1758. In drawing the plans he probably had the collaboration of Dr. John Kearsley [*q.v.*], who was a member of the building committee. The church still exists, in almost its original condition save for the addition of a spire; it is notable for its fenestration and the beauty of its interior appointments, and may probably be considered its builder's masterpiece. From this time forward Smith's services seem to have been in constant demand. He submitted plans for a building for the Carpenters' Company in 1768, and when Carpenters' Hall was built two years later his name headed the list of the building committee. He appears to have designed the Zion Lutheran Church (1766) and the Walnut Street Prison (1773); these have been destroyed, while the Third (Old Pine Street) Presbyterian Church, also his work (1766), survives in a form altered beyond recognition. Though the statement that he built the spire of Christ Church is probably unfounded, he carried out large repairs on it about 1771. There is record of his having built dwelling houses.

In 1774 he was one of a committee chosen by the "mechanics" of Philadelphia to assist in organizing agitation against the coercion of Boston, and at a mass meeting of citizens on June 18 he was appointed to the committee of correspondence that was directed to take steps for a general colonial congress (*Pennsylvania Gazette*, June 15, 22, 1774). On July 24, 1775, the Pennsylvania committee of safety approved a plan he submitted for the construction of chevaux-de-frise to· block the channel of the Delaware below Philadelphia, and accepted his offer to serve gratis in supervising the three lines that were placed in the river near Fort Mifflin. During 1776 he was employed in the preparation of similar defences, anl other works, at Billingsport, N. J., further down the river. The obstacles he devised were of a very massive nature (*The Annual Register . . . for the Year 1777,* 1778, p. 134) and embarrassed the British considerably in their efforts to open communication with Philadelphia by sea in the autumn of 1777 (*The Writings of George Washington,* edited by J. C. Fitzpatrick, vol. IX, 1933, p. 428). Smith died, however, without seeing his inventions tested in action.

In the greatest age of colonial building he was

Philadelphia's most eminent architect. Though his designs might be taxed with an excessive plainness amounting to severity (probably explicable by local circumstances), and with a tendency to repetition, he handled the contemporary Georgian style with admirable dignity combined with a sane regard for practical ends, and made a very distinguished contribution to the amenity of the city. He owned a country house as well as the one in town where he died, and the journal of his friend Jacob Hiltzheimer (*post*) testifies that in his later years he was fond of company and entertainment. He was a member of the American Philosophical Society from 1768. His wife, Esther or Hester, lived until 1783. The John Smith who was associated with her in administering her husband's estate (*Pennsylvania Gazette*, Apr. 9, 1777) may have been a son, and the Philadelphia records of the Society of Friends (*post*), to which Smith appears to have belonged, mention two girls, Martha and Rebecca, who died in 1758 and 1770 respectively, as "daughters of Robert Smith." These records give his age at his death as fifty-five; the *Pennsylvania Evening Post*, Feb. 13, 1777, states that he was in his fifty-fifth year.

[See Joseph Jackson, *Early Phila. Architects and Engineers* (1923); P. B. Wallace and W. A. Dunn, *Colonial Churches and Meeting Houses, Pa., N. J., and Del.* (1931); *Extracts from the Diary of Jacob Hiltzheimer of Phila., 1765–1798* (1893), ed. by J. C. Parsons; *Minutes of the Provincial Council of Pa.*, vols. X, XI (1852); *Pa. Archives*, 1 ser., vols. IV, V (1853); John Maclean, *Hist. of the Coll. of N. J.* (1877), vol. I; C. P. B. Jefferys, "*The Provincial and Revolutionary Hist. of St. Peter's Church, Phila., 1753–1783*"; *Pa. Mag. of Hist. and Biog.*, Oct. 1923; *An Act to Incorporate the Carpenters' Company of the City and County of Phila.* (1866), not reliable for dates prior to 1763; J. T. Scharf and Thompson Westcott, *Hist. of Phila., 1609–1884* (1884), vol. II; transcripts of vital records of Soc. of Friends, Hist. Soc. of Pa., Phila.; records of the Am. Philos. Soc. There are a few manuscript fragments by or relating to Smith in the possession of the Hist. Soc. of Pa. and the Princeton Univ. Lib.; several of his architectural books are preserved at Carpenters' Hall.]   C. P. S.

SMITH, ROBERT (Aug. 14, 1732–o.s. Oct. 28, 1801), Revolutionary patriot, first Protestant Episcopal bishop of South Carolina, was a native of Worstead, Norfolk, England, the second child of Stephen Smith, a grazier, and Hannah (Press) Smith. At the age of sixteen, having spent seven years at the Norwich grammar school under Timothy Bullimer, he was admitted sizar at Gonville and Caius College, Cambridge, matriculating in 1750. He received his bachelor's degree in 1754 and in 1755 was appointed a fellow. On Mar. 7, 1756, he was ordered deacon, and on Dec. 21 was ordained priest by the Bishop of Ely. The next year, upon the recommendation of William Mason, M.P., he was appointed assistant minister of St. Philip's Church in Charlestown, S. C., and arrived there Nov. 3, 1757. He became rector in 1759. On July 9, 1758, he married Elizabeth, the daughter of John Pagett. Ten years later, in the hope of restoring her broken health, he carried her to England, where they remained for eighteen months. She died June 8, 1771, however, some five months after their return to America. Early in 1774 he married Sarah, the daughter of Thomas Shubrick. She died July 7, 1779, and some years later he married Anna Maria (Tilghman) Goldsborough, daughter of Col. Edward Tilghman of Wye, and the widow of Charles Goldsborough, by whom she had a son Charles [*q.v.*]. She died Dec. 6, 1792. By his second wife Smith had one daughter, and by his third, two sons.

He was "a very sociable & polite clergyman" (*Publications of the Southern History Association*, vol. II, 1898, p. 138), a prodigious worker, and a powerful speaker. His position at St. Philip's also gave him importance, and in the years before the Revolution he acquired great influence. He was early an intense patriot and in November 1775 was elected to the second provincial congress, where he failed to take his seat, but became chaplain of an artillery company. Later he was chaplain of the 1st South Carolina Regiment, and also of the Continental Hospital in Charlestown. Still later, he was chaplain general of the Southern department of the Continental Army. During the siege of Charlestown he served as a private soldier, and so active was he in the American cause that his name headed the list, published Dec. 30, 1780, of those whose estates were sequestered under Cornwallis' proclamation of Sept. 6. When offered immunity if he would support the British cause, he replied, "Rather would I be hanged by the King of England than go off and hang myself in shame and despair like Judas" (letter in private hands). He had inherited the "Brabant" plantation of 3,600 acres from his first wife and had added to it by purchase, so that his loss was great; to cap his misfortune, moreover, he was imprisoned in Charlestown and later banished to Philadelphia. After a stay of some months there he went to Maryland, where he took charge of St. Paul's Parish, Queen Anne's County. He returned to Charleston in 1783.

Smith was active in many good works of peace. As rector of St. Philip's he had charge of a successful school for negroes. He was instrumental in founding the Society for the Relief of Widows and Orphans. After his return from Maryland he founded a school which in 1790 became the College of Charleston, of which he was principal until 1798. When the movement for the organization of the Protestant Episcopal Church in the United States began, Smith was chiefly responsible for the assembling of a convention in South Carolina, which sent delegates to the General Convention of 1785. He did not attend, but was present in 1786 and 1789. There was much opposition in the state to the selection of a bishop, but finally, in 1795, after the first minister chosen had declined, Smith was elected and was consecrated at Christ Church, Philadelphia, in September. He continued to be rector of St. Philip's until his death, and because of local prejudice he never administered the rite of confirmation. He is buried in St. Philip's Cemetery.

[John and J. A. Venn, *Alumni Cantabrigienses*, pt. 1, vol. IV (1927); John Venn, *Biog. Hist. of Gonville and Caius Coll.*, vol. II (1898), p. 63; *S. C. Hist. and Geneal. Mag.*, Jan. 1917, Apr. 1919, Jan., Apr., July 1920, Jan. 1924; Frederick Dalcho, *An Hist. Account of the Protestant Episcopal Church in S. C.* (1820); William Moultrie, *Memoirs of the Am. Revolution* (1802); Alexander Garden, *Anecdotes of the Am. Revolution* (1822), 2 ser. (1828); Elizabeth Poyas, *Days of Yore; or Shadows of the Past* (1870), pt. 2, pp. 1–24; H. H. Ravenel, *Charleston, the Place and the People* (1907); Edward McCrady, *The Hist. of S. C. in the Revolution, 1775–1780* (1901), *1780–1783* (1902); W. S. Perry, *The Hist. of the Am. Episc. Church, 1776–1883* (1885) and *Jours. of the Gen. Conventions of the Protestant Episcopal Church in the U. S., 1785–1833* (1874); W. B. Sprague, *Annals of the Am. Pulpit*, vol. V (1859); *News and Courier* (Charleston), Jan. 26, 1898; D. E. Huger Smith and A. S. Salley, Jr., *Reg. of St. Philip's Parish . . . 1754–1810* (1927).]
                        J. G. deR. H.

SMITH, ROBERT (Nov. 3, 1757–Nov. 26, 1842), secretary of the navy and secretary of state, brother of Samuel Smith [q.v.], was born in Lancaster, Pa. His parents were John Smith and Mary (Buchanan), daughter of Robert Buchanan. He was educated at the College of New Jersey, graduating in 1781. For a time he served as a private in the Revolution. Later, he studied law and was admitted to the bar in Baltimore. Ambitious, industrious, courteous, and amiable, he soon had the largest admiralty practice in the city. On Dec. 7, 1790, he married a distant cousin, Margaret, daughter of William Smith. Eight children were born to them, of whom only one, a son, lived to maturity.

From 1793 to 1795 Smith was a member of the Maryland Senate and then for some time a member of the House of Delegates; from 1798 to 1801 he sat in the Baltimore city council. By now he had become a loyal Republican and ardent admirer of Jefferson, who, in 1801, after first offering the post to his brother, appointed him secretary of the navy. At the beginning of Jefferson's second term Smith asked to be transferred to the attorney-general's office; and this was done, Jacob Crowninshield [q.v.] being tendered his place in the navy department. The Senate confirmed both appointments, but since Crowninshield would not accept the position, Smith continued to act as secretary of the navy and after a few months gave up the attorney-generalship, continuing at the head of naval affairs until March 1809 without being recommissioned or reconfirmed. Though greatly criticized by the secretary of the treasury, Albert Gallatin [q.v.], Smith seems to have been fairly efficient in this office. With very limited funds he maintained a blockading squadron in the Mediterranean during the war against the Barbary States; though opposed to the Embargo, he seems to have tried conscientiously to enforce it; and in 1808 it was he, and not the Secretary of State, who was Jefferson's intermediary with George Henry Rose, Canning's agent in the diplomatic discussions of impressment.

As president-elect, Madison wished Gallatin to be his secretary of state, but his desire was opposed by a faction headed by senators Samuel Smith, William Branch Giles, and Michael Leib [qq.v.]. In an effort to win their support he decided to give the treasury portfolio to Robert Smith, to be assisted in his duties by Gallatin from the State Department. Gallatin refused these terms, however, and Smith was made secretary of state. Friction developed inevitably between the Secretary and the President, for Smith sided with the Senate cabal, which continued its attack on Gallatin, and in his official capacity generally opposed the President's plans for commercial restrictions. The two men frequently disagreed over the policy to be pursued in the troubles growing from the Napoleonic wars; moreover, Madison could not endure the English in which the Secretary expressed his views, and therefore, was soon writing all of the important diplomatic communications of the administration.

Matters reached a climax when Gallatin handed in his resignation early in March 1811. Madison refused to accept it, and sent for Smith. In the ensuing interview he criticized Smith for inefficiency, breach of trust, and causing discord in administration circles. As a way out, he offered Smith the position of minister to Russia, but after some hesitation the latter refused the offer, resigned his portfolio, and returned to Baltimore. In June 1811 he published *Robert Smith's Address to the People of the United States,* an attempt at self-defense which further hurt his prestige. During the last thirty years of his life, spent in Baltimore, he filled offices in a number of private organizations. His ability was, on the whole, little more than average, and the high positions to which he attained came chiefly through the influence of his brother, Gen. Samuel Smith.

[C. C. Tansill, "Robert Smith," in S. F. Bemis, *The American Secretaries of State and Their Diplomacy*, vol. III (1927); Henry Adams, *Hist. of the U. S. A.* (9 vols., 1889–91); *Votes and Proc. of the Gen. Assembly of the State of Md.*, 1793–1800; G. E. Davies, "Robert Smith and the Navy," *Md. Hist. Mag.*, Dec. 1919; C. O. Paullin, "Naval Administration under Secretaries of the Navy Smith, Hamilton, and Jones, 1801–1814," *Proc. U. S. Naval Inst.*, vol. XXXII (Dec. 1906); *The Life and Correspondence of James McHenry* (1907), ed. by B. C. Steiner; *The Writings of Thomas Jefferson* (20 vols., 1903–04); *Letters and Other Writings of James Madison* (4 vols., 1865); *Aurora* (Phila.), May 4, 1811; *American and Commercial Daily Advertiser* (Baltimore), July 6, 1811, Nov. 28. 1842; *National Intelligencer*, Mar. 26, July 4, 6, 9, 11, 1811, Nov. 29, 1842; genealogical table of the Smith family, Wilson Miles Cary MSS. Coll., F 62, Md. Hist. Soc.; Smith Papers, MSS. Div. Library of Congress; information from the secretary of Princeton Univ.]   M. W. W.

SMITH, ROBERT ALEXANDER C. (Feb. 22, 1857–July 27, 1933), promoter, capitalist, dock commissioner, was born in Dover, England, the son of Gilbert and Emily Smith. His father was chief engineer of the Compañia Transatlantica, a steamship line operating between Spain and Cuba. From his second to his thirteenth year, Robert lived in Cadiz and then completed his education at Folkestone and London. In 1874, he came to New York. His knowledge of Spanish led him into the employ of Lyles & Gilson, who specialized in selling railroad supplies to Latin America, and for a time he was the firm's representative in Havana.

Cuba was the principal scene of Smith's activity for many years. Becoming a sort of contact man for the Ward Line and other American business interests, he was particularly active in railroads and shipping. In association with Henry G. Runkle, he is credited with the chief initiative in introducing gas, electric, and water systems to Havana. It is said that he and one J. J. McCook once formed a syndicate to free Cuba by purchase (*Herald Tribune,* July 28, 1933). During the Spanish-American War, he assisted with transport and shipping, having particular charge of the evacuation of Spanish prisoners. That same year, he organized and became head of the American Indies Company, a public utilities organization, and the American Mail Steamship Company, which secured a lucrative mail contract and soon leased its ships to the United Fruit Company. His financial activities were not limited to Cuba, however. In 1895, with Morgan backing, he and Alden M. Young formed the Gas Supply Company, later the Connecticut Railway & Lighting Company,

which secured control of some fourteen separate lighting and traction companies in that state. His interests also included sugar, coal, realty, and banking corporations and he was chairman of the board of the White Rock Mineral Springs Company.

Although through his exploits in economic imperialism he had built up a fortune and influenced the development of Cuba, his most distinctive service to his generation was his share in the development of the Port of New York. Because of his knowledge of shipping problems he was appointed chairman of a state commission "to investigate port conditions and pier extension in New York Harbor," and in 1913, before the publication of his report, he was made commissioner of docks and ferries of New York City. New York at the time was challenging London, Liverpool, and Hamburg for first place among world seaports. After the outbreak of the World War in 1914, it held a secure primacy. The port had grown, however, without any coordinated plan; something had to be done at once to accommodate the new thousand-foot liners, which were too large for the regular docks. The construction of a splendid group of North River (Hudson) piers was Smith's first achievement. In 1915, the ferries were operated at a profit for the first time in ten years of municipal ownership. Smith also urged the deepening and straightening of Hell Gate. A violent discussion arose in 1916 over the "West Side" problem, provoked by the privileges enjoyed by the New York Central, the freight tracks of which lay along the Hudson waterfront. Smith preferred improvements which would continue the Central's favored position as against those who sought more privileges for the railroads having their terminals on the New Jersey side of the river, but the question was still unsettled at the end of his administration in 1917. Smith wrote several vigorous pamphlets on various aspects of port problems. Among these were: *Commission to Investigate Port Conditions in New York Harbor . . . A Tabulation of Facts* (1915); *New York's Progress in Port Problems* (1915); *Report on the Operation of Municipal Ferries by the City of New York from 1905 to 1915* (1916); *The West Side Improvement and its Relation to all of the Commerce of the Port of New York* (1916); *Hell Gate* (1917). He was influential in calling attention to the needs which in 1921 led to the creation of the Port of New York authority.

Retiring as commissioner in 1917, he continued to serve as director in various corporations. After a period of ill health, he sailed for

England but died on board the *Majestic* just after the vessel's arrival at Southampton. In 1882 he had married Alice S. Williams of Brooklyn, who with two daughters survived him.

[*N. Y. Times* and *N. Y. Herald Tribune*, July 28, 1933; *N. Y. Times*, Aug. 17, 1933; *Directory of Directors in the City of N. Y.*, 1899–1933; *Ann. Reports of the Dept. of Docks and Ferries* (N. Y. City), 1913–17; *Joint Report with Comprehensive Plan and Recommendations: N. Y., N. J. Port and Harbor Development Commission* (1920); *Who's Who in N. Y.*, 1929.]
R. G. A.

SMITH, ROBERT BARNWELL [See RHETT, ROBERT BARNWELL, 1800–1876].

SMITH, ROBERT HARDY (Mar. 21, 1813–Mar. 13, 1878), lawyer, member of the provisional Congress of the Confederacy, was born in Camden County, N. C., the son of Robert Hardy and Elizabeth (Gregory) Smith. His grandfather, Joseph Smith, was a native of London, England; his maternal ancestors were also of English descent, but had served the American cause with distinction in the Revolutionary War. Robert received an appointment to West Point but he did not graduate. He taught school in various counties of Virginia and Alabama, studied medicine, and later turned to the law. Admitted to the bar in 1835, he settled for practice at Livingston, Ala. He was successful in his profession and was recognized as especially able in addresses to the jury. His style was clear and forceful, argumentative rather than oratorical.

In politics he was a Whig. He supported Harrison in 1840 and Clay in 1844. In 1849 he was elected to represent Sumter County in the legislature, being the only Whig chosen from that county. He was regarded as the leader of the Whigs in the Alabama House of Representatives during the session and in 1851 became a candidate for the state Senate on a platform of opposition to the Nashville Convention and defense of the compromise measures of 1850 against the State-Rights Democrats. The campaign was a bitter one and John A. Winston [*q.v.*] defeated Smith by one vote. For the next ten years he was actively interested in politics but held no office. In 1853 he moved to Mobile, where he continued the practice of law. Throughout the period he was one of the leaders of the opposition to William L. Yancey [*q.v.*] and was tireless in his efforts against the growing sentiment in the state for secession. He supported Bell and Everett in 1860 and appears to have originated the movement to fuse the Bell and Douglas forces in the state in order to defeat secession. The movement failed.

When Alabama withdrew from the Union, Smith accepted the decision loyally. He was Alabama's commissioner to confer with North Carolina on secession and was elected to the provisional Confederate Congress in 1861 as one of Alabama's two delegates at large. In the Congress he served on the committee which framed the permanent constitution for the Confederacy and took an active part in the debates. He was anxious that the wording of the constitution be clear and simple and most of his work was directed toward securing definiteness and clarity of statement. He also served on the judiciary committee and on the committee on naval affairs. In 1861 he published *An Address to the Citizens of Alabama on the Constitution and Laws of the Confederate States of America*. He organized, in 1862, the 36th Alabama Infantry and was elected colonel, but was compelled to resign before the end of the year because of poor health. Thereafter he practised law in Mobile until his death. He was married three times and had several children. His first wife, whom he married Jan. 12, 1839, was Evelina Inge. After her death in 1843, he married, Nov. 25, 1845, her sister Emily. A third wife, whom he married Apr. 9, 1850, was Helen Herndon.

[Dates are from family Bible and records; for published sources, see T. M. Owen, *Hist. of Ala. and Dict. of Ala. Biog.* (1921), vol. IV; Willis Brewer, *Ala.: Her Hist., Resources, War Record, and Public Men, 1540 to 1872* (1872); William Garrett, *Reminiscences of Public Men in Ala. for Thirty Years* (1872); *News* (Gainesville, Ala.), Sept. 3, 1870; article by Stephens Croom, in *Southern Law Jour.*, Jan. 1879, repr. in *Daily Register* (Mobile), Mar. 23, 1879; obituary in *Daily Register*, Mar. 15, 1878.]
H. F.

SMITH, ROSWELL (Mar. 30, 1829–Apr. 19, 1892), lawyer and publisher, was born at Lebanon, Conn., the son of Asher Ladd Smith and his second wife, Wealthy Pratt. Asher Smith, farmer and business man, wrote *How to Get Rich* (1856; 2nd ed., 1866), and his brother, Roswell Chamberlain Smith, was the author of numerous textbooks in grammar, arithmetic, and geography. The boy was named for this uncle, but in mature life rarely used his middle name. In 1843 he went to New York to enter the employ of his uncle's publishers, Paine & Burgess. Five years later he entered Brown University as a student in the two-year English and scientific course. The record books of the university show that his marks were consistently high; the lowest, 83, was in French. After honorable dismissal, May 6, 1850, he studied law in Hartford, under Thomas C. Perkins, and began practice in Lafayette, Ind. In 1852 he married Annie Goodrich Ellsworth, daughter of Henry Leavitt Ellsworth [*q.v.*].

In 1868, as a result of a successful practice and fortunate investments in real estate, Smith was able to retire and go to Europe. He had conceived the idea of buying a newspaper or a magazine upon his return, and when, by arrangement, he met Josiah Gilbert Holland [*q.v.*] at Geneva, the two worked out plans for a new magazine to encourage American art and literature. A warm friendship developed between them and upon their return to the United States in 1870, they joined with Charles Scribner [*q.v.*], the publisher of Holland's works, in the corporation of Scribner & Company, which in November 1870 published the first issue of *Scribner's Monthly*. Holland, as editor-in-chief, was ably seconded by Richard Watson Gilder [*q.v.*]. In 1873, Smith proposed the publication of a high-class magazine for children, and accordingly *St. Nicholas,* edited by Mary Elizabeth Mapes Dodge [*q.v.*], was sponsored by the firm. In the face of the financial panic of that year Smith held out for the purchase and merging with the new magazine of several juvenile periodicals, and the outcome completely vindicated his judgment. In 1881, Holland, in ill health, sold his interest in the company to Smith, and later Smith also purchased the Scribner interest, which gave him control of the magazine. This purchase, however, carried the requirement that he change the name of the company and of the periodical, and in this way *Scribner's Monthly* became the *Century.*

In 1882, Smith first conceived the idea of *The Century Dictionary and Cyclopedia,* which was his chief interest for the next ten years. That it was completed before his death was, to him, a great source of comfort. As work on it progressed, the project grew far beyond the proportions of the original design, which had been little more than a revision for American use of Ogilvie's *Imperial Dictionary* (2 vols., Glasgow, 1851); but Smith refused to consider proposals of economy and enabled the editors to make the *Century* the most comprehensive work of its kind in the English language up to the completion of the great Oxford Dictionary. Smith's behavior in this instance was characteristic: whatever he undertook he determined should be the best in its field, regardless of expense. As a result of this characteristic, his magazines, under Alexander Wilson Drake [*q.v.*] as art director, were a major factor in stimulating the development of American illustration. Holding the enthusiastic belief that American publications could win praise and financial success in foreign countries, Smith demonstrated his faith by spending large sums of money, personally arranging the details involved in placing his magazines before English readers. In addition to his activities as president of the Century Company, he was interested in educational work, especially in the South; Lincoln Hall, at Berea College, Ky., is an example of his generosity.

Smith's own literary work was slight. It consists of a sixteen-line poem, "What the Devil Said to the Young Man" (*Scribner's Monthly,* May 1871), and two short stories in *St. Nicholas*: "The Boy Who Worked" (January 1874), and "Little Holdfast" (January 1891). Of small value in themselves, the stories illustrate, as Smith intended, two principles that he followed rigidly: work hard; and when you make a promise, hold fast to it, regardless of consequences. Smith was tall, with a leonine head, and made a commanding appearance. He loved his home, his family, and a few friends, but he was not fond of "social life." He felt that a man should be useful in a public way, and he was too busy trying to be useful to have time for trivial pleasures. He died of Bright's disease and paralysis, at his home in New York, after an illness of three years. For eight weeks before his death he had been unable to speak, as a result of a succession of paralytic strokes. He was survived by his wife and by one daughter.

[G. W. Cable, *A Memory of Roswell Smith* (1892); *Century Magazine,* June 1892; *St. Nicholas,* June 1892; *Commercial Advertiser* (N. Y.), Apr. 19, 1892; *N. Y. Tribune, N. Y. Times, World* (N. Y.), all of Apr. 20, 1892; Record Books in Brown Univ. Library; *Hist. Cat. Brown Univ.* (1905); information from members of the family.]   H. S. R—n.

SMITH, RUSSELL (Apr. 26, 1812–Nov. 8, 1896), painter, third in a family of four boys and three girls, was born in Glasgow, Scotland. Although christened William Thompson Russell Smith, he was known simply as Russell Smith. His father, William Thompson Smith, and his mother, Margaret (Russell) Smith, a practising physician who had studied medicine in Glasgow, emigrated to America with their children in 1819 because of their political views. They settled in Indiana County, Pa., but moved to Pittsburgh in 1824. There Russell's father, who is said to have been "an ingenious mechanic, excelling in the manufacture of cutlery, artists' tools, and mathematical instruments" (Tuckerman, *post,* p. 519), established a cutlery business, and Russell began his art career by painting with house paints life-sized portraits of Gen. William Jackson, 1759–1828, and Lafayette [*qq.v.*]. He also joined a dramatic society, for which he played female parts and painted scenery. His success at the latter led to four years of study under the painter James Reid Lambdin [*q.v.*]. In 1833, when Francis Courtney Wemyss, manager of the Pittsburgh Theatre, took Edwin Forrest [*qq.v.*] to Pittsburgh, Smith was asked in an emergency to paint the scenery, although actor and producer doubted the ability of so young a man. The result was a tent scene for *Metamora* so successful that Smith attached himself to Wemyss as professional scene-painter and began an active career that was spent partly in Boston, but mostly in Philadelphia, Baltimore, and Washington. On Apr. 7, 1838, at Milestown, Pa., he married Mary Priscilla Wilson. His wife, well educated and of a cultured family, had been a teacher of French and Latin, and was a painter of flowers. They had two children, Xanthus [*q.v.*] and Mary (Sept. 25, 1842–June 6, 1878), both painters.

The years 1851–52 the family spent in Europe, returning so that Smith could produce a panorama of Mexico and California, and a diorama of the Holy Land (both exhibited in Philadelphia) as well as much operatic scenery and a number of drop-curtains, including those for Welsh's old National Theatre in Philadelphia and for the Boston Museum. When the Philadelphia Academy of Music was built, 1855–56, he was commissioned to produce its landscape drop-curtain, scenery for its operas, and additional drop-curtains, a task that stretched through the years almost until the time of his death. He painted all the scenery for the American Academy of Music in Baltimore, and drop-curtains for the principal theatrical houses in Philadelphia, Boston, and Brooklyn. These large canvases, many of them fifty feet square or more, were ordinarily painted with no more assistance than that of a color grinder who also helped to raise and lower the frame that held them. Smith believed that unless he executed the entire project himself his individuality as an artist would suffer. In 1879, after the death of his daughter Mary, he founded the Mary Smith Prize of $100, given yearly to a resident woman artist exhibiting in the annual exhibition of oil paintings at the Pennsylvania Academy of the Fine Arts. In addition to his scene painting, he devoted considerable time to illustrations for scientific lectures, drawings for geological surveys, and occasional landscapes in oil. Always interested in observing nature closely, he made sketching trips to picturesque parts of Virginia, New England, and Pennsylvania, using the resultant material in composing such landscape drop-curtains as that in the Philadelphia Academy of Music. After a vigorous old age he died in his home in Glenside, Pa.

[See H. T. Tuckerman, *Book of the Artists* (1867); Clara E. Clement and Laurence Hutton, *Artists of the Nineteenth Century* (1885); *Appletons' Ann. Cyc.*, 1896; obituary in *Pub. Ledger* (Phila.), Nov. 9, 1896; *Cat. of the Forty-Ninth Ann. Exhibition Pa. Acad. of the Fine Arts* (1878) and *Descriptive Cat. of the Permanent Colls.* (1892). For Mary Smith see *A Brief Sketch of the Life of Mary Smith, the Painter* (privately printed, 1878). Information has been supplied by Mary B. Smith, wife of Xanthus Smith.]   D. G.

SMITH, SAMUEL (July 27, 1752–Apr. 22, 1839), soldier and statesman, was born in Carlisle, Pa.; but his parents removed to Baltimore, Md., when he was seven or eight years old. His mother was Mary Buchanan of Lancaster, Pa. His father, John Smith, a native of Strabane, Ireland, of Scotch-Irish descent, was brought to Pennsylvania by his parents in 1728. He removed to Baltimore in 1760, became one of the wealthiest merchants in that city, and was active in Revolutionary politics. After two years in an academy at Elkton, Md., Samuel, then fifteen, entered his father's counting house. He was sent to Europe in 1772, spent considerable time traveling there, and upon his return resumed his work with his father.

In 1775 he organized a company of volunteers and entered the conflict against Great Britain. He participated in the battle of Long Island, covered the rear of the American army in its retreat across New Jersey, and was with Washington at Valley Forge and at the battle of Monmouth. As commander of Fort Mifflin, in the Delaware, near Philadelphia, he held out for some forty days, helping keep Howe's fleet at bay and thus contributing towards Burgoyne's surrender, which marked the turning point of the war. For this service Congress gave him a vote of thanks and a sword. After the Revolution he continued his mercantile activities in Baltimore, and engaged in land speculation in various states, becoming very wealthy. In 1791 he commanded the Maryland quota of troops sent to suppress the Whiskey Rebellion. Three years later, when war threatened with France, he was made brigadier-general of the state militia.

Meanwhile, in 1792 he had entered politics, through being elected to Congress. He was re-elected four times, serving until 1803. For a few months (Mar. 31–June 13, 1801) at the beginning of Jefferson's administration, until the appointment of his brother Robert [*q.v.*], he acted as virtual secretary of the navy while Henry Dearborn was nominal secretary *ad interim*. In this capacity he began energetic action against Tripoli. In 1803 Smith was elected to the Senate, where he remained until 1815. During the War of 1812, with the rank of major-general, he headed the land and sea forces which defended Baltimore from the British. He returned to the House, Jan. 31, 1816, serving, by reëlections, until December 1822, when he resigned to fill a vacancy in the Senate caused by the death of William Pinkney [*q.v.*]. To this seat he was reëlected in 1826, serving until 1833, and thus completing forty continuous years in Congress.

At first Federalist in his leanings, Smith soon became a stanch Jeffersonian Republican. He was tall and handsome, of proud countenance and imperious bearing, and easily attracted attention. He was also self-confident, ambitious, industrious, intelligent, and an able and forceful debater. He quickly made his influence felt both on the floor of Congress and behind the scenes. Repeatedly he was president *pro tempore* of the Senate, and he did important work as chairman of the finance committees of both houses. He was given to cabals and intrigues, was one of the leaders in opposing the nomination of Madison, and, following it, headed a group which aimed, in vain, to eliminate nominating by congressional caucus. Nevertheless, in 1816 he was chairman of such a gathering, and in 1820 he made a futile effort to secure by caucus the nomination of Clay for vice-president because he himself aspired to Clay's position as speaker of the House (J. Q. Adams, *Memoirs, post,* V, 58–60). He was one of the leaders of the faction which fought Albert Gallatin [*q.v.*] as secretary of the treasury, and did much to embarrass the administration through holding up in Congress the financial measures advocated by Gallatin. Thus, in 1811, he opposed the rechartering of the United States Bank, although in 1816 he advocated the chartering of a new United States bank, and in 1830, as chairman of the Senate committee on finance, recommended its rechartering. He was chairman of the special committee which introduced the non-importation agreements in 1806; he opposed Macon's Bill, No. 1, in March 1810; and was a member of the faction which delayed by twelve days the declaration of war against Great Britain in 1812. He favored equalization of tariff duties but fought bitterly Clay's "American system" and in 1832 even suggested dividing the Union at the Potomac to escape it (Adams, *Memoirs,* VIII, 455). Perhaps his most constructive efforts were those for the recovery of trade with the British West Indies. He was the chief sponsor of the act of Congress approved May 29, 1830, authorizing the president to undertake negotiations for the opening of British ports in those islands to American vessels.

After his last term in the Senate, Smith lived in retirement in Maryland until 1835, when, as commander of the state militia, he was called upon to quell the riots in Baltimore resulting from the failure of the Bank of Maryland, precipitated by Jackson's withdrawal of deposits. As the "savior of the City," he was elected its mayor in 1835 on the resignation of Jesse Hunt. He was reëlected in 1836 and served until 1838, dying the following year in Baltimore. Smith married in 1778 Margaret Spear of Baltimore, by whom he had eight children. His wife's sister, Dorcas, was the wife of William Patterson [*q.v.*] and the mother of Betsy Patterson who married Jerome Bonaparte, and Smith made much of this family connection with Napoleon I. In 1819 a panic in the Baltimore branch of the United States Bank caused the failure of his firm, Smith & Buchanan, and the loss of his personal fortune. Some scandal attached to his partner, but none to Smith, whose public service was uninterrupted.

[*Biog. Dir. Am. Cong.* (1928); *Memoirs of John Quincy Adams,* vols. I, IV–VIII (1874–76); J. F. Essary, *Md. in National Politics* (2nd ed., 1932); *The Life and Correspondence of James McHenry* (1907), ed. by B. C. Steiner; Annie L. Sioussat, *Old Baltimore* (1931); Henry Adams, *Hist. of the U. S. A.* (9 vols., 1889–91); *Niles Weekly Register,* Sept. 10, 24, Oct. 27, 1814; J. T. Scharf, *The Chronicles of Baltimore* (1874); *Sun* (Baltimore), Apr. 23, 1839, Apr. 16, 1911; genealogical table of the Smith family, Wilson Miles Cary MSS. Coll., F62, Md. Hist. Soc.; Smith Papers MSS. Division, Lib. of Cong.; clippings, etc., in private hands.]

M. W. W.

SMITH, SAMUEL FRANCIS (Oct. 21, 1808–Nov. 16, 1895), Baptist clergyman, editor, poet, was born in Boston, Mass., the son of Samuel and Sarah (Bryant) Smith. He graduated from the Eliot School and from the Boston Latin School, receiving at the latter in 1825 both the Franklin medal and a prize medal for a poem. He entered Harvard College in what proved to be one of its most distinguished classes, 1829, its memory prolonged by Oliver Wendell Holmes's poem, "The Boys," in which are the lines:

> "And there's a nice youngster of excellent pith:
> Fate tried to conceal him by naming him Smith."

His studies for the ministry were pursued at Andover Theological Seminary, where he was graduated in 1832.

He had met some of the cost of his education by the translation of articles for the *Encyclopaedia Americana,* edited by Francis Lieber [*q.v.*]. During the latter part of his course in the seminary he was asked by Lowell Mason [*q.v.*] to translate or compose verses for a song book to be used in schools. Among the tunes placed in his hands was one which especially appealed to him. "Being pleased with its simple and easy movement," he later wrote, "I glanced at the German words, and seeing that they were patriotic, instantly felt the impulse to write a patriotic hymn of my own to the same tune. Seizing a scrap of waste paper, I put upon it, within half an hour, the verses substantially as they stand to-day" (*Poems of Home and Country*, 1895, p. xvii). This hymn, beginning "My country, 'tis of thee," was first published in Mason's *The Choir* (1832). As it then appeared it contained five stanzas, the third of which was later discarded. It speedily was popularly adopted as the national hymn, a status never needing the support of political action, but maintained by force of sentiment.

Smith attained fame by this one enduring poem, but his career was otherwise productive and influential. Ordained to the Baptist ministry on Feb. 12, 1834, he had two pastorates at important educational centers. The first of these was at Waterville, Me., 1833–42, where he was also professor of modern languages in Waterville College (now Colby); the second, at Newton Center, Mass., which was his home from January 1842. From 1842 to 1848, in addition to his pastoral work, he edited *The Christian Review*. On Sept. 16, 1834, he married Mary White Smith of Haverhill, a grand-daughter of Dr. Hezekiah Smith [*q.v.*]; six children were born to them, one of whom, Daniel Appleton White Smith, went in 1863 as a missionary to Burma and served for forty years as president of the Karen Baptist Theological Seminary. In 1854 Smith resigned his church at Newton Center and became editorial secretary of the American Baptist Missionary Union.

He wrote much both in verse and prose. While most of the former lacked distinction, it was the outpouring of a simple, wholesome idealism, as is suggested by the title of his collected poetry, *Poems of Home and Country* (1895). "The Morning Light is Breaking" became one of the most widely sung missionary hymns, and his poem, "The Lone Star," 1868, is generally conceded to have saved the Telugu mission at Nellore, India, and a dramatic reference to it in 1925 led, in a crisis, to the strengthening of the Baptist missionary efforts in the Orient. His prose works include *Life of the Rev. Joseph Grafton* (1849); *Missionary Sketches* (1879); *History of Newton, Mass.* (1880); *Rambles in Mission-Fields* (1883), based on a tour of mission fields in Europe and Asia. He also edited, with Baron Stow [*q.v.*], *The Psalmist* (1843), which for more than thirty years was the hymn book most widely used by Baptists. The April before his death, in recognition of his authorship of "America," a great public celebration was held in Boston. A tower and a chime of bells in the First Baptist Church, Newton Center, are a memorial to him.

He died suddenly in a train at the railroad station, Boston, as he was on his way to fill a preaching engagement.

[An autobiog. sketch appears in *Poems of Home and Country,* and another by G. H. W. Whittemore in *America! Our National Hymn* (1879). See also C. M. Fuess, in *Christian Science Monitor,* May 15, 1930; H. S. Burrage, *Baptist Hymn Writers and Their Hymns* (copr. 1888); H. K. Rowe, *Tercentenary Hist. of Newton* (1930); *Boston Transcript,* Nov. 18, 1895. Parents' names have been verified by Smith's granddaughter, Miss Anna Haven Smith, Newton Center, Mass. There are a few miscellaneous papers of Smith's in the Lib. of Cong.]   W. H. A.

SMITH, SAMUEL HARRISON (1772–Nov. 1, 1845), journalist, banker, author, was the son of a Philadelphia merchant, Jonathan Bayard Smith [*q.v.*], and Susannah (Bayard) Smith. He was educated in Philadelphia, graduating at the University of Pennsylvania in 1787, and early in his life became a journalist and author. He gained the recognition of Thomas Jefferson in 1797 by tying for the first prize offered by the American Philosophical Society for the best essay on a system of education and a plan for free public schools (*Remarks on Education,* 1798). In the late summer of 1796, however, he had begun the publication of a Jeffersonian newspaper, the *New World* of Philadelphia, which he published until Aug. 16, 1797. In September 1797 he bought the *Independent Gazetteer* of the elder Joseph Gales [*q.v.*], and three months later, Nov. 16, 1797, began to issue the *Universal Gazette.* Upon the invitation of Jefferson, he followed the government to Washington, D. C., in 1800, where he continued the *Universal Gazette* as a weekly and inaugurated a tri-weekly, the *National Intelligencer and Washington Advertiser,* issuing the first number Oct. 31, 1800. On Sept. 29 of this year he had married his cousin, the brilliant and versatile Margaret Bayard [see Margaret Bayard Smith], daughter of Col. John Bubenheim Bayard [*q.v.*]. They had a son and three daughters.

Smith was thoroughly a party editor, but his calm, sound, judicial temperament kept him from being as vitriolic as some of his Republican partisans desired. The Federalists dubbed the *Intelligencer* the "National Smoothing-Plane," and to some of the Jeffersonians he was known as "Silky-Milky Smith." His admiration for Jefferson, whom he often pronounced the greatest man in America, was unbounded, and he warmly advocated every measure which Jefferson proposed. The *Intelligencer,* being the official organ of the Jefferson administration, published Jefferson's *Manual of Parliamentary Practice* (1801), the executive proclamations, and public notices. It also received half of the congressional printing. Though unwavering in his adherence to Jeffersonian principles, in his personal relations Smith may have been influenced somewhat by his Federalist wife, to whom he was devoted; she never gave up her Federalist friendships. Thus, while Smith admired Calhoun and Madison, their opponent, Henry Clay, was often welcomed into his home. The Smiths often dined with Jefferson and visited him at Monticello. In 1804 Smith bought "Turkey Thicket," a country estate which later became part of the grounds of the Catholic University. This place he named "Sidney." Whether in the country or in town, his home was the rendezvous of statesmen, authors, musicians, politicians, and editors. He set a lavish table, filled his cellar with rare wines, attended an Episcopal church regularly, enjoyed chess and whist, and drove fine horses. He owned slaves, rejoiced in the purchase of Louisiana, opposed nullification, and advocated nationalism. He admired Madison, cared little for Monroe, disliked Adams, and tolerated and feared Jackson. He sympathized with labor and the poor, but feared the result of a government by the masses. Because of ill health, he sold the *Intelligencer,* Aug. 31, 1810, to the younger Joseph Gales [*q.v.*]. In July 1813 he was appointed commissioner of revenue, and in 1828 he was chosen president of the Washington Branch of the United States Bank. He served as a director of the Washington Library, as president of the Bank of Washington nearly a decade, as treasurer of the Washington National Monument Society, and as a public school trustee. He died in Washington and was buried in Rock Creek Cemetery.

[*The First Forty Years of Washington Society* (1906), ed. by Gaillard Hunt, being family letters of Mrs. Samuel Harrison Smith; Josephine Seaton, *Wm. Winston Seaton . . . A Biog. Sketch* (1871); *Daily National Intelligencer,* Nov. 3, 1845; W. B. Bryan, *A Hist. of the National Capital* (2 vols., 1914–16); J. G. B. Bulloch, *A Hist. and Geneal. of the Families of Bayard, Houstoun of Ga. . . .* (1919); C. S. Brigham, "Bibliog. of American Newspapers: Philadelphia," *Proc. Am. Antiquarian Soc.,* n.s. XXXII (1923); Jonathan Bayard and Samuel Harrison Smith Papers and Mrs. Samuel Harrison Smith Papers, MSS. Div., Lib. of Cong.]   W. E. S—h.

SMITH, SAMUEL STANHOPE (Mar. 16, 1750–Aug. 21, 1819), Presbyterian clergyman, college president, was born at Pequea, Lancaster County, Pa., the son of the Rev. Robert and Elizabeth (Blair) Smith; one of his younger brothers was John Blair Smith [*q.v.*]. At the age of six Samuel commenced the study of Latin and Greek at the academy conducted by his father at Pequea and was so well grounded in these essentials that he was admitted when sixteen to the junior class of the College of New Jersey, at Princeton. There mathematics awakened in him

a life-long interest in natural science; there, also, he began to manifest the spirit of free inquiry that characterized ever afterward his intellectual activities. He had become infected "with the fanciful doctrines of bishop Berkeley" and it required the blandishments of a Witherspoon to wean him from the cloudy speculations of immaterialism to the clear light of common sense (*Sermons, post,* I, 7–16).

After graduating in 1769 he assisted his father at the academy for a time, but the following year was recalled to Princeton to teach the classics and to cultivate among the students a taste for belles-lettres. In 1773 he was licensed to preach by the New Castle Presbytery, and, partly because of ill health, he abandoned his books for the missionary field. In the western counties of Virginia, among his own Scotch-Irish people, he supplemented the work of his predecessor, Samuel Davies [*q.v.*], in strengthening the Presbyterian allegiance. So great was his influence that his humble adherents raised the sizable sum of $50,000 to found, in 1776, under his guidance, the Academy of Hampden-Sidney, rechartered in 1783 as the College of Hampden-Sidney. Meanwhile he married Ann, daughter of John Witherspoon [*q.v.*]; nine children were born to them. After serving as president of the Academy in addition to his pastoral work for two or three years, ill health compelled him to turn over the work to his brother John.

In 1779 he returned to the College of New Jersey as teacher of moral philosophy. Here for thirty-three years he labored, first as professor and after 1795 as president. In the absence of President Witherspoon, who was engaged in public affairs, much of the administrative work fell on Smith. The task that confronted him was herculean. Money had to be raised to repair the ravages of the Revolution; in 1802, after Smith had succeeded to the presidency, the work had to be done again, for Nassau Hall was practically destroyed by fire. Suspicion that wanton students were responsible for the damage led to the strengthening of discipline; and while the elders talked of irreligion and false notions of liberty, the students with Gallic fervor charged restraints upon their liberties. In 1807, just after the enrollment had reached 200 students, insubordination broke out. More than half the undergraduates were suspended. Smith never recovered from the strain of those days and from that time on his health waned; in 1812 he resigned. To the intellectual advancement of the college, however, he had contributed much. He raised funds for scientific apparatus and called to the college, in 1795, John Maclean [*q.v.*], the first undergraduate teacher of chemistry and natural science in the United States. For ten years a unique course that combined training in the sciences and the humanities was offered. All such innovations were bitterly opposed, however. Smith himself was subjected to hostile criticism because of his views. His position upon the subject of divine grace was not approved, and he was constrained to discontinue his original lectures upon the evidence of religion and moral philosophy.

He was a popular preacher, compounding "the sound sense and masterly argument of the English preachers," and "the spirit, fire, and vehemence of the French" (*Sermons*, I, 55). Though the three volumes of his sermons were widely read, his *Lectures on the Evidences of the Christian Religion* (1809) and his *Lectures . . . on the Subjects of Moral and Political Philosophy* (2 vols., 1812) have had a lasting influence. These works aided in perpetuating the commonsense realism of Witherspoon, which became so popular and so widely spread as to bear the legitimate claim of being distinctive American philosophy. Smith showed a willingness to liberalize many of the old and more strict data of moral philosophy. Discarding the theory of catastrophe in the affairs of men, he put forth the view, far in advance of that of his time, that "The minutest causes, acting constantly, and long continued, will necessarily create great and conspicuous differences among mankind" (*An Essay on the Causes of the Variety of Complexion and Figure in the Human Species*, 1787, p. 3). In the same essay he flatly contradicted the theory of the separate creation of the different races. Independently of revelation, he arrived at a belief in the genetic unity of mankind, ascribing the existence of racial types to the influences of climate and "the state of society." He gave much thought to the problem of slavery and devised a plan whereby, he believed, freedmen might become economically independent.

[A. J. Morrison, *Coll. of Hampden Sidney Dict. of Biog., 1776–1825* (1921); *Sermons of S. S. Smith* (1821); W. B. Sprague, *Annals Am. Pulpit*, vol. III (1858); John Maclean, *Hist. of the Coll. of N. J.*, vol. II (1877); V. L. Collins, *Princeton* (1914); Gladys Bryson, "Philosophy and Modern Social Sciences," *Social Forces*, Oct. 1932.]   J. E. P.

SMITH, SEBA (Sept. 14, 1792–July 28, 1868), political satirist under the pseudonym of Major Jack Downing, was born in a log cabin in Buckfield, Me., the son of Seba and Aphia (Stevens) Smith, and a descendant of Francis Smith, who emigrated to America in the seventeenth century and settled in Massachusetts. In 1799 his father moved with his family to Bridgton, some thirty-five miles north of Portland, and was for a time post-rider from Portland to Waterford. The toil of pioneer life left the boy Seba little time for book-learning. He worked in a grocery store, in a brick yard, and in a foundry for casting iron, but he managed to learn enough to teach school in Bridgton at eighteen. In 1815 he finally entered Bowdoin College as a sophomore, graduating in 1818 with honors. After teaching for a year in Portland he made a journey as far south as the Carolinas and across the Atlantic from Portland to Liverpool, in all probability working his passage as he went. Upon his return to Maine he assumed the assistant-editorship of the *Eastern Argus,* an important Democratic paper in Portland, and continued his connection with it until 1826. While he was editor of the *Argus,* on Mar. 6, 1823, he married Elizabeth Oakes Prince, a promising young woman of Portland who as Elizabeth Oakes Smith [*q.v.*] was later to win distinction both as a writer and as a lecturer on the lyceum platform.

In the fall of 1829 he launched the *Portland Courier,* a newspaper of his own with no political affiliation, and the first daily to be issued in Maine. This paper was the vehicle for his Downing letters, which first appeared in January 1830, written by a Yankee adventurer who had left his native village of Downingville with cheeses and other country products to trade in Portland. From bargaining Jack Downing turned to politics, wandered into the legislature, and, finding proceedings blocked by party animosities, wrote humorous accounts of the situation to the Downings at home. These letters were reprinted in Boston, and their wider circulation through New England led to a more ambitious program, suggested by two years of the spoils system under Andrew Jackson [*q.v.*]. Smith sent Jack Downing as an office-seeker to Washington, allowed him to become the confidant of the president, and viewed through his eyes the trend of national events, at the same time hinting through covert satire at the dangers threatening this emerging democracy. In the unexpectedness of such a spokesman, a threadbare hero shining in the reflected glory of Old Hickory, there was the welcome element of comedy. This plan resulted in the widespread popularity of the Downing letters and the reprinting of them in local newspapers throughout the Union. The irony of their vogue in the heyday of the new democratic era was obvious, and many spurious Jacks made political use of Seba Smith's device. Smith's freedom from party hostility sets him apart from his only serious rival among his imitators, Charles Augustus

Davis (Tandy, *post,* pp. 32–38 and Wyman, *Two American Pioneers, post,* pp. 70–82), and from such later satirists of the Jackson period as Nathaniel Beverly Tucker in *The Partisan Leader* (1836) and John Pendleton Kennedy [*q.v.*], in *Quodlibet* (1840). The popularity of the Davis letters, however, and the confusion of the public as to their true author hastened Smith's publication of his letters in 1833 as a book entitled *The Life and Writings of Major Jack Downing of Downingville.* His rather mild ridicule of parties, platforms, and national leaders is in distinct contrast to the sharp wit and pointed political application of Davis, who is more often quoted by historians. (See A. B. Hart, *American History Told by Contemporaries,* vol. III, 1901, p. 540.) But the creation of this Yankee critic— a racy figure against a rustic and picturesque New England background, yet shrewd enough to serve as counselor to the president of the United States—must be credited to Seba Smith alone.

Smith was one of the victims of the land boom that began in 1834. After a desperate and unsuccessful attempt in 1839 to retrieve his losses by going to South Carolina, where he hoped to sell cotton planters a machine for cleaning cotton, he returned from Charleston to New York with his wife and their four sons. There his wife joined him in supplying articles for the *Southern Literary Messenger* and other periodicals of the day. By 1843, however, he had resumed his rôle as editor, having connections first with the *Rover,* a weekly magazine of some dignity, 1843–45, and later for a long period of time, though intermittently, 1854–59, with Emerson's *United States Magazine.* In 1859 he established a monthly, the *Great Republic,* which lasted only a year. Of his published books, which ranged from a metrical romance, *Powhatan* (1841), to an original dissertation on geometry, *New Elements of Geometry* (1850), the one most widely circulated was a collection of quaint tales on Yankee customs and characters called *'Way Down East* (1854). In 1847 he had begun his second series of Downing letters, which were published in the *Daily National Intelligencer,* and in 1859 these appeared in book form with the best of the earlier letters under the title *My Thirty Years Out of the Senate,* a parody on Thomas Hart Benton's *Thirty Years' View* (1854–56). In 1860 Smith retired from active life to spend his last years in Patchogue, Long Island. In disposition shy and retiring, he was essentially conservative, regarding with apprehension extreme measures which might endanger the solidarity of the Union. He will be remembered as a political satirist who set a new pattern for American humor, and who led the way for a host of homely philosophers and critics from Sam Slick and Hosea Biglow to Mr. Dooley and Will Rogers.

[The date of death is from a manuscript note by Elizabeth Oakes Smith in the Colls. of the Me. Hist. Soc., Portland, Me. Smith's autobiog. in MS. is in the Bowdoin Coll. Lib., Brunswick, Me.; that of Elizabeth Oakes Smith is in the manuscript dept. of the N. Y. Pub. Lib., N. Y. City. See *Hist. of Bowdoin Coll. with Biog. Sketches of its Grads.* (1882), A. S. Packard, ed.; Mary A. Wyman, *Selections from the Autobiog. of Elizabeth Oakes Smith* (1924) and *Two Am. Pioneers, Seba Smith and Elizabeth Oakes Smith* (1927); W. P. Trent, *A Hist. of Am. Lit., 1607–1865* (1903); Jennette R. Tandy, *Crackerbox Philosophers in Am. Humor and Satire* (1925); Constance Rourke, *Am. Humor, A Study of Nat. Character* (1931); H. L. Koopman, in *Pine Tree Mag.* (Portland, Me.), Nov. 1906; death notice in *N. Y. Tribune,* July 31, 1868.]

M. A. W.

SMITH, SOLOMON FRANKLIN (Apr. 20, 1801–Feb. 14, 1869), comedian, theatre manager, generally known as Sol Smith, was born, the eighth of the eleven sons of Levi and Hannah (Holland) Smith, in Norwich, N. Y., but spent most of his early years in a log house in Solon, Cortland County, N. Y. His father, who had been a piper in a volunteer company in the Revolutionary War, at Solon was a goldsmith (Smith, *post,* p. 1). Such education as Smith obtained, except for three quarters of regular schooling, he owed to his mother. At the age of eight he was sent to work on a farm a few miles away. After staying there four years he made his way to Boston; there he worked in a store owned by one of his brothers, and in the fall of 1814 accompanied his brothers to Albany. It was then that his predilection for the stage manifested itself. He devoted his leisure hours to reading Shakespeare and many of his evenings to surreptitious visits to the theatre of John Bernard [*q.v.*], where he made the acquaintance of the actors, among them the later celebrated family of Samuel Drake [*q.v.*]. Having decided after frequent experiments that nature intended him for an actor, in 1817 he ran away and sought to join the company when it left Albany, but was compelled to return home disappointed. A year later his brothers decided to move to Cincinnati. When he failed to keep an appointed meeting with one of them, he floated alone down the river to Pittsburgh, whence he worked his way to Ohio. There he remained for a time, but he was too restless for a sedentary life, and the next three or four years he spent roaming about from town to town in Ohio, Indiana, and Kentucky, usually in pursuit of his friends the Drakes. For a time he served as a printer's apprentice in Kentucky and later as foreman of the *Western Sun and General Advertiser,* Vincennes, Ind. He joined an occasional Thespian society, acted with the Drakes, performed the duties of prompter in the Collins and Jones company in Cincinnati, and studied law. In 1822 he married Martha Therese Mathews, an amateur singer, daughter of Edwin Mathews, and in the same year started in Cincinnati the *Independent Press and Freedom's Advocate,* one of the first Ohio papers to support Andrew Jackson [*q.v.*]. But he soon tired of journalistic work, sold the paper, and, buying out Collins and Jones, embarked in 1823 on his managerial career.

During the next twelve years he traveled about the country, picking up a living as best he could, chiefly with itinerant theatrical troupes, some of which he managed. In 1827 he and his wife joined the company of James H. Caldwell of New Orleans, La., and with it made their first visit to St. Louis, Mo. After a "gagging tour" of the southern states Smith rejoined Caldwell in 1831 to play in the Mississippi river towns under the management of Noah Miller Ludlow [*q.v.*]. With four more years of independent trouping in the southeastern states, where he was by this time well known, he attained the dignity of a star, and in 1835 played engagements with Ludlow in St. Louis and at the Park Theatre in New York under Edmund Shaw Simpson [*q.v.*] and the Walnut Street Theatre in Philadelphia under Francis Courtney Wemyss. In the fall of 1835 he joined Ludlow in Mobile, Ala., and became junior partner in the firm of Ludlow & Smith, which developed rapidly into one of the most important in the West, if not in the country. For sixteen years it dominated the St. Louis stage, and in that city built the first real theatre west of the Mississippi, with scenery by John Rowson Smith [*q.v.*], the artist. It also controlled Mobile until 1840, when, having lost two theatres by fire and being threatened with the rivalry of Caldwell, the partners abandoned the town to him, but in turn invaded his home territory, New Orleans. A bitter war ensued, but in 1842 with the erection of the New St. Charles Theatre they finally drove their rival out of business. By 1851 Smith gave up the St. Louis Theatre; two years later the firm of Ludlow & Smith was dissolved. Settling in St. Louis he devoted himself to the law, which for some years he had practised occasionally, and in 1861 he was elected to the state convention which kept Missouri from secession. He died suddenly in 1869 after a paralytic stroke. He was survived by his second wife, Elizabeth Pugsley, whom he had married in 1839 after the death of his first wife, and seven sons, two of whom, Marcus [*q.v.*] and Sol, Jr., became actors. On the stage his forte

was low comedy, but one of his favorite rôles was that of Mawworm in Isaac Bickerstaffe's *The Hypocrite.* As an actor he was extremely popular, especially in the West. He was a man of the most upright character and occupied an honored place both on the stage and in the community. In his life-time he published three autobiographical works, *The Theatrical Apprenticeship* (1846), *The Theatrical Journey-Work* (1854), and *Theatrical Management in the West and South* (1868), a combination of the first two.

[The best source of information concerning Smith's life is his *Theatrical Management in the West and South* (1868), which is on the whole reliable, though dates are sometimes hard to determine. See also T. A. Brown, *Hist of the Am. Stage* (1870); G. C. D. Odell, *Annals of the N. Y. Stage,* vol. IV (1928); N. M. Ludlow, *Dramatic Life As I Found It* (1880), which is characterized by a hostile bias; and *N. Y. Times,* Feb. 16, 18, 24, 1869. Many letters, diaries, and other records are part of the estate of Smith's grandson, the late Sheridan S. Smith, Webster Groves, Mo.; a number of old programs and other papers are in the estate of Smith's daughter-in-law, the late Mrs. Thaddeus S. Smith, St. Louis, Mo.]   W. G. B. C.

SMITH, SOPHIA (Aug. 27, 1796–June 12, 1870), founder of Smith College, fourth of the seven children of Joseph and Lois (White) Smith, was born in Hatfield, Mass., a descendant of Samuel Smith who emigrated from England in 1634, and a niece of Oliver Smith [*q.v.*]. Her family was substantial, though not conspicuous except for excessive thrift. Sophia showed little of the initiative characteristic of the Smiths; her younger sister Harriet took charge of the household after their mother's death and directed activities for the shy and retiring Sophia. Harriet's death in 1859 left Sophia bereft indeed, but she leaned on her eldest brother Austin, whose parsimony and success in speculation enabled him to amass a fortune to which, on his sudden death in 1861, Sophia fell sole heir. Now sixty-five years old, diffident, deaf, she felt an overwhelming burden of loneliness and responsibility. Accustomed always to depend on others, she laid her problems before her young pastor, John Morton Greene. Hoping to give her introspective nature opportunity for expression, he advised her to keep a journal, the source now of what is known of her inner life. It reveals an anxious and suspicious spirit, battling with afflictions, bewailing her sins, praying for self-improvement and for greater perfection of character.

"This is no tale of a stout-hearted, single-minded woman, fired by great ambition, evolving a great ideal" (Hanscom and Greene, *post,* p. 10). The founding of Smith College is rather the tale of the conscientious young minister of the town Congregational Church, the loyal friend and far-sighted adviser to whom the perplexed woman turned. His was the vision, with which, through long years of thoughtful planning and consultation with educational authorities, he was to kindle the imagination of his parishioner. Unable to interest her in his own college, Amherst, or in Mount Holyoke Seminary, founded by Sophia Smith's distant cousin, Mary Lyon [*q.v.*], Greene proposed an academy and woman's college, or a deaf-mute institution. In 1862 she made a will omitting the woman's college but providing for a library, an academy, and an institution for the deaf at Hatfield. The foundation of the Clarke School for the Deaf in Northampton anticipated the latter provision, and Greene again (1868) urged her to endow a woman's college. At her request, he prepared a "Plan for a Woman's College," which was embodied in a new will providing for a college "with the design to furnish for my own sex means & facilities for education equal to those which are afforded now in our Colleges to young men" (*Ibid.,* p. 61). The location of the college, originally planned for Hatfield, was changed in her fifth and final will in 1870 to Northampton. The bequest amounted to nearly half a million dollars by 1875, when the college was opened.

Sophia Smith's own education had been elementary, though she indulged a taste for reading, especially after she became deaf. She lived a quiet life enlivened by occasional trips to watering places and once to Washington, and by visits to and from friends. One of the few luxuries she allowed herself was the building of a fashionable but ugly mansard-roofed mansion, in which she spent her last three years.

[MSS. assembled by John M. Greene in Lib. of Smith College; Sophia Smith's journ., Greene's journ., and manuscript narrative in possession of Helen French Greene; E. D. Hanscom and H. F. Greene, *Sophia Smith and the Beginnings of Smith College* (1925); *Addresses at the Inauguration of Rev. L. Clark Seelye as President of Smith College* (1875); *The Centennial of the Birth of Sophia Smith* (1896); *Celebration of the Quarter-Centenary of Smith College* (1900); G. B. Stebbins, "The Home of Sophia and Oliver Smith," *New England Mag.,* Oct. 1898.]   E. W. F.

SMITH, STEPHEN (Feb. 19, 1823–Aug. 26, 1922), surgeon and pioneer in public health, was born on a farm near Skaneateles, Onondaga County, N. Y., the son of Chloe (Benson) and Lewis Smith, and a descendant of John Smith, of Oxfordshire, England, who settled in Milford, Conn., in the seventeenth century. Stephen, a delicate child, was forced to undergo long hours of arduous toil on the farm. With his brother, Job Lewis Smith [*q.v.*], he attended the village school and later the academy at Homer in Cortland County. He then took his first course of

lectures in the Geneva Medical College, his second course at the Buffalo Medical College, and later established residence as a medical student in the hospital of the Sisters of Charity in Buffalo, N. Y. In 1850 he went to New York City to study at the College of Physicians and Surgeons where he was graduated with the M.D. degree in 1851. He was selected from ten other candidates to be interne at Bellevue Hospital in New York. While there, he wrote his first medical paper, "A Contribution to the Statistics of Rupture of the Urinary Bladder," for the *New York Journal of Medicine,* May 1851. This made such a reputation for him that he was elected to the surgical society of Paris and in 1853 was made joint editor, and later editor, of the periodical in which his paper was published. He remained a member of the surgical staff at Bellevue until 1911.

It is impossible to list his numerous offices or his many notable achievements. He was a conservative surgeon but not afraid of progress. One of his early operations was the second Syme's amputation of the foot ever done in the United States. A great advance in modern conservative surgery was effected by his amputation at the knee-joint. His *Hand-book of Surgical Operations,* published in 1862, was invaluable to Civil War surgeons, and his *Manual of the Principles and Practice of Operative Surgery* (1879, revised in 1887) was used as a standard textbook. Well known as a teacher and surgeon, his name will be remembered first of all for his efforts in promoting legislation for public health. His work in making New York City a safe and sanitary place in which to live was of incalculable value. He prepared the draft of a public health bill passed in 1866 as the Metropolitan Health Law, which became the basis of civic sanitation in the United States; he was commissioner of the new Board of Health, 1868–75; in 1868, through his efforts, the Bureau of Vaccination was formed; he helped to organize the American Public Health Association, 1871, of which he was the first president; he was instrumental in founding training schools for nurses; he drafted bills for a national board of health and a state board of health in 1878 and 1880; he was state commissioner in lunacy, 1882–88; he drafted the original bill for the State Care Act, passed in 1890; he was sent by President Cleveland as one of the three delegates to the ninth International Sanitary Conference in Paris in 1894; and he contributed active support to the passage of the bill giving the State Board of Charities authority for licensing and supervising dispensaries in 1899. He assisted in planning the

Roosevelt Hospital, New York City, and the Johns Hopkins Hospital, Baltimore, Md. He was one of the first to propose organization of the Bellevue Hospital Medical College where he taught both anatomy and surgery, and he had the distinction of being the first to introduce Lister aseptic treatment of wounds into Bellevue Hospital.

Although the later years of his life were not spent in such active service, he was vice-president of the State Board of Charities from 1903 to 1913, and was a faithful and influential member of the Board until 1918. He was president of the thirteenth New York State Conference of Charities and Corrections in 1912. From 1918 until his death he lived in quiet retirement, occasionally giving public lectures. In the spare moments of his busy life, Smith found time to contribute numerous articles to medical literature. Among these should be mentioned the monographs, "The Evolution of American Surgery," in J. D. Bryant and A. H. Buck's *American Practice of Surgery* (8 vols., 1906–11), and his "History of Surgery," in T. L. Stedman's *A Reference Handbook of the Medical Sciences* (3rd edition, 8 vols., 1913–17). A vivid description of some of Smith's public health work may be found in his *The City that Was* (1911), and in *Who is Insane* (1916). For thirty years he was the New York correspondent of the London *Lancet*. The splendid care he took of his delicate constitution in youth helped to preserve him until he reached nearly the century mark. To the end his intellect remained unclouded and his memory bright. He held himself erect and square-shouldered, never seeming to lose the vitality and energy of his youth. A keen, disciplined mind and a genial sense of humor won him the esteem and admiration of his contemporaries. A painting of him hangs in the New York Academy of Medicine. He was married to Lucy E. Culver of Brooklyn, N. Y., on June 1, 1858. They had nine children, six daughters and three sons. Smith died at the home of his daughter at Montour Falls, N. Y., after a short illness.

[*Who's Who in America*, 1920–21, 1922–23; F. L. Colver, *Colver-Culver Geneal.* (1910); John Shrady, ed., *The Coll. of Physicians and Surgeons, New York* (1903–04, vol. I); F. H. Garrison, "Dr. Stephen Smith," *Annals of Med. Hist.*, Autumn Number, 1917; J. J. Walsh, *Hist. of Med. in N. Y.* (1919), vol. V; "Stephen Smith," *State Service*, June 1918; S. W. Francis, *Biog. Sketches of Distinguished N. Y. Surgeons* (1866); *Stephen Smith, M.D., Addresses in Recognition of his Public Services* (1911); *Dinner in honour of Dr. Stephen Smith* (1911); *N. Y. Times*, Aug. 27, 1922.]
G. L. A.

SMITH, THEODATE LOUISE (Apr. 9, 1859–Feb. 16, 1914), genetic psychologist, was born at Hallowell, Me., the daughter of Thomas and Philomela (Hall) Smith. She received the degrees of B.A., 1882, and M.A., 1884, at Smith College, and the degree of Ph.D. at Yale University, 1896. Before taking her degree at Yale she taught in Gardiner, Me., 1882–84; Brooklyn Heights (N. Y.) Seminary, 1884–86; and Mount Vernon Seminary, Washington, D. C., 1886–89. In 1895–96 she was a student at Clark University. Her special work as a student of child psychology she did at Clark, where she was research assistant to Granville Stanley Hall [q.v.] from 1902 to 1909, and lecturer and librarian at the Children's Institute from 1909 to the time of her death. She not only assisted Hall in his pioneer studies in genetic psychology but gave aid to many graduate students. As librarian she brought together a vast number of pamphlets and other publications on child welfare, one of the largest collections of its kind in the world, and made them available to teachers and others. She also did a large amount of independent work, wrote articles for such magazines as the *Pedagogical Seminary* and the *American Journal of Psychology* ("On Muscular Memory," July 1896; "The Psychology of Day Dreams," October 1904; "Note on the Psychology of Shame," April 1915), and collaborated with Hall in his *Aspects of Child Life* (1907).

Her most noteworthy contribution was her interpretation of Dr. Maria Montessori's psychology and methods of child-training, which she studied in Rome. In *The Montessori System in Theory and Practice; An Introduction to the Pedagogic Methods of Mme. Montessori* (1912) she explained Mme. Montessori's practical methods of will-training and called attention to her indebtedness to Edouard Seguin [q.v.], the great master in the training of the feebleminded. Doing her work in the scientific study of children at a time when rash practical applications based on unverified inferences were likely to be made, she not only took a sane view of the results in this new subject but applied them with caution, common sense, and an appreciation of their wider relationships. Of her Dr. Hall wrote, "As a scholar, thoroughgoing and widely read; as a psychologist and student of childhood, sane and conservative; as a teacher, clear and straightforward; as a colleague, modest, helpful and generous; one did not always realize the scope of her accomplishments on account of the fact that her training was so well balanced" (*Pedagogical Seminary, post,* p. 160).

[*Pedagogical Seminary*, Mar. 1914; *Smith Alumnae Quart.*, Apr. 1914; tribute by G. Stanley Hall, in *Scientific Papers of Theodate L. Smith* (1906–14), vol. II, Clark Univ. Lib.; *Obit. Record Grads. Yale Univ.*

(1914); obituary in *Boston Transcript,* Feb. 16, 1914; date of birth supplied by the registrar of Smith Coll.]

W. H. B.

SMITH, TRUMAN (Nov. 27, 1791–May 3, 1884), lawyer, congressman, was born at Roxbury, Conn., the eldest child of Phineas and Deborah Ann (Judson) Smith and a descendant of John Smith who was in Lancaster, Mass., as early as 1653. Two of his uncles, Nathan and Nathaniel Smith [qq.v.], were lawyers and members of Congress, and it is reasonable to suppose that their careers determined the direction of his ambitions. He was reared on his father's farm and completed his preparation for college under the Rev. Daniel Parker. In 1815 he was graduated from Yale. After studying at the Litchfield Law School he was admitted to practice in 1818 and gradually won his way to the front rank of the unusually able Litchfield bar.

A habit of cultivating the friendship of all classes laid the foundation of his political career. After an apprenticeship in the state legislature, 1831–32 and 1834, he was elected to the federal House of Representatives in 1838 and served until 1843, and from 1845 to 1849. He was a presidential elector on the Whig ticket in 1844. In the House he was chiefly interested in parliamentary management in behalf of the Whig party, in which activity he was conspicuously successful. He was one of the first of the party leaders to promote the presidential candidacy of Taylor in 1848, and, as the first chairman of the Whig national committee, he directed Taylor's campaign. He declined to accept the reward of appointment as secretary of the interior, preferring to take the seat in the Senate to which he had been elected in 1849.

In accordance with good Whig doctrine he obtained a land grant to assist in the construction of the Sault Sainte Marie canal, and urged the construction of a Pacific railroad "by the central route if possible." In the absorbing controversy over slavery he refused to become a leader either of the "Cotton Whigs" or of the active free-soil men. The sectional question, in his opinion, was "an offensive cesspool." It should be settled, he thought, on the basis of the climate and topography of the regions into which it was proposed to extend slavery. On most yea and nay votes he followed the predominant views of his own section. He vigorously opposed bills to grant $100,000 to Dr. W. T. G. Morton [q.v.] for having introduced anaesthesia in surgical operations, and in 1853 published *An Examination of the Question of Anaesthesia* (reprinted in later editions under various titles), in which he sought to prove that credit for prior discovery

and application belonged to Dr. Horace Wells [q.v.] of Hartford. His speeches were straightforward presentations of facts, with sensible estimates of the effects of pending measures. He was at his best in informal colloquies.

On May 24, 1854, he resigned his seat for financial reasons and opened a law office in New York, commuting from Stamford, Conn. He appeared in a number of important cases, but resumed practice too late in life to attain the same relative rank as in his earlier professional career. In July 1862 President Lincoln appointed him a judge of the mixed court set up by the treaty with England of Apr. 7, 1862, for the trial of British and American vessels suspected of engaging in the slave trade. He served until the court was terminated in 1870. In the fall of 1872 he retired from active practice. He was twice married: first, June 2, 1832, to Maria Cook of Litchfield; she died in April 1849, and on Nov. 7, 1850, he married Mary A. Dickinson. By his first marriage he had a son and two daughters, and by his second, six sons; one of his daughters became the second wife of Orville H. Platt [q.v.].

[*Biog. Dir. Am. Cong.* (1928); W. R. Cutter and others, *Geneal. and Family Hist. of the State of Conn.* (1911), vol. II; William Cothren, *Hist. of Ancient Woodbury,* vol. I (1854); F. B. Dexter, *Biog. Sketches Grads. Yale Coll.,* vol. VI (1912); E. W. Leavenworth, *A Geneal. of the Leavenworth Family* (1873); D. C. Kilbourn, *The Bench and Bar of Litchfield County, Conn.* (1909); some MSS. in Lib. of Cong.]

E. C. S.

SMITH, URIAH (May 2, 1832–Mar. 6, 1903), religious leader, editor, was born in West Wilton, N. H., the son of Samuel and Rebekah (Spaulding) Smith, and the great-grandson of Uriah Smith, who was in Wilton as early as 1778. Samuel was a highway builder and contractor. As a youth of twelve, Uriah came into contact with William Miller [q.v.] and his followers, who expected Christ's return to earth on Oct. 22, 1844, and the religious excitement of those days made a profound impression on him. His mother embraced the views taught by the Adventists and continually strove to guide her children into a deep Christian experience. In early boyhood Uriah contracted a sickness resulting in a "fever sore" on his left leg above the knee, which, when he was fourteen, necessitated amputation of the leg. He studied at the academy at Hancock, N. H. (1846–47) and at Phillips Academy, Exeter (1848–51). Because of financial reverses which his father experienced, he was forced to relinquish his plan for a college education.

In the meantime his sister Annie had begun work in the office of the *Advent Review and Sabbath Herald,* a struggling little weekly, then being published at Saratoga, N. Y. In 1852 it was moved to Rochester and the following year Uriah also entered its employ. For their services they received only their board, room, and clothes. In 1855 the paper was again moved, this time to Battle Creek, Mich., and Smith became editor. With one slight interruption he continued in charge of it until 1898, and his editorial connection was not broken until his death. Under his direction it developed into a healthy church organ representing a growing constituency which numbered at his death over a hundred thousand. On June 7, 1857, he married Harriet Newell Stevens, an assistant in his office.

In addition to his editorial work, Smith played an important rôle in the organization of the Seventh-Day Adventist denomination. He was one of those who advocated the establishment of a General Conference, and upon its organization in 1863 he was made secretary. This important office he also filled on four subsequent occasions, serving twenty years in all. In 1874 he was ordained to the ministry and labored much in camp meetings and conferences from the Atlantic to the Pacific. Upon the establishment of Battle Creek College that same year he became lecturer on the Bible there. In 1877, in connection with editorial attention he was giving to *The Signs of the Times,* a newly founded Adventist paper on the Pacific coast, he established a Biblical Institute at Oakland, Cal., for the training of young ministers. As a General Conference official and editor of the church organ, he had a prominent part in the founding of the well-known Battle Creek Sanitarium.

Although his days were filled with various duties, he found time between nine in the evenings and midnight to write books. His most important work, perhaps, was *Thoughts Critical and Practical on the Book of Daniel and the Revelation* (1873), expanded and reprinted in 1882, and issued in subsequent editions. Another of his widely read works was *The Marvel of Nations* (1887), a history of the United States as an Adventist phenomenon. Among his other publications were *The Testimony of the Bible on the State of the Dead* (1873); *Modern Spiritualism* (1896); and *Here and Hereafter* (1897). Some of his poems appear along with his sister's in the volume published by their mother, *Poems: With a Sketch of the Life and Experiences of Annie R. Smith* (1871).

By trade Smith was a wood engraver. He had a mechanical turn of mind which enabled him to make some practical inventions. Since his cork leg caused him considerable difficulty in kneeling in prayer, he constructed an improved wooden

leg with movable foot. For this he received a patent (No. 39,361), July 28, 1863, and with the income he derived from the invention he bought a house. Later he invented a school desk with folding seat. In 1894, in the interests of his paper he visited Europe and the Near East. While in Syria he contracted a fever from the effects of which he never fully recovered. He died at Battle Creek, survived by his wife and five children.

[A. A. Livermore and Samuel Putnam, *Hist. of the Town of Wilton . . . N. H.* (1888); Harold Lincoln, "Uriah Smith," MS. in Union Coll. Lib., Lincoln, Nebr.; J. N. Loughborough, *Rise and Progress of the Seventh-Day Adventists* (1892); M. E. Olsen, *A Hist. of the Origin and Progress of Seventh-Day Adventists* (copr. 1925); *Advent Rev. and Sabbath Herald* files, 1851–1903; *Mich. Pioneer Colls.,* II (1880), 214–15, III (1881), 353, 363; *Detroit Free Press,* and *Detroit Tribune,* Mar. 7, 1903.]   E. N. D.

SMITH, WALTER INGLEWOOD (July 10, 1862–Jan. 27, 1922), congressman, jurist, was born in Council Bluffs, Iowa, the son of George Francis Smith, a building contractor, and Sarah Henrietta (Forrest). Having graduated from high school at the age of fifteen, he entered Park College, Parkville, Mo., but soon had to leave because of illness. During the following year he taught a country school and then began the study of law in the office of D. B. Dailey at Council Bluffs. Admitted to the bar in December 1882, before he was of legal age, he at once became a partner of his tutor. On July 10, 1890, he married Effie M. Moon, by whom he had four children. By November of the same year he had achieved sufficient professional distinction to be elected judge in the fifteenth judicial district of Iowa, to which office he was twice reëlected.

On Sept. 1, 1900, he resigned to accept the Republican nomination for the office of representative from the ninth congressional district, a position left vacant by the appointment of Smith McPherson [*q.v.*] to a federal judgeship. He won the seat for the unexpired term and was reëlected for the regular term by decisive majorities. Beginning his congressional career on Dec. 3, 1900, he served continuously until Mar. 15, 1911. Although he was on several special committees, including one to investigate the practice of hazing at West Point, he concentrated his attention mainly upon the work of the appropriations committee, of which he became a member in the Fifty-eighth Congress. For a number of years his chief activity was in connection with the fortifications appropriation bill. During his last term, as a member of the reorganized rules committee, he had a prominent part in the "revolution" of 1910. Even in his first term, Smith was acknowledged to be one of the ablest members of the Iowa delegation which had "a national reputation for strong men" (*Register and Leader,* Des Moines, July 24, 1902). He was not widely known at home, however. In the bitterly factional Republican state convention of 1901, though at first howled down, he later made such a sensible, good-humored speech that he won general admiration (*Dubuque Daily Times,* Aug. 8, 1901). The next year he was made temporary chairman and accomplished the difficult task of stating a tariff policy that was acceptable to both the conservatives and progressives (*Register and Leader,* Des Moines, July 31, 1902).

The elevation of Willis Van Devanter to the United States Supreme Court in December 1910, created a vacancy on the bench of the circuit court of appeals in the eighth circuit. Most of the Iowa congressional delegation signed a petition indorsing Smith for the position. Meanwhile, the Iowa legislature was deadlocked in the choice of a successor to J. P. Dolliver [*q.v.*] in the United States Senate, and Smith was mentioned for that office if insurgent opposition to his judicial appointment should develop (*Washington Post,* Jan. 18, 23, 1911). President Taft, however, was known to consider him qualified for the highest judicial position (*Shenandoah World,* Iowa, Jan. 28, 1922), and his appointment was confirmed on Jan. 31, 1911. His work on the federal bench was characterized by the same legal ability, honest judgment, and common sense that he exhibited throughout his public career. Though he rarely dissented, he wrote his share of the opinions of the court. Probably one of the most significant was his closely reasoned distinction between civil and criminal contempt of court (*Merchants' Stock and Grain Company* vs. *Chicago Board of Trade,* 201 *Federal Reporter,* 20). With the decision which held the Iowa sterilization act unconstitutional as applied to criminals he concurred, not because cruel and unusual punishment would be inflicted, but on the more technical ground of denial of due process (*Davis* vs. *Berry,* 216 *Federal Reporter,* 413). Since he dealt almost exclusively with appeals, it was natural that his judgments should be legalistic. Smith died at Council Bluffs of apoplexy, after a lingering illness.

[*Congressional Record,* 1900–11; *Federal Reporter,* 1911–22; H. H. Field, and J. R. Reed, *Hist. of Pottawattamie County, Iowa* (1907), I, 258, 259; *Proc.... Iowa State Bar Asso.,* 1922; Johnson Brigham, *Iowa: Its Hist. and Its Foremost Citizens* (1915), vol. II; *Who's Who in America,* 1920–21; *Biog. Dir. Am. Cong.* (1928); *Des Moines Capital,* Feb. 1, 1922; *Dubuque Times-Journal,* Jan. 27, 1922.]   J. E. B.

SMITH, WILLIAM (Oct. 8, 1697–Nov. 22. 1769), jurist, was born at Newport-Pagnell, Buckinghamshire, England, the eldest son of Thomas and Susanna (Odell) Smith. His father, a tallow chandler, brought his family to New York in 1715, and shortly afterward William entered Yale College. He was graduated in 1719 and received the master's degree three years later, distinguishing himself as a scholar in Hebrew, classical languages, and theology. From October 1722 to April 1724 he served as a tutor at Yale.

Though admitted to the bar in 1724, Smith soon supplemented his colonial legal training by attendance at the Inns of Court, being admitted to Gray's Inn in 1727. On his return to America, he established a lucrative practice in New York City and attained considerable eminence at the bar, identifying himself throughout his career with the radical Presbyterian faction in provincial litigation and politics. The most noted cases with which he was associated were those in which he sought to curb the governor's prerogative. In 1733, in conjunction with James Alexander [*q.v.*], he was retained by Rip Van Dam [*q.v.*] to defend the action for a division of the emoluments of office brought by Gov. William Cosby [*q.v.*] before the judges of the supreme court sitting on the equity side of the exchequer. Smith at once proceeded to attack the legality of the court, and was sustained by Chief Justice Lewis Morris [*q.v.*], Justices James De Lancey [*q.v.*] and Philipse dissenting. Action was blocked; no decision on Cosby's claim was reached, but the efforts of the opposition to get rid of the court of exchequer continued unabated. On the strength of petitions from Queens and Westchester counties that courts might be established only by statute, William Smith and Joseph Murray, an eminent legal contemporary, were called before the Assembly in 1734 to argue the question of the legality of that court as established by the prerogative. Smith's learned plea (*Mr. Smith's Opinion Humbly Offered in General Assembly of the Colony of New York,* 1734) that both English and colonial courts rested upon statutory authority seems, at least on the colonial side, the more convincing, although Sir John Randolph, who agreed with Smith, was quick to point out that both parties had fallen into a common error in regard to the extension of British statutes to the plantations (William Smith, *History of New York,* 1829, I, 314–15, note).

In the feud between the Cosby and Morris factions, Smith was one of the stalwarts of the latter group and was associated with the founding of Peter Zenger's opposition paper, the *New York Weekly Journal*. It was thus only natural that in 1735 Smith, joined with Alexander, should appear in the supreme court to defend Zenger in his trial for seditious libel. Both attorneys at once attacked the validity of the appointment of De Lancey and Philipse as judges on the ground that their commissions were granted during pleasure and contrary to legal precedent. For this they were disbarred (Livingston Rutherfurd, *John Peter Zenger*, 1904, pp. 173–90) ; but they countered with a petition to the Assembly stating their grievances, which they followed up by personal pleas before the committee of the Assembly. Two years later the decree against them was set aside by the court and they were readmitted to practice.

Smith continued his fight against the prerogative party, and, in 1737, in the election dispute between Garret Van Horne and Adolph Philipse, challenged the latter's seating on the ground that Jews had been permitted to vote for him, whereas, he claimed, history and theology denied them the franchise. Although unsuccessful in preventing the seating of Philipse, his argument was followed by a resolution of the Assembly that the Jews "ought not to be admitted to vote for representatives in this colony" (*Journal of the General Assembly*, 1764, I, 712; Smith, *History*, 1829, II, 38–40).

Smith was associated as counsel in many of the leading cases in the mayor's court of New York City, frequently acted as proctor in admiralty, and practised extensively in neighboring colonies, serving in 1743–44 as counsel for Connecticut in a case against the Mohegan Indians (*Documents, post*, VI, 258). He was appointed attorney-general in 1751 and served one year, but was not confirmed by the royal authorities (*Ibid.*, VI, 737, 766). He was a member of the Provincial Council from 1753 to 1767, and as such attended the Albany Congress in 1754, being one of the members of the committee that formulated the plan of union, which he strongly advocated (*Ibid.*, 853, 860). In this same year he served as commissioner in the boundary controversy between New York and Massachusetts. He declined the office of chief justice of New York in 1760, but became an associate justice of the supreme court in 1763, and held office until his death. In this capacity, in the case of *Cunningham* vs. *Forsey* (1764), he stoutly denied the right of appeal in questions of fact, taking the popular position, bitterly opposed by Colden, but subsequently affirmed on appeal (*Ibid.*, VII, 685; *Acts of the Privy Council of England, Colonial Series*, IV, 1911, p. 740).

One of the few college-trained members of the early New York bar, Smith took a leading rôle in behalf of public education. He was associated with the founding of the first public school in New York in 1732, was one of the incorporators of the College of New Jersey, is believed to have been largely responsible for the phraseology of its first two charters (John Maclean, *History of the College of New Jersey*, 1877, I, 87), and was a founder and trustee of the New York Society Library (A. B. Keep, *The Library in Colonial New York*, 1909, p. 163). Foremost among the proponents of a non-sectarian college in New York, Smith vigorously protested against the establishment of King's College under Episcopalian auspices (Herbert and Carol Schneider, *Samuel Johnson . . . His Career and Writings*, 1929, IV, 208–12).

Smith was twice married: first, May 11, 1727, to Mary, daughter of René and Blanche (Du Bois) Het, by whom he had fifteen children, including William, 1728–1793 [*q.v.*], and Joshua Hett, whose career became tangled in the skein of Benedict Arnold's treason; and secondly to Elizabeth (Scott) Williams, widow of the Rev. Elisha Williams [*q.v.*], fourth rector of Yale College, and daughter of the Rev. Thomas Scott of Nithern, Herefordshire, England. By this second marriage there was no issue.

[Printed materials include *The New-York Gazette, or the Weekly Post-Boy*, Nov. 27, 1769; M. L. Delafield, "William Smith," *Mag. of Am. Hist.*, Apr., June 1881 ; E. A. Jones, *Am. Members of the Inns of Court* (1924) ; F. B. Dexter, *Biog. Sketches Grads. Yale Coll.*, vol. I (1885) ; *N. Y. Geneal. and Biog. Record*, Apr. 1873, Jan. 1879, July 1880 ; E. B. O'Callaghan, *Docs. Rel. to the Col. Hist. of the State of N. Y.*, vols. VI–VII (1855) ; I. N. P. Stokes, *The Iconography of Manhattan Island*, vol. IV (1922). Smith's pleadings in the Mayor's Court are available in the court files in the office of the Commissioner of Records, New York City.]
R. B. M.

SMITH, WILLIAM (Sept. 7, 1727–May 14, 1803), educator, clergyman, first provost of the College, Academy, and Charitable School of Philadelphia, was born in Aberdeen, Scotland, the son of Thomas Smith, a gentleman of means, and Elizabeth (Duncan) Smith. After attending the parish school he was taken in charge by the Society for the Education of Parochial Schoolmasters and educated under its care until 1741, when he entered the University of Aberdeen, from which he graduated A.M. in 1747. The next few years he seems to have spent in London as agent of the Society that had sponsored him, and also, for a time, as agent of the Society for the Propagation of the Gospel.

On Mar. 3, 1751, he sailed for New York as tutor to two sons of Colonel Martin of Long Island, who were returning to their native country. He was a member of the Martin household until August 1753, during which time he prepared and published *A General Idea of the College of Mirania . . .* (1753), addressed particularly to the trustees nominated by the legislature to receive proposals relating to the establishment of a college in New York. In it he outlined the kind of institution he thought best adapted to the circumstances of a new country. The making of good men and good citizens was to be its chief objective; history, agriculture, and religion were to be most emphasized; and it was to embrace a school to meet the needs of those who were to follow the "mechanic profession," for whom time spent on the learned languages would be thrown away. Smith sent a copy of his pamphlet to Benjamin Franklin and to the Rev. Richard Peters [*qq.v.*], trustees of the Academy and Charitable School, Philadelphia. Franklin wrote Smith, expressing interest in his ideas. Accordingly, the young man visited Philadelphia, with the result that he was invited to connect himself with the Academy. So impressed with the institution was he that he addressed to the trustees *A Poem on Visiting the Academy of Philadelphia, June 1753* (1753). Before entering upon his duties, he went back to England and was ordained deacon in the Established Church on Dec. 21, 1753; two days later he was elevated to the priesthood.

On his return to Philadelphia in May of the year following, he at once became teacher of logic, rhetoric, and natural and moral philosophy in the Academy. From that time until the Revolution he was the dominant influence in its affairs. In December 1754 the trustees requested Smith and Francis Alison [*q.v.*], the rector, to prepare a clause to be incorporated in the charter, empowering the Academy to grant degrees. They drew up what was practically a new charter, adding the word college to the title of the institution, and providing for a provost and vice-provost. The charter was approved and went into effect the next year, and Smith became provost of the College, Academy and Charitable School of Philadelphia. In 1756, he presented to the trustees at their request a curriculum, prepared some two years before, which was one of the most comprehensive schemes of education which up to that time had been devised for any American college.

His duties as provost and teacher, however, offered insufficient scope for his talents and ambitions. These required a large stage upon which he could play many parts. Accordingly, as time went on, his influence came to be felt in all the affairs of the province—social, religious, scientific, literary, and political. When in England

for his ordination, he had addressed a long communication to the Society for the Propagation of the Gospel regarding the need of affording the Germans in Pennsylvania such educational facilities as would make them one with the other people. As a result, the Society appointed certain American gentlemen a board of trustees to establish and manage schools where the Germans were principally settled. Smith was made secretary of the board, and was active in its work. He was a member and official of the Masonic order, to which many of Philadelphia's most noted citizens belonged. An ardent churchman, he was prominent in ecclesiastical matters and in constant communication with Church officials in England. He strongly favored the appointment of an American bishop and undoubtedly hoped to occupy that position himself. Politically, he was a friend of the Penns and a leading supporter of the proprietary interests, by this affiliation, as well as by other actions, incurring the bitter enmity of Franklin. During the French and Indian War, he publicly condemned the Assembly for its failure to adopt aggressive military measures, publishing in 1755 *A Brief State of the Province of Pennsylvania.* As an easy plan to restore quiet and defeat the ambitions of the French, he suggested requiring members of the Assembly to take an oath of allegiance to the king declaring they would not refuse to defend their country against all his enemies, withdrawing the right to vote from the Germans until they were better acquainted with the English language, and forbidding the publication of any newspaper or periodical in a foreign tongue. The pamphlet drew forth caustic replies and in 1756 Smith published *A Brief View of the Conduct of Pennsylvania in 1755.* His enemies assailed his character in the newspapers, and accused him of teaching what was inconsistent with the charter of the college and even with religion itself. A committee appointed by the trustees of the College, July 5, 1756, investigated the charges and completely exonerated the provost.

Partly because of his interest in literature, but more especially to provide himself with a political weapon, Smith established in 1757 *The American Magazine and Monthly Chronicle of the British Colonies,* published by William Bradford, 1722–1791 [*q.v.*]. It supported the Crown against France and the interests of the Penns against the Quakers and Franklin, but also contained scientific and religious articles and papers on miscellaneous subjects. It was particularly notable for its encouragement of poetry, among its contributors being Francis Hopkinson, the younger Thomas Godfrey, and James Sterling [*qq.v.*]. The genius of young Benjamin West [*q.v.*], also, was first announced to the public through this publication. Smith himself wrote for the magazine a series of papers entitled "The Hermit," and signed Theodore, which were religious in character. The periodical was issued for only a year, however, since in December 1758 Smith's political troubles compelled him to sail for England.

These troubles arose from his association with William Moore, 1699–1783 [*q.v.*], a Pennsylvania judge and an advocate of more aggressive opposition to the French. Moore had been charged with unjust and extortionate behavior in office, and the Assembly had petitioned Gov. William Denny to remove him. In reply, after the Assembly had adjourned, Moore presented a memorial to the governor which characterized the Assembly's petition as virulent and slanderous. It was published in the *Pennsylvania Gazette* and *Pennsylvania Journal,* and at Smith's behest translated and printed in a German paper, which he had been instrumental in establishing in connection with his educational work for the Germans. The next Assembly ordered the arrest of both Moore and Smith, which was effected Jan. 6, 1758. Smith was later brought before the bar of the House, charged with promoting and publishing seditious libels, and convicted. He was ordered committed to jail and confined until he had made satisfaction. He remained there until after the Assembly had adjourned, being released by order of the supreme court on Apr. 11; in the meantime he had taught his classes at the jail. On June 3, he married Moore's daughter, Rebecca. In September he was arrested for a second time and kept in jail until the House was dissolved. During his first confinement he had appealed to the King, and early in December 1758 he sailed for England to prosecute the appeal. Here his writings and activities had brought him into great favor. The Archbishop of Canterbury and several bishops recommended him to Oxford for the degree of D.D., which the University conferred; he also received the same degree from the University of Aberdeen. The law officers of the Crown, after hearing his case, reported to the Lords of the Committee for Plantation Affairs that in their opinion Moore's address was a libel, but that since it was published after the Assembly adjourned, no subsequent Assembly had a right to consider the offense. This opinion was approved by the Privy Council.

Vindicated in his contention that his arrest had been illegal, Smith was back in Philadelphia on May 3, 1759. In February 1762, however, he again sailed for England and was away from home more than two years engaged in collecting funds for the College. This work, in which he was highly successful, was carried on jointly with James Jay [*q.v.*] under a royal brief authorizing them both to solicit subscriptions, Jay being in England at that time in the interests of King's College, New York. The funds they secured were divided between the two institutions. While he was abroad, 1763, the University of Dublin honored Smith with the degree of doctor of divinity. Upon his return he speedily resumed his various activities. At the request of Henry Bouquet [*q.v.*] and from facts supplied by him he prepared *An Historical Account of the Expedition Against the Ohio Indians in 1764* (1765), which attained much popularity abroad. From 1766 to 1777 he acted as rector of Trinity Church, Oxford, Pa. He was elected a member of the American Philosophical Society, Jan. 2, 1768, and the following year was associated with David Rittenhouse [*q.v.*] and John Lukens at the former's Norriton observatory in observing the transit of Venus. The approach of the Revolution placed him in an embarrassing predicament. He opposed the Stamp Act as "contrary to the faith of charters and the inherent rights of Englishmen," but he did not favor independence. His *Sermon on the Present Situation of American Affairs* (1775), preached at Christ Church, Philadelphia, June 28, 1775, before Congress, created a great sensation. It went through many editions and was translated into several foreign languages. It opposed British measures and awakened patriotism, but in its preface Smith professed himself as "ardently panting for a return of those Halcyon-days of harmony" and as "animated with purest zeal for the mutual interests of Great-Britain and the Colonies." He is credited, moreover, with the authorship of *Plain Truth; Addressed to the Inhabitants of America* . . . (1776) and *Additions to Plain Truth* . . . (1776), signed Candidus, which endeavored to show that "American independence is as illusory, ruinous, and impracticable, as a liberal reconciliation with Great Britain is safe, honorable, and expedient." When General Howe was advancing on Philadelphia he was among those ordered apprehended because of conduct and conversation inimical to the American cause. He gave his parole and retired to Barbados Island, which belonged to an estate he had purchased on the Schuylkill. After the evacuation of the city he returned to Philadelphia and set to work rehabilitating the College.

In 1779 the General Assembly appointed a committee to examine into the state of the College. A majority of this committee reported that the corporation had shown hostility to the government and constitution of the State and that the original principle of the institution, which required it to afford equal privileges to all religious denominations, had not been observed. Accordingly, on Nov. 27, 1779, the Assembly passed an act making void the charter of the College and creating a new corporation to be known as the Trustees of the University of the State of Pennsylvania. Smith's activities were now transferred to Maryland. He became rector of Chester Parish, Chestertown, Kent County, and established Kent School, which had 142 pupils in 1782, when it was chartered as Washington College with Smith as president. Always successful as a money-raiser, he secured more than £10,-000 for the new institution. He was president of every convention of the Episcopal churches of Maryland during his residence there, and was invariably sent as a delegate to the General Conventions, where he was one of the leaders in the organization of the Protestant Episcopal Church. As chairman of the committee appointed in 1785 to adapt the prayer book to American conditions, he performed much of the work. His ambition to be bishop was never realized, however. The Maryland Convention of 1783 elected him to that office, but the General Convention did not confirm the election. For its failure to do so there were probably several reasons, but the decisive one, doubtless, was that given by the church historian Perry. Writing of the convention of representatives of the Church held in New York, October 1784, over which Smith presided, he says: "It was at this very convention, that he was destined, alas! to make shipwreck of a lifetime's honors, and by a public indulgence . . . in intemperate habits to close to himself the coveted episcopate none labored more to secure" (*post*, II, 29). He was opposed, Perry adds, by his oldest pupils and his dearest friends.

During his residence in Maryland, Smith had kept in close touch with Philadelphia and labored to have the rights of the old College restored. Finally, his efforts and those of others were successful, the Assembly on Mar. 6, 1789, declaring the act of 1779 repugnant to justice and restoring the former charter with all its privileges. In July Smith resumed his position as provost. The University of the State of Pennsylvania still existed, however, and on Sept. 31, 1791, the two were united, John Ewing [*q.v.*] becoming provost of the new institution. On Mar. 1 of that year, in behalf of the American Philosophical Society, Smith, ironically enough, had delivered an oration on the death of Franklin, in the German Lutheran Church, before the members of Con-

gress and a great gathering of notable personages. According to a family tradition, his daughter Rebecca said to him afterward, "I don't think you believed more than one tenth part of what you said of Old Ben Lightning Rod" (H. W. Smith, *post*, II, 344); Smith made no reply. He spent the most of his remaining days on his estate at the Falls of the Schuylkill, engaged more or less in land speculation and in advocating the development of canal navigation in Pennsylvania. At the time of his death he was preparing his writings for publication in five volumes, two of which appeared in 1803. He died at the home of a daughter-in-law in Philadelphia, survived by five children.

In spite of the responsibilities that were intrusted to him and the honors he received, he never enjoyed the highest respect and confidence of many of his noted contemporaries. While this fact may be attributed in part to political and ecclesiastical differences, it was undoubtedly due, also, to defects in Smith's character. Upon meeting him for the first time, John Adams wrote, "There is an appearance of art" (C. F. Adams, *The Works of John Adams,* vol. II, 1850, p. 360). Learned and righteous Ezra Stiles [*q.v.*] had nothing but contempt for him. "Dr. Smith," he recorded in his diary, "is a haughty, self-opinionated, half-learned Character"; and on another occasion, "His moral character is very exceptionable and unbecoming a Minister of Christ, & it is even a doubt whether he is a Believer of Revelation. He is infamous for religious Hypocrisy" (F. B. Dexter, *The Literary Diary of Ezra Stiles,* 1901, vol. III, p. 350; vol. II, p. 528). Dr. Benjamin Rush [*q.v.*], who knew him well and attended him in his last illness, left a vivid portrait of him. "Unhappily," Rush says, "his conduct in all his relations and situations was opposed to his talents and profession. His person was slovenly and his manners awkward and often offensive in company . . . he early contracted a love for strong drink and became toward the close of his life an habitual drunkard. . . . His temper was irritable . . . and when angry he swore in the most extravagant manner. He seldom paid a debt without being sued or without a quarrel, he was extremely avaricious. . . . On his death bed he never spoke upon any subject connected with religion . . . nor was there a Bible or Prayer Book ever seen in his room. . . . He descended to his grave . . . without being lamented by a human creature. . . . From the absence of all his children not a drop of kindred blood attended his funeral" (*A Memorial Containing Travels Through Life or Sundry In-*

cidents in the Life of Dr. Benjamin Rush, 1905, pp. 175–79).

With all his faults, however, he was one of the ablest, most versatile, and most influential Pennsylvanians of his day. Rush himself admits that Smith possessed "genius, taste, and learning." He was a clear, forceful writer and an eloquent public speaker. The importance of his service for practically a quarter of a century during the formative period of what is now the University of Pennsylvania is incalculable, and his contribution to education in general, not inconsiderable. He imparted literary enthusiasm to a notable group of young men, aided in the publication of their work, and helped to make Philadelphia a literary center. Notwithstanding his Loyalist tendencies, he was an ardent supporter of liberty, and his political activities, while not uninfluenced by personal motives, were in the main directed by a passion for the best interests of his state and the country. Though more interested in its temporal than in its spiritual condition, he played no insignificant part in the organization of the Protestant Episcopal Church, the name of which he is said to have suggested.

[H. W. Smith, *Life and Correspondence of the Rev. William Smith, D.D.* (2 vols., 1880), is the best single source, but presents all Smith's activities in the most favorable light; for discussion of the Moore-Smith libel on the Assembly, consult W. R. Riddell, in *Pa. Mag. of Hist. and Biog.,* Apr., July, Oct. 1928; see, also, C. J. Stillé, *A Memoir of the Rev. William Smith, D.D.* (1869); J. L. Chamberlain, *Universities and Their Sons: Univ. of Pa.* (1901); F. N. Thorpe, *Benjamin Franklin and the Univ. of Pa.* (1893); H. M. Lippincott, *The Univ. of Pa.: Franklin's Coll.* (1919); W. B. Sprague, *Annals of the Am. Pulpit,* vol. V (1859); W. S. Perry, *The Hist. of the Am. Episcopal Church* (1885); C. C. Tiffany, *A Hist. of the Protestant Episcopal Church in the U. S. of America* (1895); J. T. Scharf, *Hist. of Md.* (1879); E. P. Oberholtzer, *The Lit. Hist. of Phila.* (copr. 1906); A. H. Smyth, *The Phila. Magazines* (1892); F. L. Mott, *A Hist. of Am. Magazines, 1741–1850* (1930); L. N. Richardson, *A Hist. of Early Am. Magazines, 1741–1789* (1931).]

H. E. S.

SMITH, WILLIAM (June 25, 1728–Dec. 3, 1793), jurist, historian, Loyalist, was born in New York City, the eldest son of William, 1697–1769 [*q.v.*], and Mary (Het) Smith. His legal career closely paralleled his father's. He attended Yale College, from which he was graduated in 1745, studied law in his father's office with Whitehead Hicks and William Livingston [*q.v.*], and was admitted to the bar in 1750. With Livingston as his partner, he soon established himself as a leading practitioner in the mayor's court, supreme court, and Court of Vice-Admiralty. In 1752 he and Livingston, at the request of the Assembly, published the first digest of the colony statutes in force at that time, *Laws of New York from the Year 1691 to 1751, Inclusive*; ten years

later a second volume, *Laws of New York . . . 1752–1762* (1762), appeared. Smith was concerned as counsel in some of the most important litigation in the middle colonies. One notable instance was his appearance in 1771 in behalf of Lord Dunmore in his suit against Lieut.-Gov. Cadwallader Colden [*q.v.*] for an accounting of the governor's emoluments (*Collections of the New York Historical Society, Publication Fund Series,* LVI, 1925, pp. 172–82; E. B. O'Callaghan, *Documents Relative to the Colonial History of the State of New York,* vol. VIII, 1857, p. 257). He was one of the founders and vice-president of The Moot, a select organization of the principal New York lawyers formed in 1770 for the discussion of legal problems (Moot Court Minutes, MS., New York Historical Society). His legal papers abundantly testify to his scholarship.

Prior to the Revolution Smith was a leader of the Whig Presbyterian forces in New York. With William Livingston and John Morin Scott [*q.v.*] he was one of the chief contributors to the *Independent Reflector,* 1752–53, and the *Occasional Reverberator,* September–October 1753 (see L. N. Richardson, *A History of Early American Magazines, 1741–1789,* 1931, pp. 78–84, 87–91). In 1757 the three collaborators published *A Review of the Military Operations in North America . . . 1753 . . . 1756* (reprinted in *Collections of the Massachusetts Historical Society,* 1 ser. VII, 1801). This was a defense of Gov. William Shirley [*q.v.*] of Massachusetts and contained a series of attacks on James De Lancey, Thomas Pownall, and Sir William Johnson [*qq.v.*]. Smith's chief literary contribution was *The History of the Province of New-York, from the First Discovery to the Year M.DCC.XXXII,* published in London in 1757; it was reissued in 1814, with a continuation, attributed to J. V. N. Yates, and was reprinted again, with Smith's own continuation bringing the narrative down to 1762, by the New York Historical Society in 1829, under the title, *The History of the Late Province of New York* (2 vols.). It is in large measure a political chronicle of the eighteenth century, probably the most valuable material being contained in an appendix of one hundred pages describing the economic, religious, and legal organization of the province. Smith's narrative is marred by inaccuracies and partisanship, and his adversaries were bitter in their comments. By far the most important part of the chronicle, however, both from the historical and the biographical point of view, was never published. These "Historical Memoirs," now in the New York Public Library, cover the period from the eve of the Revolution to 1783, and comprise six closely written volumes, indispensable to an understanding of New York's position during the Revolution.

Smith's career during the Revolution is unique in the annals of American Loyalism. Though an office-holder under the Crown, having become chief justice of the province in 1763 and succeeded his father as a member of the council in 1767, he was one of the foremost leaders of the popular party and a founder of the Whig Club. When violence broke out, he appears to have taken a position on the fence, gradually leaning toward the Loyalist side, never completely repudiated by the patriots, never completely accepted by his own party (*B. F. Stevens's Facsimiles of MSS. in European Archives Relating to America*, 1889, no. 487, in vol. V; *The Works of John Adams*, vol. II, 1850, pp. 353–54). Despite his anomalous position, he was the recipient of many honors, and therefore the *bête noire* of his envious colleague, Thomas Jones [*q.v.*], whose venomous *History of New York during the Revolutionary War* (edited by E. F. De Lancey, 2 vols., 1879) is devoted in no inconsiderable part to exposing his alleged duplicity. The attempts of his enemies to discredit him included the publication of a letter ascribed to him, later shown to be a forgery, conveying valuable information to General Howe in regard to the plans of the revolutionists (Peter Force, *American Archives*, 4 ser., IV, 1843, col. 1000; *Magazine of American History*, June 1881, pp. 423–24). In drafting the state constitution, the committee of the New York Provincial Convention freely consulted him, and in later years as an exile he claimed credit for influencing the federal constitutional program (Sabine, *post*, II, 312–13), apparently basing his claim on the parliamentary plan of union which he had put forth on the eve of the conflict and consistently advocated thereafter as a solution of the imperial issues (manuscript Diary, V, Oct. 31, 1777, July 17, 1778, July 1, 1780; *History of . . . New York*, 1829, I, xi–xiii). Refusing in 1777 to take the oath of allegiance to the state, he was ordered to Livingston Manor on parole. Refusing again the following year, he was banished by the commissioners for detecting and defeating conspiracies, under the act of June 30, 1778, and returned to New York City (Stokes, *post*, V, 1068, 1069, 1074; *New York Gazette*, Sept. 17, 1778), still maintaining a friendly correspondence with Gov. George Clinton [*q.v.*], although by this time he was confident that the Revolution would fail because of a popular uprising against it. Appointed chief justice of New York on May 4, 1779, to succeed

Daniel Horsmanden [*q.v.*], he took the oath of office in 1780 and strongly urged the restoration of civil government (Diary, VI, Aug. 1–5, 1779; VII, May 27, 1782; Smith MSS., fol. 194). He never actually served as chief justice, since the city remained under military control until the evacuation (Stokes, V, 1074, 1085, 1091, 1108). In the fall of 1780 he was one of the commissioners who visited General Washington in an attempt to save Major André.

On the evacuation of New York in 1783 Smith proceeded to England, remaining there until 1786, when he sailed to Canada to take the post of chief justice, to which he had been appointed on Sept. 1, 1785. This office he held until his death at Quebec, Dec. 3, 1793. Smith was married on Nov. 3, 1752, to Janet Livingston, daughter of James and Maria (Kierstedt) Livingston and first cousin of James Livingston [*q.v.*]. They had eleven children; the only son who survived infancy was William (1769–1847), the Canadian historian and jurist.

[For the unpublished chronicle and diary of Smith and other miscellaneous papers in the New York Public Library, see E. B. Greene and R. B. Morris, *A Guide to the Principal Sources for Early Am. Hist. (1600–1800) in the City of New York* (1929), pp. 102–03. Smith's pleadings in the mayor's court and supreme court are available in the office of the Commissioner of Records, New York City. Historians frequently confuse the elder William Smith with his son the historian. Useful biographical material will be found in M. L. Delafield, "William Smith—The Historian," *Mag. of Am. Hist.*, June 1881; Lorenzo Sabine, *Biog. Sketches of the Loyalists of the Am. Rev.* (1864), II, 312–13; F. B. Dexter, *Biog. Sketches Grads. Yale Coll.*, vol. II (1896); B. F. Butler, "Annual Discourse," *Trans. Albany Inst.*, I (1830), 154–56, 207–09; William Smith, "Memoir," prefixed to Smith's *Hist. of the Late Province of New-York* (1829), I, x–xvi. I. N. P. Stokes, *The Iconography of Manhattan Island*, vols. IV–VI (1922–28) makes considerable use of Smith's MSS.]   R. B. M.

SMITH, WILLIAM (*c.* 1754–Apr. 6, 1821), Episcopal clergyman, was probably born in Aberdeen, Scotland, for he is described as "a fellow countryman and townsman" of Dr. William Smith, 1727–1803 [*q.v.*] of Pennsylvania (H. W. Smith, *Life and Correspondence of the Rev. William Smith*, 1880, II, 274). He received a university education, possibly at Aberdeen, and was ordained in the Scottish Non-juring Episcopal Church before coming to America. From January to July 1785 he was in charge of Trinity Church, Oxford, and All Saints, Pequestan (now a part of Philadelphia). He then became minister of Stepney Parish, Somerset County, Md. Resigning this charge in 1787, he assumed, on July 7, the rectorship of St. Paul's Church, Narragansett, R. I. Ezra Stiles [*q.v.*] in his diary records a visit to his church on Oct. 21, 1788: "The Rev. Mr. Smith, late fr. Scotld., a non-Juror, has been about 1 y. inducted here by Dr. Seabury. He preached on Eccl.—all Vanity. An excellent Sermon" (F. B. Dexter, *The Literary Diary of Ezra Stiles,* 1901, III, 330). In 1789 Smith undertook occasional services at Trinity Church, Newport, and on Jan. 27, 1790, resigned his Narragansett charge to become rector of the Newport church. He was active in the organization of the diocese of Rhode Island, preaching the sermon (*A Discourse at the Opening of the Convention ... the 18th of November, 1790*) at its first convention.

On Apr. 12, 1797, he resigned the Newport church to become rector of St. Paul's, Norwalk, Conn. That same year, Oct. 18, he preached at the consecration of the Rev. Abraham Jarvis [*q.v.*] as second bishop of Connecticut. The publication of his sermon (*A Discourse ... Before the Ecclesiastical Convention ... Assembled ... To Witness the Consecrating of the Right Rev. Abraham Jarvis,* 1797) led to a controversy on episcopacy with the Rev. Samuel Blatchford, a Congregational minister of Bridgeport, who published *The Validity of Presbyterian Ordination Maintained, in a Letter to the Rev. William Smith, D.D.* (1798). To this Smith replied with *Dr. Smith's Answer to Mr. Blatchford's Letter* (1798). In 1800 Smith disagreed with his Norwalk flock over a proposal made by them that his tenure of office should be determined each year by the congregation, and resigned. He then went to New York City where he opened a grammar school. In 1802 the trustees of the Episcopal Academy at Cheshire, founded by Bishop Seabury, which was then undertaking work of college grade in order to prepare men for the ministry of the Episcopal Church, elected Smith as principal. The academy did not prosper under his direction, however. Following an investigation made by the diocesan convention, he resigned June 5, 1806, and returned to New York, where he engaged in private instruction. Afterwards, returning to Connecticut, he did supply work in various parishes, particularly Milford and West Haven. The frequent changes in Smith's ministerial work suggest that he did not possess the gift of commending himself to the people of his successive cures. The Hon. Gulian C. Verplanck [*q.v.*], who as a youth, in the home of his grandfather, Dr. William Samuel Johnson [*q.v.*], had seen Smith, says of him that he "was a man of extensive and diversified learning, of an ardent and fertile mind, a great and ready command of language, a flow of thought, as well extemporaneously and in conversation as on paper." He had moreover "deep religious feeling, unquestionable zeal and devotion to his duties,

whether in religious or secular instruction, and a frank, kind disposition. Yet, unhappily, he was never successful in either sphere of labour, in any proportion to his ability or acquirements" (Sprague, *post,* p. 346).

Smith was an accomplished musician and published several books intended for the use of organists and church choirs, which had a widespread and salutary influence in the development of church music, particularly in his own communion. Among them was *The Churchman's Choral Companion* (1809). He is said to have built with his own hands several small pipe organs (Updike, *post,* II, 352). His chief production, published in 1814, is entitled *The Reasonableness of Setting Forth the Most Worthy Praise of Almighty God, According to the Usage of the Primitive Church; with Historical Views of the Nature, Origin, and Progress of Metre Psalmody.* It is a refutation of eighteen objections to chanting in churches, and incidentally a violent attack on metre psalmody, the Scottish custom of singing the psalms in metrical and rhythmical versions, then prevailing throughout the Protestant churches of America. It approves, however, hymns such as those contained in the Methodist collection. Among his other publications were *Consolations from Homar, an Hermit of the East* (1789) and *The Convict's Visitor; or, Penitential Offices* (1791), the latter containing suitable devotions for use before or at the time of execution. Perhaps Smith's chief claim to remembrance is that he contributed the "Office of Institution of Ministers" to the Episcopal Book of Common Prayer. He composed this service originally at the request of the clergy of Connecticut where it was first used. Later it was adopted with slight modification by the General Convention of the Church. His wife was Magdalen Milne, by whom he had several children.

[W. B. Sprague, *Annals of the Am. Pulpit,* vol. V (1859); Wilkins Updike, *A Hist. of the Episcopal Church in Narragansett* (3 vols., 1907), ed. by Daniel Goodwin; G. C. Mason, *Annals of Trinity Church, Newport* (1890); E. E. Beardsley, *An Address ... on Occasion of the Fiftieth Anniversary of the Episcopal Acad. of Conn.* (1844); C. M. Selleck, *Address at the Centenary of St. Paul's Church, Norwalk, Conn.* (1886).]

W. P. L.

SMITH, WILLIAM (*c.* 1762–June 26, 1840), lawyer, United States senator, is said to have been born in North Carolina. He always spoke of himself as a South Carolinian, however, and his grand-daughter believed that a change of boundary lines threw his birthplace in South Carolina into North Carolina (O'Neall, *post,* I, 112). His preliminary training is supposed to have been under the Rev. Mr. Alexander at Bullock's Creek, York County, S. C., and Andrew Jackson and William H. Crawford are said to have been his schoolmates there. It is certain that he knew them both from boyhood. Later he attended Mount Zion Society school at Winnsboro. His early life is reputed to have been "wild, reckless, intemperate, rude and boisterous" (*Ibid.*, I, 107). His reformation was attributed to his wife, Margaret Duff, who was fourteen years old when he married her in 1781; they had one child, a daughter. He studied law in Charleston and was admitted to the bar. Settling in York District, he was speedily successful.

He served in the state Senate, 1802–08, and was president of that body, 1806–08. In the latter year he was elected judge of the constitutional court of appeals. He filled that office with ability until 1816, but gained a reputation for great severity. On Dec. 4, 1816, he was elected by the legislature United States senator to fill the vacancy of John Taylor [*q.v.*] and on the same day was elected for the term beginning Mar. 4, 1817. In the Senate he gained reputation as a powerful speaker, though he was far from being an orator. He was a persistent defender of state rights and slavery and as persistent an opponent of banks, capitalism, internal improvements, and the tariff. The most important of his speeches was that in the Missouri debates, delivered Dec. 18, 1820. By building up a state-rights organization in South Carolina and aligning himself with Crawford in national politics, he won the enmity of Calhoun, who declared him "narrow-minded and . . . wedded to the Georgia politicians," and suggested Hayne as a suitable successor ("Correspondence of John C. Calhoun," *Annual Report of the American Historical Association . . . 1899,* vol. II, 1900, p. 204). Defeated for reëlection in 1823 he returned home, joining with William C. Preston, Thomas Cooper, and Stephen D. Miller [*qq.v.*] in organizing the group of "Radicals" who opposed the nationalism and latitudinarianism of Calhoun. He was elected to the lower house of the state legislature in 1824 and again in 1825, and led the so-called "Revolution" of 1825 by pushing through to passage a series of resolutions declaring a protective tariff and internal improvements unconstitutional.

In 1826 he was again elected by the legislature to the United States Senate to fill a vacancy. He took his seat Dec. 7, and during the four years he served he was twice elected president *pro tem.* In 1829 he declined to accept a proffered appointment to the Supreme Court. During this term he was increasingly a strict constructionist and on Apr. 11, 1828, made an elaborate speech in opposition to the system of in-

ternal improvements as extravagant, unequal, and unjust in its operations in different sections, and as a "flagrant outrage . . . to the Constitution." He objected to the word "national" that had "crept into our political vocabulary," and declared it "a term unknown to the origin and theory of our government." On Feb. 10, 1829, he presented the protest of South Carolina against the tariff and in his speech said, "I, as Senator from South Carolina, can never consent to that doctrine, that dangerous principle that a majority shall rule. If a majority is to rule, away with your constitution at once." In 1829 he received the seven electoral votes of Georgia for vice-president.

Smith's state-rights views stopped short of nullification, however, which he thought a remedy as bad as the disease. He opposed a convention as unnecessary since the protective tariff and internal improvements system were, he thought, crumbling to destruction. He was reasonably consistent, but the same group of nationalists, who had thought him too radical in 1823, now, as the leaders of the nullification movement, thought him too broad and national, and in 1830 they secured his defeat for reëlection, Stephen D. Miller replacing him. In November he published a letter "To the Good People of South Carolina" (*Charleston Courier*, Nov. 13, 15, 1830, reprinted from the *Yorkville Pioneer*) against nullification, and was thereafter identified with the Union party as one of its strongest leaders. He hated Calhoun, who, so he said, had "sold the state twice; once for the tariff and again for internal improvements" (O'Neall, *post,* I, 119) and who wanted a grievance rather than tariff reduction. He also resented leadership in the state passing to Calhoun and to Hamilton, Hayne, and McDuffie [*qq.v.*], all of them his juniors, and thus his opposition to nullification was tinged with personal feeling.

In 1831 he was again in the state Senate and there ended his career in South Carolina. He had for years been buying land in the Southwest, and had become very wealthy. In 1833 he moved to Louisiana, and, after a brief residence there, to Huntsville, Ala. In 1836 Jackson again offered him an appointment to the Supreme Court, but he declined. In the same year he was elected to the lower house of the Alabama legislature and served until his death. A Jeffersonian Democrat of the straitest sect, able, industrious, fearless, with none of the evasions of the politician, Smith was a strong and outstanding figure. But he was a bitter and vindictive enemy, witheringly sarcastic and never conciliatory, inclined to be opinionated and prejudiced, and never gained the influence to which his talents and character entitled him.

[*Annals of Cong.*, 1817–1823, 1826–1831; *Jours. of the Senate of S. C.*, 1802–1808, 1831; *Jours. of the House of Representatives of S. C.*, 1824–1825; *Jours. of the House of Representatives of Ala.*, 1836–1839; "Diary of Edward Hooker, 1805–1808," in *Ann. Report of the Am. Hist. Asso.*, 1896, vol. I (1897); Dumas Malone, *The Public Life of Thomas Cooper* (1926); B. F. Perry, *Reminiscences of Public Men* (1883); C. S. Boucher, *The Nullification Controversy in S. C.* (1916); J. B. O'Neall, *Biog. Sketches of the Bench and Bar of S. C.* (1859); D. F. Houston, *A Critical Study of Nullification in S. C.* (1896); William Garrett, *Reminiscences of Public Men in Ala.* (1872); Gaillard Hunt, *John C. Calhoun* (1907); W. M. Meigs, *The Life of John Caldwell Calhoun* (1917); *Biog. Dir. Am. Cong.* (1928); *Daily National Intelligencer* (Washington, D. C.), July 14, 1840; *Mobile Daily Commercial Register and Patriot*, July 3, 1840.]

J. G. deR. H.

SMITH, WILLIAM (Sept. 6, 1797–May 18, 1887), congressman, governor of Virginia, Confederate soldier, was born at "Marengo" in King George County, Va., the son of Col. Caleb and Mary Waugh (Smith) Smith. His parents, who were first cousins, claimed descent from Sir Sidney Smith who emigrated from England in the reign of George I. William attended school in King George County and at fourteen, after the death of his mother, was sent to an academy at Plainfield, Conn. Called home in 1812 to prevent his enlistment in the navy, he was sent after the death of his father in 1814 to Nelson's Classical School in Hanover County. He subsequently studied law in Fredericksburg and Warrenton, and spent a few months in the office of Gen. William H. Winder in Baltimore. In 1818 he began practice in Culpeper, and in 1821 was married to Elizabeth H. Bell.

In 1827 he organized a mail-coach service from Fairfax Court House to Culpeper Court House, and by 1834 had established a daily post service from Washington, D. C., to Milledgeville, Ga. From the rapid extension of his mail service and the frequent extra payments he received from the Post Office Department, came the sobriquet, "Extra Billy Smith," bestowed on him by Senator Benjamin Watkins Leigh [*q.v.*] of Virginia in the course of an attack on Postmaster-General William T. Barry [*q.v.*]. From 1836 to 1841 Smith served in the Virginia Senate and from 1841 to 1843, in Congress, being unsuccessful in his campaign for reëlection. In 1842 he moved to Fauquier County. He was elected governor of Virginia for the term 1846–49, and on Mar. 13, 1847, signed the act accepting the retrocession to Virginia of the part of the District of Columbia south of the Potomac River. In April 1849 he took up his residence in California, where two of his sons were living. He was sent as a delegate from San Francisco to the State Democratic

Convention, was unanimously elected its chairman, and was nominated for the United States Senate, but, unwilling to forfeit his Virginia citizenship, declined the nomination. Returning to Virginia in 1852, he was again elected to Congress and served from 1853 to 1861.

At the beginning of the Civil War he was offered by Governor Letcher a commission as brigadier-general, but declined it, saying that he was "wholly ignorant of drill and tactics" and became colonel of the 49th Virginia Infantry instead. He fought at Manassas and while with his troops was elected a member of the Confederate Congress. He attended its sessions during intervals between campaigns, rejoining his command on adjournment. When the regiment was reorganized as a part of the Confederate States Army in May 1862, he was reëlected colonel and resigned his seat in Congress. He subsequently took part in the operations on the Peninsula, about Yorktown, and around Richmond, was severely wounded at Sharpsburg, and promoted brigadier-general in command of the 4th Brigade near Fredericksburg. In May 1863 he was again elected governor of Virginia, serving from Jan. 1, 1864, until after the fall of the Confederacy. In August 1863 he had received the brevet rank of major-general. His energies as governor were largely given to securing food and supplies for the Confederate troops centered in Virginia. On the fall of Richmond, he led his government first to Lynchburg and then to Danville, but after Lee's surrender returned to Richmond, was paroled, and spent the remainder of his life in farming at his estate, "Monterosa," near Warrenton, Fauquier County. When he was eighty years old, still erect and active, he was elected to the Virginia House of Delegates, and served from 1877 to 1879. He died at "Monterosa" in his ninetieth year and was buried in Hollywood Cemetery, Richmond. Of his eleven children, one daughter and two sons survived him. His wife had died in 1879.

[Sketch by R. A. Brock, in *Hardesty's Hist. and Geog. Encyc.*, Va. edition (1884); J. W. Bell, *Memoirs of Gov. William Smith of Va.* (1891); M. V. Smith, *Virginia, 1492–1892 . . . With A History of the Executives* (1893); *Biog. Dir. Am. Cong.* (1928); L. M. S. Price, *The Sydney-Smith and Clagett-Price Geneal.* (1927); *Richmond Dispatch*, May 21, 1887.]

J. E. W.

SMITH, WILLIAM ANDREW (Nov. 29, 1802–Mar. 1, 1870), clergyman, author, college president, was born in Fredericksburg, Va., the son of William Smith, English immigrant, and Mary (Porter) Smith. He was left motherless at two and fatherless at eleven years of age, his father losing both his fortune and his life at the hands of faithless trustees. After his father's death the boy was befriended by Mr. Russell Hill, a merchant of Petersburg, Va., and was given a limited education. After teaching in Madison County several years he was admitted on trial as preacher in the Methodist Episcopal Church in 1825 and in full connection in the Virginia Conference in 1827. Thereafter he served churches in Petersburg, Lynchburg, Richmond, and Norfolk, acting also as joint-editor of the *Virginia Conference Sentinel*. He was one of the great preachers of his day. Few had more sons in the gospel, many eminent ministers among them and in various denominations. A delegate to every general conference of the Methodist Episcopal Church from 1832 to 1844, at the conference of 1844 he acted as counsel in the appeal case of the Rev. F. A. Harding, who had become a slave-holder by marriage and who had been suspended from ministerial work. Smith took the position that "slavery is a great evil, but beyond our control; yet not necessarily a sin" (*Report of Debates in the General Conference, 1844, post*, p. 28); at the same time he argued that it is no part of the work of a minister to "meddle with politics." At the same conference he was a leading participant in the more important extra-judicial trial of Bishop James Osgood Andrew [*q.v.*] which led to the division of the church. He was a member of the Louisville convention which organized the Methodist Episcopal Church, South, and was a delegate to all its general conferences until his death.

In 1846 he was elected president of Randolph-Macon College, Ashland, Va., then in the darkest period of its history. He had been one of its trustees from the beginning, 1830, and in 1833, while acting as its agent, had been crippled for life by the overturning of a carriage. Under his able administration the enrollment was increased, the quality of work was improved, and an endowment fund of $100,000 was secured, most of it swept away by the Civil War. As professor of "Moral and Intellectual Philosophy" he delivered to his students a series of lectures published in 1856 under the title *Lectures on the Philosophy and Practice of Slavery as Exhibited in the Institution of Domestic Slavery in the United States, with the Duties of Masters to Slaves,* which had considerable influence in the South. He undertook to show that philosophy, natural rights, and Holy Scripture all sustained the system of domestic slavery, which was intended to be perpetual. The book called forth a reply by J. H. Power under the title *Review of the Lectures of Wm. A. Smith, D.D., on the Philosophy and Practice of Slavery* (1859). Resigning the presidency of Randolph-Macon in

1866, he became pastor of Centenary Church, St. Louis, Mo. Two years later he was elected president of Central College, Fayette, Mo., for which he raised an endowment of nearly $100,000. Ill health prevented his continuing this work, and he returned to Virginia. He died in Richmond, Mar. 1, 1870, and was buried there in Hollywood Cemetery. He was married three times: first to Mahala Miller of Delaware, second to Laura Brooking of Richmond, and third to Mrs. Eliza V. Williams of Lynchburg. He had two children by his first wife and two by his second.

[See esp. J. R. Spann, in *John P. Branch Hist. Papers of Randolph-Macon Coll.*, June 1916. See also J. C. Granberry, in *In Memoriam: Rev. Bishop James Osgood Andrew, D.D. . . . Rev. William A. Smith, D.D.* (1871), compiled by W. T. Smithson; Richard Irby, *Hist. of Randolph-Macon Coll., Va.* (n.d.); *Jour. of the Gen. Conference M. E. Church . . . 1844* (1844); *Report of Debates in the Gen. Conference M. E. Church . . . 1844* (1844); obituaries in *Richmond Daily Whig, Richmond Christian Advocate, Daily Enquirer* and *Daily Dispatch* (Richmond), Mar. 2, 3, 1870.]   R. E. B.

SMITH, WILLIAM FARRAR (Feb. 17, 1824–Feb. 28, 1903), Union soldier, engineer, was born at St. Albans, Vt., the son of Ashbel and Sarah (Butler) Smith. Family tradition held that in colonial days the name had been Smithson, the last syllable having been dropped before the family moved to Vermont from Barre, Mass. John Gregory Smith [*q.v.*] was a cousin. William received a common school education and was graduated from the United States Military Academy in 1845 as a second lieutenant of topographical engineers, standing fourth in a class of forty-one members. He was engaged in making surveys and in teaching mathematics at West Point for the next fifteen years. During a tour of duty in Florida in 1855 he suffered a severe attack of malaria which shattered his health temporarily and made him subject to recurrent seizures which at various times during his life caused him great pain and mental depression.

At the beginning of the Civil War, he was commissioned colonel of the 3rd Vermont Volunteers, and was present in the Manassas campaign. In August 1861 he was promoted to the rank of brigadier-general and was assigned to the command of the 2nd Division of the IV Corps, Army of the Potomac, which opened the Peninsular campaign in 1862. He led his division in the battle of Williamsburg and the Seven Days' battles, and, in June 1862, was brevetted lieutenant-colonel in the regular army for his services at White Oak Swamp. In July he became a major-general, commanded the 2nd Division, VI Corps, at Antietam, and was brevetted colonel for this service. After the disasters of Fredericksburg, in which he had taken part, Smith indulged in the indiscretion of writing a letter, signed also by William Buel Franklin [*q.v.*], directly to President Lincoln, expressing the dissatisfaction of the subordinate officers and the common soldiers in their leadership, objecting to the proposed advance on Richmond as impracticable, and offering an alternative plan (*Official Records, Army,* XXI, 868). Lincoln saved him from being relieved from duty, but the incident occasioned his transfer to the IX Corps. The Senate having refused to sanction to the promotion of major-general on Mar. 4, 1863, he reverted to the rank of brigadier-general.

The great call for troops to rescue Rosecrans' army after the disaster at Chickamauga took Smith to Chattanooga, Tenn., in October 1863, as chief engineer. The problem of supplying the starving army by restoring a short line of communication with Bridgeport challenged Smith's extraordinary engineering skill. The unquestioned excellence of his work in constructing pontoon bridges won extravagant praise from Grant, Sherman, and Thomas, and led to a reappointment as major-general in March 1864, but made it especially difficult for Smith to bear with equanimity an acrid controversy which was later waged over the question as to whom credit was due for opening the famous "cracker-line." Rosecrans had been occupied with the problem before Smith's arrival, but, unfortunately, was relieved by Thomas before his plan could be executed. Consequently Smith, until his death, labored under the impression that the plan, as it was successfully carried out by Thomas, was original with him. The matter was finally disposed of for all but Smith with the publication of the findings of an investigating committee in 1901. Rosecrans was credited with having planned the recovery of Lookout Valley and was said to have been long aware of the strategic importance of Brown's Ferry. At Missionary Ridge Smith took charge of the preparations for the assault, of moving troops, and of building bridges and defenses.

Grant took Smith east with him in 1864 and assigned him to the XVIII Corps under Benjamin Franklin Butler [*q.v.*]. He participated in the bloody and fruitless action at Cold Harbor and was once more moved to criticize the actions of Meade to Grant. His complaints were justified in the light of later changes of policy, but struck too close to Grant to make him acceptable as a subordinate. Smith led the attack on Petersburg in June. His delay in pushing the movement because of the fatigue of his men, and

a sudden return of his old illness, lost for him some of the reputation he had justly earned and, on July 19, Grant relieved him of his command. The confidence which Grant had demonstrated toward Smith in the west was probably never shaken, but his hand was forced by the circumstances, particularly the difficulty of keeping Butler, who was very popular, and Smith, at peace with each other. Smith was brevetted brigadier-general and major-general on Mar. 13, 1865, for distinguished services at Chattanooga, and in the Virginia campaign of 1864.

Smith resigned as a major-general of volunteers in 1865 and, two years later, from the regular army. He had, meanwhile, become president of the International Ocean Telegraph Company which was operating a cable to Cuba, and remained in this position until the controlling interest was sold in 1873. He then spent two years in Europe with his family, and returned to the United States to become president of the Board of Police Commissioners in New York City. He resigned in 1881 and for the next twenty years was employed by the government on engineering projects for river and harbor improvements, being restored to the army with the rank of major in 1889. Smith wielded a vigorous pen in support of his "cracker-line" claims in his *Military Operations Around Chattanooga* (copyright 1886), his articles for *Battles and Leaders of the Civil War* (4 volumes, 1887–88), *The Relief of the Army of the Cumberland* (1891), and *From Chattanooga to Petersburg* (1893). The last ten years of his life were spent in Philadelphia. His wife was Sarah Ward Lyon, to whom he had been married on Apr. 24, 1861. Two of their five children survived their parents.

[*Who's Who in America,* 1901–02; J. H. Wilson, article in *Ann. Reunion, Asso. of Grads. U. S. Mil. Acad.* (1903), and *Heroes of the Great Conflict* (1904); G. W. Cullum, *Biog. Reg. . . . U. S. Mil. Acad.* (1891); *Report of a Board of Army Officers upon the Claim of Maj. Gen. William Farrar Smith* (1901); *Memoirs of Gen. W. T. Sherman* (2nd ed., 1886), vol. I; *War of the Rebellion: Official Records* (*Army*), 1 ser., vols. XI, XVIII, XIX, XXX, XXXI, XXXVI, XL; *House Report No. 1813,* 50 Cong., 1 Sess.; *Public Ledger,* Philadelphia, Mar. 2, 1903.]　　　　C.H.L.

SMITH, WILLIAM HENRY (Dec. 4, 1806– Jan. 17, 1872), actor, was a native of Montgomeryshire, Wales, and is said to have been the son of an officer in the British army who was killed in Spain during the Peninsular War. At fourteen, after an unhappy childhood under the domination of a harsh stepfather, he ran away from home and joined a troupe of strolling players. On the stage he was known as W. H. Smith, but in private affairs he used his family name of Sedley. After acting in many provincial companies in theatres in Glasgow, Lancaster, and other cities of Great Britain, he came to the United States and made his début at once in Philadelphia at the Walnut Street Theatre in June 1827, appearing as Jeremy Diddler in *Raising the Wind* and as Lothair in *Adelgitha* (Wemyss, *post,* p. 130). Varied engagements followed both as actor and stage manager; in the latter capacity he revealed a skill that held him to that line of his professional work through his entire career, in Philadelphia, Boston, and other cities. It was not until 1840 that he ventured to New York, acting there for the first time in November of that year in support of Junius Brutus Booth [*q.v.*], playing Edgar to his Lear, Laertes to his Hamlet, Gratiano to his Shylock, and Mark Antony to his Brutus. His subsequent appearances on the New York stage were infrequent.

In 1843 he joined the new stock organization at the Boston Museum, becoming stage manager of the theatre, and remaining there in that capacity and also as actor for sixteen years. His making-over of *The Drunkard,* a manuscript play by another author, brought lasting popularity to the Boston Museum; after its first performance there on Feb. 12, 1844, it was acted continuously for an exceptionally long run of one hundred and forty times. Smith himself acted the rôle of Edward Middleton, the play remaining a favorite with American playgoers for several years. His life after he left Boston and the Museum in 1859 was for some time a wandering one. An interesting episode in this part of his career was his acting of David Deans in the dramatization by Dion Boucicault [*q.v.*] of *The Heart of Midlothian* at the Winter Garden in New York, May 6, 1865, at the benefit of his daughter, Mrs. Sedley Brown, who played Jeanie Deans. During his last years he was in San Francisco, and was connected with the California Theatre as actor and stage manager. He was a versatile actor in a wide range of parts, being equally successful in his younger days in juvenile characters and in his later years in the acting of comedy old men. Joseph Cowell, with whom he was associated when he first came to America, says that he was "one of those pink-looking men, with yellow hair, that the ladies always admire, and in his day was considered the best fop and light comedian on the continent" (Cowell, *post,* p. 81). Yet his art is said to have been "intellectual, truthful, conscientious, significant with thought and purpose, and warm with emotion" (Winter, *post,* p. 272). When in Boston he had married Sarah (Lapsley) Riddle of the Philadelphia theatrical family of that

name, who died in 1861 after a distinguished career on the stage. They had a son and a daughter who in later years became well known on the stage, first as Mrs. Sedley Brown, and later as Mrs. Sol Smith. His second wife, Lucy, survived him by many years.

[Joseph Sabin, *A Dict. of Books Relating to America,* pt. 122 (1930), continuation by R. W. G. Vail; F. C. Wemyss, *Wemyss' Chronology of the Am. Stage* (1852); Joseph Cowell, *Thirty Years Passed Among the Players in England and America* (1844); *Boston Museum, an Interesting Retrospect* (1880–81); W. M. Leman, *Memories of an Old Actor* (1886); William Winter, *Brief Chronicles,* pt. 3 (1890); T. A. Brown, *A Hist. of the N. Y. Stage* (1903), vol. I; G. C. D. Odell, *Annals of the N. Y. Stage,* vols. IV (1928), VII (1931); *Boston Transcript,* Mar. 6, 1915, pt. 3; obituaries in *N. Y. Times,* Jan. 20, and *Morning Bull.* (San Francisco), Jan. 19, 1872.]   E.F.E.

SMITH, WILLIAM HENRY (Dec. 1, 1833–July 27, 1896), journalist, was born at Austerlitz, Columbia County, N. Y., the son of William DeForest Smith. His father is said to have come from Litchfield County, Conn., where his ancestors settled about 1640, and his mother is said to have been a member of a family named Gott, which settled in Columbia County, N. Y., at the close of the Revolutionary War. He was taken by his parents as an infant to Homer, Ohio. After serving as a school teacher and a tutor, he began his journalistic career by acting as correspondent for Cincinnati newspapers. He early joined a group of young men—free soilers—that included Rutherford B. Hayes and John Brough [*qq.v.*]. In 1855 he was married to Emma Reynolds, who died in 1891. He became a member of the staff of the Cincinnati *Gazette,* but he gave up newspaper work for a time to act as private secretary to Governor Brough and from 1864 to 1866 to be secretary of the state of Ohio. After his second term as secretary of state, he edited the Cincinnati *Evening Chronicle.* In 1870 he took charge of the Western Associated Press, then a struggling organization with headquarters at Chicago. President Hayes, his old friend, appointed him collector of the port of Chicago, but he also continued his press association work. As collector he was instrumental in correcting certain abuses in the New York customs office that worked to the disadvantage of Chicago importers. In 1882 he effected a combination of the New York Associated Press and the Western Associated Press and was chosen general manager of the joint organization, a position he held until he was succeeded by Melville E. Stone [*q.v.*]. During his twenty-two years as head of these two press associations, a system of leased wires was established, and typewriters were used in receiving the telegraphic news reports. He also aided Whitelaw Reid [*q.v.*] in organizing and developing the Mergenthaler Linotype Company.

He was keenly interested in the history of the Middle West. He took an active part in the preservation of historical material pertaining to the Northwest Territory and was requested by the Ohio state legislature to edit the papers of Arthur St. Clair, the first governor of the territory. These were published in two volumes in 1882 under the title *The St. Clair Papers.* After 1892 he devoted his time to preparing a history of slavery in this country, particularly with reference to the anti-slavery movement in the Middle West, with which he had been identified. This work, practically completed at the time of his death, was finally published in two volumes in 1903 as *A Political History of Slavery.* He also collected some material for a volume on the life and times of President Hayes, which was to be a continuation of his history of slavery. This material was incorporated in the *Life of Rutherford Birchard Hayes* (2 vols., 1914) written by Smith's son-in-law, Charles Richard Williams [*q.v.*]. He died at his home in Lake Forest, Ill., survived by one son.

[Biographical sketch by Whitelaw Reid in *A Political History of Slavery, ante*; some details of his friendship with Hayes in Williams, *ante*; M. E. Stone, *Fifty Years a Journalist* (1921); *Ohio Arch. and Hist. Pubs.*, vol. IV (1895); *Chicago Daily Tribune*, July 28, 1896; *N. Y. Tribune*, July 28, Aug. 28, 1896.]
W. G. B—r.

SMITH, WILLIAM LOUGHTON (*c.* 1758– Dec. 19, 1812), congressman from South Carolina, diplomat, and political pamphleteer, was the great-grandson of William Smith who was in South Carolina as early as 1690 and the son of Benjamin Smith who held many provincial offices, made a fortune in trade, and gave generously to welfare work. His mother, Anne (Loughton) Smith, died when William was but two years old. At the age of twelve, a few months before his father's death, he was sent to London and entered at Hackney. On May 12, 1774, he was admitted to the Middle Temple, but from 1774 to 1778 he studied at Geneva. Returning to England in 1779, he studied law until the fall of 1782, when he left London to seek passage for America. A year later he reached Charleston, where he was admitted to the bar in January 1784 and in November was elected to the legislature. On May 1, 1786, he married Charlotte Izard, the daughter of Ralph Izard [*q.v.*]. She bore him a son and a daughter and died in 1792. After holding various local offices, he was elected to the First Congress, where his seat was contested by David Ramsay [*q.v.*] on the ground that he was not an American citizen, the first of

the congressional contested elections. He was seated and soon became a leading Federalist. A heavy speculator in government paper, he vigorously supported assumption of state debts by the federal government, and it is said that after the reading of Hamilton's report he was one of those who sent fast-sailing vessels down the coast to purchase all the certificates that could be had from discouraged holders. In the summer of 1790, he set out from New York with Washington's party for Rhode Island, an episode of which he has left an interesting journal (*post*). In 1792 he published his first pamphlet, which has been erroneously attributed to Alexander Hamilton (copy in Charleston Library Society with attribution in own handwriting, see Salley, *post,* p. 254), *The Politicks and Views of a Certain Party, Displayed,* an attack on Jefferson. In 1796 it was probably he who attacked Jefferson anonymously in *The Pretensions of Thomas Jefferson to the Presidency Examined* (originally published in *Gazette of the United States,* Oct., Nov. 1796). In the same year he received an honorary LL.D. from the College of New Jersey, now Princeton (*General Catalogue of Princeton,* 1908, p. 404, is mistaken; see Matthews, *post,* footnote 3, p. 29). His *Comparative View of the Constitutions of the Several States with Each Other, and with That of the United States* (1796) was much admired and is said to have been used as a text at Princeton. In the spring of 1794, his political enemies in Charleston expressed their dislike by burning him in effigy in the company of Arnold and the Devil. Although Hamilton rated him a man of abilities, information, industry, and integrity, both he and Washington felt that Smith's personal unpopularity debarred him from a conspicuous appointment.

However, he was elected to Congress five times and served until July 10, 1797, when he resigned to become minister to Portugal. There he entertained handsomely, worked smoothly with the British diplomats, and, as attested by voluminous letters, followed intelligently the progress of Napoleon in Europe. He was relieved on Sept. 9, 1801, but remained in Europe. Upon his return to Charleston in December 1803 he resumed the practice of law and at the next election was defeated for Congress. About this time he included his mother's name with his own to distinguish him from William Smith, *c.* 1762–1840 [*q.v.*], with whom he has usually been confused. On Dec. 19, 1805, he married Charlotte Wragg, the daughter of William Wragg [*q.v.*], by whom he had a son. In February 1806 under the name of "Phocion," he began a series of letters in the *Charleston Daily Courier* (reprinted in pamphlet form as *The Numbers of Phocion,* 1806, in Charleston and as *American Arguments for British Rights,* 1806, in London).

[Papers and letters in Lib. of Cong. and in Pickering Papers of the Mass. Hist. Soc.; some letters in *S. C. Hist. and Geneal. Mag.,* Apr. 1924–Jan. 1925, and *Sewanee Review,* Jan. 1906; sketches and bibliog. in A. S. Salley, "Wm. Smith and Some of his Descendants," *S. C. Hist. and Geneal. Mag.,* Apr. 1903, and in Albert Matthews, "Journ. of Wm. Loughton Smith, 1790–1791," *Mass. Hist. Soc. Proc.,* vol. LI (1918) and separately (1917); David Ramsay, *Observations on the Decision . . . Respecting the Eligibility of the Hon. Wm. Smith* (1789); E. A. Jones, *Am. Members of the Inns of Court* (1924); U. B. Phillips, "The S. C. Federalists," *Am. Hist. Rev.,* July 1909.] A. K. G.

SMITH, WILLIAM NATHAN HARRELL (Sept. 24, 1812–Nov. 14, 1889), representative from North Carolina and judge, was born at Murfreesboro, N. C. His father, William Lay Smith, a native of Lyme, Conn., and a half-brother of James Murdock [*q.v.*], was a Yale graduate and a physician. He removed to North Carolina in 1806, married Ann Harrell of Murfreesboro, and died in 1813. The son, prepared for college at Kingston, R. I., and Colchester, Conn., was graduated from Yale College in 1834, studied law there, and was admitted to the North Carolina bar. He immediately removed to Texas but remained there only six months. On Jan. 14, 1839, he married Mary Olivia Wise of Murfreesboro. They had three children. He was a good jury lawyer and successful in practice. Active in the campaign of 1840, he became a Whig member of the House of Commons. In 1848 he was a member of the Senate. In 1849 he was elected solicitor and served until 1857. In that year he accepted the nomination of the American party for Congress. He was, however, not a Know-Nothing, opposing frankly their proscriptive principles. He was defeated but, after serving in 1858 in the House of Commons, was elected to Congress and served from Mar. 4, 1859, to Mar. 3, 1861. In the long contest for speaker that grew out of John Sherman's indorsement of *The Impending Crisis,* Smith's election seemed certain, although he himself took no part in the contest. A believer in protection, he was apparently satisfactory to the Pennsylvania Republicans, several of whom voted for him. He received a majority of one, but, before the result was announced, E. Joy Morris of Pennsylvania demanded that the Pennsylvania delegation should dictate the organization of the ways and means committee. Smith refused to make any bargain and, three Republicans changing their votes, he failed of election.

Intellectually and temperamentally opposed to secession, he was earnest in his efforts to obtain compromise, but the call for troops ended all discussion of the matter for him. One of the very few members to serve in all three Confederate congresses, he was a hard-working, useful member, always conservative, a supporter of the administration, though not a blind one. He voted, for example, uniformly against the suspension of the writ of *habeas corpus,* but he also voted to discontinue the exemption of those who had furnished substitutes. He declined to countenance the peace movement and voted against the peace resolutions of 1864. In 1865–66 he was again a member of the state House of Commons and was particularly active in promoting the liberal legislation concerning the freedmen. He favored President Johnson's policy and was a delegate to the National Union convention in 1866. He was a leader in organizing the Conservative party to oppose Radical control of the state and was a delegate to the National Democratic Convention in 1868. In 1869 he volunteered as counsel for the members of the bar, led by B. F. Moore [*q.v.*], who had been disabled from practice before the supreme court on account of their protest against the political activity of the judges. In 1870 he removed to Norfolk but two years later established himself in Raleigh, N. C. In 1871 he was one of Governor Holden's counsel in the impeachment trial and delivered what was generally regarded as the ablest argument of the trial. In 1873 the disabilities of the Fourteenth Amendment were removed.

In 1878 he became chief justice of the state supreme court and served until his death. Though not a great judge he was a prodigious worker and as executive of the court highly successful. His opinions are scholarly, relying heavily upon precedent, partly as a result of his temperament, but more, probably, because of his modesty. They were logically reasoned but were written in a very involved style. Personally he was a courteous, retiring gentleman with many friends and no enemies. He did not lack convictions, but there was in him no trace of undue partisanship. He was an able and fluent speaker, a learned lawyer in the best sense of the term.

[*Biog. Hist. of N. C.,* vol. VII (1908), ed. by S. A. Ashe and S. B. Weeks; *N. C. Reports,* vol. CIV (1890), App. pp. 955–66; *Hist. of the Class of 1834 in Yale College* (1875); F. B. Dexter, *Biog. Sketch of the Grads. of Yale College,* vol. V (1911); J. G. deR. Hamilton, *Reconstruction in N. C.* (1914); *News and Observer* (Raleigh), Nov. 15, 1889.] J. G. deR. H.

SMITH, WILLIAM RUSSELL (Mar. 27, 1815–Feb. 26, 1896), lawyer, congressman, author, was born in Russellville, Ky., the son of Ezekiel and Elizabeth (Hampton) Smith, descendants of old Virginia families. According to tradition, both of the boy's grandfathers fought in the battle of King's Mountain. Ezekiel, a planter, left his farm to fight in the Seminole War and shortly after his return he died. His widow moved to Huntsville, Ala., and in 1820, to Tuscaloosa. Before William was ten years old she died also, leaving her children to the care of strangers. William was befriended by George W. Crabb, who recognized his ability and financed his education. In 1834, having completed three years of college work at the University of Alabama, he entered the law office of his benefactor. He was soon admitted to the bar and opened an office in Greensboro, Ala.

Throughout his life he had a wide variety of interests and turned with bewildering rapidity from one to the other. He had been practising only one year when the outbreak of a Creek War led him to abandon law for arms. He raised a company and marched to the scene of conflict only to find that the uprising had been put down. His company then moved on toward Texas with the idea of aiding the Texans in their revolt against Mexico, but was stopped at Mobile by the news of the battle of San Jacinto. Smith stayed in Mobile and began the publication of a monthly, of which only six numbers were issued. In 1837 he returned to Tuscaloosa. He edited a Whig newspaper of some merit and served as mayor in 1839. Independent and an individualist, he found it difficult to work with a party, and he was severely criticized for his many shifts in party allegiance. In 1841 and again in 1842 he was elected to the Alabama general assembly as a Whig, but he was opposed to the Whig position on the tariff and left the party in 1843. In 1844 he moved to Fayette County and from 1850 to 1851 served as circuit judge. In 1850 he was elected to Congress as a supporter of the Union and served until Mar. 3, 1857. In 1855 he allied himself with the American party and was mentioned as a vice-presidential possibility in the election of 1856, but was defeated as an American candidate for Congress in that year. After retiring from Congress he moved back to Tuscaloosa. He supported Bell and Everett in 1860 and opposed secession in the Alabama state convention of 1861, but recruited and became colonel of the 26th Alabama Regiment. Before active fighting began, however, he was elected to the Confederate House of Representatives, where he served throughout the war. He was a candidate for governor in 1865 and for Congress in 1866 and in 1878. He was defeated in 1865 and in 1878, and in 1866 he withdrew from the contest. In 1870 he was elected president of the University of Alabama by the radical board of trustees, in an attempt to secure popular support for the university. The feeling between radicals and conservatives was so strong, however, that only a few students enrolled in 1871 and the president resigned. After his resignation he practised law in Tuscaloosa until 1879, when he removed to Washington, D. C., where he practised and devoted much time to writing.

He was a prolific writer in many fields. As early as 1833 he published a volume of poetry, *College Musings, or Twigs from Parnassus*. His best known poem, *The Uses of Solitude* (1860), was read to the Tuscaloosa chapter of Phi Beta Kappa. His *The Justice of the Peace* (1841), a book for the guidance of magistrates, appeared in two subsequent editions under the titles *The Jurisdiction of Justices of the Peace in Civil and Criminal Cases* (1859, 1860). In 1861 he published *The History and Debates of the Convention of the People of Alabama . . . 1861*. His *Reports of Decisions of the Supreme Court of the State of Alabama* (10 vols., 1870–79), covering the period 1820–46, with notes, was widely known. He also wrote *Reminiscences of a Long Life* (copr. 1889). In addition he published several volumes of poetry, plays, and essays. His first wife was Jane Binion of Tuscaloosa, to whom he was married in 1843 and who died less than two years thereafter. On Jan. 3, 1847, he married Mary Jane Murray of Fayette, Ala. After her death in 1853 he married June 14, 1854, Wilhelmine M. Easby of Washington. He had children by all three wives.

[Anne Easby-Smith, *William Russell Smith of Ala.* (1931); T. M. Owen, *Hist. of Ala. and Dict. of Ala. Biog.* (1921); William Garrett, *Reminiscences of Public Men in Ala. for Thirty Years* (1872); *Biog. Dir. Am. Cong.* (1928); Willis Brewer, *Alabama* (1872); *Washington Post*, Feb. 27, 1896.]   H. F.

SMITH, WILLIAM SOOY (July 22, 1830–Mar. 4, 1916), civil engineer, Union soldier, was born in Tarlton, Pickaway County, Ohio, the son of Sooy and Ann (Hedges) Smith. His father was a local magistrate. William worked his way through Ohio University, Athens, Ohio, graduating with distinction in 1849. He immediately obtained an appointment to the United States Military Academy at West Point, where he graduated in 1853, ranking sixth in his class.

On June 19, 1854, he resigned his commission to become an assistant on construction for the Illinois Central Railway, but his career was soon interrupted by a desperate illness and he subsequently spent two years teaching in Buffalo, N. Y. Resuming engineering practice in 1857, he organized the firm of Parkinson & Smith, and made the first surveys for an international bridge at Niagara Falls. In 1859 he began the construction of a large bridge over the Savannah River for the Charleston & Savannah Railroad. In connection with this structure he made the first use in America of the pneumatic process for sinking foundations, then but recently developed in France. Finding the method cumbersome and ill-suited to his requirements, he made many fundamental changes in the design of apparatus and in construction procedure.

The project was interrupted by the outbreak of the Civil War, whereupon Smith immediately returned to his native state and enlisted in the volunteer army. On June 26, 1861, he was commissioned colonel of the 13th Ohio Infantry, and on Apr. 15, 1862, he was made a brigadier-general. He served with distinction until 1864, when a serious attack of inflammatory rheumatism completely disabled him. Resigning from the army July 15, 1864, he regained his health slowly, occupied as a farmer at Oak Park, Cook County, Ohio, and it was not until 1866 that he again took up civil engineering practice. His next project was that of building a protection for the Wagoschance lighthouse on the Straits of Mackinac. In connection with this enterprise he further developed his pneumatic caisson process for sinking foundations, and later perfected it on several railroad bridges which he constructed in the early seventies. For this work he received a prize award from the American Centennial Exposition in 1876. In 1876 he prepared plans for a tunnel under the Detroit River, which he proposed to build by sinking a continuous series of pneumatic caissons across the river. His plan received the approval of the advisory board of engineers, but it was too far in advance of the times to secure financial support.

For the next twelve years, Smith specialized in bridge construction and deep foundations. He was successively engaged, either as chief engineer or consulting engineer, on important railroad bridges over the Missouri River at Omaha, Leavenworth, Boonville, Glasgow, Plattsmouth, Sibley, and Kansas City. During this period steel was perfected to the point of competing with wrought iron, and Smith was one of the first to champion the use of the new material. Owing to his influence, it was decided to use steel throughout in the trusses of the Glasgow bridge, which became the first all-steel truss bridge in the world.

About 1890 Smith settled in Chicago and gave most of his professional attention to the subject of building foundations, which presented an extraordinarily difficult problem in that vicinity because of the great depth of rock and bad soil conditions. He was one of the first to advocate

carrying the piers of high buildings to rock instead of supporting them on rafts or grillages. He was consulted in regard to the foundations of nearly all the large buildings constructed in Chicago during the period from 1890 to 1910, in which year he retired from active practice. The remainder of his life he spent quietly in the village of Medford, Ore. His professional labors never ceased, however; at the time of his death, which followed an attack of pneumonia in his eighty-sixth year, he was completing plans for a new-type fireproof building. He was one of the founders of the Western Society of Engineers, of which he was president from 1877 to 1880, and thereafter for a number of years chairman of its committee on iron and steel. He was also an influential member of a similar committee of the American Society of Civil Engineers. To this society he contributed two important papers: "Pneumatic Foundations" (*Transactions,* vol. II, 1874) and "The Hudson River Tunnel" (*Ibid.,* vol. XI, 1882). He was married in 1854 to Elizabeth Haven of Buffalo, N. Y., by whom he had one son, Charles Sooysmith [*q.v.*]. His first wife died in 1860, and in 1862 he married Anna Durham of Bowling Green, Ky., who died in 1882; in 1884 he married Josephine Hartwell of St. Catharines, Ontario, by whom he had a son.

[G. W. Cullum, *Biog. Reg. Officers and Grads. U. S. Mil. Acad.* (1891); *Engineering News,* Mar. 30, 1916; *Jour. Western Soc. of Engineers,* Jan. 1917; *Who's Who in America,* 1914–15; *Morning Oregonian* (Portland), Mar. 6, 1916.]   J. I. P.

SMITH, WILLIAM STEPHENS (Nov. 8, 1755–June 10, 1816), Revolutionary soldier, was born in New York. His father, John Smith, was a wealthy merchant. His mother, Margaret Stephens, belonged to a Loyalist family. After graduating from the College of New Jersey (Princeton) in 1774, he studied law with Samuel Jones of New York. He entered the army at the outbreak of the Revolution, being appointed aide to General Sullivan with the rank of major in August 1776. He was present at the battle of Long Island, and when the American troops withdrew across East River on the night of Aug. 29, it is said that he was one of the last to leave, accompanying Washington in his barge. In October, although suffering from a wound received at Harlem Heights, he destroyed the bridge at Throgs Neck, and thus helped to prevent Howe from outflanking the American army. After participating in the battle of White Plains, he accompanied the Revolutionary forces on the retreat across New Jersey. Gallantry at Trenton won him a lieutenant-colonelcy in William R. Lee's regiment. In 1777 he served under Putnam in New York; in 1778, fought at Monmouth and

Newport; in 1779, marched with Sullivan against the Indians; and in 1780, took part in the battle of Springfield. After acting as inspector and adjutant to a corps of light infantry under Lafayette, he was honored in July 1781 by an appointment as aide to Washington, performed important duties at Yorktown and was charged with supervising the evacuaction of New York by the British in accordance with the treaty of peace.

He was appointed secretary of legation in London in 1785. There he met and was married, on June 12, 1786, to Abigail Amelia, daughter of the American minister, John Adams, 1735–1826 [*q.v.*]. In company with Francisco de Miranda, he toured the Continent, visiting Prussia in order to study the army organization of Frederick the Great, and was later sent on a diplomatic mission to Spain and Portugal. He returned to the United States in 1788 and plunged heavily into land speculation and politics. He held successively the offices of federal marshal, supervisor of the revenue, and surveyor of the port of New York. When war with France impended in 1798, Adams nominated him as adjutant-general, but the nomination was rejected by the Senate largely owing to the interference of Timothy Pickering (C. F. Adams, *The Life of John Adams*, 1871, II, 269), and Smith was obliged to content himself with the command of the 12th Infantry. In 1806 he was prosecuted for complicity in the fitting out of Miranda's filibustering expedition to South America and was acquitted but his political career was seriously affected. He returned to his farm in Lebanon, N. Y., where he devoted himself to agriculture until 1812 when he was elected to Congress as a Federalist, serving from 1813 until his death at Lebanon. He was one of the founders of the Society of the Cincinnati, succeeding his friend von Steuben as president of the order. He was the pattern of the eighteenth-century gentleman, handsome, brave, urbane, and equally at ease at camp or court. His wife preceded him in death. They had three children, two sons and a daughter.

[Letters to and from Smith are scattered through public and private collections, including those of his great-grandson, Mr. H. A. DeWindt, the New York and Massachusetts Historical Societies, the Library of Congress, and the Academia Nacional de la Historia (Caracas). See also *The Trials of William S. Smith and Samuel G. Ogden* (1807); *Jour. and Corresp. of Miss Adams* (2 vols., 1841, 1842); *The Lee Papers*, vol. III (1874); M. D. Raymond, in *N. Y. Geneal. and Biog. Record*, Oct. 1894; *Pubs. of the Southern Hist. Asso.*, vol. XI (1907); B. C. Steiner, *The Life and Corresp. of James McHenry* (1907); K. M. Roof, *Colonel William Smith and Lady* (1929); W. S. Robertson, *The Life of Miranda* (2 vols., 1929); *New-York Gazette & General Advertiser*, June 17, 1816.]
E. E. C.

SMITH, WILLIAM WAUGH (Mar. 12, 1845–Nov. 29, 1912), educator and college president, born at Warrenton, Va., was the son of Richard McAllister Smith and Ellen Harris Blackwell, both members of families connected with the educational development of Virginia. The father, a first cousin of Gov. William Smith, 1797–1887 [*q.v.*], was principal of the academy at Warrenton, editor of the Alexandria *Evening Sentinel* and subsequently of the *Richmond Enquirer,* and in his later life professor of natural sciences in Randolph-Macon College, Ashland, Va. Willie Waugh, as he was known in his youth, was educated in his father's academy and in the Quaker Academy at Alexandria, Va., until the outbreak of the Civil War. He was rejected twice for military service as a "little boy in knee pants," but in 1862 was accepted as a volunteer. He served in the Confederate army until 1865, acting in intervals as reporter of the Confederate Senate for his father's paper, the *Enquirer,* and rejoining his regiment at the beginning of each campaign. He was wounded at Seven Pines, at Sharpsburg and at Gettysburg, and kept through his later life the little diary, with embedded bullet, that saved his life on one occasion.

In 1867 he entered the University of Virginia and completed the course in Latin in one year, which according to accepted custom gave him the right to be a "graduate of the University of Virginia." The next year he went to Randolph-Macon College, and graduated in Greek in one year. He taught a year in Lane's University School in Richmond, returning to Randolph-Macon in 1870 and graduating with the degree of A.M. in 1871. From 1871 to 1874 he served as co-principal of Bethel Academy and as its principal from 1874 to 1878. Then called to Randolph-Macon College, he occupied there, successively, the chairs of mental and moral philosophy, Greek, and Latin. While professor of Latin in 1886 he was elected president of the college. He soon became convinced that honest college work was impossible while colleges in the South were admitting totally unprepared students with the sole requirement that they be sixteen years old. To prepare students especially for Randolph-Macon College, in 1890 he established an academy at Bedford City, Va., and another in 1892 at Front Royal. In scholastic requirements, in training of faculty, and in building and equipment, the two academies were the standard toward which the state moved and which in many particulars only the best of the modern Virginia high schools have equaled.

At the time of his inauguration as president

of Randolph-Macon College, the state had five colleges and two universities for men, but not a single standard college for women. He wrote in 1890: "We wish to establish in Virginia a college where our young women may obtain an education equal to that given in our best colleges for young men and under environments in harmony with the highest ideals of womanhood" (Harmanson, *post,* p. 6). With this end in view he launched plans that year for the erection of Randolph-Macon Woman's College at Lynchburg. Formally opened in 1893, this was the first woman's college in the South to be given general academic recognition. In the *Annual Report* of the Carnegie Foundation for 1907 it was named as one of the three Southern institutions on the accepted list. Serving as president until his death, Smith steadily enlarged the plant, secured an endowment, and saw the enrollment grow to nearly 600. From 1897 he was also chancellor of the Randolph-Macon System. That year he caused to be established an institute for girls at Danville. During his administration at the Woman's College he was bitterly attacked for having the college enrolled on the "accepted list" of the Carnegie Foundation, which required that trustees "should remain free from control of any other body." The college board of trustees was a self-perpetuating body, but had been closely identified with the Virginia conferences of the Methodist Episcopal Church, South. After enduring the attack of certain Methodist leaders for two years, Smith agreed to the passage of a resolution by the board itself that elections of trustees be approved by the Methodist conferences in Virginia. Accordingly, the college withdrew from the Carnegie list.

Smith was twice married, first, to Ella Jones, of Richmond, on Oct. 1, 1869; and after her death to Marion Love Howison of Alexandria, on Jan. 27, 1875. He had no children. Quick in thought and plan, physically and mentally energetic, he was tireless in work, devoted in purpose, inspiring in leadership. He even sold his own home to speed up an endowment subscription. He lived up to his own motto, "What must be done, can be done" (Harmanson, p. 40). He worked out for the South new standards of secondary education for boys and of higher education for women.

[Richard Irby, *Hist. of Randolph Macon Coll.* (1898?); S. T. M. Harmanson, "Recollections of Dr. W. W. Smith, in *Bulletin of Randolph-Macon Woman's Coll.,* Oct.–Dec. 1917 and "Randolph-Macon Woman's College," *Ibid.,* July–Sept., Oct.–Dec. 1923; R. E. Blackwell, "Dr. William Waugh Smith," in *Alumnae Bulletin of Randolph-Macon Woman's Coll.,* April 1931; Carnegie Foundation for the Advancement of Teaching, *Fourth Annual Report of the President and of the Treasurer* (1909); L. G. Tyler, ed., *Men of Mark in Va.,* vol. I (1906); *Who's Who in America, 1912–13; Times-Dispatch* (Richmond), Nov. 30, 1912; L. M. S. Price, *The Sydney-Smith and Clagett-Price Genealogy* (1927); family manuscripts in the possession of J. F. Howison, Richmond, Va., and R. C. Howison, Raleigh, N. C.]
J. E. W.

SMITH, WINCHELL (Apr. 5, 1871–June 10, 1933), playwright, director, was born in Hartford, Conn., son of William Brown and Virginia (Thrall) Smith. His father, a nephew of John Brown, 1800–1859 [*q.v.*], owned a flour, grain, and feed store. Educated in the Hartford public schools, young Winchell rejected college and enrolled in the school of acting at the Lyceum Theatre (later the American Academy of Dramatic Arts) in New York City. Upon completion of his course in 1892, he found sporadic employment for a decade as actor and stage manager, without attracting much attention, though he acted with William Gillette in *Secret Service.* It was not until 1904, when with Arnold Daly [*q.v.*] he produced in New York a series of plays by George Bernard Shaw, that he became prominent. The first, *Candida,* was produced with $1,000 lent by William Gillette and, with those that followed, started the Shaw vogue in America. Two years later, in collaboration with Byron Ongley, Smith tried his own hand at playwriting with a dramatization of George Barr McCutcheon's *Brewster's Millions,* which he also directed and which was a popular success. Thereafter he gave up acting entirely, and became a dramatist and director. His other original plays were *The Fortune Hunter* and *The Only Son;* all the rest were done in collaboration. With Victor Mapes he wrote *My Little Friend, The New Henrietta,* and *The Boomerang;* with Paul Armstrong [*q.v.*], *Via Wireless;* with John E. Hazzard, *Turn to the Right;* with Tom Cushing, *Thank You;* with Augustin McHugh, *Officer 666;* and with Frank Bacon [*q.v.*], the actor, *Lightnin',* which was one of the greatest popular successes ever produced in America.

He also acted as "play doctor" for numerous other scripts and almost always directed any play he worked on, as well as plays by other authors, notably Frank Craven's *The First Year,* which ran for over 700 performances on Broadway. Because of his skill in gauging public taste and his ability as a director, the percentage of popular successes on his list was phenomenally high; in consequence, his services, at a high fee, were for twenty years in great demand, which no doubt explains why he wrote so few plays entirely alone. Practically all the plays he worked on, however, were comedies in the American tradition of character types, broad effects, brisk dialogue, a "wholesome" atmosphere, and a sentimental ending. They added nothing to the development of a serious native drama nor were they experimental in technique, but they were of their kind theatrically expert and unfailingly entertaining. Though he rose to fame as a producer of Shaw, Smith never in his own playwriting betrayed any Shavian influence. One of his quaintest character creations was "George Spelvin." In an early Smith production an actor who "doubled" was given a second name, George Spelvin, on the program; thereafter the name appeared in the cast of every play with which Smith was associated, till many theatre-goers thought there actually was such a person. Smith married Grace Spencer of Troy, N. Y., on Dec. 20, 1895. They had no children. After his successes began to mount he purchased an estate in Farmington, Conn., close to the town of his birth, and gave much time to its extensive development. His fortune was now ample, and he was with increasing difficulty tempted from his country acres to Broadway; the last play he staged was *The Vinegar Tree* in 1930. He died leaving an estate estimated at a million and a half, a share of which was willed as a trust fund for the care of needy actors and dramatists. Though so successful a man of the theatre, he never lost a boyish bright simplicity and a certain Yankee tang. His smooth, alert face, behind eyeglasses, was that of a keen and kindly observer, without an actor's wrinkle or a worried managerial scowl. He was soft and pleasant spoken, with a dry but kindly wit, and he was universally liked both by his colleagues in the theatre and his neighbors in the country. The writing of popular plays was easy for him, his worldly affairs were uniformly successful, and he lived pleasantly by giving pleasure.

[According to one account—W. R. Cutter, ed., *Geneal. and Family Hist. of the State of Conn.* (1911), vol. II, p. 617—Smith's name was originally William Brown Smith. See *Who's Who in America*, 1932–33; *Who's Who in the Theatre* (1933); *Christian Sci. Monitor* (Boston), Sept. 26, 1916; *N. Y. Times*, Mar. 26, pt. 2, Nov. 19, pt. 5, and Dec. 10, 1916, pt. 2; *Hartford Courant*, Apr. 19, 1931, pt. VI; obituaries in *Hartford Courant* and *N. Y. Times*, June 11, 1933.]

W. P. E.

SMITH, XANTHUS RUSSELL (Feb. 26, 1839–Dec. 2, 1929), painter, was born in Philadelphia, Pa., the son of Russell Smith [*q.v.*] and Mary Priscilla (Wilson) Smith. Educated at home and at the University of Pennsylvania, where he studied medicine from 1856 to 1858 and gave particular attention to anatomy, he had his art training at the Pennsylvania Acad-

emy of the Fine Arts, at the Royal Academy in London, and in Europe. He received his first commission for a landscape at sixteen.

Although listed in the family Bible as Xanthus Russell Smith he did not use his middle name until he enlisted at the outbreak of the Civil War, in which he served under Samuel Francis du Pont [*q.v.*] and took part in Farragut's operations during the capture of Mobile. After the war he painted pictures of many important naval engagements and land battles. Among these are "Surrender of the *Tennessee*," "Sinking of the *Cumberland*," and "Attack on Fort Fisher" in the permanent collection of the Pennsylvania Academy of the Fine Arts; "*Monitor* and *Merrimac*" and "*Kearsage* and *Alabama*" in the Union League of Philadelphia; and "Pickett's Last Charge at Gettysburg" in the John Wanamaker collection. He also painted a picture of "John Burns' July First at Gettysburg," a portrait of John Burns in civilian dress, and portraits from life of Maj. Francis Wister, Gen. Rush Shippen Huidekoper, and Joshua Lawrence Chamberlain [*q.v.*]. Among his other paintings are "The Treaty Elm" in the Bank of North America, Philadelphia, and portraits of Washington and Walt Whitman, and several of Lincoln, whom he greatly admired, one of them being in the possession of the Union League of Philadelphia. On June 19, 1879, he married Mary Binder, daughter of George A. Binder of Philadelphia, by whom he had a daughter and two sons. Private collectors acquired many of his landscapes and marines, the latter painted off the Maine coast, where he maintained a summer home on an island in Casco Bay. In winter he lived at Edgehill, Pa., and worked in his Philadelphia studio, turning especially to portraiture in his last years. After an illness of several years he died at his home in Edgehill and was buried in Ivy Hill Cemetery.

[Necrology in *The New Internat. Year Book*, 1929; Pa. Acad. of the Fine Arts, *Descriptive Cat. of the Permanent Colls.* (1902); obituaries in *Am. Art Ann.*, 1930, *Art Digest*, mid-Dec., 1929, *Pub. Ledger* (Phila.), Feb. 27, Dec. 4, 1929, and *N. Y. Times*, Dec. 4, 1929; information from Mary B. Smith, Smith's widow.]

D. G.

SMOHALLA (*c.* 1815–1907), Indian prophet and founder of the Dreamer religion, was chief of a small tribe related to the Nez Percés, the Wanapum or Sokulk, which inhabited the region around Priest Rapids on the Columbia River, Yakima County, Wash. Soon after 1850 he achieved local celebrity as a medicine man. In the Yakima War of 1855–56 the mystical belief in dreams that he was inspiring aided in encouraging the Indian hostility to the white man.

His new prominence brought him the jealous enmity of Moses, a neighboring chief, who provoked a quarrel. In the resulting fight Smohalla, badly wounded, was left on the field for dead. However, he partially revived, made his way to a boat on the Columbia River, and cast himself adrift. Rescued by white men, he was afraid to return to the hatred of his rival, so set out on romantic wanderings down the Pacific coast into Mexico and then through Arizona, Utah, Nevada, and back home. There he reappeared as one miraculously resurrected from the dead. The resulting prestige and his new knowledge he used with skilful oratory and canny prophecy to gain, by 1872, a wide following. Though short, bald-headed, and almost hunchbacked, he possessed a high forehead, bright, intelligent eyes, and above all a fluent tongue. The Dreamer religion developed by him and his apostles appealed to Indians who, circumscribed and regulated, harassed by white encroachments and attacks, and with a life of hunting and fishing ever harder, were near despair. It taught that the Indians alone were the real people, that the whites, the negroes, and the Chinese were later created by Saghalee Tyee, "The Great Chief Above," to punish them for their apostasy from ancient customs. They had only to live as their fathers had lived and to follow the Dreamer rituals in order to get the aid of cataclysmic forces of nature and the resurrection of the myriad hordes of Indian dead to drive out or to suppress these interlopers. The ritual, based on Indian custom with additions gathered from military parades, Roman Catholic ceremonial, and Mormon practices, so utilized the hypnotic influence of beaten drums, ringing bells, and rhythmic dancing, as to bring visions and exaltation. All the Indian conflicts with the government in this region derived inspiration from Dreamer doctrines. Chief Joseph and his people during the tension with authority that eventuated in the Nez Percé war of 1877 were greatly influenced, especially through Smohalla's apostle, Toohulhulsote, though Smohalla himself was persuaded to peaceful submission. Later this religion was considered to be the principal check to civilizing influences and the peaceful acceptance of land restrictions, and it maintained an important influence for some time after the death of Smohalla.

[James Mooney, "The Ghost Dance Religion," *Fourteenth Ann. Report Bur. of Amer. Ethnology*, pt. 2 (1896); *Report of the Commissioner of Indian Affairs ... 1870* (1870), pp. 50, 54, report of A. B. Meacham of the Oregon superintendency; *Ibid. ... 1892* (1892); O. O. Howard, *Nez Percé Joseph* (1881), esp. pp. 8–9, 45–48, 64–67, 81–83; J. W. MacMurray, "The Dreamers," *Trans. Albany Institute*, vol. XI (1887); E. L.

Huggins, "Smohalla," *Overland Monthly*, Feb. 1891; S. I. Crowder, "The Dreamers," *Ibid.*, Dec. 1913.]

R. A. W.

SMYTH, ALBERT HENRY (June 18, 1863– May 4, 1907), educator, author, and editor, was born in Philadelphia, Pa., the son of William Clarke and Adelaide (Suplee) Smyth. He studied in the public schools of Philadelphia and graduated from the Central High School in 1882. After two years of desultory work on local newspapers, and some time as assistant librarian in the Mercantile Library, he was engaged in 1885 to catalogue books at the Johns Hopkins University, Baltimore, Md., where he found opportunity to pursue certain seminar courses in 1885–86, and in February 1887 received the degree of A.B. *extra ordinem*. Elected professor of English language and literature at the Central High School of Philadelphia in 1886, from 1893 till his death he was head of the department. He never married. Instead he showed a rare devotion to cultural pursuits. His active and versatile mind found an outlet in writing and in lecturing, especially in courses arranged by the Free Library of Philadelphia and by the University Extension Society. Enthusiasm for his subject, ready wit, a fine presence, a beautiful voice, and a natural gift of eloquence made him an unusually pleasing speaker. Among his earlier volumes were *American Literature* (1889), *The Philadelphia Magazines and Their Contributors* (1892), and *Bayard Taylor* (1896) in the American Men of Letters series; he edited *Edmund Burke's Letter to a Noble Lord* (1898) and *Pope: the Iliad of Homer* (1899). At the age of twenty he had become one of a small group of youths who founded *Shakespeariana*, which he continued to edit until 1886; later in his writing, teaching, and lecturing he did valuable service in encouraging a wider interest in Shakespeare and became known as a student of Shakespeare and his country. Every summer after 1886 he spent abroad, studying in foreign libraries and establishing lasting friendships with some of the leading scholars of the time. In addition to his *Shakespeare's Pericles and Apollonius of Tyre* (1898), a revision of seminar studies made at Johns Hopkins, he wrote a critical and historical introduction to a translation of *Hamlet* into modern Greek and published numerous reviews of modern Greek translations of Shakespeare. Upon invitation he even superintended a production of *Hamlet* at Phalerum, Greece.

In 1887 he was elected to the American Philosophical Society, as a delegate of which he delivered a Latin oration at Glasgow on the occasion of the 450th anniversary of the university. Two of his memorial addresses were published in the *Proceedings of the American Philosophical Society, Memorial Volume I* (1900), one on Henry Phillips, the other on Daniel Garrison Brinton [*qq.v.*]. It was undoubtedly through his interest in the Society that the most notable undertaking of his life developed, the publication of the *Writings of Benjamin Franklin* (10 vols., 1905–07). The American Philosophical Society had long had in its possession the most valuable collection in existence of Franklin's manuscripts, more than 13,000 documents in nine languages, and when plans were begun for the celebration of the bicentenary of Franklin's birth it was thought that "a revised and authoritative edition of his Works might be possibly the best and most enduring monument" to his memory (*Writings of Benjamin Franklin,* vol. I, p. viii). There had been three previous editions of Franklin's writings. William Temple Franklin in 1818 had produced an edition of his grandfather's works that was neither adequate nor satisfactory; Jared Sparks [*q.v.*] had saved many valuable papers from oblivion, but had tampered ruthlessly with spelling, grammar, style, and even substance; John Bigelow [*q.v.*] had not had available material that later came to light and occasionally accepted the defective transcripts of Sparks. Smyth's edition was made with assiduous and painstaking care that involved his personal examination of practically all the known documents in Europe and America, a careful study of eighteenth-century newspapers, and the examination of many of Franklin's private papers that had never before fallen into the hands of an editor. As a result of his extensive and thorough research he published 385 letters and 40 articles that had not appeared in previous editions, and from the discovery of many missing leaves was enabled to restore letters hitherto "mutilated" or "incomplete." Every document was faithfully reprinted from the original, "every point, capital letter, and eccentricity of spelling loyally preserved" in accordance with the desires of Franklin, who had urged his printer to observe "strictly the Italicking, Capitalling and Pointing" (*Ibid.,* p. ix). There were added a bibliography of printed material, an analysis of Franklin's writings, and an extensive index. In both the editing and annotating of this authoritative edition Smyth displayed great literary skill, historical accuracy, and good judgment. In 1906 he was decorated by the French government with the insignia of the Legion of Honor when he spoke with marked distinction as the representative of the United States at the dedi-

cation of a statue of Franklin in Paris. His plans to write a life of Franklin and to edit the writings of George Washington were frustrated by his sudden death in Germantown, Pa., of Bright's disease. On the day of his funeral the schools of Stratford-on-Avon were closed as a mark of respect. A portrait of him, painted by James B. Sword, is in the Central High School, Philadelphia.

[See *Who's Who in America,* 1906–07; F. S. Edmonds, *The Early Life of Albert Henry Smyth, 78th Class* (1912), in Hist. Ser. of the Associated Alumni of the Central High School of Phila.; J. G. Rosengarten, in *Proc. Am. Philosophical Soc.,* vol. XLVI (1907); William Winter, *Old Friends* (1909), pp. 329–36; A. S. Henry, in *Book News Monthly,* July 1907; Albert Mordell, in *Barnwell Bull.,* Mar. 1934; R. E. Thompson, *Ibid.,* Oct. 1934; obit. notice in *Pub. Ledger* (Phila.), May 5, 1907. Smyth himself gives an excellent account of his editorship in *Writings of Benjamin Franklin,* vol. I (1905).]   A. L. L.

SMYTH, ALEXANDER (1765–Apr. 17, 1830), soldier, congressman, was born in the island of Rathlin off the coast of Ireland and was brought as a child to Virginia by his father, the Rev. Adam Smyth, who became rector of the Episcopal parish of Botetourt, at Fincastle, Botetourt County. Here Alexander grew up during the American Revolution. He completed his preparatory studies at home, read law, and was appointed deputy clerk of Botetourt County when he was twenty years old. He was licensed in 1789 and began practice at Abingdon, Va. In January 1791, he married Nancy Binkley of Wythe County, and the next year established his home there, where he maintained a practice until his death. He was the father of two sons and two daughters. In 1792, 1796, 1801–02, and 1804–08, he served in the Virginia House of Delegates, and in 1808–09 in the state Senate.

Meanwhile, July 8, 1808, President Jefferson had commissioned him colonel of the Southwest Virginia rifle regiment, and on July 6, 1812, upon the outbreak of war with Great Britain, he was appointed inspector-general with the rank of brigadier-general, United States Army. In this year he published *Regulations for the Field Exercise, Manoeuvres, and Conduct of the Infantry of the United States.* At his own request he was given command of a brigade of regulars ordered to Niagara for the projected invasion of Canada. Here he quarreled with his superior officer, Gen. Stephen Van Rensselaer [*q.v.*] of the New York militia, as to whether the crossing into Canada should be made above or below the Falls. Van Rensselaer, without the cooperation of Smyth, attempted to cross below, failed for lack of support by his own forces, and was relieved of his command at his own request. His force was then turned over to Smyth, who took command at Buffalo, Oct. 24, 1812, and issued a boastful and confident address promising immediate conquest of Canada. On Nov. 25 he gave orders to prepare for crossing, at Black Rock, above Buffalo. Two detachments crossed successfully on the morning of Nov. 28, but by that afternoon it was discovered that only 1,200 of the 4,500 men could be embarked on the boats from the navy yard; Smyth, probably correctly, refused to risk fighting with less than 3,000 men, and a council of war decided to abandon the project. After one more attempt to cross, Dec. 1, the ill-organized, untrained, and ill-equipped army dissolved. One of Smyth's subordinates, Peter B. Porter [q.v.], in command of volunteers, published a letter in the *Buffalo Gazette* (Dec. 8, 1812), attributing the failure to the cowardice of Smyth, who challenged him, but after an exchange of shots on Grand Island the two men shook hands and came back to Black Rock unhurt. Smyth suffered much just ridicule for his bombast and much unjust condemnation for his failure. His answer to a committee of citizens of western New York (dated Dec. 3, 1812; see Severance, *post,* p. 235), in which he laid the blame on the miserable condition of the army and the lack of soldierly spirit in the troops, described the conditions correctly.

He asked permission to visit his family in the winter of 1812–13, which was granted by Dearborn. Before his leave expired, by an act of Congress reorganizing the staff, he was "legislated out" of the army. He sent a petition to Congress, couched in somewhat sentimental terms, asking that his name be replaced on the list of officers, that he might "die, if Heaven wills it, in the defence of his country" (*Annals of Congress,* 13 Cong., 1 Sess., p. 807), but no action was taken in the matter. His own people in Virginia retained their confidence in him, however, and sent him to the House of Delegates, 1816–17 and 1826–27, and to every Congress, except the Nineteenth (1825–27), from 1817 until his death. In his later years he wrote *An Explanation of the Apocalypse, or Revelation of St. John* (1825). In 1811 had appeared *Speeches Delivered by Alexander Smyth, in the House of Delegates and at the Bar.* He died at Washington, and was buried in the Congressional Cemetery.

[For sketches of Smyth's career see Goodridge Wilson, *Smyth County Hist. and Traditions* (1932); F. H. Severance, "The Case of Gen. Alexander Smyth," *Buffalo Hist. Soc. Pubs.,* vol. XVIII (1914); and T. N. Parmelee, "Recollections of an Old Stager: Apocalypse Smythe," *Harper's New Monthly Mag.,* June 1874. The Niagara correspondence is printed in Hezekiah Niles's *Weekly Register,* Sept. 1812–Mar. 1813, and in *The Hist. Reg. of the U. S.,* pt. 2, vol. II (1814). The treatment of Smyth by the major historians is uniformly unfavorable; see Henry Adams, *Hist. of the U. S. A.,* vol. VI (1890); J. B. McMaster, *A Hist. of the People of the U. S.,* vol. IV (copr. 1895); James Schouler, *Hist. of the U. S. A.,* vol. II (copr. 1882); B. J. Lossing, *The Pictorial Field-Book of the War of 1812* (1868). See also *Biog. Dir. Am. Cong.* (1928); *Daily National Intelligencer,* Apr. 19, 1830; *Richmond Enquirer,* Apr. 23, 1830. Copies of Smyth's speeches and family MSS. are in the possession of R. P. Johnson, Wytheville, Va.]
J. E. W.

SMYTH, EGBERT COFFIN (Aug. 24, 1829–Apr. 12, 1904), Congregational clergyman, professor at Andover Theological Seminary, was born in Brunswick, Me., the son of William Smyth [q.v.], professor of mathematics at Bowdoin College, and Harriet Porter (Coffin); Newman Smyth [q.v.] was a brother. Egbert attended Dummer Academy at Byfield, Mass., and was graduated at Bowdoin College in 1848. He taught at Farmington, N. H., 1848–49, was tutor in Greek at Bowdoin, 1849–51, and graduated at Bangor Theological Seminary in 1853. The year following he studied theology at Andover and then for two years was professor of rhetoric and oratory at Bowdoin. He was ordained at Brunswick on July 22, 1856, and served as Collins Professor of Natural and Revealed Religion at Bowdoin from 1856 to 1862. After a year spent in the study of theology at Berlin and Halle he was appointed Brown Professor of Ecclesiastical History at Andover and so continued for the rest of his life. He was also lecturer on pastoral theology, 1863–68, and president of the faculty, 1878–96.

He was a leader in the foundation, in 1884, of the *Andover Review,* a magazine conducted by the faculty in the interest of the interpretation of the old theological standards in the light of modern scholarship. In 1886 he and four other professors were brought to trial by the board of visitors for ideas expressed in the *Review,* and Smyth was removed from his chair of instruction. The trustees, who sustained the faculty, appealed to the supreme court of Massachusetts, which, Oct. 28, 1891, set aside the verdict of the board of visitors on technical grounds. A second trial before the board, the following year, resulted in the case being dismissed. As a member of the prudential committee of the American Board of Commissioners for Foreign Missions Smyth steadily championed the right of liberal interpretation standards, during the controversies in the eighties over the qualifications of candidates for appointment to the mission field. He did not affirm, as he was charged with doing, the doctrine of "future probation," but he did believe and teach that no eschatology could stand which limited God's redemptive purpose. This controversy was finally ended in 1893 by the board's adoption of a modern policy.

His especial interest in the field of ecclesiastical history was the development of Christian thought, which he pursued by the historical rather than the dogmatic method. His favorite field was the first three centuries, through which he traced the growth of the doctrines of the Trinity and the divinity of Christ with great detail and scholarly thoroughness. The other major domain of his interest was the religious thought of the eighteenth century, with especial reference to Jonathan Edwards. While Smyth produced no books, he was the author of many published sermons and a large number of scholarly monographs, the more important of which are: *Value of the Study of Church History in Ministerial Education* (1874); "The Change of the Sabbath to the Lord's Day," in *Sabbath Essays* (1880), edited by W. C. Wood; *Recent Excavations in Ancient Christian Cemeteries* (1882); *Progressive Orthodoxy* (1886), and *The Divinity of Jesus Christ* (1893), in collaboration with the other editors of the *Andover Review*; *Some Early Writings of Jonathan Edwards,* reprinted from *Proceedings of the American Antiquarian Society* (n.s., vol. X, 1896); *The Prevalent View in the Ancient Church of the Purpose of the Death of Jesus Christ* (1900); "Influence of Jonathan Edwards on the Spiritual Life of New England," in *Jonathan Edwards; a Retrospect* (1901), edited by H. N. Gardiner. He also prepared, in collaboration with Prof. C. J. H. Ropes, *The Conflict of Christianity with Heathenism* (1879), a translation of Gerhard Uhlhorn's work, and edited *Observations Concerning the Scripture Œconomy of the Trinity and Covenant of Redemption* (1880), by Jonathan Edwards.

Smyth was a member of several historical societies, a trustee and overseer of Bowdoin College, and a trustee of Dummer and Abbot academies. His nature was rich and sympathetic and his manner, quiet and self-effacing; but his indomitable will caused him to stand firm for his convictions. His wife, whom he married Aug. 12, 1857, was Elizabeth Bradford, daughter of Rev. William Theodore Dwight of Portland, Me., and a descendant of Jonathan Edwards: they had no children.

[*Congregational Year-Book*, 1905; *Congregationalist*, Apr. 23, 1904; *Andover Theological Sem., Necrology*, 1903–04; *Proc. Mass. Hist. Soc.*, 2 ser., vol. XVIII (1905); *Proc. Am. Antiquarian Soc.*, n.s. vol. XVI (1905), with full list of Smyth's publications; E. Y. Hincks, "Rev. Egbert Coffin Smyth, D.D., LL.D.," *New Eng. Hist. and Geneal. Reg.*, Jan. 1905, also printed separately (1904); H. P. Dewey, *Address at the Presentation of the Portrait of Professor Smyth to Andover Theological Seminary* (1901); *The Andover Case* (1887); C. A. Bartol, *The Andover Bottle's Burst* (1882).]
                                                          F. T. P.

SMYTH, JOHN HENRY (July 14, 1844–Sept. 5, 1908), negro lawyer, diplomat, and educator, was born in Richmond, Va., the son of Sully and Ann Eliza (Goode) Smyth. His father was a slave who had been bought from his master for $1,800 by his free-born wife. Since she could not set her husband free under the Virginia law, she willed him to her son. When eight years old John was sent to Philadelphia to be educated. He attended Quaker schools until the death of his father in 1857, when he was obliged to go to work. He is said to have been the first colored newsboy in Philadelphia and he also did errands for a dry-goods store. In 1858, when only fourteen, he entered the Pennsylvania Academy of the Fine Arts, the first colored student admitted there; later, after he had met with fair success as a landscape and figure painter, he was made a member.

In 1859 he became a student in the Institute for Colored Youth, from which he was graduated on May 4, 1862. He then taught in the Philadelphia public schools and at Wilkes-Barre and Pottsville. In 1865 he went to England with the intention of studying for the stage under Ira Aldridge [*q.v.*], the negro actor. The latter died unexpectedly so that Smyth was unable to carry out his plan. While in London he supported himself by giving Shakespearian readings. Returning to the United States in 1869, he entered Howard University Law School, Washington, D. C., and became a clerk, first in the Freedmen's Bureau, and later, in the Census Bureau. On Dec. 24, 1870, he married Fannie E. Shippen, by whom he had a son and a daughter. In 1872 Smyth graduated from Howard University and was made cashier of the Wilmington (N. C.) branch of the Freedmen's Savings & Trust Company of Washington. After the failure of this institution in 1874, he practised law and in 1875 was a delegate to the state constitutional convention. In 1876 he worked for the nomination and election of President Hayes. As a reward for these activities he was appointed, May 23, 1878, minister resident and consul general in Liberia, which position, with one brief intermission, he held until Sept. 11, 1885. He proved himself a thoroughly competent diplomat, and wrote some excellent dispatches on conditions in Liberia (see *Foreign Relations of the United States*, 1879–83).

For some years following his return to the United States he was engaged in the real estate business in Washington. This he relinquished to become editor of the *Reformer,* of Richmond, Va. Learning that delinquent colored boys were being sent to penal institutions in Virginia where they soon became hardened criminals, as the crowning work of his life he secured the establishment in 1897 of the Virginia Manual Labor School at Hanover, the necessary funds being contributed by Northern and Southern philanthropists. It was opened Sept. 12, 1899, and until his death Smyth was in charge of the institution, which has always been conducted on the lines laid down by him (see his article, "Negro Criminality," in the *Southern Workman,* November 1900). He was a handsome member of his race, dark in color with a fine head and regular features. He was large and portly, wore a moustache and a short tufted beard, and was courtly in manners.

[W. J. Simmons, *Men of Mark* (1887); *News Leader* (Richmond, Va.), Sept. 5, 1908; *Times-Dispatch* (Richmond), Sept. 6, 1908; *Southern Workman,* Oct. 1908; data supplied by a daughter, Mrs. Clara Smyth Taliaferro.]   H.G.V.

SMYTH, JULIAN KENNEDY (Aug. 8, 1856–Apr. 4, 1921), minister of the Church of the New Jerusalem, was born at New York City, the son of Joseph Kennedy and Julia Gabriella (Ogden) Smyth. He came of colonial stock, which on the paternal side was Loyalist, and on the maternal, Revolutionary. An ancestor, Francis Lewis [*q.v.*], was a signer of the Declaration of Independence. Julian's childhood years were spent in France; in America, he was educated under private tutors in his parents' home, "Boscobel," Fordham. Through his mother—her sister was Anna Cora (Ogden) Mowatt [*q.v.*]—the youth inherited dramatic talent, and was attracted about equally to the theatre, journalism, and the ministry. As a student at Urbana University, Urbana, Ohio, however, he decided for the ministry, and went there in 1877 to the New-Church Theological School, then situated at Waltham, Mass.

That same year he began his ministry at Portland, Me., and on Nov. 22 married Winogene Horr, of Urbana; two daughters were born to them. In 1882 he was called to the Roxbury (Mass.) Society of the New Church. During a ministry of sixteen years there he was also an editor (1894–98) of the *New-Church Review,* and published two books, *Footprints of the Saviour* (1886) and *Holy Names* (1891). A visit to Palestine and Egypt in the year 1892 added to his vividness as an expositor of the Bible. His abilities as an executive and his gift of leadership came to wider notice when, in 1898, he undertook the pastorate of the New York Society, where he served for the remaining twenty-three years of his life. He was elected presiding minister of the state association in 1909, and, in 1911, president of the General Convention of the New Jerusalem in the United States of America, serving in both positions to the end of his life. In the latter office he exerted a marked constructive influence throughout the Church he served. Even in the disturbing years of the World War, his energy and spirit brought unprecedented solidarity to the organization. A national sustaining fund was established, the liturgy was made uniform, and a campaign launched for the more adequate endowment of Urbana University. He was instrumental in arranging for the preparation of a new hymnal for the Church, to which he himself made a number of contributions. In connection with his parish he directed a mission, "Kennedy House." He also found time for writing and published *Swedenborg* (1911), a stirring address he had delivered the previous year at the Swedenborg Congress in London; *Religion and Life* (1911), the best illustration of his varied powers as a preacher; *The Heart of the War* (1914); *Christian Certainties of Belief* (1916); and *The Gist of Swedenborg* (1920), with W. F. Wunsch. He died in White Sulphur Springs, W. Va.

[W. O. Wheeler, *The Ogden Family in America* (1907); *New-Church Messenger,* June 1, 1921; *New-Church Rev.,* July 1921; *Jour. of the . . . General Convention of the New Jerusalem in the U. S. A.,* 1909, 1911; *N. Y. Herald,* Apr. 6, 1921.]   W. F. W—h.

SMYTH, NEWMAN (June 25, 1843–Jan. 6, 1925), Congregational clergyman, theologian, was born in Brunswick, Me., the son of William Smyth [*q.v.*], long professor of mathematics at Bowdoin College, and a brother of Egbert C. Smyth [*q.v.*]. His mother was Harriet Porter Coffin. Named by his parents Samuel Phillips Newman, he early dropped the first two appellations. At the age of twelve he entered Phillips Academy, Andover, and four years later, Bowdoin College, from which he graduated in 1863. After a brief period as librarian and assistant teacher of mathematics in the naval academy at Newport, R. I., he entered the Union army as a first lieutenant in the 16th Maine Volunteers and saw active service in the vicinity of Petersburg, Va., until the close of the Civil War. In 1867 he graduated from Andover Theological Seminary, and began his ministry in Providence, R. I., where he took charge of a mission connected with what was then the High Street Congregational Church, being ordained Jan. 29, 1868. A year later he went to Germany and pursued theological studies at the University of Berlin and the University of Halle. Upon his return he became pastor of the Congregational Church at Bangor, Me., continuing as such until 1875, and on June 20, 1871, marrying Anna M. Ayer. In 1876 he assumed charge of the

First Presbyterian Church, Quincy, Ill., in which relationship he remained until 1882, when he was called to the pastorate of the First Church of Christ (Congregational), New Haven, Conn. After serving for twenty-six years he became pastor emeritus. In 1899 he was elected a fellow of Yale University, and was active in the affairs of that institution until his death.

As a preacher Smyth's appeal was to the thoughtful. His sermons had literary style and were delivered with a quiet yet deep emotional intensity; but he had few oratorical gifts and never resorted to cheap expedients for popular effects. As a thinker and contributor to theological development, however, he exerted a strong influence both in the United States and abroad. He had a keen, logical mind and, even in his college days, a passion for reality not inhibited by fears of any kind. The New England theology as expounded by Prof. Edwards A. Park [q.v.] at Andover he repudiated as orthodox rationalism. His studies in Germany introduced him to modern Biblical criticism. He returned home to become one of the most constructive theological writers of his generation. His first book, *The Religious Feeling,* appeared in 1877. This was followed by *Old Faiths in New Light* (1878), *The Orthodox Theology of Today* (1881), *The Reality of Faith* (1884), *Christian Facts and Forces* (1887). In these his approach to spiritual truth is through a study of man in connection with his total environment, a method which, grounded in faith, "seeks to interpret results in mind and history by following with patient investigation the processes of life through which they have come to be what they are" (Smyth, "Orthodox Rationalism," *Princeton Review,* May 1882, p. 309). Upon the retirement of Professor Park from his chair at Andover in 1881, Smyth was chosen by the trustees to succeed him. Opposition to the appointment arose in the board of visitors, however, based on a statement in Smyth's writings regarding eternal punishment, and this opposition helped to precipitate the famous Andover controversy. His theological method caused him to welcome with enthusiasm the results of modern science, and he became a student in the Yale biological laboratory to gain better acquaintance with the scientific method and discoveries. The fruits of his studies appear in *The Place of Death in Evolution* (1897), *Through Science to Faith* (1902), *Modern Belief in Immortality* (1910), *Constructive Natural Theology* (1913), and *The Meaning of Personal Life* (1916). Another work, written earlier for the International Theological Library, *Christian Ethics* (1892), at once took rank among the leading treatments of that subject. During his later years he devoted himself with a zeal that no adverse winds could chill to the cause of church union, serving on various commissions and, in 1913, as chairman of a delegation to the Non-Conformist Churches of Great Britain in the interest of a world conference. He welcomed the modernist movement in the Roman Catholic Church as suggesting a possible future means of approach for the Catholic and Protestant bodies; his own activities were directed particularly to the union of the Congregational and Episcopal denominations. In 1908 he published *Passing Protestantism and Coming Catholicism*; in 1919, with Williston Walker, *Approaches Towards Church Unity*; and in 1923, *A Story of Church Unity.* Shortly before his death, which occurred in New Haven, he finished an autobiographical work, *Recollections and Reflections* (1926).

[*Recollections,* to which are appended commemorative addresses by B. W. Bacon, Peter Ainslie, and J. DeW. Perry; *Gen. Cat. of Bowdoin Coll.* (1912); *Gen. Cat. of the Theological Sem. at Andover, Mass., 1808–1908* (n.d.); *Who's Who in America,* 1924–25; J. W. Buckham, *Progressive Religious Thought in America* (1919); *Congregationalist,* Jan. 22, 1925; *New Haven Journal-Courier,* Jan. 6, 7, 1925; personal acquaintance.]

H. E. S.

SMYTH, THOMAS (June 14, 1808–Aug. 20, 1873), Presbyterian clergyman and author, was born in Belfast, Ireland, one of twelve children. His father, Samuel Smyth, of English descent and a ruling elder in the Presbyterian Church, was a successful business man who accumulated a considerable fortune but lost it all. His mother, Ann (Magee) Smyth, of Scotch descent, belonged to a rather remarkable family, one of whom founded the Magee College in Londonderry, Ireland. After his marriage the father changed the spelling of his name to Smith, but Thomas resumed the "y" in 1837. He was a frail but precocious child and won many prizes in school. For five years he attended the Academic Institution of Belfast and in 1827 entered Belfast College, where he made a brilliant record. In 1829 he enrolled at Highbury College, London, continuing his classical course and at the same time beginning the study of theology.

Because of financial reverses his family moved to the United States in 1830, and Smyth spent the year 1830–31 in Princeton Theological Seminary. On Oct. 4, 1831, he was ordained to the ministry by the Presbytery of Newark. Soon after his ordination he was called to supply the pulpit of the Second Presbyterian Church of Charleston, S. C., and on Dec. 29, 1834, was installed as its pastor. In the meantime, on July 9, 1832, he married Margaret Milligan Adger, a member of his congregation; ten children were born to them. When he came to Charleston he was a frail but scholarly young man of twenty-five. He grew rapidly in scholarship and in power as a preacher and writer, until he was one of the leading ministers in his state and denomination.

Although his health was always precarious, he was an untiring worker. His sermons were prepared with the greatest care and he was also a diligent pastor. In addition to his regular duties he was an omnivorous reader and a prolific writer. Some time after his death his writings were collected and edited by his son-in-law, Rev. J. William Flinn, D.D., and his daughter Jean Adger Flinn, and published in ten volumes under the title *Complete Works of Rev. Thomas Smyth* (1908–12). In these writings Smyth discussed with great ability many questions which were before the Church in his day. Since the majority of them have been displaced by others, his discussions do not have the same interest or value for the present generation which they had for his own; yet they constitute a vast storehouse of information and thought. His *Autobiographical Notes, Letters and Reflections*, which was published in 1914, contains much that is of historical value.

In 1850 Smyth suffered a stroke of paralysis from which he never fully recovered, but he toiled on for twenty years. "I have lived from day to day as a tenant at will," he wrote, "looking any moment for an ejectment and change of residence" (*Autobiographical Notes*, p. 510). In 1870 another stroke came and he resigned the pastorate of his church. He continued to work, however, sorting and arranging his manuscripts. From time to time he would say to his physician: "Not ready yet, Doctor." Finally all the manuscripts were arranged, and when the physician came again, Smyth said: "Doctor, I have finished, I am ready" (*Ibid.*, p. 710). That afternoon the end came. While still a student in Highbury College, London, he had developed "a voracious appetite for books." This appetite grew with the years until he had what was probably the most complete collection of theological books to be found in any private library in America. Toward the close of his life his library was turned over to the Columbia Theological Seminary, then located at Columbia, S. C., and now at Decatur, Ga., and it is still kept intact by that institution. In his will he left an endowment for this library, and also an endowment for the Smyth Lectureship at Columbia Seminary.

[G. R. Brackett, *The Christian Warrior Crowned—In Memoriam* (1873); George Howe, *Hist. of the Presbyterian Church in S. C.*, vol. II (1883); Semi-Centennial of Columbia Seminary (1884); W. C. Robinson, *Columbia Theological Seminary and the Southern Presbyterian Church* (1931); H. A. White, *Southern Presbyterian Leaders* (1911); *News and Courier* (Charleston, S. C.), Aug. 21, 1873.]

W.L.L.

SMYTH, WILLIAM (Feb. 2, 1797–Apr. 4, 1868), professor of mathematics, was born at Pittston, Me., the son of Caleb and Abia (Colburn) Smyth. In William's childhood his father moved to Wiscasset; he was a shipbuilder and also taught music. During the War of 1812 young Smyth entered the army and gave his bounty to his mother. His service consisted in acting as secretary to his colonel; it is said he was never in his life able to fire a gun (Packard, *post*, pp. 7–8). After leaving the army he became a clerk at Wiscasset and prepared himself to teach. His parents died when he was eighteen and to support a younger brother and sister he opened and taught a private school, and at the same time fitted himself for college, often studying by the light of the fire. Two years later he became an assistant at Gorham Academy and continued studying with such good results that in 1820 he entered Bowdoin College as a junior. Here he pursued his course against great obstacles, for his sight had been so much impaired that he was obliged to have his lessons read to him by his roommate. He also supported a younger brother in college, though often at his wit's end even for the bare necessities of life. Nevertheless he took the lead of an able class and graduated with the English valedictory in 1822.

After graduation he spent a year at Andover Theological Seminary and then returned to Bowdoin as instructor in Greek. Although Greek was his specialty, he soon was obliged also to take on instruction in mathematics. It is recorded that he introduced the use of the blackboard and made his course so interesting that many requested the privilege of reviewing their algebra under the new method. On succeeding to the professorship of mathematics in 1828 he began a series of textbooks, many of which were used in the leading colleges of the country and won the commendation of the foremost American scientists of the day. The earliest of these were *Elements of Algebra* and *Elements of Analytic Geometry*, both published in 1830. They were followed by others on the same subjects and on trigonometry and calculus.

In his later life Smyth showed unusual public spirit. A devoted member and officer of the Congregationalist Church of Brunswick, on one occasion when the church edifice was being rebuilt he served as tender to a mason to save expense.

He also drew the working plan for the spire. He was a vigorous supporter of the temperance movement and an opponent of slavery, his home being a station on the "underground railroad" for forwarding escaped slaves to Canada. He was particularly devoted to the college, and by his personal efforts raised the larger part of the money required to build Memorial Hall in honor of Bowdoin men who fought in the Civil War; indeed, it was his arduous labors in connection with this enterprise that led to his sudden death. He was also much interested in public education. He introduced a system of graded schools at Brunswick and often appeared before the Maine legislature on school matters. What were then liberal educational movements had his earnest support. He was an admirable example of the college professor of the old school, a competent scholar, an able teacher, precise, simple, clear, a strong Christian, a man greatly interested not merely in his students but in his community and in his state. He was married in 1827 to Harriet Porter Coffin; they had six children, two of whom were Egbert and Newman [qq.v.].

[*Vital Records of Pittston, Me., to the Year 1892* (1911); G. A. and H. W. Wheeler, *Hist. of Brunswick, Topsham, and Harpswell, Me.* (1878); A. S. Packard, *Address on the Life and Character of William Smyth, D.D.* (1868); Newman Smyth, *Recollections and Reflections* (1926); L. C. Hatch, *The Hist. of Bowdoin Coll.* (1927); *Gen. Cat. of Bowdoin Coll.* (1912); *Bangor Daily Whig and Courier,* Apr. 6, 7, 1868.]

K. C. M. S.

SNEAD, THOMAS LOWNDES (Jan. 10, 1828–Oct. 17, 1890), soldier, author, was born in Henrico County, Va., the son of Jesse and Jane J. (Johnson) Snead, the daughter of Mary (Henley) and Benjamin Johnson. He went to Richmond College, then to the University of Virginia, where he studied law for two years, 1846–48. Although admitted to the bar of Virginia in 1850, he chose St. Louis, Mo., for his future home. There he practised law and became interested in newspaper work. He was on the staff of the *Bulletin* during 1860 and 1861. There also he met Harriet Vairin Reel, the only child of John W. and Harriet Louise (Shreve) Reel, to whom he was married on Nov. 24, 1852. At the outbreak of the Civil War, he set aside editorial and legal work to become aide-de-camp to Gov. Claiborne F. Jackson. Acting as the governor's secretary, he attended the Planters' Hotel conference in June 1861, the last futile attempt of Missourians for peace. Immediately thereafter he became acting adjutant-general, with rank of colonel, of the Missouri state guard and took part in the battles of Booneville, Carthage, Wilson's Creek, and Lexington. He acted as one of Missouri's two commissioners in a military convention with the Confederate States, which was signed on Oct. 31, 1861. In 1862 he became assistant adjutant-general of the Confederate army, serving with the rank of major, chief of staff to Gen. Sterling Price in the southwest. In 1864 he was elected representative from Missouri to the Second Confederate Congress and resigned his post in the army. A faithful supporter of Jefferson Davis, he was a member of the committees on foreign affairs and on impressments and also of a special committee on increasing the military force.

After the war, on account of the severe test oath of Missouri's radical Reconstruction, he made New York City his third and last home. In 1865 he became the managing editor of the *New York Daily News.* The following year he was admitted to the bar and devoted his time to the law and to writing. His best known work is a detailed history of the war entitled *The Fight for Missouri,* published in 1886 and covering the period from November 1860 to Aug. 10, 1861. He also wrote "The First Year of the War," "With Price East of the Mississippi," and "Conquest of Arkansas" in *Battles and Leaders of the Civil War* (vols. I–III, 1887–88, ed. by R. U. Johnson and C. C. Buel). He possessed a host of friends who were attracted by his buoyant optimism and sunny disposition. He was a member of the Union Club of New York and was a charter member of the New York Southern Society. His death came suddenly from heart disease in his rooms in the Hotel Royal, New York City, and he was survived by his wife, a daughter, and a son. He was buried in Bellefontaine Cemetery, St. Louis.

[E. A. Allen, "Thomas Lowndes Snead," *Library of Southern Literature,* XI (1907), ed. by E. A. Alderman and J. C. Harris; S. B. Paul, *Memorial of Thomas Lowndes Snead* (1890); Dunbar Rowland, *Jefferson Davis, Constitutionalist* (1923), vols. VIII, X; O. V. S. Hatcher, *The Sneads of Fluvanna* (1910), pp. 111–12; *War of the Rebellion: Official Records (Army),* 1 ser., III, XVII, XXII, XLI, pt. 2, LII–LIII, 2 ser., I, 4 ser., III; H. E. Robinson, *Two Mo. Historians; a Paper . . . before the State Hist. Soc. Mo. . . . Dec. 5, 1901* (1912); *N. Y. Times, Richmond Dispatch,* and *St. Louis Globe-Democrat,* Oct. 19, 1890; *St. Louis Post-Dispatch,* Oct. 18, 1890; University of Va. records, information from I. Shreve Carter, St. Louis, Mo.]

L. L. T.

SNELLING, HENRY HUNT (Nov. 8, 1817–June 24, 1897), pioneer in photographic journalism, was born at Plattsburg, N. Y. He came of army stock—his father was Col. Josiah Snelling [q.v.]; his mother, Abigail, was the daughter of Col. Thomas Hunt—and his childhood was spent in army posts on the northern and northwestern frontiers, with Indian boys and girls and the children of other soldiers as his playfellows. Apparently his father expected him to follow a military calling, for in 1828 he was entered in a military academy at Georgetown, D. C., but upon his father's death soon afterward the family moved to Detroit, Mich., where the mother opened a boarding house, and here Henry completed his schooling and began a business career. In 1837 he married Anna L. Putnam, a sister of George Palmer Putnam [*q.v.*]. She was the author of *Kabaosa; or The Warriors of the West* (1842).

The year after his marriage Snelling moved with his wife to New York City, where he was employed for a while as librarian of the New York Lyceum and then for a time conducted a circulating library. In New York he met Edward Anthony, who was instrumental in awakening his interest in photography. When in 1843 Anthony started manufacturing and selling daguerrean supplies, Snelling became his general sales manager and devoted his energy to the forwarding of this business with such good purpose that it grew rapidly and was dominant in its field for many years. In 1849 Snelling made his first contribution to photographic literature, *The History and Practice of the Art of Photography*, published by his brother-in-law; this is said to have been the first bound volume on photography published in America. In 1850 Snelling sent out proposals for the issuance of the *Photographic Art Journal*, a pioneer in its field, and the first number appeared in January of the following year. Soon after its inception the magazine was increased to quarto size and its name was changed to *Photographic and Fine Art Journal*, the aim of the editor being to give artistic as well as technical instruction to photographers. In 1854 he published *A Dictionary of the Photographic Art*. During these years he was constantly experimenting with photographic processes. In 1852 he invented the enlarging camera; about the same time he devised a ray filter, eliminating the yellow rays by means of blue glass; in 1856 he announced a color process, but never published a description of it. In addition to his editorial and experimental labors he retained his active connection with the firm of E. & H. T. Anthony, often devoting sixteen hours a day to its business. Excessive work brought on nervous prostration, and, beginning in 1857, he was forced to spend three years in rest and idleness. About this time the *Photographic and Fine Art Journal* was sold to C. A. Seely, who had been a contributor to its pages.

Upon regaining his health, Snelling held clerical positions first with the Bureau of Internal Revenue and then with the immigration service, but suffered another breakdown, and was or-dered to the country, where he experimented with farming for a period of two years. Later he moved to Newburgh, N. Y., but after a few months responded again to the lure of editorial work and, moving to Cornwall, N. Y., conducted the *Cornwall Reflector* for a period of eight years. Again illness overtook him, this time accompanied by blindness, which brought about his complete retirement in 1887.

Snelling was described by his nephew, George Haven Putnam, as "a good-natured 'Skimpole' kind of man, who was always in need of help from his brothers-in-law" (*A Memoir of George Palmer Putnam*, 1903, I, 87). Childless and left alone by the death of his wife, he spent his last years in the Memorial Home, St. Louis. In 1889–90 he published "Photographic Entertainments" in *Wilson's Photographic Magazine*. He died at the Memorial Home in his eightieth year. A manuscript autobiography—"Memoirs of a Life"—covering the years down to 1868, is in the Newberry Library, Chicago.

[*St. Louis and Canadian Photographer*, Aug. 1890; *Wilson's Photographic Mag.*, 1889–90, and Aug. 1893; *Minn. Hist. Soc. Colls.*, vol. V (1885); E. F. L. Ellet, *Pioneer Women of the West* (1852); A. J. Olmsted, "Snelling the Father of Photographic Journalism," *Camera* (Phila.), Dec. 1934; *St. Louis Globe-Democrat*, June 25, 1897.]   A. J. O.

SNELLING, JOSIAH (1782–Aug. 20, 1828), soldier, was born in Boston, Mass., and was married there, Aug. 29, 1804, to Elizabeth Bell, who died soon after the birth of a son, William Joseph Snelling [*q.v.*]. Snelling entered the army in 1808 as a first lieutenant in the 4th, later 5th) Infantry, then being organized, and was promoted captain in 1809. He fought at the battle of Tippecanoe, and was afterwards stationed at Detroit, becoming a prisoner of the British upon the capitulation of Gen. William Hull [*q.v.*], in August 1812. Years later he published *Remarks on "General Wm. Hull's Memories of the Campaign of the Northwestern Army, 1812"* (1825). Just prior to the surrender, Snelling had married his second wife, Abigail Hunt, daughter of Col. Thomas Hunt of the 1st Infantry. After his exchange he served as major (assistant inspector general), lieutenant-colonel of the 4th Rifles, and colonel (inspector-general), taking part in the Niagara campaign. At the close of the war he became lieutenant-colonel of the 6th Infantry, and in 1819 was promoted colonel of the 5th Infantry, the regiment in which he had originally served.

In that year the regiment was assembled at Detroit and dispatched into the unexplored West to establish three military posts which should serve as centers for the expected settlement of the new country. The chief of these, and the headquarters of the regiment, was Fort St. Anthony, adjacent to the present cities of St. Paul and Minneapolis. Construction was begun by Lieutenant-Colonel Henry Leavenworth [q.v.] in August 1820 and the cornerstone was laid by Colonel Snelling, with ceremony, on Sept. 10, 1820. Some of the buildings were occupied in 1821, though the group was not completed before 1823. The fort consisted of barracks, storehouses, and officers' quarters, with a parade ground, all enclosed by a wall ten feet high, built of stone quarried locally by the soldiers. Two of its towers still survive (1935). Although untenable against troops with artillery, it was impregnable against Indian attack, and was well designed for the purposes it was to serve.

During and after the building of the fort Snelling had to be not only a military commander and a constructing engineer, but also the virtual monarch of a remote and self-contained community, completely isolated from civilization; for it was to be many years before continuous settlement extended so far. He fulfilled his duties well. The perfect type of the rough and convivial old colonel of fiction, "improvident in his habits and usually in debt," "considerate and intelligent when not under the influence of drink," he was likewise a natural leader of men. Though ruthless in discipline, he was admired and liked by his soldiers, who among themselves called him "the Prairie Hen," in consideration of his red and scanty hair. It was with good reason that the War Department in 1825 changed the name of Fort St. Anthony to Fort Snelling in honor of its builder, who remained in command until January 1828. He died in Washington a few months later, while on leave of absence, survived by his wife and four of their children, one of whom was Henry Hunt Snelling [q.v.], together with the son of his first marriage. Snelling's own summary of his career (Hansen, post, p. 219) is modest and shrewd: "I have passed through every grade to the command of a regiment. I owe nothing to executive patronage, for I have neither friend or relation connected with the government: I have obtained my rank in the ordinary course of promotion, and have retained it by doing my duty."

[M. L. Hansen, *Old Fort Snelling, 1819–1858* (1918); Charlotte O. C. Van Cleve, *"Three Score Years and Ten"* (1888); E. D. Neill, *Fort Snelling, Minn.* (1888), repr. from *Mag. of Western Hist.*, June, Aug. 1888; *Minn. Hist. Soc. Colls.*, esp. vols. I (1872), II (1889), III (1880), V (1885), VI (1894); "Abigail Snelling," in Elizabeth F. L. Ellet, *Pioneer Women of the West* (1852); F. B. Heitman, *Hist. Reg. and Dict.*

U. S. Army (1903); *Daily National Intelligencer* (Washington, D. C.), Aug. 21, 1828.]   T. M. S.

SNELLING, WILLIAM JOSEPH (Dec. 26, 1804–Dec. 24, 1848), journalist, satirist, was born in Boston, Mass., the son of Josiah Snelling [q.v.] and his first wife, Elizabeth Bell. The mother died early, and the boy was left in the hands of relatives who sent him to Dr. Luther Stearns's classical school at Medford. In 1818 he entered the United States Military Academy, but was very unhappy there and left after two years to drift westward toward his father's army post. For some time he lived among the Dakota Indians and eventually became a trapper in the vicinity of Fort Snelling. He married a French girl of Prairie du Chien, but she died during the first winter in their prairie hut; he shared in putting down the Winnebago Indian revolt of 1827 (see his paper, "Early Days at Prairie du Chien," *Wisconsin Historical Society Collections*, vol. V); his life was altogether wild and adventurous.

After the death of his father, Snelling gravitated to Boston, where he appeared in 1828 as a writer. He engaged in hack work for a while, most often under the pseudonym Solomon Bell. Then in 1831 he published *Truth: A New Year's Gift for Scribblers,* a satire on contemporary poets that rocked the small literary world of Boston for a time. He next plunged into newspaper work and made a great many powerful enemies as a reformer and social satirist. His most remarkable exploit in this direction was his crusade against gamblers, undertaken while he was an editor of the *New-England Galaxy* (see his *Exposé of the Vice of Gaming as It Lately Existed in New England,* 1833, reprinted from the *Galaxy*). He was generally successful in his reform activities but he stirred up a wasps' nest against himself. The onslaughts of his political and literary foes, combined with personal misfortunes, gradually drove him to despair, and he took refuge in drink. To the great delight of his ill-wishers, he spent four months in the House of Correction, but he emerged broken rather in health than in spirit. He continued as an independent journalist and in 1847 became the editor of the *Boston Herald,* which he conducted with great vigor for one year before he died, in Chelsea, at the age of forty-four, burned out. He was survived by his wife, Lucy Jordan, whom he had married Mar. 2, 1838, and by three daughters.

Snelling is best remembered as a satirist of his times and especially as the author of *Truth,* which is one of the best verse satires ever written in America. He is represented as a poet by one long piece, "The Birth of Thunder" (R. A.

Griswold, *Poets of America, 1842*). His *Tales of the Northwest; or, Sketches of Indian Life and Character* (1830), have both charm and authenticity; and *The Rat-Trap; or, Cogitations of a Convict in the House of Correction* (1837), written during his term in prison, is a document of unique interest. Only a few of his lesser writings have survived, since he often wrote anonymously and under pen names. He was sincere, fiery, and uncompromising, ever a champion of the oppressed and a passionate advocate of his own high ideas of "truth" and "freedom," but he dissipated his energies, neglected his education, and ruined his health in a series of mad quixotic adventures. His publications reveal a man of great talent, perhaps of genius, who found neither the leisure nor the opportunity to be a great writer.

[G. C. Beltrami, *A Pilgrimage in Europe and America* (1828), vol. II; A. E. Woodall, *William Joseph Snelling* (1933), repr. from *Univ. of Pittsburgh Bull.,* Jan. 1933; Barbara A. S. Adams, "Early Days at Red River Settlement and Fort Snelling," *Minn. Hist. Soc. Colls.,* vol. VI (1894); E. D. Neill, *Fort Snelling, Minn.* (1888); E. A. Perry, *The Boston Herald and Its Hist.* (1878); *The Jordan Memorial* (1882); comments on Snelling's *Truth* in S. G. Goodrich, *Recollections of a Lifetime* (1856), vol. II, and O. W. Holmes, *A Mortal Antipathy* (1885), Introduction; *Boston Transcript,* Dec. 26, 1848; *Minn. Hist.,* June 1928; unpublished thesis by A. E. Woodall, Univ. of Pittsburgh.]

A. E. W.

SNETHEN, NICHOLAS (Nov. 15, 1769–May 30, 1845), clergyman, one of the founders of the Methodist Protestant Church, was born at Glen Cove, then known as Fresh Pond, Long Island, the son of Barak and Ann (Weeks) Snethen. On his father's side he was of Welsh descent. Barak Snethen cultivated a farm and operated a flour mill, sending his product to New York in his own schooner. Nicholas spent much of his early life on the farm and the schooner. Later, through private study he acquired a competent knowledge of English and a usable knowledge of Greek and Hebrew. When he was about twenty-one the family moved to Staten Island, and in 1791 to Belleville, N. J. Here Snethen came under the influence of Methodism and professed conversion.

In 1794 he entered the ministry of the Methodist Episcopal Church and for four years served circuits in New England. In 1799 he was appointed to Charleston, S. C., and was ordained elder there in 1800. The following year he preached in Baltimore and in 1801–02 was traveling companion of Bishop Asbury. For the next three years he preached in Baltimore and New York. In 1804 he married Susannah Hood Worthington, daughter of Charles Worthington of Frederick County, Md., and came into posses-

sion of a farm and some slaves. Between 1806 and 1809 he retired temporarily from the active ministry, but then, until 1814 he preached at Fells Point, Md., Baltimore, Georgetown, D. C., Alexandria, Va., and Frederick, Md. While at Georgetown he became chaplain of the House of Representatives. In 1814 he retired to his farm, and in 1816 became a candidate for representative in Congress, but was defeated.

During the controversy which followed the revolt of James O'Kelly [*q.v.*] against the episcopal authority of Asbury in 1792, Snethen took Asbury's side, issuing in 1800 *A Reply* to O'Kelly's *The Author's Apology for Protesting Against the Methodist Episcopal Government* (*c.* 1798), and, a year or so later, *An Answer* to O'Kelly's *Vindication of An Apology* (1801). At the General Conference of 1812, however, he identified himself with the faction favoring lay representation in the Conferences and limitation of the powers of the bishops, declaring in the course of the debate that he would not again appear on the floor of the General Conference until he was sent there by vote of the laity as well as the ministers. When, in 1820, the *Wesleyan Repository* (Trenton, N. J.) was established to further the cause of reform, Snethen was a frequent contributor, his articles later appearing in a volume under the title *Snethen on Lay Representation: Essays on Lay Representation and Church Government* (1835). He also contributed to the reform monthly, *Mutual Rights,* published at Baltimore beginning in 1824. He prepared the memorial to the General Conference of 1828 asking for reform. That body turned a deaf ear to the request, and in November 1828 the Reformers convened in Baltimore and projected the establishment of the Methodist Protestant Church. Snethen was the leading spirit in drawing up the Articles of Association for the new organization and was elected president of the Maryland Conference.

In 1829, freeing his slaves, he moved to Sullivan County, Ind. Subsequently he removed to Louisville, and later to Cincinnati, where he continued to labor in the ministry of the Church he had helped to establish. In 1834 he returned to Baltimore to edit *Mutual Rights and Methodist Protestant* in conjunction with Asa Shinn [*q.v.*]. In 1836 he conducted a theological school in New York founded by the Methodist Protestant Church. Moving West again in 1837, he became head of a manual labor college, founded by Ohio Conference at Lawrenceburg, Ind., which survived but a year. His last activities were spent in the Territory of Iowa, where he attempted to establish a school in Iowa City known as

Snethen Seminary. Before it was fairly under way, however, he died at the home of a daughter in Princeton, Ind. Besides the works already cited, he was the author of a *Funeral Oration on Bishop Asbury* (1816); *Lectures on Preaching* (1822); *Lectures on Biblical Subjects* (1836), and *Sermons* (1846), edited by W. G. Snethen.

[*Mutual Rights and Methodist Protestant,* July 12, 1845; Abel Stevens, *Hist. of the Methodist Episcopal Church* (1867), vol. III; Matthew Simpson, *Cyc. of Methodism* (1878); W. B. Sprague, *Annals Am. Pulpit,* vol. VII (1859); T. H. Colhouer, *Sketches of the Founders of the Methodist Protestant Church* (1880).]

W. W. S.

SNIDER, DENTON JAQUES (Jan. 9, 1841–Nov. 25, 1925), author, educator, was born on a farm near the village of Mt. Gilead, Ohio, the son of John R. and Catherine (Prather) Snider. His mother died when he was six years old, and the family was separated. The boy passed an arduous childhood but attended several schools and finally entered Oberlin College, where he received the degree of A.B. in 1862. He enlisted in the Union Army, rose to be second lieutenant, served for a time under William Starke Rosecrans [*q.v.*], and resigned after a year of service because of ill health. As soon as his strength was regained he began, March 1864, to teach Greek and Latin in the College of the Christian Brothers in St. Louis, Mo. There he soon fell in with William Torrey Harris and Henry C. Brokmeyer [*qq.v.*], under whose influence he devoted himself to a six years' study of the philosophy of Hegel, although at one time he became so impatient with it that he threw the sacred *Logic* across the room. In the fall of 1866 he entered Brokmeyer's law office, chiefly, as he said, in order to become "a pupil of the University Brokmeyer in person" (*The St. Louis Movement,* p. 11). He was one of the original members of the St. Louis Philosophical Society, founded in January 1866, and a frequent contributor to the *Journal of Speculative Philosophy.* Versed in five foreign languages—Greek, Latin, French, German, and Italian—he brought to the St. Louis movement a knowledge of literature and a catholicity of outlook lacking in the older leaders. But he had neither the originality of Brokmeyer nor the organizing ability of Harris; he was essentially a spectator and critic. Drawn by Harris into the St. Louis schools, where he taught from 1867 to 1877, he declined to be made assistant superintendent, refusing to sacrifice intellectual freedom to professional advancement. In August 1867 he was married to Mary Krug, who bore him three children before her death in 1874. The years 1877–79 he spent in Europe, mainly in Greece. He then returned to St. Louis

and resumed his position in the high school but resigned after a year, unable to stomach the formalized methods of instruction. Every summer for a number of years he lectured in Harris' Concord School of Philosophy, where he rather scandalized the natives by his lack of reverence for the Concord tradition. During the same period he taught Homer, Sophocles, Herodotus, and Thucydides to persons studying kindergarten methods in the kindergarten training-school of Susan Elizabeth Blow [*q.v.*] in St. Louis, this interesting experiment being terminated by a violent quarrel with Miss Blow, whose autocratic personality and Christian fervor resented both Snider's independence and his paganizing tendencies.

He spent the next thirteen years, 1884–97, in lecture tours, chiefly in the Middle West, centering about Chicago. His chief educational achievements during this period were the establishment of a few weeks' Goethe school in Milwaukee in 1886 (with the cooperation of Harris and Brokmeyer) and the establishment of a ten weeks' literary school in Chicago (again with Harris' aid), which ran for eight successive seasons. He proved a brilliant popular lecturer. Tall, slender, with black mustache and fiery manner, he would move impetuously about the stage, checking his flow of eloquence only to chide severely the late-comers. It was he more than any other who carried the idealism of the St. Louis movement to the intellectually starved and spiritually hungry cities of the Middle West. Thus it was fitting that he should finally return in 1897 to the birthplace of the movement and spend his long declining years there, devoting his energy mainly to writing. He lived, by preference, in a boarding-house in the Ghetto, where he enjoyed the society of the immigrants and was free to indulge his numerous eccentricities. Suffering from varicose veins, he always composed while standing or walking about his room, using the back of a chair as an improvised desk. His irregular habits were momentarily interrupted by his marriage on Oct. 21, 1916, to Mrs. Augusta (Siemon) Sander, an admiring disciple forty years his junior, but they lived together only a short time and he was soon happily back in the Ghetto. His last years were passed at the home of a friend, William H. Miner, where he died in 1925, survived by his widow and one daughter by his former marriage. His grave in Bellefontaine Cemetery was for many years annually visited by the Snider Association.

With the possible exception of Harris, he was the only one of the St. Louis group to produce literary work of some permanent value. Ever unwilling to commercialize his talent, he himself published (under the name of the Sigma Publishing Company) more than forty volumes at his own expense, none of which proved or was expected to prove at all remunerative. In fact, he was accustomed to give copies away at his lectures to any who would promise to read them. The more important of his writings fall into three groups: the earliest in inception, dealing with Greece and Rome, includes in prose *A Walk in Hellas* (2 vols., 1881–82) and in verse *Delphic Days* (1880), *Agamemnon's Daughter* (1885), *Homer in Chios* (1891) and *Prorsus Retrorsus* (1892); the chief product of his middle period was a series of nine volumes of commentaries, three on Shakespeare, two each on Homer, Dante, and Goethe, published between 1877 and 1897; his final period brought forth a number of volumes fitted into a grand philosophic or, as he preferred to call it, "psychologic" system, the most significant of these being *Psychology and the Psychosis* (1890), *Ancient European Philosophy* (1903), *Modern European Philosophy* (1904), *The American Ten Years' War, 1855–1865* (1906), *Cosmos and Diacosmos* (1909), *The Biocosmos* (1911), *Music and the Fine Arts* (1913). He also wrote two autobiographical books, *A Writer of Books in His Genesis* (1910) and *The St. Louis Movement in Philosophy, Literature, Education, Psychology, with Chapters of Autobiography* (1920). He remained essentially a Hegelian until the end, *a priori* in his methods, mistaking results for causes, and hypnotized by the triadic scheme which his extensive but far from profound classical and historical scholarship enabled him to impose superficially upon the facts; and, although he correctly estimated the growing importance of psychology, his own psychologic method was outworn, taking little account of current developments. On the other hand he was an esthetic critic of acumen, sensitive to beauty, and extraordinarily gifted in catching meanings and significances, in detecting hidden relations, and in suggesting principles of interpretation. His works, particularly those on Shakespeare and Goethe, form no unimportant addition to American esthetic criticism. Dear to his own heart, though less significant, were his poems, especially *Johnny Appleseed's Rhymes* (1895), which he used to read aloud with great gusto, his bright eyes shining, his long hair tossing, and his voice rolling with Homeric laughter.

[The chief sources of information about Snider's life are his autobiographies, *A Writer of Books* (1910) and *The St. Louis Movement* (1920). See also *Who's Who in America*, 1924–25; *The St. Louis Movement in Philosophy: Some Source Material* (1930), ed. by

C. M. Perry; *A Brief Report of the Meeting Commemorative of the Early Saint Louis Movement* (1922), ed. by D. H. Harris; Lilian Whiting, in *Theosophical Path*, Nov. 1914; J. G. Woerner, *The Rebel's Daughter* (1899), a novel in which Snider appears as Dr. Taylor; A. E. Bostwick, *List of Books Written by Denton J. Snider* (1924); obituary in *St. Louis Post-Dispatch*, Nov. 27, 1925.]   E. S. B.

SNOW, ELIZA ROXEY (Jan. 21, 1804–Dec. 5, 1887), Mormon poet and woman leader, sister of Lorenzo Snow [*q.v.*], was born in Becket, Berkshire County, Mass., the daughter of Oliver and Rosetta L. (Pettibone) Snow. When she was a small child her family migrated westward, settling at Mantua, Ohio, where she received the best available education of her day. As a young woman she showed considerable ability in the practical handicrafts and in writing verse. Her poems were well received by the frontier press, and she developed a certain local prominence. Early in 1835 her mother and elder sister Leonora joined the Mormon church, and in April of that year Eliza herself was baptized in the new sect. In December 1835 she removed to Kirtland, Ohio, where she lived with the family of the Mormon Prophet, Joseph Smith [*q.v.*]. She supported herself by teaching a "select school for young ladies." Later, under her mother's and her influence, her father and her favorite brother Lorenzo became converts to Mormonism.

In 1838 the Snow family joined the general exodus of the Saints to Missouri, remaining there until forced to flee to Illinois because of religious persecution. When Nauvoo was founded in 1840 she settled there and soon became prominent among the women of her church. In 1842, when the chief Mormon women's organization, the Relief Society, was founded, she was made its first secretary. At the dispersal of the Mormons from Illinois following the death of Joseph Smith she joined the faction under Brigham Young [*q.v.*] and migrated with them, first to Iowa and thence to Utah, arriving there late in the summer of 1847, in one of the early pioneer companies.

In May 1855, she was given the responsibility of managing the women's work in the Mormon Endowment House, where the secret religious rituals of the church were performed before any temples were built in Utah. In 1866 she became president of the general (central) church organization of the Women's Relief Society, which position she held until her death. During the year 1872–73 she was a member of a missionary party headed by her brother Lorenzo which visited Palestine. She died Dec. 5, 1887, after several years of feeble health. On June 29, 1842, at Nauvoo, she was secretly married to the Prophet Joseph Smith under the new "dispensation" of plural marriage or spiritual wifery, which he and other Mormon leaders had begun to practise. In 1849, in Salt Lake City, she married Smith's successor, Brigham Young, as one of his polygynous wives. She had no children by either husband.

From the very outset of her association with Mormonism, she began to pour out poems appropriate to various religious and public occasions, and throughout her long life many of the signal disasters or successes of her church led her to commemorate the events in verse. Contemporary Mormon hymnology owes much to her writing, and one of the most popular and typical Mormon hymns, "O My Father, Thou that Dwellest," was written by her. Eliza R. Snow, in fact, served the very important function of putting Mormon history into verse on many occasions, thus helping to build the folk beliefs so important in fostering group solidarity. In addition to *Poems, Religious, Historical, and Political* (vol. I, 1856; vol. II, 1877), she published in 1884 *Biography and Family Record of Lorenzo Snow.*

[Andrew Jenson, *Latter-Day Saint Biog. Encyc.,* vol. I (1901), pp. 693–96; obituary in *Deseret Evening News,* Dec. 5, 1887.]   K.Y.

SNOW, FRANCIS HUNTINGTON (June 29, 1840–Sept. 20, 1908), naturalist, educator, was born at Fitchburg, Mass., the son of Benjamin and Mary (Boutelle) Snow. One of his paternal ancestors was Richard Warren, who came over on the *Mayflower*; his earliest American ancestor with the surname Snow was Richard Snow, who emigrated from England in 1645 and settled in Woburn, Mass. He spent his youth at Fitchburg, and graduated from Williams College in 1862 and from the Andover Theological Seminary in 1866. When in the autumn of 1866 the University of Kansas was founded at Lawrence, Kans., he was appointed to the professorship of mathematics and natural science, one of three men who made up the faculty. About two years later, on July 8, 1868, he married Jane Appleton Aiken of Andover, Mass., a grand-daughter of Jesse Appleton [*q.v.*], president of Bowdoin College, and a descendant of Samuel Symonds, deputy governor of the Massachusetts Bay Colony in 1673.

It does not appear that he was especially interested in entomology until he began his teaching work in Kansas; wishing, however, to make his department useful to the farmers of the state, he took up entomology with enthusiasm. With the help of his students and collaborators, he made very large collections in entomology, bot-

any, and geology. The year after the elder Agassiz [*q.v.*] started his famous summer school of natural history on Penikese Island in 1873, he joined the group of distinguished workers there and returned to his Kansas work broadened and encouraged. In 1883 he was appointed consulting entomologist to the state board of agriculture, a position which he filled (afterwards under the title of state entomologist) for the greater part of the rest of his life. Later he induced the legislature of the state to appropriate funds for the erection of a museum of natural history (afterwards known as the Snow Hall of Natural History) on the campus of the university, an effective and attractive building that he himself planned. After 1886, at his own request, his work was restricted to botany and entomology. In 1889 he was made president of the faculties and in 1890 chancellor of the university. When his health began to fail after twelve years of very successful executive work, he resigned the chancellorship (1901) and for the rest of his life devoted himself largely to museum work, remaining emeritus professor of organic evolution, systematic entomology, and meteorology. As chancellor he played an important part in the building of a great university. He was in executive charge at a critical period in its history, when all the educational institutions of the state, even the Kansas State Agricultural College at Manhattan, suffered at the hands of the Populist legislature, and it is acknowledged that it was almost wholly by his efforts that the funds necessary to carry on the institution were appropriated. He had an extensive personal acquaintanceship with the people of the state and a high place in their respect and affection.

He was probably the pioneer naturalist of Kansas. His personal contributions to science were principally economic, systematic, and faunistic. In 1872 he published the first checklist of Kansas birds, to which he added from year to year, but his bibliography is not extensive, although he made many important contributions to entomology. In the early nineties, having secured special appropriations from the state legislature, he made some interesting experiments involving the artificial introduction of epidemic diseases among chinch bugs, the great enemy to wheat and corn at that time. The work itself was later abandoned, but among both farmers and entomologists it aroused great interest in scientific investigations of injurious insects, and it consequently had a wide value. Snow seems also to have been a remarkable teacher, attracting and holding strong students to scientific studies. He died at Delafield, Wis.

[*Who's Who in America*, 1908–09 ; *Fiftieth Anniversary Report Williams Coll. Class of '62* (1913) ; G. C. Brackett, in *First Biennial Report of the Kan. State Horticultural Soc. . . . 1887–88* (1889) ; A. R. Grote, in *North Am. Entomologist*, Dec. 1879 ; C. E. McClung, in *Entomological News*, Dec. 1908 ; V. L. Kellogg, in *Jour. of Econ. Entomology*, Feb. 1909 ; *Auk*, Oct. 1908 ; obituary in *Topeka State Jour.*, Sept. 21, 1908.]

L. O. H.

SNOW, LORENZO (Apr. 3, 1814–Oct. 10, 1901), fifth president of the Utah branch of the Mormon church, was born in Mantua, Ohio, the son of Oliver and Rosetta L. (Pettibone) Snow, who had migrated from Massachusetts to the Western Reserve in the early years of the century. As an undergraduate at Oberlin College, Lorenzo became thoroughly disillusioned regarding religion. He is quoted as saying, "If there is nothing better than is to be found here in Oberlin College, goodbye to all religions" (*Historical Record*, Feb. 1887, p. 141). Lorenzo left college in 1836. During a visit to his sister Eliza [*q.v.*], who had joined the Mormons in 1835 and who was living at Kirtland, Ohio, he was converted to the new faith and was baptized in June 1836. Some months later, in 1837, he was busy converting others throughout Ohio to Mormonism. In 1838 he moved to Missouri and in the same year undertook a second mission, this time traveling in Missouri, Kentucky, and southern Illinois. Later in the same year he returned to Portage County, Ohio, where he taught school for two winters. In the fall of 1840 he was sent out from Nauvoo, Ill., on his third mission, this time to England. After his return in the spring of 1843, he became active in local affairs and among other projects organized a new company of the Nauvoo Legion and became its captain. In the midst of intense conflict between the Mormons and other citizens of Illinois in the spring and summer of 1844, Joseph Smith [*q.v.*] offered himself as a candidate for the presidency of the United States, and Snow, like dozens of other zealots, entered into a vigorous political campaign in his behalf. In the controversy over leadership following the death of Joseph and Hyrum Smith, Snow supported the Brigham Young faction. When the Saints were finally forced to abandon Nauvoo, Snow, in company with others, on Feb. 12, 1846, moved across the Mississippi into Iowa ; here he remained until the summer of 1848, when he trekked on westward to Salt Lake City.

On Feb. 12, 1849, Snow was made an apostle, thus taking a place among the dominant leaders of his church. In October 1849, Brigham Young [*q.v.*] sent out the first group of missionaries from Utah, and Lorenzo Snow was "set apart" to open the mission in Italy. In June 1850, Snow and his companions began their proselyting in Italy, chiefly among the Protestant Waldenses in the Piedmont. In 1851 Snow with T. B. H. Stenhouse carried this missionary work into Switzerland. He planned to open missions in Malta, Turkey, Russia, and India, but before he could fulfil all his plans he was released from his duties and returned to Utah in July 1852.

In the fall of 1852 he was elected to the territorial legislature, where he served for thirty years, for ten years being president of the upper house. After a year or so of school teaching in Salt Lake City, he was sent out to colonize in northern Utah and in 1853 he led fifty families to Brigham City, which became his residence for nearly forty years. During the winter of 1863–64, Snow, together with three others, organized the Brigham City Mercantile and Manufacturing Association, an example of the consumers' and producers' cooperative institution known in Mormondom as the "United Order." This organization grew to include more than 1500 members—almost the entire adult male population of the community. After a decade of flourishing activity it fell into competition with private industries and gradually shrank in scope and function until it disappeared.

After the passage of the Edmunds Bill early in 1882, Snow, like other prominent Mormons, was haled into court on charges of "unlawful cohabitation" with plural wives. He was convicted, disfranchised, and sent to prison in January 1886. Finally his case was reversed by the United States Supreme Court, and he was released on Feb. 8, 1887. On Apr. 7, 1889, he became president of the quorum of Twelve Apostles —a position that put him second in power in his church. On Sept. 13, 1898, shortly after the death of President Wilford Woodruff, Snow was chosen president of his church, but, already advanced in age, he died three years later. He was buried in Brigham City, Utah.

As a leader Lorenzo Snow represents a mixture of piety and a strong belief in "spiritual gifts" with a distinct practicality in managing men and affairs. He was one of the few early Mormon leaders who had any college training. He was an ardent missionary, and he will long be remembered for his efforts to make a success of the "United Order." His reaction to polygyny illustrates his loyalty to official dogmas. When Joseph Smith explained its principles to him, Snow decided to marry although he was at the time a bachelor of forty years. At his first matrimonial venture he took two wives on the same day, shortly thereafter marrying two more. Later he added five other wives to his household. Snow's principal contribution to Mormon theology is his aphorism: "As man now is, God once was; as God now is, man may be." This principle, later called "the doctrine of eternal progression," he announced privately in 1840 to his sister Eliza and to his close friend, Brigham Young. A year or so later Joseph Smith gave public approval to this idea, and the doctrine has become firmly intrenched in Mormon theology.

[Eliza R. Snow Smith, *Biography and Family Record of Lorenzo Snow* (1884); Andrew Jenson, *Latter-Day Saint Biog. Encyclopedia,* vol. I (1901), pp. 26–31; vol. III (1920), pp. 786–87; Andrew Jenson, comp., *Church Chronology,* 2nd ed. (1914); Andrew Jenson, ed., *The Historical Record,* vol. VI, no. 2, Feb. 1887, pp. 139–45; obituary in *Deseret Evening News,* Oct. 10, 1901.]   K. Y.

SNOWDEN, JAMES ROSS (Dec. 9, 1809–Mar. 21, 1878), numismatist, director of the United States mint, lawyer, was born in Chester, Pa., a son of the Rev. Nathaniel Randolph Snowden, curator of Dickinson College, and Sarah (Gustine) Snowden, daughter of Dr. Lemuel Gustine of Carlisle, Pa. He was a descendant of John Snowden, who emigrated from Nottinghamshire, England, about 1678 and settled on the site of the future Philadelphia; John Snowden is said to have been one of the few Europeans who welcomed William Penn when he made his first visit to his province. After attending Dickinson College for a time and studying law in an office in Carlisle, James Snowden was admitted to the bar at nineteen and in 1830 went to Franklin, Venango County, Pa., where he began practice. Shortly afterward he was appointed deputy attorney general (district attorney), in Venango County; from 1838 to 1844 he was a member of the Pennsylvania legislature, serving as speaker of the House of Representatives, 1842–44. Soon after his admission to the bar he became interested in the state militia and was elected colonel of a local regiment. In 1845 he presided at the state military convention at Harrisburg, Pa.

Elected treasurer of Pennsylvania in 1845, in a comparatively short term he succeeded in improving the character of state loans, and in 1848 was appointed treasurer of the United States mint and assistant treasurer of the United States in Philadelphia (appointment confirmed, Feb. 14, 1848). On Sept. 13, 1848, he was married to Susan Engle Patterson, a daughter of Gen. Robert Patterson [*q.v.*] of Philadelphia; they had two sons and three daughters. In 1850 he resumed practice as a lawyer in Pittsburgh, Pa., having been appointed solicitor of the Pennsylvania Railroad Company. From 1854 to 1861 he was director of the United States mint, Philadelphia, an appointment made by Pres. Franklin

Pierce (confirmed, Mar. 8, 1854). It was while he was actively connected with the mint that he developed an interest in numismatics, on which he wrote several books: *A Description of Ancient and Modern Coins in the Cabinet Collection at the Mint of the United States* (1860), *A Description of the Medals of Washington; of National and Miscellaneous Medals, and of Other Objects of Interest in the Museum of the Mint* (1861), *The Medallic Memorials of Washington in the Mint of the United States* (1861), and *The Coins of the Bible, and Its Money Terms* (1864). He contributed articles on the coins of the United States to the *National Almanac and Annual Record for the Year 1873,* and an article on international coinage to *Lippincott's Magazine,* January 1870, in which he urged that all nations be invited to adopt the dollar as a monetary unit, and advocated a single standard (gold) for all countries; he later published a pamphlet, *A Measure Proposed to Secure a Safe Treasury and a Sound Currency* (1857), in which he suggested the issuing of certificates on deposits of gold bullion at the mint, its branches, and the assay office, in convenient sums and payable to the bearer. As director of the mint he was instrumental in having the building made fireproof. In 1861 he was appointed prothonotary of the supreme court of Pennsylvania and held the office until 1873, when he resigned to resume the practice of law in Philadelphia. During the Civil War he was lieutenant-colonel of the 1st Regiment of the Philadelphia Home Guard. He died in his country home, Hulmeville, Bucks County, Pa.

[F. W. Leach, in *North American* (Phila.), July 14, and Dec. 8, 1912; Alfred Nevin, *Centennial Biog.: Men of Mark of Cumberland Valley, Pa., 1776–1876* (1876); *Hist. of Venango County, Pa.* (1890); C. A. Babcock, *Venango County, Pa., Her Pioneers and People* (1919), vol. I; *Proc. of the Celebration of the First Centennial of the Organization of the County of Venango, Pa., for Judicial Purposes* (1905); death notice in *Pub. Ledger* (Phila.), Mar. 23, 1878.]   J. J.

SNOWDEN, THOMAS (Aug. 12, 1857–Jan. 27, 1930), naval officer, son of Dr. Thomas Snowden and Catherine Clinton (Wood) Snowden, was born in Peekskill, N. Y. He was appointed to the United States Naval Academy in 1875 and was graduated in 1879. After five years spent in sea duty on the Atlantic, in 1884 he was ordered to the hydrographic office and in 1889 to the naval observatory. Commissioned junior lieutenant in 1892, he was assigned to the *Ranger* and spent over two years in coast survey work with her off the coast of Alaska. During the Spanish-American War he served on the cruiser *Dolphin* in the squadron under Admiral William

Thomas Sampson [*q.v.*], taking part in the bombardment of Santiago, June 6, 1898, and in the action near Caimanera, June 14. He was navigator of the battleship *Illinois* for three years, commanded the presidential yacht *Mayflower* from 1908 to 1910, and the battleship *South Carolina* in the Atlantic Fleet from 1911 to 1913. In this ship he was at Tampico and Vera Cruz for six months during the early disturbances under the Huerta régime in Mexico. He was then sent to the Naval War College for a year, after which he commanded the battleship *Wyoming*. When the United States entered the World War he was acting as hydrographer to the Navy Department; promoted to rear admiral July 1, 1917, he commanded a squadron of the battleship force of the Atlantic Fleet throughout the war, and at its close was awarded the Navy Cross "for exceptionally meritorious service in a duty of great responsibility as commander, Division Two, Battleship Force One, Atlantic Fleet" (*The Navy Book of Distinguished Service,* 1921, p. 131, edited by H. R. Stringer).

Soon after the armistice he was made military governor of Santo Domingo, with the additional duty of serving as military representative of the United States in Haiti. During his administration he worked indefatigably to place the republic on a safe and enduring foundation, establishing schools, and undertaking the construction of roads and public buildings. "No official ever served his country with greater fidelity, or an alien people . . . with a more lofty purpose than Admiral Snowden gave to the Dominicans" (*Times,* San Juan, Puerto Rico, Mar. 4, 1924). Ill health, however, forced him to relinquish his post in 1921, when he returned to the United States. He was assigned to duty on the general board of the navy but was retired on Aug. 12, 1921, and relieved of all active duty. Besides the Navy Cross he held the large cross of the order of El Sol de Peru, a decoration conferred by the Peruvian government. Though his career gave him no great opportunity for spectacular service, he was a highly capable seaman, an expert navigator, and an able administrator, and was highly popular throughout the service. He was twice married: first on June 2, 1881, to Adelaide Van Ness Smith of Peekskill, N. Y., and second on Jan. 14, 1911, to Helen Koerper of Washington, D. C., daughter of Col. E. A. Koerper, U. S. A. He had one son by his second marriage.

[*Who's Who in America,* 1928–29; H. W. Wilson, *The Downfall of Spain* (1900); Navy Dept. Registers, 1879–1921; Navy Dept., transcript of service record in archives of Bur. of Navigation; *Army and Navy Jour.,* Feb. 1, 1930; obituary in *N. Y. Times,* Jan. 29, 1930; information from correspondence with Snowden's widow and his brother.]   L. H. B.

SNYDER, EDWIN REAGAN (Sept. 2, 1872–Jan. 13, 1925), educator, was born in Scottdale, Pa., the son of Daniel and Catherine (Reagan) Snyder, of Pennsylvania German stock, whose characteristic tenacity of purpose he possessed. After spending his childhood and youth on his father's farm, at eighteen he entered the State Normal School of Colorado (later the State Teachers College) at Greeley at the same time that his brother, Zachariah Xenophon Snyder, became president of the college. Upon his graduation in 1895 he became principal of the public schools at Bald Mountain, Colo., and two years later of those in New Windsor, Colo. He became supervisor of manual training in the schools of Alameda, Cal., in 1900, and in 1902 head of the department of industrial arts in the State Normal School at San José (later the San José State Teachers College). During the year 1904–05 he served also as an assistant at Stanford University, where he received the degree of A.B. in 1905. He was research scholar at Teachers College, Columbia University, 1907–08, and fellow, 1908–09, and received the degree of Ph.D. in 1909, with a thesis on *The Legal Status of Rural High Schools in the United States* (1909), which reveals his belief in thoroughly democratic education. After two more years at San José he was elected in 1911 to the vice-presidency of the Fresno State Normal School (later Fresno State Teachers College), where he also served as assistant superintendent of city schools. For a few months in 1913 he served as superintendent of schools in Santa Barbara, but in January 1914 he became the first commissioner of vocational education in California. In this position he remained until the summer of 1923, when he became president of San José State Teachers College, a post he held until his death about a year and a half later at San José. He was married to Sara Llewellyn on Dec. 29, 1900, in San Francisco. They had a son and a daughter.

His greatest contributions to education came during his decade of service as commissioner of vocational education. His theory of education was given full expression in his first annual report to the state superintendent of public instruction: "We wish every child in the commonwealth to have the opportunity to secure such training in the school as will fit him to do as well as possible that work which he is, by nature and economic opportunity, best fitted to do" (*First Biennial Report of the State Board of Education of California,* 1915, p. 128). This lies at the root of his deep interest in vocational education and guidance, his belief in the part-time continuation school, his insistence that public high schools serve aims more democratic than the single one of preparation for higher institutions. In large measure his theory has since become practice, and no legislation which he proposed, whether it concerned vocational education specifically—he framed practically all the statutes for the administration of the vocational program in California —or the wider reaches of a state educational program, has been seriously modified. Essentially a philosopher, he was vigorously analytical and scientific in his approach to all problems; he had, too, an abiding faith in humanity and a sense of humor that never allowed the philosopher to become pedantic or the scientist to forget his limitations in dealing with human stuff.

[California State Board of Education, Reports of the Commissioner of Industrial and Vocational Education, 1914–22; *Industrial Educ. Mag.*, Sept. 1923; University of California, *Vocational Educ. News Notes*, Feb. 1925; *San José Evening News*, Jan. 14, 1925.]

E. A. L.

SNYDER, JOHN FRANCIS (Mar. 22, 1830– Apr. 30, 1921), physician, Confederate soldier, archaeologist, and author, son of Adam Wilson Snyder and Adelaide (Perry) Snyder, was born at Prairie du Pont, Saint Clair County, Ill., a mile south of Cahokia, in a log building erected in 1759 by the monks of Saint Sulpice. His mother, who was of French ancestry on both sides, was a grand-daughter of Capt. John Baptiste Saucier, the architect of Fort Chartres. His father, a son of Adam Snyder, a German soldier of the Revolution who was born in Alsace and settled in Reading, Pa., had come to Cahokia in 1817, penniless and afoot. Snyder was first educated at Belleville, Ill., at McKendree College, Lebanon, Ill., and at the St. Louis University. He was fond of books, a close observer of nature and natural history, and early began the collection of fossils, minerals, and archaeological relics. As a boy he played about the famous Cahokia mounds near his home, and in his maturer years his interest in archaeology developed and expanded. During the winter of 1849–50 he was a student at McDowell Medical College in St. Louis, and the following summer he crossed the plains to California; he visited the Sandwich Islands in 1852, returned home that year by way of the Isthmus of Panama, and arrived at Philadelphia in time to enter Jefferson Medical College, where he graduated in 1853. For a short period thereafter he was in government medical service in western territories and went over the old Santa Fé trail to Taos and Albuquerque, N. Mex.; then he resigned and began the practice of medicine at Bolivar, Mo., where on Sept. 27, 1854, he married Annie E. Sanders, daughter of

Landon Sanders of Lexington, Ky. He was admitted to the Missouri bar in 1859, but he never practised law. In June 1861 he joined the Confederates under Sterling Price [*q.v.*] and as colonel fought through the Civil War, taking active part in the battles of Wilson Creek, Lexington, Pea Ridge, Helena, Corinth, and Baldwin. Although he was reared in familiarity with a modified form of slavery (indenture of colored servants), served in the Confederate army, and was himself a slave-holder on a small scale, he always abhorred slavery, defending it only on the meager ground of expediency. Returning to Illinois after the war, he resumed the practice of medicine at Virginia. He was elected a member of the thirty-first Illinois legislature, where he gave a good account of himself, but declined further participation in party politics.

One of the founders of the Illinois State Historical Society in 1899, he became its president, 1903–05, and contributed many important papers to it. He was also affiliated with the St. Louis Academy of Sciences, the Illinois Academy of Science, and other organizations. He took part in the survey and mapping of the Cahokia mounds, 1880, and advocated their preservation. For many years he was a research correspondent of the Smithsonian Institution, which published several of his shorter papers. His most important writings are *The Field for Archaeological Research in Illinois* (1900); *Captain John Baptiste Saucier at Fort Chartres in the Illinois, 1751–1763* (1901), reprinted in *Transactions of the Illinois State Historical Society, 1919* (1920); *Adam W. Snyder and His Period in Illinois History, 1817–1842* (1903); "Prehistoric Illinois; Its Psychozoic Problems" (*Journal of the Illinois State Historical Society*, Oct. 1911), "The Kaskaskia Indians" (*Ibid.*, July 1912), and "The Great Cahokia Mound" (*Ibid.*, July 1917). He may well be considered the ranking pioneer in archaeology of the state of Illinois. He was the first to indicate cultural differences between prehistoric tribes of southern and central Illinois, and explorations by the University of Illinois in 1922–27 proved the correctness of his views. He died in Virginia, Ill., at the age of ninety-one years, in full possession of all his faculties.

[Newton Bateman and Paul Selby, eds., *Hist. Encyc. of Ill. and Hist. of Cass County* (1915), vol. II; *Jour. Ill. State Hist. Soc.*, Apr.–July 1921; *Belleville News-Democrat* (Belleville, Ill.), May 2, 1921; *Chicago Daily Tribune*, May 1, 1921.]

W. K. M.

SNYDER, SIMON (Nov. 5, 1759–Nov. 9, 1819), governor of Pennsylvania, was born at Lancaster, Pa., the son of Maria Elizabeth (Knippenburg) Kraemer Snyder and Anthony

Snyder, a mechanic who emigrated to America from the Palatinate. The boy's childhood was spent in poverty and hard work. At the age of seventeen he began an apprenticeship of four years as tanner and currier at York, where he also attended night school kept by John Jones, a Quaker. About 1784 he established himself at Selinsgrove in Northumberland, now Snyder, County. There he opened a general store, operated a mill, found frequent employment as a scrivener, and rose rapidly in the general estimation of the community. He was appointed a justice of the peace and, later, judge of the court of common pleas of Northumberland County, was a member of the state constitutional convention, 1789–90 and of the Assembly from 1797 to 1807. He was speaker three terms and, as a leader of the backcountry democracy, fought to liberalize the judiciary laws and to diminish the governor's powers. He was one of the principal agitators for the hundred-dollar act extending the jurisdiction of justices of the peace to cases not exceeding one hundred dollars and for compulsory arbitration legislation.

Tremendously popular in his district and among his faction, he was nominated for governor by the anti-judiciary Republicans in 1805, his chief mouthpiece being the *Republican Argus* in Northumberland edited by his close friend, John Binns [*q.v.*]. Unsuccessful by some five thousand votes in the bitter campaign that followed, he returned to the state house of representatives in 1806 to lead the abortive attempt to impeach Gov. Thomas McKean [*q.v.*]. In 1808 he was elected governor and was reëlected by overwhelming majorities in 1811 and 1814. He was the first representative of the German element or of the backcountry farming class to be elected governor of Pennsylvania. Unlike his predecessors he did not have a brilliant military or legal record. Exceedingly plain in his ways, he emulated Jeffersonian simplicity, and instead of delivering his message to the legislature in person sent it in writing. A state-rights man, he vigorously asserted the supremacy of the state in 1809 by calling out the militia to prevent a federal court from enforcing its decision in the Olmstead case, though he later yielded under protest to the federal government. He gave loyal support to the War of 1812, sponsored an act for public education, recommended abolition of the death penalty and modification of the law for imprisonment for debt, and advanced numerous schemes for internal improvements. In 1814 he vetoed over loud public protests "the forty bank bill" to establish banks over the state, on the grounds that it would give too much power to

"privileged orders," invite visionary speculation, and divert men from useful pursuits. The bill was passed over his veto. In 1817 he was elected to the state Senate. He was a member of the Moravian Church. He was married three times: first to Elizabeth Michael of Lancaster, second on June 12, 1796, to Catherine Antes, and third on Oct. 16, 1814, to Mary Slough Scott, a widow of Harrisburg, who survived him. He died from typhoid fever.

["Autobiographical Notes by Simon Snyder," *Pa. Mag. of Hist. & Biog.*, vol. IV (1880) ; M. K. Snyder, *Life of Gov. Simon Snyder* (n.d.) ; "Papers of Gov. Simon Snyder," *Pa. Archives*, 4 ser., vol. IV (1900) ; *Recollections of the Life of John Binns* (1854) ; J. B. Linn, *Annals of Buffalo Valley, Pa.* (1877) ; J. H. Peeling, "Governor McKean and the Pennsylvania Jacobins," *Pa. Mag. of Hist. & Biog.*, Oct. 1930 ; *Snyder Co. (Pa.) Annals*, vol. I (1919), compiled by G. W. Wagenseller ; J. H. Peeling, "The Public Life of Thomas McKean, 1734–1817" (1929), doctor's thesis (MS.) at Univ. of Chicago ; *Poulson's Am. Daily Advertiser*, Nov. 13, 19, 20, 1819.]   J. H. P.

SOBOLEWSKI, J. FRIEDRICH EDUARD (Oct. 1, 1808–May 17, 1872), conductor, composer, writer, was born in Königsberg, East Prussia, a descendant of an ancient Polish family. He received a fine musical education, eventually studying with Carl Friedrich Zelter and Carl Maria von Weber. In 1830 he was appointed director of music at the Königsberg theatre, and in 1835 became cantor at the *Altstädtische Kirche*. The *Philharmonische Gesellschaft*, a dilettante orchestra, was founded in 1838 and he was elected conductor, being similarly honored when the *Musikalische Akademie*, a mixed chorus, came into existence in 1843. In the course of his Königsberg period, he composed and produced the operas *Imogen* (1832), *Velleda* (1835), *Salvator Rosa* (1848), and *Der Seher von Khorassan* (1850). He developed literary activity, functioning as music critic of the *Ostpreussiche Zeitung,* and as correspondent, under the pseudonym J. Feski, of Robert Schumann's *Neue Zeitschrift für Musik.* Dubbed M. Hahnbüchn, he became a Davidsbündler, one of that redoubtable band gathered around Schumann to wage warfare upon the musical Philistines. He was appointed director of music at the Bremen theatre, presumably in 1854. During the Bremen period he published the pamphlets *Reaktionäre Briefe* (1854), *Oper, nicht Drama* (1857), *Debatten über Musik* (1857), and *Das Geheimniss der neuesten Schule der Musik* (1859). His opera *Komala* received its initial performance at Bremen in 1857 and was accorded the exceptional distinction of production at Weimar under the aegis of Franz Liszt the following year.

Apparently leaving Bremen at the end of the

season, Sobolewski took pasage for America, arriving in Milwaukee, Wis., before the end of July 1859. In an incredibly short time he composed the opera *Mohega*, which was given two performances by the Milwaukee *Musikverein,* Oct. 11, and Nov. 1, 1859. *Mohega* was probably the first operatic treatment of an episode from the Revolutionary War, the libretto celebrating the love and tragic end of Count Pulaski and the Indian maid Mohega at the siege of Savannah in 1779. Sobolewski became conductor of the short-lived Milwaukee Philharmonic Society, functioning at both concerts of the first (and last) season on Feb. 28 and Apr. 13, 1860. The St. Louis Philharmonic Society was organized in June 1860, and Sobolewski was engaged as conductor. He led his first concert a month before Hans Balatka directed the initial performance of the Chicago Philharmonic Society, both men laboring valiantly to prepare the way for the Messiah that was to come in the person of Theodore Thomas [*q.v.*] and his orchestra. Sobolewski conducted forty concerts of the St. Louis Philharmonic Society from Oct. 18, 1860, to Apr. 19, 1866, holding his organization together and achieving musical triumphs through the troubled years of the Civil War. He did missionary work of heroic dimensions, his orchestral programs constituting a liberal education in the appreciation of the classical and romantic schools. At the outset of the seventh season he resigned and devoted himself to teaching and composing. He remained professionally active until an apoplectic stroke cut him down in his sixty-fourth year.

Sobolewski was married three times. By his first wife, Bertha Dorn, he had four children, by his second wife, three, and by his third wife, Bertha von Kleist, six. He was an accomplished linguist, master of five languages. He contributed to the *Journal of Speculative Philosophy* the articles: "A Dialogue on Music" (1867), "The New School of Music" (1868), "Mendelssohn" (1873), and "Robert Schumann" (1874). He wrote an abundance of good music but his finest scores have become widely scattered if not irretrievably lost.

[Documentary material and data from Prof. Dr. Joseph Müller-Blattau, Königsberg, Rudolph Edward Sobolewski, Laddonia, Mo., Lillie Sobolewski Peterson, Loveland, Colo.; autograph letters of Sobolewski in the library of the author; the correspondence of Wagner and Liszt, *Gesammelte Schriften über Musik und Musiker von Robert Schumann* (5th ed., 2 vols., 1914); O. Burckhardt, *Der Musikverein von Milwaukee* (1900); E. E. Hipsher, *Am. Opera* (1927); E. C. Krohn, *A Century of Mo. Music* (1924), and *The Development of the Symphony Orchestra in St. Louis* (1924); *Mo. Republican*, May 18, 19, 20, 1872; *The Impressario,* June 1872.]   E. C. K.

SOLDAN, FRANK LOUIS (Oct. 20, 1842–Mar. 27, 1908), educator and scholar, was born in Frankfort-on-the-Main, Germany, the son of Johann Justin and Caroline (Elssman) Soldan. He attended German schools, emigrated in 1863 to the United States with his wife, Ottilie (Bernhard), settled in St. Louis, Mo., where he established a young ladies' academy, and in 1882 became a naturalized citizen.

In 1868 he began a notable career in connection with the St. Louis public school system. From instructor of modern languages in the high school, he was promoted to assistant superintendent in charge of instruction in German (1870); principal of the normal school (1871); principal of the combined normal and high schools (1887); and superintendent of instruction (1895), a position which he held until his death. Although a pioneer in city school administration, he saw clearly the principles effective in this work, and was largely influential in obtaining charter regulations which provided for appropriate and definite allocation of educational responsibilities together with the authority to meet them. The board of education was relieved of many details, and the initiative in administrative matters requiring professional insight was granted the superintendent. He revealed a surprising grasp of details, and tempered firmness of management with a tactful human interest in those under him.

Soldan's service to education was not confined to St. Louis. In 1880 he organized the first normal institute for teachers in South Carolina, thus contributing to a state-wide educational revival. From 1877 until his death, he was an active member of the National Educational Association, serving it in various official capacities. He lectured frequently and contributed numerous articles to educational periodicals and to *Western,* a journal of literature published in St. Louis. Closely associated with William Torrey Harris [*q.v.*] and others, he helped to make that city a center of culture. Among the subjects upon which he wrote were "The Darwinian Theory," "Goethe and Spinoza," "Law and Cause," "Goethe's Suleika," "Dante's Purgatorio," and "Culture and Facts." He published a couple of language books, *Grube's Method: Two Essays on Elementary Instruction in Arithmetic* (1881); and *The Century and the School, and Other Educational Essays* (1912). He was much interested in the writings of Horace, selections from which he translated. A turning lathe in his workshop and an excellent photographic equipment provided him means for gratifying other tastes. He died in the midst of his varied activities, falling dead in the street while on his way to attend a conference with his assistant superintendents. He was survived by his wife and one daughter. The St. Louis Soldan High School was named in his honor.

[*National Educ. Asso. Jour. of Proc. and Addresses* (1908); *A Memorial—Frank Louis Soldan* (1908); William Hyde and H. L. Conard, *Encyc. of the Hist. of St. Louis* (1899), vol. IV; James Cox, *Old and New St. Louis* (1894); *Mo. Hist. Rev.*, Oct. 1920, p. 92; *Outlook*, July 22, 1905, p. 739; *Educational Rev.*, May 1903, pp. 517–19, and May 1908; *St. Louis Globe-Democrat*, Mar. 28, 1908.]   J. H. C.

SOLEY, JAMES RUSSELL (Oct. 1, 1850–Sept. 11, 1911), teacher, naval writer, and lawyer, was born at Roxbury, Mass., son of John James and Elvira Codman (Dégen) Soley. He was a descendant of John Soley, an English settler at Charlestown, Mass., in the seventeenth century, and (through both parents) of Judge James Russell of Charlestown. After preparation in the Roxbury Latin School, he entered Harvard College and graduated in 1870. A year's instructorship in St. Mark's School, Southborough, Mass., was followed by his appointment, Oct. 1, 1871, as professor of ethics and English at the United States Naval Academy. Two years later, despite his youth and juniority to other instructors, he was made head of the department of English studies, history, and law, a position he held until 1882. From Aug. 18, 1876, until his resignation in 1890 he was a member of the naval corps of professors of mathematics, rising from lieutenant to commander. In 1878 he was abroad from April to December on duty connected with the American educational exhibit at the international exposition in Paris. He had also been commissioned to make a study of foreign systems of naval education, and his *Report on Foreign Systems of Naval Education* appeared as a government document in 1880. Between 1882 and 1890 he had duty in Washington, collecting and arranging the Navy Department library, and, as superintendent of the office of naval war records, supervising the publication of Civil War naval records. He also lectured on international law at the Naval War College, 1885–89, and was Lowell Institute lecturer in 1885 on American naval history and in 1888 on European neutrality in the Civil War. He had studied law in Annapolis and continued this work at Columbian (later George Washington) University, receiving his law degree in 1890. On July 16, 1890, he resigned his naval commission to become assistant secretary of the navy, and occupied this position until March 1893 with special administration of labor in naval shore establishments. Therafter he practised law in

New York City with his former naval chief, Benjamin Franklin Tracy [*q.v.*], in the firm of Tracy, Boardman, and Platt (later Boardman, Platt, and Soley). His special field was international law, and his most notable legal service was as counsel for Venezuela in the boundary dispute with Great Britain, arbitrated at Paris in 1899. Until otherwise occupied after 1890, he was a prolific and able writer, chiefly on naval subjects. His books include a *Historical Sketch of the United States Naval Academy* (1876); *The Blockade and the Cruisers* (1883), in the series called Campaigns of the Navy in the Civil War; *The Rescue of Greely* (1885), with W. S. Schley; *The Boys of 1812* (1887); *Sailor Boys of '61* (1888); and *Admiral Porter* (1903). He also edited the *Autobiography of Commodore Charles Morris* (1880), contributed the naval chapters to Justin Winsor's *Narrative and Critical History of America* (1884–89), and wrote frequently on naval and legal themes for periodicals and works of reference. He was orator in 1890 at the unveiling of the monument in Annapolis commemorating the *Jeannette* expedition, and in 1891 at a memorial service for Admiral David Dixon Porter [*q.v.*] in Tremont Temple, Boston. He was married, Dec. 1, 1875, to Mary Woolsey Howland, daughter of the Rev. Robert Shaw Howland of New York; they had a son who died in infancy and two daughters. His burial was in the Church of the Heavenly Rest, New York City.

[*Who's Who in America*, 1910–11; *Tenth Report of the Class of 1870 of Harvard Coll.* (1920); *Army and Navy Jour.*, Sept. 16, 1911; *N. Y. Tribune*, Sept. 12, 1911; letter of R. S. Howland, recommending Soley to a professorship at Columbia Univ., Stauffer Coll., N. Y. Pub. Lib.]   A. W.

SOLGER, REINHOLD (July 17, 1817–Jan. 11, 1866), scholar, author, was born in Stettin, Prussia, the son of Friedrich Ludwig Wilhelm Solger, a member of the Prussian *Reichstag*, and his second wife, Auguste Amalie Jungnickel. His full name was Reinhold Ernst Friedrich Karl Solger. He received a careful education at home and later at a military school at Züllichau, a small town east of Berlin, a place to which he referred in his later writings as his "prison." In the fall of 1837, he entered the University of Halle to study theology but exchanged this field shortly afterward for philosophy and history. Three years later he transferred to Greifswald and was awarded a doctor's degree in 1842. He was an industrious student, very active in liberal political movements, contributing numerous poems to revolutionary papers. Through a friend of his father he received an appointment as *Referendar* in Potsdam and spent there and in Berlin one year of gay social activity which gave him the profound scorn for *Junker* and bureaucrats that is characteristic of his later writings. He then decided to emigrate to America but owing to a ticket fraud got only as far as Liverpool, England. He was offered the post of tutor in the home of a country gentleman, a sinecure that enabled him to continue his studies and to begin giving public lectures in English. He made the acquaintance of Carlyle, Dickens, and Lord Lytton, who became his friends and sponsors.

In 1847 he went to Paris and moved in the circle of the political exiles, Bakunin, Herzen, Herwegh, Bernays, and others. An attempt to establish himself in Berlin failed and he returned to Paris. Here, on Feb. 19, 1848, he married a young French girl, Adèle Marie Bémere, who was his constant companion throughout his later numerous changes of residence and the mother of his four children. After the February Revolution of 1848 Solger went to Berlin, espousing the Revolution as member of a democratic club, and later, during the fighting in Baden, serving as adjutant and interpreter to General Mieroslawski, commander of the revolutionary forces. When the Baden uprising was crushed Solger fled from Germany with a price on his head. He spent two years in Berne and Zürich, some time in Paris and London, and in the spring of 1853 emigrated to America, settling in Roxbury, a suburb of Boston, Mass. As in Switzerland and in England, he supported himself by his pen and by public lectures on history and modern German philosophy. In 1857 and 1859 he delivered a series of twelve lectures at the Lowell Institute of Boston where James Russell Lowell and Louis Agassiz [*qq.v.*] were among his hearers. He became an American citizen in May 1859, and interested himself in the political questions of the day as an enthusiastic member of the new Republican party. So effective was his speaking in the elections of 1856 and 1860 that John Albion Andrew, governor of Massachusetts, said of him that he had been as influential in bringing the Germans in the East to the Republican side as Carl Schurz had been in the West (letter to John Sherman, Nov. 29, 1865). President Lincoln appointed him to the newly created office of assistant register of the treasury, an interim position created with the purpose of making him register as soon as this post was vacated. In April 1864, he had suffered a stroke of paralysis which turned his last days into painful suffering.

Solger was twice awarded a literary prize. In 1859 the committee in charge of the New York celebration of the centennial of Schiller's birth chose his eulogistic poem, "Erinnerung," for the prize. In 1862 his novel, *Anton in Amerika,* won the prize over twenty-two others in a competition arranged by the *Bellestristisches Journal* of New York. The novel, a satire of Gustav Freytag's best seller, *Soll und Haben* (1855), purports to be a sequel of this work; its theme is the problem of the adjustment of the cultured German in the American melting-pot. It was reworked and published again by Erick Ebermayer in 1928. Among other works by Solger are a humorous Byronic epic, *Hanns von Katzenfingen,* in part the story of the author's youth, and a farce in one act, *Der Reichstagsprofessor,* in which the inefficiency of the intellectual revolutionists of the Parliament of Frankfurt is pilloried. Solger was typical of the intellectual revolutionists of 1848 whose enthusiasm flowed through their pens. He was tall in stature and of very distinguished appearance.

[Personal information from Frederick R. Solger, Washington, D. C.; Friedrich Kapp, *Aus und Über Amerika* (1876), vol. I, and "Reinhold Solger," *Deutsch-Amerikanische-Monatshefte,* Feb. 1866; M. A. Dickie, *Reinhold Solger,* doctoral dissertation, 1930, see *Univ. of Pittsburgh Bull.,* Nov. 1930; S. A. Allibone, *A Critical Dict. of English Literature,* vol. II (1870); *Daily Nat. Intelligencer,* Washington, D. C., Jan. 13, 1866.]

A. E. Z.

SOLIS-COHEN, JACOB DA SILVA [See COHEN, JACOB DA SILVA SOLIS, 1838–1927].

SOLOMONS, ADOLPHUS SIMEON (Oct. 26, 1826–Mar. 18, 1910), philanthropist, was born in New York City, the son of John and Julia (Levy) Solomons. His father, who was of English birth, had emigrated to the United States in 1810, and was on the editorial staff of the *National Advocate* and the *Morning Courier and New York Enquirer*; his mother was of old New England stock. At fourteen he enlisted in the New York state militia and served for seven years. After his education in the public schools of New York City, he went into the stationery business. On June 25, 1851, he married Rachel Seixas Phillips, a descendant of the colonial patriot families of Seixas and Phillips, who bore him eight daughters and a son. In the same year Daniel Webster [*q.v.*], then secretary of state, appointed him special bearer of dispatches to Berlin. Moving his business to Washington, D. C., in 1859, he did government printing, added a book department, which became a literary headquarters for such men as Ulysses Simpson Grant and Chief Justice Salmon Portland Chase, and later established a photographic gallery in which pictures of many notable men, including the last photograph of Abraham Lincoln [*qq.v.*], were made. Characteristic of the esteem he enjoyed in Washington is the fact that when Schuyler Colfax [q.v.], vice-president of the United States, was prevented from making the address at the dedication of the Young Men's Christian Association building, Solomons, a Jew, was called upon to take his place. In 1871 he was elected to the house of delegates of the District of Columbia, and became chairman of the committee on ways and means. In 1873 Grant offered him the office of governor of the district, an honor Solomons refused, largely because his observance of the seventh-day Sabbath would be incompatible with the duties of the office. On giving up business in 1891, he served as general agent in America of the Baron de Hirsch Fund. At seventy-seven he retired and lived in Washington until his death.

Though never a man of ample means he was a creative philanthropist. He organized the first training school for nurses in Washington and the Washington Night Lodging-House Association, which supplied men with free lodging. He was an officer of the Provident Aid Society, of the Emergency Hospital, of the Society for Prevention of Cruelty to Animals, and director of the Providence Hospital, the Columbia Hospital for Women, and the Garfield Memorial Hospital, the last of which he had also helped to organize. In April 1881 the organization of the Associated Charities was projected at a meeting held in his house, and in May 1881 at another meeting there it was decided to organize the American Association of the Red Cross, of which he became an officer. In 1884 he was a representative of the United States at the Red Cross international congress in Geneva, Switzerland, and in 1903 he was one of the twelve petitioners on whose memorial Congress later reorganized the association. In New York his suggestion led to the organization of Mount Sinai Hospital and of the Montefiore Home for Chronic Invalids (later the Montefiore Hospital). A founder of the Jewish Protectory and Aid Society, and of the Russian Jews Immigration Aid Society (1881), he was acting president of the Jewish Theological Seminary Association when it was reorganized into the Jewish Theological Seminary of America, and its teachers' institute was formed solely through his initiative. His transparent sincerity, unassuming goodness, genial optimism, and willingness to serve made him a rarely beloved figure. His unswerving personal devotion was coupled with a beautiful tolerance. It has been said of him that, though he was "possessed of the grandeur of soul which pertains to a saint," he had "the simplicity of a child" and

lived a life "replete with moral beauty" (Marshall, post, pp. 169–70).

[Louis Marshall, in Pubs. Am. Jewish Hist. Soc., no. 20 (1911); Cyrus Adler, Ibid., no. 33 (1934); The Jewish Encyc., vol. IX (ed. of 1925); Samuel Joseph, Hist. of the Baron de Hirsch Fund (1935), passim; Am. Jewish Year Book, 1904–05; Jewish Comment (Baltimore, Md.), Oct. 24, Dec. 12, 1902; Evening Telegram (N. Y.), Apr. 27, 1880; Sunday Star (Washington), Oct. 28, 1906; Am. Hebrew, Mar. 25, 1910; Hebrew Standard, Apr. 29, 1910; Washington Post, Mar. 19, 1910 (obituary), and Mar. 13, 1932 (mag. section).]   D. deS. P.

SOMERS, RICHARD (Sept. 15, 1778–Sept. 4, 1804), naval officer, was born at Somers Point, N. J. His great-grandfather, John Somers, came to America from England before 1693 and the family ultimately settled in Gloucester County, N. J., in the Great Egg Harbor region, acquiring a considerable amount of land. He was the youngest of six children of Richard and Sophia (Stillwell) Somers. The elder Richard was a colonel in the militia, a county judge, and an ardent Whig. It appears that because of the exposure of Egg Harbor to Loyalist attacks during the American Revolution, Colonel Somers moved to Philadelphia soon after the British evacuation of that city. There young Richard Somers received some elementary schooling, but later attended an academy in Burlington, N. J., where he remained until about the time of his father's death in October 1794. For some time he was apparently engaged in coastwise shipping between New York and Philadelphia, but on Apr. 30, 1798, along with Stephen Decatur, 1779–1820 [q.v.], he enlisted in the navy and served as midshipman aboard the frigate United States. Her cruise began in July 1798, and was continued, chiefly in West Indian waters, during the remainder of the year. Hardly more than a twelvemonth after his enlistment Somers received a promotion to the rank of third lieutenant; then, in the autumn of 1799, he sailed on board the United States for Europe in company with the American commissioners to France. The United States was laid up after the peace of 1801, and Somers was transferred, as first lieutenant, to the frigate Boston which, during the summer of 1801, sailed for France with Chancellor Livingston on board, and later proceeded to the Mediterranean where American warships were engaged in the war with Tripoli.

Soon after the return of the Boston to America near the end of 1802, Somers was given command of the schooner Nautilus, attached to the squadron of Commodore Edward Preble [q.v.]. It was employed in convoying merchantmen, in blockading Tripoli, and in obtaining supplies from Naples. In August 1804 Somers was placed in command of one of two divisions of gunboats which had been borrowed from Naples. In each of the ensuing attacks upon Tripoli, on Aug. 3, 7, 28, and Sept. 3, he displayed great coolness and courage, and earned the high commendation of Preble. In the meantime, plans were being made to send a fireship into the harbor at Tripoli. Somers, now a captain, volunteered to prepare the craft and to take her into the harbor. The vessel employed was a ketch which had been captured from the Tripolitans and renamed the *Intrepid*. About one hundred barrels of powder were stored in her magazine, and about 150 shells were placed on her deck. Fuses were installed which were expected to burn fifteen minutes before igniting the powder, and the thirteen men who accompanied the *Intrepid* were to escape to safety by means of two small boats. The ketch entered the harbor on the night of Sept. 4, but, before reaching her intended destination, she suddenly exploded, killing all hands, and apparently failing to injure the enemy.

Somers was of middle stature and sturdy of frame. Ordinarily mild and amiable, he was on occasion, given to heroic and dramatic action. While a very young man, he once fought three duels in one day with associates who had questioned his courage. After his death a number of vessels were named in his honor, and a resolution was passed by Congress on Mar. 3, 1805, expressing regret for the loss of the gallant men who had died in the *Intrepid* venture.

[J. E. Stillwell, *Stillwell Geneal.*, vol. III (1930); E. M. Hoopes, *Richard Somers* (1933); C. W. Goldsborough, *The U. S. Naval Chronicle*, vol. I (1824); J. F. Cooper, *Lives of Distinguished Am. Naval Officers* (1846), vol. I; G. W. Allen, *Our Navy and the Barbary Corsairs* (1905); J. F. Hall, *The Daily Union Hist. of Atlantic City and County, N. J.* (1900); *Records of Officers and Men of N. J. in Wars, 1791–1815* (1909); M. E. Seawell, *Decatur and Somers* (1894); *Naval Mag.*, Mar. 1836.]   R. W. I.

SONNECK, OSCAR GEORGE THEODORE (Oct. 6, 1873–Oct. 30, 1928), musician, librarian, historian, was born in Jersey City, N. J., the son of Georg and Julia (Meyne) Sonneck. He lost his father in early childhood and settled with his mother, a woman of wide culture and brilliant mind, in Frankfort-on-the-Main, Germany, where she had been called to direct the household of a widowed banker. From 1883 to 1889 young Sonneck attended the *Gelehrtenschule* at Kiel, and the *Gymnasium* at Frankfort. He spent one semester at the University of Heidelberg, and then matriculated at the University of Munich, which he left in 1897 without wishing to take a degree. His chief teachers were Adolf Sandberger in musicology, Carl Stumpf and W. H. Riehl in philosophy, Theodor Lipps

in psychology, and M. E. Sachs in musical composition. The letters dating from his student days and two small collections of German verses, *Seufzer* (1895), and *Eine Totenmesse* (1898), give early evidence of Sonneck's singularly self-analytical and pessimistic nature. These characteristics were strangely companioned by strong ambition, an indomitable will to work, and a keen sense of humor. After leaving Munich, Sonneck concentrated for a while on his technical development as a musician. He studied piano in Frankfort under James Kwast, composition and orchestration under Iwan Knorr, and conducting under Carl Schröder in Sondershausen.

Although Sonneck had composed and published several sets of songs and piano pieces between 1896 and 1899, he deliberately shunned a career as a creative musician, realizing that his talents, mentality, and capacity for assiduous application fitted him more particularly for scholarly pursuits. He spent part of 1899 in Italy, working mainly in the libraries of Padua, Bologna, and Venice. Upon his return to America, about the end of 1899, he embarked on his searching quest for data regarding American musical life in colonial and Revolutionary times. Old newspaper files, especially, yielded much information, with the aid of which Sonneck succeeded in giving the first methodical and correct picture of musical conditions in America prior to 1800. In 1902 he offered the manuscript of his *Bibliography of Early Secular American Music* (privately printed, 1905) without recompense to the Librarian of Congress as a government publication. The offer could not be accepted but it led to his appointment as the first chief of the music division in the Library of Congress, Aug. 1, 1902. As the creator and organizer of the division he devoted almost superhuman energy and perseverance to the development of the largest and most comprehensive collection of music and books on music in the country and one of the leading music libraries in the world. He resigned on Sept. 5, 1917, to join the G. Schirmer company, music publishers of New York, in a managerial position, which he held until his death. The Washington years, however, represent best "his life of high public importance" (Putnam, *post,* p. 1).

In 1904 the Library published his model "Classification" of music and books on music (adopted December 1902, revised April 1917). In 1905 he published privately his book on *Francis Hopkinson, the First American Poet-Composer, and James Lyon, Patriot, Preacher, Psalmodist.* Among his most important historical and critical publications are: *Early Concert-life in Amer-*

ica (1907), *Report on The Star-spangled Banner, Hail Columbia, America, Yankee Doodle* (1909, followed by an enlarged and revised monograph on *The Star Spangled Banner* in 1914), *Early Opera in America* (1915) ; two volumes of essays, *"Suum cuique"* (1916), and *"Miscellaneous Studies in the History of Music"* (1921). The actual manual labor, apart from the research, performed by Sonneck in cataloguing music, in preparing his various bibliographies on dramatic music (1908), orchestral music (1912), opera librettos (2 vols., 1914), and the works of Stephen C. Foster (1915) and Edward MacDowell (1917), is well-nigh incredible. He represented the government at the musical congresses in Rome and London in 1911, and was one of the three United States delegates to the Beethoven Centenary in Vienna in 1927, representing the Beethoven Association of New York, which, with Harold Bauer, he founded in 1919. When Rudolph Edward Schirmer [*q.v.*] founded *The Musical Quarterly* in 1914 Sonneck became the editor. He was elected vice-president of the Schirmer company in 1921. In his activity as music publisher he fostered American talents of promise and advocated "clean music in good taste," regardless of purpose. He himself resumed his composing and published several sets of highly personal and polished songs. His last important work of critical research was *Beethoven Letters in America* (1927). His wife, Marie Elisabeth Ames, to whom he had been married in Washington on Nov. 9, 1904, survived him.

[Sonneck papers in the Lib. of Cong.; *Who's Who in America,* 1928–29; Carl Engel, "O. G. Sonneck, Ein Charakterbild," *Studien zur Musikgeschichte. Festschrift für Guido Adler* (1930), "A Postscript," *Musical Quart.,* Jan. 1929; *Musical America,* Jan. 13, 1923, Nov. 10, 1928; Herbert Putnam, Rubin Goldmark, articles in *Musical Quart.,* Jan. 1929; Frank Patterson, "Personal Recollections of Oscar G. Sonneck," *Musical Courier,* Nov. 15, 1928; *Vol. of Proc. of the Music Teachers Nat. Asso.,* 1928 (1929); *Grove's Dict. of Music and Musicians, Am. Supp.* (1930); A. Eaglefield-Hull, *A Dict. of Modern Music and Musicians* (1924), *N. Y. Times,* Nov. 11, 1928.]   C. E—l.

SONNICHSEN, ALBERT (May 5, 1878–Aug. 15, 1931), war correspondent, author, was born in San Francisco, Cal. His father, Nicolai Sonnichsen, a native of Copenhagen, Denmark, was a soldier in the American Civil War and later a Pacific ship-owner and Danish consul at San Francisco; his mother, Bertha (Leichardt) Sonnichsen, was of German parentage. Albert attended public schools at San Francisco, Oakland, and San José, Cal., and also had some schooling at a Jesuit monastery, but at fifteen he ran away from school and went to sea, where he spent most of his time for the next five years, the first three of them before the mast. At one

time he stopped off in Cuba for several weeks to aid the Cubans in their fight for independence from Spain; at another he spent several weeks in Tynemouth, England, studying painting, but decided that he had not the talent for it. Having a taste for knowledge, he did much reading on shipboard, and his years at sea gave him a liberal education. Some of their happenings are described in his book, *Deep Sea Vagabonds* (1903). With the beginning of the Spanish-American War in 1898, he became quartermaster on the United States transport *Zeelandia,* which sailed from San Francisco and reached Manila, P. I., in July. In the following January he was taken prisoner by the Philippine insurgents under Emilio Aguinaldo and was held for ten months, suffering greatly from privation and disease. He finally escaped in November 1899. While he was in prison he began writing the story of his experience, published as *Ten Months a Captive Among Filipinos* (1901).

Returning to the United States in 1900, he worked as a staff writer with the *New York Tribune* for six months in 1901–02. During 1903 he was employed by the New York publishing firm of McClure, Phillips & Company, and wrote special articles and feature stories for their news syndicate. War having broken out in southeastern Europe, he went to the Balkans in 1904 as special correspondent for the New York *Evening Post,* and was on the Bulgarian front for two years. Early in 1906, for the sake of adventure and of getting an "inside" story, he joined the Macedonian revolutionists, or brigands, as they were frequently called, in Turkey, being in effect one of them. In America it was reported that he had been slain by some of the rebel bands. He remained with them for nearly a year as soldier and peasant, then returned to America, and published his story as *Confessions of a Macedonian Bandit* in 1909. In 1907–08 he made a study of Slavic immigrants in the Middle West for the United States Immigration Commission, his work being embodied in the voluminous reports of the Commission, published in 1911. He had long been critical as to methods of distribution of products in the United States, and his study of the subject led to his serving as secretary of the Cooperative League of America (favoring production and distribution on the Rochdale system), 1910–15 and 1919–21, and as vice-president, 1924–26. He was editor of the *Co-operative Consumer* (later *Co-operation*) from 1914 to 1918. Meanwhile he wrote magazine articles on this and other subjects, and brought out his book, *Consumers' Co-öperation,* in 1919. He spent the last ten years of his life near Willimantic, Conn., where he operated a successful poultry farm. In 1919 he married Gladys Brooks of San Francisco, who with two sons and a daughter survived him.

[See *Who's Who in America*, 1930–31; *Cooperation* (N. Y.), Sept. 1931; obituaries in *Sun* (N. Y.), *World-Telegram* (N. Y.), *N. Y. Evening Post*, Aug. 17, and *Hartford Courant*, Aug. 16, 1931. Some information has been supplied by Sonnichsen's family; his own books give details of the adventurous portions of his career.]   A.F.H.

SOOYSMITH, CHARLES (July 20, 1856– June 1, 1916), civil engineer, was born at Buffalo, N. Y., the son of William Sooy Smith [*q.v.*] and Elizabeth (Haven) Smith. His father determined to give him the best technical training available, and he was accordingly sent to Rensselaer Polytechnic Institute, at that time the most famous engineering school in America. After his graduation, at the age of twenty, he was sent to Europe for two years' study and travel, a considerable part of which he spent at the Polytechnic Institute in Dresden, Germany. Returning to America in 1879, he entered the service of the Atchison, Topeka & Santa Fé Railway as assistant superintendent of the department of track, bridges, and buildings, but left this position in 1881 to form with his father the firm of William Sooy Smith & Son, Engineers & Contractors. Six years of association with his father served to fix the son's interests in the field of subaqueous foundations, to which he was to devote the remainder of his professional life.

Withdrawing from the partnership in 1887, he formed his own organization, Sooysmith & Company, Contractors, of which he was president. This firm during the following ten years was engaged in many of the most difficult and important foundation projects in the country. Among these may be mentioned the piers for the bridges over the Mississippi River at Keithsburg, Ill., and at Fort Madison, Iowa; and over the Missouri River at Sioux City, Iowa, East Omaha, Nebr., Kansas City, Mo., and Sibley, Mo. His company also built the Manhattan Life, the American Surety, the Empire, and the Washington Life buildings in New York City. During this period, Sooysmith acted personally as chief engineer of construction on the Central Bridge over the Harlem River in New York City, and directed the foundation construction for the Baltimore & Ohio Railroad bridge over the Schuylkill River in Philadelphia, Pa.

Sooysmith retired from contracting in 1898 and opened an office as consulting engineer in New York City, where he resided until his death. He was consulting engineer to the Underground Rapid Transit Railway of New York and a member of the Metropolitan Sewerage Commission, and was widely consulted on difficult foundation problems. While William Sooy Smith was the first to introduce the pneumatic caisson into American practice, using it widely in bridge construction, his son appears to have been the first to make extensive use of this process in the construction of high buildings. His most important and original contribution to the profession, however, was the introduction into the United States of the so-called "freezing" process of excavation in unstable soils, already practised in England and Germany. The method consisted essentially of driving a series of pipes into the soil and freezing it by a process similar to that generally used in artificial refrigeration. It was thus made possible to carry foundations through strata of boulders and quicksand which defied all ordinary methods of excavation. Sooysmith took out many patents on improvements of the process, and shortly before his death he devised and patented a variation of the method, suitable for subaqueous tunnel construction, but although this method was one of great ingenuity, it does not appear to have been widely adopted in practice.

Sooysmith's professional career was limited to a narrow field, but within that field his knowledge was profound and his authority second to none. Outside his profession, his tastes were those of a scholar and his avocation the study of languages and literature. He wrote very little; one short paper—"Concerning Foundations for Heavy Buildings in New York City" (*Transactions of the American Society of Civil Engineers*, vol. XXXV, 1896)—and a few scattered discussions constitute the whole of his contributions to the technical press. He was married, Dec. 17, 1887, to Pauline Olmsted of Hartford, Conn.

[*Who's Who in America*, 1912–13; *Hartford Courant*, Dec. 19, 1887; *Trans. Am. Soc. Civil Engineers*, LII (1904), 449; *Engineering News*, June 8, 1916; *Engineering Record*, June 10, 1916; *N. Y. Times*, June 2, 1916; personal recollections of engineering acquaintances.]   J.I.P.

SOPHOCLES, EVANGELINUS APOSTOLIDES (*c.* 1805–Dec. 17, 1883), classicist and neo-Hellenist, one of the most picturesque figures in American education, was born between 1800 and 1808 (he concealed the exact date) in Tsangarada, Thessaly, near Mt. Pelion. Even the original form of his name is uncertain. According to one report he was christened Sophocles, to which he prefixed his grandfather's name, Evangelinus. The commoner explanation gives the latter as his baptismal name; in America he added the patronymic Apostolides (after his father) and finally the surname Sophocles, first bestowed upon him by his paternal uncle

Constantius. This uncle took him to Cairo, where he was educated in the establishment belonging to the monastery of St. Catherine, on Mt. Sinai. The trips which he made thither across the desert provided him with his most exciting boyhood experiences, and throughout life he maintained friendly relations with the Sinaitic monks. Returning to Greece, he endeavored to obtain a post as teacher, but for reasons not wholly clear he yielded to the advice of the Rev. Josiah Brewer, a missionary of the American Board of Commissioners for Foreign Missions, and emigrated to Massachusetts. After studying at Monson Academy, Monson, Mass., he entered Amherst College in 1829 but withdrew on account of ill health before the end of the year. For some years he taught at Mount Pleasant Classical Institute (later Amherst Academy) at Amherst; in 1834 he was instructor in mathematics at Hartford, Conn. The next year he brought out *A Greek Grammar for the Use of Learners,* often reissued during the next thirty years. Other textbooks followed quickly: *First Lessons in Greek* (1839), *Greek Exercises* (1841), *Greek Lessons* (1843), all marked by clarity and originality and a wide range of illustration. The year 1842 was signalized by his appointment as tutor in Greek at Harvard, and by the publication of *A Romaic Grammar,* with chrestomathy and vocabulary (omitted in the edition of 1857), in which he exploded the theory of an Aeolic-Doric origin of Modern Greek, and rightly traced it to the Byzantine. This work presented new and correct theories of morphology and syntax long before the treatises of Albert Thumb and Hubert Octave Pernot; its neglect by transatlantic scholars reveals the remoteness of America at that time from the learned centers of Europe. Another useful work was his *A Catalogue of Greek Verbs* (1844). Although ill health interrupted his teaching for a time, in 1847 he resumed his post as tutor. In 1848 his *History of the Greek Alphabet* proved to be far in advance of its time, anticipating in many details regarding pronunciation the work of Friedrich Wilhelm Blass. He revisited Greece in 1849 and 1860. In 1859 he had been appointed assistant professor, and in 1860 he was elected to a unique position as professor of Ancient, Byzantine, and Modern Greek. His "A Glossary of Later and Byzantine Greek" (published in the *Memoirs of the American Academy of Arts and Sciences,* vol. VII, n.s., 1860) was expanded into his greatest work, *Greek Lexicon of the Roman and Byzantine Periods* (1870), of which a memorial edition was published at Harvard in 1887.

If Sophocles was somewhat indifferent to the wealth of scholarship Western Europe had brought to bear upon Greek art and letters, this was because his own work lay in a field not yet explored by competent scholars. Humor and epigram, scorn of ignorance and superficiality, and a wide acquaintance with literature (except possibly German), characterized his teaching. He seems to have been disappointed in the results of the Greek Revolution; a Bavarian Greece had not been his ideal of a liberated Greece. His small body was surmounted by an Olympian head covered with a shock of white hair; his dark eyes gleamed almost ferociously. But under a brusqueness which terrified the stranger he cherished a tender sympathy for his intimate friends. Little children loved him; the chickens which he tended on the ground now occupied by Radcliffe College came at the call of their own names. With seeming parsimony he saved money to build a bridge and waterworks for his native village, and he left large sums to friends and to the Harvard library. His dignity, courtesy, and frugality suggested the Greek peasant, and the solitariness of the bare room in Holworthy Hall in which he died, the monk's cell.

[Frederick Tuckerman, *Amherst Acad., A New England School of the Past, 1814–1861* (1929), p. 219; J. L. Chamberlain, *Harvard Univ.* (1900); S. E. Morison, *The Development of Harvard University . . . 1869–1929* (1930), with portrait; *Ann. Reports of the Pres. and Treas. of Harvard Coll., 1883–84* (1885), p. 4; minutes of the Harvard Faculty of Arts and Sciences, Jan. 8, 1884; G. H. Palmer, in *Atlantic Monthly,* June 1891 (reprinted in Palmer's *The Teacher,* 1908), with some inaccuracies; George Batchelor, in *Harvard Grads.' Mag.,* June 1916; C. L. Jackson, in *Harvard Alumni Bull.,* Mar. 15, 1923; D. C. Hesseling, *Evangelinos Apostolidis Sophoclis néo-helléniste* (Amsterdam, 1925), reprinted from *Koninklijke Akad. van Wetenschappen,* Deel 59, no. 7, the best account of Sophocles' scientific attainments; *Nation,* Jan. 3, 1884; obituaries in *Boston Transcript,* and *Boston Daily Advertiser,* Dec. 18, 1883; private correspondence in the Harvard Univ. Archives; a MS. diary of Christos Evangelides of Syra for 1856–60 in the Harvard Univ. Lib.]   C. B. G.

SORGE, FRIEDRICH ADOLPH (Nov. 9, 1828–Oct. 26, 1906), socialist and labor leader, was born in Bethau bei Torgau, Saxony, the son of Georg Wilhelm and Hedwig Klothilde (Lange) Sorge. An early education received from his father, a clergyman, was supplemented by instruction at the Franckeschen Stiftungen at Halle. In 1848 he took part in the revolutionary activities at Torgau and Baden, and crossed the Swiss border with the revolutionary army. With others he was interned at Freiburg, but in September was released and went to Geneva, where he supported himself by teaching music. Here he first came in contact with liberal socialists through the German Workers Educational Society, of which Karl Liebknecht was the leader. He was forced to leave Geneva in the summer of 1851 and joined his brother at Liège, where he worked in a carpenter shop and taught German in a private school, being continually under police surveillance. In March 1852 he was expelled from Belgium, and, exiled from Germany because of a death sentence imposed by a military tribunal at Torgau, he went to London. Here he first met Karl Marx and renewed a passing acquaintance with Friedrich Engels. While suffering from an attack of the cholera, he took ship supposedly for Australia, but found himself instead landed in New York City on June 21, 1852. Here he eventually established a reputation as a musician and music teacher.

In 1858 he joined the Communist Club organized by Albert Komp in New York, and in 1868 was a member of the executive committee of the Union for German Freedom and Unity, organized to support the republican movement in Germany. He associated with the radical anti-slavery wing of the Republican party during the Civil War; was secretary of the Secularists, a freethinker group, in 1868; joined in the political activity of the *Soziale Partei* in 1868; and finally, in 1869, became a member of Section 1 of the International Working-Men's Association. From 1869 to 1876, he was not only the most active and influential, but also the clearest exponent of the German-American proletariat. He attended The Hague convention of the International in 1872, came into active opposition to Bakunin, the leading anarchist factor in the International and was instrumental in the expulsion of Section 12 of the American branch, which was advocating anarchism, free love, and other doctrines foreign to the purposes of the International. After the removal of the International headquarters to New York City, he was persuaded to undertake the office of general secretary. At The Hague he became more intimately acquainted with Marx and Engels, and until his death was the authoritative representative of Marx in America. In July 1876, Sorge and Otto Weydemeyer represented the North American Federation of the International Working-Men's Association, at a convention held in Philadelphia for the purpose of unifying the American labor and socialist movements. This meeting resulted in ultimate adherence to the Socialist Labor Party, with which Sorge had little to do.

Sorge was keenly interested in bringing about a national organization of the labor union movement, and to that end he associated in 1877 with Ira Steward [*q.v.*] in the Eight-Hour League at Boston. The following year with J. P. McDonnell, he was instrumental in organizing the textile workers of New Jersey. At that time he was living in Hoboken, N. J. In 1891 Samuel Gom-

pers requested Sorge to make for European publication a fair statement of the conditions under which the American Federation of Labor was being attacked by the American Socialists, and from 1891 to 1895 he contributed a series of articles in German to the *Neue Zeit* (Stuttgart) on the labor movement in the United States. He was also the author of many propaganda pamphlets, one of which, *Socialism and the Worker,* was reprinted in 1910 in London. Following the Philadelphia meeting, he gradually withdrew from public connection with the Socialist movement, owing to the development of tendencies with which he was not in sympathy. Sorge was a tall, stout man with a bullet-shaped head, fullbearded, the moustache not large enough to cover a hare lip. He was overbearing and dictatorial, often quarreling bitterly with his associates and his family. Shortly after coming to the United States he was married to a young German girl. They had a son and a daughter. In 1877 he moved temporarily to Rochester, N. Y., later returning to Hoboken, N. J., where he resided until he died.

[Samuel Gompers, *Seventy Years of Life and Labor* (1925); Morris Hillquit, *Hist. of Socialism in the U. S.* (1903); J. R. Commons, *Hist. of Labour in the U. S.* (1921), vol. I; Hermann Schlütter, *Die Internationale in Amerika* (1918), Heft 7; G. M. Stekloff, *Hist. of the First International* (1928); *Neue Zeit,* Nov. 3, 1906.]
W. R. G.

SORIN, EDWARD FREDERICK (Feb. 6, 1814–Oct. 31, 1893), Roman Catholic priest, educator, founder of the University of Notre Dame, was born at Ahuillé, near Laval, France. Having completed his collegiate studies with high honors, he entered the diocesan seminary and was ordained priest on May 27, 1838. The Abbé Basil Antoine Moreau, a professor in the seminary at Le Mans, had recently organized a community of priests of the diocese and to this band he later added a society of lay brothers, giving to the united group the title Congregation of Holy Cross. Attracted by the ideals of the new society, Father Sorin entered it and made his profession Aug. 15, 1840.

About this time Bishop Hailandière of Vincennes, Ind., then in France, asked the new community to send missionaries to his diocese. After due consideration, the community decided to send Father Sorin and six brothers. They sailed from Havre as steerage passengers on the packet *Iowa* and arrived in New York Sept. 13, 1841. Traveling mostly by water, they arrived at Vincennes about a month later. At first they settled at St. Peter's in Daviess County, about twenty-seven miles from Vincennes. The following year Bishop Hailandière offered to Sorin a plot of land near South Bend, in St. Joseph County, on condition that he start a college within two years. Accompanied by the brothers, Father Sorin started for the new site, called by Father Badin, the original owner, Sainte Marie des Lacs. Arriving Nov. 26, 1842, he set about at once to fulfil the condition laid down by the bishop. He sent back to France for more priests and brothers and began to build. In the meantime he had obtained from the General Assembly of Indiana, Jan. 15, 1844, a charter for Notre Dame University. The first college building was completed in time for the initial commencement exercises in June 1844. Father Sorin continued as president until 1865 and he, more than any one else, shaped the traditions and spirit of Notre Dame. He also acted as provincial superior and together with his fellow religious took care of the mission posts in northeastern Illinois, northern Indiana, and southern Michigan. The college progressed steadily under his guidance despite extreme financial difficulties, several fires, and even a plague of cholera which seriously depleted the ranks of the little community.

In 1843 Father Sorin brought to America from Le Mans some Sisters of Holy Cross and the following year established them at Bertrand, Mich., about five miles from Notre Dame. Under his direction, this band of zealous women grew rapidly into a large community conducting schools in all parts of the country. In 1854 he secured the site of the present motherhouse adjacent to Notre Dame and moved there the sisters' community house and academy. He was especially instrumental in bringing to that community Eliza Maria Gillespie, who, as Mother Angela [q.v.], became to the Sisters of Holy Cross, after their separation into a distinct community, what Father Sorin was to Notre Dame. In 1865 he began the publication of Ave Maria, a family magazine of influence and importance. Immediately following the outbreak of the Civil War he sent priests and sisters to care for the soldiers. In 1868 he was elected superior-general of the Congregation of Holy Cross and as such supervised the educational and missionary activities of the community in France, Canada, and Bengal as well as in the United States. He retained, however, his presidency of the trustees of Notre Dame. The French government conferred upon him, in 1888, the insignia of Officer of Public Instruction for his service to education. In 1883 he assisted in the deliberations of the Plenary Council of Baltimore. His voluminous and important correspondence shows an acquaintanceship with the Catholic leaders of America, clerical and lay; it was at his sugges-

tion, in 1883, that the custom was established at Notre Dame of awarding the Laetare Medal annually to a distinguished Catholic layman.

[Father Sorin's journal and "Missions Attended from Notre Dame," in the Provincial archives, Notre Dame; Timothy Howard, A Hist. of St. Joseph County, Ind., vol. II (1907); A Brief Hist. of the Univ. of Notre Dame du Lac, 1842–1892 (1895); Notre Dame Scholastic, vols. XVI, XXVII, XXXIX; South Bend Daily Times, Feb. 28, Mar. 7, 14, 1898; Indianapolis Sentinel, Nov. 1, 1893; Ave Maria, Nov. 4, 1893.]

W. M.

SOTHERN, EDWARD ASKEW (Apr. 1, 1826–Jan. 20, 1881), actor, was born in Liverpool, England, seventh child in the large family of John Sothern, prosperous ship and colliery owner. He made attempts in London to study surgery and then theology, finally ending in a Liverpool ship-broker's office, but he was drawn strongly to the stage, first as an amateur, and in 1849, in Guernsey, as a professional. Though there was no acting tradition in his family, and his first attempts were failures, he persisted, acting in provincial cities under the name of Douglas Stewart, and in 1852, still under that name, set out for America. After his first engagement at the National Theatre, Boston, as Dr. Pangloss, in The Heir at Law, a part to which he was unsuited and in which he failed, he went to the old Howard Athenaeum, Boston, and then to Barnum's Museum in New York, where he toiled twice a day for a year. By 1854 he had sufficiently improved to be engaged by Lester Wallack, in whose New York company he acted for four years. During this period he assumed his own name, and acted Armand to the Camille of Matilda Agnes Heron [q.v.]. At Laura Keene's theatre in 1858 he was cast for a small part in Our American Cousin. According to the story told by Joseph Jefferson, the younger [q.v.], to E. H. Sothern (The Melancholy Tale of "Me," post, pp. 172–73), Sothern had resolved to give up the trifling part and go back to England, but Jefferson, who wished him to continue to share the expense of a stable for their riding horses, persuaded him to stay, on condition that Miss Keene permit him to build up his part. Thus was born the rôle of Lord Dundreary, Sothern's most famous creation, little noticed for the first two weeks, but as time went on gradually usurping the whole play, so that Miss Keene and Jefferson took the original version, and let Sothern organize a new company for his version. The play was produced in America, Oct. 18, 1858. In 1861, when it was produced in London at the Haymarket, it became even more widely popular, and ran for 496 performances. The part was, as Andrew Carpenter Wheeler put it, "the elaboration of a negation," in which the actor showed "the rich fulness of a vacuum" (Pemberton, *post*, p. 32). There had never been a similar British silly ass on the stage before, nor has there been since. It was *sui generis*, at once a comical burlesque and a thing of quaint and inexplicable dignity. The character had a mythical Brother Sam, whom Sothern later caused to be dramatized, as a sort of sequel. He also produced, among other plays, Thomas W. Robertson's romantic *David Garrick*, and a version of Henry J. Byron's *The Prompter's Box*, called *A Crushed Tragedian*, in which his part of the old actor was a mingling of almost burlesque character-drawing and pathos. So firmly had Sothern's Dundreary fixed him in the public mind as a comedian, however, that the pathos seldom told at its true value. After the first long run of Dundreary in London, he divided his time almost equally between the United States and England, touring through both countries with vast success, and carrying with him his entire company instead of depending on local stock companies for support. He retained a home in London, however, and there he died of what was perhaps euphemistically called a nervous collapse, the result of a combination of hard professional labors and excessive conviviality. In spite of his twenty years of success, his estate was found to be less than $50,000.

He had plentiful equipment for an actor—nervous sensibility, keen powers of observation, a lithe figure and handsome face, with keen, dominating blue eyes, a magnetic sense of fun, and in his professional work capacity for concentrated labor and minute attention to detail. His Dundreary was elaborated with the utmost care; every least gesture and inflection was studied, often from life, and welded into the whole. Nothing was left to chance. But in his personal life he was spendthrift of his time and energies; he loved to ride and hunt and to be in convivial society, and he was perhaps the most noted practical joker of the day. The most engaging of his innumerable pranks is that related by his son in *The Melancholy Tale of "Me,"* when the elder Sothern arrived in Boston, drove to the home of his friend Mrs. Vincent, Boston's best loved actress, burst in on a party she was giving, picked her up, dashed with her back to his cab, and drove frantically off, with all the guests in full pursuit of the abductor. There was no end to his invention of these jokes, which were carried out with as much acting skill, when necessary, as his stage impersonations. He married Frances Stewart, an actress, daughter of the Rev. R. I. Stewart, County Wexford, Ireland (Moses, *post*, p. 97). She bore him four children, all of whom went on the stage: Lytton Edward, Eva Mary, George, and Edward Hugh Sothern [*q.v.*]. But Sothern's personal habits were not those conducive to domestic happiness, and long before his death his wife had separated from him. She died in 1882. In spite of his habits, which included laxities more common on the stage then than now, he retained almost to the end a fresh, rosy complexion and unwrinkled face, though his hair early turned white and his shoulders were bowed, and the charm and conviviality of his company continued to be much sought.

[*The Dict. of Nat. Biog.*; *Birds of a Feather Flock Together, or Talks with Sothern* (1878), ed. by F. G. De Fontaine; T. E. Pemberton, *A Memoir of Edward Askew Sothern* (1889); Brander Matthews and Laurence Hutton, *Actors and Actresses of Great Britain and the United States* (copr. 1886), vol. IV; M. J. Moses, *Famous Actor-Families in America* (1906); William Winter, *Other Days* (1908); E. H. Sothern, *The Melancholy Tale of "Me"* (1916); obituaries in *Times* (London) and *N. Y. Tribune*, Jan. 22, 1881.]
W. P. E.

SOTHERN, EDWARD HUGH (Dec. 6, 1859–Oct. 28, 1933), actor, son of Edward Askew Sothern [*q.v.*] and Frances (Stewart) Sothern, was born at 79 Bienville St., New Orleans, La., during one of his father's American tours. He was educated in England and intended to become a painter, but the inherited call of the stage was too strong. In 1879 he joined his father in America, and on Sept. 8, at the Park Theatre, New York, he made an unfortunate début as a cabman in the farce, *Brother Sam*, produced by the elder Sothern, in which, overcome by stage fright, he was unable to utter a sound. Sent to Boston to act with the Boston Museum stock company under the kindly eye of Mrs. Mary Ann Vincent, a family friend, in the next few months he found his confidence, and joined for a time the company of John McCullough [*q.v.*], Shakespearian actor, to which he returned in 1883 after nearly two years in England. After failing dismally in his attempt to star in *Whose are They?* in 1884, he joined the company of Helen Dauvray at the Lyceum Theatre, New York, and there was discovered by Daniel Frohman, who took over the Lyceum in 1886 and made Sothern a leading man in his stock company. In the next fourteen years he built up in this company a brilliant reputation as a light comedian and as a charming romantic actor in the "cloak and sword" dramas then so popular. His *Captain Lettarblair* and *Lord Chumley* are best remembered as comedy, and his *Rudolf*, the dashing hero of *The Prisoner of Zenda*, as romance. As *Rudolf*, he toured the country and won such wide recognition that after 1899 he became a star in his own right, and with his wife, Virginia Harned, whom he married Dec. 3, 1896, acted in *The King's Musketeers* (adapted from the elder Dumas), *The Song of the Sword, The Sunken Bell,* and *Drifting Apart.* On Sept. 17, 1900, at the Garden Theatre, New York, he acted *Hamlet* for the first time, and thereafter kept it in his repertoire, alternating it during the next three or four years with such plays as *Richard Lovelace, If I Were King,* with which he opened the new Lyceum Theatre, and *The Proud Prince.* From 1904 to 1907 under the management of Charles Frohman [*q.v.*], he formed an alliance with Julia Marlowe to act chiefly in Shakespeare. In the next two years Sothern alone produced Laurence Irving's *The Fool Hath Said, Richelieu, Don Quixote,* and a revival of his father's famous impersonation of Dundreary in *Our American Cousin.* On Nov. 8, 1909, Miss Marlowe rejoined him, acting Cleopatra to his Antony, to open the New Theatre, New York. They then resumed their tours, acting some of the more familiar plays of Shakespeare, *Jeanne d'Arc,* Sudermann's *John the Baptist,* Hauptmann's *The Sunken Bell,* and occasionally *When Knighthood Was in Flower.* The Shakespearian productions, carefully and elaborately staged, were everywhere enormously popular, and during that decade in America were perhaps the leading attraction in the theatres. On Aug. 17, 1911, in London, having been divorced by his first wife, Sothern married Julia Marlow (born Sarah Frances Frost), who had been married previously to Robert Taber. In 1916 ill health forced her to retire, and Sothern, after an appearance in *The Two Virtues,* devoted the next years to war work, appearing as an entertainer in soldiers' camps. After the war, in 1919, his wife once more attempted to act but was unable to continue steadily; he appeared from time to time, however, either in plays or public readings, his last theatrical appearance in New York being at the Lyceum Theatre, Jan. 29, 1927, with Haidee Wright, in *What Never Dies.* His readings and lectures, given widely throughout the country, continued for several years more. (See Arthur Ruhl's "Second Nights" in the New York *Herald Tribune,* Nov. 17, 1929.) In his later years, with his wife, he spent his summers in England and his winters, when he was not in America, at Luxor on the Nile. His autobiography, *The Melancholy Tale of "Me"* (1916), is one of the most delightful of theatrical reminiscences. It is plainly the work of a man of culture, wit, and literary skill, and suggests that if its author had not been an actor he might have made a career as a writer. He died in New York

City of pneumonia. He was survived by his wife.

Sothern's stage personality was sufficiently impressive to conceal the fact that he was a small man. He had a sensitive, handsome face, extremely fine eyes, much bodily grace and expressive body control, quickness and litheness of movement, and a well-trained voice. He developed and perfected "a distinct, authoritative, crisp style, not unique, but neat, expert in mechanism, and felicitous in assumption of nonchalant, lacka-daisical demeanor" (Winter, *Vagrant Memories, post,* pp. 433–34). He excelled in the give-and-take of comedy repartee, and in romantic sword play and dashing heroics and amours; as a stage director he was skilful in bringing out the melodramatic structure of a story or the swing of the narrative. He was not by natural endowment a tragic actor, but he was led by ambition and by devotion to the ideal of a classic repertoire to act Hamlet, Shylock, Macbeth and Antony and by dint of hard work and keen, sensitive intelligence he gave in nearly all cases an excellent account of himself. His best Shakespearian rôle, however, was probably Malvolio, where with no loss of comic effect he presented a pathetic picture of an inherent gentleman overcome by vanity. One of his irresistibly comical performances was his reincarnation of his father's Dundreary. Those who saw Sothern act in the nineties, however, especially those who saw him in *The Prisoner of Zenda,* will most fondly remember him as the dashing, charming, alluring symbol of that pseudo-romance which had such a brief and beautiful Indian summer before the realistic new century set in. Better than any other player on either continent Sothern embodied its humor and gaiety, its chivalric love, its delicate grace, its wistfulness.

[*Who's Who in America,* 1932–33; *Who's Who in the Theatre* (1933); E. H. Sothern, *The Melancholy Tale of "Me"* (1916), with portraits, and "Why I Produce Shakespeare Plays," *Dramatic Mirror,* Jan. 18, 1911; William Winter, *Vagrant Memories* (1915) and *The Wallet of Time* (1913), vol. II; Arthur Symons, *Great Acting in English* (priv. printed, London, 1907); W. P. Eaton, in *Sun* (N. Y.), Apr. 12, 1908; Winthrop Ames, in *N. Y. Times,* sec. 9, Nov. 12, 1933; *Sunday Herald* (Boston), Apr. 5, 1903, reproductions of pictures painted by Sothern as a boy; obituary in *N. Y. Times,* Oct. 30, 1933.]   W. P. E.

SOTO, HERNANDO DE [See DE SOTO, HERNANDO, *c.* 1500–1542].

SOUCHON, EDMOND (Dec. 1, 1841–Aug. 5, 1924), anatomist, surgeon, sanitarian, was born in Opelousas, Saint Landry Parish, La., the son of Eugene Souchon, "surgeon dentist," and Caroline (Pettit) Souchon, both natives of France. He was sent at first to private schools at Saint Martinville, La., Mobile, Ala., and New

Orleans, La., but later, when his father suffered ill health and financial reverses, he went to public school and sold papers to aid his family. Reviving fortune took him in 1860 to Paris, where he studied medicine, ranked fourth among three hundred and fifty in the grilling concours for internship in Paris hospitals, and served at Charité under the famous surgeon, Alfred Armand Velpeau. His acting as interpreter for Dr. James Marion Sims on the latter's visit to Paris brought him financial aid from Sims and a letter of introduction to Dr. Tobias Gibson Richardson [qq.v.] when he afterwards returned to New Orleans. Upon his graduation in 1867 from the medical department of the University of Louisiana (later the Tulane University of Louisiana), he became Richardson's prosector and later his chief of clinic at Charity Hospital of New Orleans, and assisted him in private practice for many years. On Dec. 6, 1869, he married Corinne Lavie of New Orleans; they had three children, a son, who became a surgeon, and two daughters.

He was demonstrator of anatomy in the medical department of the University of Louisiana (Tulane), 1873–76, and from 1885 until 1908 served as professor of anatomy and clinical surgery, his aim being to teach anatomy "in its direct practical application" to the needs of the medical practitioner. He invented ingenious mechanical devices that were applied in both anatomical and surgical practice, and for the preservation of anatomical dissections devised original methods of injection and coloration. His museum of anatomy, housed in the Richardson Memorial Building at Tulane (which in 1892 he planned for the Richardson family), contained four hundred dissections. His anatomical knowledge led to his association in hospital work with Dr. Andrew Woods Smyth, who first successfully ligated the innominate artery. As a surgeon he was typical of the operators drilled in the quick French school of the sixties, and in the surgical renaissance of the seventies and the eighties he evolved his own methods in keeping with antisepsis and asepsis. Led to study aneurisms and shoulder dislocations, he wrote many monographs that are "conspicuous landmarks" in the history of these subjects, "undoubtedly the most enduring literary monuments of his surgical career" (*Transactions of the American Surgical Association, post,* p. 974). His surgical and anatomical writings began in 1866 with "Aneurisms of the Arch of the Aorta" (*New Orleans Medical and Surgical Journal,* May 1867) and continued until late in his life, two of the later articles being "Original Contri-

butions of America to Medical Sciences" (*Transactions of the American Surgical Association,* vols. XXXV and XXXVIII, 1917–20). Many others are listed in the *Index Catalogue of the Library of the Surgeon General's Office, United States Army* (1 ser., vol. XIII, 1892; 2 ser., vol. XVI, 1911; 3 ser., vol. IX, 1931). As president of the Louisiana State Board of Health, 1898–1908, he prepared a sanitary code embodying all the health laws of the state, contributed actively to the "Atlanta Regulations" adopted by the Southern states in 1898 to regulate yellow fever quarantine, and in 1903 announced warfare on the *Stegomyia* mosquito. He served as an officer of the American Medical Association, the Southern Surgical and Gynecological Society, and the American Surgical Association (1899); he was a fellow of the American Association of Anatomists, honorary fellow of the American College of Surgeons (1914), and corresponding member of the Société Nationale de Chirurgie de Paris. A man whose very positive convictions were often tinged with abruptness, he possessed many peculiarities that lent themselves to anecdote. In spite of his dominating passion for punctuality and method, he was capable of great outbursts of enthusiasm, expressed with typical French volubility and gaiety. His life was marked by loyal friendships and devoted domestic ties.

[*Who's Who in America,* 1924–25; Rudolph Matas, in *Jour. Am. Med. Assoc.,* Aug. 16, 1924, in *Surgery, Gynecology, and Obstetrics,* May 1931, and in *Trans. Am. Surgical Assoc.,* vol. XLIII (1925); I. A. Watson, *Physicians and Surgeons of America* (1896); obituary in *Times-Picayune* (New Orleans), Aug. 6, 1924.]

V. G. G.

SOULÉ, GEORGE (May 14, 1834–Jan. 26, 1926), mathematician, educator, and lecturer, was born at Barrington, N. Y., the second son of Ebenezer and Cornelia Elizabeth (Hogeboom) Soulé. His father died in 1838, and in 1842 his mother took the family to Illinois, settling some fifty miles west of Chicago. For the next ten years George lived on a farm. In 1853 he was graduated from an academy at Sycamore, Ill., and went to St. Louis, where he attended some lectures on medicine and law. Financial considerations forced him to abandon professional study, however, and he entered Jones' Commercial College, from which he graduated in 1856.

That same year he went to New Orleans, where, discovering that there was no business school, he opened Soulé College in a single room. Almost from the first the institution prospered; in 1861 it was chartered. On Sept. 6, 1860, Soulé married Mary Jane Reynolds of Summit, Miss. He entered the Confederate army Mar. 5, 1862, as captain of Company A, Crescent Regiment, Louisiana Infantry, was captured at Pittsburg Landing Apr. 7, and was exchanged Nov. 10. He then served in General Kirby-Smith's army as chief of the labor bureau. He was paroled in June 1865, at which time he was lieutenant-colonel of the Crescent Regiment.

Returning to New Orleans, he took personal charge of Soulé College. A pioneer in business education in the South, he tried to give his students something more than shorthand and book-keeping. His own interest in arithmetical processes and in systems of accounting led him to devise and to publish many textbooks. Among these were *Soulé's Analytic and Philosophic Commercial and Exchange Calculator* (1872); *Soulé's Intermediate Philosophic Arithmetic* (1874); *Soulé's New Science and Practice of Accounts* (1881); *Soulé's Introductory Philosophic Arithmetical Drill Problems* (1882); *Soulé's Philosophic Practical Mathematics* (1895); and *Soulé's Manual of Auditing* (6th ed., 1905). The most of these went through several editions. He was active in the National Commercial Teachers' Federation, before which he often spoke in behalf of better and more ethical standards. His success in commercial education was reflected in the rapid and steady growth of his college; during the seventy years of his presidency, some forty thousand students were enrolled. In the life of New Orleans he took a prominent part. He was a leader in Masonic activities, a prominent member of the Unitarian Church, and a most active and valuable member of the Rex carnival organization. He was king of the carnival in 1887 and wrote the history of the carnival for the golden anniversary of 1922. Tulane University conferred the degree of LL.D. on him in 1918.

In addition to annual addresses at Soulé College, he lectured frequently and widely. One of his chief interests was phrenology, which he enthusiastically believed to have a scientific basis in anatomy. In many respects he was far ahead of his times. He opposed child labor, favored more hygienic conditions for workers, and rebuked the city authorities for what he considered the shameful violation of architectural beauty and of hygienic principles and laws. When such subjects were taboo, he advocated studies in sex-hygiene and eugenics. To his success as a speaker, his striking appearance contributed. He was over six feet tall, erect, and keen-eyed; his hair fell down to his shoulders. Active in public affairs almost to the end of his life, he died after a brief illness, survived by four sons and two daughters.

[G. T. Ridlon, *A Contribution to the Hist., Biog., and Geneal. of the Families Named Sole, Solly, Soule, Sowle, Soulis* (1926); J. S. Kendall, *Hist. of New Orleans* (1922), II, 827–30; A. B. Booth, *Records of La. Confederate Soldiers* (1920), vol. III, bk. II, p. 651; *Who's Who in America*, 1924–25; *Times-Picayune* (New Orleans), June 6, 1918, Jan. 27, 1926; information from the Soulé family, and from Dr. Rudolph Matas.]   R. P. M.

SOULE, JOSHUA (Aug. 1, 1781–Mar. 6, 1867), bishop of the Methodist Episcopal Church, a lineal descendant of George Soule who came to America on the *Mayflower*, was born at Bristol, Me., the fifth son of Joshua and Mary (Cushman) Soule. Although his parents were Presbyterians, Joshua in 1797 joined the Methodist Episcopal Church, and in 1799, at the age of seventeen, was admitted on trial to the New England Conference. In 1802 he was ordained deacon and the following year, elder. He served as a pioneer itinerant and presiding elder in New England until 1816. In that year he was made book agent of the church and in 1818 became the first editor of the *Methodist Magazine*. Between 1816 and 1820 he was also active in the work of the American Bible Society and in 1819 he became a charter member and treasurer of the Missionary and Bible Society of the Methodist Episcopal Church in America, the pioneer missionary body of that denomination. From 1820 to 1824 he held pastorates in the New York and Baltimore conferences. He was elected bishop in 1824 and was assigned to the western and southern conferences, making his home in Lebanon, Ohio. In 1842 he was fraternal messenger to the British and Irish Wesleyan Conferences.

At the age of twenty-six, Soule wrote the constitution of the Methodist Episcopal Church. The early methods of vesting the legislative powers of the church in a quadrennial assembly of the preachers had become so unsatisfactory, that at the General Conference of 1808, a committee of which Soule was a member was appointed to prepare a more efficient plan. Without any assistance, he prepared a draft, which with only a few minor changes was adopted as the constitution of the church. His plan provided for a delegated and representative General Conference, which was, subject to six restrictive rules, to have legislative authority for the denomination. It also promoted the connectionalism of Methodism, and gave to Methodist polity democratic and stabilizing characteristics. Soule did his work so well as the "Father of the Constitution" that there has been only slight inclination on the part of Episcopal Methodism to devise new means of ecclesiastical law making. Subsequently, he affected the polity of Methodism by his views concerning the sub-episcopate. Until

1820 the presiding elders had been appointed by the bishops, but objections had arisen on the ground that this practice was undemocratic, and that it made the presiding elders amenable to the bishops and not to the preachers. Therefore, at the General Conference of 1820 it was decided that the annual conference should elect the presiding elders. At this same Conference Soule had been elected bishop, but when the vote on the sub-episcopate was announced he refused to be consecrated. He insisted that an elective presiding eldership was unconstitutional, since the fundamental law of the church instructed the bishops to oversee the business of the church. This function Soule asserted would be impossible if the presiding elders were not directly responsible to the bishops. His arguments were so pertinent that the delegates resolved to suspend the enforcement of the resolution for four years. By the time of the next General Conference (1824) the church had approved Soule's constitutional position, and he was again elected bishop. For twenty years he was a bishop of the Methodist Episcopal Church. He was an excellent administrator and was recognized as an authority on polity.

In 1844, when the General Conference sought to depose Bishop James O. Andrew [q.v.] for his connection with slavery, Soule held that it had violated the constitution which he himself had written. Therefore, when, at the Louisville Convention in 1845, the Methodist Episcopal Church, South, was organized, Soule was present and gave his approval to its work. At the first General Conference of that body in 1846 he formally adhered thereto, and thereby a man born in Maine became the senior bishop of the Southern branch of Episcopal Methodism. He now removed to Nashville, Tenn., later establishing his home on a farm outside the city. Soule was an active bishop until 1855. He died in Nashville and was buried in the old City Cemetery, but in October 1876 his remains were reinterred on the campus of Vanderbilt University. He was married in Providence, R. I., Sept. 18, 1803, to Sarah Allen, by whom he had eleven children. He was six feet tall and muscular, had wide cheek bones, a high forehead, and a head so large that it was necessary to have extra-size hats manufactured for him.

[G. T. Ridlon, A Contribution to the Hist., Biog., and Geneal. of the Families Named Sole, Solly, Soule, Sowle, Soulis (1926); H. M. DuBose, Life of Joshua Soule (1911); J. J. Tigert, A Constitutional Hist. of Am. Episcopal Methodism (1904); James Mudge, Hist. of the New England Conference (1910); J. B. McFerrin and others, Hist. of the Organization of the Methodist Episcopal Church, South (1845); Republican Banner (Nashville), Mar. 7, 1867.] P.N.G.

SOULÉ, PIERRE (Aug. 31, 1801–Mar. 26, 1870), jurist, diplomat, was born at Castillon-en-Couserans in the French Pyrenees, the youngest son of Joseph and Jeanne (Lacroix) Soulé. His father, a brilliant Napoleonic officer, was for twenty years a magistrate; his mother came of distinguished native stock. Destined for the Church, Soulé at fifteen rebelled against the rigid Jesuit discipline of the Collège de l'Esquille at Toulouse and, turning to politics, became an anti-Bourbon conspirator at Bordeaux by choice and thus an exiled shepherd in Navarre by necessity. Pardoned in 1818, he returned to Bordeaux where, the next year, he took his bachelor's degree, and then proceeded to Paris to study law. A lawyer in 1822, he soon joined in the republican movement against Charles X, publishing with others the journal, Le Nain Jaune, and thereby inviting monarchical prosecution. Arrested in April 1825, he was convicted and sentenced to prison. Preferring exile, Soulé escaped to England and on Sept. 5, 1825, arrived at Port-au-Prince, Haiti. Finding conditions there unsatisfactory, he proceeded in October to the United States, landing at Baltimore.

A stranger in Baltimore, a wanderer in New York, Soulé in November found refuge in New Orleans. To perfect his English he traveled inland in 1827, receiving Andrew Jackson's hospitality at "The Hermitage" and, after an illness, requiting the kindness of Dominican monks at Bardstown, Ky., by acting as gardener. Returning to New Orleans, in 1828, he married Armantine Mercier, a belle of the Vieux Carré and a sister of Armand and Charles Alfred Mercier [q.v.]. She bore him a son. The next twenty years witnessed his rise in varied fields of endeavor: as criminal lawyer, orator, financier, and man of affairs. He was a generous friend of French refugees, a philanthropist toward his fellow citizens, and, politically, a notable accession to the Democracy. Having spoken for Van Buren in 1840, he was chosen a delegate to the convention of 1844 for revising the state constitution; there he early gained recognition as the unofficial leader of the New Orleans delegation, although Judah P. Benjamin shattered his constitutional arguments. In the first election ensuing under the revised constitution, New Orleans, on Jan. 19, 1846, sent Soulé to the state Senate where he led the successful struggle for the abolition of compulsory capital punishment.

On the death of United States Senator Alexander Barrow in December 1846, John Slidell [q.v.], Soulé's rival, preferring a full term of six years, encompassed the latter's election for the unexpired term of three months. Although mentioned as a possible colleague of Nicholas P. Trist as peace commissioner to Mexico, Soulé, in March 1847, retired from public affairs for a time, but in the senatorial election of 1848, utilizing a Whig majority and capitalizing his opponent's Plaquemines frauds of 1844, defeated Slidell, the regular Democratic candidate, for the six-year term and control of Louisiana. He served until his resignation, Apr. 11, 1853. As senator, Soulé succeeded Calhoun as leader of the state-rights wing of the Southern Democracy, but, except for his oratory, achieved no outstanding parliamentary distinction. His senatorial career was a paradox in that he was a leader in the state-rights movement, although a sincere proponent of the democratic form of American government; a pioneer in the American movement for world republicanism, yet a strong protagonist of slavery; a sponsor of international amity, yet, withal, a stanch partisan advocate of American imperialism.

Soulé preferred Stephen A. Douglas in the Democratic National Convention at Baltimore in June 1852, but rendered services to Franklin Pierce in the campaign. Although mentioned for the attorney-generalship, he was passed over by Pierce in selections for the cabinet, and thus sought solace in the diplomatic service. The English and French missions being closed to him, the former by Buchanan's claims, the latter because of his republican hatred of Louis Napoleon, who cordially reciprocated, Soulé dreamed of St. Petersburg, only to be thwarted by the Czar, to whom his republicanism was anathema. On Apr. 7, 1853, Soulé therefore accepted the mission to Madrid, thereby deliberately revoking a pledge to secure it for his brilliant Louisiana friend, the historian Charles Gayarré [q.v.]. Soulé's qualifications included linguistic ability, a knowledge of Gallic Europe, and Catholicism. He was in complete harmony with Pierce's annexationist program as to Cuba, but his very zeal made his appointment an insult to Spain and a source of mortification to the United States. Continual errors marred his career. He lauded the Cuban Junta in New York; he visited Continental republican exiles in London; he sought to seduce France from Great Britain and Spain in Paris. In Madrid, after his arrival on Oct. 14, the condescending tenor and impertinent advice of his proposed address to the Queen led to revision and rebuke from the Foreign Office; his sartorial vagaries and belligerent pride led to two notorious duels by him and his son, and to the ostracism of his family. Despite the express prohibitory instructions of Secretary William L. Marcy [q.v.], Soulé sought the ac-

quisition of Cuba by purchase, by favor of the Queen Mother, or as collateral for a royal loan. The *Black Warrior* episode in Havana led him to exceed instructions and attempt acquisition by threat of war. On Apr. 3, 1854, Marcy at last ordered him to attempt the purchase of Cuba and, failing that, to "detach" it from Spain. Finding purchase programs futile, Soulé, that summer, strove to "detach" Cuba, first, by aiding Spanish republican revolutions, and second, by conniving with Ledru-Rollin in engendering revolution in France, involving the assassination of Louis Napoleon. Failure in both plans caused Soulé's sudden and discreet withdrawal from Madrid to his Pyrenean château.

On Aug. 16, Marcy, cancelling the project of a commission to aid Soulé, which had led the latter to threaten his resignation, directed him, James Buchanan [q.v.], minister to Great Britain, and John Y. Mason [q.v.], minister to France, to confer on Spanish-American relations with particular reference to Cuba. Buchanan, seeking annexation on strict ethical and legal bases, posited the application of economic pressure on Spain through foreign bondholders; Mason, with passive complacence, would permit expediency to outweigh ethics, but demanded a semblance of legality; Soulé, militant and embittered by past failures, sought Cuba regardless of ethics or legality. Meeting first at Ostend and then at Aix-la-Chapelle, the triumvirate on Oct. 18, 1854, signed the Ostend Manifesto, a document largely Soulé's handiwork (Ettinger, *post,* pp. 364–68), which proposed the purchase of Cuba in "open, frank, and public" negotiations with the Spanish Constituent Cortes. Should Spain refuse to sell, and should Cuba, "in the possession of Spain, seriously endanger our internal peace and the existence of our cherished Union," then and then only must it be wrested from Spain (*House Executive Document No. 93,* 33 Cong., 2 Sess.). Unknown to Buchanan, Soulé sent his own militant interpretation of this document to Marcy, who received both the Manifesto and the interpretation at a time when he was confronted by evidence of Soulé's revolutionary machinations, his untimely encounter with French officials at Calais, and decisive Democratic defeats in the congressional elections of 1854. Sheer expediency led Marcy on Nov. 13 to reject the Manifesto, thereby repudiating his own instructions on Apr. 3 to "detach" Cuba. For the seventh time Soulé had failed and, on receipt of Marcy's negatory letter, he resigned on Dec. 17, returning as scapegoat for the *volte-face* of the administration.

Retiring to private law practice, Soulé in 1857

successfully defended William Walker, the Nicaraguan filibuster, and became interested in a projected transisthmian canal in Tehuantepec, Mexico. In politics, he supported Buchanan as delegate to the Democratic Convention of 1856, and finally lost Louisiana to Slidell in 1859. The next year, although now opposed to secession, he went with his state. General Benjamin Butler's notorious régime in New Orleans found Soulé the chief adviser of Mayor Monroe and Confederate provost-marshal. Arrested in June 1862, he was sent to Fort Lafayette, N. Y., and paroled in November to Boston, whence he fled to Nassau in the Bahamas and Havana in February 1863. Successfully running the blockade to New Orleans, he tendered his services to the Confederacy at Richmond from September 1863 to June 1864, but President Davis' hostility prevented his rise to position other than a somewhat honorary brigadier-generalship. In 1865 he joined ex-Senator William M. Gwin [q.v.] of California in a project to settle Confederate veterans in Sonora. Four years later his powerful intellect gave way, and he was declared interdict. He died on March 26, 1870.

[In his last two years Soulé systematically destroyed his private papers; only a few unimportant letters remain in the Lib. of Cong., and in the possession of his grand-daughters, Mrs. A. H. Denis of New Orleans and Mme. M. G. S. de Arias-Salgado, Havre, France. Important sketches are Alfred Mercier, "Biographie de Pierre Soulé, Sénateur à Washington" (Paris, 1848), a partisan account by his brother-in-law; Jean Signorel, Pierre Soulé (Toulouse, 1911), a stirring little narrative based on documents in the possession of Leon Soulé; Leon Soulé, Notice sur Pierre Soulé, avocat à la Nouvelle Orléans, sénateur de la Louisiane à Washington (Toulouse, 1901), a memoir by his last surviving nephew; and Commandant Trespaillé, "Pierre Soulé," Revue des Pyrénées et de la France Méridionale, vol. II, (1890), pp. 540–72, highly laudatory and not based on original material. For surveys of his mission to Spain, see J. A. Reinecke, Jr., "The Diplomatic Career of Pierre Soulé," an unpublished master's thesis at Tulane University, New Orleans, 1914; H. B. Learned, "William Learned Marcy," in S. F. Bemis, ed., The American Secretaries of State and Their Diplomacy, vol. VI (1928); and R. F. Nichols, Franklin Pierce (1931). The latest study, which in ch. 3 reviews Soulé's life and which contains a full bibliography, is A. A. Ettinger, The Mission to Spain of Pierre Soulé, 1853–1855 (1932).]   A. A. E.

SOUSA, JOHN PHILIP (Nov. 6, 1854–Mar. 6, 1932), bandmaster, composer, was born in Washington, D. C., the son of Antonio and Elizabeth (Trinkaus) Sousa. Antonio Sousa's parents had been driven from Portugal during the revolution of 1822, and had moved to Spain where Antonio was born. He left Spain as a youth and emigrated to America in the early 1840's. He was a gentleman of culture, an accomplished linguist, and an amateur musician. Elizabeth Trinkaus was a native of Franconia, Bavaria, and had met Sousa while visiting friends in Brooklyn, N. Y. John Philip Sousa, one of ten children, showed an aptitude for music at an early age, and when he was six years old he entered the conservatory of John Esputa, receiving his first instruction on the violin, but later being taught to play a number of band instruments. At the end of his third year at the conservatory he won all five medals offered by the school, and while still with Esputa, organized a small orchestra to play for dancing. When he was thirteen years of age a circus manager offered him a position in his band, but his father, hearing of the plan, arranged that he enlist in the United States Marine Band, of which he himself had been a member. He played with the organization for about five years, and finally obtained a release in order to study violin, harmony, and theory with George Felix Benkert.

In the summer of 1872 he conducted an orchestra at Kernan's Théâtre Comique, a Washington variety house, and also played the violin in the orchestra of Ford's Opera House. By this time he had started to compose music, and had succeeded in publishing a few of his pieces. A march entitled "The Review," and a galop, "The Cuckoo," were sold outright by the composer to Lee & Walker, Philadelphia music publishers, for one hundred printed copies of each piece. In his early compositions he chose a form in which he was to earn international distinction; he became to the march what the Viennese, Johann Strauss, was to the waltz. About 1874 Sousa accepted an offer to join the Milton Nobles Comedy Company, as orchestra conductor on tour, but after a season returned to Ford's Opera House at Washington. When Matthew Somerville Morgan [q.v.] came to this theatre with his Living Pictures Company, the manager offered Sousa a position as conductor, and he again went on tour. His next engagement was as violinist in Jacques Offenbach's orchestra during the Philadelphia Centennial Exhibition in the summer of 1876. For Offenbach Sousa composed his "International Congress" fantasy. From 1876 to 1879 he made his headquarters in Philadelphia, playing at the Chestnut Street Theatre and at the Arch Street Theatre. During this period Sousa was invited to drill and conduct a group of Philadelphia society amateurs which became known later as the Philadelphia Church Choir Company. He composed for this organization his first comic opera, "The Smugglers," and through it met Jane Bellis, of Philadelphia, to whom he was married during the first week of 1880, while the bride was still in school.

On Sept. 30, 1880, he assumed the conductorship of the United States Marine Band, which he held for twelve years. He reorganized the band with vigor and vision and breathed the breath of life into a somnolent group. As the logical successor of Patrick S. Gilmore [*q.v.*] Sousa carried on the development of the wind band by devising an instrumentation which allowed effects as soft as those of a symphony orchestra. His leadership of the Marine organization brought fame to the band as well as to himself on tours throughout the nation. During these twelve years Sousa was active also as a composer, and wrote a variety of works including the famous "Washington Post March" (1889), "The High School Cadets" (1890), "The Gladiator" (his first great popular number, sold to the publishers for thirty-five dollars), and "Semper Fidelis" (1888), which became the official march of the United States Marine Corps. "Hands Across the Sea" (1899), "King Cotton" (1897), and the "Liberty Bell" (1893), were also well known wherever band music was played.

In the spring of 1892 Sousa accepted an offer from David Blakely which included a salary and financial backing for a band of his own. He accordingly secured a discharge from the Marine Corps, and gave the first concert of Sousa's Band in Plainfield, N. J., on Sept. 26, 1892. Although the first tour was not successful financially, Sousa, with more courage than his manager, insisted that they continue with their plans. After the first season the band proved an overwhelming success. It was engaged for important expositions, beginning with the Chicago World's Columbian Exposition, 1893, and toured the United States, visited Europe four times, and, in 1910–12, made one trip around the world. Sousa was one of few men to have the distinction of serving in three branches of military service: as musical director of the VI Army Corps during the Spanish-American War; as conductor of the United States Marine Band; and as lieutenant in charge of navy bands during the World War. In the last capacity he was a "dollar-a-year" man. He also toured the country with the Great Lakes Naval Training Station Band and drew millions of dollars into the government's treasury on Liberty Loan drives. A year after his discharge he received the rank of lieutenant-commander. Honors and decorations were showered upon him. He received the Royal Victorian Order of Great Britain, the Golden Palms and Rosette of the French Academy, and the Cross of Artistic Merit of the Academy of Arts, Sciences, and Literature of Hainault, Belgium.

Sousa composed more than a hundred marches, nearly all of them stamped with an individuality unmistakably his own. While some of the earlier marches were sold outright to Harry Coleman, Philadelphia music publisher, his later works were published on a royalty basis, and the composer derived handsome profits from their sale. From the famous "Stars and Stripes Forever," composed in 1897, he made about $300,000. He wrote ten comic operas, the best known being "The Bride-Elect" (1897), "El Capitan" (1896), and "The Free Lance" (1906). His works include more than fifty songs, six waltzes, two overtures, twelve suites, and a number of miscellaneous compositions. His vast library of music was bequeathed to the University of Illinois. Sousa also turned his hand to the writing of novels and produced *The Fifth String* (1902), *Pipetown Sandy* (1905), and *Transit of Venus* (1920).

Sousa's genial, gracious, robust wit, and handsome personal presence, always enhanced the dramatic performances of his band. Extravagant public applause followed in his wake around the world. He was an excellent horseman and trapshooter, and at one time was president of the American Trapshooter's Association. During his later years his helpful interest was widely solicited in the formation of amateur bands. He died suddenly in Reading, Pa., and his body was taken to Washington, where it lay in state until his burial in the Congressional Cemetery. His wife, a son, and two daughters survived him. The family home was at Sands' Point, Port Washington, L. I.

[*Who's Who in America*, 1930–31; J. P. Sousa, *Marching Along* (1928); *Through the Year with Sousa* (1910); *Grove's Dict. of Music and Musicians, Am. Supp.* (1930); *Music Trade News*, Mar. 1932; *Musical Courier*, Mar. 12, 1932; *Evening Star* (Washington, D. C.), Aug, 7, 1921; *Washington Post*, Mar. 6, 1932; *N. Y. Times*, Mar. 6, 1932; information from the family.]   J. T. H.

SOUTHACK, CYPRIAN (Mar. 25, 1662–Mar. 27, 1745), pioneer New England cartographer, privateer, was born in London, the son of Cyprian and Elizabeth Southack, of Stepney, Middlesex. The father was a naval lieutenant in the service of Charles II, and the son, at the age of ten, fought in the engagement at Southwold Bay (*Calendar of State Papers, Colonial Series, America and West Indies, 1689–92*, 1901, p. 337). In 1685 he came to Boston, Mass., where he resided for many years. Holding a commission from the Admiralty Board, he guarded the New England coast from the ravages of pirates and privateers. Among the vessels he commanded were the *Porcupine* (1689–90), *Mary* (1690), *William and Mary* (1692), *Friends Adventure* (1693), *Seaflower* (1703), and the Massachusetts Province Galley, between 1697 and 1714.

He was a member of Sir William Phips's unsuccessful expedition to Nova Scotia in the summer of 1690. By his heroic work on the night of Sept. 16 of that year the South Meeting House in Boston was saved when five neighboring buildings burned. In 1698 he commanded the Province Galley when it conveyed Maj. James Converse and Col. John Phillips from Boston to effect peace with the Indians at Casco Bay, and in 1704 he commanded the galley in an expedition under Col. Benjamin Church [q.v.] against the French and Indians in Maine and Nova Scotia. Sailing in August 1711 to carry supplies to Admiral Sir Hovenden Walker's ill-fated St. Lawrence River expedition, he met the returning transports and sailed back to Boston (*Ibid., 1711–12,* 1925, pp. 141–42). In 1717 Gov. Samuel Shute sent him out to take charge of a wrecked pirate fleet at Eastham on Cape Cod. On Feb. 18, 1718, he with several others was commissioned to inspect the plan of a lighthouse at the entrance to Boston harbor, to consider the proposal of a second light, and to report their findings to the governor and council; and in that same year he was one of the commissioners sent to adjust the boundaries of Nova Scotia (*Ibid., 1719–20,* 1933, pp. 67–69, 317–18). In 1720 he was selected by Governor Phillips to be a member of the Council in Nova Scotia (*Ibid., 1720–21,* 1933, p. 90). He served as a warden and vestryman of King's Chapel, Boston.

Apparently using only the log and compass, Southack made several charts during his numerous cruises along the northeast coast of North America. His *New England Coasting Pilot,* which appeared about 1720, was revised in 1734 and again about 1775. It was also issued as a map with the title, *An Actual Survey of the Sea Coast from New York to the I. Cape Briton,* about 1758 and 1770. On Feb. 26, 1694, he presented to King William III of England a copy of his *Draught of New England, Newfoundland, Nova Scotia and the River of Canada,* for which he received as reward a gold chain worth £50 and a medal. In the same year he issued *A Dravght of Boston Harbor;* in 1697, a map of the St. John River, since lost. About 1710 he drew a chart of the St. Lawrence River and in 1717 a chart of the English plantations from the mouth of the Mississippi to the St. Lawrence. In 1720 *The Harbour of Casco Bay and Islands Adjacent* and *Map of Canso Harbour* were published; in 1746, *A New Chart of the British Empire in North America,* and at an unestablished date a *Map of the Sea Coast of New England.* Southack died in Boston and was buried in the Granary Burying Ground. By his wife, Eliza-

beth, he had several children whose births are listed in the Boston records.

[*Proc. of the Bostonian Soc., Jan. 12, 1904* (1904); *Boston Weekly News Letter,* Mar. 28, 1745; *Records of the Court of Assistants of the Colony of the Mass. Bay,* vol. I (1901); J. P. Baxter, *Doc. Hist. of the State of Me.,* V (1897), 84–85, 127–30, 339–79; Thomas Hutchinson, *Hist. of the Province of Mass. Bay,* II (1767), 109; C. C. Sewall, *The Hist. of Woburn* (1868), p. 182; Benjamin Church, *The Hist. of the Eastern Expeditions . . . Against the Indians and French* (1867), ed. by H. M. Dexter, pp. 123, 175; Sir Hovenden Walker, *A Jour.: or Full Account of the Late Expedition to Canada* (1720); J. F. Jameson, *Privateering and Piracy in the Colonial Period* (1923); Justin Winsor, *The Memorial Hist. of Boston,* I (1880), 541; *Proc. Mass. Hist. Soc.,* 2 ser. VII (1892); *Mass. Hist. Soc. Colls.,* 5 ser. V (1878), 330; John Green, *Explanation of the New Map of Nova Scotia* (1755); Joseph Sabin, Wilberforce Eames, and R. G. Vail, *Bibliotheca Americana,* vol. XXII (1932); *Heraldic Journal,* July 1866, pp. 138–39, Jan. 1867, p. 47; catalogue of maps, plans and charts in the Library of the Colonial Office, London.]   C. E—i.

SOUTHALL, JAMES COCKE (Apr. 2, 1828–Sept. 13, 1897), journalist, was born at Charlottesville, Va., son of Valentine Wood Southall and his wife Martha (Cocke) Southall. He was a descendant of Darcy Southall, who came to America in 1720, and, through both his father and his mother, of Richard Cocke, who arrived in Virginia in 1634. Studious and apt from youth, upon graduating from the University of Virginia in 1846 with the degree of M.A. he was termed by Dr. James Lawrence Cabell [q.v.] "by long odds the most finished and promising student that had been educated at the University up to that time" (Ruffner, *post,* p. 99). After a year of travel in Europe, his observant impressions of which he communicated under the signature of "Solitaire" to the *Richmond Daily Whig,* he read law in his father's office and in 1849 was licensed to practise. He substituted for his father as commonwealth's attorney during part of 1850–51, performing with dignity and ability; but the law proved uncongenial, and in 1852, despite his prospects of success, he abandoned it as a profession. For several years following this he applied himself assiduously to an elaborate and far-reaching system of studies, which, as occasion permitted, he pursued throughout his active career; his deeply religious nature turned him towards theology and Biblical study, while his scholarly love of truth led him to familiarize himself with political and civil history, ethics, psychology, ethnology, biology, geology, and other related sciences. In 1858 he again went to Europe, returning in April 1860. A few months before the outbreak of war, with Green Peyton he started a newspaper called the *Charlottesville Review.* Originally a fervent Unionist, but after the gage of coercion had been cast an energetic supporter of the Confederacy, Southall contributed to the *Review* a notable series of editorials which attracted attention North and South, and more than seventy years later inspired a prominent historian to designate their author as a "Virginian Socrates and Quixote, rolled into one" (U. B. Phillips, "Southern Argument on Secession," *Virginia Quarterly Review,* Jan. 1932, p. 133). Never robust, he was bitterly disappointed at being rejected for military service but continued his journalistic labors until the *Review,* like the other Charlottesville papers, succumbed late in 1861 or early in 1862. About June 1865 he acquired the *Charlottesville Daily Chronicle* and conducted it with ability and vigor until 1868, when he was made chief editor of the *Richmond Enquirer.* In this rôle he furthered the conservative principles which he had maintained as a member of the Virginia constitutional convention assembled in December 1867, and his fearless, trenchant, and sagacious editorials helped to direct public opinion into channels beneficial to the state during the troubled reconstruction era.

At heart, however, he was a scholar rather than a journalist, and in 1874 he resigned his editorship to become assistant to the superintendent of public instruction, with shorter working hours and enlarged opportunity for study. The following year he published his important volume, *The Recent Origin of Man,* the erudition and logic of which evoked widespread scientific discussion, English and American; in 1878 he reissued this in a revised, more compact treatment, *The Epoch of the Mammoth.* Subsequent investigation and foreign travel led him to modify certain of the views set forth in these works and in his anti-evolutionary address, *Man's Age in the World* (1878), but they were provocative, influential, and for their time in many respects advanced. About 1880, with the Rev. William T. Richardson, he bought the Richmond *Central Presbyterian* and edited it until 1889; shortly after that time, his health failing, he settled in Norfolk, where on Nov. 10, 1869, he had married Eliza Frances Sharp, daughter of William Willoughby Sharp, who bore him a son and daughter. His last noteworthy publication was his "Genealogy of the Cocke Family in Virginia," printed in the *Virginia Magazine of History and Biography* in five installments between January 1896 and January 1898.

[For the Southall family, see R. A. Brock, in *Va. Hist. Soc. Colls.,* vol. V, n.s. (1886). See also W. H. Ruffner, in *Alumni Bull. of the Univ. of Va.,* Feb. 1898; *Univ. of Va.* (1904), vol. I, edited by P. B. Barringer, J. M. Garnett, and Rosewell Page; obituary in *Richmond Dispatch,* Sept. 14, 1897. Some information has been supplied by Southall's son.] A. C. G., Jr.

SOUTHARD, ELMER ERNEST (July 28, 1876–Feb. 8, 1920), neuropathologist, social psychiatrist, and teacher, was born in South Boston, Mass., the son of Martin Southard, a mill superintendent, and Olive Wentworth (Knowles) Southard. As a child he did not care for manual work but preferred books and chess, which his father taught him, a lifelong interest. Graduating from the Boston Latin School in 1893, he entered Harvard, where he received the degrees of A.B. (1897), M.D. (1901), and A.M. (1902). During his college years he played chess on the Harvard team and wrote occasionally for the *Harvard Monthly,* including in his contributions poems and short stories, forms to which he returned in his later years. Of the men at Harvard who had the most lasting influence upon him, two—William James and Josiah Royce [*qq.v.*]—stand out prominently. According to Southard, James was responsible for his interest in psychopathology and Royce for his constant effort toward logical writing and thinking; his scheme of diagnosis by orderly exclusion he attributed to the influence of Royce and to his reading of Francis Bacon. In the case of a man of his rare abilities, however, it is difficult to delineate the forces that played upon his personality and developed his motivation; essentially the exceptional drive came from his own personality, a unique combination of artist, philosopher, and scientist.

His greatest contribution to human welfare was in the field of neuropsychiatry and its social implications. His actual career began as interne in pathology in 1901 at the Boston City Hospital, where he was later an assistant physician. In 1902 he studied in Germany at Senckenberg Institute, Frankfort, and at Heidelberg. He was instructor in neuropathology at the Harvard Medical School, 1904–06, and assistant professor, 1906–09; in 1909 he was appointed to the newly created Bullard professorship, the youngest man ever to receive a full professorship there. From 1906 to 1909 he was also assistant physician and pathologist at the Danvers State Hospital, Danvers, Mass., and in 1909 he became pathologist to the Massachusetts Commission on Mental Diseases. At the opening of the Boston Psychopathic Hospital in 1912, he was made the first director and remained in this position until June 1919, when he was given the title of director of the Massachusetts Psychiatric Institute. Thus he had a rare combination of opportunities for research and teaching. His contacts with students in the Harvard Medical School and internes in the Boston Psychopathic Hospital also afforded him the means of influencing young neuropathologists and psychiatrists. Never throughout his professional life was he without a group of students under his guidance, many of whom later attained prominence. His first book, *Neurosyphilis,* written with H. C. Solomon, was published in 1917; his second, *Shell-Shock and Other Neuropsychiatric Problems,* in 1919. His publications, of which there are about two hundred, reveal his continued interest in the field of mental medicine, but in the later years show a growing concern with sociological problems. During the last four years of his life he wrote twenty-one papers in the field of social psychiatry, in which his posthumously published book, *The Kingdom of Evils* (1922), written with M. C. Jarrett, was the first textbook. He was responsible for the establishment of the out-patient clinic in psychiatric cases, and for the definition of the field of social psychiatry; it was at the Boston Psychopathic Hospital under his leadership that the term "psychiatric social work" and the program of training for such workers were evolved. He was also responsible for the establishment in 1918 of the Smith College School for Social Work. At the time of his death in New York City in 1920, he was engaged in a dozen or more comprehensive research projects of great potential scientific importance. As he was only forty-three years of age then, a man whose wealth of interests and joy in teaching and learning revealed an exuberance of spirit beyond that of ordinary men, it may be said that his was a genius never gleaned. On June 27, 1906, he married Mabel Fletcher Austin, a graduate of the Johns Hopkins School of Medicine and a lecturer in social hygiene, daughter of Horace Austin, once governor of Minnesota. They had two sons and a daughter.

[*Who's Who in America,* 1918–19; M. M. Canavan, *Elmer Ernest Southard and His Parents: A Brain Study* (priv. printed, 1925); R. C. Cabot, in *Harvard Grads.' Mag.,* June 1920; *Mental Hygiene,* July 1920; Norman Fenton, in *Jour. of Juvenile Research,* vol. XIII, 1929; William Healy, *Ibid.*; *Bull. Mass. Commission on Mental Diseases,* Feb. 1920; obituary in *Boston Transcript,* Feb. 9, 1920.]   N.F.

SOUTHARD, LUCIEN H. (Feb. 4, 1827–Jan. 10, 1881), musician, composer, was presumably born in Sharon, Vt., and according to the records of Trinity College, Hartford, Conn., which he entered in 1844, he was the "son of Dr. Alva Southard of Nantucket," Mass. The records also state that he was "dismissed for indolence" from Trinity in January 1846. Although he had originally intended to follow his father's career as a physician, he went to Boston to study music. From 1851 to 1858 he was general supervisor of music in the Boston public

schools. For the next two or three years he lived in Norfolk, Va., but found it convenient to leave that city because of his Northern sympathies. The year 1861 he spent in Hartford, where he was organist of the North Congregational Church, being succeeded in 1862 by Dudley Buck [*q.v.*]. Southard then enlisted in the Union army and served as a captain of cavalry in the Army of the Potomac. In 1865 he was wounded, and, after receiving an honorable discharge, returned to Boston. Three years later (1868) he became the first director of the music conservatory of the Peabody Institute in Baltimore, Md., and organized an orchestra at the school. From 1871 to 1875 he was again in Boston, removing in the latter year to Atlanta, Ga., where he remained until his death.

Between the years 1850 and 1870 Southard was active as a composer. Among his works were two operas: *The Scarlet Letter* (1855), and *Omano* (produced in concert form in Boston, January 1858). He wrote numerous glees, organ pieces, and compositions for the church services, among them "Ave Maria" (1867?); "Te Deum and Jubilate" (1868); and three motets—"As the Hart Pants," "My Heart Doth Find," and "Praise Waiteth for Thee" (1872). He was also industrious as an editor and compiler of music books, among which were *A Collection of Organ Voluntaries* (1849); a number of volumes in collaboration with Benjamin F. Baker [*q.v.*], including *The Haydn Collection of Church Music* (1850), *A Complete Method for the Formation and Cultivation of the Voice* (1852), *The Union Glee Book* (1852), and *Classical Chorus Book* (1853); *The Bouquet* (1855), with G. W. Pratt; *Course of Harmony* (1855); *The School Bell* (1857), with Charles Butler; *Morning and Evening* (1865), for quartet choirs; *The Offering* (1866); *Two Masses* (1867); *The Standard Singing School* (1868). He died in Augusta, Ga., survived by his wife.

[The only complete account of Southard's life is found in *Grove's Dict. of Music and Musicians, Am. Supplement* (1920), based largely on information supplied by the late Nathan H. Allen of Hartford. The author of this article is indebted to Dr. Waldo Selden Pratt for added data.]   J.T.H.

SOUTHARD, SAMUEL LEWIS (June 9, 1787–June 26, 1842), jurist, secretary of the navy, senator, governor of New Jersey, was born at Basking Ridge, N. J., the son of Henry and Sarah (Lewis) Southard. His father, who had moved from Long Island as a boy, was a congressman from 1801 to 1811 and from 1815 to 1821. Samuel attended the school conducted by the Rev. Robert Finley [*q.v.*] at Basking Ridge and in 1804 was graduated with honors at the

College of New Jersey, where he shared a room with Theodore Frelinghuysen [*q.v.*]. He then went as a tutor to Virginia, became a friend of James Monroe, studied law at Fredericksburg, and was admitted to the bar in 1809. Returning to New Jersey in 1811, he was deputy sheriff for a while, married Rebecca Harrow, a Virginian, in June 1812, and moved to Flemington in 1814, becoming prosecutor of Hunterdon County. In 1815, he was elected to the Assembly, but after sitting for a few days was appointed associate justice of the supreme court and three years later, reporter also, serving in both capacities until 1820 and editing 4–5 *New Jersey Reports.* In 1817 he was an unsuccessful candidate for attorney-general and governor. He moved to Trenton about 1820 and in 1838, to Jersey City.

In 1820 he was a presidential elector for Monroe and was appointed to the United States Senate to succeed James J. Wilson, taking his seat on Feb. 16, 1821. A week later, he and his father, whose career in the House was just closing, were elected members of the joint committee on the Missouri question. It is claimed that Samuel drafted the compromise measure by which Missouri was finally admitted (Southard's reminiscences, quoted by Elmer, *post,* p. 213). His friend Monroe appointed him secretary of the navy in September 1823, to succeed Smith Thompson of New York, and he held the office until the close of John Quincy Adams' administration. As secretary he made several foresighted recommendations, the only one to bear immediate fruit being the building of the first naval hospitals in 1828. He also urgently advocated a naval academy, a thorough charting of the coast, a naval criminal code, a rank higher than captain, reorganization and increase of the marine corps, and the establishment of regular communication across Panama. The Pensacola navy yard was started in 1825, and Southard urged a more intelligent location of such bases. The navy increased from thirty-five to fifty-two vessels during his administration, though only about sixteen of these were regularly kept on duty; the personnel rose from some 3,400 to 5,600, with an average of about 200 officers and 250 midshipmen, while the annual cost rose from about two million dollars to three. Southard also served *ad interim* as secretary of the treasury (Mar. 7–July 31, 1825) and as secretary of war (May 26–June 19, 1828).

Jackson's victory was a bitter blow to the Adams cabinet and Southard returned to Trenton in 1829, described as "very much broken . . . and . . . melancholy" (see Elmer, p. 227). He resumed his law practice and was at once made attorney-general of New Jersey, succeeding Frelinghuysen, who went to the Senate. Though he was by this time a Whig in a state that was rapidly turning to Jackson, he succeeded the Democrat Peter D. Vroom as governor in 1832. After three months in office, during which he vigorously attacked nullification before the legislature, he secured another election to the Senate, where he took his seat on Dec. 2, 1833, just as the Bank fight was approaching its climax. Strongly opposed to Jackson, he made a long speech on Jan. 8 and 10, 1834, opposing the removal of the federal deposits (*Congressional Globe,* 23 Cong., 1 Sess., pp. 87–88, 90–91). On Mar. 28, despite the fact that the New Jersey legislature had approved the presidential policy, he and Frelinghuysen were among the majority of twenty-eight voting to censure Jackson. He continued as a prominent member of the Whig minority but his relations with Clay were not always friendly. Reëlected in 1838, he became president *pro tempore* of the Senate on Mar. 11, 1841 and, after Tyler went to the White House, served as its president until his resignation, May 3, 1842, just before his death.

Never a profound scholar, Southard was a skilful advocate, earnest, lucid, and forceful. With a voice that was generally pleasing but sometimes pitched too high, he was capable of impassioned eloquence which when fully roused was "like a sea in a storm." Impressive in appearance, he thoroughly enjoyed society and was a constant favorite with the electorate, but he lacked the tact essential in a good political organizer. From 1822 until his death he was a trustee of the College of New Jersey and of Princeton Theological Seminary. After 1838, he was president of the Morris Canal & Banking Company. He died in Fredericksburg, Va., at the home of his brother-in-law, after a brief illness.

[Printed sources include L. Q. C. Elmer, in *N. J. Hist. Soc. Colls.,* vol. VII (1872); *Am. State Papers, Naval Affairs,* vols. I–III (1834–60); *Somerset County Hist. Quart.* (N. J.), Oct. 1914; J. P. Snell, *Hist. of Hunterdon and Somerset Counties, N. J.* (1881); W. H. Shaw, *Hist. of Essex and Hudson Counties* (1884), II, 1052; F. B. Lee, *N. J. as a Colony and as a State* (1902); *Biog. Dir. Am. Cong.* (1928); records in files of Gen. Biog. Cat., Princeton Univ.; *Newark Daily Advertiser,* June 28, 30, 1842; *Daily Nat. Intelligencer* (Washington, D. C.), June 28, 1842. Some miscellaneous papers of Southard are in the Lib. of Cong.]
R. G. A.

SOUTHMAYD, CHARLES FERDINAND (Nov. 27, 1824–July 11, 1911), lawyer, was born in New York, the son of Samuel Dwight Southmayd, a merchant, and Mary (Ogden) Southmayd. His formal education, begun in a private school, was terminated at the age of twelve and a half when his teacher "announced to his astonished father that he had taught the boy all that he knew and he had thoroughly mastered it" (Choate, *post,* p. 139). Fortunately a place was found for the precocious lad in the law office of Hurlbut & Owen, where he at once began his legal training. When Judge Elisha P. Hurlbut formed a partnership with Alexander S. Johnson [*q.v.*] the following year, Southmayd went with him. By dint of great diligence and the exercise of a remarkable power of concentration he soon attained such a proficiency in the law that he became known in the firm as the "Chancellor," and, in the course of time, entered into a partnership with Johnson. When this partnership was dissolved on the election of Johnson to the New York court of appeals in 1851, Charles E. Butler and William M. Evarts [*q.v.*], impressed by the legal ability Southmayd had displayed in the important case of *Iddings* vs. *Bruen* (4 *Sanford's Chancery Reports,* 223, 417) in which they were opposing counsel, asked him to join their firm. This association continued until the retirement of Butler in 1858—a resignation that proved premature since he later rejoined the firm. Some months later, Joseph H. Choate [*q.v.*] joined Evarts and Southmayd to make up the famous legal triumvirate of Evarts, Southmayd & Choate.

The brilliancy of these partners attracted to the firm many of the most important cases of that period. Although Southmayd detested trial work and never appeared in court unless the vital interests of his clients demanded his attendance, the clearness of his intellect and the soundness of his learning, as well as his unimpeachable integrity, contributed in no small measure to the deserved preëminence of the firm. Elihu Root describes him as "the typical solicitor, learned, logical, cautious, independent in judgment, stubborn in opinion, caustic in expression" (Choate, "Memorial," *post*).

Through careful savings Southmayd amassed a considerable fortune, and in 1884 he retired from practice. Unfortunately, law had absorbed him to such an extent that he had no interest to turn to during the remainder of his life. His days were filled with vague apprehensions and with the nursing of his innate conservatism, a conservatism that made him object to elevators, automobiles, elevated trains and electric street cars, and even led him to view a European trip by Choate's daughter as all nonsense. He sold his real estate holdings lest unbeknown to him his properties be used for immoral purposes and he be held accountable under the terms of a new law making landlords responsible in such cases.

Before he died, however, he was to frame one more great argument, that which he wrote in the case of *Pollock* vs. *Farmers' Loan and Trust Co.* (157 *U. S.,* 429; 158 *U. S.,* 601), resulting in the decision that held unconstitutional the income tax imposed in the Wilson-Gorman Tariff Act. Although he never appeared in court and others obtained the glory, Choate insists that it was Southmayd's brief which was the one to influence the Supreme Court in its opinion. It is characteristic that he wrote this brief ten years after he had retired from active practice, because he felt his own income threatened and that offended his conservative sense of property right. When he died in 1911 his name was already becoming a memory, for the busy world of New York had its new legal luminaries and recollected but poorly the stalwart figures of an earlier age.

[J. H. Choate, "Memorial of Charles F. Southmayd," *The Asso. of the Bar of the City of N. Y., Year Book,* 1913; reprinted separately (1912) and in *Arguments and Addresses of Joseph Hodges Choate* (1926), ed. by F. C. Hicks; *N. Y. Times,* July 12, 1911; T. G. Strong, *Landmarks of a Lawyer's Lifetime* (1914); E. S. Martin, *The Life of Joseph Hodges Choate as Gathered Chiefly from His Letters* (2 vols., 1920); B. W. Dwight, *The Hist. of the Descendants of John Dwight* (1874), vol. I; W. O. Wheeler, *The Ogden Family in America* (1907).]   L. M. Su—s.

SOUTHWICK, SOLOMON (Dec. 25, 1773–Nov. 18, 1839), journalist, was born in Newport, R. I., the son of Solomon and Ann (Gardner) Carpenter Southwick, and a descendant of Lawrence Southwick who settled in Salem, Mass., about 1630. The younger Solomon's mother, daughter of Lieutenant-Governor John Gardner of Rhode Island, died when the boy was about ten years old. His father, of Quaker ancestry, published the Newport *Mercury,* and for his ardent espousal of the cause of liberty suffered loss of property by Loyalist confiscation, so that from comfortable circumstances he and his family were reduced to poverty. Early in life Solomon went to sea. In 1791 he landed in New York City, where he became apprenticed to a printer, and in 1793 found employment in Albany as a journeyman with Robert and John Barber, who had established in 1788 the *Albany Register* to oppose Federalism. Robert Barber soon withdrew from the concern, and his brother, recognizing unusual talent in the young mechanic, promoted him to editorial duties and made him a partner. Southwick's prepossessing appearance, charming manner, and effective speech won for him the friendship and confidence of the leading Republicans, so that he held successively the positions of clerk of the Assembly, 1803–07; clerk of the Senate, 1807;

and sheriff of the city and county of Albany, 1809–10.

In 1800 he had relinquished formal connection with the *Register,* but when John Barber, whose sister Jane he had married on Mar. 31, 1795, died in 1808, Southwick became sole proprietor and editor, and was chosen state printer. He declared that no personal invective would appear in the *Register,* and that he would treat his enemies with "silent contempt." Such a policy was contrary to the prevailing journalistic style, however, and having a penchant for biting phrases and for apt allusions drawn from his wide reading, together with a vivid imagination but no sense of humor to hold it in check, he engaged in such scathing denunciation of political and editorial opponents that he became involved in a number of libel suits.

Always asserting his Republicanism, Southwick found difficulty in maintaining friendship with rival and ambitious party leaders. In 1805 he joined DeWitt Clinton and Ambrose Spencer [*qq.v.*] in opposing Morgan Lewis [*q.v.*] and the chartering of the Merchants' Bank in New York City. He supported George Clinton [*q.v.*], uncle of DeWitt, for president, to succeed Jefferson, in opposition to Madison, who was Spencer's choice. In 1812 he completely alienated Spencer by his conduct in connection with the "Six Million Bank" bill, which he upheld as vigorously as he had denounced the 1805 measure. Spencer, convinced that Southwick had been bribed to secure votes for the bill, set out to ruin his editorial influence by establishing a rival press. His first attempt, the *Albany Republican,* failed; but his purpose was accomplished when in 1813 the *Albany Argus* was inaugurated under the able and dignified editorship of Jesse Buel [*q.v.*]. In 1814 Buel supplanted Southwick as state printer. The following year Southwick was appointed postmaster at Albany. In 1817 he terminated his editorship of the *Register* in a state of political bankruptcy. He was financially insolvent as well, owing to overspeculation in Albany real estate and carelessness in keeping accounts, and for a time he was imprisoned for debt.

Twice Southwick aspired unsuccessfully to become governor; first, in 1822, when he was an independent candidate against Joseph C. Yates; and, again, in 1828, when he headed the Anti-Masonic ticket, which he supported as editor of the *National Observer.* From 1823 to 1826 he edited the *National Democrat.* In his later years he became a religious and moral enthusiast, and from 1831 to 1837 delivered lectures on the Bible, temperance, and self-improvement. In 1815–16 he edited the *Christian Visitant;* from 1819 to 1823, the *Plough Boy,* the first agricultural periodical in Albany County. In 1823 he published *The Pleasures of Poverty,* a long didactic poem; and in 1837, *Five Lessons for Young Men; by a Man of Sixty.* He and John Barber started in 1799 a circulating library of four hundred volumes, and he was one of the organizers of the Apprentices' Library. A favorite Fourth of July orator, he appeared in that rôle for the last time only a few months before his death, which came suddenly as the result of a heart attack. He was survived by four of his nine children.

[J. M. Caller and M. A. Ober, *Geneal. of the Descendants of Lawrence and Cassandra Southwick of Salem, Mass.* (1881); Joel Munsell, *The Annals of Albany,* vol. V (1854); DeAlva S. Alexander, *A Pol. Hist. of the State of N. Y.,* vol. I (1906); J. D. Hammond, *The Hist. of Pol. Parties in the State of N. Y.* (1842), vol. I; *Albany Evening Jour.,* Nov. 19, 1839; *Albany Daily Advertiser,* Nov. 22, 1839, copied from *N. Y. Commercial Advertiser.*]

E. L. J.

SOUTHWORTH, EMMA DOROTHY ELIZA NEVITTE (Dec. 26, 1819–June 30, 1899), novelist, was born near Capitol Hill, Washington, D. C., the elder daughter of Charles LeCompte Nevitte, a merchant of Alexandria, Va., and his second wife, Susanna George (Wailes) of Saint Mary County, Md. As Dorothy Emma Eliza Nevitt [*sic*] she was baptized a Roman Catholic (records of St. Peter's Church, Washington, D. C.). After the death of her father, her mother in 1826 married Joshua L. Henshaw of Boston, who about 1829 opened an academy which Emma and her sister attended. Following her graduation in 1835 she developed an insatiable interest in the traditions of Saint Mary County and acquired a thorough and sympathetic knowledge of southern life that served as a background for many of her stories later. She married Frederick H. Southworth of Utica, N. Y., on Jan. 23, 1840, and in 1841 moved with him to a farm near Prairie du Chien, Wis., where a son, Richmond, was born. The following year she taught in the public school at Platteville, Wis., and in 1843 (deserted by her husband, it was reported), she returned to Washington; her daughter, Charlotte, was born after this separation. Through friends she obtained a teaching position in the public schools of Washington, which she held until 1849 despite her own bad health and the sickness of her children.

During this period she wrote several short tales, published in the *Baltimore Saturday Visitor* and elsewhere, for the most part without compensation to her. In 1847 the *National Era* published, and paid for, her novel, *Retribution* (1849), and this success, together with the personal encouragement of John Greenleaf Whittier [*q.v.*], then a corresponding editor of the *National Era,* persuaded her to give up teaching and turn to writing. For many years she wrote serials for the *New York Ledger,* in which in 1859 appeared her great success, *The Hidden Hand* (copyright 1859). Shortly after its publication she made a visit to England, where she witnessed a theatrical production of *The Hidden Hand* with John Wilkes Booth [*q.v.*] in the rôle of Black Donald. In 1862 she returned to Prospect Cottage, her Georgetown house overlooking the Potomac, and lived there for the remainder of her life. About this time she suggested to Whittier the story that later became the ballad of Barbara Frietchie; when the poem was completed Whittier wrote her, "If it is good for anything, thee deserve all the credit of it" (S. T. Pickard, *Life and Letters of John Greenleaf Whittier,* 1894, vol. II, pp. 454–57). In 1877 a uniform edition of her novels in forty-two volumes was issued in Philadelphia. By this time she had become a celebrity and her home a rendezvous for the local literati; growing increasingly deaf, however, she spent the last busy years of her life in retirement. From being a communicant of the Episcopal Church, she turned in 1883 to Swedenborgianism. At the time of her death, which occurred in Georgetown, she had written more than sixty published novels, and she left much unfinished material in manuscript. Contemporary criticism praised her sentimental and melodramatic plots immoderately, and her large reading public, mostly women, encouraged her to an abundant production which she realized was not related to great literary art. In commenting on some unpublished work she revealed that she consciously had used materials and style "to please the taste of readers of the *Ledger*" and implied that she would have written differently if freed from financial pressure. Among the best known of her works, many of which are still reprinted in paper-back editions, are *Self-Raised* (copyright 1876), *The Fatal Marriage* (copyright 1869), *The Curse of Clifton* (copyright 1852), *The Maiden Widow* (copyright 1870), and *The Missing Bride* (1855).

[*Who's Who in America,* 1899–1900; T. H. Y., prefatory biog. sketch in Mrs. Southworth's *The Haunted Homestead* (1860); C. W. Stoddard, in *Nat. Mag.,* May 1905, with portrait; Sarah M. Huddleson, in *Records of the Columbia Hist. Soc., Washington, D. C.,* vol. XXIII (1920), with portrait; Edna Kenton, in *Bookman,* Oct. 1916; H. C. B., "A Noted Novel-Writer," *Washington Post,* Dec. 2, 1894; *Evening Star* (Washington), Sept. 6, 1890; obituaries in *Evening Star,* July 1, 1899, and in *Appletons' Ann. Cyc.,* 1899; information from the family.]
R. W. B.
B. E. G.

SOWER, CHRISTOPHER (1693–Sept. 25, 1758), printer and publisher, was born in Germany at Laasphe on the Lahn, which was then in the county of Sayn-Wittgenstein-Berleburg. Under its pious regent, the Countess Hedwig Sophia, this diminutive realm had become an asylum for sectarians and separatists from all Germany. Sower, who was of humble origin, grew to manhood buffeted by winds of doctrine blowing from every quarter and thoroughly enjoyed the gusty spiritual climate. Seeking greater economic with equal religious liberty, he emigrated to Pennsylvania in the autumn of 1724, bringing with him his wife, Maria Christina, and their three-year old son, Christopher, 1721–1784 [*q.v.*]. He worked as a tailor in Germantown until the spring of 1726 and then bought and began to farm a fifty-acre tract, now part of Leacock township, Lancaster County, in the Conestoga Valley. Here his proximity to Johann Conrad Beissel [*q.v.*], whom he had known in Germany, proved ruinous, for in 1730 Mrs. Sower was converted to Beissel's doctrines and left her husband in order to live as a hermit. As Sister Marcella she became sub-prioress of the Ephrata Community, but in 1744 she was at last persuaded to return to her family. Sower, his farming operations crippled by her desertion, went back to Germantown and formed an alliance with Christopher Witt, an English mystic, physician, and astrologer, the last survivor of the society founded by Johann Kelpius [*q.v.*]. Under Witt's tuition he learned clock-making, his principal occupation for the next few years, and tried his hand at concocting herbal medicines, but his religious scruples probably made him abstain from the darker arts practised by his master.

He bought six acres of land in Germantown, built a large house, and in 1738 began his notable career as the first German printer and publisher in America. Where he obtained his press, type, and other apparatus, and the skill to use them, is unknown. The first issue of the press was *Eine Ernstliche Ermahnung, an Junge und Alte* (1738) and was followed by *Der Hoch-Deutsch Americanische Calender . . . 1739,* his famous almanac, the last issue of which appeared in 1777. The first complete book from the press was the *Zionitischer Weyrauchs Hügel oder Myrrhen Berg* (1739), a huge hymnbook for the Ephrata Community, of which John Peter Miller [*q.v.*] was editor. The 400th hymn in the collection was the cause of a ludicrous controversy between Beissel and Sower. On Aug. 20, 1739 o.s., appeared the first number of the newspaper, *Der Hoch-Deutsch Pensylvanische Geschicht-Schreiber,* which, with various changes of title, had a career as long as the almanac. These two publications were sold throughout the colonies and made Sower and his son influential among the Germans of Pennsylvania and Maryland. Among the sectarians their influence was especially great. Very early Sower spoke out against war and slavery; in 1754, scenting a political plot in Provost William Smith's proposed charity schools among the Pennsylvania Germans, he waged a bitter, victorious war against the plan. As a result of Sower's propaganda, Michael Schlatter [q.v.], who had innocently accepted the superintendency of the schools, was thoroughly discredited and his usefulness among the German Reformed destroyed. The most famous and ambitious of all Sower's undertakings was his edition of the Bible, *Biblia; Das ist, Die Heilige Schrift Altes und Neues Testaments, Nach der Deutschen Übersetzung D. Martin Luthers* (1743). Except for the Indian version of John Eliot [q.v.], this was the first American edition of the Bible. Sower's son published editions in 1763 and 1776. His first publication in English was *Extract from the Laws of William Penn* (1740); from 1749 on, English as well as German publications regularly issued from the press. Most books bearing the Sower imprint were religious or educational. Sower made his own ink and may perhaps have cast type, although his best fonts came from the foundry of Dr. Heinrich Ehrenfried Luther at Frankfurt-am-Main; he is also said to have built a paper-mill in 1744 (Weeks, *post*, p. 31). For many years he continued to conduct a shop in which he sold medicines, clocks, and other wares. He was an agent for the Pennsylvania stoves invented by Franklin and manufactured by Robert Grace at Warwick Furnace. He was one of the leaders of the German Baptist Brethren. In his zeal for social reform and religious dissent, his thirst for practical information and handiness at many trades and crafts, and in his remarkable talent for popular journalism, he was, with certain variations, a German Daniel Defoe. He died at his home in Germantown and was buried on his own land behind his house.

[Sower's name is often spelled Saur or Sauer. See C. G. Sower, *Geneal. Chart of the Descendants of Christopher Sower, Printer of Germantown, Phila., Pa.* (1887); Oswald Seidensticker, "Die beiden Christoph Saur in Germantown," *Der Deutsche Pionier*, Apr. to June, Aug. to Dec. 1880, and Jan., Feb., Apr., June, and July 1881, reprinted with some abridgment in Seidensticker's *Bilder aus der Deutsch-pennsylvanischen Geschichte* (1885); J. F. Sachse, *The German Sectarians of Pa., 1708–1800* (priv. printed, 2 vols., 1899–1900); M. G. Brumbaugh, *A Hist. of the German Baptist Brethren in Europe and America* (1899); J. S. Flory, *Literary Activity of the German Baptist Brethren in the Eighteenth Century* (1908); J. Max Hark, tr., *Chronicon Ephratense* (1889), pp. 41–42; S. W.

Pennypacker, *Hist. and Biog. Sketches* (1883) and *Pa. in Am. Hist.* (1910); Isaiah Thomas, *The Hist. of Printing in America* (2nd ed., 2 vols., 1874); C. F. Huch, "Die erste Schriftgiesserei in den Vereinigten Staaten von Nordamerika," *Deutsch-Amerikanische Geschictsblätter*, July 1909; L. H. Weeks, *A Hist. of Paper-Manufacturing in the U. S., 1690–1916* (1916); John Wright, *Early Bibles of America* (3rd ed., rev. & enl., 1894); A. H. Cassel, "The German Almanac of Christopher Sauer," *Pa. Mag. of Hist. and Biog.*, vol. VI, No. 1 (1882); "Forges and Furnaces in the Province of Pa.," *Pubs. of the Pa. Soc. of the Colonial Dames of America*, vol. III (1914), p. 73.]

G. H. G.

SOWER, CHRISTOPHER (September 1721– Aug. 26, 1784), bishop of the Dunkers or German Baptist Brethren, printer and publisher, was born at Laasphe, Westphalia, the only child of Christopher Sower, 1693–1758 [q.v.], and Maria Christina Sower, and was brought to Pennsylvania by his parents in 1724. As a boy he received his schooling from the celebrated Christopher Dock [q.v.], whose *Eine Einfältige und gründlich abgefasste Schul-Ordnung* (1770) he later took pride in publishing; heard the preaching of Alexander Mack, the founder of the Dunker sect; and learned printing, bookbinding, ink-making, and other trades from his father. He was baptized, Feb. 24, 1737 o.s.; was made a deacon of the Germantown congregation in May 1747; became an elder on trial in June 1748; and was ordained by Peter Becker, June 10, 1753. To the very end of his life he was the leader of his sect, exerting on it an influence that continued to be felt for several generations. The power and persuasiveness of his preaching, his insight into the human heart, and his humble, charitable way of life have been a tradition among his people. Meanwhile, on Apr. 21, 1751 o.s., he married Catharine Sharpnack of Germantown, who bore him nine children and died on Jan. 8, 1777. He early took charge of the bindery in his father's publishing house in Germantown, and beginning in 1754 the English publication of the Sower press bore his imprint. On his father's death in 1758 he fell heir to the whole establishment and carried on the business with the intelligence and energy that had distinguished his father. The most notable productions of the press under his management were the second and third editions (1763 and 1776) of the Sower, or Germantown, Bible. In 1773 he built a paper-mill on the Schuylkill. In his periodicals he was a steadfast opponent of negro slavery, and berated the Germans for allowing the evil practice to take root among them. His political support went to the proprietary party. With the outbreak of the Revolution his prosperity ceased and the evil days came upon him. Like the Quakers, Mennonites, Schwenkfelders, and Moravians, the Dunkers refused to take oaths or to bear arms. As the leader of the Dunkers, Sower was suspected all the more because his sons Christopher [q.v.] and Peter were avowed Loyalists; and suspicion ripened into conviction when it was realized that he was a man of wealth whose houses, lands, and goods would enrich more than one deserving patriot. In a proclamation of May 8, 1778, he was named as under suspicion of treason and given till June 25 to appear before a magistrate. On May 23, 1778, he was arrested, maltreated, and variously abused, and was released only by the intervention of Gen. John Peter Gabriel Muhlenberg [q.v.]. His property, except what clothes he wore and a little food, was ruthlessly taken from him and was disposed of "at auction" for a fraction of its actual value. Sower might later have obtained redress, but, true to his religious convictions, he refused to go to law. His one protest was against the ignominy of being called a traitor. The few remaining years of his life were spent at Methacton, a few miles above Norristown, where he found refuge in a friend's house, and was cared for by his daughter, Catharine. He earned what money he needed by working as a bookbinder. Two weeks before his death he went on foot the twelve miles to Skippack to preach at a meeting of the Brethren. He died and was buried at Methacton.

[Like his father, Sower for a time used the spellings Saur and Sauer. See Oswald Seidensticker, "Die beiden Christoph Saur in Germantown," *Bilder aus der Deutsch-pennsylvanischen Geschichte* (1885); C. G. Sower, *Geneal. Chart of the Descendants of Christopher Sower, Printer, of Germantown, Phila., Pa.* (1887); M. G. Brumbaugh, *A Hist. of the German Baptist Brethren in Europe and America* (1899); J. F. Sachse, *The German Sectarians of Pa., 1708–1800* (priv. printed, 2 vols., 1899–1900). Seidensticker gives the date of birth as Sept. 21; Sower as Sept. 26. The date of death is from the tombstone. Information has been supplied by the Germantown Hist. Soc.]   G. H. G.

SOWER, CHRISTOPHER (Jan. 27, 1754– July 3, 1799), Pennsylvania publisher and Loyalist, was born in Germantown, Pa., the son of the second Christopher Sower [q.v.] and his wife, Catharine (Sharpnack) Sower. Reared in a family who were leaders among the Dunkers, he naturally conceived a strong antipathy to those colonial leaders—among them Benjamin Franklin, Henry Melchior Mühlenberg, the leader of the German Lutheran Church in America, and John Henry Miller [qq.v.], the publisher of *Der Wöchentliche Pennsylvanische Staatsbote*—who were bitter critics of the German sectarians and of the beliefs they held. When these men favored the Colonial party in its disagreement with the mother country, the conservatism of young Sower, accentuated by his aversion to the opponents of his family, drove him early into the ranks of those who were loyal to the British government. On Jan. 8, 1775, he was married to Hannah Knorr, sister of the wife of Zachariah Poulson [q.v.].

His public life began toward the end of 1774, when his father, without any legal formality, transferred to him the ancestral home in Germantown and the famous Sower printing establishment. Sometime between Apr. 20, 1775, and Mar. 20, 1776, the name of the firm was changed to Christopher Sower and Son; between the latter date and February 1777 it became Christopher Sower, Jr., and Peter Sower, the young man thus publicly assuming full charge. During these momentous years he apparently published in his newspaper, *Die Germantowner Zeitung,* everything favorable to the royal cause so far as the Patriot authorities allowed him, and when the British took possession of Philadelphia in September 1777, he removed to that city and continued the paper under the title, *Der Pennsylvanische Staats Courier.* On Dec. 5 he was wounded and captured by a detachment of American troops in Germantown, and on Jan. 10 of the following year he was released by exchange. At the time of the evacuation of Philadelphia by the British in 1778, he had no safe alternative but to accompany them to New York. In August the estate of the entire family, variously estimated to be worth from ten thousand to thirty thousand pounds, was confiscated and sold. With the encouragement of Sir Henry Clinton he now entered into correspondence with various men in Pennsylvania for the purpose of obtaining information and of organizing Loyalist Associations, which in February 1780 in the counties of Lancaster, York, and Northumberland professed to have an enrollment of six thousand, probably an exaggeration. He also published and distributed in the spring of 1780 a sixteen-page pamphlet with the title, *Zuschrift an die Teutschen in Pennsylvanien und benachbarten Provinzen,* a publication that may be considered the valedictory of the family as colonial printers. A year later, in the spring of 1781, he was sent by Clinton on a secret mission to Virginia. After the defeat of Cornwallis he concentrated his efforts on futile attempts to induce the British government to grant such liberal terms to the Colonies that they would willingly remain in the empire. On the British evacuation of New York he went to England to push his claims for indemnification for the losses he had sustained, and was allowed the sum of 1,289 pounds. In 1785 he went to the province of New Brunswick, where he later became deputy postmaster-general and king's printer of the province, and published the

Royal Gazette and Weekly Adveriser. Leaving New Brunswick in 1799 he went to the home of his youngest brother, Samuel, in Baltimore, Md., where he died, survived by his wife and five of his six children.

[Like his father and grandfather, Sower also used the spellings Saur and Sauer, particularly when writing in German. There are two comparatively large collections of original source material on his activities: his records, gathered at the time when he laid claim to indemnity, in the Audit Office Records found in the Pub. Records Office (Class 13, Bundle 102), London, England; and the Clinton papers in the William L. Clements Lib. Some of the London material has been transcribed and is in the N. Y. Pub. Lib. A secondary source almost as valuable as the original sources is "William McCulloch's Additions to Thomas's Hist. of Printing," ed. by C. S. Brigham, *Proc. Am. Antiquarian Soc.*... *Apr. 13, 1921,* vol. XXXI, n.s., pt. 1 (1922). See also C. G. Sower, *Geneal. Chart of the Descendants of Christopher Sower, Printer, of Germantown, Phila., Pa.* (1887); M. G. Brumbaugh, *A Hist. of the German Baptist Brethren in Europe and America* (1899); J. O. Knauss, *Social Conditions among the Pa. Germans in the Eighteenth Century, as Revealed in German Newspapers Published in America* (1922), and "Christopher Saur the Third," *Proc. Am. Antiquarian Soc.*... *Apr. 15, 1931,* vol. XLI, n.s., pt. 1 (1931).]   J. O. K.

SPAETH, ADOLPH (Oct. 29, 1839–June 25, 1910), Lutheran clergyman, was born at Esslingen, Württemberg, the eldest of the seven children of Ernst Philipp Heinrich and Rosine Elisabeth (Boley) Spaeth, and was christened Philipp Friedrich Adolf Theodor. His father, a skilful and beloved physician, a liberal in politics, died in 1856; his mother died in 1902 at her son's home in Philadelphia. Both parents were deeply religious; and although Spaeth wavered for a while in his final choice of a career, there was never any real doubt as to his vocation. He was educated at the Lateinschule of his native town, the Klosterschule of Blaubeuren, and the University of Tübingen. Having been ordained Oct. 10, 1861, at Waiblingen, he served for about a year as vicar at Bittenfeld and then, partly for the sake of his health, spent the winter of 1862–63 as a private tutor in northern Italy. The next year, one of the happiest and most significant of his life, was passed in Scotland, where he was a tutor in the family of the Duke of Argyll. The Marquis of Lorne, governor-general of Canada, 1878–83, was one of his pupils. While in Scotland Spaeth was betrothed to Maria Dorothea Duncan, daughter of the Scotch theologian, John Duncan, who at first was reluctant to give her to a man who did not subscribe to the Westminster Confession.

Through a cousin who was a member of the church council, Spaeth received a tentative call as assistant to William Julius Mann [*q.v.*] at St. Michael's and Zion's in Philadelphia. Thinking that the experience of a few years in America would be good for him, he accepted. On Oct. 16,

1864, he was formally installed as Mann's colleague. For the rest of his life Philadelphia was his home and the center of his work and influence. On May 8, 1865, he married his betrothed, who bore him five sons and a daughter and died Dec. 21, 1878. His second wife, whom he married Oct. 12, 1880, and by whom he had four sons and a daughter, was Harriett Reynolds Krauth, daughter of Charles Porterfield Krauth [*q.v.*]; she survived him and wrote his biography. In 1867 Spaeth accepted a call to the newly organized St. Johannis Church, with which he remained, with an assistant after 1893, until his death. From 1873 until his death he was a professor in the Philadelphia Lutheran Theological Seminary, his principal subject being New Testament exegesis. He was president of the General Council of the Evangelical Lutheran Church in North America, 1880–88; of the Ministerium of Pennsylvania, 1892–95; and of the General Conference of Lutheran Deaconess Motherhouses in America, 1896–1910; and an active member of many boards and committees of his denomination. Especially notable was his work in liturgics and hymnology. The bibliography of his published writings occupies thirteen pages of his biography; his books were *Saatkörner* (1893), a collection of sermon outlines; *Erinnerungsblätter* (1895), a selection, held together by a thread of biographical narrative, from the writings of William Julius Mann; *Annotations on the Gospel According to St. John* (1896), in the Lutheran Commentary Series; *Charles Porterfield Krauth* (2 vols., 1898–1909); *Die Heilige Passion* (1897); and *Order of Lutheran Worship* (1906). He had the magnetic personality, the powerful, flexible voice, the kinship with the audience and sense of its needs, of a great public speaker, and as an orator he was most widely known. In his command of English he was often compared to Carl Schurz, for whom he had a warm admiration; and the clarity, simplicity, and music of his German diction were flawless. He visited Europe ten times and traveled much in the United States; few of the leaders of his denomination were so widely known or exerted so much personal influence. In temperament he was a true Swabian, working with a tremendous will and enjoying life heartily to its close. He died at his home at Mount Airy, Philadelphia, in his seventy-first year.

[H. R. Spaeth, *Life of Adolph Spaeth, D.D., LL.D.* (1916), with a list of his publications; L. D. Reed, *The Phila. Seminary Biog. Record* (1923); *Public Ledger* (Phila.), June 27, 1910.]   G. H. G.

SPAHR, CHARLES BARZILLAI (July 20, 1860–Aug. 30, 1904), editor and economist, was born in the Methodist parsonage on Town Street, Columbus, Ohio, the son of the Rev. Barzillai Nelson Spahr and Elizabeth Jane (Tallman) Spahr. The Spahr family was originally of Swiss descent and seems to have settled in Virginia well before the Revolution; Gideon Spahr, father of Barzillai Spahr, was born in Virginia in 1788. Prepared for college in the Columbus schools, Spahr entered Amherst College and graduated with honors in 1881. After teaching in the Columbus high schools for a short time, he studied at Leipzig, 1884–85, and then took the degree of Ph.D. at Columbia in 1886. On July 5, 1892, he was married in Princeton, N. J., to Jean Gurney Fine, daughter of the Rev. Lambert S. Fine and Mary (Burchard) Fine, and sister of Henry Burchard Fine [q.v.], later dean of Princeton University, who had been a fellow-student of Spahr's in Leipzig; for the three years immediately preceding her marriage she had been the first head-worker of the New York College Settlement, of which she was one of the founders. They had five daughters.

Soon after taking his degree at Columbia he joined the editorial staff of the Outlook (then the Christian Union), with which he remained until February 1904, an associate of Lyman Abbott, Hamilton Wright Mabie [qq.v.], and Lawrence Abbott, who had been his roommate at Amherst. He also lectured at Columbia for several years during this period and was for some time an editorial writer on the New York Commercial Advertiser. In his editorial work he was largely concerned with sociological and economic problems. Though his views often brought him into conflict with the papers for which he wrote, and though he refrained rigidly from writing against his convictions, he was remarkable for his ability to remain on friendly terms with his most convinced opponents. He had a tremendous sympathy for the humble. Once he remarked: "I can't find it in my heart to have any one black my boots. Somehow, it seems to me undemocratic. And as I don't have time often to do it, the result is they go unblacked" (In Memory of Charles B. Spahr, post, p. 13). It was characteristic of him that in politics he was usually on the side of the minority. He was fond of remarking that his only successful presidential vote was cast for Cleveland and that he later regretted it; he is credited with having cast one of the three Populist votes in his election district in New York City, and in 1896 and 1900 he gave enthusiastic support to Bryan, having been from his college days an ardent advocate of free silver as a benefit to the debtor class. He was active in the Social Reform Club of New York, which he

helped to organize in the Outlook office in 1894 and of which he was president, 1896–98; he was also one of the founders and chairman of the executive committee of the Anti-Imperialist League. His writings include An Essay on the Present Distribution of Wealth in the United States (1896), America's Working People (1900), and papers on "The Taxation of Labor" (Political Science Quarterly, Sept. 1886), "The Single Tax" (Ibid., Dec. 1891), and "Giffen's Case Against Bimetallism" (Ibid., Sept. 1893). In 1904 he became owner and editor-in-chief of Current Literature, and in his new position was compelled to add to his duties the work of a business manager, with which he was unfamiliar. The nervous strain so undermined his health that in July he went abroad for a rest, traveling from Trieste through Austria and Germany to the Rhine. His health had improved and the fits of depression from which he suffered had become less frequent, when on Aug. 30 he disappeared from the ship on which he had sailed from Ostend for Dover. His body was washed ashore near Broadstairs, Kent, Sept. 21.

[Who's Who in America, 1903–05; In Memory of Charles B. Spahr (1905), with portrait; Amherst Coll. Biog. Record of the Grads. and Non-Grads. (1927), ed. by R. S. Fletcher and M. O. Young; F. H. Parsons, Thirty Years After: A Record of the Class of Eighty-One, Amherst Coll. (1911), not altogether accurate; editorials in Outlook, Jan. 30, Sept. 10, and Oct. 1, 1904; obituaries in Current Lit., Oct. 1904, N. Y. Times, Sept. 2, and N. Y. Tribune, Sept. 2, 3, 1904; report of inquest in Times (London), Sept. 24, 1904.]
J. B.

SPAIGHT, RICHARD DOBBS (Mar. 25, 1758–Sept. 6, 1802), governor of North Carolina, representative in Congress, was born in New Bern, N. C. His father, Richard Spaight, a native of Ireland, married Margaret, the sister of Gov. Arthur Dobbs [q.v.], and was a member of the colonial council under him, secretary of the colony, and paymaster of troops during the French and Indian War. Both parents died when the boy was eight years old, and he was sent to Ireland to be educated. It is said that his advanced studies were completed at the University of Glasgow. In 1778 he succeeded in returning to North Carolina, where in 1779 he was a member of the House of Commons from the borough of New Bern. Afterward, as aide to Gen. Richard Caswell commanding the state militia, he was present at the battle of Camden. There his military career ended, for he was reelected to the Commons, where he represented either New Bern or Craven County from 1781 to 1787, except 1784, and again in 1792. Young as he was in these early sessions, he won reputation, but rather in committee service and in council than in debate. In 1785 he was chosen speaker, and on Jan. 1, 1787, when the House entered upon a sweeping investigation of the state judges and of alleged official corruption, he was selected as chairman of the whole. He was defeated for the Continental Congress, but he was appointed to fill a vacancy in 1783, was elected the next year, and served until 1785, during which time he was a member of the committee to frame a temporary government for the western territory and of the committee of the states. In political faith a democrat and a strict constructionist, he was opposed to what he regarded as the usurpation by the North Carolina courts of the power to declare an act of the legislature null and void, asking, perhaps with some point, who would control the judges.

In 1787 as an advocate of a stronger federal government, he was chosen a delegate to the federal constitutional convention, where he favored the election of senators by the state legislatures, a term of seven years for senators and president, the election of the president by Congress, and the filling of congressional vacancies by the president. He voted for the Constitution and signed it. In 1787 he was defeated for governor, but he was a member of the state convention of 1788, was active in explanation and defense of the Constitution, and, in spite of his well-known democratic views, voted with the Federalists. When North Carolina finally ratified in 1789, he was the Anti-Federalist candidate for federal senator but was defeated. His health had already failed, and for four years he withdrew from public affairs and traveled widely in search of a cure. In 1792 he was elected governor and served three terms. In 1793 he was a presidential elector. As governor in 1793 he issued a proclamation enjoining neutrality in the European war, and he had several French privateers, which were being fitted out in Wilmington, seized and held. In 1795 he married Mary Leach of Holmesburg, Pa., who with three children survived him.

He was a member of Congress from Dec. 10, 1798, to Mar. 3, 1801, but declined reëlection. A stanch Republican, he favored the repeal of the Alien and Sedition Acts and in the election of president by the House voted for Jefferson. He was, however, never a narrow partisan, and, always independent, he frequently voted differently from his party. After his retirement from Congress he was elected state senator in 1801 and 1802. In 1802 he was mortally wounded in a duel with John Stanly, a prominent Federalist leader, who has ever since been depicted as the aggressor, while Spaight has been regarded as a martyr. But in fact, as appears clearly in the cor-

respondence between them, Spaight forced Stanly to the duel (R. A. Spaight, *Correspondence*, 1802). It is difficult to conceive of him in such a light, for he was normally genial, affable, and good-tempered, and had few personal quarrels and fewer enemies. In politics he was notably dispassionate. His abilities, which do not seem very striking today, were measured highly by his contemporaries.

[S. A. Ashe, *Biog. Hist. of N. C.*, vol. IV (1906); J. H. Wheeler, *Sketch of the Life of Richard Dobbs Sperry* (1880); *The State Records of N. C.*, vols. XIII, XVII–XX, XXII (1898–1907); G. J. McRee, *Life and Correspondence of James Iredell* (1858), vol. II, esp. pp. 120–22, 168–70, 273.] J. G. deR. H.

SPALDING, ALBERT GOODWILL (Sept. 2, 1850–Sept. 9, 1915), sportsman and merchant, was born on a farm in Byron, Ogle County, Ill., the son of James Lawrence and Harriet Irene (Goodwill) Wright Spalding and a descendant of Edward Spalding who became a freeman of the Massachusetts Bay Colony in 1640. He was educated in the public schools of Byron and Rockford, Ill., and at the Rockford Commercial College. His first employment was as a grocer's clerk. A crippled soldier, it is said, invalided out of the Civil War, taught the boys of Rockford how to play baseball and young Spalding became an apt pupil. At the age of seventeen his skill as a pitcher and batsman was such that he became an outstanding player with the Forest City team of Rockford. Largely through the prowess of Spalding and Ross Barnes, who also later became a National League player, this team attained a wide reputation. After the establishment of professional baseball, Spalding joined in 1871 the Boston team managed by Harry Wright [*q.v.*]. Spalding was pitcher and captain until 1875 and during that time the team won the championships of the National Association of Professional Base Ball Players from 1872 to 1875, inclusive.

In 1876 William A. Hulbert of Chicago, with Spalding as aid and adviser, formed the National League of Professional Base Ball Clubs, and Spalding became pitcher, captain, and manager of the Chicago team. In March of the same year he organized, with his brother James, a business firm to manufacture and sell baseball equipment and other sporting goods, under the name A. G. Spalding & Brother. Two years later his brother-in-law, William T. Brown, joined them and the firm name became A. G. Spalding & Brothers. In time the concern developed into the largest and most successful of its kind in the United States, with a capitalization in 1932 of $6,000,000. Spalding maintained a connection with the Chicago Club for many years, however.

Upon the death of William A. Hulbert in 1882 he became its president and continued as such until 1891, when he felt it necessary to give all his time to his sporting-goods business.

He was a big fellow physically, with a dominating personality, and a genius for organizing and directing. He was a great believer in baseball as a beneficial sport as well as an exciting public spectacle. As early as 1874 he made the arrangements for a tour of England and Ireland by two baseball teams, in an endeavor to impress the good points of the game on the followers of cricket and football. Again, in 1888–89, he organized and took personal charge of a trip around the world made by his Chicago team and another group known as the All-American players. They gave exhibitions of baseball in Australia, Ceylon, Egypt, Italy, France, and the British Isles. In Egypt a game was played on the sands near the pyramids. In these early days of professional baseball it was necessary to stamp out rowdyism and eliminate professional gamblers who sought to corrupt teams and players for their own ends. As a player and later as a club manager, president, and league official, Spalding was a forceful leader in the fight for honest play, honest players, and a wholesome and respectable atmosphere around the ball parks. He was chosen as director of the section of sports for the United States at the Olympic Games of 1900, held in connection with the World's Fair at Paris that same year. For his work in this capacity, he later received from France the rosette of the Legion of Honor. A powerful and colorful figure, he loomed large in the field of sports for many years and, through his enthusiasm, his energy, and his keenness of mind contributed largely to the success of baseball and to the spread of many other sports. From 1878 to 1880 inclusive he edited *Spalding's Official Baseball Guide,* and in 1911 published *America's National Game,* a comprehensive history of baseball. He spent the last fifteen years of his life as a resident of Point Loma, Cal., and it was there that he died of heart failure, at the age of sixty-five. His first wife, whom he married Nov. 18, 1875, was Sarah Josephine Keith and by her he had one son; she died in 1899 and in 1900 he married Mrs. Elizabeth Churchill Mayer, who survived him.

[Spalding's collection of books, pamphlets, pictures, and other material on baseball is in the N. Y. Pub. Lib. For sources of information see his *America's National Game* (1911); *Spalding's . . . Guide,* 1916; C. W. and S. J. Spalding, *The Spalding Memorial: A Geneal. Hist. of Edward Spalding . . . and His Descendants* (1897); *Who's Who in America,* 1914–15; *Literary Digest,* Sept. 25, 1915; *N. Y. Times,* Sept. 10, 11, 1915. Information as to certain facts was furnished by J. T. Doyle, Am. Sports Pub. Company.]   J.K.

SPALDING, CATHERINE (Dec. 23, 1793– Mar. 20, 1858), foundress and mother superior of the Sisters of Charity of Nazareth, was born of old Maryland stock in Charles County, Md. On the death of her father, Ralph, a kinsman of Martin J. Spalding and William H. Elder [*qq.v.*], Catherine and her sister Ann accompanied her mother and the Thomas Elder family to Kentucky. The mother died in 1801, and Catherine was reared by the Elders and their daughter, Mrs. Richard Clark, mother of the distinguished Father William E. Clark. When John B. M. David [*q.v.*] with the assistance of Bishop Flaget [*q.v.*] established the Sisters of Charity in Nazareth, Bardstown, Ky., with a rude cabin as a mother-house, Catherine Spalding and six other girls from Kentucky and Maryland joined as charter members (Jan. 21, 1813). Catherine was elected mother superior and directed the primitive community, which soon included her blood-sister, with rigid economy and noble courage. The nuns labored in the fields, spun and wove their own clothing, built a chapel (1816), and established a small boarding school at Bardstown (1818), one of the first academies on the Kentucky frontier. Under her successor, Mother Agnes Higdon (1819–25), Sister Catherine continued to be the guiding spirit of the growing community as mistress of novices, as foundress of St. Vincent's Academy in Union County, and as director of the Academy of St. Catherine's, founded in 1823 in Scott County and moved to Lexington in 1834.

She was chosen mother superior again in 1825, serving until 1831. In the latter year she established Presentation Academy, the first Catholic school in Louisville, and two years later, as a nurse in the cholera epidemic, she carried the stricken victims' orphans to her home, thus founding St. Vincent's Orphanage in Louisville, for which she obtained liberal support from Protestants as well as Catholics. In 1836 she founded St. Vincent's Infirmary at Louisville, which in 1853 was developed into the commodious St. Joseph's Infirmary. In 1850, she established the School of St. Frances at Owensboro, and in 1854 she rejoiced in the consecration of a Gothic chapel at Nazareth, then the largest church in the diocese. In her later years, although she served four more terms as mother superior, her primary concern was St. Vincent's Orphanage at Louisville. Here she died, as the result of a cold contracted while on a sick mission. Loved and revered as a humble servant of the destitute, Mother Catherine was as beautiful in character as in person.

[*Biog. Sketch of Mother Catherine Spalding* (1912); a sketch of three and a half columns in the *N. Y. Freeman's Journal*, May 15, 1858, reprinted from the *Louisville Guardian*; B. J. Webb, *The Centenary of Catholicity in Kentucky* (1884), useful but inaccurate; Anna B. McGill, *Sisters of Charity of Nazareth* (1917); annual Catholic directories.]   R. J. P.

SPALDING, FRANKLIN SPENCER (Mar. 13, 1865–Sept. 25, 1914), bishop of the Protestant Episcopal Church, was the son of Rev. John Franklin and Lavinia Deborah (Spencer) Spalding and a descendant of Edward Spalding who was made a freeman of Massachusetts Bay Colony on May 13, 1640. At the time of Franklin's birth his father was rector of St. Paul's Church, Erie, Pa., but in 1873 he was elected missionary bishop of Colorado, Wyoming, and New Mexico. The boy received his early education in the public schools of Erie and Denver, and prepared for college at Jarvis Hall in the latter city. In 1883 he entered the College of New Jersey, Princeton, where he took only fair rank as a student but was a prize debater and participated with enthusiasm in student activities, winning a place on the baseball and football teams and on the editorial board of the *Princetonian*. After graduating in 1887 he taught for a year in the Princeton Preparatory School and then entered the General Theological Seminary, New York. Upon completing the course in 1891, he returned to Colorado and on June 3 was ordained deacon by his father; the following year, June 1, he was advanced to the priesthood.

His first charge was All Saints' Church, North Denver, a newly formed parish, where, with characteristic enthusiasm, he threw himself into the work of organization and joined the communal activities. Incidentally he became known and admired for his athletic prowess, especially as the star fullback of the Denver Athletic Club's football team. From 1892 to 1896 he was master of Jarvis Hall, the diocesan school for boys. In the latter year he was called to his father's old parish, St. Paul's, Erie, Pa., where he remained until 1904, when he was elected missionary bishop of Utah, a field which included, in addition to Utah, parts of Nevada, Wyoming, and Colorado. He was consecrated in his own church on Dec. 14, and immediately removed to Salt Lake City, which was his residence until, ten years later, he was killed by an automobile while crossing the street. He never married, but with regard to the merits of celibacy expressed the opinion that "to be the husband of some woman, or the wife of some man took more grace than to be a monk or a nun, and to walk the floor with a crying baby more Christianity than the vow to poverty" (Melish, *post*, pp. 90, 91).

The district of Utah offered peculiar difficulties to an Episcopal bishop, but Spalding won the respect of all classes and displayed exceptional ability in adapting himself both to the problems of Salt Lake City and to the rough conditions of the outlying country. A thoroughgoing Churchman, he was nevertheless broad in his sympathies, progressive theologically, and not inclined to attach too much importance to elaborate ceremonials. He abhorred "begging," but was successful in raising money in the East for hospital and educational work. Glimpses of his field are given by him in articles in the *Spirit of Missions* (October, December 1912, September 1914). It was his conviction that the Church should not only minister to the individual but also direct its energies to the transformation of his environment, and outside his own communion Spalding was best known perhaps as the "socialist bishop." From the beginning of his career he took an active interest in social and political affairs. During the Presidential campaign of 1896 he made speeches in Colorado in support of free silver. At Erie he espoused the cause of the working man in labor controversies. Believing that Christian ideals cannot be realized without a revolution in the social organization, he at length avowed his belief in Marxian socialism, and in sermons and lectures uncompromisingly set forth his convictions, fearlessly challenging the Church to array itself on the side of radical reform. His views provoked opposition but his transparent sincerity and devotion to human welfare won him the regard of those who differed with him. He was a public speaker of more than ordinary effectiveness, and his addresses at the Pan-Anglican Congress, London, in 1908, and a sermon he delivered in Westminster Abbey, called forth much favorable comment. He was a prison reformer, a prohibitionist, and a pacifist, rewriting in 1914 such militant hymns as "Onward Christian Soldiers" and "Stand up, Stand up for Jesus" with the warlike terms eliminated. He even went so far as to suggest that the phrase "fight manfully under his banner" in the baptismal service be changed to "work faithfully for his cause." In the *Atlantic Monthly* for May 1913 he set forth his views on church unity. At the time of his death he was characterized as a unique combination of hero and saint.

[C. W. Spalding, *The Spalding Memorial: A Geneal. Hist. of Edward Spalding . . . and His Descendants* (1897); J. H. Melish, *Franklin Spencer Spalding, Man and Bishop* (1917); *Christian Socialist*, Nov. 9, 1911, Nov. 1914; *Spirit of Missions*, Nov. 1914; *Churchman*, Oct. 3, 10, 17, 1914; *Living Church*, Oct. 3, 10, 1914; *Outlook*, Nov. 25, 1914; *Salt Lake Tribune*, Sept. 26, 27, Nov. 2, 1914.]   H. E. S.

SPALDING, JOHN LANCASTER (June 2, 1840–Aug. 25, 1916), Catholic prelate and educator, was born in Lebanon, Ky., a son of Richard Madison and Mary Jane (Lancaster) Spalding, a nephew of Martin John Spalding [*q.v.*], and a descendant of Thomas Spalding who settled in Maryland about 1650. Educated in local schools and St. Mary's College, from which he was graduated in 1859, Spalding, in answer to the priestly vocation so common in his family, entered Mount St. Mary's Seminary of the West in Cincinnati. Subsequently, he proceeded to the American College at Rome and to the American College at Louvain. Ordained a priest by dispensation on Dec. 19, 1863, he remained in Europe two years longer engaged in advanced studies. After his return to the United States, he served as a curate of the Cathedral in Louisville, organized St. Augustine's negro parish (1869), and acted as secretary to Bishop Peter J. Lavialle and William McCloskey and as chancellor of the diocese (1871). Recognized as a scholarly theologian, he accompanied his ordinary to the Second Plenary Council of Baltimore (1866), where he was invited to preach before the assembled prelates. In 1872 he left the Louisville diocese and was stationed as an assistant at St. Michael's Church in New York. While here he published a biography of his uncle, *The Life of the Most Rev. M. J. Spalding* (1873).

Named by Pope Pius IX to the see of Peoria, Spalding was consecrated bishop by John Cardinal McCloskey in St. Patrick's Cathedral, New York, on May 1, 1877. He was associated with the liberal leaders of the Church in the Third Council of Baltimore (1884); with John Ireland in the Irish colonization movement; and with the founders and promoters of the Catholic University of America at Washington, D. C., in the establishment of which he is regarded as the moving force (see *An Address Delivered at the Laying of Corner-Stone of the Catholic University,* 1888). As an ordinary, he managed his diocese with skill, promoted education, and founded in 1898 a model boys' high school, the Spalding Institute. He was largely responsible for the Catholic educational exhibit at the World's Columbian Exposition in Chicago. As an essayist he had no peer in the priesthood, although some critics feared that he leaned toward the philosophy of Kant and Hegel. His educational essays, which appeared in the *American Catholic Quarterly Review,* the *Catholic World,* and the *Educational Review,* received high praise from impartial critics. A voluminous writer, he published a number of books treating of philosophy, religion, education, and social problems; among them are *Essays and Reviews* (1876); *Religious Mission of the Irish People* (1880); *Lectures*

and Discourses (1882); three volumes of verse— *America and Other Poems* (1885), *The Poet's Praise* (1887), *Songs Chiefly from the German* (1896)—under the pen name Henry Hamilton; *God and the Soul* (1901); *Education and the Higher Life* (1890); *Things of the Mind* (1894); *Thoughts and Theories of Life and Education* (1897); *Opportunity and Other Essays* (1898, 1900), which, translated by the Abbé Felix Klein, went through three French editions; *Means and Ends of Education* (1895); *Religion, Agnosticism and Education* (1902, 1903); *Socialism and Labor and Other Arguments* (1902, 1905); *Religion, Art, and Other Essays* (1905); *Aphorisms and Reflections* (1901); *Glimpses of Truth* (1903). In 1905 *The Spalding Year Book: Quotations from the Writings of Bishop Spalding* appeared, under the editorship of M. R. Cowan; and a long narrative poem, *A Kentucky Pioneer,* was published in 1932. A sermon touching upon Americanism which he preached at Rome in 1900 (published by the Ave Maria Press, Notre Dame University), challenged attention and was quoted at length in the *Independent* (Sept. 20, 1900), with the observation that "such a leader, who is a scholar, theologian, and poet, is an honor to his Church."

In 1902, at the suggestion of leaders of the striking miners, President Theodore Roosevelt, who believed that Spalding was "one of the very best men to be found in the entire country" (*Theodore Roosevelt: An Autobiography,* 1913, p. 509), appointed him to the anthracite coal commission (*Report to the President on the Anthracite Coal Strike of May-October 1902,* 1903). Since most of the striking miners were Catholics, Spalding's efforts and personality had great influence in bringing about a satisfactory solution of the difficulties involved. His active life was ended by a paralytic stroke in 1905. He resigned his see on Sept. 11, 1908, and lived in retirement as titular archbishop of Scitopolis until his death.

[P. H. Callahan, biographical introduction to Spalding's *A Ky. Pioneer* (1932); *Souvenir of the Episcopal Silver Jubilee of Rt. Rev. J. L. Spalding* (1903); *Ceremonies of the Golden Sacerdotal Jubilee of His Grace John Lancaster Spalding* (1913); *Catholic Univ. Bull.,* Jan. 1898; *Am. Catholic Who's Who* (1911); *Who's Who in America,* 1916–17; official Catholic directories, esp. 1917; M. F. Rutherford, *The South in Hist. and Lit.* (1906); F. J. Zwierlein, *The Life and Letters of Bishop McQuaid* (3 vols., 1925–27); J. F. Rhodes, *The McKinley and Roosevelt Administrations* (1922); Sister M. Evangela Henthorne, *The Irish Cath. Colonization Asso. of the U. S.* (1932); *Catholic Encyc.,* XI (1911), 602; *Harper's Weekly,* Oct. 25, 1902; *Dial,* Jan. 1, 1904; *Chicago Daily Tribune,* Aug. 26, 27, 1916; material from Msgr. E. L. Spalding, Alton, Ill.]

R. J. P.

SPALDING, LYMAN (June 5, 1775–Oct. 21, 1821), physician and surgeon, was born in Cornish, N. H., the son of Dyer Spalding and Elizabeth Cady (Parkhurst) Spalding, and a descendant of Edward Spalding who came to America from England before 1640. At the age of seven, he entered the academy at Charlestown, Mass., was graduated in July 1794, and almost immediately began the study of medicine under the tutelage of Nathan Smith, 1762–1829 [*q.v.*]. In the winter of the same year, he began to attend lectures at the Harvard Medical School, and the following year carried on the practice of Dr. Smith while the latter was away on a visit to Europe. He resumed his studies at Harvard and was graduated in 1797 with the degree of M.B. Later Harvard honored him with the M.D. degree and Dartmouth College with the M.B. and M.D. degrees. From 1797 to 1799, he lectured on chemistry and materia medica at the medical school which had just been organized at Dartmouth. During this time he prepared a translation of a French book on chemistry which he published in 1799 under the title *A New Nomenclature of Chemistry*. Realizing that he could not make a living by lecturing, he settled in Walpole, N. H., with the intention of establishing a practice there, but soon moved to Portsmouth where he served as a contract army surgeon for the troops stationed at the fort in the harbor. He rapidly built up an extensive private practice and was compelled to discontinue his lectures at Dartmouth. On Oct. 9, 1802, he was married to Elizabeth Coues, the daughter of Capt. Peter Coues. Five children were born to them.

Spalding practised in Portsmouth from 1799 to 1812. Early in this period, he founded a medical society which eventually became the Eastern District Branch of the New Hampshire Medical Society, and, later, an anatomical museum. He originated and distributed "bills of mortality" which gave the causes of death of all persons in Portsmouth from 1800 to 1813. He obtained a portion of the first shipment of smallpox vaccine from England to the United States and immediately began experimentation. His activity as an investigator during this period is further manifested by his invention of a galvanic battery for therapeutic use, the perfection of a method for the preparation of oxygen for inhalation, and the invention of a soda fountain. In 1810 Spalding formed a connection with an academy at Fairfield, N. Y., and lectured there on chemistry and surgery for seven years. In 1813 he was made president of the institution, which then became known as the College of Physicians and Surgeons of the Western District of New York, and filled most of the chairs until 1816. In the last year, he started the publication of a book in pamphlet form on the institutes of medicine but it was never completed. Following this period, he established a residence in New York City, practised his profession, pursued the investigations which interested him, and wrote until his untimely death. While walking down Pearl Street he was struck on the head by some rubbish thrown from a second-story window, and never fully recovered from the effects.

Spalding's most outstanding contributions to medicine during his later years were his studies on yellow fever, additional investigations in the field of vaccination, an extensive and thorough study of hydrophobia, and the founding of the United States pharmacopoeia. Of these, the last was undoubtedly his greatest achievement. As early as 1815 he had written to some of his friends, urging that a national pharmacopoeia be established, but did not receive any encouragement until two years later when he read a paper on the subject before the New York County Medical Society. A committee was appointed, with Spalding as chairman, to suggest measures for the elaboration of a national pharmacopoeia. The plan worked out by this committee provided that a national convention be held of delegates chosen from each of four sections into which the United States was divided. A convention was held in Washington, D. C., on Jan. 1, 1820, plans for the elaboration of the book were agreed upon, and Spalding was made chairman of the committee on publication. This committee set to work immediately and made such rapid progress that the book was completed and printed by Dec. 15, 1820. Spalding took an active interest in the public schools and served as a trustee of the schools of the city of New York during his residence there. He died in Portsmouth, N. H.

[S. J. Spalding, *Spalding Memorial* (1872); C. W. Spalding, *The Spalding Memorial* (1897); H. A. Kelly, W. L. Burrage, *Am. Medic. Biographies* (1920); J. A. Spalding, *Dr. Lyman Spalding* (1916), and *The Friendship of Dr. Nathan Smith and Dr. Lyman Spalding* (1906); H. M. Hurd, article in *Am. Jour. Pharmacy,* June 1919; *Proc. Am. Pharmaceutical Asso.,* vol. LII (1904); *New-Hampshire Gazette,* Nov. 6, 1821.]

A. G. D–M.

SPALDING, MARTIN JOHN (May 23, 1810–Feb. 7, 1872), Catholic prelate, was born at Rolling Fork, Ky., the son of Richard and Henrietta (Hamilton) Spalding, who had migrated with their families to Kentucky in 1790. He was a descendant of Thomas Spalding who settled in St. Mary's, Md., about 1650. Bishop John L. Spalding [*q.v.*] was a nephew. After the death of their mother, the Spalding children were reared by an unusually devout grandmother, whose influence doubtless accounts in part for the fact that two of them entered the priesthood and two others joined a convent. Martin attended a typical log-cabin school and St. Mary's College, near Lebanon, from which he was graduated in 1826. He then entered the seminary at Bardstown, where he came into contact with such Catholic pioneers as Bishop B. J. Flaget and his coadjutor, John B. M. David, and F. P. Kenrick [qq.v.]. Although delicate as a child, he developed into a large man of demonstrative spirit, with a merry ring in his laughter, a good speaking voice, and a frank, blunt address. Sent by Bishop Flaget to the Urban College, Rome, in 1830, Spalding ranked well in his examination for the doctorate in theology and won the friendship of John England [q.v.], the future Cardinals, Wiseman and Cullen, and Monsignor Capellari (Gregory XVI), connections which no doubt facilitated his later rise in the Church. Ordained, Aug. 13, 1834, by Cardinal Pedicini, he said his first mass at St. Peter's tomb and soon returned to Bardstown, Ky., as pastor of the cathedral and instructor in the seminary.

The young priest was active in making conversions, in ministering to the negroes, and in writing for the St. Joseph's College Minerva, a literary magazine, the forerunner of the Catholic Advocate (begun 1835) of which later he was editor and which was in turn succeeded (1858) by his Louisville Guardian under lay editors. In 1838, he was appointed to the rectorship of St. Joseph's College, from which he resigned in 1840, engaging thereafter in pastoral work in Lexington and, after the episcopal see was removed to Louisville in 1841, in the old Bardstown parish. About this time he commenced the career as a lecturer which brought him fame throughout the United States and Canada. He also contributed to such magazines as the Religious Cabinet, the United States Catholic Magazine, and The Metropolitan, serving the last named in an editorial capacity. In 1844 Bishop Flaget called him to Louisville to be vicar-general. Here, with Father John McGill [q.v.], he conducted a series of lectures, published as General Evidences of Catholicity (1847), and republished in several subsequent editions. At the suggestion of the aged Flaget, he was appointed by Pope Pius IX to the coadjutorship of Louisville with the right of succession as titular bishop of Lengone, though certain members of the hierarchy feared that he lacked the necessary energy and firmness for the office.

Consecrated bishop on Sept. 10, 1848, he took active charge of the diocese, although he did not formally succeed until Feb. 11, 1850. Leaving financial affairs to his brother, Rev. Benedict J.

Spalding (1812–68), whose patrimony was bequeathed to diocesan institutions, the Bishop gave zealous attention to administrative matters. He established schools, an orphanage, a house for Magdalens, and a conference of the St. Vincent de Paul Society (1854); he built churches and a cathedral (1852). In 1852 he went to Europe with aid for John Henry Newman, who was in financial difficulties because of the suit brought against him by Dr. Achilli; as a result of this trip he introduced into his diocese in 1854 the Xaverian Brothers from Bruges. He also introduced the Minor Conventuals, the Ursulines, and the Sisters of Notre Dame. In the Councils of Baltimore and Cincinnati he took an active part. His pastorals on the sacraments, on marriage, and on the school question attracted wide attention, as did his series of articles in The Catholic Guardian (1858) contrasting the liberal acceptance of religious schools in Europe with the hostility which they encountered in America. The bishop's greatest difficulty arose from the Know-Nothing agitation stirred up by the Louisville Daily Journal, then edited by George D. Prentice. A mob attacked the foreign quarters, murdered about a hundred Irish and German residents of Louisville on "Bloody Monday," Aug. 5, 1855, and drove many from town. Spalding bore himself with tactful force and displayed a courageous leadership of his people which deterred further violence (see An Address to the Impartial Public on the Intolerant Spirit of the Times, 1854, p. 45).

Interested in higher education, he and Bishop Peter Paul Lefevere [q.v.] of Detroit promoted in 1857 the American College of Louvain when most members of the hierarchy displayed little interest in the enterprise. Later, he was active in the establishment of the North American College in Rome and was one of the first prelates to urge a national Catholic university for higher studies in the United States. He found time, also, for considerable writing of an apologetic and historical nature: Sketches of the Early Catholic Missions of Kentucky (1844); D'Aubigne's 'History of the Great Reformation in Germany and Switzerland,' Reviewed (1844), which was expanded into A History of the Protestant Reformation (2 vols., 1860); Sketches of the Life, Times, and Character of the Rt. Rev. Benedict Joseph Flaget (1852); Eight Days Retreat of Father David (1864); Miscellanea (1855), a series of essays, in one of which, by a skilful use of historical evidence, he disposed of some of the charges against Catholicism brought by Samuel F. B. Morse; and an introduction and notes to A General History of the Catholic Church (4 vols., 1865–66), a translation from the French of J. E. Darras.

Though a Southerner, during the Civil War Spalding tried to be scrupulously neutral. In charities, he was assuredly so. He detailed Sisters of Charity and Sisters of Nazareth as nurses on the battle fields and in the Louisville hospitals. He visited and preached in camps; he advised against Archbishop Kenrick's proposal of a definition of the Church's position in the struggle; he influenced Governor Magoffin to veto the first test-oath bill which passed the Kentucky legislature, but when it became law he took the oath under protest that he held the act unconstitutional. His brochure, *Dissertazione nella Guerra Civile Americana* (1863), is said to have had considerable effect upon Continental opinion. After the death of Archbishop Kenrick, he was transferred on July 31, 1864, to the archepiscopal see of Baltimore, to the general satisfaction of Catholics throughout the country, despite apparent protests by Secretary Seward to Rome on the score of Spalding's doubtful loyalty to the federal cause. As archbishop, his régime was brief but noteworthy. The Second Plenary Council was held in 1866 and carried out much church legislation formulated by himself and Dr. James A. Corcoran of Charleston. He busied himself in collecting funds for the rehabilitation of the churches in the South, and displayed unusual activity in organizing conferences of the St. Vincent de Paul Society, the Catholic Protectory under the Xaverian Brothers, a home of the Good Shepherd, St. Francis School and Colored Orphanage, and the headquarters of Father Herbert Vaughan's Josephite Fathers for colored missions, which has since become an important community. He gave ample support to the Passionists, and to the Redemptorists and the Jesuits who were building their respective houses of study at Ilchester and Woodstock. In 1867–68, he was in Rome on papal invitation to celebrate the anniversary of St. Peter's martyrdom and in 1870 he took a leading part in the Vatican Council as a member of the commissions on Faith and Postulata. A strong supporter of the cause and definition of papal infallibility, he published *Pastoral Letter to the Clergy and Laity of the Archdiocese on the Papal Infallibility, Written in Rome, July 19, 1870* (1870), which has both theological and historical value, and *Lecture on the Temporal Power of the Pope and the Vatican Council . . . Philadelphia* (1870). Two years later he died and with fitting services was buried in his cathedral.

[J. L. Spalding, *The Life of the Most. Rev. M. J. Spalding* (1873), from papers left by the archbishop to his friend I. T. Hecker, C.S.P.; Spalding's printed pastoral letters; B. J. Webb, *The Centenary of Catholicity in Ky.* (1884); J. G. Shea, *Hist. of the Catholic Church in the U. S.*, vol. IV (1892); R. H. Clarke, *Lives of the Deceased Bishops of the Catholic Church in the U. S.*, vol. III (1888); *Cath. Encyc.*, vol. XIV (1912), p. 208; *Sun* (Baltimore), Feb. 8, 12, 1872.]
R. J. P.

SPALDING, THOMAS (Mar. 26, 1774–Jan. 4, 1851), planter, writer, legislator, and congressman, only child of James and Margery (McIntosh) Spalding, was born in Frederica, St. Simon's Island, Ga. His father, a noted Scotch student and trader, settled in Georgia in 1760 and built up an extensive Indian trade; being a Loyalist, he removed to Florida at the outbreak of the Revolution, but later returned to Georgia. His mother was a daughter of Col. William McIntosh, an officer in the Revolution, who had settled in Georgia in 1736. Spalding was educated in common schools in Florida and Georgia and a private school in Boston, Mass. He studied law under Judge Thomas Gibbons [*q.v.*] of Savannah and was admitted to the bar in 1795, but never practised. He married, Nov. 5, 1795, Sarah Leake, only child of the wealthy Richard Leake of Belleville, McIntosh County, Ga. He built a home on St. Simon's but soon sold his estate and spent several years in England, where he engaged in business and took great interest in Parliament. After returning to Georgia he bought a plantation on Sapelo Island and devoted himself to his family, politics, and agriculture. He was the father of sixteen children, of whom several died before reaching maturity. His home was noted, even after the death of his wife in 1843, for his lavish entertaining.

Spalding's political life was influential though not spectacular. Before going to England, he served in the constitutional convention of 1798 and as Glynn County's representative in the legislature. After his return, at several different times he represented McIntosh County in the state Senate. He successfully contested the election of Cowles Mead to Congress in 1805, but resigned in 1806. An ardent patriot, he secured arms from the federal government in 1812 and armed his slaves against the British. In 1815 he was sent by the government to Bermuda to investigate claims of American citizens against Great Britain for property destroyed and slaves carried away during the War of 1812 (for some of his letters as United States agent, see *Niles' Weekly Register*, Sept. 30, 1815). In 1826 he represented Georgia on the commission appointed to determine the boundary between Georgia and Florida; but he could not agree with the federal commissioner and the dispute remained unsettled until years later. As a member of the Milledgeville anti-tariff convention of 1832, he aided in drawing up its resolutions on the tariff. He took a moderate position on the sectional controversy over slavery. Elected president of the Georgia Convention of 1850, he favored the compromise measures of that year and was influential in getting Georgia to accept them.

Spalding had extensive agricultural interests. Owning hundreds of slaves, he was noted for his considerate treatment of them. He never sold a slave, and while in the legislature advocated a law prohibiting the sale of a slave from the estate on which he was born. He founded and was president of the Bank of Darien and its Milledgeville branch. One of the first to introduce sea island cotton into the South, he was the first to grow sugar cane and manufacture sugar in Georgia. He experimented with silk culture, imported wines, and developed vineyards and wine making. His contributions to agricultural journals were voluminous. Courteous and affable and with easy, unassuming manners, he was a fluent and energetic speaker, often in demand at the Agricultural and Sporting Club, of which he was a member. He liked neither art nor music, but loved books and collected one of the largest libraries in the South. Especially interested in history, he wrote "A Sketch of the Life of General James Oglethorpe," published in the *Collections of the Georgia Historical Society* (vol. I, 1840). Although tender, loving and generous, he was devoid of a sense of humor and sternly condemned dancing and card playing. He died at his son's home in Darien and was buried in St. Andrews Cemetery of Christ Church, Frederica.

[C. W. Spalding, *The Spalding Memorial* (1897); *Biog. Dir. Am. Cong.* (1928); L. C. Gray, *Hist. of Agriculture in the Southern U. S. to 1860* (1933), vol. II; L. J. Hill, *The Hills of Wilkes County, Ga.* (n.d.); L. L. Knight, *Georgia's Landmarks*, vol. II (1914); Caroline C. Lovell, *The Golden Isles of Ga.* (1932); W. J. Northen, *Men of Mark in Ga.*, vol. II (1910); George White, *Hist. Colls. of Ga.* (1854); C. S. Wylly, *The Seed that Was Sown in the Colony of Ga.* (1910); *Savannah Daily Republican*, Jan. 8, 1851.] F. M. G.

SPALDING, VOLNEY MORGAN (Jan. 29, 1849–Nov. 12, 1918), botanist, was born at East Bloomfield, N. Y., the son of Frederick Austin and Almira (Shaw) Spalding, and a descendant of Edward Spalding, who came from England and settled in Massachusetts before 1640. His mother was of Scotch-Irish ancestry. He attended the public schools of Gorham, N. Y., and, after the removal of his family to a farm near Ann Arbor, Mich., in 1864, prepared for college at the Ann Arbor High School. In 1869 he entered the University of Michigan, and was graduated with the degree B.A. in 1873. The next three years he served as principal of high schools at Battle Creek and Flint, Mich. In 1876 he

joined the faculty of the University of Michigan as instructor in zoölogy and botany (1876–79), and subsequently devoted himself wholly to botanical research and instruction, filling in succession the positions of assistant professor (1879–81), acting professor (1881–86), and professor of botany (1886–1904).

At intervals during his early career he studied plant physiology, anatomy, and histology at Harvard, the University of Pennsylvania, and Cornell, and later carried on advanced studies in European universities, receiving from Leipzig the Ph.D. degree in 1894. Admirably suited in character for teaching, and well-equipped by long and many-sided training in botanical fields until then little cultivated in America, he became noted for his earnest insistence upon the recognition of botany in its broadest sense as a science of the utmost utility to mankind and upon the requirement of thorough training for teachers of science in secondary schools. He was himself an uncommonly successful teacher, even-tempered, genial, and possessed to an unusual degree of the ability to impart his own deep enthusiasm to those who studied under him and went out as investigators and teachers. His textbook, *Guide to the Study of Common Plants: An Introduction to Botany* (1893), served an important purpose.

Among other subjects, forests early interested Spalding, and over the long educational period required to arouse public appreciation of their importance and value as an irreplaceable national asset he steadfastly advocated a detailed study of the manifold problems connected therewith and the development of a rational policy of forest conservation and utility. He assisted the federal government not only in planning forestry work but by carrying out extended experimental studies as well, and was the principal author of *The White Pine* (*Pinus Strobus Linnaeus*), a monograph published in 1899 by the United States Department of Agriculture. In later years his interest was directed primarily to ecology and the life relations of desert plants. Failing health compelled him to spend the winter of 1898–99 in southern California and later (1904) to resign his professorship at Michigan. The next year he joined the resident staff of the Desert Botanical Laboratory of the Carnegie Institution of Washington, at Tucson, Ariz., a region better suited to his condition. Of the results of his work here the volume *Distribution and Movements of Desert Plants* (1909) is the most important. Owing to increasingly severe rheumatism he removed in 1909 to a sanitorium at Loma Linda, Cal., where, cheerful and mentally alert although physically more and more helpless, he resided until his death. He was married in September 1876 to Harriet Hubbard of Battle Creek, Mich., and on Jan. 1, 1896, some years after her death, to Effie Almira Southworth, of Forestville, N. Y., who survived him. A bronze tablet erected at the University of Michigan in 1909 by former students fittingly commemorates his life and services.

[C. W. Spalding, *The Spalding Memorial: A Geneal. Hist. of Edward Spalding . . . and His Descendants* (1897); *Science*, Nov. 29, 1918; H. S. Reed, "Volney Morgan Spalding," in *Plant World*, XXII, 14–18 (Jan. 1919), portr.; B. A. Hinsdale, *Hist. Univ. Mich.* (1906); F. E. Bliss, *The Class of '73 of the Univ. of Mich.* (1923); *Mich. Alumnus*, May 1899; *Who's Who in America*, 1918–19; Regents' Proceedings Univ. of Mich., 1901–06; Univ. of Mich, alumni office records.]
W. R. M.

SPANGENBERG, AUGUSTUS GOTTLIEB (July 15, 1704–Sept. 18, 1792), bishop of the Moravian Church, was the youngest of four sons of George Spangenberg, Lutheran pastor at Klettenberg-Hohenstein, and his wife, Elizabeth Nesen. He was left an orphan in 1714, with a small estate, most of which was wiped out by fire. All of the children had gymnasial and university training, however, by virtue of the patient industry of the older boys, and Augustus entered the university at Jena in 1722. Here he came under the influence of Francke, Breithaupt, Freylinghausen, and Buddeus, was made a member of Buddeus' family, and was assisted by a yearly stipend. Pietism was just beginning to divide Protestant sentiment into two schools and Spangenberg's young mind was laid open to the evangelical possibilities of the new spirit. Under the influence of his distinguished foster father, he abandoned the study of law for theology, receiving the M.A. degree in 1726, and becoming an assistant in theology in the university. An acquaintance with Count Zinzendorf and the Moravians of Herrnhut about this time attracted Spangenberg's interest to the practical application of pietistic ideas to everyday life. He visited Herrnhut in 1730 and found himself in such sympathetic comradeship that he looked upon the Moravians as brethren. He meanwhile refused a profitable lectureship at Copenhagen, but was persuaded two years later by the king of Prussia to accept the chair of religious education at the University of Halle. By this time the orthodox and separatist movements in the Lutheran Church had become more antagonistic and his adherence to the Moravians resulted in dismissal from his position. He went at once to Herrnhut as an assistant to Zinzendorf and the two became lifelong friends. He was responsible for carrying out the Zinzendorf plans for the establishment of missions in Surinam and in Georgia, and the

negotiations in Amsterdam and in London proved him a patient and competent agent, and made for him strong friends in both countries.

In 1735 he started for America with some Swiss colonists and began a service of almost thirty years in Georgia and in Pennsylvania. His superlative qualities of leadership, his outstanding common sense, his vigorous but controlled evangelism, and his ability to restrain the extravagances of the pietistic attitude, made him the driving force in the organization of the Moravian work in America. He left Savannah in 1736 and went to Pennsylvania where he lived with the Schwenkfelders while he looked for a site for a Moravian mission center. In 1739, having made arrangements for the Georgia group to move north, he went to Marienborn and then to Herrnhaag, in Württemberg, where he was married to Mrs. Eva Maria (Zielgelbauer) Immig, on Mar. 5, 1740. In 1741 he founded at London the Society for the Furtherance of the Gospel to enlist the financial support of the Church of England for Moravian missions. He was consecrated bishop in 1744 at Herrnhaag and at once sailed for America to become overseer of the Bethlehem settlement, started in 1741 by Zinzendorf and David Nitschmann [*q.v.*]. An invasion from Canada had made the colonists fearful of the Indians as allies of the French, and his first move was to send all the New York converts to Bethlehem from the northern stations and to organize the American work with Bethlehem as a center. He divided his people into two alternating groups, the "Home" and the "Pilgrim" congregations, operating under a communistic order which he himself established and directed very effectively, notwithstanding the pressure of war conditions and much local opposition. In Europe, meanwhile, pietism had run wild in Moravian circles, carrying with it most of the men around Zinzendorf, and internal church politics caused Spangenberg to lose his influence. He was replaced at Bethlehem by Bishop John Nitschmann and returned to London, where, in 1750, he wrote a declaration in defense of Zinzendorf which appeared as the *Apologetische Schluss-Schrifft* at Leipzig in 1752.

After the cross-fire of pietism had burned out, he was again selected to go to Bethlehem. He found his so-called "Economy" disrupted by laziness and lack of management, and he promptly began to plan a new scheme to separate family life that should supplant the former system. His wife had died in 1751 and, on May 19, 1754, he was married to Mrs. Mary Elizabeth (Jaehne) Miksch. A short visit to London in the spring of 1753 had convinced him that plans for America must be made in accordance with existing conditions, so when he returned in 1754, he promptly began to organize a new work in North Carolina on a large tract selected from the Granville grant in 1752 and hastened the break up of the Economy at Bethlehem. He also took active part in the colonial legislation that moved the Indians to the further side of the Ohio. The anxieties and privations of these proceedings, involving much laborious travel, so undermined his health that, at last, in 1762, when the new organization was complete, he returned to Herrnhut. Here he stayed for the rest of his life as the actual leader of the group of so-called elders, recognized not only by his own, but by all Christian groups in Europe, as the dominating figure in the work of missions. He was continually called into conference by rulers and ministries as an expert in matters of colonial control. During this period of his life he produced most of his literary work. His first efforts were *Leben des Herrn Nichlaus Ludwig Grafen und Herrn Zinzendorf* (three volumes, 1772–75), and his *Idea Fidei Fratrum* (Barby, 1779). His *Kurzgefasste Historsche Nachricht von der . . . Bruederunität* was published in Frankfort in 1774, the *Reden an Kinder,* in Barby, 1782; *Das Wort von Krenz* and *Vergebung der Sünde,* in Barby, 1791–92.

Spangenberg's second wife died at Bethlehem in March 1759. He had no surviving children from either marriage. He retired from active service in 1790, but remained in full strength of mind, even though feeble in body, until his death in Berthelsdorf. He was buried at Herrnhut.

[Spangenberg papers in the Moravian archives, Bethlehem, Pa., and Herrnhut, Saxony (also photostatic copies in the Lib. of Cong.) ; manuscript mission reports, and diary of the congregation, Bethlehem; K. F. Ledderhose, *The Life of Augustus Gottlieb Spangenberg* (London, 1855) ; Gerhard Reichel, *August Gottlieb Spangenberg* (Tübingen, 1906) ; Jeremiah Rissler, *Life of Spangenberg* (Barby, 4 vols., 1794) ; *Pubs. South. Hist. Asso.,* vol. I (1879) ; *Pa. Mag. of Hist. and Biog.,* no. 4, 1878, no. 1, 1879; A. L. Fries, *Records of the Moravians in N. C., Pubs. N. C. Hist. Commission* (4 vols., 1922–30) ; J. T. Hamilton, *A Hist. of the Ch. Known as the Moravian Ch., Trans. Moravian Hist. Soc.,* vol. VI (1900) ; J. M. Levering, *A Hist. of Bethlehem, Pa.* (1903) ; *Trans. Moravian Hist. Soc.,* vols. I, III, IV (1876, 1886, 1891).]   A. G. R.

SPANGLER, EDWARD [See BOOTH, JOHN WILKES, 1838–1865].

SPANGLER, HENRY WILSON (Jan. 18, 1858–Mar. 17, 1912), engineer, educator, author, was born at Carlisle, Pa., the son of John Kerr and Margaret Ann (Wilson) Spangler. While he was attending public school in Carlisle, the United States Navy inaugurated the four-year course for engineers at the Naval Academy, an-

nouncing that twenty-five cadets would be appointed annually on competitive examination. Spangler, viewing this announcement somewhat in the light of a divine dispensation, took the examination, passed it, and received his appointment to the United States Naval Academy at the age of sixteen. His career at the Academy was brilliant; his technical aptness led him into advanced work in mathematics, and he was graduated third in the class of cadet engineers in 1878.

At that time, it was the practice of the Navy to assign young officers to engineering colleges as teachers of engineering subjects. Spangler and two of his classmates, Ira Nelson Hollis [*q.v.*] and Mortimer Elwyn Cooley, were so detailed; all three later resigned from the Navy; and all three became noted educators in the field of engineering. From 1878 to 1889 Spangler retained his affiliation with the Navy, rising to the rank of assistant engineer, and returning in 1898 for service with the rank of chief engineer during the Spanish-American War. Meanwhile, on detached service he was instructor in marine engineering (1881) and assistant professor of dynamical (mechanical) engineering from 1882 to 1884 and from 1887 to 1889 at the University of Pennsylvania, where in 1889 he was made full professor, a merited promotion which had been delayed on account of his youth. It was during the twenty-three years of service that followed, as professor of mechanical engineering, holder of the Whitney professorship of dynamical engineering, and head of the department of mechanical and electrical engineering, that Spangler brought to mature fruition those qualities of precision, initiative, leadership, and executive ability which he had so ably developed at the Naval Academy, and made his noteworthy contribution to the development of engineering education.

As an author he published standard textbooks on several subjects: *Valve-Gears* (1890) ; *Notes on Thermodynamics* (1901) ; *Elements of Steam Engineering* (1903), jointly with A. M. Greene, Jr., and S. M. Marshall; *Graphics* (1908) ; *Aplied Thermodynamics* (1910) ; and contributed a wealth of papers and reports to technical periodicals. He maintained membership in the Franklin Institute and numerous professional societies. As a teacher he was endowed with an imposing personality, a quick and brilliant mind, a stern sense of discipline, and a scathing contempt for affectation and pretense. These qualities, coupled with his genuine regard for accurate and rigorous teaching, made him feared at first and later loved by an admiring student body who manifested their affection through the kindly nickname, "Pop." He was honored with membership on the advisory council of the Engineering Congress of the World's Columbian Exposition, 1893, and membership on the jury of awards of the Buffalo exposition of 1901. A painting of him hangs in the Engineering Building at the University of Pennsylvania.

Spangler married, Dec. 1, 1881, Nannie Jane Foreman of Carlisle, Pa., and they had three children. He died of heart disease at the age of fifty-four, survived by his wife and one son.

[*Who's Who in America,* 1912–13; *Trans. Am. Soc. Mech. Engineers,* vol. XXXIV (1913); *Science,* Mar. 29, 1912; *Old Penn* (Univ. of Pa.), Mar. 23, 1912; Edgar Marburg, in *Engineering News,* Mar. 28, 1912, repr. in *Proc. Engineers' Club of Phila.,* vol. XXIX (1912); *Pub. Ledger* (Phila.), Mar. 19, 1912; *Pennsylvanian* (Phila.), Mar. 19, 1912; letter from Dean Greene; conversations with Univ. of Pa. alumni.]

F. V. L.

SPARKS, EDWIN ERLE (July 16, 1860–June 15, 1924), college president, historian, was born near Newark, Licking County, Ohio. His father, Erastus Felton Sparks, a bridge contractor and farmer, traced his lineage from a Captain Sparks who came to Virginia with the second group of colonists sent out by the London Company; some of the descendants of this colonist emigrated later to the Ohio Valley. His mother, Jane Erle (Dodd) Sparks, a well-known evangelist, was descended from a Virginia family, one branch of which moved to Ohio in 1840. After his farm boyhood he worked at a variety of odd jobs and served as a reporter on a number of Ohio newspapers until he acquired enough money to go to college. He entered Ohio Wesleyan University, Delaware, Ohio, after a year in the preparatory department there, but in 1881 he transferred to the sophomore class at the Ohio State University, Columbus, where he received the degree of B.A. in 1884.

He was assistant in history at Ohio State University, 1884–85, and principal in the public schools of Portsmouth and Martins Ferry, Ohio, 1885–90. On Jan. 1, 1890, he was married to Katharine Cotton of Portsmouth, Ohio, by whom he had a daughter. During the next six years he held the position of administrative head of the preparatory department of the Pennsylvania State College at State College, Pa., where he also taught history. In 1891 he received the degree of M.A. from Ohio State University and in June 1900 the degree of Ph.D. in history from the University of Chicago, where he was a member of the faculty, 1895–1908, rising to a professorship of American history in 1904. He was also curator of the historical museum, 1905–08, and dean of University College, 1905–07. His

extension courses in history, an innovation in the field of higher education, attracted nationwide attention. In 1908 he was called to the presidency of the Pennsylvania State College, a position in which he showed marked capacity. He expanded the work of the institution both on the campus and, by extension service, throughout the state, and effected many reforms in the interest of educational efficiency and scholastic standards. At the same time the faculty of the college was enlarged from 114 to 518, and the student body increased from 1,147 to 4,316; ten new buildings were erected, and the administrative divisions of the institution were thoroughly reorganized. He served for several years on the executive council of the American Historical Association (1909–12) and was an active member of other historical organizations. In 1920 he resigned to devote his time to teaching American history, lecturing, and organizing chapters of the scholastic honorary society, Phi Kappa Phi. Throughout his entire career he displayed rare ability as a popular lecturer on historical, scholastic and administrative topics. Among his publications are *Topical Reference Lists in American History* (1893); *The Expansion of the American People* (1900); *The Men Who Made the Nation* (1901); *Formative Incidents in American Diplomacy* (1902); *The United States of America* (2 vols., 1904); *The Capture of William Johnston* (1906); *National Development, 1877–1885* (1907); *The English Settlement in the Illinois* (1907); *Worth-While Americans* (1921); and *Worth-While Europeans* (1923).

[*Who's Who in America,* 1924–25; *In Memoriam: Edwin Erle Sparks, Pres. of the Pa. State Coll.,* 1908–1920 (1925); obituaries in *N. Y. Times* and *Pub. Ledger* (Phila.), June 16, 1924; papers of E. E. Sparks in the Pa. State Coll. lib.]

A. E. M.

SPARKS, JARED (May 10, 1789–Mar. 14, 1866), editor and historian, was born at Willington, Conn., to Eleanor Orcutt, daughter of a substantial farmer. The date is found in his own "Biographical Memoranda" (Sparks Manuscripts, 141a). In the baptismal records of the First Church of Willington, the minister wrote "Jared son of [   ] by Elinor Orcut July 1789," but crossed out "son of" and wrote "born" in the blank space (*New England Historical and Genealogical Register,* Apr. 1913, p. 123; information from Town Clerk of Willington). On Dec. 24 of the same year Eleanor Orcutt married Joseph Sparks (Manuscript Vital Statistics, Town Clerk's office, Book B., p. 84), a young Willington farmer, and subsequently bore him nine children. Local tradition has it that Joseph was Jared's father. His maternal grandmother was something of a poet and local prophetess, and his mother a reader of history and philosophy; hence we have sufficient biological explanation of the boy's talents, without recourse to other theories of his paternity.

Just before his sixth birthday, when four or five younger children were straining the resources of the Sparks household, Jared was taken in charge by a childless uncle and aunt; and the next winter he had his first schooling. With the temporarily adopted parents, he emigrated to Camden, Washington County, N. Y., in 1800. Jared spent so much time helping his shiftless uncle, that little opportunity was found for schooling; he remembered reading Guthrie's geography while feeding logs into a saw-mill, and being greatly interested in Franklin's *Autobiography*. Returning to his parents at Willington in 1805, he so quickly exhausted the resources of the local schools as to be known as "the genius." The young boy became keenly interested in astronomy, and observed the comet of 1807 with a homemade cross-staff. At the age of eighteen he worked as a journeyman carpenter in summer and school teacher in winter; at twenty, he began the study of mathematics and Latin with the minister at Willington, the Rev. Hubbell Loomis, paying in part by shingling the parson's barn. Another nearby minister, the Rev. Abiel Abbot, was so favorably impressed with Jared as to obtain him a scholarship at the Phillips Exeter Academy, whither the young man repaired on foot. After two happy and fruitful years there, he entered Harvard College in 1811. Although several years older than his classmates, and forced to work his way, Sparks was a social as well as a scholastic success. He was the first member of his class to be chosen to the leading sophomore society and with two aristocratic classmates, John G. Palfrey [*q.v.*] and William H. Eliot, he formed lifelong friendships. In order to earn money he served during sophomore year as a private tutor at Havre de Grace, Md., where he witnessed the plundering of the town by Admiral Cockburn's expedition. His employer wished him to establish a private school; but he returned to Harvard, joined the Phi Beta Kappa, won the Bowdoin prize with an essay on Newton which was regarded as setting a new high mark for undergraduate work, and delivered a commencement part at his graduation in 1815. Jared Sparks loved people, his zest for improvement was combined with delightful social qualities, and in whatever community he found himself, from earliest youth, he took a leading part and made devoted friends.

Essentially roving and adventurous in dispo-

sition, the young graduate from rustic Connecticut longed to explore Africa. The travels of Mungo Park and of John Ledyard [*q.v.*] fascinated him; in college he was already planning to cross the Sahara, visit the mysterious city of Timbuktu, sail down the Niger, and circumnavigate Africa. It is true that after graduating he conventionally took up the study of divinity, but this may have been in the hope of reaching the Dark Continent as a missionary; for in 1816 he offered his services to the African Society of London. They were not encouraging; and during the two years 1817–19, Sparks served as science tutor at Harvard while studying at the Harvard Divinity School, and for a short period editing the *North American Review*. Although brought up a Calvinist, he yielded to the Unitarian influences at Harvard. On completing his studies and taking a master's degree, the young man received three offers: a comfortable parish in Boston, a professorship at a small college, and the pulpit of the First Independent Church (Unitarian) of Baltimore. The last appealed to his adventurous nature; and the famous ordination sermon of William Ellery Channing [*q.v.*] when Sparks was installed at Baltimore (May 5, 1819), made that occasion the "Pentecost of American Unitarianism." Sparks flung himself with youthful energy into his pastoral duties, and created new ones. Regarding himself as an apostle of liberal Christianity to the South, he engaged in pamphlet controversy with conservatives, and launched sundry schemes for religious propaganda and publication. His love of travel was gratified by invitations to preach in Southern cities as far as Savannah; and for a year, as chaplain to the House, he was much in Washington. But the ministry was never more than a stepping-stone for Sparks: in April 1823, greatly to the regret of his congregation, he resigned.

It so happened that Edward Everett, editor of the *North American Review,* was at odds with the "association of gentlemen" who owned it. Sparks first proposed to move the *Review* to Philadelphia, and let Everett start a rival periodical in Boston (Manuscript Diary, 1823–26, p. 12); but Everett's restless ambition turned elsewhere. Sparks then purchased the *Review* on credit for about $10,000, and edited it for six years, when he sold it for almost double the amount. Under his vigorous management the *North American* shook off the dilettante flavor of its youth, and became an equal to the great English and French reviews, remarkable for the quality and range, both geographical and intellectual, of its articles. The editor even subscribed to South American newspapers, and learned

Spanish in order to keep his readers in touch with Latin-American affairs; and he was constantly thinking up desirable subjects for articles, and getting them written. Sparks became a leading social and literary figure in the Boston group that revolved about Prescott, Ticknor, the Eliots, and the Everetts; and *The Life of John Ledyard* (1828), republished in England, and soon translated into German, gave him an independent literary reputation. The portraits of him by Rembrandt Peale (1826), Gilbert Stuart (1828), and Thomas Sully (1831), show him to have been remarkably handsome, with dark curly hair, brown eyes, and a Roman nose; robust in physique; and having the general air of an intelligent and alert aristocrat. His tastes, however, remained simple; he made no concealment of his humble origin, and kept in touch with childhood friends.

In the meantime Sparks had begun what was destined to be his greatest life work, the publication of the writings of George Washington. Justice Bushrod Washington, the owner of the Washington manuscripts, was won over by an offer to share the profits, through the friendly mediation of Chief Justice Marshall, who also consented to take an equal share, twenty-five per cent., with the owner (Bassett, *post,* p. 80). In January 1827, Sparks found himself alone at Mount Vernon with the manuscripts. An examination of them extending over three months showed that years would be required for the undertaking; and with the owner's consent, Sparks carried off the entire collection, eight large boxes, picking up on the way to Boston a box of diplomatic correspondence from the Department of State, and the Gates manuscripts from the New York Historical Society (Manuscript Journal, June 14, 1827). Not content with these, he searched or caused to be searched public and private archives for material, questioned survivors of the Revolution, visited and mapped historic sites. In 1830, for instance, he followed Arnold's route to Quebec. The first of the twelve volumes of *The Writings of George Washington* to be published (vol. II) appeared in 1834 and the last (vol. I, containing the biography) in 1837. In the meantime Sparks had become so enthusiastic over the literary possibilities of the Revolutionary period, as to begin and partially to complete several parallel publications. These included *The Life of Gouverneur Morris* (3 vols., 1832), *The Works of Benjamin Franklin* (10 vols., 1836–40), *The Library of American Biography* (first series, 10 vols., 1834–38), to which he himself contributed several lives, and *The Diplomatic Correspondence of the American Revolution* (12

vols., 1829–30). In order to obtain material for this last work he visited Europe in 1828–29, and spent several months copying documents in the archives of England and France, which he was probably the first American to enter. He was also a pioneer purchaser and collector of manuscript Americana. From 1837 to 1840 Sparks served on the Massachusetts Board of Education; but he took slight interest in politics and held no other public office.

Only by knowing the paucity and poverty of printed material on the American Revolution before 1830 can one realize the debt that American history owes to Sparks. All his work except that on the *Diplomatic Correspondence* was done on his own responsibility, and at his own risk, without subsidies or grants or a wealthy patron. The result proved that Sparks knew his public. These formidable sets of printed letters and documents sold to such an extent as to make a handsome profit for all concerned; and they were a boon to students and writers of history for the next fifty years. Yet Sparks's editorial methods were very bad; for he treated historical documents as if they had been articles or reviews submitted to the *North American,* using the editorial blue pencil freely. He made omissions without indicating them, standardized spelling and capitalization, and undertook to improve Washington's English. These methods are partly explained by Sparks's editorial experience, partly by his sense of social responsibility. He approached history as a gentleman in the "era of good feeling," rather than a scientific historian, resolved to tell the truth however unpalatable. He wished to spare the feelings of great men's descendants, and of those who lent him documents. Justice Washington enjoined him "to avoid giving offence to the writers [of letters to Washington], or their famileis [*sic*], by publishing any which have a reference to the state of parties, and alluding to particular indeviduals [*sic*] by name"; to which Sparks replied, "I am fully aware of the delicacy you mention, and trust my judgment will guard me against any indiscretion" (Apr. 9, 17, 1827, Sparks Manuscripts; Adams, *post,* II, 15). Observing that Washington in his old age completely rewrote his early letters, Sparks felt obliged to touch up later letters when they appeared to need it; and usually he had only the rough draft, not the letter actually sent, to work from. The harsh and hasty criticism of men and measures, in which the harassed General sometimes indulged, especially those that might arouse sectional animosities, Sparks thought best to gloss over or omit; but no sectional bias was shown in the omissions. Similarly, a strong secession passage was deleted from a letter of Gouverneur Morris, published in the critical year 1832. With Lord Aberdeen, who gained him access to the Public Record Office, Sparks had a gentleman's understanding that nothing would be published from that source tending to revive angry feelings between the two countries; and the same reticence was applied to documents from the French archives that might injure the traditional friendship (Justin Winsor, *Narrative and Critical History of America,* VIII, 1889, p. 414). It was customary, in his day, to edit very freely the letters of literary and historical figures before publication; and neither the English nor the American public had acquired a taste for seeing their heroes in the buff. Thus, in editing *The Works of Benjamin Franklin,* Sparks omitted the famous definition of chastity, and all other matters of the sort. But Sparks's carelessness respecting the Washington manuscripts is inexcusable. When George Corbin Washington, Justice Washington's heir, sold the "public" papers of the General to the United States, he allowed Sparks to keep "a few autographs" (Sparks's acknowledgment to G. C. Washington, Aug. 16, 1837, Sparks Manuscripts) of the "private" papers, and from these Sparks tore out and gave away leaves to friends who desired a specimen of the great man's handwriting (J. C. Fitzpatrick, *George Washington Himself,* 1933, p. 529; *The Diaries of George Washington,* 1925, vol. I, 211; IV, 295; Ellis, *post,* p. 254). It is not fair, however, to blame all cases of missing Washington manuscripts on Sparks, for Justice Washington gave away some of the diaries, and G. C. Washington mentions in a letter to Sparks (Dec. 27, 1848, Sparks Manuscripts) "some few unimportant autographs presented to friends."

These fifteen years (1823–38) of intense activity enlarged Sparks's circle of friends, brought him fame and money, and the opportunity for a change of occupation. On Oct. 16, 1832, he married Frances Anne Allen of Hyde Park, N. Y., and brought her to live in the historic Craigie House at Cambridge. She died in 1835, but he continued to reside at Cambridge, and in 1838 was offered the Whig nomination for Congress from that district. This he declined in favor of the McLean Professorship of Ancient and Modern History at Harvard, with a salary of $2,000; he had earlier declined the Alford Professorship of Philosophy. His first course, on the American Revolution, began in March 1839; and on May 21 he married an heiress twenty years his junior, Mary Crowninshield Silsbee, daughter of Senator Nathaniel Silsbee of Salem, and

brought her to live in a large house near the College Yard. Sparks was the first professor of history other than ecclesiastical in any university of the United States; and in the conditions that he laid down for accepting the chair, he showed prophetic insight into the form that history teaching was to assume in American universities fifty years later (Adams, II, 372–75). He proposed to discard recitations on set textbooks for the upper classes, to instruct by lectures, assigned reading, and essays; he insisted that he should "not at any time be called on to instruct in any other branch than that of history," and that he should not be expected to reside and lecture more than four months in the year. These conditions, which would be liberal even today, were accepted by the College Corporation. Sparks organized a department of history, using young graduates of no special training to teach the younger students out of textbooks, while he lectured to the upper classes and to law students, mostly on American, but occasionally on Greek, history. He seems to have impressed rather than interested the students; and although we find him lecturing on "the nature of historical evidence, and the rules of historical composition," he trained no disciples, and his professorship proved to be a false dawn for modern history in American universities. It was on one of his long absences to search European archives and collections, in 1841, that Sparks discovered the copy of D'Anville's map marked by Franklin, which subsequently figured in the "Battle of the Maps" that followed the Webster-Ashburton negotiations (Adams, II, 393–413). At that time Sparks was making researches for a "formidable history of the American Revolution" (Adams, II, 378) which was never completed. On returning to America he did much lyceum and other public lecturing, at New York and elsewhere, when not in residence at Cambridge. The stenographic reports of one of these courses, in the *New York Herald,* Nov. 8–Dec. 19, 1841, show that Sparks without sacrificing dignity was a lively and entertaining lecturer.

On Feb. 1, 1849, Sparks was chosen by the governing boards, president of Harvard University. His election was welcomed by the students as a return to the "Augustan Age" of Kirkland after the asperities of the Quincy and the inanities of the Everett administrations. Quite unexpectedly, Sparks attacked the elective system of studies in his inaugural address, which Professor Longfellow considered "very substantial, but retrograde." His object appears to have been to substitute definite alternative programs for indiscriminate groupings of course units; but the result was reaction toward the rigidly prescribed course, with recitation sections determined by alphabet rather than proficiency, that had prevailed at Harvard before the reforms associated with George Ticknor [*q.v.*]. Although he encouraged a greater use of lectures in instruction, notably in the case of Louis Agassiz [*q.v.*] and of two young scholars, Josiah P. Cooke and Francis J. Child [*qq.v.*], who owed their first professorial appointments to him, the McLean chair of history remained vacant; Professor Sparks's promising historical program became President Sparks's first victim. The Harvard Observatory, the only research unit of the University at that time, was furthered by his influence, and he had the satisfaction of seeing its new plant completed. Sparks was unhappy in the presidential office. By delegating petty disciplinary duties to a lower official he had hoped to find leisure for literary pursuits; and he did manage to finish his *Correspondence of the American Revolution* (4 vols., 1853) and to reply vigorously to Lord Mahon's strictures on his editorial methods. But new duties arose to fill up the time saved; and, fearing to become completely bogged in administrative routine, he resigned early in 1853.

Except for a year in Europe (1857–58) where he was much entertained, and had the pleasure of meeting David Livingstone, and reviving the African dreams of his youth, Sparks passed the remainder of his life quietly at Cambridge. For ten years he continued to collect material for his projected history of the Revolution, but nothing was written. Time slipped away rapidly and pleasantly with old friends and new, summer travels with wife and children, and answering the questions of correspondents. One gathers that the rôle of sage was not uncongenial to Sparks. He died of pneumonia at Cambridge on Mar. 14, 1866, and was survived by his widow, one son, and three daughters.

On account of Sparks's faulty editorial methods, no one of his documentary collections can be regarded as definitive, although every one was *editio princeps*. He has an assured place as an explorer and producer of American history. His energetic search for original documents, skill in selecting and annotating them, and success in getting them published, gave the American public a new conception of their history, and provided a host of writers with material. The fruits of his original or editorial labors amounted to over one hundred volumes. If Sparks dressed his subject with too much formal dignity, it was because she was young, and frontier manners would not have recommended her

to the family of Clio. His significance lies in the fact that he did obtain that recognition for American history.

[H. B. Adams, *The Life and Writings of Jared Sparks* (2 vols., 1893) is the official biography based on Sparks's own papers. Important appraisals of Sparks's work are in Justin Winsor, *Narrative and Critical Hist. of America,* VIII (1889), 416–24, and J. S. Bassett, *The Middle Group of American Historians* (1917), Ch. II. Bassett printed some *Correspondence of George Bancroft and Jared Sparks,* which throws light on his editorial methods, in *Smith College Studies in History,* II (1917), no. 2. The best memoirs by contemporaries are those of G. E. Ellis, in *Proceedings Mass. Hist. Soc.,* X (1869), 211–310; of Brantz Mayer, *Memoir of Jared Sparks, LL.D.* (1867); and of A. P. Peabody, in *Harvard Graduates Whom I Have Known* (1890). See also Ephraim Emerton, "History," in S. E. Morison, *The Development of Harvard Univ.* (1930). The pamphlet controversies with Lord Mahon and others are covered by the Adams biography and the Ellis memoir. The Sparks MSS. are in the Harvard Coll. Lib.; there is a brief calendar of the historical MSS. by Justin Winsor in *Harvard Univ. Lib. Bibliographical Contributions,* no. 22 (1889); but this does not include the several thousand pieces of private correspondence, journals, accounts, and other MSS. referring to Sparks's life, which were used by Adams and Bassett. These have been card-catalogued. The Peale portrait and several photographs of Sparks are owned by Harvard; the photographs of the Stuart and Sully portraits, owned by descendants, are in Adams' biography.]   S. E. M.

SPARKS, WILLIAM ANDREW JACKSON (Nov. 19, 1828–May 7, 1904), lawyer, congressman, and commissioner of the General Land Office, was born near New Albany, Harrison County, Ind., the youngest of ten children of Baxter and Elizabeth (Gwin) Sparks. His ancestors on both sides were English and early settlers in Virginia; his parents had moved to Harrison County about 1805 and when William was seven they moved again, settling in Macoupin County, Ill. In 1840 the father died but William was allowed to continue his schooling in a nearby log house during the winter months. The death of his mother, when he was fifteen, forced him to seek employment on a neighboring farm. For several years he worked by day and spent his evenings in study; then he turned to teaching school. By 1847 he had saved enough of his earnings to enter McKendree College at Lebanon, Ill., where he graduated in 1850. After studying law in the office of Sidney Breese [*q.v.*] at Carlyle, Ill., he was admitted to the bar in 1851 and immediately began practice. In 1853 he was appointed receiver in the federal land office at Edwardsville, Ill. Characteristic of him is the story that upon the discovery of an apparent error of three dollars in his accounts, when he relinquished his receivership after three years, he journeyed to Washington by stage, compelled a re-examination of his books, and had them found exactly correct. While at Edwardsville, Apr. 16, 1855, he married Julia E. Parker.

After resuming his law practice at Carlyle he served in the lower house of the legislature (1856–58), and in 1863, upon the death of J. M. Rodgers, succeeded him in the state Senate. He presided at many Democratic state conventions and was a delegate to the Democratic National Convention in 1868 and 1884. Meanwhile, in 1874, he was elected to Congress from a district regarded as Republican and was returned for three successive terms. In 1882 his district is said to have been gerrymandered and he declined to seek renomination. In the House he served on the Appropriations Committee and was later chairman of the Committee on Military Affairs. He was known as a "Jacksonian" Democrat with a contempt for Civil Service. Being an able speaker, he took a prominent part in discussions, especially those on the tariff, currency, and military affairs. He was a strong advocate of government regulation of the railroads. He became excited in debate, and at one time a physical encounter between Sparks and Representative James B. Weaver was narrowly averted (*Congressional Record*, Dec. 21, 22, 1880).

After Mar. 3, 1883, Sparks returned to Carlyle and developed a wide reputation as a jury lawyer. He had built up a "liberal fortune" when on Mar. 26, 1885, President Cleveland appointed him commissioner of the General Land Office. In this position he performed his most notable public service. Public opinion had come to feel that the Land Office was dominated by the land-grant railroads, syndicates, speculators, and cattle barons, to the detriment of actual settlers; moreover the Land Office was handicapped by considerable arrears of work. To aid him in his new duties Sparks had pugnacious honesty, good health, legal training, and an independent income. His attempts to reform the land service began with special reports on urgent cases, and his famous "April 3rd" order (Apr. 3, 1885; see his *Report* for 1886, p. 43) withheld the issue of patents for certain regions. He abolished the special privileges of the land lawyers of Washington. His thoroughly able reports of 1885, 1886, and 1887 set forth needed changes in land laws with cogent reasons therefor. He was stanchly supported by President Cleveland and Secretary L. Q. C. Lamar [*q.v.*], though Congress and the partisan press proved extremely hostile. As the result of a dispute with the Secretary regarding a railroad case, however, Sparks tendered his resignation, Nov. 15, 1887, which the President accepted, while expressing cordial sympathy with his accomplishments.

After a trip abroad, Sparks again practised law at Carlyle until about 1900, when he moved

to St. Louis, where he died. He was taken to Carlyle for burial in St. Mary's Catholic Cemetery. He left no children.

[*Biog. Dir. Am. Cong.* (1928); *Ann. Reports of the Commissioner of the Gen. Land Office*, 1885, 1886, 1887; *Copp's Land Owner*, 1885–87; *Centennial McKendree Coll. with St. Clair County Hist.* (1928); *N. Y. Tribune, Index*, 1885–87; files of *N. Y. Tribune* and *N. Y. Times*; *N. Y. Tribune*, Mar. 25, 1885; *Washington Post*, Nov. 12, 13, 16, 17, 1887; St. Louis and Carlyle papers, May, 1904.]   H. H. D.

SPARROW, WILLIAM (Mar. 12, 1801–Jan. 17, 1874), Episcopal clergyman, educator, was born in Charlestown, Mass., the son of Samuel and Mary (Roe) Sparrow. His father's family had gone to Ireland from England in the time of Cromwell and settled in County Wexford. Because of participation in the rebellion of 1798, Samuel Sparrow had been obliged to leave his native land. He found refuge in Massachusetts, but in 1805 was permitted to return to Ireland, where his oldest son, William, was brought up in the home of his grandfather, William Sparrow, at Gorey. With a view to entering Trinity College, Dublin, he acquired an excellent classical education, but in 1816 his grandfather died and the following year William returned to the United States with his parents, who established themselves in Utica, N. Y. Here, in a competitive examination, he won a position as classical teacher in the academy. In 1819 he entered Columbia College, and apparently pursued studies there for two years. In the meantime his family moved to Huron County, Ohio, where his mother died in 1821, and whither he himself went the next year.

In Ohio he became associated with pioneer educational enterprises, especially with those initiated by Bishop Philander Chase [*q.v.*], whose wife's sister, Frances Greenleaf, daughter of Duncan and Susannah (Greenleaf) Ingraham, he married on Feb. 13, 1827. He first taught in the school at Worthington conducted by Bishop Chase's son and later in Cincinnati College, of which the Bishop was president. In November 1824, Miami University opened its doors with Rev. Robert H. Bishop as president and William Sparrow as professor of languages, both having been elected on July 6 preceding (*The Diamond Anniversary Volume . . . 1824–1899*, n.d., p. 80). The following year, however, Bishop Chase persuaded Sparrow that his duty to the Episcopal Church, in which he was about to take orders, required him to sacrifice his opportunity at Miami and assist in establishing a theological seminary. The school was opened on the Bishop's farm at Worthington, and upon his arrival Sparrow became principal and chief teacher. On June 7,

1826, he was ordained deacon and four days later was advanced to the priesthood. From the start the most of the work in the seminary was preparatory and collegiate, and out of it developed Kenyon College and Gambier Theological Seminary, Gambier, Ohio, whither the institution was moved in June 1828. Although Bishop Chase by virtue of his office was head of the institution, Sparrow, as vice-president, was its administrator. Interference by the former led to a controversy between him and the faculty and, in 1831, to his resignation as bishop. Changes in the organization of the institution, brought about by Bishop Charles P. McIlvaine [q.v.] in 1840, led Sparrow to accept a professorship in the Theological Seminary in Virginia, Alexandria, in 1841.

For more than ten years he had been a leading educator and official in the diocese of Ohio; now for thirty-three years he was to have a quieter but no less influential career in Virginia. Twice, in 1844 and in 1851, he was asked to return to Kenyon as president, but declined; he was also called to important churches in Boston, Cincinnati, Richmond, and Baltimore. His teaching in the Seminary, of which he was soon made dean, was chiefly in the field of theology and Christian evidences. He had great gifts as a teacher and his work was characterized by breadth of mind and the spirit embodied in his own advice to others: "Seek the truth; come whence it may, cost what it will" (Goodwin, post, p. 601). He was repeatedly a delegate to the diocesan Convention, and was regarded as one of the strongest representatives intellectually of the evangelical Low Churchmen. He died suddenly in the First National Bank of Alexandria, where he had gone to cash a check. His wife had died in the previous year; they had ten children.

[The Gen. Cat. of Miami Univ. . . . 1809–1909 (n.d.) ; G. F. Smythe, Kenyon Coll.: Its First Century (1924) ; A. R. Goodwin, Hist. of the Theolog. Sem. in Va., vol. I (1923) ; Cornelius Walker, The Life and Correspondence of Rev. William Sparrow, D.D. (1876) ; J. E. Greenleaf, Geneal. of the Greenleaf Family (1896) ; The Sou. Rev., July 1876.]   H. E. S.

SPAULDING, ELBRIDGE GERRY (Feb. 24, 1809–May 5, 1897), a substantial banker of Buffalo, N. Y., acquired the sobriquet "father of the greenbacks" during a brief period of service in the House of Representatives. He was born in Cayuga County, N. Y., whither his parents, Edward and Mehitable (Goodrich) Spaulding, had gone from New England as pioneers. His ancestor, Edward Spalding, had established the name in Massachusetts Bay by 1640. Spaulding studied law in offices at Batavia, Attica, and Buffalo, and began practice in Buffalo in the middle

thirties. He was immediately successful in his profession, and was actively concerned in the development of the city, handling business connected with its harbor, its sewage system, its gas works, and the enlargement of the Erie Canal. He married, Sept. 5, 1837, Jane Antoinette Rich, the daughter of an Attica banker, and in due course brought to Buffalo the Farmers' & Mechanics' Bank of Batavia. He served as mayor (1847), as assemblyman (1848), and as state treasurer (1853).

Spaulding's national career began with his election, as a Whig, to the Thirty-first Congress (1849–51). He declined reëlection, returning to his banking business, in which he laid the foundation of a large fortune. Turning Republican, he went again to Congress in 1859, sat on the Congressional Executive Committee, and had some part in the peace negotiations that attempted to avert the Civil War. Reëlected in 1860, he found himself in the Thirty-seventh Congress a member of the Committee on Ways and Means, and one of its sub-committee of three in charge of the problem of war loans. In the summer of 1861 the United States Treasury was on the verge of bankruptcy, with receipts from taxes inadequate and with the credit of the government too uncertain for the favorable placement of loans. Currency was scarce and in unusual demand, and on Monday, Dec. 30, 1861, the New York banks suspended specie payments (D. C. Barrett, The Greenbacks and Resumption of Specie Payments, 1862–1879, 1931, p. 14). On the same day Spaulding introduced into the House of Representatives a bill for the issuance of legal-tender treasury notes payable on demand (Congressional Globe, 37 Cong., 2 Sess., p. 181). "The bill before us is a war measure. . . ." he stated in debate upon his proposal; "We were never in greater peril than at this moment . . . the Treasury must be supplied from some source, or the Government must stop payment in a very few days" (Ibid., p. 523 f., Jan. 28, 1862). He took pride in the resulting law of Feb. 25, 1862, authorizing the issuance of the legal-tender notes, or greenbacks, to the amount of $150,000,000. As financial needs became more pressing, there was a second authorization of $150,000,000 in July 1862; and before the Thirty-seventh Congress expired, on Mar. 3, 1863, another $150,000,000 had been made available. Spaulding called himself "a somewhat prominent though humble actor in originating and maturing" the law. Its legal-tender feature was distasteful to the Secretary of the Treasury and to the banks, and was accepted only as a measure of desperation. Thaddeus Stevens [q.v.], chairman of the Committee on Ways and Means, gave it his support, however, and in the Senate John Sherman and Charles Sumner [*qq.v.*] supported it.

This was Spaulding's only important work in Congress, and with it his political career came to an end. He was thenceforth content to be a benevolent local magnate. He brought his bank into the national banking system in 1864 as the Farmers' & Mechanics' National Bank of Buffalo, and managed it until, late in his life, he turned it over to his son. After his return from Washington he compiled a volume published in 1869 under the title, *A Resource of War—The Credit of the Government Made Immediately Available: History of the Legal Tender Paper Money Issued during the Great Rebellion: Being a Loan without Interest and a National Currency*. In 1875 he decorated a Buffalo park with a monument to the Spauldings, some of them his forebears, who fought at Bunker Hill. He was three times married; after the death of his first wife, Jane Rich, in 1841, he married, Sept. 5, 1842, Nancy Selden Strong, who died May 4, 1852, leaving two sons and a daughter; two years later, May 2, 1854, he married Delia (Strong) Robinson, sister of his second wife. There were no children by the first and third marriages.

[C. W. Spalding, *The Spalding Memorial: A Geneal. Hist. of Edward Spalding . . . and His Descendants* (1897), p. 395, which gives Spaulding's name a spelling that he did not follow; *Biog. Dir. Am. Cong.* (1928); *World* (N. Y.), May 6, 1897; *Buffalo Commercial*, May 5, 1897.]   F. L. P.

SPAULDING, LEVI (Aug. 22, 1791–June 18, 1873), missionary, was born in Jaffrey, N. H., the son of Phineas and Elizabeth (Bailey) Spaulding, and a descendant of Edward Spaulding (or Spalding) who was in Massachusetts before 1640. Levi received his early education from the Rev. John Sabin of Fitzwilliam, N. H., and graduated from Dartmouth College in 1815. Having decided during his senior year to enter the Christian ministry, he proceeded to Andover Theological Seminary, was graduated in 1818, and on Nov. 18 of that year was ordained by a Congregational Council at Salem, Mass. On Dec. 10, at Antrim, N. H., he was married to Mary, daughter of Samuel and Zebiah Warren Christie of that town. Under appointment of the American Board of Commissioners for Foreign Missions, he and his wife, in company with others designated for the India service, sailed from Boston, June 8, 1819, on the brig *Indus*, bound for Calcutta around the Cape of Good Hope. The ship arrived at Calcutta Oct. 19, whence the party took passage on Nov. 10 for Ceylon, finally reaching their destination, Jaffnapatem (Jaffna), Ceylon, on Feb. 18, 1820. The

following June they settled at Uduvil Oodooville), a new station five miles from Jaffna. Except for residence in nearby Manepay, Aug. 25, 1821, to Aug. 25, 1828, and in Tellippallai, until Mar. 8, 1833, Uduvil was the permanent base of Spaulding's work until his death. He remained longer in active foreign service than had any other missionary sent out by the Board. Only once did he and his wife return on furlough to America. Coming home late in 1844 they were back again in Uduvil before the end of March 1847.

Spaulding distinguished himself as an educator and a Tamil linguist, in addition to faithful and effective service otherwise. At Manepay he received in 1823 his first convert to the Christian faith. There also he took charge of the Mission's Female Boarding School, transferred temporarily (1825–28) from Uduvil. At Tellippallai he conducted the boys' preparatory school which was united in 1832 with the Mission's seminary at Vaddukkoddai (Batticotta, in the old records). At Uduvil he was in charge of the church, the schools, and evangelistic work among the villages. Early in 1834, he made a two months' tour of southernmost India, commissioned to investigate a continental region for the extension of the Mission's Tamil work. The important Madura Mission was the ultimate outcome. Toward the close of 1838 he began a significant service as translator, reviser, proof-reader, and tract and hymn writer. He prepared in Tamil more than twenty tracts and composed many of the choicest vernacular hymns. He compiled a Bible history and translated *Pilgrim's Progress*. For the sake, incidentally, of "settling" the orthography and the definition of Tamil terms, he compiled a Tamil dictionary and the revised and enlarged *English-Tamil Dictionary* (1852). He was one of the commission, from 1847, on the Scriptures published by the Bible Society, in Madras, being largely responsible for making the Tamil Bible "idiomatic and acceptable" (*Missionary Herald*, September 1849, p. 309); from 1865 to 1871 he served as a reviser of the Tamil Old Testament. He is described as "a shrewd man, a man of humor, utterly unostentatious, and quietly industrious" (*Ibid.*, October 1873, p. 308). He died in Uduvil, survived until Oct. 28, 1874, by his wife. They had two daughters and a son.

[Spaulding's journal, letters, and reports are scattered through *The Panoplist and Missionary Herald*, which in 1820 became the *Missionary Herald*. For other biog. material, see C. W. Spalding, *The Spalding Memorial: A Geneal. Hist. of Edward Spalding and His Descendants* (1897); *Gen. Cat. Theological Sem., Andover, Mass., 1808–1908* (n.d.); *Memoirs of Am. Mission-*

aries (1833) ; H. O. Dwight and others, *The Encyc. of Missions* (1904).]   J. C. A.

SPAULDING, OLIVER LYMAN (Aug. 2, 1833–July 30, 1922), soldier and civil official, was born in Jaffrey, N. H., the son of Lyman and Susan (Marshall) Spaulding. He was seventh in descent from Edward Spalding, who settled in Braintree, Mass., before 1640; his grandfather was a brother of Levi Spaulding [*q.v.*]. Oliver attended local elementary schools, and the Melville Academy in Jaffrey. In 1851 the family moved to Medina, Mich., and he received further education at Oberlin College, where he was graduated in 1855. After teaching school in Medina and reading law for two years, he moved, in 1857, to St. Johns, Clinton County, a new village just being laid out. There he studied in the law office of James W. Ransom and in 1858 was admitted to the bar. That same year he was elected a regent of the University of Michigan for a term of six years.

He entered the Union army in 1862 as captain in the 23rd Michigan Infantry, and passed through the intermediate grades to that of colonel (Apr. 16, 1864). With his regiment he took part in the Atlanta campaign, the battles of Franklin and Nashville, the capture of Fort Anderson, N. C., and the advance from Wilmington to Goldsboro and Raleigh, N. C. Toward the close of the war he commanded his brigade, and was mustered out in 1865 as colonel and brevet brigadier-general.

He then returned to St. Johns and to the practice of law. From 1867 to 1870 he was secretary of state of Michigan. In 1871 he declined appointment as federal judge in Utah; but in 1875 he accepted appointment as special agent of the Treasury at Detroit. This office he held most of the time until 1890, retaining his residence in St. Johns and his legal connections there. For one term, 1881–83, he represented his home district in Congress. For the greater part of 1883 he was chairman of a commission appointed to investigate the workings of the Hawaiian reciprocity treaty, a task which involved a visit to Honolulu and to other places in the Islands, then not at all easy of access. As special agent of the Treasury his duties included not only the ordinary inspections of his own district, which extended from Marquette to Rochester, but special investigations of customs and immigration matters from New York to San Francisco. From 1890 to 1893, and again from 1897 to 1903, he was assistant secretary of the Treasury, having supervision of Customs, Revenue Cutter, Marine Hospital, Life Saving and Immigration services, and the Seal Islands. He was charged also with the special arrangements for handling customs affairs at the World's Columbian Exposition, Chicago, and developed procedure which has served as precedent at subsequent expositions. He was president of the first Customs Congress of the American Republics, held in New York in January 1903. In that year he resigned as assistant secretary by reason of ill health, but continued to reside in Washington until his death, serving as special agent of the Treasury there until continued ill health forced his complete retirement.

He was regarded as the leading authority in the country on customs law and administration, and until he finally relinquished his residence in Michigan, was one of the leaders of the bar of the state. In politics he was a Republican, and when not in public office was active in Michigan political affairs. For several years he was chairman of the Republican state committee. He was an active Mason, and served as grand master of the Michigan Grand Lodge and Grand Commander of the Michigan Knights Templars. He was a communicant of St. John's Episcopal Church in St. Johns, and for nearly twenty-five years was senior warden. He married, May 29, 1856, Mary Jane Mead of Hillsdale, Mich., who died the next year, and on Apr. 12, 1859, he married her sister, Martha Minerva, who died in 1861; the following year, Aug. 12, he married Mary Cecilia, daughter of John Swegles, one of the leading figures in Michigan affairs and founder of the village of St. Johns. Spaulding died at his home in Georgetown, D. C., survived by his wife, four sons, and a daughter.

[C. W. Spalding, *The Spalding Memorial: A Genealogical Hist. of Edward Spalding . . . and His Descendants* (1897) ; *Biog. Dir. Am. Cong.* (1928) ; *Who's Who in America,* 1922–23 ; *Washington Post,* Aug. 1, 1922 ; *N. Y. Times,* Aug. 1, 1922 ; manuscript memoirs of General Spaulding ; information from members of his family.]   J. W. W.

SPEAR, CHARLES (May 1, 1801–Apr. 13, 1863), Universalist minister, friend of prisoners, was born in Boston, Mass. As a child he was apparently nurtured in a religious atmosphere, for a younger brother (born in Boston, Sept. 16, 1804) was named after John Murray [*q.v.*], the founder of Universalism in America. Accordingly, although completing an apprenticeship as a printer, Charles likewise studied theology under the Rev. Hosea Ballou and was called to minister to the Universalist parish in Brewster (1828), then in Rockport (*c.* 1837), and finally in Boston (1839). On Dec. 22, 1829, he married Mrs. Frances King of Brewster. A little book, *Names and Titles of the Lord Jesus Christ,* which he compiled and printed in 1841, gained him a wider acquaintance, but his religious fervor was more a product of sentiment than of scholarship, and it was his sympathy for the fate of both condemned and discharged criminals that made his life significant. Printing his *Essays on the Punishment of Death* in 1844, Spear deserves some of the credit for the formation in that year of the Society for the Abolition of Capital Punishment, of which he became the faithful secretary. It was at this point that a squabble among the friends of prison reform in New England alienated a large faction from the dogmatic leadership of Louis Dwight of the Boston Prison Discipline Society, and Spear found the occasion propitious for the establishment of a thin weekly paper, *The Hangman,* the first issue appearing in January 1845; a year later the title was changed to *The Prisoners' Friend,* and in September 1848, on the occasion of a John Howard Festival in Boston, organized by Spear and a group of friends, the weekly was transformed into a monthly. Meanwhile, in its pages and subsequently in book form, Spear had published *A Plea for Discharged Convicts* (1846).

While Charles was issuing appeals against the irrevocable punishment of death and in behalf of the friendless discharged man, his younger brother, John Murray Spear, also a Universalist minister and collaborator in the journal, undertook a personal mission of visitation, befriending and assisting released convicts. The two brothers thus introduced Boston to the humanitarian activities later to be organized under parole laws, in which pioneering they had been preceded by Isaac Tatem Hopper [*q.v.*] in New York. Depending entirely on the philanthropy of their subscribers—numbering only 1,500 in 1845—and faced with the fact that "all do not pay up," they were fortunate in attracting a donation of $225 from Jenny Lind in 1850. Wider recognition was received in the same year when an official request from England for information concerning the laws of the states on capital punishment was referred by the authorities at Washington to Charles Spear. Interpreting this request as a providential command to go over and help Europe abolish capital punishment, he proceeded to Washington to gather information and to enlarge the circle of his backers. Securing a letter from Daniel Webster, he journeyed to England in time to attend the Congress of the Friends of Universal Peace at London in 1851, but his "Notes by the Way," sent back to his brother who was temporarily in charge of the *Prisoners' Friend,* naïvely reveal that his inspection of English and French prisons and his attempted conference with several British statesmen made very little stir in the Old World. His dream of a world association to safeguard the interests of convicts remained to be dreamed afresh by Enoch Cobb Wines [*q.v.*] in the late sixties.

Even back in Boston the friendless prisoner was becoming still more friendless as the fifties advanced, and Charles Spear, with many of his subscribers disgruntled over the cost of the editor's five-month "vacation," found the support for his paper steadily decreasing and was forced to discontinue publication in 1859 or shortly thereafter. Meanwhile John Murray Spear had been attracted to Spiritualism, and had become a medium in 1852. Perhaps because of his unorthodox interests, his later years are obscure, though publications of his indicate that he was still living in 1872. It is evident that Charles kept to the firmer path of the devout friend of the down-trodden, for in 1858, together with his second wife, Catharine Swan Brown, he engaged in missionary activities (*Missionary Labors of Mr. and Mrs. Charles Spear for the Year Ending January, 1859,* 1859), and soon after the outbreak of the Civil War he secured an appointment as hospital chaplain in Washington, where he contracted a disease and wasted away his remaining energies visiting wounded soldiers. His decease in 1863 was mourned by *The Liberator* (Apr. 24, 1863, p. 67) as that of a modest philanthropist who found "his chief happiness in laboring for others, especially for the neglected and most wretched classes of society."

[Charles Spear's publications are listed in Joseph Sabin, Wilberforce Eames, and R. W. G. Vail, *A Dict. of Books Relating to America,* XXII, 487–89; of these the volumes of the *Prisoners' Friend,* 1846–59, have the greatest value to the biographer, but see also J. G. Adams, *Fifty Notable Years: Views of the Ministry of Christian Universalism* (1882); *Boston Transcript,* Apr. 14, 22, 1863. For John M. Spear his *Labors for the Destitute Prisoner* (1851), *The Educator* (1857), and *Twenty Years on the Wing* (1873), as well as Frank Podmore, *Modern Spiritualism* (2 vols., 1902), are of assistance.]   B. McK.

SPEAR, WILLIAM THOMAS (June 3, 1834–Dec. 8, 1913), jurist, was born at Warren, Trumbull County, Ohio. He was named after a grandfather who was a soldier at Valley Forge, crossed the Delaware with the army of Washington, and was present at the surrender of Cornwallis at Yorktown. The boy's father, Edward Spear, a worker in wood, was a native of Pennsylvania; his mother, Ann (Adgate) Spear, was from Norwich, Conn. In 1819 they moved to Warren, Ohio. Here William received in the public schools and at a private academy his early education. Learning the trade of a printer, he worked as such on the local newspaper in Warren, in Pittsburgh, and in New York City. Returning to Warren, he became deputy clerk of the probate and common pleas courts and began the study of law, his preceptor being Jacob D. Cox [*q.v.*], later governor of Ohio and secretary of the interior in the cabinet of President Grant. In 1858 he was admitted to the bar and soon after went to the Harvard Law School, where he was graduated in 1859. He then formed a partnership in Warren with his old instructor, Cox, and on Sept. 28, 1864, was married to Frances E. York of Lima, N. Y. Having served as city solicitor of Warren for two terms, he was elected in 1871 prosecuting attorney of Trumbull County and reëlected for a second term. In 1878 he was elected a judge of the common pleas court, and while serving his second term in this office was in 1885 elected a member of the Ohio supreme court. He continued as such until 1912, when, on account of the "Progressive Party" split in the Republican organization, he was defeated for reëlection. This continuous tenure of over twenty-seven years as a supreme court judge was the longest in the history of the court. Leaving the bench at the age of seventy-nine, frail of body but keen of mind, he opened an office for the practice of law in Columbus, Ohio. Here within a year he died, survived by his wife and four children.

There was nothing spectacular about his career; his was the cloistered life of a deep student of the law who for thirty-four years served as a judge. He took no part in public affairs and wrote nothing of a lasting character save the 288 opinions, some of which are to be found in every volume of the *Ohio State Reports* from the 44th to the 87th inclusive, and which exceed in number those written by any other judge of the Ohio supreme court. He did not possess an unusually quick mind. "He is the hardest worker on the bench of any judge I ever knew" was the testimony of one who was for years the supreme court reporter (E. O. Randall, in *Ohio State Journal*, Dec. 9, 1913). This capacity for labor, combined with a remarkable fairness of judgment, liberality of view, and kindliness of manner, made him a truly great judge, and one of the ablest and most conscientious of those who have served on the Ohio bench.

["William T. Spear: A Memorial of His Life, Character, and Pub. Services," 89 *Ohio State Reports*, xlviii; *Western Reserve Chronicle*, Dec. 11, 1913; *Ohio State Jour.* (Columbus), Dec. 9, 1913; *Ohio Law Reporter*, May 27, 1912, Dec. 15, 1913, July 20, 1914; *Case and Comment*, May 1911; *Who's Who in America*, 1912–13.]   A. H. T.

SPEED, JAMES (Mar. 11, 1812–June 25, 1887), lawyer, federal attorney-general, was the descendant of James Speed who emigrated from England and settled in Surry County, Va., about the end of the seventeenth century. His grandfather, also James, settled near Danville, Ky., about 1783. His father, John, settled in Jefferson County, at "Farmington," five miles from Louisville, and married Lucy Gilmer Fry. There James was born. He attended school in the neighborhood, and then at St. Joseph's College in Bardstown, where he was graduated probably in 1828. The next two years he spent in the county clerk's office in Louisville. He then went to Lexington to the law department of Transylvania University. In 1833 he began the practice of law in Louisville and continued with a few interruptions as long as he lived. In 1841 he married Jane Cochran, the daughter of John Cochran of Louisville. They had seven sons. In 1847 he was elected to the state legislature. In 1849 he was defeated for the state constitutional convention by James Guthrie, on the emancipation issue. His grandfather, James, had suffered defeat for a seat in the Constitutional Convention of 1792 on the same issue, for hostility to slavery long characterized the Speed family. In 1849 Speed wrote a series of letters to the *Louisville Courier*, in which he boldly assumed a position against slavery that definitely limited his political career until the outbreak of the Civil War. For two years, from 1856 to 1858, in addition to his legal practice, he taught law in the University of Louisville.

In the secession movement he took the typical Kentucky attitude—a desire to preserve the Union and at the same time avoid war. He was a member of the Union central committee, which was set up to merge the Bell and Douglas forces, and which on Apr. 18, 1861, issued an address lauding Gov. Beriah Magoffin's refusal to respond to Lincoln's call for troops and advising the people to refuse aid to either side. In 1861 he was elected to the state Senate as an uncompromising Union man, and he continued in this position until 1863. He became a principal adviser of Lincoln on affairs in Kentucky, and in the latter part of 1864 was appointed attorney-general. He was the brother of Joshua Fry Speed, Lincoln's intimate friend. He was also a Southerner and a conservative, a man agreeing with the President's policy of moderation toward the Southern states, and a man for whom Lincoln had a personal affection. Lincoln could say of him in Washington, that he was "an honest man and a gentleman, and one of those well-poised men, not too common here, who are not spoiled by a big office" (Lord Charnwood, *Abraham Lincoln*, 1916, p. 404). As long as Lincoln lived Speed held true to the President's policy;

but when a strange fascination for the radicals developed, Charles Sumner was then able to say of him that he was the "best of the Cabinet" (J. F. Rhodes, *History of the United States, 1904*, V, 533). He favored military commissions to try the Lincoln conspirators and other persons not protected by their paroles (*Opinion of the Constitutional Power of the Military to Try and Execute the Assassins of the President, 1865*, and the *American Annual Cyclopaedia*, Appletons', 1866), though he consistently held that Jefferson Davis should be tried by the civil courts. He early began to advocate negro suffrage and was soon as critical as Stanton of President Johnson. He opposed Johnson's veto of the Freedmen's Bureau bill and favored the Fourteenth Amendment. `As time went on he found himself increasingly out of harmony with Johnson, and on July 17, 1866, he resigned. The breaking point seems to have developed over the Philadelphia convention, when, in answer to a communication sent him by the committee in charge of promoting that convention, he declared that he thoroughly disapproved of it.

He then returned to Louisville and later bought a home near the city, "The Poplars." In September 1866 he attended the Southern Radical convention in Philadelphia and was made its permanent chairman. There he made a bitter speech against Johnson, characterizing him as the "tyrant of the White House"—an expression he later changed to "tenant" (J. G. Blaine, *Twenty Years*, 1886, II, 226; G. F. Milton, *Age of Hate*, 1930, p. 726, footnote 28). Back in Kentucky he took a prominent part in Radical Republican activities. In 1867 he received forty-one votes in the Kentucky legislature for senator but was defeated; the next year the Kentucky delegates gave him their votes for vice-president; in 1870 he ran for the national House of Representatives and was defeated. In 1872 and in 1876 he was a delegate to the Republican National Convention and each time served on the committee of resolutions. As he grew older he reverted to the ways and beliefs of his earlier life. He continued his practice of law in Louisville and from 1872 to 1879 he taught law again in the University of Louisville. In 1884 he supported Grover Cleveland for the presidency. A few years before his death he became an unwilling party to a controversy with Joseph Holt, over the question of President Johnson having received the recommendation for mercy in the Mrs. Surratt case. Against the almost frantic appeals of Holt to Speed to say publicly that Johnson saw the recommendation, Speed resolutely refused on the ground of the rule against

divulging cabinet proceedings. Speed's last public appearance was at Cincinnati on May 4, 1887, when he addressed the Society of the Loyal Legion, *Address of Hon. James Speed before the ... Loyal Legion* (1888). He died at "The Poplars" and was buried in Cave Hill Cemetery at Louisville.

[James Speed, *James Speed, A Personality* (1914); *Biog. Encyc. of Kentucky* (Cincinnati, 1878); *Diary of Gideon Welles* (1911), vol. II; A. J. Beveridge, *Abraham Lincoln* (1928), vol. I; *Appletons' Ann. Cyc. ..., 1887* (1888); *War of the Rebellion: Official Records (Army)*, 2 ser., VII; Lewis and R. H. Collins, *Hist. of Ky.* (2 vols., 1874); Thomas Speed, *Records and Memorials of the Speed Family* (1892); *New York Herald*, July 17, 1866; *Louisville Commercial*, June 26, 1887; *North American Review*, July, Sept. 1888; letters in Joseph Holt Correspondence and Edwin M. Stanton MSS. in the Lib. of Congress and in the Charles Sumner MSS. in Harvard College Lib.]   E. M. C.

SPEER, EMORY (Sept. 3, 1848–Dec. 13, 1918), congressman, jurist, was born in Culloden, Ga., the son of the Rev. Eustace Willoughby and Anne (King) Speer. Both his grandfather and his father were Methodist divines of notable eloquence. The boy inherited much of their fine physique and power, and grew up alert and headstrong, moving with his parents from town to town as his father was sent to different churches. At sixteen he fell in with Lewis' Kentucky brigade of mounted infantry retreating before Sherman's advance, and volunteered enlistment in their ranks. The war over, he entered the University of Georgia and was graduated in 1869 with distinction in scholarship and oratory. The same year he was admitted to the bar. He served as state solicitor-general in 1873–76 and as congressman in 1879–83. Elected first as an Independent Democrat, and reëlected as an Independent, he affiliated with the Republicans before his second term expired, thus losing the good will of many of his constituents but gaining substantial reward. He was put on the Ways and Means Committee and on the conference committee on the tariff bill of 1883, and in that year was appointed district attorney of the North Georgia circuit by President Arthur. Despite vigorous Democratic opposition, he was promoted, Feb. 18, 1885, to the federal court of the southern district of Georgia, a position which he held until his death.

As judge he was distinguished by his dignity and formality and his ultra-courteous bearing. His enemies—and they were many—accused him of tyranny and pomposity, but politics and local interests were doubtless at the bottom of hostile criticism. In 1913 an attempt was made to divide the district, and upon its failure, a House resolution was secured appointing a committee to visit Georgia and conduct an *ex-parte* investigation of Speer's conduct, as a basis for impeachment. His defense was superb; the record fills a pamphlet of 331 pages (*House Resolution No. 234 . . . Statement and Reply of Judge Emory Speer,* n.d., probably privately printed). Upon recommendation of the investigating committee, the proceedings were dropped for lack of evidence. During the thirty-three years of his incumbency Judge Speer wrote pioneer decisions in many cases involving the expansion of federal powers. His opinions commanded respect not only for their lucidity and admirable marshaling of evidence, but for their literary excellence. They cover a wide range of cases, the most outstanding, *United States* vs. *Greene and Gaynor* (146 *Federal Reporter,* 803), being regarded as one of the greatest criminal trials ever conducted in a federal court. His later decisions proved a valuable support to the government in upholding vital statutes evoked by the World War.

Speer was dean of the Law School of Mercer University from 1893; in 1897 he published *Lectures on the Constitution of the United States.* His addresses on public occasions revealed his talents at their best, and were in constant demand; some of these were published under the title *Lincoln, Lee, Grant and Other Biographical Addresses* (1909). From 1877 to 1885 he served as alumni trustee of the University of Georgia. He was twice married; his first wife, Sallie Dearing of Athens, died while he was a member of Congress, leaving him with five small daughters, all of whom grew up, married, and survived him. While still in Congress and in his early thirties he married Eleanora D. Morgan, daughter of Dr. James E. Morgan of Washington. He began practice in Athens, removed to Atlanta in 1883, and in 1887 to Macon, where he established an attractive home, "The Cedars," identified with the rest of his life. He was buried in Riverside Cemetery at Macon.

[*Federal Reporter,* 1885–1918; *Investigation of the Behavior of Judge Emory Speer,* being *House Report No. 1176,* 63 Cong., 2 Sess.; *Conduct of Emory Speer: Hearings before a Subcommittee of the Committee on the Judiciary, House of Representatives, Sixty-third Cong.* (1914); O. A. Park, "Judge Emory Speer," *Report . . . Ga. Bar Asso.,* 1919; *Who's Who in America,* 1918–19; *Case and Comment,* Mar. 1912; *Savannah Morning News,* Dec. 14, 1918; *Atlanta Constitution,* Dec. 14, 1918; personal acquaintance.] J. H. T. M.

SPEER, WILLIAM (Apr. 24, 1822–Feb. 15, 1904), Presbyterian missionary, was born in New Alexandria, Westmoreland County, Pa. He was a great-grandson of James Speer who came from Ireland to Lancaster County, Pa., about 1759, and a grandson of the Rev. William Speer, who graduated from Dickinson College, Carlisle, Pa., and became the first chaplain at the

seat of the new government of the Northwest Territory, Chillicothe, Ohio; his parents were Dr. James Ramsey Speer, a physician of Pittsburgh, and Hetty (Morrow) Speer. William spent a year at Jefferson College, Canonsburg, Pa., and then entered Kenyon College, Gambier, Ohio, from which he was graduated in 1840. He began the study of medicine in his father's office, but having been strongly influenced toward missionary work while he was at Jefferson by Walter M. Lowrie, later known as the "martyr missionary," he began the study of theology at Allegheny Seminary, now Western Theological Seminary, Pittsburgh. On Apr. 21, 1846, he was graduated and licensed to preach, and on June 16 of the same year he was ordained to the Presbyterian ministry. Married May 7, 1846, to Cornelia Brackenridge, he sailed at once, with his wife, for missionary work in China. A child was born to them there, but under the severe climatic conditions both mother and child died.

With two colleagues, Speer organized the first Presbyterian mission work in Canton and set the program for all subsequent work in that area. Broken by the death of his wife and child and in failing health, he returned to America in 1850. On Apr. 20, 1852, he was married to Elizabeth B. Ewing, a daughter of the Hon. John H. Ewing of Washington, Pa. Chinese from Canton Province were then pouring into California in search of gold, and Speer felt called to minister to the people with whom he had labored in their native land. Accordingly, he and his wife sailed for the Pacific coast by way of the Isthmus of Panama. Arriving there, he began a varied program of religious and social work among the rapidly increasing numbers of Chinese people, chiefly in San Francisco. He organized the first Chinese church on the Western Continent, and established a weekly paper, called *The Oriental,* printed in both Chinese and English and dealing with both secular and religious matters, which did much to soften the racial antipathy that made the life of the Chinese almost intolerable. He also led in the successful agitation for the repeal of legislation in the mining regions unfavorable to the Chinese.

With his educational and organizing experience, he was well qualified for the service he was called to render when, in 1865, he was chosen secretary of the board of education of the Presbyterian Church. To this work he gave ten years of active leadership during the disordered period following the Civil War. He developed higher standards of education for the ordained ministry, encouraged the building and maintenance of church colleges and academies, and enlarged the available scholarship funds devoted to the education of worthy candidates for the Presbyterian ministry. He constantly contributed to weekly and monthly periodicals, and was the author of a number of books; among them *Semicentenary Review: A Practical Summary of the Principles and Work of the Presbyterian Church* (1869), *The Oldest and the Newest Empire: China and the United States* (1870), *The Great Revival of 1800* (1872), *God's Rule for Christian Giving* (1875). Retiring from active service in 1876, he traveled extensively throughout the Orient, reviewing the progress of the work of which he was a pioneer. He died at Washington, Pa.

[David Elliott, *The Life of the Rev. Elisha Macurdy* (1848), pp. 269–71; William Rankin, *Memorials of Foreign Missionaries of the Presbyterian Church* (1895); *Who's Who in America,* 1903–05; F. A. Virkus, *The Compendium of Am. Geneal.,* vol. V (1933); Alfred Nevin, *Encyc. of the Presbyterian Church in the U. S. A.* (1884); *Presbyterian Banner,* Mar. 3, 1904; date of death from death notice in *Pittsburgh Dispatch,* Feb. 17, 1904.]   W. C. C.

SPEIR, SAMUEL FLEET (Apr. 9, 1838–Dec. 19, 1895), physician, was born in Brooklyn, N. Y., the son of Robert Speir, a New York merchant, and Hannah (Fleet) Spier, descendant of Capt. Thomas Fleet, a retired officer of the British navy who settled on Long Island about 1660. He was educated in the Brooklyn Polytechnic Institute and in the medical department of the University of the City of New York (later New York University), from which he graduated in 1860. The following two years he spent in attendance upon European clinics, mainly in Paris. There he became interested in the recently devised plaster of Paris splint, and, returning home, he brought it to the attention of the military authorities for use upon the battlefields of the Civil War. In 1862 the Sanitary Commission fitted up for him two boats, with which he assisted in caring for the wounded of the Army of the Potomac, then engaged in the Peninsular campaign. In 1865 he went again to Europe for post-graduate study in ophthalmology and otology, afterwards returning to his practice in Brooklyn, where he spent the remainder of his life. He was married to Frances S. Hegeman, daughter of Peter Hegeman of New York, in 1869. Possessed of a handsome face and figure, with a gracious manner, he attained a success in professional practice hardly equaled in Brooklyn; for many years he was the unquestioned leader of the medical profession of the city. He served on the surgical staff of the Brooklyn Eye and Ear Infirmary and of the Brooklyn Dispensary, held the posts of physician, curator, and microscopist at the Brooklyn City Hospital, and

for a time (1864–65) was demonstrator of anatomy at the Long Island College Hospital. In 1864 he attracted the attention of the local profession by a paper, "On the Pathology of Jaundice" (*Transactions of the American Medical Association,* vol. XV, 1865, pp. 311–36), which was awarded a gold medal by the American Medical Association, and he made a notable contribution to the literature of pathology in his *The Use of the Microscope in the Differential Diagnosis of Morbid Growths* (1871). For the control of arterial hemorrhage during operations he devised an ingenious instrument called an artery constrictor, which is noted in the standard surgical works of the day, though it was soon superseded by the artery forceps, and was awarded a prize by the Medical Society of the State of New York (*Medical Record,* Apr. 1, 1871). In 1875 he published *Going South for the Winter,* a volume on the climatic treatment of tuberculosis. In addition to his county and state medical societies and the American Medical Association, he was a member of the New York Pathological Society and a fellow of the New York Academy of Medicine. Though a skilful surgeon, he was loath to resort to surgery until the aid of therapeutics had been exhausted.

He was a leader in public charity work, with original ideas on the subject. He organized the seaside Home for Children and the Helping Hand Dispensary, two examples of intelligently applied charity. Of a different character was the Robins Island Club, which he organized as a "sportsmen's seaside home." He was a lover of nature, happiest when in the fields or upon the sea. On his estate on Gravesend Bay he maintained a refuge for wild animal life, grew flowers in profusion, and collected rare and exotic plants; here too he kept a kennel of prizewinning hunting dogs and a herd of Guernsey cattle. His later years were saddened by the death of a son and a daughter, and by a protracted period of invalidism which terminated suddenly with a gastric hemorrhage probably due to a malignant growth. He was survived by his wife and one daughter.

[W. B. Atkinson, *Physicians and Surgeons of the U. S.* (1878); *Jour. Am. Medic. Asso.,* Dec. 28, 1895; Robert Ormiston, W. H. Bates, and E. W. Wright, in *Brooklyn Medic. Jour.,* May 1896, pp. 325–31, with portrait; obituary in *N. Y. Tribune,* Dec. 20, 1895.]
                                        J. M. P.

SPENCER, AMBROSE (Dec. 13, 1765–Mar. 13, 1848), congressman and jurist, second son of Philip and Abigail (Moore) Spencer, was born in Salisbury, Conn. He was descended from William Spencer, who came to New England with his brothers about 1630 and later was one of the first settlers of Hartford, Conn. Philip Spencer was an iron dealer and an ardent Whig in the Revolution who furnished cannon and supplies to the American armies. Ambrose, with his elder brother, was prepared for college under a Presbyterian minister in Canaan and in 1779 was admitted to Yale; in 1782 he transferred to Harvard, where he was graduated with honors in 1783. Until 1785 he studied law at Sharon, Conn., under John Canfield, whose daughter, Laura, he married, Feb. 18, 1784. After three years as clerk in law offices in Claverack and Hudson, N. Y., he was admitted to the bar in December 1788. In 1786 he was appointed clerk of the city of Hudson. In 1793 he was elected as a Federalist to the Assembly and in 1795 to the state Senate, where he served until 1802. In 1796 he was made assistant attorney general of Columbia and Dutchess counties, and in 1797 he was a member of the Council of Appointment. Spencer served loyally in the Federalist party until 1798, when he astounded his colleagues by announcing the transfer of his allegiance to the Republicans. Federalists attributed his action to disappointment at not being made comptroller, an accusation which Spencer denied with characteristic vehemence (*Albany Gazette,* Jan. 12, and Oct. 5, 1801; Hammond, *post,* I, 177).

Elected with DeWitt Clinton [*q.v.*] in 1800 to the all-powerful Council of Appointment, Spencer entered upon two decades of almost undisputed dictatorship of politics in New York. With a thoroughness rarely equaled in partisan politics, he and Clinton inaugurated the spoils system in New York by wholesale removals. The only high office untouched was that of attorney general; but the incumbent, Josiah Ogden Hoffman [*q.v.*], resigned in 1802 to make way for Spencer, no doubt by virtue of a bargain between the two (McBain, *post,* p. 111; Hammond, I, 182), though Spencer denied it emphatically. He was appointed to the supreme court bench, Feb. 3, 1804, and though he remained there until 1823, becoming chief justice in 1819, his power and activity in politics increased rather than abated.

His first wife, who had borne eight children, died in 1807, and shortly afterward he married Mary, sister of DeWitt Clinton and widow of Burrage Norton. She died a few months later, and in September 1809 he married her sister Catherine (Clinton) Norton, widow of Samuel, the brother of Burrage. In 1812 Spencer separated from Clinton on account of the latter's attitude toward the Bank of America, the reëlection of Gov. D. D. Tompkins [*q.v.*], and the war with Great Britain (see *The Coalition,* 1812, by Spencer and John Armstrong); possibly these

factors were augmented also by family differences occasioned by his third marriage (Spencer to James Clinton, Feb. 19, 1810, letter in New York Historical Society). To counteract the advocacy of the Bank by the *Albany Register,* Spencer established the *Albany Republican,* by means of which during the campaign he bitterly castigated Clinton, the Bank, and all those opposing him. With Clinton in retirement, Spencer's power in state politics from 1812 to 1816 was supreme. In 1816 he suddenly healed the breach with Clinton and forced him from retirement against the party's wishes. Dissatisfaction with Spencer's autocratic manner as well as his autocratic power, together with a growing feeling against judges in politics, produced a reaction against his rule which found expression in the New York constitutional convention of 1821 and in the person of Martin Van Buren. The amendments abolishing the Council of Appointment, extending the suffrage, and popularizing the judiciary were direct blows at Spencer, who, as a member of the convention from Albany, opposed them to the last. His regard for the sanctity of the eighteenth-century safeguards of property and privilege led him to refuse to sign the new constitution.

Subsequently he served two years (1824–25) as mayor of Albany, was an unsuccessful candidate for the United States Senate in 1825, was elected to Congress in 1829, saw his son John Canfield Spencer [*q.v.*] become secretary of war in Tyler's cabinet, and in 1844 served as president of the Whig Convention in Baltimore; but, as a factor to be reckoned with in New York politics, his career ended in 1823 when Gov. Joseph Yates [*q.v.*] nominated him for reappointment to the supreme court and the Senate rejected him by an almost unanimous vote.

Spencer's great ability as a jurist has been obscured by the prominence and fury of his political activities. With a trace of provincialism, Henry Adams declared that "Ambrose Spencer's politics were inconsistent enough to destroy the good name of any man in New England; but he became a Chief Justice of ability and integrity" (*History of United States,* vol. I, 1889, p. 112). Not a deep student of legal lore like James Kent [*q.v.*], he wrote brief opinions wherein citations were few and reasoning was based on commonsense realities. Frequently he disregarded settled dicta and often his dissent gave the first expression to what became accepted doctrine in New York courts, as in *Mann & Toles* vs. *Pearson* (2 *Johnson's Reports,* 37). He was accused of allowing politics to influence his decisions, as in *Tillotson* vs. *Cheetham* (3 *Johnson,* 56) and

In the Case of John V. N. Yates (4 *Johnson*, 317). His greatest contribution in the formative years of the New York judiciary was probably in domesticating the English Common Law (*e.g., Jackson* vs. *Brownson, 7 Johnson, 227*), wherein, with constructive foresight, he guided the jurisprudence of New York along lines he thought it should follow, rather than along channels marked out by judicial precedent. Somewhat in the manner of John Marshall and Theophilus Parsons [*qq.v.*], he created judicial law largely by the sheer force of his own reasoning and authority. He occasionally dissented from the opinions of Chancellor Kent and was sustained in the court of errors, as in *Anderson* vs. *Roberts* (18 *Johnson*, 515).

Of stately presence, with dark flashing eyes, energetic, domineering manner, and often vehement speech, Spencer was capable of inspiring fear, hostility, and admiration in his contemporaries. He retired in 1839 to Lyons, N. Y., where he took up agriculture, and formally accepted the Christian religion. This latter course he urged upon his lifelong friends, John Armstrong and Chancellor Kent, who, in obedience to a masterful voice, both accepted his advice.

[There are scattered letters in N. Y. State Lib., N. Y. Hist. Soc., Lib. Cong., and elsewhere. Printed sources include W. B. Sprague, *A Discourse Commemorative of the Late Hon. Ambrose Spencer* (1849); A. B. Street, *The Council of Revision of the State of N. Y. . . . and Its Vetoes* (1859); H. L. McBain, *DeWitt Clinton and the Origin of the Spoils System in N. Y.* (1907); J. D. Hammond, *The Hist. of Pol. Parties in State of N. Y.* (2 vols., 1842); D. S. Alexander, *A Pol. Hist. of the State of N. Y.*, vols. I, II (1906); D. D. Barnard, *A Discourse on the Life, Character and Public Services of Ambrose Spencer* (1849), a eulogy which is valuable for its estimate of Spencer's contribution to jurisprudence, but which, like that by W. B. Sprague, must be used carefully; Nathaniel Goodwin, *Geneal. Notes . . . of Some of the First Settlers of Conn. and Mass.* (1856); *Albany Law Jour.*, Apr. 29, 1876, Dec. 25, 1886; *Memorial of Ambrose Spencer* (1849), including resolutions and the eulogies by Sprague and Barnard as well as that by Horatio Potter, *Christian Suffering* (1849); *Pa. Law Jour.*, June 1848; C. E. Fitch, *Encyc. of Biog. of N. Y.*, vol. I (1916); L. B. Proctor, "Ambrose Spencer," *Am. Lawyer*, IV, 8–9 (1848); G. C. Verplanck, *Dick Shift or The State Triumvirate* (1819); "The Autobiography of Martin Van Buren," ed. by J. C. Fitzpatrick, *Ann. Report Am. Hist. Asso. . . . 1918*, vol. II (1920); L. B. Proctor, *The Bench and Bar of New York* (1870); N. H. Carter and W. L. Stone, *Reports of the Proc. and Debates of the Conv. of 1821 for the Purpose of Amending the Constitution of the State of New York* (1821); *Journal of the Convention* (1821); Joel Munsell, *The Annals of Albany* (10 vols., 1850–59); Wm. Johnson, *N. Y. Sup. Ct. Reports* (1804–23) and *N. Y. Chancery Reports* (1814–23); *Daily Albany Argus*, Mar. 14, 1848. A series of articles by M. D. Rudd, "Ambrose Spencer," in the *Lakeville Journal* (Lakeville, Conn.), Jan. 3, 10, 17, 23, 31, and Feb. 7, 1935, is based in part on local manuscript records.]   J. P. B.

SPENCER, ANNA GARLIN (Apr. 17, 1851– Feb. 12, 1931), journalist, minister, educator, reformer, was born in Attleboro, Mass. She came of fine old New England stock, her father, Francis Warren Garlin, being a descendant of Peter Garland [*sic*], who was in Charlestown, Mass., in 1637, and her mother, Nancy Mason (Carpenter) Garlin, a descendant of William Carpenter, one of the founders of Rehoboth, Mass., in 1643. Her education, according to her own statement, was "largely private." She began her career as a teacher in the public schools of Providence, R. I. (1870–71), and as a member of the staff of the *Providence Daily Journal* (1869–78). On Aug. 15, 1878, in Providence, she married William Henry Spencer, a Unitarian clergyman; they lived in parishes in Haverhill and Florence, Mass., and Troy, N. Y. As early as 1870 she had discovered and had begun using her remarkable abilities as a public speaker; now, under the influence of her husband, she occasionally preached in Unitarian and other liberal pulpits. On Apr. 19, 1891, she was ordained and installed as minister of the Bell Street Chapel (independent), Providence, and thus became one of the few women clergymen of America, among whom she was decidedly the most successful. Her ministry at the Bell Street Chapel, which began before her ordination, lasted fourteen years.

It was during these years that she began those multifarious labors in education, philanthropy, and humanitarian endeavor which made her a national figure. Her interests ran all the way from local charities to world movements of reform, such as woman's suffrage and international peace, and her ceaseless energies took her from pulpit and platform to college halls and administrative offices. The list of her activities is bewildering. Early in her career she enlisted in the moral education movement, and served as an officer of the American Purity Alliance, a federation of moral education societies later merged with the American Social Hygiene Association.

During the years 1903 to 1928 she lectured widely. She was associate leader of the New York Society for Ethical Culture, staff lecturer and associate director in the New York School of Philanthropy (later the New York School of Social Work), special lecturer on education and social service at the University of Wisconsin, director of the Summer School of Ethics of the American Ethical Union, director of the Institute of Municipal and Social Service, Milwaukee, Wis., acting professor of sociology and ethics at the Meadville Theological School, Meadville, Pa., lecturer at the University of Chicago, and at Teachers College, Columbia. Her offices in women's organizations for suffrage, temperance, child-labor reform, and world peace were numerous and important, and her labors for these causes nation-wide. She wrote many newspaper and magazine articles, pamphlets, hymns, and books, among them *The History of the Bell Street Chapel Movement* (1903), *Woman's Share in Social Culture* (1913), and *The Family and Its Members* (copyright 1923). In her seventy-ninth year she was serving as director of the family relations division of the American Social Hygiene Association, New York. On Feb. 10, 1931, after a full day at her desk, she attended a public dinner for world peace and was there stricken with a sudden heart attack. She died two days later, survived by her daughter. Physically diminutive, clad always in a Quaker-like garb of gray, with brilliant eyes shining beneath a crown of white hair, she was a person of exceptional intellectual and spiritual power, and her magnetism, kindled from an inner fire of moral conviction, was extraordinary. When she spoke, in a full, resonant voice that seemed to belie her tiny frame, she held attention and commanded allegiance. More strong than gentle, vibrant rather than serene, she demonstrated in many fields her capacity for public leadership.

[Anna Garlin Spencer's name appears in W. H. Spencer, *Spencer Family Record* (1907), as Anna Carpenter Garlin. See J. G. Garland, *Garland Geneal., the Descendants of Peter Garland, Mariner* (1897); *Who's Who in America*, 1901–02, and 1930–31; *Woman's Who's Who of America*, 1914–15; *Jour. of Social Hygiene*, Mar. 1931, with portrait; *Survey*, Mar. 15, 1931; *N. Y. Times*, Feb. 13 (obituary), 14, 15, 1931; manuscript bibliog. of Anna Garlin Spencer's writings, Teachers Coll., Columbia Univ.; personal acquaintance.]   J. H. H.

SPENCER, CHRISTOPHER MINER (June 20, 1833–Jan. 14, 1922), inventor, manufacturer, son of Ogden and Asenath (Hollister) Spencer, was born on his father's farm at Manchester, Conn. He attended school until he was fourteen and then entered the machine shop of the Cheney silk mills in Manchester. Upon completing his apprenticeship in 1849, he worked in the Cheney mills as a journeyman machinist until 1853, when he went to Rochester, N. Y., and found employment in a tool-building and locomotive shop with a view to acquiring familiarity with machinery other than that used in textile manufacture. For the succeeding seven years he worked successively in the Colt armory, Hartford, Conn., and in the Cheney silk mills. During this period he obtained his first patent, which was for an automatic silk-winding machine that was utilized by the Willimantic Linen Company.

By this time he had turned his attention to firearms, for which he had had a passion since boyhood, and on Mar. 6, 1860, he received patent No. 27,393 for a self-loading, or repeating, rifle.

This was immediately adopted by the United States government and a company known as the Spencer Repeating Rifle Company was organized to manufacture it. Before the Civil War was over, about 200,000 Spencer rifles had been produced. Meanwhile, he continued his inventions in firearms and in 1862 patented a breech-loader; in 1863, a magazine gun; and in 1866 obtained two additional patents for improvements on the latter. At the close of the war he went to Amherst, Mass., and became associated there with Charles E. Billings [*q.v.*] in the Roper Arms Company, established to manufacture Spencer's magazine gun. This venture was not a success, and in 1869 Spencer and Billings went to Hartford, Conn., formed the Billings & Spencer Company, and began the manufacture of drop forgings. It is said that the partners' work in this field did more for the art of drop forging, particularly with respect to the accuracy and application of the process, than that of anybody else. Spencer continued with his inventive work and perfected a machine for turning sewing machine spools. This suggested to him the idea of a machine for turning metal screws automatically. Working secretly, on Sept. 30, 1873, he obtained patent No. 143,306 for a machine for making screws. The great feature of this invention was the automatic turret lathe. Peculiarly enough, this feature, with its blank cam cylinder and flat strips adjustable for various jobs, was wholly overlooked by the patent attorney, with the result that Spencer could claim no patent rights to it. Convinced of the efficiency of his screw machine, he gave up active connection with the Billings & Spencer Company in 1874, and in 1876 formed with others the Hartford Machine Screw Company and, as superintendent, laid the foundation of one of the largest industrial enterprises in Hartford. He could not forget firearms, however, and in 1882 withdrew from the screw company in order to manufacture a new repeating shotgun that he had invented. He organized the Spencer Arms Company at Windsor, Conn., and although the gun was a success mechanically, the company failed and Spencer lost heavily. He then returned to the field of automatic lathes, and in 1893 organized the Spencer Automatic Machine Screw Company at Windsor, Conn., which, together with his directorship of the Billings & Spencer Company, consumed his entire attention until his retirement some years before his death. He was twice married: first, in June 1860, to Frances Theodora Peck, who died in 1881; second, July 3, 1883, to Georgette T. Rogers. He died in Hartford, survived by three children.

[E. S. Farrow, *Farrow's Military Encyc.* (1885), vol. III; J. W. Roe, *English and Am. Tool Builders* (1926); *Commemorative Biog. Record of Hartford County, Conn.* (1901); L. W. Case, *The Hollister Family* (1886); *Hartford Courant*, Jan. 15, 1922; Patent Office records; information from family.]

C. W. M—n.

SPENCER, CORNELIA PHILLIPS (Mar. 20, 1825–Mar. 11, 1908), author, was born in Harlem, N. Y. She was the daughter of Judith (Vermeule) and James Phillips. Her father was a teacher and Presbyterian minister who emigrated from England to the United States in 1818. Her mother (sometimes called Julia) was a member of Dutch families of distinction, whose settlement in New Jersey antedated the Revolution. Growing up in Chapel Hill, N. C., where in 1826 her father accepted the chair of mathematics at the University of North Carolina, she lived the life of that time and place though she was better educated than the average Southern girl. In addition to acquiring the customary ladylike accomplishments, she learned Latin, Greek, and mathematics, and her reading was both extensive and well-chosen. On June 20, 1855, she married James Munroe Spencer, a lawyer of Clinton, Ala., and removed to her husband's home, but after his death in 1861 she returned to Chapel Hill with her young daughter. Her first book, *The Last Ninety Days of the War in North Carolina* (1866), was written immediately after the Civil War at the request of her friend, Gov. Zebulon Baird Vance.

She distinguished herself in the years following the war by her efforts on behalf of the University of North Carolina, which was pitiably impoverished. In 1868 the reconstruction government of the state closed the institution, and then reorganized and reopened it; after a year or two this ill-advised experiment ended in failure, and the university was closed a second time. Through all these changes Mrs. Spencer remained in Chapel Hill, writing for the conservative papers of the state accounts of the inadequacy and dishonesty of the new régime. During 1869 she published a series of "Pen and Ink Sketches of the University of North Carolina As It Has Been" in the *Raleigh Sentinel* (Apr. 26–July 6, 1869). When the second closing of the university occurred she rallied the alumni, most of whom she knew personally, to the task of restoration, and by means of innumerable letters and many newspaper articles helped to crystallize public sentiment in favor of it. The reopening of the university was finally voted by the assembly of the state on Mar. 20, 1875, and soon she had the satisfaction of seeing it functioning usefully again under the presidency of Kemp

Plummer Battle [*q.v.*]. From 1869 through the seventies she contributed a weekly column to the *North Carolina Presbyterian* (Charlotte, N. C.) and in 1889 published *First Steps in North Carolina History*. During her last years she lived in Cambridge, Mass., with her daughter and son-in-law. Her journals, letters, and other papers which have been preserved reveal both her personal charm and her strength of character.

[K. P. Battle, *Hist. of the Univ. of N. C.* (2 vols., 1907–12); Hope S. Chamberlain, *Old Days in Chapel Hill: Being the Life and Letters of Cornelia Phillips Spencer* (1926); obituaries in *Boston Transcript*, Mar. 12, and *News and Observer* (Raleigh, N. C.), Mar. 13, 1908; Spencer papers in the possession of the N. C. Hist. Commission and the Univ. of N. C.]

H. S. C—in.

SPENCER, ELIHU (Feb. 12, 1721–Dec. 27, 1784), clergyman, was one of the group of sturdy Presbyterian ministers who helped to shape American religious and political history during the last half of the eighteenth century. Although his work was done in the middle colonies, he was of New England ancestry, birth, and education. His parents were Isaac and Mary (Selden) Spencer of East Haddam, Conn., where he was born; and he was a descendant of Jared or Garrard (the name is given under various spellings) Spencer, who came to Massachusetts about 1630, later went to Connecticut, and was one of the first settlers of Haddam. Elihu graduated from Yale College in 1746. David and John Brainerd [*qq.v.*] were his second cousins, and on David's recommendation the Boston commissioners of the Society for the Propagation of the Gospel appointed Spencer and Job Strong missionaries to the Indians. They passed the winter of 1747–48 with John Brainerd at Bethel, N. Y., and the following summer with Jonathan Edwards [*q.v.*] at Northampton, Mass., preparing for their work. On Sept. 14, 1748 Spencer was ordained at Boston as missionary to the Oneidas, and later proceeded to Onooguagua (Unadilla), Otsego County, N. Y. The difficulties of the work, augmented by an unfortunate choice of interpreter, so discouraged him that in the spring of 1749 he abandoned the enterprise. In the meantime he had made progress on a vocabulary of the Oneida language.

On Feb. 7, 1749/50 he was installed as pastor of the Presbyterian church, Elizabethtown, N. J., succeeding Jonathan Dickinson [*q.v.*], and on the fifteenth of October married Joanna, daughter of John and Joanna Eaton of Shrewsbury, N. J., where he also ministered to a congregation. During the early part of his pastorate at Elizabethtown, in 1752, he was elected to the board of trustees of the College of New Jersey, of which he was an active member till his death, being placed almost immediately on a committee to negotiate with the people of Princeton with regard to locating the college there. From 1756 to 1759 he served the church in Jamaica, L. I., as stated supply, and in 1758 was chaplain to the New York troops in the French and Indian wars. For six years he was in charge of the church in Shrewsbury and served smaller parishes, but when in May 1765 Rev. John Rodgers [q.v.] left St. George's, Del., Spencer was invited to supply the church there and the Forest Church, Middletown, and on Apr. 17, 1766, was installed over the two congregations. Resigning in 1769, he became pastor at Trenton, N. J., and continued as such until his death.

In addition to his parochial work his services were many and varied. In the ecclesiastical bodies to which he belonged he held important offices. With Alexander MacWhorter [q.v.], he was sent by the synod in 1764 to visit the scattered congregations of the South, especially those in North Carolina, as general adviser and counselor. They were to adjust bounds, administer the sacraments, ordain, and instruct in matters of discipline. His earlier interest in the Indians did not altogether pass, and he was an official visitor to Brainerd's Indian School. From 1770 to 1775 he was a delegate from the synod to the Congregational and Presbyterian Council. An ardent supporter of the Revolution, he was requested by the North Carolina delegates in the Continental Congress, December 1775, to visit, in company with MacWhorter, the more isolated portions of the South, inform the people there of existing conditions, and insure their support of the war. This mission they performed. His activities enraged the Loyalists, and a price of one hundred guineas was placed upon his head. During the British occupancy of Trenton he retired to St. George's, but his home and library were destroyed. On appointment of Congress he acted as chaplain to hospitals in the vicinity of Trenton from 1777 to 1781. His ability to deliver a sermon or address at short notice won for him the appellation "ready money Spencer." A letter of his to Ezra Stiles [q.v.] on Dissenting interest in the middle colonies in 1759 seems to have been printed. An addition to it is in the *Collections of the Massachusetts Historical Society* (2 ser., vol. I, 1814). His elder brother, Joseph [q.v.], was a general in the Revolution; one of his daughters married Jonathan Dickinson Sergeant [q.v.], and was the mother of John and Thomas Sergeant [qq.v.]. The inscription on the tombstone over his grave in the churchyard at Trenton describes him as "possessed of fine genius, of great vivacity, of eminent and active piety," adding, "his merits as a minister and as a man stand above the reach of flattery."

[W. H. Spencer, *Spencer Family Record* (1907); S. S. Rogers, E. S. Lane, E. V. Selden, *Selden Ancestry* (1931); Nathaniel Goodwin, *Geneal. Notes . . . of Some of the First Settlers of Conn. and Mass.* (1856); F. B. Dexter, *Biog. Sketches Grads. Yale Coll.,* vol. II (1896); E. F. Hatfield, *Hist. of Elizabeth, N. J.* (1868); John Hall, *Hist. of the Presby. Church in Trenton, N. J.* (1859); *A Hist. of Trenton, N. J., 1679–1929* (2 vols., 1929), pub. by the Trenton Hist. Soc.; Richard Webster, *A Hist. of the Presbyt. Church in America* (1857); W. B. Sprague, *Annals Am. Pulpit,* vol. III (1858); F. B. Heitman, *Hist. Reg. of Officers of the Continental Army* (1914).]   H. E. S.

SPENCER, JESSE AMES (June 17, 1816– Sept. 2, 1898), Episcopal clergyman, educator, author, was born at Hyde Park, N. Y. His father, Reuben, was a seafaring man of Connecticut stock; his mother, Mary (Ames), came from Sudbury, Mass. When Jesse was seven years old the family moved to Poughkeepsie, N. Y., and three years later, to New York City. Here he received his education and did most of his life's work. His mother died when he was thirteen and soon afterward he left school and was employed for two and a half years in a print shop in lower Manhattan, a training which was to influence his entire career. "I was steady and diligent and resolved to learn the trade thoroughly," he records in his autobiography (*Memorabilia,* p. 20). At the end of this experience he became assistant to his father, who had been appointed city surveyor. While in this position he decided to enter the Episcopal ministry. During the year 1833–34 he attended Trinity School, then entered Columbia College, where he was graduated in 1837, having received several medals for proficiency in Greek and English, and in the fall entered the General Theological Seminary, graduating in 1840. On Sept. 4 of that year he married Sarah J. E. Loutrel. Ordained deacon June 28, 1840, by Bishop B. T. Onderdonk, he became rector of St. James's Church, Goshen, N. Y., and while there he was ordained to the priesthood, July 28, 1841, by Bishop Onderdonk.

Resigning his rectorship in 1842 because of ill health, he made a tour of Europe, and on his return in 1843 supplied for several parishes, taught, wrote magazine articles, and did editorial work for publishers. In 1844 he published his first book, a volume of sermons, *The Christian Instructed in the Ways of the Gospel and the Church.* About this time he purchased the school of the Rev. C. D. Jackson, near Washington Square, New York, but for lack of capital gave it up within a few months. For several years, including this period, he edited Greek and Latin textbooks for D. Appleton & Company. In 1845 he founded a monthly magazine, *The Young Churchman's Miscellany,* which was suspended in 1848. In its pages appeared as a serial his *History of the Reformation in England,* published in book form in 1846. During these years he edited *The Four Gospels and Acts of the Apostles, in Greek, with English Notes* (n.d.; 1847?). Owing to another failure of his health, in 1848, he went abroad for two years. On his return, in 1850, he became professor of Latin and Oriental languages in Burlington College, Burlington, N. J., but resigned the following year and became editor and secretary of the General Protestant Episcopal Sunday School Union, New York, serving in this capacity until the Union, in 1857, transferred its publishing business to E. P. Dutton & Company. During the year 1856–57 he supplied the pulpit at St. Thomas' Church, New York, and in the following year assisted in Trinity Chapel, at the same time tutoring private pupils and doing editorial work for Appletons' *American Cyclopædia.* In 1863 he became rector of St. Paul's Church, Flatbush, but resigned two years later, returning to New York City and resuming his work of teaching, editing, and supplying various pulpits. He was elected secretary of the Corporation for the Relief of Widows and Children of Clergymen in the State of New York and in 1869 was appointed professor of Greek in the College of the City of New York, a position he held for ten years, on his retirement being made professor emeritus. Difficult years followed, owing to his advanced age. In 1883 he was appointed custodian of the Standard Bible of the Church.

Spencer was of the school of broad churchmanship. His point of view was established when, during his time as student at the seminary, the controversy over the Oxford Movement in England was raging. His evangelical position is emphasized in all his theological writings. His best known work was *History of the United States* (3 vols., copr. 1858), continued by B. J. Lossing, and copyrighted in 1878 as *The Complete History of the United States of America* (4 vols.). It was translated into German and Spanish. In addition to the works named, Spencer was the author of *The East: Sketches of Travel in Egypt and the Holy Land* (1850), *The Inspiration of the Holy Scriptures* (1865), *The Young Ruler Who Had Great Possessions* (1871), *Pronunciation of Ancient Greek* (1875), *Memorabilia of Sixty-five Years* (1890), *Papalism versus Catholic Truth and Right* (1896), and edited *The Woman of Early Christianity: a Series of Portraits , with Appropriate Descriptions by Several American Clergymen*

(1852). He died in his eighty-third year, survived by one son.

[Spencer's *Memorabilia of Sixty-five Years* (1890); *Churchman,* Sept. 10, 1898; *N. Y. Tribune,* Sept. 3, 1898.]   G. E. S.

SPENCER, JOHN CANFIELD (Jan. 8, 1788–May 17, 1855), lawyer, congressman, cabinet officer, was born in Hudson, N. Y., the eldest son of Ambrose Spencer [*q.v.*] and Laura (Canfield) Spencer. His father soon afterward became established in Albany; and subsequently held many important public offices—a fact of considerable significance in relation to the public career of the son. John C. Spencer entered college at Williamstown, Mass., where he remained about a year; then transferred to Union College, Schenectady, N. Y. He graduated with high honors in 1806, and during the following year became the private secretary of Gov. Daniel D. Tompkins [*q.v.*]. He also began the study of law in Albany, and in 1809 was admitted to the bar. On May 20 of that year he married Elizabeth Scott Smith, daughter of J. Scott Smith of New York City, and soon thereafter moved to Canandaigua, Ontario County, N. Y., where, with very limited funds, he began to practise law.

His rise was rapid. Within two years he became a master in chancery, and in 1813 was appointed brigade judge-advocate in active service along the frontier. He was appointed postmaster at Canandaigua in 1814, and in 1815 became assistant attorney-general and district attorney for the five western counties of the state. While holding the last-named office, he was elected to Congress by the Clintonian faction. During his term in the House (1817–19), he served on a committee which investigated and reported unfavorably on the affairs of the Bank of the United States (*House Document 92,* 15 Cong., 2 Sess.). While still in Congress, he was nominated for United States senator by the Clintonian members of the legislature, but was defeated in the ensuing election. He was next elected to the General Assembly, serving three terms, 1820, 1821, 1822, in the first as speaker. He was a member of the state Senate during four sessions, 1825–28. In 1827 Gov. DeWitt Clinton [*q.v.*] appointed him with John Duer and B. F. Butler [*qq.v.*] on a committee to revise the statutes of the state. Spencer's abilities, including an amazing grasp of detail, eminently qualified him for this task and contributed greatly to the successful revision (*The Revised Statutes of the State of New York,* 3 vols., 1829).

Having in the meantime joined the Anti-Masonic party, Spencer, in 1829, became special prosecuting officer to investigate the abduction of

William Morgan [*q.v.*], and, despite attempts to assassinate him, pursued the investigation until lack of funds necessitated his resignation in 1830. His pamphlet, *A Portrait of Free Masonry* (1832), was reprinted in John Quincy Adams' *Letters Addressed to Wm. L. Stone . . . upon the Subject of Masonry* (1833). In 1831 and 1833 he was again a member of the state Assembly. In 1837 he moved to Albany, where he spent the greater portion of his remaining years. In 1838 he edited *Democracy in America,* translated by Henry Reeves from the French of De Tocqueville. Joining the Whig party, he became secretary of state of New York in 1839, and upon the reorganization of the cabinet following the death of President Harrison in 1841, he was appointed by President Tyler as secretary of war. His adherence to Tyler cost him the friendship of the Clay Whigs, and when in January 1844 Tyler nominated him to the United States Supreme Court, the Senate rejected him. He remained in the War Department from Oct. 12, 1841, until Mar. 3, 1843; then became secretary of the treasury, but resigned, May 2, 1844, because of his opposition to the annexation of Texas. After retiring from public life, his last important legal case was the successful defense of Dr. Eliphalet Nott [*q.v.*], president of Union College, against the charge of misappropriating college funds (*Argument in Defense of the Rev. Eliphalet Nott,* 1853).

In personal appearance Spencer has been described as tall and slender; with eyes "fierce and quick-rolling," and a face bearing "the line of thought and an unpleasant character of sternness." He was considered one of the ablest lawyers of his day, but his devotion to detail often prevented his taking a broad view of public problems. He was notoriously short-tempered, and his inability to yield to or work with others kept him from acquiring the political power he desired. He died in Albany, survived by his wife and three children. One son, Philip, serving as acting midshipman under Alexander Slidell Mackenzie [*q.v.*], was executed for attempted mutiny on the brig *Somers,* in 1842, while his father was secretary of war.

[L. B. Proctor, *The Bench and Bar of N. Y.* (1870); Joel Munsell, *The Annals of Albany,* vols. III (1852), VI (1855); W. A. Butler, *The Revision of the Statutes of the State of N. Y. and the Revisers* (1889); D. S. Alexander, *A Pol. Hist. of the State of N. Y.,* vols. I, II (1906); E. A. Werner, *Civil List . . . of N. Y.* (1889); *Evening Post* (N. Y.), May 21, 1855; *N. Y. Daily Times,* May 19, 1855; *Albany Evening Atlas,* May 18, 19, 1855; *Albany Argus,* May 19, 1855.]

R. W. I.

SPENCER, JOSEPH (Oct. 3, 1714–Jan. 13, 1789), Revolutionary soldier, was the son of Isaac and Mary (Selden) Spencer, the brother of Elihu Spencer [*q.v.*], and the great-grandson of Jared (Gerard) Spencer, an English emigrant who settled in Haddam, Conn., about 1662. In that part of the town which in 1734 became East Haddam Joseph was born, related by blood and marriage to half the countryside, as he was to his second cousins John and David Brainerd [*qq.v.*] and their sister Martha, to whom he was married on Aug. 2, 1738. Throughout his adult life he enjoyed official position in the community, was probate judge from 1753 to his death, deputy to the Assembly in most of the sessions between 1750 and 1766, and assistant after 1766. In 1767 he became deacon of the Millington Congregational Church. He was an officer in the last two of the colonial wars. In 1747 he was commissioned lieutenant of the company raised in Millington Parish, became a major in 1757, lieutenant-colonel in 1759, and colonel in 1766. At the outbreak of the Revolution he was chosen brigadier-general of the Connecticut forces and was stationed at Roxbury early in May 1775. Notwithstanding his experience, his military rank in the colony, and his civil position he found himself superseded, when on June 20, 1775, the Continental Congress raised Israel Putnam [*q.v.*] to the rank of major-general, while two days later it commissioned Spencer, his superior officer in the Connecticut line, as brigadier-general. In his disappointment and resentment Spencer left the army without leave or notice to the new commander-in-chief, George Washington, and returned to Connecticut, where opinion about the propriety of his conduct was divided. Silas Deane wrote to his wife that he "once had a good opinion of him, but his leaving the forces . . . shocks it very greatly . . . I wish him to resign at once and let another take his place" (*Connecticut Historical Society Collections, post,* p. 288). On the other hand, forty-nine of his fellow officers at Roxbury addressed a letter to the Connecticut Assembly asking it to take up the matter with the Congress. The governor and council drafted a letter and appointed two members to try to reconcile Spencer to the situation. This was arranged, and he served through the siege of Boston and in New York. On Aug. 9, 1776, he became major-general. In September he was one of the three officers who advised Washington to attempt to hold New York City. Ordered to New England in December, he took up headquarters at Providence and planned a movement against the enemy. When he was criticized for his failure in the autumn of 1777 he asked for and received a court of inquiry, which exonerated him. However, he resigned on Jan. 13, 1778.

At home in Connecticut he was at once appointed to the council of safety and in 1779 was chosen a member of the Continental Congress, in which he took his seat on Mar. 27, 1779. He was also elected to the Assembly, deputy in 1778 and assistant in 1779, and he again served on the council of safety, in 1780 and 1781. He died in East Haddam, survived by his second wife, Hannah (Brown) Southmayd Spencer, to whom he was married in 1756. Of his thirteen children, Martha became the mother of Spencer Houghton Cone [q.v.] and Joseph the father of Elizabeth Spencer who married Lewis Cass [q.v.].

[Some papers in the Lib. of Cong.; C. B. Whittelsey, *Hist. Sketch of Joseph Spencer* (1904) and also in *Decennial Register of the Soc. of the Sons of the Rev. in . . . Conn.* (1913); H. B. Niles, *The Old Chimney Stacks* (1887), pp. 118–22; *The Public Records of the Colony of Conn.*, vols. IX–XV (1876–90); *The Public Records of the State of Conn.*, vols. I–III (1894–1922); *The Writings of George Washington*, vols. IV–XI (1931–34), ed. by J. C. Fitzpatrick; *Conn. Hist. Soc. Colls.*, vol. II (1870); *Am. Archives*, 4 ser., II, cols. 1585–86 (1839), ed. by Peter Force; *Jour. of the Continental Cong.*, vol. XIII (1909), ed. by W. C. Ford; L. A. Brainard, *The Geneal. of the Brainerd-Brainard Family* (1908), vol. II, pt. 7, p. 70.]   K. E. C.

SPENCER, PITMAN CLEMENS (July 28, 1793–Jan. 15, 1860), surgeon and lithotomist, was born in Charlotte County, Va., the second son of Gideon Spencer, a lieutenant in the Revolutionary War, colonel of militia, and member of the Virginia General Assembly, and Catherine Clements (or Clemens, as her son seems to have spelled it), daughter of Dr. John Clements of Essex County. The family medical tradition descended to her sons, Pitman and Mace Clements Spencer. Pitman's early education was meager, a disadvantage which he overcame in later life by diligent study. For six or seven years, beginning in 1810 and interrupted only by a brief service as surgeon's mate to a detachment at Norfolk during the War of 1812, he studied medicine under his older brother, Mace. Then he went to Philadelphia for further training, became a pupil of Wistar, Chapman, and Physick, and in April 1818 received his M.D. degree from the University of Pennsylvania. Returning to Virginia, he practised with Dr. Archibald Campbell at Nottoway for several years; but in 1827 his eagerness for wider experience took him to Europe. For three years he traveled, studying surgery and anatomy in London and Paris especially. In Paris he laid the foundation for his later fame as a specialist in urinary surgery, studying under Dupuytren and observing the operations of Civiale, who had just made public a new method of lithotrity, or stone-crushing.

He acquired in Paris a fine set of crushing instruments, and devoted many hours to acquiring skill in their use.

Upon his return to Virginia he settled in Petersburg, where he remained the rest of his life, and rapidly acquired fame as a surgeon. In August 1833 his first published article appeared in the *American Journal of the Medical Sciences,* with the title, "Case of Urinary Calculus successfully treated by Lithotrity." However, he soon abandoned stone-crushing for lithotomy, which he first performed in 1833. His article, "Results of Fifteen Operations for Lithotomy," published in the same journal, July 1850, and reprinted in the *Stethoscope,* March 1851, shows the influence of his Paris training, for he "uniformly operated with the same instrument, viz. lithotome caché . . . of Baron Dupuytren" (*Virginia Medical Journal,* July 1858). By 1858 his lithotomies totaled twenty-eight, with only two deaths, the first two he performed, a mortality of one in fourteen. The rate in Philadelphia was one in eight, and in French hospitals one in six. He also wrote on other subjects, describing a remarkable case of tumor-removal for the *American Journal of the Medical Sciences,* January 1845; a successful operation for "Occlusion of the Vagina," for the *Stethoscope,* April 1851; and "A Case of Empyema," *Virginia Medical and Surgical Journal,* January 1855.

A contemporary spoke of Spencer as "a born surgeon . . . bold to recklessness in his operations, but his success was marvelous" (Claiborne, *post,* p. 121). The success was no doubt partly due to his great care of patients before and after operation and to his free use of soap and water. His name became a household word in Virginia and North Carolina and was well known nationally. He was president of the Petersburg Medical Faculty in 1851 and vice-president of the Medical Society of Virginia in 1855. He was unmarried and died in Petersburg.

[Will Books, Essex County, Va., nos. 12, 13; article by R. M. Slaughter, in H. A. Kelly, W. L. Burrage, *Am. Medic. Biog.* (1920); G. N. Mackenzie, *Colonial Families of the U. S.,* vol. VI (1917); L. A. Burgess, *Va. Soldiers of 1776,* vol. I (1927); J. H. Claiborne, *Seventy-Five Years in Old Va.* (1904); W. B. Blanton, *Medicine in Va. in the Eighteenth Century* (1931); *Md. and Va. Medic. Jour.,* Mar. 1860; *N. Am. Medico-Chirurgical Rev.,* May 1860; *Am. Medic. Recorder,* vol. I (1818), p. 304; *Daily Richmond Enquirer,* Jan. 18, 1860.]   L. F. C.

SPENCER, PLATT ROGERS (Nov. 7, 1800–May 16, 1864), penman, was born at East Fishkill, Dutchess County, N. Y., the youngest of the eleven children of Caleb and Jerusha (Covell) Spencer. His father, a farmer and a soldier in the Revolution, was of Rhode Island stock; his mother was a native of Chatham, Mass., on Cape Cod. The Spencers moved, when Platt was about three years old, to the vicinity of Wappingers Falls and thence to Windham, Green County, where after a few years the father died. Foot-loose and hopeful, however poor, the family set out for the West and on Dec. 5, 1810, after a wagon jaunt of fifty-one days, pulled up at Jefferson, Ashtabula County, Ohio. Except for short absences occasioned by his duties as a peripatetic teacher and for two others of somewhat longer duration, Spencer lived the rest of his life in that county. From earliest childhood he had a Chinese reverence for calligraphy, which, growing to a master passion, became his mission and his livelihood and made his name familiar, like Noah Webster's and Lindley Murray's, in the schoolrooms of his country. As a small boy he studied and often criticized severely the handwriting of the notices posted on the village bulletin-board and practised his own chirography on sandbeds, snowbanks, and other available surfaces, for paper was scarce and expensive in the back settlements. In later years he enjoyed telling the story, half humorous and half pathetic, of his first piece of writing paper. By the time he was twenty years old he had developed his characteristic hand, a sloping, semi-angular style, rapid and legible, and easily lending itself to embellishment with mazy capitals and shaded lines of the sort affected by old-time writing masters. His schooling having been of the scantiest, he was practically self-taught, but a dilute Rousseauism was in the atmosphere, and to Nature Spencer gave all credit for his art, maintaining in prose and rhyme that he had found his inspiration in the graceful forms of the feathered grass, the vine, and the undulating waves of Lake Erie's shore. After a little experience as clerk in a store and supercargo on a lake vessel, he entered on his life-work as a teacher of penmanship. Besides conducting his own school in a log-house on his farm at Geneva, Ohio, he traveled around the country teaching in various academies and business colleges. His innocent, winning manner, the skill and enthusiasm of his teaching, and the conviction with which he preached the moral, esthetic, and pecuniary benefits of the gospel of penmanship made him irresistible. In 1848 he first issued copy-slips with printed instructions; copy-books followed about 1855; and soon a whole series of textbooks began to appear. His five grown sons and a favorite nephew became his chief disciples, and continued and spread his work.

Spencer was married in 1828 to Persis Duty, by whom he had six sons and five daughters. Despite his devotion to his profession, he took great delight in his family life and had several avocations. In spirit even more a reformer than a pedagogue, he was, like most reformers, too magnanimous to restrict himself to one line and gave himself generously to the temperance and anti-slavery causes. For a time he lived in Oberlin in order to enjoy congenial society. He was treasurer of his county for twelve years and secretary, from its founding in 1838, of its historical society. His wife's death in 1862 was a great affliction to him, and he survived her by less than two years. He died at his home at Geneva, Ohio.

[Biog. sketch, with an introductory note by J. A. Garfield, in *Hist. of Ashtabula County, Ohio* (1878), ed. by W. W. Williams; R. C. Spencer, *Spencer Family Hist. and Geneal.* (Milwaukee, 1889); *The Am. Ann. Cyc.*, 1864.]   G. H. G.

SPENCER, ROBERT (Dec. 1, 1879–July 10, 1931), painter, was born at Harvard, Nebr., the son of Solomon Hogue Spencer, a Swedenborgian clergyman, and Frances (Strickler) Spencer. On his father's side he was descended from Samuel Spencer, who emigrated from England and settled in Upper Dublin, Pa., prior to 1699, and on his mother's from Hollanders who early settled in Virginia. His boyhood was enlivened by close association with his father, and by their common liking for reading and the classics. Because of the movement of the family from Nebraska to Kansas, Missouri, and Virginia, his early education was somewhat desultory, but they finally remained long enough in Yonkers, N. Y., for him to be graduated in 1899 from high school. He studied at the National Academy of Design in New York, 1899–1901, and at the New York School of Art, 1903–05, where he was encouraged by William Merritt Chase [q.v.], the painter. He worked also with Robert Henri [q.v.], Francis Coates Jones, and Frank DuMond. Except for one year spent in an engineering office, he never deviated from painting as a career. Although he traveled extensively abroad, he did not study there. After his early study in New York, where he developed an interest in slum dwellers as subjects for his sketches, he lived in Frenchtown, Point Pleasant, and Lumberville, Pa., studying with Daniel Garber and painting landscape direct from nature. About 1909 he settled in New Hope, Pa., where he made his home until the end of his life. There he turned to imaginative and philosophical composition, or for subject matter drew upon the mills; in a later and final period he painted almost entirely from notes, again making use of the mills and reviving an earlier interest in portraiture. To eke out a living he tried potboilers for a time under the pseudonym of John St. John but without success. In 1914, however, his "Repairing the Bridge" was purchased by the Metropolitan Museum of Art, and he was elected an associate member of the National Academy of Design, of which he became a full member in 1920. On Feb. 27, 1914, he married a painter, Margaret A. Fulton, of Santa Barbara, Cal., by whom he had two daughters. Tall and spare, he was never robust, and suffered several nervous breakdowns that led to prolonged depression and culminated in his suicide in his home, July 10, 1931. He was survived by his wife and children.

He won numerous prizes, among them the second Hallgarten prize at the National Academy of Design (1913), the Jenny Sesnan gold medal of the Pennsylvania Academy of the Fine Arts (1914), the Inness gold medal of the National Academy of Design (1914), a gold medal at the Panama Pacific International Exposition (1915), the gold medal and purchase prize of the Boston Art Club (1915); third prize in the International Exhibition of the Carnegie Institute, Pittsburgh (1926); and a gold medal at the Sesquicentennial Exposition at Philadelphia (1926). One of his paintings, "Across the River," was purchased in 1928 by the National Academy of Design through the Ranger Purchase Fund. He is represented also in the National Arts Club, New York; the Corcoran Gallery of Art, Washington; the Art Institute of Chicago; Carnegie Institute, Pittsburgh; the Albright Art Gallery of the Buffalo Academy of Fine Arts; the Brooklyn Museum; the Detroit Institute of Arts, and the Phillips Memorial Gallery, Washington, where a number of his paintings ("The Evangelist," "Mountebanks and Thieves," "The Barracks," "Day in March," "The End of the Day," "The Seed of a Revolution," "Ship Chandler's Row," and "The Auction") may be seen.

[*Who's Who in America*, 1930–31; F. N. Price, in *Internat. Studio*, Mar. 1923, with portrait; *Am. Art Ann.*, 1929, biog. directory; E. A. Jewell, in *N. Y. Times*, July 5, 1931, sec. 9; Duncan Phillips, *A Collection in the Making* (copr. 1926); obituaries in *Art News*, Aug. 15, 1931, and *Pub. Ledger* (Phila.), July 11, 1931; information from Mrs. Robert Spencer.]

D. G.

SPENCER, SAMUEL (Mar. 2, 1847–Nov. 29, 1906), railway engineer and executive, was born in Columbus, Ga., the only child of Lambert and Vernona (Mitchell) Spencer. He was in the fifth generation of descent from James Spencer, who settled in Talbot County, Md., in 1670. Spencer obtained his early education in the elementary schools of Columbus and at the Georgia

Military Institute in Marietta, which he left in 1863 to enlist in the Confederate army. He served first as a private in the "Nelson Rangers," an independent company of cavalry, and later under Forrest, remaining in uniform until April 1865. Resuming his education, he entered the junior class of the University of Georgia at Athens, and was graduated B.A. in 1867 with first honors. He studied engineering at the University of Virginia in the two following years, and received the C.E. degree in 1869.

Spencer's lifelong railway career began with the Savannah & Memphis Railroad, on which he acquired practical engineering experience in various capacities between 1869 and 1872, ending as principal engineer. After his marriage on Feb. 6, 1872, to Louisa Vivian Benning, daughter of Henry Lewis Benning [*q.v.*], he went north and was for a few months clerk to the superintendent of the New Jersey Southern Railroad at Long Branch, N. J. He then spent four years in charge of one of the transportation divisions of the Baltimore & Ohio Railroad. For a brief period he was general superintendent of the Long Island Railroad, but in 1879 returned to the Baltimore & Ohio as assistant to the president. He rose through successive vice-presidencies to the presidency in December 1887. His incumbency of that office was brief and stormy. His central purpose was to reduce the floating debt, which had grown to over $8,000,000, by rewriting book values and by other drastic measures. In this program he met with considerable success, but his opponents forced his resignation after a year, fearing that Drexel, Morgan & Company were seeking through Spencer to gain control of the road.

In March 1889, Spencer became the railroad expert for Drexel, Morgan & Company, and by December 1890, had become a partner in the firm. In this capacity he had an important part in the Morgan railroad reorganization campaign, particularly in regard to southern railroads. He was appointed in 1893 one of the receivers for the Richmond & Danville Railroad, and for the East Tennessee, Virginia & Georgia Railway. In 1894 a Morgan reorganization created the Southern Railway out of the Richmond & Danville and other moribund southern railroads, and Spencer was made the first president. The twelve intervening years before his death saw efficient, conservative management and great expansion of this Morgan-controlled railroad. Between 1896 and 1906 the mileage of the system increased from 4,391 to 7,515, the number of passengers from 3,427,858 to 11,663,550, the tons of freight from 6,675,750 to 27,339,377, and the annual earnings from $17,114,791 to $53,641,438. The emphasis, however, had been placed on increase in volume of traffic, and the road's physical condition was not improved proportionately. In the two years preceding his death, Spencer was much in the public eye as an opponent of further legislation for rate-regulation. Although he agreed that secret, discriminatory rates were indefensible, and did not deny that the railroads were affected with a public interest, he characterized further government control as "commercial lynch law" (*New York Tribune*, Oct. 12, 1905, p. 9). He appeared before the House Committee on Interstate and Foreign Commerce as spokesman for the railroads, and carried on a vigorous campaign, public and private, against the passage of the Hepburn Act of June 29, 1906.

Spencer was one of seven persons killed in a rear-end collision of two fast passenger trains on his own road, near Lawyers, Campbell County, Va. He was survived by his wife, and by two sons and a daughter. He was regarded with affection by his employees, who erected a monument to him in front of the Southern Railway station at Atlanta. The railroad he administered was a vital factor in the economic development of the New South, and at Spencer's death he was perhaps the most outstanding southerner in the American business world.

[*In Memoriam Samuel Spencer* (1910); Rosewell Page, biog. ed., *Univ. of Va. Its History, Influence, Equipment and Characteristics* (1904), vol. I; Edward Hungerford, *The Story of the Baltimore & Ohio Railroad, 1827–1927* (1928), vol. II; Lewis Corey, *The House of Morgan* (1930); W. J. Northen, *Men of Mark in Ga.*, IV (1908); *Outlook*, Dec. 8, 1906; *Who's Who in America*, 1906–07; Samuel Spencer, "Railway Rates and Industrial Progress" in *Century Mag.*, January 1906; *Collier's*, May 4, 1917, p. 14; *Poor's Manual of the Railroads of the U. S.*, 1869–1906; *N. Y. Tribune*, Feb. 1, Oct. 12, 1905, Nov. 30, Dec. 1, 8, 1906; *Evening Star* (Washington, D. C.), Nov. 29, 30, Dec. 1, 2, 3, 1906.]

L. P. B.

SPERRY, ELMER AMBROSE (Oct. 12, 1860–June 16, 1930), engineer, inventor, was born at Cortland, Cortland County, N. Y., the son of Stephen Decatur and Mary (Burst) Sperry and a descendant of Richard Sperry who came to America from England and settled in the New Haven Colony between 1640 and 1650. From his father, who was engaged in the production, transportation, and sale of lumber, Sperry may have inherited his leaning toward machinery, and from his mother, who died soon after his birth, his keen mathematical sense. He was brought up by his paternal grandparents in Cortland. During his school days he took every opportunity to examine and study the machinery in the various shops and factories there and in the laboratories at Cornell University, not far away. For a time

he worked in a book bindery after school hours, and with the money he saved, and through an arrangement made possible by the Young Men's Christian Association, he visited the Centennial Exhibition in Philadelphia in 1876. This visit, with the inspiration he received from the mechanical exhibits he saw there, he always regarded as having determined the direction of his career.

After completing his common-school education he spent three years at the State Normal and Training School, Cortland, and a year of casual attendance at Cornell, 1878–79. Here he had his first insight into dynamo electric machinery, particularly the Gramme type of dynamo built in the University shops. He immediately saw possibilities of increasing the production of electric current by making certain alterations in the dynamo, and succeeded in interesting a Cortland manufacturer, who financed him in the construction of his improved dynamo and an arc lamp as well. These were so successful that he was sent to Syracuse immediately to build a large dynamo capable of operating a series of arc lamps. Upon completing this work early in 1880, he went to Chicago, Ill., and there founded the Sperry Electric Company to manufacture dynamos and arc lamps, and also other electrical appliances. His factory was opened on his twentieth birthday, and in two or three years many industrial plants and municipalities in the Northwest were furnished with Sperry arc light equipment. One of his most notable installations was the 40,000 candle-power electric beacon on the Board of Trade tower, 350 feet high, the highest beacon in the world at that time.

In the middle eighties, Sperry turned his attention to the application of electricity to mining, and in 1888 organized the Sperry Electric Mining Machine Company to manufacture an electrically driven, undercutting, punching machine for use in soft coal mines. He subsequently perfected a continuous chain undercutter, and designed new electric generators and electric mine locomotives, the manufacture of which was undertaken by the Goodman Manufacturing Company of Chicago. From electric mine locomotives it was but a short step to electric street-railway cars, and in 1890 Sperry founded the Sperry Electric Railway Company and established a plant for the manufacture of his cars at Cleveland, Ohio. He operated this concern until 1894, adding constantly his own patented improvements to the equipment, and then sold the plant and all his patents bearing on street railway machinery to the General Electric Company. Turning next to electric automobiles, he

454

was engaged from 1894 to 1900 in the manufacture of electric carriages of his own design, having as their particular feature an improved storage battery capable of operating a vehicle over the remarkable distance of one hundred miles. For the production of his patented storage battery the National Battery Company was organized, with works at Buffalo.

Meanwhile, Sperry had become interested in electro-chemistry, and about 1900 established in Washington, D. C., a research laboratory which he maintained for upwards of ten years. He had there as his associate C. P. Townsend, an electrochemist, and between them they evolved the so-called Townsend Process for manufacturing pure caustic soda from salt, accompanied by the production of hydrogen and chlorine compounds; this process has since been used extensively by one of the largest manufacturers of soda and chlorine products at Niagara Falls, N. Y. Another of their achievements was the chlorine detinning process, for recovering tin from old cans and scrap; this process, involving some thirty patents, was taken over by the Goldsmith Detinning Company. During these years Sperry also devised machinery for producing electric fuse wire, and established the Chicago Fuse Wire Company to manufacture it. As early as 1890 he began investigations and experiments looking toward the development of a compound internal combustion engine using low-grade fuel oil, in other words, a compound Diesel engine. This work was started in Chicago, continued in Cleveland, and after 1910, carried on in Brooklyn, N. Y.; at the time of Sperry's death eight distinct experimental engines had been produced, and the work was still in progress.

Sperry's most distinctive inventions, however, were those which put to practical use the principles of the gyroscope, which had been for several centuries merely an amazing toy. He began work on this project about 1896, and through tedious and expensive investigation and great ingenuity overcame the obstacles involved and successfully combined electrical and mechanical elements into gyroscopic compasses and stabilizers for ships and airplanes which have been great contributions to the safety and comfort of the navigation of the sea and air. The Sperry Gyroscope Company was established in Brooklyn in 1910, in which year Sperry's first compass was tried out on the battleship *Delaware* at the Brooklyn Navy Yard. The compass was shortly adopted by the United States Navy; during the World War it was used in the navies of the Allies, and subsequently by more than sixty steamship lines. The gyroscopic stabilizers for ships

appeared in 1913, and in 1914 Sperry's airplane stabilizer was awarded a first prize of 50,000 francs by the French government, through the Aero Club, in a contest for safety devices for airplanes.

In 1918 Sperry produced his high-intensity arc searchlight, 500 per cent. brighter than any light previously made; at the time of his death, it was the standard searchlight of the principal armies and navies of the world. Because of its high actinic value, it proved useful also in a totally different sphere, making possible the taking of motion pictures indoors, without the sun. In 1929 Sperry disposed of the Sperry Gyroscope Company and organized Sperry Products, Inc., to continue investigation and research in other fields. Before he died he had just completed a device for detecting flaws in railroad rails.

Sperry possessed the very unusual combination of inventive ability and clever business sense. In the course of his life he founded eight companies to manufacture his inventions, with an aggregate annual business in excess of $8,000,000. He obtained more than four hundred patents, both in the United States and in Europe, and for nearly fifty years was an unusually productive worker in a surprisingly wide field of both science and engineering. Many honors were conferred upon him. He was made a member in 1915 of the United States Naval Consulting Board, and chairman of the division of engineering and industrial research of the National Research Council. In addition to the award for his airplane stabilizer, he received in 1914 the John Scott Legacy Medal and Premium, awarded by the Franklin Institute of Philadelphia. He was awarded the Collier Trophy in 1915 and 1916; the John Fritz and the Holley medals in 1927; the American Iron and Steel Institute Medal and the Elliott Cresson Medal in 1929; two decorations from the Emperor of Japan; and two from the last Czar of Russia. Stevens Institute of Technology, Lehigh University, and Northwestern University gave him honorary degrees. He was a founder-member of the American Institute of Electrical Engineers and the American Electrochemical Society; a life member and president (1928–29) of the American Society of Mechanical Engineers; and a member of many other technical, engineering and scientific societies. He was intensely interested in promoting a better understanding between the peoples of the United States and Japan and devoted much of his time in his later years to this work. Throughout his life he was deeply grateful to the Cortland Y. M. C. A. for the opportunity afforded him to attend the Centennial

Exhibition, and in his will he bequeathed $1,-000,000 to the national organization of that body. He married Zula A. Goodman of Chicago on June 28, 1887, and at the time of his death in Brooklyn was survived by two sons and a daughter. Another son had lost his life in 1923, flying an airplane over the English Channel.

[Gano Dunn, W. L. Saunders, and B. A. Fiske, "The Engineering and Scientific Achievements of Elmer Ambrose Sperry," *Mechanical Engineering*, Feb. 1927; *Ibid.*, July, Sept. 1930; *Jour. Am. Inst. Elec. Engineers,* July 1930; *S. A. E. Jour.* (Soc. of Automotive Engineers), July 1930; *Dr. Sperry as We Knew Him* (Sperry Memorial Book Committee, Japan, 1931); *Who's Who in America*, 1926–27; H. F. Pringle, "Gadget-maker," in *New Yorker*, Apr. 19, 1930; *N. Y. Herald Tribune*, June 17, 1930; *N. Y. Times*, June 17, 1930.]   C. W. M—n.

SPERRY, NEHEMIAH DAY (July 10, 1827–Nov. 13, 1911), congressman and postmaster of New Haven, was born in Woodbridge, Conn., the third son of Enoch and Mary Atlanta (Sperry) Sperry and the descendant of Richard Sperry, an original settler in Woodbridge and one of those who aided the regicides in 1661. Nehemiah obtained a scanty education at the district school and later at a private school in New Haven, and while scarcely more than a boy taught successfully in various district schools. As a youth he learned the trade of mason and builder. In 1847 he was married to Eliza H. Sperry of Woodbridge who died in 1873 leaving two children. In 1847 also he began business as a building contractor in partnership with his brother-in-law. The firm, later known as Smith, Sperry & Treat, was successful from the start, and for more than a half century was a leading firm of contractors in New Haven. Early financial success led him into other lines of business, and he became prominent in many New Haven enterprises. He was particularly interested in transportation and among other projects organized the Fair Haven and Westville horse railroad, said to be the first street railroad in the state, obtained for it a charter from the state, and served as its president for ten years. He was also one of the promoters and incorporators of the New Haven and Derby railroad.

Although an able and successful business man, his primary interest was politics, and it is doubtful if, in length of years, his political career has been equaled in Connecticut. In 1853 he was a member of the New Haven common council, and an alderman in 1854. Originally a Whig, he threw himself into the new American or "Know-Nothing" party and was an important leader in Connecticut. As a candidate of that party he was elected secretary of state for 1855 and 1856, and only his lack of the requisite age prevented his nomination for governor in 1855. In 1856 he was a member of the platform committee of the national convention of the American party that nominated Fillmore and was one of those who bolted the convention because of its refusal to take a strong anti-slavery stand. From then on his affiliations were with the Republican party, and for many years, as chairman of the state Republican committee, he dominated Republican politics in Connecticut. He was a member and secretary of the Republican National Committee during the Lincoln administration, and one of the executive committee in charge of his reëlection. Throughout most of his life Sperry's great influence in politics was as a committeeman behind the scenes rather than as an elected officeholder. In his later life, however, he consented to run for the federal House of Representatives and was elected to eight successive congresses, 1895–1911, when he retired. In Congress his chief interests were the tariff and the postal service. He was an ardent believer in high protection, which he frequently defended on the platform, and in an efficient postal service. His particular hobby was the rural free delivery. For a quarter of a century he advocated this system in season and out. As postmaster of New Haven, 1861–86 and 1890–94, he maintained the office at such high efficiency that it was long considered a model post-office. He was offered membership on a commission to study the postal systems of Europe but declined. He died at New Haven. His second wife, Minnie B. (Newton) Sperry, to whom he was married on Dec. 3, 1874, survived him.

[E. E. Atwater, *Hist. of the City of New Haven* (1887); *Biog. Dir. Am. Cong.* (1928); *Representative Men of Conn.* (1894); *Who's Who in America*, 1910–11; *Hartford Courant, Hartford Times, New Haven Register* and *Springfield Republican*, Nov. 14, 1911; dates of service as postmaster from *Journ. of the Exec. Proc. of the Senate*, vols. XXV, XXVII (1901), XXIX (1909).]   H. U. F.

SPICKER, MAX (Aug. 16, 1858–Oct. 15, 1912), musician, conductor, composer, was born in Königsberg, Germany, the son of Alexander Spicker and his wife, Doris. He received his first musical instruction from Robert Schwalm and Louis Köhler. His parents were anxious that he become a physician, but the boy insisted on entering the Royal Conservatory at Leipzig, where, from 1877 to 1879, he studied piano with Karl Reinecke and Ernst Ferdinand Wenzel, and theory with Solomon Jadassohn. He also attended Oscar Paul's lectures on the history and esthetics of music. On completing his studies he was engaged for a concert tour of Germany and Russia with the violin virtuoso, Miska Hauser. Following this engagement, he started his career as a conductor, and on Oct. 2, 1879, directed the performance of Beethoven's music to Goethe's *Egmont* at the *Stadt-Theatre* of Heidelberg. Subsequently he appeared as conductor in the opera houses of Cologne, Aix-la-Chapelle, Kiel, and at the royal theatres in Ghent, Belgium, and in Potsdam. His health, however, was not equal to the strenuous demands of the opera house, and, when he learned that the directorate of the New York Beethoven-Männerchor was vacant, he applied for the post and received the appointment over 161 rivals. Possibly the enthusiastic recommendation of Anton Rubinstein helped to win him the position.

He came to New York in 1882 and acted as conductor of the Beethoven-Männerchor until 1888, conducting the silver jubilee concerts in 1884. From 1888 to 1895 he was director of the Brooklyn Conservatory of Music, and in the summers of 1889–90 shared the conductorship of the Brighton Beach orchestra concerts with Anton Seidl [*q.v.*]. While he was at the Brooklyn Conservatory he also conducted each winter a series of symphony concerts at the Brooklyn Academy of Music, featuring such artists as Rafael Joseffy, Arthur Friedheim, and Lilli Lehmann. From 1895 to 1907 he was head of the theory department at the National Conservatory of Music in New York, and from May 1898 until 1910 he was music director of the Temple Emanu-El. He was also connected as a reader and editor with the G. Schirmer publishing company. In 1899 he was married to Isabel Sternthal, who, with a son, survived him.

Spicker was a man of simple tastes, sincere and unaffected. An estimate of his place in American music was attempted by A. W. Kramer in an obituary article in *Musical America*, Oct. 26, 1912: in all the many capacities in which he served a musical public, he ". . . won the approval of musicians and music-lovers throughout the length and breadth of the land . . . his compositions are not epoch-making in any sense, nor were they intended to be, but they show and show very conclusively that their creator was a musician of high rank, a man of culture and of deep and scholarly make-up. . . ." Spicker's published compositions include his incidental music to Schiller-Laube's *Demetrius; Suite Moderne,* for orchestra; an arrangement for men's chorus and orchestra of the first finale from Wagner's *Rienzi; The Pilot,* for men's chorus and orchestra; a *Festival-Overture*; and many songs and shorter choral works. He edited many editions of the classics—an *Operatic Anthology* (5 volumes, 1903–04) ; *Anthology of Sacred Song* (4 volumes, 1902) ; *The Masterpieces of Vocaliza-*

tion (6 volumes, 1896) ; a *Synagogical Service* (1901) ; and *Songs of Germany* (1904), a collection of folk-songs.

[The material for this sketch has been derived largely from an account of Spicker's career published in the *New-Yorker Staats-Zeitung,* Oct. 16, 1912. See also brief accounts in *Grove's Dict. of Music and Musicians, Am. Supp.* (1930), and *Baker's Biog. Dict. of Musicians* (3rd ed. 1919).]   J. T. H.

SPIERING, THEODORE (Sept. 5, 1871– Aug. 11, 1925), violinist, conductor, and teacher, was born in St. Louis, Mo., the elder of two sons of Ernst and Theresa (Bernays) Spiering. His father, an excellent violinist, who was born in Lübeck, Germany, was brought to the United States at the age of ten and for twenty-five years was concert-master of the St. Louis symphony orchestra, as well as first violin of the Beethoven String Quartet. His mother was born in Highland, Ill., the daughter of Charles L. Bernays, a prominent newspaper man. At the age of five the boy had his first lessons on the violin from his father and at seven made his first public appearance. He attended the public schools of St. Louis until he was fifteen, when he went to Cincinnati to study for two years with Henry Schradieck [*q.v.*] at the Cincinnati College of Music. The next four years, 1888–92, he spent in Berlin, where he studied with Joseph Joachim and during his last year was concert-master of the Joachim Hochschule Orchestra. After his return to America, he was married on Oct. 2, 1895, at Arlington, N. J., to Frida Mueller, daughter of Wilhelm Mueller, New York journalist and writer.

As a result of a letter from Joachim to Theodore Thomas [*q.v.*], Spiering in 1892 became a member of the Chicago Symphony Orchestra and remained with it until 1896. During this period he frequently appeared as soloist under Thomas, especially during the World's Columbian Exposition, and organized the Spiering Quartet, which during the twelve years of its existence, 1893–1905, gave over four hundred concerts. He founded and directed the Spiering Violin School in Chicago, 1899–1902, and was a director of the Chicago Musical College, 1902–05, where he was also instructor in violin. Going abroad, he established himself as a concert artist and teacher in Berlin, 1905–09, and made successful concert tours through Germany, England, and Holland. Having attracted the attention of Gustav Mahler, he was appointed concert-master of the New York Philharmonic Society, 1909–11, and during Mahler's prolonged last illness in 1911 conducted the seventeen remaining concerts of the season, each of which added new laurels to his brilliant record as conductor. The

New York press, with rare unanimity, was enthusiastic in his praise, and it was expected that he would be chosen Mahler's successor, but the American tradition prevailed of seeking conductors in Europe. Disappointed, Spiering returned to Berlin, where he was engaged as a conductor, 1911–14, and toured Germany, Scandinavia, and Switzerland as a soloist. He was also musical adviser of the *Neue Freie Volksbühne* in Berlin and conductor of their symphony concerts, besides appearing as guest conductor of the Philharmonic and Blüthner orchestras. Always on the outlook for worthy novelties, he gave the first Berlin performances of such works as symphonies by Georges Enesco and Paul Dukas, the "Concerto in Antique Style" of Max Reger, Frederick Delius' "In a Summer Garden," Emil Reznicek's "Der Sieger" (with unusual success), and Henry Hadley's "The Culprit Fay."

After the outbreak of the World War he made his permanent home in New York, devoting himself largely to teaching (he was a born pedagogue) and to extensive editorial work. In the New York season of 1918–19 he conducted performances of Maurice Maeterlinck's "The Betrothal" with music by Eric Delamarter; in September 1923 he was once more guest conductor in Berlin and Vienna, and won renewed praise. He was appointed conductor of the Portland (Ore.) Symphony Orchestra in 1925. Partly for rest—he had always worked under the handicaps of poor health and extreme nervousness—and partly to select new works for the coming season, he went abroad again, but he was taken ill in Munich and there died, survived by his mother, his wife, and two daughters. He was buried in St. Louis. Though he was a brilliant performer and possessed deep musicianship, he was modest and unassuming in his bearing and affable in his personal relationships. He was the recipient of many honors, among them the French decoration of Officier d'Académie, conferred by the French government in 1905 in recognition of his work in introducing French music, notably chamber music, in the United States.

[*Who's Who in America,* 1924–25; *International Who's Who in Music and Musical Gazetteer,* 1918; *Musical America,* Mar. 25, 1911, the material of which was verified by Spiering's wife and mother, and Aug. 22, 1925; *Sun* (N. Y.) and *Evening Mail* (N. Y.), Feb. 27, 1911; *World* (N. Y.), Feb. 27, Mar. 12, 18, 1911, and Aug. 14, 1925 (obit.); *Brooklyn Daily Eagle,* Mar. 20, 1911; Otto Taubmann, in *Berliner Börsen-Courier,* Sept. 29, 1923; Rudolf Kastner, in *Berliner Morgenpost,* Sept. 30, 1923; Paul Ertel, in *Berliner Lokal Anzeiger,* Oct. 4, 1923; obituaries in *Musical Courier* (N. Y.), and *Musical Leader* (Chicago), Aug. 20, *Münchener Neueste Nachrichten,* Aug. 12, *Münchener Zeitung,* Aug. 14, *Münchener-Augsburger Abend Zeitung,* Aug. 15, and *N. Y. Times,* Aug. 14, 1925.]

F. L. G. C.

SPILLMAN, WILLIAM JASPER (Oct. 23, 1863–July 11, 1931), scientist, agricultural economist, eleventh of fifteen children of Nathan Cosby and Emily Paralee (Pruitt) Spilman, was born in Lawrence County, Mo. His father, a farmer and judge, had little formal education but was a leader in the community. The son earned his way through the University of Missouri, graduating in 1886 as valedictorian and three years later receiving the degree of M.S. While at the university he changed the spelling of his name. On May 20, 1889, he married Mattie L. Ramsay, who with one son survived him.

After brief periods of teaching in state normal schools of Missouri and Oregon and at Vincennes University, Spillman in 1894 joined the staff of Washington State College, Pullman, and its experiment station. The need of a wheat better adapted to conditions in Washington led him to breed new varieties. His account of his work in hybridization contained essentially an independent statement of the two chief tenets of Mendelism ("Quantitative Studies on the Transmission of Parent Characters to Hybrid Offspring," *Proceedings of . . . the Association of American Agricultural Colleges and Experiment Stations . . . 1901,* 1902). His pleas for quantitative studies in plant breeding gave considerable impetus to this kind of research. Because of his work in genetics he was appointed in 1902 as agrostologist in charge of grass and forage plant investigations in the United States Department of Agriculture. In this capacity he instituted studies of types of farming and farming methods. An office of farm management was created in 1904, and to the direction of its work he gave his major efforts thenceforth until his resignation in 1918, as the result of friction with Secretary Houston (see *Senate Document 300,* 65 Cong., 2 Sess., and *House Resolution 611,* 65 Cong., 3 Sess.). After a three-year interim during which he was associate editor of the *Farm Journal,* he returned to the Department, where he remained until his death. From 1922 he was also professor of commercial geography in the Foreign Service School of Georgetown University.

Spillman "to a very unusual degree . . . combined practical organizing ability with penetrating power of abstract reasoning" (*Journal of Farm Economics,* January 1932, p. 1). His hobby was mathematics, but "his fertile mind suggested many more things than one man could do. . . . He was an inspirer of men, not only because of his own exuberance and fertile imagination but because of his personal relationships" (*Ibid.*). Among his important achievements were the development of farm management surveys and the extensive use of this method of approach to farm problems in representative areas. In 1903 he devised the dot-map method of presenting statistics graphically. He also directed historical and geographical studies, including the preparation of atlases on agriculture. Under his ægis demonstration work and the county-agent system were begun. He discovered the mathematical form of the law of diminishing returns with relation to the results of the use of fertilizers on farms. Later he completed a means of solving arithmetically for several variables the exponential yield curve or law of biological growth. The domestic allotment plan of farm relief was outlined in detail in his book, *Balancing the Farm Output* (1927). His leadership and pioneer efforts in the field of farm management were early recognized and he was chosen the first president of the American Farm Economic Association (1910–12). He was a member of the National Academy of Sciences and many other learned bodies, and spoke frequently before both scientific and popular audiences. His unusual record of accomplishment in many and diverse fields is reflected in his writings, over three hundred in number, ranging from popular articles for the farm press to highly technical mathematical treatises.

[*Who's Who in America*, 1930–31; *Experiment Station Record*, Nov. 1931; E. N. Bressman, "Spillman's Work on Plant Breeding," *Science*, Sept. 23, 1932; Lillian Crans, *A List of the Printed and Mimeographed Publications of Dr. W. J. Spillman* (U. S. Bureau of Agric. Economics, Aug. 1931); E. F. Gaines, "The Value of the Hybrid Wheats Produced by the State College of Washington," *Northwest Science*, Mar. 1933; Earl Godwin, "Steps Back to the Farm," *Country Life in America*, Mar. 15, 1911, portr.; F. C. Kelly, "A Wonderful Question Answerer," *Am. Mag.*, Jan. 1917, portr.; *Wash. Acad. Sci. Jour.*, vol. XXI, p. 346 (Aug. 1931); articles by C. B. Smith, E. H. Thomson, and G. F. Warren, in *Jour. Farm Econ.*, Jan. 1932; *Evening Star* (Washington, D. C.), July 12, 1931; *Memorial Honoring the Late Dr. W. J. Spillman* (Wash. State Coll., 1931); *The Official Record* (U. S. Dept. Agric.), July 25, 1931; biography of Spillman (MS., 1933) by his son, Dr. Ramsay Spillman, New York City.]   E. E. E.

SPILSBURY, EDMUND GYBBON (Dec. 7, 1845–May 28, 1920), mining engineer and metallurgist, son of Francis Gybbon Spilsbury, was born in London, England. He received most of his education in Belgium, attending a preparatory school at Liège and then pursuing technical studies at the University of Louvain, where he was graduated in 1862. After a post-graduate "practical course" at Clausthal, Germany, he was for three years in the employ of the Eschweiler Zinc Company of Stolberg, Germany, which was engaged on a large scale in mining and smelting lead and zinc. In 1865 he took charge of its works in Sardinia, and subsequently was sent to the Atlas Mountains in Morocco. During his stay in Sardinia he had occasion to entertain, on behalf of the company, the Duke of Brabant, afterward King Leopold II of the Belgians, who was in the island on a hunting trip. This experience resulted in a lasting friendship. Returning to London, Spilsbury in 1867 entered the service of the British firm of McClean & Stilman, for whom he supervised construction of the iron gates for the Surrey Commercial Docks. In 1868, in the employ of J. Casper Harkort, he designed much of the detail work of the Keulenberg Bridge in Holland, and of bridges over the Danube in Vienna, and over the Rhine at Düsseldorf.

In 1870 he came to the United States in the employ of an Austro-Belgian metallurgical firm to investigate American lead and zinc resources. He spent two years in this work, then resigned to establish himself in private practice. As general manager of smelting works at Bamford, Pa., he introduced the Harz system of dressing zinc ores into Pennsylvania and New Jersey. In 1879 he built the Lynchburg Blast Furnace and Iron Works in Virginia, at about the same time acted as consulting engineer for the Coleraine Coal & Iron Company of Philadelphia, and subsequently (1883) became general manager of the Haile gold mine in South Carolina. From 1887 to 1897 he was in the employ of Cooper, Hewitt & Company of New York, serving from 1888 to 1897 as managing director of their Trenton Iron Company, Trenton, N. J. Here he introduced the Elliott locked wire rope and the Bleichert system of aerial tramways, publishing, in 1890, a thirty-five page brochure, *Wire Rope Tramways; with Special Reference to the Bleichert Patent System.* In 1893 he presided at sessions of the mining division of the International Engineering Congress, held in connection with the World's Columbian Exposition at Chicago. After 1897 he was in private practice as consulting engineer until his death, traveling in connection with his work into many parts of the world. He had but recently returned from Brazil when, in the spring of 1920, he submitted to an operation for cataract, in a New York hospital, and died of heart failure soon afterward. He had married Rosa Hooper, and was survived by three sons and a daughter.

During his career Spilsbury contributed a number of significant papers to the *Transactions of the American Institute of Mining Engineers,* among which were: "On Rock-Drilling Machinery" (vol. III, 1875); "A New Air Compressor" (vol. VIII, 1880); "Gold Mining in

South Carolina" (vol. XII, 1884) ; "Notes on the General Treatment of the Southern Gold Ores, and Experiments in Matting Iron Sulphides" (vol. XV, 1887) ; "The Chlorination of Gold-Bearing Sulphides" (vol. XVI, 1888) ; "Notes on a Novel Cable-Transfer for Railroad-Cars and the Use of the Patent Locked-Wire Rope" (vol. XX, 1892) ; "Improvements in Mining and Metallurgical Appliances during the Last Decade" (vol. XXVII, 1898) ; and "Improvement in Cyanide Process" (vol. XLI, 1911). To the *Mining and Scientific Press* he contributed two informal, entertaining articles on some of his professional experiences ("Technical Reminiscences," July 10, Aug. 28, 1915). He was active in the work of the numerous professional societies to which he belonged, being called upon frequently for service on various committees.

[*Who's Who in America*, 1920–21 ; *Trans. Am. Soc. Civil Engineers*, vol. LXXXIV (1921) ; *Trans. Am. Inst. Mining and Metallurgical Engineers*, vol. LXVI (1922) ; *Engineering and Mining Jour.*, June 5, 1920 ; *Mining and Scientific Press*, June 12, 1920 ; *N. Y. Times*, May 30, 1920.]   B. A. R.

SPINNER, FRANCIS ELIAS (Jan. 21, 1802–Dec. 31, 1890), treasurer of the United States, was born in that part of the town of German Flats, Herkimer County, N. Y., which afterwards became the village of Mohawk. He was the eldest son of the Rev. John Peter and Mary Magdalene Fidelis (Brument) Spinner. His father, a native of Werbach, Baden, had been a Roman Catholic priest in Germany, but in 1801 had renounced that faith and emigrated to America ; at the time of Francis' birth he was pastor of the Reformed Dutch Church at German Flats. Francis was a pupil in four Mohawk Valley district schools and in his old age stated that he learned nothing in any of them (letter to F. G. Barry, in *College and School*, Utica, N. Y., April 1890 ; Hartley, *post*, pp. 192–95). His father apprenticed him to a confectioner at Albany and later to a saddler at Amsterdam, N. Y. ; during his spare time he devoted himself to reading and formed an acquisitiveness of mind that persisted throughout his life.

As time went on he became a merchant in Herkimer, major-general of artillery in the state militia, cashier, director, and president of the Mohawk Valley Bank. In politics he was long known as an aggressive Democrat. He was appointed to supervise the building of the state insane hospital at Utica, and during the Polk administration was auditor of the Port of New York. Identifying himself with the anti-slavery wing of the Democratic party, he was elected to Congress from the Herkimer district in 1854. In the protracted speakership contest of 1855–56 he

refused to caucus with the House Democrats and was the only representative elected as a Democrat whose vote was cast for Nathaniel P. Banks [*q.v.*]. For the rest of that Congress he was affiliated with the Whig-Republican majority. He served on the committee that dealt with the Brooks-Sumner assault, and was a member of the conference committee in charge of the long-disputed army appropriation bill in the summer of 1856. To the two succeeding Congresses he was elected as a Republican by large pluralities. He became known as an outspoken and inflexibly honest representative who never left his colleagues long in doubt as to his stand on any public question.

A vigorous supporter of Lincoln, he was appointed treasurer of the United States in March 1861. In that capacity he served fourteen years, under three presidents. When he took office, the Treasury was paying out $8,000,000 a month ; within sixty days the expenditure amounted to $2,000,000 a day. It was Spinner's task to guard the government's money chest in a time of perils and difficulties for which there was no precedent. In connection with the issue of Treasury notes during the Civil War years, Spinner's autograph signature—the despair of would-be forgers—came to be a kind of national symbol, known to all. In the expansion of his bureau and its personnel at a time when men were needed for military service he employed a few young women, at first to count currency bills and later to take over various clerical duties, so that by the end of the war women had a definite status in the civil service. For this innovation he has always been given the chief credit.

Following his resignation in 1875, caused by friction with the department head over responsibility for appointments, Spinner went to Jacksonville, Fla., where he lived much in the open for fifteen years. At eighty he took up the study of Greek as a mental recreation. He died in his eighty-ninth year of cancer of the face, after prolonged suffering. On June 22, 1826, he had married Caroline Caswell of Herkimer ; one of three daughters survived him.

[*Biog. Dir. Am. Cong.* (1928) ; N. S. Benton, *A Hist. of Herkimer County* (1856) ; A. L. Howell, "The Life and Public Services of Gen. Francis E. Spinner," *Papers Read Before the Herkimer County Hist. Soc.*, vol. II (1902) ; W. R. Hooper, in *Hours at Home*, Sept. 1870 ; reports of Treasurer of U. S., 1861–75 ; I. S. Hartley, *Mag. of Am. Hist.*, Mar. 1891, pp. 185–200 ; Hugh McCulloch, *Men and Measures of Half a Century* (1882) ; J. C. Derby, *Fifty Years among Authors, Books and Publishers* (1884), pp. 644–46 ; M. C. Ames, *Ten Years in Washington* (1873) ; L. E. Chittenden, *Personal Reminiscences* (1893) ; S. P. Brown, *The Book of Jacksonville* (1895) ; *N. Y. Times*, Jan. 1, 1891 ; *Fla. Times-Union* (Jacksonville), Jan. 1, 1891.]   W. B. S.

SPITZKA, EDWARD ANTHONY

SPITZKA, EDWARD ANTHONY (June 17, 1876–Sept. 4, 1922), anatomist and criminologist, son of Dr. Edward Charles Spitzka [q.v.] and Catherine (Watzek) Spitzka, was born in New York City. He was educated in the College of the City of New York and obtained his medical degree in 1902 from the College of Physicians and Surgeons, Columbia University. He was assistant demonstrator of anatomy at Columbia University, 1905–06, and then became professor of general anatomy at Jefferson Medical College, Philadelphia, Pa. On June 20, 1906, he was married to Alice Eberspacher of New York. He was made director and professor of anatomy at the Daniel Baugh Institute of Anatomy at Jefferson Medical College in 1911, but in 1914 he resigned to take up the practice of nervous and mental diseases in New York. Upon the entry of the United States into the World War, he went to a medical officers' training camp at Fort Benjamin Harrison, Ind. After being assigned to duty at Camp Grant, Ill., he was promoted to the grade of lieutenant-colonel and in the summer of 1918 was sent to France in command of the sanitary train of the 86th Division. When he was discharged from the army in the following year he returned to practice in New York. A life full of early promise and of frustrated achievement had its tragic culmination three years later in his sudden death from cerebral hemorrhage at his home in Mount Vernon, N. Y. At the time of his death he held the position of medical referee with the United States Veterans' Bureau.

His most important contributions to medicine are his studies upon the human brain. These include notable studies of the size and structure of the brains of Japanese, Eskimos, and certain South Sea islanders, observations on electrocution and its effects, and studies of the brains of criminals and of noted men. He was particularly interested in the anatomical variations in the brains of criminals, and performed the autopsy on Leon F. Czolgosz, the assassin of Pres. William McKinley [q.v.], and made a detailed study of the brain. He had a special interest as well in the evolutionary development of the nervous system, which he studied comparatively in the primates and in the higher mammals. He made other notable studies upon the morphology of the ductless glands, wrote on *Resuscitation of Persons Shocked by Electricity* (1909), and edited the eighteenth American edition of Henry Gray's *Anatomy, Descriptive and Applied* (1910), which is a lasting monument to his memory. In his chosen work he had the accuracy and the zeal of the investigator together with the broader and deeper interest of the cultural scientist, and his studies show marked originality. He was tall and of heavy, powerful build. Though he was inclined to be melancholic and reticent of speech, with little inclination for ordinary social activities, he displayed when he was interested an unexpectedly good command of language, and had a gift for intimate friendships.

[*Who's Who in America*, 1922–23; *Jour. Am. Medic. Assoc.*, Sept. 16, 1922; *Jour. of Nervous and Mental Diseases* (N. Y.), Jan. 1923; *Am. Men of Sci.* (3rd edition, 1921), ed. by J. M. Cattell and D. R. Brimhall; *Dict. Am. Medic. Biog.* (edition of 1928), ed. by H. A. Kelly and W. L. Burrage; bibliog. in *Index Cat. Lib. of Surgeon Gen's. Office, U. S. Army*, 2 ser., vol. XVI (1911); obituary in *N. Y. Times*, Sept. 6, 1922.]
J. M. P.

SPITZKA, EDWARD CHARLES

SPITZKA, EDWARD CHARLES (Nov. 10, 1852–Jan. 13, 1914), neurologist and psychiatrist, was born in the city of New York to Charles Anthony and Johanna (Tag) Spitzka. His father, a watch and clock maker of Germano-Slavonic origin, had been compelled to flee from Germany following the Revolution of 1848, a cause which he had espoused. The son was educated in the public schools, and after two years in the College of the City of New York entered the medical department of the University of the City of New York (later New York University), from which he graduated in 1873. He spent the following three years in post-graduate study in Europe, first in Leipzig and later in Vienna. In Vienna he came under the instruction of Theodor Meynert, the great anatomist and psychiatrist, and of Samuel Leopold Schenk, distinguished in the field of human and comparative embryology, whose influence had much to do with shaping his future career. On June 30, 1875, he married Catherine Watzek in Vienna. A year later he began a general practice in New York, but after a few years he limited his practice to nervous and mental diseases. Immediately after his return he took up neurological work at Mt. Sinai and St. Mark's hospitals and at the Northeastern Dispensary. From pathological material collected from public and private asylums of the vicinity he produced an essay on *The Somatic Etiology of Insanity* (1882) published as a supplement to the *American Journal of Neurology and Psychiatry*, which in 1878 won the W. and S. Tuke prize offered by the British Medico-Psychological Association. In the same year he was awarded the William A. Hammond prize of the American Neurological Association for his essay on "The Anatomical and Physiological Effects of Strychnia on the Brain, Spinal Cord, and Nerves" (*Journal of Nervous and Mental Disease*, April 1879). One of the pioneers of his specialty in America, he gained a nation-wide reputation as a consultant and as a medico-legal expert in cases involving insanity and injury to the nervous system. His most noted case was that of Charles J. Guiteau, the assassin of Pres. James Abram Garfield [*q.v.*], whom he considered insane.

He filled the position of professor of comparative anatomy at the Columbia Veterinary College at different times, and was professor of anatomy and physiology of the nervous system at the New York Post-Graduate Medical School, 1882–85. Working upon the comparative and human anatomy of the nervous system throughout his career, he made many notable contributions to the knowledge of this subject. He made exhaustive studies of the central nervous system of birds and reptiles, and is credited with being the original discoverer of the so-called Lissauer tract in the spinal cord; he also devoted himself to the morbid anatomy of organic diseases of the central nervous system and to the classification of mental disorders by clinical methods. He published a textbook on *Insanity, Its Classification, Diagnosis, and Treatment* (1883) and was the author of monographs on "The Chronic Inflammatory and Degenerative Affections of the Spinal Cord," and "Anaemia and Hyperaemia of the Brain and Spinal Cord," in William Pepper's *A System of Practical Medicine* (vol. V, 1886), and on brain histology and the spinal cord in *A Reference Handbook of the Medical Sciences* (vol. VIII, 1889), edited by A. H. Buck, popularly known as Woods' Reference Handbook. Among the subjects he treated in journal articles were the relation of race and heredity to insanity, the historic rôle of mental disorders, the misconceptions regarding physical abnormality of criminals, and the legal and biologic disabilities of illegitimate children. For three years (1881–84) he was editor of the *American Journal of Neurology and Psychiatry*; in 1883–84 he was president of the New York Neurological Society, and in 1890 president of the American Neurological Association. Tall and heavily built, with a rugged, smooth-shaven face, he was an impulsive man, quick in action, thought, and speech. A contemporary wrote of him that he was "a red headed, hot-headed man, but finely trained in anatomy . . . very scornful of American work and violently antagonistic to the state methods of caring for the insane at that time—as he had a right to be" (C. L. Dana, "Early Neurology in the United States," *Journal of the American Medical Association,* May 5, 1928, p. 1422) and adds that his critical attitude was of great benefit to New York neurology. He died suddenly as the result of a cerebral hemorrhage,

leaving his wife and a son, Edward Anthony Spitzka [*q.v.*].

[*Who's Who in America*, 1912–13; E. A. Spitzka, in *Jour. of Nervous and Mental Disease* (N. Y.), Apr. 1914; *Am. Medic. Biogs.* (1920), ed. by H. A. Kelly and W. L. Burrage; N. E. Brill, *N. Y. Medic. Jour.,* May 9, 1914, with portrait; obituary in *N. Y. Times,* Jan. 14, 1914.]   J. M. P.

SPIVAK, CHARLES DAVID (Dec. 25, 1861–Oct. 16, 1927), physician, author, editor, was born in Krementchug, government of Poltava, Russia, the son of Samuel David Spivakowsky and his wife, Deborah Adel Dorfman. From his father and the Cheder, a Jewish school, he received the traditional Hebrew education, while he was self-educated in secular subjects. He took and passed successfully the examination of the local Gymnasium, and continued his private studies. In common with his revolutionary-minded contemporaries in Russia, he participated in illegal political activities, until the danger of imprisonment compelled him to leave the country. Joining the Kiev group, "Am Olam," a society of young intellectuals who planned to emigrate to America and establish themselves there as agriculturists on a communal basis, he arrived in the United States in March 1882. Ignorant of the language and without means, he started out as a laborer, loading and unloading freight in railroad yards, paving Fifth Avenue in New York City, working in wool and cotton mills in Maine, as a typesetter on the *Jewish Messenger,* and as a farm-hand in Alliance, N. J., where he later taught. Settling in Philadelphia, he studied medicine at the Jefferson Medical College, was graduated with the M.D. degree in 1890, and then attended lectures at the University of Berlin, 1891–92. Two years later he was appointed chief of the clinic for gastro-intestinal diseases at the Philadelphia Polyclinic. From 1896 to 1901 he was associate professor in the department of medicine of the University of Denver; professor of anatomy, 1897–98; and then professor of clinical medicine and chief of the clinical laboratory at Denver and Gross College of Medicine, 1900–07. He was president of the Colorado Medical Library Association, 1902; librarian of the Denver Academy of Medicine, and a member of numerous medical societies. In 1920 he was delegated by the Joint Distribution Committee of the American Funds for Jewish War Sufferers to study health and sanitation conditions among the Jews in the devastated war areas of Europe. His main achievement, however, was the founding of the Jewish Consumptives' Relief Society in 1904, for the care of tubercular patients without means, and the building of the Society's Sanatorium in Denver, Colo., acknowledged to be one of the best in the country. From the inception until his death Spivak acted as secretary and gastro-enterologist to the Sanatorium. The locality of the Sanatorium Buildings was named Spivak, Colo., in his honor after his death.

Notwithstanding his onerous professional and communal duties as physician and social worker, Spivak found time for a many-sided literary activity. He wrote with equal facility in Hebrew, Yiddish, Russian, and English. (His Hebrew and Yiddish writings appeared under his Jewish name Hayyim Spivak.) Even during his early years of struggle he contributed to the *Woskhod* (Russian) and *Hameliz* (Hebrew), both in St. Petersburg, as well as to Yiddish and Anglo-Jewish periodicals in the United States. The greater part of his writing, however, has been chiefly in the field of gastro-enterology, in which he won a national reputation (see the *Index-Catalogue of the Library of the Surgeon-General's Office, U. S. Army,* 2 ser., vol. XVI, 1911). Among his other interests were medical bibliography, linguistics, and the history of medicine, particularly of Jewish physicians and their achievements. His familiarity with the Hebrew sources led him to make many interesting contributions to the history of early medicine. He was editor of *Medical Libraries* from 1898 to 1902, and a *Longevity Almanach* (Yiddish) in 1921; compiler and editor of *Medical Coloradoana*; author of a number of bibliographies on medicine among the Jews; and a contributor to the *Annals of Medical History* and the *Jewish Encyclopedia.* Of special value were his articles on medicine in the Bible, the Talmud, and in Rabbinic literature. Two periodicals, the *Denver Jewish News,* 1915–18, and the *Sanatorium,* 1907–27, appeared in Denver under his editorship. For the *Jewish Daily Forward* of New York City he wrote a series of popular articles on hygiene and longevity from a Jewish standpoint. He had an insatiable curiosity for data bearing on medical notions in ancient Jewish folklore. Of his linguistic researches may be mentioned a *Yiddish Dictionary* (1911), compiled in collaboration with Solomon Bloomgarden [*q.v.*], containing all the Hebrew and Chaldaic elements of the Yiddish language illustrated with proverbs and idiomatic expressions.

Spivak was married to Jennie (Gittel) Charsky in Philadelphia in 1893. She survived him with one son and two daughters.

[*Who's Who in America,* 1926–27; *Who's Who in Am. Med.,* 1925; *Who's Who in Am. Jewry,* 1926; *Rocky Mountain News* (Denver, Colo.), Oct. 17, 1927; Zalmen Reisen, *Lexicon fun der Yiddisher Literatur,* vol. II (Vilna, 1927); *Am. Rev. of Tuberculosis,* Dec. 1927; A. Levinson, *Charles D. Spivak's Contribution to Medicine,* reprinted from *Medic. Life,* Jan. 1928.]
I. S.

SPOFFORD, AINSWORTH RAND (Sept. 12, 1825–Aug. 11, 1908), librarian, the son of the Rev. Luke Ainsworth and Grata (Rand) Spofford, was born in Gilmanton, N. H. He was a descendant of John Spofford who came to Massachusetts with the Rev. Ezekiel Rogers' company in 1638 and in 1643 settled in what became the town of Rowley, Mass. Ainsworth prepared under private tutors and at Williston Seminary for admission to Amherst College, but ill health prevented him from entering. Instead, he gave himself over to a course in books; through a long life they were his unnumbered and always unforgotten *almae matres.* At the age of nineteen he removed to Cincinnati, where he was successively a clerk in a bookstore, a bookseller and publisher, and, from 1859, associate editor of the *Cincinnati Commercial.* In 1856 he was a delegate to the convention in Philadelphia that nominated John C. Frémont for the presidency. Books appealed to him far more strongly than politics, however, and accordingly, while in Washington in 1861 after the battle of Bull Run, which his newspaper had sent him to report, he accepted an appointment as chief assistant to Dr. John G. Stephenson, then librarian of Congress. "With his entrance upon librarianship he put away the merely contemporary, and from that moment no one could find him partisan upon a current issue, nor, except after insistent effort, could discover his opinion upon it" (Putnam, *post*). Following Stephenson's resignation, Spofford, on Dec. 1, 1864, became the librarian-in-chief and directed the affairs of the Library of Congress until 1897. In that year, on the removal of the library from its old quarters in the Capitol to the building newly erected for it, he gave way to a younger man and once more took the chief assistant's position, continuing in that office until his death. On Sept. 15, 1852, he was married to Sarah Putnam Partridge of Franklin, Mass.; three children were born to them.

Spofford, in his day and land, was perhaps the most widely renowned of the librarians of the old school, those masters and servants at once of the books about them, who took, or seemed to take, all that was between the covers as their province, and who counted what they brought back with them from personal journeyings over endless printed pages as of greater importance in the administration of a library than bibliographical method. With Spofford, these journeyings were unceasing; his memory retained all that he found along the way, and nothing escaped him. So extraordinary was his memory that he has been likened to the celebrated Magliabecchi. For nearly half a century he was known as an unfailing source of factual knowledge to official and unofficial Washington and to an unnumbered constituency beyond. His ability to recall on the spur of the moment a fact which he had somewhere read made him a conspicuous and even unique member of various cultural and learned societies in Washington, and was an ever ready aid to him as the author and the compiler of numerous volumes. A list of his publications, brought together by his successor as chief assistant librarian, Appleton P. C. Griffin [q.v.], and printed in the pamphlet *Ainsworth R. Spofford, 1825–1908* (1909), contains no less than 184 titles. Of yet more importance to the Library, Spofford's memory seemed to carry within its recesses a complete record of the books needed in the Library collections, and never a title of the kind escaped him as he scanned the catalogues of dealers. His memory and industry together, and his astonishing success in the use of the fund for the purchase of books, which never amounted to more than $10,000 a year, enabled him to increase the collections he administered from some 60,000 items in 1861 to more than 1,000,000 items in 1897, and to lay the foundations for the National Library which he ever insisted the Library of Congress should be. Out of this notable achievement grew his other and more easily visible one, the establishment of a separate building to house the growing institution. After fully twenty years of opposition, discouragement, and delay, he prevailed upon Congress to provide for it, and in 1897 it was completed. This building (now greatly enlarged), and the many books in it which Spofford obtained are his lasting contributions to American cultural life. In choosing the quotations to be lettered here and there in the building, one that he took from Carlyle must have had its own special meaning to him: "The true university of these days is a collection of books."

[Knowledge of Spofford may be gained from his *A Book for All Readers* (1900) and from his "Washington Reminiscences," *Atlantic Monthly,* May, June 1898. See also Jeremiah and A. T. Spofford, *A Geneal. Record . . . Descendants of John Spofford* (1888); Herbert Putnam, in the *Independent,* Nov. 19, 1908, reprinted in the *Library Jour.,* Dec. 1908, presenting a striking picture of Spofford, "a soul aloof in a world ideal— the world of books"; *Records of the Columbia Hist. Soc., Washington, D. C.,* vol. XII (1909); *Evening Star* (Washington), Aug. 12, 1908. Certain facts in this sketch were supplied by Spofford's daughter, Miss Florence P. Spofford, Washington, D. C.] W. A. S—e.

SPOFFORD, HARRIET ELIZABETH PRESCOTT (Apr. 3, 1835–Aug. 14, 1921), au-

thor, was one of several children of Sarah Jane (Bridges) and Joseph Newmarch Prescott, a merchant. She was descended from John Prescott, who in 1643 was one of the first settlers of Lancaster, Mass. She lived in Calais, Me., her birthplace, until she was fourteen years of age. At about that time her father set out for the West, hoping to better his fortunes, and soon afterwards her mother removed to Newburyport, Mass., thereafter the permanent home of the family. Here Harriet Prescott attended the excellent Putnam Free School for three years. During this time one of her essays attracted the attention of Thomas Wentworth Higginson [q.v.], who encouraged her ambition to become a writer. Her formal education was completed by a brief period at the Pinkerton Academy in Derry, N. H. Her father having returned from the West fortuneless and broken in health, she began contributing to newspapers and periodicals before she was twenty in order to assist with the financial burdens of the household. She worked tirelessly but with little recognition and scant payment until her story "In a Cellar" was published in February 1859 by the newly established *Atlantic Monthly.* Mr. Higginson, proud of the "demure little Yankee girl," introduced her into the literary circles of Boston, and opportunity opened before her. In rapid succession during the next few years she published *Sir Rohan's Ghost* (1860), *The Amber Gods, and Other Stories* (1863), and *Azarian: an Episode* (1864), all characterized by highly romantic details, elaborate word-painting, and an absence of any definite moral purpose. On Dec. 19, 1865, she married Richard Smith Spofford, Jr., a talented young lawyer of Newburyport. She spent the winters of her early married life in Washington, D. C., where her husband was professionally associated with Caleb Cushing [q.v.]. One of her later works, *Old Washington* (1906), pleasantly reflects the interest she always took in the city. In 1874 Mr. Spofford bought picturesque Deer Island in the Merrimac River near Newburyport, and there, in a delightful old house of generous size, she continued her writing. During the next thirty years a succession of stories, articles, and poems made her name a familiar one to readers of the outstanding American magazines; many of these contributions were later collected into such volumes as *New-England Legends* (1871), *In Titian's Garden and Other Poems* (1897), and *Old Madame and Other Tragedies* (1900). Her interest in domestic life found expression in such works as *Art Decoration Applied to Furniture* (1878), and *The Servant Girl Question* (1881), published originally in *Harper's Bazar,* for which she wrote regularly. Her genius for friendship and her generous appraisal of others are charmingly revealed in *A Little Book of Friends* (1916), an account of eight literary contemporaries. Although she was best known to a popular audience by her fiction, she considered poetry her more significant work. The luxuriant fancy which led her to write over-opulent descriptions in her early prose finds a natural expression in the imagery of her verse.

During her later life, she spent many winters in Boston. One trip to Europe with her husband, and one after his death in 1888 were her only distant wanderings. New England and an imaginative world of romance were the regions she knew best. She took no active part in the reform movements of her time, although she was sympathetic toward them. The beauty of her island home and the companionship of congenial friends and kinsfolk brought her the great satisfactions of her life. In a poem written at the time of Richard Spofford's death ("R. S. S. at Deer Island on the Merrimac"), John Greenleaf Whittier [*q.v.*] reveals with quiet sensitiveness the happy hospitality of that home. Mrs. Spofford was a woman of distinguished presence, and all who saw her moving about in her garden, clothed in the trailing black garments she always wore as she grew older, were impressed by her serenity and grace. She died at Deer Island, in her eighty-seventh year. Her only child, a son, died in infancy.

[William Prescott, *The Prescott Memorial* (1870); *Who's Who in America,* 1920–21; Elizabeth K. Halbeisen, *Harriet Prescott Spofford* (1935), with portraits; Rose Terry Cooke, in *Our Famous Women* (1884); J. J. Currier, *"Ould Newberry"* (1896); Jeremiah Spofford, *A Geneal. Record . . . Descendants of John Spofford* (1888); review in *North Am. Review,* Jan. 1865, and one by P. E. More in *Atlantic Monthly,* Aug. 1897; obituary in *Boston Transcript,* Aug. 15, 1921; information from relatives and friends.]
B. M. S.

SPOONER, JOHN COIT (Jan. 6, 1843–June 11, 1919), senator from Wisconsin, born at Lawrenceburg, Ind., moved with his parents to Madison, Wis., in 1859. His father, Philip Loring Spooner, born in New Bedford of old Massachusetts stock, was married in 1839 to Lydia Lord Coit, of Plainfield, Conn., and lived for twenty years at Lawrenceburg, Ind. He was a lawyer, and the reporter of four volumes (XII–XV) of the *Wisconsin Reports.* John attended the University of Wisconsin, receiving his degree while on duty at the front in 1864. Mustered out with the brevet rank of major, he became colonel on the staff of Gov. Lucius Fairchild [*q.v.*], whose secretary he was; and in 1867

he was admitted to the Wisconsin bar. He married Anna E. Main of Madison, on Sept. 10, 1868, and moved in 1870 to Hudson, on the western border of the state, where he at once took rank as a brilliant lawyer. In due time he was elected to the Assembly (1872) and appointed as regent of the University of Wisconsin. His brief for the state in the case of *Schulenberg* vs. *Harriman* (21 *Wallace,* 44) helped establish the federal law as to railroad land grants, and pointed to the class of legal business for which he was fitted. As counsel for the Chicago, St. Paul, Minneapolis & Omaha Railway, and for the roads that were merged as the Chicago & Northwestern Railway, he developed marked talent, and as legislative adviser he watched proceedings at Madison, where he was described as "chief of the corporation lobbyists" (*Milwaukee Sentinel,* Jan. 16, 1885, p. 4). As a campaigner for Blaine in 1884 he established his reputation on the stump.

He was elected to the United States Senate in 1885, with the patronage of Philetus Sawyer [*q.v.*], defeating Lucius Fairchild in the caucus and William F. Vilas in the canvass. Spooner sacrificed a large private income when he became senator, but he acquired immediate reputation as an able debater, brilliant parliamentarian, and sound constitutional lawyer. When his term came to an end in 1891, Wisconsin was in the hands of the Democrats, who chose Vilas to succeed him. Spooner returned to Madison, resumed the practice of his profession without abandoning his activity in politics, and assisted as counsel in the gerrymander cases, whereby the supreme court of Wisconsin in 1892 twice set aside Democratic apportionment laws (81 *Wisconsin Reports,* 440; 83 *Wisconsin Reports,* 90). He offered himself for sacrifice in 1892 when he was defeated for governor by George W. Peck [*q.v.*]. In 1897 when the term of Vilas ended the Republicans were once more in complete control of Wisconsin, and Spooner was returned to his seat in the Senate. For the next ten years, "the day of the Elder Statesman" (Stephenson, *post,* p. 134), Spooner was a notable national figure, sharing with Nelson W. Aldrich, William B. Allison, and Orville H. Platt [*qq.v.*] the confidence of both McKinley and Roosevelt. He managed on the floor of the Senate the intricate matters of constitutional law relating to the new colonial ventures, and attached his name to the canal bill of 1902. He was essentially counsel for his party, rather than its leader, and never overcame a distaste for the manipulations of politics. So long as Henry C. Payne [*q.v.*] could direct the "stalwart" interests in Wisconsin, and could prevail over the attacks of the "half-breeds" led by Robert M. LaFollette [*q.v.*], Spooner remained the great ornament of his state in Washington, and "the most brilliant man in Congress" (Wellman, *post,* p. 167). In 1900 he talked of leaving the Senate to resume the law, but he was persuaded to accept reëlection in 1903, and he became, as caricatured, the mahout of the G. O. P. elephant, with Roosevelt on its back. In 1904 his intimacy with Roosevelt created a perplexing dilemma for the President, for LaFollette was selected as head of the regular delegation to the Republican National Convention, while Spooner was head of a bolting delegation, and Payne was both postmaster general and vice-chairman of the Republican National Committee. The Spooner delegation was seated, throwing LaFollette into bitter opposition that was dangerous even to Roosevelt. Lincoln Steffens chose this moment to attack the original election of Spooner to the Senate in 1885, as due to corrupt manipulation by Sawyer, and other "enemies of the Republic" (*McClure's Magazine,* October 1904) ; the death of Payne removed the local organizer of "stalwart" victory; and when LaFollette was elected to the Senate in place of Joseph V. Quarles in 1905, Spooner set the date at which he proposed to resume his practice. He had declined the offices of secretary of the interior and attorney general under McKinley and was later to decline the secretaryship of state under Taft. At the end of the Fifty-ninth Congress, Mar. 2, 1907, Spooner sent in his resignation, effective May 1. He left the Senate, with brevet from the *New York Times,* as "the ablest man in it" (June 12, 1919, p. 14), but without a client or an announced plan of operations. For the rest of his life his name appeared rarely in the news, but his office in New York was busy and profitable, for he was among the greatest lawyers of his day. He rarely returned to Wisconsin, and seems never to have reconciled himself to the reversal in politics that left his friends in a minority. He died in New York City, survived by his widow and three sons.

[The Spooner Papers, now in the Lib. Cong., have not yet been exploited, though some use of them was made in N. W. Stephenson, *Nelson W. Aldrich* (1930). Printed accounts are W. R. Bagby, in 174 *Wisconsin Reports* (1921), pp. lvii–lix; Walter Wellman, "Spooner of Wisconsin," *Am. Monthly Review of Reviews,* Aug. 1902; obituaries in *Milwaukee Sentinel,* June 11, 1919, and *N. Y. Times,* June 11, 12, 1919. See also F. W. Chapman, *The Coit Family* (1874) ; *Biog. Directory of the Am. Congress 1774–1927* (1928) ; *Who's Who in America,* 1918–19.]   F. L. P.

SPOONER, LYSANDER (Jan. 19, 1808–May 14, 1887), lawyer and writer on political subjects, was born at Athol, Mass., the son of Asa and Dolly (Brown) Spooner and a descendant of William Spooner who was in Plymouth, Mass., as early as 1637. Lysander remained on his father's farm until the age of twenty-five, and then read law in the office of John Davis and, later, in that of Charles Allen at Worcester, Mass. In defiance of the legal requirement that those not college graduates should read law for three years before practising, he opened an office. In 1835 he published a pamphlet, addressed to members of the legislature, which secured repeal of that requirement the following year. After six years' residence in Ohio, where he protested unsuccessfully against the draining of the Maumee River, he returned to the Atlantic seaboard and in 1844 established the American Letter Mail Company, a private agency carrying letters at the uniform rate of five cents each between Boston and New York. He soon extended the service to Philadelphia and Baltimore, but, faced with many prosecutions brought by the government, was forced to abandon the enterprise within the year. Thereupon he published a vigorous pamphlet, *The Unconstitutionality of the Laws of Congress Prohibiting Private Mails* (1844), in which he contended that the constitutional authority was permissive, not exclusive. It has been believed that Congress twice reduced postage rates within the following six years as a result of his activities.

Spooner was an uncompromising foe of slavery, and, believing that the institution had no constitutional sanction, advocated political organization with a view to its abolition. His *Unconstitutionality of Slavery* (1845, reprinted with a second part added, 1847, 1853, 1856, 1860) became campaign literature of the Liberty Party. Not only did slavery lack validation in the Constitution, he contended, but it "had not been authorized or established by any of the fundamental constitutions or charters that had existed previous to this time; . . . it had always been a mere abuse sustained by the common consent of the strongest party" (p. 65). His starting point was that "Law, . . . applied to any object or thing whatever, signifies a *natural,* unalterable, universal principle. . . . Any rule, not . . . flexible in its application, is no law" (p. 6). The last quotation discloses Spooner's dogmatic insistence upon natural rights. Gerrit Smith [*q.v.*] agreed with his legal contentions as to slavery as heartily as Wendell Phillips and William Lloyd Garrison [*qq.v.*] disapproved of them (see Wendell Phillips, *Review of Lysander Spooner's Essay on the Unconstitutionality of Slavery,* 1847). All admitted, of necessity, that he was an inexorable logician. His *A Defence for Fugitive Slaves, against the Acts . . . of 1793 and . . . 1850*

(1850) showed the same ingenuity in argument and the same intense moral purpose; the laws being unconstitutional, "it follows that they can confer no authority upon the judges and marshals appointed to execute them; and those officers are consequently, in law, mere ruffians and kidnappers" (p. 27). For his religion as for his political and legal theory, he sought a basis in nature, as is evidenced by his *The Deist's Reply to the Alleged Supernatural Evidences of Christianity* (1836). When Millerite laborers at Athol quit work to wait for the end of the world and were arrested as vagrants, he secured their release because of a flaw in the indictments. He was a bachelor and a recluse, spending much of his time in the Boston Athenaeum. Of strong convictions and positive utterance, he had few lasting friends. The range of his interests was wide, however, and his sympathies were warm. He defended the Irish against British tyranny and attacked American financiers for exploitation of the public. His *Essay on the Trial by Jury* (1852) maintained that jurors should be drawn by lot from the whole body of citizens, and that they should be judges of law as well as of fact. Among his other works were *Constitutional Law, Relative to Credit, Currency, and Banking* (1843), *A New Banking System* (1873), and *The Law of Intellectual Property* (1855).

[Thomas Spooner, *Records of William Spooner, of Plymouth, Mass., and His Descendants*, vol. I (1883); *Boston Sunday Globe*, May 15, 1887; *Boston Transcript*, May 16, 1887.]   B. M.

SPOONER, SHEARJASHUB (Dec. 3, 1809–Mar. 14, 1859), dentist, art editor, was one of the ten children of Paul and Deborah (White) Spooner. His earliest ancestor in America was William Spooner who came to New Plymouth in 1637 as an indentured apprentice. His father and grandfather were carpenters. He was born at Orwell, Vt., but his family, the following year, moved to the neighboring village of Brandon, where he attended school. For several years he worked on a farm, but at the age of eighteen he joined Dr. John Roach Spooner, one of his four brothers who became physicians, in Montreal and studied the classics and medicine. From general medicine he turned to dentistry, and in 1833 went to New York City to attend the New York Medical College. Two years later, in obtaining the degree of Doctor of Medicine from the College of Physicians and Surgeons, he presented and defended his thesis: *An Inaugural Dissertation on the Physiology and Diseases of the Teeth* (1835). The following year he published a *Guide to Sound Teeth, or A Popular Treatise on the Teeth*. His practice grew rapid-

ly and he became affluent. His last published work of importance on dentistry was *An Essay on the Art of the Manufacture of Mineral, Porcelain, or Incorruptible Teeth* (1838).

He was married, on Nov. 26, 1836, to Jane E. (Foot) Darrow, the widow of Allen Darrow. His wife possessed a modest competence and he had amassed a small fortune from his practice. Some time before 1842 he retired from dentistry to devote himself to art and to the promotion of art appreciation in America. While in Europe in 1842 he purchased the old copper plates of John Boydell's illustrations of Shakespeare. These plates were carefully restored and in 1852 he published a two-volume edition of them with original descriptions from his own pen under the title *The American Edition of Boydell's Illustrations of the Dramatic Works of Shakspeare*. He had observed in Paris in 1842 that the plates of two celebrated French works of art, the *Musée Français* and the *Musée Royal*, were for sale. He determined to make these works available to his countrymen, purchased the 522 "coppers" and brought them to New York, but found that he was unable to pay the heavy import duties. He petitioned Congress for an exemption, and finally offered them to the Smithsonian Institution, Washington, D. C., if it would agree to carry out his original plan. These appeals failed, the plates were shipped back to France, and the project collapsed. He published a pamphlet, remarkable for its elucidation of the state of the arts in contemporary America, during his fight to have the plates admitted free of duty: *An Appeal to the People of the United States, in Behalf of Art, Artists, and the Public Weal* (1854).

More successful were two other productions in the field of the arts: *Anecdotes of Painters, Engravers, Sculptors and Architects, and Curiosities of Art* (3 vols., 1850), and *A Biographical and Critical Dictionary of Painters, Engravers, Sculptors and Architects . . .* (1853). For some years these works were looked upon as standard authorities and they have not yet completely lost their value. It was in their preparation that Spooner contracted a nervous disorder which, aggravated by his difficulties in 1854, finally resulted in his death at Plainfield, N. J.

[Thomas Spooner, *Memorial of William Spooner . . .* (1871), and *Records of William Spooner, of Plymouth, Mass., and His Descendants*, vol. I (1883); *N. Y. Herald*, Mar. 18, 1859.]   F. M.

SPOTSWOOD, ALEXANDER (1676–June 7, 1740), lieutenant-governor of Virginia, son of Robert and Catherine (Mercer) Elliott Spotswood, was born in Tangier, where his father was physician to the English garrison. In 1693 he became an ensign in the Earl of Bath's regiment of foot, and, during the War of the Spanish Succession, served as lieutenant-quartermaster-general under Lord Cadogan, rising to the rank of lieutenant-colonel. He was wounded at Blenheim, and apparently captured at Oudenarde, since a month later Marlborough was negotiating his exchange. On June 23, 1710, he assumed office as lieutenant-governor of Virginia, under the nominal governor George Hamilton, Earl of Orkney. He entered upon his new duties with a vigor rather disconcerting to a people inclined to reduce governmental activity to a minimum. He sought to regulate and stabilize the fur trade and at the same time to finance an enlightened Indian policy by the erection, in 1714, of the monopolistic Virginia Indian Company with headquarters at Fort Christanna. In 1713 the governor obtained the passage of a measure requiring inspection of all tobacco designed for export or use as legal tender. Anathema to the producer and marketer of low-grade tobacco as well as to the debtor and taxpayer, who naturally favored "cheap money," the Tobacco Act, coupled in the popular mind with the Indian Act, led to a violent quarrel between governor and burgesses in 1715, a quarrel that continued, even after the Crown had repealed both acts. His land policy was designed to encourage the actual settler as opposed to the mere speculator, to render the quit-rents as profitable as possible, and to bring completeness and order to the public records. Here he achieved fair success, much that he proposed being accepted by the colony with tolerably good grace.

However, his reforms embroiled him with two prominent members of his council, William Byrd [q.v.] the receiver-general, and Philip Ludwell the deputy auditor, who resented interference and had little taste for the additional labors the governor thrust upon them. Shortly thereafter, he found himself at odds with the majority of the council, which had thitherto supported him against the burgesses. The councillors claimed that as members of the General Court they alone had the right to compose the newly created courts of oyer and terminer. The quarrel had many side currents, and underlying the specific points at issue was a struggle for power between governor and council. Similarly, the question of the governor's right to induct ministers seems to have cloaked a contest with Commissary James Blair [q.v.] for the paramount voice in church affairs. In 1718, with both council and burgesses hostile, the situation boded little good for the public life of the colony. Pressure was brought

to bear from England, and two years later harmony was restored.

From his first arrival in Virginia he was actively identified with the problems of the frontier. His name inevitably calls to mind the picture of the governor leading a company of colonial gentlemen, rangers, Indians, and servants over the Blue Ridge and down to the waters of the Shenandoah, which the Adventurers named the Euphrates. A peak of the Ridge was loyally named Mount George, and copious potations were drunk to the royal health. Romance and policy were nicely joined when Spotswood instituted the Order of the Golden Horseshoe with the evident object of cultivating among Virginians an interest in the West. The journey of 1716, however, was merely the most famous of Spotswood's excursions to and beyond the limits of settlement. He sought to protect the colony from Iroquois raids by establishing compact communities of friendly Indians, powerful enough to resist attack and convenient for the work of missionary and schoolmaster. When the repeal of the Indian Act left him unable to finance this scheme, he negotiated a treaty with the Iroquois at Albany whereby they were to keep north of the Potomac and west of the Blue Ridge. He watched with apprehension the difficulties with the Tuscarora in North Carolina in 1712 and with the Yamasee in South Carolina in 1715. The success of either of these attacks would have placed Virginia in a serious position, and the measure of assistance that he in both instances afforded the Carolinians was not pure altruism. Behind the Indians were the Spanish and the French, and Spotswood urged upon the British authorities the advisability of seizing Florida, and of taking possession of the Appalachians before the French did so. He was handicapped by a lack of precise geographical knowledge, and some of his proposals were quite impracticable. More practical was the policy of fostering settlement in the frontier districts by exempting the inhabitants from taxes and quit-rents.

During the closing years of his administration his attitude toward colonial self-assertion mellowed perceptibly. Doubtless due in part to the conviction, born of experience, that it was futile to contend against what amounted to a Virginia nationalism, the change was natural in one who had decided to make America his permanent home. Before he ceased to be governor he had acquired, by means not always above question, an estate of some eighty-five thousand acres in Spotsylvania County. In 1722, removed from office, he retired to Germanna, where he had founded, as early as 1714, a colony of Germans as part of the scheme of frontier defense, and where he was now actively engaged in the mining and smelting of iron. In the hope of adjusting his land titles that had been challenged, he went to England in 1724. He was married, the same year, to Anne Butler Brayne, the daughter of Richard and Anne Brayne of St. Margarets, Westminster, by whom he had four children. Six years later he returned with his family to Virginia, having obtained appointment as deputy postmaster-general for the American colonies. He extended the regular postal service as far south as Williamsburg. When war with Spain broke out in 1739, he proposed the recruiting of a regiment in the colonies. He was assigned the task of raising it, was made its colonel, and was appointed major-general and second in command of the expedition that Lord Cathcart was to lead against Cartagena. Entering upon such congenial duties with customary vigor, he was halted by death, the end coming at Annapolis.

[Letters and Papers, esp. in Lib. of Cong. and in Public Records Office, London; *The Official Letters of Alexander Spotswood* (2 vols., 1882–85), ed. by R. A. Brock; Leonidas Dodson, *Alexander Spotswood, Governor of Colonial Virginia, 1710–1722* (1932); *The Writings of "Col. Wm. Byrd"* (1901), ed. by J. S. Bassett, esp. intro. pp. li-lxxv; James Fontaine, *Memoirs of a Huguenot Family* (1907), ed. by Ann Maury; Hugh Jones, *The Present State of Va.* (1724); *Dict. of Nat. Biog.*; T. J. Wertenbaker, "The Attempt to Reform the Church of Colonial Va.," *Sewanee Rev.*, July 1917; Charles Campbell, *Geneal. of the Spotswood Family* (1868); *Wm. and Mary College Quart.*, Oct. 1901, pp. 143–44; mother's maiden name "Mercer" from *Va. Mag. of Hist.*, July 1905, p. 98.]   L. D.

SPOTTED TAIL (*c.* 1833–Aug. 5, 1881), a head-chief of the Lower Brulé Sioux, was born near Fort Laramie, Wyo. He had no hereditary claims on the chieftainship, and his advancement was due to his feats as a warrior. He was in the fight near Fort Laramie on Aug. 19, 1854, in which Lieut. John Grattan's command was annihilated, and after Harney's victory at Ash Hollow, Nebr., he was demanded of the tribe, with two others, for trial. To save the tribe from further punishment the three warriors voluntarily surrendered at Fort Laramie. Imprisoned for two years, they were released to find themselves acclaimed as heroes. At the Fort Laramie council in June 1866, he opposed the stand of Red Cloud [*q.v.*] and favored the government's proposals to open the road to the gold regions of Montana. He was one of the signers of the treaty of Apr. 29, 1868, providing for an Indian reservation of the western part of the present state of South Dakota and for the withdrawal of Indian opposition to railroad construction, and he was ever afterward distinguished for his friendliness to the whites. In the same year his tribe was settled on a reservation on the Missouri River,

near Fort Randall, but within a few years was moved to the newly created Spotted Tail reservation at Camp Sheridan in northwestern Nebraska, in the vicinity of the Red Cloud reservation. On the discovery of gold in the Black Hills in 1874, he joined with Red Cloud in an effort to sell the mineral rights to the government. When it was found, however, that Spotted Tail, who considered himself an astute business man, had set the price at $60,000,000, negotiations ceased, and the government permitted the miners to enter the Black Hills region without its opposition. Nevertheless, he stoutly resisted the efforts of agitators to bring his tribe into the war of 1876 and succeeded in holding most of his followers to the reservation. In the spring of 1877 he was influential in bringing about the surrender of Crazy Horse [*q.v.*], his nephew, and in the late summer was a leading figure in the dramatic episode that ended with that fiery chieftain's death. In 1880 he seems to have become for a time inflated with an undue sense of his importance and to have threatened serious trouble; but he was soon cured and, on Red Cloud's deposal from the chieftainship of the Oglalas, was recognized as head-chief at both agencies. He did not live to enjoy the honor. On leaving a council he was followed by Crow Dog, a prominent sub-chief, who shot and killed him.

According to Bourke, though a man of dignified bearing, with strong, melancholy features, he was at all times "easy and affable in manner ... sharp as a brier, and extremely witty. He understood enough English to get along at table," had good conversational powers, and his opinions, which were carefully considered, were clearly expressed. He was, in Bourke's opinion, one of the great men of this country, "bar none, red, white, black, or yellow" (*post*, pp. 400–01). Eastman, a Sioux, credited him with being one of the most brilliant of the Sioux leaders, but expressed the view that in manifesting so great a friendliness for the whites he was in some degree unfaithful to his people (*post*, pp. 35, 41).

[J. G. Bourke, *On the Border with Crook* (1891); Doane Robinson, "Hist. of the Dakota or Sioux Indians," *S. D. Hist. Soc. Colls.*, vol. II, pt. 2 (1904); Frank Huntington and Doane Robinson, *Handbook of Am. Indians*, pt. 2 (1910), ed. by F. W. Hodge; C. A. Eastman, *Indian Heroes and Great Chieftains* (1918); H. W. Wheeler, *Buffalo Days*, ch. xxiii (1925); Anson Mills, *My Story* (1918); report of J. M. Lee, agent at Spotted Tail Agency, Nebr., *Ann. Report of the Commissioner of Indian Affairs ... 1877* (1877), p. 462.]
W. J. G.

SPRAGUE, ACHSA W. (*c.* 1828–July 6, 1862) spiritualist, author, was born on a farm at Plymouth Notch, Vt., the sixth child of Charles (d. 1858) and Betsy Sprague (d. 1868). She was a connection of William Sprague, 1830–1915 [q.v.], and of the stepmother of Calvin Coolidge, who describes the family of Achsa Sprague as "very intellectual . . . but nervously unbalanced" (letter to the author). At twelve she began teaching in a rural school, but a scrofulous disease of the joints overtook her when she was about twenty, and though for a time she continued her duties in a crippled condition, she later became a bedridden invalid for about six years. In 1854, having been restored to apparently normal health through the agency of "angelic powers," she became a trance medium and later a lecturer on spiritualism, and addressed large audiences throughout the country. She is represented by tradition as having a personality of rare charm; it is plain that she had a wide following. Known as the "preaching woman," she opposed slavery, visited prisons in numerous cities and urged reforms, and condemned what she said was the contemporary belief that "woman must be either a slave or a butterfly." She abandoned the *materia medica* of the day, experimented with magnetizing processes, with galvanic bands, with hypnotism, and with sensational séances, and came finally to a belief in mental healing, which with no strange physical manifestations had raised her almost instantly from her sick bed and seemed to her "the voice of God."

She read widely in the poets and wrote voluminously, especially during the last few years of her life. Many of her compositions were produced by automatic writing—at the rate of 4,600 lines in seventy-two hours on the first draft of "The Poet"—in which she believed herself to be under the control of divine and mystic energies. Her poems, which display no careful craftsmanship, are spontaneous expressions of spiritual anguish and despair, appeals for economic justice and equality, or exultant affirmations of faith and hope. Only a very small part of what she produced is represented by her published books, *I Still Live, A Poem for the Times* (1862) and *The Poet and Other Poems* (1864). Among her unpublished writings, which include essays, journals, and a play, is an autobiographical poem of 162 pages, which she composed in six days in such a nervous state that spinning-wheel, latches, and roosters were muffled for her peace of mind. In 1861 she became a victim of her old affliction and died a year later at the age of thirty-four. She was buried at Plymouth.

[See biog. sketch by M. E. G. in A. W. Sprague, *The Poet and Other Poems* (1864); Athaldine Smith, *Achsa W. Sprague and Mary Clarke's Experiences in the First Ten Spheres of Spirit Life* (Oswego, N. Y., 1862); O. R. Washburn, in *Nat. Spiritualist*, Feb. 1, 1932; W. J. Coates, in *Drift-Wind*, Nov. 1927; death notice in *Rutland Weekly Herald*, July 24, 1862. The chief sources are materials in the possession of the author (clippings from *New England Spiritualist*, 1855–57, and other publications; diary, letters, poems, sermons, etc.), some of which are being prepared for publication.]
L. T.

SPRAGUE, CHARLES (Oct. 26, 1791–Jan. 22, 1875), banker and poet, was born in Boston, one of seven sons of Samuel and Joanna (Thayer) Sprague. His father, a native of Hingham, Mass., and a descendant of William Sprague who came to New England in 1628 and settled in Hingham in 1636, was one of the "Indians" of the Boston Tea Party. Young Sprague attended the Franklin School for a time, but his formal education was brief, and at the age of thirteen he was apprenticed to Messrs. Thayer & Hunt, importers of dry goods. At the age of nineteen he entered into partnership with a grocer; five years later, abandoning this project, he formed another partnership, which, however, lasted but four years. In 1819 he became a teller in the State Bank; with the establishment of the Globe Bank in 1824 he became its cashier, a position he held for the next forty years. As a business man, he was greatly respected and trusted. Almost never absent from his accustomed desk in the bank, "he occupied a foremost place in the financial circles of Boston" (Quincy, *post*, p. 41).

It is, however, as a poet that he will be chiefly remembered. A literary amateur in the sense that his best poetry was written in spare moments snatched from business duties, he held during the late twenties and thirties a significant place in the literary life of Boston. Like his contemporaries, William Cullen Bryant and Fitz-Greene Halleck [*qq.v.*], with whom he was frequently ranked by critics of that day, he disdained the subtleties of thought and mood which were becoming so popular in the work of Tennyson and Browning. Relying upon clarity and purity of diction, he found his chief inspiration in the poetic traditions of the preceding century. The heroic couplet is employed in five prize prologues which he wrote for the opening of new playhouses and in *Curiosity*, delivered at the Harvard Phi Beta Kappa exercises of 1829, which in recurring moods of humor, satire, and didacticism traces the course in human life of curiosity, "the power That masters man in every changing hour." A group of odes to be found in his collected works (*Writings of Charles Sprague, Now First Collected*, 1841, of which there were four later editions) is best represented by the one on Shakespeare, in which he affects with some success the dignity of Collins and Gray, and that delivered "at the Centennial Celebration of the Settlement of Boston," which introduces a panegyric on the American Indians and received the commendation of the London *Athenaeum* in the issue of Jan. 29, 1831 (reprinted in *Museum of Foreign Literature,* Apr. 1831). In many of his shorter pieces, such as "The Funeral" and "The Tomb of Emmeline," he relied too heavily on the morbid, graveyard sentimentality of Mrs. Lydia Howard Huntley Sigourney [*q.v.*], although even in some of these verses one finds at times a strain of genuine pathos. He was probably at his best, however, in the whimsical didacticism of the lines "To My Cigar," in the simple sincerity of "The Brothers," and in the quiet deism of "The Winged Worshippers." Undoubtedly much overrated as a poet by his contemporaries, he must today take his place among those minor authors without whom we should scarcely have had an early American literature.

Like Halleck, he wrote most of his poetry and achieved his greatest fame early in life. But, partly from ill health and partly from temperament, he became as time went on more and more retiring, hardly ever venturing outside the limits of Boston. His marriage on May 8, 1814, to Elizabeth Rand provided him with a happy home and four children, one of whom, Charles James, born in 1823, attained some note as a poet. Unable to leave his home during the last few years of his life, he had ample time for reading and reflection. Years before, his religious beliefs had acquired a tinge of rationalism which in later life he freely avowed to his friends.

[Hosea Sprague, *The Geneal. of the Sprague's* (*sic*) *in Hingham* (1828); W. V. Sprague, *Sprague Families in America* (1913); C. J. Sprague, in *The Poetical and Prose Writings of Charles Sprague* (1876), with portrait; Edmund Quincy, *Memoir of Charles Sprague* (1875); R. C. Waterston, *Remarks upon the Life and Writings of Charles Sprague* (1875); J. S. Loring, *The Hundred Boston Orators* (1853); E. A. and G. L. Duyckinck, *Cyc. of Am. Lit.* (1855), vol. II, pp. 132–35; R. W. Griswold, *The Poets and Poetry of America* (1850); E. P. Whipple, *Essays and Reviews* (1848), vol. I, pp. 38–44; J. T. Buckingham, *Personal Memoirs* (1852), vol. I, pp. 184–200; *New England Mag.*, Aug. 1832; reviews in *Littell's Living Age*, Jan. 12, 1850, and *North Am. Review*, July 1824, Apr. 1830; obituary in *Boston Transcript*, Jan. 22, 1875; date of death from Registry Dept., Boston, Mass.]   N. F. A.

SPRAGUE, CHARLES EZRA (Oct. 9, 1842–Mar. 21, 1912), banker, writer on accountancy, teacher, was born at Nassau, N. Y., the son of the Rev. Ezra Sprague and his second wife, Elisabeth Brown (Edgerton) Sprague. He was a descendant of Ralph Sprague who emigrated from Dorsetshire, England, and arrived in Salem, Mass., in 1628. At fourteen he entered Union College, Schenectady, N. Y., where he took all prizes for which he was eligible and was elected to Phi Beta Kappa at graduation in 1860. Later he received the degree of M.A. in course from Union University, for which he acted as

alumni trustee, 1894–98, and as life trustee from 1906 until he resigned shortly before his death. In 1862, after teaching at Greenwich Union Academy, he enlisted in the New York National Guard and saw active service in the Civil War until he was wounded at Little Round Top during the battle of Gettysburg. For meritorious service in that battle he was made a brevet colonel of the New York Volunteers. He served again in the New York National Guard, 1870–72, and 1897–1901; during the latter period he was assistant paymaster-general for the state of New York with the rank of colonel. From 1864 until 1870 he taught at Yonkers (N. Y.) Military Institute, Peekskill Military Academy, and Poughkeepsie Military Institute. He wrote numerous articles on military tactics, on which he became an expert, and because of his knowledge of British and Prussian methods was asked to aid the commandant of the United States Military Academy in revising the book of tactics used there.

In 1870 his career as a banker began. At that time his ability as an interpreter—he spoke sixteen languages, studying obscure ones and unusual dialects as a hobby—brought him a position as clerk with the Union Dime Savings Bank in New York City; seven years later he became secretary, then treasurer, and in 1892 president, the position which he held at his death. Becoming a skilled accountant during his clerkship, he was one of the first to qualify as a certified public accountant. He introduced from Great Britain the idea of having a board of examiners for public accountants and served as chairman of the New York board, 1896–98. Savings bank bookkeeping owes much to the systems which he devised or adapted. Always in search of new and more efficient ways of performing routine tasks, he introduced the use of the small check book and pass book, and loose-leaf ledger, designed the first machine (which he never patented) for the making of ledger entries, and worked out amortization methods that are widely used in savings banks. He was a moving spirit in the establishment of the New York University School of Commerce, Accounts, and Finance, and found time in the midst of numerous other activities to teach evening classes there as professor of accountancy from 1900 until his death. Since his subject was without methods, texts, or other materials, he himself provided them for his students. Between 1900 and 1910 he wrote *The Accountancy of Investment* (1904), *Extended Bond Tables* (1905), *Problems and Studies in the Accountancy of Investment* (1906), *Logarithms to 12 Places* (1910), *Amortization* (1908), *Tables of*

Compound Interest (1907), and *The Philosophy of Accounts* (1908), a fifth edition of which was published in 1922. His *The Algebra of Accounts* had appeared as early as 1880. Though he contributed articles on business to magazines and newspapers, he was interested also in such widely divergent matters as croquet, simplified spelling, Esperanto, Volapük, and the revival of Gaelic, and wrote occasional articles on them as well. His wife was Ray Ellison of New York City (d. May 17, 1931), whom he married Apr. 2, 1866. Of their four children, all daughters, two survived at his death. He died of pneumonia in New York City.

[*Who's Who in America*, 1912–13; *Who's Who in N. Y.*, 1911; Helen S. Mann, *Charles Ezra Sprague* (1931), with portraits; A. V. V. Raymond, *Union Univ.* (1907), vol. II; E. G. Sprague, *The Ralph Sprague Geneal.* (1913); obituary in *N. Y. Times*, Mar. 22, 1912.]   H. J. S. M.

SPRAGUE, HOMER BAXTER (Oct. 19, 1829–Mar. 23, 1918), educator, was born at South Sutton, Mass., the second child of Jonathan and Mary Ann (Whipple) Sprague, both of old Colonial stock. On his father's side he was descended from William Sprague, who emigrated from England with his brothers Ralph and Richard in 1628, and was one of the founders of Charlestown and later of Hingham, Mass. Although he worked as a boy in a cotton mill (where he was paid $1.50 for a sixty-six hour week), became a cobbler's apprentice, and had only desultory schooling, he entered Yale in September 1848 and graduated in 1852. After his graduation he taught Greek and Latin at Worcester, Mass., studied law, and in 1854 was admitted to the bar. On Dec. 28, 1854, he married Antoinette Elizabeth Pardee of New Haven, Conn., by whom he had four children. He served as principal of the Worcester High School from 1856 to 1859, but then returned to New Haven to practise law. At the opening of the Civil War he raised a volunteer company and was elected captain; his war experiences he described in two books, *History of the 13th Infantry Regiment of Connecticut Volunteers* (1867), and *Lights and Shadows in Confederate Prisons* (1915).

After the war he went back to educational work with renewed vigor. During 1866 and 1867 he was principal of the Connecticut State Normal School at New Britain, Conn., and in 1868 a member of the Connecticut House of Representatives, where he was chairman of the joint standing committee on education. In the fall of 1868 he became professor of rhetoric and English literature on the first faculty at Cornell University under Pres. Andrew Dickson White [*q.v.*]. Leaving Cornell in 1870, he became presi-

dent of Adelphi Academy in Brooklyn, N. Y., where his developing talents as a lyceum speaker brought him wide acclaim. He returned to New England in 1876 as headmaster of the Girls' High School of Boston, continued to lecture widely, and became a director of the Boston Watch and Ward Society. In 1879 he founded the Martha's Vineyard Summer Institute, the "first general summer school in the United States." But his spirit was not entirely content with the life of a New England headmaster. In 1885 he accepted the presidency of Mills College at Oakland, Cal., newly reorganized; two years later he assumed the same office at the University of North Dakota, which had recently been established at Grand Forks, Dakota Territory. When in 1889 North Dakota entered the Union, he prepared the article on education for the new constitution, at the unanimous request of the constituent assembly. A moderate Republican in politics and hence a member of the dominant political faction, it was only his unswerving opposition to the Louisiana lottery scheme that kept him from being elected the first United States senator from North Dakota. Retiring from active administrative work in 1891, he spent most of his later years in Newton, Mass. He gave occasional lectures at the University of Southern California, at Drew Theological Seminary, and at Cornell, and wrote a number of books, among them *Shakespeare's Alleged Blunders in Legal Terminology* (1902), *The True Macbeth* (1909), *Caesar and Brutus* (1912), *The Book of Job; the Poetic Portion Versified* (1913), which he prepared in his eighty-fourth year, and *Studies in Shakespeare, First Series* (1916). At the time of his death he left completed a second series of studies in Shakespeare. He wrote several autobiographical articles for the *Tomahawk,* published by Alpha Sigma Phi (February, May 1916), and one of reminiscences which appeared in the *Quarterly Journal of the University of North Dakota* (October 1916). In many respects he represented the best qualities in post Civil War America—its optimism, its moral earnestness, its devotion to education, and its intense belief in progress. His greatest joy was not in his personal achievement but in his friendships with those men and women all over the country who had been his "boys and girls" in their student days, and whom, with a kind of patriarchal dignity, to the day of his death he regarded as being in a peculiar sense his own.

[The principal source is Sprague's autobiog. in the *Tomahawk,* Feb., May 1916. See also his reminiscences in *Quart. Jour. of the Univ. of N. Dak.,* Oct. 1916; V. P. Squires, *Ibid.,* May 1928; *Who's Who in America,* 1916–17; *Obit. Records Grads. Yale Univ. . . . . 1918* (n.d.); *Records of the Class of 1852, Yale Coll.* (1878); A. B. R. Sprague, *Geneal. (in Part) of the Sprague Families in America* (1905); W. V. Sprague, *Sprague Families in America* (1913); obituaries in *Boston Transcript,* Mar. 23, *N. Y. Times,* Mar. 24, and *Grand Forks Herald,* Mar. 25, 1918. There is a collection of Sprague correspondence and other materials in the Alpha Sigma Phi alumni lib. at Yale Univ.]

J. D. S.

SPRAGUE, KATE CHASE (Aug. 13, 1840–July 31, 1899), political hostess, was born in Cincinnati, Ohio, the daughter of Salmon Portland Chase [*q.v.*] and his second wife, Eliza Ann (Smith) Chase. She was christened Katherine Jane. Her mother died in 1845, and seven years later her stepmother was dead, leaving a daughter. In the years that followed, the lonely father turned more and more to his elder daughter, whom he indulged greatly, and whose talents and personality he developed by participation in his own career. Her schooling was begun by him, and from 1847 to 1856 she was a pupil at the school kept by Henrietta B. Haines in New York City. In Columbus, when her father was governor of Ohio, she studied at Heyl's Seminary, where she specialized in music and languages and became proficient in French. Proficiency in German was to come later, from her travels and her residence abroad. From her sixteenth year she was her father's official hostess. At eighteen, according to Carl Schurz, "she had something imperial in the pose of her head," and "took a lively and remarkably intelligent part" in the conversation at her father's table (*The Reminiscences of Carl Schurz,* II, 1907, 169). With her pale auburn hair, white skin, pert nose, and graceful figure she was a beauty. Already she was thoroughly extravagant in clothes and personal expenditures. She went with Chase to the Republican convention in Chicago in 1860 and worked hard for his nomination as presidential candidate. When he became secretary of the treasury she established a salon in their home at Sixth and E streets. Her marriage on Nov. 12, 1863, to William Sprague [*q.v.*] was declared to be the most brilliant wedding Washington had ever seen. She was referred to as "the toast of the nation." What she wore, said, and did became national news. "The birth of her first baby,"—a son who in 1890 committed suicide—"was a national event, every woman in the country reading descriptions of the layette" (Bowers, *post,* p. 254). The Sprague country home, "Canonchet," built in 1868, became a showplace, where some of the country's greatest were entertained. The Sprague wealth became an instrument to further her political ambitions for her father. Jealous for her father's political future, she disliked Lincoln and was believed to

have known about the "Pomeroy Circular" even though Chase was ignorant until he saw it in print. From time to time newspapers noticed her political influence, and gossip was ever busy with the subject (*New York Herald,* Jan. 20, 1868; *Independent* (N. Y.), June 4, 1868; Warden, *post,* pp. 705–06). At the National Democratic Convention of 1868 in New York she waged a vigorous campaign for her father. "Competent judges have believed that had she been able to go into the convention and make her combinations on the spot she would have secured his nomination" (A. B. Hart, *Salmon Portland Chase,* 1899, p. 420).

By 1866 it had been whispered that her marriage was in difficulty, and with the stress due to Sprague's financial difficulties in 1873 the breach widened with a series of quarrels discussed in public print. In August 1879 Sprague in a jealous rage attacked with a gun his children's German tutor and Roscoe Conkling [*q.v.*]. Newspapers the next day and for days following described the scene and the details of what the parties to the quarrel said to reporters and to others. After divorce proceedings, scandalous and widely discussed, she was granted a divorce in 1882 and sailed for Europe with her three daughters. In 1886 she returned to Washington to take up a dreary existence at "Edgewood," her father's old home, where in her last years she struggled pitifully for mere existence, raising chickens, peddling milk, and always getting deeper in debt. In 1896 Henry Villard raised a fund sufficient to pay the mortage, and she died at "Edgewood."

[Consult bibliog. of sketches of father and husband; scrapbook kept by Zechariah Chafee, the estate trustee, and now in possession of Zechariah Chafee, Jr., Cambridge, Mass.; see also M. M. Phelps, *Kate Chase* (copr. 1935), inaccurate esp. in details of the financial failure and of Chafee's relations to the estate and to the family; V. T. Peacock, *Famous Am. Belles of the Nineteenth Century* (1901); C. G. Bowers, *The Tragic Era* (1929); R. B. Warden, *An Account of the Private Life and Public Services of Salmon Portland Chase* (1874); Benj. Knight, *Hist. of the Sprague Families* (1881), esp. appendix for divorce proceedings; J. C. Chase and G. W. Chamberlain, *Seven Generations of . . . Chase* (1928); *Ladies' Home Jour.,* June 1901; *N. Y. Times,* Nov. 15, 1863, Aug. 10–19, Nov. 27, 1879, Oct. 20, 29, Dec. 5, 20, 1880–Jan. 28, Feb. 26, 1881; *N. Y. Tribune,* Aug. 13, 15, May 28, 1882, Feb. 15, 1896, Aug. 1, 1899.]

J. W. M.
K. E. C.

SPRAGUE, PELEG (Apr. 27, 1793–Oct. 13, 1880), jurist, son of Seth and Deborah (Sampson) Sprague, was born in Duxbury, Mass., one of a large family of children. His father, a merchant of Duxbury and for many years a member of the Massachusetts legislature, was descended from William Sprague, who came from England to Salem in 1628 and finally settled at Hingham, Mass. Peleg Sprague graduated from Harvard

College in 1812, and, after studying law at Litchfield, Conn., was admitted to the bar in 1815 and practised first in Augusta and then in Hallowell, Me. In August 1818 he married Sarah, daughter of Moses Deming of Whitesboro, N. Y. They had three sons and one daughter.

Sprague was elected to the first legislature of Maine after its separation from Massachusetts and served in 1820–22. He represented Maine in the federal House of Representatives from 1825 to 1829, and in the United States Senate, 1829–35. He then entered the practice of law in Boston, was chosen a presidential elector as a Whig in 1840, and in the following year was appointed United States district judge for the district of Massachusetts. In this position he found his real vocation until his retirement in 1865.

From his college days, because of a nervous affection of the eyes, Sprague was unable to read much of the time. His trouble grew worse soon after he was appointed to the bench so that during most of his judicial career he was obliged to darken the courtroom and even to sit with eyes closed while listening to those addressing him. Nevertheless, he became a really great judge. His opinions, delivered orally, disclosed the full background of an exceptional mind trained in those powers of concentration which are sometimes characteristic of the blind. Upon his retirement a committee of the bar, headed by Benjamin R. Curtis and including Sidney Bartlett and Richard H. Dana, Jr. [qq.v.], paid merited tribute to his thorough legal knowledge, to his extraordinary "power of analysis . . . united with sound judgment to weigh its results," and to his possession of "that absolute judicial impartiality which can exist only when a tender and vigilant conscience is joined to an instructed and self-reliant intellect and a firm will" (2 *Sprague's Decisions*, 352).

In March 1851 he delivered a notable charge to the grand jury after a mob had broken into the federal courtrooms, and rescued a negro named Shadrach who had been arrested as a fugitive slave. Though himself regarding slavery as a great political and moral evil, he reminded the grand jury that the fact that human institutions are not perfect is no justification of forcible resistance to government and the introduction of anarchy and violence. In 1854 he delivered what has been described as an epoch-making opinion in maritime law, holding that "when a sailing vessel, going free, meets a steamer, the rule . . . requires the former to keep her course, and the latter to keep out of the way" (*The Osprey*, 1 *Sprague's Decisions*, at p. 256). This rule has survived all attacks as the guiding rule of the

sea in American courts. During the Civil War (March 1863) he delivered a charge to the grand jury on the doctrine of treason and the powers of the federal government in which he "allowed of no line beyond which the government could not follow a treasonable rebellion" (Dana, *post*, p. 10). This address, printed and circulated by the Union League, "did more to settle the minds of professional men in this part of the country . . . than anything that appeared, from whatever source, in the early stages of the controversy" (*Ibid.*).

Before his appointment as a judge, Harvard College had offered Sprague the chair of ethics and moral philosophy, which he declined. The law school repeatedly sought his services as a professor, without avail. He retired from the bench in 1865 because of failing health, and was entirely blind for the last sixteen years of his life. He died in Boston at the age of eighty-seven. His *Speeches and Addresses* (1858) contains, among others, his speeches in Congress and his charge to the grand jury in the Shadrach case; selections from his decisions were published as *Decisions of Hon. Peleg Sprague, in Admiralty and Maritime Cases* (cited as *Sprague's Decisions*), Vol. I appearing in 1861, Vol. II in 1868.

[Justin Winsor, *A Hist. of the Town of Duxbury* (1849), p. 319; Richard Soule, Jr., *Memorial of the Sprague Family* (1847); W. V. Sprague, *Sprague Families in America* (1913); *Biog. Dir. Am. Cong.* (1928); R. H. Dana, Jr., *A Tribute to Judge Sprague* (1864); *New England Mag.*, June 1835; *Chicago Legal News*, Nov. 15, 1879; *New Eng. Hist. and Geneal. Reg.*, Apr. 1881; *Boston Daily Advertiser*, Oct. 14, 1880; judicial traditions of Judge Sprague among his successors on the bench.]   F. W. G.

SPRAGUE, WILLIAM (June 5, 1773–Mar. 28, 1836), textile manufacturer, was the son of William and Isabel (Waterman) Sprague and was born on his father's farm in Cranston, R. I. He was descended from William Sprague who emigrated from England and died at Hingham, Mass., in 1675. After obtaining the education afforded by the district schools of the time and helping in the farm work, Sprague induced his father to erect a gristmill for him in Cranston because he then had but little interest in farming. He operated this for a number of years and at the same time widened his activities to include a sawmill that he erected in the same vicinity. Both of these enterprises were very successful, and about 1808 he ventured into the field of textiles, particularly the manufacture of cotton cloth. He first converted his gristmill into a factory to card and spin cotton yarn, using the crude machinery available for the purpose. As power weaving was then unknown, he arranged with the local farmers' wives and daughters to weave his yarn on their own hand looms and return the cloth to him. After bleaching it in the open air by the sun and water method he sold the finished product to merchants as far away as Baltimore, Md. This was one of the first cotton-cloth manufactories in Rhode Island, and under his management it was continued successfully for upwards of thirteen years. Meanwhile rapid developments in cotton-mill machinery had taken place, particularly in power machinery, and in 1821 he purchased one half of the water power at Natick Falls, Kent County, R. I., and erected there a forty-two-loom cotton mill as well as a building for carding and spinning. From that time the expansion of his business was phenomenal, as evidenced by the fact that five mills were constructed and put into operation in the succeeding fifteen years. Besides being one of the earliest cotton-cloth manufacturers he was also among the first calico printers of Rhode Island, for in 1824 he transformed his original mill at Cranston into a bleaching, dyeing, and printing factory and began to manufacture and market calicoes known as "indigo blues." The printing machines first used printed but two colors, additional colors being printed by hand with wood blocks. Besides his textile interests he carried on farming to a considerable extent, specializing in stock raising. He conducted, too, in the winter season quite a lumbering business. Until in his early thirties he evidenced little interest in politics. Then he became a violent anti-Mason and did everything he could to overthrow the Masonic order in Rhode Island, even running for governor in 1832 on the Anti-Masonic Ticket. He married Anna Potter of Cranston. They had five children. He died at his home in Cranston from the effects of a bone that was stuck in his throat.

[Charles Carroll, *Rhode Island* (1932), vol. I; Benj. Knight, *Hist. of the Sprague Family in R. I.* (1881); W. V. Sprague, *Sprague Families in America* (1913).]
C. W. M—n.

SPRAGUE, WILLIAM (Sept. 12, 1830–Sept. 11, 1915), governor of Rhode Island, senator, was born in Cranston, R. I., the son of Amasa and Fanny (Morgan) Sprague, the grandson of William Sprague, 1773–1836 [*q.v.*], and the descendant of William Sprague who emigrated from England and died at Hingham, Mass., in 1675. His father greatly increased the mill holdings and capital he had inherited and in 1843 was murdered, probably because he had influenced the town council to refuse a license to sell liquor near his factory. Owing to a general belief that the wrong man was convicted and executed for

his murder, capital punishment was abolished soon afterward in Rhode Island. The boy received an inadequate education in schools in East Greenwich and Scituate, R. I., and at Irving Institute, Tarrytown, N. Y. He was fifteen when he went to work in the factory store. The next year he became a book-keeper in the Sprague counting-house. When he was twenty-six, at the death of his uncle, he and his brother assumed control of the Sprague properties. He was a handsome young man, and his great wealth soon made him a prominent figure in the state. At this time he was an enthusiastic member of the Providence Marine Artillery, of which he later became colonel. In 1859 he went to Europe and returned home to find himself the Democratic nominee for governor in the impending election. After a vigorous contest, in which he was accused of astounding bribery, he won by a large majority. In 1861 he was reëlected.

The outbreak of the Civil War served to heighten his popularity and to increase fabulously his wealth from the family cotton mills. Owing to his energy and financial support, a Rhode Island regiment was one of the first to reach Washington after the call for troops. He himself served as an aide under General Burnside and in the battle of Bull Run proved his gallantry under fire. Later he was offered the rank of brigadier-general but declined. He was one of twelve war governors who met at Altoona, Pa., in 1862 to pledge themselves to support President Lincoln's policies. That same year he was reëlected governor but resigned to become federal senator. He took his seat on Mar. 4, 1863, and served until Mar. 3, 1875. On Nov. 12, 1863, Sprague was married to Kate Chase (see Sprague, Kate Chase), the very beautiful and much courted daughter of the secretary of war, Salmon P. Chase [*q.v.*]. They had four children. During his first term in the Senate he took little part in its business, but soon after his reëlection he delivered a series of five speeches (*National Affairs, Speeches . . . in the Senate . . . Mar. 15, 17, 24, 30 and Apr. 8, 1869,* 1869), attacking what he described as the grip of capital and industry upon the organs of government. Gideon Welles (*Diary,* 1911, III, 565) wrote that, in spite of efforts to answer him, "Sprague's remarks remain"; but the speeches angered many of his constituents, because of bitter personal attacks and because they thought that he betrayed a distinct lack of responsibility as a legislator. In December 1870 he introduced a resolution providing for an investigation of charges against him of illicit trading for cotton in Texas during the war. The committee appointed held the charges were not sustained by the evidence at their disposal and was discharged on the ground that the session was too short for going into the matter further (*Senate Executive Document 10,* pt. 4, 41 Cong., 2 Sess., 1871, vol. I; *Senate Report 377,* 41 Cong., 3 Sess., 1871).

About the same time his financial standing began to be questioned. With the panic of 1873, acrimonious complaints and litigation culminated in a failure involving some $20,000,000 that wiped out all but a fraction of the Sprague wealth. Domestic troubles developed also, and in 1882 he was divorced with a good deal of scandal for both sides. Moreover his name was constantly involved in the difficulties and litigation (citations, *post*) over the Sprague properties, of which Zechariah Chafee had accepted the responsibilities of trustee on Dec. 1, 1873, when the three trustees first chosen by the creditors refused to act unless the creditors should protect them against personal liability for their conduct of the business. On Mar. 8, 1883, Sprague married Dora Inez (Weed) Calvert. In 1883 he was again candidate for governor, but he was unsuccessful. He retired to "Canonchet," his large estate at Narragansett Pier, which remained a relic of his former splendor. After this house was burned to the ground, he went to live in Paris, his mind and health much shattered. He died there, and his body was brought back to his native state for burial.

[H. W. Shoemaker, *The Last of the War Governors* (1916); Charles Carroll, *Rhode Island* (1932), vol. I; Benj. Knight, *Hist. of the Sprague Families in R. I.* (1881); W. V. Sprague, *Sprague Families in America* (1913); *Latham* vs. *Chafee,* 7 *Fed. Reports,* 520, 525, *Quidnick Company* vs. *Chafee,* 13 *Rhode Island,* 367, 438, 442, and *Hoyt* vs. *Sprague,* 103 *U. S.,* 613 for litigation over estate; for divorce see bibliography of sketch of wife, Kate Chase Sprague; scrapbook kept by Zechariah Chafee, the estate trustee, and now in the possession of Zechariah Chafee, Jr., Cambridge, Mass.; W. H. Chaffee, *The Chaffee Geneal.* (1909, pp. 237–38 for brief review of trusteeship of Sprague estate; *Providence Daily Jour.,* Apr. 12, 1869, Sept. 12, 1915; *N. Y. Tribune,* Aug. 20, 1879, Dec. 25, 1882; *Sun* (N. Y.), Dec. 19, 1880.]   E. R. B.
                                                                              K. E. C.

SPRAGUE, WILLIAM BUELL (Oct. 16, 1795–May 7, 1876), clergyman, biographer, collector, was a native of rural Connecticut, having been born in a part of Hebron which is now incorporated in the town of Andover, Tolland County. He was the youngest son of Benjamin Sprague and Sibyl, daughter of William and Sibyl (Post) Buell, and a descendant of Francis Sprague who came to Plymouth in 1623, later settling at Duxbury. Having prepared for college under Rev. Abiel Abbot, minister in the nearby town of Coventry, he entered Yale College, from which he graduated in 1815. The following year he

spent at "Woodlawn," about two miles from Mount Vernon, Virginia, as tutor in the family of Maj. Lawrence Lewis, a nephew of George Washington, and the husband of Eleanor Parke Custis, grand-daughter of Martha Washington. He then entered Princeton Theological Seminary, where he was a student until 1819. On Aug. 25 of that year he was ordained and installed as a colleague of Rev. Joseph Lathrop, who just sixty-three years before had himself been installed pastor of the Congregational Church of West Springfield, Mass. Upon Dr. Lathrop's death, Jan. 31, 1820, his colleague succeeded him.

Sprague's active ministry covered a period of fifty years, ten at West Springfield, and forty at the Second Presbyterian Church, Albany, N. Y., of which he assumed the pastorate, July 26, 1829. During this time he became one of the most widely known American clergymen of his day— an able sermonizer, constantly called upon for addresses on special occasions; a scholar especially interested in history and biography; a prolific writer on a variety of subjects; and an enthusiastic collector of autograph manuscripts. A list of his publications includes more than 150 titles, to which must be added numerous contributions to periodicals. For the most part these writings are sermons and addresses, but they also include such works as *Letters on Practical Subjects From a Clergyman of New England to His Daughter* (1822); *Lectures to Young People* (1830); *Lectures on Revivals of Religion* (1832); *Lectures Illustrating the Contrast Between Christianity and Various Other Systems* (1837); *Letters to Young Men, Founded on the History of Joseph* (1844); "Life of Timothy Dwight," in Jared Sparks's *Library of American Biography* (2 ser., vol. IV, 1845); *Memoirs of the Rev. John McDowell, D.D., and the Rev. William A. McDowell* (1864), and *The Life of Jedidiah Morse, D.D.* (1874). He made two trips to Europe, the first in 1828 and the second in 1836. While on the former he wrote a series of letters which appeared in the *New York Observer* (May 17–Oct. 4), were published in book form under the title, *Letters from Europe* (1828), and reprinted in London. His *Visits to European Celebrities* appeared in 1856. Probably his most enduring work, however, is his *Annals of the American Pulpit* (9 vols., 1857–69), an invaluable compendium of information regarding Protestant ministers in America down to 1850.

Throughout his life he was an indefatigable collector, especially of pamphlets, manuscripts, and autographs. While a tutor at "Woodlawn," he was given permission by Bushrod Washington to select from General Washington's correspondence whatever letters he wanted on condition he would leave copies of them. He thus came into possession of some 1,500 letters. At his death he is said to have had the largest and most valuable collection of autographs in the United States, numbering some 40,000 (Draper, *post,* p. 15). He was the first to complete a set of autographs of the Signers of the Declaration of Independence, and later completed two more sets. His own opinion of collectors he once expressed as follows: "I would advise you to have as little to do with an autograph collector as possible, for though there are some honorable exceptions yet, as a class, I think they rank A No. 1 in point of meanness" (Joline, *post,* pp. 39–40). He himself had some reputation for fairness and even generosity, but Christopher C. Baldwin wrote regarding him: "He has so much fury about him in collecting autographs that he would carry off everything that had a name attached to it. I am heartily glad he has gone out of New England, for he is so much esteemed wherever he goes that people let him into their garrets without any difficulty, and, being a Doctor of Divinity, they never think to look under his cloak to see how many precious old papers he bears off with him" ("Diary," *post,* pp. 297–98).

After his resignation at Albany, Sprague made his home with a son at Flushing, Long Island, where he died. His first wife, to whom he was married on Sept. 5, 1820, was Charlotte Eaton of Brimfield, Mass., daughter of Gen. William Eaton [*q.v.*]. She died the following year, and on Aug. 2, 1824, he married Mary Lathrop of West Springfield, who died in 1837. His third wife was her sister, Henrietta Burritt Lathrop, to whom he was married on May 13, 1840. By the first marriage he had one child; by the second, four; and by the third, five.

[F. B. Dexter, *Biog. Sketches, Grads. Yale Coll.,* vol. VI (1912); Joel Munsell, in *Colls. on the Hist. of Albany,* vol. IV (1871); C. B. Moore, "Biographical Sketch of the Rev. William Buell Sprague, D.D., LL.D.," *N. Y. Geneal. and Biog. Record,* Jan. 1877; Albert Welles, *Hist. of the Buell Family . . .* (1881); B. W. Dwight, *The Hist. of the Descendants of John Dwight of Dedham, Mass.* (2 vols., 1874); W. V. Sprague, *Sprague Families in America* (1913); "Diary of Christopher Columbus Baldwin," *Trans. and Colls. Am. Antiquarian Soc.,* vol. VIII (1901); L. C. Draper, *An Essay on the Autographic Collections of the Signers of the Declaration of Independence and of the Constitution* (1889); A. H. Joline, *The Autograph Hunter and Other Papers* (1907); *Albany Evening Journal,* May 9, 11, 12, 1876; Sprague papers in Yale Univ. Lib.]

H. E. S.

SPRECHER, SAMUEL (Dec. 28, 1810–Jan. 10, 1906), preacher, scholar, educator, was born in Washington County, Md. His father, David Sprecher, was one of three brothers who emigrated to America from Germany before the Revolution; his mother was probably a native of Washington County. He was the youngest of ten children and of delicate constitution. He early showed unusual intellectual ability and was very religious. After clerking for a while in a store in Williamsport, Md., he entered the Gymnasium in Gettysburg, Pa., in 1830, and was a student when it was organized as Pennsylvania (now Gettysburg) College in 1832. In 1834 he entered the Lutheran Theological Seminary at Gettysburg from the junior year in college, and was under the tutelage of Samuel Simon Schmucker [*q.v.*]. He was graduated from the Seminary in 1836, and on Oct. 13 of that year he was married to Catharine, the daughter of John George Schmucker [*q.v.*]. They had nine children, six boys and three girls. He was pastor of Zion Lutheran Church, Harrisburg, Pa., from 1836 until 1840, when he resigned because of poor health and became principal of Emmaus Institute, Middletown, Pa. He was pastor at Martinsburg, W. Va., from 1842 to 1843, and at Chambersburg, Pa., 1843 to 1849. Before Dr. Ezra Keller, the first president of Wittenberg College, Springfield, Ohio, died in 1849, he chose Sprecher as his successor. The trustees acted in harmony with his suggestion, and Sprecher was president from 1849 to 1874, professor of theology and philosophy, 1874 to 1880, professor of systematic theology, 1880 to 1884, and professor emeritus until his death.

In 1849 Wittenberg College was still a pioneer educational venture and the new president acted also in the capacity of chief teacher and field agent. During his administration the first building, begun under his predecessor, was completed, the endowment fund was started, and the teaching staff and the student body were enlarged. Though he was small of stature, weak in voice, and without forceful manner, his presence was always felt. Through sheer power of personality, he exercised his peculiar talents to maintain an institution of admirable academic standing. He was a born teacher and was revered by his students in philosophy and theology. He was a persuasive and convincing preacher, though somewhat handicapped by his stature and voice. His message was conservatively evangelical; his methods were often sanely evangelistic. In spite of his aggressive intellectual urge, he was a mystic pietist, representing, as did S. S. Schmucker, the conservative movement of the American Lutheran Church, which a later generation came to consider too liberal. Administrative duties and a heavy teaching load interfered with his creative work. Early in life he planned a translation of I. A. Dorner's *Entwick-*

lungsgeschichte der Lehre von der Person Christi (1845), but this work was delayed by other more pressing tasks and was finally performed by others. Until he was in the late sixties he had published only articles in religious and theological journals. In 1879 he published *The Groundwork of a System of Evangelical Lutheran Theology,* the only volume that came from his pen. Sprecher lived to be ninety-five years of age. He spent his last years at the home of a daughter in San Diego, Cal., where he died, and is buried at Springfield, Ohio.

[P. G. Bell, ed., *Samuel Sprecher, In Memoriam* (1906); G. G. Clark, *Hist. of Wittenberg Coll.* (1887); W. H. Wynn, article in the *Luth. Quart.,* Apr. 1906; C. B. Stover, C. W. Beachem, *The Alumni Record of Gettysburg Coll.* (1932); *Ohio State Jour.* (Columbus), Jan. 12, 1906.]   S. G. H.

SPRECKELS, CLAUS (July 9, 1828–Dec. 26, 1908), sugar manufacturer and California capitalist, was born in Lamstedt, in Hanover, Germany, eldest of the six children of Diedrich and Garinna (Back) Spreckels. In 1846 he came to America and found employment in a grocery store in Charleston, S. C., eventually buying the business. Here, in 1852, he married Anna Christina Mangel. In 1855 he sold this business and removed to New York City, where he successfully ran a wholesale and retail grocery store. His brother Bernard, returning from California, induced him to dispose of his profitable New York enterprise and to move in 1856 to San Francisco. Here he again operated a grocery store, soon selling it, however, and engaging in the more profitable brewing business.

In 1863 Claus and his brother established the Bay Sugar Refining Company, getting their raw material from the Hawaiian Islands. Two years later he sold his interest, and went to Europe to study the manufacture of sugar in all its aspects. Returning to California in 1867 with new ideas and improved machinery, he organized the California Sugar Refinery, and within five years the plant had grown to large proportions, with an output of fifty million pounds a year. He invented and patented, July 28, 1874, a method of manufacturing hard or loaf sugar. Between 1881 and 1883, he completed the construction in San Francisco of the largest refinery on the Pacific Coast. Convinced of the commercial possibilities in the sugar-beet industry, he went to Europe and purchased machinery for a sugar-beet refinery, which he established at Salinas, Cal., near two large sugar-beet ranches which he had previously begun to develop. To connect these projects with San Francisco he financed the Pajaro Valley Railroad, opened in 1895 and completed in 1898. For many years he held a virtual monop-

oly of the manufacture and sale of refined sugar on the Pacific Coast, and was called the "Sugar King." Enraged at the competition and threats of the Sugar Trust, he dramatically carried the war into the enemy's country by constructing a three million dollar refinery in Philadelphia (1888–89), which he compelled the Trust to buy at his own price. He fought the transportation monopoly of the Southern Pacific Railroad by aiding in the financing of the San Francisco & San Joaquin Valley Railway, which later became a part of the Santa Fé system. By organizing the Independent Light & Power Company (1899) and the Independent Gas & Power Company (1903), he compelled the San Francisco Gas & Electric Company first to reduce rates and improve the service to the people of San Francisco and then to purchase the independent companies. By organizing a rival street railway company (1906), he attempted to prevent the United Railroads under Patrick Calhoun from setting up an overhead trolley system on San Francisco's principal streets.

Shortly after moving to California, Spreckels became deeply interested in the development of the sugar industry in the Hawaiian Islands, and eventually obtained from the King a concession of upwards of 40,000 acres. This he proceeded to develop through the Hawaiian Commercial Company. Over the control of this company and its rich plantations a family feud, which had been in existence for some time, came to a climax in 1899. After long and bitter financial and legal battles, the sons, Rudolph and Claus Augustus, defeated their father and their two brothers, Adolph and John Diedrich [*q.v.*]. They secured control of the company, reorganized its affairs, and sold their interests at a great profit. A family reconciliation was effected in 1905, and thereafter Rudolph became the active manager of his father's affairs. Claus at his death left a fortune of not less than $15,000,000, two-thirds of which was invested in real estate, including the Spreckels Building on Market Street, the first skyscraper in San Francisco. He owned several fine residences, the one on Van Ness Avenue being partially destroyed at the time of the great fire. He gave generously to the welfare of San Francisco and its institutions. He never sought office, though he was a presidential elector on the Republican ticket in 1872. He was a man of unusual force of character, endowed with boundless pluck, daring, and resourcefulness. He died in San Francisco, survived by his wife, four sons, and a daughter.

[Alonzo Phelps, *Contemporary Biog. of California's Representative Men* (1881); *The Bay of San Francisco* (1892); R. D. Hunt, *Cal. and Californians* (1926);

Who's Who in America, 1908–09; San Francisco Call, Mar. 24, 1906, Dec. 27, 1908; San Francisco Chronicle, Dec. 27, 1908; San Francisco Bulletin, Feb. 11, 1905; article in Los Angeles Express, May 19, 1906, repr. in B. K. Power, William Henry Knight (1832); N. Y. Times, Dec. 27, 1908.]
          P. O. R.

SPRECKELS, JOHN DIEDRICH (Aug. 16, 1853–June 7, 1926), sugar merchant and California capitalist, was the eldest of thirteen children born to Claus Spreckels [q.v.] and Anna (Mangel). Three years after his birth in Charleston, S. C., his parents moved to San Francisco. He was educated in the public schools, and in Oakland College, Oakland, Cal., later studying chemistry and mechanical engineering in the Polytechnic College in Hanover, Germany. Upon his return to California, he became an apprentice in the technical and business departments of his father's sugar refinery, and at the age of twenty-two was made a plant superintendent. In 1876 he went to the Hawaiian Islands and devoted a year to sugar analysis, and later superintended the erection of a sugar mill and the development of his father's sugar plantations. In 1880 he founded the J. D. Spreckels & Brothers Company, shipping and commission merchants, which in December 1881 established the Oceanic Steamship Company, operating between San Francisco and the Hawaiian Islands. Subsequently, the firm's shipping interests were extended to Australia and New Zealand.

Visiting San Diego on a pleasure trip in 1887, he became captivated with the locality and made it the chief seat of his activities for the rest of his life, contributing in many ways to the development of the city and nearby Coronado. First he built a wharf and began supplying coal to the Santa Fé Railroad; in 1887 the Spreckels Brothers' Commercial Company was organized and soon practically controlled the import and export trade of San Diego. He promoted the erection of the Coronado Beach Hotel; bought the San Diego street railway and supplanted horsepower with electricity; aided the city in obtaining an adequate supply of pure water; erected modern office buildings, a theatre, and two more hotels. He generously aided in the success of the Panama-California Exposition (1915–16), and among his best known benefactions was the gift of the great organ in Balboa Park, dedicated on the eve of the opening of the Exposition. Another of his notable benefactions was a large gift which he, a 33rd degree Mason, made to Mercy Hospital, a Catholic institution, for a much needed addition. Through his efforts, the San Diego & Arizona Railway (later part of the Southern Pacific system) was built during the World War as a link between San Diego, the Imperial Val-

ley, and the East. In most of these interests and activities he was closely associated with his brother Adolph B. Spreckels, who died in 1924.

He was president or vice-president of many business corporations, including the Oceanic Steamship Company, the Western Sugar Refining Company, the Spreckels Sugar Company, the San Diego Electric Railway, the Pajaro Valley Railroad, and the San Diego & Arizona Railway. He was a member of numerous clubs, including the Pacific Union and Bohemian Club of San Francisco and the San Francisco and San Diego yacht clubs. His magnificent yacht *Venetia* he turned over to the government during the World War. Yachting, music, and art were his favorite avocations. In 1897 he purchased the *San Francisco Call* and conducted it until 1913, when it became an evening paper, with Spreckels holding a minority interest. At one time he was a dominant figure in the Republican party of the state. In October 1877 he married Lillie C. Siebein of Hoboken, N. J.; four children were born to them. Although he owned a beautiful residence in San Francisco, his favorite home was in Coronado, where he lived during the last twenty years of his life and died.

[Who's Who in America, 1920–21; R. D. Hunt, Cal. and Californians (1926); The Bay of San Francisco (1892); San Francisco Call, San Francisco Chronicle, San Francisco Examiner, and N. Y. Times, June 8, 1926; San Francisco Bulletin, June 7, 1926; C. A. McGrew, City of San Diego and San Diego County (1922), II, 3–6; San Francisco: Its Builders, Past and Present (1913).]
          P. O. R.

SPRING, GARDINER (Feb. 24, 1785–Aug. 18, 1873), Presbyterian clergyman, was born at Newburyport, Mass., descended from John Spring who settled at Watertown, Mass., in 1634. His father was Samuel Spring [q.v.] and his mother, Hannah (Hopkins) Spring, the daughter of Samuel Hopkins, for fifty-six years minister in Hadley, Mass. Spring graduated at Yale College in 1805, entered a New Haven law office, then went to Bermuda to teach, and remained until late in 1807, except for a visit during which he was married to Susan Barney of New Haven, on May 25, 1806. Resuming his legal studies, he was admitted to the bar in December 1808 and began practice in New Haven. Before long a religious experience that had begun in college caused his decision to become a minister. In the autumn of 1809 he entered Andover Theological Seminary, where he studied for eight months. Called to the pastorate of the Brick Presbyterian Church, then located on Beekman Street at Nassau, he was ordained and installed on Aug. 8, 1810, as colleague to the aged John Rodgers, 1727–1811 [q.v.].

He took up this pastorate, his life-work, with a concentrated devotion that remained constant with him. From the first, preaching was his chief concern. In his early ministry, as always, his sermons came out of diligent study and wide reading but were definitely intended to produce conversions. He believed firmly in the revival method, which then dominated the American churches. During the twenty years preceding 1834 his church experienced repeated awakenings, resulting in a steady religious earnestness. Thereafter his preaching had a larger element of instruction. Distinctly pastoral and ethical, it had a strong theological framework. He was a thorough Calvinist, with considerable liberality of spirit. He protested strongly against the exclusion of several synods from the Presbyterian Church in 1837 because of theological differences, but when the church divided he and his congregation joined the conservative branch. After the Brick Church had suffered for ten years because of its down-town location—meanwhile held together chiefly by loyalty to its pastor—a new building was dedicated in 1858, which still (1935) stands at Fifth Avenue and Thirty-seventh Street. He had now built up a congregation remarkable for the strength of its membership, which included many people influential in the city, and for its abundant philanthropies. He held a commanding position in the life of New York and was active in all sorts of religious and charitable enterprises, local and national, especially in missionary causes. The publication of many of his sermons and addresses increased the influence gained by his preaching. His most widely circulated books were *Essays on the Distinguishing Traits of the Christian Character* (1813), *Obligations of the World to the Bible* (1839), and *The Power of the Pulpit* (1848). In 1866 he published two volumes of *Personal Reminiscences of the Life and Times of Gardiner Spring*. His wife, the mother of his fifteen children, died on Aug. 7, 1860, and on Aug. 14, 1861, he was married to Abba Grosvenor Williams.

The Civil War stirred him to intense activity. He had sympathized strongly with the South, because he held that slavery was recognized in the Constitution and had opposed the Abolitionists. But when secession impended, he committed himself to the cause of the Union. In the Old School Presbyterian General Assembly that met in May 1861 he proposed the "Gardiner Spring resolutions." By adopting these, somewhat amended, after a strenuous debate, the Assembly gave its allegiance to the Federal government— an action memorable in the relations of church and state. In the General Assembly of 1869, in his own church, though eighty-four and almost blind, he pled powerfully at a critical point for the reunion of the two branches of the Presbyterian Church, the New School and the Old School, and he saw it accomplished. Four years later he died in New York.

[J. O. Murray, *A Discourse Commemorating the Ministerial Character and Services of Gardiner Spring* (1873); F. B. Dexter, *Biog. Sketches of the Grads. of Yale College*, vol. V (1911); Shepherd Knapp, *A Hist. of the Brick Presbyterian Church in the City of New York* (1909); L. G. VanderVelde, *The Presbyterian Churches and the Federal Union, 1861–1869* (1932); *New York Observer*, Aug. 28, 1873.]   R. H. N.

SPRING, LEVERETT WILSON (Jan. 5, 1840–Dec. 23, 1917), clergyman, professor of English, and historian, was born at Grafton, Vt., the son of Edward and Martha (Atwood) Spring, and a descendant of John Spring who came from England and settled at Watertown, Mass., in 1634. He received his elementary education in Manchester, Vt., and was graduated from the Burr and Burton Academy in 1858. After taking the degree of B.A. from Williams College in 1863, he entered the Theological Institute of Connecticut at Hartford, from which he was graduated in 1866; the following year he continued his studies at the Andover Theological Seminary, and began preaching. His formal education completed, he was married on Sept. 25, 1867, to Sarah Elizabeth Thompson, daughter of Prof. William Thompson of Hartford. They had two children, a daughter, who died in 1888, and a son. He was ordained as pastor of the Rollstone Congregational Church of Fitchburg, Mass., in 1868 and continued at that charge till 1875, when he moved to Lawrence, Kan., for his health. After serving as minister of the Plymouth Congregational Church of Lawrence, 1876–81, he became professor of belles-lettres and English literature at the University of Kansas, Lawrence. During these years he wrote the book for which he is best known, *Kansas: the Prelude to the War for the Union* (1885), which he based not only upon printed sources but upon personal reminiscences collected from surviving pioneers. In this book, the first nonpartisan account of the Kansas struggle, he was eminently fair to John Brown; however, he offended the admirers of that crusader who wanted nothing printed but panegyrics, and brought forth a storm of criticism by his account of the massacre of Dutch Henry's Crossing and other rash exploits of Brown. The book nevertheless has become the basis for later critical studies of the fight for Kansas. In 1886 Spring became Morris Professor of Rhetoric at Williams, a position he held till he was retired in

1909 in his seventieth year. The remainder of his life he spent in Boston, where he died.

His later works include *Mark Hopkins, Teacher* (1888); *Williams College, Williamstown, Mass., Historical Sketch and Views* (1904); and *A History of Williams College* (1917). He also wrote various other sketches of Williams College for college publications and cooperative works. To the proceedings of the Massachusetts Historical Society he contributed a sketch of Col. Samuel Walker's visit to John Brown (vol. XLVII, 1914), "A Case of Church Discipline in the Berkshires" (vol. XLIX, 1916), and "The Singular Case of a New England Clergyman" (vol. L, 1917), and to the *American Historical Review*, April 1898, "The Career of a Kansas Politician," the subject being James Henry Lane [*q.v.*].

[See *Who's Who in America*, 1916–17; T. C. Smith, in *Proc. Mass. Hist. Soc.*, vol. LI (1918), pp. 214–19; obituary in *Boston Transcript*, Dec. 24, 1917. Information has been supplied by Prof. C. L. Maxcy of Williams Col., Prof. E. M. Hopkins of the Univ. of Kan., and Romney Spring, Boston, Mass., Spring's son.]

F. A. S.

SPRING, SAMUEL (Feb. 27, 1746 o.s.–Mar. 4, 1819), Congregational clergyman, one of the founders of Andover Theological Seminary and of the American Board of Commissioners for Foreign Missions, was a native of that part of Uxbridge, Mass., that is now known as Northbridge. He was a descendant of John Spring who settled in Watertown, Mass., in 1634; his parents were Col. John, a wealthy farmer, deacon, and slave-holder, and Sarah (Read) Spring. His father's opposition to an academic education for his son having been overcome by his mother's influence, Samuel pursued preparatory studies under Rev. Nathan Webb of Uxbridge and graduated from the College of New Jersey in 1771. The next three years he spent in the study of theology under John Witherspoon at Princeton, and under Joseph Bellamy, Samuel Hopkins [*qq.v.*], and Stephen West. In 1775 he joined the Continental Army and was chaplain of Arnold's expedition to Canada. He left the army at the close of 1776 and on Aug. 6, 1777, was ordained pastor of the North (now Central) Congregational Church of Newburyport, Mass., where he served the remainder of his life.

Spring occupied a position of commanding influence among the Congregational churches of New England and was identified with the "Hopkinsian" or extreme Calvinist wing. He was a leader in the formation of the Massachusetts Missionary Society in 1779, an organization devoted to the promotion of his type of theology, and was an editor of its organ, *The Massachusetts*

Missionary Magazine, established in 1803. He was also one of the founders of the Massachusetts General Association in 1803, a union of the two Calvinistic parties with a view to opposing more effectually the rising tide of Unitarianism. Much interested in theological education and an instructor of students for the ministry, he was one of the first to conceive of a school of divinity for New England and in 1806 took the lead in securing an endowment for a seminary of strict Hopkinsian principles to be established at West Newbury. At the same time another school was being projected by the more moderate Old Calvinist party at Andover, and after much adjustment the two movements were finally brought together, with the result that the Andover Theological Seminary was opened in September 1808. The West Newbury group, known as the "Associate Founders," were perpetuated in the Board of Visitors and their creed, formulated by Spring and destined to be productive of much mischief in the subsequent history of the Seminary, was added to the standards of the institution. Though reluctant at first, he finally became a champion of the union and was a Visitor and a stanch supporter to the end of his life.

Although a wave of missionary interest had been rising in the churches and colleges, no attempt at an organization to carry on missionary work had been made till the meeting of the Massachusetts General Association at Bradford in June 1810, when the American Board of Commissioners for Foreign Missions was founded. Spring was in large measure responsible for the inauguration of the enterprise and was its vice-president, a member of its prudential committee, and its ardent champion till his death. He was the author of about twenty-five publications which were mostly sermons for various occasions. Typical of them were his *Christian Knowledge and Christian Confidence Inseparable* (1785); *The Exemplary Pastor* (1791); *Two Discourses on Christ's Selfexistence* (1805). He was a clear thinker, a forceful preacher, and noted for his practical wisdom. John Quincy Adams wrote of him: "His sentiments are extremely contracted and illiberal, and he maintains them with the zeal and enthusiasms of a bigot, but his delivery is very agreeable, and I believe his devotion sincere" (*Life in a New England Town . . . Diary of John Quincy Adams*, 1903, p. 63). On Nov. 4, 1779, he married Hannah, daughter of Rev. Samuel Hopkins of Hadley, Mass. Their family consisted of eleven children, one of whom was Gardiner Spring [*q.v.*].

[Henry Bond, *Geneals. of . . . the Early Settlers of Watertown, Mass.* (1855); W. B. Sprague, *Annals Am. Pulpit*, vol. II (1857); *Personal Reminiscences of the*

Life and Times of Gardiner Spring (1866); *A Memorial of the Semi-Centennial Celebration of the Founding of the Theological Sem. at Andover* (1859); Leonard Woods, *Hist. of the Andover Theological Sem.* (1885); W. E. Strong, *The Story of the Am. Board* (1910); Williston Walker, *A Hist. of the Congregational Churches in the U. S.* (1894); *Columbian Centinel* (Boston), Mar. 6, 1819.]   F. T. P.

SPRINGER, FRANK (June 17, 1848–Sept. 22, 1927), lawyer, paleontologist, son of Judge Francis and Nancy (Coleman) Springer, was born at Wapella, Iowa. He was educated in the local public schools and the state university at Iowa City, receiving the degree of B.S. in 1867. He then studied law in the office of Henry Strong, and in 1869 was admitted to the bar and given the position of prosecuting attorney for the Burlington district. In 1873 he left Burlington for New Mexico, settling at Cimarron in the northern part of the territory, whence in 1883 he moved to Las Vegas, retaining his residence there until his death, though spending much of his time in Santa Fé and in Washington, D. C.

Springer early became one of the leading lawyers of the state, and "during all the years of his active career at the bar, either as trial lawyer or as counsel, was consulted in every case of any consequence which was heard in the courts of New Mexico" (Twitchell, *post*, p. 159). In 1890 he was elected president of the New Mexico Bar Association, and became leader in a movement providing for the immediate settlement by Congress, through a proper tribunal, of titles under Spanish and Mexican land grants, the bill establishing the "Court of Private Land Claims" which finally became a law, being, it is stated, drafted by him. His most conspicuous legal effort was as counsel in the case of the celebrated Maxwell Land Grant, which he fought in the United States courts for some thirty years and finally won, becoming in 1891 president of the Maxwell Land Grant Company. In 1880 and in 1901 Springer was a member of the legislative council of New Mexico; in 1889, of the constitutional convention. He was for five years (1898–1903) president of the board of regents of the New Mexico Normal University at Las Vegas, and he took a prominent part in the building of the Eagle's Nest Dam and the St. Louis, Rocky Mountain & Pacific Railroad.

While a student at the University of Iowa he became interested in the natural sciences, and under the extremely favorable conditions there afforded entered upon paleontological studies that in the end placed him in the foremost rank of students of the great group of fossil crinoids. Even after his removal to New Mexico, he returned for a number of years each summer to Burlington, where he and Charles Wachsmuth [*q.v.*] built up what became known in later years as the Wachsmuth-Springer collection, comprising over 100,000 individual specimens. Springer was not, however, a mere collector. He became a leader along the lines of systematic and morphologic work and published, alone or with Wachsmuth, fifty-eight books and papers on crinoids. Their first great joint work, *Revision of the Palaeocrinoidea,* a three-part volume of 725 pages, was published during 1880–86. This was followed in 1897 by a three-volume work, *The North American Crinoidea Camerata*; in 1920, after the death of Wachsmuth, by *Crinoidea Flexibilia* in two volumes; and in 1926, by *American Silurian Crinoids,* all comprising "the most magnificent of monographs on invertebrate paleontology published in this country" (Schuchert, *post*, p. 74). Springer early became interested in archaeology, also, and was one of the founders and active promoters of the museum of New Mexico and the school of American research in Santa Fé. He was prominent in the councils of the Archaeological Society of America and was for some years sponsor for its publications.

In the spring of 1906 he developed an organic disease of the heart, which became a cause of frequent prostrations. In 1910 he retired from his law practice but continued his studies on his crinoid collections, which became the property of the National Museum at Washington, where he did most of his work. His last publication, *American Silurian Crinoids,* he completed and saw through the press while confined to his bed at the home of his son-in-law in Philadelphia. On Oct. 10, 1876, he was married to Josephine M. Bishop of Santa Fé, who, with three sons and four daughters, survived him.

[Charles Schuchert, "Memorial of Frank Springer," in *Bull. Geological Soc. of America,* Mar. 1928; Charles Keyes, "Springer of the Crinoids," in *Pan. Am. Geologist,* Dec. 1927; addresses by E. L. Hewett, R. E. Twitchell, and others on the occasion of the presentation to the state of a bronze bust of Springer, at Santa Fé, Oct. 2, 1922, reprinted in his *Am. Silurian Crinoids*; *Who's Who in America* 1926–27; *Santa Fé New Mexican,* Sept. 23, 1927.]   G. P. M.

SPRINGER, REUBEN RUNYAN (Nov. 16, 1800–Dec. 11, 1884), philanthropist, son of Charles and Catherine (Runyan) Springer, was born in Frankfort, Ky. His father, a farmer, fought under General Wayne at the battle of Maumee (1794) and was for many years postmaster of Frankfort. Springer was educated in the local schools and at thirteen entered the post office as a clerk, succeeding his father as postmaster upon the latter's death in 1816. Two years later, he secured a position as clerk on the *George Madison,* a river boat that ran between Louisville and New Orleans; later, he held a similar position on the *George Washington,* a boat owned by Kilgour, Taylor & Company, the largest wholesale grocery house in Cincinnati. On Jan. 30, 1830, he married Jane Kilgour, the daughter of the senior member of this firm. Springer was soon admitted to partnership in the concern and for the next ten years was engaged in mercantile pursuits. In 1840 he retired from active business on account of ill health. Two years later he went to Europe, and again in 1844–45, 1849, and 1851. During his travels abroad he spent much time in visiting the art centers and in collecting valuable works of art. As a result of prudent investments in real estate and railroads, he accumulated a fortune. He was a large stockholder and a director of the Little Miami and the Pittsburgh, Fort Wayne & Chicago railroads, and a director in numerous banks and insurance companies.

Springer is best remembered as a patron of music and art and as a liberal donor to the Catholic Church, of which he was a devoted member. He interested himself particularly in the education of young men for the priesthood. In connection with music, he was largely responsible for providing Cincinnati with a music hall and a college of music. The music festivals held in 1873 and 1875 created great enthusiasm and suggested the establishment of a permanent institution devoted to music. In May 1875 Springer addressed a letter to John Shillito offering to donate $125,000 for the purpose of building a music hall, on two conditions: first, that the lot on Elm and Fourteenth streets be secured from the city at a nominal rental and free from taxation for the perpetual use of a society formed for the purpose; and second, that a further sum of not less than $125,000 be donated by the citizens. The offer was received with much acclaim but subscriptions came in slowly. Many felt that preference was being extended to the music hall at the expense of the exposition building. "We are a mechanical people, not a race of fiddlers," was the argument advanced (*Cincinnati Enquirer,* Dec. 11, 1884). Several times when the success of the project seemed to be threatened Springer came to the rescue with supplementary propositions, and it is estimated that his donations amounted to $190,500. He also secured a lot and advanced funds for the erection of a suitable building for the College of Music; gave the institution a permanent endowment; provided for the construction of the Odeon—an adjunct to the college, for recitals and student concerts; and established a fund of $5,000 for gold medals to be awarded to pupils of superior merit. His do-

nations to the college amounted in all to $200,-000. He was one of the incorporators in 1881 of the Cincinnati Museum Association, and left $20,000 to the Art School of Cincinnati. A quiet, unostentatious, modest man, he refused to have the Music Hall or the College of Music named after him. He had no children.

[*The Biog. Cyc. and Portrait Gallery . . . of the State of Ohio,* vol. II (1884); G. M. Roe, *Cincinnati: The Queen City of the West* (1895); C. T. Greve, *Centennial Hist. of Cincinnati* (1904), vol. I; *Cincinnati Enquirer,* Dec. 11, 12, 14, 16, 1884.]   R. C. McG.

SPRINGER, WILLIAM McKENDREE (May 30, 1836–Dec. 4, 1903), lawyer, congressman, was born in New Lebanon, Ind., the son of Thomas B. and Katherine Springer. When he was about twelve years old the family moved to Jacksonville, Ill. William attended the public schools in New Lebanon and Jacksonville and prepared for college under Dr. Newton Bateman [*q.v.*], who was then teaching in the latter city. He entered Illinois College, Jacksonville, but was dismissed in 1856 following some difficulty with the faculty. He immediately enrolled at Indiana University, where he was graduated in 1858. The following year he was admitted to the bar and began practising law in Lincoln, Ill. On Dec. 15, 1859, he married Rebecca, daughter of the Rev. Calvin W. Ruter of Bloomington, Ind. She became a writer of some note, publishing several novels and contributing poetry to current magazines. They had one son. In 1861 they moved to Springfield, Ill., where Springer entered into a law partnership with N. M. Broadwell and John A. McClernand [*q.v.*].

After the Civil War he admitted that he had not supported the war measures of the administration and took the position that the Southern states were never out of the Union. He further stated that he had been agreeably surprised by President Johnson's policies, having expected very little from him (speech reported in *Daily Illinois State Register,* Sept. 12, 1865). Springer's non-support of the war was not entirely passive, however; he was a member of two anti-administration organizations, the Sons of Liberty (*War of the Rebellion: Official Records, Army,* 1 ser., vol. XLV, pt. 1, p. 1083) and the Order of American Knights (*Ibid.,* 2 ser. VII, 298, 746). In 1862 he represented Logan County at a state constitutional convention held in Springfield and was chosen secretary. There was much bitterness between the northern and southern parts of the state at this time. Most of the convention officers were from the southern section and their attempt to force through a constitution led to increased animosity. The constitution finally accepted was defeated by vote of the people (Elliott Anthony, *Constitutional History of Illinois,* 1891; O. M. Dickerson, *The Illinois Constitutional Convention of 1862,* 1905). In 1868 Springer left his law practice to travel in Europe, partly for his wife's health and partly for pleasure. He returned to Illinois in 1870.

Ten years before he had been defeated on the Democratic ticket for representative in the state legislature, but in 1870 he was elected to represent Sangamon County. In 1874 he was elected to the Forty-fourth Congress from the twelfth district, and served continuously from Mar. 4, 1875, to Mar. 3, 1895. During these twenty years he was on many committees and chairman of some important ones—Claims, Territories, Elections, Ways and Means, Banking and Currency. He was always a friend of the territories and introduced bills under which Washington, Montana, and the Dakotas were admitted into the Union as states. He was interested in the tariff and as chairman of the Ways and Means Committee carried through several minor tariff revisions during the Fifty-second Congress. In the following Congress he used his influence in favor of the Wilson tariff measure which was passed in 1894. He was a parliamentarian, and as such was often more interested in the rules of procedure and debate than in the issues involved. "Uncle Joe" Cannon remarked that Springer had "a weakness for breaking into the limelight regardless of the inconvenience he caused other Members" (L. W. Busbey, *Uncle Joe Cannon: The Story of a Pioneer American,* copr. 1927, p. 342). Renominated for Congress in 1894, he was defeated. A friend, Henry Clendenin, editor of the *State Register* of Springfield, claimed that his defeat was due to his conversion to the gold standard after years of advocating the free coinage of gold and silver at the ratio of 16 to 1 (*Autobiography of Henry W. Clendenin,* 1926, p. 215). Upon the completion of his congressional career, Springer resumed his law practice in Washington, D. C., but was appointed in 1895 judge of the northern district of the Indian Territory and justice of the United States court of appeals in the Indian Territory. When his term expired, in December 1899, he again took up the practice of law in Washington. He died of pneumonia in his sixty-seventh year.

[*Hist. of Sangamon County, Ill.; Together with . . . Biogs. of Representative Citizens* (1881); biog. sketch in Springer's *Tariff Reform . . . Speeches and Writings* (1892); *Chicago Daily Tribune,* Dec. 5, 1903; *Ill. State Journal* (Springfield), Dec. 5, 1903; *Ill. State Reg.* (Springfield), Dec. 5, 1903; Joseph Wallace, *Past and Present of the City of Springfield and Sangamon County, Ill.* (1904); *Biog. Dir. Am. Cong.* (1928); *Who's Who in America,* 1901–02.]   E. B. E.

SPROUL, WILLIAM CAMERON (Sept. 16, 1870–Mar. 21, 1928), manufacturer, governor of Pennsylvania, was born at Octoraro, Lancaster County, Pa., the son of William Hall and Deborah Dickinson (Slokom) Sproul. On his father's side he was of Scotch-Irish ancestry, being descended from Charles Sproul, who came to America from Ireland in 1786; his mother's people were Quakers. When William was four years old the family removed to Negaunee, Mich., where he attended public schools. Returning to Lancaster County in 1882, the Sprouls decided soon after to settle in Chester, a rising industrial center of Delaware County, where their son completed the high-school course in 1887. He then entered Swarthmore College, and was graduated in 1891. As an undergraduate he interested himself in athletics, oratory, and journalism, among other distinctions achieving the editorship of the Swarthmore College *Phoenix.* Soon after leaving college he acquired an interest in the daily *Chester Times,* later extending his investments with unusual financial success to manufacturing, railroad, traction, real estate, and banking enterprises. On Jan. 21, 1892, he married Emeline Wallace Roach, grand-daughter of John Roach [*q.v.*] and daughter of John B. Roach who was the owner of a large shipbuilding concern on the lower Delaware River; they had two children.

Coincident with his entrance into business, Sproul engaged actively in local politics. In 1895, the first year he was eligible under the constitutional age requirement, he became a candidate for a seat in the Senate of the Commonwealth from the ninth (Delaware County) district, being elected thereto the following year and every four years thereafter to and including 1916. Early in his career as state senator (1896), he voted for John Wanamaker [*q.v.*], candidate for the United States Senate against Boies Penrose [*q.v.*]; the latter, however, was elected. He also opposed the reëlection to that body of Matthew S. Quay [*q.v.*], leader of the Republican state organization, who at the time was under indictment because of certain banking scandals. For these bold actions he was hailed as a reformer, destined perhaps to cleanse the Augean stables of Pennsylvania politics. After Quay's acquittal, in 1901, however, Sproul made his peace with the organization and supported its leader for the United States senatorship. Thereafter, while preserving, probably, as great a degree of independence as the boss-ridden condition of the state permitted, he remained essentially a regular Republican, at times making vigorous denials of the charge that he was an Insurgent or Progressive. While in the state Senate Sproul pushed highway construction vigorously, $100,000,000 being appropriated to that purpose during his long period of membership. In consequence he became widely known throughout the state as the "father of good roads."

As early as 1910 and again in 1914 Sproul's friends urged his candidacy for the governorship, his reply on both occasions being: "I have not cocked up my hay yet." In 1918, however, he entered the contest, winning the nomination in the direct primary by 205,000 votes. During the ensuing campaign he supported prohibition and woman's suffrage, both of which measures were opposed by the Democratic nominee, Eugene C. Bonniwell, whom he defeated by 247,222 votes. As governor from 1919 to 1923 Sproul continued his interest in good roads and secured a much needed reorganization of several branches of the state administration. He attracted wide attention by going outside the commonwealth for his superintendent of public instruction, appointing a well-known expert, Dr. Thomas E. Finegan, then deputy commissioner of education in New York. During the great steel strike of 1919 his administration was criticized severely by liberals because of the conduct of the state police in the areas affected. He pushed vigorously the proposal for a convention to revise the antiquated state constitution dating from 1874; but it was rejected by nearly 100,000 majority at the referendum of Sept. 20, 1921. At the Republican National Convention of 1920 Sproul was a "favorite son" candidate for the presidency, receiving the support of the entire Pennsylvania delegation and a total of eighty-four votes; after the ninth ballot he withdrew. Foregoing his own ambition, he had occasion as governor to appoint three men to vacancies caused by death in the United States Senate—William E. Crow *vice* Philander C. Knox, George Wharton Pepper *vice* Boies Penrose, and David A. Reed *vice* William E. Crow. After completing his term at Harrisburg, Sproul devoted himself to travel, to the interests of Swarthmore College—of the board of managers of which he was a member from 1902 onward and to which he had presented the Sproul Astronomical Observatory—and to the management of his large business interests. He died at "Lapidea Manor," the family residence, near Chester, Pa.

[*Smull's Legislative Handbook and Manual of the State of Pa.*, 1896–1916, 1919–25; *Address of Gov. William C. Sproul to the Gen. Assembly of Pa.* (1923); C. E. Slocum, *A Short Hist. of the Slocums, Slocumbs and Slocombs*, vol. I (1882); J. W. Jordan, *Encyc. of Pa. Biog.*, vol. IV (1915); G. P. Donehoo, *Pa.: A Hist.* (1926), vol. VII; *Who's Who in America*, 1926–27; *Pa. Mag. of Hist. and Biog.*, July 1928; *Evening Pub.*

Ledger (Phila.), Mar. 22, 1928; *Phila. Inquirer*, Mar. 22, 1928.]
               R. C. B.

SPROULL, THOMAS (Sept. 15, 1803–Mar. 21, 1892), clergyman of the Reformed Presbyterian Church and theological teacher, was born near Lucesco, Westmoreland County, Pa. Thither his parents, Robert and Mary (Dunlap) Sproull, north of Ireland people and Covenanters, had moved from Franklin County in 1796. The Sproulls maintained covenanting principles alone in their neighborhood for twenty years, until they were joined by David Houston. From these families there sprang an influential Reformed Presbyterian or Covenanter congregation. Thomas Sproull conformed to the teaching of his Church by leading his life wholly within its associations. Because of his parents' poverty he had in boyhood only an elementary education. From the age of twenty-three he studied for two years with Jonathan Gill, minister of the church at Lucesco, and then entered the senior class of the Western University of Pennsylvania, graduating in 1829. After leaving college he read theology with John Black, minister of the Reformed Presbyterian Church of Pittsburgh. On Apr. 4, 1832, he was licensed to preach by the Presbytery of Pittsburgh, and on the same day of 1833 he was ordained as a home missionary. At the General Synod of 1833 the Reformed Presbyterian Church divided into Old School and New School—Synod and General Synod. The New School allowed church members to vote and hold civil office, thus departing from the disapproving attitude toward the government of the United States maintained by the Church. Sproull, who was present at this meeting, sided with the Old School. The Pittsburgh Reformed Presbyterian Church having joined the New School, a small Old School Church was formed in Allegheny (North Pittsburgh), over which he was installed pastor on May 12, 1834. During his ministry of thirty-four years this congregation grew to be the strongest in the denomination.

At the founding of the theological seminary of the Church in Allegheny in 1838 Sproull was chosen professor of theology, and served until 1845, the institution then being moved to Cincinnati. In 1856 it was reëstablished in Allegheny and he again became professor. Twelve years later, when he resigned his office because of pastoral duties, the Synod asked him to leave his church and devote himself to the seminary; to this request he acceded. He was made professor emeritus in 1874, but carried on some teaching for seventeen years longer. His theology appears in his *Prelections on Theology* (1882) as Calvinism according to Covenanter traditions.

He was a leader of his Church in all its affairs. In 1847 he was moderator of its Synod. He was especially interested in its missionary work in China and in behalf of negroes and Indians. For two years he was one of the editors of the *Christian Witness,* an early anti-slavery paper published 1836–40. He was editor of the *Reformed Presbyterian* from 1855 to 1863, and then of the *Reformed Presbyterian and Covenanter* until 1874. For these periodicals he wrote many articles, chiefly in support of the distinctive tenets of the Reformed Presbyterians, and a series of sketches of their early history in America. In 1859 he was appointed to compose a declaration of the Church regarding slavery and secret societies. While he held rigidly to the peculiar witness of his Church, his gracious Christian influence was widely acknowledged. After teaching until he was eighty-eight, he spent his last days in Allegheny. He was married on July 1, 1834, to Magdeline Wallace of Pittsburgh, and had three sons who were Reformed Presbyterian ministers.

[W. M. Glasgow, *Hist. of the Reformed Presbyterian Church in America* (1888) ; R. D. Sproull, in *Reformed Presbyterian and Covenanter,* June 1892, and other articles, *Ibid.,* May, July 1892; Minutes of the Synod of the Ref. Presbyt. Church in *Reformed Presbyterian and Covenanter* ; O. H. Thompson, *Sketches of the Ministers of the Reformed Presbyterian Church of North America from 1888 to 1930* (1930) ; *Pittsburg Press,* Mar. 21, 1892.]   R. H. N.

SPRUNT, JAMES (June 9, 1846–July 9, 1924), business man, author, and philanthropist, was born in Glasgow, Scotland, the son of Alexander and Jane (Dalziel) Sprunt. The family emigrated to Duplin County, N. C., in 1852, and two years later removed to Wilmington. James attended school in Glasgow, in Kenansville, N. C., and in Wilmington. He began preparation for college but the needs of the family compelled him to go to work at the age of fourteen, though he still attended a night school and studied navigation. During the Civil War, his father was captured while attempting to run the blockade and heavy responsibilities were thrown upon the boy. In 1863, however, he went to Bermuda to become purser of the *North Heath,* a blockade runner; later, he became purser of the *Lilian.* After several trips through the Federal fleet, the ship was captured in 1864 and Sprunt was imprisoned at Fort Macon. Taken to Fortress Monroe for transfer to another prison, he escaped through cool daring and made his way by Boston to Halifax, Nova Scotia. While returning he was wrecked on Green Turtle Cay, but was rescued and became purser of the *Susan Beirne,* on which he served until the fall of Fort Fisher. Setting out from Green Turtle Cay in a launch for Wilmington, he was wrecked off Cape

Canaveral in Florida. He walked to Fernandina and, avoiding Federal troops, finally reached Wilmington.

He had brought through the blockade as a personal venture ten barrels of sugar, the profits from which he invested in cotton. Five bales survived the Federal occupation of the city, and with the proceeds from these the exporting firm of Alexander Sprunt & Son, dealing in naval stores and later in cotton, was established. Direct connections were established with British customers and presently Sprunt went to the Continent and formed connections in Holland, Belgium, France, Germany, Russia, Switzerland, and Italy. Untiring effort, keen business sagacity, and unquestioned integrity brought success and the firm became the largest exporter of cotton in the country, with more than fifty foreign agencies. In 1884 Sprunt succeeded his father as British vice-consul, holding the post until his death and twice receiving the formal thanks of the British government. From 1907 to 1912 he was Imperial German Consul and upon his retirement was decorated with the Order of the Royal Crown. For many years he was chairman of the board of commissioners of navigation and pilotage and accomplished much in securing river and harbor improvement for Wilmington. He was president of the North Carolina Literary and Historical Association, and of the North Carolina Folk Lore Society. He wrote many valuable biographical and historical sketches and several books, among them : *Information and Statistics Respecting Wilmington, North Carolina* (1883) ; *Tales and Traditions of the Lower Cape Fear, 1661–1896* (1896) ; *Chronicles of the Cape Fear River* (1914; 2nd ed., 1916) ; and *Derelicts* (1920). In 1900 he established a fund at the University of North Carolina for the publication of the "James Sprunt Historical Monographs," known after 1910 as the "James Sprunt Historical Publications." In 1883 he married Luola, daughter of Kenneth McKenzie Murchison.

Sprunt had a genius for friendship ; he was the soul of hospitality, and his home in Wilmington and his beautiful colonial plantation "Orton," on the Cape Fear, were known and loved by many. A wide reader, rich in personal experience, a gifted conversationalist, he was an ideal host. He viewed wealth as a trust and poured it out in wise philanthropy and charity. A devoted Presbyterian, he was untiring in church work. He built several churches, maintained two schools in China; established a loan fund at Davidson College; founded a lectureship at Union Theological Seminary, Richmond, Va. He also gave much financial assistance to hospital activities.

Crippled by an accident in early manhood, he was ever eager to relieve suffering, and sent all deformed and crippled children in the mill sections of Wilmington to Baltimore for orthopedic treatment.

[*James Sprunt: A Tribute* (1925); *Wilmington Morning Star*, July 10, 1924; biog. sketch in *Chronicles of the Cape Fear River* (1914); Walter Clark, *Histories of the Several Regiments and Battalions from N. C. in the Great War 1861–'65* (1901), V, 353–451; personal acquaintance.]   J. G. deR. H.

SQUANTO (d. 1622), Indian of the Pawtuxet tribe, was called Tisquantum. He is by some authorities identified with the Tisquantum whom George Waymouth [*q.v.*], according to Ferdinando Gorges's *Briefe Narration* (1658, see Baxter, *post*, vol. XIX, p. 8), carried off from the Maine coast in 1605 and with the Tantum whom Capt. John Smith brought out from England and set on shore at Cape Cod in 1615 (John Smith, *The Generall Historie of New England*, 1624, p. 222). However that may be, he was one of the Indians kidnapped by Capt. Thomas Hunt at Pawtuxet (Plymouth) later in the same year and sold into slavery at Malaga in Spain. He escaped to England and lived at London two years with John Slany, treasurer of the Newfoundland company, who sent him to Newfoundland. Capt. Thomas Dermer took him back to England in 1618. The next summer Squanto acted as Capt. Dermer's pilot to the New England coast but left him before reaching Cape Cod. Squanto made his way home to Pawtuxet and found himself the only surviving member of his tribe. Introduced by Samoset to the Pilgrim Fathers in March 1621, he conducted Edward Winslow to Massasoit [*q.v.*] and acted as interpreter in concluding the treaty of Plymouth with that chief and the Pilgrims. *"Squanto* continued with them, and was their interpreter, and was a spetiall instrument sent of God for their good beyond their expectation. He directed them how to set their corne, wher to take fish, and to procure other comodities, and was also their pilott to bring them to unknowne places for their profitt, and never left them till he dyed"* (Bradford, *post*, I, 202–03). The same year he took part in Winslow's hungry embassy to Massasoit, delivered the famous rattlesnake skin stuffed with bullets to Canonicus, and was rescued by Miles Standish from Corbitant. Squanto made himself obnoxious to the Indians by exploiting his friendship with the English and pretending a power to spread the plague. At Plymouth in the spring of 1622 he sounded a false alarm of impending treachery by Massasoit, who, when he heard of it, sent a messenger to demand Squanto, as one of his subjects. The Pilgrims were at the point of starvation, and Governor Bradford was about to deliver Squanto up, when a boat was seen at sea; and the Governor, thinking it might be Frenchmen in league with Massasoit, postponed his decision. By the time he had ascertained that it was an English boat, Massasoit's messengers had "departed in great heat." Squanto later made his peace with Massasoit. In November 1622 he served as guide and interpreter on Bradford's expedition around Cape Cod. At Chatham Harbor "Squanto fell sick of an Indean feavor, . . . and within a few days dyed ther; desiring the Gov[erno]r to pray for him, that he might goe to the Englishmens God in heaven, and bequeathed sundrie of his things to sundry of his English freinds, as remembrances of his love; of whom they had a great loss" (Bradford, *post*, I, 283).

[Wm. Bradford, *Hist. of Plymouth Plantation* (1912), vol. I, ed. by W. C. Ford; J. P. Baxter, "Sir Ferdinand Gorges," *Prince Soc. Pubs.*, vols. XVIII–XX (1890); L. N. Kinnicutt, "The Plymouth Settlement and Tisquantum," *Proc. Mass. Hist. Soc.*, vol. XLVIII (1914–15, pp. 103–18).]   S. E. M.

SQUIBB, EDWARD ROBINSON (July 4, 1819–Oct. 25, 1900), physician, pharmacist, and chemist, was born in Wilmington, Del., of Quaker parents, James R. Squibb and Catherine H. (Bonsal) Squibb. After his boyhood days in Wilmington, where he pursued his studies under the guidance of a tutor, he began an apprenticeship under Warder Morris, a druggist in Philadelphia, Pa., in 1837 and completed it under J. H. Sprague, another Philadelphia druggist, at the end of five years. Having graduated from Jefferson Medical College, Philadelphia, in 1845 with the degree of M.D., he practised medicine in Philadelphia for two years and held the positions of assistant demonstrator of anatomy, curator of the museum, and clerk of the clinic at Jefferson Medical College. On Apr. 26, 1847, he accepted a commission as assistant surgeon in the United States navy; he spent the next four years at sea as medical officer on the *Perry*, the *Erie*, and the *Cumberland* in Mexican and South American waters and on the Mediterranean. In 1851 he was assigned to duty at the naval hospital in Brooklyn, N. Y., where he began his career as a manufacturing pharmacist and chemist. It is believed that his experiences at sea with drugs and medicines of poor quality supplied to the navy were largely responsible for starting him on this career; it is known that he set about attempting to secure better supplies almost immediately after his arrival in Brooklyn. It was largely through his efforts that the Navy Department was authorized to establish its own laboratory, of which he became assistant director in 1852, for the manufacture of pharmaceuticals and chemicals. The equipment installed was for the most part crude, much of it having been designed and built by Squibb himself, yet the laboratory was a success from the start. Here ether was first manufactured by the use of steam heat instead of an open flame; the first Squibb still for the manufacture of anesthetic ether was built; processes were perfected for the manufacture of chloroform, fluid extracts, bismuth salts, calcium chloride, benzoic acid, aconite and ergot preparations, and methods were devised for the assay of opium, potent tinctures, and powdered extracts. From 1853 until 1857, when the laboratory was discontinued for lack of funds, Squibb was director. Within the same year he resigned from the navy and accepted the position of manufacturing co-partner in the firm of Thomas E. Jenkins & Company of Louisville, Ky., known as the Louisville Chemical Works. About this time the suggestion was made to him by Dr. Richard Sherwood Satterlee [q.v.], then chief medical purveyor of the army, that he start a laboratory of his own from which the army could purchase its drugs and chemicals with the assurance that they would be of high purity and strength. In 1858 he established in Brooklyn the first Squibb chemical and pharmaceutical laboratory under the name of Edward R. Squibb, M.D. Just as the work of the new establishment was getting well under way, it was completely destroyed by fire that resulted from an explosion of ether, and Squibb was severely burned. During his convalescence, however, he drafted plans for rebuilding, and a year later a new laboratory was erected. In 1892 he admitted his two sons to co-partnership and changed the name of the firm to E. R. Squibb & Sons. Shortly after his retirement in 1895, his health began to fail, and five years later he died at his home in Brooklyn, N. Y. He was survived by his wife, Caroline F. Lownds Cook of Philadelphia, to whom he was married on Oct. 7, 1852, and his three children, a daughter and two sons.

Squibb was a pioneer in the manufacture of pharmaceuticals and chemicals, and one of the leaders in independent chemical research in the United States. He differed from manufacturers generally in that he had no secrets in his business and was ready at all times to share with others the fruit of his ingenuity and labors. He was recognized as an authority on the *United States Pharmacopoeia*, in the revision of which he took a leading part, and he was an indefatigable investigator and writer. His studies and his work in improving the process of percolation were perhaps his greatest contribution to pure phar-

macy. Over a hundred of his papers on subjects of fundamental importance to pharmacy were published in the *American Journal of Pharmacy* alone; others appeared in various journals, including *An Ephemeris of Materia Medica, Pharmacy, Therapeutics, and Collateral Information,* published by Squibb at irregular intervals from 1882 until his death. (A list of his more important articles appears in *General Index to Volumes One to Fifty of the Proceedings of the American Pharmaceutical Association . . .,* 1904, compiled by H. M. Wilder.) He was a delegate to the pharmacopoeial conventions of 1860 and 1870, and served on the committee of revision of the *United States Pharmacopoeia* in 1880. From 1869 to 1872 he lectured at the College of Pharmacy of the City and County of New York (later part of Columbia University). He took an active interest in the affairs of the American Pharmaceutical Association, which he served as a member of various committees and as first vice-president, 1858–59, and was a member of numerous other scientific societies.

[*Proc. of the Am. Pharmaceutical Assoc.,* vol. XLIX (1901); *Am. Jour. of Pharmacy,* Dec. 1900; *Bull. of Pharmacy,* Dec. 1900; *Nat. Druggist,* Dec. 1900; obituary in *Brooklyn Daily Eagle,* Oct. 26, 1900; letters from Margaret R. Squibb of New York, grand-daughter of E. R. Squibb.]
                                                          A. G. D–M.

SQUIER, EPHRAIM GEORGE (June 17, 1821–Apr. 17, 1888), journalist, diplomat, and archaeologist, was born in Bethlehem, N. Y. His father, Joel Squier, minister of the village Methodist Church, was a descendant of Philip Squier, who emigrated from England to America after the Reformation, settling first in Boston and later in Connecticut; his mother, Catharine (Kilmer or Külmer) Squier, belonged to a prominent New York family, Palatine German in origin. He had little opportunity for formal schooling beyond the grades, but through study by himself he became a scholar of distinction. As a child he worked on a farm, and in his early youth taught school and studied civil engineering; but the panic of 1837 made engineering unprofitable, and he soon turned to journalism and literature. After some success as contributor to Albany papers, he launched the *Poets' Magazine* in Albany in the spring of 1842, but only two issues appeared. He was next associated with the *New York State Mechanic,* an organ for prison reform which ceased publication in 1843, and in 1844–45 was editor of the *Evening Journal,* Hartford, Conn., a Whig publication supporting Henry Clay [q.v.]. Through his efforts the party carried the state, but after Clay's national defeat he left the *Journal* and removed to Chillicothe, Ohio, where for some years he published the *Scioto Gazette.*

In 1847 and 1848 he was clerk of the Ohio House of Representatives. In Ohio, in collaboration with Edwin Hamilton Davis [q.v.], he studied the remains of the Mound Builders. The results of their researches appeared in the first publication of the Smithsonian Institution under the title, *Ancient Monuments of the Mississippi Valley* (Smithsonian Contributions to Knowledge, no. 1, 1847). Later he examined native remains in New York and published his chief work on the subject, *Aboriginal Monuments of the State of New-York* (1851), again through the Smithsonian Institution. These two studies were marked by observation and description so accurate and thorough that they became authoritative in their fields.

In April 1849, through the influence of William Hickling Prescott [q.v.], the historian, he was appointed for a term of about a year and a half chargé d'affaires to Central America. In this capacity he signed with Nicaragua an agreement for the American construction of an interoceanic canal. It was never ratified, but through being submitted to the Senate it caused considerable embarrassment to the British-American negotiations which finally resulted in the Clayton-Bulwer Treaty. In 1853, as secretary of the Honduras Interoceanic Railway Company, he visited Central America again to examine the proposed route for the road, which was never built. About 1860 he became chief editor of the publishing house of Frank Leslie [q.v.], and under his direction *Frank Leslie's Pictorial History of the American Civil War* (2 vols., 1861–62) was begun. From 1863 to 1865 he was United States commissioner to Peru and was successful in settling financial claims between the two countries. In 1868 he was made consul general of Honduras in New York City. Following his return from Peru he continued his work with *Leslie's* for some years, but gave it up when his health permanently failed and his mind became clouded. He died in Brooklyn, N. Y., after many years of hopeless illness. In 1858 he was married to Miriam Florence Folline [see Miriam F. F. Leslie] of New Orleans, La., who divorced him in 1873 and about a year later married Leslie.

The major results of his connection with Latin America were his published writings on the archaeological remains and the general conditions of the countries he visited. The best of these are *Nicaragua; Its People, Scenery, Monuments, and the Proposed Interoceanic Canal* (2 vols., 1852), *The States of Central America* (1858), and *Peru: Incidents of Travel and Exploration in the Land of the Incas* (1877). He wrote a number of other volumes and many arti-

cles of value, chiefly upon archaeological and ethnological subjects. He was honored at home and abroad as one of the most distinguished Americanists of the nineteenth century, and is perhaps the best single authority on the Central America of the period. He was handsome and distinguished in appearance, with waving hair, full beard, and fine features. He was sociable, somewhat fond of gayety, slightly vain, but had a saving sense of humor and a strong altruistic bent, and in the performance of duty was conscientious as well as energetic.

[C. H. Kilmer, *Hist. of the Kilmer Family in America* (1897); *Letters from Francis Parkman to E. G. Squier* (1911), edited by Don C. Seitz; *A List of Books, Pamphlets, and More Important Contributions to Periodicals, etc., by Hon. E. G. Squier* (1876); Joseph Sabin, *A Dict. of Books Relating to America*, vol. XXIII (1932–33), continued under the editorship of Wilberforce Eames and C. W. G. Vail; I. D. Travis, *The Hist. of the Clayton-Bulwer Treaty* (1899); Mary W. Williams, "John Middleton Clayton," in *The Am. Secretaries of State and Their Diplomacy*, vol. VI (1928), ed. by S. F. Bemis; Squier MSS. in Lib. of Cong.; obituary in *N. Y. Times*, Apr. 18, 1888.] M. W. W.

SQUIER, GEORGE OWEN (Mar. 21, 1865–Mar. 24, 1934), soldier, scientist, electrical engineer, was born at Dryden, Mich., the son of Almon Justice and Emily (Gardner) Squier. He entered the army as a second lieutenant of artillery upon his graduation, seventh in his class, from the United States Military Academy in June 1887. For the next six years he was stationed at Fort McHenry, Md., during part of that time studying physics, mathematics, and chemistry at the Johns Hopkins University, where he received the degree of Ph.D. in 1893. After several brief assignments in various parts of the country, he attended the Artillery School at Fort Monroe, Va., 1894–95, and from November 1895 to April 1898 was instructor in its department of electricity and mines. During the Spanish-American War he served as a signal officer, attaining the rank of lieutenant-colonel of volunteers, and upon his return to the Regular Army was assigned to the signal corps as a first lieutenant. He was in command of the cable-ship *Burnside*, 1900–02, laying submarine cables in the Philippine archipelago, and was superintendent of telegraph lines in the Philippine Islands for a year thereafter. Promoted captain in 1901 and major in 1903, he was signal officer in San Francisco, 1903–05, and assistant commandant of the Army Signal School, Fort Leavenworth, Kan., 1905–07. While engaged in studying various methods of cable and radio communication he discovered that growing trees could be utilized as receiving radio antennae, and demonstrated absorption by vegetation-covered areas of some of the electro-magnetic waves passing over them. After brief service in the office of the chief signal officer at Washington, 1911–12, he became military attaché at the United States embassy in London, being promoted to lieutenant-colonel in 1913. In 1912 he was also a delegate to the International Radio Telegraphic Conference in London.

He had become interested in aviation as early as 1908, and while in England made a study of European military aviation, after the outbreak of the World War closely observing technical developments in radio and aviation in the British army. Recalled to Washington in May 1916, he had charge of the aviation section of the signal corps until his appointment, Feb. 14, 1917, as chief signal officer of the army, with the rank of brigadier-general. At this time he also became a member of the Joint Army and Navy Board on Aeronautics, serving until Sept. 6, 1918. As chief signal officer he organized the cable and radio communications between military headquarters in the United States and the American Expeditionary Forces abroad.

He was a representative of the War Department and technical adviser to the American delegation at the International Conference on Electrical Communications held in Washington, D. C., in 1920. During the following year he represented the Department of State at the sessions of the provisional technical committee at the International Conference on Electrical Communications in Paris, France, and in the fall of 1921 served as an expert assistant to the American commission at the conference on the limitation of armament held in Washington, D. C. He was an *ex-officio* member representing the War Department on the national committee of the International Electrotechnical Commission. He continued as chief signal officer of the army, with the rank of major-general after Oct. 6, 1917, until his retirement at his own request, Dec. 31, 1923.

Squier's administrative services during the World War won him the Distinguished Service Medal of the United States and appointment as Knight Commander of the Order of Saint Michael and Saint George (Great Britain), Commander of the Order of the Crown (Italy), and Commander of the Legion of Honor (France). His attainments as a scientist brought him election as a member of the National Academy of Sciences and a fellow of Johns Hopkins University. For his researches he was awarded the Elliott Cresson Gold Medal (1912) and the Franklin Medal (1919) of the Franklin Institute and the John Scott Legacy Medal of the City of Philadelphia (1896). His important contribu-

tions to science included his researches in connection with electro-chemical effects due to magnetization; the polarizing photochronograph; the sine-wave systems of telegraphy and ocean cabling; the absorption of electro-magnetic waves by living vegetable organisms; multiplex telegraphy and telephony; and tree telegraphy and telephony. His most significant papers were published in the *Transactions of the American Institute of Electrical Engineers,* the *Journal of the Franklin Institute,* or publications of the signal corps. He was the inventor of the monophone for broadcasting over telephone wires. Of his inventions, by far the best known is "wired wireless," which includes multiple telephony, wireless telephony, long-distance telephony, and practical telephony. He was the holder of a number of patents in these fields.

After his retirement from the army he made his home at Dryden, Mich., but spent a part of each year in Washington, D. C., where he died. He never married.

[Official records, Adjutant-General's Office and Office of the Chief Signal Officer, War Dept., 1888–1934; A. E. Kenelly, in *Science,* May 25, 1934; *Who's Who in America,* 1932–33; *Who's Who in Engineering* (1925); G. W. Cullum, *Biog. Reg. Officers and Grads. U. S. Mil. Acad.,* vols. III–VII (1891–1930); *Proc. Inst. Radio Engineers,* vol. XXII (May 1934); B. J. Hendrick, *The Life and Letters of Walter H. Page,* vol. III (1925); *Washington Post,* Mar. 25, 1934.]

I. J. C—r.

SQUIERS, HERBERT GOLDSMITH (Apr. 20, 1859–Oct. 20, 1911), soldier, diplomat, was born of American parents at Madoc, Canada, the son of John T. and Elizabeth J. Squiers. He attended Canandaigua Academy, Canandaigua, N. Y., and the Minnesota Military Academy at Minneapolis, graduating in 1877 and securing appointment as second lieutenant in the 1st United States Infantry. After two and a half years' service he obtained a transfer to the Artillery School at Fortress Monroe, Va. While here, Oct. 11, 1881, he married Helen Lacy Fargo, daughter of William George Fargo [*q.v.*]. On completing his course, May 1, 1882, he pleaded for and obtained assignment to the cavalry, but after three years in this branch, again sought change and got himself assigned to St. John's College, Fordham, N. Y., as teacher of military science. A memorandum issued from the Adjutant-General's Office at this time (July 8, 1885) reveals the irritation Squiers' love of change provoked in the bosom of authority: "There is not probably a young officer in the service who has been more indulged in his personal requests than has Lieutenant Squiers. . . . He has not shown one particle of military spirit but rather the reverse." His wife, having borne a son and three daughters, died in 1886, and in 1889 he married Harriet Bard Woodcock of Bedford Hills, N. Y., daughter of Dr. William P. and Mary (Bard) Woodcock. To this marriage three sons were born.

Repeated endeavors to have Squiers return to active service proved unavailing and he remained at St. John's College until the fall of 1890, when an Indian uprising in South Dakota led him to ask for duty in the field. He was promptly ordered West, was promoted to first lieutenant, Dec. 17, and twelve days later took part in the battle of Wounded Knee. The following summer he was granted a month's leave, and after the month was up delayed returning to duty so long that finally he was ordered to return at once or resign. He resigned, Nov. 28, 1891, in a letter justifying his conduct on the ground of urgent private business.

In person Squiers was handsome and attractive, and despite his restlessness had superior qualities of mind and character, including a robust will to work. Throughout life he was a student, with a passion for history but interested in many fields. His personality and talents were much better adapted to the new career which opened for him on Nov. 15, 1894, with appointment as second secretary to the United States embassy at Berlin. Here he remained until May 1897, when he resigned. A year and a half later he reëntered the diplomatic service as secretary to the legation at Peking. During the Boxer uprising of 1900, his previous military training caused Sir Claude MacDonald to select him as chief of staff. The courage and competence with which he discharged his duties won for him the thanks of the British government and commendation by President McKinley. Lord Lansdowne, British foreign minister, in a note to the ambassador at Washington said: "Sir Claude mentions that his [Squiers's] earlier services in the U. S. Army were of great use in the defence and that he cannot speak too highly of his zeal and ability. The barricades on the Tartar Wall were designed and carried out by him and under Sir Claude's orders he drew the plan for the entry of the troops which was conveyed to General Gaselee by a messenger let down from the wall" (Dec. 11, 1900; State Department Archives).

From May 1902 until November 1905, Squiers filled with distinguished success the arduous and difficult post of United States minister to the newly constituted Republic of Cuba. At the outset he made clear his special status as the representative of the United States, claiming the right to deal with the president of Cuba directly instead of through the secretary of state. The treaty containing the Platt Amendment was ratified during his incumbency, and he was instructed to impress upon the Cuban government the dangers of insolvency and to urge the importance of carrying out the suggested sanitation plans. From 1906 until failing health caused by tropical fevers forced his retirement in 1910, he was minister to Panama. He died in London in 1911. One of his daughters married Harry Harwood Rousseau [q.v.]. His wife, Harriet B. W. Squiers, engaged actively in work for the wounded during the World War; she died in New York, June 18, 1935.

[Archives of the War and State departments; *The Times* (London), Oct. 19, 1900; *Outlook,* July 5, 1902; F. B. Heitman, *Hist. Reg. and Dict. U. S. Army* (1903); *Papers Relating to the Foreign Relations of the U. S.,* 1902–05; *Who's Who in America,* 1910–11; H. F. Guggenheim, *The U. S. and Cuba* (1934); *N. Y. Herald,* Oct. 21, 1911; correspondence with Squiers's son; obituary of Mrs. Squiers, *N. Y. Times,* June 19, 1935.]
W. E. S—a.

SQUIRE, WATSON CARVOSSO (May 18, 1838–June 7, 1926), capitalist, governor of the Territory of Washington, United States senator, was born at Cape Vincent, N. Y. His father, the Rev. Orra Squire, a Methodist Episcopal clergyman, and his mother, Erreta (Wheeler) Squire, were both of New England stock. He attended public schools, Falley Seminary, Fulton, N. Y., and Fairfield Seminary in Herkimer County. In 1859 he graduated from Wesleyan University, Middletown, Conn., and during the year following was principal of Moravia Institute at Moravia, N. Y. He began the study of law at Herkimer, but soon after the outbreak of the Civil War he enlisted as a private in Company F, 19th New York Volunteer Infantry, and was later promoted to first lieutenant. Mustered out in October 1861, he went to Cleveland, Ohio, graduated from the Cleveland Law School in 1862, and was admitted to the bar. He then organized the 7th Independent Company of Ohio Sharpshooters, of which he became captain. The company operated with the Western divisions during the remainder of the war. In 1864–65 Squire served as judge advocate on Rosecrans' staff. He had been promoted to major and was subsequently brevetted lieutenant-colonel and colonel.

After the war he returned to New York State and accepted a position with E. Remington & Sons, manufacturers of firearms. On Dec. 3, 1868, he married Ida, daughter of Philo Remington [q.v.]; they had four children. He soon attained managerial rank in the company and negotiated important sales to France, during the Franco-Prussian War, and to other powers. His business necessitated extensive travel in Europe, also a winter's sojourn in Mexico. In the spring of 1879, property interests took him to the Puget Sound country, and from that year Seattle became his permanent residence. Besides acquiring extensive real-estate holdings, he interested Eastern capitalists, chiefly Henry Villard [*q.v.*], in the Territory's railroads and coal mines.

Affiliated with the Republican party, he leaned toward the Stalwart or regular wing. Appointed governor of Washington Territory in 1884, he distinguished himself for his firmness in maintaining law and order during the anti-Chinese riots of 1885–86. In 1887 he resigned to devote himself to his private business, but in 1889 he was called to preside over the convention held at Ellensburg for the purpose of drafting a state constitution. Statehood attained, Squire was elected senator. As a member and twice as chairman of the committee on coast defenses, he secured material enlargements in these defenses. Among his other important interests were Alaska, for which he secured the government geological survey and special reconnaissances of its mineral resources; and the Isthmian canal, for which he favored the Nicaraguan route. For his state he secured the naval station and dry dock at Bremerton, extensive harbor and river improvements, and the initial appropriation for the Lake Washington Canal. When he first entered the Senate, drawing with the other new arrivals from the omnibus states, Squire secured a two-year term, but he was reëlected in 1891; in 1897, however, the strength of the free-silver movement eliminated him, a gold-standard man, from candidacy for reëlection. He returned to business and became president of the Union Trust Company and of the Squire Investment Company. He died in Seattle.

[*Alumni Record of Wesleyan Univ. . . . 1921* (n.d.); *Hist. of the Remington Armory. E. Remington & Sons* (1872); C. B. Bagley, *Hist. of Seattle from the Earliest Settlement to the Present Time* (1916), vol. III; F. J. Grant, *Hist. of Seattle, Wash.* (1891); W. F. Prosser, *A Hist. of the Puget Sound Country* (1903), vol. II; C. A. Snowden, *Hist. of Wash.* (1911), vols. IV, V; *Who's Who in America,* 1924–25; *Biog. Dir. Am. Cong.* (1928); *Seattle Daily Times,* June 8, 1926.] H. J. D.

STAGER, ANSON (Apr. 20, 1825–Mar. 26, 1885), telegraph pioneer, was born in Ontario County, N. Y., but was brought up in Rochester, where his father was engaged as an edged-tool maker. At the age of sixteen, upon completing his education in the public schools, he became a printer's devil in the office of the *Rochester Daily Advertiser,* owned and published by Henry O'Reilly [*q.v.*]. By 1845 Stager had become the *Advertiser's* bookkeeper. About this time O'Reilly contracted with Samuel F. B. Morse [*q.v.*] and

his associates to raise the capital to build a line of Morse's electro-magnetic telegraph from Philadelphia to the Middle West. His activities undoubtedly aroused Stager's interest, and while O'Reilly was constructing the first link of the telegraph line to Pittsburgh, the younger man was learning telegraphy in his spare time, and upon the opening of the telegraph office at Lancaster, Pa., in 1846, he was installed as operator. In the succeeding three months he was transferred to Chambersburg and from there to Pittsburgh, serving as manager of the latter office during most of 1847.

With the extension of the O'Reilly lines to Cincinnati late in that year, Stager was made manager of the operating department of the Pittsburgh, Cincinnati & Louisville Telegraph Company. During the succeeding four years he conducted the office skilfully and originated the system by which telegraph wires were worked from a common battery on a closed circuit. His reward came in 1852 when he was appointed general superintendent of the New York & Mississippi Valley Printing Telegraph Company. With the formation of the Western Union Telegraph Company in 1856, Stager was immediately appointed its general superintendent and assigned the work of rearranging the many telegraph lines, strengthening the organization, and establishing favorable relations with the great railroad interests. He was the originator of the cunningly devised contract which for many years gave the Western Union an iron-bound monopoly of the privilege of stringing wires along the railroads.

After 1856 Stager made his headquarters at Cleveland, Ohio, and upon the outbreak of the Civil War he was asked to take the management of the telegraphs in the military department of the Ohio. Appointed captain and assistant quartermaster general on Nov. 11, 1861, he was placed on duty in Washington as chief of the United States military telegraphs. On Feb. 26, 1862, he was promoted to colonel and subsequently assigned as aide-de-camp to General Halleck at the War Department. After 1864 his headquarters were in Cleveland, Ohio, and continued there until he was honorably mustered out Sept. 1, 1866. For his meritorious services, which included the originating and development of the military telegraph cipher system, he had been brevetted brigadier-general of volunteers on Mar. 13, 1865.

He had not broken his connection with the Western Union Telegraph Company, and upon its reorganization following the war he was tendered the general superintendency of the whole system. When he refused the offer, the system was divided into three great divisions, Central, Eastern, and Southern, and Stager accepted the superintendency of the Central Division, with headquarters at Cleveland. In 1869 these were transferred to Chicago, Ill., and there Stager lived for the remainder of his life. He became a vice-president of the Western Union, which office he resigned in 1881. He was the leading Western representative of the Vanderbilt interests, and took an active part in all electrical progress of the time. He helped found the Western Electric Manufacturing Company and was its president until a few months before his death. He was prominent in furthering the telephone business in Chicago and the Northwest generally, as well as in the introduction of the electric light, serving as president of the Western Edison Electric Light Company from its formation until his death. On Nov. 14, 1847, he married Rebecca Sprague of Buffalo, and at the time of his death in Chicago was survived by three children.

[J. D. Reid, *The Telegraph in America* (1879); W. R. Plum, *The Military Telegraph During the Civil War in the U. S.* (1882), vols. I and II; *Electrical World,* Mar. 28 and Apr. 4, 1885; *Electrician and Electrical Engineer,* Apr. 1885; *Journal of the Telegraph,* Apr. 20, 1885; records of Adjutant-General's Office, War Dept., Washington, D. C.; *Chicago Daily Tribune,* Mar. 26, 1885.]   C. W. M—n.

STAHEL, JULIUS (Nov. 5, 1825–Dec. 4, 1912), soldier and consular officer, son of Andreas and Barbara (Nagy) Stahel (Hungarian name Számvald), was born in Szeged, Hungary. He received a classical education at Budapest. In the struggle for Hungarian independence in 1848 he espoused the patriotic cause, became a lieutenant in the forces of Louis Kossuth, was wounded and decorated for bravery. With the triumph of Austrian arms in 1849, however, he was forced to flee the country. He then maintained himself in Berlin and London by teaching and journalism until 1856, when he came to America and settled in New York City. There he continued a journalistic career until the outbreak of the Civil War, at which time he was on the staff of the *New York Illustrated News.*

When Lincoln called for volunteers in April 1861, Stahel at once responded, helped organize the 8th New York Infantry, and became its lieutenant-colonel. On July 21, 1861, when the Union army was routed at Bull Run, Stahel, then in command of his regiment, was with a brigade in reserve at Centerville; ordered to cover the retreat, the brigade performed its task so well that the Confederate commander, General Johnston, in his report on the battle stated that "the apparent firmness of the U. S. troops at Centreville ... checked our pursuit" (*War of the Rebellion:*

Official Records, Army, 1 ser. II, 478). The following month Stahel was promoted to colonel and soon thereafter assigned to command a brigade. On Nov. 12, 1861, he was appointed brigadier-general of volunteers. He fought under General Frémont in the Shenandoah Valley in the spring of 1862, particularly distinguishing himself at Cross Keys on June 8, when his brigade bore the brunt of the fighting. At the second battle of Bull Run, Aug. 30, 1862, he temporarily commanded a division and was commended for gallantry. In October 1862 he was assigned to command a division in the Army of the Potomac, and for a short time during the next winter he commanded the XI Corps. Promoted to major-general on Mar. 14, 1863, he was given command of the cavalry division in front of Washington. In the spring of 1864 he was transferred to a cavalry division in the department of West Virginia and led General Hunter's advance in the Shenandoah Valley gallantly until June 5, 1864, when he was badly wounded in the arm while personally leading a successful charge against the Confederate flank. For his bravery on this occasion he was awarded the Congressional Medal of Honor in 1893. After recovering from his wound he served on court-martial duty in Washington, and in the Middle Department until Feb. 8, 1865, when he resigned his commission. He was soon given opportunity to show his abilities in a new field of public service, being appointed in 1866 consul at the important post of Yokohama. He returned to the United States in 1869, and for the next eight years engaged in mining operations. On Oct. 25, 1877, he was nominated as consul to Osaka and Hiogo, the nomination being confirmed on Feb. 6, 1878. He held this post until 1884, when he was made consul at Shanghai, China. The next year he resigned because of ill health, thus ending an eventful public career which throughout was characterized by ability and the highest standards of honor and duty. He returned to New York, where for a number of years he held an executive position with the Equitable Life Assurance Company. He was never married.

[*War of the Rebellion: Official Records* (Army); Eugene Pivany, *Hungarians in the Am. Civil War* (1913); *The Union Army* (1908), vol. VIII; *A Record of the Commissioned Officers, Non-Commissioned Officers, and Privates of the Regiments ... Organized in the State of New York* (1864); F. B. Heitman, *Hist. Reg. and Dict. U. S. Army* (1903); *Military Order of the Loyal Legion of the U. S. ... State of New York, Circular 19, Series of 1913*; *Who's Who in America,* 1912–13; *N. Y. Times,* Dec. 5, 1912; *New-Yorker Staats-Zeitung,* Dec. 5, 1912.]   S. J. H.

STAHLMAN, EDWARD BUSHROD (Sept. 2, 1843–Aug. 12, 1930), railroad official, publisher, was born at Güstrow, in the German grand duchy of Mecklenburg-Schwerin, the fourth son of Frederick and Christine (Lange) Stahlman. His only formal education was secured in the primary school taught by his father at Güstrow. In 1854 the family emigrated to the United States and settled at West Union, Doddridge County, Virginia (now West Virginia). Soon afterward the father died, leaving his wife and children destitute. In spite of the fact that a school-room accident had left him permanently crippled, Edward aided in supporting the family until the mother remarried. In 1863 he went to Nashville, Tenn., where he entered the employ of the Louisville & Nashville Railroad Company. Three years later he became the Nashville representative of the Southern Express Company, and in 1871 returned to the service of the Louisville & Nashville Railroad as freight agent. Rising rapidly, he was made a vice-president of the company in 1884, after having held a similar position with the Louisville, New Albany & Chicago Railway (Monon Route) from 1883 to 1884. Withdrawing from the Louisville & Nashville in 1890, he served until 1895 as commissioner for the Southern Railway and Steamship Association, in which capacity he was an important representative of the transportation interests of the South during the period of the creation and adjustment of the Interstate Commerce Commission.

His real life work began, however, in 1885, when he purchased the *Nashville Banner,* then a small paper with little influence and less financial standing. Throughout the next thirty-five years the editorial policy of this paper was a direct reflection of the personality and convictions of its owner, with the result that it became one of the best-known journals of the South. He was seldom neutral on an issue, making vigorous use of both news and editorial columns to promote any cause which he espoused. Thus he unhesitatingly threw himself into a fight to prevent the citizens of Nashville from voting a proposed bond issue for the Tennessee-Midland Railroad in 1885, and against a similar plan put forward by the Tennessee Central Railroad in 1901–02; into the fight to preserve an independent judiciary for the state in 1910; and into another in 1925 to protect the power resources of the state from seizure and exploitation by the power trusts. In such contests he fought both brilliantly and bitterly, arousing, as a result, an intense antagonism on the part of his opponents which usually led to recriminatory attacks.

Through his connection with transportation interests he became a powerful political factor in the state. Proceeding on an avowed belief that

independence is essential to the highest usefulness of a paper, he was never willing to affiliate permanently with a political party or faction. He was, nevertheless, a shrewd worker in the field of practical politics, and participated in many state and local contests, frequently sponsoring the candidacy of a promising young leader only to turn against him as he later became absorbed into the regular party organization. Although he never held important public offices, he exercised a dominating influence in the municipal affairs of Nashville as a member of the board of education, as a promoter of chamber of commerce activities, and as a leader in real-estate and building development. He was twice married: first, Oct. 4, 1866, to Mollie T. Claiborne of Nashville, by whom he had three children; she died in 1915, and on Aug. 23, 1920, he married Sarah Shelton, of Erin, Tenn., by whom he had a son.

[*Who's Who in Tennessee* (1911); *Who's Who in America,* 1930–31; *Nashville Banner,* Aug. 12, 13, 1930, and *Nashville Tennessean,* Aug. 13, 1930.]

W. C. B.

STAHR, JOHN SUMMERS (Dec. 2, 1841– Dec. 21, 1915), clergyman, educator, was born near Applebachsville, Bucks County, Pa., the son of John and Sarah(Summers or Sommer) Stahr. The family name had been originally Stoehr, his ancestors having come from the Palatinate in 1739 to settle in Bucks County. He received his early education in the public schools and became a teacher when he was but sixteen years of age. He prepared for college during the summer months at the Bucks County Normal and Classical School and finally entered the junior class of Franklin and Marshall College, Lancaster, Pa., in 1865, graduating *summa cum laude* in 1867. He had then intended to enter the theological seminary of the Reformed Church at Mercersburg, Pa., but he was urged to accept a position as tutor in German and history at his alma mater, and, at the same time, to study theology under the direction of John Williamson Nevin [*q.v.*]. In 1868 he was made adjunct professor of the natural sciences and German, and in three years rose to a full professorship in the natural sciences and chemistry, with additional work in German and political economy. He held this position until 1887 when he became temporary financial agent for the college. In 1889 he was the acting president and professor of philosophy, and president from 1890 until he retired in 1909. He retained the professorship of philosophy, however, until he died.

In 1872 he was ordained to the holy ministry and served as assistant pastor of the First Reformed Church at Reading, Pa., but declined a call to the pastorate. He was a member of the Eighth Council of the Alliance of Reformed Churches which met at Liverpool in 1904, and at the Tenth Council at Aberdeen in 1913. In 1914 he was elected president of the General Synod of the Reformed Church. From 1890 to 1908 he served as a member of the International Sunday School Lesson Committee, representing it at a convention in Rome in 1907. His linguistic accomplishments led to an appointment to the editorial staff of the Funk & Wagnall Standard Dictionary, and for forty-five years he was a frequent contributor to the *Mercersburg Review* and its successors, the *Reformed Church Quarterly* and the *Reformed Church Review,* on which he served as a managing editor from 1906. Stahr spoke and wrote a pure English, and, with the same ease, a faultless German. He showed in his opening address of the college year of 1870 on "Pennsylvania German," *Mercersburg Review,* October 1890, its proper place in the realm of the Germanic languages. He wrote on education, science, philosophy, ethics, and theology, and when Darwin's *Origin of Species* was still vehemently opposed by the leading churchmen, he discussed in another opening address "Evolution Theories and Theology," in which he stoutly maintained that the theory of evolution and the tenets of genuine Christianity did not conflict (*Ibid.,* July 1872). His position became even more definite in his eloquent and profoundly scholarly refutation of A. Wilford Hall's *The Problem of Human Life Here and Hereafter* (1880), for the *Reformed Church Quarterly,* July 1883. His chief interest, however, was in the study of philosophy. He was the last of the master exponents of the Mercersburg Philosophy (see his article, "Philosophy as a Factor in the Educational System of the Reformed Church," *Reformed Church Review,* January 1898).

A recital of his experiences as administrator of college funds, "The Financial Development of Franklin and Marshall College" (*Reformed Church Review,* April 1903), reveals an infinite capacity for work and a zealous and practical interest in business matters. He procured for the college legacies and gifts, one immediate result of his financial mission being the building and equipment of the first chemical laboratory under his supervision. He was one of six men who founded the Pennsylvania-German Society in 1891 and he acted as president in 1903–04. On July 23, 1872, he was married to Francina Elmira Andrews, the daughter of Hugh Andrews of Lancaster County. She, with three of their five children, survived him.

[Information from the family; *Who's Who in America,* 1914–15; a brief autobiography in the *Student Weekly of Franklin and Marshall Coll.,* Feb. 3, 1916; Profs. Mull, Richard, and Herman, "In Memoriam," *Proc. and Addresses, Pa.-Ger. Soc.,* vol. XXVI (1918); J. H. Dubbs, *Hist. of Franklin and Marshall Coll.* (1903); *Public Ledger,* Philadelphia, Dec. 22, 1915.]
R. C. S.

STALEY, CADY (Dec. 12, 1840–June 27, 1928), civil engineer, the son of Harmanus and Evaline (Darrow) Staley, was born in Florida township, Montgomery County, N. Y., and spent his boyhood on a farm. He received his early education in a district school, in Jonesville Academy, and in the Classical Institute in Schenectady, then studied civil engineering at Union College, under Prof. William M. Gillespie [*q.v.*]. He was graduated A.B. with honors in 1865 and the following year received the degree of C. E. Soon afterward, he crossed the plains as an ox-driver with a wagon train, spent some months in prospecting for gold, then went to work for the Central Pacific Railroad as a civil engineer, being engaged in tunnel construction.

In 1867 he returned to Union College as an instructor in civil engineering, and the following year, upon the death of Gillespie, became professor of civil engineering and president of the faculty. In December 1869, at Waterford, N. Y., he married Kate, daughter of Elvin and Philetta (Hall) Holcomb. He was dean of the faculty from 1876 to 1886, when he resigned to become professor of civil engineering and president of the faculty of Case School of Applied Science, Cleveland, Ohio. Bringing to his new post well-defined ideas of organization and administration, the result of his years of experience at Union, he insisted upon assuming the direction of the work of the school, although he allowed the department heads full power in their several fields. His method proved eminently successful and Case School remains a monument to his administrative ability. In addition to his teaching, until some time after he went to Case, Staley practised his profession, specializing in sanitary engineering. He was a pioneer in promoting the separate system of sewerage; collaborated with George S. Pierson in publishing *The Separate System of Sewerage* (1886); and was associated with him in designing and superintending the construction of such systems in West Troy and Schenectady, N. Y., and in Dayton, Ohio. Because suitable textbooks on stresses in framed structures were lacking, he wrote *Notes on Bridge Engineering* (1875); *Strength of Materials and Stability of Structures* (1876); and *Elements of Truss Bridges* (1878). He edited Gillespie's *Treatise on Levelling, Topography, and Higher Surveying* (1870; 1877), and compiled

The Teachings of Jesus, Selected from the Gospels (copyright 1889).

As a teacher, Staley was informal and sympathetic; as an executive he had the welfare of the individual at heart, and never hesitated to make exceptions in general rules for the benefit of individuals. Thus in many cases he made it possible for a student who was slow or poorly prepared to achieve an engineering education.

In his prime Staley had a magnificent physique. He was tall, broad-shouldered, and heavily built. He was a great lover of horses, and for a time owned a stock farm in the West, where he hoped after his retirement to raise heavy draft horses from imported Percheron stock. A series of unsuccessful years discouraged him, however, and he disposed of his farm and stock. During his summer vacations, after going to Case, Staley and his wife traveled a great deal, and in 1902 Staley retired so as to spend more time in foreign travel. With his wife he made a trip around the world, then made his home on a farm at Minaville, N. Y., but continued to spend much time in travel. By 1907, however, he had tired of having no definite work to do, and from then until 1917 spent the fall term of each year at Case as professor of political economy. He died at Minaville, in his eighty-eighth year.

[*Proc. Am. Soc. Civil Engineers,* vol. LV (1929); *Who's Who in America,* 1920–21; *Who's Who in Engineering,* 1925; *Union College . . . Commemoration . . . of the One Hundredth Anniversary* (1897); *Cleveland Plain Dealer,* June 28, 1928; records of Case School of Applied Science; personal acquaintance.]

F. H. N.

STALLO, JOHANN BERNHARD (Mar. 16, 1823–Jan. 6, 1900), lawyer, scientist, minister to Italy, was born at Sierhausen, Oldenburg, Germany, the son of Johann Heinrich and Maria Adelheid (Moormann) Stallo. He was of Frisian descent, his ancestors for many generations having been schoolmasters. Under his grandfather's tutelage he learned to read and cipher before he was four years old, and later learned English and the classical languages, while his father taught him French. At the age of thirteen he entered the normal school at Vechta and then the Gymnasium, but his father lacked means for his further education, and to avoid becoming a village schoolmaster he emigrated to America at sixteen years of age. At Cincinnati, Ohio, where an uncle had settled previously, the studious boy procured a position as teacher in a Catholic school. He published a primer, *ABC, Buchstabier und Lesebuch, für die deutschen Schulen Amerikas* (1840), as well as some poems which betray a philosophical interest in nature, and until 1844 was a student at St. Xavier's College in Cincinnati, teaching German and the classical languages at the same time. He employed all his spare time in the study of chemistry and physics and was appointed professor of these sciences in St. John's College, Fordham, N. Y., from 1844 to 1847. Here he studied philosophy and prepared his *General Principles of the Philosophy of Nature* (1848), introducing American readers to the philosophical views of Kant, Hegel, Fichte, Schelling, and Lorenz Oken. While it served its purpose in this respect, Stallo later disavowed the book as having been written "under the spell of Hegel's ontological reveries" (see the introduction to *Concepts, post,* p. 11).

Stallo then returned to Cincinnati, studied law, and was admitted to the bar in 1849. After practising for some time he was appointed judge in the Hamilton County Court of Common Pleas from 1853 to 1855. One of his most famous cases was his defense of the Cincinnati School Board in a mandamus suit in which Protestant clergymen tried to force it to retain the singing of hymns and the reading of the Bible as part of the school curriculum. His brilliant plea before the superior court of Cincinnati won the day for religious freedom (see *The Bible and the Public Schools,* Cincinnati, 1870). Throughout the years of his law practice Stallo continued his study of philosophy, physics, and mathematics. He gave lectures on scientific subjects, was a frequent contributor to periodicals, and collected an enormous library containing some rare first editions of Kepler annotated by the scientist himself. For seventeen years he was examiner of candidates for teaching positions, was on the Board of Curators of the University of Cincinnati, and in many ways showed his interest in education. He published *The Concepts and Theories of Modern Physics* in Appleton's *International Scientific Series* (vol. XXXVIII, 1882), which was translated into French, German, Spanish, Italian, and Russian. It was primarily an essay in epistemology with results similar to Ernst Mach's, and attempted to define the contemporary position of science.

Stallo was a great admirer of Jefferson and belonged to the Democratic party until the question of slavery became acute, when he helped found the Republican party. In 1856 he was an elector for Frémont. At the outbreak of the Civil War he eloquently called on the Germans of Cincinnati to form a regiment, the 9th Ohio Infantry, sometimes called "Stallo's Turner Regiment." When corruption became rife within the Republican party he joined the group of reformers who attempted to nominate Charles Francis Adams at the convention in Cincinnati in 1872.

In speeches and letters Stallo always favored the interests of the people against monopolies, and was an opponent of the protective tariff. In 1885 in recognition of his activity in political reform, Cleveland appointed him minister to Italy. After four years in Rome he settled in Florence where he spent the remainder of his life with his books. He published his German writings under the title *Reden, Abhandlungen und Briefe* in 1893. Stallo's home was a seat of rare culture in letters, science, and music, and was open only to a few people. He was a born scholar, a keen and liberal thinker whose works anticipated the studies of Darwin. In 1855 he had been married to Helene Zimmermann, of Cincinnati, who survived him with two of their seven children.

[H. A. Rattermann, *Johann Bernhard Stallo* (1902); shorter accounts in Gustav Körner, *Das deutsche Element in den Vereinigten Staaten* (1880); T. J. McCormack, biographical article in *Open Court*, May 1900; *Popular Sci. Monthly*, Feb. 1889; Hans Kleinpeter, "J. B. Stallo als Erkenntniskritiker," *Vierteljahrsschrift für wissenschaftliche Philosophie*, Nov. 1901; autobiographical items in preface to Stallo's *Die Begriffe und Theorien der Modernen Physik* (1882); *Cincinnati Enquirer*, Jan. 7, 1900.]   A. E. Z.

STANARD, MARY MANN PAGE NEWTON (Aug. 15, 1865–June 5, 1929), Virginia historian, was born in Westmoreland County, Va., of prominent stock, daughter of the Rt. Rev. John Brockenbrough Newton and his wife Roberta Page (Williamson) Newton. She was a descendant of John Newton who emigrated from Hull, Yorkshire, first to Maryland and then to Westmoreland County about 1675. She attended first the ordinary schools near her home, later graduating from the Leache-Wood School in Norfolk, but she grew up in a literary atmosphere and early developed scholarly instincts; throughout her life, despite her sociable and companionable nature and her none too robust health, she remained essentially the student. On Apr. 17, 1900, she married William Glover Stanard [q.v.] of Richmond, Va., corresponding secretary of the Virginia Historical Society, and thereby associated herself permanently with the city whose history she was so lovingly to record. Reared to venerate Virginia's past and to believe in its present, her residence in Richmond enabled her to gratify her interest in both. From the creation of the office until her death she was historian of the Association for the Preservation of Virginia Antiquities; she served as vice-president of the Virginia Society of the Colonial Dames of America and as president of the Richmond Woman's club; and she was a member of the Virginia Writers' club, of the executive committee of the Edgar Allan Poe Shrine, and of the Virginia War History commission.

Her first volume was her original and meritorious study, *The Story of Bacon's Rebellion* (1907), although she had previously collaborated with her husband in the laborious and highly valuable compilation, *The Colonial Virginia Register* (1902); this she followed with *The Dreamer; a Romantic Rendering of the Life-Story of Edgar Allan Poe* (1909), in which particular emphasis was laid on the poet's early life in Richmond. More significant, and likely to prove her most enduring works, are her detailed and interesting social histories, *Colonial Virginia, Its People and Customs* (1917) and *Richmond, Its People and Its Story* (1923), both abounding in excellent word pictures of noteworthy and influential people and events. Besides numerous magazine articles and short stories, she published two other brief volumes, *John Marshall* (1913), and *John Brockenbrough Newton* (1924), first published serially in the *Virginia Churchman*, a biographical sketch of her father, at one time rector of Monumental Episcopal Church in Richmond and later bishop coadjutor of Virginia; she edited, most capably, the *Edgar Allan Poe Letters Till Now Unpublished, in the Valentine Museum, Richmond, Va.* (1925), and in 1928 published her last book, *The Story of Virginia's First Century*. She died in Richmond, survived by her husband. They had no children. While not primarily concerned with discovering new facts or correcting minutiae, she wrote enjoyable and authoritative books on Virginia history for the general reader, more than passingly accurate despite their disregard of footnotes or bibliographies. All of her work shows a sense of order and arrangement, of discriminating selection, graphic detail, and graceful charm; it is local history, definitely restricted in compass, but there is little of it that will need to be done again.

[*Who's Who in America*, 1928–29; Daniel Grinnan, in *Va. Mag. of Hist. and Biog.*, July 1929; obituary in *Richmond Times-Dispatch*, June 6, 1929; date of birth supplied by a relative of Mrs. Stanard.]   A. C. G., Jr.

STANARD, WILLIAM GLOVER (Oct. 2, 1858–May 6, 1933), editor and antiquarian, was born in Richmond, Va., of substantial and well-connected stock (the Stanard family had settled in Middlesex County before 1700), son of Capt. Robert Conway and Virginia M. (Cowan) Stanard. His father, who was a captain in the Confederate Army, died in 1861, and his mother later married William B. Wooldridge. Educated at McGuire's School, Richmond, at the College of William and Mary, 1875–76, and at Richmond College (later part of the University of Richmond), 1876–80, during his young manhood he worked at various occupations, including those of surveyor and of reporter for the *Richmond Daily Whig,* but early developed a taste for historical and genealogical study, and began to contribute occasional articles to the *Critic* (Richmond) and other periodicals. In October 1898 he succeeded Philip A. Bruce as corresponding secretary of the Virginia Historical Society and editor of the *Virginia Magazine of History and Biography,* continuing in this dual capacity until his death. Barring his marriage, Apr. 17, 1900 (see Stanard, Mary Mann Page Newton) and the publication of his two useful and meritorious volumes, *The Colonial Virginia Register* (1902), compiled with the assistance of his wife, and *Some Emigrants to Virginia* (1911), there were few milestones in the remaining portion of his career. The record of his later days was that of faithful and painstaking devotion to the routine tasks of collecting and preserving whatever bore upon the history of Virginia, as colony or as commonwealth, and of extending the sphere of the society whose efficient officer he was. He printed little in book form, despite his industry, his power of easy, direct composition, and the astonishing extent of his information—it has been said that "he knew more of the history of Virginia than any other man has ever known" (quoted in Munford, *post*) ; self-effacing and generous, he employed no little of his private research in supplying material for the narratives his wife wrote, while with gentle and patient courtesy he gave unstintingly of his time and knowledge to the numberless students who, seldom fruitlessly, sought historical or genealogical aid from him. The thirty-five volumes of the *Virginia Magazine of History and Biography* which he published, however, remain a monument to his scholarly and authoritative editorship at the same time that they abound in valuable contributions from his pen, most of them with characteristic modesty left unsigned.

[*Who's Who in America, 1932–33*; R. B. Munford, Jr., *In Memoriam: William Glover Stanard* (1934); with portrait, reprinted from the *Va. Mag. of Hist. and Biog.,* July 1933; obituaries in *Richmond Times-Dispatch,* May 7, 8, and *News-Leader* (Richmond), May 8, 1933.]   A. C. G., Jr.

STANBERY, HENRY (Feb. 20, 1803–June 26, 1881), lawyer, attorney-general of the United States, was born in New York City, the son of Dr. Jonas and Ann Lucy (Seaman) Stanbery. In 1814 his parents removed to Ohio and settled in Zanesville. Henry showed unusual gifts as a student and was graduated from Washington College (later, Washington and Jefferson) in Pennsylvania at the age of sixteen. He then read law with Ebenezer Granger and Charles B. Goddard and upon reaching his majority was admit-

ted to the bar. That same year he was invited into partnership with Thomas Ewing [*q.v.*] of Lancaster, Ohio, one of the ablest attorneys in the state, and continued in association with him until Ewing entered the United States Senate in 1831. Stanbery early developed into a thoroughly well-rounded lawyer, learned in both the technicalities and the general principles of the law, and won for himself a place at the front rank of the Ohio bar, then renowned for its distinguished practitioners. His election to the newly created office of attorney-general of Ohio in 1846 necessitated his removal from Lancaster to Columbus, and for the next few years he was engaged in organizing the new department of justice and in expanding his practice in the United States courts and in the Ohio supreme court. He was among the most influential members of the constitutional convention of 1850 and ably contributed out of his broad learning and experience to the improvement of the organic laws of the state. In 1853 he transferred his law office to Cincinnati and continued his practice there until appointed attorney-general of the United States in 1866.

A handsome man of imposing presence, kindly manner, and unsullied character, Stanbery was universally respected. His clear and forceful reasoning, persuasiveness, and finished eloquence combined to make him effective on the stump as well as in the court room, but he was not an office-seeker and seldom took a conspicuous part in political campaigns. He identified himself with the Whig and later the Republican party and was an ardent supporter of the Lincoln administration. The moderate policy of reconstruction begun by Lincoln and carried forward by Johnson appealed to him strongly, and after entering the cabinet of the latter, July 23, 1866, he interpreted the reconstruction legislation as liberally as the language of the acts permitted. Gideon Welles thought him too much a man of precedents and too timid when action seemed appropriate (*Diary, post,* III, 221, 308–09), but Johnson placed a high estimate upon his judgment and wisdom and apparently relied much upon him in the preparation of his veto messages. When the impeachment proceedings against the President were begun, Stanbery resigned as attorney-general (Mar. 12, 1868) to serve as Johnson's chief counsel. After the opening days, in which he bore the main burden of the defense, illness forced him to withdraw, but he returned to make the final argument. His summation glowed with loyalty and praise for the harassed executive. At the close of the trial Johnson renominated him as attorney-general, but the Senate, as in the case of his nomination to the United States Supreme Court in April 1866, refused to confirm his appointment. In both instances the Senate's action was undoubtedly dictated by hostility to the President rather than by any question as to the nominee's fitness. After his rejection in 1868 Stanbery resumed his practice in Cincinnati with distinguished success, but failing sight obliged him to retire about 1878. He died in New York City. He was married twice: first, in 1829, to Frances E. Beecher of Lancaster, Ohio, who died in 1840 after having borne him five children; subsequently, he married Cecelia Bond, who survived him.

[G. I. Reed, *Bench and Bar of Ohio* (1897), vol. I; *Biog. and Hist. Cat. of Washington and Jefferson Coll.* (1902); *Trial of Andrew Johnson* (3 vols., 1868); *Diary of Gideon Welles* (1911), vols. II, III; Charles Warren, *The Supreme Court in U. S. Hist.* (1928), vol. II; E. P. Oberholtzer, *A Hist. of the U. S. Since the Civil War,* vol. II (1922); W. H. Safford, in *Ohio State Bar Asso. Reports,* vol. IV (1884); *N. Y. Times,* June 27, 1881; *Cincinnati Commercial,* June 27, 1881; information from grandson.] A. H. M.

STANCHFIELD, JOHN BARRY (Mar. 30, 1855–June 25, 1921), lawyer, son of John King and Glorvina (Smith) Stanchfield, was a descendant of John Stinchfield who came to Gloucester, Mass., from Leeds, England, in 1735, and later settled at New Gloucester, Me. The boy's father was a native of Maine, a graduate of the medical department of Bowdoin College, and for thirty years a physician at Elmira, N. Y. Upon taking up his residence in that place, apparently, he changed his name from Stinchfield to Stanchfield. John the younger was born there and was educated at the Elmira Free Academy and at Amherst. His record in his studies was only average, but he excelled in debating, rowing, and baseball. He is credited with being one of the first to use the "curve ball" in pitching. After his graduation in 1876, he attended some lectures at the Harvard Law School and then, returning to Elmira, studied in the office of David Bennett Hill [*q.v.*], under whose guidance he learned much about law and acquired a taste for politics. He was admitted to the bar in 1878 and became Hill's partner the following year. He served as district attorney of Chemung County, 1880–86, and as mayor of Elmira, 1886–88. After a few years, during which he devoted himself exclusively to law and obtained a good practice throughout most of western New York, his ambition for a political career led him to enter the New York Assembly in 1895. He was minority leader the following year and in 1898 was the unsuccessful candidate of Hill's faction for the Democratic nomination for governor. He was nominated in 1900, but was defeated through the opposition of organized labor and the unpopularity of his party's national candidates.

The experience was at least valuable in making him well known throughout the state. After the election he opened an office in New York City, where he at once gained favorable reputation through his conduct of several criminal cases, notably the defense of members of the Metropolitan Turf Association charged with violating laws against bookmaking, and of F. A. Heinze, charged with misappropriating funds of the Mercantile National Bank. During the last ten years of his life he was engaged in probably more cases which attracted public interest than any other member of the New York bar. He was counsel for friends of Harry K. Thaw in obtaining his release from Matteawan, for Duveen Brothers in cases concerning duties on works of art, for forty-one individuals and sixty-nine corporations charged with conspiracy in restraining trade in bituminous coal, for the Assembly committee in the impeachment of Governor Sulzer, and in family lawsuits of the Goulds and the Guggenheims. Though often retained as advisory counsel, he was generally engaged for work in the courtroom, where his erect, imposing figure, resonant voice, power of concise statement, courage, and resourcefulness in emergencies showed to great advantage.

On public affairs his convictions were conservative; his expressions, positive. It was he who, at the Democratic National Convention of 1912, called Bryan a "money-grabbing, selfish, office-seeking, favor-hunting, publicity-loving marplot." In 1915 he was a delegate to the state constitutional convention, in which he took little part. He was active in the National Security League, publishing an address in 1916, entitled, *Some Suggestions on the Perils of Espionage,* in which he recommended that Congress create a new offense, which he called misprision of espionage or misprision of treachery, and extend protection to systems of communications, mines, and factories, as well as to government property. His last appearance in public proceedings was in 1920 as counsel for the New York Assembly in the expulsion of five Socialist members. On Sept. 2, 1886, he married Clara, daughter of Henry C. Spaulding of Elmira; they had a son and a daughter.

[J. C. Stinchfield, *Hist. of the Town of Leeds . . . Me.* (n.d.); *The Asso. of the Bar of the City of N. Y., Year Book,* 1922; D. S. Alexander, *Four Famous New Yorkers* (1923); *Who's Who in America,* 1920–21; *Obit. Record, Grads. . . . of Amherst Coll.,* 1922; Ausburn Towner, *Our County and Its People: A Hist. of the . . . County of Chemung* (1892); *N. Y. Times,* June 26, 1921; information as to certain facts from Stanchfield's son.] E. C. S.

STANDERREN, ANN LEES [See LEE, ANN, 1736–1784].

STANDISH, MYLES (*c.* 1584–Oct. 3, 1656), Pilgrim father and captain, is said to have been born in Lancashire, England, and affirmed in his will that he was descended from the important Roman Catholic family, Standish of Standish, and had been fraudulently deprived of his inheritance, but no confirmation of this descent and no details of his early life have been discovered by extended modern research. He served in the Low Countries as soldier of fortune and in 1620 was hired by the Pilgrims to accompany them, sailing from London on the *Mayflower*. The only man with practical experience in camping, he was their mainstay in the first explorations of Cape Cod and was one of the small party who made the first landing at Plymouth on Dec. 11/21, 1620. During the general sickness of the first winter he was the only man except William Brewster, 1567–1644 [*q.v.*], who escaped, and with Brewster he rendered most important service to the sick. Probably it was this incident which made him one of the Pilgrims in fact and not merely their employee. Their first relations with the Indians he handled expertly, and, soon learning the Indian dialects, he became their chief resource in "foreign relations." Almost single-handed he suppressed the early conspiracies against them, designed and superintended the erection of the fort, and devised their measures of defense. So well did he work that after 1623 the colony experienced no real danger for half a century. This was one of the most important contributions to the welfare and success of Plymouth. In 1624 he became one of the five assistants then appointed for the first time. Four years later he broke up the settlement of Thomas Morton [*q.v.*] at Merry Mount and shipped the offender to England. Certainly by 1625 he was established as one of the Pilgrims, for at that time he was selected for a difficult mission. Isaac Allerton and Edward Winslow, 1595–1655 [*qq.v.*], had failed to complete satisfactory arrangements with the Merchant Adventurers or with the Council for New England, and the Pilgrims were as yet without rights in the new world to land or property. Standish was chosen to return to England bearing credentials to negotiate on their behalf. With the Council he had some success, with the merchants very little; but he did secure further loans and purchased supplies of great importance. He returned in April 1626. The following year he became one of the Undertakers who assumed the debts of the colony, and in 1630 was the attorney for the Council for

New England to deliver to the Pilgrims their land under the new grant. In later years he continued one of the chief men in all affairs, for six years treasurer and for twenty-nine an assistant. He and John Alden [*q.v.*] founded Duxbury in 1631, later set off as the first new town in their jurisdiction (1637), and there he lived for the remainder of his life.

His wife, Rose, having died in the sickness of the first winter, he married in 1624 his second wife, Barbara, who had come in the *Anne* in 1623. They had six children, of whom a son and a daughter died young. There is no historical basis for the story of John Alden's proposal to Priscilla on Standish's behalf or for other incidents in Longfellow's *The Courtship of Miles Standish* (A. E. Alden, *Pilgrim Alden,* 1902). There is some doubt whether he was ever a member of the Pilgrim church (Goodwin, *post,* p. 449), but the better view seems to be that he became a convert soon after reaching Plymouth. On his death in 1656 he left a considerable property in land and cattle, and one of the largest libraries at Plymouth. He was survived by his wife and four sons. Short, plump, and sturdy in appearance, he was called by Thomas Morton "Captaine Shrimp," a "quondam Drummer" (C. F. Adams, *The New English Canaan of Thomas Morton,* 1883, pp. 285–87), and by William Hubbard [*q.v.*], he was compared for his "very little stature" and his "hot and angry temper" to "a little chimney . . . soon fired" (*A General History of New England from the Discovery to MDCLXXX,* 1815, p. 111). He was nevertheless a man of great physical endurance and high courage.

[The chief authority is William Bradford, *Hist. of Plymouth Plantation, 1620–1647* (2 vols., 1912), ed. by W. C. Ford. See also R. G. Usher, *The Pilgrims and Their Hist.* (1918); J. A. Goodwin, *The Pilgrim Republic* (1888); Tudor Jenks, *Captain Myles Standish* (1905); T. C. Porteus, *Captain Myles Standish, His Lost Lands and Lancashire Connections* (1920); Myles Standish, *The Standishes of America* (1895), which gives Standish's will; C. E. Banks, *The English Ancestry and Homes of the Pilgrim Fathers* (1929).]

R. G. U.

STANFORD, JOHN (Oct. 20, 1754–Jan. 14, 1834), preacher, teacher, humanitarian, the son of William and Mary Stanford, was born at Wandsworth, in Surrey, England. He received his early education at a seminary in Wandsworth. At the age of sixteen he began to study medicine but his studies were interrupted by the death of his parents and he subsequently took charge of a boarding school in Hammersmith. Reared an Anglican he turned to the Baptist faith, began to write and distribute tracts before there were any Tract Societies, organized a Baptist church in Hammersmith, and was ordained as its first minister in 1781. Five years later he emigrated to the United States and, after a brief period of teaching in Norfolk, Va., and in New York City, he served as pastor of the First Baptist Church of Providence, R. I., in 1788–89, afterwards returning to teaching in New York City. In 1795 he erected a building for combined use as a church, school, and residence on Fair (now Fulton) Street, and acted as pastor until the yellow fever scourge of 1798 disrupted his congregation and a fire in 1801 reduced his church building to ashes. Stanford never held a fixed pastorate thereafter. For a decade he was known to his friends as a professor of theology although he preached frequently in Baptist churches in New York, New Jersey, Pennsylvania, and Connecticut. He spoke occasionally before the inmates of Bellevue Hospital and the New York State Prison, and in 1812 was appointed chaplain of the Prison. He called his charges at the latter institution his "Greenwich congregation." His services in a similar capacity in municipal institutions began the following year without formal appointment by any city authority, but he was compensated annually by the Common Council by special resolution. It was "for his zeal in administering to the spiritual wants of the poor and afflicted in the Alms House Gaol—and City Prison" (*Minutes Common Council, post,* VIII, 400), that the original annual stipend of $250 was increased to $300 in 1816, and to $500 in 1830.

Unfortunates of every description found a friend in Stanford, but the youthful inmates of institutions were particularly his concern. With a zeal reminiscent of John Howard he pled with the city magistrates to separate young offenders from the hardened criminals, and, as a result, the House of Refuge, called by Governor DeWitt Clinton the "best penitentiary institution . . . [which had] ever been devised by the wit and established by the beneficence of man" was dedicated by Stanford with a discourse in 1825 (*Journal of the Assembly of the State of New York,* 1826, p. 15). He organized the "Paupers' School" in the Alms House and drew up the necessary "regulations." He wrote a unique catechism for these children and persuaded the city to pay for the preparation and printing. In addition to many tracts and printed discourses, dedicated to the welfare of youth, Stanford wrote *The Aged Christian's Cabinet* (1829). He was married on June 16, 1790, to Sarah Ten Eyck who died during the fever scourge of 1798, leaving two sons and two daughters.

[Stanford's diary, 5 vols., manuscript, 1816–31, and his Letter Book, 1795–1821, autographed copies of his annual reports as Chaplain of the State Prison, 1819–26, and of New York City institutions, 1819–30, are preserved in the archives of the N. Y. Hist. Soc.; C. G. Sommers, *Memoir of the Rev. John Stanford, D.D.* (1835), with portrait, is based on the diary and Letter Book but contains many unfortunate changes in phraseology; "A Brief Sketch of the Life of the Rev. John Stanford, D.D.," is to be found in *Aged Christian's Companion* (1855, 4th edition of the *Cabinet*). See also Enoch Hutchinson's biographical sketch in *The Bapt. Memorial and Monthly Record,* vol. VIII (1849); *Minutes of the Common Council of the City of N. Y., 1784–1831,* 21 vols. (1917–30); original letters and reports in city clerk's archives; brief references in David Benedict, *A Gen. Hist. of the Bapt. Denomination* (1813), vol. I, and *A Brief Hist. of the Am. Tract Soc.* (1857); H. W. George, "The Ten Eyck Family in New York," *N. Y. Geneal. and Biog. Record,* July 1932; *New-York American,* Jan. 15, 1834.]　　A. E. P.

STANFORD, LELAND (Mar. 9, 1824–June 21, 1893), railroad builder, governor of California, and United States senator, was born in Watervliet, N. Y. Originally his name was Amasa Leland (Clark, *post,* p. 14), but he never used the full form after he was mature. His father, Josiah Stanford, a native of Massachusetts and a man of means, was a descendant of Thomas Stanford who settled at Charlestown, Mass., in the seventeenth century. His mother was Elizabeth Phillips, whose parents were once residents of Boston, moving thence to Vermont, and later to New York. Leland Stanford was the fourth son of a family of seven sons and one daughter. The daughter died in infancy, and one son in early life. The remaining children were, in the order of their ages, Josiah, Charles, Asa Phillips, Leland, De Witt Clinton, and Thomas Welton. The boys helped their father upon the farm, and perhaps also with various contracts for road and bridge construction in which he was interested. Leland attended school until the age of twelve. He was then taught at home for three years. After an interval of two years he returned to school, attending Clinton Liberal Institute, Clinton, N. Y., and Cazenovia Seminary at Cazenovia, and at the age of twenty-one entered the law office of Wheaton, Doolittle and Hadley at Albany. Three years later he was admitted to the bar. He can thus be said to have received a fair education for his place and time. When the young man began the practice of the law in 1848 at Port Washington, Wis., his father presented him with a law library that was said to be the best in that part of the United States north of Milwaukee.

While Leland Stanford entered upon a professional career, his brothers migrated to California, attracted by the commercial opportunities in that rapidly developing community. Under the leadership of the younger Josiah, who led the way, the five brothers prospered in the mercantile business, with a wholesale house in Sacramento and retail stores at Mormon Island and Michigan Flat, all more or less connected, and one brother as a purchasing agent in New York (Clark, p. 51). It is not improbable that Leland may have considered joining them, for Port Washington was a small place, and his legal ability was in no way conspicuous. The change did not occur, however, until 1852. In the meantime, on Sept. 30, 1850, he married Jane Elizabeth Lathrop, daughter of a respected merchant at Albany, N. Y., Dyer Lathrop, and his wife, Jane Ann Shields. Two years later his office at Port Washington, with his law library, was burned. The newly married couple were jolted out of their accustomed routine, and, instead of settling down again, decided to follow the other younger members of the Stanford family to the Pacific Coast. They returned to Albany, where Mrs. Stanford remained with her father while her husband went ahead to prepare the way.

In 1852, accordingly, Leland Stanford was in California, visiting at first his brother in Sacramento. J. M. Bassett, who knew him well, and who was likely to be acquainted with the facts, says that he came to California poor as a church mouse, and that his brothers set him up in business in El Dorado County, at Cold Springs, with a stock of miners' supplies (San Francisco *Daily Report,* Mar. 21, 1896). Capt. Nicholas T. Smith, later treasurer of the Southern Pacific, was his partner. Bassett says, further, that Stanford was popular with the miners and did a good business. He and Smith thought they were making money until they found out that the San Francisco firm with which they dealt was charging them interest on unpaid balances. This absorbed their profit, and they went out of business with very little cash. Whether for this reason or because the mining at Cold Springs petered out, Stanford started a new store at Michigan Bluff the following spring, and is said to have done well.

Michigan Bluff was a central business point for the Placer County mining territory, and well located for the distribution of miners' supplies. Whether Stanford, in addition to merchandising, profited by successful mining operations at this time is not certain, but if he did engage in mining it was probably upon a small scale. In 1855 he returned to Albany for his wife and the next year he moved to Sacramento to join his brothers in business there. Meanwhile his attention had been drawn to politics. In Michigan Bluff he had been justice of the peace. During the state campaign of 1857 he was the Republican candidate for state treasurer, but went down to

defeat with his party. In 1859 he was nominated for governor and made a thorough canvass, only to be decisively beaten by Milton S. Latham [*q.v.*]. In 1860 he was chosen delegate to the Republican National Convention, but did not attend. These various activities made him known, and in 1861 when the outbreak of the Civil War split the Democratic party of the state in two, the tenacious Stanford, again a candidate, was elected governor, although he received less than the combined vote of his two Democratic opponents. His success was due to his personal popularity, and to his strong Union and Republican convictions, for he had had no opportunity to distinguish himself in public service. In 1863 he was not renominated, and he held no other public office until his election as United States senator in 1885.

The chief task of Stanford's administration as governor was to hold California safely in the Union, and this he accomplished to the satisfaction of the Union party and of the state legislature. He had, in addition, to cope with difficulties caused by a serious flood upon the Sacramento at the very outset of his gubernatorial career. In addition to providing for sufferers from the flood of 1861, and promoting minor administrative and legislative reforms, Stanford approved, during his term of office, several public grants to the transcontinental railroad via Truckee, Cal. This was the enterprise which brought him wealth, and upon which his reputation chiefly rests. His connection with the transcontinental railroad project, like that of Collis Potter Huntington [*q.v.*], seems to have been due to the promotion activity of Theodore Dehone Judah [*q.v.*]. When he became interested, Stanford subscribed, with others, a sufficient amount to finance instrumental surveys which gave satisfactory evidence of the feasibility of the proposed railroad line, and then to permit the organization of the Central Pacific Railroad on June 28, 1861. Only a small amount of capital was available to the associates; most of the necessary funds for the building of the road were procured by means of subscriptions and grants of a public nature.

Ground was broken at Sacramento in January 1863, and in April Stanford as governor signed four acts affording considerable assistance to the new enterprise. One of these instructed the board of supervisors of Placer County to order a special election to consider a county subscription of $250,000 to the Central Pacific capital stock. A second provided for a similar election in the City and County of Sacramento to approve a subscription for 3,000 shares. A third act directed the supervisors of the City and County of San Francisco to submit a proposal to the voters to subscribe $600,000 to the stock of the Central Pacific and $400,000 to the stock of the Western Pacific Railroad. The last act authorized the comptroller of the state to draw warrants in favor of the Central Pacific to the extent of $10,-000 per mile. The warrants were to be issued when the first twenty miles, the second twenty miles, and the last ten out of fifty miles were finished. They were to bear seven per cent. interest if the state proved unable to cash them when presented. It should be added that this law was repealed in the following year, when the legislature proposed, instead of drawing warrants, to assume the interest on 1,500 of the company's bonds bearing seven per cent. interest and running for twenty years. From these various acts the Central Pacific ultimately realized some $825,000, besides the interest payments contemplated by the act of 1864. Stanford had no scruples about taking official action as governor where his private interests as railroad president were engaged, or he overcame such as may have occurred to him by reflecting upon the public importance of a railroad connection with the East.

When his term of office expired in 1863, Stanford left the governorship to devote his whole time to railroad construction. He then occupied an important position in the little group that was responsible for the transcontinental railroad, and he worked hard during the next ten years to make this project a success. He was president and director of the Central Pacific Railroad from the beginning until his death in 1893. He was director of the Southern Pacific Company from 1885 to 1893, and president of the company from 1885 to 1890. He was director of the Southern Pacific Railroad in 1889 and in 1890. At all times he was a shareholder in and contributor to the resources of the construction companies, such as the Contract & Finance Company, which built the Central Pacific, the Southern Pacific, and their allied properties. The course pursued, in connection with the construction of the Central Pacific, was described by the Pacific Railway Commission as "indefensible" (*Report of the . . . United States Pacific Railway Commission,* 1887, p. 72; see also Carman and Mueller, *post*). While Huntington was the financial representative, purchasing agent, and chief lobbyist in the East, and Charles Crocker [*q.v.*] took charge of construction, Stanford seems to have handled the financial affairs and looked after the political interests of the Central Pacific in the West. He was widely known and personally of good credit, and although he sold no Central Pacific stock in the early days, and never succeeded in persuading other men of wealth to join with him and his associates, he was able to borrow considerable sums when they were needed in anticipation of receipts, and so to insure the essential continuity of construction work.

The importance of the Central Pacific Railroad, the obvious difficulties of topography and of climate which it overcame, the dramatic speed at which the work was done, the picturesque personalities and subsequent great wealth of the promoters and their relations with national and local governments, have since attracted great attention to this particular exploit. The Central Pacific was not, at the beginning, particularly well built, and it was not located upon the easiest route over the Sierras. The present Feather River route of the Western Pacific Railroad has lower grades and less snow. While the engineering difficulties were serious, the railroad was built almost entirely with or on the security of public funds, so that Stanford and his friends risked less of their own capital in the undertaking than has sometimes been supposed. Nevertheless, the associates risked their own personal fortunes, whether large or small, in building a transcontinental railway, they assembled the force and created the organization with which the work was done, and they contributed energy and courage and assumed responsibility for decisions which determined the success of the undertaking.

After the completion of the Central Pacific Railroad on May 10, 1869, by its junction with the Union Pacific near Ogden, Utah, Stanford was definitely committed to a railroad career. His business life thereafter was devoted to the strengthening and expansion of his railroad properties. In this he continued to work in close cooperation with his former associates; indeed, the continued unity in management of Central Pacific and Southern Pacific affairs was an important element in the later success of these companies as operating organizations. This same unity makes it impossible to determine Stanford's separate contribution to Central Pacific policy except in a few special instances; but it permits one to assume that he had a fair share in whatever results his organizations achieved. Notable among these was the acquisition of satisfactory terminal facilities for the new company upon San Francisco Bay, the purchase in 1871 of the competing line of the California Pacific Railroad Company from Sacramento to Vallejo, the purchase of the San Francisco and San Jose Railroad, probably in 1868, and the organization of the Southern Pacific Railroad. This last named company was incorporated in October 1870, to construct and operate a railroad from San Francisco to the Colorado River. It eventually was built from Gilroy to Tres Pinos, and from Goshen in the San Joaquin Valley to Los Angeles, Fort Yuma, and to the Needles, all in California. With connecting companies under the same control it provided a through line from San Francisco to New Orleans. In 1884, on Stanford's suggestion, the Stanford-Huntington group organized the Southern Pacific Company under the laws of Kentucky and caused it, in 1885, as a holding company, to lease the Southern Pacific Railroad, the Central Pacific Railroad, and other system properties. After this, the Southern Pacific Company became the dominant unit in the organization. The principal object of the change was to continue undisputed control of the Central Pacific in the hands of the associates in spite of sales of considerable quantities of Central Pacific stock to English and other buyers.

There has never been a public accounting of the profits which Stanford and his friends drew from the construction of the Central and Southern Pacific Railroads. We know they were great, because the associates died very rich men. Mark Hopkins engaged in no important enterprises outside of his hardware business except in railroad construction and operation, and yet in 1878 he left an estate appraised at over $19,000,000. Eleven years later, Charles Crocker's estate was estimated at c. $24,000,000. Stanford's estate was not appraised in 1893, and Huntington did not die until long afterwards, but both shared equally with Hopkins and Crocker in the results of the tasks which they undertook together.

It was this great personal fortune, as well as the backing of the Southern Pacific, which enabled Stanford to indulge his tastes in matters not strictly connected with his business. In this he showed a wider range of interests than his colleague Huntington, who remained in harness until the end of his life. Stanford, on the other hand, bought land in Tehama County, where he maintained extensive vineyards, and a large ranch, "Palo Alto," where he bred and ran fine racing stock. He did much to raise the grade of California horses and achieved records in eastern fields. His original methods of training were widely adopted. He was interested in photography as a means of studying animal locomotion, and in this connection sponsored some of the first successful experiments with instantaneous photography (Clark, chs. x, xi).

He interested himself greatly in the education of his son, a bright affectionate boy, and suffered cruelly when the lad died in 1884 at the age of fifteen years and ten months. Stanford desired to raise a fitting memorial to his son, and out of this grew Leland Stanford Junior University, founded in 1885 and opened in 1891, an institution, generously endowed, which has acquired high standing among the universities of the United States. For ten years after his death, his wife devoted herself to the problem of caring for the young institution.

Stanford also turned to politics. In a sense, indeed, he had never left politics. After the expiration of his term as governor in 1863, he was naturally the man in the Central Pacific group best fitted to resist the attempts to pass hostile legislation, as well as the one most likely to be able to secure new favors at Sacramento and elsewhere. After the completion of the transcontinental line in 1869, he continued to observe the local situation. His attitude was, as might have been expected, entirely opposed to interference with railroad business by public bodies, for by character and training he was entirely unfitted to understand the movement for public control of quasi-public enterprises which began to gain momentum in the early seventies. Many of Stanford's expressions with respect to railroad regulation have been preserved. The California constitution of 1879 displeased him greatly. He declared that *Munn* vs. *Illinois* and the other Granger cases seemed to recognize the "communistic" idea of the distribution of property and the absolutism of control by a majority of the people, and he advocated a return to the "civilized" government of the fathers which gave protection to the individual and made him truly a free and independent citizen. Stanford justified certain types of discrimination; he defended consolidation; he alluded to the efforts of the railroad to build up the state; and he asserted its right to protect itself by political action when attacked. "There is no foundation in good reason," he said to his stockholders in his annual report for 1878, "for the attempts made by the General Government and by the State to especially control your affairs. It is a question of might, and it is to your interest to have it determined where the power resides" (*Annual Report of the Board of Directors of the Central Pacific Railway to the Stockholders . . . 1878,* 1879, p. 5.).

The general belief in California was that the Southern Pacific Company gave practical effect to Stanford's views by active and persistent interference in the politics of the state, and there is evidence in support of this opinion. Stanford himself held no political office until his return from a trip to Europe in November 1884, after the death of his son Leland. A Republican legislature was to assemble in January 1885, and was to elect a successor to James T. Farley, Democrat, chosen by the legislature of 1877–78. The logical candidate for the position was A. A. Sargent, previously a representative and senator from California, but Stanford allowed his name to be used and was elected by a strict party vote soon after the legislature convened. The decision to accept public office was, on Stanford's part, undoubtedly a mistake. In the first place, it profoundly offended Collis P. Huntington, who was a friend of Sargent and believed that the latter's interests had been betrayed. The difference between Huntington and Stanford remained concealed for several years, but it broke out openly in 1890, when Huntington bitterly criticized Stanford for his political activity, and succeeded in supplanting him as president of the Southern Pacific Company. In the second place, election to the senatorship projected Stanford into a field for which he had no proper training, and for which his abilities were inadequate. He was not an easy speaker, except perhaps on a limited range of subjects connected with his personal experience, he had little talent for sustained thought on difficult problems of a general sort, and his reading in economics seems rather to have confused than to have clarified his mind. In the Senate he found himself assigned, on the whole, to committees of minor importance. His most significant committee, that on naval affairs, dealt with a subject of which he knew nothing. Nor did he try to exert influence upon the floor of the Senate. Between March 1885, when Stanford first appeared in Congress, and June 1893, when he died, the national legislature passed laws providing for the regulation of interstate commerce, for the purchase of silver, for the revision of the tariff, and for the exclusion of Chinese. These were perhaps the most important subjects considered during this period. Stanford was absent from the Senate when the Interstate Commerce Act in its first form was voted on, and when the Senate finally approved the conference report upon the measure in January 1887 he was again absent, though paired against the bill. He was likewise absent when the tariff act of 1890 and the Silver Purchase bill of the same year were passed, although paired in favor of both measures. In neither of the two last-named cases did he participate in the debates, and his contributions to the consideration of the Interstate Commerce Act were unimportant. Stanford said nothing in the Senate with reference to the exclusion of Chinese laborers in 1888, and the record fails to show whether or not he took part in the final vote. The one proposal in which he showed a real interest was a suggestion of his own, that the federal government issue paper money to borrowers on the security of mortgages upon real estate up to fifty per cent. of the assessed value of the property and at a rate of interest of two per cent. The economic theory underlying the scheme was complex but unsound, and Congress gave it scant attention; but the bill was approved by the National Grange of the Patrons of Husbandry as a step in the direction of cheap money, and brought Stanford some political backing. It is not too much to say that this legislative record shows lack of interest or lack of capacity—probably lack of both; his senatorship satisfied Stanford's vanity and increased his prestige in California, but it did not add to his reputation.

Stanford was five feet eleven inches tall, and in later years weighed as much as 268 pounds. During his prime he possessed unusual energy, working sometimes day and night without cessation, and enduring the hardships incident to railroad construction without complaint. Mentally he was slow, susceptible to flattery, and given to somewhat ponderous platitudes concerning human life and the economic conditions and organizations required for national success. He was elected by the California legislature to succeed himself in the United States Senate on Jan. 14, 1891, but by this time he was an ill man, more concerned with recovery of his health than with political or economic programs. He sought relief in America and abroad from various types of healers, but grew steadily worse, and at last died suddenly at his home in Palo Alto on June 21, 1893. The immediate cause of his death was paralysis of the heart, but the disease from which he had long suffered was diagnosed as locomotor ataxia. He left two brothers, Thomas Welton Stanford, then resident in Australia, and Asa Phillips Stanford, of New York, besides a number of nieces and nephews. The bulk of the estate passed to Mrs. Stanford, apart from a gift of $2,500,000 to Leland Stanford Junior University, and minor bequests to relatives and friends. Mrs. Stanford died in 1905.

[T. H. Hittell, *Hist. of California*, vol. IV (1897); H. H. Bancroft, *Hist. of California*, vol. VII (1890); Stuart Daggett, *Chapters on the Hist. of the Southern Pacific* (1922); Gustavus Myers, *Hist. of the Great American Fortunes*, vol. III (1910); G. T. Clark, *Leland Stanford* (1931); Bertha Berner, *Incidents in the Life of Mrs. Leland Stanford* (1934); Matthew Josephson, *The Robber Barons* (1934); G. C. Quiett, *They Built the West* (1934); H. J. Carman and C. H. Mueller, "The Contract and Finance Company and the Central Pacific Railroad," *Miss. Valley Hist. Rev.*, Dec.

1927; "Testimony Taken by the U. S. Pacific Railway Commission," *Senate Executive Document 51, 50 Cong., 1 Sess.* (1887), vol. V; *Report . . . of the U. S. Pacific Railway Commission* (1887); *California Hist. Soc. Quart.*, Oct. 1923, pp. 203–10; June 1926, pp. 178–83, containing reminiscences and letters; obituary notices in San Francisco *Daily Evening Bulletin* and *Morning Call*, June 21, and the San Francisco *Examiner*, June 21, 22, 23, 24, 1893; A. W. Stanford, *Stanford Genealogy* (1906).]   S. D.

STANG, WILLIAM (Apr. 21, 1854–Feb. 2, 1907), Roman Catholic prelate and educator, son of Francis Joseph and Frances (Bellm) Stang, was born in Langenbrücken, Baden, Germany, where he attended a local gymnasium. In the *petit séminaire* of Saint-Nicolas, Belgium, he prepared for his theological studies at the American College in Louvain. Ordained priest, June 15, 1878, he accepted the call of Bishop Thomas F. Hendricken (1827–86) to Providence, R. I., where he served as a curate in the Cathedral of SS. Peter and Paul. Six years later, he became rector of St. Anne's Church at Cranston, R. I., from which he was soon recalled to the rectorship of the cathedral and chancellorship of the diocese. In the latter capacity he largely inspired the erection of St. Joseph's Hospital in 1892. A thorough student and an exceptional linguist, he found time to publish *The Life of Martin Luther* (1883), *The Eve of the Reformation* (1885), *More about the Huguenots* (1886), and *Germany's Debt to Ireland* (1889). While not learned works, they evidenced wide reading on the part of the author, as well as a scientific spirit of toleration. In 1895 he was appointed vice-rector of the American College in Louvain, where he was honored by the Belgian hierarchy with election in 1898 to the chair of moral theology in the University of Louvain. During his tenure he wrote or compiled solid volumes, *Pastoral Theology* (1896), and *Historiographia Ecclesiastica* (1897). In 1899 he returned to Providence as superior of the diocesan apostolate, which included the direction of missions to non-Catholics, and in 1901 became pastor of St. Edward's Church as well.

Recognized as a spiritual priest and as a capable administrator who could handle racial questions intelligently and sympathetically, on Mar. 12, 1904, he was named by Pope Pius X as bishop of the newly created diocese of Fall River, which had over a hundred priests, of whom fifty were attending French, Polish, Italian, and Portuguese parishes. Consecrated on May 1, 1904, by Bishop Matthew Harkins of Providence (1845–1921), whom he had served so wholeheartedly, he began a brief episcopate. In 1907 he underwent an unsuccessful operation at St. Mary's Hospital, Rochester, Minn., on the eve

of which he gave orders for a simple and inexpensive funeral such as became an impoverished scholar. His later publications, aside from articles in the *American Ecclesiastical Review* (later the *Ecclesiastical Review*) and thoughtful pastoral letters on *Christian Marriage* and *Christian Education* (1907), included a handy *Business Guide for Priests* (1899), *The Devil: Who He Is and What He Is* (1900), *Spiritual Pepper and Salt* (1902), an apologetic treatise for missionaries, *Socialism and Christianity* (1905), *Medulla Fundamentalis Theologiae Moralis* (1907), and *The Holy Hour of Adoration* (1907).

[*Jour. American-Irish Hist. Soc.*, vol. VII (1907); *Cath. Encyc.*, vol. V (1909), p. 771; ann. official Cath. directories; F. J. Bradley and M. V. McCarthy, *A Brief Hist. of the Diocese of Fall River* (1931); sketch by Joseph Stang, *Pastoral-blatt* (St. Louis), Jan. 1920; obituary in *Boston Post*, Feb. 3, 1907.]   R. J. P.

STANLEY, ALBERT AUGUSTUS (May 25, 1851–May 19, 1932), educator, conductor, and composer, was born in Manville, R. I., the younger of two sons of Dr. George Washington and Augusta Adaline (Jefferds) Stanley. He was the seventh in line of descent from Matthew Stanley, founder of the second immigration of Stanleys from England and first mentioned in Lynn, Mass., in 1646. In 1856 his parents moved to Slatersville, R. I., where the father practised medicine for over thirty years and the son obtained his only formal schooling. As a child he exhibited unusual musical ability, doubtless inherited from his mother, who was fond of music and possessed a fine contralto voice. He early manifested a decided preference for the organ; at fourteen he became organist of the Congregational church in Slatersville, and at seventeen organist of the Church of the Mediator in Providence. Going to Germany in 1871, he studied at the Leipzig conservatory under Ernst Ferdinand Wenzel (piano), Benjamin Robert Papperitz (organ), Ernst Friedrich Richter (theory), Carl Heinrich Reinecke, and Oscar Paul. His scholarship was so excellent that during his last year he assisted Richter in the theory classes and was substitute organist at the Nikolai-Kirche. Upon his graduation in 1875, he returned to America, taught one year at Ohio Wesleyan College, Delaware, Ohio, and then went to Providence as organist of Grace Church (1876–88). In 1888 he was called to fill the chair of music at the University of Michigan, a position he retained till his death, becoming emeritus professor in 1921. A man of boundless energy, he displayed great ability for organization, combined with a contagious enthusiasm for whatever he had in hand. He welded together the various university and local musical activities, reorganized the earlier Ann Arbor School of Music as the University School of Music with well-rounded courses of study and a larger faculty, and in 1894 established the Ann Arbor May Festival. This annual music festival, which greatly broadened the cultural influence of the music department, under his energetic development (he was conductor until 1921) became one of the most influential of its kind. He was also conductor of the Choral Union (1888–1921), which from 1893 on maintained an average membership of about three hundred. He took an active interest in association work as well. He was secretary, treasurer, and in 1886 president of the Music Teachers' National Association, president of the Michigan Music Teachers Association, one of the founders of the American College of Musicians (1884) and of the American Guild of Organists (1896); president of the American Section of the Internationale Musikgesellschaft (1906–12), representing America at several important European musical congresses; and honorary vice-president of the Musical Association (Great Britain).

In his earlier years he was a brilliant organist, but he gradually abandoned this field for the more urgent activities of university life. His more important compositions include a symphony "The Soul's Awakening"; a symphonic poem, "Attis"; a choral work, "Chorus Triumphalis"; and three works for chorus and orchestra, "A Psalm of Victory" (1906), "Fair Land of Freedom" (1919), and "Laus Deo." For various academic performances in Ann Arbor he wrote incidental music, employing ancient modes and suggesting ancient instrumentation, to Percy Mackaye's *Sappho and Phaon* (first performed with Stanley's music, 1907), Euripides' *Alcestis* (1912) and *Iphigenia among the Taurians* (1917), and Plautus' *Menaechmi* (1916). The last four, with elaborate annotations, were published as *Greek Themes in Modern Musical Settings* (University of Michigan Studies, Humanistic Series, vol. XV, 1924). His love for details found expression in a scholarly and exhaustive *Catalogue of the Stearns Collection of Musical Instruments* (1918), a collection presented to the university in 1898. On Dec. 27, 1875, he married Emma F. Bullock, of Randolph, Mass., who died July 9, 1911. Their only child, Elsa, died May 14, 1910. His second wife was Dorothea Oestreicher of Ann Arbor, Mich., whom he married Dec. 1, 1921. He died in Ann Arbor, survived by his wife.

[*Who's Who in America*, 1932–33; *Grove's Dict. of Music and Musicians: Am. Supp.* (rev. ed., 1930); C. A. Sink, in *Mich. Alumnus*, June 4, 1932; obituary in *Detroit News*, May 19, 1932; Stanley's memoirs, in MS., in the School of Music of the Univ. of Mich.; information about ancestry from Stanley's widow.]

R. G. C.

STANLEY, ANN LEE [See LEE, ANN, 1736–1784].

STANLEY, DAVID SLOANE (June 1, 1828–Mar. 13, 1902), soldier, was born at Cedar Valley, Ohio, the son of John Bratton and Sarah (Peterson) Stanley, and a descendant of Thomas Stanley who came to Massachusetts from England in 1634. David was educated in a log school house until he was fourteen years old, when he was apprenticed to study medicine. In 1848 he entered the United States Military Academy, at West Point, N. Y., graduating in 1852 as second lieutenant of dragoons. His first assignments were in Texas and California. On Apr. 2, 1857, he married Anna Maria, daughter of J. J. B. Wright, an army surgeon. In 1856 he was active in the Kansas disturbances, and the next year in operations against Cheyenne Indians.

The commencement of the Civil War found him a captain of cavalry at Fort Smith, Ark. He was offered the colonelcy of an Arkansas regiment in the Confederate service, but declined and in May 1861 escaped from Southern territory by a hazardous march to Kansas. Later in the same year he served in the Missouri campaign, receiving and accepting a commission as brigadier-general of volunteers in October 1861. In November he broke his leg and was forced to quit the field. The following spring he took a prominent part in the battles of New Madrid and Island No. 10. He next participated in the capture of Corinth, Miss. When the Confederates attempted to retake that city in October, Stanley counter-attacked at the head of his troops, and drove the enemy back. For this victory, he was given command of a cavalry division in Tennessee, becoming a major-general in April 1863, his commission being dated Nov. 29, 1862. He ably seconded the campaigns of Rosecrans during 1863. At the end of that year, he was assigned to the 1st Division, IV Corps, guarding communications. In 1864 he took part in Sherman's Atlanta operations, being particularly commended for gallant conduct at Resaca, Ga. On July 27 he succeeded to the command of the IV Corps, and in September was wounded at Jonesboro, Ga. Although criticized by Sherman (see B. H. Liddell Hart, *Sherman*, 1930, p. 301), Stanley led his troops with vigor. In November 1864 his corps arrived at Pulaski, Tenn., just in time to save Thomas' army from the advance of Hood. Falling back, Stanley next fought the battle of Spring Hill, enabling the balance of the army to retreat north. On Nov. 30, Thomas was heavily attacked by Hood at Franklin, Tenn. Once again Stanley personally led a counter-attack, restoring the battle to the Federals. He was painfully wounded and his active career in the Civil War came to an end.

In June 1865 Stanley's IV Corps was sent to Texas to support diplomatic representations against French interference in Mexico. In February 1866 Stanley was mustered out of the volunteer service as a major-general, and on July 28, 1866, became colonel, 22nd Infantry, in the Regular Army. He was now sent to the Indian frontier. In 1873 he led the expedition into the Yellowstone area (see his *Report on the Yellowstone Expedition, 1874*), and between 1879 and 1882 he settled several Indian disturbances in Texas. On Mar. 24, 1884, he was promoted to the rank of brigadier-general, United States Army, and subsequently commanded in Texas until he retired, June 1, 1892. He was governor of the Soldiers' Home, Washington, from Sept. 13, 1893 to Apr. 15, 1898, and thereafter lived in Washington until his death.

His great service was his thirty-four years spent in the opening of the West. He was a master in handling Indians. He possessed the esteem of his associates, but was disliked by some on account of his deep prejudices, which his kindly appearance failed sometimes to conceal. He contributed an article to *Battles and Leaders of the Civil War* (vol. II, 1888), edited by R. U. Johnson and C. C. Buel, and an incomplete autobiography, *Personal Memoirs of Major-General D. S. Stanley, U. S. A.*, was published in 1917. His wife died in 1895, and of seven children four daughters and a son survived him.

[*War of the Rebellion: Official Records (Army)*; G. W. Cullum, *Biog. Reg. Officers and Grads. U. S. Mil. Acad.* (1891); I. P. Warren, *The Stanley Families of America* (1887); *Who's Who in America,* 1901–02; *Evening Star* (Washington), Mar. 13, 1902; *Washington Post*, Mar. 14, 1902; family information from Stanley's son, Col. D. S. Stanley.]   C. H. L.

STANLEY, FRANCIS EDGAR (June 1, 1849–July 31, 1918), inventor, manufacturer, was born in Kingfield, Me., the son of Solomon and Apphia (French) Stanley. His father was a teacher and a farmer, a descendant of Matthew Stanley who emigrated from England to Lynn, Mass., about 1646. Stanley attended public school in Kingfield and graduated in 1871 from the Farmington State Normal and Training School. For a number of years he taught school in various towns in Maine; at the same time, having a talent for crayon portraiture, he

built up a portrait business. In 1874 the demands of this work led him to give up teaching, and he removed to Lewiston, Me., where he believed a larger opportunity lay. In the course of the succeeding nine years, which were successful ones, he added photography to his business and became one of the leading portrait photographers of New England. Having begun about 1883 to experiment with photographic dry plates, he devised a formula for a dry-plate firm which seemed to have such possibilities that in partnership with his twin brother, Freelan O. Stanley, he organized the Stanley Dry Plate Company and established a manufactory in Lewiston. Their products, which were of very good quality, soon came into general use in the United States and foreign countries, and in 1890 the Stanleys established a new plant at Newton, Mass., where better railroad facilities were to be had. In 1905, the brothers sold their business to the Eastman Kodak Company of Rochester, N. Y.

Meanwhile Francis had become interested in steam automobiles, and early in 1897 began a series of experiments which resulted in the production by the brothers in that year of the first steam motor car to be successfully operated in New England. For this he designed a very efficient high-pressure steam boiler, light in weight and yet with ample storage capacity. This he combined with a new design of light weight, reversing, two-cylinder steam engine, and produced a very successful steam automobile. Having organized a company to manufacture their machine, the brothers in 1898 began the construction of one hundred cars, all with standard parts, but before completing them they sold the entire business, including the patents, to John Brisben Walker of New York, who subsequently organized the Mobile Company of America and was interested in the establishment of the Locomobile Company of America. In 1902, however, the Stanley brothers repurchased their original patents from the Locomobile Company and organized the Stanley Motor Carriage Company, with Francis as president, and continued to conduct the affairs of the company until their retirement in 1917. In the last years of his life Francis Stanley was engaged in developing a "unit steam engine" to be applied to the running of individual steam cars on interurban railroad lines. With his brother he also invented a process for manufacturing illuminating gas from gasoline. As an avocation he gave much attention to the theory and practical science of violin construction. He was an ardent student of economics, and was a member of economic associations and clubs, as well as of literary clubs. A collection of his addresses and essays presented to these organizations during his life was privately printed after his death under the title *Theories Worth Having* (1919). He married Augusta May Walker, daughter of William Walker of New Portland, Me., on Jan. 1, 1870, and at the time of his death, which occurred as the result of an automobile accident, was survived by his widow and three children.

[E. S. Stackpoole, *Hist. of Winthrop, Mass., with Geneal. Notes* (1925); biog. sketch in F. E. Stanley, *Theories Worth Having* (1919); *Automobile Trade Jour.,* Dec. 1, 1924; obituary in *Boston Transcript,* Aug. 1, 1918; Patent Office records.]   C. W. M—n.

STANLEY, HENRY MORTON (1841–May 10, 1904), explorer, was born at Denbigh, Wales, the son of a small farmer named Rowlands, who died soon after the boy's birth. His mother's maiden name was Parry. Until his adoption in America in 1859, he was known as John Rowlands. The confusion about the date of his birth, taken into consideration with the marked heartlessness of his mother and uncles toward him, has led some students of his history to suspect that he was illegitimate. He lived with his mother's father till the latter died in 1847; with him, departed the last vestige of humane treatment the child was to know. One day the son of the family with whom his uncles boarded him told him he would be taken on a journey to visit his Aunt Mary, whom he had never seen (*Autobiography,* p. 10). He set out happily and was delighted to see the imposing house where the cart finally stopped. He ran in looking for his aunt, to meet with mockery and taunts. The building was St. Asaph Union Workhouse. John now came under the discipline of the boys' schoolmaster, James Francis, a fanatically brutal man who ended his own days in a madhouse. Stanley has related briefly and movingly how he and a comrade stole into the room where a boy, who had been popular with all his companions, lay dead, and how one of them, presumably himself, turned down the sheet and saw the marks of the blows which had caused his death (*Ibid.,* p. 22). His treatment by his family and the years of horror at St. Asaph are described intimately and with much detail in his *Autobiography,* which was written, as he indicates, out of a desire to make his nature and character comprehensible to the world which knew him in the day of his fame. At St. Asaph his only comforter was the God revealed to him in his Bible as the Divine Father and the friend of the helpless. Out of his experiences with the scriptures and with prayer grew the faith in "A God at hand and not afar off" which

so strongly influenced him in later years, and which infuses his narratives of his great exploits and some of his letters.

He was about fifteen years old when, one day, he turned on the brutal master and, to his own astonishment, worsted him in the bout. Seeing the tyrant laid low by his prowess brought a rush of conflicting emotions on the boy: fears for his life mingled with the sudden proud knowledge that he had had the courage to rebel and the muscular strength to conquer. He ran away from the workhouse in May 1856 and at last, tired and hungry, reached the house of his paternal grandfather, a well-to-do farmer, who callously showed him the door. He found refuge with a cousin, a schoolmaster at Brynford, who needed the help of a pupil-teacher, for which post Stanley's earnest application to study, while at St. Asaph, had qualified him. The same curious family resentment was evident here, too, and a year later he was sent to an uncle in Liverpool. This relative was not unkind but he was very poor. Stanley worked first for a haberdasher and then for a butcher, but he saw no prospect of advance in Liverpool so he shipped as cabin boy on a vessel bound for Louisiana in 1859. He found work in New Orleans with a merchant named Henry Morton Stanley, who became deeply interested in him, and presently adopted him rather informally and gave him his name (December 1859, *Autobiography,* p. 120). In the fall of 1860 he was sent to a country store in Arkansas to begin his experience as a merchant. Meanwhile, the elder Stanley went to Cuba on business and died there in 1861. He had made no legal provision for his adopted son, who did not even know of his death until some years later.

In 1861 Stanley enlisted in the Dixie Grays, and in April 1862 was taken prisoner at the battle of Shiloh. He has written a vivid description of the hardships endured by those Confederate prisoners, who did not die under them, at Camp Douglas, Chicago. After two months' experience of them, he enrolled in the Federal artillery but his physical condition was so bad as to render him useless, and he was discharged within the month. He worked his way back to England and sought out his mother, who showed him plainly that, like the rest of his relatives, she wanted nothing to do with him. He returned to America in 1863, enlisted in the United States Navy the next year and was present at the attack on Fort Fisher, N. C.

Given the talent for narration and description, the habit of close observation and the thoughtful mind, it was natural that Stanley should turn to journalism, after the war, at a time when so much American territory, and so many colorful phases of American life, were still undiscovered literary material. He crossed the plains to Salt Lake City, Denver, and other western parts, sending to various newspapers accounts of his journeys which were eagerly read by the public. Apparently there was a career for him as a press correspondent. In 1866 he was in Asia Minor; the next year the *Weekly Missouri Democrat* of St. Louis sent him with General Hancock's army against the Indians and his reports of this expedition brought him a commission from the *New York Herald* to accompany the British forces against the Emperor Theodore of Abyssinia in 1868. Stanley distinguished himself by sending through the first account of the fall of Magdala. This was, in newspaper parlance, a brilliant "scoop" for the *Herald*. The younger James Gordon Bennett, 1841–1918 [*q.v.*], took note of the young journalist and commissioned him to travel wherever matters of dramatic interest seemed to be looming and to report on them for the *Herald*. In 1868 Stanley went to Crete, then in rebellion, and later to Spain, where he reported the state of affairs following on Isabella's flight and the Republican uprising (1869).

In response to a wire he joined Bennett in Paris in October 1869, and was informed that his next task would be to lead an expedition into the heart of Africa to find David Livingstone (*Autobiography*, p. 245). There had been agitation in Great Britain for some time over the probable fate of the Scotch missionary, and the general belief now was that he had perished. Bennett may have shared this opinion, while still seeing the expedition as spectacular publicity for the *Herald,* for he gave Stanley other assignments which delayed him en route so that he did not reach Zanzibar till Jan. 6, 1871. Newspaper enterprise of this sort was new to England: it roused a storm of fury which was to break later about Stanley's head. The Royal Geographical Society was inspired to take up the search for Livingstone, subscriptions poured in, and an expedition was launched. Meanwhile, Stanley had seen the opening of the Suez Canal, visited Philae, Jerusalem, Constantinople, and the scenes of the Crimean War, had traversed the Caucasus and crossed Persia to the sea at Abu-Shehr, sailed thence to Bombay, and from Bombay to Africa. On Mar. 21 he set off for the interior. In this wild land, wholly strange to him, he was to go through hardships and perils for which his past experiences had little prepared him, and which would test his full equip-

ment of intelligence and moral force. But, in due course, he raised his helmet to a frail, gray-haired, white man in the native village of Ujiji, and spoke the greeting which has passed into the history of humor, as well as of exploration: "Dr. Livingstone, I presume?" The meeting occurred on Nov. 10. Livingstone's report of it is less restrained: "I am not of a demonstrative turn; as cold, indeed, as we islanders are usually reputed to be, but this disinterested kindness of Mr. Bennett, so nobly carried into effect by Mr. Stanley, was simply overwhelming. . . . Mr. Stanley has done his part with untiring energy; good judgment in the teeth of very serious obstacles" (*The Last Journals of David Livingstone,* 1874, vol. II, 156). Stanley had brought a tent and other comforts and necessaries for Livingstone, as well as a supply of trading goods. In company with Livingstone he explored the northern shore of Lake Tanganyika, where the discovery was made that the river Rusizi flowed into, not out of, the lake and therefore was not one of the Nile's headwaters. The discovery was of great importance at that time when the problem of the sources of the Nile was uppermost in the minds of geographers.

In 1872 Stanley was back in London, bearing Livingstone's journals and letters to his children and friends. In that year he published his account of the adventure, *How I Found Livingstone*. In the meantime the English expedition had come to nothing. The fury of resentment which burst upon the young explorer, from certain quarters, is difficult to understand, however much American newspaper methods may have been disliked by conservative Englishmen of that period. It was loudly asserted that Stanley was a cheat and his story a lie, that he had not found Livingstone, that he had not made the journey to Ujiji, which was a feat not possible of achievement by a young man of his total inexperience in Africa; as to Livingston's journals and letters, Stanley had forged them. Investigation brought to light these shocking facts as proofs of his fraudulence: his name was not Stanley, it was John Rowlands, and he was a "workhouse brat" from Wales. However, Livingstone's son verified his father's handwriting in the journals, the letters were declared genuine by himself and by friends who had received them; and Queen Victoria sent Stanley her thanks for the great service he had rendered, and a gold snuff box set with brilliants.

Later in the year Stanley lectured successfully in the United States; and in 1873 the *Herald* sent him as special correspondent with the army of Viscount Wolseley, on the Ashanti campaign.

He was at the island of St. Vincent, Cape Verde Islands, on his way home next year when he heard of Livingstone's death. Stanley went on to England and sought sympathy and support for plans, which he had been formulating, to carry on Livingstone's work against slavery and to settle geographical problems which his death had left unsolved. The latter were uppermost in his mind. John Hanning Speke, discoverer of Victoria Nyanza, the second largest lake in the world, believed rightly that he had discovered the source of the Nile but his conclusions were not yet considered final by geographers. He had not explored Victoria's shores, hence the point was still unsettled whether this was one vast body of water, or one of a group of lakes. Furthermore, there was Livingstone's belief that the Lualaba, or Congo, was the upper Nile. Such an expedition required a good deal of money to back it, as well as a spirit that was not looking chiefly to journalistic profits, since its purposes were purely scientific. Stanley discussed his project with Sir Edwin Arnold, the poet, then a writer on the staff of the London *Daily Telegraph,* a man keenly interested in Africa. Arnold's interest, happily for Stanley, was shared by his chief, Edward Levy (later Levy-Lawson and Lord Burnham), editor of the *Daily Telegraph,* who persuaded Bennett to join him in raising funds for an Anglo-American exploring expedition in Africa, under Stanley's command.

Stanley sailed for Africa in October of that same year, 1874, not to return until the fall of 1877, after a journey which was outstanding in its discoveries, and was to prove momentous in its commercial and political results. In short, on this exploration Stanley had accomplished more than had any other single expedition in Africa. From Jan. 17, 1875, to Apr. 7, 1876, he had been engaged in tracing the extreme southern sources of the Nile from the marshy plains and uplands, where they rise, down to the immense reservoir of Victoria Nyanza. He had circumnavigated Victoria's entire expanse, explored its bays and creeks by boat and, on foot, had traveled hundreds of miles along its northern shore, discovered Albert Edward Nyanza, and also explored the territory between Victoria and Edward. By proving that mighty Victoria was one single lake and not five, he insured to Speke, its discoverer, "the full glory of having discovered the largest inland sea on the continent of Africa" (*Through the Dark Continent,* 1878, vol. I, 482).

After his exploration of the Nile's headwaters, Stanley made as complete a survey of Lake Tanganyika and then turned his attention to the Congo. From Zanzibar he reached the Con-

go at Nyangwe, the place of Livingstone's death, and there launched upon the unknown stream of the second largest river in the world. He forced his way through the territory where Arab hostility had turned Livingstone back, and followed the long course of the river to its sea mouth at Boma, where he arrived in August 1877. The journey was one of terrible hardship owing to natural obstacles, fever, and unfriendly natives. Stanley's three white companions died in the jungle; his own powerful constitution was sapped, his face lined, and his hair nearly white, when he again reached civilization. The next year, 1878, he published *Through the Dark Continent* (2 vols.). His talent for the apt phrase gave Africa what amounted to a new name, for "Dark Continent" caught the imagination of scientists as well as of press writers and the general public. While the solution of geographical problems was of immense value, Stanley's journey resulted significantly in other ways. From Uganda he sent letters to England emphasizing the importance of sending missionaries to the court of Mtesa; and the immediate response was the first step in bringing the territory of the Nile's headwaters under British protection. During his stay with Livingstone, Stanley had adopted the missionary's recent conviction, namely, that it was impracticable to Christianize natives who were utterly at the mercy of the Arab slave traders, and never free from fear of raids. Protection in some form must be established first, and the cruel trade abolished, before the gospel could be preached. Also the new region which Stanley had traversed held immense commercial possibilities in its rubber and ivory; to open it up to commerce and civilization needed only swift-moving and stubborn enterprise. It was the American Stanley, the man who had seen the wheel-ruts of pioneer wagons on the western prairie and young sturdy towns on the recent Indian battle-grounds, who looked at the Congo region and saw nothing there to daunt determined men thoroughly equipped with the means and methods of civilization.

His news reached Europe ahead of him, and Leopold II of Belgium caught the vision, in its commercial hues at least; his commissioners were at Marseilles when Stanley's ship docked, with proposals that he return to the Congo in Belgian employ. Stanley refused and continued his journey home. He was worn out and needed to recuperate and also he wished Great Britain, not some other power, to make use of his discoveries. To his great disappointment British interest was not aroused. In November 1878, at Leopold's repeated request, Stanley went to

Brussels and agreed to lead an expedition for study of the region which he had discovered. He arrived on the river in August 1879. He remained for five years and established twenty-two stations on the Congo and its tributaries, put four small steamers on the upper river, and built a road past the long cataract of Stanley Falls. The natives, watching the arduous work of road-building go forward under the inflexible will of the white man, gave him a name meaning the strong one, the rock-breaker—"Bula Matari." It is carved on the rough stone pillar which marks his grave. On the basis of Stanley's work the Congo Free State was formed. In 1885 Stanley published his book, *The Congo and the Founding of Its Free State* (2 vols.). During the Berlin Conference of 1884–85, which dealt with African affairs, he acted as technical adviser to the American delegates. He lectured in several German cities, where he found the people much more interested in Africa than were the English, who remained curiously indifferent to the vast interests at stake—or, perhaps, blindly and stubbornly resentful against the "American journalist," still an American citizen, who trod on their traditions of good form and modesty and always finished successfully whatever enormous task he set himself. He was "Bula Matari" in a symbolic sense long before a group of wondering blacks so christened the first road-builder in their forest.

In 1887 Stanley sailed for Africa again on a three-fold mission. He was to further plans for the establishment of a British protectorate in East Equatorial Africa; to give help to the Congo Free State, which was seriously menaced by Tippu Tib and his Arab tribesmen from Zanzibar; and to proceed to the relief of Emin Pasha, governor of the Equatorial Province of Egypt, who was cut off after the fall of Khartoum (1885) by the fanatical force of the Mahdi. As to its outlined purposes, the expedition proved somewhat abortive. Seeing the strength of the wily Tippu Tib, Stanley resorted to the bold expedient of creating him governor of Stanley Falls station for the Congo Free State and then arranged with him for carriers on the march to relieve Emin, who, as it turned out, did not wish to be relieved, nor to abandon his province, and who felt that Stanley's arrival had caused him to lose face with his people. In achieving this unsatisfactory result Stanley crossed the densest area of the Ituri, or Great Congo, Forest three times. The expedition crawled at a snail's pace, covering only three or four hundred yards in an hour, among densely packed trees which rose a hundred and fifty feet with interlaced

branches hung with vines that shut out the sun's rays. Underbrush twice a man's height clogged the path, which lay over swampy ground, the breeding place of innumerable insects and of fever. Stanley nearly died of fever himself and he brought out of the forest only a third of the men he took in with him. This adventure, with descriptions of the forest and its animal life, as well as both vivid and valuable ethnological data regarding the Pigmy tribes, forms the content of *In Darkest Africa* (2 vols.), which was published in 1890 in six languages. On his way from the vast shadow where so many of his men had met death Stanley discovered the Ruwenzori or "Mountains of the Moon." He also traced the Semliki River to its source in Albert Edward Nyanza.

He was greeted warmly in England. Among numerous honors he received the degree of D.C.L. from Oxford and of LL.D. from Cambridge and from Edinburgh. He was then about fifty years of age. On July 12, 1890, he married Dorothy, second daughter of Charles Tennant, at one time member of Parliament from St. Albans. He spent two years lecturing in Australia and New Zealand and in America, where he revisited the scenes of his youth. His roving career had been a long one and his African journeys had taken toll of his vitality, but his mind was as restless and eager as ever. Chiefly to provide an outlet for his mental energies, his wife persuaded him to run for Parliament as the Liberal-Unionist candidate for North Lambeth in 1892, after his renaturalization as a British subject in 1892; he was defeated by a small majority. In the next election, 1895, he was successful; but representing an English constituency failed to interest the former Congo State builder, and he did not campaign again in 1900. The year of his election he published *My Early Travels and Adventures in America and Asia* (2 vols., 1895). In 1897 Stanley went on his last journey to Africa, as the guest of the British South Africa Company, to speak at the opening of the railway from the Cape to Bulawayo. In his last volume, *Through South Africa* (1898), he described his tour to the Victoria Falls of the Zambezi, and enriched the gallery of vivid portraits which his books present with a lifelike and penetrating study of Paul Kruger. In 1899 he was made a Knight Grand Cross of the Bath. His health was failing and he retired to his small country estate called "Furze Hill," near Pirbright. He died on May 10, 1904, at his London house in Richmond Terrace, Whitehall, after a paralytic stroke. Services for him were held in Westminster Abbey, although the Dean refused him a resting place there. He was buried at Pirbright. He left one son, Denzil, apparently adopted. Three years later his widow married Henry Curtis, F.R.C.S.

The extent of his geographical discoveries alone places Stanley's name first among African explorers, even when one considers the great contribution made by Livingstone during his many years in Africa. In addition to his qualities as an explorer, Stanley possessed the vision and organizing ability of the true pioneer builder. He believed wholly in the superiority of his race and civilization; and, as organizer of the Congo Free State (Belgian Congo), never doubted that he was bringing good to the natives. He saw himself pushing on Livingstone's work and adding to it the benefits of a vast commerce. As a westerner he looked at the Congo and, as a westerner, he sped on to the tasks of Bula Matari in Leopold's employ when the British rejected the empire in embryo which he offered them. His disappointment over later developments in the Congo is suggested by his phrase, "a moral malaria." Moral force was strong in him. It was rooted deeply in his faith in God; and, in resisting the common vices to which he was early subjected, it was aided by his innate fastidiousness. In his teens he thought drunkenness and licentiousness both repulsive and stupid, and he never changed this opinion. His strong will was invoked not only to overcome external obstacles but, less happily, to suppress his naturally affectionate and trusting temperament and all desire for affection from others. Though he had to fight his way through hostile regions, at times, in Africa, he was generally successful in winning the friendship of the natives. But in civilized countries he had no tact. Self-schooled to live without illusions and emotional expression, he never understood the offended clamor aroused by his criticisms of the methods of other men in Africa who had perished and become heroes. He himself did not think that mistakes detracted from these men's personal nobility, and he believed that their errors should be seen and avoided by their successors; but the public called him a brute. To say that he was egotistical and ambitious is to state the obvious: his loneliness made him introspective and self-absorbed; and his energy and pride drove him on to win a fame that should wipe out the stigma of his despised origin. His total lack of humor possibly has been overstressed; it is a question whether humor develops later in any one whose youth has been without laughter. Three tragic episodes of his younger life were continuously with him: the day he entered St. Asaph's, his mother's cold

dismissal of him years later when he sought her out, and the treatment he received in England on his return from finding Livingstone. Harsh and narrow in his judgments of those who wronged him, he forgave nothing and his wounds were always fresh. A Welsh writer has said of his countrymen that they are "narrow, but dangerously deep," and Stanley was Welsh. His unfinished *Autobiography,* begun chiefly in the desire to make his character understood, shows him still bewildered by the chicaneries and cruelties he relates. He was preëminently the man of action, ever on the move from one exacting labor to another, yet there was a metaphysical cast to his mind that probed for answers beyond the actualities of his life and career. It may have shaped his last conscious thought. As the watchers by his bed heard Big Ben strike, Stanley opened his eyes and said, "How strange!—So that is time." He died two hours afterwards.

[*The Autobiography of Sir Henry Morton Stanley* (1909), ed. by his wife, Dorothy Stanley; J. S. Keltie, ed., *The Story of Emin's Rescue as Told in Stanley's Letters* (1890); H. M. Stanley, *My Dark Companions and Their Strange Stories* (1893); H. M. Stanley, *Slavery and the Slave Trade in Africa* (1893); A. J. A. Symons, *H. M. Stanley* (1933); J. S. Keltie, "Stanley and the Map of Africa," in *Annual Report of . . . the Smithsonian Institution . . . 1890* (1891), first published in *Contemporary Review,* Jan. 1890; Ethel Jameson, ed., *The Story of the Rear Column of the Emin Pasha Relief Expedition* (1891); W. G. Barttelot, *The Life of Edmund Musgrave Barttelot* (1890); A. J. M. Jephson, *Emin Pasha and the Rebellion at the Equator* (1890); Jakob Wassermann, *H. M. Stanley—Explorer* (1932), first pub. in Germany (1932) and in the U. S. (1933) as *Bula Matari;* Herbert Ward, *My Life with Stanley's Rear Guard* (1891); J. R. Troup, *With Stanley's Rear Column* (1890); S. J. Low, in *Dict. of Nat. Biography,* 2 supp. (1912), vol. III, with good bibliographical note; obituary and account of funeral, *Times* (London), May 11, 18, 1904.]   C.L.S.

STANLEY, JOHN MIX (Jan. 17, 1814–Apr. 10, 1872), painter of Indians, was born at Canandaigua, N. Y. He was orphaned when he was fourteen and spent his boyhood in Naples and Buffalo, N. Y., as apprentice to a wagon maker. At twenty he went to Detroit, where he painted portraits and landscapes; by 1838–39, when he lived in Chicago and Galena, Ill., he had begun painting the Indians near Fort Snelling. After spending the next few years in New York City, Troy, N. Y., Philadelphia, Pa., and Baltimore, Md., he went in 1842 with Sumner Dickerman of Troy to Arkansas and New Mexico, sketching and painting Indians and Indian scenes, and during the next ten or twelve years he traveled widely in the West, painting wherever he went. In June 1843, having gone with Pierce Mason Butler [*q.v.*] to a council with the chiefs of many Cherokee tribes, he made numerous sketches and paintings of the Cherokee chiefs, whose caprice and superstition made them at first somewhat unwilling to serve as subjects. After spending part of 1845 in New Mexico, with Dickerman he exhibited eighty-three canvases in Cincinnati and Louisville in January 1846, but returned to the West in May 1846. He visited Keokuk at his lodge, painted portraits of Sauk chiefs and of the wife of Black Hawk, and in the fall of 1846, at Santa Fé, joined the expedition of Stephen Watts Kearny [qq.v.] overland to California. Less than a year later he was on his way from California to Oregon, which he reached by July. There he journeyed nearly a thousand miles on the Columbia River by canoe, made sketches of Mount Hood and of scenes on the river, and later painted two pictures of Mount Hood. From San Francisco, to which he returned, he took ship for New York, but stopped at Honolulu and remained there during most of 1848. The portraits he painted at that time of King Kamehameha III and his queen hang in the government museum, Honolulu, formerly the royal palace.

In 1850 he exhibited about a hundred and fifty pictures at Troy and Albany, N. Y., and in 1851 at New Haven and Hartford, Conn., and Washington, D. C. This collection, which is described by the painter as containing accurate portraits painted from life of "forty-three different tribes of Indians, obtained at the cost, hazard, and inconvenience of a ten years' tour through the South-western Prairies, New Mexico, California, and Oregon," was deposited in the Smithsonian Institution in 1852. All but five of the pictures were destroyed by fire in 1865, but a full list (there seem to have been no additions) is given in the catalogue, *Portraits of North American Indians, with Sketches of Scenery, etc., Painted by J. M. Stanley, Deposited with the Smithsonian Institution,* which appeared in 1852. In 1853, when he was appointed artist of the expedition sent by the United States government to explore a route for the Pacific Railroad from St. Paul, Minn., to Puget Sound, he was sent on a special mission to the Piegan Indians and brought back about thirty of their chiefs to a council with Isaac Ingalls Stevens [q.v.] at Fort Benton. He had taken with him a daguerreotype apparatus (probably the first taken up the Missouri River), and made both daguerreotypes and paintings of the Indians, much to their pleasure and admiration. After spending nine years, 1854–63, in Washington, D. C., he went to Buffalo for a year. There he began "The Trial of Red Jacket," a picture containing about a hundred figures, his most important work. He died in Detroit, Mich., of heart disease. His work was characterized

by such spirit, accuracy of observation, and attention to detail that the destruction of the pictures in the Smithsonian was an irreparable loss to students of history and ethnology.

[D. I. Bushnell, Jr., in *Ann. Report of the Board of Regents of the Smithsonian Institution,* 1924, with portrait, reproductions of Stanley's paintings, and an account of his life written by his son; Bertha L. Heilbron, in *Minn. Hist.: A Quart. Mag.,* June 1926; obituaries in *Detroit Free Press,* Apr. 11, and *N. Y. Times,* Apr. 14, 1872.]   R.P.T.

STANLEY, WILLIAM (Nov. 22, 1858–May 14, 1916), electrical engineer, inventor, was the son of William and Elizabeth Adelaide (Parsons) Stanley, and was born in Brooklyn, N. Y., where his father practised law. He was a descendant of John Stanley who arrived in Boston in 1634. He was educated in the schools of Great Barrington, under private tutors in Englewood, N. J., which was his home during most of his boyhood, and at Williston Academy, Easthampton, Mass. At seventeen he entered Yale College with the class of 1881. The pre-law classical course, however, so irked him that he left in three months, went to New York, and obtained a job with a manufacturer of telegraphic apparatus. A while later, with money borrowed from his father, he purchased a partnership in a nickel-plating business and for a little more than a year did a thriving business. About 1880 he gave it up to become research assistant to Hiram Stevens Maxim [q.v.] in the United States Electric Lighting Company in New York. When the company purchased the Western Arc Light Company, he became assistant to Edward Weston and thus gained in two years an invaluable experience in both incandescent and arc electriclighting. In 1882 he went to Boston to carry on experimental work for the Swan Electric Light Company. There he made his first invention, a perfected method of exhausting incandescent lamp bulbs. A year later he returned to Englewood and established his own research laboratory, where for two years he engaged in experimental work on storage batteries, on the manufacture of incandescent lamps, and on other electrical problems, obtaining three patents in these fields.

In 1885 he accepted the position of chief engineer of the Westinghouse Electric and Manufacturing Company of Pittsburgh, Pa., contracting at the same time to undertake certain investigations which were to be taken up as business enterprises by Westinghouse if successful. During his first year he devised the multiple system of alternating current distribution together with its equipment (patent No. 372,942 issued Nov. 8, 1887), but Westinghouse refused to finance its development until Stanley at his own expense had put the system into regular commercial service in Great Barrington, installing it in several stores. Thereupon in the fall of 1886 Westinghouse financed the installation of a similar plant at Buffalo, N. Y. In 1888 Stanley resigned his position of chief engineer, continuing, however, as a general consultant; in 1890 he severed this connection and established in Pittsfield, Mass., the Stanley Laboratory Company and the Stanley Electric Manufacturing Company in association with C. C. Chesney and J. F. Kelly. The partners together worked out the famous "S.K.C." system of long-distance transmission of alternating current from the inductor type of generator, and in 1894 put into operation a plant in which they had installed equipment of their own manufacture to supply electric power to textile mills at Housatonic and Great Barrington. In 1905, after directing the affairs of his company for eleven years, Stanley sold it to the General Electric Company. Among his many inventions were condensers, two-phase motors, generators, and an alternating-current watt-hour meter employing magnetic suspension of its moving parts, the manufacture of which was undertaken by the Stanley Instrument Company, established at Great Barrington in 1898. For his alternating-current system of long-distance transmission of electrical energy he was awarded the Edison Medal in 1912 by the American Institute of Electrical Engineers, of which he served as a vice-president from 1898 to 1900. He married Lila Courtney Wetmore of Englewood on Dec. 22, 1884, and at the time of his death in Great Barrington was survived by his widow and nine children.

[I. P. Warren, *The Stanley Families* (1887); *Who's Who in America*, 1916–17; Harry Douglas, *William Stanley, A Short Biog.* (1903), with a list of Stanley's patents; *Proc. Am. Institute Electrical Engineers*, vol. XXXV (1916); *Electrical Rev. and Western Electrician*, May 20, 1916; obituary in *Boston Transcript*, May 15, 1916.]   C. W. M—n.

STANLY, EDWARD (July 13, 1810–July 12, 1872), congressman, a native of New Bern, N. C., was the son of John Stanly, a Federalist leader and member of Congress, from whom he acquired the nationalistic opinions and intense hatred of the Democratic party which shaped his public life. His mother was the daughter of Martin Frank of Jones County. His education in the American Literary, Scientific, and Military Academy at Middletown, Conn., where he was a student from 1827 to 1829, tended to strengthen his Federalism. Having taken up the study of law, he was admitted to the bar in 1832 and began practice in Beaufort County, N. C.

Soon thereafter he married a daughter of Dr. Hugh Jones of Hyde County. She died about 1850, and some ten years later he married Cornelia, a sister of Joseph G. Baldwin [*q.v.*], then an associate justice of the supreme court of California.

Stanly was a successful lawyer, but his ambitions were almost wholly political, and in 1837 he was elected to Congress as a Whig. He served three terms, distinguishing himself by his eloquence, his readiness in debate, and his numerous quarrels. His temper was passionate, and his sarcastic and unrestrained tongue spared neither friend nor foe. He became, as John Quincy Adams expressed it, "the terror of the Lucifer party" (*Memoirs,* vol. XI, 1876, p. 19). Several times he engaged in personal encounters on the floor of the House, and he fought a duel with S. W. Inge of Alabama. By virtue of his ability, however, he became a leader of his party in the House. Defeated for reëlection to Congress in 1843, he was a delegate to the Whig convention in Baltimore in 1844, and was elected to the House of Commons, being reëlected in 1846. At both sessions he was speaker. In 1847 be became attorney general of the state, but resigned the next year to return to the legislature. Again elected to Congress in 1848, he supported the compromise measures of 1850. Making his campaign on the abstract issue of secession and declaring his readiness to vote men and money to whip any seceding state back into the Union, he was returned to Congress by an increased majority. Defeated for reëlection in 1853, he removed to California the following year, and in San Francisco won instant success in his profession. He supported Frémont in 1856 as a choice of evils, and in 1857, although he was still a slaveholder, and scarcely in accord with the party, he was nominated for governor by the Republicans, but was defeated.

Secession brought only anger and horror to Stanly's mind, and, unaware of the change of sentiment, he could not rid himself of the belief that the withdrawal of North Carolina from the Union was the result of Democratic deception of the people, and that, if they could be informed of the purposes of the North by one in whom they had confidence, they would renew their allegiance. He expressed to Lincoln his readiness to undertake such a mission, and to his amazement the latter in May 1862 made him military governor of the state, to foster Union sentiment and promote the establishment of a loyal civil government. Stanly assumed office on May 26, and quickly discovered that he had an impossible task. He could get no hearing and was despised as a traitor. Soon, moreover, he was in trouble with the abolitionists, and, through them, the ire of Charles Sumner, who had never forgiven Stanly for a bitter speech against him in 1852, was freshly aroused. He found himself unable to protect private property from what he characterized as "the most shameful pillaging and robbery that ever disgraced an army in any civilized land." The last straw was the Emancipation Proclamation, to which he was bitterly opposed, and on Jan. 15, 1863, he resigned, returning to California in March. After the war he opposed congressional reconstruction with his accustomed vehemence, and in 1867 left the Republican party to canvass the state against the policy. His death, following a stroke of apoplexy, occurred in San Francisco.

[S. A. Ashe, *Biog. Hist. of N. C.,* vol. V (1906); *A Military Governor among Abolitionists; a Letter from Edward Stanly to Charles Sumner* (1865); J. G. deR. Hamilton, *Reconstruction in N. C.* (1914); J. H. Wheeler, *Reminiscences and Memoirs of N. C.* (1884); C. C. Baldwin, *The Baldwin Geneal. Supp.* (1889); G. M. Dodge and W. A. Ellis, *Norwich Univ.* (1911), II, 226; *Biog. Dir. Am. Cong.* (1928); *Morning Bulletin* (San Francisco), July 15, 1872.]   J. G. deR. H.

STANSBURY, HOWARD (Feb. 8, 1806–Apr. 17, 1863), soldier, explorer, was born in New York City, the son of Arthur Joseph and Susanna (Brown) Stansbury, and a grandson of Joseph Stansbury [*q.v.*]. He was educated as a civil engineer. On Sept. 1, 1827, he married Helen Moody of Detroit. In October of the following year he was placed in charge of a series of surveys in connection with the project of uniting Lake Erie and Lake Michigan with the Wabash River by canals. Between 1832 and the end of 1835 he surveyed the route of the Mad River & Lake Erie Railroad and the mouths of the Cumberland, Vermilion, and Chagrin rivers, and had charge of a number of public works in Indiana. In 1836, as a preliminary to the project of improving the harbor of Richmond, Va., he surveyed the lower part of the James River, and in the early part of 1838 was engaged in the survey of a proposed railroad route from Milwaukee to the Mississippi.

He entered the army on July 7, 1838, as a lieutenant of topographical engineers, and on July 18, 1840, was made a captain. His work during the next eight years included various surveys of the lake regions and a minute survey of the harbor of Portsmouth, N. H. In 1849 he was put in command of an exploring and surveying expedition to the Great Salt Lake region. With a party of eighteen men, including Lieut. John Williams Gunnison [*q.v.*] as second in command, he left Fort Leavenworth on the last day of May and proceeded by South Pass to Fort Bridger.

Here he divided his party and, engaging James Bridger [*q.v.*] as his guide, explored a new route to the lake midway between the Bear River and the Echo Canyon trails. Reuniting the two sections of his party near Salt Lake City and dismissing Bridger, he marched northward and after some months circled the lake. For various reasons the work was not completed as planned, and in the summer of the following year he started on his return. At Fort Bridger, Sept. 5, 1850, again employing Bridger as guide, he determined upon the exploration of a route to the settlements more direct than that by way of South Pass. Proceeding directly eastward, he traversed the course subsequently followed by the Overland Stage and, in the main, by the Union Pacific Railway; and though not the first to use it was the first to recommend its feasibility and to make it widely known. His report, "Exploration and Survey of the Valley of the Great Salt Lake of Utah, Including a Reconnoissance of a New Route through the Rocky Mountains" (printed in 1852 as *Senate Executive Document 3, 32 Cong.,* special session of the Senate) won immediate popularity in England as well as in the United States, and during the next four years was several times reprinted by the Lippincotts. During the next ten years he was engaged in surveys in the lake region and in the construction of military roads in Minnesota. In 1861 he was ordered to Columbus, Ohio, as mustering officer for that locality, and on Aug. 6 was made a major. On Sept. 28, 1861, he was retired, but he later reëntered the service and was appointed mustering and disbursing officer for Wisconsin, with station at Madison, where he died. He was survived by his wife, a son, and a daughter.

[F. H. Wines, *The Descendants of John Stansbury of Leominster* (1895); F. B. Heitman, *Hist. Reg. and Dict. of the U. S. Army* (1903), vol. I; J. C. Alter, *James Bridger* (1925); *The Am. Ann. Cyc.,* 1863; obituary in *Wis. State Jour.* (Madison), Apr. 17, 1863.]
W. J. G.

STANSBURY, JOSEPH (Jan. 9, 1742 o.s. ?–Nov. 9, 1809), Loyalist, was the son of Samuel and Sarah (Porter) Stansbury. He was born in London, where his father was a mercer and haberdasher. Joseph was a pupil at St. Paul's School, not on the foundation, but in 1753 he was withdrawn and apprenticed to a trade. On Apr. 2, 1765, he married Sarah Ogier, a Huguenot, and, embarking in 1767 for America, they landed at Philadelphia on Oct. 11. He at once opened a china store and entered with instant sympathy into the cultivated social life of the city. He was intelligent and vivacious and, among other talents, possessed the ability to write and to sing songs. When the Revolution impended, he sympathized with the colonists but opposed independence by writing songs about race kinship and race glory. In 1776 he suffered a brief imprisonment for his loyalty, but during the British occupation of Philadelphia he was held in favor and appointed to several minor offices. As his whole nature was opposed to war and violence, he steered a peaceful middle course, paid for substitutes in the Philadelphia militia, and even signed the oath of allegiance and abjuration. He was permitted to remain in the city until the end of 1780. Arrested then on the suspicion that he was carrying on a secret correspondence with the enemy, he sought and obtained permission to retire with his family within the British lines. The suspicions against him were well grounded; it was he who carried Benedict Arnold's first proposals to British headquarters and who, during the entire correspondence, was Arnold's go-between, as Jonathan Odell [q.v.] was André's ("André-Arnold Treason," Sir Henry Clinton Papers, William L. Clements Library). For his secret services he received lodgings in New York, rations, and a stipend. Meanwhile he continued to write festive political songs and to satirize with playful humor the inconsistencies of the Whigs. As a writer of satirical verse, free from hatred or bitterness, he was "without a rival among his brethren" (Tyler, post, II, 80). Many years later The Loyal Verses of Joseph Stansbury and Doctor Jonathan Odell was edited by Winthrop Sargent (1860).

His animosity ended with the war; he burned all his political poems he could find and tried to resume his old life in Philadelphia. Those he had satirized were not so tolerant; he was again imprisoned and forced to return to New York. In August 1783 he sought refuge in Nova Scotia, whose cold wilderness he found uninviting. The next year he spent in England seeking compensation for his secret services but, because of the oath of allegiance and abjuration, did not succeed. In 1786 he was permitted to resume his business in Philadelphia. However, not prospering as before, in 1793 he removed his family to New York. There he was for many years secretary of the United Insurance Company. He died in New York, survived by his widow and seven of their nine children. Caroline Matilda Kirkland and Howard Stansbury [qq.v.] were grandchildren and Joseph Kirkland [q.v.] was a great-grandson.

[MSS. of Mrs. V. C. Sanborn, Lake Forest, Ill., and Frederick S. Tyler, Washington, D. C.; Am. Loyalists Transcripts, N. Y. Pub. Lib.; manuscript biographical sketch by Arthur Joseph Stansbury, a son, Tyler Papers, Cornell Univ. Lib.; M. C. Tyler, The Literary Hist. of the Am. Rev. (2 vols., 1897); Malcolm Decker, Benedict Arnold (1932), p. 484; F. H. Wines, The

Descendants of John Stansbury of Leominster (1895); F. S. Tyler, The Hist. and Connection of the Stansbury-Tyler-Adee Families (1933); The Admission Registers of St. Paul's School from 1748 to 1876 (1884), ed. by R. B. Gardiner; N. Y. Gazette & General Advertiser, Nov. 11, 1809.]   J.C.

STANTON, EDWIN McMASTERS (Dec. 19, 1814–Dec. 24, 1869), attorney-general and secretary of war, a native of Steubenville, Ohio, was the eldest of the four children of David and Lucy (Norman) Stanton. His father, a physician of Quaker stock, was descended from Robert Stanton, who came to America between 1627 and 1638, and, after living in New Plymouth, moved to Newport, R. I., before 1645, and from the latter's grandson, Henry, who went to North Carolina between 1721 and 1724 (W. H. Stanton, post, pp. 27–34). His mother was the daughter of a Virginia planter. The death of Dr. Stanton in 1827 left his wife in straitened circumstances and Edwin was obliged to withdraw from school and supplement the family income by employment in a local bookstore. He continued his studies in his spare time, however, and in 1831 was admitted to Kenyon College at Gambier, Ohio. During his junior year his funds gave out and he was again obliged to accept a place in a bookstore, this time in Columbus. Unable to earn enough to return to Kenyon for the completion of his course, he turned to the study of law in the office of his guardian, Daniel L. Collier, and in 1836 was admitted to the bar. His practice began in Cadiz, the seat of Harrison County, but in 1839 he removed to Steubenville to become a partner of Senator-elect Benjamin Tappan.

Stanton's ability, energy, and fidelity to his profession brought him quick recognition and a comfortable income. To give wider range to his talents he moved to Pittsburgh in 1847 and later, in 1856, he became a resident of Washington, D. C., in order to devote himself more to cases before the Supreme Court. His work as counsel for the state of Pennsylvania (1849–56) against the Wheeling & Belmont Bridge Company (13 Howard, 518; 18 Howard, 421) gave him a national reputation and resulted in his retention for much important litigation. He was one of the leading counsel in the noted patent case of McCormick vs. Manny (John McLean, Reports of Cases . . . in the Circuit Court of the United States for the Seventh Circuit, vol. VI, 1856, p. 539) and made a deep impression upon one of his associates, Abraham Lincoln, because of his masterly defense of their client, Manny (A. J. Beveridge, Abraham Lincoln, 1928, vol. I, 581). Stanton's practice was chiefly in civil and constitutional law, but in 1859 in defending

Daniel E. Sickles [*q.v.*], charged with murder, he demonstrated that he was no less gifted in handling criminal suits. More important than any of these cases, however, was his work in California in 1858 as special counsel for the United States government in combatting fraudulent claims to lands alleged to have been deeded by Mexico to numerous individuals prior to the Mexican War. It was a task requiring prodigious and painstaking research in the collection of data and the most careful presentation, but Stanton proved equal to the occasion and won for the government a series of notable victories. It has been estimated that the lands involved were worth $150,000,000. His services in this connection were undoubtedly the most distinguished of his legal career. As a lawyer Stanton was capable of extraordinary mental labor; he was orderly and methodical, mastering with great precision the law and the facts of his cases, and he was able apparently to plead with equal effectiveness before judges and juries.

It was his success in the California land cases, together with the influence of Jeremiah S. Black [*q.v.*], that won for him the appointment of attorney-general on Dec. 20, 1860, when Buchanan reorganized his cabinet. Prior to that time Stanton had taken little part in politics and had held only two minor offices, those of prosecuting attorney of Harrison County, Ohio (1837–39), and reporter of Ohio supreme court decisions (1842–45). Jacksonian principles enlisted his sympathies while an undergraduate and he appears to have adhered quite consistently to the Democratic party from that time until his entrance into Lincoln's cabinet in 1862. He favored the Wilmot Proviso, however, and was critical of the domination of the Southern wing of the party during the two decades before 1860. Like his forebears he disapproved of the institution of slavery, but he accepted the Dred Scott decision without question and contended that all laws constitutionally enacted for the protection of slavery should be rigidly enforced. He supported Breckinridge's candidacy for the presidency in 1860 in the belief that the preservation of the Union hung on the forlorn hope of his election (Gorham, *post,* I, 79). Above all Stanton was a thorough-going Unionist.

In Buchanan's cabinet he promptly joined with Black and Joseph Holt [*q.v.*] in opposition to the abandonment of Fort Sumter and was zealous in the pursuit of persons whom he believed to be plotting against the government. Since he was of an excitable and suspicious temperament, his mind was full of forebodings of insurrection and assassination, and, while he hated the "Black Republicans," he collogued with Seward, Sumner, and others in order that they might be apprised of the dangers he apprehended to be afoot. The disclosure of this later resulted in the charge that he had betrayed Buchanan (*Atlantic Monthly* and *Galaxy, post*). If Stanton was at odds with the President at that time he gave him no indication of it for Buchanan wrote in 1862: "He was always on my side and flattered me *ad nauseam*" (G. T. Curtis, *Life of James Buchanan,* 1883, vol. II, 523).

During the early months of Lincoln's presidency, Stanton, now in private life, was utterly distrustful of him and unsparing in his criticism of "the imbecility of this administration" (*Ibid.,* II, 559). When George B. McClellan [*q.v.*] took over the control of the operations of the army in 1861, Stanton became his friend and confidential legal adviser and expressed to him his contempt for the President and his cabinet. Oddly enough, soon afterwards he also became legal adviser to Secretary of War Simon Cameron [*q.v.*] and aided in framing the latter's annual report recommending the arming of slaves (*Atlantic Monthly,* Feb. 1870, p. 239; Oct. 1870, p. 470). It was this proposal, offensive to Lincoln, which hastened Cameron's departure from the War Department and inadvertently helped to pave the way for Stanton's succession to the post. Although he had had no personal contacts of any kind with Lincoln since Mar. 4, 1861, Stanton was nominated for the secretaryship, confirmed on Jan. 15, 1862, and five days later entered upon his duties. Various plausible explanations for his selection by Lincoln have been given. Gideon Welles firmly believed that Seward was responsible for it, but Cameron claimed the credit for himself (*American Historical Review,* Apr. 1926, pp. 491 ff.; Meneely, *post,* pp. 366–68). The true circumstances may never be known.

Stanton was generally conceded to be able, energetic, and patriotic, and his appointment was well received. It presaged a more honest and efficient management of departmental affairs and a more aggressive prosecution of the war. In these respects the new secretary measured up to the public expectations. He immediately reorganized the department, obtained authorization for the increase of its personnel, and systematized the work to be done. Contracts were investigated, those tainted with fraud were revoked, and their perpetrators were prosecuted without mercy. Interviews became public hearings; patronage hunters received scant and usually brusque consideration; and the temporizing replies of Cameron gave way to the summary judgments of his successor. At an early date Stanton persuaded Congress to authorize the taking over of the railroads and telegraph lines where necessary, and prevailed upon the President to release all political prisoners in military custody and to transfer the control of extraordinary arrests from the State to the War Department. Also he promptly put himself in close touch with generals, governors, and others having to do with military affairs, and especially with the congressional Committee on the Conduct of the War.

For a few months after entering office Stanton continued his friendly relations with McClellan and assured the general of his desire to furnish all necessary *matériel*, but he became impatient when McClellan proved slow in accomplishing tangible results. Despite the Secretary's professions of confidence and cooperation, McClellan soon became distrustful and suspected Stanton of seeking his removal. The withdrawing of McDowell's forces from the main army in the Peninsular campaign was attributed to Stanton and editorial attacks upon him began to appear in the New York press which were believed to have been inspired by McClellan (Gorham, I, 415–21). Both men were too suspicious, jealous, and otherwise ill-suited to work in harmony; trouble between them was inevitable. Stanton was particularly irked by McClellan's disobedience to orders and in August 1862 joined with Chase and others in the cabinet in seeking to have him deprived of any command (Welles, *Diary*, I, 83, 93, 95–101; "Diary and Correspondence of Salmon P. Chase," *Annual Report of the American Historical Association for the Year 1902*, 1903, vol. II, 62–63).

Although McClellan constantly complained of a shortage of men, supplies, and equipment, Stanton appears to have made vigorous efforts to meet his requisitions. The same was true with respect to other commanders in the several theatres of operations. His dispatch of 23,000 men to the support of Rosecrans at Chattanooga (September 1863) in less than seven days and under trying circumstances was one of the spectacular feats of the war. Quickness of decision, mastery of detail, and vigor in execution were among Stanton's outstanding characteristics as a war administrator, and he became annoyed when his subordinates proved deficient in these qualities. He was frequently accused of meddling with military operations and was probably guilty of it on many occasions; but Grant had no complaint to make of him in this respect. His severe censorship of the press was also a source of much criticism in newspaper circles, and his exercise of the power of extraordinary arrest was often capricious and harmful. Soldiers and civilians alike found him arrogant, irascible, and often brutal and unjust. Grant said that he "cared nothing for the feeling of others" and seemed to find it pleasanter "to disappoint than to gratify" (*Personal Memoirs*, vol. II, 1886, p. 536). A noted instance of his harshness was his published repudiation of General Sherman's terms to the defeated Johnston in May 1865. That Sherman had exceeded his authority was generally admitted, but the severity of the rebuke was as unmerited as it was ungrateful. Again, Stanton's part in the trial and execution of Mrs. Surratt, charged with complicity in Lincoln's assassination, and his efforts to implicate Jefferson Davis in the murder of the President were exceedingly discreditable (Milton, *post*, Ch. x; DeWitt, *post*, pp. 232–34, 272–76). His vindictiveness in both instances was probably owing in part to a desire to avenge the death of his chief, whose loss he mourned. Intimate association for three years had gradually revealed Lincoln's nature and capacities to Stanton, and while he was sometimes as discourteous to him as to others, there developed between the two men a mutual trust and admiration.

At the request of President Johnson, Stanton retained his post after Lincoln's death and ably directed the demobilization of the Union armies. At the same time he entered upon a course with respect to reconstruction and related problems that brought him into serious conflict with the President and several of his colleagues. During the war he appears to have been deferential and ingratiating in his relations with the radical element in Congress, particularly with the powerful congressional Committee on the Conduct of the War, and when peace came he began almost immediately to counsel with leading members of that faction as to the course to be pursued in reconstruction. Although he expressed approval in cabinet meetings of the President's proclamation of May 29, 1865, initiating a reasonable policy of restoration under executive direction, it was soon suspected by many of Johnson's supporters that Stanton was out of sympathy with the administration and intriguing with the rising opposition. In this they were not mistaken (Beale, *post*, pp. 101–06). When Charles Sumner in a speech on Sept. 14, 1865, denounced the presidential policy, insisted on congressional control of reconstruction, and sponsored negro suffrage, Stanton hastened to assure him that he indorsed "every sentiment, every opinion and word of it" (Welles, II, 394).

From the summer of 1865 onward, upon nearly every issue he advised a course of action which would have played into the hands of the Radicals and fostered a punitive Southern policy. He urged the acceptance of the Freedmen's Bureau and Civil Rights bills of 1866, and while he was evasive regarding the report of the Stevens committee on reconstruction, he subsequently expressed approval of the Military Reconstruction bill based upon it which was passed over the President's veto on Mar. 2, 1867 (Welles, III, 49; Gorham, II, 420). Stanton actually dictated for Boutwell [*q.v.*] an amendment to the army appropriation act of 1867 requiring the president to issue his army orders through the secretary of war or the general of the army and making invalid any order issued otherwise (G. S. Boutwell, *Reminiscences of Sixty Years in Public Affairs,* 1902, vol. II, 107–08; Milton, p. 378). He was also responsible for the supplementary reconstruction act of July 19, 1867, which exempted military commanders from any obligation to accept the opinions of civil officers of the government as to their rules of action (Gorham, II, 373). The one important measure in the rejection of which the Secretary concurred was the Tenure of Office bill which was chiefly intended to insure his own retention in the War Department. He was emphatic in denouncing its unconstitutionality and "protested with ostentatious vehemence that any man who would retain his seat in the Cabinet as an adviser when his advice was not wanted was unfit for the place" (Welles, III, 158; J. D. Richardson, *A Compilation of the Messages and Papers of the Presidents,* 1897, vol. VI, 587). He aided Seward in drafting the veto message.

For more than a year Johnson had been importuned by his supporters to remove Stanton and he repeatedly gave the Secretary to understand "by every mode short of an expressed request that he should resign" (Richardson, *ante,* VI, 584), but Stanton ignored them and with fatal hesitation the President permitted him to remain. In doing so he virtually gave his opponents a seat in the cabinet. By the beginning of August 1867, however, Johnson could tolerate his mendacious minister no longer. He had become convinced that the insubordination of General Sheridan and other commanders in the military districts was being encouraged by the Secretary and he was now satisfied that Stanton had plotted against him in the matter of the reconstruction legislation. Consequently, on Aug. 5, he called for his resignation, but Stanton brazenly declined to yield before Congress reassembled in December, contending that the Tenure of Of-

fice bill had become law by its passage over the veto and Johnson was bound to obey it. A week later he was suspended, but in January 1868 he promptly resumed his place when the Senate declined to concur in his suspension. Johnson then resolved to dismiss him regardless of the consequences and did so on Feb. 21, 1868. Stanton with equal determination declared that he would "continue in possession until expelled by force" (Gorham, II, 440), and was supported by the Senate. He ordered the arrest of Adjutant-General Lorenzo Thomas, who had been designated secretary *ad interim,* and had a guard posted to insure his own occupancy and protect the department records from seizure. For several weeks thereafter he remained in the War Department building day and night, but when the impeachment charges failed (May 26, 1868) he accepted the inevitable and resigned the same day.

Over-exertion during his public life, together with internal ailments, had undermined Stanton's health and he found it necessary after leaving the department to undergo a period of rest. During the fall of 1868 he managed to give some active support to Grant's candidacy and to resume to a limited extent his law practice, but he never regained his former vigor. He was frequently importuned to be a candidate for public office, but steadfastly refused. His friends in Congress, however, prevailed upon Grant to offer him a justiceship on the United States Supreme Court and this he accepted. His nomination was confirmed on Dec. 20, 1869, but death overtook him before he could occupy his seat.

With the gradual rehabilitation of Andrew Johnson's reputation Stanton's has suffered a sharp decline. His ability as a lawyer and his achievements as a tireless and versatile administrator during the Civil War have not been seriously questioned, but his defects of temperament and the disclosures of his amazing disloyalty and duplicity in his official relations detract from his stature as a public man. In 1867 he explained his remaining in the War Department by contending that his duties as a department head were defined by law and that he was not "bound to accord with the President on all grave questions of policy or administration" (Gorham, II, 421; J. F. Rhodes, *History of the United States,* 1920, VI, 210, note 3); but shortly before his death he is said to have admitted that "he had never doubted the constitutional right of the President to remove members of his Cabinet without question from any quarter whatever," and that in his reconstruction program Johnson advocated measures that had been favorably considered by Lincoln (Hugh McCulloch,

Men and Measures of Half a Century, 1888, pp. 401–02). Stanton was encouraged in his disloyalty and defiance by Republican politicians, newspapers, and Radical protagonists generally, but his conduct has found few defenders among modern students of the post-war period. Whether he was motivated by egotism, mistaken patriotism, or a desire to stand well with the congressional opposition is difficult to determine.

In appearance Stanton was thick-set and of medium height; a strong, heavy neck supported a massive head thatched with long, black, curling hair. His nose and eyes were large, his mouth was wide and stern. A luxuriant crop of coarse black whiskers concealed his jaws and chin. Altogether he was a rather fierce looking man; there was point to Montgomery Blair's characterization, the "black terrier." Stanton was twice married. Mary Ann Lamson of Columbus, Ohio, with whom he was united on Dec. 31, 1836, died in 1844. On June 25, 1856, he married Ellen M. Hutchison, the daughter of a wealthy merchant of Pittsburgh. Two children were born of the first union; four of the second. His biographers assure us that in his family life Stanton was a model husband and father, and for his mother, who survived him, he appears to have cherished a lifelong filial devotion.

[There is no satisfactory biography of Stanton. G. C. Gorham, *The Life and Public Services of Edwin M. Stanton* (2 vols., 1899), and F. A. Flower, *Edwin McMasters Stanton* (1905) contain much useful data, but both are extremely laudatory. The *Diary of Gideon Welles* (3 vols., 1911), although hostile, is a very serviceable documentary source. The writings and biographical literature of other public men of the day contain numerous references to Stanton. Of especial value for the war period are J. G. Nicolay and John Hay, *Abraham Lincoln: A History* (10 vols., 1890), and *Complete Works of Abraham Lincoln* (12 vols., Gettysburg ed., 1905). See also A. H. Meneely, *The War Department—1861* (1928). G. F. Milton, *The Age of Hate: Andrew Johnson and the Radicals* (1931), and H. K. Beale, *The Critical Year* (1930) are the most scholarly of the recent studies of the reconstruction era. D. M. DeWitt, *The Impeachment and Trial of Andrew Johnson* (1903), is the standard book on the subject and has a sharply critical chapter on Stanton's public career. Revealing disclosures of his conduct while in Buchanan's cabinet are to be found in the Black-Wilson controversy in the *Atlantic Monthly*, Feb., Oct. 1870, and the *Galaxy*, June 1870, Feb. 1871, reprinted as *A Contribution to History* (1871). The papers of Stanton and many of his associates are deposited in the Lib. of Cong.; these, together with *War of the Rebellion: Official Records* (Army), and other government publications pertaining to the war and reconstruction problems are the basic sources for the study of Stanton's official life. Genealogical material is in W. H. Stanton, *A Book Called Our Ancestors the Stantons* (1922). For an obituary, see *N. Y. Daily Tribune*, Dec. 25, 1869.]   A. H. M.

STANTON, ELIZABETH CADY (Nov. 12, 1815–Oct. 26, 1902), reformer and leader in the woman's rights movement, was born in Johnstown, N. Y. Her parents were Daniel Cady [q.v.] and Margaret (Livingston) Cady, daughter of Col. James Livingston [q.v.]. A stern religious atmosphere pervaded her home, and as a child Elizabeth feared rather than loved her parents, who seem to have had little positive influence upon the shaping of her personality and character. Simon Hosack, minister of the Presbyterian church to which the Cady family belonged, had a larger share in her affections and did much to give a serious, purposeful bent to her life. Her education was superior to that of most girls of her time. Encouraged by Simon Hosack, she studied Greek, Latin, and mathematics with classes of boys in the academy in Johnstown, where she spent several years, and took second prize in Greek. At the age of fifteen she was sent to the famous seminary of Emma Willard [q.v.] at Troy, N. Y., from which she graduated in 1832. For a time she studied law with her father. She early learned that she was living in an imperfect world. As a small child, hearing women in her father's law office pour forth recitals of wrongs supported by existing law, she was troubled by the handicaps and discriminations existing against her sex. In her young womanhood, under the influence of her cousin Gerrit Smith [q.v.] of Peterboro, N. Y., she likewise became deeply interested in temperance and anti-slavery, but it was not until somewhat later that she was fully launched as a reformer.

It is significant that on May 10, 1840, when she married Henry Brewster Stanton [q.v.], the word "obey" was at her insistence omitted from the ceremony. Stanton, who later became known as a lawyer and journalist, was already a noted abolitionist and immediately after his wedding went as a delegate to the world anti-slavery convention held in London in the summer of 1840. There his wife, who accompanied him, met Lucretia Coffin Mott [q.v.] and was much influenced by conversations with her. When Mrs. Mott and a few other American women who were delegates to the anti-slavery gathering were refused official recognition by the convention on the ground of their sex, Mrs. Mott and Mrs. Stanton resolved to hold a woman's rights convention upon their return to the United States. Though the execution of this resolve was delayed, Mrs. Stanton began to work for temperance and abolition, and used her influence for the passage of the married woman's property bill of New York State, which finally became a law in 1848. Two years before this she moved with her husband and their children from Boston, where they had been living, to Seneca Falls, N. Y., and the handicaps she was aware of in this small frontier-like community made her thoughts turn more seriously to the hard, circumscribed lot of woman. Her mind was full of the subject when, on July 13, 1848, she again met Lucretia Mott. To Mrs. Mott and a few others she poured out her indignation at the established order and succeeded in so rousing herself as well as the others that a week later, July 19 and 20, they held a woman's rights convention in the Wesleyan Methodist Church in Seneca Falls. Mrs. Stanton, who made the opening speech, read a "Declaration of Sentiments," modeled after the Declaration of Independence, setting forth the grievances of women against existing law and custom, and she was wholly responsible for a resolution demanding suffrage. When Lucretia Mott protested against the last, "Why, Lizzie, thee will make us ridiculous," the author of the resolution defended it as the key to all other rights for women, and with the help of Frederick Douglass [q.v.] it was adopted with ten other resolutions.

The Seneca Falls convention, which promptly became the object of sarcasm, ridicule, and denunciation from press and pulpit, formally launched the modern woman's rights movement. Other conventions devoted to the same purpose soon followed, and in many of them Mrs. Stanton played a leading part. In addition she gave much time to writing articles, protests, and petitions, lecturing in public, and speaking before legislative bodies in the interest of temperance, abolition, and woman's rights, but as the years passed she devoted more and more of her time to the cause of women. From 1851, when she first met Susan B. Anthony and induced her to enlist in the crusade for woman's rights, the two women worked together, a remarkably efficient pair whose association ended only with Mrs. Stanton's death. Together they planned campaign programs, organization work, and speeches and addresses; together they appeared upon public and convention platforms, and before legislative bodies and congressional committees to plead for woman's rights. Miss Anthony had the greater persistence and was the better organizer and executive, but her colleague was the more eloquent and graceful speaker and writer, and in general had a more charming and persuasive personality. Both were hard fighters and both were long considered rather dangerous radicals, though Mrs. Stanton was at first more conspicuous in this latter regard because of her pioneer stand for suffrage and her demand a little later that women be permitted to secure divorce on the grounds of drunkenness and brutality. Though she hated war as stupid and wicked, she saw the Civil War as a struggle for the abolition of slavery, and helped to organize and became president of the Women's Loyal National League, which supported the Union and fostered the complete emancipation of slaves. The war ended, she and her colleagues first strove to secure suffrage for women in connection with the enfranchisement of negro men, but they later renewed and enlarged their earlier activities directly in behalf of woman's rights. When in May 1869 the National Woman Suffrage Association was founded, she was chosen president, an office which for the most part she held until 1890; at that time the organization was united with the American Woman Suffrage Association to form the National American Woman Suffrage Association, of which she was also elected president. These twenty-one years at the head of the more radical of the two woman's rights organizations covered the period of Mrs. Stanton's greatest activity for the cause to which she had dedicated herself. Partly from a suggestion of hers came the first International Council of Women, held in Washington in 1888 under the auspices of the National Woman Suffrage Association, and it was she who sent out the call, and made the opening and closing addresses before the Council.

In addition to her suffrage work, from 1869 to 1881 she devoted eight months annually to lyceum lecturing throughout the country, usually on family life and the training of children, of whom she had borne and reared seven. She also found time to write for publication. In 1868 she and Parker Pillsbury [q.v.] as joint editors started the *Revolution*, a weekly devoted especially to woman's rights, and many of the best articles and editorials appearing during her connection of about two years with the publication were from her pen. She was largely responsible, too, for the *Woman's Bible*, published in two parts in 1895 and 1898. To newspapers and magazines, especially the *North American Review*, she contributed many articles. In 1898 she published her reminiscences, *Eighty Years and More*. But her monumental undertaking was the compilation, in conjunction with Susan B. Anthony and Matilda Joslyn Gage [q.v.], of the first three ponderous volumes of the *History of Woman Suffrage* (1881–86). In the cause of woman's rights she was undoubtedly one of the most influential leaders of her day. Her strong and undaunted manner made her very impressive, though she was short in stature, not exceeding five feet three inches. Her skin was fresh and fair, and the good-natured expression of her face was accentuated by the merry twinkle rarely absent from her clear, light blue eyes. In youth her curly hair was black, but it began early to turn gray and by middle age was snowy white. She died at her New York City home when she was closing her eighty-seventh year. She was survived by six of her children.

[See O. P. Allen, *Descendants of Nicholas Cady of Watertown, Mass., 1645–1910* (1910), where Mrs. Stanton's name is given as Elizabeth Smith Cady; *Who's Who in America*, 1901–02; *Elizabeth Cady Stanton as Revealed in Her Letters, Diary and Reminiscences* (2 vols., 1922), ed. by Theodore Stanton and Harriot Stanton Blatch; *Hist. of Woman Suffrage* (6 vols., 1881–1922), ed. by E. C. Stanton, etc.; Alice S. Blackwell, *Lucy Stone, Pioneer of Woman's Rights* (1930); obituary in *N. Y. Times*, Oct. 27, 1902. In the Lib. of Cong., Washington, D. C., are some unpublished letters of minor importance.]   M. W. W.

STANTON, FRANK LEBBY (Feb. 22, 1857–Jan. 7, 1927), journalist, poet, son of Valentine Stanton, a printer, and Catherine Rebecca (Parry) Stanton, was born in Charleston, S. C. His formal education was interrupted by the death of his father. At the age of twelve he moved to Savannah, Ga., with his family and became copy-boy on the Savannah *Morning News,* edited by William Tappan Thompson [*q.v.*]. His verses, which he had begun writing at the age of eleven ("To Lizzie"), attracted the attention of Joel Chandler Harris [*q.v.*], then a member of the editorial staff, who encouraged him to write. He served as reporter and feature writer until 1887, when he became owner and editor of the weekly *Smithville News* of Smithville, Ga. He continued to write verses that were copied in many newspapers. On Jan. 15, 1887, he married Leona Jossey, who inspired some of his best poems and was a gifted reader of his poetry. A year later he joined the staff of the *Tribune of Rome,* published in Rome, Ga., under the editorship of John Temple Graves [*q.v.*], and a year after that, persuaded by Joel Chandler Harris, went to the *Atlanta Constitution.* After serving as reporter and feature writer for a short time, he began his "Just from Georgia" column, one of the first American newspaper columns, to which for nearly forty years he contributed daily anecdotes, brief essays, and poems, many of them in negro and Georgia cracker dialects. His philosophy was a simple, idealistic one, and he wrote unaffectedly about his own thoughts and feelings.

In 1892 his great popularity as a "scrap-book poet" encouraged him to publish a collection of his poems, *Songs of a Day and Songs of the Soil.* Other volumes, in which there is a wide range of lyrical forms, followed at intervals: *Comes One with a Song* (1898), *Songs from Dixie Land* (copyright 1900), *Up from Georgia* (1902), *Little Folks Down South* (1904), and

Frank L. Stanton's Just from Georgia (1927), a posthumous collection compiled by his daughter, Mrs. Marcelle Stanton Megahee. They are characterized by spontaneity, humor, kindly tolerance, and a bright, optimistic tone. These qualities, and his use of simple emotions and subjects of such universal appeal as love, beauty, childhood, nature, patriotism, and democracy endeared this "Riley of the South" to a wide circle of readers. He was honored at home by his appointment on Feb. 22, 1925, as poet laureate of Georgia, and abroad by the translation of his poems (as songs) into many languages. Ethelbert Woodbridge Nevin [*q.v.*], Carrie Jacobs Bond, and Edward Kneisel set some of his songs to music; his "Georgia Land" is a sort of unofficial state song. Since he wrote one or more poems every day for nearly forty years, they were naturally of unequal merit. But he wrote a surprisingly large number of good ones. He will be remembered, however, chiefly for a small group of poems in which his lyrical gift finds its happiest expression: "St. Michael's Bells," "A Song of Harvest," "One Country," "My Study," "Marcelle," " 'Nearer to Thee,'" "Oh, Christmas Skies in Blue December," on the death of Henry W. Grady, and "Going Home," a poem of stately repose of spirt. His last published poems appeared in his column on Christmas morning, 1926. He died on Jan. 7, 1927, after an illness of a few weeks. He was survived by his wife and three children.

[See *Who's Who in America*, 1916–17; *Lib. of Southern Lit.*, vol. XI (1909), edited by E. A. Alderman, J. C. Harris, and C. W. Kent; Mildred L. Rutherford, *The South in Hist. and Lit.* (copr. 1906); Walter Chambers, in *Am. Mag.,* Feb. 1925, with portrait; L. L. Knight, *Reminiscences of Famous Georgians,* vol. I (1907); "The Poet of Georgia," *Nation,* Jan. 19, 1927; "A Columnist of the South," *Outlook,* Jan. 19, 1927; papers in the Joel Chandler Harris collection, Emory Univ.; *Atlanta Constitution,* Jan. 8 (obituary), 9–11, 16, 1927. Information has been supplied by Mrs. Marcelle Stanton Megahee, Stanton's daughter.]   J. M. S., Jr.

STANTON, FREDERICK PERRY (Dec. 22, 1814–June 4, 1894), congressman and acting governor of Kansas Territory, was born in Alexandria, then a part of the District of Columbia, the son of Richard and Harriet (Perry) Stanton. Richard Henry Stanton [*q.v.*] was an older brother. The boy was taught the bricklayer's trade by his father, and attended the private school conducted by Benjamin Hallowell [*q.v.*]. Later he taught in this same school, and also at Occoquan and at Portsmouth Academy in Virginia. After receiving the degree of A.B. from Columbian College (now George Washington University) in 1833, he served for two years as principal of Elizabeth City Academy in North

Carolina. Meantime he read law, was admitted to the Alexandria bar, and joined the Democratic party. In 1835 he removed to Somerville, Tenn., and some two years later to Memphis, where he practised his profession and contributed political editorials to the *Gazette*. On Dec. 25, 1835, he married Jane Harriet Sommers Lanphier of Alexandria. They had nine children, five of whom died in infancy. In 1845 Stanton entered Congress from the Memphis district and served until Mar. 3, 1855. He was assigned to the committee on naval affairs, and became its chairman in December 1849. His speeches reveal a wealth of scientific nautical information. He contended that replacements rather than additions would promote efficiency in the navy, advocated the use of heavier ordnance and the screw propeller, and proposed regular itineraries for both the Atlantic and the Pacific fleets. In the speakership contest of 1849 he introduced the resolution to substitute the plurality for the majority rule which resulted in the election of Howell Cobb [*q.v.*]. During the crisis of 1850 he threatened secession unless a satisfactory compromise was effected, and he voted against the District of Columbia slave trade bill, and against the admission of California as a free state. In discussing the Kansas-Nebraska measure, he assured the North that slavery could not exist in either territory, and that the bill was of no practical importance to the South "except for the principle of non-intervention." During his last term he served as chairman of the judiciary committee.

After a decade in Congress Stanton retired voluntarily but continued to reside in Washington, where he practised law. On Mar. 10, 1857, President Buchanan appointed him secretary of Kansas Territory, and he went there with a natural pro-slavery prejudice. From his arrival at Lecompton on Apr. 15 until he was relieved by Robert J. Walker [*q.v.*] on May 27, he served as acting governor. He urged a general political amnesty, promised a safeguarded franchise, and pledged enforcement of the territorial laws. With inadequate information on conditions in Kansas, he apportioned delegates to the Lecompton convention under an incomplete and inequitable census. Practical experience in the territory developed open-mindedness, and in the summer of 1857 both Walker and Stanton promised a fair vote in the October election for members of a legislature. They redeemed their pledge by rejecting sufficient fraudulent votes to change the party character of both houses. This act cost Walker his position and Stanton again became acting governor (Nov. 16–Dec. 21). At the re-

quest of Free-State men he convened the newly chosen legislature in extra session to provide a referendum on the whole Lecompton constitution. His removal for this act completed his transition to the Free-State party, and in the winter of 1858 he toured the North to lay its cause before the people. After Kansas was admitted into the Union in 1861, Stanton was defeated for the United States Senate. A few months later, when Senator James H. Lane [*q.v.*] accepted a brigadiership, Gov. Charles Robinson appointed Stanton to the supposed vacancy; but the Senate decided that none existed.

Soon after his arrival in Kansas, Stanton purchased a tract of land near Lecompton and erected a commodious stone house. In 1862 he removed to "Farmwell," in Virginia, and resumed law practice in Washington. Years later (1886) he settled in Florida. At the height of his congressional career, Buchanan characterized him as persevering, industrious, faithful, and able, credited him with "practical sense and sound judgment," and designated him as "the most promising" young man in the lower house (U. B. Phillips, "The Correspondence of Robert Toombs, Alexander H. Stephens, and Howell Cobb," *Annual Report of the American Historical Association . . . 1911,* vol. II, 1913, p. 181). He died at Stanton, near Ocala, Fla.

[A few of Stanton's speeches are preserved in pamphlet form in the Lib. of Cong., and his correspondence with Cass while acting governor is available in *Sen. Ex. Doc. 8*, 35 Cong., 1 Sess.; see also *Cong. Globe*, 1845–55; *Trans. Kan. State Hist. Soc.,* vol. V (1896); D. W. Wilder, *The Annals of Kan.* (1875); W. E. Connelley, *A Standard Hist. of Kan. and Kansans* (1918), vol. II; *Frank Leslie's Illustrated Newspaper,* Mar. 27, 1858; *U. S. Mag. and Democratic Rev.,* June 1850; *Biog. Dir. Am. Cong.* (1928); *Florida Times Union* (Jacksonville), June 5, 1894; information concerning family and children from a descendant.]   W. H. S.

STANTON, HENRY BREWSTER (June 27, 1805–Jan. 14, 1887), lawyer, reformer, journalist, was born in Griswold, Conn. His father, Joseph, a woolen manufacturer and merchant, traced his ancestry to Thomas Stanton who emigrated to America from England, and about 1637 settled in Connecticut. He was Crown interpreter of the Indian tongues in New England and judge of the New London county court. Henry's mother, Susan Brewster, was a descendant of William Brewster [*q.v.*] who arrived on the *Mayflower*. After studying at the academy in Jewett City, Conn., Henry went to Rochester in 1826 to write for Thurlow Weed's *Monroe Telegraph,* which was then supporting Henry Clay for the presidency. In 1828 he delivered addresses and wrote for the *Telegraph* in behalf of John Quincy Adams. The next year he became deputy clerk of Monroe County, N. Y., and continued in that office until 1832, meanwhile studying law and the classics. Converted by Charles G. Finney [*q.v.*], and having come into contact with Theodore D. Weld [*q.v.*], he then entered Lane Theological Seminary, in Cincinnati, where in the fall of 1834 he helped organize an anti-slavery society. This the trustees, who tried to prevent all discussion of the question, opposed, and in consequence about fifty students left, including Stanton (*Liberator*, Jan. 10, 1835), who at once associated himself with James G. Birney [*q.v.*] in his anti-slavery work. Soon he was made agent of the American Anti-Slavery Society, and was later a member of its executive committee.

For many years thereafter he devoted practically all of his time to this reform. He wrote for the *Liberator* and other abolitionist journals, for religious publications, and for some political papers, including the *National Era* of Washington and the *New York American*. He also appeared before many legislative commissions, and made platform speeches from Maine to Indiana. As a speaker he was quick-witted, eloquent, and impassioned, capable of making his hearers laugh as well as weep, and was ranked by many as the ablest anti-slavery orator of his day. His handsome, distinguished appearance, personal charm, and rare conversational powers added to his general popularity. His thunderous denunciations of human bondage subjected him, however, to scores of mob attacks. From 1837 to 1840 he busied himself with trying to get the abolitionists to form a strong political organization, a project which William Lloyd Garrison [*q.v.*] opposed, thereby causing a permanent break in the relation of the two men. On May 10, 1840, he married Elizabeth Cady [see Elizabeth Cady Stanton], daughter of Judge Daniel Cady [*q.v.*] of Johnstown, N. Y.; seven children were born to them.

Immediately after his marriage Stanton sailed with his wife for London to attend the World Anti-Slavery Convention, to which he was a delegate. Later, he traveled through Great Britain and Ireland delivering many speeches on the slavery question. One result of this tour was his *Sketches of Reforms and Reformers, of Great Britain and Ireland* (1849). Upon his return to the United States he studied law with his father-in-law, was admitted to the bar, and began practising in Boston. Finding the Massachusetts winters too severe for his health, he removed about 1847 to Seneca Falls, N. Y., making this place his home for the next sixteen years. He was successful at the law, but his continued interest in abolition led him into increased political

activity. In 1849 he was elected to the state Senate from Seneca Falls. He was one of the senators who resigned to prevent a quorum in the Senate and the passage of the bill appropriating millions of dollars for the enlargement of the canals. In 1851 he was reëlected but was not again a candidate. He helped draft the Free-Soil platform at Buffalo in 1848; in 1855 he helped organize the Republican party in New York State; and in 1856 he campaigned for Frémont. He remained a Republican until Grant's administration, during which he joined the Democrats. After the Civil War he gave most of his time to journalism, being connected with the *New York Tribune* under the editorship of Greeley, and with the *Sun* from 1869 to his death. He died in New York City.

[H. B. Stanton, *Random Recollections* (3rd ed., 1887); *Elizabeth Cady Stanton, as Revealed in her Letters, Diary, and Reminiscences* (copr. 1922), ed. by Theodore Stanton and Harriot Stanton Blatch; *Letters of Theodore Dwight Weld, Angelina Grimke Weld and Sarah Grimke* (2 vols., copr. 1934); annual reports of the Am. Anti-Slavery Soc., 1835 ff.; N. Y. Senate *Journal* and *Documents*, 1850–51; William Birney, *James G. Birney and His Times* (1890); W. A. Stanton, *A Record . . . of Thomas Stanton, of Connecticut, and His Descendants* (1891); *Liberator* (Boston), Jan. 10, 1835; N. Y. *Tribune* and N. Y. *Sun*, Jan. 15, 1887.]

M. W. W.

STANTON, RICHARD HENRY (Sept. 9, 1812–Mar. 20, 1891), congressman, jurist, and legal writer, was born at Alexandria, D. C. (now Va.), the son of Richard and Harriet (Perry) Stanton; Frederick P. Stanton [*q.v.*] was a younger brother. He received his elementary education at the academy in Alexandria conducted by Benjamin Hallowell [*q.v.*]. In early youth he assisted his father in his occupation as a brick-mason, but devoted his spare time to reading law. In 1835 he moved to Kentucky, taking up his residence at Maysville the following year, and in 1839 was admitted to the bar. He was a ready writer and edited the *Maysville Monitor* until 1841, when he entered regularly upon the practice of law. In later years, in association with Thornton F. Marshall, he published the *Maysville Express,* and afterwards was for some time editor of the *Maysville Bulletin*.

Appointed postmaster at Maysville in 1845, he held the position until 1849. In that year he was elected to Congress and was twice reëlected. During his second term he was chairman of the committee on public grounds and buildings and was instrumental in advancing the construction and improvement of the Capitol. In his last term, he was chairman of the committee on elections and of the select committee on the military supervision of civil works. It was upon his motion and insistence that the territory (now the state) of Washington received its name by congressional enactment in February 1853. During his congressional career he is said to have been "the ablest and most popular Democrat in the district" (Collins, *post*, II, 117). Stanton, the county seat of Powell County (established in 1852) was named in his honor.

In 1857 he was appointed commonwealth's attorney for what was then the tenth judicial district of Kentucky. To this office he was elected in 1858, and retained the post until 1862, when he resigned. In 1868 he was elected judge of the circuit court for the fourteenth judicial (Maysville) district, and served the full term of six years. Always an ardent Democrat, he was a delegate to the Baltimore Convention of 1844, by which James K. Polk was nominated for the presidency, and was also a delegate to the Baltimore Convention of 1852, which nominated Franklin Pierce. In 1856 he was a presidential elector from Kentucky and cast his vote for James Buchanan. On account of his anti-administration attitude and outspoken Southern sympathies, in October 1861 he was arrested and temporarily confined in Camp Chase, at Columbus, Ohio, but was soon transferred to Fort Lafayette, New York City, where he remained a prisoner for some time. He was a member of the Union Convention which met in Philadelphia in 1866, and of the New York Convention of 1868, which nominated Horatio Seymour for president. In February 1867 he was an unsuccessful candidate for the Democratic nomination for governor of Kentucky, and, a year later, he failed to secure nomination for senator in the Democratic caucus of the Kentucky legislature.

As a newspaper editor and contributor, he was a writer "of marked versatility and vigor" (Collins, II, 561). Of his earlier speeches, that delivered at Maysville on Dec. 18, 1847, "In Defence of the Mexican War," is, perhaps, the best example, and his speech in the House of Representatives, on June 14, 1854, "Against Military Superintendency of Civil Works," is a good illustration, in style and substance, of his political sentiments. He ranked high as a jurist. He was methodical, painstaking, and laborious; solid, safe, and thorough, rather than original or brilliant. His works as a law-writer comprise the following publications, which were extensively used: *Code of Practice in Civil and Criminal Cases for the State of Kentucky* (1859); *The Revised Statutes of Kentucky* (2 vols., 1860); *The Revised Statutes of Kentucky* (2 vols., 1867); *A Practical Treatise on the Law Relating to the Powers and Duties of Justices of the Peace, Clerks of the Circuit and County Courts, Sher-*

iffs, *Constables, Jailers, and Coroners in the State of Kentucky* (1875); *A Practical Manual for the Use of Executors, Administrators, Guardians, Trustees . . . in Kentucky* (2nd ed., 1875); *A New Digest of the Decisions of the Court of Appeals of Kentucky* (2 vols., 1877).

In 1833 he was married, in Alexandria, to Asenath Throop, of Fairfax County, Va. She was a daughter of Rev. Phares and Elizabeth (Bonner) Throop. Nine children were born to them, of whom three sons and four daughters grew to maturity. The eldest, Maj. Henry Thompson Stanton (June 30, 1834–May 8, 1898), was a lawyer and journalist; he served as an officer in the Confederate army and achieved considerable reputation as a novelist and poet.

[*The Biog. Encyc. of Ky.* (1878); Lewis and R. H. Collins, *Hist. of Ky.* (2 vols. 1874); *Evening Bull.* (Maysville, Ky.), Mar. 21, 1891; *Maysville Bull.*, May 22, 1924; *Cong. Globe*, 32nd Cong., 2 Sess.; *Biog. Dir. Am. Cong.* (1928); information from Stanton's family and from family MSS.]   S. M. W.

STANWOOD, EDWARD (Sept. 16, 1841–Oct. 11, 1923), editor, historian, was born in Augusta, Me., the son of Daniel Caldwell and Mary Augusta (Webster) Stanwood. He came of a family long settled in Essex County, Mass.; his ancestor Philip Stanwood having been a citizen of Gloucester as early as 1652. His father, at the age of fourteen, went to Augusta to live with an uncle, who had moved thither from Massachusetts (Ethel S. Bolton, *post*). Daniel Caldwell Stanwood became a man of some mark in Augusta; he was a book-seller by occupation, and served as city clerk and as major in the state militia. Edward Stanwood was educated in the public schools of the city, and at Bowdoin College, from which he graduated in 1861. Among his fellow students at Bowdoin was Thomas B. Reed, in later years speaker of the House of Representatives. From boyhood, Stanwood was deeply interested in public affairs, and strongly drawn to the profession of journalism. At seventeen he was reporting the proceedings of the Maine legislature for the Augusta *Age*; and after his graduation from college he was similarly employed on the staff of the *Kennebec Journal*, of which James G. Blaine [*q.v.*] was for some years the editor. Blaine had married a cousin of Stanwood's and the relations of the two men were close for many years. For a time in 1863–64 he was Blaine's secretary in Washington, shortly returning to Augusta to continue his newspaper work.

In 1867 the attention of the editor of the Boston *Daily Advertiser* was attracted to Stanwood, and he offered the young man a position on the *Advertiser* staff. For sixteen years Stanwood was connected with this paper, rising to the post of editor-in-chief. During these years he contributed articles to many magazines, published a book called *Boston Illustrated* (1872), and wrote for Justin Winsor's *The Memorial History of Boston* a chapter on the topography and landmarks of the city (vol. IV, 1881). In December 1883 Stanwood resigned the editorship of the *Advertiser* and shortly afterward joined the staff of the *Youth's Companion*. First as managing editor and then, after the death of Daniel Sharp Ford [q.v.], as editor, he remained for twenty-seven years with this famous household weekly; and after his retirement from the editorship he continued to contribute to its editorial page almost to the end of his life. He was in responsible charge of its conduct during its period of greatest popularity and prosperity. He maintained faithfully the policies and traditions by which, under the direction of Ford, the *Youth's Companion* had become one of the journalistic institutions of the United States. Its carefully selected combination of wholesome and entertaining fiction with articles of information and reminiscence by eminent writers, and a great variety of anecdote, both humorous and instructive, amply justified the esteem in which the paper was held in half a million households all over the land.

In 1884, Stanwood published *A History of Presidential Elections,* a valuable political handbook, of which several editions appeared. In 1898 it appeared in enlarged form as *A History of the Presidency,* and under that title was several times reissued. In 1903 Stanwood published his *American Tariff Controversies in the Nineteenth Century* (5 vols.). Written by a convinced adherent of the policy of protection to industry through tariff duties, the book may be found to lack thorough impartiality; but it assembles a great body of facts not available elsewhere in collected form. In 1905 appeared Stanwood's *James Gillespie Blaine,* written for the American Statesmen series. The long and close friendship between the author and his subject gives this book a certain personal as well as biographical interest. As is natural from the circumstances of the case, it takes a view consistently favorable to Blaine. For years Stanwood was identified with the affairs of the cotton industry. He was secretary and treasurer of the Arkwright Club, special agent for cotton manufactures in the preparation of the census of 1900 (*Census Reports. Twelfth Census. . . . Manufactures, Textiles,* 1902); and for textiles in 1905 (*Department of Commerce and Labor. Bureau of the Census. Bulletin 74. Census of Manufactures: 1905. Textiles,* 1907). For years he was a contributing editor to the *Statesman's Year Book,* dealing with American affairs. From 1903 to the year of his death he was a member of the Massachusetts Historical Society, and most of that time its recording secretary.

He was married on Nov. 16, 1870, to Eliza Maxwell Topliff of Boston, daughter of Samuel Topliff, and was the father of three children, two of whom, a daughter and a son, survived him. He died at his home in Brookline, Mass., on Oct. 11, 1923.

[This article is based in part on personal acquaintance. The best account of Stanwood's life is the memoir of his son-in-law, C. K. Bolton, in *Mass. Hist. Soc. Proceedings,* vol. LVII (1924). For genealogy and a list of his writings to 1899, see *A Hist. of the Stanwood Family* (1899) by his daughter, Ethel Stanwood Bolton. A character sketch, by Geoffrey Bolton, in manuscript, is in the library of the Boston Athenaeum. See also *The Class of 1861, Bowdoin College* (1897), compiled by Stanwood; obituary in *Boston Evening Transcript,* Oct. 11, 1923; and passages in E. P. Mitchell, *Memoirs of an Editor* (1924).]

H. S. C—an.

STAPLES, WALLER REDD (Feb. 24, 1826–Aug. 20, 1897), Confederate congressman, Virginia jurist, was born at Stuart, Patrick County, Va., the son of Col. Abram Penn and Mary (Penn) Staples. At sixteen he entered the University of North Carolina, and after two years there transferred to the College of William and Mary, where he was graduated with honors in 1846. He studied law under Judge Norbonne Taliaferro in Franklin County, and in 1848 began practice in Montgomery County, Va., as the junior associate of his kinsman, William Ballard Preston [q.v.]. Preston's appointment within a few months to the post of secretary of the navy under President Taylor was of great professional advantage to the younger man. He became a Whig in politics and served as a delegate from Montgomery County in the House of Delegates, 1853–54.

In the crisis of 1860–61 Staples opposed immediate secession and worked with the conservatives to avert the disruption of the Union, but when Virginia adopted the ordinance of secession he volunteered for service in the state forces. He was appointed to the staff of Col. Robert C. Trigg, but was soon chosen, together with W. C. Rives, R. M. T. Hunter [qq.v.], and John Brockenbrough on the commission sent to represent Virginia in the provisional Confederate Congress at Montgomery, Ala. He served in that body until the end of its existence in February 1862, and then, having been elected by a large majority, took his seat in the House of Representatives of the new Confederate Congress. He was reëlected in 1863 and served till the end of the war.

After the war he resumed his practice in Montgomery County, regained his place as a leader at the bar, and in 1870 was elected a justice of the Virginia supreme court of appeals. His most notable opinion as a member of this court was his dissent in the "Coupon Case" in 1878 (*Antoni* vs. *Wright, 63 Va. Reports,* 833) which led to the forming of the Readjuster party and to the partial repudiation of a portion of the state debt. Staples, dissenting, held that the Virginia law of 1871 making coupons of bonds issued in that year receivable for all state taxes was invalid as applied to school taxes for which a special fund had been set aside by the state constitution. After the Readjuster period his opinion on this point was upheld by the supreme court of Virginia (*Commonwealth* vs. *McCullough, 90 Va.,* 597) and by the United States Supreme Court (*Vashon* vs. *Greenhow, 135 U. S.,* 713). He sat on the supreme bench for a full term of twelve years, but when the Readjuster party secured a majority in the legislature he and his associates were not reëlected. During his judicial service he was offered at different times the Democratic nominations for governor, attorney-general, and United States senator, but he declined political office, though he canvassed the state for the nominees and was twice a Democratic presidential elector.

In 1884 Staples, Judge E. C. Burks, a former colleague on the bench, and Maj. John W. Riely, later a member of the same court, were appointed to prepare *The Code of Virginia,* approved and published in 1887. For two years Staples was counsel for the Richmond & Danville Railroad Company, resigning this position to devote himself to a lucrative practice as senior member of the Richmond law firm of Staples & Munford. During this same period he was president of the Virginia Bar Association. As attorney in two significant cases before the Virginia supreme court of appeals (*Fifield* vs. *Van Wyck, 94 Va.,* 557 and *Munford, Trustee,* vs. *McVeigh, 92 Va.,* 446), he won reversals of former decisions of the supreme court.

Above medium height, of strong, athletic build, with a persuasive voice, Staples was a polished orator but also enjoyed a "knock down and drag out" legal fight. He was never married. He died at his Christiansburg home, in Montgomery County, at the age of seventy-one.

[Frederick Johnston, *Memorials of Old Va. Clerks* (1888) ; 94 *Va. Reports,* xxi–xxvi ; *Va. Law Reg.,* Feb. 1898; *Report . . . Va. State Bar Asso.,* 1898; *Green Bag.,* Sept. 1893, pp. 407, 409 ; *Richmond Dispatch,* Aug. 21, 1897; parents' names from a nephew, Hon. A. P. Staples.]   J. E. W.

STAPLES, WILLIAM READ (Oct. 10, 1798–Oct. 19, 1868), historian, was born in Providence, R. I., the youngest son of Samuel and Ruth (Read) Staples. He graduated from Brown University in 1817. After reading law in the office of a local attorney, he was admitted to practice in 1819, and although at the bar and on the bench he maintained a successful association with the law for nearly half a century, he impressed one of his contemporary biographers as being "not especially fond of his profession" (Guild, *post,* p. xvii). He entered public life in 1832 as a member of the common council of Providence, served as a police justice of the city for two years, and in June 1835 took his seat by appointment as an associate justice of the supreme court of Rhode Island. Elected chief justice of that court in 1854, he was compelled through loss of health to resign his office in March 1856. Thereafter, except for a few months in 1856 as state auditor, he devoted himself largely to unofficial public service and to the development of his interest in the history of his native state. From the eulogies of his professional associates at the time of his death, one learns that it was not profound legal knowledge that gave him distinction among Rhode Island jurists so much as a faculty for dealing systematically and promptly with the business of the court and unusual readiness in discerning the bearing of general principles of law upon particular cases.

He was one of the incorporators of the Rhode Island Historical Society in 1822. He was chosen at once to act as its librarian and cabinet keeper, one of the several offices that he held in the society in the course of his long membership. He edited for the society an edition of *Simplicities Defence* by Samuel Gorton [*q.v.*] in *Rhode Island Historical Society Collections* (vol. II, 1935). His annotation of that confused narrative and his documentary additions to it indicate the possession of a more than respectable knowledge of early New England and a conception of editorial responsibility seldom attained by the untrained antiquarians of his day. In his *Annals of the Town of Providence,* published in 1843 (also in *Rhode Island Historical Society Collections,* vol. V, 1843), he claimed with too much modesty that his purpose was only "to collect facts for the future historian," but in that book he arranged economically a great store of facts, collected from numerous original sources, into a vigorous, reliable narrative covering two centuries of the city's life. At the instance of the Assembly he performed in his closing years a similar task of research and presentation in his *Rhode Island in the Continental Congress,* a work that was brought out by the state in 1870 under the editorship of Reuben Aldridge Guild [*q.v.*]. He edited also *The Documentary History of the Destruction of the Gaspee* (1845) and, at different periods of his life, certain works of legal utility of no general interest. His closest religious affiliation was with the Friends, though he does not seem to have been a member of that society. He was married in November 1821 to Rebecca M. Power who died in 1825. They had two children both of whom died in childhood. In October 1826 he was married to his second wife, Evelina Eaton of Framingham, Mass., who survived him with six of their eleven children.

["Preface" and the "Introductory Memoir" by R. A. Guild, in *Rhode Island in the Continental Congress,* ante; *Hist. Cat. of Brown Univ.* (1914); S. G. Arnold, *Greene-Staples-Parsons* (1869); *Providence Daily Journ.,* Oct. 20, 1868.]   L. C. W.

STARIN, JOHN HENRY (Aug. 27, 1825–Mar. 22, 1909), transportation owner, congressman, was of old Dutch stock, a descendant of Nicholas Ster, who emigrated from Holland to New Amsterdam in 1696 and about 1705 moved up the Mohawk Valley to a settlement called German Flats. He was born in Sammonsville, N. Y., fifth of the eight children of Myndert and Rachel (Sammons) Starin. His father developed extensive manufacturing interests in Sammonsville and was the founder of Fultonville. After attending Esperance Academy, he began to study medicine with Dr. C. C. Yates, an Albany doctor, but, preferring business, returned in 1845 to his brother's drug store at Fultonville, where he served also as postmaster, 1850–53. In 1856 he moved to New York and began to manufacture toilet articles. There the difficulties he met in shipping his products called his attention to the complete lack of system in handling freight around New York. The situation was a chaotic one, the result of the insular position of Manhattan, accentuated by the fact that several railroads started on the Jersey side of the Hudson. In 1859 he organized a general freight agency, the Starin City River and Harbor Transportation Lines, and soon won the support of Vanderbilt and other railroad officials, who realized that a centralized system would mean economy. At first he used canal boats for transshipping freight. During the Civil War the government relied on his organization for the moving of men, munitions, and supplies, and it is said that his quick work once saved a regiment from starvation. After the war he rapidly increased his equipment of lighters and tugs. In 1866 he in-

vented the car float, by which a freight train could be broken into parts and the cars carried across the harbor—a system that, with few modifications, is still extensively used. He was, in fact, responsible for most of the important solutions of the problem of handling freight down to the time of his death. He devised special facilities for handling grain and coal, and built up the largest "harbor marine" in the country, if not in the world. In addition, he owned and operated passenger and freight lines on Long Island Sound. Having purchased Glen Island (formerly Locust Island), off New Rochelle on the Sound, he made it into a summer resort intended to rival Coney Island and linked it to New York City with a line of excursion steamers, on which he annually gave free trips to war veterans, police, firemen, newsboys, poor women, and other groups from the city. To build and repair his "navy" he had a shipyard, iron works, and drydock on Staten Island. Until the very end he kept active daily control of his wide-spread activities from his office on Pier 13, North River.

He also deserves much credit for establishing New York's subway system. He was an original member of the Rapid Transit Commission of the city, 1894–1907, and served as vice president, 1895–1907. Opposed to the building of more elevated and surface lines, he fought hard for the subways, construction of which was begun on Mar. 24, 1900. It is said, too, that by his firm stand against all the rest of the board he prevented the traction interests from securing a monopoly of the franchises. A strong Republican, he sat in Congress for an upstate district from 1877 to 1881, declining a third term. More than once he was prominently mentioned for governor. He was president of the Saratoga Monument Association and its most active supporter, president of the Holland Society, 1901–02, vice president of the Union League Club, and a member of many other organizations. He had several estates, one at his old home in Fultonville, another in a remote part of the Adirondacks on Hamilton Lake, and a third, "Folly Island," on the South Carolina coast, where he had a herd of 4,000 Angora goats. He married Laura M. Poole of Oriskany, N. Y., on Jan. 27, 1846. He died in New York City. He was survived by a son and two daughters, his wife and two sons having predeceased him.

[See W. L. Stone, *The Starin Family in America* (1892), with portraits; *Who's Who in America,* 1908–09; *Biog. Directory Am. Cong., 1774–1927* (1928); J. H. Mowbray, *Representative Men of N. Y.* (1898), vol. II; *Year Book Holland Soc. of N. Y.,* 1909; *Report of the Board of Rapid Transit Railroad Commissioners . . . City of N. Y. . . . 1902* (1903). The N. Y. harbor transportation situation is best described, without specific reference to Starin, in *Joint Report with Comprehensive Plan and Recommendations; N. Y., N. J. Port and Harbor Development Commission* (1920).]

R. G. A.

STARK, EDWARD JOSEF (Apr. 29, 1858–Apr. 22, 1918), cantor, composer of synagogue music, was born at Hohenems, Austria, to Josef and Josepha (Pollak) Stark. From his father, a synagogue cantor who had been a pupil of the world-famed Salomon Sulzer, he derived his knowledge and love of Jewish religious music. After a childhood spent for the most part at Ichenhausen, Bavaria, he came with his parents in 1871 to the United States, where his older brothers were already in business. Young Stark received his musical education in New York City and in European conservatories, whither he was sent by a wealthy friend. On his return to America, he spent a short time in business before becoming cantor in the Beth Elohim Synagogue in Brooklyn, N. Y. This position he held until October 1893, when he was called to be cantor in Temple Emanu-El, San Francisco. He served in this capacity until, in August 1913, owing to failing health, he was made honorary cantor emeritus. On Apr. 1, 1884, in New York City, he married Rosa Weinberger, who bore him two sons and two daughters.

His was the uneventful life of a synagogue cantor and composer devoted to his calling. He possessed a rich, magnetic, baritone voice which he used with dramatic feeling. While his principal works are in the field of sacred music, he also wrote light operettas for the Progress Club (1884) and the Germania Quartett Club in New York (1885), and for celebrations in the Sunday School of Temple Emanu-El in San Francisco (1895 and 1906). Many of his numerous sacred compositions have gained wide recognition in American synagogues. They include the four collections (each under the Hebrew title *Sefer Anim Zemiroth*) *Musical Service for Sabbath Evening* (New York, 1911, third printing 1931), *Musical Service for Sabbath Morning* (1909, second printing 1926), *Musical Service for the Eve and Day of New Year* (1910, third printing 1930), *Musical Service for the Eve of Atonement and for the Day of Atonement* (1913), besides anthems, adaptations, and a number of unpublished works. His anthem "The Lord is my light" won the Schirmer prize in the national contest of 1905; "Day of God," sung on the eve of the Day of Atonement, is often regarded as his finest composition. He was a prolific worker, sometimes sitting all night composing at the organ. A feature of some of his work, which is unusual in synagogue music, is its orchestral setting for string and wind instruments.

"He was gifted with considerable creative talent, and with power and depth of Jewish expression" (Idelsohn, *post*, p. 326–27). His synagogue music, especially that for the New Year and the Day of Atonement, using Jewish modes and showing both the influence of Sulzer and of the classic oratorio, disciplines Jewish traditional motifs and modes by the constraints of the organ and of Western musical conventions. This combination of traditionalism and modernism makes his compositions particularly well adapted for reform Jewish temples. He aimed to preserve the traditional character of the synagogue service in which the main elements of the ritual are rendered by the cantor in recitatives and solos, with the choral and hymnal elements constituting a superstructure on this foundation. His influence in this direction was the greater and more needed because he came into the field at a time when the tendency in American reform Judaism had been towards the entire elimination of the plaintive, emotional Eastern Jewish traditional motifs in favor of operatic airs, or the stately devotional Western music borrowed, or at least copied, from that of the dominant Church.

[*Emanu-El* (San Francisco), Apr. 26, 1918; A. Z. Idelsohn, *Jewish Music* (1929); *The Am. Jewish Year Book . . . 1903–1904* (1903), p. 102, which gives date of birth as Mar. 29, 1863; unpublished records in possession of Stark's children.]   D. deS. P.

STARK, JOHN (Aug. 28, 1728–May 8, 1822), Revolutionary soldier, was born at Londonderry, N. H., the son of Archibald Stark and his wife, Eleanor Nichols. The elder Stark was a Scotsman who, after residing some years in Ulster County, Ireland, emigrated to New Hampshire in 1720 with a party of compatriots. Brought up in a frontier community where fishing, hunting, and Indian-fighting were the chief occupations, Stark developed a physique well adapted to endure the risks and rigors of military life. He became familiar with the New Hampshire wilderness and guided exploring expeditions into remote regions. During the French and Indian War he saw extensive service with Rogers' Rangers and attained a captaincy by gallantry on the field. He took part in the operations resulting in the defeat of Baron Dieskau in 1755. In January 1757, en route with a scouting party to Lake Champlain, he distinguished himself by walking forty miles in deep snow, after a day's fighting and a night's marching, in order to bring succor to the wounded. He was present during Rigaud's attack upon Fort William Henry, and in 1758 participated in Abercromby's futile assault upon Ticonderoga. He concluded this chapter of his military career, by serving under Amherst at the reduction of Crown Point and Ticonderoga in 1759, and then returned to his farm and his mills, and devoted himself to the settlement of a new township, at first called Starkstown but later Dunbarton. On Aug. 20, 1758, he was married to Elizabeth, the daughter of Capt. Caleb Page.

When the news of the battles of Lexington and Concord came, he promptly mounted horse and set out for Cambridge, Mass. A regiment of New Hampshire patriots presently assembled at Medford and Stark was appointed colonel. In the battle of Bunker Hill his men defended the rail fence on the American left. After the siege of Boston, he assisted in planning the defenses of New York, and in May 1776 went to Canada and accompanied the American forces on their retreat southward. He played a conspicuous part in the battles of Trenton and Princeton, but resigned his commission in March 1777 because Congress had promoted junior officers over his head (see *Proceedings of the Massachusetts Historical Society,* LVII, 1924, p. 334).

When Burgoyne invaded the province of New York, the Vermont council of safety, anticipating a raid into the region west of the Connecticut River, largely unprotected after the fall of Ticonderoga, appealed to the authorities of New Hampshire for help. On July 18 the general court authorized the mobilization of a force to assist Vermont, and elected Stark to command it with the rank of brigadier-general. Within twenty days he raised and equipped a brigade of about 1,400 men, crossed the mountains, and arrived at Manchester, Vt., where he conferred with Seth Warner, Benjamin Lincoln [*qq.v.*], and the Vermont leaders. On Aug. 8, he moved southward to Bennington with the intention of cooperating with Schuyler in a movement to harass Burgoyne's flank. On the next day the British commander dispatched Colonel Baum with 500 men to test the sentiment of the Hampshire Grants and to secure supplies of cattle, horses, and wagons. On Aug. 16 Stark attacked Baum on the Walloomsac River, about five miles northwest of Bennington, and captured almost his entire force. As he led his men into action, he is alleged to have exclaimed, "There, my boys, are your enemies, the red-coats and tories; you must beat them or my wife sleeps a widow tonight" (Caleb Stark, *post,* p. 60). Later in the day, Stark and Warner repulsed reënforcements under Breymann hastening to Baum's assistance. Stark received the thanks of Congress three days later, after having been censored for disregarding orders for a different movement of his men.

On Oct. 4, 1777, he was promoted to the rank of brigadier-general in the Continental service. After capturing Fort Edward, he helped to effect the surrender of Burgoyne by blocking his line of retreat across the Hudson. His services during the remainder of the war were interesting and significant. He twice commanded the northern department; served with Gates in Rhode Island in 1779; participated in the battle of Springfield in 1780; and acted on the board of general officers appointed to try Major André. He was brevetted a major-general in September 1783.

After the war he retired to his estate, eschewing public office and devoting himself to the cares entailed by a large farm and a family of eleven children. He was buried with military honors in a cemetery upon his own land, the site being marked by a granite obelisk erected in 1829, on the anniversary of the battle of Bennington. He was a man of medium height, bold features, keen, light-blue eyes, and compressed lips. While the phraseology of his celebrated sayings in battle has been disputed, there is no doubt that he possessed a gift for picturesque expression which served to enhance the dramatic quality of his martial exploits.

[Sources include N. H. Hist. Soc. collection of published and unpublished letters and papers of John Stark; George Stark, *Origin of the Stark Family* (1887); C. E. Potter, *The Hist. of Manchester* (1856); Caleb Stark, *Memoir and Official Corres. of Gen. John Stark* (1860); Isaac Jennings, *Memorials of a Century* (1869); *N. H. State Papers,* vols. VII–VIII (1873–74); *Proc. in Cong. upon the Acceptance of the Statues of John Stark and Daniel Webster, Sen. Misc. Doc., 64,* 53 Cong., 3 Sess. (1895); Henry Boynton in *Granite Monthly,* Oct. 1902; F. B. Sanborn in *Proc. N. H. Hist. Soc.,* vol. III (1902); H. D. Foster & T. W. Streeter, *Stark's Independent Command at Bennington* (1918); John Spargo, *The Bennington Battle Monument* (1925); *Natl. Standard* (Middlebury, Vt.), May 28, 1822. Stark's stirring adventures among the Indians served as a basis for a novel, *The Hero of the Hills* (1901), by G. W. Browne.]   E. E. C.

STARR, ELIZA ALLEN (Aug. 29, 1824–Sept. 7, 1901), writer, lecturer on art, the second of four children of Oliver and Lovina (Allen) Starr, was born in a rangy old house at Deerfield, Mass. On both sides her family traced descent from early English emigrants to the Bay Colony and found satisfaction in their long residence in Deerfield. Her father, a dyer, was a descendant of Dr. Comfort Starr, who emigrated from Kent, England, to Boston in 1635. Uneducated but intelligent, the Starrs encouraged Eliza to go beyond the district school, and even the local academy, to Boston, where she took lessons in art and painting from the wife of Richard Hildreth [*q.v.*], the historian. In some way about 1845 her Unitarian beliefs were upset by a sermon of Dr. Theodore Parker [*q.v.*], and her religious yearnings were not satisfied until in 1854 she joined the Roman Catholic Church, influenced by her association with Bishops Francis Patrick Kenrick and John Bernard Fitzpatrick, and her cousin, George Allen [*qq.v.*], a convert and a professor of Latin and Greek at the University of Pennsylvania. Her conversion was the central fact in a life dedicated to painting, poetry, and writing where religion provided the motif. Finding the climate disagreeable in Boston, where she had a studio, she taught art in private schools in Brookyn, N. Y., and Philadelphia, Pa., became a tutor in a wealthy family of Natchez, Miss., and finally settled in Chicago, Ill., about 1856 as one of its first teachers of art and the first to instruct her pupils from nature and casts.

Her early success was partly due to Bishop Kenrick, with whom she kept up a long correspondence, to Bishop James Duggan of Chicago, and to such pioneer patrons of art in Chicago as William Butler Ogden [*q.v.*], Walter Loomis Newberry [*q.v.*], Jonathan Young Scammon [*q.v.*], and Leander James McCormick [*q.v.*]. In addition to private teaching she gave for a score of years an annual series of lectures, which contributed to the cultural life of the first families of the city, on painting, architecture, and the great artists of the Renaissance. After her studio burned in the great fire of 1871, she spent a few years at St. Mary's Academy (later College), South Bend, Ind., under Mother Angela [*q.v.*], organizing an art department. She became widely known as a lecturer in Catholic circels and convent schools, and as a writer of poems and popular essays on art in the *Catholic World, Ave Maria, New York Freeman's Journal, London Monthly,* and other magazines. In 1875 she traveled extensively in Europe, drawing upon her experiences later for her *Pilgrims and Shrines* (2 vols., 1885). Other books, always devotional, which she herself usually illustrated, followed in rapid succession: *Patron Saints* (1 ser., 1871; 2 ser., 1881), *Songs of a Life-Time* (copyright 1888), *Isabella of Castile* (1889), *Christian Art in Our Own Age* (1891), *The Seven Dolors of the Blessed Virgin Mary* (1898), *The Three Archangels and the Guardian Angels in Art* (1899), and *Three Keys to the Camera Della Segnatura of the Vatican* (1895). She received a medallion from Pope Leo XIII in appreciation of her work; a Laetare Medal (1885), awarded annually by the University of Notre Dame to an outstanding Catholic contributor to the church and nation; and a gold medal at the World's Columbian Exposition of 1893 in Chicago for her work as a teacher. She died at the home of a brother in Durand, Ill., and was buried from the Cathedral of the Holy Name, Chicago, in Calvary Cemetery.

[See B. P. Starr, *A Hist. of the Starr Family* (1879), which gives Eliza Starr's name as Eliza Ann ('Allen') Starr; *Who's Who in America,* 1901–02; *The Cath. Encyc.,* vol. XIV (copr. 1912); J. J. McGovern, *Life and Letters of Eliza Allen Starr* (1905); *N. Y. Freeman's Jour.,* Sept. 3, 1887; W. S. Clarke, in *Cath. World,* Nov. 1897; W. S. Merrill, *Ibid.,* Feb. 1902; Frances E. Willard and Mary A. Livermore, *A Woman of the Century* (1893), with portrait; obituary in *Chicago Daily Tribune,* Sept. 9, 1901.]   R. J. P.

STARR, FREDERICK (Sept. 2, 1858–Aug. 14, 1933), anthropologist, was born in Auburn, N. Y., the fourth of the seven children of the Rev. Frederick Starr, a Presbyterian minister, and Helen Strachan (Mills) Starr. He was a descendant of Dr. Comfort Starr, who emigrated from Kent, England, to Boston in 1635. He spent his boyhood in the East and in 1882 graduated from Lafayette College, Easton, Pa., where in 1885 he received the degree of Ph.D. He was professor of biology at Coe College, Cedar Rapids, Iowa, 1883–87, and registrar and professor of geography at Chautauqua University, Chautauqua, N. Y., 1888–89. From 1889 to 1891 he was engaged in arranging, labelling, and classifying the collections in the department of ethnology in the American Museum of Natural History, New York. In 1891 he became professor of geology and anthropology, and dean of the science department in Pomona College, Claremont, Cal., but in the following year he was called to organize the work of anthropology at the newly established University of Chicago, under William Rainey Harper [*q.v.*], where in 1895 he became associate professor. During his thirty-one years there he was probably the most popular instructor in the university. Though his classes were crowded and he was the only instructor in his subject, he refused to add others, remaining, as he said, "the Lone Star." He had numerous personal idiosyncrasies. He refused to wear an overcoat, never used a telephone, and usually walked about the campus with an open book in his hands, while his apartment was a labyrinth of books stacked on the floors of various rooms. His frankness and fearlessness in the expression of opinion often made him enemies; on the other hand, his informality and camaraderie in the classroom created a loyalty seldom met with between students and professor. When he retired from the university in 1923 his former students presented him with a large purse, which enabled him to purchase a house in Seattle, Wash., a location convenient for his frequent trips to Japan.

Throughout his career he traveled widely for the sake of making anthropological studies. In preparation for the Louisiana Purchase Exposition at St. Louis, Mo., in 1904, he visited northern Japan and brought back with him a representative group of Ainu; he also visited various parts of the United States and Mexico, the Philippines, Korea, and Africa, returning several times to the last two. During these visits he lived the life of the people, and in Japan, at least, he wore native dress. Keenly interested in the intimate life of those he met, he was always inclined to take the part of minority or unpopular groups. While the world was condemning the African policy of King Leopold II, he visited the Congo and came forward with a vigorous defense of Belgian rule; while "imperialism" was at its height in America he advocated Philippine independence. Mexico found in him an ardent advocate, and shortly before his death he defended Japan in the Manchukuo dispute. He was a chevalier of the Order of the Crown of Italy, a member of the Third Order of the Sacred Treasure of Japan, an officer of the Order of Leopold II (Congo), and had been awarded medals by Holland, Belgium, and Liberia, as well as the palms of Officer of Public Instruction by the French government. His best known writings are *Some First Steps in Human Progress* (1895), *American Indians* (copyright 1898), *Indians of Southern Mexico* (1898), *Strange Peoples* (1901), *Readings from Modern Mexican Authors* (1904), *The Truth about the Congo* (1907), *In Indian Mexico* (1908), *Philippine Studies* (1909), *Japanese Proverbs and Pictures* (1910), *Congo Natives* (1912), *Liberia* (1913), *Korean Buddhism* (1918), *Fujiyama, the Sacred Mountain of Japan* (1924). His greatest contribution to anthropology lies, however, in the wide interest he personally created in the subject, and in the appreciation of other peoples which he engendered in his students. In 1923 he went through the earthquake that devastated Tokio and claimed many of his closest friends. Ten years later he died of bronchial pneumonia in the same city. He was unmarried.

[B. P. Starr, *A Hist. of the Starr Family* (1879); *Who's Who in America*, 1932–33; *Am. Men of Sci.* (1933), edited by J. M. and Jaques Cattell; *Biog. Cat. of Lafayette Coll., 1832–1912* (1913); *Univ. Record* (Chicago), Oct. 1933; *Am. Anthropologist*, Apr.–June 1934; *Am. Jour. of Sociology*, Nov. 1933; obituaries in *Japan Advertiser* (Tokio) and *N. Y. Times*, Aug. 15, 1933, personal acquaintance.]   F.-C. C.

STARR, LOUIS (Apr. 25, 1849–Sept. 12, 1925), physician, was born in Philadelphia, Pa., the son of Isaac and Lydia (Ducoing) Starr. The line of his paternal ancestors was estab-lished in America by Isaac Starr, an English Quaker, who settled in Wilmington, Del., in 1710. Eight generations remained in the Quaker faith and married within the bounds of their religious convictions until Starr's father, a banker, took as his wife a French girl, Lydia Ducoing, who was a refugee from the slave insurrections of Santo Domingo and a descendant of a family which had originally come from Bordeaux, France. Louis graduated from Haverford College in 1868 with the degree of B.A., studied medicine at the University of Pennsylvania, and obtained the degree of M.D. in 1871. After acting as the resident physician for the Episcopal Hospital, he entered general practice in Philadelphia, where his personal charm, diligence, and, doubtless, his excellent social position made him a very successful practitioner. Nevertheless, he turned to a special field and by 1882 was recognized as a pediatrician of note. He was visiting physician to the Episcopal Hospital, 1875–84, and to the Children's Hospital, 1879, and held numerous other such appointments. In 1884 he became clinical professor of the diseases of children in the University of Pennsylvania, a position he held until 1890. For fifty years he was a fellow of the College of Physicians of Philadelphia, at various times a member of its council, and later a censor; he was also a fellow of the Royal College of Physicians of London. He first appeared in scientific literature in 1885–86 as an assistant to Dr. William Pepper [*q.v.*] in the editing of *A System of Practical Medicine* (5 vols., 1885–86). Subsequently he published several textbooks on pediatric subjects. His most successful publication was *Hygiene of the Nursery* (1888), one of the first popular expositions of nursery care, and his most ambitious *The American Text-book of Diseases of Children by American Teachers* (1894).

On Sept. 16, 1882, in Kent, England, he married Mary Parrish of Philadelphia, grand-daughter of Joseph Parrish [*q.v.*]. They had three children. At the age of sixty-two, when he was forced to retire from all official and professional activities because of serious cardiac disease, he took up residence with his family in England, but the leisure of his retirement was soon interrupted by the World War. When his younger son, Dillwyn, was killed in the battle of the Somme as a lieutenant of the Coldstream Guards, he sought respite from his sorrow in the cultivation of an artistic talent which had hitherto lain dormant. Some of his etchings were later shown at an exhibition of the Pennsylvania Academy of the Fine Arts in Philadelphia and are said to have won favor in authoritative circles. The death of his older son, Louis, in 1921 caused him to leave the scene of so much affliction, and he repaired to Dinard, on the coast of Brittany, where he spent the last years of his life in pursuit of his artistic inclinations. He died after a short illness, survived by his wife and daughter.

[*Who's Who in America*, 1914–15; T. S. Westcott, *Trans. Coll. of Physicians of Phila.*, 3 ser., vol. XLVIII (1926); *Jour. Am. Medic. Assoc.*, Oct. 10, 1925; obituary in *Pub. Ledger* (Phila.), Sept. 14, 1925.]

H. S. R—e.

STARR, MERRITT (Feb. 27, 1856–Aug. 2, 1931), corporation lawyer, was born at Ellington, Chautauqua County, N. Y. His father, James Comfort Starr, later a proprietor of the Moline Paper Company, was a descendant of Dr. Comfort Starr, of Ashford, Kent, who emigrated from England to Massachusetts in 1635; his mother, Cynthia Cordera (MacKoon), was a descendant of Roger Williams. Merritt Starr spent his boyhood in Rock Island, Ill. He attended Griswold College at Davenport, Iowa, for two years, and in 1873 entered Oberlin College as a junior, receiving the degree of A.B. from Oberlin in 1875 and from Griswold (*ad eundem*) in 1876. Ambitious for a legal career, he read law in the office of the attorneys for the Chicago, Burlington & Quincy Railroad Company, entered the Harvard Law School in 1878 and Harvard College, as a junior, in 1879, and was graduated A.B. and LL.B. in 1881.

Establishing residence in Chicago, he was admitted to the Illinois bar Jan. 11, 1882. He began his career by preparing briefs for his fellow attorneys and publishing valuable contributions to legal literature. In 1883 appeared his *Index-Digest of the Wisconsin Reports* and his chapters on practice in *A Treatise on the Law of Waters* by John Melville Gould. Shortly afterward he began a collaboration with R. H. Curtis in compiling *Annotated Statutes of the State of Illinois* (1st ed., 2 vols., 1885, with supplements 1887, 1892; 2nd ed., 3 vols., 1896). He also digested the *Illinois Cases* for the *Northeastern Reporter*, from 1885 to 1888.

Meanwhile he was becoming well known in the field of corporation law. During the suspension of the Indiana banks in 1883, he conducted the litigations in Chicago on behalf of their creditors and "established in the Supreme Court of Illinois the then novel doctrine that banks must hold the entire funds of the garnished depositor for the benefit of all the creditors who may thereafter perfect a claim" (*Chicago Legal News*, Jan. 18, 1896, p. 169). From 1890 until his death he was associated with John S. Miller, under a succession of firm names and with several other individuals as partners. In Washington, D. C.,

he maintained offices from 1925 to 1931, as a member of the firms of Hopkins, Starr & Hopkins, and (1926–29) Hopkins, Starr, Hopkins & Hamel.

Starr was a trustee of Oberlin College, 1893–1924, and a trustee of the National College of Education, Evanston, Ill., 1922–31, being president of its board, 1926–31. To the latter institution he gave most of his valuable library, and he contributed unstintingly of his time and legal counsel to both Oberlin and the National College of Education. He was a member of the board of managers of the Chicago Law Institute, 1888–90, and its president, 1896–97; a member of the executive committee of the Civil Service Reform Association of Chicago, 1884–1914; and president of the Chicago Literary Club, 1910–11. Much interested in local affairs, he was village attorney of Winnetka, Ill., 1894–95, a member of the Winnetka board of education, 1899–1907, and its president, 1900–05. On Sept. 8, 1885, he married Leila Wheelock, whom he had met at Oberlin College. They had four children, three of whom survived him.

[B. P. Starr, *A Hist. of the Starr Family of New England* (1879); *The Past and Present of Rock Island County, Ill.* (1877); J. M. Palmer, *The Bench and Bar of Ill.* (1899), I, 100; *Chicago Legal News*, Jan. 18, 1896; *Who's Who in Jurisprudence*, 1925; *Chicago Literary Club: Yearbook*, 1932–33; *Chicago Bar Asso. Record*, Jan.–Mar. 1932; *Our Guidon* (Nat. Coll. of Educ.), Aug. 1931; *Oberlin College Alumni Necrology*, 1930–31; *Who's Who in Chicago*, 1931; *Twenty-fifth Anniversary Report . . . Class of 1881 of Harvard College* (1906); *Ann. Report Ill. State Bar Asso.*, 1932; *Who's Who in America*, 1930–31; *Chicago Daily Tribune*, Aug. 4, 1931.]

J. K. W.

STARR, MOSES ALLEN (May 16, 1854–Sept. 4, 1932), neurologist, was born in Brooklyn, N. Y. He was the son of Egbert and Charlotte Augusta (Allen) Starr, of Middlebury, Vt. His first American ancestor was Dr. Comfort Starr of Ashford, County Kent, England, who came to Boston, Mass., in 1635 and settled in Warren, Conn. His early education was received in a private school in Orange, N. J., and he received the B.A. degree from Princeton University in 1876. During the whole period of his undergraduate study he was second honor man and after his graduation he was offered a professorship of history. With the intention of pursuing this subject he studied in Germany under Mommsen and Curtius, but he also attended the lectures of Helmholz and McCosh, developing a special interest in psychology and the functions of the nervous system, and upon his return to America he decided to prepare for a medical career. He entered the College of Physicians and Surgeons in New York City, received the M.D. degree in 1880, and spent the next two years as an interne in Bellevue Hospital. After this he again went to Germany and became a student of the renowned neurologists, Erb and Schultze, in Heidelberg, later continuing his studies in Vienna with Nothnagel and Meynert. His first important publication appeared soon after his return to America. The article, "The Sensory Tract in the Central Nervous System," was awarded the Alumni Association Prize of the College of Physicians and Surgeons in May 1884, and was published in the *Journal of Nervous and Mental Disease,* July 1884.

In 1884 he was appointed professor of anatomy and physiology at the New York Polyclinic Medical College and in 1886 was made Professor of Nervous Diseases. He retained this position for three years and then resigned to accept the professorship of diseases of the mind and nervous system in the College of Physicians and Surgeons, a chair which he held with distinction until 1915 when he became professor emeritus. His early work as an investigator was on cerebral localization, a field in which he was one of the American pioneers. He contributed to the localization of visual function, and of the senses of touch, pain, and temperature in the parietal region, and also to the problem of aphasia. He was one of the first in America to investigate brain tumors and with Dr. Charles McBurney published in 1895 an analysis of fifty brain tumors: *Tumor of the Corpus Callosum.* His *Atlas of Nerve Cells* (1896) received favorable reviews in all parts of the world. He also published one hundred special articles covering a wide range of neurological subjects and several important systematic works, *Familiar Forms of Nervous Disease* (1890), *Brain Surgery* (1893), *Organic and Functional Nervous Diseases* (1903). He held many important hospital positions as consultant, among them the Presbyterian Hospital, St. Vincent's, St. Mary's Free Hospital for Children, St. John's Hospital, Yonkers, the New York Eye and Ear Infirmary, and the Neurological Institute of New York. He was president of the New York Neurological Society, 1894–97, of the American Neurological Association, 1896–97, and was a vice-president of the New York Academy of Medicine, 1903–06. He was an honorary member of the Neurological Section of the Royal Society of London, and of French, German, and Austrian neurological and psychological societies. He also received many academic honors during his active career. Starr was particularly noted as a teacher, and his clinics at the College of Physicians and Surgeons were famous in a day when neurology was in its early evolution as a special

field of medicine. He was married to Alice Dunning on June 7, 1898, and one of their two children survived him.

[Personal acquaintance; *Who's Who in America,* 1930–31; B. P. Starr, *A Hist. of the Starr Family* (1879); Frederick Tilney, article in the *Jour. of Nervous and Mental Disease,* Feb. 1933; Frederick Peterson, in *Bull. of the N. Y. Acad. of Med.,* Nov. 1932; L. Casamajor, in *Arch. of Neurology and Psychiatry,* Dec. 1932; John Shrady, ed., *The Coll. of Physicians and Surgeons* (n.d.), vol. I; *N. Y. Times,* Apr. 5, 1912, Sept. 5, 1932.]   J. R. H.

STARRETT, LAROY S. (Apr. 25, 1836–Apr. 23, 1922), inventor, manufacturer, was born on his father's farm at China, Me., one of the twelve children of Daniel D. and Anna (Crummett) Starrett, both of Scotch ancestry. He worked on the farm in his youth, attended public school during the winter months, and developed a marked interest in mechanics. When he was seventeen years old he went to work on a stock farm at Vassalboro, Me., and later on a dairy farm at Newburyport, Mass., to help support the family. After about eight years he acquired for himself a six-hundred acre stock farm in Newburyport, which he operated for four years. He tried his hand at invention during this time and devised among other things a meat chopper, for which he was granted patent No. 47,875 on May 23, 1865. Shortly after obtaining the patent he made an arrangement with the Athol Machine Company, Athol, Mass., to manufacture his chopper while he undertook its sale in Maine. His success was so great that three years later he sold his farm, moved to Athol, purchased a controlling interest in the manufacturing company, and reorganized it for the special purpose of manufacturing his meat chopper, as well as a washing machine and a butter worker which he had patented in 1865 (patents No. 48,458 and 49,953).

In the period of more than ten years in which he served as superintendent of the Athol Machine Company, he invented a number of hand tools useful in the building trades. The first of these was a combination square which contained a steel rule, graduated into small parts of an inch on both sides, with a sliding head capable of being moved along the rule or detached entirely from it; with the aid of the head it could be used as a square or mitre, as a bevel, and as a plumb bob. Shortly after patenting this (May 6, 1879), he established a business of his own on a small scale to manufacture it, and experienced slow but positive success. During the eighties he devised and patented a center try-square, a surface gauge, a bevelling instrument, a micrometer caliper square, and a new type of dividers, manufacturing each as it was patented.

Since the products were marketed and sold in increasing numbers, he was obliged to enlarge his plant a number of times. In 1882 the establishment of agencies in England, Germany, France, and other countries helped to increase his business materially and to establish his name the world over as a maker of fine tools. By 1906 he was employing about one thousand people in a great general manufacturing plant in Athol and in a caliper manufacturing plant at Springfield, Mass. He manufactured steel rules in a large variety of styles, and in both English and metric graduations; many different styles of squares; almost two hundred varieties of calipers and dividers; and such articles as bevels, surface and depth gauges, levels, steel tapes, plumb bobs, hacksaw frames and blades, as well as a number of unique precision instruments. In 1912 his company was incorporated with a capital stock of $3,500,000 as the L. S. Starrett Company, of which he was president until his death. His whole life was centered in his business and in the Methodist Church, his outstanding contribution to the latter being the gift of a new parsonage, a pipe organ, and a church building in Athol. He married Lydia W. Bartlett of Newburyport, Mass., on Apr. 20, 1861. At the time of his death at his winter home in St. Petersburg, Fla., he was survived by four children.

[L. B. Caswell, *Athol, Mass., Past and Present* (1899); D. H. Hurd, *Hist. of Worcester County, Mass.,* vol. II (1889); E. B. Crane, *Hist. of Worcester County, Mass.,* vol. II (1924); obituary in *Boston Transcript,* Apr. 24, 1922; Patent Office records.]   C. W. M—n.

STARRETT, WILLIAM AIKEN (June 14, 1877–Mar. 26, 1932), engineer, financier, builder, architect, was born in Lawrence, Kan., one of seven children of William Aiken and Helen (Ekin) Starrett. His grandfather and great-grandfather (of Scotch origin) had been carpenters and stone masons in and near Pittsburgh and Allegheny, Pa. His father, Presbyterian minister though he was, did not lose touch with the building tradition; he had, it is said, built his church, shared in the building of the first structure of the University of Kansas, and not only built but designed his own house. All five of his sons in their turn became builders of importance. Educated in local schools, in Chicago, and at the University of Michigan (1893–95), Starrett worked for a time in a wholesale grocery house, became a timekeeper for the George A. Fuller Company, general contractors, of which his brother Paul was a member, and by 1899 had risen to the position of a superintendent. From 1901 to 1913 he was vice-president of the famous Thompson-Starrett Company, New York, found-

ed by his brothers Theodore and Ralph, for many years one of the two or three largest and most successful firms engaged in constructing skyscrapers, large commercial buildings, and factories. For five years, 1913–18, he was a partner in the architectural firm of Starrett and Van Vleck, which designed numerous commercial buildings, among them the Kaufmann and Baer department store in Pittsburgh (1915), and the Lasalle and Koch store in Toledo (1916).

In 1917 he was appointed head of the emergency construction section of the War Industries Board, charged with the construction of camps, hospitals, army bases, flying fields. With the building industry in a chaotic state, to build $150,000,000 worth of cantonments in three months seemed almost impossible; yet under his direction the buildings began to rise all over the country with amazing rapidity. Nominal profits of contractors were held within 3⅔ per cent., an extraordinary achievement. Construction under these conditions was of necessity extremely costly, however, and after the war was the subject of congressional investigation, in the course of which inexcusable and unwarranted accusations were made against Starrett, only to be proved groundless. After his discharge from the army, a colonel in the quartermaster corps, he became vice-president of the George A. Fuller Company, and directed the construction of a number of large office buildings in Tokio, especially designed to resist earthquakes. In 1922 with two of his brothers and Andrew J. Eken he founded the contracting firm of Starrett Brothers, Inc. (later Starrett Brothers and Eken, Inc.), builders of some of the most important American skyscrapers of the time, among them the nineteen-story Starrett Lehigh Terminal Building in New York, the Carew Tower in Cincinnati, Ohio, the forty-story Ramsey Tower in Oklahoma City, Okla., the seventy-story 40 Wall Street Building in New York, and the Empire State Building in New York. Starrett was perhaps the chief financial and business executive in this work. When the Starrett Corporation (N. Y.) was formed to handle the Starretts' large interests, which had branched out from pure construction to financing, he became president and as such coordinator of all their companies. He died in Madison, N. J., where he made his home. He was survived by his wife, Eloise Gedney of East Orange, N. J., whom he had married on June 14, 1900, and by a son and a daughter. He was a member of the Society of Military Engineers, the American Society of Civil Engineers, the American Society of Mechanical Engineers, and from 1914 to 1918 of the

American Institute of Architects. In 1917 he received the degree of B.S. in civil engineering as of the class of 1897 from the University of Michigan.

A gifted and persuasive writer, he contributed from time to time to magazines such things as "Marked 'Shop'" (*Atlantic Monthly,* July 1917), a story; "Building for Victory" (*Scribner's Magazine,* Nov. 1918), a description of his government work; and "New Construction in an Ancient Empire" (*Scribner's Magazine,* Sept. 1923), an account of his work in Japan. His *Skyscrapers and the Men Who Build Them* (1928) contains a brief history of the skyscraper, a vivid description of the tremendous complexity and the careful organization necessary in the building industry, and a simple exposition of the various trades and their part in the erection of a modern steel-frame structure. Perhaps the best popular exposition of the subject that has been produced, it is written with verve, drive, power. Of Starrett himself it reveals much. The chapters devoted to the financing of large buildings make strange and ironical reading in a time of depression. He seemed completely oblivious to all city-planning values except the financial, and quite overlooked the danger of unchecked speculation. Thus he writes, "There are opportunities in New York, Chicago, or any other large metropolis, for an enterprising operator to run a shoe-string into a fortune legitimately in one enterprise" (*Skyscrapers and the Men Who Build Them,* p. 110). He has been called "a great business executive with an engineering background" (*New York Times,* Mar. 27, 1932), and in all his connections—contracting, governmental, architectural—it was his power as an executive that distinguished him. As long as there was a job to do, to the doing of it he brought tremendous energy and clear vision; his imagination in his own line was vivid, his judgment acute and sure. But in the wider implications of the job, he had, apparently, little interest. He was essentially an executive, not a designer; a man of action rather than a man of thought.

[*Who's Who in America,* 1930–31; *Who's Who in Engineering,* 1931; A. R. Palmer, in *Trans. Am. Soc. of Civil Engineers,* vol. XCVIII (1933); "The Contributors' Column," in *Atlantic Monthly,* July 1917; *Architectural Record,* Apr. 1932, with portrait; letter signed G. C., in *N. Y. Times,* Mar. 31, 1932; obituary in *Herald Tribune* (N. Y.), Mar. 27, 1932; information from Ernest A. Van Vleck.]   T. F. H.

STATLER, ELLSWORTH MILTON (Oct. 26, 1863–Apr. 16, 1928), hotel owner, was born in Somerset County, Pa., the son of William Jackson and Mary (McKinney) Statler. His father, a German Reformed clergyman, tried to piece out his income by farming, but the family was large and the living was still hard. When Ellsworth was five his family moved to Bridgeport, Ohio, and at nine the boy went to work in a glass factory across the river in Wheeling, W. Va., where he endured intense heat for a wage of fifty cents—rising later to ninety cents—a day. At thirteen he found a position as bell-boy in a hotel in Wheeling, the McClure House. There he began polishing his manners and his language, taking the hotel bartender as his model at first, and advanced to the position of night clerk, then to that of day clerk; meanwhile he studied bookkeeping and the details of hotel management. He was not yet of age when he took over the billiard room and railroad-ticket concession in the hotel. A little later he opened a combination lunch room, billiard hall, and barber shop in Wheeling, from which he derived a comfortable yearly income.

In 1896 he bought the restaurant concession in the Ellicott Square Building, Buffalo, N. Y., and prospered with it. During the Pan-American Exposition in Buffalo, he built and operated a temporary frame hotel of 2,100 rooms near the exposition grounds. Though he made no profit on the venture, he acquired both reputation and experience, and in 1904 won the privilege of erecting the famous Inside Inn on the grounds of the Louisiana Purchase Exposition in St. Louis, Mo., upon which he cleared $280,000 profit. Before the summer was over he began building a hotel in Buffalo, the Statler (later the Buffalo), the first in the country in which each room had running ice-water and a bath. The cardinal rule of the house, and afterwards of his entire business, was "The guest is always right." He later built the New Statler in Buffalo and in rapid succession a Statler hotel each in St. Louis, Mo., Cleveland, Ohio, and Detroit, Mich., and took over the management of the Hotel Pennsylvania in New York. His last achievement was the Hotel Statler of Boston, opened in March 1927. He originated the practice of slipping a morning newspaper under the door of each guest's room, and is said to have been the first to install a radio connection in every room of a hotel. Several other devices to promote the ease and good will of guests were his, and his name became a symbol for comfort, courtesy, and efficient service. At his death his hotel properties were the largest owned by one man, their annual receipts being estimated at $25,000,000. In 1926 he was decorated by the French government with the Cross of the Legion of Honor. He was for several years president of the Hotel Men's Mutual Benefit Association of the United States and Canada. He was married twice: on Apr. 16, 1895, to Mary I. Manderbach (d. 1925) of Akron, Ohio, and on Apr. 30, 1927, to Alice M. Seidler, who had been his secretary for many years. He died in New York City of pneumonia, survived by his wife and by three of the four children he and his first wife had adopted.

[*Who's Who in America*, 1926–27; Walter Tittle, in *World's Work*, Nov. 1927; E. M. Statler, in *Am. Mag.*, May 1917, and *Mag. of Business*, Sept. 1927; *N. Y. Times*, May 1, 1927 (second marriage), Apr. 17, 18 (obituary and editorial), May 19 (will), 1928; obituaries and editorials in *N. Y. Herald Tribune* and *World* (N. Y.), Apr. 17, 1928.]   A. F. H.

STAUFFER, DAVID MCNEELY (Mar. 24, 1845–Feb. 5, 1913), civil engineer, editor, collector, author, was born in Richland, now the borough of Mount Joy, Lancaster County, Pa. His father, Jacob Stauffer, a patent lawyer and naturalist of reputation, was a descendant of John Stauffer, who emigrated from Switzerland to Pennsylvania in 1710; his mother, Mary Ann Knox McNeely, was of a Scotch-Irish family that settled in Pennsylvania about 1721. Graduating from the high school at Lancaster in 1862, at the head of his class, David was granted a scholarship in Franklin and Marshall College, but on Sept. 12, 1862, enlisted for service in the Civil War and saw action almost at once in the Antietam campaign. He subsequently attended classes for a while at the college, but could not remain out of the service, and early in 1864 was appointed a master's mate in the United States Navy and ordered to the *Alexandria* in the Mississippi Squadron under Rear Admiral David Dixon Porter [*q.v.*]. As mate he later commanded the same vessel, in May 1865 he was listed as acting ensign, and on Nov. 1, 1865, was honorably discharged.

At once he began his engineering career as rodman on surveys for the Columbia & Port Deposit Railroad in eastern Pennsylvania. He continued on surveys and construction work successively as assistant engineer of the Philadelphia & Reading Railroad and division engineer of the Allentown Railroad from 1868 until 1870, when the boom in railroad construction collapsed. Subsequently, from August 1870 until its completion in February 1876, he served as assistant engineer and consultant in the construction of the South Street Bridge over the Schuylkill River, Philadelphia. In this work he used compressed-air caissons in sinking foundations, a method which at the time was comparatively new to the United States, and his paper, "The Use of Compressed Air in Tubular Foundations" (*Journal of the Franklin Institute*, November

1872), based on study of the French and English practice, was used for a time as a textbook in several engineering schools. A fuller description of the work at South Street Bridge was published after its completion in the *Transactions of the American Society of Civil Engineers* (vol. VII, 1878). Meanwhile, as assistant chief engineer on the Bound Brook line of the Philadelphia & Reading Railroad, Stauffer had special charge of the construction of the Delaware Bridge, and upon its completion, June 1, 1876, he engaged in private practice, during which he made bridge plans for the City of Philadelphia. Beginning on Apr. 15, 1877, he was construction engineer for the Philadelphia Water Department, building the Frankford reservoir and pumping stations. Late in 1879 with the contractor R. A. Malone, he undertook the construction of the Dorchester Bay sewage tunnel at Boston, an inverted siphon some 9,000 feet long, with a bottom 180 feet below sea level. The seepage through the rock roof was so great that an enormous pumping plant involving large expense was necessary. The engineering problems he encountered are described in Stauffer's paper, "Shaft Sinking Under Difficulties at Dorchester Bay Tunnel" (*Transactions of the American Society of Civil Engineers*, vol. X, 1881). In December 1880, when the tunnel was nearly finished, he sold his interest in the contract to his partner, returned to Philadelphia, and was associated with the Philadelphia Bridge Works until September 1882, when he resigned and opened an office in New York as consulting engineer. In January 1883, he bought an interest in *Engineering News*, with which he was connected in an editorial capacity until he sold his interest in 1907. In addition to his contributions to the technical magazines and transactions of professional societies, he was the author of *Modern Tunnel Practice* (1906).

Stauffer will be remembered for his avocations almost as much as for his professional success. He traveled extensively and was an enthusiastic collector of autographic and illustrative material relating to the colonial and revolutionary history of America, and in connection with his collecting made thousands of pen-and-ink and water-color drawings. He designed a number of bookplates (see *D. McN. Stauffer: His Bookplates*, n.d.). Many of the illustrations in *Engineering News* were from his pen. Early in his career he began a collection of thousands of prints illustrating the first four centuries of the art of engraving on wood and copper, and in his later years this hobby absorbed most of his time and energy. In 1907 he published *American Engrav-*

ers upon Copper and Steel (2 vols.), which remains a standard work in its field. He was also interested in public affairs, and was long a member of the Palisades Interstate Park Commission for the preservation of the Palisades of the Hudson River. On Apr. 19, 1892, he married Florence Scribner, daughter of G. Hilton Scribner, secretary of state of New York under Governor Dix. He died at his home in Yonkers.

[*Who's Who in America*, 1912–13; J. W. Jordan, in *Pa. Mag. of Hist. and Biog.*, Apr. 1913; *Engineering News*, Feb. 13, 1913; *Sun* (N. Y.), Feb. 7, 1913.]
B. A. R.

STAUGHTON, WILLIAM (Jan. 4, 1770–Dec. 12, 1829), Baptist minister and educator, was born at Coventry, Warwickshire, England, the oldest child of Sutton and Keziah Staughton. At seventeen he entered Bristol Baptist College, where he showed such promise that in 1793 he was called to the church at Northampton to succeed Dr. John Ryland, who became president at Bristol. He early looked to America as his future field of labor, so when Dr. Richard Furman [*q.v.*] wrote to Dr. John Rippon of London asking him to suggest "a young man of promise and character" (Lynd, *post*, p. 27) for South Carolina, he went supported by strong commendations. He arrived at Charleston, S. C., in the fall of 1793 and there married Maria Hanson before January 1794. They had six children. For about a year and a half he supplied at Georgetown, S. C., a church soon being formed. In the summer of 1795 he went to New York, became head of an academy at Bordentown, N. J., and on June 17, 1797, was ordained there. Moving in 1798 to Burlington, where there was a larger academy, he organized a small Baptist church which he served as pastor. He edited several works in the classics and for his talents received the degree of Doctor of Divinity from the College of New Jersey (later Princeton). After a tour in the West, where he considered settling, he was called in 1805 to the First Baptist Church in Philadelphia. Although several groups were dismissed to form other churches, there was a relatively large increase in membership. In 1811, partly on account of some internal tension over his English birth (superficially indicated by the remark of the sexton regarding a smoking stove, "There must be an Englishman in the stovepipe"), he became pastor of what was known as the Sansom Street Baptist Church, a new church in the western part of the city. In 1814 he took an active part in organizing the Triennial Convention and as its corresponding secretary until 1826, was concerned with the constant and varied problems of the foreign missionary enterprise.

As the need for better-trained ministers stirred the Baptists to provide schools for their education, it was to Staughton they turned for practical leadership. For many years he had been taking young men into his home in Philadelphia to begin their theological education; with the formation in 1812 of the Baptist Education Society of the Middle States, he was designated its tutor. So intimate was his connection with it that the educational institution could hardly be distinguished from his home. His reputation as a classical scholar was heightened by his editions of *The Works of Virgil . . . To Which is Added a Large Variety of Botanical, Mythological, and Historical Notes,* and of Edward Wetenhall's *A Compendious System of Greek Grammar,* both published in 1813. When the Triennial Convention took up its educational task more definitely in 1817, the incipient institution at Philadelphia was recognized as its theological department, with Staughton as principal and Irah Chase [*q.v.*] as professor of languages and Biblical literature. More definite plans for the organization of what was soon called Columbian College (later George Washington University) were adopted in 1818, but the transfer to Washington, D. C., was not made until September 1821. Staughton remained most of the time in Philadelphia until the fall of 1823, although he was installed as president on Jan. 9, 1822, with professorial responsibilities in "General History, Belles Lettres, Rhetoric and Moral Philosophy" in the classical department, and in "Divinity and Pulpit Eloquence" in the theological department. From the beginning he visualized a university of national scope rendering service broader than that required by denominational needs, a conception which found its correlate in the world-mission ideal so dominant in Luther Rice [*q.v.*], the chief financial agent for the college. The effective forces in the development of collegiate education during that period, however, were largely stimulated by denominational loyalties and local economic considerations, rarely entirely divorced from speculative land interests. Competing educational institutions were rapidly forming, financial complications arose, and in 1829 Staughton resigned the presidency. He was soon chosen president of Georgetown College in Kentucky. Starting for his new field, he died as he was passing through Washington. A few months before his death, on Aug. 27, 1829, he married Anna Claypoole Peale [*q.v.*], who survived him. Hampered as he was later at Columbian College, he nevertheless achieved a far-reaching and significant educational influence during the years at Philadelphia, when largely through his own direct personal instruction he trained young men who became outstanding leaders in religion and education.

[The standard work on Staughton is that by his son-in-law, the Rev. S. W. Lynd, *Memoir of the Rev. William Staughton, D.D.* (1834), which contains much source material; little is added in W. B. Sprague, *Annals Am. Pulpit,* vol. VI (1860), and William Cathcart, *The Baptist Encyc.* (1881). For a few other details, see a letter by Irah Chase, in *Baptist Memorial,* Apr. 15, 1842, and obituary in *Daily Nat. Intelligencer* (Washington, D. C.), Dec. 14, 1829.]   W. H. A.

STAYTON, JOHN WILLIAM (Dec. 24, 1830–July 5, 1894), jurist, was born in Washington County, Ky., the son of Robert G. and Harriet (Pirtle) Stayton, both descendants of early settlers of the state. When he was two years old the family removed to Paducah in the western part of Kentucky, a region then sparsely settled. The death of his father two years later placed the burden of his support and education on his mother. Her death in 1844 left him an orphan at the age of fourteen. The next four years were spent on his grandfather's farm, where he performed farm labor during the summer and attended the country schools in the autumn and winter. He also read all the books he could find.

At the age of seventeen he made up his mind to prepare himself for the bar. Since his guardian was unwilling that he should spend his meager resources on a college education, he left the farm and apprenticed himself to a blacksmith in order to learn the trade and earn the money to pay for his legal training. Upon attaining his majority he continued to work at his trade and at the same time carried on a systematic course of study. At twenty-four he began reading law under the written direction of his mother's brother, Henry Pirtle of Louisville, Ky. In the fall of 1855 he entered the law school of Louisville University, from which he was graduated the following March with the degree of bachelor of laws. In November 1856 he removed to Texas, settling the following year at Pleasanton, south of San Antonio, where for a time he operated a blacksmith shop and conducted a law office. His law practice, however, soon absorbed all his time and energies. In 1858 he was elected to the office of district attorney and was reëlected in 1860. At the end of his term of office he enlisted in the Confederate army as a private in Capt. Lewis Maverick's company, but later he was commissioned to raise a company of cavalry, which he commanded during the remainder of the war. Immediately after the war, since the courts were all closed, he earned a livelihood by teaching school for a year. In 1866, in partnership with Samuel C. Lackey, he opened a law office at Clinton, Tex., then the county seat of DeWitt County. In 1871 Maj. A. H. Phillips of Victoria was admitted to the partnership, the firm name becoming Phillips, Lackey & Stayton, and Stayton removed with his family to Victoria. Phillips in 1878 retired and two years later Stayton's son, Robert Weldon, and R. J. Kleberg joined the firm, which was thereafter known as Staytons, Lackey & Kleberg. In 1875 Stayton served as a member of the constitutional convention. Gov. O. M. Roberts appointed him associate justice of the supreme court in 1881 to fill the vacancy caused by the resignation of Chief Justice George F. Moore, and he was elected for a full term the following year. In 1888, upon the retirement of Asa H. Willie [*q.v.*], he became chief justice. In this position he served most acceptably until his death some six years later at the home of his daughter, at Tyler.

In 1856, immediately after his graduation from law school, he married Eliza Jane ("Jennie") Weldon, daughter of Abraham and Mary Jane (Rutter) Weldon, and grand-niece of United States Attorney-General Felix Grundy [*q.v.*]. They had one son and two daughters, all of whom survived him. A grandson, Robert Weldon Stayton, served for several years on the commission of appeals of the supreme court, and became professor of law at the University of Texas.

[87 *Texas Reports,* v–xviii; J. D. Lynch, *The Bench and Bar of Tex.* (1885); L. E. Daniell, *Personnel of Tex. State Gov., with Sketches of Representative Men of Tex.* (1892), pp. 80–81; J. H. Davenport, *The Hist. of the Supreme Court of the State of Tex.* (copr. 1917); *Dallas Morning News,* and *Houston Post,* July 6, 1894; information from grandson.]   C. S. P—s.

STEARNS, ABEL (Feb. 9, 1798–Aug. 23, 1871), California pioneer, was born in Lunenburg, Mass., the son of Levi and Elizabeth (Goodrich) Stearns, and a descendant of Isaac Stearns who emigrated from England to Salem, Mass., in 1630. About 1826 he went to Mexico, where he became naturalized. In July 1829 he arrived at Monterey, expecting to obtain a land grant. Suspected by the Mexican governor, Manuel Victoria, of some political design, he was banished, but in 1831 he returned and joined in the movement by which Victoria was overthrown. Two years later he settled in Los Angeles as a trader in hides and liquors, and grew prosperous, though he was often in trouble with the authorities because of alleged smuggling. He was chosen *sindico* (fiscal agent) of the village in 1836. Ordered by Gov. Mariano Chico to leave the country, he joined in a revolution which placed Juan Bautista Alvarado in power and made California for two years (1836–38) an independent republic. About 1840 he married Maria Francisca Paula Arcadia Bandini, a woman of great beauty and charm, and soon afterward acquired the extensive Los Alamitos ranch. In November 1842, more than five years before the discoveries on the American River, he sent to the Philadelphia mint twenty ounces of gold taken from the San Feliciano placers, near the present Newhall. He engaged in stock-raising, bought more lands, and by the time of the conquest was doubtless the wealthiest man in California. He built the most imposing residence in the village, which he named *El Palacio,* and entertained lavishly. In 1844–45 he took part in the revolution which expelled Gov. Manuel Micheltorena. Hating the Mexicans but admiring the Californians, he sided with the party that was attempting to bring California into the Union by peaceful means. With the outbreak of hostilities in 1846, however, he remained neutral, and in the following year, under American rule, became again the village *sindico.* He was a member of the constitutional convention of 1849. In 1858 he built the Arcadia block, the largest and most expensive structure south of San Francisco. Although during the drought of 1864 he suffered staggering losses, before his death seven years later he managed to recover much of his former wealth. He died suddenly at the Grand Hotel in San Francisco and was buried in Los Angeles. His wife survived him; there were no children.

He was a tall, well-formed man, with a homely visage which won him the nickname of *Cara de Caballo,* "Horse-Face." A personal encounter in 1835 had left him with a scar about the mouth and an impediment in his speech. He was quick-tempered, with strong prejudices, but was hospitable and generous. At various times he held local political office. He was deeply interested in education, and just before his death had planned to establish a foundation at the projected University of Southern California.

[A. S. Van Wagenen, *Geneal. and Memoirs of Isaac Stearns and His Descendants* (1901); H. H. Bancroft, *Hist. of Cal.,* vol. V (1886), pp. 732–33; *Sixty Years in Southern Cal.* (2nd ed., 1926), ed. by M. H. and M. R. Newmark; *A Hist. of Cal. and an Extended Hist. of Los Angeles and Environs* (1915), vol. III, ed. by J. M. Guinn; C. D. Willard, *The Herald's Hist. of Los Angeles City* (1901); H. D. Barrows, "Don Abel Stearns," *Hist. Soc. of Southern Cal. Pubs.,* vol. IV (1897–99); obituary in *Daily Alta California* (San Francisco), Aug. 24, 1871.]   W. J. G.

STEARNS, ASAHEL (June 17, 1774–Feb. 5, 1839), lawyer, descended from Isaac Stearns who became a freeman of Watertown, Mass., in 1631, was born in Lunenburg, Worcester County, Mass., the son of the Hon. Josiah and Mary (Corey) Stearns and a first cousin of Abel

Stearns [*q.v.*]. After graduating from Harvard College in 1797 he studied law in the office of Timothy Bigelow, of Groton. In 1800 he married Frances Wentworth (Whitney) Shepard, daughter of Benjamin Whitney of Hollis, N. H., and widow of Daniel Shepard. They had a son and a daughter who grew to maturity.

Settling after his marriage in that part of Chelmsford which is now Lowell, Mass., Stearns practised law there until 1815, when he moved to Charlestown. In 1813 he had been appointed district attorney for Middlesex County, in which position he served until 1832, except for the period 1815–17, when he represented his district in Congress. In 1817–18 he served also as representative in the General Court, and in 1830–31 as state senator.

By 1817 his character and attainments as a sound and scholarly lawyer had so impressed the community that when in that year the Harvard Law School was established under Chief Justice Isaac Parker [*q.v.*] Stearns was appointed University Professor of Law. He accepted the appointment with diffidence; the venture was an experiment, and in practice it amounted to the opening of an office by Stearns in connection with the university, in which he devoted part of his time to delivering lectures, conducting moot courts, and otherwise supervising the work of the students. Although he was not very successful, he retained the post of professor until the reorganization of the law school in 1829, when under Joseph Story and John Hooker Ashmun [*qq.v.*] its real history as an educational force began. Stearns's professorship was not wholly unproductive, however, for in connection with his teaching he prepared a series of lectures, the substance of which he published in 1824 under the title, *A Summary of the Law and Practice of Real Actions.* This work proved to be one of the notable early American law books and was welcomed by a bar in need of accurate available information on technical procedure.

While Stearns was not successful as a pioneer law professor, his reputation as a sound lawyer continued, and in 1832 he was appointed one of the commissioners under the chairmanship of Charles Jackson [*q.v.*] to make the first real revision of the Massachusetts statutes. Adopted, with few changes, by the legislature on Nov. 4, 1835, *The Revised Statutes of the Commonwealth of Massachusetts* (1836) set a standard for such work and, with the commissioners' notes accompanying their report, remains of great practical value to the courts and to the bar. Stearns had previously, as joint commissioner with Lemuel Shaw [*q.v.*], compiled the fourth and fifth volumes (1823) of *Private and Special Statutes of . . . Massachusetts*. His health began to fail about 1836 and although in 1837 he presided over a board of arbitration of an important case from the state of Maine, he gradually retired from active work and died in 1839. In addition to his professional activities, he was an officer in various banks and in 1833 was treasurer of the Society for Propagating the Gospel Among the Indians.

[A portrait of Stearns by Harding is in the possession of the Harvard Law School. For biog. data see *Law Reporter*, Apr. 1839; *The Centennial Hist. of the Harvard Law School, 1817–1917* (1918); A. P. Peabody, *Harvard Reminiscences* (1888); *Biog. Dir. Am. Cong.* (1928); A. S. Van Wagenen, *Geneal. and Memoirs of Isaac Stearns and His Descendants* (1901); *Boston Daily Advertiser*, Feb. 8, 1839.]   F. W. G.

STEARNS, EBEN SPERRY (Dec. 23, 1819–Apr. 11, 1887), educator, was born in Bedford, Mass., the youngest son of the Rev. Samuel and Abigail (French) Stearns. He was descended from a long line of clergymen and teachers, the original ancestor in America having been Isaac Stearns, who came from England and settled in Watertown, Mass., in 1630. Three of his brothers also became clergymen, one of whom was William Augustus Stearns [q.v.]. Eben, who gave up the use of his name Ebenezer for the shorter form early in youth, was graduated from the Phillips Academy, Andover, Mass., in 1837, and received the B.A. degree from Harvard in 1841. He taught in a school for young women at Ipswich, Mass., and at Portland, Me., before receiving the M.A. degree from Harvard in 1846. Afterwards he organized and acted as principal of the Newburyport, Mass., Female High School until 1849, when he succeeded Cyrus Peirce [q.v.] as principal of the normal school at West Newton. He remained as principal when the school, the first of its kind in the United States, was moved to Framingham in 1853. Two years later he was elected principal of the Albany (New York) Female Academy, where he remained until he was appointed the first president of the Robinson Female Academy at Exeter, N. H., in 1869. A strict disciplinarian, he often quoted to students and visitors that "order is heaven's first law." In addition to the usual normal and classical studies, he inaugurated and taught personally a class in household science.

In September 1875 he was selected by officials of the Peabody Fund as first president of the new State Normal School at Nashville, Tenn., and a few months later he was appointed, by the board of trust, Chancellor of the University of Nashville. At his inauguration the school had thirteen pupils; when he died it had over two hun-

dred. At the beginning any prospective teacher, regardless of previous training, could enter the school if he could pass an elementary examination, but he soon raised that standard so that high school graduates only were admitted. Stearns was an ardent missionary of popular education, and emphasized in many speeches that free government was based on the intelligence of its people. He rapidly prepared teachers to meet the new demand in the South and kept in close touch, through correspondence and occasional tours, with Southern schools and county superintendents of education, all of his work being accomplished under the close supervision of the Peabody Fund. He also made a vigorous effort to beautify Southern colleges, and tree-planting became a yearly rite at Nashville. He prevented the removal of the State Normal College, as it came to be known in 1878, to Georgia in 1880, and secured from a reluctant legislature the first grant of aid to the state normal school. A colorless but efficient administrator, Stearns left small imprint of his own personality on the school. The first two years he taught didactics; after that he was concerned only with administrative problems. In that field he was highly successful, leaving the school in good financial condition. He was indefatigable in trying to raise educational standards throughout the South. He was married to Ellen Augusta Kuhn, of Boston, on Aug. 27, 1854; she died in 1873. He was again married in 1880 to Betty Irwin, of Marianna, Fla. Their only child died in infancy, but his widow and three children of his first wife survived him. He is buried at Boston, Mass.

[Information from the family; Stearns's scrapbook and correspondence in the Peabody College Library, Nashville, Tenn.; Avis Stearns Van Wagenen, *Geneal. and Memoirs of Isaac Stearns and His Descendants* (1901); R. C. Winthrop, *Tribute to Eben Sperry Stearns* (1887); C. M. Fuess, *Men of Andover* (1928); E. S. Stearns, *Hist. Sketch of the Normal Coll.* (1885); L. S. Merriam, *Higher Education in Tenn., Bur. of Education, Circular of Information, No. 5* (1893); R. H. White, *Development of the Tenn. State Educ. Organization* (1929); *Daily American*, Nashville, Apr. 12, 1887.]   E. W. P.

STEARNS, FREDERIC PIKE (Nov. 11, 1851–Dec. 1, 1919), civil engineer, son of William Henry Clark Stearns and Mary (Hobbs) Hill Stearns, was born at Calais, Me. He was a descendant of Isaac Stearns, who became a freeman of Watertown, Mass., in 1631. After attending the Calais public schools he worked for a short time for a local business concern, but when he was eighteen went to Boston, found a job with the city engineering department, and began to study civil engineering. Here he came under the influence of such able engineers as James B. Francis and Hiram F. Mills [qq.v.], and by his diligence and power of application gained proficiency in his field and laid a solid foundation for later achievement.

By 1872 he was engaged in responsible work upon the Sudbury River water supply of Boston and in 1880 he became division engineer on the sewage tunnel under Dorchester Bay. In 1886 Stearns was called by the State Board of Health to become its chief engineer. This board, newly reorganized, had been placed in charge of the state's inland waters, and empowered to advise the various municipalities with regard to sanitation and water supply. This was pioneer work, requiring great sense and soundness in making decisions, and the influence which the Board acquired was due largely to the good judgment, tact, and fairness of its chief engineer. His exhaustive studies of water supplies and the means of controlling and improving them have become the basis for practice in many other states. He also made plans for the sewerage of the Mystic and Charles River valleys which were adopted and carried out, and planned the improvement of the Charles River Basin—later carried out with his advice as consultant—by which the foul tidal estuary of the Charles was converted into a beautiful fresh-water basin.

His most notable piece of work as engineer for the State Board of Health was the design, utilizing the Nashua River, for the metropolitan water supply of Boston and its vicinity. When this plan was adopted in 1895, he became chief engineer of the new metropolitan water board which carried it to completion in 1907 at a cost of $40,000,000. These water works were widely recognized as examples of the best practice in this field. They included as an innovation a provision by which the fall of water into the aqueduct was utilized for the development of power, a feature productive of increased revenue for the metropolitan water district.

After completion of the Boston metropolitan water supply, Stearns withdrew as chief engineer and became consultant for the board as well as for many other municipalities. His more important projects included water-supply problems of New York City, Baltimore, Los Angeles, Hartford, Conn., Providence, R. I., Rochester, N. Y., Worcester, Mass., and Winnipeg, Manitoba, and sewerage for Baltimore, Chicago, and Pittsburgh. He also did much important consultation work upon dams and other difficult structures. In 1905 he was appointed by President Theodore Roosevelt as a member of the board of consulting engineers to consider plans for the Panama Canal. He was one of the minority who advocated a lock canal, the type which

was adopted. He later served upon another board appointed by President Roosevelt to accompany Secretary of War William H. Taft [q.v.] to Panama and subsequently to revise the plans for the Gatun dam.

Stearns published many important papers in the engineering field, among the more significant of which were the following: "Description of Some Experiments on the Flow of Water Made during the Construction of Works for Conveying the Water of Sudbury River to Boston," with Alphonse Fteley (*Transactions of the American Society of Civil Engineers,* vol. XII, 1883); "On the Current-Meter" (*Ibid.*); "Experiments on the Flow of Water in a 48-Inch Pipe" (*Ibid.,* vol. XIV, 1885); "Disposal of Sewage in Massachusetts" (*Ibid.,* vol. XVIII, 1888); "The Effect of Storage upon the Quality of Water" (*Journal of the New England Water Works Association,* March 1891); "The Selection of Sources of Water Supply" (*Ibid.,* March 1892); "The Development of Water Supplies and Water-Supply Engineering" (*Transactions of the American Society of Civil Engineers,* vol. LVI, 1906). He also contributed many discussions of other papers and was chairman of the special committee of the American Society of Civil Engineers which reported upon methods of evaluating public utilities (*Transactions,* vol. LXXXI, 1918, p. 1311), as well as of the committee upon yield of drainage areas of the New England Water Works Association (*Journal,* December 1914), which presented a report of much value that has been widely used. He was active in professional organizations and served as president of the American Society of Civil Engineers and of the Boston Society of Civil Engineers.

On June 21, 1876, Stearns married Addie C. Richardson of Framingham, Mass., who died two years before her husband. He was survived by two sons, both engineers.

[A. S. Van Wagenen, *Geneal. and Memoirs of Isaac Stearns and His Descendants* (1901); *Trans. Am. Soc. Civil Engineers,* vol. LXXXIII (1921); *Jour. of the New England Water Works Asso.,* Mar. 1920; *Who's Who in America,* 1920–21; *Boston Transcript,* Dec. 2, 1919.]
                                                    H. K. B.

STEARNS, GEORGE LUTHER (Jan. 8, 1809–Apr. 9, 1867), Free-Soiler, was born in Medford, Mass., the eldest son of Luther and Mary (Hall) Stearns and the descendant of Charles Stearns who became a freeman of Watertown, Mass., in 1646. Such formal education as the boy received was in a preparatory school for boys established by his father, a physician. At the age of fifteen he began his business career in Brattleboro, Vt., in 1827 entered a shipchandlery firm in Boston, and in 1835 returned to Medford to manufacture linseed oil and to marry, on Jan. 31, 1836, Mary Ann Train. He became a Unitarian and was prominent in church activities. After the death of his wife in 1840, he reëntered business in Boston, at first with a ship-chandlery company but later, very successfully, as a manufacturer of lead pipe. By 1840 he felt strongly enough on the subject of slavery to support James G. Birney and the Liberty party. His marriage, on Oct. 12, 1843, to Mary Elizabeth Preston probably furthered his interest in the anti-slavery cause for his wife was a niece of Lydia Maria Child [q.v.]. In 1848, as a Conscience Whig, he liberally supported the Free-soil campaign with his money. He was greatly disturbed by the passage of the Fugitive Slave Law in 1850 and is known to have aided at least one slave to escape. He was among the leaders in the movement that put Charles Sumner in the federal Senate, and later, as a member of the famous Bird Club, he played a considerable part in the rise of the Republican party in Massachusetts, becoming particularly interested in the political fortunes of his friend John A. Andrew.

He was in the group that, in 1856, raised a subscription to equip the free state forces in Kansas with Sharpe's rifles. The subsequently successful operations of the Kansas committee of Massachusetts, of which he became chairman, were largely due to the willingness with which he contributed his time and money. In 1857 he met John Brown and made him the committee's agent to receive the arms and ammunition for the defense of Kansas and also aided in purchasing a farm for the Brown family at North Elba, N. Y. Indeed, from this time on Stearns practically put his purse at Brown's disposal. That he ever appreciated Brown's responsibility for the murders on the Potawatomi is doubtful, but in March 1858 Brown confided to him the general outline of his proposed raid into Virginia, an enterprise that Stearns approved, as did S. G. Howe, Theodore Parker, T. W. Higginson and Franklin B. Sanborn [qq.v.]. These five men constituted an informal committee in Massachusetts to aid Brown in whatever attack he might make on slavery. Stearns acted as treasurer for the enterprise in New England. Gerrit Smith of New York and Martin F. Conway of Kansas were also in the secret. Stearns, however, does not appear to have known just when and where Brown proposed to strike, and the blow at Harpers Ferry took him by surprise. On learning of Brown's capture he authorized two prominent Kansas jayhawkers to go to Brown's relief if they thought they could effect his rescue. Stearns

himself, becoming somewhat apprehensive of the attitude of the Federal government, fled with Howe to Canada. He soon returned, however, and appeared before the Mason committee of the Senate that was investigating the Brown conspiracy. No further action was taken by the government respecting Stearns.

During the Civil War, upon Governor Andrew's authorization he recruited many negro soldiers for the 54th and 55th Massachusetts regiments, especially from the middle and western states. So satisfactory were his efforts that in the summer of 1863 Secretary Stanton commissioned him as major with headquarters in Philadelphia and directed him to recruit colored regiments for the Federal government. A few months later he was sent to Nashville, where he successfully continued his work until a misunderstanding with Stanton led him to resign from the army early in 1864. In 1865 he established the *Right Way,* a paper that supported radical Republican policies, particularly negro suffrage, and attained a circulation of 60,000, largely at his expense. He died of pneumonia while on a business trip to New York.

[F. P. Stearns, *The Life and Public Services of George Luther Stearns* (1907) and *Cambridge Sketches* (1905); O. G. Villard, *John Brown* (1910); J. F. Rhodes, *Hist. of the U. S.,* vol. II (1892); *Sen. Report, No. 278,* 36 Cong., 1 Sess. (1860); A. S. Van Wagenen, *Geneal. and Memoirs of Charles and Nathaniel Stearns, and Their Descendants* (1901).]   W. R. W.

STEARNS, HENRY PUTNAM (Apr. 18, 1828–May 27, 1905), physician, was born in Sutton, Mass., the son of Asa and Polly (Putnam) Stearns, and a descendant of Charles Stearns, who became a freeman in Watertown in 1646. He was fitted for college in Monson, Mass., and received the B.A. degree from Yale in 1853, the M.D. degree two years later, studied medicine at Harvard, and finally completed his medical studies at the University of Edinburgh, Scotland. He was married to Annie Elizabeth Storrier of Dumfries, Scotland, on Aug. 29, 1857, and they had three children. On his return to the United States Stearns established himself in private practice in Marlboro, Mass., and remained there for three years before going to Hartford, Conn., where he made his home until his death. He achieved some distinction as a general practitioner, and when the Civil War broke out he was made surgeon of the 1st Connecticut Regiment. After three months he became surgeon of volunteers, was on the staff of General Grant, and was discharged from service in August 1865. During the greater part of that period, he was medical director of United States hospitals, stationed for the most part at St. Louis, Mo., Nashville, Tenn., and Paducah, Ky.

He spent eight years in general professional work in Hartford after the war, and in 1874 was appointed to succeed Dr. J. S. Butler and Eli Todd [q.v.], as superintendent of the Hartford Retreat for the Insane. He went abroad to familiarize himself with theory and practice in France and Great Britain, and at Cheadle, England, observed the successes of the "cottage system" which he later established at the Hartford institution. This system permitted patients to be treated without unnecessary limitation of their activities. During his years at the Retreat, he found time for numerous reports and monographs on various phases of insanity, which attracted wide comment. *Insanity, Its Causes and Prevention* was published in 1883, and *Lectures on Mental Diseases* in 1893. *Physiology vs. Philosophy* (1880) appeared first as an article in the *New Englander*, July 1880; *The Care of Some Classes of the Chronic Insane* (1881), in the *Archives of Medicine*, February 1881; and *Heredity, a Factor in the Etiology of Insanity* (1897), in the *American Journal of Insanity*, October 1897. Stearns classified mental disease according to causes and pathology. He suggested the appointment of physicians to the National Board of Health, and advocated education of the public in the prevention of insanity. For eighteen years he lectured at Yale on mental disease. He was a member of the Connecticut Medical Society and served as president 1898–99; he was a charter member of the Hartford Medical Society and of the New England Psychological Society, a member of the Association of Medical Superintendents of American Institutions for the Insane, and honorary member of the British Psychological Society and the Boston Medico-Psychological Society.

[Unpublished notes on Stearns by Dr. Henry Barnard; *Who's Who in America*, 1906–07; A. S. Van Wagenen, *Geneal. and Memoirs of Charles and Nathaniel Stearns, and Their Descendants* (1901); H. A. Kelly, W. L. Burrage, *Am. Medic. Biographies* (1920); *Obit. Records of Grads., Bull. of Yale Univ.*, July 1905; G. W. Russell, article on Stearns in *Proc. Conn. State Medic. Soc.* (1906); *New England Medic. Monthly*, Aug. 1885; *Am. Jour. of Insanity*, Oct. 1890; *Hartford Times*, May 27, 1905.]   C. C. B—e.

STEARNS, IRVING ARIEL (Sept. 12, 1845– Oct. 5, 1920), mining engineer, was born in Rushville, Ontario County, N. Y., the son of George Washington and Miranda (Tufts) Stearns. He was a descendant of Charles Stearns, an Englishman, who was admitted a freeman at Watertown, Mass., May 6, 1646. His father, a farmer and county judge, moved to Michigan in 1867 and subsequently became editor of the Coldwater *Semi-Weekly Republican*. Stearns was educated at Rushville Academy, Benedict's Collegiate Institute, Rochester, N. Y., and Rens-

selaer Polytechnic Institute, Troy, where he was graduated in 1868. He remained at the Institute for one year as assistant in analytical chemistry, then spent two years in Wilkes-Barre, Pa., as engineer in the office of Richard P. Rothwell [q.v.]. In 1871 he became superintendent of the McNeal Coal & Iron Company of Schuylkill County, Pa., and the following year, when Rothwell moved to New York, succeeded to the latter's business. As consulting engineer he examined and reported on mining properties in Pennsylvania, Virginia, West Virginia, Arkansas, Colorado, California, Wyoming, Idaho, and Utah. He was concerned with the building of bridges at Shickshinny and Pittston, Pa., and surveyed and mapped a great number of mines in the anthracite region. He was in charge of designing and carrying out for the Lehigh Valley Railroad Company improvements at Buffalo, N. Y., including canals, docks, and coal-stocking plant.

His prominence as a mining engineer brought him appointment in 1885 as manager of the coal interests of the Pennsylvania Railroad. He managed these properties with great efficiency, installing at Shamokin the first high-pressure boilers in the anthracite region; introducing electricity for underground haulage at the Lykens Valley colliery in 1886—its first use for such a purpose in the United States; and introducing high pressure compressed air for haulage in 1895. He also made radical improvements in the processes of mining and preparing anthracite coal. He retained the managership of the Pennsylvania's coal properties until July 1897, when he was chosen president of the Cross Creek Coal Company, of Coxe Brothers & Company, Inc., of the Delaware, Susquehanna & Schuylkill Railroad Company, and of Coxe Iron Manufacturing Company. He headed these organizations until the Coxe properties were bought in 1905 by the Lehigh Valley Coal Company, of which he became a director.

Retiring at this time from active business, he accepted in November 1906 election as first president of the Wilkes-Barre Park Commission, throwing himself enthusiastically into its work and during his ten years' incumbency securing almost the entire park system through gifts to the city. He had been one of the organizers of the American Institute of Mining Engineers, and retained his membership until the end of his life. At Wilkes-Barre, Nov. 20, 1872, he married Clorinda Shoemaker, daughter of Lazarus Denison and Esther (Wadhams) Shoemaker. He had two sons and one daughter, but only the latter survived him. His death occurred at Wilkes-Barre in his seventy-sixth year.

[*Trans. Am. Inst. Mining and Metallurgical Engineers*, vol. LXVI (1921) ; *Mining and Metallurgy*, Nov. 1920 ; *Coal Age*, Oct. 28, 1920 ; A. S. Van Wagenen, *Geneal. and Memoirs of Charles and Nathaniel Stearns, and Their Descendants* (1901) ; *Proc. and Colls. Wyoming Hist. and Geol. Soc.* (Pa.), vol. XVIII (1923) ; *Public Ledger* (Phila.), Oct. 6, 1920.]   B. A. R.

STEARNS, JOHN NEWTON (May 24, 1829–Apr. 21, 1895), temperance reformer, born at New Ipswich, N. H., was the son of Jesse and Lucinda (Davis) Stearns and a descendant of Isaac Stearns who came to New England in 1630. Jesse Stearns was a school-teacher ; many of his family became reformers. John graduated from New Ipswich Academy, but poor health prevented his attending college. At the age of seven he joined the celebrated "Cold Water Army," donned its blue and white uniform, and paraded the streets of New Ipswich singing "The Teetotalers Are Coming." This refrain became the battle-cry of his whole existence. He joined the Cadets of Temperance in 1839, the Band of Hope in 1842, and was among the first members of the Order of the Sons of Temperance in 1848. The last, a fraternal order designed to strengthen reformed (though backsliding) inebriates, sought to promote temperance by forbidding its members all alcoholic potations.

Thus far Stearns had taught school in his natal village, but about 1850 he settled in New York City and became a magazine salesman. He was soon conspicuous in Sunday school and temperance movements, especially in Brooklyn, liberally distributing buttons, badges, and temperance pledges. In December 1853 he purchased *Merry's Museum*, a children's magazine founded by S. G. Goodrich [*q.v.*], and the following year, while canvassing for his magazine in Utica, N. Y., he met and married Matilda C. Loring.

In 1865 he was chosen publishing agent of the National Temperance Society and editor of the *National Temperance Advocate*, the first issue of which appeared in January 1866. In that year he was made Most Worthy Patriarch of the National Division of North America, the highest office in the Sons of Temperance. During twenty-seven years he edited the *National Temperance Almanac and Teetotaler's Year Book*. Active in every prohibition group, he held from 1876 to 1878 the office of Most Worthy Templar of the Supreme Council of the Templars of Honor and of Temperance of North America. For thirty years he was responsible for a flood of prohibitionist propaganda : books, almanacs, hymn-books, pamphlets. All were paste-pot compilations, bombastic and vacuous. He estimated that $1,500,000 had been collected and spent in printing and distributing the publications which he edited. Among these were the *Temperance*

Hymn-Book (1869) ; *The Temperance Speaker* (1869) ; *Water Spouts* (1878) ; *National Temperance Hymn and Song Book* (1880) ; *Prohibition Does Prohibit; or, Prohibition Not a Failure* (1882) ; *The Prohibition Songster* (1884) ; *Foot-Prints of Temperance Pioneers* (1885) ; *Temperance in All Nations* (2 vols., 1893), reprinting speeches delivered at the World's Temperance Congress at Chicago in June 1893, which he had eagerly organized. He died in Brooklyn of heart failure, resulting from bronchial asthma.

[*N. Y. Tribune*, Apr. 22, and *N. Y. Times*, Apr. 23, 1895 ; *A Noble Life ... A Memorial Pamphlet* (undated, unsigned ; copy in N. Y. Pub. Lib.) ; excellent collection of Stearns's works in N. Y. Pub. Lib. ; J. A. Krout, *The Origins of Prohibition* (1925) ; A. S. Van Wagenen, *Geneal. and Memoirs of Isaac Stearns and His Descendants* (1901) ; information from Charles Montague of Ithaca, N. Y., and Frank Ryan of New York City.]   F. M.

STEARNS, OLIVER (June 3, 1807–July 18, 1885), Unitarian clergyman and theologian, born in Lunenburg, Mass., was through his father, Maj. Thomas Stearns, descended from Isaac Stearns, who was admitted freeman of Watertown, Mass., in 1631. Through his mother, Priscilla, daughter of Hon. Charles Cushing of Hingham, Mass., he was a descendant of Charles Chauncy [*q.v.*], the second president of Harvard College. He was a nephew of Asahel Stearns [*q.v.*], and uncle of Luther Stearns Cushing [*q.v.*]. Educated in the Lunenburg district school with added tutoring from the local clergyman and a term in the academy at New Ipswich, N. H., he entered Harvard College at the age of fifteen and graduated in 1826, ranking second in his class. After a year of teaching in a private school in Jamaica Plain, he was influenced by William Ellery Channing [*q.v.*] to enter the Harvard Divinity School, combining study there with the office, for two years, of tutor in mathematics in the college. Graduating in 1830, he was ordained pastor of the Second Congregational Society (Unitarian), Northampton, Mass., and remained there until Apr. 1, 1839, when, on account of ill health, he resigned. Unable, because of his health, to accept a call to Newburyport, he later became pastor of the Third Congregational Society in Hingham, Mass., where he was installed in April 1840, and where he remained sixteen years. As a minister Stearns won distinction by a profundity of thought matured in studious seclusion and by the ethical passion of his anti-slavery utterances. One of the earlier of his infrequent publications was *The Gospel as Applied to the Fugitive Slave Law* (1851). There were occasions when irritated listeners walked out while he was preaching.

During his Hingham pastorate he developed a theological method reconciling the older Unitarian thought with the newer Transcendentalism, and he found his truer vocation when, in 1856, he became president of the Meadville Theological School, Meadville, Pa. His eminent success in that office led in 1863 to his appointment to the Parkman Professorship of pulpit eloquence and pastoral care in the Harvard Divinity School, in succession to Convers Francis [q.v.], and to a lectureship in Christian theology in succession to George E. Ellis [q.v.]. Here, in association with Frederic Hedge and James Freeman Clarke [qq.v.], he modernized the older Unitarian tradition of the school. When President Eliot reorganized the school in 1870, Stearns was given the office of dean, and under the title of Parkman Professor of Theology, taught systematic theology and ethics. In 1878, aged seventy-one, he resigned, and lived in retirement in Cambridge until his death. On May 14, 1832, he was married to Mary Blood, daughter of Hon. Thomas H. and Mary (Sawyer) Blood of Sterling, Mass.; she died on June 10, 1871, and on July 2, 1872, he married Mrs. Augusta Hannah (Carey) Bailey. By his first wife he had six sons and two daughters.

Stearns was probably the first theologian in America to profess belief in evolution as a cosmic law, even before Herbert Spencer's adoption of the idea, though his own interest was in establishing a theory of historical development for Christian thought. His purpose was to unite the old dependence on Biblical revelation with the Transcendentalist reliance on present intuition, and at the same time, to find a relative justification of doctrines elaborated in stages of Christian history. After a preliminary effort in "Peace Through Conflict" (*Monthly Religious Magazine,* November 1851) he published further articles (*Christian Examiner,* September 1853, September 1856), in which he asserted that this progressive development is a story of intuitive reason interpreting revelation, with a safeguard against private aberration by the intention to seek truth in the light of the Holy Catholic Church. This development is more than a human process. The divine is immanent in it. Man's growing spiritual experience is an "evolution of the divine life through human nature." In support of this view, in 1856 he adopted from *Earth and Man* (1849), by Arnold Guyot [q.v.], the formulation due to von Baer, that "in the evolution of nature, the point of departure is a *homogeneous unit,* that the progress is *diversification,* that the end is an *organic* or harmonic unit" (*Christian Examiner,* September 1856, p. 174).

The same law, Stearns held, governed the history "not only of Christian theology, but of that Christian life which gives theology the law of its form and the sap of its growth" (*Ibid.*). In his Meadville instruction, he applied this thought with imperfect consistency and with a version of Christian beginnings now supplanted by modern criticism. In his Harvard period, ever receptive to new currents of thought, he assimilated some of that criticism, as is evidenced in a paper dealing with the Messianic consciousness of Jesus ("The Aim and Hope of Jesus," *Christianity and Modern Thought,* 1872), the last of his rare publications.

[A. S. Van Wagenen, *Geneal. and Memoirs of Isaac Stearns and His Descendants* (1901); A. P. Peabody, *Harvard Reminiscences* (1888); *Unitarian Rev.,* Oct. 1885; *Christian Reg.,* July 30, 1885; S. A. Eliot, *Heralds of a Liberal Faith* (1910), vol. III; F. A. Christie, *The Makers of the Meadville Theological School* (1927); *Boston Transcript,* July 20, 22, 1885.]

F. A. C.

STEARNS, ROBERT EDWARDS CARTER (Feb. 1, 1827–July 27, 1909), naturalist, was born in Boston, Mass., the son of Charles and Sarah (Carter) Stearns. His paternal grandfather was the Rev. Charles Stearns of Lincoln, mentioned by Holmes in *The Autocrat of the Breakfast Table,* and his first American ancestor was Charles Stearns who became a freeman at Watertown in 1646. His love of nature, intense from childhood, was fortunately appreciated and shared by his father and the two were frequently tramping and hunting companions. His education in the Boston public schools, often interrupted by poor health, was followed by mercantile training, but his artistic bent led him, in 1849, to paint a panorama of the Hudson River in a canvas 900 feet long and eight feet wide. He was married to Mary Ann Libby, the daughter of Oliver Libby of Boston, on Mar. 28, 1850. About this time he engaged in the investigation of certain Indiana coal fields, and in 1854 became resident agent for several copper mines in northern Michigan. But mining proved a passing interest, and after he lost his income in the panic of 1857, Stearns sold his Dover farm and migrated to California. He became a partner in a San Francisco printing business and later attempted independent publication, his first paper in 1859 being a prophetic article on the value of the sugar-beet for California. As acting editor of the *Pacific Methodist* he strongly upheld the Union cause in the Civil War and exerted an influence in the state said to have been far from negligible. Possessing considerable administrative capacity he became deputy clerk of the California supreme court, 1862–63, and secretary to the State Board of Harbor Commissioners, 1863–

68. Resigning because of ill health he spent the next two years in the East. Stearns returned to California to serve as secretary to the Board of Regents of the University of California in 1874, and supervised the dignified landscaping of the old campus until illness again impelled his retirement.

Even as a boy Stearns had become interested in collecting shells. His first zoölogical publication was a list of mollusks of Bolinas Bay (*Proceedings of the California Academy of the Natural Sciences,* vol. III, 1868). He likewise actively participated in the work of the young and struggling Academy of Natural Sciences, which he joined in 1864, holding many of its offices, and helping to prevent its dissolution after the earthquake of 1868. Thenceforth his scientific labors, particularly in the study of conchology, were unremitting. In 1869 he participated in a zoölogical expedition to Florida, and after another ten years again went east. In 1882 he was engaged in research for the United States Commission of Fish and Fisheries. In 1884 he was appointed paleontologist to the United States Geological Survey by John Wesley Powell, and assistant curator of mollusks in the National Museum by Spencer F. Baird [*qq.v.*]. In 1892 he settled in Los Angeles where he lived in semi-invalidism until his death. He was survived by one daughter.

Essentially a naturalist of the old school he will long be remembered as one of that group of earnest pioneer students of the Californian fauna which included Joseph Le Conte, James G. Cooper, William H. Dall [*qq.v.*], and others. A bibliography of his writings lists about 160 titles, mainly concerning molluscan systematics and distribution, but including several on coelenterates and others appertaining to ethnology, agriculture, and forestry. His was the foundational work on the interesting fossil land-snails of the John Day beds in Oregon. Although he suffered often from depression, Stearns's outstanding characteristics were vivacity, enthusiasm, versatility, a lively sense of humor, and a deep attachment to friends, especially exemplified in an intense and enduring love for his father. He became a fellow of the American Association for the Advancement of Science in 1874. Numerous mollusca and other animals, living and extinct, commemorate his name. His collection of mollusks was acquired by the National Museum.

[*Who's Who in America,* 1908–09; Avis Stearns Van Wagenen, *Geneal. and Memoirs of Charles and Nathaniel Stearns, and Their Descendants* (1901); M. R. Stearns, *Robert Edwards Carter Stearns,* privately printed (n.d.), and "Bibliography of Scientific Writings of R. E. C. Stearns," with a biographical sketch by W. H. Dall, *Smithsonian Misc. Colls.,* vol. LVI (1912);

W. H. Dall, "Dr. R. E. C. Stearns," *Nautilus,* Oct. 1909; *Los Angeles Daily Times,* July 29, 1909.]
S. S. B.

STEARNS, SHUBAL (Jan. 28, 1706–Nov. 20, 1771), Baptist clergyman, was born in Boston, Mass., the son of Shubael (*sic*) and Rebecca (Larrabee or Lariby) Stearns and a descendant of the Charles Stearns who was admitted a freeman of Watertown, Mass., in 1646. In 1715 the family moved to Tolland, Conn., where the father was one of the original land grantees and became the second town clerk. On Mar. 6, 1726/27, Shubal married Sarah Johnson of Lexington, Mass. Coming under the influence of the Great Awakening, he attached himself to the New Lights (Separatists) in 1745 and became a preacher among them. In 1751 he became convinced that believer's immersion was the New Testament baptism and was immersed by the Rev. Wait Palmer, who also participated on May 20, 1751, in his ordination as a Baptist minister. Although he continued to preach in New England for two years or more, he had a compelling inward conviction that he was called to a work outside that region.

Accordingly, with several married couples from the community, including some relatives, he went southward to Virginia, sojourning first at Opequon Creek and then at Cacapon. Here his brother-in-law, Daniel Marshall [*q.v.*], who had married Shubal's gifted sister, Martha, joined them and soon the group moved to Sandy Creek, N. C. There, in 1755, they organized a Baptist church, Stearns being chosen pastor, a position he retained during the rest of his life. Like the Regular Baptists of the Southern colonies, these Separate Baptists, as they were known, were Calvinists, but they had an evangelistic zeal which was their most distinctive character. Stearns himself as a preaching evangelist had been rated by some as next to Whitefield in effectiveness. The extent of his influence upon the Baptists of the wide area in which he and the ministers stimulated by him moved—the Carolinas, Georgia, and Virginia—is incalculable, but it was certainly dominant for a decade and was a primary factor in the astounding growth of the Baptists during the 1760's in those colonies. Both directly and indirectly he prepared the way for the union of the Regular and Separatist Baptists, producing the blend of Calvinistic orthodoxy and evangelistic fervor—particularly effective with the Scotch-Irish population—which has been a special mark of Southern Baptists. He was one of the principal founders of the Sandy Creek Association, in which churches of a wide area were united. Morgan Edwards has given the classic description of him: "He was but a little man but of good natural parts, and sound judgment. Of learning he had but a small share, yet was pretty well acquainted with books. His voice was musical and strong. . . . His character was indisputably good. . . . In his eyes was something very penetrating—there seemed to be a meaning in every glance" (Paschal, *post*, 286–87). He died in his sixty-fifth year.

[W. B. Sprague, *Annals of the Am. Pulpit*, VI (1860), 60; R. B. Semple, *Hist. of the Rise and Progress of the Baptists in Va.* (1810); David Benedict, *A Gen. Hist. of the Baptist Denomination in America* (2 vols., 1813); G. W. Purefoy, *A Hist. of the Sandy Creek Baptist Asso.* (1859); G. W. Paschal, *Hist. of N. C. Baptists* (1930); A. S. Van Wagenen, *Geneal. and Memoirs of Charles and Nathaniel Stearns, and Their Descendants* (1901).]   W. H. A.

STEARNS, WILLIAM AUGUSTUS (Mar. 17, 1805–June 8, 1876), Congregational clergyman, president of Amherst College, was born at Bedford, near Concord, Mass., his parents being the Rev. Samuel Horatio and Abigail (French) Stearns. Eben Sperry Stearns [*q.v.*] was a younger brother. Through his father his ancestry ran back to Isaac Stearns who emigrated to Salem in 1630 and was admitted freeman of Watertown, Mass., in 1631. Descended through both parents from distinguished leaders of the Congregational Church, he early felt himself destined to the ministry. The family consisted of eleven children who lived to reach adult estate and the problem of giving the five boys and six girls the benefit of "the New England system of education in ministers' families, viz: pure air, simple diet and a solid training in knowledge, human and divine" (Tyler, *Discourse, post,* p. 12) on an annual stipend which never exceeded five hundred dollars, in almost forty years of service, must have been a great one, but it was successfully met. The boys were all sent to Phillips Academy, Andover, Mass., and four of them were later graduated at Harvard College, William in the class of 1827. He then entered Andover Theological Seminary, where he became one of a group of unusually able young men, all of whom later fulfilled their early promise.

While he was still a student at Andover he preached occasionally to a small and weak congregation in Cambridgeport, and on his graduation he was invited to become its pastor. His friends protested that his talents entitled him to a more important charge, but, interpreting the call as evidence of divine will, he accepted it and was ordained Dec. 14, 1831. The pastorate lasted twenty-three years and was singularly successful, the weak and despised mission becoming one of the most prosperous and efficient of all the churches in the vicinity of Boston. The period

was characterized by increasing heat over the slavery issue and the young clergyman brought much obloquy on himself by condemning the extreme measures of the abolitionists although he preserved a consistent attitude of opposition to slavery.

His success as a pastor and especially the fruitfulness of his work among his younger parishioners led, in 1854, to his selection as the fourth president of Amherst College, a call he was moved to accept in spite of many misgivings. Thus he began his long term of service in the field of education which was to last until his sudden death at Amherst twenty-two years later. His kindly and urbane manner and the very evident sincerity of his moral character combined to captivate and hold the affections of faculty and students alike. He proved to be an exceptionally strong administrator and greatly increased the material wealth of the College while at the same time the curriculum was enriched and broadened. He was in great demand as a preacher on notable occasions and his sermons were generally printed at the request and expense of his hearers. He also wrote a considerable number of pamphlets on educational and missionary affairs. His only books were: *Life of Rev. Samuel H. Stearns* (3rd and enlarged edition, 1846), *Infant Church-Membership, or the Relation of Baptized Children to the Church* (1844), and *Adjutant Stearns* (copr. 1862), a short life of a son, Frazar Augustus, killed in the Civil War. He was a member of the Massachusetts Board of Education, and a trustee of Phillips Academy, and of Andover Theological Seminary. He held the presidency of the Massachusetts Home Missionary Society from 1859 to 1876 and was influential in the counsels of the American Board of Commissioners for Foreign Missions.

On Jan. 10, 1832, he married Rebecca Alden Frazar of Duxbury, Mass., by whom he had three sons and three daughters; after her death, July 19, 1855, he married, in August 1857, Olive Coit Gilbert of Providence, R. I.

[A. S. Van Wagenen, *Geneal. and Memoirs of Isaac Stearns and His Descendants* (1901); W. S. Tyler, *Discourse Commemorative of the Late President Stearns* (1877) and *A Hist. of Amherst College* (1895); C. M. Fuess, *Men of Andover* (1928); *Springfield Daily Republican*, June 9, 1876; *Congregational Quart.*, July 1877, pp. 425–26; information from descendants.]   F. L. T.

STEBBINS, HORATIO (Aug. 8, 1821–Apr. 8, 1902), Unitarian clergyman, was born at South Wilbraham, Mass., the son of Calvin and Amelia (Adams) Stebbins, and a descendant of Rowland Stebbins who emigrated from England to Massachusetts in 1634 and settled successively in Roxbury, Springfield, and Northampton. Horatio's mother died when he was six years old and his father married again. The boy's early education, broken by periods of farm work and teaching, was completed at Phillips Academy, Exeter, N. H., in 1846. Entering Harvard, he graduated in the class of 1848. While there he made a hundred dollars by raising a crop of potatoes on a plot of ground where one of the college buildings now stands. He remained at Harvard as a student in the Divinity School until 1851, in which year, June 3, he married Mary Ann, daughter of Samuel and Mary (Bowman) Fisher of Northboro, Mass. On the fifth of the following November he was ordained and installed as colleague of Rev. Calvin Lincoln at the Unitarian Church, Fitchburg, Mass. After a successful ministry here, he became on Jan. 31, 1855, the associate of Dr. Ichabod Nichols at the First Church, Portland, Me., succeeding him as pastor when Nichols died in 1859.

After the death, in 1864, of Thomas Starr King [q.v.], one of the most influential and beloved men on the Pacific Coast, the members of the Unitarian Church in San Francisco chose Stebbins to succeed him. Accepting the call, Stebbins left his comfortable and well established Portland parish for the more primitive conditions of the Far West. Sailing for California by the way of Panama, he arrived on Sept. 7, 1864, and for the next thirty-five years was an acknowledged force in the development of the state. After more than three decades of service he said with truth: "I have not withheld my hand or my heart as a minister, a man, or a citizen from any human interest, within the reach of limited capacity and prescribed duty" (*Thirty-one Years of California,* 1895, pp. 21, 22). Though quite different from the magnetic King, he was himself a striking personality. His physical appearance attracted attention everywhere, for he was a big, towering man, dignified in bearing and polished in manners. Independent, intellectually honest, direct and forceful in speech, and possessing an organ-like voice, he was likely to be the principal speaker at any important gathering. He had, furthermore, the faith, the patience, the indifference to both praise and censure, and the broad culture needed in the California leaders of his time. His influence stands out most conspicuously in the educational field. The year after his arrival in San Francisco he was made a trustee of the College of California and soon became president of the board. He strongly supported the establishment of a state university, and when the Agricultural, Mining, and Mechanical Arts College was projected, the trustees of the College of California offered to cede its property to the state

with the condition that a college of liberal arts be maintained. Without Stebbins' "planning wisdom and public skill the acceptance of the proposals . . . would probably not have been gained from the State" (Ferrier, *post,* p. 467). He was given a place on the first board of regents of the University and had an important part in its management until 1894. He was a friend and adviser of Leland Stanford [q.v.], helped in the formation of Stanford University, and became one of its trustees. Named by the will of James Lick [q.v.] as a trustee of the California School of Mechanical Arts, he was for many years active in the affairs of that institution. A serious heart trouble compelled him to resign his pastorate in January 1900. Returning to the East, he died in Cambridge, Mass., a little more than two years later, his body being taken to Portland, Me., for burial. His first wife, by whom he had three children, died in February 1875 and on Nov. 9, 1876, he married Lucy Ward, daughter of Doliver and Eliza Ann (Wilbray) Ward of Chicago, by whom he had a son and a daughter. Several of his addresses were published and selections from his writings are contained in *Horatio Stebbins: His Ministry and Personality* (1921), by Charles A. Murdock.

[In addition to the two works mentioned above, see R. S. and R. L. Greenlee, *The Stebbins Geneal.* (1904); *Unitarian Year Book,* 1902; S. A. Eliot, *Heralds of a Liberal Faith* (1910), vol. III; W. W. Ferrier, *Origin and Development of the Univ. of Cal.* (1930); *Univ. Chronicle,* July 1902; *Christian Register,* Apr. 17, 1902; *San Francisco Chronicle,* Apr. 10, 1902.]   H. E. S.

STEBBINS, RUFUS PHINEAS (Mar. 3, 1810–Aug. 13, 1885), Unitarian clergyman, was a descendant of Rowland Stebbins, or Stebbing, a native of Cambridge, England, who in 1634 emigrated to Roxbury, Mass., and later moved to Springfield. A descendant, Stephen, became a farmer in South Wilbraham in 1741, and his great-grandson Rufus Phineas, second son of Luther and Lucina (Stebbins) Stebbins, was born there. Meager schooling with farm labor was the lot of his athletic and buoyant youth, when, as his cousin Horatio Stebbins [q.v.] reports, "he could spring upon a horse's back from the ground, and ride like the wind without pad or saddle" (*Unitarian Review, post,* p. 437). After belated preparation in Wilbraham Academy, he graduated with distinction from Amherst College in 1834, and after three years in the Harvard Divinity School was ordained as pastor of the Congregational Church in Leominster, Mass., Sept. 20, 1837, nine days after his marriage to Eliza Clarke Livermore of Cambridge. In his own later words, he came to the parish "all ablaze with enthusiasm, flaming with zeal to correct all evils and perfect all good in a day . . . restless, dissatisfied, aggressive, belligerent" (*Reverend Calvin Lincoln: Sermon Preached . . . September 18, 1881,* 1882), and the energy of his denunciation of slavery, intemperance, and war provoked some temporary opposition. This vanished in view of his religious fervor and pastoral efficiency, and though austere in censure of innocent youthful amusements, he developed a crowded Sunday school, for whose forty-one teachers he conducted fortnightly training classes. He also received private pupils in his home, among them his cousin Horatio, and Thomas Hill [*q.v.*], afterwards president of Harvard University.

In 1844 Stebbins became the first president of the Theological School of Meadville, Pa., then founded in the interest of the Unitarians and the Christian Connection, serving also as pastor of the Meadville Unitarian Church until 1849. Robust energy of body and mind enabled him to accomplish a creative work in administration and teaching. He had a magisterial comprehension of the full range of knowledge, which found expression in an initial address in Meadville, Oct. 24, 1844, and in *Academic Culture* (1851), an address delivered before the students of Allegheny College. Resigning in 1856, he sought rest in Cambridge, but on Apr. 30, 1857, he began a new pastorate in Woburn, Mass. Here his notable public service on the school board of the town and the emotional power and ethical emphasis of his pulpit eloquence won adherents to his church, but for reasons now obscured he suddenly resigned, Nov. 28, 1863. He then took up his residence in Cambridge and devoted his time to preaching in various pulpits and to his duties as president of the American Unitarian Association. Early in 1865 he raised by personal effort over a hundred thousand dollars for the work of the Association—an amount unparalleled at that time—and in May accepted temporarily the administrative office of secretary. From 1871 to 1878 he built up the struggling Unitarian Church of Ithaca, N. Y., winning to its friendship Ezra Cornell [*q.v.*]; then, returning to New England, he organized, Apr. 21, 1878, the Unitarian Church of Newton Center, Mass., which he served until his death in Cambridge seven years later.

With little interest in philosophy, Stebbins based his thought solely on the Bible read with the Unitarian exegesis taught him by his Harvard teachers. He remained unaffected by the Transcendentalist movement of German Biblical criticism. In his *Study of the Pentateuch* (1881) he still upheld Mosaic authorship. The Bible, he maintained, was a revelation, even though divine illumination of its authors was not always verbal inspiration and though the revealed truth was often expressed in poetical form with imaginative coloring and emotional rather than logical terms. Strenuous in denial of Trinitarian doctrine (see *Christian Examiner,* July 1851, June, September 1853), he found in Jesus, not only the Messiah commissioned to proclaim the Gospel, but an ever present agent in the affairs of the world, spiritually present when the bread was broken in the holy communion, and a constant saving presence to support and comfort men in the vicissitudes of life.

He contributed articles to the *Christian Examiner,* the *Christian Palladium,* the *Christian Repository,* of which he was one of the founders and editors, and the *Unitarian Review.* He also published, in addition to numerous sermons and other addresses, *An Historical Address Delivered at the Centennial Celebration . . . of the Town of Wilbraham* (1864), which comprises, with appendix and index, 317 pages.

[*Unitarian Rev.,* Nov. 1885; *Christian Reg.,* Aug. 20, 27, 1885; Joseph Allen, *The Worcester Asso. and Its Antecedents* (1865); S. A. Eliot, *Heralds of a Liberal Faith* (1910), vol. III; E. M. Wilbur, *A Hist. Sketch of the Independent Congregational Church, Meadville, Pa.* (1902); F. A. Christie, *The Makers of the Meadville Theological School* (1927); R. S. and R. L. Greenlee, *The Stebbins Geneal.* (2 vols., 1904).]

F. A. C.

STECK, GEORGE (July 19, 1829–Mar. 31, 1897), piano manufacturer, was born in Cassel, Germany. In his youth and early manhood he studied piano making with Carl Scheel of Cassel, who had worked for Erard, the Paris piano manufacturer, from 1837 to 1846. Steck emigrated to America in 1853, and after a period of employment by other piano makers in New York City founded his own business in 1857. The firm of George Steck & Company prospered almost immediately, and in 1865 retail warerooms were opened on Clinton Place, New York, under the name of Steck Hall. A larger establishment was opened on East Fourteenth Street in 1871. Steck was particularly interested in designing scales for pianos, and it is said that his scales for both grand and upright pianos were often copied and imitated by other manufacturers (Dolge, *post,* p. 318). In 1873 he was awarded the first prize of merit for pianofortes at the Great Vienna Exposition. He presented one of his grand pianos to Richard Wagner in 1876, and the manufacturers of the Steck piano exhibited this instrument in the United States, stating that it was the piano Wagner used at Villa Wahnfried, in Bayreuth, when he composed *Parsifal.* Steck was something of a philanthropist, concerned with the welfare of his employees. In 1884 he incorporated his business and alloted shares of stock to the men who worked for him. He retired from active participation in the firm in 1887, and devoted the last ten years of his life to experimentation in constructing a piano which would stay permanently in tune. In 1904 George Steck & Company was consolidated with the Aeolian Company of New York. A widow and two daughters survived him at his death in New York City.

[George Steck is briefly mentioned in *Grove's Dict. of Music and Musicians, Am. Supp.* (1930). The most complete account of his career is in Alfred Dolge, *Pianos and Their Makers,* vol. I (1911). An obituary is to be found in the *N. Y. Times,* Apr. 2, 1897.]

J. T. H.

STEDMAN, EDMUND CLARENCE (Oct. 8, 1833–Jan. 18, 1908), poet, critic, editor, was born in Hartford, Conn., the son of Maj. Edmund Burke Stedman and Elizabeth Clementine (Dodge) Stedman, who as Elizabeth C. D. Stedman Kinney [*q.v.*] became known as a poet and essayist. On his father's side he was descended from Isaac Stedman, a London merchant who came to Scituate, Mass., about 1637. His mother was the great-grand-daughter of the Rev. Aaron Cleveland [*q.v.*]. Edmund Stedman, who was a lumber merchant, died when his son was two years old, and the boy, until he was six, was brought up on his maternal grandfather's farm at Plainfield, N. J. He then passed under the care of his uncle, James Stedman, an austere and puritanical lawyer of Norwich, Conn., and received his early education at the "Old Brick Schoolhouse" and the "Old Academy" in Norwich. Although of small and frail physique, he showed boyish prowess in fighting, running, and swimming. He also wrote much juvenile poetry under the influence of the Romanticists and later of Tennyson, who became a lifelong admiration. He entered Yale in 1849, the youngest member of his class. Four principles of conduct were inscribed in his notebook: to obey all the rules and regulations of the institution; to come to every recitation with lessons carefully prepared; to abstain from profane swearing, gaming, drinking, or disorderly behavior; to follow duty in all things. These resolutions he carried out during his first year in college; in the second, beer, skittles, and other amusements caused his downfall. Although he won the sophomore prize in English composition with a poem, "Westminster Abbey," he neglected his class work and was rusticated at the end of the year to study under a tutor at Northampton, Mass., where instead of studying he fell in love with a neighboring damsel. He and another student started to tour New England as "the well-known tragedian Alfred

Willoughby, and his sister Miss Agnes Willoughby"; their exposure after the first performance caused his expulsion from Yale. He next studied law for several months in the office of his uncle, and then in 1852, in partnership with Charles B. Platt, bought the *Norwich Tribune,* which he edited for about half a year until it expired. Meanwhile he and Platt had fallen in love with the same woman, Laura Hyde Woodworth, daughter of a Norwich dyer, and wrote her a joint letter, offering her the choice of marriage between them. She chose Stedman, and they were married on Nov. 3, 1853. In Feb. 1854, in partnership with Stephen A. Hubbard, Stedman bought the *Mountain County Herald* at Winsted, Conn., which he edited until April 1855. Convinced by his experience that newspaper publishing was merely a form of business like any other and less profitable than most forms, he moved to New York and became a partner with E. A. Ingraham in the firm of Ingraham and Stedman, clockmakers. The partnership lasted for only one year, and there followed a financially precarious period for the Stedmans during which they lived at the "Unitary Home" on East Fourteenth Street, a cooperative venture inspired by Stephen Pearl Andrews [*q.v.*].

In the fall of 1859 the marriage of Frances Bartlett, a New York girl in her teens, to an aged but wealthy Cuban, Don Estaban de Santa Cruz de Oviedo, caused much unfavorable public comment, and Stedman made it the theme of a satiric poem, "The Diamond Wedding," which, published in the *New-York Daily Tribune,* Oct. 18, 1859, gained wide attention and commendation. Unwise threats of legal prosecution by the Bartlett family increased Stedman's *réclame,* further augmented by the publication of his popular "Ballad of Lager Bier," "John Brown's Invasion," and "Honest Abe of the West," thought to be the first Lincoln campaign song. These poems also brought him the acquaintance, ripening into intimate friendship, of Bayard Taylor, Richard Henry Stoddard, Thomas Bailey Aldrich, and William Winter [*qq.v.*]. He joined the staff of the New York *World* in August 1860, and during the same year published his first volume, *Poems Lyrical and Idyllic.* The outbreak of the Civil War sent him to the front as correspondent for the *World,* in which capacity he followed the campaigns of 1861. Being a violent partisan of the North, he thought he could do more efficient service for its cause by accepting a position in the attorney-general's office, in which he remained during 1862–63. Then, returning to New York, he entered the banking firm of Samuel Hallett and Company, but the next year opened his own brokerage office, which he retained for the rest of his life. Although he affected to regard the stock exchange as a mere means of livelihood, there can be no doubt that he had a real liking for business and thoroughly enjoyed the battles of the market. At the same time his love of literature was even more genuine, and after daily spending six hours on his feet in the stock exchange he devoted much of the night to writing.

His later life was uneventful, except for his successive publications: *Alice of Monmouth, an Idyl of the Great War, with Other Poems* (1864); *The Blameless Prince, and Other Poems* (1869), in which "Anonyma" caused an amusing attack on him for "immorality"; *The Poetical Works of Edmund Clarence Stedman* (1873), a complete edition; *Victorian Poets* (1875); *Poets of America* (2 vols., 1885); *A Library of American Literature from the Earliest Settlement to the Present Time* (11 vols., 1889–90); *The Nature and Elements of Poetry* (copyright 1892), the substance of lectures delivered on the Percy Turnbull Memorial Foundation at the Johns Hopkins University; *The Works of Edgar Allan Poe* (10 vols., 1894–95), edited in collaboration with George E. Woodberry; *Poems Now First Collected* (1897); *A Victorian Anthology, 1837–1895* (1895); and *An American Anthology, 1787–1899* (1900). Two trips to the Caribbean Sea, 1875 and 1892, inspired some of the best of his later poetry. In 1883 he bought an estate, "Kelp Rock," at Newcastle, N. H., as a summer residence, but he was rarely able to get away from his business to enjoy it. He took great delight, however, in his attractive colonial house in an artists' colony at Lawrence Park in Bronxville, N. Y. Generous, kindly, and idealistic, he was quick to join any efforts to promote the prestige of literature or alleviate the hard lot of authors. He was one of the founders of the Authors' Club, president of the American Copyright League, chairman of the American Committee of the Keats-Shelley Memorial Association, president of the National Institute of Arts and Letters, a member of the American Academy of Arts and Letters, and president of the New England Society. He died in New York, survived by one son and a grand-daughter. Always immaculately dressed, with fine features and beautiful white beard, he was easily the most popular and most highly esteemed member of the New York literary circle of his day. Time has dealt harshly with his poetry, which for all its technical merits was largely imitative, and with his works of criticism, which were narrowly Victorian in taste, but he brought an unusually thor-

ough and conscientious scholarship to the task of editing, and through his numerous anthologies, as well as through his own writings, he exercised a great influence on the American culture of the period.

[*Who's Who in America*, 1906–07; *Obit. Record Grads. Yale Univ.* (1910); Laura Stedman and G. M. Gould, *Life and Letters of Edmund Clarence Stedman* (2 vols., 1910), with portrait and full bibliog.; *In Memory of Edmund Clarence Stedman, a Meeting Held at Carnegie Lyceum, N. Y.* (1909); Margaret W. Fuller, *A New England Childhood* (1916); Theodore Dreiser, in *Munsey's Mag.*, Mar. 1899; obituary in *N. Y. Times*, Jan. 19, 1908.]   E. S. B.

STEEDMAN, CHARLES (Sept. 20, 1811– Nov. 13, 1890), naval officer, son of Charles John Steedman and Mary (Blake) Steedman, was born in the Parish of Saint James, Santee, S. C. His grandfather, James Steedman, had emigrated from Scotland to America before the Revolution. Entering the navy as a midshipman, Apr. 1, 1828, he was promoted to the grade of passed midshipman, Jan. 14, 1834, and later, through successive grades, to that of rear-admiral, May 25, 1871. His early service, mainly in the West Indies, was without special incident. In 1835 he was ordered to the *Constitution,* and in her joined the Mediterranean Squadron, where he remained until June 1838. He spent the next four years largely in West Indian duty. In 1843 he was ordered to duty on the coast survey brig *Washington.* The next year he joined the corvette *St. Mary's,* and in her participated in the naval operations on the Gulf coast during the Mexican War, commanding the *St. Mary's* launch in the capture of the Mexican schooner *Pueblana* inside Tampico bar, Nov. 14, 1846. He also commanded an eight-inch gun of a naval shore battery in the bombardment of Vera Cruz and San Juan d'Ulloa, Mar. 24–27, 1847. After two years at the Naval Observatory, in 1850 he was again ordered to the Mediterranean Squadron. In the Paraguay expedition under William Branford Shubrick [*q.v.*] he commanded the brig *Dolphin,* returning to the United States in December 1860.

Though he was a South Carolinian, he remained loyal to the Union when the Civil War began. He was at once ordered to duty in Chesapeake Bay, keeping communications open and transporting troops from Havre de Grace to Annapolis while the railroad bridges between Baltimore, Md., and Philadelphia, Pa., were being repaired. Thence he was ordered to duty with Andrew Hull Foote [*q.v.*] on the Mississippi, but was soon recalled and given command of the *Bienville,* in which he participated in the Port Royal expedition of November 1861, his vessel leading the second attacking column. After the battle he blockaded the Georgia coast, participating in the capture of all the ports south of Savannah. In June 1862 he was transferred to the steamer *Paul Jones,* and with her silenced the batteries on St. John's Bluff, Fla. On Apr. 13, 1863, he was transferred to the *Powhatan,* doing blockade duty off Charleston, S. C., until September 1863, when he towed the captured ram *Atlanta* to Philadelphia. He was at once given command of the *Ticonderoga* and ordered to cruise against Confederate commerce raiders, particularly the *Florida.* After an unsuccessful search for this vessel off the Brazilian coast, he returned to Philadelphia in October 1864 in his ship with broken-down engines. In command of the same ship he took part in both attacks on Fort Fisher, N. C. In November 1865, after extensive repairs to the *Ticonderoga,* he joined the European Squadron of Louis Malesherbes Goldsborough [*q.v.*], returning home in the *Colorado* in September 1867. He was in charge of the Boston navy yard from 1869 to 1872, and of the South Pacific Squadron from Oct. 10, 1872, until Sept. 22, 1873, retiring Sept. 24, 1873. His record in two wars was an honorable one. His courtly bearing and polished manner were never disturbed amid the excitement of battle; a comrade said of him, "He was as cool under fire as on parade." He married Sarah Bishop of Philadelphia on Feb. 7, 1843, and had two sons and four daughters. After an extended tour of Egypt, Palestine, and Europe following his retirement, he settled in Washington, where he spent his declining years.

[*Memoir and Correspondence of Charles Steedman, with his Autobiog. and Private Journals* (1912), ed. by A. L. Mason; *War of the Rebellion: Official Records (Navy),* 1 ser., vols. I–IV (1894–97), VII (1898), XI–XVI (1900–03), XXII (1908); *Report of the Secretary of the Navy* (1859); G. F. Emmons, *The Navy of the U. S. from the Commencement 1775 to 1853* (1853); J. H. Smith, *The War with Mexico* (1919), vol. I; *Army and Navy Jour.,* Nov. 22, *Bangor Weekly Courier,* Nov. 21, *Evening Star* (Washington, D. C.), Nov. 14, and *Washington Sunday Herald,* Nov. 16, 1890.]

L. H. B.

STEEDMAN, JAMES BLAIR (July 29, 1817–Oct. 18, 1883), soldier and politician, was born in Northumberland County, Pa., the son of Mellum and Margaret (Blair) Steedman. He was left an orphan in childhood, and his education was limited to a few months in the district school. Learning the printer's trade, he worked in newspaper offices in Lewisburg, Pa., and Louisville, Ky.; later he served for a time in the Texan army and finally settled in Ohio. There he took an active part in politics; he was elected in 1847 to the state legislature, where he served two terms, and was frequently a delegate at party conventions. In the gold rush of 1849 he went to California but returned the next year to Toledo, where he made his permanent home, and resumed newspaper work. He was appointed public printer in 1857 during Buchanan's administration. A strong Douglas Democrat, he was a delegate at the Charleston and Baltimore conventions in 1860, and an unsuccessful candidate for Congress that year.

He entered the military service, Apr. 27, 1861, as colonel of the 14th Ohio Infantry, which he raised in Toledo; he was mustered out, Aug. 13, 1861, and again mustered in, Sept. 1, 1861. On Mar. 1, 1862, Lincoln nominated him to be brigadier-general of volunteers, but objection to his confirmation was made in the Senate on account of an editorial in his newspaper, the *Toledo Times,* which presented arguments in favor of the right of secession. Though these arguments were published only that they might be refuted in a later issue, the incident caused a long delay in Steedman's confirmation, and it did not take place until July 17, 1862. He commanded a brigade first in the (old) Army of the Ohio, and then in the Army of the Cumberland (Perryville and Murfreesboro), and finally a division in the latter (Tullahoma campaign). His greatest distinction was earned in the battle of Chickamauga, where he commanded a division of Granger's corps which came to the rescue of George Henry Thomas [*q.v.*], standing as the "rock of Chickamauga" when all the rest of the army had been swept away. In twenty minutes Steedman's division lost a fifth of its strength. Though his horse was shot under him and he was severely bruised, he retained command and himself headed the attack, carrying the colors of one of his regiments. One moment he gave to personal concerns, when he directed a staff officer to see that the newspaper obituaries spelled his name *Steedman* and not *Steadman,* a form he hated. He was appointed major-general of volunteers, Apr. 20, 1864. At the battle of Nashville he commanded a "detachment" of troops from various sources, the equivalent of a division. Resigning from the army, Aug. 18, 1866, he was collector of internal revenue at New Orleans, La., until 1869, when he returned to Toledo. He edited the *Northern Ohio Democrat,* served in the state Senate, was chief of police of the city, and was otherwise active in public affairs up to the time of his death. A man of great size and strength, he was aggressive, determined, fearless of responsibility, at his best in great emergencies. He was married three times: first, in 1838 at Napoleon, Ohio, to Miranda Stiles, recently of New Jersey; second, to Rose Barr; and third, Sept. 16, 1878, at Monroe, Mich., to Margaret, daughter of John Gildea.

[*War of the Rebellion: Official Records (Army)*; *Battles and Leaders of the Civil War* (4 vols., 1887–88) ; J. C. Smith, *Oration at the Unveiling of the Monument Erected to the Memory of Maj. Gen. James B. Steedman* (1887) ; J. M. Killits, *Toledo and Lucas County, Ohio* (1923), vol. I ; Clark Waggoner, *History of the City of Toledo and Lucas County* (1888) ; Harvey Scribner, *Memoirs of Lucas County and the City of Toledo* (1910), vol. II ; obituary in *Cincinnati Enquirer*, Oct. 19, 1883 ; unpublished records in the War Dept. ; letter from Steedman's widow confirming statements as to full name, date of birth, parentage, and marriages.]

T. M. S.

STEELE, DANIEL (Oct. 5, 1824–Sept. 2, 1914), Methodist Episcopal clergyman, teacher, author, was born at Windham, N. Y., in the Catskills, a son of Perez and Clarissa (Brainerd) Steele and a descendant of George Steele who came to Massachusetts in 1631/32, later settling in Connecticut. During his entire preparatory course at Wesleyan Academy, Wilbraham, Mass., he supported himself by teaching school as he did also during his freshman year at Wesleyan University, Middletown, Conn., where he was graduated, second in his class, in 1848. For the next two years he was a tutor in mathematics at Wesleyan, and during this period, 1849, he joined the New England Conference of the Methodist Episcopal Church, of which he remained a member till 1906, when he assumed a retired relation. From his ordination in 1850 until 1861, he served churches in the following places in Massachusetts: Fitchburg, Leominster, Boston, Malden, Springfield, and Holliston. Leaving the pastorate in the latter year, he was from 1862 to 1869 professor of ancient languages in Genesee College, Lima, N. Y., and from 1869 to 1871 was acting president of that institution. When the college was moved to Syracuse and became Syracuse University in 1871, he held the chair of mental and moral philosophy there for a year and also served as vice-president of the college of liberal arts in 1871–72, and as acting chancellor of the university in 1872. Again resuming the pastorate, he ministered continuously to churches in Massachusetts from 1872 to 1888, serving in Boston, Auburndale, Lynn, Salem, Peabody, Reading, and again in Boston. While pastor in Reading in 1884 he became instructor in New Testament Greek and exegesis in Boston University. From 1886 to 1899 he taught in the New England Deaconess' Training School, and then devoted the remainder of his life to literary work.

He was the author of a commentary on the Book of Joshua which appeared in 1873 as the third volume in D. C. Whedon, *Commentary on the Old Testament*; and in addition published *Binney's Theological Compend Improved* (1875) ; *Love Enthroned* (1875), his most widely known and influential work ; *Milestone Papers* (1878) ; a commentary on Leviticus and Numbers (1891), in the Whedon Series ; *Half-Hours with St. Paul* (1895) ; *Defense of Christian Perfection* (1896) ; *Gospel of the Comforter* (1897) ; *Jesus Exultant* (1899) ; *A Substitute for Holiness; or, Antinomianism Revived* (1899) ; *Half-Hours with St. John's Epistles* (1901) ; *Steele's Answers* (1912). He was a constant contributor to the religious press, was associate editor of *Divine Life*, 1889–93, and of the *Christian Witness*, 1896. His weekly contribution to *Zion's Herald*, known as "Daniel Steele's Column" was eagerly read for many years.

Steele was a leader in his denomination and active in the principal reform movements of his day. He was a stanch opponent of slavery and a persistent advocate of temperance and woman's rights. He was a man of scholarly attainments and saintly character ; but with his earnest piety he combined the saving grace of a delightful sense of humor. His outlook was broad and he was in full sympathy with the liberal scientific and theological opinion of his time. He had a wide circle of friends both within and beyond the confines of his own denomination. He died at his home in Milton, Mass., in his ninetieth year. On Aug. 8, 1850, he was married to Harriet, daughter of Rev. Amos Binney of Wilbraham, Mass., and two sons and two daughters survived him.

[*Official Minutes . . . New England Conference of the Methodist Episcopal Church*, 1915 ; *Zion's Herald*, Sept. 9, 1914 ; *Boston Transcript*, Sept. 3, 1914 ; *Who's Who in America*, 1914–15 ; D. S. Durrie, *Steele Family* (1859) ; *Alumni Record of Wesleyan Univ.* (1911).]

F. T. P.

STEELE, FREDERICK (Jan. 14, 1819–Jan. 12, 1868), soldier, was born at Delhi, Delaware County, N. Y., the son of Nathaniel Steele, and a descendant of John Steele of Essex, England, who emigrated to Newtown (Cambridge), Mass., in 1631/32 and was later one of the founders of Hartford, Conn. Frederick was appointed a cadet at West Point, July 1, 1839, and upon his graduation, July 1, 1843, was commissioned second lieutenant in the 2nd Infantry, with which he served in the Mexican War, in action at Ocalaca, Contreras, Churubusco, Molino del Rey, and Chapultepec. He was twice brevetted for gallant conduct (Contreras and Churubusco). Promoted first lieutenant on June 6, 1848, he served in California for the next five years, and from 1853 to 1861 in Minnesota, Nebraska, and Kansas. He was promoted captain, 2nd Infantry, Feb. 5, 1855, and on May 14, 1861, was appointed major in the 11th Infantry, one of the new regular regiments created by presidential proclamation and later confirmed by act of Congress. (Out of it, in later reorganizations, were formed the

16th and 20th Infantry of the present army; the present 11th Infantry has no connection with the older regiment so designated.)

During the first year of the Civil War Steele commanded a brigade at the battle of Wilson's Creek and in the other operations in Missouri. He was appointed colonel, 8th Iowa Infantry, Sept. 23, 1861, and brigadier-general of volunteers, Jan. 29, 1862. As a division commander in Curtis' Army of the Southwest he participated in the Arkansas campaign of 1862, and was appointed major-general of volunteers, Nov. 29, 1862. He commanded a division of the XIII Corps in the operations against Chickasaw Bluffs and Arkansas Post, and a division of the XV (Sherman's) Corps in the Vicksburg campaign. Immediately after the surrender of the city he was placed in command of the forces in Arkansas and charged with completing the conquest of that state. This task he substantially accomplished within a few months, defeating or driving back the small Confederate forces which might have menaced the flank of the greater operations east of the Mississippi. The portion of the state remaining in Confederate hands was too remote to affect the course of the war in any respect. When Banks started on his Red River campaign, Steele was directed to assist by operating against the Confederate forces before him, which orders he carried out at a heavy cost in men and animals and without other result. In actual combat he was successful enough, but it was impracticable to maintain the long line of communications which was necessary. The responsibility rests with the superiors who ordered the impossible, and not with Steele. He remained in charge in Arkansas through 1864, and then took part in Canby's campaign against Mobile, which ended with the capture of that city in April 1865. Though a good division commander, Steele was never entrusted with a large command. The Army of Arkansas, though operating independently, never exceeded about fourteen thousand men.

After the war he commanded the Department of the Columbia, in the northwest, until shortly before his death. He was not mustered out as major-general of volunteers until Mar. 1, 1867, having meanwhile been promoted lieutenant-colonel in the regular army, Aug. 26, 1863, and colonel, July 28, 1866. While on leave at San Mateo, Cal., he was stricken with apoplexy, fell from the carriage in which he was driving, and died instantly.

[D. S. Durrie, *Steele Family* (1859); *War of the Rebellion: Official Records (Army)*; *Battles and Leaders of the Civil War* (4 vols., 1887–88); G. W. Cullum, *Biog. Reg. Officers and Grads. U. S. Mil. Acad.* (3rd ed., 1891); *Evening Bulletin* (San Francisco), Jan. 14, 1868; unpublished records in the War Dept.]
T. M. S.

STEELE, JOEL DORMAN (May 14, 1836–May 25, 1886), educator and textbook writer, son of the Rev. Allen and Sabra (Dorman) Steele, was born in Lima, N. Y., a descendant of John Steele, one of the founders of Hartford and Farmington, Conn. His early schooling was irregular, for his father was an itinerant Methodist minister, but he had two years under Charles Anthon [*q.v.*] at the Boys' Classical Institute in Albany, and two years at the Boys' Academy in Troy. After a year in clerical positions in New York City, he entered Genesee College (later part of Syracuse University) and was graduated in 1858. To defray his college expenses, he worked summers on his father's farm or taught district school. He became instructor (1858–59), then principal at Mexico Academy, Mexico, N. Y. His marriage on July 7, 1859, to Esther Baker, teacher of music at the academy, daughter of the Rev. Gardner Baker, proved one of rare intellectual and spiritual companionship. In 1861 he resigned to raise the 81st New York Volunteers, of which he was captain. He was severely wounded at the battle of Seven Pines, Fairoaks, Va., and his life hung in the balance for weeks, but in the following autumn he was well enough to become principal of the high school at Newark, N. Y. In 1866 he became principal of the Elmira Free Academy, where he found discipline sadly demoralized; he soon had the situation under control, however, and introduced the honor system with extraordinary success. "I had become convinced," he said, "that the germinal idea of discipline was self-control; and that the true aim of the schoolmaster was not to teach the pupil how to be governed by another, but how to govern himself" (Palmer, *post,* p. xxvii).

At Elmira he taught only science, always his favorite subject. He took careful notes of effective classroom procedure, largely abandoned use of the cumbersome textbooks of the period, and substituted outlines of his own. These developed into his famous "Fourteen Weeks" series of textbooks in the sciences, the first of which was published in 1867. In 1872, at the insistent urging of his intimate friend and publisher, Alfred Cutler Barnes, he resigned his principalship to devote the rest of his life to writing textbooks. He had begun the year before, in collaboration with his wife, to write textbooks in history, known as the Barnes Brief History Series, the most popular of which was *A Brief History of the United States for Schools* (1871). No authors' names appeared on the history textbooks until after Steele's death, since he felt that to acknowledge the authorship of books in a field not his own would injure his prestige in science. His contribution in these scientific and historical textbooks lay in his ability to present facts comprehensibly and with interest; his success is attested by the fact that five of his science textbooks and two of his histories were still in print in 1928. Through them he popularized science as a secondary school subject, introduced simple laboratory exercises and the study of specimens, and urged departure from memoriter recitations. He had the advantage, as he often said, of a devoted wife who assisted him from the beginning in all his writing, and who continued to revise editions after his death. In his memory she erected the Steele Memorial Library in Elmira. He was all his life profoundly religious. His interest in reconciling science and religion is evidenced in his textbooks, in his bequest of $50,000 to Syracuse University to found a chair of "theistic science," and in the inscription his wife had placed on his tombstone: "His true monument stands in the hearts of thousands of American youth, led by him to 'look through Nature up to Nature's God.'"

[Anna C. Palmer, *Joel Dorman Steele: Teacher and Author* (1900) with autobiog. introduction; J. B. Pratt, *Seventy-five Years of Book Publishing* (1913); D. S. Durrie, *Steele Family: A Geneal. Hist. of John and George Steele (Settlers of Hartford, Conn.), 1635–36, and Their Descendants* (1859); obituary in *Jour. of Proc. and Addresses Nat. Educ. Asso., Session of 1886* (1887); *Appletons' Ann. Cyc.*, 1886.]   E. W. F.

STEELE, JOHN (Nov. 16, 1764–Aug. 14, 1815), congressman from North Carolina, comptroller of the treasury, the son of William and Elizabeth (Maxwell) Gillespie Steel or Steele, both from Pennsylvania, was born in Salisbury, N. C. There his parents, and after his father's death in 1773 his mother, kept a tavern well known in the Piedmont region of the Carolinas. The boy was educated in Salisbury and at "Clio's Nursery," conducted by James Hall [*q.v.*]. He then engaged in a mercantile business in Salisbury, establishing soon afterward a connection with Robert Cochran, a wealthy merchant of Fayetteville, whose daughter-in-law, Mary Nesfield, he married Feb. 9, 1783. Three daughters lived to adult life. In 1784 he was assessor of the town of Salisbury, in 1787 was a town commissioner, and in the same year was elected as a borough member to the House of Commons, where he served two terms. The legislature made him a commissioner to treat with the Cherokee and Chickasaw in 1788. He was a Federalist member of the Hillsboro convention, called to consider the federal Constitution, and attracted much favorable attention by his part in the debates. The convention failed to ratify, and he was a delegate to the Fayetteville convention of 1789 that carried the state into the Union. He was at once elected to the House of Representatives of the First Congress and served with some distinction for two terms. Nominally a Federalist, he showed considerable independence in his whole course, regarding with disfavor the powers granted the president, opposing, in spite of his admiration and personal friendship for Alexander Hamilton, the latter's plan of assumption of state debts, and objecting to the maintenance of a standing army of any size. Later he was warmly hostile to the extension of judicial power, criticizing Marshall's decision in the *Marbury* vs. *Madison* case as a usurpation of power. He was not reëlected in 1792 owing to the reaction against the Federalists, and he was the same year an unsuccessful candidate for the federal Senate.

Returning to North Carolina he was a member of the House of Commons in 1794 and 1795. In the last session he was the unsuccessful candidate of the Federalists for federal senator. In 1794 he was commissioned a major-general of militia. In 1796 Washington appointed him comptroller of the treasury, and he served in that office until 1802, when, over the earnest protest of Jefferson who desired to retain him in office, he resigned, chiefly on account of illness in his family. In 1805 and in 1812 he was a member of the commission to determine the boundary between North Carolina and South Carolina, and in 1807 of the commission to settle the boundary dispute between North Carolina and Georgia. An extensive land-owner, after his return from Washington he devoted the greater part of his time to agriculture and the breeding and racing of blooded horses. He was again a member of the House of Commons in 1806, 1811 to 1813, and he was elected in 1815 but died before taking his seat. He was chosen speaker in 1811 to fill a vacancy.

[Papers in possession of N. C. Hist. Soc. and N. C. Hist. Commission; "The Papers of John Steele," *N. C. Hist. Commission Pubs.* (2 vols., 1924), ed. by H. M. Wagstaff; "Letters of Nathaniel Macon, John Steele and Wm. Barry Grove," with sketches by K. P. Battle, *James Sprunt Hist. Monograph*, no. 3 (1902); E. H. Bean, "Gen. John Steele," *Davidson College Studies in Hist.*, vol. I (1898); Archibald Henderson, "John Steele" and "Elizabeth Maxwell Steel," *N. C. Booklet*, Jan., Apr. 1919, Oct. 1912; date of birth from intro. to "Papers," *ante*, p. xxv.]   J. G. deR. H.

STEENDAM, JACOB (1616–c. 1672), eulogist and first poet of New Netherland, was born in the Netherlands, perhaps in Amsterdam, perhaps in Enkhuizen. He signed his poems with the device *Noch Vaster*, meaning "still firmer" than a stone dam. According to the *Formulier-boek* of the Amsterdam Classis, Dec. 3, 1640, Jacob Jacobss. van Steendam was "to go to the West Indies as a comforter of the sick" (*De Indische Gids,* September 1907, p. 1461); but instead, he spent eight years on the Gold Coast, returning to Holland in 1649 with a large collection of poems, which he published under the title of *Den Distelvink* (3 vols., 1649–50). He was an industrious rhymester with a good memory for Bible texts, but his poems contained little that was worth preserving. During a brief residence in Amsterdam he married Sara de Rosschou, and in 1652 he was settled in New Netherland as a merchant and trader. In that year he bought a farmstead at Amersfoort (Flatlands), and in the following year two houses at New Amsterdam and a farm at Mespath. He contributed to the fund raised for the defense of New Amsterdam against the Indians in 1653 and 1655; in 1655 he was orphan master, and in 1660 he and other burghers petitioned the Governor and Council for a license to import slaves and other commodities from the Gold Coast (O'Callaghan, *post,* p. 210).

As a business man Steendam was interested in the prosperity of New Amsterdam. Accordingly, seeing its welfare neglected by the West India Company and its future imperiled by the scarcity of colonists, he published in 1659 *Klacht van Nieuw Amsterdam in Nieuw Nederlandt tot Haar Moeder* (Complaint of New Amsterdam in New Netherland to Her Mother), a poem addressed to the mother city in Holland. This poem was followed in 1661 by *'T Lof van Nuw Nederland,* an extravagant eulogy of the many attractions of the colony. The burgomasters of Amsterdam shortly afterward financed a scheme of Pieter Corneliszen Plockhoy to plant a Mennonite settlement on the South (Delaware) River. A pamphlet by Plockhoy, *Kort en Klaer Ontwerp* (1662), in which he set forth the conditions for participation in his enterprise, contained *"Prickel-Vaerzen"* ("Spurring Verses") by Steendam, descriptive of the advantages of settlement in that far country.

When this pamphlet saw the light, Steendam was evidently back in Holland. In April 1663 he petitioned for permission to fence in his land at Mespath Kil, but he never returned to New Netherland. Instead, resuming the profession of comforter of the sick, he sailed for the East Indies in 1666 in the company of his wife and children. The Consistory at Batavia sent him to Bengal, but on Aug. 16, 1667, appointed him orphan master at Batavia. Here, in 1671, he published *Zeede-Zangen voor de Batavische*

Jonkheyt (Moral Songs for the Batavian Youth). He died, evidently, before September 1673, for a resolution of the Governor-General and Council of Sept. 5 of that year states that, since J. Steendam's widow had died, it was resolved to employ her daughter Vredegund Steendam and her betrothed Cornelis Wadde of Ooltgensplaat, for a trial period of two or three months.

[A small portrait of Steendam by J. M. Quinkhard is in the Rijksmuseum at Amsterdam; another, engraved by Coomans, is reproduced in H. C. Murphy's memoir, *Jacob Steendam, Noch Vaster* (1861), which contains the three poems on New Amsterdam and New Netherland, in the original Dutch and in English translation. This work is reprinted in Murphy's *Anthology of New Netherland* (1865). See also *De Indische Gids,* Sept. Oct. 1907; *De Navorscher,* XIV (1864), 305–06; *De Nieuwe Taalgids,* vols. XIII (1919) and XIV (1920); Gerrit Kalff, *Geschiedenis der Nederlandsche Letterkunde,* IV (1909), 465–67; W. L. Andrews, *Jacob Steendam* (1908); Berthold Fernow, *The Records of New Amsterdam* (1897), vols. I–III; E. B. O'Callaghan, *Calendar of Hist. MSS. in the Office of the Secretary of State, Albany, N. Y.,* vol. I (1865).]

A.J.B.

STEENWIJCK, CORNELIS VAN [See STEENWYCK, CORNELIS, d. 1684].

STEENWYCK, CORNELIS (d. 1684), colonial merchant, was born in Holland, probably in Haarlem, and appeared in New Amsterdam as early as 1651, coming as mate of a trading vessel. He engaged in trade and rose to prominence, ultimately sending his vessels to Virginia and the West Indies. In 1655, when fear of English encroachment was aroused in New Netherland, he contributed 100 guilders for the defense of the city; in 1656 he was the victim of a piece of gossip which resulted in a suit for slander which in turn brought about an extension of the power of the lower courts (Stokes, *post,* IV, 174). He was one of those who signed a petition, dated May 3, 1660, in which a number of merchants of New Amsterdam sought permission to trade for slaves along the west coast of Africa (O'Callaghan, *Calendar, post,* p. 210). A schepen in 1658 and 1660, burgomaster in 1662 and at later periods, he was chosen in 1663 to represent the interests of the colony in the mother country, an honor which he felt obliged to decline. In 1664, however, he was engaged as a commissioner for the colony in the diplomatic transactions which foreshadowed the English conquest. His mental poise is conspicuous in his proceedings with the swashbuckling Capt. John Scott, who as a commissioner for Hartford, Conn., urged the English claim (O'Callaghan, *Documents, post,* II, 399–401). Steenwyck took part in the negotiations which followed the appearance of the English fleet in the harbor of New Amsterdam, and his name is one of those attached to the articles by which New Netherland was surrendered. His oath of allegiance to the new government rested on the assurance that the rights of Dutch subjects would be preserved as guaranteed by the articles. Trusted and honored by the English governors, he remained throughout a stanch defender of those rights.

Richard Nicolls [*q.v.*], the first English governor, made Steenwyck mayor of New York, an office in which he was retained for more than two years (1668–70). Gov. Francis Lovelace [*q.v.*] admitted him to his council; and, when the Governor was called away on public affairs, he chose Steenwyck and Thomas Delavall "to take ye managery of such Affaires as shall happen here within ye City of New Yorke or places adjacent."

The restoration of Dutch authority in the colony by no means excluded Steenwyck from places of trust. By Gov. Anthony Colve he was appointed councilor with executive functions; he commanded militia and was otherwise employed in preparations for the city's defense, being also custodian of the accounts and journals of the insolvent Dutch West India Company in New Netherland. He was one of three commissioners who visited the eastern towns of Long Island to present to the English inhabitants the oath of allegiance to the States General. The English settlers, viewing themselves as subjects of Charles II, rejected the demand, and had the bearers of the summons exercised their powers in the spirit of Captain Scott, tragic incidents must have been added to the annals of Long Island.

No hint of political pliancy appears in Steenwyck's second acceptance of English rule; for, if he welcomed Sir Edmund Andros, the new governor, he met imprisonment at Andros' hands by insisting on recognition of the treaty claims of Dutch subjects. A reconciliation followed, however, and Steenwyck thenceforth was granted a serene official life. In 1682–83 he was mayor once more, and in this capacity presided over the newly established court of general sessions.

Steenwyck's commercial activities brought him wealth. In 1674 his estate was appraised at 50,-000 florins, exceeded in the colony only by that of Frederick Philipse (*Documents*, II, 699). His house, at the corner of Whitehall and Bridge (Brugh) streets, was furnished in a style luxurious for that period and he was reputed the best dressed, most polite, and most popular man in New Amsterdam (Valentine, *post*, 1858, p. 512, 1874, pp. 662–64). On June 5, 1658, he married Margaretha de Riemer, by whom he had seven children, none of whom, apparently, lived to maturity. He was an elder in the Reformed Dutch

Church in the city, and one of his last acts was to bequeath the Manor of Fordham to that communion.

[Berthold Fernow, *The Records of New Amsterdam* (7 vols., 1897) and *N. Y. State Lib. Bull. No. 58 . . . Calendar of Council Minutes, 1668–1783* (1902); V. H. Paltsits, *Minutes of the Exec. Council of the Province of N. Y.* (1910), vol. II; E. B. O'Callaghan, *Calendar of Hist. MSS. in the Office of the Secretary of State, Albany, N. Y.*, vol. I, Dutch (1865), vol. II, English (1866), and *Docs. Rel. to the Col. Hist. of the State of N. Y.*, vols. II (1858), III (1853), XI (1861); Berthold Fernow, *Docs. Rel. to the Col. Hist. of the State of N. Y.*, vol. XIV (1883); I. N. P. Stokes, *The Iconography of Manhattan Island* (6 vols., 1915–28); D. T. Valentine, *Manual of the Corporation of the City of N. Y.*, 1853, 1858, 1864; W. E. De Riemer, *The De Riemer Family* (1905); a portrait in the N. Y. Hist. Soc.]

R. E. D.

STEERS, GEORGE (July 20, 1820–Sept. 25, 1856), naval architect, yacht designer, inherited much of his ability from his father, Henry Steer, a successful British shipbuilder, who emigrated to the United States from Devonshire in 1819, added a final "s" to the family name, and became one of the leading naval constructors of his time. His third son, George, one of thirteen children, was born in Washington, D. C., and grew up in his father's shipyard at the foot of East Tenth Street, New York City. When ten years of age he built a scow which his brothers broke up as unsafe, and at sixteen he turned out a sloop whose success brought him to the attention of John C. Stevens, one of the leading citizens in New York, and his lifelong friend and patron. Steers's first larger boat, the twenty-seven-ton sloop, *Manhattan*, built in his father's yard in 1839, was followed by the fast pilot boat, *William G. Hagstaff*, the 250-ton schooner *St. Mary the First*, three steamers for the Great Lakes, and a small ship, *Sunny South*, which subsequently became a slaver.

In his early productions Steers adhered to the accepted "cod's-head-and-mackerel-tail" theory of design, but in 1849 he turned out a schooner, *Mary Taylor*, in which the forefoot was boldly rounded away, the bows moderately hollowed, with a clean afterbody and well balanced ends. The almost instantaneous success of the *Mary Taylor* as a fast pilot boat, and others of similar lines, soon made the New York pilot fleet the talk of the shipping world. Through his intimate acquaintance with the Stevens brothers, John Cox, Robert Livingston, and Edwin Augustus Stevens, Steers was enabled to keep in close touch with the most progressive ideas of the day in steam engineering, marine propulsion, railroading, and other mechanical devices. Under the name of Hathorn & Steers he had charge of a boatyard on the Williamsburg side of the East River from 1845 to 1849, when he formed a partnership with his brother, James R. Steers. They built a number of notable vessels including the steamship, *Adriatic,* for the Collins line, and the warship, *Niagara,* which helped to lay the first transatlantic cable.

Steers became well known as a builder of pleasure craft such as the schooners *Syren, Sybil, Una, Ray, Julia, Cygnet, Cornelia,* and *Haze*— all of which were prominent in yacht races before and even after the Civil War. But his most famous craft was the *America.* He received the order for this boat from a syndicate of six members of the New York Yacht Club, John Cox Stevens, Edwin Augustus Stevens, Col. James A. Hamilton, George L. Schuyler, Hamilton Wilkes, and John K. Beekman Finlay, while engaged in the yard of William H. Brown at the foot of East Twelfth St. Steers is credited with both her design and construction. His clients were sharp business men who held him to his contract to build an unbeatable boat and paid him twenty instead of thirty thousand dollars after the *America* had been defeated by the sloop *Maria,* a much larger craft, in her first test of speed. Unchagrined by the seeming failure, Steers crossed the ocean on the *America* and sailed her in the memorable race of Aug. 22, 1851, around the Isle of Wight. At one time during her course, no second boat was in sight of the American craft. Although the *America* revolutionized yacht design on both sides of the Atlantic, Steers seems to have been forgotten in the festivities which followed the winning of the 100 guinea cup of the Royal Yacht Squadron, and it was not until some years later that his great creations received their just due. His death at the early age of thirty-seven resulted from injuries received in a runaway accident near his home at Great Neck, L. I.

[W. M. Martin, W. P. Stephens, W. U. Swan, *The Yacht "America"* (1925) ; W. M. Thompson, *The Lawson Hist. of the America's Cup* (1902) ; H. L. Stone, *The "America's" Cup Races* (1914) ; Nigel Lindsay, *The America's Cup* (London, 1930), *N. Y. Herald,* Sept. 26, 27, 1856.]   W. U. S.

STEHLE, AURELIUS ALOYSIUS (Apr. 30, 1877–Feb. 12, 1930), Roman Catholic cleric, fourth archabbot of St. Vincent, Latrobe, Pa., was born at Pittsburgh, Pa., the fourth child of Richard Stehle of Binsdorf, Württemberg, Germany, and Rose (Niggel) Stehle of Butler, Pa. He received his early education at St. Paul's parochial school, Pittsburgh, and on Mar. 17, 1885, he was sent with his older brother Joseph to St. Vincent College, Latrobe, Pa. Here in spite of his youth he soon ranked high in his classes. After completing the Latin course in 1892, he decided to study for the church and to

become a Benedictine. On July 11, 1893, following his year of probation, he made his first vows, and during the next five years studied philosophy and theology in St. Vincent Seminary. After a papal dispensation had been obtained because he had not reached his canonical age, he was ordained priest on Sept. 8, 1899, by Bishop Regis Canevin of Pittsburgh. Having always shown a great love for classical languages, he was appointed professor of Latin in the seminary, and he gradually achieved in that tongue such perfection that he could use it in daily conversation. He also became secretary to Archabbot Leander Schnerr [*q.v.*] and made special studies in the liturgy of the church, which resulted in the publication of *The Manual of Episcopal Ceremonies* (1914), a book extensively used by the prelates of the Catholic Church in the United States. In 1911 he was appointed vice-rector of St. Vincent Seminary. It was chiefly through his efforts that the institution in 1914 was raised by the Roman authorities to the rank of a pontifical seminary, with the right of granting all ecclesiastical degrees in philosophy and theology. On June 25, 1918, by the vote of the capitulars of St. Vincent Archabbey, he was chosen coadjutor-abbot of the monastery with the right of succession; on Sept. 3, 1920, upon the death of Archabbot Leander Schnerr, he became the fouth archabbot of St. Vincent.

His administration is noteworthy for the extension and perfection of the course of studies at St. Vincent College, and for the founding of the Catholic University at Peking, China. With the addition of pre-medical, pre-legal, educational, and aeronautical courses to the existing curriculum of St. Vincent College the number of students was nearly doubled. The plan for a university in China, which began in a very modest manner in 1918, grew by leaps and bounds to unexpected proportions. Believing that the founding of a Benedictine abbey in China would contribute much toward the conversion of that nation, Father Aurelius and Dr. Barry O'Toole, a professor in St. Vincent Seminary, by degrees arrived at the decision to found a Benedictine university there and in 1922 secured the approval of the Congregation de Propaganda Fide in Rome. Two years later, June 10, 1924, the first Benedictines left St. Vincent for the Far East. In 1925 Archabbot Aurelius, who had been appointed chancellor of the new institution by Rome, went to China and procured the perpetual lease of Prince Ts'ai T'ao's palace, which became the first building of the university. In 1929 a large modern structure in Chinese architecture was built. Meanwhile the educational board of the Chinese republic also approved the course of studies and granted the institution the right of conferring academic honors. In 1929 the Archabbot went to Rome to consult the ecclesiastical authorities about the extension of the work and to obtain material assistance. His labors, especially those connected with this American foundation in the Far East, gradually sapped the strength of the affable, tireless, and talented churchman, whose health was never of the best. In January 1930, while addressing a meeting of churchmen in Cleveland on behalf of his beloved project, he was stricken with a nervous breakdown, and shortly thereafter died in St. Francis Hospital, Pittsburgh, Pa.

[*Who's Who in America*, 1930–31; files of *St. Vincent Coll. Jour.*, 1892–1930, and *Bull. of the Cath. Univ. of Peking*, 1926–30; letters and docs. in archives of St. Vincent Archabbey; obituary in *Pittsburgh Sun-Telegraph*, Feb. 13, 1930.]   F. F.

STEIN, EVALEEN (Oct. 12, 1863–Dec. 11, 1923), poet, author, and artist, was born in Lafayette, Ind., and spent her entire life there. Her father, John Andrew Stein (1832–1886), a Pennsylvania farmer by birth, practised law in Lafayette from his twenty-third year until his death; as a member of the Indiana Senate he drafted the bill which founded Indiana Agricultural College (later Purdue University). Her mother, Virginia (Tomlinson) Stein (1840–1924), was born at Logansport, Ind., of a pioneer family that had moved westward from Virginia. After being educated in the public schools of Lafayette, she studied at the Art Institute of Chicago and did creditable work as a decorative designer, exhibiting illuminated manuscripts at the Society of Arts and Crafts in Chicago, and in other midwestern cities. It is, however, as a poet and as a writer of children's stories that she gained widest recognition. Her home associations stimulated literary ambitions. Her father contributed verse and essays to local newspapers; her mother was the author of a few short stories for children; and her brother, Orth, was a professional newspaper man and magazine writer. After her father's death, she became assistant to her mother, who for over thirty years was librarian of the Lafayette public library.

At twenty-three she began contributing verse to the *Indianapolis Journal* and the *St. Nicholas* magazine. Her first book of poetry, *One Way to the Woods* (1897) was followed five years later by a second, *Among the Trees Again,* and some years later by a book of verse for children, *Child Songs of Cheer* (1918), and two volumes of translations, *Little Poems from Japanese Anthologies* (1925) and *Poems of Giovanni Pascoli* (1923). The majority of her poems describe with accurate and keenly-observed detail the seasons and the moods of nature, and express a sincere and ardent joy in natural objects; the best of them have a lilting cadence, as in "By the Kankakee," or a rush and sweep of verse, as in "A Song of Thought." In January 1900 she published in *St. Nicholas* a Christmas story for children, entitled "Felix"; three years later she included it in *Troubadour Tales,* the first of a number of children's books. Her knowledge of the art of illuminating manuscripts is evident in the second of these, *Gabriel and the Hour Book* (1906), and her interest in medieval France, awakened by her study of the art of illumination, appears in *A Little Shepherd of Provence* (1910), *The Little Count of Normandy* (1911), *Pepin: A Tale of Twelfth Night* (1924), and several of her short stories. Many of her stories are legends and fairy stories retold with clarity, simplicity, and charm. In 1915 she published *Our Little Norman Cousin of Long Ago,* one of four books written for a series introducing young readers to the people and customs of vanished nations. Unfortunately in these books, written to instruct rather than to entertain, she failed to exhibit the artistry of the legends and her usual ease in story-telling. She also wrote *The Christmas Porringer* (1914), *Rosechen and the Wicked Magpie* (1917), *When Fairies were Friendly* (1922), and *The Circus Dwarf Stories* (1927). Gentle and quiet in manner, she spent her leisure among books, cultivating her garden, or enjoying the natural beauties of the countryside. In 1907 she traveled in Europe for a few months, but except for this tour and an earlier trip to California she scarcely left Indiana.

[R. P. De Hart, *Past and Present of Tippecanoe County, Ind.* (2 vols., 1909); *Lafayette Jour. Courier,* Dec. 12, 1923, and Nov. 8, 1924; undated newspaper clippings in the possession of Florence G. Ruger, librarian of the Albert A. Wells Memorial Lib., Lafayette, Ind.]   V. L. S.

STEINER, BERNARD CHRISTIAN (Aug. 13, 1867–Jan. 12, 1926), teacher, librarian, and historian, was born at Guilford, Conn., the son of Sarah Spencer (Smyth) and Lewis Henry Steiner [*q.v.*]. He was the descendant of Jacob Stoner or Steiner who settled in Frederick County, Md., before 1736. He prepared for college at the academy at Frederick, Md., received the degrees of A.B. and A.M. from Yale in 1888 and in 1890, and received the doctor's degree in history from The Johns Hopkins University in 1891. In 1894 he received the LL.B. degree from the University of Maryland. He began his active career as instructor of history at Williams College for the year 1891–92. Excellently fitted, through training and interest, for teaching or for the bar, he would doubtless have adopted one or the other as his profession but for his election in 1892 at the age of twenty-five to the librarianship of the Enoch Pratt Free Library in succession to his father. As instructor in history, and later as associate, he gave courses in constitutional history at Johns Hopkins from 1893 to 1911. During this period he acted also, 1897–1900, as dean and professor of constitutional law in the short-lived Baltimore University, and, 1900–1904, as dean and professor of public law in the Baltimore Law School. These academic interests were subordinate to his work as librarian of the Enoch Pratt Free Library, the municipal public library of Baltimore. His conduct of that institution was marked by conservatism in methods of administration coupled with extraordinary aggressiveness in broadening its field of influence through the establishment of branch libraries in every neighborhood of an expanding city, increasing the number of these in his thirty-three-year tenure of office from six to twenty-five. His creed, "The Library is the continuation school of the people" was frequently on his lips and constantly in his mind, and its strict application in practice gave an element of austerity to his administration that sometimes placed him at variance with popular conceptions of the function of a public library. He kept abreast of the departmental development of the modern public library, however, in spite of an equipment and income adapted to the simpler needs of the late nineteenth century.

His interest in historical study, especially in the history of Maryland and Connecticut, the history of education in America, and religious and constitutional history, found constant expression in authorship. From 1891 to 1926 he made almost ninety contributions in the form of books and articles to the history of Maryland alone, and, under the direction of the Maryland Historical Society, he edited for the state with comprehensive introductions, volumes XVIII, XXXVI–XLV of the *Archives of Maryland* (1900, 1916–27), displaying in this task skill in the handling of archival material and breadth in its interpretation. His biographies were, perhaps, his most significant productions. For the subjects of these books he chose deliberately men of real importance in their own times who, falling short of the highest achievement, were in danger of being forgotten. Of these the most important are "Life and Administration of Sir Robert Eden," *Johns Hopkins University Studies in History and Political Science*, 16 ser., nos. 7–9 (1898); *Life and Correspondence of James McHenry* (1907); *Life of Reverdy Johnson* (1914);

Life of Henry Winter Davis (1916); "Life of Henry Barnard," *U. S. Bureau of Education Bulletin*, no. 8 (1919); and *Life of Roger Brooke Taney* (1922). Other important writings are "History of Education in Connecticut," *U. S. Bureau of Education Circular of Information*, no. 2 (1893); "History of Education in Maryland," *Ibid.*, no. 2 (1894); *Citizenship and Suffrage in Maryland* (1895); *History of . . . Guilford, Conn.* (1897); *Institutions and Civil Government of Maryland* (1899). Notable among his personal characteristics were his convinced Republicanism, his enthusiasm for civic and social service, and an intense religious conviction, expressed formally through active membership in the Presbyterian Church. All these interests were carried into his daily life and into his conversation, with the enthusiasm that was one of his noteworthy possessions. At his death he was survived by a son and by his widow, Ethel Simes (Mulligan) Steiner, to whom he was married Nov. 7, 1912.

[*Quarter-Century Record of the Class of 1888, Yale College* (1914), comp. by B. C. Steiner (1914); L. H. and B. C. Steiner, *The Geneal. of the Steiner Family* (1896); *Who's Who in America*, 1924–25; intro. by L. C. Wroth to *Archives of Md., ante*, vol. XLV with list of writings on Md. compiled by W. R. Steiner; *Proc. Am. Antiquarian Soc.*, Apr. 1926; *Sun* (Baltimore), Jan. 13, 1926.]   L. C. W.

STEINER, LEWIS HENRY (May 4, 1827–Feb. 18, 1892), physician and librarian, was born in Frederick, Md., the son of Christian Steiner, a general merchant, and Rebecca (Weltzheimer), his cousin. He was of German descent, his first American ancestor on his father's side being Jacob Steiner who was in Frederick County before 1736. Lewis was educated in Frederick Academy and in Marshall College at Mercersburg, Pa., where he was graduated in 1846. Three years later he took his degree in medicine at the University of Pennsylvania. He began practice in Frederick, but removed to Baltimore in 1852 to take a teaching position in a private medical institute. Always interested in the natural sciences, particularly in chemistry and botany, he decided in 1855 to give up the practice of medicine and devote his whole time to the teaching of these subjects.

He was professor of chemistry and natural history at Columbian College and of chemistry and pharmacy at the National Medical College, both located in Washington, D. C., from 1853 to 1855; lecturer on chemistry and physics at the College of St. James at Hagerstown, Md., from 1854 to 1859; and lecturer on applied chemistry at the Maryland Institute in 1855 and 1856. He was one of a group that, in 1856, reorganized the Maryland College of Pharmacy, in which he held the chair of chemistry until 1861. With the outbreak of the Civil War he returned to Frederick and entered the service of the United States Sanitary Commission. He was chief of that service with the Army of the Potomac during the campaigns of 1863 and 1864. His experiences are recorded in two reports issued in 1862 and 1863, and in 1866 he published a short history of the Sanitary Commission.

He was chosen president of the Frederick County school board, in 1865, in which capacity he interested himself particularly in providing school facilities for negro children. From 1871 to 1883 he represented his native county in the state Senate as a Republican, delivering there, Feb. 23, 1876, a notable address published under the title, *The Louisiana Legislature and States Rights* (1876). He was a delegate to the Republican National Convention in 1876, which nominated Hayes for the presidency. From 1873 to 1884 he was political editor of the *Frederick Examiner*.

When, in 1884, Enoch Pratt [*q.v.*] of Baltimore endowed and built the free library which bears his name, he brought Steiner from Frederick to be its librarian. It was opened to the public in 1886, and from that time until his sudden death from apoplexy in 1892 Steiner guided its destinies. He was succeeded as librarian by his son, Bernard Christian Steiner [*q.v.*], who held the position for thirty-four years until he in turn died in 1926. Steiner's publications were numerous and varied. Among his pamphlets are *Physical Science* (1851), *Report on the Progress of Medical Chemistry* (1855), *Report on Strychnia* (1856), *The Medical Profession and Modern Chemistry* (1856), *The Marvelous in Modern Times* (1860), *The Divining Rod* (1861), *Table Movings and Spirit Rappings* (1861), and *Animal Magnetism and Hypnotism* (1861). He was an elder of the Reformed Church of Frederick and a member of the Potomac synod. For its publishing house he made translations from the German of a number of children's stories, notably *The Adventures of Leo Rembrandt* (1869), and *The Story of Father Miller* (1869), both by Franz Hoffmann. He also published *Outlines of Chemical Analysis,* a translation, made in collaboration with David Breed, from the German of Heinrich Will. As a member of the synod he collaborated in the preparation of a hymn-book, *Cantate Domino* (1859), *A Catechism of Christian Religion; Commonly Called the Heidelberg Catechism* (1860), and *Order of Worship* (1866). From 1859 to 1861 he was assistant editor of the *American Medical Monthly* of New York.

In addition to his affiliations with medical societies he was a member of the Maryland Academy of Science, the Philadelphia Academy of Natural Science, the American Association for the Advancement of Science, and the American Public Health Association. He was one of the founders in 1876 of the American Academy of Medicine, and its president in 1878. On Oct. 30, 1866, he married Sarah Spencer Smyth, daughter of Judge Ralph D. Smyth of Guilford, Conn.; they had three sons and three daughters. Steiner edited and published a *History of Guilford, Connecticut* (1877) from manuscript left by his father-in-law.

[L. H. and B. C. Steiner, *The Geneal. of the Steiner Family* (1896); E. F. Cordell, *Univ. of Md.* (1907); *Bull. Am. Acad. Medicine* (1892), pp. 216–18; J. R. Quinan, *Medic. Annals of Baltimore* (1884); H. A. Kelly and W. L. Burrage, *Am. Medic. Biogs.* (1920); *Sun* (Baltimore), Feb. 19, 1892.]   J. M. P.

STEINERT, MORRIS (Mar. 9, 1831–Jan. 21, 1912), collector of musical instruments, was born of Jewish parents, Heyum Löb Steinert and Esther Steinert, in Scheinfeld, a small Bavarian village. His early education was necessarily meager, but later he came under the influence of a man named Kleinschrod and under his guidance made extensive studies in the German classics and philosophy. Moritz (his given name) showed from the beginning an aptitude for music. He first learned to play, not on the pianoforte, but on the clavier, and grew naturally to understand the older types of instruments and the music of the Mozart-Haydn period written for them. This affection for the antique in music led to the development of his taste for collecting instruments in his later years. He learned also to play the violoncello and many times his mastery of both keyboard and bowed instruments served him well in his struggle to make a living as a musician. Music was not, however, his first profession. At the age of twelve he worked in the shop of a maker of optical instruments at Coblenz. He was then sent out by his employer as a salesman at Bad-Ems, where he remained for three years. The interruption of business by the Revolution of 1848 necessitated his return to his home for a time, and thus the record of his life for a number of years thereafter is one of wandering from city to city in an attempt to make his way as an optician. His business took him first to Switzerland, then to Germany and Russia. He settled for short periods in 1855 at Berlin, Helsingfors, and St. Petersburg successively. His experiences during this time of his career were not always pleasant, for life in cold, police-ridden Russia was exceedingly difficult, even hazardous.

Throughout these earlier years Steinert's love

for music became intensified as he heard the then "new" music of Beethoven, Schubert, and Schumann, and the German and Italian operas. Shortly after 1855 he emigrated to America, and after several years of selling optical instruments at Sharon Springs, N. Y., he settled in New Haven, Conn. The musical profession, however, gradually took the place of his trade, and the records show him as a violoncellist in Maretzek's orchestra in New York City, and as pianist with a traveling minstrel's troupe. After a short period of residence in Savannah and Thomasville, Ga., the opening of the Civil War sent him North and he settled permanently in New Haven. From 1861 until his death his work was identified with New Haven, and his most memorable activities were those that contributed to the musical development of that city. He founded the Mathushek Pianoforte Company, and later the M. Steinert and Sons Company, which maintained stores for the sale of pianos in Boston Providence, New Haven, and other cities.

In his later years Steinert became greatly interested in collecting old musical instruments, purchasing the first examples in and near his native village of Scheinfeld. His skill in discovering and restoring them was soon recognized, and he was invited to exhibit his collection at the Vienna exposition of music and drama in 1892, and at the World's Columbian Exposition in Chicago in 1893. He donated the greater part of the collection in 1900 to Yale University. There are few more important collections of the kind, containing as it does many rare examples of clavichords, harpsichords, early pianofortes, and viols (see Steinert's *The M. Steinert Collection of Keyed and Stringed Instruments*, 1893). In 1892 Steinert founded the New Haven Symphony Orchestra, one of the oldest symphonic organizations in America. He was married to Caroline Dreyfuss on Jan. 7, 1857, and there were nine children. Shortly before her death in 1899, he wrote *Reminiscences of Morris Steinert* (1900), a book which reflects in a delightfully natural way the rare good humor of its author and which gives a vivid picture of an unusually eventful life.

[Information from the family, and Steinert's *Reminiscences.* See also: *Grove's Dict. of Music and Musicians, Am. Supp.* (1930) ; W. S. Pratt, ed., *The New Encyc. of Music and Musicians* (1929) ; T. B. Willson, *Hist. Cat. of the M. Steinert Coll. of Musical Instruments* (1913) ; *New Haven Evening Register*, Jan. 22, 1912.]

D. S. S.

STEINITZ, WILLIAM (May 17, 1836–Aug. 12, 1900), chess player, was born at Prague, the son of middle-class Jewish parents. When he was twenty years old he registered as a student in the Polytechnicum in Vienna and there in the cafés became enamored of chess. Turning briefly to journalism as a means of livelihood, he perfected himself in the royal game. In 1862, when he participated in the international tournament in London, he placed sixth. In the same year he defeated Serafino Dubois in the first of some thirty important matches, all won except the final two of 1894 and 1896. By his defeat of Adolph Anderssen in 1866 he achieved general recognition as chess champion of the world, a title which he held for twenty-eight years and justified by a fine record of successes in matches and tournaments. He was never defeated in any even match until he met Emanuel Lasker ; though he was not at his best in tournament play ; in fifteen major tournaments he was nine times first and only once as low as sixth. He spent twenty years (1862–82) in England, where from January 1873 to August 1882 he edited the chess column in the English journal, *Field*. Though he had become a British citizen, in 1883 he came to America and a year later acquired American citizenship. In America he edited the *International Chess Magazine*, 1885–91, *The Book of the Sixth American Chess Congress . . . 1889* (1891), the chess column in the *New York Tribune* (Sunday edition), Oct. 19, 1890–Aug. 6, 1893, and for a brief time the columns in the *Sunday Herald* (Baltimore) and the *New York Herald*. His most notable literary achievement was *The Modern Chess Instructor* (2 pts. 1889–1895), which contributed to the theory of chess a somewhat new point of view. In chess tactics he represented the beginning of the modern school in which the accumulation of small advantages plays the greatest rôle. In 1894 and again in 1896 he was defeated by Emanuel Lasker in a match for the championship of the world. The defeat was a blow not only to his prestige but to his means of livelihood. Undoubtedly his mental troubles, which began shortly after this time, were due to the circumstances caused by his defeat. In 1897, while in Saint Petersburg (later Leningrad) at a tournament, he was adjudged insane and was confined for a time. Spells of insanity recurred until his death at the Manhattan State Hospital, Ward's Island, New York. In 1900 he published a small tract, an ill-natured appeal for money : *My Advertisement to Antisemites in Vienna and Elsewhere by "A Schacherjude" (Mercenary Jew) : or, An Essay on Capital, Labor, and Charity.*

He was short in stature, heavy set, and slightly lame. His infirmity in later life gave him a hunchbacked and gnomelike aspect, to which his ruddy beard and large head contributed. In disposition he was inclined to be disagreeable, and the trait carried over into some of his chess commentaries.

He expressed himself vigorously and pictur-esquely, with less restraint as he grew older. He must early have appreciated that there was a possibility for him to attain in chess an eminence not likely in business. Certainly both his long career as champion of the world and his literary activity amply vindicated his choice of a career. By matches, by exhibitions, by play for money in clubs, by occasional engagements in the mechanical player at the Eden Museum in New York, and by literary work, he was able to make a living, albeit a somewhat precarious one, at the game of chess. He was twice married, once in England and once in America; his first wife, Caroline, died May 27, 1892 (dedication to *My Advertisement*). A daughter whom he had adopted in England died in New York in 1888; there was one son born to the American wife, who was much younger than her husband.

[The date of birth is from Devidé, who knew Steinitz long and intimately; it is given as May 18, 1837, by the Czechoslovakian legation, Washington, D. C. Sources include Charles Devidé, *A Memorial to William Steinitz* (1901); Ludwig Bachmann, *Schachmeister Steinitz: Ein Lebensbild des ersten Weltschachmeisters, dargestellt in einer vollständigen Sammlung seiner Partien* (vols. I–IV, 1910–20) and *Schachjahrbuch für 1900* (Ansbach, 1901), pp. 197–203; P. W. Sergeant, *A Century of British Chess* (1934); obituaries in *Deutsche Schachzeitung*, Sept. 1900, *British Chess Mag.*, Sept. 1900, *N. Y. Tribune*, Aug. 14, and *Times* (London), Aug. 15, 1900; correspondence with Charles Devidé and Hermann Helms; personal acquaintance.]

L. C. K.

STEINMETZ, CHARLES PROTEUS (Apr. 9, 1865–Oct. 26, 1923), mathematician, electrical engineer, the only child of Karl Heinrich Steinmetz and his first wife, Caroline (Neubert) Steinmetz, was born in Breslau, Germany, where his father was employed as a lithographer in the railroad office. His given name, which he used for about the first twenty-five years of his life, was Karl August Rudolf, but in his application for American citizenship he anglicized his first name to Charles and substituted for the other two the name Proteus, a nickname given him when he joined the student mathematical society in Breslau. Although deformed from birth, he was a normally inquisitive, mischievous boy but badly spoiled by his grandmother, who mothered the family after the death of Charles's mother when he was a year old. It was evident early in his school career that he had a keen mind, and when he had completed the course in the gymnasium his father willingly sent him to the University of Breslau instead of apprenticing him to a trade. He entered the university in 1883, his eager, penetrating mind just beginning to open to the stimulus of study and his whole nature a questioning one. He was decidedly versatile and had an astonishing capacity for study. During his six years at the university he never missed a class, took a prodigious number of notes, and even undertook independent investigations at home. From the very first he selected difficult technical subjects. Beginning with mathematics and astronomy, he expanded his studies so that in his sixth year he was taking theoretical physics, chemistry, electrical engineering, specialized work in higher mathematics, and medicine. In addition, he was a student of economics and kept up his reading of the classics. At the same time he was a friendly, sociable fellow who was ready to join in lively, carefree student parties at almost any hour. About 1884 he joined the student Socialist group and in the course of the succeeding four years became most active, serving for a time as ghost editor of the *People's Voice,* published by the Socialists of Breslau. This proved his undoing; for, as a result of a most daring editorial published early in 1888, he had to flee from Germany to avoid arrest and imprisonment just as he had completed his university work and his thesis for his doctor's degree, which was never conferred upon him. Fleeing to Switzerland, where he lived a year in Zürich in straitened circumstances, he spent six months in attendance at the Polytechnic School, and occasionally wrote an article on some phase of electrical engineering for a German technical journal.

In the late spring of 1889, on the spur of the moment, he sailed steerage for the United States, financed by a student friend who accompanied him. He landed in New York on June 1 and within two weeks found employment as a draftsman for Rudolf Eickemeyer [*q.v.*] at Yonkers, N. Y., to whom he had gone with a letter of introduction (Hammond, *post,* p. 155). Eickemeyer, who was then engaged in research and in the development of electrical machinery, soon found Steinmetz, with his keen mathematical and technical mind, of the greatest help, and before very long established him in an experimental laboratory of his own. Here he applied himself earnestly not only to the electrical problems given him but also, in characteristic fashion, to the problem of Americanizing himself. He mastered the language, applied for citizenship, and even joined the American Institute of Electrical Engineers and the New York (later American) Mathematical Society. At the time electrical engineers were concerned with reducing the losses of efficiency in electrical apparatus due to alternating magnetism (hysteresis). The laws of this power loss were entirely unknown, and many engineers doubted its existence. Steinmetz, however, having been given the task of calculating and designing an alternating current commutator motor, and wishing to calculate the hysteresis loss, derived the law of hysteresis mathematically from existing data. He followed this with an elaborate series of tests on any and every sample of iron obtainable to prove the law and simplify its application, and in 1892 read two papers on the subject before the American Institute of Electrical Engineers. These at once established his reputation as a new thinker possessed of a powerful, analytical mind. Publicly acclaimed on every hand, he became widely known among electrical scientists, and his mathematical genius was recognized as far above the ordinary. Shortly after the organization of the General Electric Company in 1892, he joined the staff of the calculating department and went first to Lynn, Mass., and then to Schenectady, N. Y. After completing his second year with the company he was made consulting engineer, a position he held throughout the rest of his life. While he was engaged in his studies of magnetism at Yonkers, he had begun studies of alternating electric current phenomena, which were then little understood and most complex. Through the application of pure mathematics involving a degree of intricate work bewildering to the layman, he found a mathematical method of reducing the alternating current theory to a basis of practical calculation, and presented a rather complicated outline of the new method to the International Electrical Congress in session at Chicago, Ill., in 1893. Lack of funds prevented its publication at that time, but four years later he published the original paper, as well as a series of articles bringing out the practical side of his method, as a textbook under the title, *Theory and Calculation of Alternating Current Phenomena* (1897), with Ernst J. Berg as co-author. He found himself in unapproachable intellectual solitude, however, for practically no one could understand his theory or use his method. Gradually, however, through the publication of several textbooks— *Theoretical Elements of Electrical Engineering* (1901), *Engineering Mathematics* (1911)— and the expansion of his first book into three volumes—*Theory and Calculation of Alternating Current Phenomena* (5th ed., 1916), *Theory and Calculation of Electric Circuits* (1917), and *Theory and Calculations of Electrical Apparatus* (1917)—he brought about a clear understanding of his symbolic method, which is now universally used in alternating current calculations. His third and last great research undertaking had to do with the phenomena which are centered in lightning. As electric transmission lines spread over the country, lightning, an old enemy,

became more formidable, and protection from lightning most important. In an effort to learn more about it, Steinmetz began a systematic study of the general equation of the electric current and of "transient electrical phenomena," as lightning is scientifically called, publishing the results periodically from 1907 onward. This work culminated in 1921 with the dramatic experiments yielding man-made lightning in the laboratory. Though this was not the end of the investigation, it was left uncompleted at Steinmetz's death.

In addition to his consulting work and his writing, he was professor of electrical engineering, 1902–13, and professor of electrophysics, 1913–23, at Union University, Schenectady, N. Y., and lectured on electrical subjects throughout the country. He served on the board of education of Schenectady, of which he was president for two terms, and on the common council. The numerous honors conferred on him included the presidency of the American Institute of Electrical Engineers, 1901–02; the award of the Elliott Cresson gold medal, made by the Franklin Institute, Philadelphia; and membership in the American Academy of Arts and Sciences and the American Philosophical Society. He patented a large number of inventions, many of them basic, and wrote several books in addition to those mentioned, among them *Theory and Calculation of Transient Electric Phenomena and Oscillations* (1909); *General Lectures on Electrical Engineering* (copyright 1908), compiled and edited by J. L. Hayden; *Radiation, Light and Illumination* (1909); and *Elementary Lectures on Electric Discharges, Waves and Impulses, and Other Transients* (1911), all of which went through several editions. He never married but legally adopted as his son and heir Joseph Le Roy Hayden, who survived him.

[*Who's Who in America,* 1922–23; *Who's Who in Engineering,* 1922–23; J. W. Hammond, *Charles Proteus Steinmetz, A Biog.* (copr. 1924); J. T. Broderick, *Steinmetz and His Discoverer* (copr. 1924); J. N. Leonard, *Loki: The Life of Charles Proteus Steinmetz* (1929), a popular biog.; and "Steinmetz, Jove of Science," *World's Work,* Feb. 1929; Mary V. Hun, in *Forum,* Feb. 1924; obituaries in *Trans. Illuminating Engineering Soc.,* vol. XVIII (1923), H. M. H., in *Jour. Institution of Electrical Engineers* (London), vol. LXII (1924), *Jour. Am. Inst. of Electrical Engineers,* Nov. 1923; obituary and editorial in *N. Y. Times,* Oct. 27, 1923.]   C. W. M—n.

STEINMEYER, FERDINAND [See FARMER, FATHER, 1720–1786].

STEINWAY, CHRISTIAN FRIEDRICH THEODORE (Nov. 6, 1825–Mar. 26, 1889), piano manufacturer, was born in Seesen, Germany, the eldest child of Henry Engelhard Steinway [*q.v.*] and Juliane (Thiemer) Steinway,

As a youth he was musically talented, and in 1839 sufficiently accomplished as a pianist to be given the task of demonstrating his father's pianos at a fair in Brunswick. He was educated at Jacobsohn College in Seesen, where he became interested in the study of acoustics and was commissioned by his instructor, who took a particular interest in his brilliant pupil, to make the models needed for the lectures. When he completed his college course and went to work at a bench in his father's piano factory, he brought his scientific training to bear on the design and construction of pianofortes. In 1851, when his father and brothers left Germany for America, he stayed in Seesen, ostensibly to close the family business affairs and later to follow his kin to New York. He remained in Germany, however, for fourteen years after the departure of his family. On Oct. 10, 1852, he married Johanna Frederika Karolina Magdalena Luederman, and moved the piano business to Wolfenbüttel. In 1858 he admitted Friedrich Grotrian to partnership, and in the following year moved the firm's headquarters to Brunswick. Following the death of two of his brothers in 1865, he received an appeal from his father to come to New York to assist in the conduct of the Steinway business in America (the family name, originally Steinweg, had been legally changed to Steinway in 1864). He accordingly sold his business at Brunswick to his partners, Grotrian, Helfferich, and Schulz, and departed for New York. He immediately took charge of the construction department of the factory of Steinway & Sons, by this time a flourishing enterprise, and while his brother William [*q.v.*] devoted himself to the business management and sales department of the firm, he applied modern science to the problems of piano building. He investigated and tested the relative qualities of various woods; he continued his study of chemistry to determine the best ingredients of glue, varnish, and oils; and he experimented in metallurgy to find a proper alloy for casting iron plates strong enough to bear the strain of 75,000 pounds from the strings of the concert grand piano he wished to build.

He remained in America for only five years. He never enjoyed his surroundings in New York and sincerely wished to return to Germany. Moreover, he was anxious to be near Hermann Ludwig Ferdinand von Helmholtz, the distinguished physicist who had established a sure physical foundation for the phenomena manifested by musical tones. After leaving America in 1870, however, he was continuously in the employ of the American firm until his death in Brunswick. He continued his research and experiments, traveled extensively in Europe to meet and confer with eminent scientists, and made frequent trips to New York. Utilizing the discoveries of Helmholtz and of John Tyndall, the author of *Sound* (1867), he demonstrated that scientific study and research are as necessary to piano design and manufacture as empirical methods. A musician and pianist himself, he knew the demands made on the piano by the music of such composers as Franz Liszt and Anton Rubinstein, and he made it his business to construct an instrument which would meet the requirements of nineteenth-century virtuosi.

[In addition to the sources referred to in the article on Henry Engelhard Steinway, see William Geppert, in *Musical Courier*, Oct. 19, 1929, and *N. Y. Tribune*, Mar. 27, 31, 1889. Information has been supplied by Theodore Steinway.]   J.T.H.

STEINWAY, HENRY ENGELHARD (Feb. 15, 1797–Feb. 7, 1871), piano manufacturer, originally named Steinweg, was born in Wolfshagen, Germany. The names of his parents are not noted in the family records. In his boyhood and youth he endured many hardships. During the Napoleonic invasion of Germany several of his brothers were killed and the Steinweg house was burned, and when he was fifteen his father and remaining brother were killed in an accident. In 1815 he was drafted for the army and is said to have taken part in the battle of Waterloo. Though he was without musical training and manual instruction, he had a talent for craftsmanship and an interest in the making of musical instruments. His first instrument, made after his return from the war, was a zither. In 1818 he entered the shop of an organ builder at Seesen, and became the organist of the village church; two years later he became interested in piano-making. Though his first piano is given various dates between 1825 and 1835, one account relates that it was his wedding-gift to his bride (Dolge, *post*, p. 300). According to family records, his marriage occurred in February 1825, and the bride was Juliane Thiemer. Seven children were eventually born to the Steinwegs: Christian Friedrich Theodore [*q.v.*], Doretta, Charles, Henry, Wilhelmina, William [*q.v.*], and Albert.

Steinweg's piano business prospered. In 1839 he exhibited a grand piano and two square pianos at a fair in Brunswick, Germany, where he was awarded the first prize, a gold medal, but in 1848 and 1849 the revolutions in Central Europe ruined his business, and two years later he decided to emigrate to America, where his son Charles had already gone. With his wife and daughters, and all of his sons but Theodore, he embarked from Hamburg on the *Helene Sloman,* and arrived in New York, June 9, 1851. For about two years he and his sons worked in various piano factories in New York. On Mar. 5, 1853, they joined forces again to start their own business. A year later they were awarded a medal for a square piano they exhibited at the Metropolitan Fair in Washington, D. C. In 1855 Steinweg exhibited an innovation in piano-making at the American Institute, New York, a square piano with cross- or over-strung strings, and a full cast-iron frame. For five years after coming to America he concerned himself with building square pianos only, but in 1856 he manufactured a grand piano and in 1862 an upright. Meanwhile the factory quarters on Walker Street, New York, became too small for the growing business, and in 1860 a new factory was completed on Fourth (Park) Avenue at Fifty-third Street. On Apr. 30, 1861, he and his son signed their first co-partnership agreement, and in July 1864 had their name legally changed to Steinway.

Soon after this event tragedy visited the family, for in 1865 two of the sons died. The organization was so crippled that Steinway persuaded his eldest son, Theodore, to come to America and join the business, and aid him in the technical supervision of building pianos. In 1866 he built Steinway Hall on Fourteenth Street (formally opened in 1867), a building containing retail warerooms and offices for the firm, and a concert hall that became one of the centers of New York's musical life. A few years later he died in New York, survived by his daughters and three of his sons. In his piano business, which has continuously remained in the possession of his descendants and still bears his name, he established an enterprise in which manufacturing has been regarded in the old fashion: as a craft, not as a mere commercial undertaking.

[The most complete account of Steinway and his family appears in Alfred Dolge, *Pianos and Their Makers,* vol. I (1911). See also *The Steinways of Today,* a pamphlet issued by Steinway & Sons, from which the date of birth is taken; "Lineal Descendants of Henry Engelhard Steinway" in *Clef* (Kansas City, Mo.), vol. III, no. 8, 1916; Elbert Hubbard, *The Story of the Steinways* (1911), an account that stresses the picturesque; *Fortune,* Dec. 1934, and *Music,* Jan. 1897. For an obituary see *N. Y. Tribune,* Feb. 8, 1871.]

J. T. H.

STEINWAY, WILLIAM (Mar. 5, 1835–Nov. 30, 1896), piano manufacturer, was born in Seesen, Germany, the sixth child and fourth son of Henry Engelhard Steinway [*q.v.*] and Juliane (Thiemer) Steinway. The family name was originally Steinweg. Like his eldest brother, Christian Friedrich Theodore [*q.v.*], he

studied at Jacobsohn College in Seesen, where his father was engaged in manufacturing pianos. He lacked the scientific mind of his brother, and his interest lay in the study of languages and music rather than in acoustics from the standpoint of the physicist. When the family moved to New York in 1851 he was offered the choice of studying music or of learning the piano-making craft. He chose the latter and was apprenticed to the firm of William Nunns & Company, one of the leading piano manufacturers of the time. In 1853 he joined his father in business. After several years at a workman's bench he turned his attention to the commercial side of the business, and at the death of two of his brothers in 1865 he was equipped to take full charge of the financial and commercial departments of the firm.

With his brother Theodore in full charge of the scientific and manufacturing departments, he was able to devote his attention to selling the pianos his father and brother made. Realizing that the more interested Americans became in music, the more likely they would be to buy pianos, he urged his father to build and open Steinway Hall on Fourteenth Street, inaugurated in 1867 with a concert given by Theodore Thomas [*q.v.*] and his orchestra; he became one of the financial backers of the Thomas orchestra, and interested himself in the opera at the Academy of Music; he encouraged distinguished foreign pianists and musicians to visit America, and often provided the funds to guarantee the success of their tours. He also started an aggressive advertising campaign that was revolutionary in the piano industry and shocking to some of his conservative competitors. Having won an international standing for the Steinway firm by inducing foreign artists to play Steinway pianos, he opened a Steinway hall in London in 1876, and in 1880 established a factory at Hamburg, Germany, to supply the European demand for the product of his firm. When Steinway & Sons was incorporated, May 17, 1876, he was elected president, and continued in that office until his death twenty years later.

Although he was primarily interested in the affairs of his business and in music, he was active also in public affairs. He was the first chairman of the Rapid Transit Commission of New York City, which planned the construction of New York's first subway. It was he who planned and started the subway under the East River from Forty-second Street to Long Island City, and when this project was later purchased and completed by August Belmont it was named the Steinway tunnel in his memory. In 1880 he purchased four hundred acres of land on Long Island Sound and established the town of Steinway, L. I., where the present factories of Steinway & Sons are. He was also a member of the German Turn Verein in New York, and for fourteen years president of Der Deutscher Liederkranz (New York). He was married on Apr. 23, 1861, in Buffalo, N. Y., to Johanna Roos, by whom he had a son and a daughter; and on Aug. 16, 1880, in Hamburg to Elizabeth Raupt, by whom he had a daughter and two sons. He died in New York City, survived by his five children.

[The date of Steinway's birth, which is sometimes given as 1836, has been supplied by the family. In addition to the sources referred to in the article on Henry Engelhard Steinway, see *N. Y. Tribune*, Dec. 1, 6, 11, 1896. Information has been supplied by Theodore Steinway.]   J. T. H.

STEPHENS, ALEXANDER HAMILTON (Feb. 11, 1812–Mar. 4, 1883), congressman, Confederate vice-president, was born on his father's farm in that part of Wilkes County, Ga., that later became Taliaferro County. Known by his constituents as "Little Ellick," he was of average stature, but in weight seldom if ever attained a hundred pounds. A shrill voice, a sallow complexion, recurrent illness, and occasional melancholia gave evidence of organic defects; but his mind was not often morbid, and his will was always robust. Alexander Stephens, an immigrant from England to Pennsylvania, said to have been a Jacobite who came after the failure of the rising in 1745, had married a ferryman's daughter on the Susquehanna before drifting to the Georgia Piedmont, where he lived and died as a farmer of small scale. His youngest son, Andrew Baskins Stephens, made his home nearby, supplementing the meager earnings of his farm by conducting a country school. Andrew's first wife, Margaret Grier, died after bearing a daughter and two sons, and her place was filled by Matilda Lindsey, who added five more to the tale of the Stephens children. The deaths of Andrew and Matilda in 1826 brought a dispersal of the brood into the homes of such relatives as could give them shelter. But Alexander, the youngest of the first group, managed in after years to set the feet of Linton [q.v.], youngest of all, upon the path to prominence as a jurist.

Before his father's death Alexander, despite his frail physique, was doing a plowman's work, with brief terms at school interspersed. The fate which sent him to an uncle's care was kind, for the schooling was better, and the youth's earnestness prompted a patron to send him to an academy in the Georgia village of Washington. Here his admiration for his teacher, the

Rev. Alexander Hamilton Webster led the boy to adopt Hamilton as a middle name. Here also a Presbyterian educational society lent him funds for a course at the University of Georgia with a view to his preparation for the ministry should he so determine. After four happy years at Athens he graduated in 1832 at the head of his class, and having decided against a church career, cast about for a livelihood and the means to repay the charges of his education. A year and a half of rural teaching proved so full of rough episodes and so fatiguing that he read law, was admitted to the bar in 1834, and began practice at Crawfordville within a few miles of his birthplace.

The University of Georgia was in the time of Stephens' residence a place of lively debate among the students, with sentiment strong against protective tariffs and in favor of state rights. As a graduate Stephens was already primed to address his fellow-citizens on such themes; and this he did at Crawfordville on July 4, 1834, preceding his admission to the bar on July 22. Nullification he deprecated; but the right of a state to secede he upheld as a doctrine essential for keeping the central government within the bounds of constitutionality, moderation, and equity (Johnston and Browne, *post*, pp. 87–88). Within two years after that speech he was elected to the Georgia legislature; and, except for one term when he abstained from candidacy (1841), he was returned to one or the other of its houses until he went to Congress. His outstanding advocacy in this period was the project of the Western & Atlantic Railroad, to be built by the state as an avenue of commerce between Georgia and the grain region of the Northwest. The party with which Stephens had cast his lot embraced in the main the well-to-do folk whether on the seaboard or in the uplands. In its early phases a personal following successively of James Jackson, William H. Crawford, and George M. Troup [qq.v.], it adopted "State Rights" as its official designation in the later 'twenties, only to merge in the 'thirties with similar elements in other states under the Whig banner. The local opposition altered its name synchronously from Clark (see sketch of John Clark) to Union, then to Democratic, without material change of constituency. There were few substantial issues between the two except that on financial questions the Troup-State Rights-Whig party was the more conservative. It was not love of Henry Clay or indorsement of his nationalist program which led this group of Georgians into the Whig ranks, but rather a wish to link their local unit with a country-wide organization and to resist the Jacksonian surge. Stephens in particular sought in 1840 to promote the nomination of Troup for the presidency, and failing in this he declared for Harrison against Van Buren as "the choice of evils." Then and thereafter he found party restraint irksome.

Entering Congress in 1843, Stephens for a long time spoke only upon questions of large importance. His first notable speech was made at the beginning of 1845 on the Texas question. Annexation, he said, while tending to lessen the prosperity of the cotton states already in the Union, would give the South a greatly needed political weight, "thus preserving a proper balance between the different sections of the country" (Cleveland, *post*, pp. 301–02). He collaborated with Milton Brown of Tennessee to frame the resolution which prevailed against rival measures and was adopted. The next year he denounced the dispatch of troops to the Rio Grande and the consequent precipitation of war with Mexico; and in 1847, deprecating the Democratic project of expansion, he censured the Wilmot Proviso particularly, saying that if its policy were pursued the harmony of the Union would give place to a "prospect of desolation, carnage and blood" (*Ibid.*, p. 334). In July 1848, he said that had he "a voice that would echo from the mountain tops to the remotest plains and valleys of the country he would rouse the people from their slumbers to a sense of these outrages upon the great fundamental principles upon which their government was founded, and upon which their liberties rested" (*Congressional Globe*, 30 Cong., 1 Sess., p. 912). The occasion was a bill to deny to Texas the Santa Fé region although it lay within the Rio Grande limits. In the next month, without such lyricism but with great elaboration, he resisted the Clayton compromise bill, as a denial of Southern rights by indirection. This bill, to organize the territories of New Mexico and California with a reference of the question of slavery therein to the courts, was indorsed by the bulk of the Whigs, but Stephens caused enough defection to effect its defeat.

Thus the middle of the century came, with a miscellany of questions at loose ends. When Clay's plan for adjusting all these was before the House, Stephens contented himself in the main with votes of indorsement, though in August he blazed forth in defiance of the North: "Whenever this Government is brought in hostile array against me and mine, I am for disunion—openly, boldly and fearlessly, for *revolution*. . . . I am for conciliation if it can be accomplished upon

any reasonable and just principles. . . . You may think that the suppression of an outbreak in the southern States would be a holiday job for a few of your northern regiments, but you may find to your cost, in the end, that seven millions of people fighting for their rights, their homes, and their hearth-stones cannot be 'easily conquered'" (*Congressional Globe*, 31 Cong., 1 Sess., Appendix, pp. 1083–84).

Like Robert Toombs and Howell Cobb [*qq.v.*], Stephens was using strong words at Washington in order that if the result were favorable he might give soft counsel at home. In fact when the compromise measures were enacted, these three hastened to canvass Georgia in indorsement of the Union-saving legislation. For a convention which had been summoned with power to take unlimited action in the name of the state, Unionist delegates were now chosen at the polls in great majority; and the convention adopted the "Georgia Platform" approving the national compromise but with a threat of secession in case Congress or the Northern states failed to maintain it in letter and spirit. Stephens claimed the authorship of this platform, "on all turning points" (*Recollections*, p. 27). To improve the prospect of intersectional peace he, Toombs, and Cobb—two Whigs and a Democrat—undertook to discard their accustomed connections and launch jointly a Constitutional Union party. The lack of response in distant quarters brought a collapse of this project in Georgia and the return of Stephens and Toombs to an uneasy membership in their old party. When Winfield Scott was nominated as the Whig presidential candidate in 1852, Stephens framed a public letter which several other Southern Whig congressmen signed with him, repudiating the ticket on the ground of Scott's free-soil proclivities. The Know-Nothing movement soon captured a large part of the disintegrating Whig party; but Stephens, denouncing vigorously the proscription of immigrants and Catholics, made a shift to the Democratic organization without losing his seat in Congress.

In the welter of issues and the miscellany of men at Washington, Stephens found in Stephen A. Douglas a man to admire and indorse because of his urbane spirit, his fondness for "principles," and his opposition to congressional prohibition of slavery in the territories. The Kansas-Nebraska bill of course met his prompt approval; and when it reached the House he became the floor manager in its behalf. Not only did he share in the debates, but when these threatened to become interminable in committee of the whole, he procured closure by a shrewd motion to strike out the enacting clause. Under existing rules, as few but he were aware, this motion took precedence of pending amendments, and its adoption had the effect of causing the committee to report the bill unfavorably to the House. To get it reported in any manner without amendment was the essential purpose; and its friends who seemingly had killed the bill in committee promptly revived it by having the House disagree with the committee's report. Thereupon, by narrow margin, they promptly carried its enactment. Then and for years afterward Stephens was not merely proud of his personal feat but convinced that the bill was admirable (*American Historical Review,* October 1902, pp. 91–97). "The moral effect of the victory on our side," said he, "will have a permanent effect upon the public mind, whether any positive advantages accrue by way of the actual extension of slavery or not" (*Annual Report of the American Historical Association . . . 1911,* II, 344). Moreover, the bill embodied a principle; and however ambiguous and ineffective it might prove in operation, to the principle Stephens would cling.

But the disorders in Kansas, the party platforms, the Dred Scott decision, and the ceaseless wrangles over them gave even Stephens his fill of tweedledum and tweedledee; and he turned his thoughts mainly from the question of slavery in the territories to negroes and slavery at large. In 1845, denying that he was a defender of slavery in the abstract, he had said he would rejoice to see all men free "if a *stern necessity* . . . did not in some cases interpose and prevent" (Cleveland, p. 301). But within a decade he was praising the Southern system as the best in the world for the sustenance, advancement, and happiness of negroes (*Ibid.,* p. 429); in 1857 he was defending slavery on biblical grounds (*Ibid.,* pp. 557, 560); and in 1859 he was discussing with implications of approval the project of reopening the trade with Africa to procure more slaves in order to make more slave states. "African slavery with us," he now said, "rests upon principles that can never be successfully assailed by reason or argument" (*Ibid.,* p. 647). He was ready to meet Seward on his own ground: "I, too, believe in the higher law—the law of the Creator as manifested in his works and his revelation. . . . We must stand on the higher law, as well as upon the constitution." Since order is nature's first law, he continued, and gradations and subordination are essential in order, enslavement of an inferior race is right: "The principle will ultimately prevail. The wickedest of all follies, and the absurdest of all crusades are those

which attempt to make things equal which God in his wisdom has made unequal" (*Ibid.,* p. 649). These remarks of 1859 were made in a rather vainglorious speech at Augusta telling his constituents that he would represent them in Congress no longer. The main burden of this speech was the victory of the South at all important points, the placidity of the prospect within the Union, and the consequent lack of need for such watchmen as he at Washington. In his claim of all the virtues modesty was ignored; but if he had said merely that his conscientious best was always at call in the public service, none then or now could say him nay.

After his retirement from Congress, as previously between sessions, he plied a lucrative practice in the Georgia courts, and in leisure kept open house at "Liberty Hall" in Crawfordville, with a widowed sister presiding in default of a wife. He was a kindly master to his slaves, a generous patron of youths desiring college education, and a sociable companion when health permitted. Reciprocally, a multitude, including many negroes, held him in warmest esteem. Sometimes, however, his temper had proved brittle. Quarrels with William L. Yancey and Herschel V. Johnson brought him near to duels in the middle 'forties; and an affray with Judge Francis N. Cone in 1848, at a hotel in Atlanta, nearly cost him his life. In 1856 a joint debate with Benjamin H. Hill resulted in a challenge which Hill declined, saying privately that he had a family to support and a soul to save, while Stephens had neither. Stephens then posted Hill in the newspapers as "not only an impudent braggart but a despicable poltroon besides" (Pendleton, *post,* pp. 86–87).

Though he little thought it, Stephens was but a product of his time. A sensitive soul requiring himself to be high-minded, when he found a cause to champion he sought a principle to buttress every policy. This rationalizing of his conduct, while giving him great satisfaction, produced an exaltation of the technical and the trivial. Strategy was of little moment if his tactics were expert. His essential concern, often and sincerely proclaimed, was the preservation of Southern security within a placid Union of all the states; but his inability to yield on a detail or to suffer an opponent to score a point, his relish of victory for the sake of prestige and partisan morale, paralyzed him for the greater purpose. This is the more curious in the light of his complete lack of rancor and his essential kindliness toward all men.

The retirement to "Liberty Hall" and the courts of law could not divorce him from politics. As the campaign approached in 1860 he besought his correspondents to maintain Democratic solidarity. His preference for the presidency was R. M. T. Hunter [*q.v.*], with Douglas as a second choice. When the party split he clung to Douglas as against Breckinridge, and despite his own prior intention of abstinence, took the stump in a consciously forlorn effort to carry Georgia for the ticket. The Georgia legislature was in session when Lincoln was elected; and Gov. Joseph E. Brown promptly recommended that a convention be summoned for action upon the question of secession. In this crisis the Assembly invited several prominent citizens to give their advice. On the night of Nov. 12, Thomas R. R. Cobb spoke for secession forthwith. Toombs on the next evening proposed a quick plebiscite and secession by the legislature if the referendum should give warrant. Stephens took the rostrum on the third night, advocating not only a convention of Georgia but a conference of all the Southern states. Realizing that a policy of mere delay would be rejected, he proposed that the future convention demand of the several Northern states that they repeal their "personal liberty laws" and that Georgia retaliate in some manner upon such as might refuse. Beyond this he contemplated mere watchful waiting, with hope that the benefits of the Union might be retained but with readiness for drastic recourse if Lincoln or Congress invaded Southern rights or violated the constitution. Appealing to the spirit of Georgia's official motto, "Wisdom, Justice and Moderation," he said: "My position, then, in conclusion, is for the maintenance of the honor, the rights, the equality, the security, and the glory of my native state in the Union, if possible, but if these cannot be maintained in the Union, then I am for their maintenance, at all hazards, out of it" (*War Between the States,* II, 299). Toombs, seated on the platform, made interjections during the speech, and was answered in each instance. When Stephens ended he went to the desk and said with even more than his usual vigor: "Fellow citizens, we have just listened to a speech from one of the brightest intellects and purest patriots that now lives. I move that this meeting now adjourn, with three cheers for Alexander H. Stephens of Georgia!" (Pendleton, p. 163). The Damon-and-Pythias friendship of these twain was universally known; and this gesture of undiminished esteem during their brief divergence was received with great applause.

The publication of the speech brought Stephens a flood of letters, including one from Lincoln requesting a revised copy. In his reply Stephens alluded to the responsibility resting upon Lincoln in the crisis. To this Lincoln answered that he felt the weight of this, and said that any fears by the people of the South "that a Republican administration would directly, or *indirectly,* interfere with their slaves, or with them about their slaves" was groundless. He concluded: "I suppose, however, this does not meet the case. You think slavery is *right* and ought to be extended; while we think it is *wrong* and ought to be restricted. That I suppose is the rub. It certainly is the only substantial difference between us." Stephens rejoined, saying that the gravamen against the Republicans was their purpose "to put the institutions of nearly half the States under the ban of public opinion and national condemnation." He then turned to a more critical matter, for South Carolina had now seceded. Ultimate sovereignty residing always in the separate states, he said, "there is no rightful power in the general government to coerce a State in case any one of them should . . . resume the full exercise of her sovereign powers. Force may perpetuate a Union. That depends upon the contingencies of war. But such a Union would not be the Union of the constitution. It would be nothing short of a consolidated despotism" (Cleveland, pp. 150–54).

Meanwhile the Georgia legislature had summoned a convention, and the delegates elected were known to be secessionist in majority. When it met at the middle of January, Stephens, who was a delegate, spoke but once and briefly, supporting a resolution which as a substitute for a pending ordinance of secession proposed a Southern convention to consider the state of affairs and determine a course of action. Expressing a persistent hope of securing Southern interests within the Union, and urging negotiations to this end, he concluded: "My judgment, as is well known, is against the policy of immediate secession for any exciting causes. It cannot receive the sanction of my vote; but . . . if a majority of the delegates in this Convention shall, by their votes, dissolve the compact of union . . . to which I have been so ardently attached, and have made such efforts to continue and to perpetuate on the principles upon which it was founded, I shall bow in submission to that decision." (Johnston and Browne, pp. 381–82. A fraudulent version was issued in 1863 by the Union League of Philadelphia in *The Rebuke of Secession Doctrines by Southern Statesmen,* and reprinted in many places after as well as before Stephens denounced it in his *War Between the States,* I, 23. L. L. Mackall discussed this forgery in the book section of the *New York Herald-Tribune,* Nov. 9, 1924.) When the convention rejected this resolution and adopted the ordinance, Stephens signed the document without further demur.

The project in hand was centripetal as well as centrifugal. The Georgia convention, pursuing a plan already prepared, elected delegates to a convention at Montgomery, Stephens among them, to form a union of the seceded states. In this assemblage he met no substantial opposition to his own specific desire to frame a government upon the model of that of the United States. Under the quickly devised Provisional Constitution, which converted the convention into a Provisional Congress and empowered that body to choose the executives, Jefferson Davis was elected as president of the Confederate States of America and Stephens as vice-president, both of these on Feb. 9, 1861, without overt opposition. The vice-president under this régime had no regular functions, for until the Permanent Constitution went into effect the next year there was no Senate over which he might preside. Stephens merely continued as a member of the single house and lent a hand in affairs outside as occasion invited. His most notable expression in this period was the "corner-stone speech" at Savannah, Mar. 21. In this he surveyed the conditions of the Confederacy, praised its Constitution, and appealed for wise and patriotic support of the cause. As to negro slavery, he said that the architects of American independence, as exemplified in Jefferson, had contemplated a theoretical equality of races; but, he continued: "Our new government is founded upon exactly the opposite idea; its foundations are laid, its corner-stone rests upon the great truth that the negro is not equal to the white man; that slavery—subordination to the superior race—is his natural and normal condition" (Cleveland, p. 721). In the same speech he said: "We are now the nucleus of a growing power, which if we are true to ourselves, our destiny, and high mission, will become the controlling power on this continent" (*Ibid.,* p. 726). But how to procure a prosperous or a peaceful future neither he nor any other Confederate could say. To solve the specific impasse concerning the seaboard forts, a cannonade reduced Sumter on Apr. 15, whereupon Lincoln called upon the several states for troops and Virginia, North Carolina, Tennessee, and Arkansas took steps for a junction with the original seven in the Confederacy. Stephens went as a commissioner and addressed the Virginia convention to hasten this process. This was his last official mission until the Hampton Roads Conference.

His fondness for scruples and constitutional restraint made Stephens an unhappy member of a wartime government, for exigencies were as naught in the face of his principles. Many of Davis' early appointments, and his course concerning cotton as a factor in foreign relations, were ill-judged in Stephens' opinion. But these were minor matters. The conscription of troops, the suspension of *habeas corpus,* and the establishment of military government in sundry localities all seemed to him outrageous invasions of civil rights. In 1862, when the Permanent Constitution gave him a Senate over which to preside, he became in a sense the leader of the opposition. His official duties, however, yielded him so little satisfaction that at one period he stayed away from Richmond for a year and a half. In public and private letters and occasional speeches he alternated censures of the administration and gloomy prognostications with appeals for support of the Confederate cause. In particular he stimulated Gov. Joseph E. Brown [*q.v.*] to challenge the power of Davis to conscript Georgia citizens.

The war itself was keenly distressing to Stephens, and particularly the sufferings of the wounded and the prisoners on both sides. He visited hospitals and stockades often, to give such relief or solace as he might, and he concerned himself zealously with promoting systematic exchange and parole of prisoners of war. In June 1863, Stephens procured a sanction from Davis to try to open negotiations with Lincoln to regularize exchanges and perhaps to reach some arrangement for ending the war. A refusal of Lincoln to receive such a mission killed the project for the time being. In September of the next year General Sherman, having captured Atlanta, sent oral messages to Stephens and to Brown inviting them to a conference with him with a view to possible arrangements for terminating the war. Stephens, while saying that he would gladly serve as a channel for an authoritative overture, declined the invitation to a personal conference (Johnston and Browne, p. 472). Brown answered to the same effect, and the war dragged on.

At the beginning of 1865 a bill to continue the suspension of *habeas corpus* passed the Confederate House and met a tie vote in the Senate. Stephens announced that it was his duty to cast the deciding vote, and said that before doing so he would state the reasons which influenced him. His right to make the proposed speech was challenged, and after sundry proceedings it was permitted only in secret session. The remarks he then made (summarized in *War Between the States,* II, 587–89) concluded with an expression of hope for independence through negotiation. Soon afterward Francis P. Blair, Sr., came from

Washington with Lincoln's permission to sound the Confederate authorities on a project of his for a truce and a joint expedition against Maximilian in Mexico. Davis broached this in confidence to Stephens, who leaped at the chance to confer with Lincoln. With R. M. T. Hunter and John A. Campbell [*qq.v.*] as fellow commissioners, he met Lincoln and Seward on shipboard near Fortress Monroe, Feb. 3, only to find an armistice unattainable and a basis of peace impossible between those who stipulated Confederate independence and those who required acquiescence to the Federal laws. The commissioners returned from Hampton Roads to Richmond in failure. Stephens went sadly home; and upon the collapse of the Confederacy he was not surprised when a detail of Federal troops arrested him, May 11, at "Liberty Hall." Taken eastward in custody, he was held prisoner at Fort Warren in Boston Harbor, diminishing the tedium by writing a narrative of recent events and a diary (printed in Avary, *Recollections*). Released on parole, Oct. 12, he was greeted warmly by throngs at New York, Washington, and Atlanta as he traveled homeward. At "Liberty Hall" he dwelt much as before, with former slaves of his continuing to serve him.

In January 1866 he was elected to the Senate of the United States, only to meet exclusion along with all others from the "rebel" states. On Washington's birthday he made a speech before the Georgia legislature in response to a request for his views on public affairs. In the deep adversity he counseled self-discipline, patience, and forbearance from recrimination. The total change in Southern internal polity, he said, ought to be given a fair trial, with the good will toward the negroes which their fidelity in times past had merited: "It is an ethnological problem, on the solution of which depends not only the best interests of both races, but it may be the existence of one or the other, if not both" (Johnston and Browne, p. 589). Specifically, he recommended support of the policies of President Andrew Johnson. In April he testified before the congressional joint committee on reconstruction. Questioned as to the sentiments prevailing among the people of Georgia, he said that they, while not repudiating the theoretical right of secession, were convinced by the failure of their effort and were cherishing no thoughts of such recourse in future. He described likewise a general acquiescence in the abolition of slavery and a somewhat surprising accord between the two races on the new legal and industrial basis. But as to pending projects of reconstruction by Congress he said the sentiments of Georgians, and his own, were opposed to the vesting of the suffrage in the negroes or to any constitutional amendment while a number of states were deprived of representation. In fact he denied the constitutional power of the federal government to impose conditions precedent to the restoration of the late Confederate states to their functions in the Union (*Ibid.,* pp. 594–607). Congress proceeded with its drastic program; and Stephens accepted a publisher's invitation to write *A Constitutional View of the Late War Between the States.*

The first of these bulky volumes was published in 1868, the second in 1870. In an ill-judged attempt at enlivening its 1,200 pages of text, the book was cast in colloquies between Stephens and sundry men of straw whom he politely but continuously knocked down. It is a tedious rationalization, obscuring the historic problem of negro slavery by refinements of doctrine on the sovereignty of the states. Dull as the book may be to readers in the twentieth century, it was a sensation in its day, evoking attacks by Northern and Southern champions of causes upon which it impinged and yielding its author some $35,000 in royalties. Stephens not only replied to critics of every sort, but assembled the reviews, rejoinders, sur-rejoinders and rebuttals in a volume, *The Reviewers Reviewed* (1872), which is more dull than its predecessor. Afterward he wrote a school history of the United States (*A Compendium of the History of the United States,* 1872) which met some success, and a stout illustrated work (*A Comprehensive and Popular History of the United States,* 1882), which deservedly fell flat. In 1869 Stephens was offered a professorship of political science and history at the University of Georgia, but declined it. The next year he participated in a lease of the Western & Atlantic Railroad from the state of Georgia; but upon receiving a remonstrance from Toombs, pointing to the dubious quality of his colleagues and the questionable character of the procedure, Stephens transferred to the state his share of stock in the corporation. In 1871 he bought an interest in the *Southern Sun,* an Atlanta newspaper, and the next year filled its editorial page with endless arguments against the junction of the Democrats with the Liberal Republicans to support Horace Greeley. A few years of such ponderous journalism forced his withdrawal at a heavy loss.

Though reduced by rheumatism to crutches and a wheeled chair, Stephens in 1872 declared himself a candidate for the United States Senate. He was defeated by John B. Gordon, but before the end of that year he was elected to the lower house of Congress. At Washington a journalist

ense cloak, a high hat,
 of the middle a thin,
r continued: "How
d sorrowful could
gia is a wonder.
th any instant
ere laid out
fferent, only
hose burn-
offer the
proves
in his
. 387).
, now
Con-
oice
ill a
of the
ed acqui-
commission
in favor of
course, with fire
rom all quarters.
e practice of law, he
1882, only to find idle-
n entered a successful
norship of Georgia; but
fter inauguration. When
state "Little Ellick" had al-
dition as one who had served
n fair times and foul with con-
ce, and unflagging zeal.

ens, A Constitutional View of the Late
he States (2 vols., 1868–70), and M. L.
ecollections of Alexander H. Stephens
part autobiographical. R. M. Johnston
Browne, Life of Alexander H. Stephens
full biography, though not extending to his
s Pendleton, Alexander H. Stephens (1908),
Henry Cleveland, Alexander H. Stephens in
Private (1866) is a collection of his princi-
es to the date of publication, preceded by a
sketch. "The Correspondence of Robert
Alexander H. Stephens, and Howell Cobb," ed.
Phillips, is in Ann. Report of the Am. Hist.
. 1911 (1913), vol. II, with a calendar of letters
ly published. Certain letters alleged to have
etween Stephens and Abraham Lincoln in Janu-
o, were printed in a pamphlet by Judd Stewart,
incoln Correspondence with Southern Leaders
he Outbreak of the Civil War (1909). The
of these is effectively challenged by W. C. Ford
Mass. Hist. Soc., LXI (1928), 183–95; but the
s-Lincoln correspondence at the close of that
nted in crude facsimile in Cleveland's book, is
estioned authenticity. Eudora R. Richardson,
eck; A Life of Alexander H. Stephens (1932),
t biography. See also J. D. Waddell, Biog.
f Linton Stephens (1877); U. B. Phillips,
and State Rights," Ann. Report of the Am.
. . . .1901 (1902), vol. II; R. H. Shryock,
d the Union in 1850 (1026); obituary in
nstitution, Mar. 4, 5, 1883.]   U. B. P.

NS, ALICE BARBER (July 1,
13, 1932), illustrator, was born on a
e Salem, N. J., eighth of the nine

children of Samuel C. Barber, a Quaker farmer whose forebears had emigrated to America from England more than three generations before, and Mary (Owen) Barber, of Welsh descent, whose ancestors had settled in Wading River, L. I., before the Revolution. She was educated in a New Jersey country school and in the public schools of Philadelphia, and studied art from an early age. At fifteen she began to earn her own living by selling wood engravings, which she had learned to make under Edward Dalziel. Intermittently between 1870 and 1876 she studied at the School of Design for Women in Philadelphia, where she later conducted life and portrait classes, and then worked under Thomas Eakins [q.v.] at the Pennsylvania Academy of the Fine Arts. Although her professional career began with wood engravings for Scribner's Monthly, Harper's Weekly, Harper's Young People, and other magazines, about 1876 she turned to illustrating. She spent the years 1886 and 1887 abroad, studying at the Académie Julian in Paris and in the studio of Filippo Colarossi, and traveling in Italy. In 1890 she won the Mary Smith prize at the Pennsylvania Academy of the Fine Arts for her "Portrait of a Boy." In June of the same year she married Charles Hallowell Stephens, artist and collector of Indian relics, by whom she had one child, a son. Her illustrations for George Eliot's Middlemarch and paintings for Dinah Maria Mulock Craik's John Halifax, Gentleman won a gold medal at the exhibition of women's work held at Earl's Court, London, in 1899; a year later she won a bronze medal at the Exposition Universelle in Paris and illustrated a special two-volume edition of Hawthorne's The Marble Faun. For fifteen months during the years 1901 and 1902 she traveled and studied in the art galleries of England and the Continent. Returning to Philadelphia, she settled with her husband and child in Rose Valley, Pa., where she lived for the rest of her life in a stone barn, "Thunder Bird," that she remodelled as a house and studio. Throughout her career she fought against ill health, often aggravated by pressure of work. By 1926 her active professional career was at an end, though she painted landscapes and still life until her last year. She died at Rose Valley and was buried in West Laurel Hill Cemetery.

During her career she illustrated books by George Eliot, Louisa May Alcott, Bret Harte, Sir Arthur Conan Doyle, and Hawthorne, and supplied illustrations for numerous periodicals. Though she used both oils and watercolors for these, after 1900 she worked almost exclusively in charcoal, sometimes with a color wash. She painted landscapes for recreation and executed a few portraits, and produced numerous sketches and paintings of Quakers and the Pennsylvania Germans. She excelled in pictures of quiet scenes and incidents, which are characterized by simplicity of expression and technical assurance. In 1929 a comprehensive exhibition of her work was held at the Plastic Club, Philadelphia, of which she had been a founder. About seventy original illustrations and sketches are in the possession of the Library of Congress, Washington, D. C., among them most of the *Middlemarch* and *Marble Faun* drawings as well as various magazine illustrations.

[See *Who's Who in America*, 1932–33; *Woman's Who's Who of America*, 1914–15; F. B. Sheafer, in *Brush and Pencil*, Sept. 1900, with portrait; *Press* (Phila.), Sept. 26, 1915; *Woman's Progress*, Nov. 1893; Julius Moritzen, in *Twentieth Century Home*, Dec. 1904; obituaries in *Art News*, Aug. 13, and *Evening Bull.* (Phila.), July 14, 1932. Information, including date of death, has been supplied by D. Owen Stephens, Mrs. Stephens' son. The statement made in various obituaries that Mrs. Stephens painted a portrait of the queen mother of Spain is false.]   D. G.

STEPHENS, ANN SOPHIA (1813–Aug. 20, 1886), author and editor, was born in the town of Derby, Conn., the daughter of John and Ann Winterbotham. Her father emigrated from England to America in 1806 at the request of David Humphreys [*q.v.*] to act as manager of the woolen mills newly established in this region. There she spent her childhood. She learned to read, sew, and knit at a tender age in a dame's school and later received further training in South Britain. She listened to her father read aloud to his large family in the evenings and early tried her own hand at composition. Occasionally she attended plays written by Humphreys for the operatives in his factory and was strengthened in her determination to become an author. In 1831 she married Edward Stephens of Plymouth, Mass. They removed to Portland, Me., which remained their home until 1837. There in 1834 they established a literary monthly, the *Portland Magazine,* especially directed to "the Ladies of Maine." For the next two years she acted as editor of this paper, contributing to it a large part of the poems, sketches, literary notices, and romantic historical tales that made up its contents. In 1836 she edited *The Portland Sketch Book,* a collection of material from the works of local writers. The following year after winning a prize for a story of pioneer life, she accepted an invitation to act as associate editor of the New York *Ladies' Companion.* Her historical tales, florid in style but always full of action, promptly increased the popularity of the periodical. During the forties she became one of the best known of the New York literati. She was often to be

met at literary soirée [*q.v.*], much admired lively conversation. her at this time as embonpoint," wit of blonde hair *Magazine* an promising t ries should *than,* a w band, th *Lady's* her wo upon beca her ber of he serial ev traveled in persons and e ed to her. Aft magazine of her *New Monthly* (185

Between 1854 and than twenty-five books poems, and articles cons odicals. Of these the mos *and Famine* (1854) and (1855). Her publishers decl were always successful becau "heightening, coloring, and en In novels like *The Rejected Wi* many earlier works she dealt freely can history, supplying strange epi careers of notable personages. Eng attracted her even more, and she deligh tray royal figures in the midst of purp oriental pearls, ivory caskets, and snow In 1860 she supplied Beadle & Company first of its famous "dime novel" series—*M* an Indian tale, expanded from one of h short stories. She contributed to this sam *Ahmo's Plot* (1863), *The Indian Queen* and other lively accounts of Western adv Stories from her pen continued to app *Peterson's* for several years after her dea Walter Scott and Fenimore Cooper had r devoted follower in America than this e romancer. She died in Newport, R. I home of Charles J. Peterson [*q.v.*], her friend and publisher. Her two children her.

[Samuel Orcutt and Ambrose Beardsley *of the Old Town of Derby, Conn.* (1880) *The Literati* (1850), ed. by R. W. Griswo in *Godey's Mag.*, May–Oct. 1846; S. J. Ha *Record* (rev. ed. 1876); *Frank Leslie*

described him as "an imm
and peering somewhere out
pale, sad face." The write
anything so small and sick a
get here all the way from Geo
If he were to draw his last brea
you would not be surprised. If he
in his coffin, he need not look any di
then the fires would have gone out in t
ing eyes. . . . That he is here at all to
counsels of moderation and patriotisn
how invincible is the soul that dwells
shrunken and aching frame" (Pendleton,
This "queer-looking bundle," this pallid face
seamed with "a thousand lines," remained in
gress for a decade, this cracked falsetto v
rising now and again to prove its owner st
master parliamentarian and a guardian
public interest. In particular he counse'
escence in 1877 when the electoral
decided the presidential contest
Hayes, and he defended his own
on occasion, against criticism

Long since disabled for th
resigned from Congress in
ness a burden. He soo
candidacy for the gover
he died a few months a
his poor body lay in
ready become a tra
his people throug'
science, eloquen

[A. H. Stephe
War Between t
Avary, ed., R
(1910) are ir
and W. H.
(1878), is a
death; Loui
is briefer.
Public and
pal speech
eulogistic
Toombs,
by U. B.
Asso. . .
previous
passed b
ary 186
Some L
before
validity
in Proc.
Stephen
year, pri
of unque
Little Ale
is a recer
Sketch of
"Georgia
Hist. Asso
Georgia an
Atlanta Co

**STEPHE
1858–July
farm outsid

s of Anne Lynch Botta
for her high spirits and
Edgar Allan Poe described
"tall and slightly inclined to
brilliant blue eyes and masses
(*post*, p. 63). In 1842 *Graham's*
nounced her as one of its editors,
at her "life-like and thrilling sto-
appear in its columns. *Brother Jona-*
eekly newspaper published by her hus-
e *Lady's Wreath*, and the *Columbian*
nd *Gentleman's Magazine*, all featured
k during the decade. In 1843 she entered
a connection with the magazine that later
e *Peterson's Magazine*. This lasted until
eath. She contributed to almost every num-
of the journal during the last twenty years
life, and regularly supplied it with a new
ery January. From 1850 to 1852 she
Europe, meeting many distinguished
njoying the courtesies they extend-
er her return she undertook a
wn, *Mrs. Stephens' Illustrated*
6–58).

1880 she published more
in addition to the serials,
tantly appearing in peri-
t popular were *Fashion*
The Old Homestead
ared that her works
se of her skill in
larging nature."
e (1863) and
with Ameri-
sodes in the
lish history
ted to por-
le velvet,
y plumes.
with the
alaeska,
r early
e series
1864),
enture.
ear in
th. Sir
o more
nergetic
., at the
faithful
survived

The Hist.
E. A. Poe,
d, pub. first
le, *Woman's*
s *Illustrated*

Newspaper (with portrait), Aug. 16, 1856; *N. Y. Tribune*, Aug. 21, 1886.]   B. M. S.

STEPHENS, CHARLES ASBURY (Oct. 21, 1844–Sept. 22, 1931), author, was born in Norway Lake, Me., the only child of Simon and Harriet N. (Upton) Stevens. He adopted the spelling Stephens as being the ancestral form of his name. On both sides he was descended from a line of successful and keen-minded farmers; his paternal line went back probably to John Stevens, who settled in Andover, Mass., about 1645. He was fitted for college in the local school known as the Norway Liberal Institute and graduted from Bowdoin College with the degree of B.A. in 1869. For some time after his graduation he taught school. In college, however, he had been influenced by Elijah Kellogg [*q.v.*] to attempt the field of juvenile literature, and while he was still an undergraduate (1868) he contributed to *Our Flag of Boston* and wrote a serial called "Guess" for *Ballou's Monthly Magazine* (Boston). In 1870 he was engaged by Daniel Sharp Ford [*q.v.*] to write under a regular contract for the *Youth's Companion,* a connection that he maintained for more than sixty years. Under Ford's influence he traveled a great deal in Canada, the West Indies, Mexico, Panama, Europe, and Alaska for the sake of material; and attended the School of Medicine at Boston University, from which he graduated with the degree of M.D. in 1887. He once estimated that he had written more than three thousand short stories or sketches for the *Youth's Companion* and over a hundred serials. His knack of verisimilitude and circumstantiality was very great, and many of his stories were accepted as a true record of experience. His most popular contributions to juvenile literature were *Camping Out* (1872), *Lynx-Hunting* (1872), *Left on Labrador* (1872), *On the Amazons* (1872), *The Knockabout Club Alongshore* (copyright 1882) and others in the series, *When Life Was Young* (copyright 1912), and *Katahdin Camps* (1928).

In 1883 he removed from his birthplace, a farm at Upton's Ridge, to a site on Lake Pennesseewassee, Norway Lake, Me., where he erected a large laboratory, and began a systematic course of study and of original research in the field of cell life. Out of this study he developed a theory of the possibility of the indefinite extension or maintenance of cell life in the human being by systematic renewal of the biogen transmitted with the ovum by inheritance. Upon his researches at the Norway Lake laboratory he founded a series of books, beginning with *Living Matter: Its Cycle of Growth and Decline in Animal Organisms* (copyright 1888), asserting the possibility of eventual human control of the conditions of life. He rejected all but material conditions, finding in the individual no soul apart from the tissues of living organisms. His scientific books include *Pluri-cellular Man* (1892); *Natural Salvation* (1903), later issued under the title, *Salvation by Science (Natural Salvation) Immortal Life on the Earth*. He was twice married: on Apr. 30, 1871, to Christine Stevens, his second cousin, by whom he had two daughters, and on Dec. 26, 1912, to Minnie Scalar Plummer. He died in Norway, survived by his second wife and one of his two daughters.

[Though *Who's Who in America,* 1914–15, gives the date of Stephens' birth as 1847, the town clerk of Norway, Me., reports it as 1844. Other sources are C. F. Whitman, *A Hist. of Norway, Me.* (1924); obituaries in *Publishers' Weekly,* Oct. 3, and *Boston Transcript,* Sept. 22, 1931; recollections of Don C. Seitz, New York City; information supplied by Mrs. Stephens; personal acquaintance.]   J. E. C.

STEPHENS, EDWIN WILLIAM (Jan. 21, 1849–May 22, 1931), editor, publisher, son of James Leachman and Amelia (Hockaday) Stephens, was born in Columbia, Mo., where he lived and died. His grandfather, Elijah Stephens, a Kentucky farmer, settled in Boone County, Mo., near Columbia, in 1819, and in 1843 Edwin's father, a dry-goods merchant, introduced a chain-store system in central Missouri, consisting of three cash mercantile establishments in as many county seats. The boy entered the University of Missouri soon after Union soldiers broke barracks on the campus. Graduated at the age of eighteen, he went to Jones Commercial College, St. Louis, and then reported speeches in a congressional campaign. In 1870 he purchased a half interest in the *Boone County Journal*. Within a year he bought out his associates, changed the paper's name to *Columbia Herald,* and edited it for thirty-five years. Trenchant writing and clean typography made it known as "America's Model Weekly" (*Missouri Historical Review, post,* p. 546). Meanwhile, he founded printing companies in Jefferson City and Columbia, which built up court and state record business of national proportions. In 1890 he was president of the National Editorial Association and of the Missouri Press Association; in 1905 he was elected vice-president of the International Press Congress at Liège. He performed an outstanding service to his state as chairman of the commission which had charge of the erection of the $4,000,000 Missouri capitol, completed in 1918 on a site overlooking the Missouri River. A Democrat appointed by a Republican governor, Herbert S. Hadley [*q.v.*], he was chosen chairman by his three fellow commissioners. The construction time, seven years, was shorter than that of any capitol of like size, and so scrupulously were the funds handled that it was possible to devote a large surplus to making the edifice a treasury of painting and sculpture.

Stephens was a leading Baptist layman and filled numerous offices in that denomination, including the chairmanship of the Missouri Baptist Board of Home and Foreign Missions for twenty-six years, of the Missouri Baptist General Association for twenty years, and of the Southern Baptist Association for three years. For almost half his life he headed the board of curators of Stephens College, Columbia, named for his father, and he served in the same capacity for the University of Missouri from 1885 to 1887. As early as 1896 he proposed that the state support a school of journalism and when it was opened in 1908, he had the pleasure of seeing as its dean Walter Williams, whom as a young man he had engaged to help him with the *Herald*. He had a deep interest in local history, dating from his youth when he wrote the story of Boone County, published as a series of articles in the *Boone County Atlas* in 1875, and in book form in 1882, with the title, *History of Boone County, Missouri*. He helped found the State Historical Society of Missouri in 1898 and was its first president, serving for six years. Hard roads and many other progressive enterprises had his enthusiastic support. Friends urged him to become a candidate for governor, senator, and other offices, but he always declined. In 1909 he published *Around the World*, an account of his own travel experiences. He died at his home in Columbia of the infirmities of age in his eighty-third year, survived by his widow, formerly Laura Moss, whom he married Sept. 26, 1871, together with three sons and a daughter, six children having previously died. His body lay in state at Stephens College and at the University of Missouri flags were lowered in his honor.

[*"In Memoriam Edwin William Stephens, 1849-1931," Mo. Hist. Rev.,* July 1931; *St. Louis Post-Dispatch,* May 22, 23 (editorial), 1931; "The Story of a Columbian," autobiographical, in *Columbia Missourian,* May 23, 25, 26, 27, 1931; autobiographical data in *Hist. of Boone County, Mo.* (1882); R. S. Douglass, *Hist. of Mo. Baptists* (1934); *Columbia Daily Tribune,* May 22, 1931; *State of Mo.: Official Manual,* 1923–24; *Who's Who in America,* 1930–31; information from a daughter, Mrs. Ashley Gray of St. Louis, and from friends.]

I. D.

STEPHENS, HENRY MORSE (Oct. 3, 1857–Apr. 16, 1919), historian and educator, was born in Edinburgh, Scotland, the son of John Edward Stephens, who belonged to an old army family and served as an army medical officer in India, and of Emma (Morris) Stephens, the

daughter of John Carnac Morris, whose family was prominent in the Indian civil service. He entered Haileybury College, near Hertford, in 1871, and Balliol College, Oxford, in 1877, and he obtained a first class in modern history in 1880 and a third in jurisprudence in 1881. He was admitted to the degree of B.A. in 1882. In 1881 he was enrolled at Lincoln's Inn and later attended lectures at the universities of Bonn and Paris. For several years he was engaged in journalism, but historical studies were his prime interest, and when only twenty-eight years of age he published the first volume of his *History of the French Revolution* (1886), which established his reputation. After assisting William Wilson Hunter, the historian of India, with several works, he served from 1887 to 1890 as librarian of the Leeds library, of which he issued a printed catalogue. As one of the principal contributors to the *Dictionary of National Biography,* he provided for its first twenty volumes (1885–89) more than two hundred articles, principally of military biography. Besides numerous other items he furnished for the ninth edition of the *Encyclopaedia Britannica* the historical account of Portugal, which was later enlarged as a volume, *The Story of Portugal* (1891), in the Story of the Nations Series. The second volume of his *History of the French Revolution* (1891) was promptly followed by an edition of *The Principal Speeches of the Statesmen and Orators of the French Revolution, 1789–1795* (2 vols., 1892), and by *Europe, 1789–1815* (1893) as volume VII in A. Hassall's Periods of European History Series. Meanwhile he edited *India, a Journal for the Discussion of Indian Affairs,* 1890 to 1894, contributed to the Rulers of India Series a volume on *Albuquerque* (1892), and was teacher in Indian history at the University of Cambridge in connection with the Board of Indian Civil Service studies. After considerable earlier experience on the lecture platform, he served as a lecturer in the Oxford University extension system from 1890 to 1894. The extraordinary amount, scope, and high character of these scholarly contributions, produced in a little more than a dozen years after leaving Oxford, revealed his prodigious capacity for work and placed him in the front rank of historical scholarship in England.

He was chosen for the chair of modern European history at Cornell University, which he held from 1894 to 1902. In the latter year he accepted a call to the University of California as head of the department of history, where he remained until his death. From 1902 to 1909 he was also director of university extension and, from 1917 to 1918, dean of the faculty of letters and science. His methods of teaching were developed from his experience as an extension lecturer. He customarily prepared extended printed syllabi for his courses to recite the facts that were admirably illuminated in his lectures. To an unusual degree he became the confidant and trusted adviser of the students in both their individual and collective interests; he encouraged athletics and, at California, promoted the movement for student self-government. His generous and stimulating assistance to advanced students was given a new direction and a marked impetus as a result of his success in obtaining for the University of California the collection of works, relating to Spanish colonization and to the Pacific coast, gathered by Hubert Howe Bancroft [q.v.]. As an historian he was a thorough-going realist and insisted on a rigorous scientific method. His work, however, both as a writer and as a lecturer, was permeated by an intense interest both in individuals and in humanity in general. His heritage and training were reflected in his interest in military history and in the history of the British empire, especially in India. As early as 1898 he devoted one of his courses to the history of British colonization.

The heavy burdens of teaching, administration, and lecturing that he assumed in America hampered but did not stop his literary productivity. Only one of his several later publications, an essay on "History," contributed to the volume *Counsel upon the Reading of Books* (1900), may be selected for special mention because it expounds his own position as an historian. The scope of his activities, of his unusual gifts for friendship, and of his inspiring encouragement of younger scholars extended far beyond the precincts of his own university. He was a member of many clubs, notably the Bohemian Club of San Francisco, and of various historical societies, especially the American Historical Association in which he was one of the most prominent and active figures and of which he was president in 1915. He took an important part in founding the *American Historical Review* in 1895 and was a member of the board of editors during its first decade. An illness in December 1916 seriously undermined his health but did not lessen his devotion to his work, and his death came without warning. He left his estate, including his book collections, to the University of California, where he is commemorated by a memorial hall which is the center of student activities.

[*Who's Who in America,* 1918–19; *The Balliol College Register* (1914), ed. by Edward Hilliard; *Cornell Alumni News,* Mar. 19, 1902; *Nation* (N. Y.), Apr. 26, 1919; *American Historical Review,* esp. July 1919 and Oct. 1920; *University of California Chronicle,* esp. vol. XXI (1919), "Univ. Record," pp. 62–69; private information.]
         G. M. D.

STEPHENS, JOHN LLOYD (Nov. 28, 1805–Oct. 12, 1852), traveler, author, steamship and railroad executive, was born in Shrewsbury, N. J., the son of Benjamin and Clemence (Lloyd) Stephens. He was graduated at Columbia College, in 1822, and then read law with Daniel Lord and attended the law school at Litchfield, Conn., then conducted by James Gould [q.v.]. At the age of twenty he gratified his incurable wanderlust for the first time by journeying to Arkansas, to visit an aunt. Returning to New York, he was soon admitted to the bar, practised law for eight years, and gained some repute as a Tammany orator.

The law bored him, however, and when in 1834 his doctor suggested a sea voyage as a cure for an affection of the throat, he gladly followed the prescription and spent the next two years seeking the unusual in the Mediterranean and in eastern Europe. Some of his letters, appearing in Hoffman's *American Monthly Magazine,* were so well received that in 1837 he published *Incidents of Travel in Egypt, Arabia Petraea, and the Holy Land,* in two volumes; this was followed by *Incidents of Travel in Greece, Turkey, Russia, and Poland* (2 vols., 1838). He was a born raconteur, had a zest for exploring the unusual, and wrote "with a quick and keen observation, an appreciative and good-natured sense of the ludicrous, and a remarkable facility of retaining vividly to the last the freshness of first impressions" (Hawks, *post,* pp. 66–67). Overnight, he became known as "the American traveler."

A Democrat, he was sent by Van Buren in 1839 on a confidential and rather hazy diplomatic mission to Central America. His friend Francis L. Hawks [q.v.] claims the credit for urging him to investigate the ancient civilizations reported by Antonio del Rio, Guillaume Dupaix and Frederick de Waldeck, in accounts published between 1822 and 1838. Accordingly, he took with him Frederick Catherwood, an English artist with experience in archeology. He "travelled over all Guatemala looking for the government to which he was accredited, and which he never could find" (Hawks, p. 67). His main interest was in the ruins in Honduras, Guatemala, and Yucatán. At Copán, Uxmal, Palenque, and elsewhere, Catherwood with his pencil and Stephens in words portrayed the ancient ruins. Stephens lacked the thorough scholarly background necessary for sound speculations upon their origin; his chief function was to advertise them in attractive form and thus arouse further interest. Always whimsical, he purchased all of Copán for fifty dollars and considered moving some of the monuments to New York. A result of this trip was his *Incidents of Travel in Central America, Chiapas, and Yucatan* (2 vols., 1841), with sixty-five plates by Catherwood. In 1841 they returned for a more intensive study and published in 1843 two further volumes, *Incidents of Travel in Yucatan*. It is said that by the time of Stephens' death, there had been published 21,000 copies of the *Egypt*; 12,000 of the *Greece*; 15,000 of the *Central America* and 9,750 of the *Yucatan* (*Ibid.*, p. 65).

Stephens next became a promoter and director of the Ocean Steam Navigation Company, which started a line to Bremen in 1847 and was the first to take advantage of the government subsidies to mail steamships. Stephens went to Bremen on the maiden voyage of the *Washington*. The company was soon eclipsed by the subsidy line of Edward K. Collins [*q.v.*]. Stephens was also an active supporter of the Hudson River Railroad. His last great work was in connection with the Panama Railroad, in the establishment of which William H. Aspinwall [*q.v.*], Henry Chauncey, and he were the prime movers. Elected vice-president of the company at its start in 1849, Stephens handled the necessary negotiations at Bogotá. He then succeeded Thomas W. Ludlow [*q.v.*] as president and threw himself whole-heartedly into the enterprise, spending two winters in personally supervising the surveys and the preliminary work. Returning in the spring of 1852, he was attacked by a disease doubtless contracted in that dangerous climate, and died in New York City. A monument to him was erected at the highest point on the railroad, which was opened early in 1855.

[In addition to his own works, and a biog. sketch by Catherwood in some editions of the *Incidents of Travel in Central America*, see F. L. Hawks in *Putnam's Monthly Mag.*, Jan. 1853; *No. Am. Rev.*, Oct. 1841, pp. 479–506; F. N. Otis, *Illustrated Hist. of the Panama Railroad* (1861); W. R. Scott, *The Americans in Panama* (1912), pp. 31–34; *N. Y. Herald* and *N. Y. Tribune*, Oct. 14, 1852.]   R. G. A.

STEPHENS, LINTON (July 1, 1823–July 14, 1872), legislator, jurist, and soldier, was born near Crawfordville, Ga., the grandson of Alexander Stephens who emigrated to Pennsylvania from England in 1746, was a captain in the Revolution, and removed to Georgia in 1795. His father, Andrew Baskins Stephens, was a farmer and teacher and his mother, Matilda S. (Lindsey) Stephens, was the daughter of John Lindsey, a Scotch-Irish Revolutionary soldier of Wilkes County, Ga. Linton was the youngest of his father's eight children. Both parents died in 1826, and the boy was reared by his maternal

relatives until 1837, when he went to live with his half-brother, Alexander Hamilton Stephens [*q.v.*], in Crawfordville. Having attended the Culloden and Crawfordville academies, he entered Franklin College, now a part of the University of Georgia, in 1839 and graduated in 1843. He spent the winter of 1843–44 in Washington visiting Congress and the Supreme Court. He studied law under Robert Toombs, received the degree of bachelor of laws at the University of Virginia in 1845, and attended Joseph Story's lectures at Harvard for a short time. Admitted to the bar in 1846, he immediately gained prominence and, as a partner of Richard M. Johnston [*q.v.*], was a leader of the bar.

As a Whig, he was elected to the legislature in 1849 from Taliaferro County and served until his removal to Sparta in 1852. An able and fearless speaker, he loved the Union and supported the compromises of 1850. He aided his brother, Toombs, and Cobb in organizing the Constitutional Union party but returned to the Whig party in 1852. Representing Hancock County in the Senate, 1853–55, he introduced the Nebraska resolution opposing the Kansas-Nebraska Bill. As a candidate opposed to the Know-Nothings he was defeated for Congress in 1855 and again in 1857. As a Democrat he attended the Cincinnati convention of 1856 and helped to write the state Democratic platform of 1857. A delegate to the Southern Commercial Convention at Montgomery in 1858, he took an extreme position, favoring secession unless Kansas were admitted as a slave state. Governor Brown appointed him to the state supreme court in 1859, and he won recognition as an able jurist. Because of lack of health, he resigned in 1860. He supported Douglas in 1860, hoping to defeat Breckinridge in the South and thus avert revolution. A member of the convention of 1861, he voted against secession but, when the war began, raised a company and as lieutenant-colonel of the 15th Georgia Volunteers saw service in Virginia, 1861–62. Because of the failure of his health he resigned but was commissioned a colonel in the state cavalry in 1863 and served around Atlanta. A member of the legislature again in 1863, he opposed conscription and the suspension of the writ of *habeas corpus*. He introduced the famous resolutions justifying the Confederacy and the peace resolutions of 1864. He also opposed the grant of unconstitutional powers to Governor Brown.

After the war, he practised law and refused to reënter politics. He condemned the Radical party and aided in the overthrow of the bullock régime. He denounced the Fourteenth and Fifteenth admendments and the Reconstruction acts as nullities, subversive of American liberties. He resisted the Enforcement Act of 1870, was arrested and tried before a federal commission in Macon. Pleading his own case he denounced the entire Reconstruction program, and the case was dropped. In a famous speech in Atlanta he bitterly opposed Southern support for Horace Greeley in 1872. He was twice married: first, in January 1852, to Emmeline (Thomas) Bell, the daughter of James Thomas of Sparta, who bore him three daughters and died in 1857, and, second, in June 1867, to Mary W. Salter, the daughter of R. H. Salter of Boston, Mass., who also bore him three children. Devoted to his family, his brother, and his friends, he preferred home life to active politics. Positive, independent, and aggressive, he was unbending in his convictions; yet honest and sympathetic, he was loved and esteemed by the people of Georgia. He was an earnest student, a critic of literature, with a brilliant intellect, a scholar and philosopher rather than a man of action. Buried at his home in Sparta, he was reinterred in 1914 at "Liberty Hall," near Crawfordville, Ga.

[J. D. Waddell, *Biog. Sketch of Linton Stephens* (1877); L. L. Knight, *Reminiscences of Famous Georgians* (2 vols., 1907–08); I. W. Avery, *The Hist. of . . . Ga.* (1881); *Men of Mark in Ga.*, vol. III (1912), ed. by W. J. Northen; *Atlanta Daily Sun*, July 16, 1872].   F. M. G.

STEPHENS, URIAH SMITH (Aug. 3, 1821– Feb. 13, 1882), pioneer labor leader, was born near Cape May, N. J. It was his original intention to become a Baptist minister, but the panic of 1837 brought reverses to his family and terminated his studies. He was then indentured to a tailor, from whom he derived both a trade and mercantile wisdom. Meanwhile he became a student of economics, one of his teachers and companions being Rev. John L. Lenhardt. After completing his apprenticeship, he taught school for a short time in New Jersey. In 1845 he moved to Philadelphia, and in 1853 began an extended trip, through the West Indies, Central America, and Mexico, to California, where he remained nearly five years. After his return to Philadelphia he agitated for a westward workers' migration. An abolitionist, he supported Frémont in 1856 and Lincoln in 1860. In 1861 he was present at the national convention of workingmen opposed to the Civil War. He was a Mason, an Odd Fellow, and a member of the Knights of Pythias. There is no evidence to bear out the legend that he came under direct Marxist influence. His political interest was confined to Greenbackism.

In 1862 he helped organize the Garment Cut-

ters' Association of Philadelphia. The difficulties which that organization encountered from the pressure of the employers led Stephens and six others, upon its dissolution in 1869, to found the Noble Order of the Knights of Labor, an organization destined to become the most powerful labor body of its day, with a membership in 1886 of over three quarters of a million. After being defeated on the Greenback ticket for Congress from the fifth district of Pennsylvania in 1878, he resigned as Grand Master Workman of the Knights. He was reëlected *in absentia,* and resigned again in 1879. The principles which Stephens and his associates laid down for the Knights were secrecy, union of all trades, education, and cooperation. The secrecy aspect, with its attendant rituals, was introduced by Stephens. The practical unification of trades in a national organization was a unique and invaluable contribution to the labor movement. Unity was also an internal policy vigorously extended to include skilled and unskilled, women and men, negro and white. Education became agitation of the principles of cooperative organization. Cooperative ownership of the means of production was one of the ideas of the time, a facet of utopian socialism, and Stephens conceived of the Knights of Labor not simply as a trade-union, but as a nucleus for building a cooperative commonwealth. The lack of *class* consciousness which underlay the cooperative movement led to the use of the boycott (consumer action) rather than the strike as an economic weapon, though strikes occurred.

The ruthless crushing of the Molly Maguires after the great strikes of the middle seventies, the Knights' retarded growth, the active opposition of the Catholic Church (mainly in the person of Terence V. Powderly [*q.v.*], Stephens' successor), gave strength to an anti-secrecy faction which, soon after Stephens' resignation in 1879, overthrew District Assembly 1, which had controlled the General Assembly. In 1881, after a bitter fight between Stephens and Powderly, the principle of secrecy was repudiated. Stephens thus tasted defeat on his basic idea of labor organization, but he is nevertheless justly revered as one of the great pioneer labor leaders of America. After his death, in Philadelphia, the Richmond convention of the Knights (1886) granted $10,000 for his family.

[J. R. Commons and others, *Hist. of Labour in the U. S.* (1918), vol. II; G. E. McNeill, *The Labor Movement: The Problem of To-day* (1887); T. V. Powderly, *Thirty Years of Labor, 1859–1889* (1889); Selig Perlman, *A Hist. of Trade Unionism in the U. S.* (1922); N. J. Ware, *The Labor Movement in the U. S., 1860– 1895* (1929); C. D. Wright, "An Hist. Sketch of the Knights of Labor," in *Quart. Jour. of Economics,* Jan.

1887; A. C. Stevens, *The Cyc. of Fraternities* (1899); *Pub. Ledger* (Phila.), Feb 15, 1882.]   H. So—w.

STEPHENSON, BENJAMIN FRANKLIN (Oct. 3, 1823–Aug. 30, 1871), physician, founder of the Grand Army of the Republic, was born on a farm in Wayne County, Ill., one of the eleven children of James Stephenson, a native of South Carolina, and Margaret (Clinton) Stephenson. The family early moved to a farm in Sangamon County, where Benjamin grew to manhood. He had had only the advantages of education in the local schools when he went to study medicine with an older brother at Mount Pleasant, Iowa. Later he attended lectures at Columbus, Ohio, and graduated from Rush Medical College in Chicago in 1850. He settled for practice at Petersburg, Ill., and on Mar. 30, 1855, he was married at Springfield to Barbara B. Moore, recently from Kentucky. From 1855 to 1857 he was lecturer on general, special, and surgical anatomy in the medical department of the State University of Iowa at Keokuk. In June 1861 he went to Jacksonville where the 14th Illinois Volunteers was being organized and was appointed surgeon of the regiment. He served three years in the western armies of Grant and Sherman, reached the grade of major, and was mustered out with the regiment on June 24, 1864. He is credited with having been a capable surgeon, held in high confidence by the regiment which he served. After his release from the army he joined a drug firm in Springfield, but the next year he formed a partnership with one of the leading physicians of the city.

During his war service he and the regimental chaplain, W. J. Rutledge, of Petersburg, had frequently discussed the project of forming a national association of Union veterans and he now commenced developing it. He originated the name and wrote the ritual and the constitution with some help from his old regimental friend. Though the early work of organization was done at Springfield, Stephenson's plans met with little favor there, and it was at Decatur, Ill., that Post No. 1 of the Grand Army of the Republic was formed on Apr. 6, 1866. Here the name, ritual, and constitution were adopted, and Stephenson mustered in the newly elected officers and gave the post a charter, signing himself commander of the department of Illinois. He was grievously disappointed when the representatives of the new society met in Springfield in July 1866 to form a department organization and selected another for the honor of department commander. As organizer of the order he had assumed the title of commander-in-chief and in this capacity he issued the call for a national convention to meet at Indianapolis on Nov. 20, 1866. A second disappointment awaited him when Stephen A. Hurlbut [*q.v.*] was chosen as commander and he was given the subordinate place of adjutant-general. At the second national convention at Philadelphia on Jan. 15, 1868, he failed of election to any office. Though he had conceived and launched the new order it was generally realized that he was not one to make of it a great success. An enthusiast in a new enterprise, he lacked steadiness of purpose and had a distaste for routine duties and responsibilities. His administration as national adjutant-general was notably inefficient. Through these years the Grand Army had occupied his thoughts to the detriment of everything else. His usefulness as a physician had become seriously impaired without bringing him any substantial return for his sacrifices. Impoverished, and broken in health and spirit by repeated slights, he moved his family in the winter of 1870–71 to Rock Creek where he died, leaving a widow, a son, and two daughters.

His last years were further embittered by the thought that his labors had been fruitless, for at that time the Grand Army had almost ceased to exist in the section where it had originated. Years were to pass before it became the organization of his dreams, and he did not live to see that day. In 1882 his remains were moved from the village where he died to the soldiers' plot in Rose Hill Cemetery, overlooking the Sangamon River at Petersburg, by the Grand Army post of that town. A monument, erected to his honor in Washington, D. C., was dedicated in 1909.

[M. H. Stephenson, *Dr. B. F. Stephenson, Founder of the G. A. R., A Memoir* (1894); *Proc. . . . Stephenson Grand Army Memorial*, Sen. Doc. 857, 61 Cong., 3 Sess. (1911); H. A. Kelly and W. L. Burrage, *Am. Med. Biographies* (1920), a sketch by G. H. Weaver; O. M. Wilson, *The G. A. R.* (1905); R. B. Beath, *Hist. of the G. A. R.* (1888); J. A. M. Passmore, *Ancestors and Descendants of Andrew Moore* (1897), vol. I; *Ill. State Jour.* (Springfield), Sept. 1, 1871.]   J. M. P.

STEPHENSON, ISAAC (June 18, 1829–Mar. 15, 1918), pioneer lumberman, congressman, and United States senator, was born in Maugerville, New Brunswick, son of Isaac Stephenson, of Scotch-Irish descent, and Elizabeth (Watson). Isaac went to Milwaukee at the age of sixteen, already competent to cruise for timber and to manage gangs of workmen in the woods. He worked at odd jobs in eastern Wisconsin, made a farm at Janesville, filed claims in the Escanaba country, Michigan, contracted for the moving of logs up the lake, and acquired an interest in steamers on Lake Michigan. He settled at Marinette, Wis., in 1858 as a member of the firm of N. Ludington & Company, and thereafter he was connected with every operation in the Menominee River valley. His fortune grew with each phase of the industry in wood and wood manufacture. He turned out railroad ties, broom handles, pails, and other wooden articles from his factories at Peshtigo, as well as saw-logs and lumber for the Chicago and Milwaukee markets. The profits from his industry were turned into banks, mining companies, and rail-roads.

On Oct. 8, 1871, forest fires wiped away his factory town of Peshtigo, and the way in which he met this disaster established his reputation as the strong man of his community. Already he had held local office, and had twice been a member of the Wisconsin Assembly (1866, 1868). Three times, in 1882, 1884, and 1886, he was sent to Congress; but since his party was in the minority, he had little chance to shine as a legis-lator. He watched local appropriations and took care of private pension bills, but Senator Phile-tus Sawyer [q.v.] of Wisconsin was the more striking figure. Stephenson declined renomina-tion in 1888, and for a decade devoted himself to his large private interests. In 1899 he coveted the seat of John L. Mitchell in the Senate, but was mortified when the regular Republican man-ager, guided as Sawyer wished, bestowed it upon Joseph V. Quarles. Now, for the first time, Stephenson said, he realized "the power and devious ways of the 'machine'" (Recollec-tions, post, p. 201). His feeling that he had been betrayed led him to join forces with the rebel-lious half-breeds and to finance the campaign of Robert M. LaFollette [q.v.] for governor in 1900. The Milwaukee Free Press (1901) was launched with his money in their behalf. He would have been pleased to take his reward when Quarles retired in 1905, but LaFollette himself then chose to go to the Senate. When John C. Spooner [q.v.] resigned in 1907, Stephenson announced his candidacy at once, and was elect-ed with less help from Senator LaFollette than he expected. In 1908, seeking reëlection, he dis-bursed more than $107,000 in the primary cam-paign, and before the legislature was ready to ballot for senator he was under fire. The pro-gessive associates of LaFollette, with John J. Blaine in the lead, attacked his use of money; while one of the stalwart leaders, E. L. Philipp [q.v.], complained that "through the agency of the primary the state of Wisconsin offers its rich old men an opportunity to buy the senator-ship as sort of a floral tribute to themselves" (Wisconsin State Journal, Sept. 12, 1908, p. 1). Stephenson was nevertheless elected after a fight drawn out from Jan. 27 until Mar. 4, 1909. The next legislature sent a resolution to Washington,

June 26, 1911, challenging his right to sit; but the Senate declined to unseat him, Mar. 27, 1912, after a debate in which Elihu Root character-ized the case against Stephenson as "an extreme of fantastical whimsicality" (Congressional Rec-ord, 62 Cong., 2 Sess., p. 3820). At the close of his term he retired to Marinette. When he died there he was survived by his widow (a third wife), and six of his eight children.

[In his autobiography, Recollections of a Long Life, 1829–1915 (1915), Stephenson defended himself against an adverse view of his activities presented in LaFollette's Autobiog.: A Personal Narrative of Po-litical Experiences (1913). The materials upon his senatorial contest are in Report of the Senate Members of the Joint Senatorial Primary Investigation Commit-tee (Madison, 1911), and "Election of Isaac Stephen-son: Report of the Committee on Privileges and Elec-tions, U. S. Senate," Sen. Doc. 312, 62 Cong., 2 Sess. See also, Biog. Dir. Am. Cong. (1928); Who's Who in America, 1916–17; Wis. State Jour. (Madison), Mar. 15, 1918; Madison Democrat, Mar. 16, 1918.]
F. L. P.

STEPHENSON, JOHN (July 4, 1809–July 31, 1893), pioneer street-car builder, was born in County Armagh, Ireland, and was the son of James and Grace (Stuart) Stephenson, who were respectively of English and of Scotch de-scent. When he was two years old his parents emigrated to the United States, settling in New York City, and there he was educated in the pub-lic schools and in Wesleyan Seminary. At six-teen he became a clerk in a store but in 1828, having developed a marked mechanical taste and inclination, he apprenticed himself to a coach-maker, Andrew Wade, of Broome Street, New York. During his apprenticeship of two years he devoted all of his evenings to learning me-chanical drawing and tried his hand at the de-signing of vehicles. Upon the completion of his apprenticeship he found employment as repair-man for a liveryman, Abram Brower. A year later, in May 1831, he opened his own shop to engage in the repair of all kinds of vehicles, and in the course of the year designed and built the first omnibus made in New York. Brower pur-chased this and established the city's first omni-bus line, which became so popular that he had Stephenson build three additional busses imme-diately. In the same year he was employed to build a horse-drawn car for the newly organized New York & Harlem Railroad to use on its Fourth Avenue line. His car was used when the railroad was opened on Nov. 26, 1832, and thus he gained the honor of designing and build-ing the first car for the first street railway in the world. The "'John Mason," as it was called in honor of the president of the company, resem-bled a great omnibus mounted on four flange wheels. So satisfactory was it that in the succeeding three years Stephenson received orders for cars not only for this original line but for newly established street-car lines in several cities in the East. The financial panic of 1837, however, was disastrous to him, and he was compelled to close down his factory. Nevertheless, in six years he had paid all his creditors and had once more undertaken manufacturing, this time of coaches and omnibuses exclusively. He continued in this profitably until 1852, when the establishment of horse-car lines in many cities of the world brought with it a great demand for cars. At that time he altered his plant for the manufacture of cars and for many years thereafter was recognized as the chief street-car builder of the world. He made horse cars, cable, electric, and open cars, his plant in 1891 employing five hundred men and producing about twenty-five cars a week. He directed all of the affairs of his company and devised many improvements in the design of cars. In addition to his initial patent of Apr. 22, 1833, he secured about ten others in the course of his life, all on street cars. During the Civil War his factory was devoted to the construction of gun carriages and pontoons for the government, and ran up a record of seventy completed pontoons in seventeen days. Stephenson, who was very fond of music, was an active member of the New York Sacred Music Society and the Harmonic Society of New York. In 1833 he married Julia A. Tiemann, and at the time of his death in New Rochelle, N. Y., where he had resided since 1865, he was survived by two sons and a daughter.

[Waldemar Kaempffert, *A Popular Hist. of Am. Invention* (1924), vol. I; *Am. Railroad Jour.*, Nov. 17, Dec. 1, 1832; *Am. Engineer and Railroad Jour.*, Sept. 1893; "The Original Carbuilder," *N. Y. Tribune*, May 10, 1891; obituaries in *N. Y. Tribune* and *N. Y. Times*, Aug. 1, 1893; Patent Office records.]   C. W. M—n.

STERETT, ANDREW (Jan. 27, 1778–Jan. 9, 1807), naval officer, and son of John and Deborah (Ridgley) Sterett, was born in Baltimore, Md. His paternal grandfather, also named Andrew, emigrated from Ireland to America, and settled temporarily at Bradford, Mass., but later moved to Lancaster, Pa., and eventually, to Baltimore, Md. John Sterett became active in public life, serving as captain of a company during the Revolution, and later, as a member of the Maryland state legislature. He was also a successful shipping merchant, was interested in iron-works, and owned a 1646 acre estate, together with a considerable number of slaves. Deborah (Ridgley) Sterett was a sister of Gen. Charles Ridgley, owner of the large country estate "Hampton" near Baltimore.

Beyond the facts that Andrew was the fourth of ten children, that he inherited a considerable amount of property from his father, and that at an early age he became interested in maritime affairs, little seems to be known about the first years of his career. His emergence from obscurity really begins with his entering the navy as a lieutenant on Mar. 25, 1798. For a time thereafter he served as the executive officer of the frigate *Constellation,* commanded by Thomas Truxtun [*q.v.*]. On Feb. 9, 1799, the *Constellation,* after a battle lasting one hour and fourteen minutes, captured the French frigate *Insurgente* off the island of Nevis, West Indies. In this engagement only two Americans were killed, and three wounded—one of the former being slain by Sterett himself. "One fellow," he said, "I was obliged to run through the body with my sword, and so put an end to a coward. You must not think this strange, for we would put a man to death for even looking pale on board this ship" (Frost, *post*, p. 130). The *Constellation* won another signal victory on Feb. 2, 1800, by capturing a powerful French frigate, *La Vengeance*. Sterett was at the time first lieutenant on board the *Constellation,* and took an active part in the action. Later in the year he was given command of the schooner *Enterprise,* and in December 1800 captured the *L'Amour de la Patrie,* a vessel of six guns and seventy-two men, in the West Indies.

He performed the most brilliant exploit of his career soon after the outbreak of war between the United States and Tripoli. He took the *Enterprise* to the Mediterranean in 1801, and on Aug. 1 of that year, while en route to Malta, sighted a Tripolitan polacca, the *Tripoli*. The latter vessel, finding escape impossible, finally resorted to boarding tactics, in which the Tripolitans were reputed to excel, but the skilful maneuvering of the *Enterprise* kept the enemy at a distance and enabled the Yankee gunners to fire sweeping broadsides which brought the captain of the polacca to throw his colors into the sea and to surrender his vessel after three hours of fighting (Allen, *post*, pp. 95, 96). Because of his victory Sterett received words of appreciation and a sword from Congress. He was also promoted to the rank of master commandant, and was placed in command of a brig which was under construction at Baltimore. On June 29, 1805, soon after the contest with Tripoli ended, he resigned his commission and entered the merchant marine (*Maryland Historical Magazine, post,* p. 246). One United States destroyer was named after Sterett in recognition of his contribution to the upbuilding of the morale and prestige of the navy.

[Materials relating to Sterett's ancestry have been provided by one of his collateral descendants, Mr. Wm. B. Marye, of Baltimore, who has the Sterett family records. See also G. W. Allen, *Our Navy and the Barbary Corsairs* (1905); C. W. Goldsborough, *The U. S. Naval Chronicle* (1824); H. H. Frost, *We Build a Navy* (1929); *The St. Mémin Coll. of Portraits* (1862); *Md. Hist. Mag.*, Sept. 1917.]   R. W. I.

STERKI, VICTOR (Sept. 27, 1846–Jan. 25, 1933), physician, conchologist, was born in Solothurn, Switzerland, the son of Anton and Magdalena (Müller) Sterki. His early education was received in a country school and at the Gymnasium. After two years in the college of Solothurn, he studied medicine at the University of Bern and, later, at the University of Munich. A serious illness during this period left its marks upon him for life. Having passed an examination at Munich which gave him the privilege of practising medicine, he served as polyclinical and clinical assistant in the hospital of the University of Bern, and in 1874 went into practice for himself. In 1878, at the age of thirty-two, he received the degree of doctor of medicine. He had been engaged in a careful study of the *Infusoria (Protozoa)*, and his doctor's dissertation, *Beiträge zur Morphologie der Oxytrichinen* (1878), brought favorable comment from leading zoölogists of that time. On Feb. 2, 1875, he married Mary Lanz, of Huttwyl, Switzerland. Emigrating to the United States in 1883, he settled in New Philadelphia, Ohio, and engaged in the practice of medicine.

He was always keenly interested in the phenomena of nature and in his youthful days made extensive collections of the fauna and flora of his neighborhood. His study of the *Protozoa* in college and university was another expression of this interest. In America a new field opened to him, and all the time that he could spare from his medical practice he devoted to it. *Protozoa*, mosses, and other groups claimed some of his attention, but to the *Mollusca*, especially the smaller forms, he was chiefly attracted. The small gastropods, especially the *Pupillidae*, were the first he studied, and he at once began a systematic examination of the rich fauna of this group living in America, bringing to light many new species and races and providing the basis for a comprehensive nomenclature of the peculiar folds and plications found within the aperture of these tiny mollusks. A distinguished authority on the land fauna of the United States says of his work: "In 1888 Dr. Victor Sterki published the first of a long series of studies upon American *Pupidae*, which have marked a great advance in our knowledge of the group, not alone in the increased number of species, but in the more just appreciation of their interrelationships" (*Proceedings of the Academy of Natural Sciences of Philadelphia*, vol. LII, 1901, p. 582). Other small forms of mollusks, such as the *Zonitidae*, attracted his interest, as did also the great group of *Naiades*, or freshwater mussels, and to knowledge of the anatomy and physiology of these he made valuable contributions.

The group of *Mollusca* to which his name will be attached for all time, however, is the *Sphaeriidae*, small freshwater bivalves. These he began to study early in his American residence and they principally engaged his attention to the time of his death. He amassed the largest collection of this family ever assembled and studied literally hundreds of thousands of specimens from all parts of America as well as from other sections of the world. A hundred or more species have been added to the American fauna and many yet remain to be described. This collection, together with other mollusks acquired during his lifetime, has been deposited in the Carnegie Museum at Pittsburgh, Pa., in which institution he was an assistant (*in absentia*) in the department of invertebrates from 1909 until his death. Sterki was an able writer and more than 150 papers appeared under his name. His contributions were published in *The Nautilus*, the official organ of the conchologists of America; the *Proceedings of the United States National Museum* at Washington; *Proceedings of the Academy of Natural Sciences of Philadelphia*; *Proceedings of the Ohio State Academy of Science*; and the *Annals of the Carnegie Museum*.

One of Sterki's most notable characteristics was his willingness to help others, especially beginners in the science, and during his residence in America he examined thousands of specimens sent to him for determination by all classes of students—the adolescent amateur and the distinguished professional. He was a man of genial and hospitable nature, and always unpretentious in his manner. A son and two daughters survived him, a third daughter having predeceased her father by a few weeks.

[S. T. Brooks, in *The Nautilus*, Apr. 1933, and in *Annals of the Carnegie Museum*, vol. XXII (1934), with bibliog.; *Who's Who in America*, 1918–19; *N. Y. Times*, Jan. 27, 1933.]   F. C. B.

STERLING, GEORGE (Dec. 1, 1869–Nov. 17, 1926), lyric poet, was born in Sag Harbor, N. Y., the eldest of nine children of George Ansel and Mary Parker (Havens) Sterling. He was a descendant of William Sterling, an Englishman who settled in Haverhill, Mass., in 1662. From the Havens he inherited his splendid physique, handsome features (his resemblance to Dante was often noted), his sprightly and restless spirit. His maternal grandfather, Wickham

Sayre Havens, sailed from the port of Sag Harbor between 1820 and 1840 as captain of a whaling vessel. His paternal forefathers were men of some intellectual attainment, but the line carried a taint of emotional instability that was quite manifest in the elder Sterling, a physician. In middle life Sterling's father was converted to the Roman Catholic faith. An ardent proselyte, he induced his son to enter the second year of high school at St. Charles' College, Ellicott City, Md. At St. Charles', from which he graduated in 1889, Sterling came to know as instructor and friend Father John Bannister Tabb [q.v.]. Before completing his course, however, he renounced the church, and for the rest of his life he remained consistently irreverent. His philosophic views crystallized in the simple conviction that the total of human happiness is unalterably fixed, varying only in details actually irrelevant, and that the part of wisdom is to choose pleasure and avoid pain. After leaving school, he went to live in Oakland, Cal., where he was employed as private secretary by his uncle, Frank C. Havens, a wealthy man of affairs, from 1890 until 1908.

In the summer of 1892 he first met Ambrose Bierce [q.v.]. Promptly proclaiming Bierce his master, he submitted to him for criticism and correction nearly every poem he wrote from that time until Bierce's disappearance at the end of 1913. The manuscript of one poem indicates that of twenty-five suggestions noted by Bierce all but two were adopted. Nor was this instance exceptional. Association with Bierce was a major experience in Sterling's life and undeniably stimulating. Drawn throughout his life to characters stronger than his own, it is doubtful if he would ever have attained poetic maturity had it not been for Bierce. On Feb. 7, 1896, he married Caroline Rand of Oakland, Cal., daughter of David H. Rand of New Hampshire. They moved in 1908 from Oakland to Carmel, Cal., where Sterling became, in Bierce's phrase, "the High Panjandrum" of the artist colony then assembling in Carmel. Divorced by his wife on Feb. 5, 1915, he lived for a time in the East but returned to California in 1918 when informed of her death, a suicide. Between 1903 and 1926 he published ten volumes of verse, five separately published poems, a blank verse translation of Hugo von Hofmannsthal's *Everyman* (in collaboration with Richard Ordynski), four dramatic poems, much uncollected magazine prose and verse, and *Robinson Jeffers, the Man and the Artist* (1926). A volume of sonnets, *Sonnets to Craig* (1928), was posthumously published. His reputation was still local when, in 1907,

Bierce induced the *Cosmopolitan* to publish "A Wine of Wizardry." Extravagant praise by Bierce and much consequent publicity gave the poet and the poem an unenviable notoriety. A victim of an aroused "cismontane criticism," it was not until 1923 that he found an eastern publisher.

As much by his personal influence as by his poetry, Sterling revived the early literary traditions of California, which by 1892 verged on extinction. The remarkable range and the intimate quality of his acquaintance, coupled with his long residence in the West, gave a cultural significance to his career quite apart from his writing. He was an incurable romanticist and indefatigable Bohemian, and his poetry and character came in time to reveal the strain of an insupportable exertion after the elusive phrase, the delectable experience. The ambitious poems done in his grandiose early style will not be remembered as long as such charming lyrics as "Autumn in Carmel," "Willy Pitcher," "The Last Days," "Beyond the Breakers," "Spring in Carmel," which carry the unmistakable accent and quality of his personal manner, and a few magnificent sonnets. He left much unpublished manuscript. There has been no collected edition of his work, although *Selected Poems* (1923) contains most of his best work. "Saintly, whimsical, vagabondish," Sterling was a person of manifold contradictions; mild of manner but vehement of expression; riotously witty but momentarily morose and penitent; prodigal but capable of a painstaking practicality. A passion for action and an unbridled generosity were perhaps the only traits of his nature that were wholly free from contradiction. On Nov. 17, 1926, he committed suicide in his rooms at the Bohemian Club in San Francisco.

[The date of death is from the Dept. of Pub. Health, San Francisco. There is no biog. of Sterling. See A. M. Sterling, *The Sterling Geneal.* (1909), vol. II; Upton Sinclair, in *Sonnets to Craig* (1928) and *Bookman*, Sept. 1927; Mary Austin, in *Am. Mercury*, May 1927; *Overland Monthly*, Nov., Dec. 1926; *San Francisco Review*, Nov., Dec. 1926; H. S. R., in *Authors Today and Yesterday* (1933), ed. by S. J. Kunitz; *San Francisco Water*, July 1928, a pamphlet edited by E. F. O'Day, Spring Valley Water Company; Cecil Johnson, *A Bibliog. of the Writings of George Sterling* (1931); obituaries in *San Francisco Chronicle* and *San Francisco Examiner*, Nov. 18, 1926. See also the character of Russ Brissenden in Jack London's *Martin Eden* (copr. 1908) and, particularly, *The Letters of Ambrose Bierce* (1921), ed. by Bertha C. Pope, with a memoir by Sterling. There are colls. of Sterling's letters in the possession of the author, Mrs. Madeleine Diamond of Los Angeles (Sterling's sister), James Hart of San Francisco, James Hopper of Carmel, and others.]

C. McW.

STERLING, JAMES (1701?–Nov. 10, 1763), Anglican clergyman, author, and colonial customs official, was born at Dowrass, Kings County, Ireland, the son of James Sterling, a half-pay captain of the British army. He was graduated (B.A.) from Trinity College, Dublin, in 1720, and much later, in 1733, proceeded to the M.A. degree in that institution. His literary career began with the publication in London in 1722 of the *Rival Generals,* a play with which the author claimed he "first awak'd the Irish Muse to Tragedy." The *Parricide* (1736) had a short run at Goodman's Fields, but neither this nor the earlier play sufficed to bring him the fame he sought as dramatist. He was not more fortunate as a lyric poet with his translation from Musaeus, *The Loves of Hero and Leander* (1728), and the *Poetical Works of the Rev. James Sterling* (1734). No trace remains of the political writing he is reputed to have done for the Opposition in these years, unless it be found in the favor with which certain proposals of his were met by eminent members of the party after they had come into office. About 1733 he entered Holy Orders and became a regimental chaplain, and it was probably just before this time that he lost his first wife, who had been a popular and accomplished Dublin actress.

A few years after ordination his attention was turned toward service in the colonies by his "near relation," Robert Auchmuty, d. 1750 [*q.v.*]. In 1737 he took the King's Bounty for Maryland, where he held successively the rectorships of All Hallows Parish, Anne Arundel County, of St. Ann's, Annapolis, and of St. Paul's, Kent County. Inducted to the last of these on Aug. 26, 1740, he remained its rector until his death in 1763. He was not content, however, with the limited duties and aspirations of a parish priest. He held a conviction that the future greatness of Britain was wrapped up in the development of her American colonies, and he gave expression to his imperialistic dream in a long poem of 1600 lines with the incongruous title, *An Epistle to the Hon. Arthur Dobbs,* which, written in Maryland in 1748, was published for him in London and Dublin in 1752, when he visited England. He published in 1755, in Annapolis and in London, an Assembly sermon, entitled in its English edition, *Zeal against the Enemies of our Country Pathetically Recommended,* a vigorous and well-informed piece of propaganda directed against the French aggression in America. Before returning to America in 1752, he obtained appointment as collector of customs at Chester, a customs district created by the treasury upon his unsupported recommendation that it was needed for the protection and development of the "Maryland Trade." This need was denied and

his appointment opposed by Governor Sharpe, the Maryland customs officials, and a strong group of London merchants trading with Maryland, but despite their continuous opposition his influence at the treasury remained strong enough to keep him in office as long as he lived. His literary efforts seem to have come to an end with the publication of a group of poems, not all clearly identified, in the *American Magazine,* established in 1757 by William Smith, 1727–1803 [*q.v.*]. On Sept. 19, 1743, he was married to Rebecca (Hynson) Holt, the widow of a fellow clergyman; their daughter, Rebecca, became the wife of William Carmichael [*q.v.*]. After his second wife's death he was married, on Sept. 7, 1749, to Mary Smith. Both of these wives were women of property and position. The poetical epitaph and the eulogy of Sterling published in the *Maryland Gazette* (Annapolis) for Nov. 17, 1763, indicate that he had gained the affection of his neighbors in the same degree that he had impressed them with his varied and exceptional abilities.

[L. C. Wroth, "James Sterling," *Am. Antiquarian Soc. Proc.,* Apr. 1931, with citations to sources in Md. and in England; *Dict. Nat. Biog.*; *Archives of Md.,* vols. VI (1888), pp. 8, 67, IX (1890), XLVI (1929); G. D. Burtchaell and T. U. Sadleir, *Alumni Dublinenses* (1924); *Md. Gazette, ante.*]   L. C. W.

STERLING, JOHN WHALEN (July 17, 1816–Mar. 9, 1885), educator, was born in Blackwalnut, Wyoming County, Pa., a descendant of William Sterling who settled in Haverhill, Mass., in 1662. He was one of twenty children of Daniel Sterling, lumberman and government contractor, by the last two of three wives, his mother being the third wife, Rachel (Brooks) Sterling. Educated in the public school of his town and the academies of Hamilton and Homer, N. Y., he read law for two years in Wilkes-Barre, Pa., after which he entered the sophomore year of the College of New Jersey (later Princeton) and graduated there with honors in 1840. During the following year he was principal of Wilkes-Barre Academy. In 1841 he entered the Princeton Theological Seminary and during his three years there officiated as tutor in the College of New Jersey. He spent about a year as Presbyterian missionary in the Pennsylvania county in which he was born, taught in Carroll College, newly established under Presbyterian auspices at Waukesha, Wis., in 1846, and in 1847 opened a private school in Waukesha. Early in 1849 he became professor of mathematics, natural philosophy, and astronomy at the University of Wisconsin, and principal of the preparatory department. For about two years thereafter he and his preparatory school pupils, with the chancellor, formed the faculty and student body of the infant university.

After the resignation of the first chancellor, John Hiram Lathrop [q.v.], which took effect in January 1859, the internal administration of the university till the installation in July 1859 of the new chancellor, Henry Barnard [q.v.], was largely in the hands of Sterling, whom the regents made acting chancellor. Because of Barnard's ill health and frequent absence he continued to take much of the administrative responsibility until 1860, when Barnard's chancellorship came to an end, and during the next seven years, when the university was without a chancellor, he was the chief administrative officer, dean till 1865 and thereafter vice-chancellor. In the reorganization of the faculty under Paul Ansel Chadbourne [q.v.] in 1867, he was one of three retained from the old professional group, his title being professor of natural philosophy and astronomy. After Chadbourne resigned in 1870, the routine of administration was again placed in his capable hands, where it remained till the appointment of a new president a year later. The regents had conferred on him in 1869 the office and title of vice-president, which he held to the time of his death. In 1874 he became professor of mathematics; in 1883 professor emeritus. When his health weakened in 1874 under his double load of administration and teaching, he was given a six months' leave of absence, three months of which he spent in Europe. On Sept. 3, 1851, he had married Harriet Dean, daughter of Eliot Byram Dean of Raynham, Mass. He died in Madison, survived by his wife and three of their eight children. Characteristic of him were deep piety, unfailing kindliness, high standards of scholarship, great energy, and steadfast faith that, as he declared in a commencement address, his university would some day be "the chief pride of the state and its glory abroad." Because of this faith of his, which brought inspiration to others, and the thirty-six years of devoted service he rendered, he is regarded as the chief builder and the guiding spirit of the university in its early years. In 1921 the name Sterling Hall was bestowed by the regents of the university on a new building dedicated to the interests of physics and economics.

[A. M. Sterling, *The Sterling Geneal.* (1909), vol. I, with portrait; R. G. Thwaites, *The Univ. of Wis.* (1900); *Wis. State Jour.*, Mar. 9, 11, 14, 1885; *Univ. Press*, Mar. 14, 1885; *Wis. Alumni Mag.*, June–July 1904; information from Sterling's daughter, Susan Adelaide Sterling.]   W. J. C.

STERLING, JOHN WILLIAM (May 12, 1844–July 5, 1918), lawyer, philanthropist, was born at Stratford, Conn., the son of John William and Catharine Tomlinson (Plant) Sterling. His father was a sea captain, but retired from that calling before he was forty years old. He was a descendant of William Sterling who came to America before 1660, settling in Haverhill, Mass., and later moving to Lyme, Conn. Having prepared for college at Stratford Academy, John entered Yale in the fall of 1860. After graduation with the class of 1864, he remained at college for a year, reading under the guidance of Noah Porter [q.v.], chiefly in the fields of general literature and history. In October 1865 he went to New York to enter the Columbia Law School, then directed by Theodore W. Dwight [q.v.]. He was chosen valedictorian of his class (1867) and soon was engaged as a clerk (at first without pay) in the office of David Dudley Field [q.v.], who at that time probably had the largest law practice in New York. Within eighteen months Sterling was admitted to the new firm of Field & Shearman as junior partner.

All his life a man who hated and dreaded publicity, Sterling figured in sensational news that could not be kept out of the daily headlines, for his firm, as counsel for Jay Gould and James Fisk [qq.v.] in their control of the Erie Railway, was active for years in hard-fought litigation. Sterling himself obtained from Justice Barnard (later impeached) the mysterious order putting the Albany & Susquehanna Railroad into a receivership. After the famous "Black Friday" in Wall Street (Sept. 24, 1869), nearly a hundred suits were begun against Gould and Fisk as a result of their attempt to corner gold. A great part of the office drudgery in each case fell to the lot of the junior counsel. Sterling had not wished to be an "office lawyer," merely, but the logic of events made him that and the time came when he was fully reconciled to such an outcome; for the advance of "big business" demanded the kind of service that he was equipped to give—at the office desk rather than at the counsel table in court.

As early as 1873 the firm dissolved co-partnership, Thomas G. Shearman [q.v.] and Sterling setting up an office of their own. Their first important case was the defense of Henry Ward Beecher [q.v.] in the suit brought by Theodore Tilton. For this work, continuing for a year and a half, no compensation was received. Sterling's knowledge of business practice, not less than his mastery of the law, made his advice priceless to an increasing number of important clients. The National City Bank and Standard Oil groups, with many railroad corporations, availed themselves of his counsel. At Shearman's death in 1900 the firm name was retained, with Sterling as senior partner, others having from time to time been admitted to membership. His fees in the organization of combines and mergers, as well as in the settlement of estates, were very large, and the money so received was profitably invested. He toiled early and late, subjecting himself to a routine that for most men would have been painful. He had never married and only one or two of his friends knew that he had a definite objective in amassing a fortune. When he was about sixty years of age he said to at least one of those in his confidence that he had from the first cherished the ambition of making money which after his death should enrich Yale University. In hinting at the size of this prospective addition to Yale's resources he used the word "fabulous."

The only philanthropy in which he was known during his lifetime to be interested was the Miriam Osborn Memorial Home for old ladies at Harrison, N. Y., established by a friend of whose will he was executor. This also contributed to Yale indirectly, since tracts of land in Westchester County, N. Y., and in Connecticut, that he acquired while he was building the Osborn Home, were deeded by him to the University. While salmon fishing, as had long been his custom, at Lord Mount Stephen's lodge, Grand Metis, Que., he died suddenly from a heart attack. His will left his residuary estate to Yale University, under the direction of a board of trustees. Provision was made for the erection of buildings and the founding of professorships, fellowships, and scholarships. Yale has received from the trustees funds for the erection of the Sterling Memorial Library and other buildings, including a chemistry laboratory, a hall of medicine, law buildings, dormitories (Trumbull College), a hall of graduate studies, the Divinity School quadrangle, and a tower for the Sheffield Scientific School. The funds for buildings and maintenance and for endowments total many millions. This single benefaction doubled Yale's resources.

[A. M. Sterling, *The Sterling Genealogy* (2 vols., 1909); Samuel Orcutt, *A Hist. of the Old Town of Stratford and the City of Bridgeport, Conn.* (1886), vol. II; *Who's Who in America*, 1918–19; *N. Y. Times*, July 7, 1918; J. A. Garver, *John William Sterling . . . a Biog. Sketch* (1929); A. P. Stokes, unpublished reminiscences; A. R. Burr, *The Portrait of a Banker: James Stillman, 1850–1918* (1927); J. K. Winkler, *The First Billion: The Stillmans and the National City Bank* (1934), pp. 91–95; F. A. Vanderlip in *Sat. Eve. Post*, Jan. 5, 1935; *Yale Univ. Obit. Record . . . 1919* (1920); *Addresses at the Dedication of Sterling Memorial Library at Yale Univ.* (1931); *Charges of the Bar Asso. of N. Y. Against George G. Barnard and Albert Cardozo, Justices of the Supreme Court: Testimony before Judiciary Com. of Assembly* (1872), pp. 580–611.]   W. B. S.

STERN, JOSEPH WILLIAM (Jan. 11, 1870–Mar. 31, 1934), song-writer, music publisher, was born in New York City, the son of Charles and Theresa (Katz) Stern. His parents had both been born in Germany, his father in Cologne and his mother in Frankfort. After he had completed his elementary education Stern was put to work as a traveling salesman in his father's neckwear business (C. Stern & Mayer); his chief interest, however, was not in the selling of neckties but in music, which absorbed him. Since he had a gift for composing tunes, he decided to start a music-publishing business in partnership with a friend, Edward B. Marks. To Stern and Marks publishing songs meant writing them as well, and so together they produced their first song, "The Little Lost Child," with words by Marks and music by Stern. With this their sole product they opened offices as Joseph W. Stern & Company at 304 East Fourteenth St. in 1894. Partly because it was one of the sentimental narrative songs then in great vogue, and partly because Stern and Marks displayed great enterprise in promoting it, "The Little Lost Child" proved a tremendous success. It was one of the first songs to be sung with illustrated "song slides," which the authors themselves ordered made. The slides were used with stereopticons in hundreds of auditoriums, music halls, and theatres, and Stern and Marks became virtual pioneers in the art of "song plugging." Weekly they visited the principal resorts where music was performed, to persuade singers, pianists, and orchestra leaders to include Stern songs in their repertoires. In 1896 they wrote "My Mother Was a Lady, or, If Jack Were Only Here," a rather maudlin effort as successful as their first, suggested by an incident that occurred in a German restaurant when a waitress spoke indignantly in the words of the title to a patron who annoyed her by his attentions.

By ascertaining popular trends and observing public demand they secured from other writers compositions that achieved wide circulation, and they soon stood among the leading publishers of current successes. For many years Stern went abroad annually, bringing back with him the American rights to such foreign songs as the English popular song, "Elsie from Chelsea," which they published in 1896, Paul Lincke's "Glow Worm," and "The Parade of the Wooden Soldiers," which was published in 1911 but did not achieve popularity until it was used in the *Chauve-Souris* in 1922. Among the American popular songs issued by the firm were "A Hot Time in the Old Town" (later called "There'll Be a Hot Time in the Old Town Tonight"),

"Sweet Rosie O'Grady," "Under the Bamboo Tree," "Everybody Works But Father," and many others. When the craze for dancing swept America in the years just before the World War, Stern and Marks were quick to put their firm in the lead as publishers of dance music for the latest steps. In 1920 Stern retired from the business and devoted himself largely to raising prize flowers at his home in Brightwaters, Long Island. A few weeks before his death, which occurred at Brightwaters, he had decided to re-enter the song publishing business. He was survived by his wife, Leona Lewis, a singer, whom he had married in 1899.

[E. B. Marks, *They All Sang* (1934); Isaac Goldberg, *Tin Pan Alley* (1930); Sigmund Spaeth, *Read 'Em and Weep* (1926); obituaries in *Variety* and *N. Y. Herald Tribune,* Apr. 3, and *N. Y. Times,* Apr. 1, 3, 1934; information from Stern's widow.]   J. T. H.

STERNBERG, CONSTANTIN IVANOVICH, Edler von (July 9, 1852–Mar. 31, 1924), pianist, composer, teacher, was born in St. Petersburg (later Leningrad), Russia. After the death of his father, Ivan von Sternberg, when Constantin was three, and the remarriage of his mother, he was reared by his grandmother and a French governess in somewhat pampered fashion. At six he spoke four languages and was beginning the study of music. After a few years in the St. Petersburg Lutheran School, which he left at eleven, and a year at school in Weimar, Germany, he was taken to Leipzig in 1865 upon the recommendation of Franz Liszt to become a pupil of Ignaz Moscheles, Coccius, and Ernst Friedrich Richter at the conservatory. In 1866, the cholera epidemic having sent the family to Dresden, he studied piano with Friedrich Wieck, father-in-law of Robert Schumann, who refused all payment for lessons. Upon returning to Leipzig, he directed an orchestra of forty and a chorus of twenty-four in *Martha, Stradella,* and *Fra Diavolo,* although he was not yet fifteen years old. His duties as conductor took him to Berlin, where in 1872 he formed a friendship with Moritz Moszkowski and, through Moszkowski, with Theodor Kullak. Under Kullak, who invited him to become his pupil and practically supported him for two years, he modernized his piano method and overcame the restrictions imposed by the more pedantic style of Moscheles. In February 1875 he made his début as a pianist in Berlin, and won the admiration and friendship of Anton Rubinstein. In the same year he was appointed court pianist at Schwerin, Mecklenburg-Schwerin, and head of the Academy Music School. At various times he acted as chorusmaster at the Stadt-Theater in Berlin, as summer conductor at Würzburg and Kissingen, and

as conductor at the court opera in Neustrelitz. In addition he found time for a number of lessons with Franz Liszt. In 1877 he was engaged for a tour as pianist with Madame Désirée Artôt, a celebrated singer, and spent the season of 1877–78 in concerts with her in Europe, Russia, Siberia, Asia Minor, and Egypt. A performance he gave on Mar. 22, 1880, before Kaiser Wilhelm I, led to engagements at embassies and palaces of the aristocracy, and to a tour of more than one hundred concerts in the United States, 1880–81. His first tour was followed by further engagements in successive years, some of them undertaken in conjunction with August Wilhelmj, the violinist, and others with Minnie Hauk, the singer. He was married in the year following his first American visit, and in 1886 settled in Atlanta, Ga., and became an American citizen. In 1890, moving to Philadelphia, Pa., he established the Sternberg School of Music, which he conducted until his death. He died in Philadelphia, survived by his wife, Tyl.

He had a position of importance in the musical life of America, principally as a teacher, although he was prominent also as a composer and pianist. His distinguished pupils included Olga Samaroff, Robert Armbruster, Gustave Becker, Robert Braun, and the modernistic composer, George Antheil. His compositions include a "Humoresque," five "Concert-Études," an "Impromptu," "Caprice Hippique," "Nuit Arabe," "En Bohème," and three "Preludes," all for piano; six trios for piano, violin, and violoncello; and many choral works and songs. Some of his music was played in concert by Josef Hofmann, Leopold Godowsky, Fannie Bloomfield Zeisler, and other pianists. His writings include *Ethics and Esthetics of Piano-Playing* (copyright 1917) and *Tempo Rubato and Other Essays* (copyright 1920). He wrote many articles for musical magazines; three autobiographical articles, "The Making of a Musician as Shown in the Reminiscences of Constantin von Sternberg," appeared in the *Musician,* December 1913, and January and February 1914.

[The most complete account of von Sternberg's life and career is given in his articles in the *Musician* in 1913 and 1914. See also *Grove's Dict. of Music and Musicians: Am. Supp.* (1926); *Baker's Biog. Dict. of Musicians* (3rd edition, 1919), ed. by Alfred Remy; W. R. Murphy, in *Musical America,* Apr. 5, 1924; obituary in *Pub. Ledger* (Phila.), Apr. 1, 1924.]

J. T. H.

STERNBERG, GEORGE MILLER (June 8, 1838–Nov. 3, 1915), bacteriologist, epidemiologist, and surgeon-general of the United States army, was born at Hartwick Seminary, Otsego County, N. Y., where he spent most of his childhood. His father, Levi Sternberg, a Lutheran clergyman who later became principal of Hartwick Seminary, was descended from a German family from the Palatinate, which had settled in the Schoharie valley in the early years of the eighteenth century. His mother, Margaret Levering (Miller) Sternberg, was the daughter of George B. Miller, also a Lutheran clergyman and professor of theology at the seminary, a Lutheran school. The eldest of a large family, George was early compelled to lighten his father's burden by gainful work. His studies at Hartwick Seminary were interrupted by a year of employment in a bookstore in Cooperstown and by three years of teaching in rural schools. During his last years at Hartwick he taught mathematics, chemistry, and natural philosophy, and devoted his leisure hours to the study of anatomy and physiology under Dr. Horace Lathrop of Cooperstown. After medical courses first in Buffalo and then at the College of Physicians and Surgeons (later part of Columbia University), where he received the degree of M.D. in the spring of 1860, he settled for practice in Elizabeth, N. J., and remained there until the outbreak of the Civil War. He was appointed assistant surgeon, United States Army, on May 28, 1861, and on July 21 of the same year he was captured at Bull Run while serving with Gen. George Sykes's division in the Army of the Potomac. Escaping, he joined his command in front of Washington, and later participated in the battles of Gaines's Mill and Malvern Hill (Peninsular campaign). He contracted typhoid fever at Harrison's Landing and was sent north on a government transport. The remaider of his Civil War service he rendered mainly in military hospitals at Portsmouth Grove, R. I., and at Cleveland, Ohio. He received brevet commissions of captain and major for faithful and meritorious service during the war. From the close of the Civil War until 1879 he served at various army posts, first in Kansas, then on the Atlantic seaboard, and later in the Pacific northwest. In 1868–69 he took part in several expeditions against hostile Cheyennes along the upper Arkansas River in Indian Territory and western Kansas. During his service at Fort Barrancas, Fla., 1872–75, which was marked by frequent contact with yellow fever, he noted the efficacy of moving inhabitants out of an infected environment and successfully applied the method to the Barrancas garrison. About this time he published two articles in the *New Orleans Medical and Surgical Journal* ("An Inquiry into the Modus Operandi of the Yellow Fever Poison," July 1875, and "A Study of the Natural History

of Yellow Fever," March 1877) which gave him a definite status as an authority upon yellow fever. He was stricken with the disease himself in the summer of 1875, and recovered only after a critical illness and a long convalescence. Later, while serving at Fort Walla Walla, Wash., he participated in the Nez Percés campaign of 1877. In these days he was utilizing the time not taken up by his military duties in the studies and experiments which were the foundation for his later work. He perfected an anenometer and in 1870 patented an automatic heat regulator which has had wide use.

In April 1879 he was ordered to Washington, D. C., and detailed for duty with the Havana Yellow Fever Commission, his medical associates being Dr. Stanford Chaillé of New Orleans and Dr. Juan Guiteras [*q.v.*] of Havana. In the distribution of work, Sternberg was given the problems relating to the nature and natural history of the cause of the disease, which involved microscopical examination of blood and tissues of yellow fever patients. In these investigations he was one of the first to employ the newly discovered process of photomicrography, and he developed high efficiency in its use. During three months which he passed in Havana he was intimately associated with Dr. Carlos Juan Finlay [*q.v.*], the proponent of the theory of transmission of yellow fever by the mosquito. At the end of its year's work, however, the Commission came to the conclusion that the solution of the cause of the disease must wait upon further progress in the new science of bacteriology. Sternberg was next sent to New Orleans to investigate the conflicting discoveries of the *Plasmodium malariae* by Alphonse Laveran and of the *Bacillus malariae* by Arnold Carl Klebs and Corrado Tommasi-Crudeli. His report, made in 1881, stated that the so-called *Bacillus malariae* had no part in the causation of malaria. In this same year, simultaneously with Louis Pasteur, he announced his discovery of the pneumococcus, now recognized as the pathogenic agent in pneumonia, though it remained for Karl Frankel to show its relationship to the disease. In the United States he was the first to demonstrate the plasmodium of malaria (1885) and the bacilli of tuberculosis and typhoid fever (1886). His interest in bacteriology naturally led to an interest in disinfection, and with him and Koch scientific disinfection had its beginning. In 1878, using putrefactive bacteria, he had begun to experiment on disinfectants. He continued his experiments in Washington and in the laboratories of the Johns Hopkins Hospital at Baltimore under the auspices of the American Public Health Association. His essay, *Disinfection and Individual Prophylaxis against Infectious Diseases* (1886), received the Lomb prize and was translated into several foreign languages. During the Hamburg cholera epidemic of 1892 he was attached to the New York quarantine station as consultant upon disinfection as applied to ships and quarantine stations. Though the disease reached American shores, no case developed within the country.

In the meantime he was ascending in military grade. He was made captain in 1866, major in 1875, lieutenant-colonel in 1891, and on May 30, 1893, surgeon-general of the army with the rank of brigadier-general. His nine years' tenure of that office was marked by the establishment of the Army Medical School in 1893, the organization of the army nurse corps and the dental corps, the creation of the tuberculosis hospital at Fort Bayard and of many general hospitals during the Spanish-American War. His own early difficulties in acquiring the knowledge for which he thirsted led to a liberal-minded policy in the establishment of laboratories in the larger military hospitals where medical officers could engage in scientific research. In 1898, led by similar motives, he established the Typhoid Fever Board made up of Majors Walter Reed, Victor Clarence Vaughan [*qq.v.*], and Edward O. Shakespeare, which introduced new points of view for the prevention of this disease, and in 1900 he established the Yellow Fever Commission, headed by Reed, which fixed the transmission of yellow fever upon a particular species of mosquito. After his retirement from active duty in the army in 1902, he devoted his later years to social welfare activities in Washington, particularly to the sanitary improvement of habitations and to care of the tuberculous. He died at his home in Washington. His monument in Arlington Cemetery bears the inscription : "Pioneer American Bacteriologist, distinguished by his studies of the causation and prevention of infectious diseases, by his discovery of the microorganism causing pneumonia, and scientific investigation of yellow fever, which paved the way for the experimental demonstration of the mode of transmission of the disease." His name will survive as that of the American bacteriologist, contemporary of Pasteur and of Koch, who first brought the fundamental principles and technique of the new science within the reach of American physicians. From 1875, when he published his first articles on yellow fever, he was a frequent contributor to periodical literature of medicine. In 1892 he brought out his *A Manual of Bacteriology,* the first exhaustive treatise on the subject published in the United States. His books, reports, and articles number not less than one hundred and fifty.

He was a man of reverent piety and practical Christianity, modest and unassuming, gentle in manner and in speech, whose career was marked by devotion to duty and untiring industry. Faced in the Spanish-American War with great difficulties, he bore without reply the burden of much criticism, either unfounded or the result of conditions not of his making. He was short in stature, with a moderate stoutness in his later years. His portraits show how the smooth-faced youth of abundant dark hair changed to the middle-aged man of full beard, and finally to the retired officer with white mustache and fringe of white hair. Marked in them all are the high intelligent forehead and the keen speculative dark eyes. He was married on Oct. 19, 1865, to a daughter of Robert Russell of Cooperstown, N. Y., Louisa Russell, who died in 1867 from cholera at Fort Harker, Kan. On Sept. 1, 1869, he was married at Indianapolis, Ind., to Martha L. Pattison, daughter of Thomas T. N. Pattison of that city. There were no children.

[*Who's Who in America,* 1914–15; Martha L. Sternberg, *George Miller Sternberg* (1920), with portraits and bibliog.; *Addresses Delivered at the Complimentary Banquet to Gen. George M. Sternberg . . . on his Seventieth Birthday* (1908), ed. by G. M. Kober; A. C. Abbott, in *Trans. Coll. of Physicians of Phila.,* 3 ser., vol. XXXVIII (1916); H. A. Kelly and W. L. Burrage, *Am. Medic. Biogs.* (1920); obituary in *Evening Star* (Washington, D. C.), Nov. 3, 1915.]
J. M. P.

STERNE, SIMON (July 23, 1839–Sept. 22, 1901), lawyer and civic reformer, was a son of Henry and Regina Sterne. He was born in Philadelphia and attended the public schools there. Later, he traveled in Europe and for a short period studied at the University of Heidelberg. On his return he began preparation for the practice of law in the offices of George Sharswood and John H. Markland. In 1859 he was graduated from the University of Pennsylvania with the degree of LL.B., and the same year was admitted to the bar in Philadelphia.

Moving to New York in 1860, he was admitted to the bar there and began a successful practice and an active and varied career in promoting civic improvement. In 1863 he gave a series of lectures on economics at Cooper Institute. He wrote leading articles for the New York *Commercial Advertiser,* the property of one of his clients, and in 1865 he became editor of the *New York Social Science Review.* While in England in 1865 he obtained permission from Thomas Hare to adapt his ideas of representation to American conditions. The result was the founding of the Personal Representation Society, which advocated cumulative voting and induced the Illinois constitutional convention of 1870 to adopt it. He was the hard-working secretary of the Committee of Seventy which overthrew the "Tweed ring." In 1875 he assisted, as a member of Governor Tilden's commission, in devising a uniform plan of government for the cities of New York state. He served on a commission appointed by Governor Morton in 1895 to suggest improvements in the methods of legislation. In the interest of free trade he made numerous campaign speeches for the Democratic party from 1876 to 1888.

As his practice developed it tended to center in cases involving common carriers, and after 1875 his most important activities, both public and legal, were in this field. He believed that the common law of railroads, which had been adapted from the rules relating to highways and canals, was inadequate to guarantee proper service to the public and safety to investors. When the Hepburn committee of the New York Assembly met to inquire into alleged abuses (1879), he appeared as counsel for the board of trade and transportation and the chamber of commerce and practically conducted the investigation. The report of this committee was followed by the passage of the state railroad commission act of 1882, which he drafted. He later drafted essential provisions of the federal Interstate Commerce Act of 1887, incorporating the results of an extensive private investigation into the relations between railroads and the state in western Europe. He was employed as counsel by the Interstate Commerce Commission; by several large railway systems; by Northern friends of Jefferson Davis in 1865; by the bondholders of Louisiana in their suit in the Supreme Court against the state; and by Mark Twain and Joaquin Miller in copyright cases. In the course of his practice he secured important additions to the common law of New York—that elevated railroad companies are liable for damages for obstructing the passage of light and air; that the existence of a strike is no excuse for a common carrier to refuse to receive and forward freight; and that telephone service is analogous to that rendered by a common carrier.

He was the author of *On Representative Government and Personal Representation* (1871); *Constitutional History and Political Development of the United States* (copr. 1882); several articles for Lalor's *Cyclopædia of Political Science, Political Economy, and of the Political History of the United States* (3 vols., 1881–84); and many essays published in American and foreign periodicals, the best of which were republished in book form in 1912 under the title *Railways in the United States*. His writings, though marred by prolixity, show originality of thought and keen analysis of contemporary conditions. His most prominent personal traits were large sympathy, determination, intellectual enthusiasm, and mental agility. He died from an apoplectic stroke in his sixty-third year and was buried from Temple Emanu-El in New York City. His widow, the former Mathilde Elsberg, whom he married June 8, 1870, together with a daughter, survived him.

[John Foord, *The Life and Public Services of Simon Sterne* (1903); *Biog. Dir. of the State of N. Y.* (1900); *Who's Who in America,* 1899–1900; A. S. Gitterman, *Memorial Exercises at the Unveiling of a Small Fountain . . . 1902* (n.d.); introduction to *Railways in the U. S.* (1912); *N. Y. Times,* Sept. 23, 24 (editorial), 1901; *N. Y. Herald,* Sept. 23, 1901; *Jewish Messenger,* Oct. 6, 1901; *Hist. of the Bench and Bar of N. Y.* (1897), II, 360–62; *Asso. of the Bar of the City of N. Y.; Ann. Reports,* 1903.]   E. C. S.

STERNE, STUART [See Bloede, Gertrude, 1845–1905].

STERRETT, JAMES MACBRIDE (Jan. 13, 1847–May 31, 1923), Protestant Episcopal clergyman, philosopher, was born in Howard, Pa., the son of Robert and Sarah E. (MacBride) Sterrett. He graduated from the University of Rochester in 1867 and from the Episcopal Theological Seminary at Cambridge, Mass., in 1872. In the latter year he was ordained deacon and became assistant minister at Lawrence, Mass. Elevated to the priesthood in 1873, he served as rector of the church in Wellsville, N. Y., until 1877, marrying, Jan. 20, 1876, Adlumia Dent of Brookland, Pa. His next parish was in Bedford, Pa., where he ministered from 1879 to 1882. He was then called to the Seabury Divinity School, Faribault, Minn., as professor of philosophy, which position he held for the ensuing ten years, at the end of which time he assumed a similar professorship at Columbian (now George Washington) University, Washington, D. C. He was made professor emeritus in 1909. From 1892 to 1911 he served also as assistant minister of the Church of the Epiphany, Washington. Becoming rector of All Soul's Parish in 1911, he continued as such until 1917, and thereafter he was associate rector. During a period of ill health he committed suicide by shooting; he was survived by his wife and five sons.

As a philosopher, Sterrett's distinctive contribution to American thought was along the line of the development of idealistic philosophy, notably the idealism of Hegel. His close relation to William T. Harris [*q.v.*], the leading spirit of what is known as the "St. Louis School," would perhaps entitle him to be classed as an adherent of this school. He was especially interested in the field where philosophy and religion touch. Free from the implied pantheism of some idealists, and no slavish follower of Hegel, he turned his thought to the philosophical principles which underlie the intellectual aspect of religion. The titles of his several books indicate the line his interest followed: *Studies in Hegel's Philosophy of Religion* (1890), *Reason and Authority in Religion* (1891), *The Ethics of Hegel* (1893), *The Freedom of Authority* (1905), and *Modernism in Religion* (1922). His *Freedom of Authority* is a collection of essays, significant as showing his stanch defense of religion against attacks made by those of opposite mind. He was, however, never unfair to opponents nor did he criticize them for the mere sake of criticism.

His ethical viewpoint was the social one. It was his conviction that man finds his truest ethical life in conjunction with other men. The freedom of authority is the philosophical justification of authority in that under law one finds the best of one's own nature. Law is the expression of one's own moral self, whether this fact be consciously realized or not. Authority is real freedom; indeed, freedom is best actualized under and through authority. Thus freedom is given an ethical meaning. This was one of Sterrett's outstanding ideas and, applied to historical religion, became a plea for the episcopate, which seemed to him to be rationally justified and which he regarded as conducive to the best interests of the Church.

As a teacher he was enthusiastic in the presentation of his subject. He loved philosophy as men love an ideal and consistently followed the light that it yielded. He was eager to impress others with its knowledge and to make it a living force. As the leader of a church he was devoted to the spiritual welfare of those who looked to him for guidance, a fact especially evinced in the closing years of his life, when, after retirement from teaching, he assumed the active work of the ministry and wrought devotedly and effectively. His great work was in the field of philosophy, however, in which his clear, yet profound, thinking helped to give idealism a better standing as against the empirical pragmatic trend so pronounced in some quarters.

[Sterrett spelled his middle name with a small "b," though his mother's name was MacBride. Sources for this sketch include *Who's Who in America*, 1922–23; *Living Church*, June 9, 1923; *Washington Post*, June 1, 1923; personal acquaintance.]   E. E. R.

STERRETT, JOHN ROBERT SITLINGTON (Mar. 4, 1851–June 15, 1914), archaeologist, was born at Rockbridge Baths, Va., of Scotch-Irish ancestry, the son of Robert Dunlap and Nancy Snyder (Sitlington) Sterrett. From 1868 to 1871 he was a student in the University of Virginia, and then went abroad, where he studied at Leipzig, Berlin, and Munich, receiving the degree of Ph.D. from the University of Munich in 1880. He was a student at the American School of Classical Studies at Athens, from 1882 to 1883, and its secretary from 1883 to 1884.

Returning to the United States, he became professor of Greek at Miami University in 1886, retaining that position for two years and then holding a similar position at the University of Texas until 1892. Called to Amherst College, he was professor of Greek there until 1901, when he became head of the Greek department at Cornell University, remaining as such until his death. In 1896–97 he also served as professor in the American School of Classical Studies in Athens, Greece. On Mar. 1, 1892, he was married to Josephine Mosely Quarrier of Charleston, W. Va., by whom he had four children.

The ruling passion of Sterrett's life was exploration and archaeological research in Asia Minor and Babylonia, whither he led several expeditions, the fruits of which are contained in his publications. His unbounded enthusiasm for archaeology is evinced by the fact that he spent all his limited patrimony upon it. His main object was to explore the least known, and therefore the most dangerous, regions. On the Wolfe Expedition in 1885, for example, with a subsidy of only a thousand dollars, and with but two native servants, he was able—thanks to his economy, tact, personality, and knowledge of the Turkish language—safely to visit the unknown regions of Pisidia, Cilicia, Lycaonia, and Isauria and by his observations and measurements to reconstruct Heinrich Kiepert's maps of those countries. Sterrett's chorographic work is to be seen in the two subsequent maps made by Kiepert himself. In addition to the host of inscriptions which Sterrett published, he identified the sites of scores of important cities, among them the Lystra of St. Paul's travels. At the age of thirty-five he had made remarkable contributions to the fields of chorography and epigraphy.

His published works include: *Qua in re Hymni Homerici quinque maiores inter se differant* (1881); *Inscriptions of Assos, Inscriptions of Tralles* (1885); *An Epigraphical Journey in Asia Minor* (1888), containing 398 inscriptions; *The Wolfe Expedition to Asia Minor* (1888), containing 651 inscriptions;

Leaflets from the Notebook of an Archaeological Traveler (1889); *The Torch-Race at Athens* (1902); *Homer's Iliad: First Three Books and Selections* (copr. 1907), edited for school use; *The Outline of a Plan for the Exploration of Asia Minor, Syria, and the Cyrenaica* (1907); *A Plea for Research in Asia Minor and Syria* (1911).

Before his untimely death Sterrett had in mind the completion of three great tasks: an historical geography of the New Testament; a translation of Strabo's work on geography; and a two-year expedition to Asia Minor and Cyrenaica. He had collected material for the first task, had begun the second (see Preface to H. L. Jones, *The Geography of Strabo*, vol. I, 1917), and had started a campaign for $100,-000 to finance the third. He was a man of large physique and commanding personality, an inspiring teacher, and an indefatigable worker. Although uncompromising in his settled beliefs, he was modest and tolerant to a fault. He was intensely religious, caring only for the things of the spirit. When upon unearthing an inscribed stele at Tarsus it suddenly dawned upon him that the Apostle Paul had often beheld it, he burst into tears.

[Twenty-nine notebooks kept on the expeditions to Asia Minor, 1884–85, in Cornell Univ. Lib.; *Who's Who in America*, 1914–15; *Bull. of the Univ. of Tex.* (1889); *Boston Post*, May 8, 1888, *Independent*, May 10, 1888, *Nation* (N. Y.), May 10, 1888; *Classical Rev.*, July 1889; *Evening Post* (N. Y.), June 17, 1914.]   H. L. J.

STETEFELDT, CARL AUGUST (Sept. 28, 1838–Mar. 17, 1896), inventor and metallurgist, was born at Holzhausen, Gotha, Germany. He was the only son of August Heinrich Christian Stetefeldt and Friederika Christiane (Credner) Stetefeldt. His father was a Lutheran clergyman, who moved in 1847 to Hörselgau, where he kept a private school in addition to performing his clerical duties. Under his tutelage his son was prepared to enter the Gymnasium at Gotha at the age of fourteen. His career there was chiefly marked by a conflict that ended in his being permitted to give up the study of Hebrew, and by the founding of a natural history society among the students. After Gotha he spent two years at the university at Göttingen, entering the school of mines at Clausthal in 1860 and graduating in 1862. He received the highest rating in his class in all metallurgical and mining subjects and was immediately commissioned to make some investigations of metallurgical processes in the government works in the Harz. After a brief experience managing a small copper smelting

plant in Bohemia he came to the United States in 1863 and was immediately engaged as assistant to Charles A. Joy, professor of chemistry in Columbia College, New York City. The next year he became an assistant to the consulting firm of Adelberg & Raymond of which Rossiter W. Raymond [*q.v.*] was a member, and, in 1865, formed a partnership with John H. Boalt to operate an assay office and consulting business at Austin, Nev. He built the first lead blast furnace in the district at Eureka, Nev., but the enterprise failed because of the nature of the ore deposit.

Stetefeldt had taken out a patent on an improvement on the Gerstenhöfer roasting furnace soon after he came to America, and he followed it by developing the design known as the Stetefeldt furnace, the first successful one being built at Reno, Nev. It has since been superseded, but the advance it marked in the metallurgical processes for dealing with sulphide ores containing gold and silver by the chlorination process won for its inventor a high place in the history of metallurgy. Stetefeldt devoted most of his life thereafter to the construction and operation of his furnaces and to auxiliary processes, but he also did much to improve and recommend the Russell lixiviation process. He contributed more than a score of papers to the *Transactions of the American Institute of Mining Engineers* (see *Transactions*, vol. XXVI, pp. 542–43), and was twice vice-president of the Institute. He went to Europe in 1870 but returned to San Francisco in 1872, and was married there on Dec. 31, 1872. He had no children and his wife died before him. He resided in New York City from 1882 until 1889, and then returned to California, spending the rest of his life in Oakland studying general science. His book, *The Lixiviation of Silver-ores with Hyposulphite Solutions*, was published in 1888. He was a worthy representative of the group of German-trained metallurgists who contributed so much to the development of metallurgy in the United States in the latter half of the nineteenth century.

[Biographical article by R. W. Raymond, *Engineering and Mining Jour.*, Mar. 28, 1896; *Trans. of the Am. Institute of Mining Engineers*, vol. XXVI (1897); *San Francisco Chronicle*, Mar. 18, 1896.]
T. T. R.

STETSON, AUGUSTA EMMA SIMMONS (*c.* 1842–Oct. 12, 1928), Christian Science leader, daughter of Peabody and Salome (Sprague) Simmons, and a descendant of Moses Simmons, who came to Plymouth in 1621, was born in Waldoboro, Me. During her infancy the family moved to Damariscotta, Me., where her father was an architect. She early showed musical and elocutionary talent. Her education at the Damariscotta High School and in the Lincoln Academy, New Castle, Me., was adequate for the period. In 1864 she married Capt. Frederick J. Stetson, a ship-builder associated with Baring Brothers, London. Like his wife, he was of early New England ancestry, being a descendant of Robert Stetson who was living at Scituate, Mass., in 1634. His business took them to England, then to Bombay, and finally to Akyab, British Burma. His health, however, had been permanently injured by privations suffered in Libby Prison during the Civil War, and after a few years in the Orient it broke down completely. He and his wife returned to America and settled in Boston, where Mrs. Stetson undertook to support them as an elocutionist. Large and ample-bosomed, with a good voice and an ingratiating manner, she was well equipped for the rôle, and her elocutionary studies were of great assistance in her later career. While engaged in them she attracted the attention of Mary Baker Eddy [q.v.], who persuaded her to enter one of her classes. Immediately on completion of the three weeks' course she began to practise as a Christian Science healer. Her success in this and in preaching the new doctrine was so great that in November 1886 Mrs. Eddy sent her to New York City to open up the field there. The work at first moved slowly, but by February 1888 Mrs. Stetson was able to legally incorporate a church of seventeen members. The congregation met in a hall over Caswell and Massey's drug store at Fifth Avenue and Forty-seventh Street; the next year it moved to Crescent Hall at 123 Fifth Ave., and later to Hardman Hall at Fifth Avenue and Nineteenth Street. These changes of location were dictated by the increasing size of the congregation, which in 1894 made necessary a further move to Scottish Rite Hall, and in 1896 led to the purchase of the old Rutgers Presbyterian Church at 143 West Forty-eighth St. In 1899 property was secured at Ninety-sixth Street and Central Park West, where a magnificent building was erected which at its completion in 1903 was without mortgage although it had cost over a million dollars. Most of this sum was raised through the personal exertions of Mrs. Stetson. She herself lived on a lavish scale commensurate with her dwelling—a gift from her followers which cost about $100,000 and was adorned with a marble staircase, expensive rugs and tapestries, six grandfather's clocks, and other luxurious objects.

Her disciple's remarkably successful career

had now aroused the jealousy of Mrs. Eddy, and various by-laws were promulgated by her which aimed to limit the sphere of Mrs. Stetson's influence but still left her in actual control of her own church. In the summer of 1909, however, the Board of Directors of the Mother Church, at Mrs. Eddy's prompting, began to investigate certain charges against Mrs. Stetson, of which the chief were that she taught the sinfulness of physical procreation and endeavored by means of mental suggestion to bring illness and even death upon her enemies. These charges were found to be well grounded, and in November 1909 Mrs. Stetson was formally excommunicated. Refusing to admit that her leader had turned against her, Mrs. Stetson continued to proclaim Mrs. Eddy's semi-divinity and, after the latter's death in 1910, she prophesied her speedy resurrection. She published three volumes dealing largely with their mutual relations: *Reminiscences, Sermons and Correspondence* (1913), *Vital Issues in Christian Science* (1914), *Sermons and Other Writings* (1925). A fervent believer in the Anglo-Israelite theory, she became a violent Jingoist during the World War. Toward the close of her life she spent as much as $250,000 annually in self-advertising in the press or on the radio. She also formed a choral society which gave notable public performances during 1918–26, specializing in what she called "spiritual music." Shortly before her death, she announced that she would never die.

[L. A. Simmons, *Hist. of the Simmons Family* (1930), not altogether dependable; *Who's Who in America,* 1928–29; autobiog. passages in Mrs. Stetson's writings; E. F. Dakin, *Mrs. Eddy* (1928); Fleta C. Springer, *According to the Flesh* (1930); A. K. Swihart, *Since Mrs. Eddy* (1931); obituary in *N. Y. Times,* Oct. 13, 1928.]   E. S. B.

STETSON, CHARLES AUGUSTUS (Apr. 1, 1810–Mar. 28, 1888), hotel proprietor, the son of Prince and Hepzibeth or Hepzibah (Patch) Stetson, was born at Newburyport, Mass. He was a descendant of Robert Stetson, probably of England, who emigrated to America before 1634. His father was a tavern-keeper in that city, and in 1824, when he entertained Lafayette, young Charles acted as *valet de chambre* to the distinguished guest. In 1829 the famous Tremont House in Boston, then newly built, opened its doors with Charles Stetson, then nineteen years of age, as clerk and bell-boy. He was married to Lucy Ann Brown of Newburyport on Mar. 14, 1832. The Astor House in New York was completed in 1836, and Astor first leased it to the Boydens of Boston, owners of the Tremont House. His relations with them, however, were unsatisfactory, and in July 1838 Stetson took over the hotel, having at first as his partner, Robert B. Coleman, who presently retired. For nearly thirty years Stetson was the proprietor and literally the host of the Astor, probably the most famous host and hostelry in America at the time. In his first conversation with Astor, Stetson called himself a hotel-keeper, rather than a tavern landlord who merely "knows how to go to market, and how to feed so many people." "A hotel keeper," he declared, "is a gentleman who stands on a level with his guests" (Smith, *post*, p. 313).

Stetson was appointed a quartermaster-general of New York State on the staff of Governor Washington Hunt in 1851, and was known thereafter as "General" Stetson—a title which he used to best advantage as Mine Host. All celebrities who visited New York in the middle of the nineteenth century stopped at the Astor and were greeted by Stetson as if they had been guests in his own home. A sumptuous dinner to the Prince de Joinville at the Astor in 1840 was long considered a milestone in the city's history. Louis Kossuth addressed hordes of admirers from its windows in 1851. Room No. 11 was long the New York home of Thurlow Weed, and many a political deal, many a "slate" was arranged there. A certain suite of two rooms was always ready, even at a moment's notice, for Daniel Webster, a warm friend of Stetson's. "If I were shut out of the Astor," remarked Webster, "I would never go to New York again" (*New York Times*, Jan. 22, 1928). But notwithstanding Stetson's genius and hospitality, the Astor House was gradually outmoded by newer and larger hotels, and when he gave up its management in 1868 it was losing its fashionable preëminence. His son Charles operated it until 1875. During the last twenty-five years of his life, Stetson lived in quiet retirement. His home was at Swampscott, Mass., but he died at the home of one of his eight children in Reading, Pa.

[*Vital Records of Newburyport, Mass.* (2 vols., 1911); J. S. Barry, *A Geneal. and Biog. Sketch of the Name and Family of Stetson* (1847); N. M. Stetson, *Stetson Kindred of America* (1914); E. V. Smith, *Hist. of Newburyport* (1854); M. H. Smith, *Sunshine and Shadow in N. Y.* (1868); Jefferson Williamson, *The Am. Hotel* (1930); *Boston Daily Courier*, Oct. 19, 1829, on opening of Tremont House; *N. Y. Times*, Jan. 13, 1875, May 11, 1913, on history of Astor House; *N. Y. Times*, Mar. 30, 1888.]   A. F. H.

STETSON, CHARLES WALTER (Mar. 25, 1858–July 20, 1911), painter, born at Tiverton Four Corners, R. I., was the youngest of four children of the Rev. Joshua Augustus and Rebecca Louisa (Steere) Stetson. His father, a Free Will Baptist minister, was stationed suc-

cessively at Tiverton, Taunton, Mass., and Providence. Stetson had a high-school education in Providence and as a youth taught himself to draw and paint. Sending a picture to the Pennsylvania Academy of the Fine Arts, where it was well hung, he had encouragement from the critic, James Jackson Jarves, who visited Providence especially to meet the young artist, and from Benjamin Champney [*q.v.*]. He held a successful one-man show in 1884 at the Providence Art Club, of which he was one of the founders, and later an exhibition in Boston which was praised by John Boyle O'Reilly [*q.v.*]. He also made many etchings, exhibited at the Boston Museum of Fine Arts in 1913.

In 1884 he married Charlotte A. Perkins (later Charlotte Perkins Gilman), who won distinction as a lecturer and writer on social topics. They had one daughter, who became an artist. The marriage was unsuccessful, however, and in 1894 they were divorced. On June 11, 1894, Stetson married Grace Ellery Channing, a literary woman, grand-daughter of the Rev. William Ellery Channing [*q.v.*]. They lived for a time in southern California, whose landscape Stetson painted with keen appreciation of its beauty of line and romantic atmosphere. In 1897 they settled in Italy, where Mrs. Stetson studied and wrote much about the peasants while her husband painted them and their surroundings. John Elliott [*q.v.*] wrote of his pictures, which were exhibited in London and in Rome; "His chief charm is that he is American, pure and simple, with a sweet new-world sentiment and feeling for colour" (Maud H. Elliott, *John Elliott*, 1913, p. 78), and an Italian critic found in them "an artistic personality and the soul of a poet" (*American Art News*, May 6, 1905). Stetson, always a frail man, died at Rome, survived by his wife and his daughter by the first marriage. Shortly before his death he wrote, "I think I have learned my trade; now if I have even three years more, I will paint something" (*Stetson Kindred, post*, p. 14). In his early years he painted several official portraits; one of Henry Lippitt [*q.v.*], governor of Rhode Island; one of Judge George Moulton Carpenter of the United States district court; and one of Arthur Doyle, mayor of Providence. He became known, however, through his landscapes of California and Italy. He is best represented at the Rhode Island School of Design, Providence Museum of Art.

[See *Stetson Kindred of America*, no. 4 (1914), compiled by N. M. Stetson, with portrait; *Who's Who in America*, 1910–11; *A Catalogue of the Pictures . . . Exhibited by Charles Walter Stetson, at . . . the Providence Art Club . . .* (1884); obituaries in *Providence Daily Jour.*, July 21, and *Il Giornale d'Italia* (Rome),

July 23, 1911. An important coll. of Stetsoniana is owned (1933) by William A. Brown, Providence, R. I.]
F. W. C.

STETSON, FRANCIS LYNDE (Apr. 23, 1846–Dec. 5, 1920), lawyer, was born in Keeseville, N. Y., the son of Lemuel and Helen (Hascall) Stetson. His father, besides being a lawyer of distinction, was at one time in Congress (1843–45) and was an active member of the Democratic party of New York. After receiving his secondary education in the public schools of Plattsburg, Francis entered Williams College, graduating with honors in 1867. He then attended Columbia Law School, completing his course by 1869.

Following a short interval of practice with his uncle, William S. Hascall, he fell under the eye of William C. Whitney [*q.v.*] and was appointed assistant corporation counsel for the City of New York, remaining in this office until 1880. In this year he formed a partnership with Francis N., Francis S., and Charles W. Bangs under the name of Bangs & Stetson which was eventually succeeded by the firm of Stetson, Jennings & Russell. Although Stetson was a good trial lawyer, the importance of this phase of his work was overshadowed by the part he played in the organization and reorganization of corporate entities. It is of interest that he has been credited with first suggesting the use of the form of no par value stock (F. W. Wegenast, *The Law of Canadian Companies*, 1931, p. 452). Through Charles E. Tracy, at one time his partner, his firm acquired the business of J. Pierpont Morgan [*q.v.*], Tracy's brother-in-law, and ultimately Stetson became his personal counsel. "Morgan's attorney general," as he was jocularly known on Wall Street, was called upon to handle the legal details incident to the creation of the United States Steel Corporation, to play a large, if unostentatious rôle in the financier's efforts to reorganize the railroads of the continent, and to act as legal adviser to the many Morgan-controlled transportation and industrial concerns. As Morgan's counsel he appeared in the case of *Northern Securities Co.* vs. *United States* (193 U. S., 197), one of the most important cases under the Sherman Anti-Trust Act. Naturally this work brought him to the forefront of the New York bar both in prestige and in financial rewards. There was a rumor that he received $50,000 annually from Morgan merely to insure first call on his services (Ivy Lee, in *World's Work*, June 1904, p. 4880).

In the broader field of politics Stetson was likewise prominent, having been a member of the Young Men's Democratic Club (which did effective work in the overthrow of the "Tweed ring") and an ardent supporter of Samuel J. Tilden. As such he presented to the electoral commission the Democratic side of the Florida election returns in the Hayes-Tilden controversy. He was a friend and adviser of Cleveland, who sought his counsel both as governor and president and, had Stetson not wished otherwise, he would have been offered a cabinet position. This friendship was accentuated when Cleveland, between his presidential terms, was associated with Stetson's firm. To Stetson large credit must be given for Cleveland's policy of sound money. As Morgan's counsel, he attended the meeting at the White House at which the Morgan-Belmont syndicate offered to sell gold to the government to stem the drain on the waning gold reserves. In conjunction with Assistant Secretary Curtis he later framed the contract between the government and the syndicate. Although it is generally considered that a hard bargain was driven (and at the time scurrilous rumors pointed to the Cleveland-Stetson friendship as indicative of fraud), Stetson construed his action as high patriotism. To a Senate committee he stated: "I shall always consider it the most useful public service I could render" (*Senate Document 187, 54 Cong., 2 Sess., p. 281*).

Stetson was "one of the most cultivated attorneys in the city, . . . a lifelong student, an omnivorous reader and man of exquisite courtesy and social grace" (Nevins, *post*, p. 451). It is not strange, in view of his affiliations with wealthy corporations and of his own ample means, that his economic views were of the most conservative nature. His article, "The Government and Corporations" (*Atlantic Monthly,* July 1912) is an amazing apologetic. (See also letter in *Outlook,* Feb. 16, 1907; *McClure's Magazine,* October 1908; and Stetson's article, "Control of Corporations Engaged in Interstate Commerce," *Case and Comment,* February 1912.) It is notable that he joined with Joseph H. Choate and others in opposing the sixteenth (income tax) amendment to the Constitution.

In private life he was friendly and generous. His marriage with Elizabeth Ruff, celebrated on June 26, 1873, having proved childless, he adopted his wife's secretary, Margery H. Lee, as daughter. Aside from law and politics his two great interests were the Episcopal Church and Williams College. He was credited with having framed the Episcopal canon on divorce, and as permanent trustee and benefactor of Williams his services were unflagging. So deep was his attachment to this institution that at his death he was interred in Williamstown beside the college campus.

Stetson

Stetson

[G. C. Holt, "Memorial of Francis Lynde Stetson," *The Asso. of the Bar of the City of N. Y., Year Book*, 1921; S. B. Griffin, "Francis Lynde Stetson," in *Obit. Record, Soc. of Alumni, Williams Coll.*, 1920–21; E. C. Hill (editor), *The Hist. Reg.* (1920), p. 231; *Who's Who in America*, 1920–21; *Who's Who in N. Y.*, 1918; *Who's Who in Finance* (1911); *Outlook*, Dec. 15, 1920; A.T. Clearwater, in *Proc. N. Y. State Bar Asso.*, 1920; Allan Nevins, *Grover Cleveland* (1933); *N. Y. Times*, Dec. 6, 1920.] L. M. Su—s.

STETSON, JOHN BATTERSON (May 5, 1830–Feb. 18, 1906), hat manufacturer, philanthropist, was born at Orange, N. J., one of the twelve children of Stephen and Susan (Batterson) Stetson, who were both of New England descent. His father and several of his brothers were hatters, having acquired the trade in Connecticut, their native state. After the family's removal to New Jersey shortly before John's birth, the Stetsons helped build up a new center of the hat industry and the boy's school days were cut short that he might serve an early apprenticeship to the trade. John proved an apt worker, but after reaching his majority his business prospects as a junior partner in the family firm did not seem alluring and he decided to strike out for himself. Ill health, however, compelled him to quit work for a time and in an effort to recuperate he went to Illinois, Missouri, and later, during the gold-seeking period of the sixties, to Colorado. Outdoor life on the plains and in the foothills restored his health, and he returned to the East robust and energetic.

In 1865 he opened a one-man hat factory in Philadelphia. The hats, made by hand, he peddled among the local retailers. During the first six months he never sold as many as a dozen hats in a single order. Concluding that his product lacked distinction of style, he proceeded to make his own models instead of slavishly following the prescribed fashions of the period. Continuing as salesman-producer, he took and filled orders for larger and larger quantities until his fame as a hatter began to spread beyond the city. Besides renewing his health and strength, Stetson's journey to the Rocky Mountains had extended his knowledge of Americans and their ways. Having noted with interest the head gear then in vogue in the West, he was able to supply a type of hat that quickly became popular there. To build up his business he relied not on advertising, but wholly on the quality of his goods. The hats, he felt, must advertise themselves; in looks and wear they must appeal to buyers. With the increase in sales, Stetson never departed from the fixed-price policy with which he started.

As the demand for his product grew his manufacturing facilities kept pace; machinery was introduced, and gradually a great industrial plant was organized on the outskirts of Philadelphia, later to be surrounded by the growing city. By 1906 the Stetson works, equipped for every process involved in the making of high-grade fur-felt hats, employed 3500 hands and turned out 2,000,000 hats a year, which were distributed throughout the civilized world. An apprentice system with bonus was early established, to be followed in later years by annual gift distributions at Christmas, bonus awards for continuous services, stock allotments to employees, a home-building association, savings and benefit funds, and other welfare features. An auditorium was built primarily for Sunday-school purposes. A hospital with a capacity of 20,000 patients a year, served by a large permanent staff, was erected. The company was opposed to organized labor, and these paternalistic activities brought against it the charge of "benevolent feudalism" and the destruction of "the spirit of independence and liberty" (*American Federationist,* May 1916, pp. 383–85).

In 1888 Stetson, who had long been a generous giver to Baptist churches and benevolences, became interested in an academy at DeLand, Fla., where for many years he passed his winters. The name of the institution was changed to John B. Stetson University and Stetson gave liberally to it in money and buildings. He died of apoplexy at his DeLand home, leaving his entire estate, of approximately $5,000,000 to his family. He was twice married; by his first wife he had a daughter, and by his second, Sarah Elizabeth Shindler, two sons.

[Henry Whittemore, *The Founders and Builders of the Oranges* (1896); *Hat Review*, Mar. 1906; Elbert Hubbard, *A Little Journey to the Home of John B. Stetson* (1911); E. P. Oberholtzer, *Phil., a Hist. of the City and Its People* (n.d.), vol. IV; *Moody's Mag.*, Feb. 1914; A. T. Freeman, in *Annals Am. Acad. Pol. and Soc. Sci.*, Nov. 1903; *Profit-Sharing by Am. Employers* (1916), pub. by Welfare Dept., Nat. Civic Federation; *Who's Who in America*, 1906–07; *Pub. Ledger* (Phila.), Feb. 19, 1906.] W. B. S.

STETSON, WILLIAM WALLACE (June 17, 1849–July 1, 1910), educator, was born in Greene, Me., the son of Reuben and Christiana (Thompson) Stetson, and a descendant of Robert Stetson who settled in Scituate, Mass., in 1634. The boy's early years were spent on his father's farm. He attended the local school and academy, and at the age of fifteen was appointed teacher in a district school. For some years he taught winters and worked for his father when not so engaged.

Deciding to use his savings in search of opportunities in the West, he left home in 1868, and in 1870 took a position as clerk in a combination drug and book store in Peoria, Ill. At the same time he enrolled in the preparatory department of Monmouth College and later entered the commercial department, withdrawing at the close of the academic year to accept an appointment as teacher in a local academy. Shortly before entering upon his new duties, he married, July 4, 1871, Rebecca Jane, daughter of William and Jane (Nicol) Killough, of Morning Sun, Iowa.

In 1880 he was appointed superintendent of schools in Rockford, Ill., a position which he held for four years. During this period he reorganized the city school system, and effected reforms in methods of instruction. His success and his popularity as a lecturer before teachers' meetings and institutes brought him recognition as a progressive administrator. He took an active part in the work of the Northern Illinois Teachers' Association, and was elected its president in 1883.

In 1884 he returned to Maine, to become principal of the Webster Grammar School in Auburn. A year later he was elected superintendent of schools. His unusual executive ability was immediately demonstrated; he regraded the schools, improved their equipment, established modern courses of study, and effected various reforms in methods of teaching. During the ten years of his administration his achievements, and his wise counsel on educational matters, made him widely known. He was president of the Maine Pedagogical Society, 1890–91, and president of the American Institute of Instruction, 1894–95. In 1895 he was elected state superintendent of public schools in Maine, which office he held until his retirement from active professional life in 1907. Among his accomplishments while in this position were the abolition of the district system, and the establishment of the present township system of school administration; the reclassification and consolidation of schools; the institution of free conveyance of pupils; the adoption of the free textbook system; the extension of free tuition privileges in secondary schools to all the pupils of the state; the improvement of courses of instruction in teacher-training institutions; the state certification of teachers; and the adoption of a plan of union supervision, designed to extend the advantages of expert guidance to the schools of all towns in the state. His reports from 1895 to 1907, widely recognized for their constructive suggestions, enhanced his reputation as a leader in educational reforms. In 1905, he was elected president of the department of superintendence of the National Education Association, an organization in which he had played an active rôle for

many years. He resigned as state superintendent in 1907 and spent the rest of his life in Auburn, Me. He was the author of *History and Civil Government of Maine* (copr. 1898), and of numerous articles and pamphlets in the field of educational administration. In 1911 *Ideals and Essentials of Education,* comprising selections from his publications and manuscripts, was issued by his wife.

[G. T. Little, *Genealogical and Family Hist. of the State of Maine* (1909), vol. I; *Reports of the State Superintendent of Pub. Schools of the State of Maine, 1895–1906;* Payson Smith, "William Wallace Stetson," in *Nat. Educ. Asso. of the U. S.: Jour. of Proceedings and Addresses, 1911; Who's Who in America, 1910–11; Lewiston Evening Jour.,* July 2, 1910; information from a brother, Dr. Herbert Lee Stetson, Kalamazoo, Mich.]   R. F. S.

STETTINIUS, EDWARD RILEY (Feb. 15, 1865–Sept. 3, 1925), industrialist, assistant secretary of war, was born at St. Louis, Mo., a son of Joseph and Isabel (Riley) Stettinius. The father had come of Maryland German stock and after a venture in river steam-boating had been employed for many years by a wholesale grocery firm at St. Louis. He died when Edward was only three years old. The boy was a student at St. Louis University, in the preparatory and collegiate departments, from 1874 through 1881. Then followed several years of employment by local business concerns and banks and after that one or two only partially successful personal ventures. His mother died in 1891 and in the following year he went to Chicago, becoming treasurer of Stirling & Company, manufacturers of machinery. Later he became vice-president and general manager and in a reorganization that occurred in 1905 he was made president; after a consolidation in 1906 with Babcock & Wilcox, he was made vice-president. Outside a small group of business associates, Stettinius was comparatively unknown when in 1909, at the age of forty-four, he was made president of the Diamond Match Company, of which in 1908 he had become treasurer. A single act of his administration brought him widespread prominence. On Jan. 28, 1911, his corporation freely dedicated to the public a patent (of Nov. 15, 1898) for a substitute for the poisonous white phosphorous used in the manufacture of matches. This generous action eventually removed the specter of slow poisoning from the employees of rival match factories the country over (*Scientific American,* Feb. 11, 1911).

After the Allies, in 1915, had retained the banking firm of J. P. Morgan & Company to handle their purchases of war supplies in the United States, the firm made a nation-wide canvass in search of a man able to control and bring to fruition so vast and unprecedented a business. The choice finally fell upon Stettinius, who after a few months resigned the Diamond Match presidency. His task was not merely to make contracts with persons and corporations offering products and materials desired by the Allies; he had to see that war munitions in enormous quantities should be produced in record time from remodeled and often improvised plants, whose owners were at first quite unversed in the munitions industry. Yet many such plants turned out within a stipulated period large consignments of shells that fully met the technical requirements set up by the Allied governments. This was accomplished so promptly and satisfactorily that Stettinius, almost over night, became an outstanding figure in the war. How his success impressed his immediate business associates is indicated by the announcement in January 1916 of his admission as a member of the Morgan firm. Within two years the total of Allied purchases through his agency reached $3,000,000,-000—truly a record for such transactions.

After the entry of the United States into the war, Stettinius was appointed surveyor-general of purchases, and, on Apr. 16, 1918, as second assistant secretary of war. Secretary Newton D. Baker saw him as "a man of great exactness and of an almost terrifying sense of responsibility" (quoted by Frederick Palmer, *Newton D. Baker,* 1931, vol. II, p. 396). In July 1918 he was sent to France as special representative of the Secretary of War in the matter of foreign orders for war materials placed by the American Expeditionary Force. Returning to New York after the Armistice, Stettinius left the government service in January 1919 and remained with the Morgan firm until his death at Locust Valley, L. I. On Oct. 18, 1894, he had married Judith Carrington of Richmond, Va.; she and their two sons and two daughters survived him.

[J. W. Ridings, "Edward R. Stettinius, Assistant Secretary of War," in *Mo. Hist. Rev.,* Oct. 1918; B. C. Forbes, "The Biggest Buyer in the World," *American Mag.,* Sept. 1917; Donald Wilhelm, "Stettinius, Master Buyer," *Am. Rev. of Reviews,* Mar. 1918; G. B. Clarkson, *Industrial America in the World War* (1923), pp. 53, 339; Benedict Crowell and R. F. Wilson, *Demobilization* (1921), pp. 297–98, 305–06; T. W. Lamont, *Henry P. Davison: The Record of a Useful Life* (1933), pp. 227–30; newspaper files and directories in St. Louis Pub. Lib.; *Who's Who in America,* 1924–25; obituary in *N. Y. Times,* Sept. 4, 1925.]

W. B. S.

STEUBEN, FRIEDRICH WILHELM LUDOLF GERHARD AUGUSTIN, Baron von (Sept. 17, 1730–Nov. 28, 1794), professional soldier, military expert, inspector general of the Continental Army, was given this name at his christening, seven days after his birth, in the German Reformed Church of Magdeburg. Later in life he changed it to Friedrich Wilhelm August Heinrich Ferdinand; and in America he was known as Frederick William Augustus von (or de) Steuben. His parents were Wilhelm Augustin von Steuben and Maria Dorothea von Jagow. His grandfather, Augustin Steube, a minister of the German Reformed Church, inserted the "von" in the family name about 1708. He was born in the fortress of Magdeburg, where his father was stationed as a lieutenant of engineers in the army of King Frederick William I of Prussia. He spent his early childhood in Russia, where his father served for several years in the army of the Czarina Anne. In his tenth year he returned to Germany with his father and received his education in the Jesuit schools in Breslau.

In his seventeenth year Steuben entered the officer corps of the Prussian army and served therein with credit throughout the Seven Years' War, first as a regimental officer of infantry and then as a staff officer. In 1761, after active service on the staffs of Generals von Mayer and von Hülsen he became a general staff officer and soon thereafter was promoted to the grade of captain. In January and February 1762, while serving at Königsberg, he received two personal letters from the King, Frederick the Great, thanking him for transmitting news of the death of the Czarina Elizabeth. These letters, an unusual compliment to a junior officer, are in the Prussian Archives. A few weeks later, Steuben went to St. Petersburg with Count von der Goltz, the new Prussian ambassador, and was engaged on confidential duties in connection with the peace negotiations between Prussia and Russia. Upon his return from St. Petersburg, in May 1762, and until the end of the war, he served at the Royal Headquarters as a general staff officer and as one of the aides-de-camp to the King. The significance of Steuben's general staff training and service has not been sufficiently appreciated. This is partly because the German word "Quartiermeister," signifying a general staff officer with troops, has been erroneously translated into English as "quartermaster." That Frederick the Great should select Steuben for general staff duty at the Royal Headquarters in time of war is the highest tribute to his professional standing. It was this specific training for and experience in the duties of the general staff, an agency then litttle known outside of Prussia, that so peculiarly equipped Steuben for his invaluable services to the cause of American independence. He brought to Washington's staff a technical training and equipment that was unknown in either the French or the British armies at that time.

Steuben was still a captain when he was discharged from the Prussian army shortly after the Peace of Hubertusburg in the spring of 1763. The circumstances attending his discharge at the early age of thirty-three, and so soon after gaining the royal favor, are obscure. His retirement left him without employment. In 1764, after unsuccessful negotiations to enter the Sardinian army, he was appointed chamberlain (*Hofmarschall*) at the Court of Hohenzollern-Hechingen upon the recommendation of Prince Henry of Prussia and his niece, the Princess Sophie Dorothea Fredericka of Württemberg. While at Hechingen he attained the rank of baron (*Freiherr*) and became a knight of the Margrave of Baden's Order of Fidelity. In 1771 the Prince of Hohenzollern-Hechingen, on account of financial embarrassment, decided to close his court and to reside abroad, incognito. Steuben was the only member of the court to accompany his patron and resided with him in France, principally at Montpellier. But the financial objects of the journey were not accomplished and in 1775 the Prince returned to Hechingen more embarrassed than ever. Steuben, who was always improvident, now found himself seriously in debt and sought employment elsewhere. Early in 1776 he entered into an unsuccessful negotiation to form a German regiment for the French army. Later he failed in an effort to enter the Austrian army and in April 1777 he visited Karlsruhe where he was again disappointed in an effort to enter the service of the Margrave of Baden. But while in Baden the Baron met a friend and correspondent of Benjamin Franklin who drew his attention to the American war as a field for his talents (Ebeling, *post*, p. 154). Accordingly, early in the summer of 1777, he set out for Paris with letters to Franklin and others.

Fortunately for Steuben, his high professional reputation as a trained Prussian staff officer had long been known to Count de St. Germain, the French minister of war. Just at that time St. Germain was making an unsuccessful effort to reform the French army by the introduction of Prussian methods of military efficiency and discipline. He recognized in Steuben an accomplished graduate from the school of Frederick the Great who was peculiarly qualified to give the American authorities much needed advice on military training, organization, and administration. He therefore commended Steuben to Beaumarchais, who was giving secret aid to the American colonies through the commercial cor-

poration, Hortalez & Company, which he had formed with the connivance of the French government. Beaumarchais, Franklin, and Silas Deane recognized Steuben's merits and the importance of securing his services, but at first the negotiations failed because the American commissioners were not empowered to assure him adequate rank and pay or to make any contract with him in behalf of the Continental Congress. Later, however, it was decided that Hortalez & Company should advance the expenses of the journey and that the Baron should go purely as a distinguished volunteer and trust to fortune for a suitable opening for his recognized talents after his arrival in America. As his actual military rank of captain did not carry sufficient prestige to assure the success of this rôle, it was decided that he should assume the glamor of high rank. He was accordingly given letters from Franklin, Deane, and Beaumarchais to Washington, Henry Laurens, Robert Morris, and others in which he was introduced as a lieutenant-general. Indeed, in his letter to Washington, Franklin presented him as "a Lieutenant General in the King of Prussia's service" (Sept. 4, 1777, Kapp, *post*, p. 652). There could be no higher military prestige in the last quarter of the eighteenth century, and without this prestige Steuben could not have succeeded in his American mission.

The new "lieutenant-general," accompanied by a military secretary and an aide-de-camp, sailed from Marseilles on Sept. 26 and arrived at Portsmouth, N. H., on Dec. 1, 1777. After a sojourn of several weeks at Boston, where he was entertained as became his distinguished rank, he made the overland journey to York, Pa., the temporary seat of government, where he arrived on Feb. 5, 1778. He was received with high honors by the Continental Congress. When a special committee waited upon him to ascertain his aims, he waived all claim to rank or pay and asked only that his expenses should be paid while acting as a volunteer with the army. He proposed that if his services should contribute to the eventual success of the American cause, he would then expect compensation for his sacrifices in leaving Europe and such reward as Congress might be pleased to grant him, but that if the cause should fail, or if his services should not prove beneficial, he would make no claim whatever. This proposal to stake his fortunes upon the success of the cause made a deep impression upon the Congress. His services were accepted and he was directed to report to Washington at Valley Forge where he arrived on Feb. 23.

Steuben made a profound impression upon

the officers and men of the Continental Army. His professional reputation, so well advertised by his exalted rank, was supported by his martial bearing, his adaptability, and his picturesque personality. Washington was so favorably impressed by his practical knowledge and experience that he prevailed upon him to serve as acting inspector general and to undertake the training of the army. This involved serious difficulties as the Baron spoke no English and was required to act through interpreters. There was no time for the preparation and publication of a complete new drill manual. Steuben therefore prepared his drill instructions in brief installments. These were translated into English and issued to the regiments from time to time as the drills progressed. Fortunately, he had the tact to rely upon the power of example. He formed a model company of 100 selected men and undertook its drill in person. The rapid progress of this company under his skilled instruction made an immediate appeal to the imagination of the whole army. Drill became the fashion and within a few weeks the new gospel, imparted day by day to the model company, had spread throughout the army. This is perhaps the most remarkable achievement in rapid military training in the history of the world. The Baron's success was so speedy that on April 30 Washington recommended his appointment as inspector general with the rank of major-general. On May 5 the appointment was confirmed by the Continental Congress. The value of Steuben's instruction was soon manifested on the battlefield of Monmouth. There and thereafter throughout the war the Continental Army proved itself, battalion for battalion, the equal in discipline and skill of the best British regulars. Immediately before the battle Steuben served Washington as a general staff officer. He reconnoitered the enemy's position near Allentown and was first to report that his objective was Monmouth Courthouse. After the disastrous retreat of Charles Lee, in the ensuing battle, Steuben reformed Lee's disordered troops and led them back to the battlefield.

During the winter of 1778–79, Steuben prepared his *Regulations for the Order and Discipline of the Troops of the United States.* This manual of drill and field service regulations contained the essentials of military instruction and procedure adapted to the needs of the American citizen soldier. It was popularly known as the "blue book" and became the military bible of the Continental Army. No important book has ever been produced under greater difficulties. The Baron first wrote each passage in his practical but inelegant French. One of his staff officers then transposed it into literary French. Another translated it literally into English and a third then transposed it into correct and simple English. During most of 1779 and 1780 Steuben was busy with his duties as inspector general, perfecting the training and discipline of the army and developing his system of property accountability that went far to check the waste of public property which had formerly prevailed in the American army. During this period he grew steadily in popularity throughout the army and grew more and more in Washington's confidence. He was consulted upon all questions of strategic and administrative policy and performed all of the essential functions of a modern general staff. During the winter of 1779–80 he was Washington's representative with the Continental Congress in the efforts to reorganize the army.

In the autumn of 1780, when Greene was sent to the Carolinas to replace Gates after the disastrous defeat at Camden, Washington sent Steuben with the new commander to assist in reorganizing the southern army. Upon their arrival at Richmond, Greene realized that most of his replacements and supplies must come from Virginia. He therefore left Steuben in command in that state. Steuben immediately took comprehensive measures to make Virginia a base of supply for Greene's army. But his efforts were thwarted to a large extent by the invading forces under Benedict Arnold and Phillips which were effectively supported by British ships in James River. With his limited forces of ill-armed militia, Steuben could offer but limited resistance to the invaders. Many of his stores were captured and many more were dispersed and wasted by the successive drafts of ill-disciplined short-service militia. Greene, however, appreciated Steuben's difficulties and gratefully acknowledged that his support from Virginia, limited as it was, had been indispensable to the success of his campaign in the Carolinas. In April 1781 Lafayette took command in Virginia and Steuben served under his orders during Cornwallis' invasion. When Washington's army was assembled before Yorktown, Steuben was assigned to the command of one of the three divisions and served in that capacity until after the surrender. He also contributed materially to the success of the final campaign by virtue of the extensive experience in siege warfare which he had acquired during the Seven Years' War.

In the interval between the surrender of Cornwallis and the final conclusion of peace Steuben continued his duties as inspector general and as Washington's trusted adviser in all military affairs. In the spring of 1783 he assisted Washington in the preparation of a plan for the future defense of the United States and in the arrangements for demobilizing the Continental Army. This was published as *A Letter on the Subject of an Established Militia* (1784). At the same time he took a leading part in forming the Society of the Cincinnati. In August, Washington sent him to Canada to receive the frontier posts from the British, but his mission was unsuccessful as the British commander, General Haldimand, had not been authorized to treat with him. When Washington relinquished command of the army, Dec. 23, 1783, he deliberately made it his last official act to write a letter to the Baron commending his invaluable services to the United States throughout the war (Jared Sparks, *The Writings of George Washington,* VIII, 1833, pp. 503–04; W. C. Ford, *The Writings of George Washington,* X, 1891, p. 338). Steuben was honorably discharged from the army Mar. 24, 1784. He became an American citizen, by act of the Pennsylvania legislature in March 1783 and by act of the New York legislature in July 1786.

After Steuben's retirement from the army he made his residence in New York and became one of the most popular figures in the social life of the city and state. He was the president of the German Society and of the New York branch of the Cincinnati. In 1787 he was elected one of the regents of the University of the State of New York. Always careless in his business affairs and extravagant in his charities and hospitalities, he went heavily in debt in anticipation of the grant of about $60,000 for his military services which he claimed from Congress. In 1786 the State of New York granted him 16,000 acres of wild land near the present town of Remsen, north of Utica. In June 1790 the new federal government granted him a pension of $2500 per year instead of the lump sum which he had expected. Later in the year, through a friendly mortgage of his New York lands, Alexander Hamilton and other influential friends were able to settle the Baron's debts and to relieve him from bankruptcy. During the remaining years of his life he spent his winters in New York City and his summers on his estate in the Mohawk country. There he finally died of apoplexy on Nov. 28, 1794, and there his tomb now is. He was never married. In his will he left his estates in America to his former aides-de-camp, William North and Benjamin Walker (will in Kapp, p. 702).

Steuben's likeness is preserved in contemporary portraits by Charles Willson Peale, Ralph Earle, and Pierre Eugene du Simitiere and in the equestrian figure of him in John Trumbull's "The Surrender of Cornwallis," in the national capitol. He was of middle height. He had a fine soldierly bearing and his manners were graceful and courtly. His picturesque personality made a strong impression upon his contemporaries and the anecdotal history of the Revolution presents him as one of the most conspicuous figures in the esteem and affections of the rank and file of the Continental Army. Through his influence in converting the American army into an effective and highly disciplined military force he was an indispensable figure in the achievement of American independence. Here he performed an essential service that none of his contemporaries in America was qualified to perform.

[The generally accepted history of Steuben's early life in Europe is taken from Friedrich Kapp, *Leben des Amerikanischen Generals Friedrich Wilhelm Steuben* (Berlin, 1858), translated as *The Life of Frederick William von Steuben* (N. Y., 1859), and is largely apocryphal. Kapp did not have access to the documents in the Prussian Archives relating to Steuben's service in the Prussian army or to those in the Archives in Hechingen and Karlsruhe relating to his subsequent life in Hohenzollern-Hechingen, the south of France, and Baden, and was therefore unable to check the official records against certain questionable documents which he found in the "Steuben Papers" in the library of the N. Y. Hist. Soc. The contemporary German evidence is given by C. D. Ebeling in the "Nachrichten von den Lebensumständen des Baron von Steuben," in the *Amerikanisches Magazin* (Hamburg, 1796), Vol. I, pt. 3, pp. 148–63. Steuben's ancestry and family history are given by A. B. C. Kalkhorst in the *Neue Zeit,* New Ulm, Minn., Sept. 8–15, 1923, and by Hermann Stöbe, "General Steubens Herkunft," in *Jahrbuch der Historischen Kommission für die Provinz Sachsen und für Anhalt* (Magdeburg, 1931). An account of his Prussian military service is contained in A. B. C. Kalkhorst, "Steubens Dienstzeit in Preussischen Heere," *Erie Tageblatt,* Sept. 8, 1923. This article gives full references from the Prussian Archives. Kapp's history of Steuben after his arrival in America contains many excerpts from official documents and, in general, is reliable, but much of Steuben's voluminous personal correspondence and other valuable materials were not then accessible. There is much Steuben material in the Washington Papers and the Papers of the Continental Congress in the Lib. of Cong. and in the Old Records Division of the War Dept. His personal papers (16 vols.) are in the library of the N. Y. Hist. Soc. Letters from Steuben, both official and personal, are to be found in almost every public and private collection of manuscripts relating to the Revolutionary period. His correspondence with his aides-de-camp, William North and Benjamin Walker, now widely scattered, gives an intimate picture of his personality and of his financial indiscretions and difficulties after the Revolution. Much material relating to his New York estate is in the collection of the Oneida Hist. Soc., Utica, N. Y. J. B. Doyle, *Frederick William von Steuben and the American Revolution* (1913), is based on Kapp. J. McA. Palmer has chapters on Steuben in *Washington, Lincoln, Wilson* (1930), and is preparing a full biography.]

J. McA. P.

STEVENS, ABEL (Jan. 17, 1815–Sept. 11, 1897), Methodist Episcopal clergyman, editor, and historian, was the third child of Samuel and Mary (Hochenmeller) Stevens. He was born in Philadelphia, where his father, a native of Needham, Mass., had settled as a copperplate printer and engraver. Eight years after Abel's birth his father died, leaving the mother with five young children. The estate was mismanaged by the custodian and the family forced to undergo numerous hardships, but Abel was sent to Wesleyan Academy, Wilbraham, Mass., and later entered Wesleyan University, Middletown, Conn., though his stay at the latter institution was short, owing to his feeble health. The records of the University indicate, however, that he had completed the scientific course when he left college. Five years later (1839) Brown University conferred upon him the degree of M.A. While a very young man he displayed extraordinary ability as a speaker and at nineteen was financial agent of Wesleyan University. In 1834 he was admitted to the New England Conference on trial, was ordained deacon in 1836, and elder in 1838. From 1835 to 1837 he served the Church Street Church and the Bennet Street Church in Boston. He visited Europe in 1837 and his published letters from abroad attracted attention. Upon his return he became the minister of the Methodist church in Providence, R. I. At the age of twenty-five, on the recommendation of President Wilbur Fisk [q.v.] of Wesleyan University, he was made editor of *Zion's Herald,* an influential Methodist journal published in Boston. This position he held for twelve years.

In 1852 he became the editor of a new literary venture of the Methodists called the *National Magazine,* which position he held until June 1856. He again visited Europe in 1855 and on his return was chosen editor of the *Christian Advocate and Journal* in New York. Here he again displayed the highest degree of editorial ability. By this time the Methodist Episcopal Church had divided over the slavery issue, though there still remained in the Northern branch numerous slave-holding members. Stevens contended that nothing should be done to embarrass the border churches. He argued that the slave-holders had a constitutional right to church membership and protested against the attempt to expel them. He maintained, however, that he was an abolitionist. His position alienated the radicals and at the General Conference of 1860 he was not reëlected editor. To support the position of Stevens and other New York leaders on the slavery issue an independent journal was established in 1860 called *The Methodist,* which from the beginning had Stevens' substantial aid, and of which he was associate editor, 1871–74. From 1861 to 1865 he served two churches in the New York East Conference, to

which he had transferred on his removal to New York. For some years he was also constantly employed in writing and speaking in the interest of lay representation in the General Conference, and much of his writing in *The Methodist* was devoted to this subject.

Throughout his life Stevens was a tireless worker and a prolific writer. His first book, entitled *An Essay on Church Polity,* was published in 1847. This was followed in 1848 by the first volume of his *Memorials of the Introduction of Methodism into the Eastern States,* the second volume appearing in 1852. His most important works were the seven volumes dealing with the history of English and American Methodism. The *History of the Religious Movement of the Eighteenth Century, Called Methodism,* in three volumes, appeared between the years 1858 and 1861; the *History of the Methodist Episcopal Church in the United States,* in four volumes, between the years 1864 and 1867. These works, founded on extensive research and written with remarkable literary attractiveness, take high rank among denominational histories. He also published *Life and Times of Nathan Bangs* (2 vols., 1863). His last book was *Madame De Staël, A Study of her Life and Times* (2 vols., 1881). The books mentioned represent only his major publications.

At fifty years of age Stevens retired from active participation in the affairs of the Church, and after he had finished his histories took up his residence in Geneva, Switzerland, where he served as the minister of the Union Church and corresponded with several American newspapers. In 1888 he returned to the United States and made his home in San José, Cal., where he died suddenly of heart failure at the age of eighty-two. He had been married three times: in 1838, to Marguerite, daughter of the Rev. Bartholomew Otheman of Roxbury, Mass.; on Sept. 8, 1869, at Clinton, N. Y., to Amelia Dayton, who died within a year; and in 1871 to Frances C. Greenough, who, with three of the six children of his first marriage, survived him.

[Sources include *Christian Advocate* (N. Y.), Sept. 16, 23, 1897; *The New Schaff-Herzog Encyc. of Religious Knowledge,* vol. XI (1911); *Zion's Herald,* Sept. 15, 1897; *The Call* (San Francisco), Sept. 12, 1897. The date of birth sometimes appears as Jan. 19, but is given as Jan. 17 in the general catalogues of Brown and Wesleyan universities. Information regarding Stevens' family was obtained through the courtesy of Dr. James R. Joy.]   W. W. S.

STEVENS, ALEXANDER HODGDON (Sept. 4, 1789–Mar. 30, 1869), surgeon, was born in New York City, the third son of Ebenezer and Lucretia (Ledyard) Sands Stevens, and a brother of John Austin Stevens, 1795–1874 [*q.v.*]. His father, a descendant of John Stevens who came from Cornwall, England, to Boston about 1638, was a member of the group who took part in the Boston Tea Party. His mother was a native of Hartford, Conn., and a half-sister of William Ledyard [*q.v.*]. As a boy he studied at home until the age of twelve, when he entered the school of John Adams, 1772–1863 [*q.v.*], in Plainfield, Conn.; he graduated from Yale College in 1807. At eighteen he began the study of medicine in the office of Dr. Edward Miller [*q.v.*], professor of clinical medicine at the College of Physicians and Surgeons (later part of Columbia University), New York. He soon left, however, for the University of Pennsylvania, where he received the degree of M.D. in 1811. His thesis, *A Dissertation on the Proximate Cause of Inflammation, with an Attempt to Establish a Rational Plan of Cure* (1811), was highly commended by Benjamin Rush [*q.v.*]. After graduation he spent seven months in the surgical service of the New York Hospital. In 1812, on his way to Europe as a carrier of dispatches, he was captured and imprisoned in England. When he was released, he studied under John Abernethy and Sir Astley Cooper, and in Paris under Alexis Boyer, whose book on surgery he later translated as *A Treatise on Surgical Diseases and the Operations Suited to Them* (2 vols., 1815–16). His days in Paris brought him in close touch with such men as Félix Hyppolyte Larrey, Alfred Velpeau, and Guillaume Dupuytren. On his way home he once more became a prisoner of war, but was soon able to return home to act as army surgeon. From 1815 to 1826 he was professor of surgery at Queen's College (later Rutgers), where he was considered an excellent clinical teacher, following the methods of Hermann Boerhaave; in 1826 he became professor of surgery at the College of Physicians and Surgeons. His lectures were clear, comprehensive, familiar in style, quaint in expression, but emphatic and impressive. He began in 1817 his long career as surgeon to the New York Hospital, a post which he filled for the greater part of his life. A trustee of the College of Physicians and Surgeons, 1820–37, he served as president, 1843–55. In the meantime he had built up a large practice which, with his outside work, proved too much for his health, and in 1831 he was forced to go abroad for a rest. On his return he was plunged into the battle against the cholera epidemic of 1832, in which he played a notable part. Three years later, his health failing again, he took Dr. John Watson as a partner to relieve him of part of his practice and moved to Astoria, Long Island. He devoted much of his time there to agriculture and in 1849 became president of the state agricultural society. Nevertheless he still maintained his interest and influence in medical matters. In 1842, when the Society for the Relief of Widows and Orphans was organized, he became a member; he was one of the leading spirits in the founding of the New York Academy of Medicine, of which he was president in 1851; and he served also as president of the American Medical Association, 1848, and of the Medical Society of the State of New York, 1849–51.

He was a stern, religious man with no sympathy for the ideas of Darwin, Spencer, or Huxley. Conservative, he cast aside the Brunonian theory under which he had been educated. He was a deliberate and cautious surgeon who preferred to treat surgical diseases rather than to resort to the knife. Accurate in diagnosis and prognosis, his therapeutics were rarely unsound, although he was often criticized for his lack of interest and persistence in following out details of protracted cases. He was unassuming and courteous, but firm in his decisions. His interest in medical education led him to institute in 1865 the Stevens Triennial Prize in the College of Physicians and Surgeons, for the best essay on a medical subject. His own writings were of no great value. His portrait was painted by Henry Inman, the original going to the New York Hospital and a facsimile to the College of Physicians and Surgeons. He was married three times: in 1813 to Mary Jane Bayard (d. 1817), daughter of John Murray Bayard of Millstone, N. J.; in April 1825 to Catherine Morris, daughter of James Morris of Morrisania, N. Y.; in 1841 to Phoebe Coles Lloyd, daughter of John Nelson Lloyd of Lloyd's Neck, Long Island. He had a son by his first wife, a daughter by his second, and two sons by his third.

[E. S. Barney, *The Stevens Geneal.* (1907); F. A. Virkus, *The Abridged Compendium of Am. Geneal.,* vol. II (1926); J. G. Adams, *Discourse Commemorative of the Life and Character of Alexander Hodgdon Stevens* (1871); S. W. Francis, *Biog. Sketches of Distinguished Living Surgeons* (1866); *The Coll. of Physicians and Surgeons, N. Y., A Hist.* (n.d.), vol. I, ed. by John Shrady; *N. Y. Medic. Gazette,* June 1853; *N. J. Medic. Reporter,* June 1854; *Obit. Record Grads. Yale Coll.* (1869); obituary in *Medic. Record* (N. Y.), May 1, and *N. Y. Tribune,* Apr. 1, 1869.]   G. L. A.

STEVENS, BENJAMIN FRANKLIN (Feb. 19, 1833–Mar. 5, 1902), bookman and antiquary, was born in Barnet, Vt., brother of Henry Stevens [*q.v.*], and tenth of the eleven children born to Henry and Candace (Salter) Stevens. His father, a descendant of Cyprian Stevens who emigrated to New England before 1671, was not only a farmer, postmaster, innkeeper, and mill-owner, but a book-collector and antiquarian as well, founder and first president of the Vermont Historical Society. After attending Peacham Academy and Newbury Seminary, Benjamin in 1850 was assistant state librarian of Vermont, in 1852 deputy secretary of state, and in 1853–54 a student at the University of Vermont. In 1858–59 he worked in the Astor Library in New York City, where he acted also as an agent for Henry, then well established as a London bookseller. He sailed in 1860 to join Henry as partner, London being thereafter his home and bookselling his calling. In 1864 he left Henry to join another brother, Simon, but left him in 1866 to set up for himself, and so continued until 1899, when he took Henry J. Brown as partner. He came to know the Whittinghams of the Chiswick Press, and on Jan. 28, 1865, married Charlotte (d. July 22, 1903), daughter of Charles Whittingham (1795–1876). He was appointed United States dispatch agent, June 23, 1866, a post he filled until his death, which occurred at Surbiton, Surrey. This appointment brought him into contact with American diplomatic, consular, and naval officers passing through London and with many on the Continent. As bookseller, acting as agent for many American libraries and private buyers, he became one of the familiar personalities of the London trade. Though he took part in many business, social, and public activities, and was at his death recognized as one of the leading spirits in the American colony at London, he was first of all a bookman and antiquarian.

Early in life he had begun to help his father copy and index documents in American archives (he had been sent to Albany, N. Y., at fourteen to copy manuscripts), and this interest he carried to England. There it led him to make an index in 180 manuscript volumes (now in the Library of Congress, Washington, D. C.) to the manuscripts in foreign archives relating to America, 1763–83. (See Stevens' *Introduction to the Catalogue Index of Manuscripts in the Archives of England, France, Holland, and Spain Relating to America, 1763 to 1783,* 1902.) He made extensive transcripts for the Library of Congress, the New Hampshire, Pennsylvania, and New York Historical societies, and the New York Public Library. Between 1889 and 1895 he published twenty-four portfolios, *B. F. Stevens's Facsimiles of Manuscripts in European Archives Relating to America, 1773–1783,* with an index published in 1898. His other publications include *The Campaign in Virginia, 1781: An Exact Reprint of Six Rare Pamphlets on the Clinton-Cornwallis Controversy* (1888); *General Sir William Howe's Orderly Book ... 1775*

(1890); *Christopher Columbus, His Own Book of Privileges, 1502: Photographic Facsimile of the Manuscript in the Archives of the Foreign Office in Paris* (1893); "Calendar of American Papers in the Earl of Dartmouth's Collection," in *Great Britain Historical Manuscripts Commission: Fourteenth Report: Appendix, Part X* (1895); *Facsimile of the Unpublished British Headquarters Coloured Manuscript Map of New York and Environs, 1782* (1900); and *Report on American Manuscripts in the Royal Institution of Great Britain* (4 vols., 1904–09, edited by H. J. Brown).

[F. P. Wells, *Hist. of Barnet, Vt.* (1923); G. M. Fenn, *Memoir of Benjamin Franklin Stevens* (priv. printed, 1903); S. S. Green, *Proc. Am. Antiquarian Soc.,* n.s., vol. XVI (1905); *Times* (London), Mar. 7 (death notice), Mar. 10 (obituary), and *Athenaeum,* Mar. 15, 1902.]   H. M. L.

STEVENS, CLEMENT HOFFMAN (Aug. 21, 1821–July 25, 1864), Confederate soldier, though born in Norwich, Conn., was of Southern parentage, his father being Lieut. Clement W. Stevens, United States Navy, and his mother, Sarah J. (Fayssoux) Stevens, a daughter of Dr. Peter Fayssoux [*q.v.*], Revolutionary surgeon-general of South Carolina. Leaving the navy, Lieutenant Stevens soon removed his family to Florida, and thence, in 1836, to Pendleton, S. C. Clement, after enjoying several years of travel and adventure as secretary to his kinsmen, Commodore William B. Shubrick [*q.v.*] and Commodore William Bee, in 1842 forsook the sea to enter the Planters' & Mechanics Bank, in Charleston, eventually becoming cashier. Enterprising and energetic, he also joined the firm of Hacker and Pickens, pioneer railroad contractors, and by 1861 was a successful business man. Meantime, through marriage with his cousin, Annie Bee, he had several children, of whom one son lived to maturity.

His invention and construction, early in 1861, of a land battery faced with iron and, later, of portable ovens for supplying his troops with fresh bread, justified an intimate associate in declaring, after the war, to one of Stevens' nieces: "Your Uncle Clem was a genius. Had he lived, the world would have heard of him." (Letter from Mrs. Helen Capers Stevens DuPré.) This battery, built on Morris Island, was shielded with railroad T-iron. It was perhaps the first armored fortification ever constructed, and was used successfully in the bombardment of Fort Sumter. As a volunteer aide to his brother-in-law, Gen. Barnard E. Bee [*q.v.*], Stevens was severely wounded at Manassas. Recovering, he commanded a militia regiment at Charleston, but was soon elected colonel of the 24th South Carolina Infantry, of which Ellison Capers [*q.v.*] was lieutenant-colonel. Stevens' skilful handling of flank detachments contributed greatly to the Confederate victory at Secessionville, June 16, 1862, and in 1863 he fought with Gist's brigade through the Vicksburg campaign. Transferred to Bragg's army, he led his regiment with reckless bravery at Chickamauga and was again badly wounded. Gen. S. R. Gist [*q.v.*] eulogized him as "the iron-nerved," while his division commander, Gen. W. H. T. Walker [*q.v.*], declared: "From what I know of his capacity, as an officer, from his gallantry in the field, and from his devotion to the cause, he would grace any position that might be conferred" (*War of the Rebellion: Official Records, Army,* 1 ser., vol. XXX, pt. 2, p. 242).

Although physically shattered, he was promoted brigadier-general Jan. 20, 1864, and commanded a Georgia brigade with distinguished ability through the Atlanta campaign, earning from his soldiers the affectionate nickname, "Rock" Stevens. Toward evening of July 20, 1864, in the headlong attack of his troops at Peach Tree Creek, he was mortally wounded. His horse, mangled by the same shot, hearing the call for battle formation, dragged himself to his accustomed place ahead of the line, and fell dead, mute witness to his master's habitual valor. Stevens died five days later. Of forceful but winning personality, he carried into his military career the earnestness and enthusiasm which had earned him success in civil life. These qualities enabled him to inspire in others his own devotion to principles and undeviating performance of duty.

[Ellison Capers, in C. A. Evans, *Confederate Mil. Hist.* (1899), V, 419–20; details regarding battery, *Ibid.*, pp. 16–17; *War of the Rebellion, Official Records (Army),* 1 ser., vols. XIV, XXX, XXXVIII; manuscript reminiscences of C. H. Steinmeyer; letters from Mrs. Helen Capers Stevens DuPré.]

J.M.H.

STEVENS, EDWIN AUGUSTUS (July 28, 1795–Aug. 7, 1868), engineer, financier, inventor, the sixth son of John [*q.v.*] and Rachel Cox Stevens, was born at "Castle Point," Hoboken, N. J. After receiving his education under private tutors, he engaged in the experiments and business enterprises of his father and older brothers until he was twenty-five, developing, meanwhile, a keen business sense and unusual organizing ability. He came to be regarded, in fact, as the family "fly-wheel," and in 1820, by family agreement, his father made him trustee of practically the whole of his estate. Although

the responsibility was great for so young a man, he succeeded admirably and, in addition, occasionally assisted both his father and his brother Robert L. Stevens [*q.v.*] in their engineering work. With the latter, he invented and patented, Aug. 23, 1821, a plow which was extensively used for years.

In 1825 he took charge of the Union Line, which operated freight and passenger stages between New York and Philadelphia. Two years later it became the property of himself and his brothers Robert and John Cox, Edwin continuing as business manager. When, in 1830, the Camden & Amboy Railroad & Transportation Company was chartered, he was made treasurer and manager. With his great business and organizing ability this first railroad project in New Jersey succeeded in an incredibly short time, and during the whole of his management, extending over thirty-five years, the stock of the company constantly appreciated in value and no dividend was passed. Occasionally, Stevens would try his hand at invention. For example, he designed a wagon body with removable sides, extensively used for many years in New York for hauling refuse and known as the "two horse dump wagon"; he also helped his brother Robert in designing the "closed fire-room" system of forced draft, patented Apr. 1, 1842, and first applied on Robert's steamboat *North America.*

As early as 1814 Stevens had become interested with his father and brother in armored naval vessels and had carried on experiments in which projectiles from a six-pounder cannon were fired against iron plating. Little public interest could be aroused at that time, however. The prospect of serious trouble with Great Britain in 1841 prompted Edwin to conduct a new series of experiments at Bordentown. He then applied to the United States Navy Department for permission to build an armored vessel, the design to be largely that of his brother Robert, and on Apr. 14, 1842, Congress authorized the Secretary of the Navy to enter into a contract with him. His struggle to build the *Stevens Battery,* as it was called, was of some years' duration, chiefly because of changes in Navy administration and improvements in ordnance. Not until 1854 were the ship's floor timbers actually laid, and two years later Robert, the leader in the undertaking, died. Edwin then assumed the whole burden, although he realized that the Navy Department had little belief that iron-clad vessels would ever come into general use. He met with small success in arousing any real interest until 1861, when, influenced by newspaper and periodical suggestions, the navy board condescended to make an examination of the Stevens plans. Its report to Congress was adverse, however. Undaunted, Stevens built, at his own expense, a small iron-clad, twin-screw steamer, the *Naugatuck,* to demonstrate the practicality of his plans. Even though this vessel saw considerable service in and about Hampton Roads and proved the feasibility of the novel features it contained, the government's attitude remained unchanged. Stevens bequeathed it to the state of New Jersey together with one million dollars for its completion. The money was spent in 1869 and 1870 without finishing the vessel, and in 1881 it was dismantled and sold for junk.

Stevens' father had always hoped that some of his estate might be devoted to founding an "academy" for teaching fundamental subjects and science. Edwin kept this purpose always before him and particularly after he inherited much of his brother Robert's fortune. Accordingly, in his will he bequeathed both land and money sufficient to establish the Stevens Institute of Technology at Hoboken. He was twice married: first, in 1836, to Mary B. Picton of West Point, N. Y., who died in 1841; second, Aug. 22, 1854, to Martha Bayard Dod of Princeton, N. J., daughter of Prof. Albert Dod [*q.v.*]. By his first wife he had two children, and by the second, seven. His daughter Mary Picton Stevens became the wife of Muscoe Russell Hunter Garnett [*q.v.*]. Stevens' death occurred in Paris, France.

[A. D. Turnbull, *John Stevens, An Am. Record* (1928); R. H. Thurston, "The Messrs. Stevens of Hoboken," *Jour. Franklin Inst.,* Oct. 1874; J. E. Watkins, *Biog. Sketches of John Stevens, Robert L. Stevens, Edwin A. Stevens* (1892), and *The Camden and Amboy Railroad* (n.d.); *The Stevens Iron-clad Battery* (1874); *Jour. Franklin Inst.,* Sept. 1874; J. P. Baxter, Jr., *The Introduction of the Ironclad Warship* (1933); *N. Y. Geneal. and Biog. Record,* Jan. 1881, pp. 20, 28; *N. Y. Tribune,* Aug. 10, 1868; *N. Y. Times,* Aug. 11, 1868; Patent Office records.]
                                                    C. W. M—n.

STEVENS, EMILY (Feb. 27, 1882–Jan. 2, 1928), actress, was born in New York City, daughter of Robert E. Stevens and Emma (Maddern) Stevens. Her grandfather on her mother's side was Richard Maddern, an English musician who came to America in mid-nineteenth century with a large family, and organized a traveling concert company composed of his own children. She was educated at the Institute of the Holy Angels, Fort Lee, N. J., and at Saint Mary's Hall, Burlington, N. J., and when she was twenty played Miriam with her cousin, Minnie Maddern Fiske, in the latter's production of *Mary of Magdala.* She remained with Mrs.

Fiske for some years, playing Lady Blanche in a revival of *Becky Sharp,* and Berta in *Hedda Gabler* early in the century. Leaving her cousin's company, she acted with George Arliss in *The Devil* in 1908, and in *Septimus,* 1909. But it was not till the season of 1915–16 that she became a "featured" player. In 1914–15 she made an unsuccessful attempt in a fairy play called *The Garden of Paradise,* by Edward Brewster Sheldon, with scenery by Joseph Urban which rather over-topped the frail play. When she appeared in New York, Oct. 9, 1915, in *The Unchastened Woman,* by Louis Kaufman Anspacher, however, she was widely acclaimed. Her rôle was that of a witty, worldly, rather neurasthenic woman, restless and cruel, yet charming; and she made a minute and effective character study of the part. The play was very successful. An equally good new rôle was not forthcoming for some time, but she won attention with a revival of *Hedda Gabler.* On Mar. 3, 1924, at the Garrick Theatre, New York, she appeared as Mathilde Fay in the Theatre Guild's production of *Fata Morgana,* by Ernest Vajda, which enjoyed a long and prosperous run. Here again she was a woman of the world—restless, somewhat predatory, bored, subtle—and again she made of the rôle a fascinating character study. The next season she appeared in *The Makroupoulos Secret,* by Karel Čapek, based on the legend of the woman who has eternal youth. That was her last prominent rôle. She died in New York. She never married.

Strikingly fair in appearance, with a mass of gold hair, with brilliant eyes and coloring, she could assume the rôle of beautiful and alluring women without difficulty. She was herself witty, with an ironical twist of humor, which further fitted her for the parts in which she excelled. Her methods of acting had, quite naturally, been shaped by observation of her cousin when she was in Mrs. Fiske's company, and at times her voice and inflection echoed the older player's startlingly. But there the likeness ceased. Her playing was neither so brilliant nor so brittle as her cousin's; her stage personality was much less intellectual and much more alluringly feminine, though she was unable to suggest emotional depth. Her strength lay in depicting with minute understanding modern women of the world, witty, charming, and sexually restless.

[Emily Stevens' full name is said to have been Emily Mary Stevens. See *Who's Who in the Theatre* (1925); W. P. Eaton, *Plays and Players* (1916); George Arliss, *Up the Years from Bloomsbury* (1927); Burns Mantle and G. P. Sherwood, *The Best Plays of 1909–19* (1933); *N. Y. Times,* Jan. 3 (obituary), Jan. 4 (editorial), Jan. 15 (letter from Evelyn O'Connor in "The Dramatic Mail Bag," sec. 8), and obituary in *Herald*

Tribune (N. Y.), Jan. 3, 1928; theatre collections in the N. Y. Pub. Lib. and the Widener Lib., Harvard Univ.]   W. P. E.

STEVENS, GEORGE BARKER (July 13, 1854–June 22, 1906), theologian and educator, was born in Spencer, Tioga County, N. Y., the son of Thomas Jackson and Weltha (Barker) Stevens. Three years in Ithaca Academy prepared him to enter Cornell University in 1873. After two years he transferred, for pecuniary reasons, to the University of Rochester, graduating from that institution in 1877. For a year he studied in the Rochester Theological Seminary, then entered the middle class of Yale Divinity School, where he completed his course in 1880. He was ordained and installed over the First Congregational Church of Buffalo, N. Y., on Sept. 28, 1880, and on Nov. 23 of the same year was married to Kate A. Mattison of Oswego, N. Y. After two years of service in Buffalo he became pastor of the First Presbyterian Church of Watertown, N. Y., but continued his theological studies and received the degree of doctor of philosophy from Syracuse University in 1883. Two years later he was granted leave of absence by his parish to study in Germany. Here he displayed such marked proficiency that the faculty of the University of Jena encouraged him to submit a thesis ("The Rational Grounds of Theism") and stand an examination for the degree of doctor of divinity, which was granted him in 1886.

His brilliant record as a student led to his election, in the autumn of the same year, to the Buckingham Professorship of New Testament Criticism and Interpretation in Yale Divinity School, succeeding Timothy Dwight [*q.v.*], who was entering on his duties as president of Yale College. After some six years of intensive study in the field of exegesis, his vigorous mind produced in rapid succession works which attracted wide attention—*A Short Exposition of the Epistle to the Galatians* (1890, 1894), *The Pauline Theology* (1892, 1918), *The Johannine Theology* (1894), *Doctrine and Life* (1895). In 1895 he was appointed to the more congenial chair of systematic theology, succeeding Samuel Harris [*q.v.*], but his new duties and extensive preaching engagements did not abate his literary productivity. In 1896 appeared *The Life, Letters, and Journals of the Rev. and Hon. Peter Parker* (1896), followed by *The Epistles of Paul in Modern English* (1898), *The Theology of the New Testament* (1899), *The Messages of Paul* (1900), *The Messages of the Apostles* (1900), *The Teaching of Jesus* (1901), *The Christian Doctrine of Salvation* (1905). In what appeared

a slight illness he died suddenly on June 22, 1906, in the fifty-second year of his age.

As a theologian Stevens was chiefly interested in the reinterpretation of religious truth in the light of the best scholarship of his day. His mind, eminently clear, balanced and energetic, neither clouded nor illumined by mysticism, made him a successful expounder of his substantial learning. His abounding vitality, his ability to kindle his own intellectual fires, his ready command of his acquisitions, enabled him almost at will to do his daily stint of writing and produce so many volumes of solid merit. A certain radiant healthfulness won him friends and strongly influenced his pupils.

[*Who's Who in America,* 1906–07; Williston Walker, *Professor George Barker Stevens, D.D., LL.D., An Address . . . Dec. 7, 1906* (n.d.); *Report of the President of Yale Univ.* (1907); *Obit. Record Grads. Yale Univ.,* 1907; *New Haven Evening Reg.,* June 23, 1906.]   C. A. D.

STEVENS, GEORGE WASHINGTON (Jan. 16, 1866–Oct. 29, 1926), educator, art museum director, author, was born at Utica, N. Y., the son of George and Elizabeth (Garripy) Stevens. Educated in the Utica schools and the Utica Academy, where he specialized in the natural sciences, he first became a reporter on the *Utica Press.* In 1889 he went to Ohio. A year later, after a short time on the Springfield *Republican-Times,* he went to Toledo, where he lived for the rest of his life. For five years he was on the staff of the *Toledo Bee.* From 1896 for a number of years he devoted his time to advertising, a field in which he was an early entrant. Later, while he was a member of the editorial staff, he conducted a column of original matter for the *Toledo Times,* 1900–03. At the same time he contributed to such popular magazines of the time as *Outing Magazine, Recreation, Smart Set, Success,* and *Ainslee's Magazine,* and wrote numerous poems, which were collected and published as *The King and the Harper Together with Other Poems* (1900) and *Things* (1903). One of his poems, "Be glad you're poor," was widely reprinted in newspapers in the years 1929–33.

Of unusual talent in both music and art, he had developed a great interest in painting as a pastime. He studied under the eminent landscapist, John Francis Murphy [*q.v.*], in 1896 in the Catskills and spent many summers painting in Holland, France, and Italy. He was a member of the Western Society of Artists, and exhibited in various museums and exhibitions in the country. In 1903 he became the first director of the Toledo Museum of Art, which had been founded two years before, and thereupon entered into close association with its great patron, Edward Drummond Libbey [*q.v.*]. Libbey had foreseen tremendous opportunities and possibilities in the field of art education, and it remained for Stevens, in company with his wife, Nina de Garmo Spalding of Port Huron, Mich., whom he had married, June 12, 1902, to develop a plan and policy for the future of the museum and to put it into effect. With a broad concept of art, which he defined as "that science whose laws applied to all things made by man make them most pleasing to the senses," and an ideal of a museum of usefulness and helpfulness, he was able to completely revolutionize museum practice in America and to influence it throughout the rest of the world. Under his guidance the Toledo Museum of Art became the first to admit freely children of all ages, the first to embark upon a policy of art education for all people, the first to maintain a free school of design, and among the first to accord to music equal rank with the other arts. As a result of his liberal policies, public interest in the Toledo Museum of Art attained such remarkable proportions that for many years it had the largest per capita attendance among art museums in American cities. His ideas for the building of museum collections are best exemplified in the George W. Stevens Gallery of Books and Manuscripts in the Toledo Museum. For it he acquired material which shows the development of writing and printing from the first crude beginnings of the alphabet through the early illuminated manuscripts and block books to the earliest printed books, the typographical masterpieces of later printers, and the art of the illustrator and the binder.

A man of broad civic interests, he served on the boards of the chamber of commerce and other civic institutions, and was a member of the city plan commission under which Toledo's zoning ordinances were perfected. He was an honorary secretary of the Egypt Exploration Fund; vice-president of the Faculty of Arts, London, England, 1908–10; president of the American Federation of Photographic Societies, 1909–10; and from 1919 until his death president of the Association of Art Museum Directors. He was also interested in astronomy and maintained a perfectly equipped observatory at his home.

[*Who's Who in America*, 1926–27; *Am. City*, Apr. 1916; *Outlook*, June 21, 1916; *Woman's Home Companion* (picture sec.), Sept. 1916; Nina S. Stevens, in *Am. Mag. of Art*, Dec. 1920; A. D. Albert, in *Collier's*, Jan. 8, 1921; Gardner Teall, in *Arts and Decoration*, Nov. 1921; Nell L. Jaffe, in *Fine Arts Rev.* (Cleveland, Ohio), May 1922; *Art News* (N. Y.), Nov. 6, 1926, and Feb. 12, 1927; *Art Digest*, Mar. 1, 1927; *Museum News* (Toledo Museum of Art), Feb., Mar., Dec. 1908, Jan. 1909, Oct. 1914, Dec. 1915, Feb., Dec. 1921, Jan. 1923, Apr. 1927; *Museum News* (Am. Asso.

of Museums), Nov. 15, 1926; *Bull. Minneapolis Inst. of Art*, Nov. 13, 1926; *Toledo News-Bee*, Dec. 7, 1922, Oct. 29–Nov. 2, 1926; *Toledo Blade* and *Toledo Times*, Oct. 29–Nov. 2, 1926; *Utica Press*, Oct. 30, 1926.]
B.–M.G.

STEVENS, HENRY (Aug. 24, 1819–Feb. 28, 1886), bookman, was born in Barnet, Vt., third child and second son of Henry and Candace (Salter) Stevens, and brother of Benjamin Franklin Stevens [*q.v.*]. On the title page of his *Recollections of Mr. James Lenox of New York and the Formation of His Library* (1886) he describes himself as "Bibliographer and Lover of Books," member of various historical and scientific societies, "Patriarch of Skull & Bones of Yale . . . as well as Citizen of Noviomagus et cetera." According to his own account he was at Middlebury College, 1839; in Washington as a clerk in the Treasury Department and the Senate, 1840; at Yale College, 1841–43, where he took the degree of B.A.; and at Harvard, 1844, where he studied law, "all the while dabbling in books and manuscripts by way of keeping the pot boiling." During his vacations he hunted through New England and the middle states for "historical nuggets" for Peter Force [*q.v.*] and his *American Archives*. "In July 1845," he relates, "I found myself in London, a self-appointed missionary, on an antiquarian and historical book-hunting expedition, at my own expense and on my own responsibility, with a few Yankee notions in head and an ample fortune of nearly forty sovereigns in pocket" (*Recollections of Mr. James Lenox*, pp. 15–16).

London was his home until his death and the world of books his life. He reached England just as Sir Anthony Panizzi began his development of the book stock of the British Museum, and had much to do with museum purchases of books relating to the New World. In America he helped build up the collections of John Carter Brown of Providence, R. I., James Lenox [*qq.v.*] of New York City, the Smithsonian Institution, and the Library of Congress, to mention but a few of his outstanding American customers. He came to hold high rank as an authority in the bibliographical history of the English Bible, and in the geographical and historical literature of the western world. As early as Nov. 14, 1846, in a letter to Lenox, he urged transcription of documents in European archives for the use of American scholars, and he was a pioneer in the use of photography to supplement bibliography (see his *Photo-bibliography*, 1878). His publications, which were for the most part annotated catalogues of items in his collections or reprints of rare documents, include *Historical Nuggets* (1862), a catalogue of the rarities in his library;

Bibliotheca Historica (1870); and *The Bibles in the Caxton Exhibition, MDCCCLXXVII* (1878). Though he agreed to make a catalogue of the Lenox library, he never fulfilled the promise. His conflicts with such men as Henry Harrisse and Justin Winsor were frequent. Characterized by Richard Garnett (*post,* pp. 65–69) as genial, expansive, sanguine, and as both crafty and candid, he was called "an enigma" by so restrained and careful a man as George Henry Moore (manuscript letter to John Russell Bartlett, Mar. 20, 1873, in the John Carter Brown Library). On Feb. 25, 1854, he married in London Mary (Newton) Kuczynski, a descendant of Sir Isaac Newton, widow of Vincent Kuczynski of H. M. State Paper Office. The bookselling business he founded was continued in London by his son and his grandson. He was buried in Hampstead Cemetery, London, where a monument, a block of Barre granite, cut at Montpelier, Vt., was erected to his memory by the Society of Noviomagus.

[Stevens' *Recollections of Mr. James Lenox* (1886) serves well for both author and subject. See also F. P. Wells, *Hist. of Barnet, Vt.* (1923); Richard Garnett, in *Lib. Chronicle* (London), May 1886; F. B. Dexter, *Obit. Record Grads. Yale Coll.* (1886); G. P. Winship, *The John Carter Brown Lib.; A Hist.* (1914); obituary in *New England Hist. and Geneal. Reg.,* July 1886; death notice and obituary in *Times* (London), Mar. 2, 5, 1886. There are manuscript letters from Stevens to Lenox and Brown in the N. Y. Pub. Lib. and the John Carter Brown Lib., Providence, R. I. Stevens' most important pubs. are listed in Joseph Sabin, *Bibliotheca Americana: A Dict. of Books Relating to America,* vol. XXIII (1923–33), continued under the editorship of R. W. G. Vail, and in M. D. Gilman, *The Bibliog. of Vt.* (1897).]   H. M. L.

STEVENS, HIRAM FAIRCHILD (Sept. 11, 1852–Mar. 9, 1904), lawyer, was born in St. Albans, Vt., the son of Dr. Hiram Fairchild and Louise I. (Johnson) Stevens. His father was an army surgeon during the Civil War and several times a member of the Vermont legislature; his career, however, was short, and his death in 1866 threw upon Hiram, the eldest son, the burden not only of his own support but, in part, that of the family. Nevertheless, the boy was able to work his way through Kimball Union Academy, Meriden, N. H., and to spend several terms at the University of Vermont. He then studied law with Judge John K. Porter of New York City, attended lectures at Columbia Law School with the class of 1874, and returned to practise his profession in St. Albans. He was one of the group which organized the American Bar Association at Saratoga in 1878.

In 1879 Stevens went to St. Paul, Minn., where he became a member of the law firm of Warner, Stevens & Lawrence. This connection he maintained until 1886, when he became counsel for the St. Paul Real Estate Title Insurance Company. Not long afterward, he was the head of a new firm, Stevens, O'Brien, Cole & Albrecht. In St. Paul he helped to organize the Ramsey County Bar Association and also the Minnesota State Bar Association, of which he was president in 1901. From 1892 to 1900 he lectured on real property at the law school of the University of Minnesota. This phase of law work especially engaged his interest and led him to take a leading part in launching the St. Paul College of Law in 1900; as its president he functioned until his death.

For a dozen years Stevens was especially active in politics. As a Republican he was elected in 1888 to the lower house of the state legislature from a strongly Democratic district, and in 1890 and 1894 he was elected to the state Senate. His leadership was recognized by his selection as chairman of the committee on the judiciary, a position from which he dominated the legislative body during the last half of his term of service. In 1901 he was made the chairman of a commission to revise the Minnesota statutes, but his death occurred before the task was completed.

A fluent speaker, he was much in demand for occasional addresses. He wrote frequently on law subjects. He edited and wrote portions of the *History of the Bench and Bar of Minnesota* (2 vols., 1904), an expansion of his chapter on "The Bench and Bar of St. Paul" in C. C. Andrews' *History of St. Paul* (1890). The range of his interests was wide; he was prominent in the St. Paul Chamber of Commerce, a member and president of the park commission, and a member of several fraternal orders—in short, he qualified as a "good mixer." On Jan. 26, 1876, he married Laura A. Clary of Massena, N. Y.; they had no children.

[E. V. Smalley, *A Hist. of the Republican Party . . . [and] a political Hist. of Minn.* (1896); C. C. Andrews, *Hist. of St. Paul, Minn.* (1890); *Proc. Minn. State Bar Asso.,* 1904; *Report . . . Am. Bar Asso.,* 1904; *Who's Who in America,* 1903–05; *Daily Pioneer-Press* (St. Paul), Mar. 10, 1904; *St. Paul Dispatch,* Mar. 10, 1904; *St. Paul Globe,* Mar. 10, 1904.]
L. B. S.

STEVENS, ISAAC INGALLS (Mar. 25, 1818–Sept. 1, 1862), soldier, governor of Washington Territory, was born at Andover, Mass., the son of Isaac and Hannah (Cummings) Stevens, and a descendant of John Stevens who was living in Andover as early as 1641. During his boyhood he helped on the farm and outstripped all his fellows in study. After a year and four months at Phillips Academy, where he excelled in mathematics, he entered the United States

Military Academy, graduating first in his class in 1839. Commissioned a second lieutenant of engineers, he was engaged for several years in the construction or repair of fortifications on the New England coast. While stationed at Newport, R. I., he met Margaret Hazard, whom he married Sept. 8, 1841. A son and four daughters were born to them.

During the Mexican War he was engineer adjutant on Scott's staff in Mexico, and at Contreras, Churubusco, and Chapultepec displayed a combination of judgment and cool daring for which he was brevetted captain and major. After the war, while recovering from wounds received in the capture of the city of Mexico, he was assigned once more to engineering duties in coastal fortifications until 1849, when Alexander D. Bache [q.v.] appointed him executive assistant in the United States Coast Survey at Washington. Here he demonstrated high talent for administration. He remained till 1853, meanwhile taking a deep interest in army reorganization and other questions calling for arguments before the departments, congressional committees, and the president. His clarity and breadth of thought, sound practical judgment, dignity, and power of statement made him an ideal worker for such ends. In 1851, partly as a critique of Major Roswell S. Ripley's *The War with Mexico* (1849), he published *Campaigns of the Rio Grande and of Mexico*. He desired to see historical justice done to Generals Scott and Taylor, who at the time were the victims of partisan prejudice. Yet, as a Democrat, in 1852 he campaigned for Pierce.

Early in Pierce's administration, upon the enactment of the law providing for Pacific Railway surveys, Stevens sought and secured appointment as director of exploration for the northern route. Just previously he had secured the governorship of Washington Territory, resigning from the army (Mar. 16, 1853) in order to accept it. Under the circumstances, precedent would have denied him assistants from the army; nevertheless, several young officers, including George B. McClellan [q.v.], volunteered for his survey and were permitted to serve under him. This survey, and the later effort to get the route he recommended accepted by government and people, constituted thereafter Stevens' most engrossing interest. Secretary Davis withheld the funds required for completing the work but Stevens used his meager resources as governor to bring it gradually to perfection, and in 1858 he dictated his final report, which is considered his masterpiece (*House Executive Document 56*, vol. XII, bks. I, II).

Meanwhile, the governorship of the Territory had proved a nightmare. Faced with the problem of opening 100,000 square miles of land to white settlement, Stevens began by making a series of Indian treaties. He was probably lacking in the requisite patience, and as usual, the negotiations caused restiveness among the tribes which eventuated in widespread and desolating Indian wars. Gen. John E. Wool [q.v.], commander of the army on the Pacific, refused to coöperate with the people of Washington and Oregon and even thwarted their military undertakings. The correspondence between Stevens and the General was long and bitterly controversial. A stormy episode resulting from the Indian troubles was the Governor's proclamation of martial law, the subsequent arrest of a federal judge, Edward Lander [q.v.], and the arrest of the Governor for contempt of court. In his great work, however, the endeavor to pacify the Indians, he succeeded partially.

Although subjected to a flood of criticism, from both within and without the Territory, Stevens was elected territorial delegate to Congress for the term beginning Mar. 4, 1857. Here he urged the ratification of his Indian treaties, winning against the bitter opposition of Wool's friends. He was returned to his delegate's seat for the following term. In 1860 he assumed the chairmanship of the Breckinridge and Lane national committee, Lane being a close personal friend. This action alienated the Douglas Democrats so that he failed of renomination as delegate to Congress, and when on the outbreak of the Civil War he proffered his services to the Federal government, the response was slow and grudging He finally accepted the colonelcy of the 79th Regiment of New York Volunteers ("The Highlanders"), was promoted to brigadier-general in September, and major-general as of July 4, 1862. He was gallantly leading a charge at Chantilly when a bullet in the temple instantaneously terminated his career.

In appearance Stevens was slight and undersized, but with a massive head, and great dignity both of bearing and speech. He was deeply serious and somewhat deficient in humor. Politically, he once called himself a "Democratic Abolitionist." He sincerely believed that Breckinridge's success in the election of 1860 would prevent a rupture of the Union. His loyalty was never questioned. In addition to the *Campaigns* and the report mentioned above, he published *A Circular Letter to Emigrants Desirous of Locating in Washington Territory* (1858) and *Address on the Northwest* (1858), delivered before the American Geographical and Statistical Society.

[Hazard Stevens, *The Life of Isaac Ingalls Stevens* (2 vols., 1900) is the best biography, though somewhat eulogistic; see also S. H. Paradise, "Isaac I. Stevens," *Phillips Bull.*, Oct. 1932; O. J. Victor, *Men of the Time* (3 vols., 1862–63); G. W. Cullum, *Biog. Reg. Officers and Grads., U. S. Mil. Acad.* (1891), vol. I; *Biog. Dir. Am. Cong.* (1928); *Harper's Weekly*, Sept. 20, 1862; *Daily Nat. Intelligencer*, Sept. 8, 1862; Ezra Meeker, *Pioneer Reminiscences of Puget Sound* (1905), contains a criticism of Stevens as a negotiator of Indian treaties.]   J. S.

STEVENS, JOHN (1749–Mar. 6, 1838), engineer, inventor, pioneer in the field of mechanical transportation, was born in New York City, the son of John Stevens, whose father, John, had come to America in 1699 at the age of sixteen as an indentured law clerk. The boy's mother was Elizabeth, daughter of James Alexander [*q.v.*] and sister of William [*q.v.*]. His father, a ship owner and master and a merchant, gradually acquired extensive land areas in New Jersey and in his later years entered politics. He served as treasurer of New Jersey, as president of various legislative meetings during the Revolution, and as president of the New Jersey convention which ratified the federal Constitution. His residence was at Perth Amboy, N. J., and here young John grew up, receiving his primary education from tutors and at Kenersley's College near Woodbridge. In 1760 his parents removed to New York, and after completing his school work in 1762 John joined the family there. Four years later he entered King's College (now Columbia), graduated in 1768, and during the next three years studied law. In 1771 he received his appointment as an attorney but did not practise his profession; instead he joined his father in his political activities in New Jersey, undertaking various commissions for the latter and an occasional service as special aide to Gov. William Franklin.

With the outbreak of the Revolutionary War he offered his services to General Washington and was immediately commissioned a captain and appointed loan commissioner for Hunterdon County, N. J., to collect money for the Continental Army. A few months later he was appointed treasurer of New Jersey, in which capacity he served for the duration of the war, advancing gradually in grade to colonel. In 1782–83 he held the office of surveyor-general for the eastern division of New Jersey, with headquarters in Trenton, and then returned to his home in New York, having married, Oct. 17, 1782, Rachel, daughter of Col. John Cox of Bloomsbury, N. J. In 1784 he bought at auction a large tract of land in New Jersey on the west side of

the Hudson River, which included most of what is now Hoboken, and for the succeeding three years he was busily engaged in developing the estate and building a home.

About 1788 his attention was drawn to the work of John Fitch and James Rumsey [*qq.v.*] in the development of the steamboat, and from that time until his death Stevens veritably gave himself, his family, and his fortune to the advancement of mechanical transport both on water and on land. Up to the moment he saw Fitch's steamboat on the Delaware River, he had given but little thought to engineering, though he had always been a great reader of science and natural philosophy. Now, thoroughly aroused, he concentrated his reading on steam. Soon he was working out on paper designs of boilers and engines unique for the time, and on Feb. 9, 1789, he petitioned the New York legislature for the exclusive privilege of building steamboats. Rumsey, however, had already submitted a similar petition to that body and received the grant. Stevens then turned to the federal government, which had not as yet formulated any patent laws. Through his friends in Congress and elsewhere he brought about the framing of the act establishing the first patent laws, which act was passed in April 1790, and in August 1791 he was among the first dozen citizens to receive United States patents. His inventions were an improved vertical steam boiler and an improved Savery-type steam engine, both intended for steamboats, and an application of steam to the working of bellows.

Upon the death of his father in 1792 it became Stevens' lot to administer the former's vast estate, and although an extremely busy man, he found time in the next five years to continue his steam-engine experiments. His greatest difficulty lay in his inability to get satisfactory work done. He had no skill of his own in this field and there were no mechanical shops nor competent workmen to be had. About 1797, however, he met Nicholas J. Roosevelt [*q.v.*], who was interested in a foundry at what is now Belleville, N. J., and had several workmen just "out" from England, and the prospects of actually building a steam engine and boat became brighter. Stevens now aroused the latent interest of his brother-in-law, Chancellor Robert R. Livingston [*q.v.*] of Clermont, N. Y., in the project, with the result that Stevens, Roosevelt, and Livingston became actively associated. Livingston succeeded in having the lapsed grant of Fitch for the exclusive privilege of steamboat operation on the waters of New York State transferred to him in 1798, and with this incentive the partners set to work with added vigor. An experimental boat, the

Polacca, was built and tried on the Passaic River, but proved unsuccessful. Experiments continued, however, during the succeeding two years, interpersed with alternate disagreements and compromises between the associates with respect to engine and boat design and methods of propulsion. In 1800 a definite twenty-year agreement of partnership between them was consummated. Shortly after, Livingston became American minister to France and his active part in the experiments ceased. About this time Stevens became consulting engineer for the Manhattan Company, organized to furnish an adequate water supply to New York City. He succeeded in convincing the directors that steam pumping engines should be used and installed such equipment of his own design, but it was not efficient and a Boulton & Watt type of engine was later substituted. He and Roosevelt went forward with their experiments, Stevens being determined to build a small steamboat to ferry him across the Hudson. He had also become greatly interested in promoting adequate transportation facilities generally, and devoted much time to educating the public on the subject. In 1802 he became president of the Bergen Turnpike Company, organized to construct suitable roads across Bergen County in New Jersey.

By Apr. 11, 1803, he had advanced sufficiently with his experiments to secure on that date a United States patent for a multitubular boiler, and the following year his small steamboat, operated by twin screw propellers and called *Little Juliana,* was taken back and forth across the Hudson by two of his sons. The steam engine and boiler of this boat are preserved in the National Museum at Washington. The successful performance of *Little Juliana* now spurred Stevens to greater effort. His goal was to inaugurate an adequate steam ferry system across the Hudson between Hoboken and New York and to operate a regular line of steamboats on the Hudson between New York and Albany and on other inland rivers. He gave what time he could during the next two or three years toward further experiment, and in 1806 began his plans for a 100-foot steamboat, the *Phoenix,* designed for passenger and freight service. Before this vessel was completed, however, Fulton's steamboat *Clermont* made in 1807 its successful voyage to Albany and return. The achievement was discouraging to Stevens in that the trip was made under a monopoly granted to Livingston and Fulton. He was later given the opportunity to join them but refused because of his agreement with Roosevelt and his firm belief that the monopoly was unconstitutional. Furthermore, he

would have had to submerge his own accomplishments and inventions at the cost of partnership. Bitter debates ensued, and numerous proposals and counter proposals were made during the next seventeen years by Stevens and the monopolists, for each side had something the other could use to advantage; but the deadlock was never broken. Since he was restricted from using the Hudson River, he sent the *Phoenix,* completed in 1808, to Philadelphia in June 1809. It made the sea trip successfully and established for itself the record of being the first sea-going steamboat in the world. Thereafter, plying between Philadelphia and Trenton, it served as a unit in the cross-state transportation system controlled and managed by Stevens' sons. Still determined to develop a steam ferryboat system across the Hudson, he purchased a ferry license in New York in 1811 and built the *Juliana.* He then sublet the lease and a regular ferry system was soon inaugurated. Threats from Fulton and Livingston, however, compelled Stevens, who could not afford the expense of lawsuits, to remove the *Juliana* after a few months, whereupon it was sent to Connecticut and used in regular service on Long Island Sound.

Leaving steam navigation in the hands of his sons, about 1810 he began giving close attention to the adaptation of the steam engine as the motive power for railways. In letters to his political friends he urged the adoption of such means of conveyance rather than canals. His correspondence on this subject was voluminous but the results were far from satisfactory. Accordingly, in 1812, he published *Documents Tending to Prove the Superior Advantages of Rail-ways and Steam-carriages over Canal Navigation,* in which every conceivable phase of railway transportation was considered, engineering features explained, and construction costs worked out. All his friends conceded that his proposals were ingenious but, privately, they considered them the dreams of a visionary projector. He approached the state legislatures of New York, New Jersey, Virginia, North Carolina, and Pennsylvania with memorials asking them to open the way for railroads, and finally, on Feb. 6, 1815, the New Jersey Assembly created a company "to erect a rail road from the river Delaware near Trenton to the river Raritan at or near New Brunswick" (*Votes and Proceedings,* 1815, p. 193). This was the first American railroad act. After eight years' additional hammering at the Pennsylvania legislature, on Mar. 31, 1823, "on a memorial and representation of John Stevens," an iron railroad was authorized by that body. The bill allowed Stevens to form a company to erect a railroad from Philadelphia to Columbia, Pa., and upon the organization of the company Stevens was empowered to build it. The necessary funds could not be raised, however, and in 1826 the act was repealed, but another authorizing a railroad was passed. In 1828 the legislature appropriated $2,000,000 to construct the Philadelphia & Columbia Railroad, opened in 1834 and later acquired by the Pennsylvania Railroad. Since Stevens called his company of 1823 The Pennsylvania Railroad, he may be regarded as the founder of the Pennsylvania system (W. B. Wilson, *History of the Pennsylvania Railroad,* 1899, I, 10). Two years later the New Jersey legislature chartered the Camden & Amboy Railroad & Transportation Company and Stevens' sons Robert Livingston and Edwin Augustus [*qq.v.*] were elected president and treasurer, respectively. In neither of these legislative acts was the kind of motive power indicated, and Stevens, in an effort to convince the popular mind of the feasibility of the steam locomotive, designed and built in 1825, when seventy-six years old, an experimental locomotive and operated it on a circular track on his estate in Hoboken. This was the first American-built steam locomotive, although it was never used for actual service on a railroad, and on its completion Stevens brought his active engineering work to a close.

For the remaining years of his life he devoted his time to study, and wrote many essays on metaphysical subjects, political economy, and education, which, however, were not published. In addition to his pioneer work in the field of transportation, he and his sons put forward the idea of an armored navy as early as 1815. He developed plans for the protection of New York City; drew up the design of a bridge across the Hudson from New York to Hoboken; and proposed a vehicular tunnel under the Hudson as well as an elevated railroad system for New York. At the time of his death in Hoboken he was survived by his widow and seven children. His eldest son, John Cox Stevens, was a founder of the New York Yacht Club and head of the group which sent the *America* to England to compete for the international cup. Robert Livingston and Edwin Augustus, already mentioned, were engineers and inventors. One of his daughters, Mary, married Joshua R. Sands [*q.v.*] and after her death her sister Harriet married him.

[Collection of Stevens' papers and letters in the Lib. of the Stevens Institute of Technology, Hoboken, N. J.; A. D. Turnbull, *John Stevens, An American Record* (1928); J. K. Finch, *Early Columbia Engineers* (1929); R. H. Thurston, "The Messrs. Stevens of Hoboken," *Jour. Franklin Institute,* Oct. 1874; J. E. Watkins,

Biog. Sketches of John Stevens, Robert L. Stevens, Edwin A. Stevens (1892), and *The Camden and Amboy Railroad* (n.d.); Charles King, *Progress of the City of N. Y.* (1852); *N. Y. Geneal. and Biog. Record,* Jan., Apr. 1881; *Morning Herald* (N. Y.), Mar. 8, 1838; Patent Office Records.]

C. W. M—n.

STEVENS, JOHN AUSTIN (Jan. 22, 1795– Oct. 19, 1874), banker, was born in New York City, the son of Lucretia (Ledyard) Sands Stevens and Ebenezer Stevens, of Boston, an officer of the Continental Army and later a prosperous importer in New York. Four of the sons graduated from Yale College, Alexander Hodgdon Stevens [*q.v.*] in 1807 and John Austin, the youngest, in 1813. Five years later John became a partner in his father's importing house, and he achieved business success. In 1824 he was married to Abby, the daughter of Benjamin Weld of Brunswick, Me., and Boston. One of their sons was John Austin Stevens, 1827–1910 [*q.v.*].

When, in the efforts to regain financial stability after the depression of 1837, a new state banking law was enacted, a group of New York capitalists and lawyers organized the Bank of Commerce in 1839. They installed Stevens as its first president and issued capital stock to the amount of $5,000,000, divided among 624 stockholders, and in 1856 increased the capital to $10,000,000. In the second year of its existence the bank took $1,000,000 of federal bonds at par and was made agent for government moneys collected in New York, and, having weathered the crisis of 1857, it was recognized at the outbreak of the Civil War as perhaps the strongest financial institution in the country. In the summer of 1861 he joined the other New York bankers in taking the federal government's loan of $50,000,000 and thereafter until the end of hostilities gave the Lincoln administration unwavering support. He was president of the Associated Banks of New York, Philadelphia, and Boston. He even led a group of bankers in advocating the Legal Tender Bill in 1861 (J. W. Schuckers, *Life and Public Services of Salmon P. Chase,* 1874, p. 243). His advice was more than once sought by the treasury department. In 1866 he resigned the bank presidency and passed the remaining eight years of his life in retirement. For half a century he had been an important figure in the life of the metropolis, as president of the Merchants' Exchange, as secretary of the Chamber of Commerce, and as excellent public speaker, devoted to literature. He died in New York City.

[F. B. Dexter, *Biog. Sketches of the Grads. of Yale College,* vol. VI (1912); *Appletons' Annual Cyc.,* 1874; *The N. Y. Geneal. and Biog. Record,* vol. VII (1876), p. 13; *Evening Post* (N. Y.), Oct. 19, 1874; information from the National Bank of Commerce.]

W. B. S.

STEVENS, JOHN AUSTIN (Jan. 21, 1827–June 16, 1910), financier, author, was born in New York City, the son of Abby (Weld) and John Austin Stevens [q.v.]. He was educated in the local schools and was graduated from Harvard College in 1846. He became cashier and had charge of the entire correspondence of Spofford, Tileson & Co., a mercantile firm of New York. In 1852 he went into partnership with John Storey, of Cuba, and carried on an extensive Cuban importing business until the Civil War. On June 5, 1855, he married Margaret Antoinette Morris, the daughter of William Lewis Morris and great-grand-daughter of Richard Morris [q.v.]. They had one son and two daughters. During the panic of 1857 he was secretary of the exchange committee that was appointed by the banks to buy produce bills. He was a stanch Republican and in 1860 helped to organize a meeting at the Merchants' Exchange to rally men of all parties to the support of Abraham Lincoln. In 1863 he was a leader in organizing the Loyal National League, which pledged unconditional loyalty to the federal government and support of its war efforts. He was active in recruiting the 51st New York Volunteers and in obtaining money to maintain it in the field. He was manager and director of the Loyal Publication Society, secretary of the National War Committee, and in 1862 secretary of the treasury note committee that obtained the loan to the government of $150,000,000 in gold coin. He was offered and declined the positions of commissioner of internal revenue and register of the treasury, as well as the post of consul-general at Paris. He was secretary of the Chamber of Commerce, 1862–68, and began the collection of its gallery of portraits. He resigned the secretaryship to visit Europe, where he remained five years, mostly in Paris. He was in London for a year, was Jay Cooke's agent there for a Pacific railroad by the northern route, and in 1872 went to Alsace and Lorraine to try to arrange for extensive emigration to the United States.

He contributed to the *New York Times* in September and October 1873 a series of articles signed "Knickerbocker," afterward published as *Resumption of Specie Payment* (1873). As a delegate to the convention of the boards of trade at Baltimore in 1874, he delivered an address on the national finances. In 1876 he was elected librarian of the New York Historical Society and served for two years. He was one of the founders of the Sons of the Revolution in 1876, and in 1883 was chairman of the committee in charge of the centenary celebration of the evacuation of New York. His portrait, owned by the Sons of the Revolution, hangs (1935) in Fraunces Tavern in New York City. In 1877 he founded the *Magazine of American History*, which he edited until 1881, and in which a number of his articles were printed. He wrote the chapter on "The English in New York, 1664–1689" for Justin Winsor's *Narrative and Critical History* (vol. III, 1885) and contributed several chapters to *The Memorial History of the City of New York*, edited by James Grant Wilson (4 vols., 1892–93). Among his separate publications were *The Valley of the Rio Grande* (1864), *Colonial Records of the New York Chamber of Commerce . . . with . . . Historical and Biographical Sketches* (1867); *Progress of New York in a Century, 1776–1876* (1876); *The Burgoyne Campaign* (1877); and *Albert Gallatin*, in the American Statesmen Series (1884). He died at his home in Newport, R. I., where he had lived since 1886.

[Notebooks, esp. on horse racing in America and New York taverns, and typewritten historical addresses in possession of N. Y. Hist. Soc.; manuscript biog. by his daughter, Mary Morris Stevens, Newport, R. I.; *Sons of the Revolution . . . of N. Y. Reports and Proc. . . . 1909–10* (1911); *Who's Who in America*, 1910–11; *N. Y. Times*, June 17, 1910.]   A. J. W.

STEVENS, JOHN HARRINGTON (June 13, 1820–May 28, 1900), pioneer and "first citizen" of Minneapolis, the son of Gardner Stevens and Deborah (Harrington), was born at Brompton Falls, Quebec, a transplanted New England community just over the Vermont border. At the age of fifteen, after the family had gone back to Vermont, Stevens joined an elder brother at White Oak Springs, Wis. Pursuing lead-mining ventures, the boy found himself at Galena where he joined the militia called out to repress the Winnebago Indians. It was then that he met Governor Dodge who later was influential in securing for him a captain's commission in the quartermaster's department of the army on the outbreak of the Mexican War. He served through the war, and resigned in 1848 to return to Texas where he had preëmpted some land. He was turned from this course by John Catlin, former secretary of Wisconsin Territory, who told him of a new territory to be organized about the Falls of St. Anthony. This region, said Catlin, "was well known . . . to be the best climate in the world for such invalids" as Stevens who had come back from Mexico with "serious lung difficulties" (Stevens, *post*, pp. 2, 3). The following spring Stevens was in St. Paul where Franklin Steele, sutler at Fort Snelling, employed him to help in his store.

Steele advised Stevens to squat on land on the west bank of the Mississippi at the Falls where the latter obtained 160 acres. He built a cottage, destined to be the first dwelling in the city of Minneapolis, in the autumn of 1849, and brought to it his bride, Frances Helen Miller, of Westmoreland, N. Y., to whom he had been married on May 1, 1850. They had six children. In the course of the next few years Stevens plotted his land and sold lots to newcomers, but as the settlement grew he turned over to Steele the remainder of his holdings, realizing but a very modest sum for what was to become the business district of Minneapolis. Ever a pioneer he obtained, in 1855, forty-five acres in Glencoe, McLeod County, which had just been opened to settlement. Here, among other enterprises, he edited the *Glencoe Register* from 1857 to 1863. As brigadier-general of militia he took an important part in the suppression of the Indian uprising during the last months of 1862, being for a time in charge of a long strip of the frontier. In September 1863 he was one of the commissioners to take the Minnesota soldier vote in the southern department, and, shortly afterward, he settled once more in Minneapolis where he lived for the remainder of his life. He engaged in various occupations, but his interest lay chiefly in the promotion of agriculture; he edited such papers as the *Farmers' Tribune, Farmer and Gardner,* and *Farm, Stock, and Home*; for many years was president of the Minnesota State Agricultural Society; and was keenly interested in the agricultural department of the University of Minnesota. In 1890 he published his *Personal Recollections of Minnesota and Its People,* a mine of information about early Minneapolis in which he "seems to have remembered everybody but himself" (Folwell, *post,* IV, 85n). He collaborated with Isaac Atwater in producing a *History of Minnesota* (1895), editing and writing portions of the part dealing with Hennepin County.

Stevens took no very active part in the politics of his day, although he was a member of the first state legislature, 1857–58, and that of 1876; he was state senator in 1859–60, but declined to contest a similar position in 1877 with Charles A. Pillsbury [*q.v.*]. While a good enough business man in a routine way, he apparently lacked that quality which many of his contemporaries utilized to build up a fortune through the exploitation of a new country, or else he was genuinely indifferent to the acquisition of great wealth, for he died a comparatively poor man.

[Stevens Papers, Steele Papers, Minnesota Historical Society; J. H. Stevens, *Personal Recollections of Minnesota and Its People* (1890); W. W. Folwell, *A Hist. of Minn.* (1921–30), vols. I, II, IV; C. E. Flandreau, *Encyc. of Biog. of Minn. and Hist. of Minn.*

(1900), vol. I; D. S. Hall and R. I. Holcombe, *Hist. of the Minn. State Agricultural Soc.* (1910); H. W. B., in *Farm Students' Rev.,* July 1899; D. B. Johnston, "Journalism in the Territorial Period," *Colls. Minn. Hist. Soc.,* vol. X (1905), pt. 1; *Minneapolis Times,* Dec. 28, 1898; *Minneapolis Tribune,* May 29, 1900.]
L. B. S.

STEVENS, JOHN LEAVITT (Aug. 1, 1820–Feb. 8, 1895), journalist and diplomat, was born at Mount Vernon, Me., where his father, John Stevens, a native of New Hampshire, settled in 1805. His mother was Charlotte (Lyford) Stevens. The son was educated at Maine Wesleyan Seminary and Waterville Classical Institute, entered the Universalist ministry in 1845, and for ten years held pastorates in Maine and New Hampshire. On May 10, 1845, he married Mary Lowell Smith, daughter of Daniel Smith of Hallowell, Me. Becoming interested in the antislavery cause and feeling that he could aid it best through newspaper writing, he joined with James Gillespie Blaine [*q.v.*] in acquiring the *Kennebec Journal,* of Augusta, Me., which he edited continuously from 1855 until 1869, and thereafter occasionally during intervals in his diplomatic service. He was minister to Paraguay and Uruguay from 1870 to 1874, to Norway and Sweden from 1877 to 1883, and to Hawaii from 1889 to 1893, at first as minister resident, later as envoy extraordinary and minister plenipotentiary.

The annexation of Hawaii by the United States, first seriously proposed in 1853 and again in 1854, when Kamehameha III negotiated for its admission as a state, became a live issue once more during the reign of Kalakaua. The extravagance and dishonesty of the government gradually led many men, genuinely attached to the monarchy, to the conviction that it must eventually be abolished; opinion was divided as to whether the establishment of a republic or annexation to the United States should follow. The death of Kalakaua in 1891 and the accession of his sister, Liliuokalani, gave a momentary hope of good government, which the new queen soon disappointed. The end came in January 1893, when the queen announced her intention of abrogating the constitution and proclaiming a new one which would increase her power. A committee of safety, composed of leading citizens, proclaimed a provisional government, of which Sanford Ballard Dole [*q.v.*] became head, and occupied the public buildings in Honolulu. On Feb. 1 Stevens recognized it, and upon his request the commander of the cruiser *Boston,* which was lying in the harbor at Honolulu, landed forces for the protection of life and property in case of riot. The queen, yielding, asserted that she had been dispossessed by force of American arms and appealed for redress to the president of the United States, to whom the provisional government also sent commissioners to negotiate for annexation. So much is history. As to Stevens' part in the proceedings there is dispute. Certainly he was always an open advocate of annexation, and it is claimed that he "overstepped the limits proper to a diplomatic representative in a friendly and peaceable country" (*The American Secretaries of State and Their Diplomacy,* vol. VIII, p. 244, S. F. Bemis, editor). But James Henderson Blount [*q.v.*], sent to Hawaii by President Cleveland as special commissioner, further alleged that Stevens had entered into a conspiracy with the revolutionists, that the use of American forces to overthrow the royal government had been promised in advance, and that otherwise the revolution would not have taken place. In reliance upon Blount's report, Cleveland endeavored by every means short of actual force to restore the queen to the throne, though without success. In passing upon the validity of the charges, not only Blount's temperament but the peculiarly one-sided character of his investigation must be considered. Most of those whose testimony he took were royalists, and of the small number of sympathizers with the revolution whom he examined few had taken prominent part in it. He interviewed only two of the thirteen members of the committee of safety, one of the four members of the executive committee, three of the fourteen members of the advisory committee; some of them offered him their testimony and were turned away. Nor did he seek information from Stevens himself, there present. An investigation conducted in 1894 by a Senate committee was more thorough. Stevens, who was questioned under oath at great length, denied all complicity. The sworn statements of nearly all persons concerned with the revolution—including all those who were alleged to be ringleaders—were obtained, and an ironclad oath taken by members of the committee of safety declared that "neither prior to nor after our appointment as such committee, did we or either of us, individually or collectively, have any agreement or understanding, directly or indirectly, with . . . Mr. Stevens . . . [to] assist in the overthrow of the monarchy or the establishment of the Provisional Government" (*Senate Report 227, post,* p. 590). No "plot" is necessary to explain the revolution. The endurance of men who wanted decent government had been strained too long. At last it snapped. After his return to the United States Stevens lived in Augusta, where he died, survived by one of his four children, a daughter.

Aside from his journalistic writings he was the author of a *History of Gustavus Adolphus* (1884) and *Picturesque Hawaii* (copyright 1894), republished as *Riches and Marvels of Hawaii* (copyright 1900).

[An authoritative account of Stevens' career is given in the *Daily Kennebec Jour.* (Augusta, Me.), Feb. 9, 1895, reprinted in part in *Representative Citizens of the State of Me.* (1903). See also W. D. Alexander, *Hist. of Later Years of the Hawaiian Monarchy* (copr. 1896), the best general account of the Hawaiian revolution; *Hawaii's Story by Hawaii's Queen* (1898), the standard royalist version, sponsored by Liliuokalani; Lucien Young, *The "Boston" at Hawaii* (1898), republished as *The Real Hawaii* (1899), the personal experiences of a naval officer; J. W. Pratt, "The Hawaiian Revolution: a Re-Interpretation," *Pacific Hist. Rev.,* Sept. 1932, an elaboration of the plot theory, which, however, the author discards in a later (unpublished) article; *Foreign Relations of the U. S., 1894; App. II, Affairs in Hawaii* (1895); *House Exec. Doc. 47,* 53 Cong., 2 Sess., the Blount report; and *Sen. Report 227,* 53 Cong., 2 Sess., the Senate Committee's investigation, which appeared as *Hawaiian Islands: Report of the Committee on Foreign Relations, U. S. Senate* (2 vols., 1894), with appendices containing all the diplomatic correspondence of the revolutionary period. The Univ. of Mich. has transcripts of unpublished material in both the Washington and Honolulu archives.]
T. M. S.

STEVENS, ROBERT LIVINGSTON (Oct. 18, 1787–Apr. 20, 1856), engineer, naval architect, inventor, the second son of John [*q.v.*] and Rachel (Cox) Stevens, was born on his father's estate, "Castle Point," Hoboken, N. J. He was educated under private tutors and at the same time assisted his father in his experimental engineering work, his first undertaking being the operation in 1804 of the steamboat *Little Juliana* on its journeys back and forth across the Hudson. In 1808 he helped in the design and construction of the *Phoenix,* introducing her concave water lines, and was master, under Capt. Moses Rogers [*q.v.*], on her pioneer sea voyage from New York to Philadelphia in 1809. For several years thereafter, with headquarters in Trenton, he managed the operation of the *Phoenix,* placed in service on the Delaware River and plying between Philadelphia and Trenton. While thus engaged, he helped his father build the ferryboat *Juliana,* which on Oct. 11, 1811, went into regular service between New York and Hoboken, thus establishing the world's first steam-ferry system.

By this time he had become wholly engrossed in naval architecture and for the succeeding twenty-five years was widely recognized as a leader of that profession. He designed and had built upwards of twenty steamboats and ferries, incorporating in them his successive inventions. Among these were the method of installing knees of wood and iron inside the ship's frame; a "cam-board" cut-off for steam engines; and balanced poppet valves. He replaced the old cast-iron walking beam with the wrought-iron skeleton type; shortened the length of the beam and added a wooden gallows frame; and introduced a forced-draft firing system under boilers, the split paddle wheel, "hog-framing" for boats, and the present type of ferry slip. He also increased the strength of steam boilers until pressures of fifty pounds per square inch could be safely carried, and was the first to perfect a marine tubular boiler. In addition to these activities he played an important part with his father and brothers in the cross-state transportation business, and upon the establishment, in 1830, of the Camden & Amboy Railroad & Transportation Company out of the Union Line (practically controlled by the Stevenses) Robert was elected president and chief engineer. That same year he went to England to study English locomotives then in service or under construction, with a view to purchasing one and ordering iron rails. On the way he designed the T-rail (the standard section on all American railroads), which, after much difficulty, he succeeded in having rolled in England. He designed at the same time the "hook-headed spike" (substantially the railroad spike of to-day), and the "iron tongue" (now the fish plate), as well as the bolts and nut to complete a rail joint. He purchased the locomotive *John Bull*, which on its trial trip at Bordentown, N. J., Nov. 12, 1831, with Stevens at the throttle, inaugurated the first steam railway service in New Jersey. He also designed the earliest locomotive pilot. During the succeeding fifteen years he divided his time between railroading and steam navigation. In the company's railroad shops in Hoboken he devised a double-slide cut-off for locomotives, designed and built several types of locomotives, improved boilers, and successfully burned anthracite coal under boilers.

Toward the close of the War of 1812, Stevens had perfected for naval use a bomb that could be fired from a cannon. He invented, too, an elongated percussion shell and sold large quantities to the federal government as well as the secret of its construction. This work led Stevens, his father, and brothers to give their attention to the introduction of armor on ships of war and brought into being plans for an unusual armored steamer for harbor defense, the design based upon extensive experiments which they had conducted. After submitting their plans to Congress they waited thirty years for authorization to construct a war steamer "shot and shell proof." Work was then started by Robert in a newly built drydock at Hoboken. Coincident with this undertaking began a great improvement in ordnance in all the principal navies of the world,

and as Stevens had contracted to build "shot and shell proof," he was compelled year after year to alter his plans, and before the vessel was finished he died. Besides constructing steamboats he designed and built a number of sailing vessels, the most famous of which was the yacht *Maria* (1850), the fastest sailing vessel of her day. It was this yacht that defeated the *America,* a few months before the latter won the memorable race in England. Stevens lived practically the whole of his life in Hoboken and New York, entering into the social activities of the metropolis and being prominent in musical circles. He never married, however, and died at Hoboken at the age of sixty-nine.

[A. D. Turnbull, *John Stevens, An American Record* (1928); R. H. Thurston, "The Messrs. Stevens of Hoboken," *Jour. Franklin Inst.,* Oct. 1874; J. E. Watkins, *Biog. Sketches of John Stevens, Robert L. Stevens, Edwin A. Stevens* (1892), and *The Camden and Amboy Railroad* (n.d.); Charles King, *Progress of the City of N. Y.* (1852); J. P. Baxter, 3rd, *The Introduction of the Ironclad Warship* (1933); *N. Y. Tribune,* Apr. 22, 1856; Patent Office records.]

C. W. M—n.

STEVENS, THADDEUS (Apr. 4, 1792–Aug. 11, 1868), lawyer, congressman, political leader, was born in Danville, Vt., of a family which had migrated from Massachusetts a few years earlier. His father, Joshua Stevens, an unthrifty shoemaker, died or disappeared at an undetermined date, leaving the mother, Sally (Morrill) Stevens, and four small sons in dire poverty. She was fortunately a woman of fine ideals and great industry, and made many sacrifices to educate Thaddeus, who as the youngest child, and lame and sickly from birth, required special care. The family soon removed to Peacham, Vt., to gain the advantages of the academy which had been established there in 1795. This village, just above the junction of the Connecticut and Passumpsic rivers in north central Vermont, was still part of a semi-frontier community, and the boy grew up in a ruggedly democratic society. He was early trained to hard work and an independent outlook, and though a chance visit to Boston at the age of twelve gave him an ambition some day "to become rich" (McCall, *post,* p. 7), he imbibed a strong feeling for the poor and an intense dislike of aristocracy and of caste lines.

Completing his course at Peacham Academy, Stevens entered Dartmouth College as a sophomore in 1811, and graduated in 1814. However, he spent one term and part of another at the University of Vermont. There are early evidences of his headstrong nature: at Peacham Academy he joined other students in presenting a tragedy in the evening, both the dramatic entertainment and the hour being infractions of the rule, and at the University of Vermont he is said to have killed a cow. At the latter institution he also wrote a drama on "The Fall of Helvetic Liberty" and helped enact it. The instruction at Dartmouth and Vermont was limited and thorough, emphasizing Greek, Latin, higher mathematics, and ethics. From his classical training Stevens undoubtedly drew much of the clarity, exactness, and force which later characterized his public speaking, and which led Blaine to say that he rarely uttered a sentence that would not meet the severest tests of grammar and rhetoric (J. G. Blaine, *Twenty Years of Congress*, I, 1884, p. 325). He had determined to practise law, and began reading it in Vermont. On taking his degree he obtained a post as instructor in an academy at York, Pa., and continued his law studies under David Casset, leader of the local bar. Apparently to evade a time requirement in Pennsylvania, he took his bar examinations at Bel Air, Md., passing with ease when he proved that in addition to a little law he knew how to order Madeira for his examiners and to lose money at cards to them. He then removed to Gettysburg, Pa., in 1816 to practise.

For several years a struggling lawyer of narrow income, Stevens used his leisure to do much profitable reading in history and belles-lettres. But an important case in which he defended a man accused of murder on the then unusual plea of insanity gave him a large fee, said to have been $1500 (Hensel, *post*, p. 5), and a reputation. Thereafter from 1821 to 1830 he appeared in almost every important case at the county bar and won almost all of his numerous appeals to the state supreme court (Woodburn, *post*, p. 12). Since his county adjoined Maryland, Stevens saw much of the slavery system and of runaway negroes, and his instinctive New England dislike of slavery grew into a fierce hatred. It is said that he once spent $300 which he had saved to make additions to his law library in purchasing the freedom of a negro hotel-servant who was about to be sold away from his family (Hensel, pp. 7, 8). He defended numerous fugitive slaves without fee, and displayed great skill in gaining their freedom.

After practising law for ten years in Gettysburg, Stevens also entered the iron business by becoming in 1826 a partner in James D. Paxton & Company, which at once built Maria Furnace in Hamilton-ban Township, Adams County. The company, which became Stevens & Paxton in 1828, first tried to manufacture stoves and other light castings, but the metal was "cold-short" and the product frequently too brittle to

have a value. Stevens and Paxton therefore bought property near Chambersburg, where they built Caledonia Forge (probably named after Stevens' native county in Vermont), and mixed pig iron from Maria Furnace with other ores. In 1837 they also built Caledonia Furnace, and finding ample supplies of superior ore near it, the next year gave up their first furnace entirely. They confined themselves chiefly to the sale of blooms. The Caledonia establishment was never very profitable even in the earlier years. When it met the competition of more effective and economical iron works, Stevens kept it up primarily because he did not wish to deprive the surrounding community of its principal means of livelihood. From his manufacturing enterprise sprang Stevens' interest in protective tariff.

It was natural for a man who felt with his burning intensity on public questions to push into politics. In 1830 he was described as "a firm and undeviating Federalist" and "a violent opponent of General Jackson" (quoted, Woodburn, p. 13). But already the Anti-Masonic movement had attracted him, and he emerged into political prominence in 1831 at the Anti-Masonic Convention in Baltimore which nominated William Wirt for president, and at which he delivered a notable arraignment of secret orders. Two years later he was elected to the Pennsylvania House on the Anti-Masonic ticket, taking his seat in the last weeks of 1833. As a member of the legislature Stevens quickly became known as one of the most fiery, most aggressive, and most uncompromising leaders in Pennsylvania affairs. He served until 1841. For some years he introduced or supported much legislation striking at Masonic influences, and in 1835 was chairman of a committee which made abortive attempts to investigate the evils of Free-Masonry. But his range of interests was wide. He was a warm advocate of the act of 1834 extending the free school system of Philadelphia over the whole state. The next year, when in a reaction against the taxes that were required an effort was made to repeal this law, he sprang into statewide fame by a brilliant defense of free education,—a defense "which produced an effect second to no speech ever uttered in an American legislative assembly" (McCall, p. 38). His denunciation of class-hostility toward free public schools, his excoriation of the repeal as "an act for branding and marking the poor" (Woodburn, p. 45), and his panegyric of a democratic system of instruction, completely won the hostile House. What was more, it caused the Senate to reverse its position. Stevens also labored for larger appropriations for colleges, including Pennsylvania College (now Gettysburg College) at Gettysburg. He argued in behalf of the right of petition, appealed for a constitutional limit on the state debt, and defended the protective tariff and the United States Bank. In 1838 a disputed election in Philadelphia County brought on at Harrisburg the "Buckshot War," with the Whig and Anti-Masonic members of the House endeavoring to organize in opposition to the Democrats. Stevens was the chief leader in this attempt, showing the fierce fighting spirit and uncompromising disposition which marked him through life. At one time he escaped from a mob in the state capitol by leaping from a window. His faction was defeated, and the Democrats declared his seat vacated, but he was at once reëlected. In 1836–37 he offered a resolution in favor of abolishing slavery and the slave-trade in the District of Columbia. In the state constitutional convention of 1837 he displayed great bitterness in debate, opposing everything that smacked of privilege or class distinctions, and refusing to sign the constitution finally adopted because it limited suffrage to white citizens (McCall, p. 48). At his retirement from the legislature the Harrisburg *Pennsylvania Telegraph* pronounced him "a giant among pigmy opponents" (E. B. Callender, *Thaddeus Stevens, Commoner,* 1882, p. 51), and every one recognized him as one of the strongest men in the state.

His decision to quit politics was only temporary, for as the contest over slavery grew heated he was irresistibly drawn toward the arena. Pique over his failure to gain a place in the cabinet of Harrison, whom he had supported in 1836 and 1840, may have played a part in his retirement. His business had not prospered, and he had debts variously estimated at from $90,000 to $217,000 to pay off (Woodburn, p. 66). Removing in 1842 to Lancaster, he at once gained a place at its bar worth from $12,000 to $15,000 a year. As he repaired his fortunes he turned toward public life and in 1848 was elected on the Whig ticket to the Thirty-first Congress. Here he immediately took a leading place among the little band of free-soilers, surpassing such men as Joshua R. Giddings and G. W. Julian [*qq.v.*] in fieriness of temper as in general parliamentary versatility. He was willing to make no compromise whatever with slavery in the territories, and predicted that if ringed about by "a cordon of freemen," all slave states would within twenty-five years pass laws "for the gradual and final extinction of slavery" (Feb. 20, 1850, *Congressional Globe,* 31 Cong., 1 Sess., Appendix, p. 142). He denounced slavery as "a curse, a

shame, and a crime"; he compared it to the horrors of Dante's *Inferno* (June 10, 1850, *Ibid.,* Appendix, p. 767). He taunted men of the lower South as slave-drivers, and Virginians for devoting their lives "to selecting and grooming the most lusty sires and the most fruitful wenches to supply the slave barracoons" (Feb. 20, 1850, *Ibid.,* Appendix, p. 142). His invective was bestowed as harshly upon Northerners who condoned slavery as upon Southerners who practised it. He assailed the compromise measures of 1850, and did his utmost to defeat the Fugitive Slave Act. Southern members expressed horror at his gross language, which they declared too indecent for print, and at his reckless and incendiary sentiments. Reëlected in 1850, he renewed his assaults upon slavery and his warnings to the South against secession. He also spoke for increased tariffs. In March 1853, disgusted with the moderation of most Whigs, he quit Congress but not politics. For within a year Douglas had prepared his Kansas-Nebraska scheme, and the moment was ripe for a leader of Stevens' unsurpassed powers of agitation and denunciation.

In the formation of the Republican party in Pennsylvania, Stevens played a vigorous part. He helped organize Lancaster County in 1855, and in 1856 attended the National Convention at Philadelphia as a supporter of Justice McLean. His impassioned appeals at this gathering led Elihu B. Washburne to say that he had "never heard a man speak with more feeling or in more persuasive accents" (E. B. Washburne, ed., *The Edwards Papers,* 1884, p. 246, note). In 1858 he was reëlected to Congress and, with fire unabated at the age of sixty-eight, entered the last debates before the Civil War. His harshness of speech was as great as ever. An early colloquy with Crawford of Georgia almost provoked a riot on the floor (Woodburn, pp. 135–36). He also renewed his pleas for a protective tariff. In 1860 he again was a delegate to the Republican National Convention, and though he was constrained to support Cameron and preferred McLean, finally voted for Lincoln. Returning to Congress, he opposed any concessions to the Southerners as "the coward breath of servility and meanness"; he warned the South to secede at its peril, saying that if it tried to break up the Union "our next United States will contain no foot of ground on which a slave can tread, no breath of air which a slave can breathe" (Jan. 29, 1861, *Congressional Globe,* 36 Cong., 2 Sess., p. 624). He called upon Buchanan to exert the Federal authority sternly against those who were flouting the national government. In one memorable debate he denounced the plotters of "treason" so violently that the excitement, according to Henry L. Dawes, "beggared all description," and his friends formed a hollow square to protect him from the menaces of hostile members (McCall, pp. 127–28).

Stevens was again mentioned for a cabinet post, and when Lincoln chose Simon Cameron instead he criticized the cabinet as representing political expediency rather than efficiency. But he soon found himself in a position of greater power than if he had taken Cameron's place. He was made chairman of the ways and means committee, which gave him wide authority over all revenue bills and most other congressional measures dealing with the prosecution of the war; while as Blaine states, in everything he was "the natural leader, who assumed his place by common consent" (Blaine, *ante*, I, 325). Upon nearly all aspects of the war he had stern and positive views, and his ideas of policy diverged sharply from Lincoln's. In the field of finance he fortunately gave the administration loyal support. He was prompt in carrying through the House all necessary legislation authorizing Secretary Chase to float loans. He and his committee acted with expedition and nerve in devising new taxes and making them effective. He pressed the income tax against urban objection, the direct tax on real estate against rural objection. The internal revenue act of 1862 showed especial ingenuity in reaching almost every source of revenue, and for this he as well as Justin S. Morrill, chairman of the sub-committee on taxation, deserves credit. On the legal-tender legislation that became a matter of hard necessity following the suspension of specie payments he held doctrines possibly derived in large part from Eleazar Lord (McCall, p. 259; W. C. Mitchell, *A History of the Greenbacks,* 1903, pp. 47 ff.). He favored a uniform nation-wide paper currency issued directly by the United States without mediation of the banks, legal tender for all purposes, and interchangeable with six per cent. United States bonds (Woodburn, pp. 257–58). The act finally passed with numerous compromises, and the amendment which required the interest on government bonds to be paid in coin and not greenbacks was highly repugnant to Stevens. In his opinion it changed a "beneficent" measure into one "positively mischievous" by establishing one currency for the rich bondholder and another for the plowholder and fighter (Feb. 20, 1862, *Congressional Globe,* 37 Cong., 2 Sess., p. 900).

On the conduct of the war Stevens took a harsh and aggressive position. He was one of the two House members who in 1861 voted against the Crittenden resolution declaring that the war was not fought for conquest or subjugation, or to interfere with the established institutions of the South. From the early months he urged confiscation of all property used for insurrectionary purposes and the arming of slaves (Aug. 2, 1861, *Congressional Globe,* 37 Cong., I Sess., pp. 414–15). He bitterly criticized Lincoln for overruling Frémont and Hunter on military emancipation, and termed the President's proposal for compensated emancipation "diluted milk and water gruel" (*Ibid.,* 37 Cong., 2 Sess., p. 1154). In language often acrid and abusive he called upon Lincoln to turn out Seward, shake loose from the Blairs and other border-state politicians, and use every possible method of attack against the South. "Oh, for six months of stern old Jackson!" was one of his exclamations (Woodburn, p. 220). He helped make the committee on the conduct of the war, formed after Ball's Bluff, a thorn in the side of the administration. As the conflict progressed he asked ever-sterner measures. Believing the Constitution no longer applicable to the South, he had no difficulty in justifying demands for wholesale arrests, confiscations, and capital punishments. Early in 1862 he told the House that the war would not end till one party or the other had been reduced to "hopeless feebleness" and its power of further effort had been "utterly annihilated" (Jan. 22, 1862, *Congressional Globe,* 37 Cong., 2 Sess., p. 440). He went so far by 1864 as to speak of the necessity of seeing the "rebels" exterminated, and more than once spoke of desolating the section, erasing state lines, and colonizing it anew. It was charged that his shrill demands for vengeance after 1863 were prompted in part by the destruction of his iron works near Chambersburg in Lee's invasion of that year (Rhodes, *post,* V, 544). Confederate troops spent several days at the Caledonia iron works, where they removed all stores and supplies, then burning most of the settlement. In a letter Stevens describes the destruction in indignant terms. They "took all my horses, mules, and harness, even the crippled horses"; they seized two tons of his bacon, with molasses, other contents of the store, and $2,000 worth of grain; they burnt the furnace, rolling-mill, sawmill, two forges, bellows-houses, and other parts of the works; they "even hauled off my bar-iron, being as they said convenient for shoeing horses, and wagons about $4,000 worth"; and they destroyed fences and about eighty tons of hay (Stevens Papers, Library of Congress, vol. II). Stevens was forced to provide for the indigent families of the vicinity.

But his chief quarrel with Lincoln was upon reconstruction. He earnestly opposed Lincoln's ten per cent. plan, objected to the seating of congressmen from Louisiana under it, and in a notable speech on reconstruction laid down the rule that the South was outside the Constitution and that the law of nations alone would limit the victorious North in determining the conditions of restoration (Jan. 22, 1864, *Congressional Globe,* 38 Cong., 1 Sess., pp. 317–19). The Wade-Davis bill, embodying a rigorous scheme of reconstruction, did not go far enough for him, but when Lincoln gave this bill a pocket veto with an explanatory proclamation Stevens called the action "infamous" (Woodburn, p. 321). Though he supported Lincoln for reëlection in 1864 it was probably with secret hostility (G. W. Julian, *Political Recollections,* 1884, p. 243; Woodley, *post,* p. 405), and his sorrow over the President's assassination was not keen. Temporarily he hoped that Johnson would take the radical road. But within a month he saw that the new President was following Lincoln, and wrote Sumner in angry horror: "I fear before Congress meets he will have so be-devilled matters as to render them incurable" (Beale, *post,* p. 63). With Sumner, he at once prepared to give battle to Johnson for the purpose of reducing the South to a "territorial condition," making it choose between negro suffrage and reduced representation, imposing other harsh conditions, and fixing Republican supremacy—for which he appreciated economic as well as political arguments (Beale, pp. 73, 152, 206, 403–05). Like Sumner, he also set about promoting schism in Johnson's cabinet (Oberholtzer, *post,* I, 164).

As soon as Congress met, the two houses, on motion of Stevens, appointed a joint committee on reconstruction (Dec. 4, 1865, *Congressional Globe,* 39 Cong., 1 Sess., p. 6), of which he as chairman of the House group was the dominant member. A fortnight later (Dec. 18, 1865), he again asserted that rebellion had obliterated the Southern states and that the section was a "conquered province" with which Congress could do as it pleased. He also frankly avowed that one aim of representation was "to divide the representation, and thus continue the Republican ascendency" (*Ibid.,* pp. 73–74). The first open rupture with the President came in February 1866, on the Freedmen's Bureau Bill which Stevens belligerently pushed and Johnson vetoed. Beginning with Johnson's speech on Washington's birthday, the two men exchanged bitter attacks, and Stevens succeeded in passing both the Civil Rights Bill and a revised Freedmen's Bureau Bill over Johnson's veto. On Apr.

30, 1866, the joint committee reported the Fourteenth Amendment, which with a few changes Congress adopted, and a bill declaring that when the amendment became part of the Constitution any state lately in insurrection which ratified it and adopted a constitution and laws in conformity with its terms should be admitted to representation in Congress. But this bill never passed. It did not go as far as Stevens wished and on the last day of the session he tried to amend it to require full negro suffrage. Johnson opposed the congressional plan, the South with his apparent approval refused to accept the Fourteenth Amendment, and the whole issue went before the people in the congressional election of 1866. Economic factors strengthened Stevens' hands, for large elements feared loss of tariff advantages, railway grants, free homesteads, and gold bond-redemptions, with all of which the Republican party was identified (Beale, pp. 225–99). A sweeping victory that fall gave Stevens the whip-hand over Johnson and the South.

The first use which he made of his success was to impose military reconstruction and the Fifteenth Amendment upon the South. He had expected it to reject the Fourteenth Amendment and thus give him an opening, and he was prepared to make the most of a defiance which he had deliberately inspired and encouraged (Woodburn, pp. 436–37). His new measure, introduced Feb. 6, 1867, and passed in March, provided for temporary military rule while the states were remade in the South on the basis of negro suffrage and the exclusion of leading ex-Confederates. He pushed it through a reluctant House by invective, sarcasm, threats, taunts, and cracking of the party whip (Rhodes, VI, 17, 18). Having accomplished this, he turned to the chastisement of the President. He declared during the summer of 1867 that he would willingly help impeach Johnson but that he did not believe the measure would succeed (July 19, 1867, *Congressional Globe,* 40 Cong., 1 Sess., pp. 745–46). In December he did vote for an impeachment resolution which failed by nearly two to one. When Johnson summarily removed Stanton as secretary of war Stevens saw his chance, and the very next day reported an impeachment resolution based on the President's supposed disregard of the Tenure of Office Act (Feb. 22, 1868, *Ibid.,* 40 Cong., 2 Sess., p. 1336). He was made a member of the committee to draft articles of impeachment, and also one of the managers to conduct the case before the Senate. But his health had now hopelessly failed, and he took little part in the trial itself. Deeply disappointed by the President's acquittal, he sank so rapidly that when Congress recessed he could not be taken back to Lancaster, but died in Washington. He had never married, and only his nephew and colored housekeeper were at his bedside. By his own wish he was buried in a small graveyard in Lancaster. His tombstone bears an inscription prepared by himself: "I repose in this quiet and secluded spot, not from any natural preference for solitude, but, finding other cemeteries limited by charter rules as to race, I have chosen this, that I might illustrate in my death the principles which I advocated through a long life—Equality of Man before his **Creator**" (Woodburn, p. 609; Callender, p. 163).

Stevens was an intense partisan, and his career was marred throughout by a harsh and vindictive temper which in his last years made him frankly vengeful toward the South. Within a brief time after his death it was evident that he had fallen short of the measure of a statesman. His radical and bitter policy, offered as a means of obtaining equality and justice for the negro, aroused fierce resentment, accentuated racial antagonism, cemented the Solid South, and postponed for many decades any true solution of the race problem. He had rare parliamentary talents. Well-read, with a quick and lucid mind, of indomitable courage, a master of language and past master of invective, gifted with a sardonic humor and nimble wit, he was almost invincible on the floor. His private life was far from saintly, for gambling was but one of several habitual vices. But his leonine spirit, his terrible earnestness, his gay resourcefulness, and his fine intellectual equipment always inspired respect. Had tolerance and magnanimity been added to his character, he might have been a brilliant instead of sinister figure in American history.

[The best biography is J. A. Woodburn, *The Life of Thaddeus Stevens* (1913), though S. W. McCall, *Thaddeus Stevens* (1899) in the American Statesmen Series offers an incisive characterization, and there is material of value in T. F. Woodley, *Thaddeus Stevens* (1934). Much material on Stevens is also to be found in W. U. Hensel, *Thaddeus Stevens as a Country Lawyer* (1906), reprint from *Report . . . of the Pa. Bar Asso. . . . 1906* (1906); J. F. Rhodes, *Hist. of the U. S. from the Compromise of 1850*, vols. V, VI (1904–06); James Schouler, *Hist. of the U. S. of America under the Constitution*, vol. VII (1913); E. P. Oberholtzer, *A Hist. of the U. S. Since the Civil War*, vol. I (1917); H. K. Beale, *The Critical Year* (1930); G. F. Milton, *The Age of Hate: Andrew Johnson and the Radicals* (1930); C. G. Bowers, *The Tragic Era* (1929); and the reminiscences of many of Stevens' associates in public life. See also J. M. Swank, *Hist. of the Manufacture of Iron* (1884); E. B. Westling, "Old Iron Works of the Cumberland Valley," *Papers Read Before the Kittochtinny Hist. Soc.*, vol. X, no. 1 (1922); H. R. Mueller, *The Whig Party in Pa.* (1922); B. B. Kendrick, *The Journal of the Joint Committee of Fifteen on Reconstruction* (1934). No collection of his speeches exists, and they must be sought in the *Cong.*

Globe. Edward MacPherson made a collection of Stevens letters and papers which is in the Lib. of Cong.]
                                                                A. N.

STEVENS, THOMAS HOLDUP (Feb. 22, 1795–Jan. 21, 1841), naval officer, was born in Charleston, S. C. Left an orphan in early childhood, he was adopted by Col. Daniel Stevens of Charleston, and was also greatly befriended by Lieut. Ralph Izard, of the Charleston family of that name, the warm affection between the youth and these older officers being evident in letters still retained by the family. In place of his original surname Holdup, in 1815 by legislative enactment he took that of Stevens. He was warranted midshipman in the U.S.S. *Hornet* at Charleston in February 1809, and at the outbreak of the War of 1812 was in the *John Adams* at New York. Volunteering for lake service, he went to the Niagara frontier, and in a night assault on the enemy works opposite Black Rock, Nov. 27–28, 1812, was one of the leaders of a detachment which captured two enemy guns and dislodged an enemy force by firing their barracks. A canister shot through his right hand in this action inflicted permanent injury. Remaining after the retreat of his main party, he later with seven others recrossed the Niagara at great hazard in a leaky canoe. In recognition of his gallantry, Commodore Isaac Chauncey [*q.v.*] made him acting lieutenant (confirmed July 24, 1813). In April 1813 he joined Oliver Hazard Perry [*q.v.*] at Erie. In the battle of Lake Erie he commanded the sloop *Trippe* (one long 32-pounder), last in the line, which passed the *Tigress* and *Porcupine* to engage the *Queen Charlotte*, and after the action assisted the *Scorpion* in the pursuit and capture of two escaping enemy vessels. That he was not specifically mentioned in Perry's dispatches, Stevens attributed to differences with Jesse Duncan Elliott [*q.v.*], second in command, under whom he had served previously in the *Niagara*. He received the silver medal awarded by Congress to officers in the action, and a sword from his native city. In the summer of 1814 he was first lieutenant in the *Niagara* on Lake Huron, and in the autumn he was selected by Perry to join him in the *Java*, fitting for the Mediterranean. Her departure being delayed till after peace, however, he did not sail in her, but secured a furlough and was married in November or December 1815 to Elizabeth Read Sage (Andrews, *post*, p. 160), daughter of Ebenezer Sage, a prominent merchant of Middletown, Conn. His home in later years was in Middletown. In 1818–20 he had duty in the *Alert* and the *Constellation* at Norfolk, and from January 1823 to June 1824 he commanded successively the schooners *Jackal* and *Shark* of the West India Squadron under David Porter [*q.v.*] in energetic campaigns against the West Indies pirates. Made master commandant, Mar. 3, 1825, his next and last command afloat was the *Ontario,* Mediterranean Squadron, 1829–31. He had charge of the Boston naval rendezvous, 1832–36; was made captain, Jan. 27, 1836; and at the time of his sudden death had held command of the Washington navy yard for nearly a year. A miniature by Peale, owned by his descendants, pictures him as of strong and pleasing features, marked by a scar on the right cheek. Surgeon Usher Parsons [*q.v.*], a friend and fellow-officer of the lake campaign, speaks of him as "the very soul of chivalry, generous, high-minded," lively in conversation, being a "loud and free talker," and with "literary talent . . . of a high order" (Parsons, *post,* p. 13). He had three daughters and three sons, but of the sons only one, Thomas Holdup, 1819–1896 [*q.v.*], lived to mature years. Buried first in the Congressional Cemetery, his body was later removed to Arlington.

[In addition to general naval sources, of which J. F. Cooper, *The Hist. of the Navy of the U. S. of America* (1839), is the fullest, see Usher Parsons, *Brief Sketches of Officers Who Were in the Battle of Lake Erie* (1862); H. F. Andrews, *Geneal. of Capt. Giles Hamlin of Middletown, Conn.* (1900); letters, etc., in the possession of Stevens' great-grand-daughter, Mrs. Frederick C. Hicks, Washington, D. C., and in the Navy Lib., where the Personnel Files contain detailed references; obituary in *Daily Nat. Intelligencer* (Washington, D. C.), Jan. 22, 1841.]   A. W.

STEVENS, THOMAS HOLDUP (May 27, 1819–May 15, 1896), naval officer, son of Commodore Thomas Holdup Stevens, 1795–1841 [*q.v.*], and Elizabeth Read (Sage) Stevens, was born in Middletown, Conn. As a youth he spent a year or more in the counting-house of his mother's cousin, Guerdon Hubbard, in Chicago, but then, following his early predilection, entered the navy as midshipman, Dec. 14, 1836. After a cruise in the Brazil Squadron he studied for several months at the Philadelphia naval school, ranking third in his class upon promotion to passed midshipman, July 1, 1842. Brief service as aide to President Tyler was followed by survey duty in the Gulf of Mexico and an assignment to the *Michigan,* Lake Erie, 1843–44. On Nov. 2, 1844, occurred his marriage at Erie, Pa., to Anna Maria Christie. He was afterwards naval storekeeper at Honolulu, 1845–48. Returning home with his wife and his daughter Ellen in the Chilean ship *Maria Helena,* he was wrecked, Jan. 4, 1848, on Christmas Island, the passengers and crew re-

maining there nearly three months before they were rescued. Stevens' account of this, *Narrative of the Wreck of the Chilean Ship Maria Helena* (1849), was reprinted in pamphlet form from the *Polynesian.* Subsequent service included duty at Sacketts Harbor, 1849; in the *Michigan,* Great Lakes, 1849–51; in west coast survey work, 1852–55; and in the *Colorado,* Home Squadron, 1858–60.

In the Civil War, commanding the gunboat *Ottawa,* he participated in the capture of Port Royal, Nov. 7, 1861, and in later operations on the southeast coast, commanding the first expedition up the St. John's River, March–April 1862, which resulted in the occupation of Jacksonville and other towns and fortified points, and the capture of the yacht *America,* then owned by the Confederacy. This vessel was turned over for naval use without claims for prize-money. Later in 1862 he engaged in numerous operations in Virginia waters, opening up the Pamunkey River in the *Maratanza,* May 12, in support of George Brinton McClellan [*q.v.*], capturing the gunboat *Teazer,* July 4, and commanding the *Monitor* in the James River in August during McClellan's withdrawal from the Peninsula. Transferred to the *Sonoma* in cruising operations, he chased the *Florida* thirty-four hours on the Bahama Banks, captured five prizes, and off Bermuda held up the steamer *Gladiator,* though convoyed by H. M. S. *Desperate,* until he was satisfied of her character, both naval vessels clearing for action. He commanded the monitor *Patapsco* in frequent actions around Charleston, August-September 1863, and, despite his unfavorable opinion of its success, was given charge of a desperate night boat attack, Sept. 8, on Fort Sumter, which was repulsed with 124 casualties in his force of about four hundred (see his account of "The Boat Attack on Sumter" in *Battles and Leaders of the Civil War,* vol. IV, 1888). In 1864 he commanded the *Oneida* of the Gulf Squadron, transferring temporarily to the monitor *Winnebago* in the battle of Mobile and later operating off Texas, where in July 1865 he was senior officer. From superiors, during this almost continuous active war service, he received uniformly high commendation for initiative and dependability (Hamersly, *post*). Made captain (1866), commodore (1872), and rear admiral (1879), he was assigned service as lighthouse inspector, 1867–70; command of the *Guerrière,* European Squadron, 1870–71; varied duties at Norfolk, 1873–80; and command of the Pacific Squadron, 1880–81. After retirement, May 27, 1881, he lived in Washington, D. C., occupying his leisure in part with writing on naval and other subjects. One of his articles, "Service under Du Pont," appeared in the *Times* (Philadelphia), Jan. 10, 1886. Of his family of three daughters and six sons, the eldest son became a rear admiral, and two others were officers respectively in the army and marine corps. He died at Rockville, Md., at the home of his daughter and was buried in Arlington Cemetery.

[*United Service* (Phila.), May 1891, with portrait; L. R. Hamersly, *Records of Living Officers U. S. Navy and Marine Corps* (4th edition, 1890); *War of the Rebellion: Official Records* (*Navy*); obituary in *Evening Star* (Washington, D. C.), May 15, 1896; papers in the possession of Stevens' granddaughter, Mrs. Frederick C. Hicks, Washington, D. C.]   A. W.

STEVENS, WALTER HUSTED (Aug. 24, 1827–Nov. 12, 1867), Confederate soldier, was born at Penn Yan, N. Y., the son of Samuel Stevens. He entered West Point as a cadet in 1844, graduated in 1848, fourth in his class, and was commissioned in the corps of engineers. Practically all of his service from then until the Civil War was in Louisiana and Texas, where he did some engineering work upon rivers and harbors, acted as lighthouse inspector for four years, and supervised the construction and repair of fortifications at Galveston and New Orleans. He was promoted first lieutenant in 1855. His life in the South and his marriage to a resident of Louisiana had made him entirely southern in sentiment, and after Texas passed the ordinance of secession he accordingly sent in his resignation from the army, Mar. 2, 1861. Without waiting for it to be forwarded to Washington, he offered his services to Texas and assisted in preparation for the war. The War Department accordingly withheld action on the resignation, and eventually he was dismissed, May 2, 1861, on the technical ground of failure to render his accounts. Meanwhile he had been appointed a captain of engineers in the Confederate army, accredited to the state of Texas. He served on the staff of Gen. Pierre Gustave Toutant Beauregard [*q.v.*] at the battle of Bull Run, and was then promoted major and assigned to duty as chief engineer of the Army of Northern Virginia, continuing in the field with it during the Peninsular campaign. When Lee succeeded Johnston in the command of the army, Stevens, now a colonel, was put in charge of the defenses of Richmond. These resembled field works rather than a fortress, being constructed on a much more modest scale than the contemporary fortifications of Washington, but they were of value in releasing troops for service at the front and proved of some direct use in checking the Kilpatrick-Dahlgren cavalry raid in 1864. Ste-

vens was appointed brigadier-general with rank from Aug. 28, 1864, and again became chief engineer of the Army of Northern Virginia, with which he served until the surrender. The defensive lines before Petersburg were constructed under his direction. It is said that on the evacuation of Richmond he turned back into the flames of the burning bridge over which the troops were marching in order that he might be the last soldier to leave the city he had defended so long. Paroled at Appomattox, he went to Mexico, apparently intending to make it his permanent home, and became superintendent and constructing engineer of a railroad between Vera Cruz and the city of Mexico. He died at Vera Cruz.

[*War of the Rebellion: Official Records* (*Army*); C. A. Evans, *Confederate Mil. Hist.* (1899), vol. III, pp. 664–65; G. W. Cullum, *Biog. Reg. Officers and Grads. U. S. Mil. Acad.* (1891), vol. II, p. 346; J. G. Barnard, *A Report on the Defenses of Washington* (1871), app. D. and F; *Confederate Veteran,* July 1922; unpublished records in the War Dept.]   T. M. S.

STEVENS, WILLIAM ARNOLD (Feb. 5, 1839–Jan. 2, 1910), New Testament scholar, was born at Granville, Ohio, son of the Rev. John and Mary (Arnold) Stevens. His father was for many years a professor at Denison University and an active factor in Baptist education in Ohio; his mother, the daughter of William Arnold of Charlestown, Mass., was a woman possessing to an unusual degree the gift of discernment and the grace of piety. William received his early education at Granville, spent three years of business experience at Cincinnati, where under the influence of Ezekiel Gilman Robinson [*q.v.*] he united with a Baptist church, and was graduated A.B. at Denison University in 1862. After a year in the short course at Rochester Theological Seminary, he returned to Denison as tutor in the classics, 1863–65, during which time he served for a while with the Christian Commission. Enrolling at Harvard in the fall of 1865 as a student of philology and theology, he studied under the eminent Greek, Professor E. A. Sophocles [*q.v.*], and, residing at the Newton Theological Institution, simultaneously pursued some studies there. In 1867–68 he was in Germany, at Leipzig and Berlin, and for the next nine years was professor of the Greek language and literature at Denison. In 1876 he published *Select Orations of Lysias*.

The most distinctive part of his career began with his call to Rochester Theological Seminary in 1877, where he was professor of New Testament interpretation for the rest of his life. An able and inspiring teacher, he helped equip more than a generation of Baptist ministers, whose preaching and pastoral work were partially shaped by his instruction. His greatest influence has been ascribed to the downright honesty and sincerity of his thinking. As a theological conservative but a truly scholarly student of the New Testament, he both worked harmoniously with his associates and encouraged methods of New Testament study which carried some of his students—notably Ernest DeWitt Burton and Walter Rauschenbusch [*qq.v.*]—to more liberal positions. Most of his published writings lay in the field of New Testament study. In 1887 he published *A Commentary on the Epistles to the Thessalonians,* in the American Commentary on the New Testament edited by Alvah Hovey, and in 1894 a *Life of the Apostle Paul.* He collaborated with E. D. Burton in an *Outline Handbook of the Life of Christ* (1892) and in *A Harmony of the Gospels for Historical Study* (1894), which years later remains the most widely used book of its kind. He was a man of broad culture, well read, especially in biography and poetry, with a wide range of classical and Biblical lore. In demeanor he was quiet and reserved. Especially appreciative of nature, he spent his vacations for many years on the Maine coast, particularly at Mount Desert, with its remarkable combination of wooded hills and ocean stretches. He was married, Apr. 5, 1876, to Caroline A. Clarke of Springfield, Ohio.

[*Who's Who in America,* 1908–09; *Memorial Volume of Denison Univ., 1831–1906* (1907); *The Record* (Rochester Theological Seminary), Feb. 1910; *Democrat and Chronicle* (Rochester), Jan. 3, 1910.]

W. H. A.

STEVENS, WILLIAM BACON (July 13, 1815–June 11, 1887), Episcopal bishop, historian, was born in Bath, Me., the youngest of three surviving children of William Stevens, a captain in the War of 1812, and his wife Rebecca, daughter of J. W. Bacon. The family soon moved to Boston where young Stevens received his first education in the city schools. At the age of fifteen he entered Phillips Academy, Andover, where he remained two years. Frail since birth, he now set out on a horseback trip through the Middle West in the hope of building up his strength, and upon his return took passage for Savannah, thence to the Sandwich Islands, and thence westward around the globe, visiting Java, China, and the Philippines. After his return to America he was called upon frequently to lecture on the missionary activities he had observed in China and the Sandwich Islands.

Though greatly improved in health, he determined as a precaution to settle in the South, and in the fall of 1836 entered the Medical College of the State of South Carolina in Charleston.

The following spring he returned to Savannah to continue his studies with Dr. Edward Coppée, whose daughter, Alethea, subsequently became his wife. In the summer he visited his home in Boston, and, deciding to finish his medical studies at Dartmouth, received the degree of M.D. from that institution in 1837. After visiting Florida, he returned to Savannah and entered a partnership with his father-in-law. His success was immediate; he was made physician and surgeon for the orphan asylum and for the Central of Georgia Railroad, and was appointed health officer for the port. He was also elected secretary of the Georgia Medical Society and in 1840 was sent as a delegate to the National Medical Convention in Washington. Upon settling in Savannah he had joined the Georgia Hussars in order to enlarge his social acquaintanceship and to secure release from militia and jury service.

Becoming interested in the history of the state, he was instrumental in founding the Georgia Historical Society in 1839, being elected its first recording secretary and later its librarian. He delivered the Georgia Day address before the Society in 1841, and set forth so eloquently the need for a history of the state that the Society commissioned him to write one. Accordingly, he published *A History of Georgia from Its First Discovery by Europeans to the Adoption of the Present Constitution in MDCCXCVIII,* the first volume appearing in 1847 and the second in 1859. Writing with precision and accuracy and using the documentary sources, he produced a history which has not yet been supplanted. Also he edited the first two volumes of the *Collections of the Georgia Historical Society* (1840, 1842).

Stevens, who was always of a religious bent, soon after he began his medical career found himself haunted by the feeling that he should enter the ministry. Though born into a Congregationalist family, he was early attracted by the Episcopal Church, and in Savannah he joined that communion. Under the dynamic influence of Bishop Stephen Elliott, he pursued a course of study, maintaining himself meanwhile by writing editorials for the *Georgian,* the principal newspaper in the city. On Feb. 26, 1843, he was ordered deacon and was appointed a missionary at Athens, Ga., the seat of the state university. Advanced to the priesthood, Jan. 7, 1844, he became rector of the Episcopal church in Athens. He had previously been appointed to the board of visitors of the university and elected (1843) to the new chair of oratory and belles-lettres, the duties of which he assumed, in addition to his rectorship, in January 1844. In 1847 he was appointed a delegate to the General Convention of his Church in New York, and the next year was persuaded to accept a call to St. Andrew's Church, Philadelphia. He visited the Holy Land and western Europe in 1857, and in the fall of 1861 was made professor of liturgics and homiletics in the Philadelphia Divinity School, established that year. In 1862 he became assistant bishop of the diocese of Pennsylvania, and three years later, on the death of Bishop Alonzo Potter [q.v.], he was made bishop. In 1868 he was given charge of the American churches in Europe, and for years thereafter he spent much time abroad, preaching in many of the churches and cathedrals of England and of other countries. He was chosen in 1876 to preach in St. Paul's Cathedral, London, the closing sermon of the Pan-Anglican Conference.

Stevens was instrumental in founding Lehigh University, of which his brother-in-law, Henry Coppée [q.v.], became president, and in 1869 he was made a trustee. He was also a trustee of the University of Pennsylvania from 1866 until his death. He was a member of nearly two dozen literary and historical societies. Besides his historical works, he wrote a great many books and pamphlets on religious subjects, the best known of which are: *The Bow in the Cloud; or, Covenant Mercy for the Afflicted* (1854); *The Parables of the New Testament Practically Unfolded* (1855); *Home Service: A Manual* (1856); *The Lord's Day* (1857); *The Past and Present of St. Andrew's* (1858); *Sabbaths of the Lord* (1872); *Early History of the Church in Georgia* (1873); *Sermons* (1879). Stevens was simple, modest, and unpretending, a forceful orator, tall and graceful in appearance. His first wife, Alethea Coppée, bore him three children. After her death he married, in 1869, Anna, daughter of J. N. Conyngham of Wilkes-Barre, Pa., and by her had a son and a daughter.

["Autobiog. of Bishop Stevens," *Church Magazine* (Phila.), Nov., Dec. 1887; A. L. Hull, *A Hist. Sketch of the Univ. of Ga.* (1894); A. D. Candler and C. A. Evans, *Georgia* (1906), III, 372; minutes of the trustees of the Univ. of Ga., 1835–57 (MS.); minutes of the vestry of Emmanuel Parish, 1843–93 (MS.); G. W. J. De Renne, *Observations on Doctor Stevens's Hist. of Ga.* (1849); *Hartford Courant*, May 9, 1840; *Galignani's Messenger* (Paris), June 13, 1887; *Evening City Item* (Phila.), June 12, 1871; S. F. Hotchkiss, *A Memoir of the Rt. Rev. William Bacon Stevens* (1899); M. A. De W. Howe, *A Discourse Commemorative . . . of the Rt. Rev. William Bacon Stevens* (1888); biog. sketch in *The Parables* (ed. of 1887); *Churchman*, June 18, 1887; *Pub. Ledger* (Phila.), June 13, 1887.]

E. M. C.

STEVENSON, ADLAI EWING (Oct. 23, 1835–June 14, 1914), congressman from Illinois, vice-president, was born in Christian County, Ky., the son of John Turner Stevenson and Eliza (Ewing) Stevenson, both of whom were Scotch-Irish Presbyterians. His father was a small planter and slave-owner. In 1852 the Stevensons emigrated to Bloomington, Ill., where their conditions of life were not so primitive as to deny young Stevenson fair educational advantages. He taught country school, attended Illinois Wesleyan University as a preparatory student, and even spent two years at Centre College, Danville, Ky. There he met his future wife, to whom he was married on Dec. 20, 1866—Letitia, the daughter of Lewis W. Green [q.v.], the president of the college. Adlai left college before graduation because of the death of his father, read law, was admitted to the bar, and in 1858 opened an office at Metamora, Ill. A fortunate court appointment as master in chancery, and an even more fortunate election as state's attorney, gave him the needed start in his profession; and in 1868 he found it possible to return to Bloomington as the law partner of James S. Ewing. Like most country lawyers of the period, he never became a specialist along any particular line, but he did acquire a wide and varied practice. He was a successful advocate, prepared his cases carefully, and tried them well.

Always an ardent Democrat, he campaigned for Douglas against Lincoln in 1858 and 1860, and in 1864 he ran for elector on the McClellan ticket. He was unexpectedly swept into Congress on the Democratic tidal wave of 1874, was a candidate for reëlection in 1876 and lost, ran once more in 1878 with Greenback support and won. During his two rather undistinguished terms in Congress he made his low-tariff and soft-money views well known; but he was far from belligerent in pressing them, and he made hosts of friends, even among those who were opposed to his political principles. When Cleveland became president in 1885, it was well understood that thousands of fourth-class Republican postmasters would have to be removed to make way for deserving Democrats. The first assistant postmaster-general, to whom the duty of making these removals would fall, must therefore be a man of tact, who could serve his party's interests well and yet give as little offense as possible to the opposition. Stevenson was chosen for this place, and he made some forty thousand removals as painlessly as any one could have done it. Naturally his course provoked scathing denunciation, although very little of the criticism came from the men actually removed from office. In 1889 Cleveland would have rewarded him for his service by making him justice of the supreme court of the District of Columbia, but the Republican majority in the Senate, still smarting from the wounds his course in the post-office had inflicted on them, turned the nomination down. In 1892 he headed the Illinois delegation to the Democratic national convention and helped nominate Cleveland. Thereafter, when a man was sought on whom all factions of the party could unite for vice-presidential nomination, he was chosen for second place. Elected to preside over a Senate that only recently had refused to confirm him for a minor office, he displayed his usual good humor, won many friends, and made no enemies. On the money question he was known to be out of sympathy with the administration, but he was never guilty of embarrassing it. When he retired from office in 1897, President McKinley promptly appointed him a member of the monetary commission to Europe that sought unsuccessfully to pave the way for international bimetallism.

Twice after this his availability made him a candidate for office. In 1900 he was Bryan's running mate, with "Imperialism" as the paramount issue. In 1908 the Democrats of Illinois thought that in spite of his advanced age he was the best man to defeat Charles S. Deneen for the governorship, and he came within twenty-two thousand votes of election. During his declining years he put together a book of reminiscences and addresses, *Something of Men I Have Known* (1909). The book tells little of Stevenson's own career, but it reveals well his natural modesty, his capacity for friendship, and his great personal charm. He died in Chicago.

[J. W. Cook, "The Life and Labors of Hon. Adlai Ewing Stevenson," *Jour. of Ill. State Hist. Soc.*, July 1915; J. S. Ewing, "Mr. Stevenson, the Democratic Candidate for Vice-President," in *Review of Reviews* (N. Y.), Oct. 1900; F. E. Leupp, "Mr. Bryan's Running Mate," *Independent*, Sept. 6, 1900; *In Memoriam: Letitia Green Stevenson, Adlai Ewing Stevenson* (191–?); *Chicago Sunday Tribune*, June 14, 1914.]   J. D. H.

STEVENSON, ANDREW (Jan. 21, 1784– Jan. 25, 1857), congressman from Virginia, speaker of the House of Representatives, and minister to Great Britain, was the son of James and Frances (Littlepage) Stevenson and the nephew of Lewis Littlepage [*q.v.*]. He was born in Culpeper County, Va., where his father was rector of St. Mark's Parish, and was educated at the College of William and Mary. Later he studied law, was admitted to the bar, and began practice in Richmond. He was a member of the House of Delegates from 1809 to 1821, excepting the year 1817. He was speaker of this body from 1812 until 1815. In 1814 and again in 1816 he ran for Congress but was defeated. The next year he became a director of the Richmond

branch of the Bank of the United States. He finally was successful in his campaign for Congress and served from 1821 to 1834, when he resigned. During this period his political influence became important on the federal theatre. Being an early supporter of Van Buren, he went over into the Jackson camp with his chief and became a member of the "Richmond Junto," which, beside himself, consisted of Spencer Roane, Thomas Ritchie, and William C. Rives. In 1827, with the support of Van Buren, he was elected speaker of the federal House of Representatives and served until 1834. Adams accused him of double dealing on the tariff question (Adams, *post,* VII, 369), and he immediately won the hatred of the opposition by appointing committees on a strictly partisan basis, thus breaking with the policy established by his immediate predecessors in office.

When the nullification controversy arose, he took the side of the Union and was one of the few congressmen of that persuasion who weathered the storm in Eastern Virginia. His stand was an important factor in preventing Virginia from following the lead of South Carolina in this matter. In 1832 he supported Van Buren for the vice-presidency and in 1835 was chairman of the Baltimore convention that nominated Van Buren for the presidency. In 1834 Stevenson was nominated by President Jackson as minister to Great Britain. The Senate refused to confirm his nomination at the time, but Jackson made no other appointment, and finally in 1836 Stevenson's appointment was confirmed. While serving in this capacity, he brought embarrassment upon himself by advising certain British investors that he believed the attack upon the Bank of the United States would fail. His service in England was terminated in 1841 by the Whig triumph of the previous year. Returning to Virginia, he made his home at "Blenheim" in Albemarle County, an estate that he had purchased in 1836. Ritchie tried to obtain his return to active political life when Polk was elected to the presidency, but the Polk administration did not accept the suggestion. In 1845 Stevenson was elected president of the Virginia Society of Agriculture and became a member of the board of visitors of the University of Virginia. In 1856 he was chosen rector of the university. He died at "Blenheim" and lies buried at "Enniscorthy," the estate of John Coles, his father-in-law, in Albemarle County.

He was married three times: first, to Mary Page White, the daughter of John White and the grand-daughter of Carter Braxton [*q.v.*], second, in 1816, to Sarah Coles, and third, to Mary Schaff, of Georgetown, D. C. His son was John White Stevenson [*q.v.*]. He is reputed to have been a courtly and talented man; but he was a machine politician, and his career lacks the stamp of a strong personality.

[47 vols. of his papers in Lib. of Cong.; *Memoirs of John Quincy Adams,* vols. VI–XII (1875–77); C. G. Bowers, *The Party Battles of the Jackson Period* (1922); J. S. Bassett, *The Life of Andrew Jackson* (1911), II; C. H. Ambler, *Sectionalism in Va.* (1910) and *Thomas Ritchie* (1913); J. B. McMaster, *A Hist. of the People of the U. S.,* vol. VI (1906); B. H. Wise, *The Life of Henry A. Wise* (1899); H. E. Hayden, *Va. Geneal.* (1891); Edgar Woods, *Albemarle County* (1901), p. 319.]   T. P. A.

STEVENSON, CARTER LITTLEPAGE (Sept. 21, 1817–Aug. 15, 1888), Confederate general, was born near Fredericksburg, Va., the son of Carter Littlepage and Jane (Herndon) Stevenson. He was the nephew of Andrew Stevenson [q.v.] and the grand-nephew of Lewis Littlepage [q.v.]. Entering West Point in 1834, he graduated in 1838, was commissioned second lieutenant in the 5th Infantry, and promoted to be first lieutenant in 1840. Before the Mexican War he served in Florida, Wisconsin, and Michigan. His wife, Martha P. Griswold, was a Michigan woman. He fought at Palo Alto and Resaca de la Palma, was promoted to the rank of captain in 1847, and, serving chiefly on the frontier until the Civil War, participated in several skirmishes with Indians and in the Utah expedition of 1858. On June 6, 1861, he presented his resignation to his commanding officer and departed on leave of absence, intending to offer his services to his native state; but his commanding officer left the same day for the same purpose, forgetting to forward the resignation. Finally it was found by the succeeding commanding officer, who sent it on to Washington, where it arrived a month after it had been written (Old Files Section, Adjutant-General's Office, War Department). Meanwhile, on June 25, an order for Stevenson's dismissal had been issued, "it having been ascertained . . . that he had entertained and expressed treasonable designs against the Government of the United States" (Cullum, *post,* pp. 727–28).

In July he was commissioned lieutenant-colonel of infantry in the Confederate Army and colonel of the 53rd Virginia Infantry. On Beauregard's recommendation he was appointed brigadier-general in February 1862 and sent to duty in the West, where he served in Tennessee and Kentucky. He was commissioned major-general in October 1862. In December his division was transferred from Bragg's command to Pemberton's and fought at Champion's Hill and Big Black Ridge in the Vicksburg campaign. He personally commanded the Confederate forces during their retreat into the city, while Pemberton hastened ahead to organize the defense. He

was in charge of the right of the Confederate lines during the siege and was paroled along with his division at the surrender in July 1863. The Confederate government declared the division exchanged and returned it to duty in September, an action the Union authorities insisted was a violation of the terms of the cartel. An acrimonious correspondence followed, but the division was not withdrawn from field service. Whether his government's action may be justified or not, Stevenson had no responsibility in the matter. He fought at Missionary Ridge in Hardee's corps and in Hood's through the Atlanta campaign, notably at Resaca and Kenesaw Mountain. When Hood was assigned to the command of the Army of Tennessee, Stevenson succeeded him temporarily as corps commander, until the assignment of S. D. Lee. His division was not engaged at Franklin but suffered heavily at the battle of Nashville and in covering the retreat. He again had temporary command of the corps when S. D. Lee was wounded. In 1865, with the remnant of his division, he was transferred to the east, where he served through the campaign of the Carolinas and at the battle of Bentonville. After the war he was a civil and mining engineer. He died in Caroline County, Va.

[G. W. Cullum, *Biog. Register of . . . Grads. of . . . West Point,* 3rd ed., vol. I (1891); *War of the Rebellion: Official Records (Army)*; R. U. Johnson and C. C. Buel, *Battles and Leaders of the Civil War,* vols. III, IV (1887–88); C. A. Evans, *Confederate Military Hist.* (1899), vol. III; H. E. Hayden, *Va. Geneal.* (1891); MS. in the War Department files.] T. M. S.

STEVENSON, JAMES (Dec. 24, 1840–July 25, 1888), ethnologist, explorer, was born in Maysville, Ky., and educated in private schools. Coming into contact with the engineering corps of the government at sixteen, he engaged in explorations in the Northwest and afterwards became a member of the United States Geological Survey of the Territories under Dr. Ferdinand Vandiveer Hayden [q.v.]. With Dr. Hayden he explored the Missouri, Columbia, and Snake rivers to their sources. Inclination, training, and character made him an efficient aid in the conduct of the expeditions, and this meant much on the early wild frontiers. In 1871 he "took an active part in the survey of the Yellowstone region and was instrumental in having the heart of this 'wonderland' made a national park" (*American Anthropologist, post,* p. 558). In 1872 he was in charge of a division of Hayden's party that explored the Snake River in Idaho and Wyoming territories. During the surveys he came to know the Blackfeet and other Indians of Dakota, and grew interested in their languages, names, and customs, a preparation for his studies in the

Southwest. On the survey of 1872 he climbed the Great Teton, the first white man known to have reached the ancient Indian altar on its summit. Though he interrupted the work of exploration to join the Union army in 1861 and saw service in the 13th New York Volunteers, in 1866 he resumed the ethnological studies he had begun in previous years. He continued with these on the passing of the survey to the directorship of Major John Wesley Powell [*q.v.*], and at the inception of the Bureau of Ethnology in 1879 he engaged in research for it in the Southwest, where explorations were carried on among the Pueblo Indians and the remains of their former settlements. On Apr. 18, 1872, he married Matilda Coxe Evans of Washington [see Matilda Coxe Evans Stevenson], who became his associate in the Southwestern work. He outfitted and conducted expeditions of Frank Hamilton Cushing [*q.v.*], Mindeleff, and other explorers of the bureau investigating the ancient ruins and the living Navaho, Zuñi, Hopi, and other tribes. Gathering large collections of culture material, both ancient and modern, he prepared the first illustrated catalogues of specimens from the Southwest (*Second Annual Report of the Bureau of Ethnology ... 1880–'81*, 1883, and *Third Annual Report ... 1881–'82*, 1884), classified according to tribes, materials, and uses. These primer catalogues have a continuing use. He also made the first studies among the Navaho, "Ceremonial of Hasjelti Dailjis and Mythical Sand Painting of the Navajo Indians" (*Eighth Annual Report of the Bureau of Ethnology ... 1886–'87*, 1891). He died in New York City as he was returning from Gloucester, Mass., to Washington, D. C. He was survived by his wife.

Although Stevenson amassed voluminous notes as the result of his observations, he was a man of action, irked by writing, and gladly turned over most of his material to his wife. He was wont to say that he was not a scientific man, little realizing that his great collection of material would remain a valuable and in most respects unique contribution to science. A pioneer making the ways straight for subsequent workers, he belonged to the type of American who prefers the freedom and adventure of the wilds to the life of cities, and he found his work in Washington on maps and field notes but a tedious prelude to his real life in the summer in the mesas and canyons of the West. Though he displayed the reserve and reticence of the frontiersman, his speech was as pointed as it was brief, and in action usually secured him what he wanted, a quality that made him invaluable to his department.

He was a man above medium height, meager of frame, with brown hair and beard.

[G. P. Merrill, *The First One Hundred Years of Am. Geology* (1924); *Tenth Ann. Report of the Bureau of Ethnology ... 1888–89* (1893); *Sci.*, Aug. 10, 1888, pp. 63–64; *Am. Anthropologist*, Oct.–Dec. 1916; obituaries in *Evening Star* (Washington), July 26, and *Nat. Tribune* (Washington), Aug. 2, 1888; personal recollections.]   W. H.

STEVENSON, JOHN JAMES (Oct. 10, 1841–Aug. 10, 1924), geologist, was born in New York City. His father, the Rev. Andrew Stevenson, who was born in Ballylaw, Ireland, emigrated to America in 1831; his mother, Ann Mary (Willson) Stevenson, a native of Bedford, Pa., was a descendant of Zaccheus Willson who came to America in 1711. Educated in private schools in New York City and at the University of the City of New York (later New York University), from which he graduated in 1863, he first essayed teaching mathematics and natural science in the academy at Mexico, N. Y., but shortly resigned to take charge, in September 1864, of a school for boys at Astoria, N. Y. There he also edited the *American Educational Monthly*. In 1867, when he received the degree of Ph.D. from the University of the City of New York, he undertook professional work in western mining regions and contracted tuberculosis, from which he did not fully recover for several years. He was professor of chemistry and natural sciences in West Virginia University, 1869–71; assistant to Dr. John Strong Newberry [*q.v.*] on the geological survey of Ohio, 1871–72, and part-time professor of geology in the University of the City of New York, 1872. In 1873 he was appointed geologist on the surveys under Col. George Montague Wheeler west of the 100th meridian, and in 1875 was assistant geologist to Prof. Peter Lesley [*qq.v.*] in charge of the geological survey of Pennsylvania, where he was given charge of the work in Greene and Washington counties, and in 1876 and 1877 of Fayette and Westmoreland counties. In 1878 he rejoined the Wheeler survey in Colorado. In 1879, 1880, and 1881 he was engaged a part of the time in expert work in southwest Virginia and New Mexico, but returned to work on the Pennsylvania survey in 1881, and became professor of geology in New York University, holding the position until 1909 when he retired as professor emeritus.

As a teacher he was eminently successful. He had in a marked degree the ability to make his subject interesting, to hold the attention of his students, and to encourage and stimulate them. In addition to his scientific papers he contributed many articles on college problems and on the place of science in education to such magazines as *School and Society* and *Popular Science Monthly*. As a working geologist he covered a wide field, though he gave his greatest attention to stratigraphic problems and to those relating to coal. Apart from his publications in the reports of the Wheeler survey of 1875 and 1881 (*United States Geographical Surveys West of the 100th Meridian,* vol. III, 1875; supplement, 1881) and in reports of the Pennsylvania survey (*Second Geological Survey of Pennsylvania, 1875 ... Greene & Washington District,* vol. K, 1876; *Second Geological Survey of Pennsylvania, 1876 ... 1877 ... Fayette & Westmoreland District,* KK–KKK, 1877–78, and *Second Geological Survey of Pennsylvania ... The Geology of Bedford and Fulton Counties,* 1882), his best known studies are "Lower Carboniferous of the Appalachian Basin" (*Bulletin of the Geological Society of America,* vol. XIV, 1903) and "Carboniferous of the Appalachian Basin" (*Ibid.,* vols. XV, 2904, XVII, 1906, XVIII, 1907); "The Formation of Coal Beds" (*Proceedings of the American Philosophical Society,* vols. L–LII, 1911–13); and *Interrelation of the Fossil Fuels* (1921). Of particular interest were his conclusions that the New Mexican coal fields were cretaceous, and that the Laramie section of King and the Fort Union of Hayden were composite successions of the cretaceous age; he showed too that each coal bed of the Pennsylvania field had peculiarities of its own by which any particular bed could be recognized over wide areas.

Kindly and courteous, but incisive in expression, he was a man keenly and forcefully alert, capable of thoroughly enjoying a good fight when it was honorably conducted, whoever might be the victor. He was a good conversationalist and a delightful companion, being gifted with an unusual sense of humor. He was the first secretary of the Geological Society of America, which he had been active in establishing, and president in 1899; he was also president of the New York Academy, 1896–98; acting vice-president for the United States at the International Geological Congress in 1903, and a member of numerous scientific societies at home and abroad. He was twice married, first on Apr. 13, 1865, to Mary A. McGowan, who died in 1871, and second on Jan. 1, 1879, to Mary C. Ewing. There were three children by the first marriage and two by the second. Although his output of work was checked by failing eyesight during his last two years, he was mentally active until the last. He died of pneumonia in New Canaan, Conn., in his eighty-third year.

[*Who's Who in America,* 1922–23; I. C. White, in *Bull. Geological Soc. of America,* Mar. 1925, with bibliog.; Charles Keyes, in *Pan Am. Geologist,* Oct. 1924; *Gen. Alumni Cat. of N. Y. Univ., 1833–1905* (1906); obituary in *N. Y. Times,* Aug. 11, 1924; personal recollections.]

G. P. M.

STEVENSON, JOHN WHITE (May 4, 1812–Aug. 10, 1886), senator and representative in Congress and governor of Kentucky, was born in Richmond, Va., the only child of Andrew Stevenson [*q.v.*] and Mary Page (White) Stevenson. His mother dying at his birth, he was taken in charge and given his earliest training by his grandmother, Judith White. His first formal schooling was provided by private tutors in Virginia and also in Washington where he spent much time with his father. He attended Hampden-Sidney College, 1828–29, before entering the University of Virginia, where he graduated in 1832. He read law with Willoughby Newton, a prominent Virginia lawyer, and on the advice of James Madison decided to grow up in the West. He began the practice of law in Vicksburg, Miss., but in 1841 he settled in Covington, Ky., where he made his home throughout the rest of his life. His success as a lawyer was soon assured. In 1845 he was elected as a representative from Kenton County to the state legislature, and he was reëlected in 1846 and 1848. The next year he represented his county in the constitutional convention which met in Frankfort and remade the state constitution. With M. C. Johnson and James Harlan, he prepared for the state a *Code of Practise in Civil and Criminal Cases* (1854). He was a delegate to the National Democratic Conventions of 1848, 1852, and 1856, and was elected to the Thirty-fifth and Thirty-sixth congresses, serving from 1857 to 1861. He failed of reëlection to the following Congress.

On Jan. 30, 1861, he made his principal speech, regarding the perilous situation created by the secession movement. Imbued with a strong feeling for the Union, characteristic of Kentuckians, he called upon the Republicans to recede from the extreme policies of their platform and help to preserve the common country. Decrying the passions of the hour, he blamed the Republicans for the failure of the Crittenden propositions and all other compromises, and declared that "the slave states have a right to resist the execution of a policy at war with their interests, destructive of their peace, injurious to their rights, and subversive of the ends and objects for which the Union was formed" (*Congressional Globe,* 36 Cong., 2 Sess., Appendix, p. 144). Though strongly sympathizing with the Confederacy, he managed to keep out of war and free from Federal prisons, and not until 1865 did his name become prominent again. This year he attended as a delegate the Union Convention in Philadelphia called to indorse President Johnson's policy of reconstruction. In August 1867 he was elected lieutenant-governor of Kentucky and the next month succeeded to the governorship, on account of the death of Gov. John L. Helm [*q.v.*]. The next year he was elected to this position by a majority of more than four to one over his Republican opponent. He was a constructive and sane governor, using his influence and power to break up violent gangs of "Regulators," and aiding the development of a common-school system. He became entangled in a bitter controversy with Senator Thomas C. McCreery and Thomas L. Jones over charges and countercharges relative to a recommendation for the appointment to a federal office of Stephen G. Burkridge, a Union officer violently hated by Kentuckians. This controversy seems to have been preparatory to the contest between Stevenson and McCreery for the senatorship a few months later. Stevenson won and in February 1871 he resigned the governorship to serve a term in the United States Senate. For the next six years he tenaciously upheld a political faith from which he had never swerved —a faith which he had imbibed from Jefferson and Madison, both of whom he had known in their homes. He opposed the rivers and harbors appropriations bill of 1875 and in a speech against it declared that he clung to the "doctrines of close construction and rigid adherence to all the limitations of the Constitution upon congressional or executive power with greater tenacity now than ever, as the palladium of political safety" (*Congressional Record,* 44 Cong., 1 Sess., p. 4836). In the disputed election of 1876, he went to New Orleans as one of the visiting statesmen and became thoroughly convinced that the election had been fair in Louisiana.

On the expiration of his term he returned to Covington to resume the practice of law, and at the same time he accepted a position in the Cincinnati Law School to teach criminal law and contracts. In 1880 he was made chairman of the National Democratic Convention in Cincinnati, and four years later he was elected president of the American Bar Association. In 1842 Stevenson had married Sibella Winston, of Newport, Ky., and to them were born five children, three daughters and two sons. He was somewhat reserved in demeanor, was a great lover of the law, and was strongly religious. He was a member of the Episcopal Church and often attended its conventions. He died in Covington, Ky., and was buried in Spring Grove Cemetery, Cincinnati.

[*Biog. Directory of the Am. Congress, 1774–1927* (1928); *The Biog. Encyc. of Ky.* (1878); Lewis and R. H. Collins, *Hist. of Ky.* (2 vols., 1874); *Cincinnati Commercial Gazette,* Aug. 11, 1886; memoir in *Report of the Ninth Ann. Meeting of the Am. Bar Asso. . . . 1886* (1886), pp. 528–36. The principal speeches Stevenson made in Congress were reprinted as follows: *Speech of Hon. J. W. Stevenson, of Kentucky, on the State of the Union* (1875); *Tax and Tariff* (1875); *River and Harbor Appropriations* (1876); *The Electoral Vote* (1876). The Stevenson Papers, 1849–82 (9 vols.), are in the MS. Division, Lib. of Cong., and a few Stevenson letters are to be found in the Joseph Holt Papers in the same place.]   E. M. C.

STEVENSON, MATILDA COXE EVANS (*c.* 1850–June 24, 1915), ethnologist, was born in San Augustine, Tex., the daughter of Alexander H. and Maria Matilda (Coxe) Evans. Her parents moved in her infancy to Washington, D. C., and she was educated in Miss Anable's school in Philadelphia, Pa. Her marriage, Apr. 18, 1872, to James Stevenson [*q.v.*] of the United States Geological Survey, led to the beginning of her career as an ethnologist. She accompanied her husband on various expeditions into the Southwest and early became interested in the Zuñi Indians, who were more accessible, less modified, and more amenable to study than most. Her first work resulted in a paper almost unique in American studies, "The Religious Life of the Zuñi Child" (*Fifth Annual Report of the Bureau of Ethnology . . . 1883–84,* 1887). In 1888 she published an important paper on "Zuñi Religions" (*Science,* Mar. 23, 1888). Working among the Sia Pueblo Indians of the Rio Grande at an opportune time for ethnological studies, she produced some years later a paper, "The Sia" (*Eleventh Annual Report of the Bureau of Ethnology . . . 1889–'90,* 1894), the closest study of a Rio Grande Pueblo. One of her especially noteworthy discoveries was the existence of a Snake Society and ceremonial among the Sia. The Sia paper, full of social and material culture-elements, was a forerunner of her encyclopedic study of the Zuñi, "The Zuñi Indians: Their Mythology, Esoteric Fraternities, and Ceremonies" (*Twenty-third Annual Report of the Bureau of American Ethnology, 1901–1902,* 1904). Her fortitude in carrying out the work necessary for this study is almost unexampled among ethnologists, and her success in winning the confidence of the Indians was a triumph of character. The Zuñi, who loved her and called her "Mother," realized that a record of their civilization should be made, and expedited her work in every way, permitting her to observe the most secret ceremonies. As the result of later studies dealing with phases of Zuñi material culture she produced "Ethnobotany of the Zuñi Indians" (*Thirtieth Annual Report of the Bureau of American Ethnology . . . 1908–1909,* 1915), her last major work. She found time to write several less important articles, which appeared in the *American Anthropologist* at various dates, on more general aspects of the Pueblo Indian subject. Following her laborious work at Zuñi, she continued studies among the Rio Grande Pueblo Indians from 1904 to 1910, concentrating her attention especially on the Tewa and the difficult Taos Indians. In this her experience with the Zuñi and other tribes cleared away obstacles. Among her papers on these Indians were "Strange Rites of the Tewa Indians" (*Smithsonian Miscellaneous Collections,* vol. LXIII, 1914) and "The Sun and Ice People among the Tewa Indians of New Mexico" (*Ibid.,* vol. LXV, 1916). She made numerous collections of objects of material culture from the Pueblo Indians, being deputized to collect such objects for the Louisiana Purchase Exposition in 1903.

The scientific investigations carried on in anthropology at the time were not based on the more comprehensive and accurate methods of the modern school, but the necessity of careful observation and record was clearly recognized. Mrs. Stevenson's work rests on abundant and careful data, and, seen in perspective, it places her in a secure position in ethnological science. Since the Indians have changed greatly in the intervening years, her work has unique value. She was one of the founders of the Woman's Anthropological Society of Washington, and a member of a number of scientific societies.

[*Who's Who in America,* 1914–15; *Science,* July 9, 1915; W. H. Holmes, in *Am. Anthropologist,* Oct.–Dec., 1916; death notice in *Evening Star* (Washington, D. C.), July 24, 1915; personal acquaintance.]
W. H.

STEVENSON, SARA YORKE (Feb. 19, 1847–Nov. 14, 1921), archaeologist, was born in Paris, France. Through her father, Edward Yorke, a business man and banker, she was descended from Thomas Yorke who emigrated from England to what is now Berks County, Pa., about 1728. Her mother Sarah (Hanna) Yorke was the daughter of a planter in Louisiana. During her childhood she lived in Paris, where she was educated at the Cours Remy and the Institut Descauriet. She also spent a summer in Newport, a winter in New Orleans, and five years, 1862 to 1867, in Mexico. Her memories of the French intervention she later published in a book called *Maximilian in Mexico* (1899). Since her family had suffered severe financial losses, she went to Philadelphia to live in the quiet household of an aunt and two uncles. There she met Cornelius Stevenson to whom she was married on June 30, 1870. Their son Wil-

liam was born in 1878. Her dinners were notable, and she was a spirited and vivacious social leader. Rarely gifted, she possessed a magnetic personality, assured executive ability, and indomitable energy. The result was a record of unusual achievement.

She became interested in the Educational Home for Indian Boys and Girls, and then in the Depository and Philadelphia Exchange for Woman's Work, which afforded means of self-help to indigent gentlewomen. She helped found the Archaeological Association of the University of Pennsylvania, which became the University Museum, and was secretary for ten years and then president of the board of managers. It was she who started the museum building scheme. As early as 1894 she lectured at the University of Pennsylvania and at the Peabody Museum of Harvard University. At the World's Columbian Exposition in Chicago she was vice-president of the jury of awards for ethnology. In 1897 she made a trip to Rome for the department of archaeology and paleontology of the University of Pennsylvania and in 1898 to Egypt for the American Exploration Society and the city of Philadelphia. Besides a number of addresses and articles that she published on Egyptian archaeology and other subjects, one on *Insurance and Business Adventure in the Days of Shakespeare and in Those of William Penn* (1913) was republished and widely translated. She was president of the Pennsylvania branch of the Archaeological Institute of America from 1899 to 1903, had the honor of being elected a member of the American Philosophical Society, and was the first woman given an honorary degree by the University of Pennsylvania. Meanwhile she was enthusiastic in obtaining wider fields of opportunity for women and was the first president of the Equal Franchise Society of Pennsylvania. As first president of the Civic Club she helped inaugurate a movement that did much for the improvement of Philadelphia and soon became national. She was appointed to several important citizen's committees and from 1894 to 1901 was trustee of the Commercial Museum. She was a charter member and for twenty-five years president of the Acorn Club. The war brought her still more responsibility, for she was vice-chairman of the emergency aid and chairman of the French war relief committee, which raised $1,500,000. In recognition of her services the French government awarded her the academic palms as Officier d'Instruction Publique in 1916 and made her a Chevalier of the Legion of Honor in 1920. From 1908 until her death, she was literary editor of the *Public Led-*

ger as well as the contributor of "Peggy Shippen's Diary." Her keen wit, wide acquaintance, and rich experience enabled her to wield extensive influence. She was as merciless in opposing falsehood or dishonesty as she was courageous in championing what she believed to be right.

[*Sara Yorke Stevenson, 1847–1921, A Tribute from the Civic Club of Philadelphia* (1922); *Sara Yorke Stevenson, 1847–1921. Addresses made at Meeting in Her Memory Held in the Auditorium of the University Museum . . . Apr. 29, 1922* (n.d.); *Who's Who in America,* 1920–21; J. W. Jordan, *Colonial Families of Philadelphia* (1911), vol. II; *Public Ledger,* Nov. 15, 1921.]

             A. L. L.